T0077212

Programming Languages

Computer scientists often need to learn new programming languages quickly. The best way to prepare is to understand the foundational principles that underlie even the most complicated industrial languages.

This text for an undergraduate programming-languages course distills great languages and their design principles down to easy-to-learn "bridge" languages implemented by interpreters whose key parts are explained in the text. The book goes deep into the roots of both functional and object-oriented programming, and it shows how types and modules, including generics/polymorphism, contribute to effective programming.

The book is not just about programming languages; it is also about programming. Through concepts, examples, and more than 300 practice exercises that exploit the interpreters, students learn not only what programming-language features are common but also how to do things with them. Substantial implementation projects include Milner's type inference, both copying and mark-and-sweep garbage collection, and arithmetic on arbitrary-precision integers.

Norman Ramsey is Associate Professor of Computer Science at Tufts University. Since earning his PhD at Princeton, he has worked in industry and has taught programming languages, advanced functional programming, programming language implementation, and technical writing at Purdue, the University of Virginia, and Harvard as well as Tufts. He has received Tufts's Lerman-Neubauer Prize, awarded annually to one outstanding undergraduate teacher. He has also been a Hertz Fellow and an Alfred P. Sloan Research Fellow. His implementation credits include a code generator for the Standard ML of New Jersey compiler and another for the Glasgow Haskell Compiler.

Programming Languages
Build, Prove, and Compare

Norman Ramsey
Tufts University, Massachusetts

CAMBRIDGE
UNIVERSITY PRESS

University Printing House, Cambridge CB2 8BS, United Kingdom

One Liberty Plaza, 20th Floor, New York, NY 10006, USA

477 Williamstown Road, Port Melbourne, VIC 3207, Australia

314–321, 3rd Floor, Plot 3, Splendor Forum, Jasola District Centre, New Delhi – 110025, India

103 Penang Road, #05–06/07, Visioncrest Commercial, Singapore 238467

Cambridge University Press is part of the University of Cambridge.

It furthers the University's mission by disseminating knowledge in the pursuit of education, learning, and research at the highest international levels of excellence.

www.cambridge.org
Information on this title: www.cambridge.org/highereducation/isbn/9781107180185
DOI: 10.1017/9781316841396

First published 2023

A catalogue record for this publication is available from the British Library.

ISBN 978-1-107-18018-5 Hardback

Additional resources for this publication at www.cambridge.org/ramsey

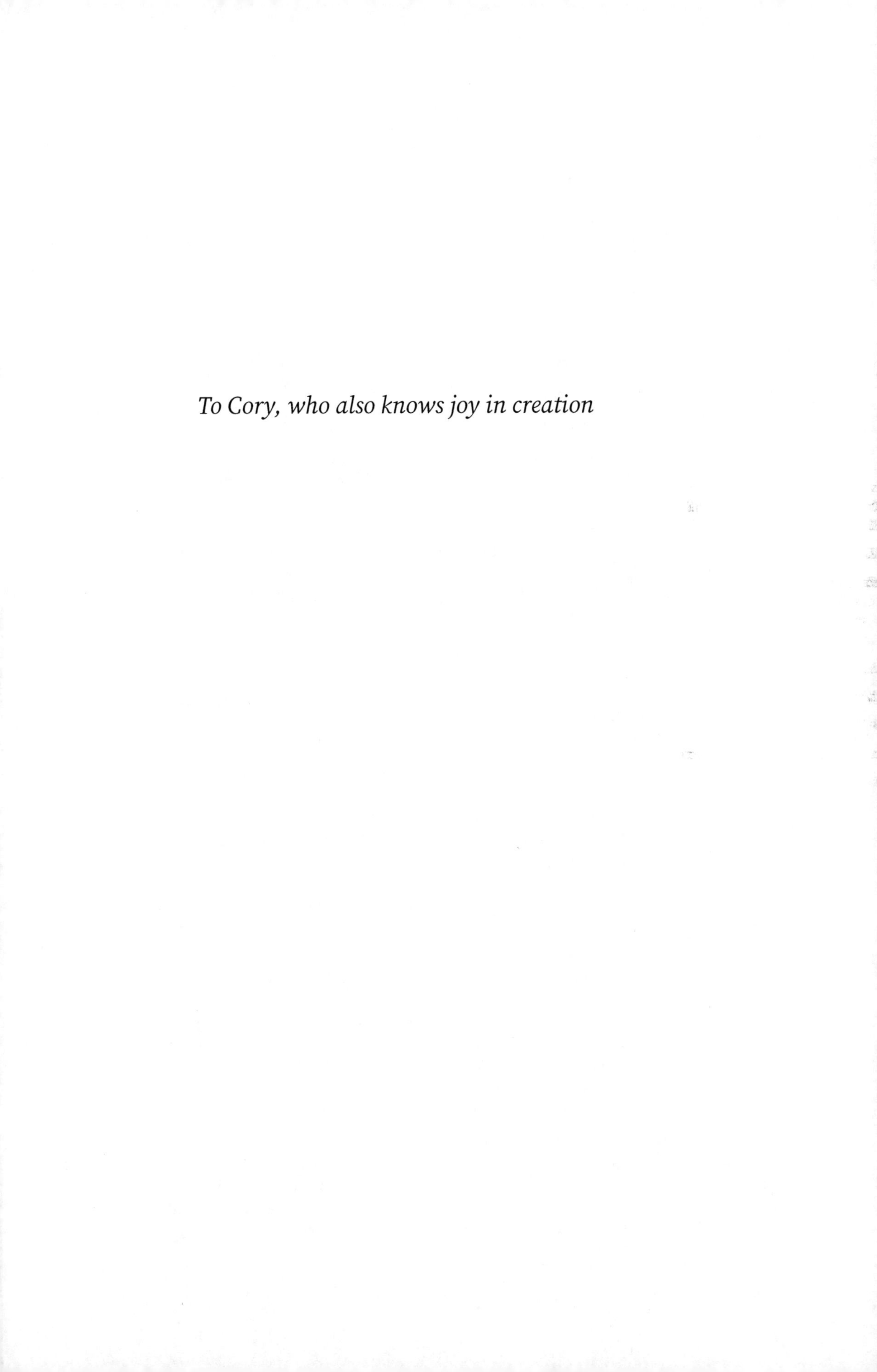

To Cory, who also knows joy in creation

Contents

Preface

This textbook, suitable for an undergraduate or master's-level course in programming languages, is about great language-design ideas, how to describe them precisely, and how to use them effectively. The ideas revolve around functions, types, modules, and objects. They are described using formal semantics and type theory, and their use is illustrated through programming examples and exercises.

The ideas, descriptive techniques, and examples are conveyed by means of *bridge languages*. A bridge language models a real programming language, but it is small enough to describe formally and to learn in a week or two, yet big enough to write interesting programs in. The bridge languages in this book model Algol, Scheme, ML, CLU, and Smalltalk, and they are related to many modern descendants, including C, C++, OCaml, Haskell, Java, JavaScript, Python, Ruby, and Rust.

Each bridge language is supported by an interpreter, which runs all the examples and supports programming exercises. The interpreters, which are presented in depth in an online Supplement, are carefully crafted and documented. They can be used not only for exercises but also to implement students' own language-design ideas.

The book develops these concepts:

- Abstract syntax and operational semantics
- Definitional interpreters
- Algebraic laws and equational reasoning
- Garbage collection
- Symbolic computing and functional programming
- Parametric polymorphism
- Monomorphic and polymorphic type systems
- Type inference
- Algebraic data types and pattern matching
- Data abstraction using abstract types and modules
- Data abstraction using objects and classes

The concepts are supported by the bridge languages as shown in the Introduction (Table I.2, page 5), which also explains each bridge language in greater detail (pages 3 to 7).

The book calls for skills in both programming and proof:

- As prerequisites, learners should have the first-year, two-semester programming sequence, including data structures, plus discrete mathematics.

- To extend and modify the implementations in Chapters 1 to 4, a learner needs to be able to read and modify C code; the necessary skills have to be learned elsewhere. C is used because it is the simplest way to express programs that work extensively with pointers and memory, which is the topic of Chapter 4.

To extend and modify the implementations in Chapters 5 to 10, a learner needs to be able to read and modify Standard ML code; the necessary skills are developed in Chapters 2, 5, and 8. Standard ML is used because it is a simple, powerful language that is ideally suited to writing interpreters.

- To prove the simpler theorems, a learner needs to be able to substitute equals for equals and to fill in templates of logical reasoning. To prove the more interesting theorems, a learner needs to be able to write a proof by induction.

DESIGNING A COURSE TO USE THIS BOOK

Some books capture a single course, and when using such a book, your only choice is to start at the beginning and go as far as you can. But in programming languages, instructors have many good choices, and a book shouldn't make them all for you. This book is designed so you can choose what to teach and what to emphasize while retaining a coherent point of view: how programming languages can be used effectively in practice. If you're relatively new to teaching programming languages and are not sure what to choose, you can't go wrong with a course on functions, types, and objects (Chapters 1, 2, 6, 7, and 10). If you have more experience, consider the ideas below.

Programming Languages: Build, Prove, and Compare gives you interesting, powerful programming languages that share a common syntax, a common theoretical framework, and a common implementation framework. These frameworks support programming practice in the bridge languages, implementation and extension of the bridge languages, and formal reasoning about the bridge languages. The design of your course will depend on how you wish to balance these elements.

- To unlock the full potential of the subject, combine programming practice with theoretical study and work on interpreters. If your students have only two semesters of programming experience and no functional programming, you can focus on the core foundations in Chapters 1 to 3: operational semantics, functional programming, and control operators. You can supplement that work with one of two foundational tracks: If your students are comfortable with C and pointers, they can implement continuation primitives in μScheme+, and they can implement garbage collectors. Or if they can make a transition from μScheme to Standard ML, with help from Chapter 8, they can implement type checkers and possibly type inference.

  If your students have an additional semester of programming experience or if they have already been exposed to functional programming, your course can advance into types, modules, and objects. When I teach a course like this, it begins with four homework assignments that span an introduction to the framework, operational semantics, recursive functions, and higher-order functions. After completing these assignments, my students learn Standard ML, in which they implement first a type checker, then type inference. This schedule leaves a week for programming with modules and data abstraction, a couple of weeks for Smalltalk, and a bit of time for the lambda calculus.

  A colleague whose students are similarly experienced begins with Impcore and μScheme, transitions to Standard ML to work on type systems and type inference, then returns to the bridge languages to explore μSmalltalk, μProlog, and garbage collection.

  If your students have seen interpreters and are comfortable with proof by induction, your course can move much more quickly through the foundational material, creating room for other topics. When I taught a course like this, it explored everything in my other class, then added garbage collection, denotational semantics, and logic programming.

- A second design strategy tilts your class toward programming practice, either de-emphasizing or eliminating theory. To introduce programming practice in diverse languages, *Build, Prove, and Compare* occupies a sweet spot between two extremes. One extreme "covers" N languages in N weeks. This extreme is great for exposure, but not for depth—when students must work with real implementations of real languages, a week or even two may be enough to motivate them, but it's not enough to build proficiency.

  The other extreme goes into full languages narrowly but deeply. Students typically use a couple of popular languages, and overheads are high: each language has its own implementation conventions, and students must manage the gratuitous details and differences that popular languages make inevitable.

  Build, Prove, and Compare offers both breadth and depth, without the overhead. If you want to focus on programming practice, you can aim for "four languages in ten weeks": μScheme, μML, Molecule, and μSmalltalk. You can bring your students up to speed on the common syntactic, semantic, and implementation frameworks using Impcore, and that knowledge will support them through to the next four languages. If you have a couple of extra weeks, you can deepen your students' experience by having them work with the interpreters.

- A third design strategy tilts your class toward applied theory. *Build, Prove, and Compare* is not suitable for a class in pure theory—the bridge languages are too big, the reasoning is informal, and the classic results are missing. But it is suitable for a course that is primarily about using formal notation to explain precisely what is going on in whole programming languages, reinforced by experience implementing that notation. Your students can do metatheory with Impcore, Typed Impcore, Typed μScheme, and nano-ML; equational reasoning with μScheme; and type systems with Typed Impcore, Typed μScheme, nano-ML, μML, and Molecule. They can compare how universally quantified types are used in three different designs (Typed μScheme, nano-ML/μML, and Molecule).

- What about a course in interpreters? If you are interested in *definitional* interpreters, *Build, Prove, and Compare* presents many well-crafted examples. And the online Supplement presents a powerful infrastructure that your students can use to build more definitional interpreters (Appendices F to I). But apart from this infrastructure, the book does not discuss what a definitional interpreter is or how to design one. For a course on interpreters, you would probably want an additional book.

All of these potential designs are well supported by the exercises (345 in total), which fall into three big categories. For insight into how to use programming languages effectively, there are programming exercises that use the bridge languages. For insight into the workings of the languages themselves, as well as the formalism that describes them, there are programming exercises that extend or modify the interpreters. And for insight into formal description and proof, there are theory exercises. Model solutions for some of the more challenging exercises are available to instructors.

A few exercises are simple enough and easy enough that your students can work on them for 10 to 20 minutes in class. But most are intended as homework.

- To introduce a new language like Impcore, μScheme, μML, Molecule, or μSmalltalk, think about assigning from a half dozen to a full dozen programming exercises, most easy, some of medium difficulty.
- To introduce proof technique, think about assigning around a half dozen proof problems, maybe one or two involving some form of induction (some metatheory, or perhaps an algebraic law involving lists).
- To develop a deep understanding of a single topic, assign one exercise or a group of related exercises aimed at that topic. Such exercises are provided for continuations, garbage collection, type checking, type inference, search trees, and arbitrary-precision integers.

Contents and scope

Because this book is organized by language, its scope is partly determined by what the bridge languages do and do not offer relative to the originals on which they are based.

- μScheme offers `define`, a `lambda`, and three "let" forms. Values include symbols, machine integers, Booleans, `cons` cells, and functions. There's no numeric tower and there are no macros.
- μML offers type inference, algebraic data types, and pattern matching. There are no modules, no exceptions, no mutable reference cells, and no value restriction.
- Molecule offers a procedural, monomorphic core language with mutable algebraic types, coupled to a module language that resembles OCaml and Standard ML.
- μSmalltalk offers a pure object-oriented language in which everything is an object; even classes are objects. Control flow is expressed via message passing in a form of continuation-passing style. μSmalltalk provides a modest class hierarchy, which includes blocks, Booleans, collections, magnitudes, and three kinds of numbers. And μSmalltalk includes just enough reflection to enable programmers to add new methods to existing classes.

Each of the languages supports multiple topical themes; the major themes are programming, semantics, and types.

- *Idiomatic programming* demonstrates effective use of proven features that are found in many languages. Such features include functions (μScheme, Chapter 2), algebraic data types (μML, Chapter 8), abstract data types and modules (Molecule, Chapter 9), and objects (μSmalltalk, Chapter 10).
- *Big-step semantics* expresses the meaning of programs in a way that is easily connected to interpreters, and which, with practice, becomes easy to read and write. Big-step semantics are given for Impcore, μScheme, nano-ML, μML, and μSmalltalk (Chapters 1, 2, 7, 8, and 10).
- *Type systems* guide the construction of correct programs, help document functions, and guarantee that language features like polymorphism and data abstraction are used safely. Type systems are given for Typed Impcore, Typed μScheme, nano-ML, μML, and Molecule (Chapters 6 to 9).

In addition the major themes and the concepts listed above, the book addresses, to varying degrees, these other concepts:

- Subtype polymorphism, in μSmalltalk (Chapter 10)
- Light metatheory for both operational semantics and type systems (Chapters 1, 5, and 6)
- Free variables, bound variables, variable capture, and substitution, in both terms and types (Chapters 2, 5, and 6)
- Continuations for backtracking search, for small-step semantics, and for more general control flow (Chapters 2, 3, and 10)
- The propositions-as-types principle, albeit briefly (Chapter 6 Afterword)

A book is characterized not only by what it includes but also by what it omits. To start, this book omits the classic theory results such as type soundness and strong normalization; although learners can prove some simple theorems and look for interesting counterexamples, theory is used primarily to express and communicate ideas, not to establish facts. The book also omits lambda calculus, because lambda calculus is not suitable for programming.

The book omits concurrency and parallelism. These subjects are too difficult and too ramified to be handled well in a broad introductory book.

And for reasons of space and time, the book omits three engaging programming models. One is the pure, lazy language, as exemplified by Haskell. Another is the prototype-based object-oriented language, made popular by JavaScript, but brilliantly illustrated by Self. The third is logic programming, as exemplified by Prolog—although Prolog is explored at length in the Supplement (Appendix D). If you are interested in μHaskell, μSelf, or μProlog, please write to me.

SOFTWARE AND OTHER SUPPLEMENTS

The software described in the book is available from the book's web site, which is `build-prove-compare.net`. The web site also provides a "playground" that allows you to experiment with the interpreters directly in your browser, without having to download anything. And it holds the book's PDF Supplement, which includes additional material on multiprecision arithmetic, extensions to algebraic data types, logic programming, and longer programming examples. The Supplement also describes all the code: both the reusable modules and the interpreter-specific modules.

Acknowledgments

I was inspired by Sam Kamin's 1990 book *Programming Languages: An Interpreter-Based Approach.* When I asked if I could build on his book, Sam gave me his blessing and encouragement. *Programming Languages: Build, Prove, and Compare* is narrower and deeper than Sam's book, but several programming examples and several dozen exercises are derived from Sam's examples and exercises, with permission. I owe him a great debt.

In 1995, the Computer Science faculty at Purdue invited me to visit for a year and teach programming languages. Without that invitation, there might not have been a book.

An enormous book is not among the typical duties of a tenured computer-science professor. Kathleen Fisher made it possible for me to finish this book while teaching at Tufts; I am profoundly grateful.

Andrea Schuler and Jack Davidson helped me get permissions for the epigraphs that appear at the beginning of each chapter.

Russ Cox helped bootstrap the early chapters, especially the C code. His work was supported by an Innovation Grant from the Dean for Undergraduate Education at Harvard.

Many colleagues contributed to the development of Molecule. Matthew Fluet's insights and oversight were invaluable; without him, Chapter 9 would never have been completed. And Andreas Rossberg's chapter review helped get me onto the right track.

Robby Findler suggested that the control operators in μScheme+ be lowered to the `label` and `long-goto` forms. He also suggested the naming convention for μScheme+ exceptions.

David Chase suggested the garbage-collector debugging technique described in Section 4.6.2.

Matthew Fluet found some embarrassing flaws in Typed Impcore and Typed μScheme, which I repaired. Matthew also suggested the example used in Section 6.6.8, which shows that if variable capture is not avoided, Typed μScheme's type system can be subverted.

Benjamin Pierce taught me how to think about the roles of proofs in programming languages; Section 1.7 explains his ideas as I understand them.

Chris Okasaki opened my eyes to a whole new world of data structures.

The work of William Cook (2009) shaped my understanding of the consensus view about what properties characterize an object-oriented language. Any misunderstandings of or departures from the consensus view are my own.

Christian Lindig wrote, in Objective Caml, a prettyprinter from which I derived the prettyprinter in Appendix J.

Sam Guyer helped me articulate my thoughts on why we study programming languages.

Matthew Flatt helped me start learning about macros.

Kathy Gray and Matthias Felleisen developed `check-expect` and `check-error`, which I have embraced and extended.

Cyrus Cousins found a subtle bug in μScheme+.

Mike Hamburg and Inna Zakharevich spurred me to improve the concrete syntax of μSmalltalk and to provide better error messages.

Andrew Black examined an earlier design of μSmalltalk and found it wanting. His insistence on good design and clear presentation spurred innumerable improvements to Chapter 10.

Pharo By Example (Black et al. 2010) explained Smalltalk metaclasses in a way I could understand.

Dan Grossman read an early version of the manuscript, and he not only commented on every detail but also made me think hard about what I was doing. Kathleen Fisher's careful reading spurred me to make many improvements throughout Chapters 1 and 2. Jeremy Condit, Ralph Corderoy, Allyn Dimock, Lee Feigenbaum, Luiz de Figueiredo, Andrew Gallant, Tony Hosking, Scott Johnson, Juergen Kahrs, and Kell Pogue also reviewed parts of the manuscript. Gregory Price suggested ways to improve the wording of several problems. Penny Anderson, Jon Berry, Richard Borie, Allyn Dimock, Sam Guyer, Kathleen Fisher, Matthew Fluet, William Harrison, David Hemmendinger, Tony Hosking, Joel Jones, Giampiero Pecelli, Jan Vitek, and Michelle Strout bravely used preliminary versions in their classes. Penny found far more errors and suggested many more improvements than anyone else; she has my profound thanks.

My students, who are too numerous to mention by name, found many errors in earlier drafts. Students in early classes were paid one dollar per error, from which an elite minority earned enough to recover the cost of their books.

Individual chapters were reviewed by Richard Eisenberg, Mike Sperber, Robby Findler, Ron Garcia, Jan Midtgaard, Richard Jones, Suresh Jagannathan, John Reppy, Dimitrios Vytiniotis, François Pottier, Chris Okasaki, Stephanie Weirich, Roberto Ierusalimschy, Matthew Fluet, Andreas Rossberg, Stephen Chang, Andrew Black, Will Cook, and Markus Triska.

Larry Bacow inspired me to do the right thing and live with the consequences.

Throughout the many years I have worked on this book, Cory Kerens has loved and supported me. And during the final push, she has been the perfect companion. She, too, knows what it is to be obsessed with a creative work—and that shipping is also a feature. Cory, it's time to go adventuring!

Credits

In the epigraph for the Introduction, Russ Cox is quoted by permission.

The epigraph for Chapter 1 is from John Backus 1978. Can programming be liberated from the von Neumann style? A functional style and its algebra of programs. *Communications of the ACM,* 21(8):613–641. Used by permission.

The epigraphs for Chapters 2 and 4 are from Richard Kelsey, William Clinger, and Jonathan Rees 1998. *Revised^5 Report on the Algorithmic Language Scheme.* Used by permission.

The epigraph for Chapter 3 is from Peter J. Landin 1964. The mechanical evaluation of expressions. *Computer Journal,* 6(4):308–320. Used by permission.

In the epigraph for Chapter 5, David Hanson and the unnamed student are quoted by permission.

The first epigraph for Chapter 6 is from John C. Reynolds 1974. Towards a theory of type structure. In *Colloque sur la Programmation, Paris, France, LNCS,* volume 19, pages 408–425. Springer-Verlag. Used by permission.

In the second epigraph for Chapter 6, Arvind is quoted by permission.

The epigraph for Chapter 7 is from Robin Milner 1983. How ML evolved. *Polymorphism—The ML/LCF/Hope Newsletter,* 1(1). Used by permission.

The epigraph for Chapter 8 is from Frederick P. Brooks, Jr. 1975. *The Mythical Man-Month.* Addison-Wesley. Used by permission.

The epigraph for Chapter 9 is from Barbara Liskov and Stephen Zilles 1974. Programming with abstract data types. *SIGPLAN Notices,* 9(4):50–59. Used by permission.

The first epigraph for Chapter 10 is from Alan C. Kay 1993. The early history of Smalltalk. *SIGPLAN Notices,* 28(3):69–95. Used by permission.

The second epigraph for Chapter 10 is from Kristen Nygaard and Ole-Johan Dahl 1978. The development of the SIMULA languages. *SIGPLAN Notices,* 13(8):245–272. Used by permission.

Judgment forms, important functions, & concrete syntax

Evaluation judgments

Language	*Expression or related form*	*Page*	*Definition*	*Page*
Impcore	$\langle e, \xi, \phi, \rho \rangle \Downarrow \langle v, \xi', \phi, \rho' \rangle$	30	$\langle d, \xi, \phi \rangle \rightarrow \langle \xi', \phi' \rangle$	37
μScheme	$\langle e, \rho, \sigma \rangle \Downarrow \langle v, \sigma' \rangle$	144	$\langle d, \rho, \sigma \rangle \rightarrow \langle \rho', \sigma' \rangle$	151
μScheme+	$\langle e/v, \rho, \sigma, S \rangle \rightarrow \langle e'/v', \rho', \sigma', S' \rangle$	215	$\langle d, \rho, \sigma \rangle \rightarrow \langle \rho', \sigma' \rangle$	222
Typed Impcore	(as in Impcore)	30		37
Typed μScheme	$\langle e, \rho, \sigma \rangle \Downarrow \langle v, \sigma' \rangle$	380	(as in Impcore)	151
nano-ML	$\langle e, \rho \rangle \Downarrow v$	405	$\langle d, \rho \rangle \rightarrow \rho'$	405
μML	$\langle e, \rho \rangle \Downarrow v$	491	(as in nano-ML)	405
	$\langle p, v \rangle \rightarrowtail r$ (pattern match)	490		

μSmalltalk		
definition	$\langle d, \xi, \sigma, \mathcal{F} \rangle \rightarrow \langle \xi', \sigma', \mathcal{F}' \rangle$	684
expression finishes	$\langle e, \rho, c_{\mathsf{super}}, F, \xi, \sigma, \mathcal{F} \rangle \Downarrow \langle v; \sigma', \mathcal{F}' \rangle$	679
expression returns	$\langle e, \rho, c_{\mathsf{super}}, F, \xi, \sigma, \mathcal{F} \rangle \Uparrow \langle v, F'; \sigma', \mathcal{F}' \rangle$	679
expressions return	$\langle [e_1, \ldots, e_n], \rho, c_{\mathsf{super}}, F, \xi, \sigma, \mathcal{F} \rangle \Uparrow \langle v, F'; \sigma', \mathcal{F}' \rangle$	679
expressions finish	$\langle [e_1, \ldots, e_n], \rho, c_{\mathsf{super}}, F, \xi, \sigma, \mathcal{F} \rangle \Downarrow \langle [v_1, \ldots, v_n]; \sigma', \mathcal{F}' \rangle$	679
primitive	$\langle p, [v_1, \ldots, v_n], \xi, \sigma, \mathcal{F} \rangle \Downarrow_p \langle v; \sigma', \mathcal{F}' \rangle$	679
method dispatch	$m \rhd c \mathbin{@} imp$	681

Typing judgments

Language	*Expression or related form*	*Page*	*Definition*	*Page*
Typed Impcore	$\Gamma_\xi, \Gamma_\phi, \Gamma_\rho \vdash e : \tau$	335	$\langle d, \Gamma_\xi, \Gamma_\phi \rangle \rightarrow \langle \Gamma'_\xi, \Gamma'_\phi \rangle$	336
Typed μScheme	$\Delta, \Gamma \vdash e : \tau$	363	$\langle d, \Gamma \rangle \rightarrow \Gamma'$	366
nano-ML	$\Gamma \vdash e : \tau$ (nondeterministic)	413	$\langle d, \Gamma \rangle \rightarrow \Gamma'$	416
	$\theta\Gamma \vdash e : \tau$ (with substitutions)	418	$\langle d, \Gamma \rangle \rightarrow \Gamma'$	416
	$C, \Gamma \vdash e : \tau$ (with constraints)	418	$\langle d, \Gamma \rangle \rightarrow \Gamma'$	416
μML	(as in nano-ML)	418	(as in nano-ML)	416
	$\Gamma, \Gamma' \vdash p : \tau$ (pattern)	496		
Molecule	(14 judgment forms are shown in Chapter 9, Figure 9.14)			565

Well-formedness judgments

Language	*Form*	*Judgment*	*Page*
Typed Impcore	Type	τ is a type	334
Typed μScheme	Kind	κ is a kind	354
	Type	$\Delta \vdash \tau :: \kappa$	355

Evaluation and type-checking functions

Language	*Evaluation* *Exp.*	*Page*	*Def.*	*Page*	*Type checking and elaboration* *Exp.*	*Page*	*Def.*	*Page*
Impcore	`eval`	48	`evaldef`	53				
μScheme	`eval`	155	`evaldef`	159				
μScheme+	`eval`	227	`evaldef`	159				
μScheme (in ML)	`eval`	309	`evaldef`	311				
Typed Impcore	`eval`	S397	`evaldef`	S398	`typeof`	338	`typdef`	341
Typed μScheme	`eval`	S411	`evaldef`	S412	`typeof` ($\mathcal{E}$)	366	`typdef` ($\mathcal{E}$)	366
nano-ML	`eval`	S429	`evaldef`	S430	`typeof`	437	`typdef`	439
μML	`ev`	492	`evalDataDef`	490	`ty`	497	`typeDataDef`	489
μSmalltalk	`eval`	688	`evaldef`	693				

Other judgments

Language	*Concept*	*Judgment*	*Page*
μScheme	Primitive equality	$v_1 \equiv v_2$	150
μScheme+	Tail position	e is in tail position	253
μScheme	Free term variable	$y \in \text{fv}(e)$	316
Typed μScheme	Free type variable	$\alpha \in \text{ftv}(\tau)$	371
Typed μScheme	Type equivalence	$\tau \equiv \tau'$	369
Typed μScheme	Capture-avoiding substitution	$\tau'[\alpha \mapsto \tau] \equiv \tau''$	374
Nano-ML	Constraint satisfied	C is satisfied	428

Tables relating judgments and functions

Language	*Evaluation*	*Type checking*
Impcore	page 40	—
μScheme (C code)	page 153	—
μScheme (ML code)	page 304	—
Typed Impcore	—	page 338
Typed μScheme	—	page 367
nano-ML	—	page 432
μML	page 492	page 491

Concrete syntax

Language	*Page*	*Language*	*Page*
Impcore	18	nano-ML	404
μScheme	93	μML	467
μScheme+	203	Molecule	536
Typed Impcore	330	μSmalltalk	628
Typed μScheme	353		

Symbols and notation, in order of appearance

Impcore

$::=$ defines a syntactic category in a grammar, page 17
$|$ separates alternatives in a grammar, page 17
$\{\cdots\}$ repeatable syntax in a grammar, page 17
ξ global-variable environment ("ksee"), page 28
ϕ function environment ("fee"), page 29
ρ value environment ("roe"), page 29
x object-language variable, page 29
v value, page 29
$\mapsto$ shows binding in function or environment, page 29
y object-language variable, page 29
$\{\}$ empty environment, page 29
d definition, page 30
e expression, page 30
$\langle\cdots\rangle$ brackets wrapping abstract-machine state, page 30
$\oplus$ object-language operator, page 30
$\Downarrow$ relates initial and final states of big-step evaluation ("yields"), page 30
dom domain of an environment or function, page 32
$\in$ membership in a set, page 32
f name of object-language function, page 36
$\rightarrow$ relates initial and final states in evalution of definitions, page 37
$\triangleq$ defines syntactic sugar, page 66
$[\![\cdots]\!]$ brackets used to wrap syntax ("Oxford brackets"), page 81
$[\cdots]$ optional syntax in a grammar, page 86

μScheme

$\mathcal{P}$ in a mini-index, marks a primitive function ("primitive"), page 95
$O(\cdots)$ asymptotic complexity, page 100
k a key in an association list, page 105
a an attribute in an association list, page 105
$\{\cdots\}$ justification of a step in an equational proof, page 114
$(\!|\cdots|\!)$ a closure, page 122
$\circ$ function composition ("composed with"), page 125
$::$ infix notation for `cons` ("cons"), page 128
$\vee$ disjunction ("or"), page 139
$\neg$ Boolean complement ("not"), page 139
σ the store: a mapping of locations to values ("sigma"), page 144
$\subseteq$ the subset relation, reflexively closed ("subset"), page 181

μScheme+

$[]$ an empty stack ("empty"), page 210
F frame on an evaluation stack ("frame"), page 210
S evaluation stack, page 210
$\bullet$ a hole in an evaluation context ("hole"), page 211
$e \rightsquigarrow e'$ lowering transformation ("lowerexp"), page 214

$\rightarrow$	the reduction relation in a small-step semantics ("steps to"), page 215
e/v	abstract-machine component: either an expression or a value, page 215
$\rightarrow^*$	the reflexive, transitive closure of the reduction relation ("normalizes to"), page 215
C	an evaluation context in a traditional semantics, page 241
λ	the Greek way of writing `lambda`, page 242

Garbage collection

H	the size of the heap, page 260
L	the amount of live data, page 261
γ	the ratio of heap size to live data ("gamma"), page 262

Type systems

τ	a type ("tau"), page 333
Γ	type environment; maps term variable to its type ("gamma"), page 333
$\rightarrow$	in a function type, separates the argument types from the result type ("arrow"), page 334
$\times$	in a function type, separates the types of the arguments ("cross"), page 334
$\vdash$	in a judgment, separates context from conclusion ("turnstile"), page 335
$e : \tau$	ascribes type τ to term e ("e has type τ"), page 335
$\rightarrow$	relates type environments before and after typing of definition, page 336
μ	a type constructor ("mew"), page 347
$\times$	forms pair types or product types (multiplication is $\cdot$ on page S15) ("cross"), page 348
$+$	used to form sum types, page 349
$[\![\tau]\!]$	the set of values associated with type τ, page 350
κ	a kind, which classifies types ("kappa"), page 354
$*$	the kind ascribed to types that classify terms ("type"), page 354
$\Rightarrow$	used to form kinds of type *constructors* ("arrow"), page 354
$\tau :: \kappa$	ascribes kind κ to type τ ("τ has kind κ"), page 354
Δ	a kind environment ("delta"), page 354
α, β, γ	type variables ("alpha, beta, gamma"), page 356
$\forall$	used to write quantified, polymorphic types ("for all"), page 356
$(\tau_1, \ldots, \tau_n)\ \tau$	τ applied to type parameters $\tau_1, \ldots, \tau_n$, page 357
$\equiv$	type equivalence, page 369
$\cap$	set intersection, page 374
$\emptyset$	the empty set ("empty"), page 374

Type inference

σ	a type scheme ("sigma"), page 408
θ	a substitution ("THAYT-uh"), page 409
$\leqslant$	the instance relation ("instance of"), page 410
θ_I	the identity substitution, page 411
$\tau \sim \tau'$	simple type-equality constraint ("τ must equal τ'"), page 418
C	type-equality constraint, page 418
$\mathbf{T}$	the trivial type-equality constraint, page 420
$\equiv$	equivalence of constraints, page 432

Abstract data types

$\wr\cdots\int$	bag brackets, page 550
$<:$	the subtype relation, page 561

Introduction

The implementation exercises, for all my frustration while doing them, are tremendously valuable. I find that actually implementing something like type inference or continuations greatly enhances my understanding of it, and testable programs are much easier to play with and build intuition about than are pages of equations.

Russ Cox

This book is about programming languages—and also about programming. Each of these things is made better by the other. If you program but you don't know about programming languages, your code may be longer, uglier, less robust, and harder to debug than it could be. If you know about programming languages but you don't program, what is your knowledge for? To know a language is good, but to use it well is better.

What should you know? Not as many languages as possible. Master a few language-design ideas of lasting value: learn what they are, how to recognize them, and how to use them. Focus on the best the field has to offer.

The field of programming languages is about more than just programming; it offers rigorous, formal techniques for describing *all* computational processes, for analyzing language features, and for proving properties of programs. The formal tools are used by professionals to communicate their ideas concisely and effectively. Practice with formal tools will help you to see past superficial differences in programming languages, to recognize old ideas when they appear in new languages, to evaluate new programming languages, and to choose and use programming languages intelligently. But formalism is in second place here; programming comes first.

What you will learn and how

Programming Languages: Build, Prove, and Compare helps you *use* programming languages effectively, *describe* programming languages precisely, and *understand* and *enjoy* the diversity of programming languages. You will learn by experimenting with and comparing code written in different languages. You will use important programming-language features to write interesting code, understand how each feature is implemented, and see how different languages are similar and how each one is distinctive.

You will code in and experiment with small *bridge languages,* which illuminate essential features that you will see repeatedly throughout your career. Each bridge language is small enough to learn, but big enough to act as a bridge to the real thing. The main bridge languages—μScheme, μML, Molecule, and μSmalltalk—are rich enough to write programs that are interesting, and they are distilled from languages whose greatness is widely acknowledged: designers behind Scheme, ML, CLU, and Smalltalk have all won ACM Turing Awards, which is the highest professional honor a computer scientist can receive. Their designs have influenced many languages that are fashionable today, including Racket, Clojure, Rust, Haskell, Python, Java, JavaScript, Objective C, Ruby, Swift, and Erlang.

Four other bridge languages are suitable for writing toy programs only: Impcore, Typed Impcore, Typed μScheme, and nano-ML are intended for conveying ideas, not for programming.

All the bridge languages share the same, simple concrete syntax, in which every expression is wrapped in parentheses. Uniform syntax helps you ignore superficial differences and focus on essentials. Each bridge language is also implemented by an interpreter, which runs the code you write. The interpreter helps you master the abstract world of formalism—in each chapter, you can compare mathematical descriptions of language ideas with the code that implements those ideas. And you can use the interpreters to create your own language designs. Whether your own design explores a variation on one of mine or goes in a completely different direction, trying new design ideas for yourself—and programming with the results—will give you a feel for the problems of language design, which you can't get just by studying existing languages. Don't let other people have all the fun!

The book helps you learn in three ways:

- *Build, and learn by doing.* You will learn by building and modifying programs. You will write code in the bridge languages, and you will modify the interpreters.

  Once you build things, you may want to share them with others, such as potential employers. My own students' work is more than worthy of a professional portfolio. But if you share your work using a public site like Github or Bitbucket, please share this part of your portfolio only with individuals that you name—please don't put your work in a public repository.

- *Prove, to keep things simple and precise.* A proof enables an expert to know that an optimized program behaves the same as the original, or that no program in a safe language can ever result in an unexplained core dump. Practice with proof will help you understand what you can and can't count on from a language and its implementation. Try some exercises in language metatheory (Chapter 1), equational reasoning (Chapters 2 and 8), and type-system metatheory (Chapters 6 and 7).

- *Compare, and find several ways to understand.* We all learn more easily when we compare new ideas with what we already know—and with each other. You will learn syntax, for example, by seeing it in two forms: concrete and abstract. (Concrete syntax says how a language is written; it's something every programmer learns. Abstract syntax, which may be new to you, says what the underlying structure of a language is; it's the best way to think about what a language can say.) You can compare these two ways of writing one syntax, and you can also compare the syntaxes of *different* languages. The syntax of each new bridge language uses a new form only when it is needed to express a new feature; if a feature is found in multiple bridge languages, it is written using the same syntax each time. Things look different only when they *are* different.

  To learn about the meanings of language constructs, you can compare an interpreter with an operational semantics. Learning about interpretation and operational semantics together is easier than learning about each separately.

To learn powerful programming techniques, including recursion, higher-order functions, and polymorphism, you can compare example programs both large and small. At first you'll compare example programs written in a single language, but eventually you will also compare examples written in different languages.

You'll accomplish all this by doing exercises. In each chapter, exercises are organized by the skills they require or develop, with cross-reference to the most relevant sections. And the exercises are preceded by short questions intended for "retrieval practice," which helps bring knowledge to the front of your mind. Doing exercises will help you learn how a semantics is constructed, how an interpreter works, and most important, how to write great code. Each of these avenues to learning reinforces the others, and you can emphasize what suits you best.

THE BOOK IN DETAIL

Don't try to read this book cover to cover. Instead, choose languages and chapters that work for you. To help you choose, I introduce the languages and chapters here. The introductions sometimes use jargon like "operational semantics," "polymorphism," or "garbage collection," because such jargon tells an expert exactly what's here. If you're not expert yet, don't worry—there are also some longer explanations. And use the figures! Figure I.1 (on the next page) shows how the later chapters depend on earlier ones, and Tables I.2 and I.3 summarize, respectively, the main theory concepts and programming techniques for each language. All three, like the book, are divided into two parts: foundational features and features for programming at scale.

Foundations

Technical study starts with *abstract syntax* and *operational semantics,* which specify what a language is and what it does. These specifications are implemented by *definitional interpreters.* The first specifications and implementation are presented in the context of a tiny procedural language, *Impcore,* which is the subject of Chapter 1. Impcore includes the familiar imperative constructs that are found at the core of mainstream programming languages: loops, conditionals, procedures, and mutable variables. Impcore doesn't introduce any new or unusual language features; instead it introduces the professional way of thinking about familiar language features in terms of abstract syntax and operational semantics. Impcore also introduces the interpreters.

Using abstract syntax, operational semantics, and a definitional interpreter, *μScheme* (Chapter 2) introduces two new language features. First, it introduces *S-expressions,* a recursive datatype. S-expressions are most naturally processed using recursion, not iteration; this change has far-reaching effects on programming style. μScheme also introduces *first-class, nested functions,* which are treated as values, can be stored in data structures, can be passed to functions, and can be returned from functions. Functions that accept or return functions are called *higher-order functions,* and their use leads to a concise, powerful, and distinctive programming style: *functional programming.* μScheme is used to explore simple recursive functions, higher-order functions, standard higher-order functions on lists, continuation-passing style, and equational reasoning. These new ideas require only a handful of new language features and primitive functions: μScheme extends Impcore by adding `let`, `lambda`, `cons`, `car`, `cdr`, and `null?`.

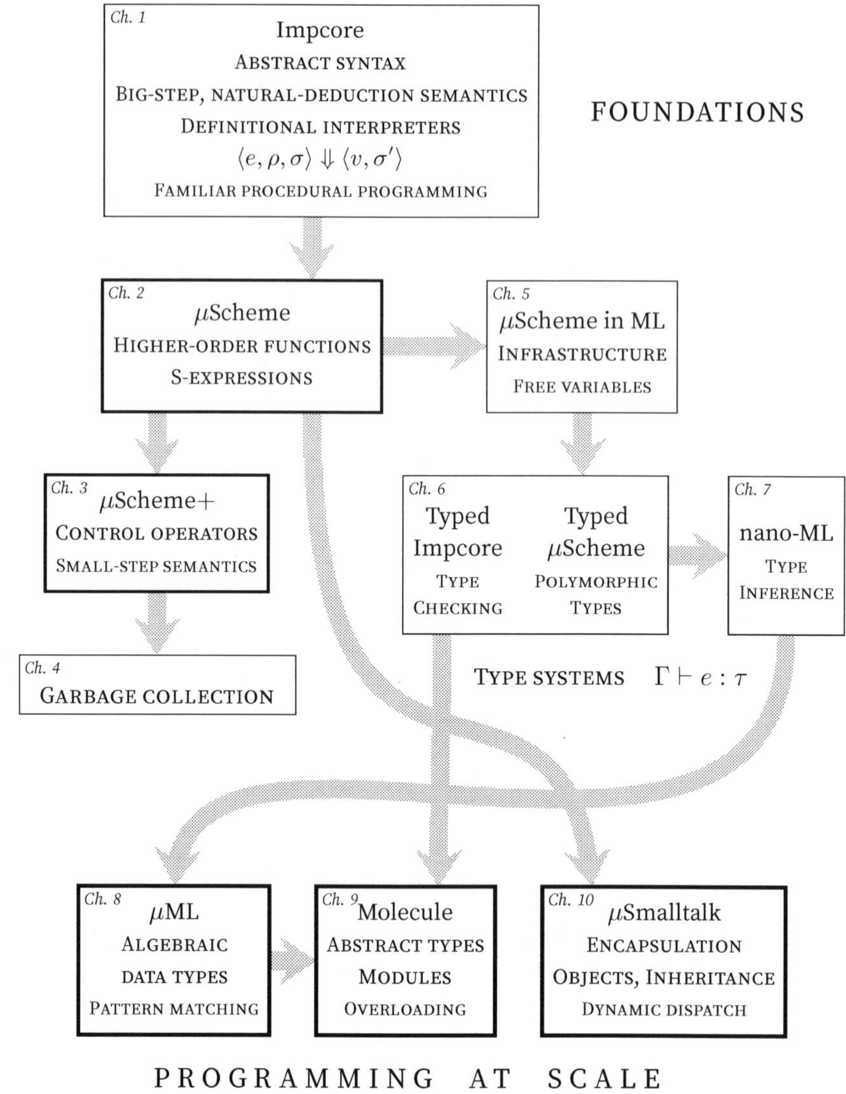

Figure I.1: Topics and languages in this book

Impcore and μScheme underlie everything else. The subsequent foundational chapters are divided into two independent parts: one focused on memory management and one focused on types. *μScheme+* (Chapter 3) extends μScheme with *control operators*: `break`, `continue`, `return`, `try-catch`, and `throw`. Control operators are supported by a *small-step operational semantics* and a different style of definitional interpreter; both are based on a so-called CESK machine, which uses an explicit stack for evaluation. The new semantics and interpreter are the primary reasons to study Chapter 3; you'll learn how exceptions can be implemented, and you'll see a semantics that can model interaction and nontermination. And in Chapter 4, you can extend the interpreter with *garbage collectors*.

Table I.2: Theory and concepts in each bridge language

Language	*New theory or concepts*
Impcore	Abstract syntax, big-step operational semantics
μScheme	Mutable locations, capturing environment in a closure, algebraic laws
μScheme+	Control operators, small-step semantics, garbage collection
Typed Impcore	Typechecking a monomorphic language
Typed μScheme	Parametric polymorphism
nano-ML	Type inference using equality constraints
μML	Algebraic data types
Molecule	Abstract types, modules, bounded polymorphism, separately compiled interfaces, and operator overloading
μSmalltalk	Objects, classes, and inheritance

Garbage collection enables programs written in Scheme and other safe languages to allocate new memory as needed, without worrying about where memory comes from or where it goes. Garbage collection simplifies both programming and interface design, and it is a hallmark of civilized programming. It supports all the other languages in the book. In Chapter 4, you can learn about garbage collection by building both mark-and-sweep and copying garbage collectors for μScheme+. You can even build a simple generational collector. If you master Chapters 1 to 4, you will have substantial experience connecting programming-language ideas to interpreters.

Independent of μScheme+ and garbage collection, you can proceed directly from μScheme to *type systems*. Type systems demand a change in the implementation language: while C is a fine language for writing garbage collectors, it is not so good for writing type checkers or sophisticated interpreters. Such tools are more easily implemented in a language that provides algebraic data types and pattern matching. The simplest, most stable, and most readily available such language is Standard ML, which is used from Chapter 5 onward. To acclimate you to Standard ML, Chapter 5 reimplements μScheme using Standard ML. That reimplementation provides infrastructure used in subsequent chapters, including chapters on type systems.

In Chapter 6, type systems are presented for two languages: *Typed Impcore,* a monomorphic, statically typed dialect of Impcore, and *Typed μScheme,* a polymorphic, statically typed dialect of μScheme. Both type systems illustrate formation rules, introduction rules, and elimination rules, with connections to logic. And in the exercises, both systems can be implemented by *type checkers.* A type checker embodies the rules by using type annotations, on formal parameters and elsewhere, to determine the type of every expression in a program.

Typed μScheme is super expressive, and its type system, when suitably specialized or extended, can describe many real languages, from the simple Hindley-Milner types of Standard ML to complex features like Haskell type classes or Java generics. But considered as a programming language, Typed μScheme is most unpleasant: it requires a type annotation not just on every function definition, but on every *use* of a polymorphic function. A better approach is to add type annotations automatically, using *type inference.*

Table I.3: Programming technique in each bridge language

Language	New programming technique
Impcore	Untyped procedural programming
μScheme	Recursive functions on lists and S-expressions; higher-order functions; continuation-passing style
μScheme+	Coding with `break`, `continue`, `return`, `try-catch`, `throw`
Typed Impcore	Typed procedural programming with numbers, arrays, and Booleans
Typed μScheme	Polymorphic functions with explicit types and explicit generalization and instantiation
nano-ML	Polymorphic functions with inferred types and implicit generalization and instantiation
μML	Algebraic data types and pattern matching
Molecule	Abstract data types and modules; operator overloading
μSmalltalk	Control structured using dynamic dispatch and continuations

Type inference is demonstrated in Chapter 7, using the language nano-ML. Nano-ML is derived from untyped μScheme, and it uses almost the same data: numbers, symbols, Booleans, lists, and functions. But like Typed μScheme, nano-ML is type-safe, and yet it does not need to be annotated—the type of every parameter, variable, and function is inferred. Type inference helps make code short, simple, reusable, and reliable. And in Chapter 7, you can learn how type inference works by implementing it for yourself. I recommend an algorithm based on conjunctions of type-equality constraints, which can be solved by unification.

Programming at scale

Operational semantics, functions, and types are everywhere. These concepts provide a foundation for the second part of the book, which presents mechanisms that programmers rely on when working at scale. These mechanisms revolve around *data abstraction,* which hides representations that are likely to change. Data abstraction enables components of large systems to be built independently and to evolve independently.

Representations worth hiding need more ways of structuring data than just the arrays, lists, and atomic types found in Typed Impcore, Typed μScheme, and nano-ML. To structure arbitrarily sophisticated representations, a language needs grouping (like `struct`), choice (like `union`), and recursion. All three capabilities are combined in inductively defined *algebraic data types.* In Chapter 8, algebraic data types are demonstrated using *μML.* μML can define algebraic data types and can inspect their values using *case expressions* and *pattern matching.* These ideas are central to languages like Haskell, Standard ML, OCaml, Scala, Agda, Idris, and Coq/Gallina.

Once defined, representations can usefully be hidden using abstract data types, objects, or both. In Chapter 9, abstract data types are demonstrated using *Molecule,* which builds on μML's algebraic data types. Abstract types are defined inside *modules,* and they hide information using types: a representation of abstract type can be accessed only by code that is in the same module as the type's definition. Access is controlled by a polymorphic type checker like the one in Typed μScheme. Abstract types and modules are found in languages as diverse as CLU, Modula-2, Ada, Oberon, Standard ML, OCaml, and Haskell. (Molecule is a new design inspired by Modula-3, OCaml, and CLU.)

In Chapter 10, objects are demonstrated using *μSmalltalk*. Objects hide information using names: the parts of an object's representation can be named only by code that is associated with that object, not by code that is associated with other objects. Unlike such hybrid languages as Ada 95, Java, C#, C++, Modula-3, Objective C, and Swift, μSmalltalk is *purely* object-oriented: every value is an object, and the basic unit of control flow is message passing. Any message can be sent to any object. Objects are created by sending messages to *classes*, which are also objects, and classes *inherit* state and implementation from parent classes, which enables new forms of code reuse. The mechanisms are simple, but remarkably expressive.

Parting advice

This book is not a meal; it's a buffet. Don't try to eat the whole thing. Pick out a few tidbits that look appetizing, taste them, and do a few exercises. Digest what you've learned, rest, and repeat. If you work hard, then you, like my students, will be impressed at how much skill and knowledge you develop, and how you'll be able to apply it even to languages you will have never seen before.

Part I. Foundations

Chapter 1 contents

1 An imperative core

Von Neumann programming languages use variables to imitate the computer's storage cells; control statements elaborate its jump and test instructions; and assignment statements imitate its fetching, storing, and arithmetic... Each assignment statement produces a one-word result. The program must cause these statements to be executed many times in order to make the desired overall change in the store, since it must be done one word at a time.

John Backus, *Can Programming Be Liberated from the von Neumann Style?*

In your prior programming experience, you may have used a *procedural* language such as Ada 83, Algol 60, C, Cobol, Fortran, Modula-2, or Pascal. Or you may have used a procedural language extended with object-oriented features, such as Ada 95, C#, C++, Eiffel, Java, Modula-3, Objective C, or Python—although these hybrid languages support an object-oriented style, they are often used procedurally. Procedural programming is a well-developed style with identifiable characteristics:

- Code is organized into *procedures*; a procedure is a sequence of *commands*, each of which tells the computer, "do something!" ("Command" is what we said in the 1960s; these days, we say "statement.") A command is executed for its *effects* on the state of the machine; procedures continually change the "mutable state" of the machine—the values contained in the various machine words—by assignment.

  Each command in a procedure can itself be implemented by another procedure, and so on; procedures can be designed from the top down using *stepwise refinement* (Wirth 1971).

- Data is processed one word at a time; words are commonly organized into arrays or records. An array is typically processed by a loop, and a record is typically processed by a sequence of commands; these control constructs reflect an element-by-element approach to data processing. Loops are typically written using "structured" looping constructs such as `for` and `while`; recursive procedures are not commonly used.

- Both control and data mimic machine architecture. The control constructs `if` and `while` combine conditional and unconditional jump instructions in simple ways; `goto`, when present, exposes the machine's unconditional jump. Arrays and records are implemented by contiguous blocks of memory. Pointers are addresses; assignment is often limited to what can be accomplished by a single load or store instruction.

Mimicking a machine has its advantages: costs can be easy to predict, and a debugger can be built by adapting a machine-level debugger.

The procedural style can be embodied in a language. In this chapter, that language is *Impcore*. Impcore is named for the standard imperative core—assignments, loops, conditionals, and procedures—that is found in almost all programming languages, including not only "imperative" or "procedural" languages but also many "functional" and "object-oriented" languages. Impcore is best explained by example, so let's start by defining a global variable n, which is initialized to 3:

12a. ⟨*transcript* 12a⟩≡ 12b ▷

```
-> (val n 3)
3
```

The arrow "-> " is the interpreter's prompt; text following a prompt is my input; and text on the next line is the interpreter's response:[1]

To continue, let's define a function, which I'll name x-3-plus-1. It multiplies a number k times 3, then adds 1 to the product:

12b. ⟨*transcript* 12a⟩+≡ ◁ 12a 12c ▷

```
-> (define x-3-plus-1 (k)
      (+ (* 3 k) 1))                ;; returns 3 * k + 1
```

The syntax may look different from what you are used to, including the dashes in the function's name, but before we dive into the differences, let's compute with the variable n and function x-3-plus-1 that I just defined. I use them in a loop that tries to reduce n to 1 by halving n when it is even and replacing it with $3n + 1$ when it is odd. (This loop is believed to terminate for any positive n, but at press time, no proof is known.) In the loop, each line of Impcore code is commented with analogous C code on the right; if you know C, C++, Java, JavaScript, or something similar, the comments should help you interpret Impcore's syntax.

12c. ⟨*transcript* 12a⟩+≡ ◁ 12b 21a ▷

```
-> (begin                                  ;; {
      (while (> n 1)                       ;;   while (n > 1)
         (begin                            ;;     {
            (println n)                    ;;       printf("%d\n", n);
            (if (= (mod n 2) 0)            ;;       if (n % 2 == 0)
                (set n (/ n 2))            ;;         n = n / 2;
                (set n (x-3-plus-1 n)))))) ;;       else n = x_3_plus_1(n); }
      n)                                   ;;   return n; }
3
10
5
16
8
4
2
1
```

In these examples, you might notice that

- Where C uses curly brackets, Impcore uses begin.
- Impcore doesn't use else or return keywords.
- Impcore uses a lot of ugly parentheses, but no commas.
- Impcore puts operators like +, *, >, =, and / in places that might look strange.

[1] Most of the examples in this book are written using the Noweb system for *literate programming*. Bold labels such as **12a** identify chunks of examples or code, and pointers such as "12b ▷" point to subsequent chunks. Noweb is explained more fully in Section 1.6 on page 39.

Impcore, like every other language in this book, uses *fully parenthesized, prefix* syntax, in which each operator precedes its arguments. C uses *infix* syntax; each binary operator appears between its arguments. In C's infix syntax, order of evaluation is determined by "operator precedence," which is fine for stuff you use every day—but not so good when you have to figure out whether & and && have the same precedence and where they both stand with respect to |. In Impcore's prefix syntax, order of evaluation is determined by parentheses; it might be ugly, but you don't have to remember any operator precedence. Prefix parenthesized syntax, which is used in Scheme, Common Lisp, Emacs Lisp, Racket, Clojure, and the many other languages of the Lisp family, puts every operator and every programmer on the same footing—the parentheses eliminate any possible ambiguity.

These examples show Impcore, which is going to help us look at programming languages in a deep, systematic way. But first, let's get the big picture of what aspects we will look at.

1.1 LOOKING AT LANGUAGES

A program is ultimately formed from the individual characters of its code. And before code runs, it passes through several different phases, each of which is governed by its own rules. Phases and their rules can be hard to identify, but for any programming language, three sets of rules are essential. They tell us

- How code is formed
- What checking it undergoes before it is deemed OK to run
- What happens when it runs

To highlight these rules, let's look at some code that breaks them. Because some of the rules involve type checking, we'll look at some C code. (If C is not so familiar, try thinking about Java, which has the same kinds of rules.)

Imagine that I have a two-dimensional point on the plane, and that I want to add 3 to its x coordinate. In C, a point p can be defined like this:

```
struct { int x; int y; } p;
```

To add 3 to p's x coordinate, I write an assignment statement. But if a letter x is deleted by a cat that walks across my keyboard, the cat might leave this code:

```
p. = p.x + 3;
```

This code is rejected by the C compiler, which reports a *syntax error*. The compiler might flag the = sign after the dot, where it would prefer a name. The code is *ill formed*.

I know I want the = sign, and if I'm programming after midnight, I might just remove the dot:

mod 27c

```
p = p.x + 3;
```

This code is well formed, but a C compiler will report a *type error*: p is not the type of thing you can assign a number to. The code is *ill typed*.

The code I meant to write is

```
p.x = p.x + 3;
```

This code is well formed and well typed, and the compiler is happy. But a happy compiler doesn't guarantee a happy program. Suppose I write

```
int n = 0;
p.x = p.x / n;
```


This code is also well formed and well typed, so it makes the compiler happy, but when it runs, nothing good will happen. The best I can hope for is that my operating system will report a *run-time error*, maybe a "floating-point exception." (The example exhibits what the C standard calls "undefined behavior," which the system is not obligated to report.) The code is *ill behaved.*

Useful code is well formed, well typed, and well behaved. Learning precisely what that means, for several different languages, is half of this book. (The other half is learning how to use the languages effectively.) The key concepts are as follows:

- Code is formed according to two sets of rules: Characters are clumped into groups called *tokens* according to *lexical* rules, and tokens are grouped into definitions, statements, and so on according to *syntactic* rules. The syntactic rules are the important ones. Syntax is so important that we talk about two varieties: *concrete syntax,* which is how we write the code, and *abstract syntax,* which is how we think about the code's structure. Impcore's concrete and abstract syntax are presented in Sections 1.2 and 1.3, respectively.

- Although there are myriad ways that code can be checked before it is deemed OK to run, the most practical method is *type checking,* which follows the rules of a *static type system.* Impcore does not have a static type system; type checking and its companion, *type inference,* are not explored in depth until Chapters 6 and 7.

- The behavior of running code is specified by its *semantics* (sometimes called *dynamic semantics*). Semantics can be written in several different styles, but this book uses *operational semantics,* a style that has dominated the field since the 1990s. Operational semantics has a learning curve, and to help you climb it, each language in this book is implemented by an *interpreter.* The interpreter demonstrates what the language's semantics is trying to tell us, and by enabling us to run code, it also helps us learn to use the language effectively.

  The operational semantics of Impcore is presented in Section 1.5. In Section 1.6, the operational semantics is used to guide the construction of Impcore's interpreter, and in Section 1.7, the operational semantics is used to prove properties of Impcore code.

To understand *any* language's operational semantics or type system, you must first know how its programs are formed. To learn, try this approach:

1. Understand the lexical structure, especially of things like comments and string literals.

2. Look for familiar *syntactic categories* (page 16), like definitions, declarations, statements, expressions, and types.

3. In each category, look for familiar *forms*: loops, conditionals, function applications, and so on. To identify what's familiar, mentally translate concrete syntax into abstract syntax.

This approach calls for an understanding of lexical structure, grammars, and the two varieties of syntax.

Lexical structure

Lexical structure rarely requires much thought. If you can spot comments, string literals, and token boundaries, you're good to go. For example, in C, you need to see `3*n+1` as 5 tokens, `"3*n+1"` as a single token (a string literal), and `/*3*n+1*/` as no tokens at all (just a comment). In this book's bridge languages, a comment begins with a semicolon, there are no string literals, and token boundaries are found only at brackets or whitespace. For example, in Impcore, `3*n+1` is a single token (a name).

Grammars

Concrete syntax is specified using a *grammar*, which tells us what sequences of tokens are well formed. For example, the following toy grammar shows four ways to form an expression *exp*:

$$exp ::= \textit{variable-name} \mid \textit{numeral} \mid exp + exp \mid exp * exp.$$

The grammar says that an expression may be a variable, a numeral, the sum of two expressions, or the product of two expressions. Each alternative is a *syntactic form*.

This grammar, like any grammar, can be used to *produce* an expression by replacing *exp* with any of the four alternatives on the right-hand side, and continuing recursively until every *exp* has been replaced with a variable or a numeral. For example, the C expression `3 * n + 1` can be produced in this way.

The toy grammar is *compositional*: big expressions are made by composing smaller ones. Every interesting programming-language grammar supports some kind of composition; even an assembly language allows you to compose long sequences of instructions by concatenating shorter sequences. Compositional syntactic structure is part of what makes something a programming language. More compositional structure can be found in the grammar for Impcore (page 18).

Two varieties of syntax

When we *write concrete* syntax, we should be *thinking* about *abstract* syntax. For example, concrete syntax tells us that the "$3n + 1$" loop is written using a `while` keyword, and that in C the loop condition goes between round brackets (parentheses). But we should be thinking "`while` loop with a condition and a body," which is what abstract syntax tells us: it names the form (WHILE) and says that a WHILE loop is formed from an expression (the condition) and a statement (the body). Abstract syntax ignores syntactic markers like keywords and brackets.

Abstract syntax helps us recognize familiar forms even when they are clothed in unfamiliar concrete syntax. For example, you can probably recognize loops written in C, Icon, Impcore, Python, Modula-3, Scala, and Standard ML:

```
while (n > 1) n = n / 2;
while n > 1 do n := n / 2
(while (> n 1) (set n (/ n 2))
while n > 1: n = n / 2
WHILE n > 1 DO n := n / 2 END
while (n > 1) { n = n / 2; }
while !n > 1 do n := !n div 2
```

Each language uses a different concrete syntax, but abstract syntax provides a kind of X-ray vision: under their clothes, all these loops are the same.

Abstract syntax is not just a tool for thought. It also gives us *abstract-syntax trees*, the data structure used to represent code in most compilers and interpreters.

In this book, abstract-syntax trees appear in C code (Chapters 1 to 3) and in Standard ML code (Chapters 5 to 10). Abstract syntax also provides a compact notation for operational semantics and type systems. Using such a notation, all the `while` loops above would be written the same way: WHILE(e, s), where e stands for the condition and s stands for the body.

Familiar syntactic categories and forms

Abstract syntax is rarely specified explicitly; you'll almost always infer it by reading a grammar that describes concrete syntax. A real grammar will have many left-hand sides like *exp*; these symbols are called *nonterminal symbols*, or just *nonterminals*. Sometimes the nonterminals tell you exactly what the important phrases in a language are, but if the grammar has been engineered primarily to help a compiler to convert its input into an abstract-syntax tree, many nonterminals will be annoying or distracting. For example, a nonterminal like *explist1* (a list of one or more expressions separated by commas) adds nothing to our understanding.

To understand the structure of a grammar, search the nonterminals for *syntactic categories*. A syntactic category is a group of syntactic forms that share an important role; for example, the role of an expression is to be evaluated to produce a value (and possibly also have a *side effect*). Typically, two phrases in the same syntactic category can be interchanged without affecting the well-formedness of a program. For example, any of these expressions could be used on the right-hand side of the assignment to `p.x`:

```
p.x + 3            p.x / n            p->next            2 * p
```

Assigning any of these expressions to `p.x` would be well formed, but as shown above, the division `p.x / n` might not be well behaved, and the assignments of `p->next` and `2 * p` aren't well typed.

Syntactic categories aren't arbitrary, and in any programming language, there are at least four common categories worth looking for:

- A *definition* introduces a new thing and gives it a name. Forms to look for include forms that define functions, variables, and maybe types; Impcore marks its function-definition and variable-definition forms with keywords `define` and `val`.
- A *declaration* introduces a new thing, with a name, but doesn't yet define the thing—instead, a declaration promises that the thing is defined elsewhere. Because anything that can be declared eventually has to be defined, the forms to look for are forms for declaring things that can be defined. In C and C++, declaration forms are mostly found in `.h` files. Impcore has no declaration forms; in this book, declaration forms aren't used until Chapter 9.
- An *expression* is evaluated to produce a value, and possibly also have a side effect. Forms to look for include variables, literal values, function applications, maybe infix operators, and hopefully a conditional form (like C's ternary expression e_1 `?` e_2 `:` e_3). Impcore has all these forms except infix operators.
- A *statement* is executed for side effect; it doesn't produce a value. Side effects might include printing, changing the value of a variable, or changing some value in memory, among others. Forms to look for include loops (`while`, `for`), conditionals (`if`), sequencing (`begin`), and if you're lucky, a `case` or `switch` statement. Impcore doesn't actually have statements; its `while` and `if` forms are expressions.

Impcore's lack of statements might surprise you, but it's a well-known design choice. Providing loops and conditionals as expressions, not statements, makes a language *expression-oriented*. All functional languages are expression-oriented; among procedural languages, Icon is expression-oriented (Griswold and Griswold 1996); and among languages with object-oriented features, Scala is expression-oriented (Odersky, Spoon, and Venners 2019). Making a language expression-oriented simplifies the syntax a bit; for example, an expression-oriented language needs only one conditional form, whereas a language like C has both a conditional statement and a conditional expression.

With your eye out for familiar definition and expression forms, you're ready to be fully introduced to Impcore.

1.2 THE IMPCORE LANGUAGE

An Impcore program is a sequence of *definitions*, each of which contains at least one *expression*. Definitions come in two main forms: a definition of a variable, such as `(val n 5)`, and a definition of a function, such as `(define double (x) (+ x x))`. Impcore is implemented by an interactive interpreter, and because it's wonderfully convenient to be able to type in an expression, have it evaluated, and see the result, Impcore also counts an expression, such as `(+ 2 2)`, as a "definition"—in this case, a definition of the global variable `it`. The global variable `it` thereby "remembers the last expression typed in." (The variable `it` has played this special role in interactive interpreters for over thirty years.)

With the big picture of definitions and expressions in mind, we're ready to look at the complete lexical and syntactic structure of Impcore—how programs are formed—and some more examples.

1.2.1 Lexical structure and concrete syntax

Impcore fits the model described on page 14: the rules for forming programs are divided into lexical rules and syntactic rules. The lexical rules, with only minor variations, are the same for all the languages in the book:

- A semicolon starts a comment, which runs to the end of the line on which it appears.
- Each bracket character—`(`, `)`, `[`, `]`, `{`, or `}`—is a token by itself. Impcore uses only the round and square brackets, not the curly ones.
- Other characters are clumped into tokens that are as long as possible; a token ends only at a bracket, a semicolon, or whitespace.
- Aside from its role in delimiting tokens, whitespace is ignored.

If you're used to C or Java, these rules may surprise you in a one small way: inputs like `x+y` and `3rd` are *single* tokens—in Impcore, each is a valid name!

In this book, syntactic rules—that is, grammars—are written using Extended Backus-Naur Form, usually abbreviated as EBNF. EBNF is based on plain BNF, which is ubiquitous. BNF has been extended in many different ways, and the EBNF I use is best understood through an example: the grammar for Impcore, which appears in Figure 1.1 on the next page. (ENBF is explained more fully in Appendix A.)

Figure 1.1, like any other grammar, lists nonterminal symbols like *def*, *unit-test*, *exp*, and so on. Each nonterminal is followed by the ::= symbol (pronounced "produces"), followed by the forms of the phrases that the nonterminal can produce. Alternative forms are separated by vertical bars, as (one thing | another). In each

def	::=	`(val` *variable-name exp*`)`
	|	*exp*
	|	`(define` *function-name* `(`*formals*`)` *exp*`)`
	|	`(use` *file-name*`)`
	|	*unit-test*
unit-test	::=	`(check-expect` *exp exp*`)`
	|	`(check-assert` *exp*`)`
	|	`(check-error` *exp*`)`
exp	::=	*literal*
	|	*variable-name*
	|	`(set` *variable-name exp*`)`
	|	`(if` *exp exp exp*`)`
	|	`(while` *exp exp*`)`
	|	`(begin` {*exp*}`)`
	|	`(`*function-name* {*exp*}`)`
formals	::=	{*variable-name*}
literal	::=	*numeral*
numeral	::=	token composed only of digits, possibly prefixed with a plus or minus sign
any *-*name*	::=	token that is not a bracket, a *numeral*, or one of the "reserved" words shown in `typewriter font`

Any syntactic form that is written with a matching pair of round brackets `(` ⋯ `)` may equally well be written with a matching pair of square brackets `[` ⋯ `]`. They mean the same.

Figure 1.1: Concrete syntax of Impcore

syntactic form, a token that is supposed to appear literally (like `val` or `while`) is written in `typewriter font`; a name that stands for a token or for a sequence of tokens (like *def*, *variable-name*, or *exp*) is written in *italic font*. Finally, a phrase that can be repeated is written in curly brackets, like the {*exp*} in the `begin` form; a `begin` may contain any number of *exp*s, including zero.

Figure 1.1 confirms that Impcore's concrete syntax is fully parenthesized; wherever a sequence of tokens appears, that sequence is wrapped in brackets. You may find this syntax unattractive, especially in complex expressions. But when you're learning multiple languages, it's great not to have to worry about operator precedence. And when you must write a deeply nested expression with a ton of brackets, you can reveal its structure by mixing round and square brackets—as long as round matches round and square matches square, the two shapes are interchangeable.

Figure 1.1 begins with definitions. The definition form `(val x` e`)` defines a new global variable `x` and initializes it to the value of the expression e. A global variable must be defined before it is used or assigned to. Next, any expression *exp* may be used as a definition form; it defines or assigns to the global variable `it`. And the definition form `(define f (`$x_1 \cdots x_n$`)` e`)` defines a function `f` with formal parameters x_1 to x_n and body e.

The `val`, *exp*, and `define` forms are what I call *true definitions*; these forms should be thought of as part of a program. The remaining forms, which I call *extended definitions*, are more like instructions to the interpreter. The `(use` *file-name*`)` form tells the interpreter to read and evaluate the definitions in the named file. A `check-expect`, `check-assert`, or `check-error` form tells the interpreter to remember a test and to run it *after* reading the file in which the test appears.

The expression forms, which all appear in the example `while` expression at the beginning of the chapter, constitute a bare minimum needed for writing imperative or procedural code. The forms can express a literal value, a variable, an assignment (`set`), a conditional (`if`), a loop (`while`), a sequence (`begin`), and a function application (any other bracketed form).

Variables and functions are named according to liberal rules: almost any non-bracket token can be a name. Only the words `val`, `define`, `use`, `check-expect`, `check-assert`, `check-error`, `set`, `if`, `while`, and `begin`, are *reserved*—they cannot be used to name functions or variables. And a *numeral* always stands for a number; a numeral cannot be used to name a function or a variable.

When Impcore starts, some names are already defined. These include *primitive* functions `+`, `-`, `*`, `/`, `=`, `<`, `>`, `println`, `print`, and `printu`, and also *predefined* functions `and`, `or`, `not`, `<=`, `>=`, `!=`, `mod`, and `negated`. A set of defined names forms a *basis;* the set of names defined at startup forms the *initial basis.* The concepts of primitive, predefined, and basis are explained in Section 1.2.6 (page 26).

1.2.2 Talking about syntax: Metavariables

Once we know how code is formed, we can talk about what happens when it is run. To talk about *any* well-formed code, not just particular codes, we use names called *metavariables.* In this chapter, the metavariables used to talk about code are as follows:

e	Any expression
d	Any definition
n	Any numeral
x	Any name that is meant to refer to a variable or a parameter
f	Any name that is meant to refer to a function

To talk about more than one expression or name, we use subscripts. For example, we write an `if` expression as (`if` e_1 e_2 e_3). Because each subexpression might be different from the other two, each one is referred to by its own metavariable.

Metavariables are distinct from *program variables.* Program variables *appear in* source code; metavariables *stand for* source code. Metavariables are written in $math\ italics$ and program variables in `typewriter font`. For example, `x` is a program variable: it is a name that can appear in source code. But x is a metavariable: it stands for *any* name that could appear in source code. Metavariable x might stand for `x`, but it might also stand for `y`, `z`, `i`, `j`, or any other program variable. To illustrate the difference, when we write `(val x 3)`, we mean the definition of global program variable `x`. But when we write (`val` x e), we mean a template that can stand for *any* definition of *any* global variable.

Metavariables differ from program variables in one other crucial respect: a metavariable can't be renamed without changing its meaning. So although you can write `(define double (n) (+ n n))` and it means *exactly* the same thing as `(define double (x) (+ x x))`, you *cannot* write (`val` m g) and have it mean the same thing as (`val` x e): (`val` x e) is a template for an expression, but because m and g mean nothing when used as metavariables, (`val` m g) is gibberish. If you want a distinct name for a new metavariable, the most you can do is decorate the original name in some way—traditionally with a prime or a subscript. For example, (`val` x' e_4) is also a template for an expression, and it's an expression that might be different from (`val` x e).

- To evaluate a literal expression, which in Impcore takes the form of a numeral n, we return the 32-bit integer that n stands for.
- To evaluate an expression that takes the form of a variable name x, we find the variable that x refers to, which must be be either a function parameter or a global variable defined with `val`, and we return the value.
- To evaluate an expression of the form `(set` x e`)`, we evaluate e, assign its value to the variable x, and return the value. Variable x must be a global variable or a formal parameter.
- To evaluate an expression of the form `(if` e_1 e_2 e_3`)`, we first evaluate e_1. If the result is nonzero, we evaluate e_2 and return the result; otherwise we evaluate e_3 and return the result.
- To evaluate an expression of the form `(while` e_1 e_2`)`, we first evaluate e_1. If the result is not zero, we evaluate e_2, then start evaluating the loop again with e_1. We continue until e_1 evaluates to zero. When e_1 evaluates to zero, looping ends, and the result of the `while` loop is zero. (The result of evaluating a `while` expression is *always* zero, but because `while` is typically evaluated for its side effects, we usually don't care.)
- To evaluate an expression of the form `(begin` $e_1 \cdots e_n$`)`, we evaluate expressions e_1 through e_n in that order, and we return the value of e_n.
- To evaluate an expression of the form `(`f $e_1 \cdots e_n$`)`, we evaluate expressions e_1 through e_n in that order, calling the results $v_1, \ldots, v_n$. We then apply function f to $v_1, \ldots, v_n$ and return the result. Function f may be *primitive* or user-defined; if f names a user-defined function, we find f's definition, let the names in the *formals* stand for $v_1, \ldots, v_n$, and return the result of evaluating f's body. If f names a primitive function, we apply it as described Section 1.2.4 (page 23).

Figure 1.2(a): Rules for evaluating expressions

1.2.3 *What the syntactic forms do*

Metavariables enable us to talk about *any* definition or expression of a certain form. And what we most want to say is *operational*: what happens when a form is evaluated. To explain the evaluation of Impcore's syntactic forms, I want to draw on your experience and intuition, so I use informal English. But informal English lacks precision, so in Section 1.5 (page 29), I also provide a precise, formal semantics.

I start with the most fundamental syntactic category: expressions. When an expression is evaluated, it returns a value. A value is not code, so to refer to a value, we need another metavariable:

v	Any value

In Impcore, all values are integers. Evaluating an expression produces a value and may also have a *side effect*; in Impcore, possible side effects include printing something or changing the value of a variable.

A literal 3 evaluates to the value 3.

21a. ⟨*transcript* 12a⟩+≡ ◁12c 21b▷

```
-> 3
3
```

The global variable n defined earlier in the chapter evaluates to its value:

21b. ⟨*transcript* 12a⟩+≡ ◁21a 21c▷

```
-> n
1
```

A set changes a variable's value:

21c. ⟨*transcript* 12a⟩+≡ ◁21b 21d▷

```
-> (set n -13)
-13
-> n
-13
```

A conditional evaluates to a value that depends on the condition. For example, a conditional can compute the absolute value of n:

21d. ⟨*transcript* 12a⟩+≡ ◁21c 21e▷

```
-> (if (< n 0) (negated n) n)
13
```

A loop's value is always 0, but its evaluation can change the values of variables:

21e. ⟨*transcript* 12a⟩+≡ ◁21d 21f▷

```
-> (while (< n 0) (set n (+ n 10)))
0
-> n
7
```

A begin is used to sequence expressions for their side effects, like printing:

21f. ⟨*transcript* 12a⟩+≡ ◁21e 21g▷

```
-> (begin (printu 169) (println 2021) -1)
©2021
-1
```

Function application may call a primitive, predefined, or user-defined function, like <, negated, +, printu, println, or x-3-plus-1.

Figure 1.2(b): Examples of evaluating expressions

Expressions are evaluated according to the rules in Figure 1.2(a), and corresponding examples appear in Figure 1.2(b)—except for calls and names, because examples of calls and names won't fit in the figure. To illustrate calls and names, I show what the Impcore interpreter does with two function definitions and calls. After evaluating a function's definition, the interpreter echoes the function's name.

negated 27c
printu *B*

21g. ⟨*transcript* 12a⟩+≡ ◁21f 22a▷

```
-> (define add1 (n) (+ n 1))
add1
-> (define double (n) (+ n n))
double
-> (add1 4)
5
-> (double (+ 3 4))
14
```

A user-defined function is called much as in C: first the arguments are evaluated; their values are the *actual parameters*. Then the function's body is evaluated with each actual parameter "bound to" (which is to say, named by) the corresponding *formal parameter* from the *formals* in the function's definition. In the first example, the actual parameter is 4, and `(+ n 1)` is evaluated with 4 bound to `n`. In the second, the actual parameter is 7, and `(+ n n)` is evaluated with 7 bound to `n`.

In Impcore, a function call behaves nicely only if the number of actual parameters is exactly equal to the number of formal parameters in the function's definition. Otherwise, the call goes wrong:

22a. ⟨*transcript* 12a⟩+≡ ◁21g 22b▷

```
-> (add1 17 12)
Run-time error: in (add1 17 12), expected 1 argument but found 2
```

In our examples so far, as in C, the name `n` means different things in different contexts. For example, functions `add1` and `double` use the name `n` as a formal parameter, and inside each function, `n` refers to that parameter. But outside any function, `n` continues to refer to the global variable defined on page 12. The meaning of any occurrence of any name is determined by the context in which the name occurs: If a variable x occurs in a function definition, and if the function has a formal parameter named with the same x, then x refers to that formal parameter. Otherwise x refers to a global variable. (Impcore has no local variables; to provide them is the object of Exercise 30.) If x occurs in a top-level expression, outside of any function definition, it necessarily refers to a global variable.

Let's contrive an example:

22b. ⟨*transcript* 12a⟩+≡ ◁22a 23a▷

```
-> n                                     ;; the global n
7
-> (define addn (n m) (set n (+ n m)))   ;; mutates the parameter
addn
-> (addn n 1)                            ;; the parameter is set to 8
8
-> n                                     ;; the global n is unchanged
7
```

Within the body of `addn`, the two occurrences of `n` refer to the formal parameter. But in the top-level expressions `n` and `(addn n 1)`, `n` refers to the global variable. And in the body of `addn`, where `n` is set, changing the formal `n` does not affect anything in the calling context; we say that Impcore passes parameters *by value*. No assignment to a formal parameter ever changes the value of a global variable.

With the details of expressions explored, we turn our attention to definitions. When a definition is evaluated, no value is returned; instead, evaluating a definition updates some part of the interpreter's state, causing it to "remember" something. The Impcore interpreter can remember global variables, function definitions, and pending unit tests.

- To evaluate a definition of the form `(val` x e`)`, we first check to see if a global variable named x exists, and if not, we create one. We then evaluate e and assign its value to x.
- To evaluate a definition that takes the form of an expression e, we evaluate e and store the result in the global variable `it`.
- To evaluate a definition of the form `(define` f `(`$x_1 \cdots x_n$`) e)`, like the definitions of `add1` or `double`, we remember f as a function that takes arguments $x_1, \ldots, x_n$ and returns e.

- To evaluate a definition of the form (use *filename*), we look for a file called *filename*, which should contain a sequence of Impcore definitions. We read the definitions and evaluate them in order. And after reading the file, we run any unit tests it contains.

- To evaluate a definition of the form (check-expect e_1 e_2), we remember this test: at the end of the file containing the definition, evaluate both e_1 and e_2. If their values are equal, the test passes; if not, the test fails.

- To evaluate a definition of the form (check-assert e), we remember this test: at the end of the file containing the definition, evaluate e. If its value is nonzero, the test passes; if not, the test fails.

- To evaluate a definition of the form (check-error e), we remember this test: at the end of the file containing the definition, evaluate e. If evaluating e triggers a run-time error, like dividing by zero or passing the wrong number of arguments to a function, the test passes; if not, the test fails.

1.2.4 *What the primitive functions do*

Not every function is defined using define; some are built into the interpreter as *primitives*. Each primitive function takes two arguments, except the printing primitives, which take one each. The arithmetic primitives +, -, *, and / do arithmetic on integers, up to the limits imposed by a 32-bit representation. Each of the comparison primitives <, >, and = does a comparison: if the comparison is true, the primitive returns 1; otherwise, it returns 0.

The printing primitives demand detailed explanation. Primitive println prints a value and then a newline; it's the printing primitive you'll use most often. Primitive print prints a value and *no* newline. Primitive printu prints a Unicode character and no newline. More precisely, printu takes as its argument an integer that stands for a Unicode *code point*—that means it's an integer code that stands for a character in one of a huge variety of alphabets. Primitive printu then prints the UTF-8 byte sequence that represents the code point. In most programming environments, this sequence will give you the character you're looking for. For example, (printu 955) prints the Greek letter λ. Each printing primitive, in addition to its side effect, also returns its argument.

When used interactively, the printing primitives can be confusing, because whenever an expression is evaluated, its value is printed automatically by the interpreter. Don't be baffled by effects like these:

23a. ⟨*transcript* 12a⟩+≡ ◁ 22b 23b ▷

```
-> (val x 4)
-> (println x)
4
4
```

add1 21g

The 4 is printed twice because println is called with actual parameter 4 (the value of x), and println first *prints* 4, accounting for the first 4, then *returns* 4. The second 4 is printed because the interpreter prints the value of *every* expression, including (println x).

23b. ⟨*transcript* 12a⟩+≡ ◁ 23a 24a ▷

```
-> (val y 5)
5
-> (begin (println x) (println y) (* x y))
4
5
20
```

True definitions and extended definitions: A design compromise

If you want to learn to use programming languages well and also to describe them precisely, what languages should you study? Not big industrial languages—you can write interesting programs, but it's hard to say how programs behave, or even what programs are well behaved. And not a tiny artificial language (or a "core calculus" like the famous *lambda calculus*)—its behavior can be described very precisely, but it's hard to write any interesting programs. That's why I've designed the bridge languages: to bridge the gap between industrial languages and core calculi.

The bridge languages are small enough to be described precisely, but big enough for interesting programs. (I won't pretend you can write interesting programs in Impcore, but you *can* write interesting programs in μScheme, μML, Molecule, and μSmalltalk.) But a few features are too complicated to define precisely, yet too useful to leave out. They are the "extended definitions": the `use`, `check-expect`, `check-assert`, and `check-error` forms. The `val`, `define`, and top-level expression forms, which *are* defined precisely, are the "true definitions." The true definitions are part of the language, and the extensions are there to make you more productive as a programmer.

If you happen to use `print` instead of `println`, you can get some strange output:

24a. ⟨*transcript* 12a⟩+≡ ◁23b 25b▷

```
-> (begin (print x) (print y) (* x y))
4520
```

Because the interpreter automatically prints the value of each expression you enter, you'll use printing primitives rarely—mostly for debugging. I typically debug using `println`, but when I want fancier output, I also use `printu` and `print`.

1.2.5 Extended definitions: Beyond interactive computation

The examples above show transcripts of my interactions with the Impcore interpreter. But interactive code disappears as soon as it is typed; to help you write code that you want to edit or keep, the Impcore interpreter, like all the interpreters in this book, enables you to put it in a file. And when you put code in a file, you can add *unit tests*. For example, the file `gcd.imp` tests a function that computes greatest common denominators:

24b. ⟨*contents of file* `gcd.imp` 24b⟩≡ 25a▷

```
(val r 0)
(define gcd (m n)
  (begin
    (while (!= (set r (mod m n)) 0)
      (begin
        (set m n)
        (set n r)))
    n))

(check-expect (gcd 6 15) 3)
```

Since the code is in a file, there are no arrow prompts. But there is a unit test, our first: the `check-expect` says that if we call `(gcd 6 15)`, the result should be 3.

The file includes more unit tests:

25a. ⟨*contents of file* gcd.imp 24b⟩+≡ ◁24b

```
(check-expect (gcd 15 15) 15)
(check-expect (gcd 14 15) 1)
(check-expect (gcd 14 1)  1)
(check-expect (gcd 72 96) 24)
(check-error (gcd 14 0))
```


The last unit test says that if we evaluate `(gcd 14 0)`, we expect a run-time error.

Unit tests aren't run until after a file is loaded. Then the interpreter summarizes the test results:

25b. ⟨*transcript* 12a⟩+≡ ◁24a 25d▷

```
-> (use gcd.imp)
0
gcd
All 6 tests passed.
```

A unit test can appear *before* the function it tests. This trick can be a great way to plan a function, or to document it. I've written an example using *triangular numbers*. A triangular number is analogous to the square of a number: just as the square of n is the number of dots needed to form a square array with a side of length n, the nth triangular number is the number of dots needed to form an equilateral triangle with n dots along one side.

```
1  =    *

3  =    *
       * *

        *
6  =   * *
      * * *
```

A triangular number can be computed using the `sigma` function in Exercise 2 on page 74, but there's a shortcut:

25c. ⟨*triangle.imp* 25c⟩≡

```
(check-expect (triangle 1) 1)
(check-expect (triangle 2) 3)
(check-expect (triangle 3) 6)
(check-expect (triangle 4) 10)

(define triangle (n)
  (/ (* n (+ n 1)) 2))
```

25d. ⟨*transcript* 12a⟩+≡ ◁25b 26a▷

```
-> (use triangle.imp)
triangle
All 4 tests passed.
```

mod 27c

When writing `triangle`, I botched my first attempt. My unit tests caught the botch. The botched code, preceded by tests, looked like this:

25e. ⟨*botched-triangle.imp* 25e⟩≡

```
(check-expect (triangle 1) 1)
(check-expect (triangle 2) 3)
(check-expect (triangle 3) 6)
(check-expect (triangle 4) 10)

(define triangle (n)    ; botched version
  (/ (* n (- n 1)) 2))
```

The unit tests caught the botch:

26a. ⟨*transcript* 12a⟩+≡ ◁25d 26c▷

```
-> (use botched-triangle.imp)
triangle
Check-expect failed: expected (triangle 1) to evaluate to 1, but it's 0.
Check-expect failed: expected (triangle 2) to evaluate to 3, but it's 1.
Check-expect failed: expected (triangle 3) to evaluate to 6, but it's 3.
Check-expect failed: expected (triangle 4) to evaluate to 10, but it's 6.
All 4 tests failed.
```

The `check-expect` form provides what you'll need to test most Impcore code: because every Impcore value is an integer, your unit tests can usually just say what value you expect. But in Chapter 2 and beyond, you'll have access to more structured values, like records and lists, and you'll want to talk about *properties*, like "the list is sorted." For that purpose, each of the bridge languages includes a `check-assert` form, which is intended for use with Booleans. As examples, here are a few assertions about properties of products.

26b. ⟨*arith-assertions.imp* 26b⟩≡

```
(check-assert (< (* 1 2) (+ 1 2)))    ; product is smaller than sum
(check-assert (> (* 2 3) (+ 2 3)))    ; product is bigger than sum
(check-assert (not (< (* -1 -1) 0))) ; product of negatives is not negative
```

Function `not` is predefined; its definition appears in Figure 1.3 (page 27).

26c. ⟨*transcript* 12a⟩+≡ ◁26a 29▷

```
-> (use arith-assertions.imp)
All 3 tests passed.
```

1.2.6 *Primitive, predefined, and basis; the initial basis*

Programmers like big languages with lots of data types and syntactic forms, but implementors want to keep primitive functionality small and simple. (So do semanticists!) To reconcile these competing desires, language designers have found two strategies: translation into a *core language* and definition of an *initial basis*.

Using a core language, you stratify your language into two layers. The inner layer defines or implements its constructs directly; it constitutes the core language. The outer layer defines additional constructs by translating them into the core language; these constructs constitute *syntactic sugar*. In this chapter, the core language is Impcore, and as an example of syntactic sugar, a `for` expression can be defined by a translation into `begin` and `while` (Section 1.8).

To be useful to programmers, a language needs to be accompanied by a standard library. In the theory world, a library contributes to a *basis*; basis is the collective term for all the things that can be named in definitions. In Impcore, these things are functions and global variables. A language's *initial basis* contains the named things that are available in a fresh interpreter or installation—the things you have access to even before evaluating your own code.

Like the Impcore language, Impcore's initial basis is stratified into two layers, one of which is defined in terms of the other. The inner layer includes all the functions that are defined directly by C code in the interpreter; these are called *primitive*. The outer layer includes functions that are also built into the interpreter, but are defined in terms of the primitives using Impcore source code; they are user-defined functions and are called *predefined*.

Stratifying the initial basis makes life easy for everyone. Implementors make their own lives easy by defining just a few primitives, and they can make programmers' lives easy by defining lots of predefined functions. Predefined functions are

Boolean connectives are defined using `if` expressions.

27a. ⟨*predefined Impcore functions* 27a⟩≡ 27b ▷

```
(define and (b c) (if b c b))
(define or  (b c) (if b b c))
(define not (b)   (if b 0 1))
```

Unlike the similar constructs built into the syntax of many languages, these versions of and and or always evaluate both of their arguments. Section G.7 shows how you can use syntactic sugar to define *short-circuit* variations that evaluate a second expression only when necessary.

Only comparisons <, =, and > are primitive; the others are predefined.

27b. ⟨*predefined Impcore functions* 27a⟩+≡ ◁27a 27c ▷

```
(define <= (x y) (not (> x y)))
(define >= (x y) (not (< x y)))
(define != (x y) (not (= x y)))
```

Primitive arithmetic includes +, -, *, and /, to which the predefined functions add modulus and negation.

27c. ⟨*predefined Impcore functions* 27a⟩+≡ ◁27b

```
(define mod (m n) (- m (* n (/ m n))))
(define negated (n) (- 0 n))
```

These functions are installed into the initial basis by the C code in chunk ⟨*install the initial basis in* `functions` S297b⟩, which is continued in chunk S297d.

Figure 1.3: Predefined functions in Impcore's initial basis

just ordinary code, and writing them is lots easier than defining new primitives. Impcore's predefined functions are defined by the code in Figure 1.3.

Just like any other function, a primitive or predefined function can be redefined using `define`. This trick can be useful—for example, to count the number of times a function is called. But if you redefine an initial-basis function, don't change the results it returns! (You'll introduce bugs.)

Before going on to the next sections, work some of the exercises in Sections 1.10.2 to 1.10.4, starting on page 73.

1.3 ABSTRACT SYNTAX

In every interpreter in this book, programs are represented as *abstract-syntax trees* (ASTs). And as noted in Section 1.1, abstract syntax isn't just a great representation; abstract-syntax trees are the best way to *think* about syntax. Alas, in C, AST representations are a pain to code. To ease the pain, the representations in this book are generated from a little language that is used only to describe abstract-syntax trees. This language also helps with our thinking. As an example, the language describes the abstract syntax of an Impcore definition like this:

27d. ⟨*simplified example of abstract syntax for Impcore* 27d⟩≡ 28 ▷

```
Def = VAL          (Name, Exp)
    | EXP          (Exp)
    | DEFINE       (Name, Namelist, Exp)
```

This description defines `Def` as a category of abstract-syntax tree, which includes only the true definitions; extended definitions are `XDef`s. Each form of `Def` is named (`VAL`, `EXP`, or `DEFINE`), and following the name of the form is a comma-separated list showing what values or subtrees each form is made from.

The same language is used to specify the abstract representation of an expression, which has more forms:

28. ⟨*simplified example of abstract syntax for Impcore* 27d⟩+≡ ◁27d

```
Exp = LITERAL (Value)
    | VAR     (Name)
    | SET     (Name, Exp)
    | IF      (Exp, Exp, Exp)
    | WHILE   (Exp, Exp)
    | BEGIN   (Explist)
    | APPLY   (Name, Explist)
```

This description is worth comparing this with the description of *exp* in the grammar for Impcore (Figure 1.1, page 18).

An abstract-syntax tree for a given form is usually drawn with the form's name at the root and with its subtrees connected to it by solid lines. When a form has no subtrees, like `LITERAL` or `VAR`, its single node can be drawn with the associated `Value` or `Name` just underneath. For example, the abstract-syntax tree for the Impcore expression `(set i (- (+ (* 2 j) i) (/ k 3)))` can be drawn like this:

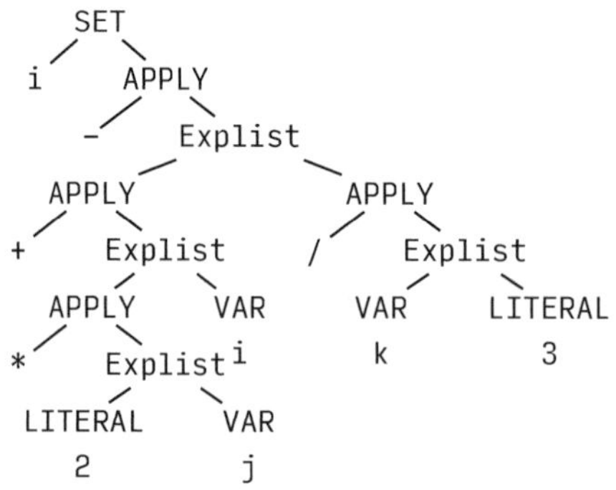

```
            SET
           /   \
          i     APPLY
               /     \
              -       Explist
                    /         \
            APPLY                 APPLY
           /     \               /     \
          +       Explist       /       Explist
                 /       \             /       \
            APPLY         VAR       VAR         LITERAL
           /     \         i         k            3
          *       Explist
                 /       \
            LITERAL       VAR
               2           j
```

An abstract-syntax tree is much easier to analyze, manipulate, or interpret than source code. And ASTs focus our attention on structure and semantics. Concrete syntax becomes a separate concern; one could easily define a version of Impcore with C-like concrete syntax, but with identical abstract syntax.

Abstract syntax is created from concrete input by a *parser*, which also identifies and rejects ill-formed phrases such as `(if x 0)` or `(val y)`. Parsing is covered in a large body of literature; for textbook treatments, try Appel (1998) or Aho et al. (2007). A parser for Impcore, which you can easily extend, can be found in Appendix G.

1.4 Environments and the meanings of names

An expression like `(* x 3)` cannot be evaluated by itself; to know its value, we must know what `x` is. Similarly, to know the effect of evaluating an expression like `(set x 1)`, we must know whether `x` is a formal parameter, a global variable, or something else entirely. In programming-language theory, knowledge about names is kept in an *environment*, which is usually a mapping from names to meanings. Environments are often implemented as hash tables or search trees, and in an implementation, an environment is sometimes called a *symbol table*.

Knowing what can be in an environment tells us what kinds of things a name can stand for, which is a good first step in understanding a new programming language. To understand Impcore, we need to know about three environments, each of which is written using its own metavariable:

- Environment ξ (xi, pronounced "ksee") holds values of global variables.

- Environment ϕ (phi, pronounced "fee") holds definitions of functions.
- Environment ρ (rho, pronounced "roe") holds values of a function's parameters.

Environments ξ and ϕ are global and shared, but there is a distinct ρ for every function call. Together, the contents of the three environments comprise Impcore's *basis*.

A name can be defined in all three environments at once. But it's a bad idea:

29. ⟨*transcript* 12a⟩+≡ ◁26c 64▷

```
-> (val x 2)
2
-> (define x (y) (+ x y))    ; pushing the boundaries of knowledge...
-> (define z (x) (x x))      ; and sanity
-> (z 4)
6
```

The `val` definition introduces a global variable `x`, which is bound to value 2 in environment ξ. The first `define` introduces a function `x` that adds its argument to the global variable `x`; that function is bound to name `x` in environment ϕ. The second `define` introduces function `z`, which passes its formal parameter `x` to the function `x`; when `z` is called, parameter `x` is bound to 4 in environment ρ. This example should push you to understand the rules of Impcore; to follow it, you have to know not only that Impcore has three environments but also how the environments are used. Of course, no sane person programs this way; production code is written to be *easy* to understand, even by readers who may have forgotten details of the rules.

Mathematically, an environment is a function with a finite domain, from a name to whatever. In Impcore, environments ξ and ρ map each defined name to a value; ϕ maps each defined name to a function. Whatever a name is mapped to, all environments are manipulated using the same notation, which is mostly function notation. For example, whatever is associated with name x in the environment ρ is written $\rho(x)$. The set of names bound in environment ρ is written $\operatorname{dom} \rho$. An extended environment, ρ plus a binding of the name x to v, is written $\rho\{x \mapsto v\}$. In an extended environment, the new binding hides previous bindings of x, so lookup is governed by this equation:

$$\rho\{x \mapsto v\}(y) = \begin{cases} v, & \text{when } y = x \\ \rho(y), & \text{when } y \neq x. \end{cases}$$

Finally, an empty environment, which does not bind any names, is written $\{\}$.

One environment can be combined with another, but because combining environments is not useful in Impcore, the notation is deferred to Chapter 2.

1.5 OPERATIONAL SEMANTICS

Earlier in this chapter, Impcore is defined informally and concisely, if imprecisely (Section 1.2). For a precise understanding of what Impcore is, we could consult the implementation (Section 1.6), but an implementation is much longer and harder to understand than an informal description. An implementation also lacks focus; code embodies many irrelevant decisions, including decisions about the *representations* of names, environments, and abstract syntax. Those decisions are part of the implementation, not part of the language.

In this section, Impcore is defined using a technique that is concise, focused, and precise: formal *operational semantics*. Operational semantics specifies behavior precisely while hiding implementation details. Although the notation can be

Table 1.4: Metavariables of Impcore's operational semantics

e, e_i	An expression
d	A definition
x, x_i	A name that refers to a variable or a parameter
f	A name that refers to a function
v, v_i	A value
$\xi, \xi', \ldots$	A global-variable environment
$\phi, \phi', \ldots$	A function-definition environment
$\rho, \rho', \ldots$	A formal-parameter environment

intimidating at first, with practice operational semantics becomes as easy to read as informal English.

Impcore's operational semantics defines an *abstract machine* and rules for its execution. The semantics defines the machine's states, including its start state and its acceptable final states, and it presents rules for making transitions from one state to another. By applying these rules repeatedly, the machine can go from a start state like "I just turned on and have this program to evaluate" to an accepting state like "the answer is 42."

A machine may reach a state from which it cannot make progress; for example, a machine evaluating `(/ 1 0)` probably cannot make a transition. When a machine reaches such a state, we say it "gets stuck" or "goes wrong." An implementation might indicate a run-time error.

An Impcore machine's states and transitions are described using the metavariables from Sections 1.2 and 1.4, which describe syntax, values, and semantics (Table 1.4). The state of an Impcore machine has four parts: a *definition* d or *expression* e being evaluated; a value environment ξ, which holds the values of global variables; a function-definition environment ϕ; and a value environment ρ, which holds the values of formal parameters. Definitions do not appear inside functions, so when the machine is evaluating a definition d, there are no formal parameters, and its state is written as $\langle d, \xi, \phi \rangle$. When the machine is evaluating an expression e, its state is written as $\langle e, \xi, \phi, \rho \rangle$. When the machine is resting between evaluations, it remembers only the values of global variables and the definitions of functions, and its state is written as $\langle \xi, \phi \rangle$.

Environments ξ and ρ store values, which in Impcore are integers. Environment ϕ stores both primitive functions and user-defined functions. A primitive function is written as $\text{PRIMITIVE}(\oplus)$, where $\oplus$ stands for a name like $+$, $=$, or $*$. A user-defined function is written as $\text{USER}(\langle x_1, \ldots, x_n \rangle, e)$, where the x_i's are the formal parameters and e is the body.

In the initial state of the Impcore machine, $\xi = \{\}$, because there are no global variables defined. But $\phi = \phi_0$, where ϕ_0 is preloaded with the definitions of primitive functions as well as the user-defined functions in the initial basis (Figure 1.3 on page 27).

1.5.1 *Judgments and rules of inference*

State transitions are described using *judgments*, which take one form for definitions and another form for expressions. The judgment for the evaluation of an expression, $\langle e, \xi, \phi, \rho \rangle \Downarrow \langle v, \xi', \phi, \rho' \rangle$, means "evaluating expression e produces value v." More precisely, it means "in environments ξ, ϕ, and ρ, evaluating e produces a value v, and it also produces new environments ξ' and ρ', while leaving ϕ

unchanged."[2] This judgment uses eight metavariables; e stands for an expression, ξ, ϕ, and ρ stand for environments, and v stands for a value. Different metavariables are distinguished by giving them subscripts, or as with the environments, by using primes.

The *form* of the judgment $\langle e, \xi, \phi, \rho \rangle \Downarrow \langle v, \xi', \phi, \rho' \rangle$ tells us a few things:

- Evaluating an expression always produces a value, unless of course the machine gets stuck. Even expressions like SET and WHILE, which are typically evaluated only for side effects, produce values.[3]
- Evaluating an expression might change the value of a global variable (from ξ) or a formal parameter (from ρ).
- Evaluating an expression never adds or changes a function definition (because ϕ is unchanged).

The form of the judgment *doesn't* tell us whether evaluating an expression can introduce a new variable. (It can't, but we can be certain of this only if we study the full semantics and write an inductive proof, which is Exercise 24 on page 83.)

The form of the evaluation judgment also gives this semantics part of its name: no matter how much computation is required to get from e to v, the judgment $\langle e, \xi, \phi, \rho \rangle \Downarrow \langle v, \xi', \phi, \rho' \rangle$ encompasses all that computation in one big step. It is therefore called a *big-step* judgment and is part of a *big-step* semantics.

The judgment for a definition is simpler; $\langle d, \xi, \phi \rangle \rightarrow \langle \xi', \phi' \rangle$ means "evaluating definition d in the environments ξ and ϕ yields new environments ξ' and ϕ'." The different arrow helps distinguish this judgment from an expression judgment.

Not all judgments describe real program behaviors. For example, unless some joker changes the binding of the name + in ϕ, $\langle$`(+ 1 1)`$, \xi, \phi, \rho \rangle \Downarrow \langle 4, \xi, \phi, \rho \rangle$ doesn't describe how Impcore code behaves. To say which judgments describe real behaviors, an operational semantics uses *rules of inference*. Each rule has the form

$$\frac{\textit{premises}}{\textit{conclusion}}. \qquad \text{(NAME OF RULE)}$$

If all the premises hold, so does the conclusion.

For example, the rule

$$\frac{\langle e_1, \xi, \phi, \rho \rangle \Downarrow \langle v_1, \xi', \phi, \rho' \rangle \qquad v_1 \neq 0 \qquad \langle e_2, \xi', \phi, \rho' \rangle \Downarrow \langle v_2, \xi'', \phi, \rho'' \rangle}{\langle \text{IF}(e_1, e_2, e_3), \xi, \phi, \rho \rangle \Downarrow \langle v_2, \xi'', \phi, \rho'' \rangle}, \qquad \text{(IFTRUE)}$$

which is part of the semantics of Impcore, says that whenever $\langle e_1, \xi, \phi, \rho \rangle$ evaluates to some nonzero value v_1, the expression $\text{IF}(e_1, e_2, e_3)$ evaluates to the result of evaluating e_2. Because e_2 is evaluated in the environment produced by evaluation of e_1, if e_1 contains side effects, such as assigning to a variable, the results of those side effects are visible to e_2. Expression e_3 is not mentioned, because when $v_1 \neq 0$, e_3 is never evaluated.

[2] A judgment describes a relation, not a function. In principle, it is possible to have two different values $v_1 \neq v_2$ such that $\langle e, \xi, \phi, \rho \rangle \Downarrow \langle v_1, \xi', \phi, \rho' \rangle$ and also $\langle e, \xi, \phi, \rho \rangle \Downarrow \langle v_2, \xi', \phi, \rho' \rangle$. A language that permits such ambiguity is *nondeterministic*. All the languages in this book are deterministic, but multithreaded languages like Java or C# can be nondeterministic. Programs written in such languages can produce different answers on different runs. Languages that do not specify the order in which expressions are evaluated, like C, can also be nondeterministic. Programs written in such languages can produce different answers when translated with different compilers. (See also Exercise 27, page 84.)

[3] This property distinguishes an expression-oriented language like Impcore (or ML, Scheme, or Smalltalk) from a statement-oriented language like C. Both have imperative constructs that are evaluated only for side effects, but only in C do these constructs produce no values.

The rule specifies that e_1 is evaluated before e_2. How do we know? By looking at which environments go where. The side effects of e_1 are captured in environments ξ' and ρ', and these are the environments used to evaluate e_2. Order of evaluation is determined not by the order in which the premises are written, but by the flow of data (in this case, the environments) through the computation. That said, the rule's premises are written in the same order as the evaluations they describe. Any other order would be, shall we say, discourteous.

The rules of Impcore's semantics belong to a larger family of reasoning techniques called *natural deduction*. This family gives Impcore's semantics the rest of its name: it is a *big-step, natural-deduction* semantics.

Rules of inference can be translated into code. A complete example is done for you in Section 1.6: Impcore's expression-evaluation judgment is implemented by function `eval`. Calling `eval`(e, ξ, ϕ, ρ) returns v and has side effects on ξ and ρ with the result that $\langle e, \xi_{before}, \phi, \rho_{before}\rangle \Downarrow \langle v, \xi_{after}, \phi, \rho_{after}\rangle$. Function `eval` looks at the form of e and considers rules that have e's of that form in their conclusions. It then looks at premises; each evaluation judgment in a premise is implemented by a recursive call. For example, to evaluate an IF expression, `eval` first makes a recursive call to itself to find v_1, ξ', and ρ' such that $\langle e_1, \xi, \phi, \rho\rangle \Downarrow \langle v_1, \xi', \phi, \rho'\rangle$. Then if $v_1 \neq 0$, `eval` makes another recursive call to find v_2, ξ'', and ρ'' such that $\langle e_2, \xi', \phi, \rho'\rangle \Downarrow \langle v_2, \xi'', \phi, \rho''\rangle$. Having satisfied all the premises of rule IFTRUE, it then returns v_2 and the modified environments.

The rules for every possible form of expression (and definition) are presented in the rest of this section.

1.5.2 Literal values

A literal value evaluates to itself, without changing any environments:

$$\frac{}{\langle \text{LITERAL}(v), \xi, \phi, \rho\rangle \Downarrow \langle v, \xi, \phi, \rho\rangle}. \quad \text{(LITERAL)}$$

This rule has no premises, so at a LITERAL node, the recursive implementation of `eval` terminates.

1.5.3 Variables

If a name is bound in the parameter or global environment, then evaluating the variable with that name produces the value associated with it in the environment. Otherwise, no rules apply, the machine gets stuck, and the computation does not continue.

Parameters hide global variables. Name x is a parameter if $x \in \operatorname{dom} \rho$, where $\operatorname{dom} \rho$ is the domain of ρ, i.e., the set of names bound by ρ.

$$\frac{x \in \operatorname{dom} \rho}{\langle \text{VAR}(x), \xi, \phi, \rho\rangle \Downarrow \langle \rho(x), \xi, \phi, \rho\rangle} \quad \text{(FORMALVAR)}$$

$$\frac{x \notin \operatorname{dom} \rho \qquad x \in \operatorname{dom} \xi}{\langle \text{VAR}(x), \xi, \phi, \rho\rangle \Downarrow \langle \xi(x), \xi, \phi, \rho\rangle} \quad \text{(GLOBALVAR)}$$

These rules have premises that involve only membership tests on environments, not other evaluation judgments, so at a VAR node, the recursive implementation of `eval` terminates.

Notation can imply "may differ" or "must equal" but not "must differ"

When we specify evaluation using a judgment form, we are using a form of mathematical logic, which uses primes and subscripts in ways that can be hard to learn. When primes or subscripts differ, the metavariables they decorate *may or may not* differ, like the ξ and ξ' in these examples:

- *The general form of judgment* $\langle e, \xi, \phi, \rho \rangle \Downarrow \langle v, \xi', \phi, \rho' \rangle$

  The general form uses ξ on the left and ξ' on the right. Environments ξ and ξ' look different, but the notation means only that they *may differ*. The form says, "evaluating an unknown expression e *may* change a global variable." What actually happens depends on what rules you use and what judgment you prove.

- *Conclusion of* LITERAL $\langle \text{LITERAL}(v), \xi, \phi, \rho \rangle \Downarrow \langle v, \xi, \phi, \rho \rangle$

  The LITERAL rule proves a judgment that uses ξ on both the left and the right. Because ξ *must equal* ξ, the judgment says, "evaluating a literal expression LITERAL(v) *does not* change or add a global variable."

- *Conclusion of* GLOBALASSIGN $\langle \text{SET}(x, e), \xi, \phi, \rho \rangle \Downarrow \langle v, \xi'\{x \mapsto v\}, \phi, \rho' \rangle$

  Environments ξ and $\xi'\{x \mapsto v\}$ look like they must differ. But it's not so: ξ may equal ξ', and ξ' may map x to v. In that case, ξ and $\xi'\{x \mapsto v\}$ are equal. Imagine evaluating `(set x 0)` when `x` is *already* zero.

Our notation can imply only that two environments "may differ" or "must equal" each other. For example, in the rule for IFTRUE on page 34, ξ may equal ξ', which may equal ξ'', as in `(if (> n 0) n (- 0 n))`. Or ξ may equal ξ', but they may both differ from ξ'', as in `(if (> n 0) (set sign 1) (set sign -1))`.

What if ξ and ξ' *must differ*? That can't be said with primes or subscripts; primes and subscripts can say only "may differ" or "must equal." To say that two things must differ, write an explicit premise, like "$v_1 \neq 0$" or "$\xi \neq \xi'$."

The notation is most important when you write your own derivations. Beginners often write primes or subscripts as they appear in rules. But a prime or subscript says "I don't know; it may differ," and in a derivation, this is almost always wrong—we *do* know. Here's an invalid derivation, intended to describe the evaluation of `(if (> n 0) n (- 0 n))` when `n` is 7 (I've taken a minor liberty with the notation):

$$\frac{\dfrac{\cdots}{\langle \texttt{(> n 0)}, \xi, \phi, \rho \rangle \Downarrow \langle 1, \xi, \phi, \rho \rangle} \qquad 1 \neq 0 \qquad \dfrac{\cdots}{\langle \texttt{n}, \xi, \phi, \rho \rangle \Downarrow \langle 7, \xi, \phi, \rho \rangle}}{\langle \text{IF}(\texttt{(> n 0)}, \texttt{n}, \texttt{(- 0 n)}), \xi, \phi, \rho \rangle \Downarrow \langle 7, \xi'', \phi, \rho'' \rangle}.$$

The conclusion is bogus. Because ξ'' appears only in the conclusion, there is nothing that ξ'' must equal, and that means the judgment says, "evaluating the `if` expression produces 7, and afterward, global variables have *arbitrary* values." (The same goes for ρ''.) To avoid this problem, remember that in any judgment that you prove, the elements of the final state *must equal* something that you specify. Do that and you'll write good derivations.

1.5.4 Assignment

Evaluating an assignment changes the value of a variable, and it produces the value of the right-hand side. Assignment, like variable lookup, prioritizes parameters: if the name x is bound in the parameter environment ρ, its binding is changed there; otherwise, x had better be bound in the global environment ξ.

$$\frac{x \in \operatorname{dom} \rho \qquad \langle e, \xi, \phi, \rho \rangle \Downarrow \langle v, \xi', \phi, \rho' \rangle}{\langle \text{SET}(x, e), \xi, \phi, \rho \rangle \Downarrow \langle v, \xi', \phi, \rho'\{x \mapsto v\} \rangle} \qquad \text{(FORMALASSIGN)}$$

$$\frac{x \notin \operatorname{dom} \rho \qquad x \in \operatorname{dom} \xi \qquad \langle e, \xi, \phi, \rho \rangle \Downarrow \langle v, \xi', \phi, \rho' \rangle}{\langle \text{SET}(x, e), \xi, \phi, \rho \rangle \Downarrow \langle v, \xi'\{x \mapsto v\}, \phi, \rho' \rangle} \qquad \text{(GLOBALASSIGN)}$$

Each of these rules has a premise that shows an evaluation of the right-hand side e, so at a SET node, the recursive implementation of `eval` always makes a recursive call. And even though there are two rules with SET in the conclusion, only one can apply at one time, because the premises $x \in \operatorname{dom} \rho$ and $x \notin \operatorname{dom} \rho$ are mutually exclusive. This property enables the implementation to know exactly what to do with a SET node, and it keeps the evaluation of Impcore programs deterministic.

Because of the premises $x \in \operatorname{dom} \rho$ and $x \in \operatorname{dom} \xi$, only a previously defined variable may be assigned to; given a SET node where $x \notin \operatorname{dom} \rho$ and $x \notin \operatorname{dom} \xi$, the machine gets stuck. In many languages, like Awk for example, assignment to an undefined and undeclared variable creates a new global variable (Aho, Kernighan, and Weinberger 1988), as specified by the following rule:

$$\frac{x \notin \operatorname{dom} \rho \qquad \langle e, \xi, \phi, \rho \rangle \Downarrow \langle v, \xi', \phi, \rho' \rangle}{\langle \text{SET}(x, e), \xi, \phi, \rho \rangle \Downarrow \langle v, \xi'\{x \mapsto v\}, \phi, \rho' \rangle}. \qquad \text{(GLOBALASSIGN for Awk)}$$

In Impcore, a new global variable can be created only by a VAL definition, as shown below in rule DEFINEGLOBAL (page 37). To spot such subtleties, you have to read inference rules carefully.

1.5.5 Control flow

Conditional evaluation

The expression $\text{IF}(e_1, e_2, e_3)$ first evaluates the expression e_1 to produce value v_1. If v_1 is nonzero, the IF expression produces the result of evaluating e_2; otherwise, it produces the result of evaluating e_3. Each case is described by its own rule.

$$\frac{\langle e_1, \xi, \phi, \rho \rangle \Downarrow \langle v_1, \xi', \phi, \rho' \rangle \qquad v_1 \neq 0 \qquad \langle e_2, \xi', \phi, \rho' \rangle \Downarrow \langle v_2, \xi'', \phi, \rho'' \rangle}{\langle \text{IF}(e_1, e_2, e_3), \xi, \phi, \rho \rangle \Downarrow \langle v_2, \xi'', \phi, \rho'' \rangle} \qquad \text{(IFTRUE)}$$

$$\frac{\langle e_1, \xi, \phi, \rho \rangle \Downarrow \langle v_1, \xi', \phi, \rho' \rangle \qquad v_1 = 0 \qquad \langle e_3, \xi', \phi, \rho' \rangle \Downarrow \langle v_3, \xi'', \phi, \rho'' \rangle}{\langle \text{IF}(e_1, e_2, e_3), \xi, \phi, \rho \rangle \Downarrow \langle v_3, \xi'', \phi, \rho'' \rangle} \qquad \text{(IFFALSE)}$$

Like the two rules for SET, these rules have mutually exclusive premises ($v_1 \neq 0$ and $v_1 = 0$). Evaluation is deterministic, and by examining v_1, the implementation knows which rule to apply.

Loops

A WHILE loop first evaluates the condition e_1 to produce value v_1. If v_1 is nonzero, evaluation continues with the body e_2, and then the WHILE loop is evaluated again.

$$\frac{\begin{array}{c}\langle e_1, \xi, \phi, \rho\rangle \Downarrow \langle v_1, \xi', \phi, \rho'\rangle \qquad v_1 \neq 0 \\ \langle e_2, \xi', \phi, \rho'\rangle \Downarrow \langle v_2, \xi'', \phi, \rho''\rangle \qquad \langle \mathrm{WHILE}(e_1, e_2), \xi'', \phi, \rho''\rangle \Downarrow \langle v_3, \xi''', \phi, \rho'''\rangle\end{array}}{\langle \mathrm{WHILE}(e_1, e_2), \xi, \phi, \rho\rangle \Downarrow \langle v_3, \xi''', \phi, \rho'''\rangle} \quad \text{(WHILEITERATE)}$$

In this rule, the value v_2, which is produced by evaluating the body e_2, is thrown away. We can tell by looking at the final state of the judgment in the conclusion of the rule. That state has elements v_3, ξ''', ϕ, and ρ''', and if you study the rule carefully, you'll see that none of these elements depends on or uses v_2. A WHILE loop evaluates its body e_2 only for its side effects, i.e., for the new environments ξ'' and ρ''. They are then used to make the final environments ξ''' and ρ'''.

If the condition in a WHILE loop evaluates to zero, the loop terminates, and the loop also evaluates to zero.

$$\frac{\langle e_1, \xi, \phi, \rho\rangle \Downarrow \langle v_1, \xi', \phi, \rho'\rangle \qquad v_1 = 0}{\langle \mathrm{WHILE}(e_1, e_2), \xi, \phi, \rho\rangle \Downarrow \langle 0, \xi', \phi, \rho'\rangle} \quad \text{(WHILEEND)}$$

If the evaluation of a WHILE loop terminates, it always produces zero, even when rule WHILEITERATE is used (Exercise 23 on page 83). A WHILE loop is therefore executed for its side effects.

Sequential execution

A nonempty BEGIN evaluates its subexpressions left to right, producing the result of the final expression e_n.

$$\frac{\begin{array}{c}\langle e_1, \xi_0, \phi, \rho_0\rangle \Downarrow \langle v_1, \xi_1, \phi, \rho_1\rangle \\ \langle e_2, \xi_1, \phi, \rho_1\rangle \Downarrow \langle v_2, \xi_2, \phi, \rho_2\rangle \\ \vdots \\ \langle e_n, \xi_{n-1}, \phi, \rho_{n-1}\rangle \Downarrow \langle v_n, \xi_n, \phi, \rho_n\rangle\end{array}}{\langle \mathrm{BEGIN}(e_1, e_2, \ldots, e_n), \xi_0, \phi, \rho_0\rangle \Downarrow \langle v_n, \xi_n, \phi, \rho_n\rangle} \quad \text{(BEGIN)}$$

Values v_1 to v_{n-1} are ignored, but the environments ξ_1 and ρ_1, which result from evaluating e_1, are used to evaluate e_2, and so on. The use of ξ_1 and ρ_1 to evaluate e_2 implies that e_1 is evaluated before e_2. Order of evaluation is determined by this "threading" of environments, not by the order in which the premises are written. For example, the BEGIN rule might equally well have been written this way:

$$\frac{\begin{array}{c}\langle e_n, \xi_{n-1}, \phi, \rho_{n-1}\rangle \Downarrow \langle v_n, \xi_n, \phi, \rho_n\rangle \\ \langle e_{n-1}, \xi_{n-2}, \phi, \rho_{n-2}\rangle \Downarrow \langle v_{n-1}, \xi_{n-1}, \phi, \rho_{n-1}\rangle \\ \vdots \\ \langle e_1, \xi_0, \phi, \rho_0\rangle \Downarrow \langle v_1, \xi_1, \phi, \rho_1\rangle\end{array}}{\langle \mathrm{BEGIN}(e_1, e_2, \ldots, e_n), \xi_0, \phi, \rho_0\rangle \Downarrow \langle v_n, \xi_n, \phi, \rho_n\rangle}. \quad \text{(equivalent BEGIN)}$$

This equivalent rule still specifies that e_1 is evaluated before e_2, and so on, but when the rule is written this way, it is not as easy to understand.

A BEGIN might be empty, in which case it evaluates to zero.

$$\frac{}{\langle \mathrm{BEGIN}(), \xi, \phi, \rho\rangle \Downarrow \langle 0, \xi, \phi, \rho\rangle} \quad \text{(EMPTYBEGIN)}$$

1.5.6 *Function application*

In the rules for function application, operational semantics first starts to show its advantages: the description is precise, and it is much more concise than an implementation.

User-defined functions

Application of a user-defined function f evaluates argument expressions e_1 to e_n, then evaluates the body of f in a new environment that binds each formal parameter to the value of the corresponding argument.

$$\frac{\begin{array}{c}\phi(f) = \text{USER}(\langle x_1, \ldots, x_n \rangle, e) \\ x_1, \ldots, x_n \text{ all distinct} \\ \langle e_1, \xi_0, \phi, \rho_0 \rangle \Downarrow \langle v_1, \xi_1, \phi, \rho_1 \rangle \\ \vdots \\ \langle e_n, \xi_{n-1}, \phi, \rho_{n-1} \rangle \Downarrow \langle v_n, \xi_n, \phi, \rho_n \rangle \\ \langle e, \xi_n, \phi, \{x_1 \mapsto v_1, \ldots, x_n \mapsto v_n\} \rangle \Downarrow \langle v, \xi', \phi, \rho' \rangle \end{array}}{\langle \text{APPLY}(f, e_1, \ldots, e_n), \xi_0, \phi, \rho_0 \rangle \Downarrow \langle v, \xi', \phi, \rho_n \rangle} \quad (\text{APPLYUSER})$$

As in the BEGIN rule, expressions e_1 through e_n are evaluated in order. Their values v_1 to v_n are used to create a new, unnamed formal-parameter environment that maps each formal parameter x_i to the corresponding v_i. This environment is used as a ρ to evaluate e, the body of the function.

The rule has these implications:

- The behavior of a function doesn't depend on the function's name, but only on the definition to which the name is bound.
- The body of a function can't get at the formal parameters of its caller, since the body e is evaluated in a state that does not contain $\rho_0, \ldots, \rho_n$.
- If a function assigns to its own formal parameters, its caller can't get at the new values, because the caller has no access to the environment ρ'.
- After the body of a function is evaluated, the environment ρ' containing the values of its formal parameters is thrown away. This fact matters to implementors of programming languages, who can use temporary space (in registers and on the stack) to implement formal-parameter environments.

In short, the formal parameters of a function are private to that function—neither its caller nor its callees can see them or modify them. The privacy of formal parameters is an essential part of what language designers call "functional abstraction," which both programmers and implementors rely on.

Primitive functions

Application of a primitive function resembles the application of a user-defined function. The arguments are evaluated, and the application produces the result of performing a primitive operation on their values. In principle, each primitive is describe by its own rule or rules, but this book shows only a few representatives.

The arithmetic primitives are represented by addition:

$$\frac{\begin{array}{c}\phi(f) = \text{PRIMITIVE}(\texttt{+}) \\ \langle e_1, \xi_0, \phi, \rho_0 \rangle \Downarrow \langle v_1, \xi_1, \phi, \rho_1 \rangle \\ \langle e_2, \xi_1, \phi, \rho_1 \rangle \Downarrow \langle v_2, \xi_2, \phi, \rho_2 \rangle \\ -2^{31} \le v_1 + v_2 < 2^{31}\end{array}}{\langle \text{APPLY}(f, e_1, e_2), \xi_0, \phi, \rho_0 \rangle \Downarrow \langle v_1 + v_2, \xi_2, \phi, \rho_2 \rangle}. \qquad \text{(APPLYADD)}$$

The final condition on the sum $v_1 + v_2$ ensures that the result can be represented in a 32-bit signed integer.

Comparison primitives are represented by equality. Like the `if` expression, the equality primitive is specified by a pair of rules which have mutually exclusive premises ($v_1 = v_2$ and $v_1 \neq v_2$):

$$\frac{\begin{array}{c}\phi(f) = \text{PRIMITIVE}(\texttt{=}) \\ \langle e_1, \xi_0, \phi, \rho_0 \rangle \Downarrow \langle v_1, \xi_1, \phi, \rho_1 \rangle \\ \langle e_2, \xi_1, \phi, \rho_1 \rangle \Downarrow \langle v_2, \xi_2, \phi, \rho_2 \rangle \\ v_1 = v_2\end{array}}{\langle \text{APPLY}(f, e_1, e_2), \xi_0, \phi, \rho_0 \rangle \Downarrow \langle 1, \xi_2, \phi, \rho_2 \rangle}, \qquad \text{(APPLYEQTRUE)}$$

$$\frac{\begin{array}{c}\phi(f) = \text{PRIMITIVE}(\texttt{=}) \\ \langle e_1, \xi_0, \phi, \rho_0 \rangle \Downarrow \langle v_1, \xi_1, \phi, \rho_1 \rangle \\ \langle e_2, \xi_1, \phi, \rho_1 \rangle \Downarrow \langle v_2, \xi_2, \phi, \rho_2 \rangle \\ v_1 \neq v_2\end{array}}{\langle \text{APPLY}(f, e_1, e_2), \xi_0, \phi, \rho_0 \rangle \Downarrow \langle 0, \xi_2, \phi, \rho_2 \rangle}. \qquad \text{(APPLYEQFALSE)}$$

The printing primitives are represented by `println`. These primitives have an important behavior that can't be expressed by our formal evaluation judgment: they print. Because this behavior is omitted, the rule makes `println` look like the identity function.

$$\frac{\begin{array}{c}\phi(f) = \text{PRIMITIVE}(\texttt{println}) \\ \langle e, \xi, \phi, \rho \rangle \Downarrow \langle v, \xi', \phi, \rho' \rangle\end{array}}{\langle \text{APPLY}(f, e), \xi, \phi, \rho \rangle \Downarrow \langle v, \xi', \phi, \rho' \rangle \quad \text{while printing } v} \qquad \text{(APPLYPRINTLN)}$$

The printing primitives could be modeled formally without much trouble; for example, we could extend the abstract-machine state to include a sequence of all characters ever printed. I prefer, however, not to clutter our semantics with such a list. Leaving the specification of printing informal is OK because our semantics is intended to convey understanding, not to nail down every last detail.

1.5.7 *Rules for evaluating definitions*

The rules above specify the effects of evaluating expressions. The effects of evaluating definitions are different: evaluating a definition does not produce a value, but unlike an expression, it may introduce a new global variable or a new function. New variables are added to ξ and new functions are added to ϕ, so the evaluation of a definition is described by a judgment of the form $\langle d, \xi, \phi \rangle \rightarrow \langle \xi', \phi' \rangle$. Below, this judgment is used in rules for *true* definitions, which are implemented by the `evaldef` function in Section 1.6.2. *Extended* definitions aren't formalized.

Variable definition

The definition $\text{VAL}(x, e)$ introduces a global variable x. It adds the binding $x \mapsto v$ to the global environment ξ', where v is the result of evaluating e. A definition does not appear in the body of a function, so e is evaluated without any formal parameters (ρ is $\{\}$). The DEFINEGLOBAL rule closely resembles the GLOBALASSIGN rule, but the DEFINEGLOBAL rule does not require $x \in \operatorname{dom} \xi$. It is OK if x is already a global variable, in which case $\text{VAL}(x, e)$ behaves just like $\text{SET}(x, e)$.

$$\frac{\langle e, \xi, \phi, \{\}\rangle \Downarrow \langle v, \xi', \phi, \rho'\rangle}{\langle \text{VAL}(x, e), \xi, \phi\rangle \to \langle \xi'\{x \mapsto v\}, \phi\rangle} \quad \text{(DEFINEGLOBAL)}$$

Function definition

The definition $\text{DEFINE}(f, \langle x_1, \ldots, x_n\rangle, e)$ introduces a function f. The function is represented as $\text{USER}(\langle x_1, \ldots, x_n\rangle, e)$, where $x_1, \ldots, x_n$ are the names of the formal parameters and e is the body. No two parameters may have the same name.

$$\frac{x_1, \ldots, x_n \text{ all distinct}}{\langle \text{DEFINE}(f, \langle x_1, \ldots, x_n\rangle, e), \xi, \phi\rangle \to \langle \xi, \phi\{f \mapsto \text{USER}(\langle x_1, \ldots, x_n\rangle, e)\}\rangle} \quad \text{(DEFINEFUNCTION)}$$

Top-level expression

An expression e, when entered at the read-eval-print loop, also serves as a definition. This "definition" does not introduce any new names into ξ or ϕ; e is evaluated for its side effect, and its value is stored in the global variable `it`. Therefore, evaluating an expression as a definition can modify the global-variable environment ξ but not the function environment ϕ.

$$\frac{\langle e, \xi, \phi, \{\}\rangle \Downarrow \langle v, \xi', \phi, \rho'\rangle}{\langle \text{EXP}(e), \xi, \phi\rangle \to \langle \xi'\{\texttt{it} \mapsto v\}, \phi\rangle} \quad \text{(EVALEXP)}$$

Evaluating the "definition" $\text{EXP}(e)$ has exactly the same effects as evaluating the more conventional definition $\text{VAL}(\texttt{it}, e)$.

Extended definitions

As mentioned in the sidebar on page 24, Impcore's extended-definition forms `use`, `check-expect`, `check-assert`, and `check-error` aren't specified formally. Evaluating `use` evaluates the definitions contained in the file named by the `use`, then runs that file's unit tests. And evaluating a `check-expect`, a `check-assert`, or a `check-error` remembers a unit test. Specifying `use` formally would require a model of files with names and contents. Specifying unit tests would require adding a set of pending unit tests to our abstract machine, plus judgments and inference rules that would describe what it means for a test to succeed or fail. Such things would distract us from what the semantics is meant to do: help us understand and compare programming languages.

To understand these issues for yourself, try designing rules for extended definitions. Start by defining the success or failure of `check-expect` (Exercise 17) or the success of `check-error` (Exercise 21). To specify `check-error`, you will need to design a proof system that says what it means for evaluation to halt with an error.

1.6 THE INTERPRETER

A bridge language like Impcore is meant to be small enough to learn, small enough to specify, small enough to implement, and yet big enough to write interesting programs in. (Or in the case of Impcore, not quite big enough.) To write programs requires an implementation, but why talk about it? Why not bury the implementation in a repository somewhere? Because the implementation of an interpreter can illustrate a language and its semantics in a way that nothing else can. And when you want to experiment with alternative language designs, you can build on or change my code. To make such experiments possible, I can't just hand you the code; I have to explain it. But I can't explain all of it—the explanations would add over 300 pages to this book. In this chapter, I explain just the most important parts.

A language is embodied by the data structures for its crucial abstractions (environments and abstract-syntax trees) and by the functions that evaluate expressions and definitions. They are all explained in this chapter. The crucial code is built on top of infrastructure: error handling, parsing, printing, test reporting, and so on. That infrastructure is lovingly described in a Supplement to this book, which is available from `build-prove-compare.net`. The interpreter requires only a standard C library, and with that and the Supplement, you can understand as much or as little as you wish.

The code is presented using the Noweb system for *literate programming*. Noweb extracts code directly from the text, so the code in the book is the code that runs. Noweb splits code into named "code chunks," which are surrounded by textual explanations. The code chunks are written in an order designed to support good explanations, not the order dictated by a C compiler.

Code chunks can mix source code with references to other chunks. References are italicized in angle brackets, as in ⟨*evaluate* `e->ifx` *and return the result* 49c⟩. The label "49c" shows where to find the definition: the number identifies a page, and when the page contains more than one chunk, each chunk gets its own lowercase letter, which is appended to the page number. The label also appears on the first line of the definition, in bold. Each chunk definition is shown using the $\equiv$ sign. A definition can be continued in a later chunk; Noweb concatenates the contents of all definitions of the same chunk. A definition that continues a previous definition is showing using the $+\equiv$ sign in place of the $\equiv$ sign. When a chunk's definition is continued, the right margin displays pointers to the previous and next definitions, written "◁ 48a" and "S296a ▷." The notation "(48b)" shows where a chunk is used.

To help you find relevant chunks, Noweb provides a *mini-index* in the margin of each right-hand page. For example, the mini-index on page 49 reveals that function `bindval` is defined in chunk 45b on page 45. It also reveals that type `Exp` is not defined by hand-written code; it is generated automatically. In any mini-index, $\mathcal{A}$ stands for automatically generated code, and $\mathcal{B}$ stands for a basis function from C's standard library. And $\mathcal{P}$, which is used from Chapter 2 onward, stands for a *primitive* function that is defined in an interpreter.

In most chapters, Noweb's information is supplemented by a table that relates semantics, concepts, and code, like Table 1.5 on the next page. This table will help you learn the important parts of the code, which all relate to metavariables and math symbols from Section 1.5.

The code will be clearer to you if you know my programming conventions. For example, when I introduce a new type, I use `typedef` to give it a name that begins with a capital letter, like `Name`, or `Exp`, or `Def`. The representation of such a type is often *exposed*, in which case you get to see all of the type's definition, and you get access to fields of structures and so on. A type whose representation is exposed is called *manifest*; for example, types `Exp` and `Def` are manifest. A type might also be *abstract*, in which case you *can't* get at its representation. In C, an abstract type is always a pointer to a named `struct` whose fields are not specified. For example, type `Name` is abstract; you can store a `Name` in a field or a variable, and you can pass a `Name` to a function, but you can't look inside a `Name` to see how it is represented. (Strictly speaking, *you* can see everything; as explained in Chapter 9, it is your client code, and mine, that cannot see the representations of abstract types.)

Table 1.5: Correspondence between Impcore semantics and code

Semantics	*Concept*	*Interpreter*
d	True definition	`Def` (page 42)
e	Expression	`Exp` (page 42)
x, f	Name	`Name` (page 43)
v	Value	`Value` (page 43)
$\text{USER}(\cdots)$	Function	`Userfun` (page 42), `Func` (page 44)
$\text{PRIMITIVE}(\oplus)$	Function	`Name` (page 43), `Func` (page 44)
ξ, ρ	Value environment	`Valenv` (page 44)
ϕ	Function environment	`Funenv` (page 44)
$\langle e, \xi, \phi, \rho \rangle \Downarrow \langle v, \xi', \phi, \rho' \rangle$	Expression evaluation	`eval(`e`, `ξ`, `ϕ`, `ρ`)` $= v$, with ξ and ρ updated to ξ' and ρ' (page 48)
$\langle d, \xi, \phi \rangle \rightarrow \langle \xi', \rho' \rangle$	Definition evaluation	`evaldef(`e`, `ξ`, `ϕ`, echo)` updates ξ to ξ' and ϕ to ϕ' (page 53)
$x \in \text{dom}\,\rho$	Definedness	`isvalbound` (page 45)
$f \in \text{dom}\,\phi$	Definedness	`isfunbound` (page 45)
$\rho(x), \xi(x)$	Lookup	`fetchval` (page 44)
$\phi(f)$	Lookup	`fetchfun` (page 44)
$\rho\{x \mapsto v\}$	Binding	`bindval` (page 45)
$\phi\{f \mapsto \cdots\}$	Binding	`bindfun` (page 45)

I write the names of functions using lowercase letters only, except for some automatically generated functions used to build lists.

To the degree that C permits, I distinguish interfaces from implementations. An interface typically includes some or all of these elements:

- Types, which may be manifest or abstract
- Invariants of manifest types, if any
- Prototypes of functions
- Documentation explaining how the types and functions should be used

An *atypical* interface might also include declarations of global variables, macros, or other arcana. But no interface, typical or atypical, ever includes the implementations of its functions.

Interface documentation explains not only how to use functions but also what happens when a function is used incorrectly; in particular, it explains who is responsible for detecting or avoiding an error. A *checked run-time error* is a mistake that the implementation guarantees to detect; a typical example would be passing a `NULL` pointer to a function. The implementation need not *recover* from a checked error, and indeed, many of my implementations simply halt with assertion failures.

An *unchecked* run-time error is more insidious; this is a mistake that it is up to the C programmer to avoid. If client code causes an unchecked run-time error, the implementation provides no guarantees; anything can happen. Unchecked run-time errors are part of the price we pay for programming in C.

Once you've read and understood an interface, you should be able to use its functions without needing to look at their implementations. But of course the cru-

Run-time errors and safety

A language in which all errors are checked is called *safe*. Safety is usually implemented by a combination of compile-time and run-time checking. Popular safe languages include Awk, C#, Haskell, Go, Java, JavaScript, Lua, ML, Perl, Python, Ruby, Rust, Scheme, and Smalltalk. A safe language might be characterized by saying that "there are no unexplained core dumps"; a program that halts always issues an informative error message.

A language that permits unchecked errors is called *unsafe*. Unsafe languages put an extra burden on the programmer, but they provide extra expressive power. This extra power is needed to write things like garbage collectors and device drivers; systems programming languages, like Bliss and C, have historically been unsafe. C++ is an anomaly: it is ostensibly intended for high-level problem-solving, but it is nevertheless unsafe.

A few well-designed systems-programming languages are safe by default, but have unsafe features that can be turned on explicitly at need, usually by a keyword `UNSAFE`. The best known of these may be Cedar and Modula-3.

cial implementations, of functions like `eval` and `evaldef`, are intended for you to look at. When you look at them, you'll see that they respect these conventions:

- Within reason, each local variable is declared in the region in which it is used; local variables typically don't scope over an entire function definition.
- When possible, each variable is initialized where it is declared, making its declaration resemble a `val` definition in Impcore.

On to the code! The presentation begins with the interfaces in Section 1.6.1. These interfaces include not only the interfaces associated with the evaluator, but also some interfaces associated with general-purpose utility code from the Supplement (Appendix F). These interfaces are necessary building blocks, but they aren't the main event; the main event is the implementation of Impcore's operational semantics in Section 1.6.2, which starts on page 48.

1.6.1 *Interfaces*

Everything comes together in the evaluator, which implements the operational semantics. That evaluator is supported by interfaces for the central structures of a programming language: syntax, names, values, environments, and lists thereof. It is also supported by interfaces used for printing and for reporting errors.

Interface to abstract syntax: Manifest types and creator functions

The abstract-syntax interface exposes the representations of definitions, expressions, and so on. It also provides convenient *creator functions* which are used to build abstract-syntax trees.

An abstract-syntax tree is a value of a *sum type*; such a type is also called a *discriminated-union type*. A sum type specifies a list of alternative forms; every value of the type takes the form of one of the alternatives. Sum types play an essential role in symbolic computing, but they are not directly supported in C. C provides only an *undiscriminated* union, sometimes also called an "unsafe" union. A C union specifies a list of alternative forms, called "members," but from the union alone, you can't tell what form a value or variable is intended to have. To represent a sum type in C requires not only a union but also a *discriminant* (a "tag"), which says which form of the union is in use. In this book, the tag and the union are placed together in a C struct. The tag is called alt (for "alternative"), and the union is unnamed. A tag is referred to by name, as in e->alt, and in the union, each alternative is referred to by name, as in e->var or d->define. An alternative may itself have multiple named parts; for example, if d represents a val definition, the name of the variable being defined is d->val.name, and the expression that gives it its initial value is d->val.exp.

The name of each alternative appears in two places: in an enumeration type that defines the possible values of alt, and in the union type, which lists the possible forms of the union. And in keeping with common C practice, each enumeration literal is written using all capital letters, and each member of the union is written in lower case.

Our first complete example is the true definition Def, a simplified version of which appears in chunk ⟨*simplified example of abstract syntax for Impcore* 27d⟩. A Def is a sum type with three alternatives, called VAL, EXP, and DEFINE.

42a. ⟨*type and structure definitions for Impcore* 42a⟩≡ 44c ▷

```
typedef struct Userfun Userfun;
struct Userfun { Namelist formals; Exp body; };

typedef struct Def *Def;
typedef enum { VAL, EXP, DEFINE } Defalt;
struct Def {
    Defalt alt;
    union {
        struct { Name name; Exp exp; } val;
        Exp exp;
        struct { Name name; Userfun userfun; } define;
    } ;
};
```

Such type definitions and creator functions are hard to write and maintain by hand. So I generate them automatically, using an ML program that appears in Appendix J. That program generates the Def type and associated functions from the following descriptions:

42b. ⟨*definition.t* 42b⟩≡

```
Userfun = (Namelist formals, Exp body)
Def*    = VAL          (Name name, Exp exp)
        | EXP          (Exp)
        | DEFINE       (Name name, Userfun userfun)
```

A valid Userfun satisfies the invariant that the names in formals are all distinct.

The abstract syntax for Exp, which you might wish to compare with the concrete syntax given for *exp* on page 18, is described as follows:

42c. ⟨*exp.t* 42c⟩≡

```
Exp* = LITERAL (Value)
     | VAR     (Name)
     | SET     (Name name, Exp exp)
     | IFX     (Exp cond, Exp truex, Exp falsex)
     | WHILEX  (Exp cond, Exp exp)
     | BEGIN   (Explist)
     | APPLY   (Name name, Explist actuals)
```

The descriptions above[4] are slightly elaborated versions of ⟨*simplified example of abstract syntax for Impcore* 27d⟩. Similar descriptions are used for much of the C code in this book.

True definitions and expressions are the essential elements of abstract syntax; once you understand how they work, you will be ready to connect the operational semantics and the code. Impcore's *extended* definitions, including unit tests, are described in the Supplement.

Interface to names: An abstract type

Programs are full of names. To make it easy to compare names and look them up in tables, I define an abstract type to represent them. Although each name is built from a string, the abstract type hides the string and its characters. Unlike C strings, names are immutable, and two names are equal if and only if they are the same pointer.

43a. ⟨*shared type definitions* 43a⟩≡ (S295a)

```
typedef struct Name *Name;
typedef struct Namelist *Namelist;    // list of Name
```

A name may be built from a string or converted to a string.

43b. ⟨*shared function prototypes* 43b⟩≡ (S295a) 46b ▷

```
Name strtoname(const char *s);
const char *nametostr(Name x);
```

These functions satisfy the following algebraic laws:

`strcmp(s, nametostr(strtoname(s))) == 0`
`strcmp(s, t) == 0` if and only if `strtoname(s) == strtoname(t)`

The first law says if you build a name from a string, `nametostr` returns a copy of your original string. The second law says you can compare names using pointer equality.

Because `nametostr` returns a string of type `const char*`, a client of `nametostr` cannot modify that string without subverting the type system. Modification of the string is an unchecked run-time error. New values of type `Name*` should be created only by calling `strtoname`; to do so by casting other pointers is a subversion of the type system and an unchecked run-time error.

Interface to values

The value interface defines the type of value that an expression may evaluate to. In Impcore, that is always a 32-bit integer. A `Valuelist` is a list of `Values`.

43c. ⟨*type definitions for Impcore* 43c⟩≡ (S295a) 44a ▷

```
typedef int32_t Value;
typedef struct Valuelist *Valuelist;    // list of Value
```

[4]The alternatives for `if` and `while` are named `IFX` and `WHILEX`, not `IF` and `WHILE`. Why? Because corresponding to each alternative, there is a field of a union that uses the same name in *lower* case. For example, if `e` is a `LITERAL` expression, the literal `Value` is found in field `e->literal`. But a structure field can't be named `if` or `while`, because the names `if` and `while` are *reserved words*—they may be used only to mark C syntax. So I call these alternatives `IFX` and `WHILEX`, which I encourage you to think of as "`if`-expression" and "`while`-expression." For similar reasons, the two branches of the `IFX` are called `truex` and `falsex`, not `true` and `false`. And in Chapter 2, you'll see `LETX` and `LAMBDAX` instead of `LET` and `LAMBDA`, so that I can write an interpreter for μScheme in μScheme.

Interface to functions, both user-defined and primitive

In the Impcore interpreter, the type "function" is another sum type. This type specifies two alternatives: user-defined functions and primitive functions. Following the operational semantics, which represents a user-defined function as USER($\langle x_1, \ldots, x_n \rangle, e$), a user-defined function is represented as a pair containing formals and body. A primitive is represented by its name.

44a. ⟨*type definitions for Impcore* 43c⟩+≡ (S295a) ◁43c 44e▷

```
typedef struct Funclist *Funclist; // list of Func
```

44b. ⟨*fun.t* 44b⟩≡

```
Func = USERDEF   (Userfun)
     | PRIMITIVE (Name)
```

This description is used to generate these type and structure definitions:

44c. ⟨*type and structure definitions for Impcore* 42a⟩+≡ ◁42a

```
typedef struct Func Func;
typedef enum { USERDEF, PRIMITIVE } Funcalt;
struct Func { Funcalt alt; union { Userfun userdef; Name primitive; } ; };
```

Also generated automatically are these prototypes for creator functions.

44d. ⟨*function prototypes for Impcore* 44d⟩≡ (S295a) 44f▷

```
Func mkUserdef(Userfun userdef);
Func mkPrimitive(Name primitive);
```

Interface to environments: More abstract types

In the operational semantics, the environments ρ and ξ hold values, and the environment ϕ holds functions. Each kind of environment has its own representation.[5]

44e. ⟨*type definitions for Impcore* 43c⟩+≡ (S295a) ◁44a

```
typedef struct Valenv *Valenv;
typedef struct Funenv *Funenv;
```

A new environment may be created by passing a list of names and a list of associated values or function definitions to `mkValenv` or `mkFunenv`. For example, calling `mkValenv`($\langle x_1, \ldots, x_n \rangle, \langle v_1, \ldots, v_n \rangle$) returns $\{x_1 \mapsto v_1, \ldots, x_n \mapsto v_n\}$. Passing lists of different lengths is a checked run-time error.

44f. ⟨*function prototypes for Impcore* 44d⟩+≡ (S295a) ◁44d 44g▷

```
Valenv mkValenv(Namelist vars, Valuelist vals);
Funenv mkFunenv(Namelist vars, Funclist  defs);
```

A value or a function definition is retrieved using `fetchval` or `fetchfun`. In the operational semantics, the lookup `fetchval`(x, ρ) is simply $\rho(x)$.

44g. ⟨*function prototypes for Impcore* 44d⟩+≡ (S295a) ◁44f 45a▷

```
Value fetchval(Name name, Valenv env);
Func  fetchfun(Name name, Funenv env);
```

[5] By defining one C type for environments that hold a `Value` and another for environments that hold a `Func`, I ensure type safety—but at the cost of having to write two essentially identical versions of each function. In C, the only alternative is to define a single C type for environments, which would hold a `void*` pointer, which would then be cast to a `Value*` or `Func*` as needed. This choice duplicates no code, but it is unsafe; if we accidentally put a `Value*` in an environment intended to hold a `Func*`, it is an error that neither the C compiler nor the run-time system can detect. In the interests of safety, I duplicate code. Chapter 5 shows how in another implementation language, ML, we can use *polymorphism* to achieve type safety without duplicating code. Similar results can be obtained using C++, Java, and other languages.

If the given name is not bound in the environment, calling `fetchval` or `fetchfun` is a checked run-time error. To ensure that fetching is safe, first call `isvalbound` or `isfunbound`; these functions return `1` if the given name is in the environment, and `0` otherwise. Formally, `isvalbound(`x`, `ρ`)` is written $x \in \text{dom}\, \rho$.

45a. ⟨*function prototypes for Impcore* 44d⟩+≡ (S295a) ◁ 44g 45b ▷

```
bool isvalbound(Name name, Valenv env);
bool isfunbound(Name name, Funenv env);
```

To add new bindings to an environment, use `bindval` and `bindfun`. Unlike the previous six functions, `bindval` and `bindfun` are not pure: instead of returning new environments, `bindval` and `bindfun` *mutate* their argument environments, replacing the old bindings with new ones. Calling `bindval(`x`, `v`, `ρ`)` is equivalent to performing the assignment $\rho := \rho\{x \mapsto v\}$. Because ρ is a *mutable* abstraction, modifications to the environment are visible to whatever code calls `bindval`.

45b. ⟨*function prototypes for Impcore* 44d⟩+≡ (S295a) ◁ 45a 45c ▷

```
void bindval(Name name, Value val, Valenv env);
void bindfun(Name name, Func  fun, Funenv env);
```

These functions can be used to replace existing bindings or to add new ones.

Interface to the evaluator

The evaluator works with abstract syntax and values, whose representations are exposed, and with names and environments, whose representations are not exposed. Its interface exports functions `eval` and `evaldef`, which evaluate expressions and true definitions, respectively. (Extended definitions are evaluated by function `readevalprint`, which is described in the Supplement.) Function `eval` implements the $\Downarrow$ relation in our operational semantics. For example, `eval`(e, ξ, ϕ, ρ) finds a v, ξ', and ρ' such that $\langle e, \xi, \phi, \rho\rangle \Downarrow \langle v, \xi', \phi, \rho'\rangle$, assigns $\rho := \rho'$ and $\xi := \xi'$, and returns v. Function `evaldef` similarly implements the $\rightarrow$ relation.

45c. ⟨*function prototypes for Impcore* 44d⟩+≡ (S295a) ◁ 45b

```
Value eval   (Exp e, Valenv globals, Funenv functions, Valenv formals);
void  evaldef(Def d, Valenv globals, Funenv functions, Echo echo_level);
```

Just as the forms of the evaluation judgments tell us something about the operational semantics, the types of the evaluation functions tell us something about the implementation. The result types confirm that evaluating an `Exp` produces a value but evaluating a `Def` does not. Both kinds of evaluations can have side effects on environments. Finally, the `echo_level` parameter, which has no counterpart in the semantics, controls printing: when `echo_level` is `ECHOING`, `evaldef` prints the values and names of top-level expressions and functions. When `echo_level` is `NOT_ECHOING`, `evaldef` does not print.

type `Def` $\mathcal{A}$
type `Echo` S293f
type `Exp` $\mathcal{A}$
type `Func` $\mathcal{A}$
type `Name` 43a
type `Namelist` 43a
type `Userfun` $\mathcal{A}$
type `Value` 43c
type `Valuelist` 43c

Interface to lists

The evaluator's data structures include many lists: names, values, functions, expressions, and unit tests are all placed in lists. For safety, each list has its own type: `Namelist`, `Valuelist`, `Funclist`, `Explist`, and `UnitTestlist`. Each of these types is recursive; a list is either empty or is a pointer to a pair (`hd`, `tl`), where `hd` is the first element of the list and `tl` is the rest of the list. An empty list is represented by a null pointer. Each list type is defined in the same way, as in this example:

45d. ⟨*example structure definitions for Impcore* 45d⟩≡

```
struct Explist {
    Exp hd;
    struct Explist *tl;
};
```

The type definitions are generated by a Lua script, which searches header files for lines of the form

```
typedef struct Foo *Foo; // list of Foo
```


For each type of list, the script also generates a length function, an extractor, a creator function, and a print function. These functions are named `lengthTL`, `nthTL`, `mkTL`, and `printTL`, where *T* is the first letter of the list type. The length of the `NULL` list is zero; the length of any other list is the number of its elements. Elements are numbered from zero, and asking for `nthTL(xs, n)` when `n` $\geq$ `lengthTL(xs)` is a checked run-time error. Calling `mkTL` creates a fresh list with the new element at the head; it does not mutate the old list.

The list functions have prototypes like these:

46a. ⟨*example function prototypes for Impcore* 46a⟩≡

```
int     lengthEL(Explist es);
Exp     nthEL   (Explist es, unsigned n);
Explist mkEL    (Exp e, Explist es);
Explist popEL   (Explist es);
```

Definitions and function prototypes for all the list types can be found in the interpreter's `all.h` file. Because of the repetition, this code is tedious to read, but generating the code automatically makes the tedium bearable. And ML's polymorphism enables a simpler solution (Chapter 5).

Interface to infrastructure: Printing

After evaluating a definition, the interpreter prints a name or a value. And when an error occurs, the interpreter may need to print a faulty expression or definition. Strings and numbers can easily be printed using `printf`, but expressions and definitions can't. So instead, the interpreter uses functions `print` and `fprint`, which replace `printf` and `fprintf`. These functions, which are defined in the Supplement, support direct printing of `Exp`s, `Def`s, `Name`s, and so on.

46b. ⟨*shared function prototypes* 43b⟩+≡ (S295a) ◁ 43b 47a ▷

```
void print (const char *fmt, ...);  // print to standard output
void fprint(FILE *output, const char *fmt, ...);  // print to given file
```

By design, `print` and `fprint` resemble `printf` and `fprintf`: the `fmt` parameter is a "format string" that contains "conversion specifications." Our conversion specifications are like those used by `printf`, but much simpler. A conversion specification is two characters: a percent sign followed by a character like `d` or `s`, which is called a *conversion specifier*. Unlike standard conversion specifications, ours don't contain minus signs, numbers, or dots. The ones used in the Impcore interpreter are shown here in Table 1.6. By convention, lowercase specifiers print individual values; uppercase specifiers print lists. Most specifiers are named for the initial letter of what they print, but the specifier for a `Def` must not be `%d`: the `%d` is too firmly established as a specifier for printing decimal integers. Instead, `Def` is specified by `%t`, for "top level," which is where a `Def` appears.
Functions `print` and `fprint` are *unsafe*; if you pass an argument that is not consistent with the corresponding conversion specifier, it is an *unchecked* run-time error.

Interface to infrastructure: Error handling

When it encounters a fault, the Impcore interpreter complains and recovers by calling a function in an error-handling interface. In general, a fault occurs whenever

Table 1.6: Conversion specifiers for impcore

%%	Print a percent sign
%d	Print an integer in decimal format
%e	Print an Exp
%f	Print a Func
%E	Print an Explist (list of Exp)
%n	Print a Name
%N	Print a Namelist (list of Name)
%p	Print a Par (see Appendix K)
%P	Print a Parlist (list of Par)
%s	Print a char* (string)
%t	Print a Def (t stands for "top level", which is where definitions appear)
%v	Print a Value
%V	Print a Valuelist (list of Value)

a program is ill formed, ill typed, or ill behaved, but Impcore has no static type system, so faults are triggered only by ill-formed and ill-behaved programs:

- When it detects an ill-formed program during parsing, the interpreter signals a *syntax error* by calling synerror.
- When it detects an ill-behaved program at run time, the interpreter signals a *run-time error* by calling runerror.

Before initiating error recovery, each error-signaling function prints a message. For that reason, an error-signaling function's interface resembles print. But because different information is available at parse time and at run time, synerror and runerror have different interfaces.

The simpler of the two is runerror. During normal operation, runerror prints to standard error and then longjmps to errorjmp.

47a. ⟨*shared function prototypes* 43b⟩+≡ (S295a) ◁46b 47b▷

```
void runerror (const char *fmt, ...);
extern jmp_buf errorjmp;         // longjmp here on error
```

During unit testing, runerror operates in *testing* mode, and it behaves a little differently (Section F.5.1, page S182).

Function synerror is like runerror, except that before its format string, it takes an argument of type Sourceloc, which tracks the source-code location being read at the time of the error. The location can be printed as part of the error message.

47b. ⟨*shared function prototypes* 43b⟩+≡ (S295a) ◁47a 47c▷

```
void synerror (Sourceloc src, const char *fmt, ...);
```

type Exp $\mathcal{A}$
type Sourceloc S293h

Error *handling*, as opposed to error signaling, is implemented by calling setjmp on errorjmp. Function setjmp must be called before any error-signaling function. It is an unchecked run-time error to call runerror or synerror except when a setjmp involving errorjmp is active on the C call stack.

One common run-time error is that an Impcore function is called with the wrong number of arguments. That error is detected by function checkargc. Its parameter e holds the call in which the error might occur.

47c. ⟨*shared function prototypes* 43b⟩+≡ (S295a) ◁47b

```
void checkargc(Exp e, int expected, int actual);
```

1.6.2 *Implementation of the evaluator*

The evaluator implements Impcore's semantics. It comprises functions `eval` and `evaldef`, which evaluate expressions and true definitions.

Evaluating expressions

Function `eval` implements the $\Downarrow$ relation from the operational semantics. Calling `eval`(e, ξ, ϕ, ρ) finds a v, ξ', and ρ' such that $\langle e, \xi, \phi, \rho \rangle \Downarrow \langle v, \xi', \phi, \rho' \rangle$, assigns $\rho := \rho'$ and $\xi := \xi'$, and returns v. Because Greek letters aren't customary in C code, I use these English names:

ξ	`globals`
ϕ	`functions`
ρ	`formals`

Function `eval` is mutually recursive with a private helper function, `evallist`:

48a. ⟨*eval.c* 48a⟩≡ 48b ▷

```
static Valuelist evallist(Explist es, Valenv globals, Funenv functions,
                          Valenv formals);
```

Evaluation of an expression e begins by discovering its syntactic form, using a `switch` on the tag `e->alt`.

48b. ⟨*eval.c* 48a⟩+≡ ◁ 48a 51b ▷

```
Value eval(Exp e, Valenv globals, Funenv functions, Valenv formals) {
    switch (e->alt) {
    case LITERAL: ⟨evaluate e->literal and return the result 48c⟩
    case VAR:     ⟨evaluate e->var and return the result 49a⟩
    case SET:     ⟨evaluate e->set and return the result 49b⟩
    case IFX:     ⟨evaluate e->ifx and return the result 49c⟩
    case WHILEX:  ⟨evaluate e->whilex and return the result 50a⟩
    case BEGIN:   ⟨evaluate e->begin and return the result 50b⟩
    case APPLY:   ⟨evaluate e->apply and return the result 50c⟩
    }
    assert(0);
}
```

The assertion at the end of `eval` might seem superfluous, but it isn't; it helps protect me, and you, from mistakes, and it convinces the C compiler that every possible case is covered.

Function `eval` proceeds by case analysis over the syntactic forms of `Exp`. Each case is written in consultation with the operational semantics: for each syntactic form, `eval` implements the rules that have the form on the left-hand sides of their *conclusions*.

The LITERAL form appears in the conclusion of just one rule.

$$\frac{}{\langle \text{LITERAL}(v), \xi, \phi, \rho \rangle \Downarrow \langle v, \xi, \phi, \rho \rangle} \qquad (\text{LITERAL})$$

The implementation returns the literal value.

48c. ⟨*evaluate* `e->literal` *and return the result* 48c⟩≡ (48b)

```
return e->literal;
```

The VAR form appears in the conclusions of two rules.

$$\frac{x \in \operatorname{dom} \rho}{\langle \text{VAR}(x), \xi, \phi, \rho \rangle \Downarrow \langle \rho(x), \xi, \phi, \rho \rangle} \qquad (\text{FORMALVAR})$$

$$\frac{x \notin \operatorname{dom} \rho \qquad x \in \operatorname{dom} \xi}{\langle \text{VAR}(x), \xi, \phi, \rho \rangle \Downarrow \langle \xi(x), \xi, \phi, \rho \rangle} \qquad (\text{GLOBALVAR})$$

A rule can be used only if its premises hold, so the interpreter checks $x \in \operatorname{dom} \rho$, which is implemented by calling `isvalbound(e->var, formals)`. If $x \notin \operatorname{dom} \rho$ and $x \notin \operatorname{dom} \xi$, the operational semantics gets stuck—so the interpreter issues an error message. Less formally, the interpreter looks for x in the formal-parameter environment first, then the global environment.

49a. ⟨*evaluate* `e->var` *and return the result* 49a⟩≡ (48b)

```
if (isvalbound(e->var, formals))
    return fetchval(e->var, formals);
else if (isvalbound(e->var, globals))
    return fetchval(e->var, globals);
else
    runerror("unbound variable %n", e->var);
```


The call to `runerror` illustrates the convenience of the extensible printer; it uses `%n` to print a `Name` directly, without needing to convert the `Name` to a string.

The SET form is very similar. Again there are two rules, and again they are distinguished by testing $x \in \operatorname{dom} \rho$.

$$\frac{x \in \operatorname{dom} \rho \qquad \langle e, \xi, \phi, \rho \rangle \Downarrow \langle v, \xi', \phi, \rho' \rangle}{\langle \mathrm{SET}(x, e), \xi, \phi, \rho \rangle \Downarrow \langle v, \xi', \phi, \rho'\{x \mapsto v\} \rangle} \quad \text{(FORMALASSIGN)}$$

$$\frac{x \notin \operatorname{dom} \rho \qquad x \in \operatorname{dom} \xi \qquad \langle e, \xi, \phi, \rho \rangle \Downarrow \langle v, \xi', \phi, \rho' \rangle}{\langle \mathrm{SET}(x, e), \xi, \phi, \rho \rangle \Downarrow \langle v, \xi'\{x \mapsto v\}, \phi, \rho' \rangle} \quad \text{(GLOBALASSIGN)}$$

Because both rules require the premise $\langle e, \xi, \phi, \rho \rangle \Downarrow \langle v, \xi', \phi, \rho' \rangle$, the code evaluates e (`e->set.exp`) first, then puts its value in `v`.

49b. ⟨*evaluate* `e->set` *and return the result* 49b⟩≡ (48b)

```
{
    Value v = eval(e->set.exp, globals, functions, formals);

    if (isvalbound(e->set.name, formals))
        bindval(e->set.name, v, formals);
    else if (isvalbound(e->set.name, globals))
        bindval(e->set.name, v, globals);
    else
        runerror("tried to set unbound variable %n in %e", e->set.name, e);
    return v;
}
```

The IF form appears in the conclusions of two rules.

$$\frac{\langle e_1, \xi, \phi, \rho \rangle \Downarrow \langle v_1, \xi', \phi, \rho' \rangle \qquad v_1 \neq 0 \qquad \langle e_2, \xi', \phi, \rho' \rangle \Downarrow \langle v_2, \xi'', \phi, \rho'' \rangle}{\langle \mathrm{IF}(e_1, e_2, e_3), \xi, \phi, \rho \rangle \Downarrow \langle v_2, \xi'', \phi, \rho'' \rangle} \quad \text{(IFTRUE)}$$

$$\frac{\langle e_1, \xi, \phi, \rho \rangle \Downarrow \langle v_1, \xi', \phi, \rho' \rangle \qquad v_1 = 0 \qquad \langle e_3, \xi', \phi, \rho' \rangle \Downarrow \langle v_3, \xi'', \phi, \rho'' \rangle}{\langle \mathrm{IF}(e_1, e_2, e_3), \xi, \phi, \rho \rangle \Downarrow \langle v_3, \xi'', \phi, \rho'' \rangle} \quad \text{(IFFALSE)}$$

Both rules have the same first premise: $\langle e_1, \xi, \phi, \rho \rangle \Downarrow \langle v_1, \xi', \phi, \rho' \rangle$. To get v_1, ξ', and ρ', the code calls `eval(e->ifx.cond, globals, functions, formals)` recursively. This call may mutate the `globals` and `formals` environments, but regardless of whether $v_1 = 0$, the mutation is safe, because the third premises of *both* rules use the new environments ξ' and ρ'. Comparing v_1 with zero determines which rule should be used: the implementation ends with a recursive call to evaluate either e_2 (`e->ifx.truex`) or e_3 (`e->ifx.falsex`).

49c. ⟨*evaluate* `e->ifx` *and return the result* 49c⟩≡ (48b)

```
if (eval(e->ifx.cond, globals, functions, formals) != 0)
    return eval(e->ifx.truex, globals, functions, formals);
else
    return eval(e->ifx.falsex, globals, functions, formals);
```

The WHILE form appears in the conclusions of two rules.

$$\frac{\begin{array}{c}\langle e_1, \xi, \phi, \rho \rangle \Downarrow \langle v_1, \xi', \phi, \rho' \rangle \qquad v_1 \neq 0 \\ \langle e_2, \xi', \phi, \rho' \rangle \Downarrow \langle v_2, \xi'', \phi, \rho'' \rangle \qquad \langle \text{WHILE}(e_1, e_2), \xi'', \phi, \rho'' \rangle \Downarrow \langle v_3, \xi''', \phi, \rho''' \rangle\end{array}}{\langle \text{WHILE}(e_1, e_2), \xi, \phi, \rho \rangle \Downarrow \langle v_3, \xi''', \phi, \rho''' \rangle} \quad \text{(WHILEITERATE)}$$

$$\frac{\langle e_1, \xi, \phi, \rho \rangle \Downarrow \langle v_1, \xi', \phi, \rho' \rangle \qquad v_1 = 0}{\langle \text{WHILE}(e_1, e_2), \xi, \phi, \rho \rangle \Downarrow \langle 0, \xi', \phi, \rho' \rangle} \quad \text{(WHILEEND)}$$

In the first rule, the premise $\langle \text{WHILE}(e_1, e_2), \xi'', \phi, \rho'' \rangle \Downarrow \langle v_3, \xi''', \phi, \rho''' \rangle$ could be implemented as a recursive call to `eval(e, ...)`. But `e` is always a while loop, so I have optimized the code by turning the recursion into iteration. This optimization prevents a long WHILE loop from overflowing the C stack.

50a. ⟨*evaluate* `e->whilex` *and return the result* 50a⟩≡ (48b)

```
while (eval(e->whilex.cond, globals, functions, formals) != 0)
    eval(e->whilex.exp, globals, functions, formals);
return 0;
```

The BEGIN form appears in the conclusions of two rules.

$$\frac{}{\langle \text{BEGIN}(), \xi, \phi, \rho \rangle \Downarrow \langle 0, \xi, \phi, \rho \rangle} \quad \text{(EMPTYBEGIN)}$$

$$\frac{\begin{array}{c}\langle e_1, \xi_0, \phi, \rho_0 \rangle \Downarrow \langle v_1, \xi_1, \phi, \rho_1 \rangle \\ \langle e_2, \xi_1, \phi, \rho_1 \rangle \Downarrow \langle v_2, \xi_2, \phi, \rho_2 \rangle \\ \vdots \\ \langle e_n, \xi_{n-1}, \phi, \rho_{n-1} \rangle \Downarrow \langle v_n, \xi_n, \phi, \rho_n \rangle\end{array}}{\langle \text{BEGIN}(e_1, e_2, \ldots, e_n), \xi_0, \phi, \rho_0 \rangle \Downarrow \langle v_n, \xi_n, \phi, \rho_n \rangle} \quad \text{(BEGIN)}$$

A nonempty BEGIN is implemented by iterating over its subexpressions, leaving the last value in variable `lastval`. If `lastval` is initialized to zero, the same code also implements the empty BEGIN.

50b. ⟨*evaluate* `e->begin` *and return the result* 50b⟩≡ (48b)

```
{
    Value lastval = 0;
    for (Explist es = e->begin; es; es = es->tl)
        lastval = eval(es->hd, globals, functions, formals);
    return lastval;
}
```

Function application appears in the conclusion of the APPLYUSER rule, and also in every rule that describes a primitive function. The rule to be implemented depends on the form of the function, which may be `USERDEF` or `PRIMITIVE`. Given a function named f (`e->apply.name`), the interpreter discovers its form by looking at $\phi(f)$, which it stores in local variable `f`.

50c. ⟨*evaluate* `e->apply` *and return the result* 50c⟩≡ (48b)

```
{
    Func f;
    ⟨make f the function denoted by e->apply.name, or call runerror 51a⟩
    switch (f.alt) {
    case USERDEF:   ⟨apply f.userdef and return the result 51c⟩
    case PRIMITIVE: ⟨apply f.primitive and return the result 52a⟩
    default:        assert(0);
    }
}
```

If f is not defined as a function, the result is a run-time error.

51a. ⟨*make* `f` *the function denoted by* `e->apply.name`*, or call* `runerror` 51a⟩≡ (50c)

```
if (!isfunbound(e->apply.name, functions))
    runerror("call to undefined function %n in %e", e->apply.name, e);
f = fetchfun(e->apply.name, functions);
```

When f is a user-defined function, applying it has something in common with `begin`: arguments $e_1, \ldots, e_n$ have to be evaluated. But where `begin` keeps only result v_n (in variable `v` in chunk 50b), function application keeps *all* the result values, which it binds into a new environment.

$$\frac{\begin{array}{c}\phi(f) = \text{USER}(\langle x_1, \ldots, x_n\rangle, e) \\ x_1, \ldots, x_n \text{ all distinct} \\ \langle e_1, \xi_0, \phi, \rho_0\rangle \Downarrow \langle v_1, \xi_1, \phi, \rho_1\rangle \\ \vdots \\ \langle e_n, \xi_{n-1}, \phi, \rho_{n-1}\rangle \Downarrow \langle v_n, \xi_n, \phi, \rho_n\rangle \\ \langle e, \xi_n, \phi, \{x_1 \mapsto v_1, \ldots, x_n \mapsto v_n\}\rangle \Downarrow \langle v, \xi', \phi, \rho'\rangle\end{array}}{\langle \text{APPLY}(f, e_1, \ldots, e_n), \xi_0, \phi, \rho_0\rangle \Downarrow \langle v, \xi', \phi, \rho_n\rangle} \quad (\text{APPLYUSER})$$

Values $v_1, \ldots, v_n$, are returned by auxiliary function `evallist`, which is given $e_1, \ldots, e_n$ along with ξ_0, ϕ, and ρ_0. It evaluates $e_1, \ldots, e_n$ in order, and it mutates the environments so that when it is finished, `globals` is ξ_n and `formals` is ρ_n. Finally, `evallist` returns the list $v_1, \ldots, v_n$.

51b. ⟨*eval.c* 48a⟩+≡ ◁48b 53b▷

```
static Valuelist evallist(Explist es, Valenv globals, Funenv functions,
                          Valenv formals)
{
    if (es == NULL) {
        return NULL;
    } else {
        Value v = eval(es->hd, globals, functions, formals);
        return mkVL(v, evallist(es->tl, globals, functions, formals));
    }
}
```

The rules of Impcore require that `es->hd` be evaluated before `es->tl`. To ensure the correct order of evaluation, `eval(es->hd, ...)` and `evallist(es->tl, ...)` are called in separate C statements. Writing both calls as parameters to `mkVL` would not guarantee the correct order.

The APPLYUSER rule requires that the application have exactly as many arguments as f is expecting: the list of formal parameters and the list of argument expressions both have length n. But in general, they might be different: the formals $x_1, \ldots, x_n$ are stored in `xs` and the actual values $v_1, \ldots, v_m$ are stored in `vs`. When both are the same length, as confirmed by `checkargc`, they are used to create the fresh environment `mkValenv(xs, vs)`, which is $\{x_1 \mapsto v_1, \ldots, x_n \mapsto v_n\}$. This environment is used to evaluate f's body.

51c. ⟨*apply* `f.userdef` *and return the result* 51c⟩≡ (50c)

```
{
    Namelist  xs = f.userdef.formals;
    Valuelist vs = evallist(e->apply.actuals, globals, functions, formals);
    checkargc(e, lengthNL(xs), lengthVL(vs));
    return eval(f.userdef.body, globals, functions, mkValenv(xs, vs));
}
```

Each primitive function is applied by code that is specialized to that primitive. A primitive is identified by comparing its name to a name made from a known string. More general techniques for implementing primitives, which are appropriate for larger languages, are shown in the Chapter 2 (page 154).

52a. ⟨*apply* `f.primitive` *and return the result* 52a⟩≡ (50c)

```
{
    Valuelist vs = evallist(e->apply.actuals, globals, functions, formals);
    if (f.primitive == strtoname("print"))
        ⟨apply Impcore primitive print to vs and return 52b⟩
    else if (f.primitive == strtoname("println"))
        ⟨apply Impcore primitive println to vs and return S299c⟩
    else if (f.primitive == strtoname("printu"))
        ⟨apply Impcore primitive printu to vs and return S299d⟩
    else
        ⟨apply arithmetic primitive to vs and return 52c⟩
}
```

Only `print` is implemented here; `println` and `printu` are in Appendix K.

52b. ⟨*apply Impcore primitive* `print` *to* `vs` *and return* 52b⟩≡ (52a)

```
{
    checkargc(e, 1, lengthVL(vs));
    Value v = nthVL(vs, 0);
    print("%v", v);
    return v;
}
```

Each arithmetic primitive expects exactly two arguments, which the code puts in C variables `v` and `w`. The characters of the primitive's name go in `s`.

52c. ⟨*apply arithmetic primitive to* `vs` *and return* 52c⟩≡ (52a)

```
{
    checkargc(e, 2, lengthVL(vs));
    Value v = nthVL(vs, 0);
    Value w = nthVL(vs, 1);
    const char *s = nametostr(f.primitive);
    ⟨if operation s would overflow on v and w, call runerror 53a⟩
    ⟨return a function of v and w determined by s 52d⟩
}
```

Ignoring the possibility of overflow, each Impcore primitive can be implemented by the corresponding operation in C. The primitive's name is synonymous with its first character, `s[0]`.

52d. ⟨*return a function of* `v` *and* `w` *determined by* `s` 52d⟩≡ (52c)

```
assert(strlen(s) == 1);
switch (s[0]) {
case '<':    return v < w;
case '>':    return v > w;
case '=':    return v == w;
case '+':    return v + w;
case '-':    return v - w;
case '*':    return v * w;
case '/':    if (w == 0)
                 runerror("division by zero in %e", e);
             return v / w;
default:     assert(0);
}
```

But the interpreter cannot ignore the possibility of overflow. The rules of Impcore are different from the rules of C, and if the result of an arithmetic operation does not fit in the range -2^{31} to 2^{31}, the operation causes a checked run-time error.

The error is detected and signaled by function checkarith, which is defined in Appendix F.

53a. ⟨*if operation* s *would overflow on* v *and* w, *call* runerror 53a⟩≡ (52c)

```
checkarith(s[0], v, w, 32);
```

Evaluating true definitions

As noted on page 24, definitions are divided into two forms: The true definitions can differ in each language; Impcore's true definitions include val and define. The extended definitions are shared across languages; they include use and check-expect. True definitions have an operational semantics; extended definitions don't. And true definitions are evaluated by code that is explained here; extended definitions are evaluated by code in the Supplement.

The $\rightarrow$ relation on the true definitions is implemented by function evaldef. Calling evaldef(d, ξ, ϕ, echo) finds a ξ' and ϕ' such that $\langle d, \xi, \phi\rangle \rightarrow \langle \xi', \phi'\rangle$, and evaldef mutates the C representation of the environments so the global-variable environment becomes ξ' and the function environment becomes ϕ'. If echo is ECHOING, evaldef also prints the interpreter's response to the user's input. Printing the response is evaldef's job because only evaldef can tell whether to print a value (for EXP and VAL) or a name (for DEFINE).

Just like eval, evaldef looks at the syntactic form of d and implements whatever rules have that form in their conclusions.

53b. ⟨*eval.c* 48a⟩+≡ ◁51b

```
void evaldef(Def d, Valenv globals, Funenv functions, Echo echo) {
    switch (d->alt) {
    case VAL:
        ⟨evaluate d->val, mutating globals 53c⟩
        return;
    case EXP:
        ⟨evaluate d->exp and possibly print the result 54a⟩
        return;
    case DEFINE:
        ⟨evaluate d->define, mutating functions 54b⟩
        return;
    }
    assert(0);
}
```


A VAL form updates ξ.

$$\frac{\langle e, \xi, \phi, \{\}\rangle \Downarrow \langle v, \xi', \phi, \rho'\rangle}{\langle \text{VAL}(x, e), \xi, \phi\rangle \rightarrow \langle \xi'\{x \mapsto v\}, \phi\rangle} \qquad \text{(DEFINEGLOBAL)}$$

The premise shows that value v and environment ξ' are obtained by calling eval. This call uses an empty environment as ρ. In the conclusion, the new environment ξ' is retained, and the value of the expression, v, is bound to x in it. Value v may also be printed.

53c. ⟨*evaluate* d->val, *mutating* globals 53c⟩≡ (53b)

```
{
    Value v = eval(d->val.exp, globals, functions, mkValenv(NULL, NULL));
    bindval(d->val.name, v, globals);
    if (echo == ECHOING)
        print("%v\n", v);
}
```

An EXP form also updates ξ, just as if it were a definition of `it`.

$$\frac{\langle e, \xi, \phi, \{\}\rangle \Downarrow \langle v, \xi', \phi, \rho'\rangle}{\langle \text{EXP}(e), \xi, \phi\rangle \rightarrow \langle \xi'\{\texttt{it} \mapsto v\}, \phi\rangle} \qquad \text{(EVALEXP)}$$

54a. ⟨*evaluate* `d->exp` *and possibly print the result* 54a⟩≡ (53b)

```
{
    Value v = eval(d->exp, globals, functions, mkValenv(NULL, NULL));
    bindval(strtoname("it"), v, globals);
    if (echo == ECHOING)
        print("%v\n", v);
}
```

A DEFINE form updates ϕ. The implementation may print the name of the function being defined.

$$\frac{x_1, \ldots, x_n \text{ all distinct}}{\langle \text{DEFINE}(f, \langle x_1, \ldots, x_n\rangle, e), \xi, \phi\rangle \rightarrow \langle \xi, \phi\{f \mapsto \text{USER}(\langle x_1, \ldots, x_n\rangle, e)\}\rangle} \qquad \text{(DEFINEFUNCTION)}$$

54b. ⟨*evaluate* `d->define`*, mutating* `functions` 54b⟩≡ (53b)

```
bindfun(d->define.name, mkUserdef(d->define.userfun), functions);
if (echo == ECHOING)
    print("%n\n", d->define.name);
```

The evaluator does not check to see that the $x_1, \ldots, x_n$ are all distinct—the x_i's are checked when the definition is parsed, by function `check_def_duplicates` in chunk S208e.

1.6.3 *Implementation of environments*

An environment is represented by a pair of lists; one holds names and the other holds the corresponding values. The lists have the same length. (A search tree or hash table would be enable faster search but would be more complicated.)

54c. ⟨*env.c* 54c⟩≡ 54d ▷

```
struct Valenv {
    Namelist  xs;
    Valuelist vs;
    // invariant: lists have the same length
};
```

Given the representation, creating an environment is simple. To prevent the invariant from being violated, the code asserts that `xs` and `vs` have equal length.

54d. ⟨*env.c* 54c⟩+≡ ◁ 54c 55a ▷

```
Valenv mkValenv(Namelist xs, Valuelist vs) {
    Valenv env = malloc(sizeof(*env));
    assert(env != NULL);
    assert(lengthNL(xs) == lengthVL(vs));
    env->xs = xs;
    env->vs = vs;
    return env;
}
```

The list of names `xs` is searched by three functions: `fetchval`, `isvalbound`, and `bindval`. Behind the scenes, that search is implemented just once, in private function `findval`. Given a name `x`, it searches the environment. If it doesn't find `x`, it returns `NULL`. If it does find `x`, it returns a pointer to the *value* associated with `x`.

The pointer can be used to test for binding (`isvalbound`), to fetch a bound value (`fetchval`), or to change an existing binding (`bindval`).

55a. ⟨*env.c* 54c⟩+≡ ◁ 54d 55b ▷

```
static Value* findval(Name x, Valenv env) {
    Namelist  xs;
    Valuelist vs;

    for (xs=env->xs, vs=env->vs; xs && vs; xs=xs->tl, vs=vs->tl)
        if (x == xs->hd)
            return &vs->hd;
    return NULL;
}
```


A name is bound if there is a value associated with it.

55b. ⟨*env.c* 54c⟩+≡ ◁ 55a 55c ▷

```
bool isvalbound(Name name, Valenv env) {
    return findval(name, env) != NULL;
}
```

A value is fetched through the pointer returned by `findval`, if any.

55c. ⟨*env.c* 54c⟩+≡ ◁ 55b 55d ▷

```
Value fetchval(Name name, Valenv env) {
    Value *vp = findval(name, env);
    assert(vp != NULL);
    return *vp;
}
```

A new binding could be added to an environment by inserting a new name and value at the beginning of `xs` and `vs`. But I can get away with an optimization. If $x \in \operatorname{dom} \rho$, instead of extending ρ by making $\rho\{x \mapsto v\}$, I overwrite the old binding of x. This optimization is safe only because no program written in Impcore can tell that it is there. Proving that the optimization is safe requires reasoning about the rules of the operational semantics, which show that in any context where $\rho\{x \mapsto v\}$ appears, the old $\rho(x)$ can't affect any evaluations (Exercise 29 on page 85).

55d. ⟨*env.c* 54c⟩+≡ ◁ 55c

```
void bindval(Name name, Value val, Valenv env) {
    Value *vp = findval(name, env);
    if (vp != NULL)
        *vp = val;              // safe optimization
    else {
        env->xs = mkNL(name, env->xs);
        env->vs = mkVL(val,  env->vs);
    }
}
```

`bindfun`	45b
`bindval`	45b
`echo`	53b
`eval`	45c
`functions`	53b
`globals`	53b
`lengthNL`	$\mathcal{A}$
`lengthVL`	$\mathcal{A}$
`mkNL`	$\mathcal{A}$
`mkUserdef`	44d
`mkValenv`	44f
`mkVL`	$\mathcal{A}$
type `Name`	43a
type `Namelist`	43a
`print`	S176d
`strtoname`	43b
type `Valenv`	44e
type `Value`	43c
type `Valuelist`	43c

The code above implements *value* environments. To preserve type safety, the same data structure and operations are implemented a second time using `Func` instead of `Value`. That code appears in Appendix K.

1.7 Operational semantics revisited: Proofs

Calling `eval`(e, ξ, ϕ, ρ) is supposed to return a value v if and only if there is a *proof* of the judgment $\langle e, \xi, \phi, \rho\rangle \Downarrow \langle v, \xi, \phi, \rho\rangle$ using the rules from Section 1.5. Proofs in programming languages are not very interesting; or rather, they are interesting primarily when they are wrong. Like a bug in a program, a wrong proof tells you that you made a mistake (in your language design, not your code). And a good proof doesn't have to be interesting, because it conveys *certainty*. A proof can guarantee that your program or your programming *language* does what you think it does.

1.7.1 Proofs about evaluation: Theory

A proof about the evaluation of code—that is, about a call to `eval` or `evaldef`—takes the form of a *derivation*. This form of proof, which is borrowed from formal logic, is a tree in which each node is an *instance* of an inference rule; an instance of a rule is obtained by substituting for the rule's metavariables. If every substitution is done consistently, and if, in the resulting derivation, every proposition holds, then the derivation is *valid*. A valid derivation justifies the judgment claimed in the conclusion of its root. These concepts are illustrated in the next few pages.

How do we write derivations?

A derivation is also called a *proof tree*; the root contains the conclusion, and each subtree is also a derivation. A derivation tree is written with its root at the bottom; as in a single rule, the conclusion of a derivation appears on the bottom, below a horizontal line. The leaf nodes appear at the top; each leaf node is an instance of an inference rule that has no evaluation judgments among its premises, like the LITERAL rule or the FORMALVAR rule (page 32). A leaf node corresponds to a computation in which `eval` returns a result without making a recursive call.

Each node in a derivation tree is obtained by *instantiating* a rule and then deriving that rule's premises. Instantiation may substitute for none, some, or all of a rule's metavariables. Substitution that replaces all metavariables, leaving only complete environments, syntax, and data, describes a single run of `eval`. For example, suppose a literal 83 is evaluated in a context where there are no global variables, no functions, and no formal parameters:

```
eval(mkLiteral(83),
     mkValenv(NULL, NULL), mkFunenv(NULL, NULL), mkValenv(NULL, NULL));
```

The resulting run can be described by an instance of the LITERAL rule. The rule appears in the semantics as follows:

$$\frac{}{\langle \text{LITERAL}(v), \xi, \phi, \rho \rangle \Downarrow \langle v, \xi, \phi, \rho \rangle}. \qquad \text{(LITERAL)}$$

The instance that describes the run is obtained by substituting 83 for v, $\{\}$ for ξ, $\{\}$ for ϕ, and $\{\}$ for ρ:

$$\frac{}{\langle \text{LITERAL}(83), \{\}, \{\}, \{\} \rangle \Downarrow \langle 83, \{\}, \{\}, \{\} \rangle}.$$

Because the LITERAL rule has no premises above the line, this instance is a complete, valid derivation all by itself.

The preceding example is awfully specific. In practice, a literal 83 evaluates to 83 *regardless* of the presence of functions or variables—and the evaluation does not change the values of any variables. To prove that, I create a different instance of LITERAL, in which I substitute only for v, leaving ξ, ϕ, and ρ as they are written in the rule:

$$\frac{}{\langle \text{LITERAL}(83), \xi, \phi, \rho \rangle \Downarrow \langle 83, \xi, \phi, \rho \rangle}.$$

This instance is also a complete, valid derivation, and it describes the evaluation of a literal 83 in any possible environment.

A complete derivation tree *ends* in a single rule, but if that rule has evaluation judgments above the line, like the APPLY rules, then each of those judgments—the premises—must be derived as well. A complete derivation follows this schema:

$$\boxed{\textit{Derivation}} = \frac{\boxed{\textit{Derivation of first premise}} \quad \cdots \quad \boxed{\textit{Derivation of last premise}}}{\boxed{\textit{Conclusion}}}.$$

This schema assumes that every premise is justified by a derivation. In practice, only an evaluation judgment can be justified by a derivation. Other premises, like $x \in \operatorname{dom} \rho$ or $\rho(x) = 3$, are justified by appealing to what we know about x and ρ.

As an example of a derivation tree with more than one node (which is wide enough to extend into the margin), I describe the evaluation of (+ (* x x) (* y y)), which computes the sum of two squares. It's evaluated in an environment where ρ binds x to 3 and y to 4.

$$\textsc{ApplyAdd}\ \dfrac{\textsc{ApplyMul}\ \dfrac{\textsc{FormalVar}\ \dfrac{\mathtt{x} \in \operatorname{dom}\rho \qquad \rho(\mathtt{x}) = 3}{\langle \mathrm{VAR}(\mathtt{x}), \xi, \phi, \rho\rangle \Downarrow \langle 3, \xi, \phi, \rho\rangle} \qquad \dfrac{\mathtt{x} \in \operatorname{dom}\rho \qquad \rho(\mathtt{x}) = 3}{\langle \mathrm{VAR}(\mathtt{x}), \xi, \phi, \rho\rangle \Downarrow \langle 3, \xi, \phi, \rho\rangle}\ \textsc{FormalVar}}{\langle \mathrm{APPLY}(*, \mathrm{VAR}(\mathtt{x}), \mathrm{VAR}(\mathtt{x})), \xi, \phi, \rho\rangle \Downarrow \langle 9, \xi, \phi, \rho\rangle} \qquad \cdots}{\langle \mathrm{APPLY}(+, \mathrm{APPLY}(*, \mathrm{VAR}(\mathtt{x}), \mathrm{VAR}(\mathtt{x})), \mathrm{APPLY}(*, \mathrm{VAR}(\mathtt{y}), \mathrm{VAR}(\mathtt{y}))), \xi, \phi, \rho\rangle \Downarrow \langle 25, \xi, \phi, \rho\rangle}$$

Each node is labeled with the name of the rule to which it corresponds. Because derivation trees take so much space, I've elided the subtree that proves

$$\langle \mathrm{APPLY}(*, \mathrm{VAR}(\mathtt{y}), \mathrm{VAR}(\mathtt{y})), \xi, \phi, \rho\rangle \Downarrow \langle 16, \xi, \phi, \rho\rangle.$$

Derivation trees can get big, and to fit them into small spaces, we often take liberties with notation. For example, instead of writing abstract syntax like APPLY(*, VAR(y), VAR(y)), we can write concrete syntax like (* y y). The resulting notation is easier to digest, but it is less obvious that each node is an instance of a semantic rule:

$$\textsc{ApplyAdd}\ \dfrac{\textsc{ApplyMul}\ \dfrac{\textsc{FormalVar}\ \dfrac{\mathtt{x} \in \operatorname{dom}\rho \qquad \rho(\mathtt{x}) = 3}{\langle \mathtt{x}, \xi, \phi, \rho\rangle \Downarrow \langle 3, \xi, \phi, \rho\rangle} \qquad \dfrac{\mathtt{x} \in \operatorname{dom}\rho \qquad \rho(\mathtt{x}) = 3}{\langle \mathtt{x}, \xi, \phi, \rho\rangle \Downarrow \langle 3, \xi, \phi, \rho\rangle}\ \textsc{FormalVar}}{\langle \mathtt{(*\ x\ x)}, \xi, \phi, \rho\rangle \Downarrow \langle 9, \xi, \phi, \rho\rangle} \qquad \cdots}{\langle \mathtt{(+\ (*\ x\ x)\ (*\ y\ y))}, \xi, \phi, \rho\rangle \Downarrow \langle 25, \xi, \phi, \rho\rangle}.$$

Even if I use a smaller font and don't label the nodes, the full derivation tree sticks even further into the margin:

$$\dfrac{\dfrac{\dfrac{\mathtt{x} \in \operatorname{dom}\rho \quad \rho(\mathtt{x}) = 3}{\langle \mathtt{x}, \xi, \phi, \rho\rangle \Downarrow \langle 3, \xi, \phi, \rho\rangle} \quad \dfrac{\mathtt{x} \in \operatorname{dom}\rho \quad \rho(\mathtt{x}) = 3}{\langle \mathtt{x}, \xi, \phi, \rho\rangle \Downarrow \langle 3, \xi, \phi, \rho\rangle}}{\langle \mathtt{(*\ x\ x)}, \xi, \phi, \rho\rangle \Downarrow \langle 9, \xi, \phi, \rho\rangle} \quad \dfrac{\dfrac{\mathtt{y} \in \operatorname{dom}\rho \quad \rho(\mathtt{y}) = 4}{\langle \mathtt{y}, \xi, \phi, \rho\rangle \Downarrow \langle 4, \xi, \phi, \rho\rangle} \quad \dfrac{\mathtt{y} \in \operatorname{dom}\rho \quad \rho(\mathtt{y}) = 4}{\langle \mathtt{y}, \xi, \phi, \rho\rangle \Downarrow \langle 4, \xi, \phi, \rho\rangle}}{\langle \mathtt{(*\ y\ y)}, \xi, \phi, \rho\rangle \Downarrow \langle 16, \xi, \phi, \rho\rangle}}{\langle \mathtt{(+\ (*\ x\ x)\ (*\ y\ y))}, \xi, \phi, \rho\rangle \Downarrow \langle 25, \xi, \phi, \rho\rangle}.$$

What is a valid derivation?

A derivation is *valid* if every node is obtained by instantiating a rule and every premise is justified (either by a valid subderivation or by other means). To explain validity, it helps to name the rule that is instantiated at the root. A derivation $\mathcal{D}$ is a valid derivation ending in an application of rule $\mathcal{R}$ when all of these conditions hold:

- The derivation is obtained by substituting for the metavariables in $\mathcal{R}$. Substitution must respect the intent of the metavariables: only a well-formed expression may be substituted for e, a value for v, a well-formed environment for ρ, and so on. While whatever is substituted must be well formed, it need not be completely specified: whatever is substituted for a metavariable may itself contain metavariables. For example, $\text{IF}(e_1, e_2, e_3)$ may be substituted for e.

- Rule $\mathcal{R}$ may include evaluation judgments above the line, as premises. After substitution, each of these premises must be justified by a derivation of its own.
- After substitution, every other premise in rule $\mathcal{R}$ must also be justified. Premises that aren't evaluation judgments are usually justified by set theory, arithmetic, or appeal to assumptions.

As an example, if `n` is a formal parameter, evaluating `(set n 0)` sets `n` to zero and returns zero. I want to derive the judgment

$$\langle \text{SET}(\mathsf{n}, \text{LITERAL}(0)), \xi, \phi, \rho \rangle \Downarrow \langle 0, \xi, \phi, \rho\{\mathsf{n} \mapsto 0\} \rangle.$$

This goal judgment is derived by a derivation $\mathcal{D}$ that ends in rule FORMALASSIGN, which I reproduce here:

$$\frac{x \in \operatorname{dom} \rho \qquad \langle e, \xi, \phi, \rho \rangle \Downarrow \langle v, \xi', \phi, \rho' \rangle}{\langle \text{SET}(x, e), \xi, \phi, \rho \rangle \Downarrow \langle v, \xi', \phi, \rho'\{x \mapsto v\} \rangle}. \qquad \text{(FORMALASSIGN)}$$

To get the conclusion of FORMALASSIGN to match the goal, I substitute `n` for x, $\text{LITERAL}(0)$ for e, ξ for ξ', 0 for v, and ρ for ρ'. With that substitution, my derivation in progress looks like this:

$$\frac{\mathsf{n} \in \operatorname{dom} \rho \qquad \langle \text{LITERAL}(0), \xi, \phi, \rho \rangle \Downarrow \langle 0, \xi, \phi, \rho \rangle}{\langle \text{SET}(\mathsf{n}, \text{LITERAL}(0)), \xi, \phi, \rho \rangle \Downarrow \langle 0, \xi, \phi, \rho\{\mathsf{n} \mapsto 0\} \rangle}.$$

To complete the derivation, I derive judgment $\langle \text{LITERAL}(0), \xi, \phi, \rho \rangle \Downarrow \langle 0, \xi, \phi, \rho \rangle$, with a new derivation $\mathcal{D}_1$. Derivation $\mathcal{D}_1$ ends in rule LITERAL, and to construct $\mathcal{D}_1$, I substitute 0 for v in rule LITERAL. Rule LITERAL has no premises, so that substitution completes $\mathcal{D}_1$:

$$\mathcal{D}_1 = \frac{}{\langle \text{LITERAL}(0), \xi, \phi, \rho \rangle \Downarrow \langle 0, \xi, \phi, \rho \rangle}.$$

Plugging $\mathcal{D}_1$ into my previous work completes $\mathcal{D}$:

$$\mathcal{D} = \frac{\mathsf{n} \in \operatorname{dom} \rho \qquad \overline{\langle \text{LITERAL}(0), \xi, \phi, \rho \rangle \Downarrow \langle 0, \xi, \phi, \rho \rangle}}{\langle \text{SET}(\mathsf{n}, \text{LITERAL}(0)), \xi, \phi, \rho \rangle \Downarrow \langle 0, \xi, \phi, \rho\{\mathsf{n} \mapsto 0\} \rangle}.$$

For derivation $\mathcal{D}$ to be valid, premise $\mathsf{n} \in \operatorname{dom} \rho$ must also be proved. It's true by assumption: `n` is a formal parameter, which is what $\mathsf{n} \in \operatorname{dom} \rho$ means.

How do we construct valid derivations?

A derivation is valid if we substitute consistently for each metavariable, replace every evaluation premise with a valid derivation, and can prove the other premises. But how do we know what to substitute? There's an algorithm, and it's the same algorithm that's used in `eval` to interpret code. That's no surprise—every derivation tree is intimately related to an application of `eval`. The derivation expresses, in a data structure, the steps that `eval` goes through to interpret the code.

To construct a derivation, we start with an initial state—the left-hand side of an evaluation judgment. We usually know some or all of the syntax, and we may know something about environments as well. The algorithm works like this:

1. Find a rule $\mathcal{R}$ whose *conclusion* matches the left-hand side we are interested in. By "matches," I mean that the left-hand side we are interested can be obtained by substituting for metavariables in the conclusion of $\mathcal{R}$. For example, in the derivation for the SET expression above, only two rules can conclude in a SET expression: FORMALASSIGN and GLOBALASSIGN.

   In the Impcore interpreter, the "find a rule" step corresponds to the main `switch` statement in function `eval` (chunk 48b), which identifies possible rules by looking at `e->alt`.

2. Substitute in $\mathcal{R}$ so that the left-hand side of the conclusion is equal to the initial state of interest. Now look at each of $\mathcal{R}$'s premises.

3. If a premise does not involve an evaluation judgment, see if it is provable. If so, continue building the derivation. If not, try some other rule.

   In an interpreter, provability corresponds to a check on run-time data. Premises like $x \in \operatorname{dom} \xi$ or $x \notin \operatorname{dom} \rho$ are checked by calling `isvalbound`, and premises like $v_1 \neq 0$ or $v_1 = 0$ are checked by comparing a run-time value with 0.

4. If a premise *does* involve an evaluation judgment, recursively build a derivation of that judgment, starting with the right-hand side. In the Impcore interpreter, recursively building a derivation corresponds to a recursive call to `eval`.

This algorithm eventually dictates what needs to be substituted on the right-hand side of the evaluation judgment. An example appears in Figure 1.7, which constructs a derivation for `(set n (+ n 1))` in an environment in which `n` is 7. Figure 1.7 shows a sequence of snapshots; in each one, the partially constructed derivation is shown in black and the parts that are not yet constructed are shown in gray. The derivation begins with the expression `(set n (+ n 1))` and an environment ρ in which $\rho(\mathtt{n}) = 8$. (Because ξ and ϕ do not take part and do not change, they are omitted to save space.) Each step fills something in; first, check $\mathtt{n} \in \operatorname{dom} \rho$; next, evaluate `(+ n 1)`, and so on. The sketch should suggest that the derivation, which is a data structure, is a spacelike representation of a timelike computation. This is true of every derivation.

What can we do with derivations?

If we know something about the environments, we can use derivation trees to answer questions about the evaluation of expressions and definitions. One example is the evaluation of the expression in Exercise 12 on page 77. This kind of application of the language semantics is called the *theory* of the language. But we can answer much more interesting questions if we *prove facts about derivations*. For example, in Impcore, the expression `(if x x 0)` is always equivalent to `x` (Exercise 13 on page 77). Because a computation is a sequence of events in time, proving facts about computations can be difficult. But if every terminating computation is described by a derivation, a derivation is just a data structure, and proving facts about data structures is much easier. Reasoning about derivations is called *metatheory*.

1.7.2 *Proofs about derivations: Metatheory*

If you already know that you want to study metatheory, you'll soon need another book. This book only suggests what metatheory can do, so you can figure out if you want to study it more deeply.

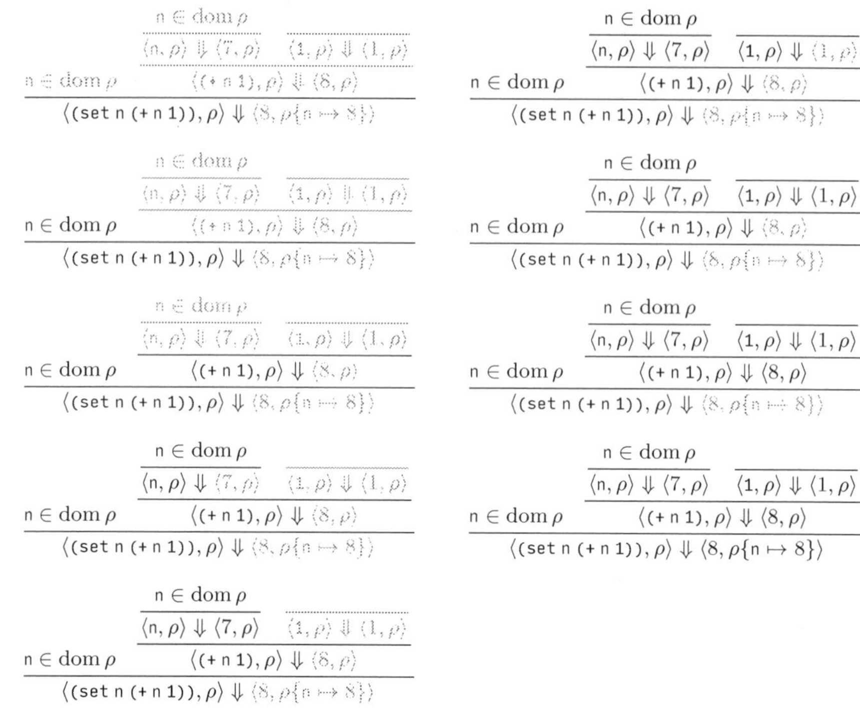

Figure 1.7: Construction of a derivation (omitting unchanging ξ and ϕ)

Metatheory can determine the validity of a claim like this: in any Impcore program, the expression `(+ x 0)` can be replaced by just `x`, and this replacement doesn't change any output of the program. This claim could be important to a compiler writer, who might use it to create an "optimization" that improves performance. If you're going to create an optimization, you must be certain that it doesn't change the meaning of any program. Certainty can be supplied by a metatheoretic proof.

What can we prove about a program that evaluates `(+ x 0)`? If a derivation exists, it will contain a judgment of the form

$$\langle \texttt{(+ x 0)}, \xi, \phi, \rho \rangle \Downarrow \langle v, \xi', \phi, \rho' \rangle.$$

That judgment will be the root of a subderivation. That subderivation must apply a rule that permits the application of the `+` primitive on the left-hand side of its conclusion. So just like the interpreter code in chunk 48b, a proof has to consider inference rules whose conclusions can contain APPLY(+, ...).

Two such rules appear in Section 1.5.6: APPLYUSER and APPLYADD. And the claim is false! If $\phi(+)$ refers to a user-defined function, the APPLYUSER rule kicks in, and it is *not* safe to replace `(+ x 0)` with `x`. Here's a demonstration:

60. ⟨*terrifying transcript* 60⟩≡

```
-> (define + (x y) y)          ; no sane person would do this
-> (define addzero (x) (+ x 0))
-> (addzero 99)
0
-> (define addzero2 (x) x)
-> (addzero2 99)
99
```

If a compiler writer wants to be able to replace an occurrence of `(+ x 0)` with `x`, they will first have to prove that the environment ϕ in which `(+ x 0)` is evaluated *never* binds `+` to a user-defined function. (Compilers typically include lots of infrastructure for proving facts about environments, but such infrastructure is beyond the scope of this book.)

Proving facts about derivations is metatheory. Metatheory enables you to prove properties like these:

- Expression `(if x x 0)` is equivalent to `x` (Exercise 13).
- If evaluation of a `while` loop terminates, its value is zero (Exercise 23).
- Evaluating an expression can't create a new variable (Exercise 24).
- In Impcore, evaluating an expression in the same context always produces the same result—which isn't true of languages that support parallel execution (Exercise 27).
- Impcore programs can be evaluated using a stack of mutable environments, as the implementation in Section 1.6 does (Exercise 29).

Results like these are useful, but one requires a long, detailed proof.

1.7.3 *How to attempt a metatheoretic proof*

A metatheoretic proof works by induction on the structure of valid derivations. A derivation is a tree, and a proof can assume that an induction hypothesis holds for any proper subtree. Or, if you prefer, a metatheorem can be proved by induction on the height of a derivation tree.

A valid derivation can end in any rule, so a proof by induction on a derivation's structure has a case for every rule. In a language as big as Impcore, that's a lot of cases. In this book, each case is presented in exactly the same way. As an example, here's a case from the proof that evaluating an expression doesn't create any new global variables. The theorem, which is also the induction hypothesis, says that if derivation $\mathcal{D}$ proves $\langle e, \xi, \phi, \rho \rangle \Downarrow \langle v, \xi', \phi, \rho' \rangle$, then $\operatorname{dom} \xi = \operatorname{dom} \xi'$:

- When the last rule used in $\mathcal{D}$ is FORMALASSIGN, the derivation must have the following form:

$$\mathcal{D} = \frac{x \in \operatorname{dom} \rho \qquad \dfrac{\mathcal{D}_1}{\langle e_1, \xi, \phi, \rho \rangle \Downarrow \langle v, \xi', \phi, \rho' \rangle}}{\langle \text{SET}(x, e_1), \xi, \phi, \rho \rangle \Downarrow \langle v, \xi', \phi, \rho'\{x \mapsto v\} \rangle} \;\text{FORMALASSIGN}$$

  The form of e is $\text{SET}(x, e_1)$. Our obligation is to prove that the induction hypothesis holds for the judgment below the line. We must therefore prove that $\operatorname{dom} \xi = \operatorname{dom} \xi'$. But because derivation $\mathcal{D}_1$ is smaller than derivation $\mathcal{D}$, we are permitted to assume the induction hypothesis, which tells us that $\operatorname{dom} \xi = \operatorname{dom} \xi'$. Our obligation is met.

This example, like all the cases in my metatheoretic proofs, uses the following template:

1. When the last rule used in $\mathcal{D}$ is RULENAME, and RULENAME has conclusion C and premises P_1 to P_n, the derivation must have the following form:

$$\mathcal{D} = \frac{P_1 \quad \cdots \quad P_n}{C} \;\text{RULENAME}$$

Commentary: The conclusion C is the evaluation judgment of which $\mathcal{D}$ is a proof. If any particular P_i is also an evaluation judgment, I write its *derivation above it, as in*

$$\mathcal{D} = \cfrac{\cfrac{\mathcal{D}_1}{P_1} \quad \cdots \quad \cfrac{\mathcal{D}_i}{P_i} \quad \cdots \quad \cfrac{\mathcal{D}_n}{P_n}}{C} \;\textsc{RuleName}$$

A premise like "$x \notin \operatorname{dom} \rho$" is not an evaluation judgment and is not supported by a subderivation.

2. The form of e is *syntactic form*, and *whatever additional analysis goes with that syntactic form and with rule* RULENAME.

3. Our obligation is to prove that the induction hypothesis holds for the judgment below the line. We must therefore prove *whatever it is.*

4. *Identifying each premise P_i that is an evaluation judgment,* because derivation $\mathcal{D}_i$ is strictly smaller than derivation $\mathcal{D}$, we are permitted to assume that the induction hypothesis applies to derivation $\mathcal{D}_i$. This assumption gives us *whatever it gives us.*

5. From the truth of premises P_1 to P_n, plus the information from the induction hypothesis, we show that *the induction hypothesis holds for the judgment below the line.*

6. Our obligation is met.

This template has served me well, but part of it may surprise you: it doesn't distinguish between "base cases" and "inductive cases." The distinction exists—a base case is one that has no evaluation judgments above the line—but in a programming-language proof, the distinction is not terribly useful. For example, base cases might or might not be easy, and they might or might not fail.

The template is instantiated for every case in a proof. As a demonstration, I instantiate the template to try to prove the metatheoretic conjecture,

> If an expression e is evaluated successfully, then every variable in e is defined.

(This conjecture isn't true, but that's a good thing—we learn the most from the things we try to prove that aren't so. To maximize your own learning, you might pause and think about which case or cases of the proof are going to fail.)

To begin, I state my conjecture formally. And that means I must formalize the idea of "every variable in e." I use the function $\operatorname{fv}(e)$, short for "free variables of e," which is defined in Figure 1.8 on the facing page. Figure 1.8 uses a simplified dialect of Impcore, which makes the metatheoretic proof a little easier:

- Simplified Impcore has no `begin` expression.
- In Simplified Impcore, every function application has exactly two arguments.

(You can work out how to eliminate `begin` in Exercise 14 on page 79.) Informally speaking, $\operatorname{fv}(e)$ is the set of variables mentioned in e. A variable can be mentioned directly only in a VAR expression or in a SET expression. In other forms of expression, the free variables are the free variables of the subexpressions.

$$
\begin{aligned}
\text{fv}(\text{LITERAL}(v)) &= \emptyset \\
\text{fv}(\text{VAR}(x)) &= \{x\} \\
\text{fv}(\text{SET}(x, e)) &= \{x\} \cup \text{fv}(e) \\
\text{fv}(\text{IF}(e_1, e_2, e_3)) &= \text{fv}(e_1) \cup \text{fv}(e_2) \cup \text{fv}(e_3) \\
\text{fv}(\text{WHILE}(e_1, e_2)) &= \text{fv}(e_1) \cup \text{fv}(e_2) \\
\text{fv}(\text{APPLY}(f, e_1, e_2)) &= \text{fv}(e_1) \cup \text{fv}(e_2)
\end{aligned}
$$

Figure 1.8: Free variables of an expression in Simplified Impcore

Now I can state my conjecture precisely and formally: if $\mathcal{D}$ is a valid derivation of $\langle e, \xi, \phi, \rho\rangle \Downarrow \langle v, \xi', \phi, \rho'\rangle$, then $\text{fv}(e) \subseteq \text{dom}\,\xi \cup \text{dom}\,\rho$. This conjecture is also my induction hypothesis.

I now instantiate the proof template for each rule of Simplified Impcore. (Rules are listed in Figure 1.11 on page 78.)

- When the last rule used in $\mathcal{D}$ is LITERAL, the derivation must have the following form:

$$\mathcal{D} = \frac{}{\langle \text{LITERAL}(v), \xi, \phi, \rho\rangle \Downarrow \langle v, \xi, \phi, \rho\rangle} \quad \text{LITERAL}$$

  The form of e is $\text{LITERAL}(v)$. Our obligation is to prove that the induction hypothesis holds for the judgment below the line. We must therefore prove $\text{fv}(\text{LITERAL}(v)) \subseteq \text{dom}\,\xi \cup \text{dom}\,\rho$. According to the definition of fv in Figure 1.8, $\text{fv}(\text{LITERAL}(v)) = \emptyset$, and the empty set is a subset of any set. Our obligation is met.

- When the last rule used in $\mathcal{D}$ is FORMALVAR, the derivation must have the following form:

$$\mathcal{D} = \frac{x \in \text{dom}\,\rho}{\langle \text{VAR}(x), \xi, \phi, \rho\rangle \Downarrow \langle \rho(x), \xi, \phi, \rho\rangle} \quad \text{FORMALVAR}$$

  The form of e is $\text{VAR}(x)$. Our obligation is to prove that the induction hypothesis holds for the judgment below the line. We must therefore prove $\text{fv}(\text{VAR}(x)) \subseteq \text{dom}\,\xi \cup \text{dom}\,\rho$. According to the definition of fv in Figure 1.8, $\text{fv}(\text{VAR}(x)) = \{x\}$. And from the first and only premise of the derivation, we know that $x \in \text{dom}\,\rho$. Therefore

$$\text{fv}(\text{VAR}(x)) = \{x\} \subseteq \text{dom}\,\rho \subseteq (\text{dom}\,\rho \cup \text{dom}\,\xi).$$

  Our obligation is met.

- When the last rule used in $\mathcal{D}$ is GLOBALVAR, the derivation must have the following form:

$$\mathcal{D} = \frac{x \notin \text{dom}\,\rho \qquad x \in \text{dom}\,\xi}{\langle \text{VAR}(x), \xi, \phi, \rho\rangle \Downarrow \langle \xi(x), \xi, \phi, \rho\rangle} \quad \text{GLOBALVAR}$$

  The form of e is $\text{VAR}(x)$. Our obligation is to prove that the induction hypothesis holds for the judgment below the line. We must therefore prove $\text{fv}(\text{VAR}(x)) \subseteq \text{dom}\,\xi \cup \text{dom}\,\rho$. According to the definition of fv in Figure 1.8,

$\text{fv}(\text{VAR}(x)) = \{x\}$. And from the second premise of the derivation, we know that $x \in \text{dom}\,\xi$. Therefore

$$\text{fv}(\text{VAR}(x)) = \{x\} \subseteq \text{dom}\,\xi \subseteq (\text{dom}\,\rho \cup \text{dom}\,\xi).$$

Our obligation is met.

- When the last rule used in $\mathcal{D}$ is FORMALASSIGN, the derivation must have the following form:

$$\mathcal{D} = \dfrac{x \in \text{dom}\,\rho \qquad \dfrac{\mathcal{D}_1}{\langle e_1, \xi, \phi, \rho\rangle \Downarrow \langle v, \xi', \phi, \rho'\rangle}}{\langle \text{SET}(x, e_1), \xi, \phi, \rho\rangle \Downarrow \langle v, \xi', \phi, \rho'\{x \mapsto v\}\rangle} \;\text{FORMALASSIGN}$$

The form of e is $\text{SET}(x, e_1)$. Our obligation is to prove that the induction hypothesis holds for the judgment below the line. We must therefore prove that $\text{fv}(\text{SET}(x, e_1)) \subseteq \text{dom}\,\xi \cup \text{dom}\,\rho$. According to the definition of fv in Figure 1.8, $\text{fv}(\text{SET}(x, e_1)) = \{x\} \cup \text{fv}(e_1)$. It therefore suffices to prove the following two inclusions:

(a) $\{x\} \subseteq \text{dom}\,\xi \cup \text{dom}\,\rho$.

(b) $\text{fv}(e_1) \subseteq \text{dom}\,\xi \cup \text{dom}\,\rho$.

From the first premise of the derivation, we know that $x \in \text{dom}\,\rho$, and as before, that implies (a). From the second premise of the derivation, we can apply the induction hypothesis to $\mathcal{D}_1$, which gives us (b). Our obligation is met.

- When the last rule used in $\mathcal{D}$ is GLOBALASSIGN, the reasoning is so similar to what we have already done that it's not worth repeating.

- When the last rule used in $\mathcal{D}$ is IFTRUE, the derivation must have the following form:

$$\mathcal{D} = \dfrac{\dfrac{\mathcal{D}_1}{\langle e_1, \xi, \phi, \rho\rangle \Downarrow \langle v_1, \xi', \phi, \rho'\rangle} \qquad v_1 \neq 0 \qquad \dfrac{\mathcal{D}_2}{\langle e_2, \xi', \phi, \rho'\rangle \Downarrow \langle v_2, \xi'', \phi, \rho''\rangle}}{\langle \text{IF}(e_1, e_2, e_3), \xi, \phi, \rho\rangle \Downarrow \langle v_2, \xi'', \phi, \rho''\rangle,} \;\text{IFTRUE}$$

The form of e is $\text{IF}(e_1, e_2, e_3)$. Our obligation is to prove that the induction hypothesis holds for the judgment below the line. We must therefore prove $\text{fv}(\text{IF}(e_1, e_2, e_3)) \subseteq \text{dom}\,\xi \cup \text{dom}\,\rho$. According to the definition of fv in Figure 1.8, $\text{fv}(\text{IF}(e_1, e_2, e_3)) = \text{fv}(e_1) \cup \text{fv}(e_2) \cup \text{fv}(e_3)$. It therefore suffices to prove the following three inclusions:

(a) $\text{fv}(e_1) \subseteq \text{dom}\,\xi \cup \text{dom}\,\rho$.

(b) $\text{fv}(e_2) \subseteq \text{dom}\,\xi \cup \text{dom}\,\rho$.

(c) $\text{fv}(e_3) \subseteq \text{dom}\,\xi \cup \text{dom}\,\rho$.

By applying the induction hypothesis to $\mathcal{D}_1$, we get (a). By applying the induction hypothesis to $\mathcal{D}_2$, we get (b). But there is no subderivation corresponding to the evaluation of e_3. And in fact we cannot prove that $\text{fv}(e_3) \subseteq \text{dom}\,\xi \cup \text{dom}\,\rho$, because it isn't true! Expression e_3 is not evaluated, and its free variables might not be defined. Here's an example:

64. ⟨*transcript* 12a⟩+≡ ◁29

```
-> (if 1 7 undefined)
7
```

Our obligation cannot be met.

- I could continue with the other cases. The proof fails for IFFALSE as well as IFTRUE, but it succeeds for EMPTYBEGIN, BEGIN, and APPLYUSER. Analysis of rules WHILEITERATE and WHILEEND is left for Exercise 26.

The conjecture isn't actually a theorem, and in the process of working out a proof, I found a counterexample. To guarantee that every variable in an expression is defined, we would need something stronger than a successful evaluation. Like a type checker, for example (Chapter 6).

1.7.4 *Why bother with semantics, proofs, theory, and metatheory?*

What's up with all the Greek letters and horizontal lines? What's the point? Isn't it easier just to look at the code? No, because an operational semantics leaves out all sorts of "implementation details" that would otherwise impede our understanding of how a language works. For example, to a compiler writer, the representation of an environment is super important—where values are stored has a huge impact on the performance of programs. But if we just want to understand how programs behave, we don't care. And once you get used to the Greek letters and horizontal lines, you'll find them easier to read than code—*much* easier. The point of operational semantics is to combine precision and understanding. That's why when you find a new idea in a professional paper, the idea is usually nailed down using operational semantics. When you can read operational semantics, you'll be able to learn about new ideas for yourself, direct from the sources, instead of having to find somebody to explain them to you.

What about proof theory and metatheory? Theory involves making derivations—typically one derivation at a time. It can guide an implementor, because it tells them just what each construct is supposed to do. In principle, theory could also guide a programmer, who also needs to know what programs are supposed to do. But in practice, operational semantics works at too low a level. A programmer can more effectively use something like the *algebraic laws* in the next chapter. The programmer—or perhaps a specialist—uses operational semantics to show that the laws are sound, and after that, programming proceeds by appealing to the laws, not to the operational semantics directly.

So theory is good for building implementations and for establishing algebraic laws, both of which are useful for programmers. What is metatheory good for? Metatheory involves *reasoning about derivations.* In particular, metatheory can reveal universal truths about derivations, which correspond to facts about all programs in a given language. Such truths might interest implementors, programmers, or even policy makers. For example,

- If you're implementing C or Impcore, you can keep the local variables and formal parameters of *all* functions on a stack (Exercise 29). This stack is called the *call stack.*

- In Impcore, no function can change the value of a formal parameter (or local variable) belonging to any other function.

- In C, a function *can* change the value of a formal parameter (or local variable) belonging to another function, but only if at some point the & operator was applied to the parameter or variable in question—or if somebody has exploited "undefined behavior" with pointers.

- If an ordinary device driver fails, it can take down a whole operating-system kernel, resulting in a "blue screen of death." But if a device driver is written in the special-purpose language Sing#, the worst it can do is take away its device—metatheory guarantees that the operating-system kernel and the other drivers are unaffected.

Serious metatheory is well worth learning; this book provides just a taste. Doing a few of the exercises can show you the difference between theory and metatheory, give you an idea of how a metatheoretic proof is structured, and give you an idea of what metatheory can do.

1.8 EXTENDING IMPCORE

Impcore is a "starter kit" for learning about abstract syntax, operational semantics, and interpreters. It's not a useful programming language—useful languages offer more values than just machine integers. (New values are coming in Chapter 2.) But even with only integer values, Impcore can still be extended in two useful ways: with local variables and with looping constructs.

Any language that even pretends to be useful offers some species of local variables. Impcore can offer them too (Exercise 30 on page 86). Local variables can be used to define functions like the one shown in Figure 1.9 on the next page, which adds up the odd numbers from 1 to `n`.

Adding local variables requires you to *change* the abstract syntax of `Userfun` so that it includes not only a body and a list of formal parameters, but also a list of local variables. And to account for the semantics of local variables, you'll need to change the evaluator. But other kinds of extensions, including new looping constructs, can be implemented *without* touching the abstract syntax or the evaluator. You add only concrete syntax, which is implemented in terms of the abstract syntax you have already. This kind of new concrete syntax is called *syntactic sugar*.

As examples of syntactic sugar, I suggest several new ways to write loops. Let's begin with an ordinary `while` loop, like this one:

```
(while (<= i n)
  (begin
    (set sum (+ sum i))
    (set i (+ i 2))))
```

The `begin` might seem like a lot of syntactic overhead. I imagine a new syntactic form, which I'll call `while*`, in which the condition is still a single expression, but the body is a *sequence* of expressions. Now the `begin` is no longer necessary:

```
(while* (<= i n)
  (set sum (+ sum i))
  (set i (+ i 2)))
```

The `while*` loop can be defined as syntactic sugar:

$$\texttt{(while*}\ \mathit{condition}\ e_1\ \cdots\ e_n\texttt{)} \triangleq \texttt{(while}\ \mathit{condition}\ \texttt{(begin}\ e_1\ \cdots\ e_n\texttt{))}$$

As another example, C's `do...while` loop executes the body first, then the condition. In Impcore, we might define a `do-while` as syntactic sugar:

$$\texttt{(do-while}\ \mathit{body}\ \mathit{condition}\texttt{)} \triangleq \texttt{(begin}\ \mathit{body}\ \texttt{(while}\ \mathit{condition}\ \mathit{body}\texttt{))}$$

Finally, C's complicated four-part `for` loop can also be defined as syntactic sugar:

$$\texttt{(for}\ \mathit{pre}\ \mathit{test}\ \mathit{post}\ \mathit{body}\texttt{)} \triangleq \texttt{(begin}\ \mathit{pre}\ \texttt{(while}\ \mathit{test}\ \texttt{(begin}\ \mathit{body}\ \mathit{post}\texttt{)))}$$

67. ⟨*answer transcript* 67⟩≡
```
-> (define add-odds-to (n)
     [locals i sum]
     (begin
       (set i 1)
       (set sum 0)
       (while (<= i n)
         (begin
           (set sum (+ sum i))
           (set i (+ i 2))))
       sum))
-> (add-odds-to 3)
4
-> (add-odds-to 5)
9
-> (add-odds-to 7)
16
```

Figure 1.9: Programming with local variables

All these alternatives can be implemented just by modifying Impcore's parser (Exercise 34, page 87). An example can be found in the Supplement (Section G.7, page S209).

1.9 Summary

Impcore is a toy, but its simple, imperative control constructs—procedure definitions, conditionals, and loops—model the structure of all procedural languages. These constructs are also found in many other languages, including some that describe themselves as "object-oriented," "scripting," or even "functional." More important, Impcore serves as a tiny, familiar medium with which to introduce two foundational ideas: abstract syntax and operational semantics. Finally, Impcore introduces the most distinctive feature of this book: the definitional interpreter.

1.9.1 *Key words and phrases*

ABSTRACT MACHINE An abstraction used to evaluate programs in OPERATIONAL SEMANTICS. An abstract machine has a state formed from mathematical objects; typical objects include ENVIRONMENTS, ABSTRACT SYNTAX, values, and *stores* (Chapter 2). The state of an abstract machine undergoes transitions that are described by an OPERATIONAL SEMANTICS.

ABSTRACT SYNTAX The underlying *tree* structure of a program's source code. It is "abstract" in part because it abstracts away from such details as whether source code is written using round brackets and square brackets or whether it is written using semicolons and curly braces. Abstract syntax expresses the important truth about a program. Compare it with CONCRETE SYNTAX.

BASIS A *basis* comprises all the information available about a *particular* set of names. In Impcore, a basis is a pair of environments $\langle \phi, \xi \rangle$. A basis provides the context used to evaluate a definition, and evaluating a definition typically extends or alters the current basis. The basis available at startup is called the INITIAL BASIS.

What is syntactic sugar and who benefits?

Syntactic sugar is a means of defining syntax in terms of other syntax, without any operational semantics. Some examples appear in the text: C's `do...while` and C's `for` loop can be defined as syntactic sugar for various combinations of `while` and `begin` (page 66). Such syntactic sugar can benefit programmers, implementors, designers, theorists, and other tool builders.

Programmers benefit most from syntactic sugar when they don't know it's there. Syntactic sugar is defined by translation, which is not easy to think about—if every time you want to use a `do-while` you first have to mentally translate it into something else, that's not an aid; it's a stumbling block.

Implementors can benefit from syntactic sugar. If you implement a *desugaring* transformation on your syntax, then without any other change to your compiler or interpreter, you have a new language feature (Exercise 34). But as soon as your implementation gets serious—say you want to check types, as in Chapter 6, or you want to provide source-level-debugging—the syntactic sugar is not so useful, because you need to report errors or state in terms of the syntax the user wrote originally, not the desugared form.

Language designers and theorists benefit the most from syntactic sugar. For example, let's say you've completed Exercise 29: you've proven that Impcore can be evaluated on a stack. Now you want to add `do-while`, `for`, `while*`, or some other shiny new syntactic form. If the new form is just sugar—that is, if it is defined by translation into the original syntax, which you used in your proof—then you know the new, extended Impcore can *still* be evaluated on a stack. You don't have to consider any new cases in your proof, and you don't have to revisit any cases that you've already proven. This scenario describes a very effective use of syntactic sugar: a careful language designer benefits from small language, which is easy to prove things about, but the users benefit from a larger language, which is more attractive and makes it easier to say things idiomatically. Using syntactic sugar, a designer can have both.

I have assumed that new syntactic sugar can be created only by a language designer or implementor. This assumption holds for most languages, including C and Impcore. the vast majority of other languages. But using Lisp, Scheme, and related languages, new syntactic sugar can be created by ordinary programmers. This capability gives programmers many of the same powers as language designers (Section 2.14.4, page 171).

BIG-STEP SEMANTICS A species of OPERATIONAL SEMANTICS in which each JUDGMENT FORM expresses, in one step, the evaluation of syntax to produce a result. For example, a judgment $\langle e, \xi, \phi, \rho \rangle \Downarrow \langle v, \xi, \phi, \rho \rangle$ shows how an expression is evaluated to produce a value, or a judgment $\langle d, \xi, \phi \rangle \to \langle \xi', \phi' \rangle$ shows how a definition is evaluated to produce a new ENVIRONMENT. Big-step semantics is well aligned with the way we think about programs. Compare it with SMALL-STEP SEMANTICS.

COMPILER A language implementation that works by translating syntax into machine code. The machine code may be for a real hardware machine made by a manufacturer like Intel or ARM, in which case the compiler is called a *native-code* compiler. Or the machine code may be for a *virtual machine* like the Java Virtual Machine or the Squeak virtual machine.

CONCRETE SYNTAX The means by which a program's source code is written, as a *sequence* of characters or tokens. Concrete syntax specifies such details as what shape of brackets to use and where to use commas or semicolons. Concrete syntax is what we use when presenting a program to a computer or talking about programs with other people. Compare it with ABSTRACT SYNTAX.

DEFINITIONAL INTERPRETER A language implementation that is intended to implement the language's theory "directly," or that is otherwise intended to illustrate a language's theory. Almost sure to include a PARSER and EVALUATOR. All the interpreters in this book are definitional.

ENVIRONMENT An mapping that stores information about names. For example, in Impcore, the environment ξ stores the value of each global variable. In old-school COMPILERS, an environment may be referred to as a SYMBOL TABLE.

EVALUATION What a pointy-headed theorist talks about instead of "running code."

EVALUATOR A part of a language implementation that evaluates code directly. In this book, the evaluators evaluate ABSTRACT SYNTAX, but an evaluator may also evaluate intermediate code, virtual-machine code, or even machine code.

EXPRESSION-ORIENTED LANGUAGE A programming language in which conditional constructs, control-flow constructs, and assignments, like `if`, `while`, `begin`, and `set`, are expressions, not statements—and evaluating each produces a value. Not usually associated with PROCEDURAL PROGRAMMING.

GRAMMAR A set of formal rules that enumerates all the SYNTACTIC FORMS in each SYNTACTIC CATEGORY. A grammar produces the set of all programs that are grammatically well formed. A grammar can be designed to support a simple decision procedure that tells if a particular utterance was produced by the grammar, and if so, how. Such a decision procedure is embodied in a PARSER.

INITIAL BASIS The BASIS used when first evaluating a user's code. The initial basis contains all the PRIMITIVE FUNCTIONS and PREDEFINED FUNCTIONS.

JUDGMENT A claim in a formal system of proof. In programming languages, a judgment often describes the evaluation of some syntactic form; for example, $\langle \texttt{(+ 2 2)}, \xi, \phi, \rho \rangle \Downarrow \langle 4, \xi, \phi, \rho \rangle$ describes the evaluation of a function application. (Judgments about types are introduced in Chapter 6.)

JUDGMENT FORM A template for creating JUDGMENTS. For example, the form of the evaluation judgment for Impcore is $\langle e, \xi, \phi, \rho \rangle \Downarrow \langle v, \xi', \phi, \rho' \rangle$. A judgment form is transformed into to a JUDGMENT by substituting ABSTRACT SYNTAX, values, ENVIRONMENTS, or other entities for its METAVARIABLES.

METATHEORETIC PROOF A proof of a fact that is true of all valid derivations. Normally proceeds by STRUCTURAL INDUCTION on derivations.

METATHEORY Theorems about proofs. More broadly, mathematical tools for showing properties that are true for the execution of any program. Example properties might be that evaluating an expression never introduces a new global variable, or that Impcore can be evaluated on a stack, or that a secure language does not leak information. Compare it with THEORY.

METAVARIABLE A variable that stands for something used in a JUDGMENT FORM or elsewhere in a THEORY. Metavariables used in this book include

e for an expression
d for a definition
x for a *program* variable
v for a value
ρ for an ENVIRONMENT
σ for a *store* (Chapter 2)

The name of a metavariable tells a reader what kind of thing it stands for, but unfortunately, no two authors agree on names. Many authors, like Harper (2012), use a mix of Greek and Roman letters, but both Pierce (2002) and Cardelli (1989) use only Roman letters.

NATURAL DEDUCTION A style of proof which is expressed using INFERENCE RULES with JUDGMENTS in the premises and conclusion. (In mathematical logic, these judgments would be called "propositions.") This is the style of our BIG-STEP SEMANTICS; it supposedly accords with a "natural" way of reasoning. Natural deduction is associated with the mathematician Gerhard Gentzen.

OPERATIONAL SEMANTICS A precise way of describing the evaluation of a program. Usually comprises PROOF RULES for JUDGMENTS about program evaluation. The operational semantics gives enough information to write an EVALUATOR for a language. Varieties in this book include BIG-STEP SEMANTICS and SMALL-STEP SEMANTICS.

PARSER The part of a language's implementation that translates CONCRETE SYNTAX to ABSTRACT SYNTAX. (A parser may also translate concrete syntax directly to intermediate code.)

PARSING The process of transforming CONCRETE SYNTAX into ABSTRACT SYNTAX. More generally, the process of recognizing concrete syntax. (Some compilers and interpreters skip abstract syntax and instead generate code directly in the PARSER.)

PREDEFINED FUNCTION A function that is available to every program written in a language, because by the time a user's code is examined, the function's definition has already been evaluated. Like the `mod` function in Impcore. A predefined function is not part of its language; it can be defined using PRIMITIVE FUNCTIONS.

PRIMITIVE FUNCTION A function that is built into a language or its implementation, like the `+` function in Impcore. A primitive function typically cannot be defined using the other parts of its language, so it is considered a sort of a part of its language.

PROCEDURAL PROGRAMMING A style in which programs are built by composing side-effecting SYNTACTIC FORMS in sequence. The forms typically produce no values and are called *commands* or *statements*. They are usually grouped into *procedures*. Procedural programs operate primarily on mutable data, and they tend to manipulate one machine word at a time. Impcore's only data type, the machine integer, does fit in one word, but because it is immutable, Impcore is not a very good example of a procedural programming language.

READ-EVAL-PRINT LOOP An interactive mechanism by which a programmer can run code. A definition or an extended definition is first *read* from standard input; then it is evaluated and its result is printed. And then the implementation loops, waiting for the next definition. A read-eval-print loop enables a programmer to easily use or explore any function or variable. Alternatives that don't support interactive exploration include command-line batch development, where a programmer uses operating-system commands to compile and run code, and app development, where code is developed and packaged on one platform and then shipped to run on another platform.

SMALL-STEP SEMANTICS A species of OPERATIONAL SEMANTICS in which each JUDGMENT FORM expresses the smallest possible increment of computation. Such a semantics exposes the intermediate steps of the computation. An example appears in Chapter 3. Small-step semantics can express more kinds of program behaviors than BIG-STEP SEMANTICS, and the METATHEORETIC proof techniques used with small-step semantics tend to be simpler.

SYMBOL TABLE A compiler writer's word for ENVIRONMENT.

SYNTACTIC CATEGORY A group of SYNTACTIC FORMS that are *grammatically* interchangeable. Examples of common syntactic categories include expressions, definitions, statements, and types.

SYNTACTIC FORM A template for creating a phrase in a programming language, like (set x e).

SYNTACTIC SUGAR A means of extending CONCRETE SYNTAX without changing ABSTRACT SYNTAX. Syntactic sugar is concrete syntax that is translated into existing abstract syntax. Syntactic sugar can appear in a program, but it doesn't make it to a theory or an EVALUATOR. Syntactic sugar can be used to add new loop forms to Impcore, for example (Section 1.8, page 66).

THEORY Theorems about programs. More broadly, mathematical tools that specify meaning and behavior of programs. Theory can be used to prove facts about individual programs and to specify an EVALUATOR or type checker. In this book, the theory of a language is its operational semantics plus, in Chapters 6 to 9, its type system. A language's theory may be used to create a DEFINITIONAL INTERPRETER. Compare it with METATHEORY.

1.9.2 *Further reading*

Literate programming was invented by Knuth (1984); Noweb is described by Ramsey (1994).

The term "basis" is taken from the Definition of Standard ML (Milner et al. 1997), where it refers to a collection of environments binding not only values but types, "signatures," and other entities.

Operational semantics got a big boost from Plotkin (1981), who describes a style of operational semantics that is better suited to proving properties of programs than the natural-deduction style that we use. The natural-deduction style was introduced by Kahn (1987); it is better suited to specifying evaluators.

The notations used to describe grammars and semantics aren't standardized: the ideas are universal, but details vary. Common variations are ably described by Steele (2017), who also explains why the variations are mostly harmless.

The first extensible printer for C programs that I know of was created by Ken Thompson; his implementation appeared in Ninth Edition Research Unix. Another implementation can be found in Chapter 14 of Hanson (1996).

Table 1.10: Synopsis of all the exercises, with most relevant sections

Exercises	*Section*	*Notes*
1 to 5	1.2	Writing Impcore syntax; simple functions that could use loops or recursion.
6 to 8	1.2	Simple functions that demand recursion; functions that manipulate decimal or binary representations.
9	1.3	Syntactic structure and syntactic categories.
10 and 11	1.4, 1.5	Reading and writing judgments of operational semantics.
12 to 14	1.7	Using operational semantics to prove facts about the evaluation of particular expressions.
15 to 17	1.5	Writing new rules of operational semantics, for new features or for features not specified in the chapter.
18 to 21	1.5	Writing new proof systems for new forms of judgment.
22 to 27	1.7	Using metatheory to prove facts about all expressions.
28 and 29	1.6, 1.7	Using metatheory to prove facts about the implementation.
30 to 32	1.6	Implementing new semantics for variables.
33 and 34	1.6, 1.8	Extend the interpreter with a new primitive or new syntax.
35 and 36	1.6	Improving the performance or error behavior of the interpreter.

A nice example of metatheory can be found in the Singularity project, which uses metatheory to guarantee the behavior of its device drivers (Hunt and Larus 2007).

1.10 Exercises

If you read this book without doing any of the exercises, you'll miss most of what it has to offer. But don't try to do *all* the exercises; you'll die of overwork. Choose your exercises well and you'll have a great experience.

To help you find exercises, I've organized them by the skill they demand. In each chapter, you'll find a table of exercises that lists each group of exercises along with the skills they develop and the reading that is most necessary. Skills often include programming in a bridge language, working with a semantics, and modifying an interpreter—but there are others as well. In this chapter, the skills are listed in Table 1.10.

Each chapter's exercises are preceded by *highlights*. The highlights list exercises that are my personal favorites, or that I think are the best, or that I often assign to my students. And each chapter's exercises begin with questions that support *retrieval practice*. These very short questions will help you keep the essential ideas at the surface of your mind, so you can do the exercises fluently. And if you are a student in a university course, they may help you study for exams.

The highlights of this chapter's exercises are as follows:

- Of all the exercises on programming with numbers, my favorite is "convert decimal to binary" (Exercise 8 on page 76). The exercise has a clean, minimal solution, but to find it, you have to develop some insight into the inductive structure of numerals. If you have trouble, start with Exercise 7 on page 75.

- You can do a little language design: What if variables didn't have to be declared before use? (Exercise 16 on page 80)

- You should write at least one derivation (Exercise 12 on page 77). To start reasoning about derivations, follow up with Exercise 13 or 23 on pages 77 or 83.

- You can do some metatheory. The very best of the metatheoretic exercises are Exercises 25 and 29 (pages 83 and 85). You may have to work up to them, but if you tackle either, or better yet both, you will understand which rules of the operational semantics are boring and straightforward and which rules have interesting and important consequences. Exercises 24 and 27 on pages 83 and 84 are significantly easier but also worthwhile.

- To get some practice with the interpreter, add local variables to Impcore (Exercise 30). It will help you think about the connection between semantics and implementation.

1.10.1 *Retrieval practice and other short questions*

A. What's the difference between function `-` and function `negated`?

B. What does `check-expect` do?

C. What is the value of the global variable `it`?

D. What is the difference between concrete syntax and abstract syntax?

E. An example on page 28 shows an example expression along with its abstract-syntax tree. The expression shown in the example uses the syntactic forms SET, APPLY, VAR, and LITERAL. What syntactic forms are used in the expression `(if (< x 0) (negated x) x)`?

F. What syntactic forms are used in the expression `(* (+ x y) (- x y))`?

G. What do the metavariables e and d stand for?

H. What does the metavariable x stand for?

I. When you evaluate `(print 4)`, why does the interpreter print `44`? What should you evaluate instead?

J. Which Greek letter holds the values of all the global variables?

K. Which Greek letter holds the values of all of a function's formal parameters?

L. What does $\rho\{x \mapsto v\}$ stand for?

M. How should you pronounce $\rho\{x \mapsto v\}$?

N. What aspect of the implementation does $\langle e, \xi, \phi, \rho \rangle \Downarrow \langle v, \xi', \phi, \rho' \rangle$ stand for?

O. What is being claimed by a rule of the form $\dfrac{J_1 \quad \cdots \quad J_n}{J}$, where each J is some kind of judgment?

1.10.2 *Simple functions using loops or recursion*

Some of the exercises in these first three sections are adapted from Kamin (1990, Chapter 1), with permission.

1. *Understanding scope, from C to Impcore.* The scope rules of Impcore are identical to that of C. Consider this C program:

   74. ⟨*mystery.c* 74⟩≡
   ```
   int x;

   void R(int y) {
       x = y;
   }

   void Q(int x) {
       R(x + 1);
       printf("%d\n", x);
   }

   void main(void) {
       x = 2;
       Q(4);
       printf("%d\n", x);
   }
   ```

   (a) For each occurrence of `x` in the C program, identify whether the occurrence refers to a global variable or a formal parameter.

   (b) Say what the C program prints.

   (c) Write, in Impcore, a sequence of four definitions that correspond to the C program. Instead of `printf`, call `println`.

2. *Sums of consecutive integers.* Define a function `sigma` satisfying the equation (`sigma` $m\ n$) $= m + (m + 1) + \cdots + n$. The right-hand side is the sum of the elements of the set $\{i \mid m \leq i \leq n\}$.

3. *Exponential and logarithm.* Define functions `exp` and `log`. When base `b` and exponent `n` are nonnegative, (`exp` $b\ n$) $= b^n$, and when $b > 1$ and $m > 0$, (`log` $b\ m$) is the smallest integer n such that $b^{n+1} > m$. On inputs that don't satisfy the preconditions, your implementation may do anything you like—even fail to terminate.

4. *The* n*th Fibonacci number.* Define a function `fib` such that (`fib` n) is the nth Fibonacci number. The Fibonacci numbers are a sequence of numbers defined by these laws:

   (`fib 0`) $= 0$

   (`fib 1`) $= 1$

   (`fib` n) $=$ (`fib (-` n `1))` $+$ (`fib (-` n `2))` when $n > 1$

5. *Prime-number functions.* Define functions `prime?`, `nthprime`, `sumprimes`, and `relprime?` meeting these specifications:

   (`prime?` n) is nonzero ("true") if n is prime and 0 ("false") otherwise.

   (`nthprime` n) is the nth prime number. Consider 2 to be the first prime number, so (`nthprime 1`) $= 2$, so (`nthprime 2`) $= 3$, and so on.

   (`sumprimes` n) is the sum of the first n primes.

   (`relprime?` $m\ n$) is nonzero ("true") if m and n are relatively prime—that is, their only common divisor is 1—and zero ("false") otherwise.

Functions `prime?` and `sumprimes` expect nonnegative integers. Functions `nthprime` and `relprime?` expect *positive* integers.

1.10.3 *A simple recursive function*

6. *Binomial coefficients without arithmetic overflow.* Define a function `choose` such that (`choose` n k) is the number of ways that k distinct items can be chosen from a collection of n items. Assume that n and k are nonnegative integers. The value (`choose` n k) is called a *binomial coefficient,* and it is usually written $\binom{n}{k}$. It can be defined as $\frac{n!}{k!(n-k)!}$, but this definition presents computational problems: even for modest values of n, computing $n!$ can overflow machine arithmetic. Instead, use these identities:

$$\begin{aligned}
\binom{n}{0} &= 1 && \text{when } n \geq 0, \\
\binom{n}{n} &= 1 && \text{when } n \geq 0, \\
\binom{n}{k} &= \binom{n-1}{k} + \binom{n-1}{k-1} && \text{when } n > 0 \text{ and } k > 0.
\end{aligned}$$

These identities guarantee that if the answer is small enough to fit in a machine word, then the results of all of the intermediate computations are also small enough to fit in a machine word.

1.10.4 *Working with decimal and binary representations*

7. *Properties of decimal representations.* In this exercise, you write functions that take numbers apart and look at properties of their decimal digits. You'll need to understand how to define decimal representations inductively, as described in Exercise 18 below.

   (a) Write a function `given-positive-all-fours?`, which when given a positive number, returns 1 if its decimal representation is all fours and 0 otherwise.

   75a. ⟨*exercise transcripts* 75a⟩≡ 75c ▷

   ```
   -> (given-positive-all-fours? 4)
   1
   -> (given-positive-all-fours? 44444)
   1
   -> (given-positive-all-fours? 44443)
   0
   ```

   (b) Write a function `all-fours?`, which when given *any* number, returns 1 if its decimal representation is all fours and 0 otherwise. You could define a function like this:

   75b. ⟨*unsatisfying answer* 75b⟩≡

   ```
   (define all-fours? (n)
     (if (> n 0) (given-positive-all-fours? n) 0))
   ```

   But that's unsatisfying; instead, define just one function `all-fours?`, which you could then use *in place of* `given-positive-all-fours?`.

   75c. ⟨*exercise transcripts* 75a⟩+≡ ◁ 75a 76a ▷

   ```
   -> (all-fours? 0)
   0
   -> (all-fours? -4)
   0
   -> (all-fours? 4)
   1
   ```

(c) Define a function all-one-digit?, which when given a number, returns 1 if the decimal representation of that number uses just one of the ten digits, and zero otherwise.

76a. ⟨*exercise transcripts* 75a⟩+≡ ◁75c 76b▷

```
-> (all-one-digit? 0)
1
-> (all-one-digit? -4)
1
-> (all-one-digit? 44443)
0
-> (all-one-digit? 33)
1
```

(d) Define a function increasing-digits?, which when given a number, returns 1 if in the decimal representation of that number, the digits are strictly increasing, and returns zero otherwise.

76b. ⟨*exercise transcripts* 75a⟩+≡ ◁76a

```
-> (increasing-digits? 1)
1
-> (increasing-digits? 1123)
0
-> (increasing-digits? 12435)
0
-> (increasing-digits? 489)
1
```

If you feel bold, try Exercise 6 in Chapter 2 (page 179).

8. *Decimal-to-binary conversion.* Define a function binary such that (binary m) is the number whose decimal representation looks like the binary representation of m. For example (binary 12) $= 1100$, since $1100_2 = 12_{10}$. An ideal implementation of binary will work on any integer input, including negative ones. For example, (binary -5) $= -101$.

   This exercise, like the previous one, will be easier if you can define decimal and binary representations inductively, as described in Exercise 18 below.

1.10.5 *Understanding syntactic structure*

9. *Syntactic categories in another language.* Here's a discussion problem: Pick your favorite programming language and identify the syntactic categories.

   - What syntactic categories are there?
   - How are the different syntactic categories related? In particular, when can a phrase in one syntactic category be a direct part of a phrase in another (or the same) syntactic category?
   - Do all the phrases in each individual syntactic category share a similar job? What is that job?
   - Which syntactic categories do you have to know about to understand how the language is structured? Which categories are details that apply only to one corner of the language, and aren't important for overall understanding?

   (The question continues on the next page.)

In Impcore, these questions might be answered as follows:

- The syntactic categories of Impcore are definitions and expressions.
- A definition may contain an expression, and an expression may contain another expression, but an expression may not contain a definition.
- In Impcore, the job of an expression is to be evaluated to produce a value. The job of a definition is to introduce a new name into an environment.

1.10.6 *The language of operational semantics*

10. *Understanding what judgments mean.* Take each of the following formal statements and restate it using informal English.

    (a) Either $x \in \text{dom}\,\rho$ or $x \in \text{dom}\,\xi$.

    (b) If $x \in \text{dom}\,\xi$, then $\langle e, \xi, \phi, \rho \rangle \Downarrow \langle \texttt{0}, \xi', \phi, \rho' \rangle$.

    (c) $\langle e, \xi, \phi, \rho \rangle \Downarrow \langle v, \xi', \phi, \rho' \rangle$.

    (d) $\langle e, \xi, \phi, \rho \rangle \Downarrow \langle v, \xi, \phi, \rho \rangle$.

    (e) If $\langle e_1, \xi, \phi, \rho \rangle \Downarrow \langle v_1, \xi_1, \phi, \rho_1 \rangle$ and $\langle e_2, \xi, \phi, \rho \rangle \Downarrow \langle v_2, \xi_1, \phi, \rho_1 \rangle$, then $v_1 = v_2$.

11. *Translating English into formal judgments.* Take each of the following informal statements and restate it using the formalism of operational semantics.

    (a) Expression e can be evaluated successfully even if global variable x is not defined.

    (b) The result of evaluating e doesn't depend on the value of global variable x.

    (c) Evaluating e doesn't change the values of any global variables.

    (d) Evaluating e does not define any new global variables.

    (e) Unless function `prime?` is defined, expression e cannot evaluate successfully.

    (f) The evaluation of e terminates and the result is zero.

    (g) If the evaluation of e terminates, the result is zero.

1.10.7 *Operational semantics: Facts about particular expressions*

To help you with the operational-semantics exercises, the rules of Impcore's operational semantics are summarized in Figures 1.11 and 1.12.

12. *Proof of the result of evaluation.* Use the operational semantics to prove that if you evaluate `(begin (set x 3) x)` in an environment where $\rho(\texttt{x}) = 99$, then the result of the evaluation is 3. In your proof, use a formal derivation tree like the example on page 57.

13. *Proof of equivalence of two expressions.* Show that expression `(if x x 0)` is *observationally equivalent* to just `x`. That is, show that the two expressions can be interchanged in any program, and if we run both variants, we won't be able to observe any difference in behavior.

$$\frac{}{\langle \text{LITERAL}(v), \xi, \phi, \rho \rangle \Downarrow \langle v, \xi, \phi, \rho \rangle} \quad \text{(LITERAL)}$$

$$\frac{x \in \operatorname{dom} \rho}{\langle \text{VAR}(x), \xi, \phi, \rho \rangle \Downarrow \langle \rho(x), \xi, \phi, \rho \rangle} \quad \text{(FORMALVAR)}$$

$$\frac{x \notin \operatorname{dom} \rho \qquad x \in \operatorname{dom} \xi}{\langle \text{VAR}(x), \xi, \phi, \rho \rangle \Downarrow \langle \xi(x), \xi, \phi, \rho \rangle} \quad \text{(GLOBALVAR)}$$

$$\frac{x \in \operatorname{dom} \rho \qquad \langle e, \xi, \phi, \rho \rangle \Downarrow \langle v, \xi', \phi, \rho' \rangle}{\langle \text{SET}(x, e), \xi, \phi, \rho \rangle \Downarrow \langle v, \xi', \phi, \rho'\{x \mapsto v\} \rangle} \quad \text{(FORMALASSIGN)}$$

$$\frac{x \notin \operatorname{dom} \rho \qquad x \in \operatorname{dom} \xi \qquad \langle e, \xi, \phi, \rho \rangle \Downarrow \langle v, \xi', \phi, \rho' \rangle}{\langle \text{SET}(x, e), \xi, \phi, \rho \rangle \Downarrow \langle v, \xi'\{x \mapsto v\}, \phi, \rho' \rangle} \quad \text{(GLOBALASSIGN)}$$

$$\frac{\langle e_1, \xi, \phi, \rho \rangle \Downarrow \langle v_1, \xi', \phi, \rho' \rangle \qquad v_1 \neq 0 \qquad \langle e_2, \xi', \phi, \rho' \rangle \Downarrow \langle v_2, \xi'', \phi, \rho'' \rangle}{\langle \text{IF}(e_1, e_2, e_3), \xi, \phi, \rho \rangle \Downarrow \langle v_2, \xi'', \phi, \rho'' \rangle} \quad \text{(IFTRUE)}$$

$$\frac{\langle e_1, \xi, \phi, \rho \rangle \Downarrow \langle v_1, \xi', \phi, \rho' \rangle \qquad v_1 = 0 \qquad \langle e_3, \xi', \phi, \rho' \rangle \Downarrow \langle v_3, \xi'', \phi, \rho'' \rangle}{\langle \text{IF}(e_1, e_2, e_3), \xi, \phi, \rho \rangle \Downarrow \langle v_3, \xi'', \phi, \rho'' \rangle} \quad \text{(IFFALSE)}$$

$$\frac{\begin{array}{c}\langle e_1, \xi, \phi, \rho \rangle \Downarrow \langle v_1, \xi', \phi, \rho' \rangle \qquad v_1 \neq 0 \\ \langle e_2, \xi', \phi, \rho' \rangle \Downarrow \langle v_2, \xi'', \phi, \rho'' \rangle \qquad \langle \text{WHILE}(e_1, e_2), \xi'', \phi, \rho'' \rangle \Downarrow \langle v_3, \xi''', \phi, \rho''' \rangle\end{array}}{\langle \text{WHILE}(e_1, e_2), \xi, \phi, \rho \rangle \Downarrow \langle v_3, \xi''', \phi, \rho''' \rangle} \quad \text{(WHILEITERATE)}$$

$$\frac{\langle e_1, \xi, \phi, \rho \rangle \Downarrow \langle v_1, \xi', \phi, \rho' \rangle \qquad v_1 = 0}{\langle \text{WHILE}(e_1, e_2), \xi, \phi, \rho \rangle \Downarrow \langle 0, \xi', \phi, \rho' \rangle} \quad \text{(WHILEEND)}$$

$$\frac{}{\langle \text{BEGIN}(), \xi, \phi, \rho \rangle \Downarrow \langle 0, \xi, \phi, \rho \rangle} \quad \text{(EMPTYBEGIN)}$$

$$\frac{\begin{array}{c}\langle e_1, \xi_0, \phi, \rho_0 \rangle \Downarrow \langle v_1, \xi_1, \phi, \rho_1 \rangle \\ \langle e_2, \xi_1, \phi, \rho_1 \rangle \Downarrow \langle v_2, \xi_2, \phi, \rho_2 \rangle \\ \vdots \\ \langle e_n, \xi_{n-1}, \phi, \rho_{n-1} \rangle \Downarrow \langle v_n, \xi_n, \phi, \rho_n \rangle\end{array}}{\langle \text{BEGIN}(e_1, e_2, \ldots, e_n), \xi_0, \phi, \rho_0 \rangle \Downarrow \langle v_n, \xi_n, \phi, \rho_n \rangle} \quad \text{(BEGIN)}$$

$$\frac{\begin{array}{c}\phi(f) = \text{USER}(\langle x_1, \ldots, x_n \rangle, e) \\ x_1, \ldots, x_n \text{ all distinct} \\ \langle e_1, \xi_0, \phi, \rho_0 \rangle \Downarrow \langle v_1, \xi_1, \phi, \rho_1 \rangle \\ \vdots \\ \langle e_n, \xi_{n-1}, \phi, \rho_{n-1} \rangle \Downarrow \langle v_n, \xi_n, \phi, \rho_n \rangle \\ \langle e, \xi_n, \phi, \{x_1 \mapsto v_1, \ldots, x_n \mapsto v_n\} \rangle \Downarrow \langle v, \xi', \phi, \rho' \rangle\end{array}}{\langle \text{APPLY}(f, e_1, \ldots, e_n), \xi_0, \phi, \rho_0 \rangle \Downarrow \langle v, \xi', \phi, \rho_n \rangle} \quad \text{(APPLYUSER)}$$

Figure 1.11: Summary of operational semantics (expressions)

$$\frac{\langle e, \xi, \phi, \{\}\rangle \Downarrow \langle v, \xi', \phi, \rho'\rangle}{\langle \text{VAL}(x, e), \xi, \phi\rangle \rightarrow \langle \xi'\{x \mapsto v\}, \phi\rangle} \quad \text{(DEFINEGLOBAL)}$$

$$\frac{x_1, \ldots, x_n \text{ all distinct}}{\langle \text{DEFINE}(f, \langle x_1, \ldots, x_n\rangle, e), \xi, \phi\rangle \rightarrow \langle \xi, \phi\{f \mapsto \text{USER}(\langle x_1, \ldots, x_n\rangle, e)\}\rangle} \quad \text{(DEFINEFUNCTION)}$$

$$\frac{\langle e, \xi, \phi, \{\}\rangle \Downarrow \langle v, \xi', \phi, \rho'\rangle}{\langle \text{EXP}(e), \xi, \phi\rangle \rightarrow \langle \xi'\{\texttt{it} \mapsto v\}, \phi\rangle} \quad \text{(EVALEXP)}$$

Figure 1.12: Summary of operational semantics (definitions)

(a) Use the operational semantics to show that if there exist environments ξ, ϕ, and ρ (and ξ', ρ', ξ'', and ρ'') such that

$$\langle \text{IF}(\text{VAR}(\mathtt{x}), \text{VAR}(\mathtt{x}), \text{LITERAL}(0)), \xi, \phi, \rho\rangle \Downarrow \langle v_1, \xi', \phi, \rho'\rangle$$

and

$$\langle \text{VAR}(\mathtt{x}), \xi, \phi, \rho\rangle \Downarrow \langle v_2, \xi'', \phi, \rho''\rangle$$

then $v_1 = v_2$.

(b) Now use the operational semantics to show that there exist environments ξ, ϕ, ρ, ξ', and ρ' and a value v_1 such that

$$\langle \text{IF}(\text{VAR}(\mathtt{x}), \text{VAR}(\mathtt{x}), \text{LITERAL}(0)), \xi, \phi, \rho\rangle \Downarrow \langle v_1, \xi', \phi, \rho'\rangle$$

if *and only if* there exist environments ξ, ϕ, ρ, ξ'', and ρ'' and a value v_2 such that

$$\langle \text{VAR}(\mathtt{x}), \xi, \phi, \rho\rangle \Downarrow \langle v_2, \xi'', \phi, \rho''\rangle.$$

Give necessary and sufficient conditions on the environments ξ, ϕ, and ρ such that both expressions evaluate successfully.

(c) Finally, extend your proof in the first part to show that not only are the results equal, but the final environments are also equal.

14. *Proof that* `begin` *can be eliminated.* Impcore can be simplified by eliminating the `begin` expression—every `begin` can be replaced with a combination of function calls. For this problem, assume that ϕ binds the function `second` according to the following definition:

```
(define second (x y) y)
```

I claim that if e_1 and e_2 are arbitrary expressions, you can always write `(second` e_1 e_2`)` instead of `(begin` e_1 e_2`)`.

(a) Using evaluation judgments, take the claim "you can always write `(second` e_1 e_2`)` instead of `(begin` e_1 e_2`)`" and restate the claim in precise, formal language.

Hint: The claim is related to the claims in Exercise 13.

(b) Using operational semantics, prove the claim.

(c) Define a translation for `(begin` $e_1 \cdots e_n$`)` such that the translated code behaves exactly the same as the original code, but in the result of the translation, every remaining `begin` has exactly two subexpressions.

For example, you might translate

```
(begin e1 e2 e3)
```

into

```
(begin e1 (begin e2 e3))
```

If you apply the translation recursively, then replace every `begin` with a call to `second`, you can eliminate `begin` entirely.

1.10.8 *Operational semantics: Writing new rules*

15. *Operational semantics of a `for` loop.* Give operational semantics for a C-like $\text{FOR}(e_1, e_2, e_3, e_4)$. Like a `while` expression, a `for` expression is evaluated for its side effects, so the value it returns is unimportant. Choose whatever result value you like.

16. *Extending Impcore to allow references to unbound variables.* In Impcore, it is an error to refer to a variable that is not bound in any environment. In Awk, the first use of such a variable (either for its value or as the target of an assignment) implicitly creates a new global variable with value 0. In Icon, the rule is similar, except the implicitly created variable is a local variable, whose scope is the entire procedure in which the assignment appears.

    (a) Change the rules of Impcore as needed, and add as many new rules as needed, to give Impcore Awk-like semantics for unbound variables.

    (b) Change the rules of Impcore as needed, and add as many new rules as needed, to give Impcore Icon-like semantics for unbound variables.[6]

    (c) Which of the two changes do you prefer, and why?

    (d) Create a program that can distinguish standard Impcore semantics from the Awk-like and Icon-like extensions described above. In particular, create a source file `awk-icon.imp` containing a sequence of definitions with the following properties:

       - Every definition in the sequence is *syntactically* valid Impcore.
       - If you present the sequence of definitions to a standard Impcore interpreter, the result is a checked run-time error.
       - If you present the sequence of definitions to an Impcore interpreter that has been extended with the Awk-like semantics, the last thing the interpreter does is print 1.
       - If you present the sequence of definitions to an Impcore interpreter that has been extended with the Icon-like semantics, the last thing the interpreter does is print 0.

17. *Formal semantics of unit tests.* The semantics of extended definitions hasn't been formalized. But some of the pieces can be formalized easily enough:

    (a) Design a judgment form to express the idea that "a `check-expect` test succeeds." Your judgment form should include environments ϕ and ξ. Write a proof rule for the new judgment form.

    (b) Design a judgment form to express the idea that "a `check-expect` test *fails*." Write a proof rule for it.

[6] Impcore has top-level expressions, and Icon does not. For purposes of this problem, assume that every top-level expression is evaluated in its own, anonymous procedure.

(c) Design a judgment form to express the idea that "a `check-error` test *fails*." Write a proof rule for it.

The *success* of a `check-error` test is another matter entirely: it requires more than just a single rule. For that, look at Exercise 21.

1.10.9 *Operational semantics: New proof systems*

18. *Meanings of numerals.* A *numeral* is what we use to write numbers. Like an Impcore expression or definition, a numeral is syntax. Decimal numerals can be defined using a grammar: a decimal numeral N_{10} is composed of decimal digits d:

$$d \;::= \texttt{0} \mid \texttt{1} \mid \texttt{2} \mid \texttt{3} \mid \texttt{4} \mid \texttt{5} \mid \texttt{6} \mid \texttt{7} \mid \texttt{8} \mid \texttt{9}$$

$$N_{10} ::= d \mid N_{10}d$$

In informal English, we might say that a decimal numeral is either a single decimal digit, or it is a (smaller) decimal numeral followed by a decimal digit.

The *meaning* of a numeral is a *number*—a numeral is syntax, and a number is a value. The numerals above are written in typewriter font; the numbers below are written in ordinary math font. The meaning of a *decimal* numeral N_{10} can be specified by a function $\mathcal{D}$. Function $\mathcal{D}$ is specified by a set of recursion equations, each of the form $\mathcal{D}[\![N_{10}]\!] = e$, where e is a mathematical formula. (The $[\![\cdots]\!]$ symbols are called "Oxford brackets," and they are used to wrap syntax.) Each equation corresponds to a syntactic form: one for each decimal digit and one for the form in which a numeral is followed by a digit.

$$\mathcal{D}[\![\texttt{0}]\!] = 0 \qquad \mathcal{D}[\![\texttt{2}]\!] = 2 \qquad \mathcal{D}[\![\texttt{4}]\!] = 4 \qquad \mathcal{D}[\![\texttt{6}]\!] = 6 \qquad \mathcal{D}[\![\texttt{8}]\!] = 8$$

$$\mathcal{D}[\![\texttt{1}]\!] = 1 \qquad \mathcal{D}[\![\texttt{3}]\!] = 3 \qquad \mathcal{D}[\![\texttt{5}]\!] = 5 \qquad \mathcal{D}[\![\texttt{7}]\!] = 7 \qquad \mathcal{D}[\![\texttt{9}]\!] = 9$$

$$\mathcal{D}[\![N_{10}d]\!] = 10 \cdot \mathcal{D}[\![N_{10}]\!] + \mathcal{D}[\![d]\!]$$

(The expression $10 \cdot \mathcal{D}[\![N_{10}]\!]$ means "10 times $\mathcal{D}[\![N_{10}]\!]$"; as described in Appendix B, this book uses the $\times$ symbol only for type theory.) In this exercise, you write a similar specification for binary numerals.

   (a) Define precisely what is a binary digit.

   (b) Write an inductive definition of binary numerals.

   (c) Using a meaning function $\mathcal{B}$, write recursion equations that define the meaning of a binary numeral.

19. *Proof systems for program analysis: having* `set`. Impcore is an *imperative* core because it uses side effects. Of these side effects, the most important is *mutation*, also known as assignment.[7] In Impcore, assignment is implemented by `set`. In this exercise, you use proof theory to reason about a very simple property: whether an expression has `set` in it. Looking forward, in Exercise 25, you can see what you can prove if you know an expression *doesn't* have a `set`.

    To see if an expression has `set`, you can just look at it. But that's a plan for a person, not an algorithm for a computer or a set of rules for a proof. The idea

[7] The other side effects are printing and `use`.

of "expression e has a set in it" can be made precise by introducing a judgment form $\boxed{e \text{ has SET}}$. The judgment is defined by this proof system:

$$\textsc{Set}\ \frac{}{\text{SET}(x, e) \text{ has SET}}$$

$$\textsc{If1}\ \frac{e_1 \text{ has SET}}{\text{IF}(e_1, e_2, e_3) \text{ has SET}} \qquad \textsc{If2}\ \frac{e_2 \text{ has SET}}{\text{IF}(e_1, e_2, e_3) \text{ has SET}} \qquad \textsc{If3}\ \frac{e_3 \text{ has SET}}{\text{IF}(e_1, e_2, e_3) \text{ has SET}}$$

$$\textsc{While1}\ \frac{e_1 \text{ has SET}}{\text{WHILE}(e_1, e_2) \text{ has SET}} \qquad \textsc{While2}\ \frac{e_2 \text{ has SET}}{\text{WHILE}(e_1, e_2) \text{ has SET}}$$

$$\textsc{Begin}\ \frac{e_i \text{ has SET}}{\text{BEGIN}(e_1, \ldots, e_n) \text{ has SET}}, i \in \{1, \ldots, n\}$$

$$\textsc{Apply}\ \frac{e_i \text{ has SET}}{\text{APPLY}(f, e_1, \ldots, e_n) \text{ has SET}}, i \in \{1, \ldots, n\}$$

The proof system has some notable properties:

- There are no rules for variables or for literal values. And no wonder: variables and literal values are expressions that don't have `set`.
- There's no premise on the rule for SET. A `set` expression definitely has `set`, no matter what's true about its subexpressions.
- Any other expression has `set` if and only if one of its proper subexpressions has `set`. Expressing that idea requires a rule for each subexpression. For IF and WHILE, the necessary rules can be written explicitly, but BEGIN and APPLY require *rule schemas*. The notation $i \in \{1, \ldots, n\}$ means that a rule is repeated n times: once for each value of i.

Solve the following two problems:

(a) Prove that the expression

```
(while (> x 1)
  (if (= 0 (mod x 2))
      (set x (/ x 2))
      (set x (+ (* 3 x) 1))))
```

has `set`.

(b) Show that *having* `set` isn't the same as *evaluating* `set`. Give an example of an expression e such that e has SET, but you can guarantee that evaluating e never evaluates a `set`.

20. *Proof systems for program analysis: lacking* `set`. When an expression has `set`, the proof system in the previous problem tells us. But if an expression *doesn't* have `set`, that proof system tell us nothing! To know that expression *doesn't* have `set` requires another proof system. Develop a proof system for yet another judgment form: $\boxed{e \text{ hasn't SET}}$. Your proof system should derive "e hasn't SET" exactly when expression e doesn't have a `set` in it.

Your proof system's structure should be related to the structure of the proof system for "e has SET." The relationship is what a mathematician would call *dual*:

- Where "e has SET" lacks proof rules, such as for literals and variables, "e hasn't SET" will have trivial proof rules with no premises.
- Where "e has SET" has a trivial proof rule with no premises, such as for `set`, "e hasn't SET" will lack proof rules. (There's no way you can prove that a `set` expression doesn't have `set`.)
- Where e has subexpressions, for "e has SET" it is sufficient to prove that *any* of e's subexpressions has a `set`. But for "e hasn't SET" it is necessary to prove that *all* of e's subexpressions have *not* got `set`. (This duality is an instance of DeMorgan's Law.)

Your proof system will be correct if every expression either has SET or it doesn't (Exercise 22).

21. *Proof system for checked run-time errors.* To show when a `check-error` test succeeds, we need to be able to show when evaluation of an expression terminates with an error. Such a conclusion requires a pretty big proof system: not quite as big as the complete operational semantics of Impcore, but bigger than the proof systems for e has SET and e hasn't SET in Exercises 19 and 20.

    (a) Design a judgment form to express the idea that evaluation of an expression terminates with an error. Your form will need all the same environments as the form for evaluating an expression that produces a value.

    (b) Write a proof system for this judgment form.

    (c) Design a judgment form to express the idea that "a `check-error` test *succeeds*." Using your proof system from part (b), write a proof rule for your new judgment form.

    (d) If a run-time error occurs during the evaluation of a `check-expect` test, that test is deemed to fail. To cover this possibility, write additional proof rules for the judgment that "a `check-expect` test fails."

1.10.10 Metatheory: Facts about derivations

22. *An expression either has* SET *or it doesn't.* Show that the two judgments in Exercises 19 and 20 are mutually exclusive and cover all cases. That is, for any expression e, there is a valid derivation of exactly one of the two judgments e has SET and e hasn't SET. Try proof by induction on the syntactic structure of e.

23. *A* WHILE *expression evaluates to zero.* Prove that the value of a WHILE expression is always zero. That is, given any ξ, ϕ, ρ, e_1, and e_2, if there exist a ξ', ρ', and v such that there is a derivation of $\langle \text{WHILE}(e_1, e_2), \xi, \phi, \rho\rangle \Downarrow \langle v, \xi', \phi, \rho'\rangle$, then $v = 0$. Use structural induction on the derivation.

24. *Expression evaluation doesn't add or remove global variables.* Prove that the execution of an Impcore expression does not change the set of variables bound in the global environment. That is, prove that if $\langle e, \xi, \phi, \rho\rangle \Downarrow \langle v, \xi', \phi, \rho'\rangle$, then $\text{dom}\,\xi = \text{dom}\,\xi'$.

25. *Program analysis and expression evaluation: does lacking* SET *guarantee unchanged variables?* Is it true or false that evaluating an expression without a SET node does not change any environment? Use metatheory to justify your answer. To be sure you understand what it means to have a SET node, see Exercise 19.

26. *Does evaluation guarantee defined variables?* Section 1.7.3 on page 61 shows how to attempt a metatheoretic proof, and it examines the conjecture "if expression e evaluates, all its variables are defined." Section 1.7.3 addresses every rule except for WHILEITERATE and WHILEEND.

    (a) For derivations ending in WHILEITERATE, either prove the conjecture or show an expression whose evaluation is a counterexample.

    (b) For derivations ending in WHILEEND, either prove the conjecture or show an expression whose evaluation is a counterexample.

    (c) Explain in informal English what is going on with `while` loops—when, whether, and how do we know if a `while` loop's variables are defined?

27. *Impcore is deterministic.* Prove that Impcore is deterministic. That is, prove that for any e and any environments ξ, ϕ, and ρ, there is at most one v such that $\langle e, \xi, \phi, \rho \rangle \Downarrow \langle v, \xi', \phi, \rho' \rangle$.

    You'll reason about two potentially different derivations, each describing its own evaluation of e. Think carefully about your induction hypothesis. For example, to prove that expression `(begin` e_0 `x)` evaluates to at most one v, what do you need to know about the evaluation of e_0?

1.10.11 *Advanced metatheory: Facts about implementation*

28. *Updating environments in place.* In the judgment $\langle e, \xi_0, \phi, \rho_0 \rangle \Downarrow \langle v, \xi_n, \phi, \rho_n \rangle$, the subscripts suggest that between the initial state $\langle e, \xi_0, \phi, \rho_0 \rangle$ and the final state $\langle v, \xi_n, \phi, \rho_n \rangle$ there are n steps of computation. A variable is evaluated in one step, an expression like `(set x 3)` in two steps, and so on. I conjecture that once a step is complete, the environments in its initial state can be discarded. As an example, here is a derivation $\mathcal{D}$ for `(set x 3)`:

$$\frac{x \notin \operatorname{dom} \rho_0 \quad x \in \operatorname{dom} \xi_0 \quad \dfrac{\xi_1 = \xi_0 \quad \rho_1 = \rho_0}{\langle 3, \xi_0, \phi, \rho_0 \rangle \Downarrow \langle 3, \xi_1, \phi, \rho_1 \rangle} \quad \xi_2 = \xi_1\{\mathtt{x} \mapsto 3\} \quad \rho_2 = \rho_1}{\langle \mathtt{(set\ x\ 3)}, \xi_0, \phi, \rho_0 \rangle \Downarrow \langle 3, \xi_2, \phi, \rho_2 \rangle}.$$

Now $\mathcal{D}$ can be a subderivation in a larger derivation for `(set y (set x 3))`:

$$\frac{y \in \operatorname{dom} \rho_0 \quad \dfrac{\mathcal{D}}{\langle \mathtt{(set\ x\ 3)}, \xi_0, \phi, \rho_0 \rangle \Downarrow \langle 3, \xi_2, \phi, \rho_2 \rangle} \quad \xi_3 = \xi_2 \quad \rho_3 = \rho_2\{\mathtt{y} \mapsto 3\}}{\langle \mathtt{(set\ y\ (set\ x\ 3))}, \xi_0, \phi, \rho_0 \rangle \Downarrow \langle 3, \xi_3, \phi, \rho_3 \rangle}.$$

In these derivations, each part of each state is given a name. For example, in the first derivation, the environment $\xi_1\{\mathtt{x} \mapsto 3\}$ is named ξ_2. The subscripts on the metavariables may help you see that, for example, ξ_0 and ρ_0 are used multiple times, but that after judgment $\langle 3, \xi_0, \phi, \rho_0 \rangle \Downarrow \langle 3, \xi_1, \phi, \rho_1 \rangle$ is proved, only ξ_1 and ρ_1 are used thenceforth—environments ξ_0 and ρ_0 are never used again. The transition from ξ_1 and ρ_1 to ξ_2 and ρ_2 is similar, and so on. This observation suggests an optimization that is used in this chapter: where the derivation says something like $\xi_2 = \xi_1\{\mathtt{x} \mapsto 3\}$, the implementation needn't build a fresh environment ξ_2. It can instead simply update a data structure: first the data structure holds ξ_1, then after the update, it holds ξ_2.

Show that this optimization does not affect the semantics:

    (a) Prove that in any valid derivation, evaluation judgments can be totally ordered by their use of the global-variable environment. That is, the premises required to prove any judgment can be ordered in such a way that after the proof of every evaluation judgment, each of which takes the form $\langle e_i, \xi_i, \phi, \rho_i \rangle \Downarrow \langle v_i, \xi_{i+1}, \phi, \rho_{i+1} \rangle$, global-variable environment ξ_i is never used again and can be discarded.

This metatheorem justifies using `bindval(e->set.name, v, globals)` to *overwrite* the `globals` environment when `set` is evaluated.

(b) Show that uses of the formal-parameter environment *cannot* be totally ordered: Exhibit a valid derivation containing a judgment of the form $\langle e_i, \xi_i, \phi, \rho_i \rangle \Downarrow \langle v_i, \xi_{i+1}, \phi, \rho_{i+1} \rangle$, such that the next evaluation judgment has an initial state of the form $\langle e, \xi_{i+1}, \phi, \rho \rangle$, where ρ is independent of ρ_{i+1}, and furthermore, some *other* evaluation judgment has an initial state that depends on ρ_{i+1}. Formal-parameter environments cannot simply be mutated in place. Their optimization is the topic of the next exercise.

29. *Keeping environments on a stack.* Formal-parameter environments can be kept on a stack. To show this, you will *imagine* an implementation that uses an explicit stack of environments. And write a semantics for it. You will imagine an implementation halfway between the operational semantics of this chapter and a stack machine that is described in Chapter 3.

Your semantics will describe an abstract machine that will be almost identical to the Impcore machine, except the last element of the state will be a *nonempty stack* of formal-parameter environments. A nonempty stack should be written as $\rho :: S$, where S is a (possibly empty) stack of formal-parameter environments. Each rule will affect only the top of the stack, so the judgment form will be $\langle e, \xi, \phi, \rho :: S \rangle \Downarrow \langle v, \xi', \phi, \rho' :: S \rangle$.

(a) Rewrite the semantics of Impcore to use this new judgment form. Ensure that if it is necessary use some other environment and also to remember ρ, that the new environment is pushed on top of the stack $\rho :: S$.

In `eval`, the implementation of every proof rule that ends in the judgment form $\langle e, \xi, \phi, \rho :: S \rangle \Downarrow \langle v, \xi', \phi, \rho' :: S \rangle$ can be implemented by popping ρ off the stack, doing some computation, and pushing ρ' onto the stack. (It is possible that $\rho' = \rho$.) The computation in the middle may include pushes, pops, and recursive calls to `eval`. And once ρ is popped off the stack, it is used only to make ρ' and not in any other way—so it is safe to compute ρ' by mutating ρ in place.

(b) Prove that if $\rho' = \rho$, then the only copy of ρ is the one on top of the stack. If $\rho' \neq \rho$, then once ρ is popped off the stack, it is thrown away and never used again. In particular, no environment ever needs to be copied anywhere except on the stack; that is, every environment that might ever be needed is present on the stack.

Use structural induction on a derivation of the evaluation judgment $\langle e, \xi, \phi, \rho :: S \rangle \Downarrow \langle v, \xi', \phi, \rho' :: S \rangle$. The base cases are the rules that have no evaluation judgments in the premises, such as the LITERAL or FORMALVAR rules. The induction steps are the rules that *do* have evaluation judgments as premises, such as FORMALASSIGN.

This lemma implies that the operation "pop ρ; push ρ'" can be replaced by the operation "mutate ρ in place to become ρ'." In particular, $\rho\{x \mapsto v\}$ can be implemented by mutating an existing binding; building a new environment is not necessary. The mutation is safe *only* because the sole copy of ρ is on top of the stack.

This theorem justifies my implementation of `bindval`, as referred to in Section 1.6.3. The stack is the C call stack.

1.10.12 *Implementation: New semantics for variables*

30. *Adding local variables to Impcore.* Extend function definitions so that an Impcore function may have local variables. That is, change the concrete and abstract syntax of definitions to:

    (define *function-name* (*formals*) [(locals *locals*)] *expression*)
    Userfun = (Namelist formals, Namelist locals, Exp body)

    where *locals*, having the same syntax as *formals*, names the function's local variables. The square brackets in "[(locals *locals*)]" means that the `locals` declaration can be omitted; when the concrete syntax has no `locals` declaration, the abstract syntax has an empty list of locals.

    If a local variable has the same name as a formal parameter, then in the body of the function, that name refers to the local variable. And before the body of the function is evaluated, each local variable must be initialized to zero.

    You will have to change the definitions of `struct Userfun` and function `mkUserfun`, as well as the relevant case in `reduce_to_xdef` in chunk S196a in Section G.2. But you will focus on the evaluator in `eval.c`. Make sure that after your changes, the interpreter still checks that the number of actual parameters is correct.

    An example function that uses local variables appears in Figure 1.9 (page 67).

31. *Extending Impcore to work with unbound variables.* Implement your solutions to Exercise 16. Use your implementation to test the code you write to distinguish the new semantics.

32. *Passing parameters by reference.* Change the Impcore interpreter to pass parameters by *reference* instead of by value. For example, if a variable `x` is passed to a function `f`, function `f` can modify `x` by assigning to a formal parameter. If a non-variable expression is passed as an argument to a function, assignments to formal parameters should have no effect outside the function. (In particular, it should not be possible to change the value of an integer literal by assignment to a formal parameter.)

    To implement this change, change the return type of `eval` and `fetchval` to be `Value*`, and make `Valuelists` hold `Value*`s rather than `Values`. Type checking in your C compiler should help you find the other parts that need to change. No change in syntax is needed.

    Explore your implementation by writing a function that uses call by reference. A good candidate is a function that wants to return multiple values, like a division function that wants to return both quotient and remainder. Then address these questions:

    (a) Is the `bindval` function in the environment interface still necessary?

    (b) How does call by reference affect the truth of the assertion (page 22): "no assignment to a formal parameter can ever change the value of a global variable"?

(c) What are the advantages and disadvantages of reference parameters? Do you prefer Impcore with call by reference or call by value? If arrays were added to Impcore, as in Chapter 6, how would your answers change?

Justify your answers, preferably using examples and scenarios.

1.10.13 Extending the interpreter

If you intend to do some of the interpreter exercises in Chapters 2 to 4, the exercises below will help you get started (as will Exercise 30 above).

33. *Adding a new primitive.* Add the primitive `read` to the Impcore interpreter and the initial basis. Function `read` is executed for its side effect; it takes no arguments, reads a number from standard input, and returns the number.

34. *Adding new concrete syntax.* Using syntactic sugar, extend Impcore with the looping constructs discussed in Section 1.8:

    (a) Implement the C-style `do-while`.

    (b) Implement `while*`, which allows you to code a loop that does multiple operations, without `begin`.

    (c) Implement the C-style `for` loop, described as FOR in Exercise 15.

    Emulate the code in Section G.7 on page S209 of the Supplement.

35. *Recovering lost file descriptors.* The implementation of `use` in chunk ⟨*evaluate* `d->use`*, possibly mutating* `globals` *and* `functions` S296c⟩ leaks open file descriptors when files have bugs. Explain how you would fix the problem.

1.10.14 Interpreter performance

36. *Profiling.* Write an Impcore program that takes a long time to execute. Profile the interpreter.

    (a) Approximately what fraction of time is spent in linear search? Approximately how much faster might the interpreter run if you used search trees? What about hash tables?

    (b) Download code from Hanson (1996). and use it to implement names and environments. (The code can likely be found at its archival site, `https://www.cs.princeton.edu/software/cii`.) How much speedup do you actually get?

    (c) What other "hot spots" can you find? What is the best way to make the interpreter run faster?

    An Impcore "program" is simply a sequence of definitions.

CHAPTER 2 CONTENTS

2 Scheme, S-expressions, and first-class functions

Programming languages should be designed not by piling feature on top of feature, but by removing the weaknesses and restrictions that make additional features appear necessary. Scheme demonstrates that a very small number of rules for forming expressions, with no restrictions on how they are composed, suffice to form a practical and efficient programming language that is flexible enough to support most of the major programming paradigms in use today.

Jonathan Rees and William Clinger (eds.),
The Revised^3 Report on the Algorithmic Language Scheme

Scheme combines power and simplicity. Scheme is derived from Lisp, which John McCarthy developed—inspired in part by Alonzo Church's work on the *λ-calculus*—while exploring ideas about computability, recursive functions, and models of computation. McCarthy intended Lisp for computing with symbolic data he called *S-expressions*. S-expressions are based on lists, and the name "Lisp" was formed from "list processing." Lisp programs can be concise and natural programs, and they often resemble mathematical definitions of the functions they compute. Lisp has been used heavily in artificial intelligence for over fifty years, and in 1971, McCarthy received ACM's Turing Award for contributions to artificial intelligence.

Lisp spawned many successor dialects, of which the most influential have been Common Lisp and Scheme. Common Lisp was designed to unify many of the dialects in use in the 1980s; its rich programming environment has attracted many large software projects. Scheme was designed to be small, clean, and powerful; its power and simplicity have attracted many teachers and authors like me.

Scheme was created by Guy Steele and Gerry Sussman, who introduced the main ideas in a classic series of MIT technical reports in the late 1970s, all bearing titles of the form "LAMBDA: The Ultimate (blank)." And Scheme may have been made famous by Abelson and Sussman (1985), who show off its ability to express many different programming-language ideas and to build programs in many different styles.

So what is Scheme? To answer such a question, set aside the syntax; the essence of a language lies in its values. If the essence of C is pointer arithmetic, the essence of Perl is regular expressions, and the essence of Fortran is arrays, the essence of Scheme is *lists* and *functions*.[1]

[1] Today, any list of Scheme's essential aspects would also include hygienic macros. But hygienic macros were developed relatively late, in the 1980s and 1990s, well after the other foundations of Scheme were laid down. And unlike those foundations, macros have not colonized other languages. In this book, macros, substitution, and hygiene are just barely touched on.

Lists come from original Lisp. Lists can contain other lists, so they can be used to build records and trees. Lists of key-value pairs can act as tables. Add numbers and symbols, and lists provide everything you need for symbolic computation.

In addition to lists, Scheme provides first-class, higher-order, *nested* functions. Nested functions are created at run time by evaluating `lambda` expressions, which should dramatically change our thinking about programming and computation.

Scheme was meant to be small, but full Scheme is still too big for this book. Instead, we use μScheme (pronounced "micro-Scheme"), a distillation of Scheme's essential features. In this book, "Scheme" refers to ideas that Scheme and μScheme share. "Full Scheme" and "μScheme" refer to the large and small languages, respectively.

2.1 Overview of μScheme and this chapter

Scheme shares some central ideas with Impcore, which you know:

- Scheme encourages interactive programming with functions. Scheme programmers don't "write a program"; they "define a function." They don't "run a program"; they "evaluate an expression."
- Scheme has simple, regular syntax. It has no infix operators and therefore no operator precedence.

μScheme goes beyond Impcore in five significant ways:

- μScheme makes it easy to define local variables, which are introduced and initialized by `let` expressions.
- In addition to machine integers, μScheme provides Booleans values, symbols, functions, lists of values, and a species of record structure.
- Instead of loops, Scheme programmers write recursive functions.[2]
- μScheme's functions, unlike Impcore's functions, are values, which can be used in the same ways as any other value. In particular, functions can be passed as arguments to other functions and returned as results from other functions; they can also be assigned to variables and even stored in lists. Such functions are said to be *first class.*

  Functions that accept functions as arguments or return functions as results are called *higher-order functions*; functions that accept and return only nonfunctional values are called *first-order functions.* Only first-order functions are found in Impcore.
- Anonymous, nested functions are defined by a new form of expression, the `lambda` expression.

These language changes wind up changing our programming style:

- Much as arrays, loops, and assignment statements lead to a procedural style of programming, S-expressions, recursive functions, and `let` binding lead to a new, *applicative* style of programming.

[2]Although mathematicians have used recursion equations for centuries, computer scientists took a long time to recognize recursion as *practical.* Alan Perlis said that when some of the world's leading computer scientists met in 1960 to design the language Algol 60, "We really did not understand the implications of recursion, or its value, ... McCarthy did, but the rest of us didn't" (Wexelblat 1981, p. 160).

Values	*Rules*
Ordinary S-expressions	1 and 2
Fully general S-expressions	1, 2, and 4
Values	1 to 4

1. A symbol, number, or Boolean is a value.
2. A list of values is a value.
3. A function is a value.
4. If v_1 and v_2 are values, `(cons` v_1 v_2`)` produces a value.

Figure 2.1: Summary of rules for μScheme values

- The ability to define first-class, *nested* functions leads to a powerful new programming technique: *higher-order programming*.

The addition of nested functions, with the ability of one function to change an enclosing function's variables, requires a change in the semantics:

- In Impcore, environments map names to values, and assignment (`set`) is implemented by binding new values. In μScheme, environments map names to mutable *locations*, which contain values. Assignment is implemented by changing the contents of locations (Section 2.7.1).

Details are found throughout the chapter, organized as follows:

- S-expressions and other values are formed according to four simple rules (Section 2.2).
- Recursion exemplifies applicative programming (Section 2.3).
- List elements are addressed by position; to enable us to refer to an element by its name, μScheme provides a `record` construct. Records in turn are used to represent trees (Section 2.4).
- Applicative code is clearly and succinctly specified by *algebraic laws*. Algebraic laws are much easier to work with than operational semantics; we can prove facts about applicative code using just simple algebra (Section 2.5).
- Local names are introduced by `let` bindings (Section 2.6).
- First-class, nested functions are created by `lambda` expressions (Section 2.7). They support list processing (Section 2.8), code reuse via *polymorphism* (Section 2.9), and backtracking search via *continuation passing* (Section 2.10).
- μScheme's run-time behavior is specified by an operational semantics (Section 2.11) and implemented by an interpreter (Section 2.12).
- Conveniences like `record`, short-circuit conditionals, and other conditional forms can be implemented as syntactic sugar. Making the sugar work correctly requires attention to *substitution* and *hygiene* (Section 2.13).

2.2 Language I: Values, syntax, and initial basis

Scheme's values include not only integers but also Booleans, functions, *symbols*, and *lists* of values, all of which are described below. The ones that can easily be written down—the ones that don't involve functions—are called *S-expressions*, which is short for "symbolic expressions."

Scheme's least familiar sort of value is the *symbol*; a symbol is a value that is a name. To paraphrase Kelsey, Clinger, and Rees (1998), what matters about symbols is that two symbols are identical if and only if their names are spelled in the same way. That is, symbols behave like `Name` values from the Impcore interpreter. And like `Names`, symbols are often used to represent identifiers in programs. They are also used in the same way that enumeration literals are used in C, C++, or Java.

The other forms of μScheme value are more familiar: numbers, Booleans, lists, and functions. They are described by three inductive rules, which are summarized in Figure 2.1 on the previous page:

1. A symbol is a value, and so is a number. The Boolean values `#t` and `#f` are values; `#t` and `#f`, not 1 and 0, canonically represent truth and falsehood.

   Values defined by this rule are *atomic*: like atoms in the ancient Greek theory of matter, they have no observable internal structure and cannot be "taken apart." Atomic values are also called *atoms*.

2. If $v_1, \ldots, v_n$ are values, then that list of n values is also a value, and it is written $(v_1 \;\cdots\; v_n)$. Even when $n = 0$, the empty list, which is written `()`, is a value. And the empty list is considered to be an atom as well as a list.

3. Every function is a value.

Although rules 1 to 3 cover the common cases, μScheme provides one more form of value, which can be explained only by referring to μScheme's `cons` primitive, which is described below.

Values formed by rules 1 and 2 are *ordinary S-expressions*, usually called just "S-expressions." Examples might include the following:

```
3 10 -39 44              ; numbers
#t #f                    ; Booleans
hello frog               ; symbols
(80 87 11)               ; list of numbers
(frog newt salamander) ; list of symbols
(10 lords a-leaping)     ; list of mixed values
((9 ladies dancing) (8 maids a-milking)) ; list of S-expressions
```

An ordinary S-expression can be written directly in source code, preceded by a quote mark.

From values we move to syntax, which is shown in Figure 2.2 on the facing page. Much of the core syntax should be familiar from Impcore; new forms include the `let` family (Section 2.6), `lambda` (Section 2.7), and lots of new *literals*. Some syntactic sugar is also new. Record definitions, short-circuit conditionals, and the `cond` form are expanded as described in Section 2.13; `when` and `unless` are expanded as described in Chapter 3 (Figure 3.3, page 204).

After values and syntax, the last element of the language is the initial basis, starting with the primitives.

- Primitives shared with Impcore include `+`, `-`, `*`, `/`, `<`, and `>`, which implement arithmetic and comparisons. The comparisons return Booleans, not numbers: `#t` if the condition holds, and otherwise, `#f`. Applying any of these functions to a non-number is a checked run-time error, as is division by zero.

Primitives that are new with μScheme include *type predicates*, which are used to identify a value's form.

- Each type predicate, `symbol?`, `number?`, `boolean?`, `null?`, or `function?`, returns `#t` if its argument is of the named form, `#f` otherwise. Predicates

```
def         ::= (val variable-name exp)
              | exp
              | (define function-name (formals) exp)
            ★ | (record record-name [{field-name}])
              | (use file-name)
              | unit-test

unit-test   ::= (check-expect exp exp)
              | (check-assert exp)
              | (check-error exp)

exp         ::= literal
              | variable-name
              | (set variable-name exp)
              | (if exp exp exp)
              | (while exp exp)
              | (begin {exp})
              | (exp {exp})
              | (let-keyword ({[variable-name exp]}) exp)
              | (lambda (formals) exp)
            ★ | (&& {exp}) | (|| {exp})
            ★ | (cond {[question-exp answer-exp]})
            ★ | (when exp {exp}) | (unless exp {exp})

let-keyword ::= let | let* | letrec

formals     ::= {variable-name}

literal     ::= numeral | #t | #f | 'S-exp | (quote S-exp)

S-exp       ::= symbol-name | numeral | #t | #f | ({S-exp})

numeral     ::= token composed only of digits, possibly prefixed with a plus
                or minus sign

*-name      ::= token that is not a bracket, a numeral, or one of the "re-
                served" words shown in typewriter font
```

Tokens are as in Impcore, except that if a quote mark `'` occurs at the beginning of a token, it is a token all by itself; e.g., `'yellow` is two tokens.

Each quoted S-expression (*S-exp*) is converted to a literal value by the parser. And each `record` definition is expanded to a sequence of true definitions, also by the parser; in other words, a `record` definition is syntactic sugar (Section 1.8, page 68), as marked by the ★. Five forms of conditional expression are also syntactic sugar. All the other forms are handled by the `eval` function.

Figure 2.2: Concrete syntax of μScheme

`symbol?`, `number?`, `boolean?`, and `null?` identify atoms—`null?` asks if the value is an empty list. Predicate `function?` identifies functions.[3]

Other new primitives support lists:

- Function `cons` adds one element to the *front* of a list. If vs (pronouced "veez") is the empty list, then `(cons` v vs`)` is the singleton list `(`v`)`. If vs is the nonempty list `(`$v_1 \cdots v_n$`)`, then `(cons` v vs`)` is the longer list `(`$v\ v_1 \cdots v_n$`)`.

In Scheme, `cons` has a quirk not common in other functional languages: it can be applied to any two values, not just to an element and a list. This quirk demands a fourth rule for the formation of μScheme values:

4. If v_1 and v_2 are values, then `(cons` v_1 v_2`)` produces a value.

Scheme values formed by rules 1, 2, and 4 are called *fully general S-expressions*.

Calling `(cons` v_1 v_2`)` always produces a value, but the result a *list* of values if and only if v_2 is a list of values. Values made with `cons` are identified by type predicate `pair?`.

- Calling `(pair?` v`)` returns `#t` if and only if v is a value produced by `cons`.

Lists are interrogated by other primitives:

- Function `null?` is used to distinguish an empty list from a nonempty list.
- Function `car` returns the first element of a *nonempty* list; if vs is the nonempty list `(`$v_1 \cdots v_n$`)`, then `(car` vs`)` is v_1. If vs is any other value made with `cons`, like `(cons` v_1 v_2`)`, then `(car` vs`)` is also v_1. If vs is `()` or is not made with `cons`, applying `car` to it is a checked run-time error.
- Function `cdr` returns the remaining elements of a *nonempty* list. If vs is the nonempty list `(`$v_1 \cdots v_n$`)`, then `(cdr` vs`)` is the list `(`$v_2 \cdots v_n$`)`, which contains all the elements of vs except the first. If vs is the singleton list `(`v_1`)`, `(cdr` vs`)` is `()`. If vs is any other value made with `cons`, like `(cons` v_1 v_2`)`, then `(cdr` vs`)` is v_2. If vs is `()` or is not made with `cons`, applying `cdr` to it is a checked run-time error.

  The word "`cdr`" is pronounced as the word "could" followed by "er."

Primitives `car` and `cdr` can safely be applied to any value made with `cons`.

The name `cons` stands for "construct," which makes some kind of sense. The names `car` and `cdr`, by contrast, stand for "contents of the address part of register" and "contents of the decrement part of register," which make sense only if we are thinking about the machine-language implementation of Lisp on the IBM 704. In the Racket dialect of Scheme, `car` and `cdr` are called by the more sensible names `first` and `rest` (Felleisen et al. 2018).

μScheme includes an equality primitive that works on more than just numbers:

- Function `=` tests atoms for equality. Calling `(=` v_1 v_2`)` returns `#t` if v_1 and v_2 are the same *atom*. That is, they may be the same symbol, the same number, or the same Boolean, or they may both be the empty list. Given any two values that are not the same atom, including any functions or nonempty lists, `(=` v_1 v_2`)` returns `#f`. (To compare nonempty lists, we use the non-primitive function `equal?`, which is shown in chunk 104a.)

[3]If you already know Scheme, or if you learn Scheme, you'll notice some differences. For example, in full Scheme, functions are called "procedures." S-expressions are called "datums." The syntax of the `define` form is different, and the `val` form uses the `define` keyword. The `=` primitive works only on numbers, and it is complemented by other equality functions like `eq?`, `eqv?`, and `equal?`. Full Scheme's `and` and `or` forms are syntax, not functions, so they short-circuit, like μScheme's `&&` and `||`.

Last, the printing primitives are like Impcore's printing primitives. Primitives print and println work with any value.

- Calling (print v) prints a representation of v, but what you normally want is (println v), which prints the value and a newline. With either one, if v is a fully general S-expression, then the primitive prints everything known about it. But when v is a function, the primitives print only "<function>."
- Function printu prints UTF-8: If n is a number that corresponds to a Unicode code point, (printu n) prints the UTF-8 encoding of the code point. Code points newline, space, semicolon, quotemark, left-round, right-round, left-curly, right-curly, left-square, and right-square are predefined.

As in Impcore, only println, print, and printu have side effects; other primitives compute new values without changing anything. For example, applying cons, car, or cdr to a list does not change the list.

The primitives that μScheme shares with Impcore are demonstrated in Chapter 1. The list primitives are demonstrated below, by applying them to values that are written as *literals*. Literals include numerals, Boolean literals, and *quoted* S-expressions (Figure 2.2, page 93). Using quoted S-expressions, we can demonstrate cons, car, and cdr:

95a. ⟨*transcript* 95a⟩≡ 95b ▷

```
-> (cons 'a '())
(a)
-> (cons 'a '(b))
(a b)
-> (cons '(a) '(b))
((a) b)
-> (cdr '(a (b (c d))))
((b (c d)))
-> (car '(a (b (c d))))
a
```

Primitive null? finds that the empty list is empty, but it finds that a singleton list *containing* the empty list is not empty:

95b. ⟨*transcript* 95a⟩+≡ ◁ 95a 98 ▷

```
-> (null? '())
#t
-> (null? '(()))
#f
```

In more complex examples, the primitives' definitions have to be used carefully; a literal S-expression might look like a long list even when it's not. For example, list (a (b (c d))) looks long, but it has only two elements: the symbol a and the list (b (c d)). Its cdr is therefore the single-element list ((b (c d))).

car	$\mathcal{P}$ 162a
cdr	$\mathcal{P}$ 162a
cons	$\mathcal{P}$ S313d
null?	$\mathcal{P}$ 162a

Primitives cons, car, and cdr are often explained with diagrams. Any non-empty list can be drawn as a box that contains two pointers, one of which points to the car, and the other to the cdr. This box helps explain not only the behavior but also the cost of running Scheme programs, so it has a name—it is a *cons cell*. If the cdr of a cons cell is the empty list, there's nothing to point to; instead, it is drawn as a slash. Using these conventions, the list (a b c) is drawn like this:

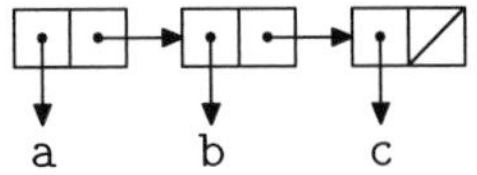

The car or cdr of a nonempty list is found by following the arrow that leaves the left or right box of the first cons cell. As another example, the S-expression (a (b (c d))) is drawn like this:

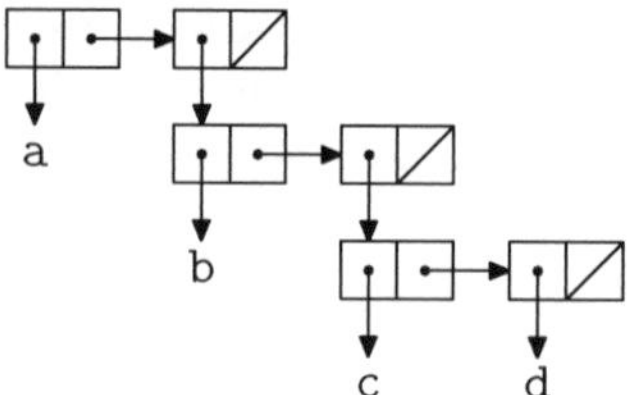

Its cdr is simply what the first cell's right arrow points at, which is, as above, ((b (c d))):

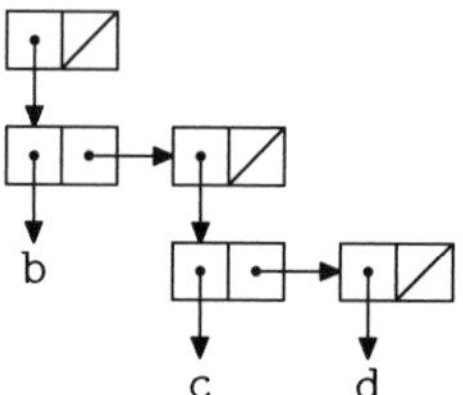

When complex structures are built from cons cells, car and cdr are often applied several times in succession. Such applications have traditional abbreviations:

96a. ⟨*predefined μScheme functions* 96a⟩≡ 96b ▷

```
(define caar (xs) (car (car xs)))
(define cadr (xs) (car (cdr xs)))
(define cdar (xs) (cdr (car xs)))
```

These definitions appear in chunk ⟨*predefined μScheme functions* 96a⟩, from which they are built into the μScheme interpreter itself and are evaluated when the interpreter starts. Definitions are built in for all combinations of car and cdr up to depth five, ending with cddddr, but the others are relegated to the Supplement.

If applying car or cdr several times in succession is tiresome, so is applying cons several times in succession. Common cases are supported by more predefined functions:

96b. ⟨*predefined μScheme functions* 96a⟩+≡ ◁ 96a 99b ▷

```
(define list1 (x)     (cons x '()))
(define list2 (x y)   (cons x (list1 y)))
(define list3 (x y z) (cons x (list2 y z)))
```

More cases, for list4 to list8, are defined in the Supplement. In full Scheme, all possible cases are handled by a single, variadic function, list, which takes any number of arguments and returns a list containing those arguments (Exercise 56).

Three predefined functions are similar but not identical to functions found in Impcore: the Boolean functions and, or, and not. Instead of Impcore's 1 and 0, they return Boolean values.

96c. ⟨*definitions of predefined μScheme functions* and, or, *and* not 96c⟩≡

```
(define and (b c) (if b  c  b))
(define or  (b c) (if b  b  c))
(define not (b)   (if b #f #t))
```

Functions and and or inconveniently evaluate both arguments, even when the first argument determines the result. To evaluate only as much as is needed to make a decision, use the syntactic forms && and || (Exercise 53).

Table 2.3: The initial basis of μScheme

`=`, `!=`	Equality and inequality on atoms
`equal?`	Recursive equality on fully general S-expressions (isomorphism, not object identity)
`/`, `*`, `-`, `+`, `mod`	Integer arithmetic
`>`, `<`, `>=`, `<=`	Integer comparison
`lcm`, `gcd`, `min`, `max`	Binary operations on integers
`lcm*`, `gcd*`, `max*`, `min*`	The same operations, but taking one nonempty list of integers as argument
`not`, `and`, `or`	Basic operations on Booleans, which, unlike their counterparts in full Scheme, evaluate all their arguments
`symbol?`, `number?`, `boolean?`, `null?`, `pair?`, `function?`	Type predicates
`atom?`	Type predicate saying whether a value is an atom (not a function and not a pair)
`cons`, `car`, `cdr`	The basic list operations
`caar`, `cdar`, `cadr`, `cddr`, ...	Abbreviations for combinations of list operations, including also `caaar`, `cdaar`, `caadr`, `cdadr`, and so on, all the way to `cddddr`.
`list1`, `list2`, `list3`, `list4`, ...	Convenience functions for creating lists, including also `list5` to `list8`
`append`	The elements of one list followed by the elements of another
`revapp`	The elements of one list, reversed, followed by another
`reverse`	A list reversed
`bind`, `find`	Insertion and lookup for association lists
`filter`	Those elements of a list satisfying a predicate
`exists?`	Does any element of a list satisfy a predicate?
`all?`	Do all elements of a list satisfy a predicate?
`map`	List of results of applying a function to each element of a list
`takewhile`	The longest prefix of a list satisfying a predicate
`dropwhile`	What's not taken by `takewhile`
`foldl`, `foldr`	Elements of a list combined by an operator, which associates to left or right, respectively
`o`	Function composition
`curry`	The curried function equivalent to some binary function
`uncurry`	The binary function equivalent to some curried function
`println`, `print`	Primitives that print one value
`printu`	Primitive that prints a Unicode character
`error`	Primitive that aborts the computation with an error message

The functions above are all part of μScheme's initial basis. The entire basis, including both primitive and predefined functions, is summarized in Table 2.3 on the preceding page. The primitives are discussed above, and predefined functions that are unique to μScheme are shown in this chapter in code chunks named ⟨*predefined μScheme functions* 96a⟩. Other predefined functions are defined exactly as in Impcore; their definitions are relegated to the Supplement.

2.3 PRACTICE I: RECURSIVE FUNCTIONS ON LISTS OF VALUES

Primitives `null?`, `car`, and `cdr` are used to write functions that inspect lists and their elements. In Scheme, such functions are typically recursive. Even functions that iterate are usually written recursively; Scheme programmers rarely use `set` or `while`. To become fluent in writing your own recursive functions, you can imitate the many examples in this section:

- Functions that are agnostic about the types of list elements
- Functions that operate on lists of numbers
- Functions the operate on lists of lists—that is, S-expressions
- Functions that use lists to represent sets or finite maps

2.3.1 *Basic principles of programming with lists*

In Scheme, a list is created in one of two ways: by using `'()` or `cons`. In the style of the preceding section,

L1. The empty list `'()` is a list of values.

L2. If v is a value and vs is a list of values, (`cons` v vs) is a list of values.

Like any other data type that can be created in multiple ways, a list is normally consumed by a function that begins with case analysis. Such a function distinguishes cases using `null?`, and when the list is not null—it was created by using `cons`—a typical function calls itself recursively on the rest of the list (the `cdr`).

One of the simplest such functions finds the length of a list of values:

98. ⟨*transcript* 95a⟩+≡ ◁95b 99a▷

```
-> (define length (xs)
     (if (null? xs)
         0
         (+ 1 (length (cdr xs)))))
```

The `length` function typifies recursive functions that *consume* lists: when it sees an empty list, its recursion stops (the *base case*); when it sees a nonempty list, it calls itself recursively on (`cdr xs`) (an *induction step*). The name `xs` (pronounced "exes") suggests a list of elements of unknown type; a single `x` suggests one such element.

The behavior of `length` can be summarized in two equations: one for each form that its argument can take (forms L1 and L2 above).

$$\begin{aligned}\texttt{(length '())} &= \texttt{0}\\ \texttt{(length (cons } v\ vs\texttt{))} &= \texttt{(+ 1 (length } vs\texttt{))}\end{aligned}$$

These equations are *algebraic laws* (Section 2.5). Algebraic laws often tell us exactly what to do with each possible form of input, making them a great way to plan an implementation. In practice, algebraic laws are also used for specification, proof, optimization, and testing.

The algebraic laws for `length` specify exactly what `length` does; if you want to *use* `length` and you understand the laws, you never need to look at the code. But if it's not obvious how the code works, it might help to look more closely at an example call. When `(length '(a b))` is evaluated, here's what happens:

- In the initial call, `xs` = `(a b)`.
- The list `(a b)` is not the empty list, so `(null? xs)` returns `#f`.
- The expression `(+ 1 (length (cdr xs)))` is evaluated, where `xs` = `(a b)`. Calling `(cdr xs)` returns list `(b)`. When `length` is applied to `(b)`,
  - List `xs` = `(b)`.
  - List `(b)` is not the empty list, so `(null? xs)` returns `#f`.
  - Expression `(+ 1 (length (cdr xs)))` is evaluated. Calling `(cdr xs)` returns the empty list. When `length` is applied to the empty list,
    * List `xs` = `()`.
    * `(null? xs)` returns `#t`.
    * `length` returns 0.
  - The call `(length (cdr xs))` returns 0, so `length` returns 1.
- The call `(length (cdr xs))` returns 1, so `length` returns 2.

As another example of recursive code specified using algebraic laws, let's look at the predefined function `append`. Function `append` takes two lists, xs and ys, and it returns a list that contains the elements of xs followed by the elements of ys:

99a. ⟨*transcript* 95a⟩+≡ ◁98 100a▷

```
-> (append '(moon over) '(miami vice))
(moon over miami vice)
```

Interestingly, `append` never looks at ys; it inspects only xs. And like any list, xs is formed using either `'()` or `cons`. If xs is empty, `append` returns ys. If xs is `(cons` z zs`)`, `append` returns z followed by zs followed by ys. The behavior of `append` can be specified precisely using two algebraic laws:

`(append '()` ys`)` = ys

`(append (cons` z zs`)` ys`)` = `(cons` z `(append` zs ys`))`

In the code, argument `xs` holds xs, argument `ys` holds ys, z is `(car xs)`, and zs is `(cdr xs)`:

99b. ⟨*predefined μScheme functions* 96a⟩+≡ ◁96b 100b▷

```
(define append (xs ys)
  (if (null? xs)
    ys
    (cons (car xs) (append (cdr xs) ys))))
```

cdr P 162a
null? P 162a

2.3.2 *List reversal and the method of accumulating parameters*

Algebraic laws can also help us design a list-reversal function—and make it efficient. To clarify the design, I condense the notation used to write laws, eliminating keywords and parentheses:

Concept	*μScheme*	*Condensed form*
Empty list	`'()`	ϵ
Element followed by list	`(cons` z zs`)`	$z \cdot zs$
List followed by list	`(append` xs ys`)`	$xs \cdot ys$
List reversed	`(reverse` xs`)`	$R(xs)$

In condensed form, the append laws look like this:

$$\begin{aligned} \epsilon \cdot ys &= ys \\ (z \cdot zs) \cdot ys &= z \cdot (zs \cdot ys) \end{aligned}$$

And the reversal laws look like this:

$$\begin{aligned} R(\epsilon) &= \epsilon \\ R(z \cdot zs) &= R(zs) \cdot z \end{aligned}$$

Translated back to Scheme, the reversal laws are

```
(simple-reverse '())          = '()
(simple-reverse (cons z zs)) = (append (simple-reverse zs) (list1 z))
```

The code looks like this:

100a. ⟨*transcript* 95a⟩+≡ ◁99a 100d▷

```
-> (define simple-reverse (xs)
      (if (null? xs)
         xs
         (append (simple-reverse (cdr xs)) (list1 (car xs)))))
-> (simple-reverse '(my bonny lies over))
(over lies bonny my)
-> (simple-reverse '(a b (c d) e))
(e (c d) b a)
```

This `simple-reverse` function is expensive: `append` takes $O(n)$ time and space, and so `simple-reverse` takes $O(n^2)$ time and space, where n is the length of the list. But list reversal can be implemented in linear time. In Scheme, reversal is made efficient by using a trick: take *two* lists, xs and ys, and return the reverse of xs, followed by (unreversed) ys. List xs is either empty or is z followed by zs, and the computation obeys these laws:

$$\begin{aligned} R(\epsilon) \cdot ys &= ys \\ R(z \cdot zs) \cdot ys &= (R(zs) \cdot z) \cdot ys = R(zs) \cdot (z \cdot ys) \end{aligned}$$

Translated back to Scheme, the laws for "reverse-append" are

```
(revapp '() ys)          = ys
(revapp (cons z zs) ys) = (revapp zs (cons z ys))
```

The code looks like this:

100b. ⟨*predefined μScheme functions* 96a⟩+≡ ◁99b 100c▷

```
(define revapp (xs ys) ; (reverse xs) followed by ys
  (if (null? xs)
     ys
     (revapp (cdr xs) (cons (car xs) ys))))
```

Function `revapp` takes time and space linear in the size of `xs`. Using it with an empty list makes predefined function `reverse` equally efficient.

100c. ⟨*predefined μScheme functions* 96a⟩+≡ ◁100b 103a▷

```
(define reverse (xs) (revapp xs '()))
```

100d. ⟨*transcript* 95a⟩+≡ ◁100a 101a▷

```
-> (reverse '(the atlantic ocean))
(ocean atlantic the)
```

The trick used to make reversal efficient also applies to other problems. Because the parameter ys is used to accumulate the eventual result, the trick is called the *method of accumulating parameters.* In full Scheme, a recursive function with accumulating parameters is typically compiled into a very tight loop.

2.3.3 *Lists of numbers: Sorting*

Functions like `length`, `append`, and `reverse` don't inspect the elements of any list—so they work on all lists of values. But other recursive functions may inspect elements and use the values to make decisions. As an example, I present a function that works only on lists of numbers: insertion sort.

Insertion sort considers one case for each form of input: an empty list of numbers is sorted, and a nonempty list `(cons` m ms`)`, where m is a number and ms is a list of numbers, is sorted by recursively sorting ms, then inserting m into its proper position in the sorted list.

Inserting m into its proper position is not trivial. Function `insert` must inspect the list of numbers into which m is inserted, so it too is recursive. Its behavior, which can depend on the relative order of two numbers m and k, is described by these laws:

`(insert` m `'())` = `(list1` m`)`
`(insert` m `(cons` k ks`))` = `(cons` m `(cons` k ks`))`, when $m < k$
`(insert` m `(cons` k ks`))` = `(cons` k `(insert` m ks`))`, when $m \geq k$

In the code, if `sorted` is `(cons` k ks`)`, then k is `(car sorted)` and ks is `(cdr sorted)`.

101a. ⟨*transcript* 95a⟩+≡ ◁100d 101b▷

```
-> (define insert (m sorted)
     (if (null? sorted)
       (list1 m)
       (if (< m (car sorted))
         (cons m sorted)
         (cons (car sorted) (insert m (cdr sorted))))))
```

Function `insert` is now used, in `insertion-sort`, to insert m into a recursively sorted list:

`(insertion-sort '())` = `'()`
`(insert (cons` m ms`))` = `(insert` m `(insertion-sort` ms`))`

101b. ⟨*transcript* 95a⟩+≡ ◁101a 102a▷

```
-> (define insertion-sort (ns)
     (if (null? ns)
       '()
       (insert (car ns) (insertion-sort (cdr ns)))))
-> (insertion-sort '(4 3 2 6 8 5))
(2 3 4 5 6 8)
```

`append`	*B* 99
`car`	*P* 162a
`cdr`	*P* 162a
`cons`	*P* S313d
`list1`	*B* 96
`null?`	*P* 162a

2.3.4 *Lists of prime numbers*

As another example of a recursive function that uses the values of list elements, I implement a well-known algorithm for finding prime numbers. The algorithm starts with a sequence of numbers from 2 to n, and it produces a prime p by taking the first number in the sequence, then continuing recursively after removing all multiples of p. Because it identifies a multiple of p by trying to divide by p, the algorithm is called *trial division.*[4]

The sequence of numbers from 2 to n is created by (seq 2 n); in general, (seq m n) returns a list containing numbers $m, m+1, m+2, \ldots, n$. A multiple of p is identified by calling (divides? p n).

102a. ⟨*transcript* 95a⟩+≡ ◁101b 102b▷

```
-> (define seq (m n)
     (if (> m n) '() (cons m (seq (+ 1 m) n))))
-> (seq 3 7)
(3 4 5 6 7)
-> (define divides? (p n) (= (mod n p) 0))
```

Multiples of p are removed by calling (remove-multiples p ns), which returns those elements of ns that are not multiples of p. It considers both possible forms of ns: '() and (cons m ms). And when the input is (cons m ms), the behavior depends on a relation between p and m:

(remove-multiples p '()) = '()
(remove-multiples p (cons m ms)) = (remove-multiples p ms), when p divides m
(remove-multiples p (cons m ms)) = (cons m (remove-multiples p ms)), otherwise

The code looks like this:

102b. ⟨*transcript* 95a⟩+≡ ◁102a 102c▷

```
-> (define remove-multiples (p ns)
     (if (null? ns)
       '()
       (if (divides? p (car ns))
         (remove-multiples p (cdr ns))
         (cons (car ns) (remove-multiples p (cdr ns))))))
-> (remove-multiples 2 '(2 3 4 5 6 7))
(3 5 7)
```

Removal of multiples is the key step in trial division. The algorithm iterates over a sequence of numbers that contains a *smallest* prime p and no multiples of any prime smaller than p. Removing p and its multiples produces a prime, plus a new, smaller sequence with the same properties as the original sequence. Iteration proceeds until there are no more primes, as described by these algebraic laws:

(primes-in (cons p ms)) = (cons p (primes-in (remove-multiples p ms)))
(primes-in '()) = '()

The code looks like this:

102c. ⟨*transcript* 95a⟩+≡ ◁102b 102d▷

```
-> (define primes-in (ns)
     (if (null? ns)
       '()
       (cons (car ns) (primes-in (remove-multiples (car ns) (cdr ns))))))
```

Applying primes-in to (seq 2 n) produces all the primes up to n.

102d. ⟨*transcript* 95a⟩+≡ ◁102c 103b▷

```
-> (define primes<= (n) (primes-in (seq 2 n)))
-> (primes<= 10)
(2 3 5 7)
-> (primes<= 50)
(2 3 5 7 11 13 17 19 23 29 31 37 41 43 47)
```

[4]This algorithm is sometimes called the Sieve of Eratosthenes, but don't be fooled: O'Neill (2009) will convince you that this algorithm is not what Eratosthenes had in mind.

2.3.5 *Coding with S-expressions: Lists of lists*

Even more recursion happens when a list element is itself a list, which can contain other lists, and so on. Such lists, together with the atoms (rule 1, page 92), constitute the *ordinary S-expressions*.

An ordinary S-expression is either an atom or a list of ordinary S-expressions.[5] An atom is identified by predefined function atom?:

103a. ⟨*predefined μScheme functions* 96a⟩+≡ ◁100c 104a▷

```
(define atom? (x)
  (or (symbol? x) (or (number? x) (or (boolean? x) (null? x)))))
```

When an ordinary S-expression sx is passed to a function, that function must consider all possible forms of sx. As an example, function has? tells if an ordinary S-expression sx "has" an atom a.

- If sx is an atom, then sx "has" a if and only if sx *is* a. Equality of atoms is tested using the primitive function =.
- If sx is the empty list of S-expressions, it doesn't have a.
- If sx is the nonempty list (cons y ys), then sx has a if either y has a or ys has a.

This specification is best written using algebraic laws:

$$\begin{aligned}\texttt{(has?}\ sx\ a\texttt{)} &= \texttt{(=}\ sx\ a\texttt{)},\ \text{when } x \text{ is an atom}\\ \texttt{(has? (cons}\ y\ z\texttt{)}\ a\texttt{)} &= \texttt{(has?}\ y\ a\texttt{)}\ \text{or}\ \texttt{(has?}\ z\ a\texttt{)}\end{aligned}$$

These laws work with *fully general* S-expressions, which can be formed using value rule 4, not just rules 1 and 2 (Figure 2.1, page 91). That's why, in the law, the cons cell is written (cons y z) and not (cons y ys).

In the code, if sx is (cons y z), then y is (car sx) and z is (cdr sx).

103b. ⟨*transcript* 95a⟩+≡ ◁102d 103c▷

```
-> (define has? (sx a)
     (if (atom? sx)
         (= sx a)
         (or (has? (car sx) a) (has? (cdr sx) a))))
```

This code calls has? twice. It could be made faster by using an if expression instead of or, or by using short-circuit operator || (Section 2.13.3, page 164).

Function has? can search a list of lists of symbols:

103c. ⟨*transcript* 95a⟩+≡ ◁103b 104b▷

```
-> (val pangrams    ;; www.rinkworks.com/words/pangrams.shtml, June 2018
     '((We promptly judged antique ivory buckles for the next prize.)
       (The quick red fox jumps over a lazy brown dog.)
       (Amazingly few discotheques provide jukeboxes.)
       (Heavy boxes perform quick waltzes and jigs.)
       (Pack my box with five dozen liquor jugs.)))
-> (has? pangrams 'fox)
#t
-> (has? pangrams 'box)
#t
-> (has? pangrams 'cox)
#f
```

car	𝒫 162a
cdr	𝒫 162a
cons	𝒫 S313d
mod	ℬ
null?	𝒫 162a
or	ℬ

[5] The empty list '() is *both* an atom *and* a list of ordinary S-expressions.

2.3.6 *Inspecting multiple inputs: Equality on S-expressions*

Functions like `length`, `append`, `insert`, and `has?` inspect only *one* list or one S-expression. A function that inspects *two* S-expressions must prepare for all forms of both inputs, for a total of four cases. As an example, function `equal?` compares two S-expressions for equality—they are equal if they are formed from the same atoms in the same way. Breaking the inputs down by cases, two atoms are equal if they are the same, as tested with primitive `=`. Two lists are equal if they contain (recursively) equal elements in equal positions. An atom and a nonempty list are never equal.

(equal? sx_1 sx_2) = (= sx_1 sx_2), if sx_1 is an atom and sx_2 is an atom
(equal? sx_1 (cons w z))) = #f, if sx_1 is an atom
(equal? (cons x y) sx_2) = #f, if sx_2 is an atom
(equal? (cons x y) (cons w z)) = (and (equal? x w) (equal? y z))

These laws call for four cases, but in an implementation, the first two laws can be combined: the second law calls for `equal?` to return `#f`, but when sx_1 is an atom and sx_2 is (cons w z), (= sx_1 sx_2) always returns false, so *both* cases where sx_1 is an atom may use `=`:

104a. ⟨*predefined μScheme functions* 96a⟩+≡ ◁103a 106a▷
```
(define equal? (sx1 sx2)
  (if (atom? sx1)
    (= sx1 sx2)
    (if (atom? sx2)
        #f
        (and (equal? (car sx1) (car sx2))
             (equal? (cdr sx1) (cdr sx2))))))
```
The expected behavior is easily confirmed:

104b. ⟨*transcript* 95a⟩+≡ ◁103c 105a▷
```
-> (equal? 'a 'b)
#f
-> (equal? '(a (1 3) c) '(a (1 3) c))
#t
-> (equal? '(a (1 3) d) '(a (1 3) c))
#f
-> (equal? '(a b c) '(a b))
#f
-> (equal? #f #f)
#t
```
More rigorous testing confirms both `#f` and (when possible) `#t` results for all four cases.

2.3.7 *Lists that represent sets*

In Scheme, as in any other language, a list with no repeated elements can represent a set. As long as the set is small, this representation is efficient, and the set operations are easy to write and to understand. Operations `emptyset`, `member?`, `add-element`, `size`, and `union` are shown below; their algebraic laws are shown in comments. Other operations appear at the end of the chapter (Exercise 3).

Function member? requires explicit recursion.

105a. ⟨*transcript* 95a⟩+≡ ◁104b 105b▷

```
-> (val emptyset '())
-> (define member? (x s)        ; (member? x '())         = #f
     (if (null? s)              ; (member? x (cons x ys)) = #t
       #f                       ; (member? x (cons y ys)) = (member? x ys),
       (if (equal? x (car s))   ;                      when x differs from y
         #t
         (member? x (cdr s)))))
```

Function add-element might be implemented recursively, but instead it calls member?.

105b. ⟨*transcript* 95a⟩+≡ ◁105a 105c▷

```
-> (define add-element (x s)   ; (add-element x s) = xs, when x is in s
     (if (member? x s)          ; (add-element x s) = (cons x xs),
       s                        ;                       when x is not in s
       (cons x s)))
-> (val s (add-element 3 (add-element 'a emptyset)))
(3 a)
-> (member? 'a s)
#t
```

Functions size and union, like member?, are recursive.

105c. ⟨*transcript* 95a⟩+≡ ◁105b 105d▷

```
-> (define size (s)             ; (size '())          = 0
     (if (null? s)              ; (size (cons x xs)) = (+ 1 (size xs))
       0
       (+ 1 (size (cdr s)))))
-> (define union (s1 s2)        ; (union '() s2)           = s2
     (if (null? s1)             ; (union (cons x xs) s2) =
       s2                       ;             (add-element x (union xs s2))
       (add-element (car s1) (union (cdr s1) s2))))
-> (union s (add-element 2 (add-element 3 emptyset)))
(a 2 3)
```

Because member? tests for identity using equal?, it can recognize a list as an element of a set:

105d. ⟨*transcript* 95a⟩+≡ ◁105c 106d▷

```
-> (val t (add-element '(a b) (add-element 1 emptyset)))
((a b) 1)
-> (member? '(a b) t)
#t
```

If member? used = instead of equal?, this last example wouldn't work; I encourage you to explain why (Exercise 4).

2.3.8 Association lists

A list of ordered pairs can represent a classic data structure of symbolic computing: the *finite map* (also called *associative array*, *dictionary*, and *table*). Finite maps are ubiquitous; for example, in this book they are used to represent the *environments* found in operational semantics and in interpreters. (In an interpreter or compiler, an environment is often called a *symbol table*.)

A small map is often represented as an *association list*. An association list has the form ((k_1 a_1) ⋯ (k_m a_m)), where each k_i is a symbol, called a *key*, and each a_i is an arbitrary value, called an *attribute*. A pair (k_i a_i) is made

car	P 162a
cdr	P 162a
cons	P S313d
null?	P 162a

with function `make-alist-pair` and inspected with functions `alist-pair-key` and `alist-pair-attribute`:

```
(alist-pair-key       (make-alist-pair k a)) = k
(alist-pair-attribute (make-alist-pair k a)) = a
```

The pair is represented by a two-element list, so the three `alist-pair` functions are implemented as follows:

106a. ⟨*predefined μScheme functions* 96a⟩+≡ ◁104a 106b▷

```
(define make-alist-pair      (k a)    (list2 k a))
(define alist-pair-key       (pair)   (car  pair))
(define alist-pair-attribute (pair)   (cadr pair))
```

A list of these pairs forms an association list, and when an association list is nonempty, the key and attribute of the first pair are retrieved by these auxiliary functions:

106b. ⟨*predefined μScheme functions* 96a⟩+≡ ◁106a 106c▷

```
(define alist-first-key       (alist) (alist-pair-key       (car alist)))
(define alist-first-attribute (alist) (alist-pair-attribute (car alist)))
```

An association list is operated on primarily by functions `bind` and `find`, which add bindings and retrieve attributes. Their behavior is described by these laws:

```
(bind k a '())                             = (cons (make-alist-pair k a) '())
(bind k a (cons (make-alist-pair k  a') ps)) = (cons (make-alist-pair k a) ps)
(bind k a (cons (make-alist-pair k' a') ps)) =
                          (cons (make-alist-pair k' a') (bind k a ps)),
                                    when k and k' are different

(find k '())                              = '()
(find k (cons (make-alist-pair k  a) ps)) = a
(find k (cons (make-alist-pair k' a) ps)) = (find k ps)
                                    when k and k' are different
```

A missing attribute is retrieved as `'()`.

106c. ⟨*predefined μScheme functions* 96a⟩+≡ ◁106b 125a▷

```
(define bind (k a alist)
  (if (null? alist)
    (list1 (make-alist-pair k a))
    (if (equal? k (alist-first-key alist))
      (cons (make-alist-pair k a) (cdr alist))
      (cons (car alist) (bind k a (cdr alist))))))
(define find (k alist)
  (if (null? alist)
    '()
    (if (equal? k (alist-first-key alist))
      (alist-first-attribute alist)
      (find k (cdr alist)))))
```

Function `bind` is illustrated by this contrived example, which shows how the attribute for I is replaced by `bind`-ing I a second time:

106d. ⟨*transcript* 95a⟩+≡ ◁105d 107a▷

```
-> (val demo-alist (bind 'I 'Ching '()))
((I Ching))
-> (val demo-alist (bind 'E 'coli demo-alist))
((I Ching) (E coli))
-> (val demo-alist (bind 'I 'Magnin demo-alist))
((I Magnin) (E coli))
-> (find 'I demo-alist)
Magnin
```

As a more realistic example, an association list can store the locations of groceries. Association list aisles shows where to find yams and butter, but not milk:

107a. ⟨*transcript* 95a⟩+≡ ◁106d 107b▷

```
-> (val aisles (bind 'nog 'dairy '()))
((nog dairy))
-> (val aisles (bind 'apple 'produce aisles))
((nog dairy) (apple produce))
-> (val aisles (bind 'yam 'produce aisles))
((nog dairy) (apple produce) (yam produce))
-> (val aisles (bind 'butter 'dairy aisles))
((nog dairy) (apple produce) (yam produce) (butter dairy))
-> (val aisles (bind 'chex 'cereal aisles))
((nog dairy) (apple produce) (yam produce) (butter dairy) (chex cereal))
-> (find 'yam aisles)
produce
-> (find 'butter aisles)
dairy
-> (find 'milk aisles)
()
```


2.4 Records and trees (more data)

S-expressions can code all forms of lists and trees: a lot of structured data. But when all data are S-expressions, every interesting structure is made with cons cells. Such structures are traversed with combinations of `car` and `cdr`, and using `car` and `cdr` for everything is too much like programming in assembly language.

Functions like `car` and `cdr` are perfect for data whose size or structure may vary. But many data structures store a fixed number of elements in known locations, like a C `struct`. In Scheme, such structures can be represented by *records*. In this section, records are introduced by example, then used to represent binary trees.

2.4.1 Records

As an example of a record, a "frozen dinner" is a container that holds these parts:

- A `protein`
- A `starch`
- A `vegetable`
- A `dessert`

In μScheme, such a record is defined like this:

107b. ⟨*transcript* 95a⟩+≡ ◁107a 108a▷

```
-> (record frozen-dinner [protein starch vegetable dessert])
```

The record is a lot like a C `struct` or a Java object:

- Like a C `struct`, a `frozen-dinner` record always holds exactly four values: the protein, the starch, the vegetable, and the dessert. As in C, these values are called the *members* or *fields* of the record.

- As in C, each field is accessed by using its name. But where C uses *dot notation*, writing `.starch` after a `struct` (or quite commonly, `->starch` after a pointer to a `struct`), μScheme uses an *accessor function*, applying `frozen-dinner-starch` to a record.

μScheme records are allocated and initialized differently from C `structs`. A `struct` is allocated by `malloc` (or in C++, `new`), and each individual field is initialized by an individual assignment. A μScheme record is allocated *and* initialized by a *constructor function*, which receives the initial values of *all* the fields as its arguments. The constructor function is a bit like a constructor in C++ or Java, except its behavior is determined by the language and cannot be changed by the programmer. The constructor function expects one argument per field of the record, in the order in which they appear, as follows:

108a. ⟨*transcript* 95a⟩+≡ ◁107b 108b▷

```
-> (make-frozen-dinner 'steak 'potato 'green-beans 'pie)
(make-frozen-dinner steak potato green-beans pie)
-> (make-frozen-dinner 'beans 'rice 'tomatillo 'flan)
(make-frozen-dinner beans rice tomatillo flan)
-> (frozen-dinner-starch it)
rice
```

The accessor functions and constructor function are defined automatically by the `record` definition form, which also defines a type predicate. The type predicate `frozen-dinner?` may receive *any* value, and it returns `#t` if and only if the value was built using constructor function `make-frozen-dinner`:[6]

108b. ⟨*transcript* 95a⟩+≡ ◁108a 108c▷

```
-> (frozen-dinner? (make-frozen-dinner 'beans 'rice 'tomatillo 'flan))
#t
-> (frozen-dinner? '(beans rice tomatillo flan))
#f
```

When a `record` form is evaluated, the interpreter prints the names of the functions that it defines:

108c. ⟨*transcript* 95a⟩+≡ ◁108b 108d▷

```
-> (record frozen-dinner [protein starch vegetable dessert])
make-frozen-dinner
frozen-dinner?
frozen-dinner-protein
frozen-dinner-starch
frozen-dinner-vegetable
frozen-dinner-dessert
```

A long name like `frozen-dinner-protein` is necessary because some other record might also have a `protein` field:

108d. ⟨*transcript* 95a⟩+≡ ◁108c 109a▷

```
-> (record nutrition [protein fat carbs])
make-nutrition
nutrition?
nutrition-protein
nutrition-fat
nutrition-carbs
```

A short name like `.protein` won't work in Scheme, because there is no type system to tell us *which* record is meant. Long names, like `nutrition-protein` and `frozen-dinner-protein`, say explicitly which record is meant (nutritional-information records and frozen-dinner records, respectively).

[6]Not quite: In μScheme, but not in full Scheme, the type predicate can be fooled by a record that is forged using `cons` (Section 2.13.6).

Functions defined by record satisfy algebraic laws, which say that we get out what we put in:

$$\begin{aligned}
&\texttt{(frozen-dinner? (make-frozen-dinner } p\ s\ v\ d\texttt{))} &&= \texttt{\#t}\\
&\texttt{(frozen-dinner? } v\texttt{)} &&= \texttt{\#f},\\
&\qquad\qquad \text{where } v \text{ is not made by } \texttt{make-frozen-dinner}\\
&\texttt{(frozen-dinner-protein (make-frozen-dinner } p\ s\ v\ d\texttt{))} &&= p\\
&\texttt{(frozen-dinner-starch (make-frozen-dinner } p\ s\ v\ d\texttt{))} &&= s\\
&\texttt{(frozen-dinner-vegetable (make-frozen-dinner } p\ s\ v\ d\texttt{))} &&= v\\
&\texttt{(frozen-dinner-dessert (make-frozen-dinner } p\ s\ v\ d\texttt{))} &&= d
\end{aligned}$$

2.4.2 Binary trees

Records, like C structs, make great tree nodes. For example, in a binary tree, a node might contain a tag and two subtrees. A binary tree is either such a node or is empty. A node can be represented as a node record, and the empty tree can be represented as #f.

109a. ⟨*transcript* 95a⟩+≡ ◁ 108d 109b ▷

```
-> (record node [tag left right])
make-node
node?
node-tag
node-left
node-right
```

The node functions obey these laws:

$$\begin{aligned}
\texttt{((node?) (make-node } t\ \mathit{left}\ \mathit{right}\texttt{))} &= \texttt{\#t}\\
\texttt{((node?) } \mathit{atom}\ \texttt{)} &= \texttt{\#f}\\
\texttt{(node-tag (make-node } t\ \mathit{left}\ \mathit{right}\texttt{))} &= t\\
\texttt{(node-left (make-node } t\ \mathit{left}\ \mathit{right}\texttt{))} &= \mathit{left}\\
\texttt{(node-right (make-node } t\ \mathit{left}\ \mathit{right}\texttt{))} &= \mathit{right}
\end{aligned}$$

The set of tagged binary trees can be defined precisely, by induction. The set $\mathit{BINTREE}(T)$ contains tagged binary trees with tags drawn from set T:

$$\frac{}{\texttt{\#f} \in \mathit{BINTREE}(T)}$$

$$\frac{l \in T \qquad t_1 \in \mathit{BINTREE}(T) \qquad t_2 \in \mathit{BINTREE}(T)}{\texttt{(make-node l t1 t2)} \in \mathit{BINTREE}(T)}.$$

Such a tree is either built with make-node or is #f, as in this example:

109b. ⟨*transcript* 95a⟩+≡ ◁ 109a 110a ▷

```
-> (val example-sym-tree
      (make-node 'A
         (make-node 'B
             (make-node 'C #f #f)
             (make-node 'D #f #f))
         (make-node 'E
             (make-node 'F
                (make-node 'G #f #f)
                (make-node 'H #f #f))
             (make-node 'I #f #f))))
```

The example tree might be drawn as follows:

```
            A
          /   \
        B       E
       / \     / \
      C   D   F   I
             / \
            G   H
```

Tagged binary trees are consumed by functions whose internal structure follows the structure of the input. Just as a list-consuming function must handle two forms, `cons` and `'()`, a tree-consuming function must handle two forms: `make-node` and empty. The forms can be distinguished by predicate `empty-tree?`:

110a. ⟨*transcript* 95a⟩+≡ ◁ 109b 110b ▷

```
-> (define empty-tree? (tree) (= tree #f))
```

One example tree-consuming function is a classic tree traversal: the preorder traversal:

110b. ⟨*transcript* 95a⟩+≡ ◁ 110a 118a ▷

```
-> (define preorder (tree)
     (if (empty-tree? tree)
         '()
         (cons (node-tag tree)
               (append
                 (preorder (node-left tree))
                 (preorder (node-right tree))))))
-> (preorder example-sym-tree)
(A B C D E F G H I)
```

Inorder and postorder traversals are left for you to implement (Exercise 11).

2.5 Combining theory and practice: Algebraic laws

Throughout this chapter, functions are described by algebraic laws. The laws help us understand what the code does (or what it is supposed to do). Algebraic laws also help with design: they can show what cases need to be handled and what needs to be done in each case. Translating such laws into code is much easier than writing correct code from scratch.

Algebraic laws have many other uses. Any algebraic law can be turned into a test case by substituting example data for metavariables; for example, QuickCheck (Claessen and Hughes 2000) automatically substitutes a random input for each metavariable. Algebraic laws are also used to specify the behavior of abstract types, to simplify code, to improve performance, and even to prove properties of code.

Algebraic laws work by specifying equalities: in a valid law, whenever values are substituted for metavariables, the two sides are equal. (The values substituted must respect the conditions surrounding the law. For example, if ns stands for a list of numbers, we may not substitute a Boolean for it.) The substitution principle extends beyond values; a valid law also holds when *program variables* are substituted for metavariables, and even when *pure expressions* are substituted for metavariables. A pure expression is one whose evaluation has no side effects: it does not change the values of any variables and does not do any input or output. And for our purposes, a pure expression runs to successful completion; if an expression's evaluation doesn't terminate or triggers a run-time error, the expression is considered impure.

The equality specified by an algebraic law is a form of *observational equivalence*: if $e_1 = e_2$, and a program contains e_1, we can replace e_1 with e_2, and the program won't be able to tell the difference. That is, running the altered program will have the same observable effect as the original. Replacing e_1 with e_2 may, however, change properties that can't be observed by the program itself, such as the time required for completion or the number of locations allocated. When an algebraic law is used to improve performance, changing such properties is the whole point.

In the sections above, algebraic laws are used only to show how to implement functions. In this section, they are also used to specify *properties* of functions and of combinations of functions, and to *prove* such properties.

2.5.1 Laws of list primitives

Algebraic laws can be used to specify the behaviors of primitive functions. After all, programmers never need to see implementations of `cons`, `car`, `cdr`, and `null?`; we just need to know how they behave. Their behavior can be specified by operational semantics, but operational semantics often gives more detail than we care to know. For example, if we just want to be able to use `car` and `cdr` effectively, everything we need to know is captured by these two laws:

$$\texttt{(car (cons } x\ y\texttt{))} = x$$
$$\texttt{(cdr (cons } x\ y\texttt{))} = y$$

These laws also tell us something about `cons`: implicitly, the laws confirm that `cons` may be applied to *any* two arguments x and y, even if y is not a list (rule 4, page 91). Use of cons cells and `'()` to represent lists is merely a programming convention.

To capture `cons` completely also requires laws that tell us how a cons cell is viewed by a type predicate, as in these examples:

$$\texttt{(pair? (cons } x\ y\texttt{))} = \texttt{\#t}$$
$$\texttt{(null? (cons } x\ y\texttt{))} = \texttt{\#f}$$

The laws above suffice to enable us to use `cons`, `car`, and `cdr` effectively. Nothing more is required, and any implementation that satisfies the laws is as correct as any other. To develop an unusual implementation, try Exercise 39.

2.5.2 Developing laws by classifying operations

How many laws are enough? To know if we have enough laws to describe a data type T, we analyze the functions that involve values of type T.

- A function that makes a new value of type T is a *creator* or a *producer*. A creator is either a value of type T all by itself, or it is a function that returns a value of type T without needing any arguments of type T. As an example, `'()` is a creator for lists. A producer is a function that takes at least one argument of type T, and possibly additional arguments, and returns a value of type T. As an example, `cons` is a producer for lists.

  Creators and producers are sometimes grouped into a single category called *constructors*, but "constructor" is a slippery word. The grouping usage comes from algebraic specification, but "constructor" is also used in functional programming and in object-oriented programming—and in each community, it means something different.

- A function that takes an argument of type T and gets information out of it is an *observer*. An observer "looks inside" its argument and produces some fact about the argument, or perhaps some constituent value, which may or

append	$\mathcal{B}$ 99
cons	$\mathcal{P}$ S313d
example-sym-tree	109b
node-left	109a
node-right	109a
node-tag	109a

may not also be of type T. Observers are sometimes also called *selectors* or *accessors*. As examples, primitives `car`, `cdr`, `pair?`, and `null?` are observers for lists.

- Creators, producers, and observers have no side effects. A function that has side effects on an existing value of type T is a *mutator*. Mutators, too, can fit into the discipline of algebraic specification. An explanation in depth is beyond the scope of this book, but a couple of simple examples appear in Section 9.6.2 (page 547). For more, see the excellent book by Liskov and Guttag (1986).

This classification of functions tells us how many laws are enough: there are enough laws for type T if the laws specify the result of every permissible combination of observers applied to creators and producers. By this criterion, our list laws aren't yet complete; they don't specify what happens when observers are applied to the empty list. Such observations are specified by these laws:

```
(pair? '()) = #f
(null? '()) = #t
```

Not all observations of the empty list are permissible. An observation would cause an error, like `(car '())`, isn't specified by any law, and so it is understood that the observation is impermissible. This convention resembles the convention of the operational semantics, where if an evaluation causes an error, no rule applies.

Laws for rich data structures can be extensive. Because S-expressions include both lists and atoms, they have lots of creators, producers, and especially observers. Laws for all combinations would be overwhelming; only a few Boolean laws are sketched below.

2.5.3 Boolean laws

For the Booleans, values `#t` and `#f` act as creators, the syntactic form `if` acts like an observer, and the predefined function `not` is a producer. Their interactions are described by these laws:

```
(if #t x y) = x
(if #f x y) = y
(if (not p) x y) = (if p y x)
(if p #f #t) = (not p)
```

If p is guaranteed to be Boolean, one more law is valid:

```
(if p #t #f) = p
```

This law, which is frequently overlooked, is also valid if the result of the `if` expression is used only as a condition in other `if` expressions (or `while` expressions). Whenever possible, it should be used to simplify code.

2.5.4 Abstract finite-map laws

Laws for association lists (Section 2.3.8) tell us that `find` returns the most recent property added with `bind`:

`(find` k `(bind` k a m`))` $= a$
`(find` k `(bind` k' a m`))` $=$ `(find` k m`)`, when k is different from k'

These laws are justified by appealing to the implementations in Section 2.3.8. But when a finite map gets large, those implementations aren't good enough; we need a more efficient data structure, like a binary search tree or even a red-black tree. These data structures, or any data structure that obeys the same laws, can serve as a drop-in replacement for the less efficient association list. (In another data structure, application of `find` to the empty map might cause an error, so no law for that case is included.)

2.5.5 *Laws that state properties of functions*

Not every set of laws fully specifies the behavior of the functions it describes. Sometimes a law states a property that a function ought to have, without nailing down its behavior in every case—as in the following examples:

$$
\begin{aligned}
(\texttt{and}\ p\ q) &= (\texttt{and}\ q\ p)\\
(\texttt{and}\ p\ \texttt{\#t}) &= p\\
(\texttt{and}\ p\ \texttt{\#f}) &= \texttt{\#f}\\
(\texttt{or}\ p\ q) &= (\texttt{or}\ q\ p)\\
(\texttt{or}\ p\ \texttt{\#t}) &= \texttt{\#t}\\
(\texttt{or}\ p\ \texttt{\#f}) &= p\\
(\texttt{append (cons}\ x\ \texttt{'())}\ xs) &= (\texttt{cons}\ x\ xs)\\
(\texttt{append (append}\ xs\ ys)\ zs) &= (\texttt{append}\ xs\ (\texttt{append}\ ys\ zs))\\
(\texttt{reverse (reverse}\ xs)) &= xs
\end{aligned}
$$

These laws, which I often use in my own programming, are great for simplifying code. They also make excellent laws for "property-based" testing (Claessen and Hughes 2000).

2.5.6 *Laws and proof*

Algebraic laws enable a new, elegant form of proof. What good is a new form of proof? It proves more interesting facts with less work then operational semantics.

In principle, anything we might prove about a μScheme program can be proved using the operational semantics. But using operational semantics to prove properties of programs is like using assembly language to write them: it operates at so low a level that it's practical only for small problems. Operational semantics is best used only to prove laws about primitive functions and syntactic forms. Those laws can then be used to prove laws about functions, which can be used to prove laws about other functions, and so on. In proof, laws play a similar role to the role that functions play in coding: they enable us to break problems down hierarchically.

These hierarchical proofs are founded on proofs about primitives and syntax. Unfortunately, the foundational proofs can be quite challenging; for example, although no program can tell the difference between the two expressions `(let ([x 1983]) x)` and just `1983`, they do not have exactly the same semantics: one allocates a fresh location and the other doesn't. The extra location can't be observed, but to prove it requires techniques that are far beyond the scope of this book.

What we do in this book is freely substitute one pure expression for another, provided they always evaluate to equal values—even if they don't have identical effects on the store. This *substitution of equals for equals* is a simple, powerful proof technique, and it works not just on primitives and simple syntactic forms, but also on function applications. To substitute for a function application, we expand the body of the function by replacing each formal parameter with the corresponding actual parameter. As long as there are no side effects, this too is substitution of equals for equals.

Substitution is justified by algebraic laws: an algebraic law says, "these two sides are equal, and so one may be freely substituted for the other." This technique is called *equational reasoning*, and the resulting proofs are sometimes called *calculational proofs*. It is demonstrated in the next section.

2.5.7 *Using equational reasoning to write proofs*

Equational reasoning can be used to prove the laws for append and length given in Section 2.3.1. The first append law on page 99 says that (append '() *ys*) = *ys*. To prove it, I first substitute for append's formal parameters, then apply the "null-empty" law from Section 2.5.2 and the "if-true" law from Section 2.5.3:

```
(append '() ys)
  = {substitute actual parameters '() and ys in definition of append}
(if (null? '())
    ys
    (cons (car '()) (append (cdr '()) ys)))
  = {null-empty law}
(if #t
    ys
    (cons (car '()) (append (cdr '()) ys)))
  = {if-#t law}
ys
```

Each step in the proof is a single equality, presented in this form:

$$\begin{aligned}&term_1\\&\quad = \{\textit{justification that } term_1 = term_2\}\\&term_2\end{aligned}$$

These steps are chained together to show that every term is equal to every other term, and in particular that the first term is equal to the last term. In the example above, the chain of equalities establishes that (append '() *ys*) = *ys*. The append-cons law, (append (cons *z zs*) *ys*) = (cons *z* (append *zs ys*)), is proved in similar fashion.

The key step in the proof is the expansion of the definition of append. As another example of such an expansion, I prove that the length of a cons cell is one more than the length of the second argument:

(length (cons *y ys*)) = (+ 1 (length *ys*))

Again the expansion is the first step: in the definition of length, the actual parameter (cons *y ys*) is substituted for the formal parameter xs:

```
(length (cons y ys))
  = {substitute actual parameter in definition of length}
(if (null? (cons y ys))
    0
    (+ 1 (length (cdr (cons y ys)))))
  = {null?-cons law}
```

```
(if #f
    0
    (+ 1 (length (cdr (cons y ys)))))
  = {if-#f law}
(+ 1 (length (cdr (cons y ys))))
  = {cdr-cons law}
(+ 1 (length ys))
```


Expanding a function's definition works, but it can make a proof long, verbose, and hard to follow. A function's definition should be expanded as little as possible—just enough to prove the laws that describe its implementation. Then, in future proofs, only those laws are needed. As an example of using such a law, I prove that appending a singleton list is equivalent to cons. I still substitute actual parameters, but now instead of substituting them for the formal parameters of append, I substitute them for the metavariables of the append-cons law on the preceding page. The key step is again the first step, where I substitute x for z and '() for zs, leaving ys unchanged:

```
(append (cons x '()) ys)
  = {substitute actual parameters in the append-cons law}
(cons x (append '() ys))
  = {apply the append-empty law, substituting the right-hand side for the left}
(cons x ys)
```

The examples above prove properties about the application of append or length to a list that is known to be short (empty or singleton). But useful properties aren't limited to short lists; for example, appending two lists adds their lengths, even when the first argument to append is arbitrarily long. The computation involves a recursive call to append, and proving general facts about recursive functions usually demands proof by induction. In particular, laws about lists and S-expressions are proved by *structural induction*:

- Prove the law holds for every base case. In the case of a list, prove that the law holds when the list is empty.
- Prove every induction step by assuming the law holds for the constituents. Again in the case of a list, prove the case for a nonempty list (cons z zs) by assuming the induction hypothesis for the smaller list zs.

As an example, I prove the law

(length (append xs ys)) = (+ (length xs) (length ys))

The proof is by structural induction on xs. In the base case, xs is empty:

```
(length (append '() ys))
  = {append-empty law}
(length ys)
  = {zero is the additive identity}
(+ 0 (length ys))
  = {length-empty law, from right to left}
(+ (length '()) (length ys))
```

In the induction step, xs is not empty, and therefore there exist a z and zs such that xs = (cons z zs).

(length (append xs ys))
 = {by assumption that xs is not empty, xs = (cons z zs)}
(length (append (cons z zs) ys))
 = {appeal to the append-cons law}
(length (cons z (append zs ys)))
 = {appeal to the length-cons law}
(+ 1 (length (append zs ys)))
 = {apply the **induction hypothesis**}
(+ 1 (+ (length zs) (length ys)))
 = {associativity of +}
(+ (+ 1 (length zs)) (length ys))
 = {length-cons law, from right to left}
(+ (length (cons z zs)) (length ys))
 = {by the initial assumption that xs = (cons z zs)}
(+ (length xs) (length ys))

These examples should teach you enough so that you can do Exercises 16 to 26 starting on page 183.

2.5.8 *Source of the induction principle: Inductively defined data*

For a law like (length (append xs ys)) = (+ (length xs) (length ys)), what cases need to be proved? One for each possible way that xs can be constructed. Since xs is a list of values, I claim there are only two ways: '() and cons. This claim can be made precise with the help of a proof system that says what a list is.

"List" is a *parametric* abstraction; for example, there are "lists of numbers," "lists of Booleans," "lists of values," and so on. To notate the set of all lists whose elements are in set A, I write $LIST(A)$. This set can be defined by a proof system for set membership. The judgment form is $v \in LIST(A)$, and it is proved by showing that v is either '() or a suitable cons cell:

$$\textsc{EmptyList}\quad \frac{}{\texttt{'()} \in LIST(A)} \qquad \textsc{ConsList}\quad \frac{a \in A \quad as \in LIST(A)}{(\texttt{cons}\ a\ as) \in LIST(A)}.$$

A value v is in $LIST(A)$ if and only if there is a proof of $v \in LIST(A)$.

Now let's prove that some property P holds for every v in $LIST(A)$. Formally that means, "if there is a derivation of $v \in LIST(A)$, then $P(v)$." The proof is a metatheoretic proof! It's just like the metatheoretic proofs in Chapter 1 (page 59), except the underlying proof system isn't the operational semantics of Impcore—it's the proof system for $v \in LIST(A)$. But the structure is the same; in particular, a proof about $LIST(A)$ needs a case for each rule in the proof system for $v \in LIST(A)$, and that means one case for '() and one for cons.

Metatheoretic proof techniques apply to other sets of values, provided those sets are defined inductively, by a proof system. For example, S-expressions can be defined by a proof system. The forms of S-expression that are of most interest to Scheme programmers are the *ordinary S-expressions* $SEXP_O$ (the ones that can be written with quote) and the *fully general S-expressions* $SEXP_{FG}$ (the ones that are made with atoms and cons). To write their proof systems, I write SYM, NUM, and $BOOL$ for primitive sets of atoms. An ordinary S-expression is either an atom or a list of S-expressions, and its judgment form is $v \in SEXP_O$:

$$\frac{v \in SYM}{v \in SEXP_O} \qquad \frac{v \in NUM}{v \in SEXP_O} \qquad \frac{v \in BOOL}{v \in SEXP_O} \qquad \frac{v \in LIST(SEXP_O)}{v \in SEXP_O}.$$

A fully general S-expression is either an atom or a pair of S-expressions:

$$\frac{v \in SYM}{v \in SEXP_{FG}} \qquad \frac{v \in NUM}{v \in SEXP_{FG}} \qquad \frac{v \in BOOL}{v \in SEXP_{FG}} \qquad \frac{}{\texttt{'()} \in SEXP_{FG}}$$

$$\frac{v_1 \in SEXP_{FG} \qquad v_2 \in SEXP_{FG}}{\texttt{(cons } v_1\ v_2\texttt{)} \in SEXP_{FG}}.$$

Not all fully general S-expressions can be written with μScheme's `quote` form; for example, the result of evaluating `(cons 2 2)` cannot be written with a quote.

Inductively defined data is so common that it's useful to have a shorthand notation for it. The most common notations, including the `datatype` definition forms of Standard ML (Chapter 5) and μML (Chapter 8), are related to *recursion equations*. For example, the simplest recursion equation for $LIST(A)$ looks like this:

$$LIST(A) = \{\texttt{'()}\} \cup \{\, \texttt{(cons } v\ vs\texttt{)} \mid v \in A \wedge vs \in LIST(A)\,\}.$$

This equation can't quite be taken as a definition, unless we say that $LIST(A)$ is the *smallest* set that satisfies the equation.

S-expressions can be described by similar equations:

$$\begin{aligned} SEXP_O &= SYM \cup NUM \cup BOOL \cup LIST(SEXP_O) \\ SEXP_{FG} &= SYM \cup NUM \cup BOOL \cup \{\texttt{'()}\} \cup \\ &\qquad \{\, \texttt{(cons } v_1\ v_2\texttt{)} \mid v_1 \in SEXP_{FG} \wedge v_2 \in SEXP_{FG}\,\}. \end{aligned}$$

2.6 LANGUAGE II: LOCAL VARIABLES AND `let`

While a lot can be done with just formal parameters, big functions need local variables. In a procedural language like C or Impcore, local variables can be introduced without being initialized, and they are often assigned to more than once. But in a functional language like Scheme, local variables are *always* initialized when introduced, and afterward, they are rarely assigned to again.

In Scheme, local variables are introduced by *let binding*. A let binding is often hand-written as "**let** $x = e'$ **in** e," which means "evaluate e', let x stand for the resulting value, and evaluate e." In Scheme, the same binding is written `(let ([`x e'`]) `e`)`. In general, Scheme's `let` form binds a *collection* of values:

`(let ([`x_1 e_1`]` $\cdots$ `[`x_n e_n`]) `e`)`

This `let` expression is evaluated as follows: First evaluate the *right-hand sides* e_1 through e_n; call the results $v_1, \ldots, v_n$. Next, *extend* the local environment so that x_1 stands for v_1, and so on. Finally, in the extended environment, evaluate the *body* e; the value of the body becomes the value of the entire `let` expression.

The `let` form helps us avoid repeating computation, and it helps make code readable. To enhance its readability, I write its bindings in square brackets. (In μScheme, in full Scheme, and in all the bridge languages, square brackets mean the same as round brackets ("parentheses"). I typically use round brackets to wrap expressions, definitions, and lists of formal parameters; I use square brackets to wrap other kinds of syntax, like binding pairs or local-variable declarations.)

A `let` form can be thought of as *naming the result of a computation*. As an example, let's compute the roots of the quadratic equation: $ax^2 + bx + c = 0$. From the quadratic formula, the roots are $x = \frac{-b \pm \sqrt{b^2 - 4ac}}{2a}$. Although this formula is not much use without real numbers, it can still be implemented in μScheme, and it can compute roots of such equations as $x^2 + 3x - 70 = 0$. Decent candidates to be named with `let` are the values of subformulas $-b$, $\sqrt{b^2 - 4ac}$, and $2a$:

118a. ⟨*transcript* 95a⟩+≡ ◁110b 118b▷

```
⟨definition of sqrt S318b⟩
-> (define roots (a b c)
     (let ([minus-b      (negated b)]
           [discriminant (sqrt (- (* b b) (* 4 (* a c))))]
           [two-a        (* 2 a)])
       (list2 (/ (+ minus-b discriminant) two-a)
              (/ (- minus-b discriminant) two-a))))
-> (roots 1 3 -70)
(7 -10)
```

In a `let` expression, all of the right-hand sides are evaluated before any of the x_i's are bound. It is often more useful to evaluate and bind one expression at a time, in sequence, so that right-hand side e_i can refer to the values named $x_1, \ldots, x_{i-1}$. Sequential binding is implemented by the `let*` form. This form has the same structure as `let`, but after evaluating the first right-hand side e_1, it extends the environment by binding the result to x_1. Then it evaluates e_2 in the extended environment, binds the result to x_2, and so on.

The difference between `let` and `let*` can be illustrated by a contrived example:

118b. ⟨*transcript* 95a⟩+≡ ◁118a 118c▷

```
-> (val x 'global-x)
-> (val y 'global-y)
-> (let
     ([x 'local-x]
      [y x])
     (list2 x y))
(local-x global-x)
```

In this example, because the right-hand sides in a `let` are evaluated in the original environment, the `x` in `[y x]` refers to the *global* definition of `x`. Using `let*`, the same structure works differently:

118c. ⟨*transcript* 95a⟩+≡ ◁118b 119a▷

```
-> (val x 'global-x)
-> (val y 'global-y)
-> (let*
     ([x 'local-x]
      [y x])
     (list2 x y))
(local-x local-x)
```

In this example, because the right-hand sides in a `let*` are evaluated and bound in sequence, the `x` in `[y x]` refers to the *local* definition of `x`.

Any `let*` expression can be simulated with a nested sequence of `let` expressions, but `let*` is more readable and more convenient. As evidence of `let*`'s utility, I show a *level-order traversal* (also called breadth-first traversal) of a binary tree. This traversal visits every node on one level before visiting any node on the next level. In effect, it visits nodes in order of distance from the root. For example, level-order traversal of the tree on page 109 visits the nodes in the order `(A B E C D F I G H)`.

Level-order traversal uses an auxiliary data structure: a queue of nodes not yet visited. Traversal starts with a queue containing only the root, and it continues until the queue is empty. When the queue is not empty, the traversal visits the node at the front of the queue, then enqueues the node's children at the end. The implementation needs queue operations emptyqueue, front, without-front, and enqueue:

119a. ⟨*transcript* 95a⟩+≡ ◁118c 119b▷

```
-> (val emptyqueue '())
-> (define front          (q) (car q))
-> (define without-front (q) (cdr q))
-> (define enqueue (t q)
     (if (null? q)
       (list1 t)
       (cons (car q) (enqueue t (cdr q)))))
-> (define empty? (q) (null? q))
```


This implementation of queues is woefully inefficient—it has the same cost as append—but it's simple. I encourage you to do better (Exercise 13) and also to describe the queue's behavior using algebraic laws (Exercise 14).

The traversal is performed recursively by auxiliary function level-order-of-q, which receives an initial queue that contains only the tree to be traversed. It uses let* to bind the first element to the name hd, which is then used both to make a new queue newq and to make the result in the body.

119b. ⟨*transcript* 95a⟩+≡ ◁119a 119c▷

```
-> (define level-order-of-q (queue)
     (if (empty? queue)
       '()
       (let* ([hd   (front         queue)]
              [tl   (without-front queue)]
              [newq (if (empty-tree? hd)
                        tl
                        (enqueue (node-right hd)
                                 (enqueue (node-left hd) tl)))])
         (if (node? hd)
             (cons (node-tag hd) (level-order-of-q newq))
             (level-order-of-q newq)))))
-> (define level-order (t)
     (level-order-of-q (enqueue t emptyqueue)))
-> (level-order example-sym-tree)
(A B E C D F I G H)
```

The example code names three queues: queue, tl, and newq. Picking the wrong one can cause an error; for example, if queue is used place of tl, the function will loop. In an idiomatic imperative function, such an error wouldn't occur; the function would use just one variable, queue, whose value would change over time. In an idiomatic applicative function, the same error can *also* be avoided; by clever use of let*, the name queue can be repeatedly *rebound* so that it always refers to the queue of interest:

119c. ⟨*transcript* 95a⟩+≡ ◁119b 120a▷

```
-> (define level-order-of-q (queue)
     (if (empty? queue)
       '()
       (let* ([hd    (front         queue)]
              [queue (without-front queue)]
              [queue (if (empty-tree? hd)
                         queue
                         (enqueue (node-right hd)
                                  (enqueue (node-left hd) queue)))])
         (if (node? hd)
             (cons (node-tag hd) (level-order-of-q queue))
             (level-order-of-q queue)))))
```

car	$\mathcal{P}$ 162a
cdr	$\mathcal{P}$ 162a
cons	$\mathcal{P}$ S313d
empty-tree?	110a
example-sym-tree	109b
list1	$\mathcal{B}$ 96
list2	$\mathcal{B}$ 96
negated	$\mathcal{B}$ 650
node-left	109a
node-right	109a
node-tag	109a
node?	109a
null?	$\mathcal{P}$ 162a
sqrt	S318b

120a. ⟨*transcript* 95a⟩+≡ ◁119c 120b▷

```
-> (define level-order (t)
      (level-order-of-q (enqueue t emptyqueue)))
-> (level-order example-sym-tree)
(A B E C D F I G H)
```

Both the imperative and the applicative idioms accomplish the same goal: they use just one name, `queue`, and at each point in the program, it means the right thing.

The `let` and `let*` forms have a recursive sibling, `letrec`, which has yet a third set of rules for the visibility of the bound names x_i. In a `let` expression, none of the x_i's can be used in any of the e_i's. In a `let*` expression, each x_i can be used in any e_j with $j > i$, that is, an x can be used in all the e's that follow it. In a `letrec` expression, all of the x_i's can be used in all of the e_i's, regardless of order. The `letrec` form is used to define recursive functions. A simple example appears on page 135, but a detailed explanation is best deferred to the formal treatment of `lambda` and closures (Section 2.11.2).

2.7 LANGUAGE III: FIRST-CLASS FUNCTIONS, `lambda`, AND LOCATIONS

In Impcore, as in C, functions can be defined only at top level. And in Impcore, functions are not values. In C, functions are not quite values either, but a *pointer* to a function is an ordinary value, and it can be used like other values. In Scheme, functions are values, and a function can be defined anywhere—even inside another function. A function is defined by evaluating a new form of expression: the *lambda expression.*

The expression

$$\texttt{(lambda (}x_1\ x_2 \cdots\ x_n\texttt{)}\ e\texttt{)}$$

denotes the function that takes values $v_1, v_2, \ldots, v_n$ and returns the result of evaluating e in an environment where x_1 is bound to v_1, x_2 is bound to v_2, and so on. Together with the LET expressions, the `lambda` expression is what distinguishes μScheme syntax from Impcore syntax; roughly speaking, μScheme is Impcore plus LET expressions, LAMBDA expressions, and S-expression data. The `lambda` expression is the key to many useful programming techniques, the most important and widely used of which are presented in this chapter.

By itself, `lambda` is not obviously powerful; one `lambda` is simple and innocuous. For example, `(lambda (x y) (+ (* x x) (* y y)))` denotes the function that, given values v and w, returns $v^2 + w^2$. Its only novelty is that it is *anonymous*; unlike Impcore functions and C functions, Scheme functions need not be named.

120b. ⟨*transcript* 95a⟩+≡ ◁120a 121a▷

```
-> ((lambda (x y) (+ (* x x) (* y y))) 3 4)
25
-> ((lambda (x y) (+ (* x x) (* y y))) 707 707)
999698
-> ((lambda (x y z) (+ x (+ y z))) 1 2 3)
6
-> ((lambda (y) (* y y)) 7)
49
```

The `lambda` looks like a new way of defining functions, so you might think that μScheme has two kinds of functions, one created with `lambda` and one created with `define`. But `define` is an abbreviation—another form of syntactic sugar. A `define` form can be *desugared* into a combination of `val` and `lambda`:

$$\texttt{(define}\ f\ \texttt{(}x_1\ \cdots\ x_n\texttt{)}\ e\texttt{)} \triangleq \texttt{(val}\ f\ \texttt{(lambda (}x_1\ \cdots\ x_n\texttt{)}\ e\texttt{))}.$$

As described in the sidebar on page 68, this kind of syntactic sugar is popular; it gives programmers a nice big language to use, while keeping the core language and its operational semantics (and the proofs!) small.

The `define` form can be desugared into a `val` only because in μScheme, a function is just another kind of value—and all values, including functions, are bound in the same environment (Section 2.11). In Impcore, where functions and values are bound in different environments, `define` could not be desugared into a `val`.

Desugaring `define` into `val` is one way to exploit the idea that a function defined with `lambda` is just another value. Besides putting it on the right-hand side of a `val`, what else can you do with such a function? What you can do with any other value:

- Pass it as an argument to a function.
- Return it from a function.
- Store it in a global variable, using `set`.
- Save it in a data structure, using `cons` or a record constructor.

These capabilities can help you assess the role of any species of value in any programming language; if you can do all these things with a value, that value is sometimes said to be *first class*. "First-class functions" is a phrase sometimes used to characterize Scheme and other functional languages, but it's not quite right: what's essential about Scheme is that it provides first-class, *nested* functions.

To see what difference nesting makes, let's start with a non-nested example. Because functions are first class, a μScheme function (defined with `define` or with `lambda`) can be passed as an argument to another function. What can the function that *receives* the argument do? All the standard things listed above, which it can do with any first-class value. And one more—the only *interesting* thing to do with a function: *apply* it. As a simple example, function `apply-n-times` receives a function `f`, an integer `n`, and an argument `x`, and it returns the result of applying `f` to `x` `n` times:

121a. ⟨*transcript* 95a⟩+≡ ◁120b 121b▷

```
-> (define apply-n-times (n f x)
     (if (= 0 n)
       x
       (apply-n-times (- n 1) f (f x))))
-> (apply-n-times 77 not #t)
#f
-> (apply-n-times 78 not #t)
#t
```

Applying `n` times is more interesting with numbers:

121b. ⟨*transcript* 95a⟩+≡ ◁121a 122▷

```
-> (define twice  (n) (* 2 n))
-> (define square (n) (* n n))
-> (apply-n-times 2 twice 10)
40
-> (apply-n-times 2 square 10)
10000
-> (apply-n-times 10 twice 1)
1024
-> (apply-n-times 10 square 1)
1
```


A function like `apply-n-times` is described by a handy piece of jargon: a function that takes another function as an argument is called a *higher-order function*. The term "higher-order function" is inclusive; it also describes a function that *re-*

turns another function. Functions like `twice` and `square`, which neither take functions as arguments nor return functions as results, are called *first-order functions*.

Not all higher-order functions are created equal. Some, like `apply-n-times`, could be implemented in C just as easily as in Scheme. What *can't* be implemented in C is a function that evaluates a *nested* `lambda` expression inside its own body, then returns the result of that evaluation, which is called a *closure*. Such a function creates a new function anonymously, "on the fly"; the closure is the *representation* of the new function. As a toy example, function `add` returns a closure:

122. ⟨*transcript* 95a⟩+≡ ◁121b 123a▷

```
-> (val add (lambda (x) (lambda (y) (+ x y))))
-> (val add1 (add 1))
-> (add1 4)
5
```

Function `add` is defined by the outer `lambda` expression, which takes `x` as an argument. It's not so interesting. What's interesting is inner `lambda`, which takes `y` as an argument: every time it is evaluated, it creates a new function. The two `lambda`s work together: when `add` receives argument m, it returns a function which, when it receives argument n, returns $m + n$. (Therefore, `add1` is a one-argument function which adds 1 to its argument.) Applying `add` to different integers can create *arbitrarily many* functions. Not only `(add 1)` but `(add 2)` and `(add 100)` can be functions. Even an expression like `(add (length xs))` creates a function.

New functions can be created because `(lambda (y) (+ x y))` is nested inside the outer `lambda` that defines `add`. Every time `add` is called, the inner `lambda` is evaluated, and in Scheme, every time a `lambda` expression is evaluated, a new function is created. In languages like Impcore and C, which don't have `lambda`, a new function can be created only by writing it explicitly in the source code.

2.7.1 *How* `lambda` *works: Closures with mutable locations*

The expression `(lambda (y) (+ x y))` can be evaluated to produce more than one function. Such a function is represented by pairing the `lambda` expression with an environment that says what `x` stands for. This pair forms the closure, which we write in "banana brackets," as in ⦇`(lambda (y) (+ x y))`, {`x` ↦ 1}⦈. The banana brackets emphasize that a closure cannot be written directly using Scheme syntax; the closure is a value that Scheme builds from a `lambda` expression. A closure is the simplest way to implement first-class, nested functions.

A closure is defined as a pair: code and an environment. In μScheme, the code is a `lambda` expression, but what is the environment? In Impcore, an environment maps a name to a value (or a function). But in Scheme, an environment maps a name to a *mutable location*. You can think of a mutable location as a box containing a value, which can change, or you can wear your C programmer's hat and think of it as a location in memory, which the environment can point to.

A Scheme environment maps each name to a mutable location because in a world where there are closures, this is the easiest way to express the way assignment (`set`) works. In Impcore, `set` simply replaces an old environment with a new one (and can even update the environment in place). But `set` can be implemented in this way only because no environment is ever copied. In Scheme, by contrast, an environment can be copied into any number of closures, and there is no easy way for `set` to update them all. Instead, when a name is assigned to, `set` updates the mutable location associated with that name.

In the following example, `set` updates a mutable location that is accessible only from within a `lambda`. The inner `lambda` evaluates to a closure in which `n` points to a mutable location. That closure is stored in global variable ten, and every time ten is called, it updates n and returns the new value:

123a. ⟨*transcript* 95a⟩+≡ ◁122 123b▷

```
-> (val counter-from
     (lambda (n)
        (lambda () (set n (+ n 1)))))
-> (val ten (counter-from 10))
<function>
-> (ten)
11
-> (ten)
12
-> (ten)
13
```

When ten is defined, counter-from is applied, and that application allocates a location ℓ to hold the value of n, which is 10. The environment in which the inner lambda is evaluated therefore binds n to ℓ, and the inner lambda evaluates to the closure $(\!|$(lambda () (set n (+ n 1))), $\{$n $\mapsto \ell, \ldots\}$ $|\!)$, which is the value of ten.[7]

A mutable location can be shared among multiple closures, which can communicate with each other by mutating it. For example, a mutable number n can be shared by counter and reset functions, which are stored in a counter record:

123b. ⟨*transcript* 95a⟩+≡ ◁123a 123c▷

```
-> (record counter [step reset])
-> (val resettable-counter-from
     (lambda (n)                          ; create a counter
        (make-counter (lambda () (set n (+ n 1)))
                      (lambda () (set n 0)))))
```

The two innermost lambda expressions refer to the *same* n, so that when a counter's reset function is called, its step function starts over at 0. And two *different* applications of resettable-counter-from refer to *different* n's, so that two independent counters never interfere.

A counter is stepped or reset in two steps: extract a function from the counter record, then apply it.

123c. ⟨*transcript* 95a⟩+≡ ◁123b 123d▷

```
-> (val step  (lambda (counter) ((counter-step  counter))))
-> (val reset (lambda (counter) ((counter-reset counter))))
```

The double applications are easy to overlook. A function is taken from the counter record in an inner application, such as (counter-step counter). That function, which takes no parameters, is called in an outer application, such as ((counter-step counter)).

In the following transcript, two counters, hundred and twenty, count independently and are reset independently.

123d. ⟨*transcript* 95a⟩+≡ ◁123c 124a▷

```
-> (val hundred (resettable-counter-from 100))
-> (val twenty  (resettable-counter-from 20))
-> (step hundred)
101
-> (step hundred)
102
-> (step twenty)
21
```

[7] As suggested by the ellipsis, the environment contains other bindings, but the only bindings that affect computation are the binding of n to ℓ and of + to a location containing the primitive addition function.

Resetting hundred doesn't affect twenty.

124a. ⟨*transcript* 95a⟩+≡ ◁123d 124b▷

```
-> (reset hundred)
0
-> (step hundred)
1
-> (step twenty)
22
```


The mutable n that the step and reset function share is an example of *shared mutable state*. Shared mutable state isn't new; it's available in any language that has mutable global variables. But the shared mutable state provided by lambda is more flexible and better controlled than a global variable.

- It's more flexible because the amount of shared mutable state isn't limited by the number of global variables.
- It's better controlled because not every piece of code has access to it—the only code that has access is code that has the relevant variables in a closure.

The mutable state that is stored in a closure is *private* to a function but also *persistent* across calls to that function. Private, persistent mutable state is sometimes provided as a special language feature, usually called "own variables." An own variable is local to a function, but its value is preserved across calls of the function. The name comes from Algol 60, but own variables are also found in C, where they are defined using the keyword static.

As another example of private, persistent mutable state, I define a simple random-number generator.[8] It's a higher-order function that takes a next function as parameter, and it keeps a private, mutable variable seed, which is initially 1:

124b. ⟨*transcript* 95a⟩+≡ ◁124a 124c▷

```
-> (define mk-rand (next)
     (let ([seed 1])
        (lambda () (set seed (next seed)))))
```

Parameter next can be any function that takes a number and returns another number. To make a *good* random-number generator requires a function that satisfies some sophisticated statistical properties. A simple approximation uses the *linear congruential* method (Knuth 1981, pp. 9–25) on numbers in the range 0 to 1023:

124c. ⟨*transcript* 95a⟩+≡ ◁124b 124d▷

```
-> (define simple-next (seed) (mod (+ (* seed 9) 5) 1024))
```

This generator is not, in any statistical sense, good. For one thing, after generating only 1024 different numbers, it starts repeating. But it's usable:

124d. ⟨*transcript* 95a⟩+≡ ◁124c 125b▷

```
-> (val irand (mk-rand simple-next))
-> (irand)
14
-> (irand)
131
-> (irand)
160
-> (val repeatable-irand (mk-rand simple-next))
-> (repeatable-irand)
14
-> (irand)
421
```

[8]Technically a generator of *pseudorandom* numbers.

Function irand has its own private copy of seed, which only it can access, and which it updates at each call. And function repeatable-irand, which might be used to replay an execution for debugging, has *its* own private seed. So it repeats the *same* sequence $[1, 14, 131, 160, 421, \ldots]$ no matter what happens with irand.

2.7.2 Useful higher-order functions

The lambda expression does more than just encapsulate mutable state; lambda helps express and support not just algorithms but also *patterns of computation.* What a "pattern of computation" might be is best shown by example.

One minor example is the function mk-rand: it can be viewed as a pattern that says "if you tell me how to get from one number to the next, I can deliver an entire sequence of numbers starting with 1." This pattern of computation, while handy, is not used often. More useful patterns can make new functions from old functions or can express common ways of programming with lists, like "do something with every element." Such patterns are presented in the next few sections.

Composition

One of the simplest ways to make a new function is by composing two old ones. Function o (pronounced "circle" or "compose") returns the composition of two one-argument functions, often written $f \circ g$. Composition is described by the algebraic law $(f \circ g)(x) = f(g(x))$, and like any function that makes new functions, it returns a lambda:

125a. ⟨*predefined μScheme functions* 96a⟩+≡ ◁106c 126c▷

```
(define o (f g) (lambda (x) (f (g x))))          ; ((o f g) x) = (f (g x))
```

Function composition can negate a predicate by composing not with it:

125b. ⟨*transcript* 95a⟩+≡ ◁124d 125c▷

```
-> (define even? (n) (= 0 (mod n 2)))
-> (val odd? (o not even?))
-> (odd? 3)
#t
-> (odd? 4)
#f
```

In large programs, function composition can be used to improve modularity: an algorithm can be broken down into functions that are connected using composition.

Currying and partial application

A lambda can be used to change the interface to a function, as in the example of add (page 122):

125c. ⟨*transcript* 95a⟩+≡ ◁125b 126a▷

```
-> (val add (lambda (x) (lambda (y) (+ x y))))
```

hundred	123d
mod	$\mathcal{B}$
reset	123c
step	123c
twenty	123d

Function add does what + does, but add takes one argument at a time, whereas + takes both its arguments at once. For example, (add 1) is a function that adds 1 to its argument, while (+ 1) is an error. Similarly, (+ 1 2) is 3, while (add 1 2) is an error. But add and + are really two forms of the same function; they differ only in the way they take their arguments. The forms are named: add is the *curried* form, and + is the *uncurried* form. The names honor the logician Haskell B. Curry.

Any function can be put into curried form; the curried form simply takes its arguments one at a time. If it needs more than one argument, it takes the first argument, then returns a lambda that expects the remaining arguments, also one at a time. As another example, the curried form of the list3 function uses three lambdas:

126a. ⟨*transcript* 95a⟩+≡ ◁125c 126b▷

```
-> (val curried-list3 (lambda (a) (lambda (b) (lambda (c) (list3 a b c)))))
-> (curried-list3 'x)
<function>
-> ((curried-list3 'x) 'y)
<function>
-> (((curried-list3 'x) 'y) 'z)
(x y z)
```


Curried functions don't mesh well with Scheme's concrete syntax. Defining one requires lots of lambdas, and applying one requires lots of parentheses.[9] If currying is so awkward, why bother with it? To get *partial applications*. A curried function is *partially applied* when it is applied to only *some* of its arguments, and the resulting function is saved to be applied later. If the function's arguments are expected in the right order, partial applications can be quite useful. For example, the curried form of < can be partially applied to 0, and the resulting partial application takes any m and says whether $0 < m$:

126b. ⟨*transcript* 95a⟩+≡ ◁126a 126d▷

```
-> (val <-curried (lambda (n) (lambda (m) (< n m))))
-> (val positive? (<-curried 0))
-> (positive? 0)
#f
-> (positive? 8)
#t
-> (positive? -3)
#f
```

Functions needn't always be curried by hand. Any binary function can be converted between its uncurried and curried forms using the predefined functions curry and uncurry:

126c. ⟨*predefined μScheme functions* 96a⟩+≡ ◁125a 129▷

```
(define curry   (f) (lambda (x) (lambda (y) (f x y))))
(define uncurry (f) (lambda (x y) ((f x) y)))
```

126d. ⟨*transcript* 95a⟩+≡ ◁126b 126e▷

```
-> (val zero? ((curry =) 0))
-> (zero? 0)
#t
-> (val add1 ((curry +) 1))
-> (add1 4)
5
```

Functions curry and uncurry obey these algebraic laws:

$$\texttt{(((curry f) x) y)} = \texttt{(f x y)}$$
$$\texttt{((uncurry f) x y)} = \texttt{((f x) y)}$$

As can be proved using the laws, the two functions are inverses; for example, if I curry +, then uncurry the result, I get + back again:

126e. ⟨*transcript* 95a⟩+≡ ◁126d 127a▷

```
-> (val also+ (uncurry (curry +)))
-> (also+ 1 4)
5
```

[9] More recently developed functional languages, like Standard ML, OCaml, and Haskell, use notations and implementations that encourage currying and partial application, so much so that in OCaml and Haskell, function definitions produce curried forms by default. For partial application in Scheme, see the proposal by Egner (2002).

If currying makes your head hurt, don't panic—I expect it. Both currying and composition are easier to understand when they are used to make functions that operate on values in lists.

2.8 Practice III: Higher-order functions on lists

If higher-order functions embody "patterns of computation," what are those patterns? The patterns you're best equipped to appreciate are patterns of computation on lists. Some of the most popular and widely reused patterns can be described informally as follows:

- Pick just some elements from a list.
- Make a new list from an existing list by transforming each element.
- Search a list for an element.
- Check every element of a list to make sure it is OK.
- Visit every list element, perform a computation there, and accumulate a result. Or more loosely, "do something" to every element of a list.

These patterns, and more besides, are embodied in the higher-order functions `filter`, `map`, `exists?`, `all?`, and `foldr`, all of which are in μScheme's initial basis. (If you've heard of Google MapReduce, the Map is the same, and Reduce is a parallel variant of `foldr`.)

2.8.1 *Standard higher-order functions on lists*

Function `filter` takes a predicate `p?` and a list `xs`, and it returns a new list consisting of only those elements of `xs` that satisfy `p?`:

127a. ⟨*transcript* 95a⟩+≡ ◁126e 127b▷

```
-> (define even? (x) (= (mod x 2) 0))
-> (filter even? '(1 2 3 4 5 6 7 8 9 10))
(2 4 6 8 10)
```

As requested in Exercise 27, function `filter` can be used to define a concise version of the `remove-multiples` function from Section 2.3.4.

Function `filter` must receive a predicate as its first argument, but `map` works with any unary function; `(map f xs)` returns the list of results formed by applying function `f` to every element of list `xs`.

127b. ⟨*transcript* 95a⟩+≡ ◁127a 128a▷

```
-> (map add1 '(3 4 5))
(4 5 6)
-> (map ((curry +) 5) '(3 4 5))
(8 9 10)
-> (map (lambda (x) (* x x)) '(1 2 3 4 5 6 7 8 9 10))
(1 4 9 16 25 36 49 64 81 100)
-> (primes<= 20)
(2 3 5 7 11 13 17 19)
-> (map ((curry <) 10) (primes<= 20))
(#f #f #f #f #t #t #t #t)
```


`add1`	122
`filter`	$\mathcal{B}$ 129
`list3`	$\mathcal{B}$ 96
`map`	$\mathcal{B}$ 130
`mod`	$\mathcal{B}$
`primes<=`	102d

Functions `filter` and `map` build new lists from the elements of old ones—a common pattern of computation. Another common pattern is linear search. In μScheme, linear search is implemented by two functions, `exists?` and `all?`.

Each takes a predicate, and as you might expect, exists? tells whether there is an element of the list satisfying the predicate; all? tells whether they all do.

128a. ⟨*transcript* 95a⟩+≡ ◁127b 128b▷

```
-> (exists? even? '(1 2 3 4 5 6 7 8 9 10))
#t
-> (all? even? '(1 2 3 4 5 6 7 8 9 10))
#f
-> (all? even? (filter even? '(1 2 3 4 5 6 7 8 9 10)))
#t
-> (exists? even? (filter (o not even?) '(1 2 3 4 5 6 7 8 9 10)))
#f
```

When called on the empty list, an important "corner case," exists? and all? act like the mathematical $\exists$ and $\forall$.

128b. ⟨*transcript* 95a⟩+≡ ◁128a 128c▷

```
-> (exists? even? '())
#f
-> (all? even? '())
#t
```

Higher-order functions on lists can make programs wonderfully concise, because they relieve you from writing the same patterns of recursion over and over again. Writing common recursions in a concise, standard way helps not just the person who writes the code but also the people who read it. A reader who sees a recursive function has to figure out what is called recursively and how it works. But one who sees map, filter, or exists? already knows how the code works.

A very general pattern of recursion is to combine the car of a list with the results of a recursive call. This pattern is embodied in the higher-order function foldr. Function foldr expects a combining operator (a two-argument function), which I'll call $\oplus$; a starting value, which I'll call $\aleph$; and a list of values, which I'll call vs. Using $\oplus$, foldr combines ("folds") all the values from vs into $\aleph$. For example, if $\oplus$ is +, $\aleph$ is 0, and vs is a list of numbers, then (foldr $\oplus$ $\aleph$ vs) is the sum of the list of numbers.

The general case of foldr is most easily understood when written using infix notation. I'll write ($\oplus$ x y) as $x \oplus y$ and (cons v vs) as $v :: vs$. In this notation, if vs has the form $v_1 :: v_2 :: \cdots :: v_n ::$ '(), then (foldr $\oplus$ $\aleph$ vs) is $v_1 \oplus v_2 \oplus \cdots \oplus v_n \oplus \aleph$. In effect, every cons is replaced with $\oplus$, and '() is replaced with $\aleph$.

What if $\oplus$ is not associative? The r in foldr means that $\oplus$ associates to the right. The right operand of $\oplus$ is always either $\aleph$ or the result of applying a previous $\oplus$:

$$(\texttt{foldr}\ \oplus\ \aleph\ \texttt{'}(v_1\ v_2 \cdots\ v_n)) = v_1 \oplus (v_2 \oplus (\cdots \oplus (v_n \oplus \aleph))).$$

Function foldr has a companion function, foldl, in which $\oplus$ associates to the left, and $\aleph$ is combined with v_1, not with v_n. Because each result becomes a right operand of $\oplus$, foldl is effectively foldr operating on a reversed list:

$$(\texttt{foldl}\ \oplus\ \aleph\ \texttt{'}(v_1\ v_2 \cdots\ v_n)) = v_n \oplus (v_{n-1} \oplus (\cdots \oplus (v_1 \oplus \aleph))).$$

For example, (foldl - 0 '(1 2 3 4)) is $(4 - (3 - (2 - (1 - 0)))) = 2$. On the same list, (foldr - 0 '(1 2 3 4)) is $(1 - (2 - (3 - (4 - 0)))) = -2$.

128c. ⟨*transcript* 95a⟩+≡ ◁128b 131a▷

```
-> (foldl - 0 '(1 2 3 4))
2
-> (foldr - 0 '(1 2 3 4))
-2
```

More applications of foldr and foldl are suggested in Exercises 8, 29, and 30.

2.8.2 *Visualizations of the standard list functions*

Which list functions should be used when? Functions `exists?` and `all?` are not hard to figure out, but `map`, `filter`, and `foldr` can be more mysterious. They can be demystified a bit using pictures, as inspired by Harvey and Wright (1994).

A generic list `xs` can be depicted as a list of circles:

xs = ○ ○ ○ ○ ○ ··· ○

If `f` is a function that turns one circle into one triangle, as in `(f` ○`)` = △, then `(map f xs)` turns a list of circles into a list of triangles.

xs = ○ ○ ○ ○ ○ ··· ○

↓ ↓ ↓ ↓ ↓ ↓

(map f xs) = △ △ △ △ △ ··· △

If `p?` is a function that takes a circle and returns a Boolean, as in `(p?` ○`)` = b, then `(filter p? xs)` selects just some of the circles:

xs = ○ ○ ○ ○ ○ ··· ○

↓ × ↓ ↓ × ↓

(filter p? xs) = ○ ○ ○ ··· ○

Finally, if `f` is a function that takes a circle and a box and produces another box, as in `(f` ○□`)` = □, then `(fold f`□`xs)` folds all of the circles into a single box:

xs = ○ ○ ○ ○ ○ ··· ○

↓

(foldr f □ xs) = □

The single box can contain any species of value—even another sequence of circles.

2.8.3 *Implementations of the standard list functions*

Most of the higher-order list functions are easy to implement and easy to understand. Each is a recursive function with one base case (which consumes the empty list) and one induction step (which consumes a cons cell). All are part of the initial basis of μScheme. Except for `app`, they are described by the algebraic laws in Figure 2.4 on the following page.

all?	$\mathcal{B}$ 130
even?	127a
exists?	$\mathcal{B}$ 130
foldl	$\mathcal{B}$ 131
foldr	$\mathcal{B}$ 131

Function `filter` is structured in the same way as function `remove-multiples` from chunk 102b; the only difference is in the test. Filtering the empty list produces the empty list. In the induction step, depending on whether the `car` satisfies `p?`, `filter` may or may not cons.

129. ⟨*predefined μScheme functions* 96a⟩+≡ ◁ 126c 130a ▷

```
(define filter (p? xs)
  (if (null? xs)
    '()
    (if (p? (car xs))
      (cons (car xs) (filter p? (cdr xs)))
      (filter p? (cdr xs)))))
```

```
(filter p? '())                          = '()
(filter p? (cons y ys))                  = (cons y (filter p? ys)), when (p? y)
(filter p? (cons y ys))                  = (filter p? ys), when (not (p? y))
(map f '())                              = '()
(map f (cons y ys))                      = (cons (f y) (map f ys))
(exists? p? '())                         = #f
(exists? p? (cons y ys))                 = #t, when (p? y)
(exists? p? (cons y ys))                 = (exists? p? ys), when (not (p? y))
(all? p? '())                            = #t
(all? p? (cons y ys))                    = (all? p? ys), when (p? y)
(all? p? (cons y ys))                    = #f, when (not (p? y))
(foldr combine zero '())                 = zero
(foldr combine zero (cons y ys))         = (combine y (foldr combine zero ys))
(foldl combine zero '())                 = zero
(foldl combine zero (cons y ys))         = (foldl combine (combine y zero) ys)
```

Figure 2.4: Algebraic laws of pure higher-order functions on lists

Function map is even simpler. There is no conditional test; the induction step just applies f to the car, then conses.

130a. ⟨*predefined μScheme functions* 96a⟩+≡ ◁129 130b▷

```
(define map (f xs)
  (if (null? xs)
    '()
    (cons (f (car xs)) (map f (cdr xs)))))
```

Function app is like map, except its argument is applied only for side effect. Function app is typically used with printu. Because app is executed for side effects, its behavior cannot be expressed using simple algebraic laws.

130b. ⟨*predefined μScheme functions* 96a⟩+≡ ◁130a 130c▷

```
(define app (f xs)
  (if (null? xs)
    #f
    (begin (f (car xs)) (app f (cdr xs)))))
```

Each of the preceding functions processes every element of its list argument. Functions exists? and all? don't necessarily do so. Function exists? stops the moment it finds a satisfying element; all? stops the moment it finds a *non*-satisfying element.

130c. ⟨*predefined μScheme functions* 96a⟩+≡ ◁130b 131b▷

```
(define exists? (p? xs)
  (if (null? xs)
    #f
    (if (p? (car xs))
      #t
      (exists? p? (cdr xs)))))
(define all? (p? xs)
  (if (null? xs)
    #t
    (if (p? (car xs))
      (all? p? (cdr xs))
      #f)))
```

Function all? could also be defined using De Morgan's law, which says that $\neg\forall x.P(x) = \exists x.\neg P(x)$. Negating both sides gives this definition:

131a. ⟨*transcript* 95a⟩+≡ ◁128c 131c▷

```
-> (define alt-all? (p? xs) (not (exists? (o not p?) xs)))
-> (alt-all? even? '(1 2 3 4 5 6 7 8 9 10))
#f
-> (alt-all? even? '())
#t
-> (alt-all? even? (filter even? '(1 2 3 4 5 6 7 8 9 10)))
#t
```


Finally, foldr and foldl, although simple, are not necessarily easy to understand. Study their algebraic laws, and remember that (car xs) is always a first argument to combine, and zero is always a second argument.

131b. ⟨*predefined μScheme functions* 96a⟩+≡ ◁130c

```
(define foldr (combine zero xs)
  (if (null? xs)
    zero
    (combine (car xs) (foldr combine zero (cdr xs)))))
(define foldl (combine zero xs)
  (if (null? xs)
    zero
    (foldl combine (combine (car xs) zero) (cdr xs))))
```

2.9 Practice IV: Higher-order functions for polymorphism

A function like filter doesn't need to know what sort of value predicate p? is expecting. For example, filter can be used with function even? to select elements of a list of numbers; or it can be used with function (o even? alist-pair-attribute) to select elements of an association list that contains symbol-number pairs; or it can be used with infinitely many other combinations of predicates and lists. The ability to be used with arguments of many different types makes filter *polymorphic* (see sidebar on the next page). Functions exists?, all?, map, foldl, and foldr are also polymorphic. By contrast, a function that works with only one type of argument, like <, is *monomorphic*. Polymorphic functions are especially easy to reuse. In this section, polymorphism is demonstrated in examples that implement set operations and sorting.

As shown in chunks 105a and 105c above, set operations can be implemented using recursive functions. But they can be made more compact and (eventually) easier to understand by using the higher-order functions exists?, curry, and foldl.

cons	$\mathcal{P}$ S313d
curry	$\mathcal{B}$ 126
equal?	$\mathcal{B}$ 104
even?	127a
filter	$\mathcal{B}$ 129

131c. ⟨*transcript* 95a⟩+≡ ◁131a 133a▷

```
-> (val emptyset '())
-> (define member?      (x s) (exists? ((curry equal?) x) s))
-> (define add-element  (x s) (if (member? x s) s (cons x s)))
-> (define union       (s1 s2) (foldl add-element s1 s2))
-> (define set-of-list   (xs) (foldl add-element '() xs))
-> (set-of-list '(a b c x y a))
(y x c b a)
-> (union '(1 2 3 4) '(2 4 6 8))
(8 6 1 2 3 4)
```

These set functions work on sets of atoms, and because member? calls equal?, they also work on sets of lists of atoms. But they won't work on other kinds of sets, like sets of sets or sets of association lists; equal? is too pessimistic.

Three kinds of polymorphism

When programmers can say "code reuse" with a fancy Greek name, they sound smart. What's less smart is that at least three different programming techniques are all called "polymorphism."

- The sort of polymorphism we find in the standard list functions is called *parametric polymorphism.*[a] In parametric polymorphism, the polymorphic code always executes the same algorithm in the same way, regardless of the types of the arguments. Parametric polymorphism is the simplest kind of polymorphism, and although it is most useful when combined with higher-order functions, it can be implemented without special mechanisms at run time. Parametric polymorphism is found in some form in every functional language.

- Object-oriented languages such as Smalltalk (Chapter 10) enjoy another kind of polymorphism, which is called *subtype polymorphism.* In subtype polymorphism, code might execute *different* algorithms when operating on values of different types. For example, in a language with subtype polymorphism, squares and circles might be different types of geometric shapes, but they might both implement `draw` functions. However, the circle would `draw` differently from the square, using different code. Subtype polymorphism typically requires some sort of object or class system to create the subtypes; examples can be found in Chapter 10.

- Finally, in some languages, a single symbol can stand for unrelated functions. For example, in Python, the symbol + is used not only to add numbers but also to concatenate strings. A number is not a kind of string, and a string is not a kind of number, and the algorithms are unrelated. Nonetheless, + works on more than one type of argument, so it is considered polymorphic. This kind of polymorphism is called *ad hoc polymorphism,* but Anglo-Saxon people tend to call it *overloading.* It is described, in passing, in Chapter 9.

In object-oriented parts of the world, "polymorphism" by itself usually means subtype polymorphism, and parametric polymorphism is often called *generics.* But to a dyed-in-the-wool functional programmer, *generic programming* means writing recursive functions that consume *types.*[b] If you stick with one crowd or the other, you'll quickly learn the local lingo, but if your interests become eclectic, you'll want to watch out for that word "generic."

[a] The word "parametric" might look like it comes from a function's parameter or from passing functions as parameters. But the polymorphism is called "parametric" because of *type parameters,* which are defined formally, as part of the language Typed μScheme, in Chapter 6.

[b] You are not expected to understand this.

To address the issue, let's focus on sets of association lists. Two association lists are considered equal if they each have the same keys and attributes, *regardless of how the key-attribute pairs are ordered.* In other words, although an association list is *represented* in the world of code as a *sequence* of key-attribute pairs, what it stands for in the world of ideas is a *set* of key-value pairs. Therefore, two association lists are equal if and only if each contains all the key-value pairs found in the other:

133a. ⟨*transcript* 95a⟩+≡ ◁131c 134c▷

```
-> (define sub-alist? (al1 al2)
      ; all of al1's pairs are found in al2
      (all? (lambda (pair)
                (equal? (alist-pair-attribute pair)
                        (find (alist-pair-key pair) al2)))
            al1))
-> (define =alist? (al1 al2)
      (and (sub-alist? al1 al2) (sub-alist? al2 al1)))
-> (=alist? '() '())
#t
-> (=alist? '((E coli) (I Magnin) (U Thant))
            '((E coli) (I Ching)  (U Thant)))
#f
-> (=alist? '((U Thant) (I Ching) (E coli))
            '((E coli)  (I Ching) (U Thant)))
#t
```

Function =alist? makes it possible to implement sets of association lists, but it doesn't dictate *how*. The wrong way to do it is to write a new version of member? which uses =alist? instead of equal?; it could be called al-member?. Then because add-element calls member?, we would need a new version of add-element, which would use al-member? instead of member?. And so on. The wrong path leads to a destination at which everything except emptyset is reimplemented. And then if anyone wants sets of sets, all the operations have to be reimplemented again. The destination is a maintainer's hell, where there are several different implementations of sets, all using nearly identical code and all broken in the same way. For example, the implementation above performs badly on large sets, and if better performance is needed, any improvement has to be reimplemented N times. Instead of collecting monomorphic implementations of sets, a better way is to use higher-order functions to write one implementation that's polymorphic.

2.9.1 *Approaches to polymorphism in Scheme*

In Scheme, polymorphic set functions can be implemented in three styles. All three use higher-order functions; instead of using equal?, the set functions use an equality predicate that is stored in a data structure or passed as a parameter. The style is identified by the location in which the predicate is stored:

- In the simplest style, a new parameter, the equality predicate my-equal?, is added to *every* function. The modified functions look like this:

  133b. ⟨*polymorphic-set transcript* 133b⟩≡ (S320c) 134a▷

  ```
  -> (define member? (x s my-equal?)
        (exists? ((curry my-equal?) x) s))
  member?
  -> (define add-element (x s my-equal?)
        (if (member? x s my-equal?) s (cons x s)))
  add-element
  ```

  Passing an equality predicate to every operation, as in (member? x s equal?) or (add-element x s =alist?), is the responsibility of the client code. That's a heavy burden. Client code must keep track of sets *and* their equality predicates, and it must ensure the same equality predicate is always passed with the same set, consistently, every time.

alist-pair-attribute $\mathcal{B}$ 106
alist-pair-key $\mathcal{B}$ 106
all? $\mathcal{B}$ 130
and $\mathcal{B}$
cons $\mathcal{P}$ S313d
curry $\mathcal{B}$ 126
equal? $\mathcal{B}$ 104
exists? $\mathcal{B}$ 130
find $\mathcal{B}$ 106

- This burden can be relieved by storing a set's equality predicate with its elements. In the second style, a set is represented by a record with two fields: an equality predicate and a list of elements.

134a. ⟨*polymorphic-set transcript* 133b⟩+≡ (S320c) ◁133b 134b▷

```
-> (record aset [eq? elements])
-> (val emptyset (lambda (my-equal?) (make-aset my-equal? '())))
-> (define member? (x s)
       (exists? ((curry (aset-eq? s)) x) (aset-elements s)))
-> (define add-element (x s)
       (if (member? x s)
           s
           (make-aset (aset-eq? s) (cons x (aset-elements s)))))
```

For sets of association lists, these operations are used as follows:

134b. ⟨*polymorphic-set transcript* 133b⟩+≡ (S320c) ◁134a

```
-> (val alist-empty (emptyset =alist?))
-> (val s (add-element '((U Thant) (I Ching) (E coli)) alist-empty))
(make-aset <function> (((U Thant) (I Ching) (E coli))))
-> (val s (add-element '((Hello Dolly) (Goodnight Irene)) s))
(make-aset <function> (((Hello Dolly) (Goodnight Irene)) ((U Thant)...
-> (val s (add-element '((E coli) (I Ching) (U Thant)) s))
(make-aset <function> (((Hello Dolly) (Goodnight Irene)) ((U Thant)...
-> (member? '((Goodnight Irene) (Hello Dolly)) s)
#t
```

The best feature of this style is that a predicate is supplied only when constructing an empty set.

- The second style imposes embarrassing run-time costs. Each set must contain the equality predicate, which adds extra memory to each set, and which requires a level of indirection to gain access either to the equality predicate or to the elements. The second style also imposes a lesser but still nontrivial burden on client code, which has to propagate the equality predicate to each point where an empty set might be created.

  In the third style, these issues are addressed by storing the equality predicate in the *operations*. Each operation is represented by a closure, and the equality function is placed the environment of that closure. In this style, no extra memory is added to any set, a set's elements are accessed without indirection, and the equality predicate is cheaper to fetch from a closure than it would be from a set. And client code has to supply each equality predicate only once, to create the specialized operations that work with that predicate.

  In a third-style implementation of sets, the equality predicate is placed into closures by function `set-ops-with`, which returns a record of set operations. Each operation is specialized to use the given equality.

134c. ⟨*transcript* 95a⟩+≡ ◁133a 135a▷

```
-> (record set-ops [member? add-element])
-> (define set-ops-with (my-equal?)
       (make-set-ops
          (lambda (x s) (exists? ((curry my-equal?) x) s)) ; member?
          (lambda (x s) ; add-element
              (if (exists? ((curry my-equal?) x) s) s (cons x s)))))
```

Specialized operations for a set of association lists are created by applying `set-ops-with` to predicate `=alist?`.

135a. ⟨*transcript* 95a⟩+≡ ◁134c 135b▷

```
-> (val alist-set-ops (set-ops-with =alist?))
-> (val al-member?     (set-ops-member?     alist-set-ops))
-> (val al-add-element (set-ops-add-element alist-set-ops))
```

These operations can be used without mentioning the equality predicate.

135b. ⟨*transcript* 95a⟩+≡ ◁135a 135c▷

```
-> (val emptyset '())
-> (val s (al-add-element '((U Thant) (I Ching) (E coli)) emptyset))
(((U Thant) (I Ching) (E coli)))
-> (val s (al-add-element '((Hello Dolly) (Goodnight Irene)) s))
(((Hello Dolly) (Goodnight Irene)) ((U Thant) (I Ching) (E coli)))
-> (val s (al-add-element '((E coli) (I Ching) (U Thant)) s))
(((Hello Dolly) (Goodnight Irene)) ((U Thant) (I Ching) (E coli)))
-> (al-member? '((Goodnight Irene) (Hello Dolly)) s)
#t
```


2.9.2 Polymorphic, higher-order sort

Another widely used, polymorphic algorithm is sorting. Good sorts are tuned for performance, and when code is tuned for performance, it should be reused. And a sort function can be reused in the same way as the set functions: just as sets require an equality function that operates on set elements, sorting requires a comparison function that operates on list elements. So like the set operations, a sort function should take the comparison function as a parameter. For example, the polymorphic, higher-order function `mk-insertion-sort` takes a comparison function `lt?`, and returns a function that sorts a list of elements into nondecreasing order (according to function `lt?`). The algorithm is from chunk 101a.

135c. ⟨*transcript* 95a⟩+≡ ◁135b 135d▷

```
-> (define mk-insertion-sort (lt?)
     (letrec ([insert (lambda (x xs)
                        (if (null? xs)
                            (list1 x)
                            (if (lt? x (car xs))
                                (cons x xs)
                                (cons (car xs) (insert x (cdr xs))))))]
              [sort   (lambda (xs)
                        (if (null? xs)
                            '()
                            (insert (car xs) (sort (cdr xs)))))])
       sort))
```

This definition includes our first example of `letrec`, which is like `let`, but which makes each bound name visible to all the others. Internal functions `sort` and `insert` are both recursive, and because both are defined in same `letrec`, either one can also call the other.

Function `mk-insertion-sort` makes sorting flexible and easy to reuse. For example, when used with appropriate comparison functions, it can make both increasing and decreasing sorts.

135d. ⟨*transcript* 95a⟩+≡ ◁135c 137a▷

```
-> (val sort-increasing (mk-insertion-sort <))
-> (val sort-decreasing (mk-insertion-sort >))
-> (sort-increasing '(6 9 1 7 4 3 8 5 2 10))
(1 2 3 4 5 6 7 8 9 10)
-> (sort-decreasing '(6 9 1 7 4 3 8 5 2 10))
(10 9 8 7 6 5 4 3 2 1)
```


=alist?	133a
car	$\mathcal{P}$ 162a
cdr	$\mathcal{P}$ 162a
cons	$\mathcal{P}$ S313d
curry	$\mathcal{B}$ 126
emptyset	105a
exists?	$\mathcal{B}$ 130
list1	$\mathcal{B}$ 96
null?	$\mathcal{P}$ 162a

Function mk-insertion-sort implements the same pattern of computation as mk-rand, only more useful: "if you tell me when one element should come before another, I can sort a list of elements." It can equally well sort lists by length, sort pairs lexicographically, and whatever else you need. That's the power of higher-order, polymorphic functions.

2.10 PRACTICE V: CONTINUATION-PASSING STYLE

In the examples above, higher-order functions use lambda to capture *data* in a closure. Such data may include counters, predicates, equality tests, comparison functions, and more general functions. Using these functions as data doesn't really affect the *control flow* of our computations; for example, no matter what comparison function is passed to insertion sort, the insertion-sort code executes in the same way. But higher-order functions can also be used for control flow. A function call is used in the same way that a C programmer or an assembly-language programmer might use a goto: to transfer control and never come back. A function used in this way is called a *continuation*. And a continuation is even more powerful than a goto, because a continuation can take arguments![10]

As an initial example, continuations can be used to represent the exits from a computation. To develop the example, let's return to association lists. As noted in Section 2.3.8, find has a little problem: it cannot distinguish between a key that is bound to '() and a key that, like milk in the aisle, is not bound at all. Solving this problem requires a change in the interface. One possibility is to change only the value returned. For example, as in full Scheme, find could return a key-value pair if it finds the key and #f if it finds nothing. Or like Lua, it could always return a pair, one element of which would say if it found anything and the other element of which would be what it found. But the conditional logic required to tests these kinds of results can be annoying.

A more flexible alternative is to pass two *continuations* to the find routine: one to tell the find routine what to do next ("how to continue") if it succeeds, and one in case of failure. That is, when (find-c k alist succ fail) is called, one of two things must happen. If key k is found in al, then find-c calls succ with the associated value. If k is not found, find-c calls fail with no arguments:

(find-c k alist succ fail) = (succ v), when (find k alist) = v;
(find-c k alist succ fail) = (fail), otherwise.

The code looks like this:

136. ⟨*definition of* find-c 136⟩≡ (137a)

```
(define find-c (key alist success-cont failure-cont)
   (letrec
      ([search (lambda (alist)
                  (if (null? alist)
                      (failure-cont)
                      (if (equal? key (alist-first-key alist))
                          (success-cont (alist-first-attribute alist))
                          (search (cdr alist)))))])
     (search alist)))
```

[10] Your teachers probably hated goto. Maybe they considered it harmful. Or maybe they didn't even *tell* you about goto—trying to find goto in an introductory programming book can be like trying to find Trotsky in a picture of early Soviet leaders. If you've been unfairly deprived of goto, Knuth (1974) can remedy the injustice.

As an example, find-c can be used to code a "pair-or-symbol" response:

137a. ⟨*transcript* 95a⟩+≡ ◁135d 137b▷

```
-> ⟨definition of find-c 136⟩
-> (find-c 'Hello '((Hello Dolly) (Goodnight Irene))
           (lambda (v) (list2 'the-answer-is v))
           (lambda ()  'the-key-was-not-found))
(the-answer-is Dolly)
-> (find-c 'Goodbye '((Hello Dolly) (Goodnight Irene))
           (lambda (v) (list2 'the-answer-is v))
           (lambda ()  'the-key-was-not-found))
the-key-was-not-found
```


More usefully, find-c can implement a table with a default element.

137b. ⟨*transcript* 95a⟩+≡ ◁137a 137c▷

```
-> (define find-default (key table default)
     (find-c key table (lambda (x) x) (lambda () default)))
```

Before going deeper into continuations, let's exercise find-default.

Function find-default can be used to count frequencies of words, using a table with default value zero. The table maps each word to the number of times it occurs, and it's used in function freq, which finds the frequencies of all the words in a list and lists the most frequent first. In freq, words are visited by foldr, which is passed add, which looks up a word's count in the table and increases the count by 1.

137c. ⟨*transcript* 95a⟩+≡ ◁137b 137d▷

```
-> (define freq (words)
     (let
         ([add (lambda (word table)
                 (bind word (+ 1 (find-default word table 0)) table))]
          [sort (mk-insertion-sort
                 (lambda (p1 p2) (> (cadr p1) (cadr p2))))])
       (sort (foldr add '() words))))
-> (freq '(it was the best of times , it was the worst of times ! ))
((it 2) (was 2) (the 2) (of 2) (times 2) (best 1) (, 1) (worst 1) (! 1))
```

As another example, find-default can help find out what words follow another word. (Statistics about sequences of words are sometimes used to characterize authorship.) This time, the table maps each word to a set containing the words that follow it; the default element is the empty set. Because the follow-set function operates on more than one word at a time, a foldr would be a bit hard to read; instead, the code defines an auxiliary recursive function, walk:

137d. ⟨*transcript* 95a⟩+≡ ◁137c 138▷

```
-> (define followers (words)
     (letrec
       ([add  (lambda (word follower table)
                (bind word
                      (add-element follower (find-default word table '()))
                      table))]
        [walk (lambda (first rest table)
                (if (null? rest)
                    table
                    (walk (car rest)
                          (cdr rest)
                          (add first (car rest) table))))])
      (walk (car words) (cdr words) '())))
-> (followers '(it was the best of times , it was the worst of times ! ))
((it (was)) (was (the)) (the (worst best)) (best (of)) (of (times)) ...
```

add-element 131c
alist-first-attribute $\mathcal{B}$ 106
alist-first-key $\mathcal{B}$ 106
bind $\mathcal{B}$ 106
cadr $\mathcal{B}$ 96
car $\mathcal{P}$ 162a
cdr $\mathcal{P}$ 162a
equal? $\mathcal{B}$ 104
foldr $\mathcal{B}$ 131
list2 $\mathcal{B}$ 96
mk-insertion-sort 135c
null? $\mathcal{P}$ 162a

The answer doesn't fit on the page, so let's show just the words that are followed by more than one word. They can be selected by using the curried form of `filter` to accept only elements that have more than one word in their `cadr`.

138. ⟨*transcript* 95a⟩+≡ ◁137d 142b▷

```
-> (define more-than-one? (xs)
     (if (null? xs) #f (not (null? (cdr xs)))))
-> (val multi-followers
      (o
       ((curry filter) (lambda (p) (more-than-one? (cadr p))))
       followers))
-> (multi-followers
      '(it was the best of times , it was the worst of times ! ))
((the (worst best)) (times (! ,)))
-> (multi-followers
      '(now is the time for all good men to come to the aid of the party))
((the (party aid time)) (to (the come)))
```

2.10.1 *Continuation-passing style and direct style*

A function like `find-c` is said to be written in *continuation-passing style*: not only does it take continuations as arguments, but it can return only what the continuations return.[11] Continuation-passing style is easily identified by looking at a function's algebraic laws: if every right-hand side is a call to a parameter, the function is written in continuation-passing style. Continuation-passing style can also be identified by looking at the code: a function written in continuation-passing style ends either by calling a continuation or by calling another function written in continuation-passing style (including itself).

A function written in continuation-passing style is inherently polymorphic: the type of its result is whatever the continuations return, and if it's given different continuations, it can return values of different types. When the function is defined but not yet used, the continuations are not yet known, so the type of the result isn't yet known. But that type is still useful to refer to, so it is referred to abstractly as the *answer type*. The answer type can help you design appropriate continuations; for example, in `find-default`, the answer type is the type of `default`, but it is also the type of `(lambda (x) x)` applied to a value in `table`—so the type of `default` must be the same as the types of the values in `table`.

Unlike `find-c`, `find-default` is *not* written in continuation-passing style: it does not take any continuations, so it cannot return the result of calling one. A function like `find-default` is written in *direct style*. Direct style is usually easier to understand, but continuation-passing style is more flexible and powerful.

2.10.2 *Continuations for backtracking*

When it succeeds or fails, `find-c` exits. But continuations can also more sophisticated control flow, like the ability to backtrack on failure. In direct-style imperative code, backtracking is hard to get right, but using continuations and purely functional data structures, it's easy. And a backtracking problem can demonstrate the virtues of leaving the answer type unknown.

One classic problem that can be solved with backtracking is *Boolean satisfaction*. The problem is to find an assignment to a collection of variables such that a Boolean formula is satisfied, that is, a *satisfying assignment*. This problem has many

[11] Properly speaking, continuation-passing style is a representation of programs in which *all* functions, even primitive functions, end by transferring control to a continuation (Appel 1992).

applications, often in verifying the correctness of a hardware or software system. For example, on a railroad, if the signals are obeyed, no two trains should ever be on the same track at the same time, and this property can be checked by solving a very large Boolean-satisfaction problem.

The satisfaction problem can be simplified by considering only only formulas in *conjunctive normal form.* (General Boolean formulas are the subject of Exercise 41.) A conjunctive normal form is a conjunction of disjunctions of literals:

$$\begin{array}{lll} CNF & ::= D_1 \wedge D_2 \wedge \cdots \wedge D_n & \text{conjunction,} \\ D & ::= l_1 \vee l_2 \vee \cdots \vee l_m & \text{disjunction,} \\ l & ::= x \mid \neg x & \text{literal.} \end{array}$$

The x is a metavariable that may stand for any Boolean variable.

A CNF formula is satisfied if *all* of its disjunctions D_i are satisfied, and a disjunction is satisfied if *any* of is literals l_i is satisfied. A literal x is satisfied if x is true; a literal $\neg x$ is satisfied if x is false. A formula be satisfied by more than one assignment; for example, the formula $x \vee y \vee z$ is satisfied by 7 of the 8 possible assignments to x, y, z. Satisfying assignments can be found by a backtracking search. Because the satisfaction problem is NP-hard, a search might take exponential time.

The search algorithm presented below incrementally improves an *incomplete* assignment. An incomplete assignment associates values with some variables—all, none, or some number in between. An incomplete assignment is represented by an association list in which each key is the name of a variable and each value is `#t` or `#f`. A variable that doesn't appear in the list is *unassigned.*

Given disjunction D_i and an incomplete assignment `cur`, the search algorithm tries to *extend* `cur` by adding variables in such a way that D_i is satisfied. If that works, the algorithm continues by trying to extend the assignment to satisfy D_{i+1}. But if it can't satisfy D_i, the algorithm doesn't give up; instead it *backtracks* to D_{i-1}. Maybe D_{i-1} can be satisfied in a *different* way, such that it becomes possible to satisfy D_i. As an example, suppose $D_1 = x \vee y \vee z$, and the search algorithm finds the assignment $\{x \mapsto$ `#t`$, y \mapsto$ `#f`$, z \mapsto$ `#f`$\}$, which satisfies it. If $D_2 = \neg x \vee y \vee z$, the search has to go back and find a different assignment to satisfy D_1. The search can be viewed as a process of going back and forth over the D_i's, tracing a path through this graph:

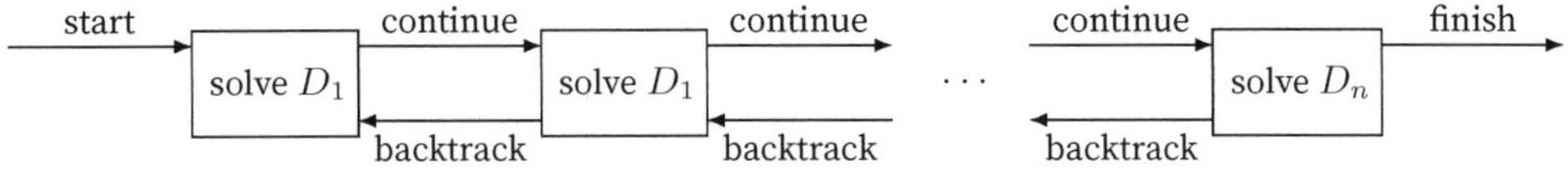

The graph is composed of solvers that look like this:

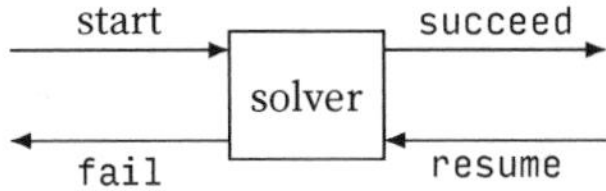

cadr	$\mathcal{B}$ 96
cdr	$\mathcal{P}$ 162a
curry	$\mathcal{B}$ 126
filter	$\mathcal{B}$ 129
followers	137d
null?	$\mathcal{P}$ 162a

Thanks to the graph structure, a solver can just tackle an individual D_i without keeping track of what it's supposed to do afterward. Its future obligations are stored in two continuations, `succeed` and `fail`, which it receives as parameters. The third continuation in the diagram, written as `resume`, is the failure continuation for the next solver: if the next solver can't succeed, it calls `resume` to ask the current solver to try something else.

The graph structure and its continuations are used to solve formulas in all three forms: CNF, D, and l. Each form is solved by its own function. For example, a CNF formula $D_1 \wedge \cdots \wedge D_n$ is solved by a function that receives the formula, an incomplete assignment `cur`, and continuations `succeed` and `fail`. When the solver is called, as represented above by the arrow labeled "start," it acts as follows:

- If `cur` cannot possibly satisfy the first disjunction D_1, call `fail` with no parameters.
- If `cur` can satisfy D_1, or if it can be extended to satisfy D_1, then compute the (possibly extended) satisfying solution, and pass it to `succeed`. In addition, because D_1 might have *more than one* solution, also pass `resume`, which `succeed` can call if it needs to backtrack and try an alternative solution.

To make this story precise requires precise specifications of the solver functions and of a representation of formulas.

The representation of CNF, the set of formulas in conjunctive normal form, is described by the following equations, which resemble the recursion equations in Section 2.5.8:

$$\begin{aligned} CNF &= LIST(D), \\ D &= LIST(LIT_{\mathcal{B}}), \\ LIT_{\mathcal{B}} &= SYM \cup \{\, \texttt{(list2 'not } x\texttt{)} \mid x \in SYM \,\}. \end{aligned}$$

In conjunctive normal form, the symbols $\wedge$ and $\vee$ are implicit. The $\neg$ symbol is represented explicitly using the Scheme symbol `not`.

In the code, the forms are referred to by names `ds`, `lits`, and `lit`. Assignments and continuations are also referred to by conventional names:

`ds`	A list of disjunctions in CNF
`lits`	A list of literals in D
`lit`	A single literal in $LIT_{\mathcal{B}}$
`cur`	A current assignment (association list)
`fail`	A failure continuation
`succeed`	A success continuation

A failure continuation takes no arguments and returns an answer. A success continuation takes two arguments—an assignment and a failure continuation—and returns an answer.

Each of the three solver functions is written in continuation-passing style.

- Calling `(find-cnf-true-assignment ds cur fail succeed)` tries to extend `cur` to an assignment that satisfies the list of disjunctions `ds`.
- Calling `(find-D-true-assignment lits cur fail succeed)` tries to extend `cur` to an assignment that satisfies any literal in the list `lits`.
- Calling `(find-lit-true-assignment lit cur fail succeed)` tries to extend `cur` to an assignment that satisfies literal `lit`.

Each function calls `succeed` on success and `fail` on failure. The specifications can be made precise using algebraic laws.

The laws for any given solver function depend on what species of formula the function solves. Each species is solved by a different algorithm, which depends on how a formula in the species is satisfied. For example, a CNF formula is satisfied if all its disjunctions are satisfied. There are two cases:

- If there are no disjunctions, then `cur` trivially satisfies them all. And when `cur` is passed to `succeed`, nothing else can be done with an empty list of disjunctions, so the resumption continuation is `fail`.

- If there is a disjunction, it should be solved by calling the solver for disjunctions: `find-D-true-assignment`. If that call fails, nothing more can be done, so its failure continuation should be `fail`. But if that call succeeds, the search needs to continue by solving the remaining disjunctions. So the *CNF* solver creates a new continuation to be passed as the success continuation. The new continuation calls `find-cnf-true-assignment` recursively, and if the recursive call fails, it backtracks by transferring control to `resume`.

Each case is described by a law:

```
(find-cnf-true-assignment '()          cur fail succeed)) = (succeed cur fail)
(find-cnf-true-assignment (cons d ds) cur fail succeed)) =
  (find-D-true-assignment d cur fail
    (lambda (cur' resume) (find-cnf-true-assignment ds cur' resume succeed)))
```

The flow of control is characteristic of continuation-passing style: in the nonempty case, only the disjunction solver knows whether `d` can be solved, but it's the *CNF* solver that decides what to do—and that decision is embodied in the continuations that are passed to the disjunction solver.

The disjunction solver works in almost the same way, except that a disjunction is satisfied if any one of its literals is satisfied. So in the nonempty case, the roles of the success and failure continuations are reversed: if a literal succeeds, the solver succeeds, but if a literal fails, the solver must try the other literals.

```
(find-D-true-assignment '()              cur fail succeed)) = (fail)
(find-D-true-assignment (cons lit lits) cur fail succeed)) =
  (find-lit-true-assignment lit cur
    (lambda () (find-D-true-assignment lits cur fail succeed))
    succeed)
```

You might be concerned that if the first literal is solved successfully, the later literals will never be examined, and some possible solutions might be missed. But those later literals `lits` are examined by the failure continuation that is passed to `find-lit-true-assignment`, which is eventually passed to `succeed` as a resumption continuation. If anything goes wrong downstream, that resumption continuation is eventually invoked, and it calls `(find-D-true-assignment lits ··· )`.

The last of the three solver functions solves a literal. It needs to know what variable appears in a literal and what value would satisfy the literal.

141a. ⟨*utility functions for solving literals* 141a⟩≡ 141b ▷

```
-> (define variable-of (lit)
     (if (symbol? lit)
        lit
        (cadr lit)))
-> (define satisfying-value (lit)
      (symbol? lit))  ; #t satisfies 'x; #f satisfies '(not x)
```

cadr 𝓑 96
find-c 136
symbol? 𝒫 162a

Because an ordinary literal is a symbol and a negated literal is a list like `(not x)`, the value that satisfies a literal `lit` is always equal to `(symbol? lit)`.

A literal is satisfied if and only if the current assignment binds the literal's variable to a satisfying value. The test uses `find-c` with a Boolean answer type.

141b. ⟨*utility functions for solving literals* 141a⟩+≡ ◁ 141a 142a ▷

```
-> (define satisfies? (alist lit)
      (find-c (variable-of lit) alist
              (lambda (b) (= b (satisfying-value lit)))
              (lambda () #f)))
```

The last solver function, find-lit-true-assignment, succeeds either when the current assignment already satisfies its literal, or when it can be made to satisfy the literal by adding a binding. There is at most one way to succeed, so the resumption continuation passed to succeed is always fail.

(find-lit-true-assignment lit cur fail succeed) = (succeed cur fail),
when cur satisfies lit

(find-lit-true-assignment lit cur fail succeed) = (succeed (bind x v cur) fail),
when x is lit's variable, cur does not bind x, and lit is satisfied by $\{x \mapsto v\}$

(find-lit-true-assignment lit cur fail succeed) = (fail), otherwise

To determine that cur does not bind x, the solver function uses find-c with yet another pair of continuations:

142a. ⟨*utility functions for solving literals* 141a⟩+≡ ◁ 141b

```
-> (define binds? (alist lit)
       (find-c (variable-of lit) alist (lambda (_) #t) (lambda () #f)))
```

All three solver functions are coded in Figure 2.5 on the facing page. And they can be used with different continuations that produce answers of different types. For example, the *CNF* solver can be used to tell whether a formula is satisfiable, to produce one solution, or to produce all solutions. To see if a formula has a solution, use find-cnf-true-assignment with a success continuation that returns #t and a failure continuation that returns false:

142b. ⟨*transcript* 95a⟩+≡ ◁ 138 142c ▷

```
-> (define satisfiable? (formula)
       (find-cnf-true-assignment formula '()
                                 (lambda () #f)
                                 (lambda (cur resume) #t)))
```

As an example, the formula

$$(x \vee y \vee z) \wedge (\neg x \vee \neg y \vee \neg z) \wedge (x \vee y \vee \neg z)$$

has a solution.

142c. ⟨*transcript* 95a⟩+≡ ◁ 142b 142d ▷

```
-> (val sample-formula '((x y z) ((not x) (not y) (not z)) (x y (not z))))
-> (satisfiable? sample-formula)
#t
```

To actually solve a formula, use a success continuation that returns cur:

142d. ⟨*transcript* 95a⟩+≡ ◁ 142c 142e ▷

```
-> (define one-solution (formula)
       (find-cnf-true-assignment formula '()
                                 (lambda () 'no-solution)
                                 (lambda (cur resume) cur)))
-> (one-solution sample-formula)
((x #t) (y #f))
```

This formula is satisfied if x is true and y is false; the value of z doesn't matter.

To find all solutions, use a success continuation that adds the current solution to the set returned by resume. (To avoid adding duplicate solutions, cur is added using al-add-element, not cons.) The failure continuation returns the empty set.

142e. ⟨*transcript* 95a⟩+≡ ◁ 142d 143b ▷

```
-> (define all-solutions (formula)
       (find-cnf-true-assignment
           formula
           '()
           (lambda () emptyset)
           (lambda (cur resume) (al-add-element cur (resume)))))
```

143a. ⟨*solver functions for CNF formulas* 143a⟩≡

```
-> (define find-lit-true-assignment (lit cur fail succeed)
     (if (satisfies? cur lit)
         (succeed cur fail)
         (if (binds? cur lit)
             (fail)
             (let ([new (bind (variable-of lit) (satisfying-value lit) cur)])
               (succeed new fail)))))
-> (define find-D-true-assignment (literals cur fail succeed)
     (if (null? literals)
        (fail)
        (find-lit-true-assignment (car literals) cur
           (lambda () (find-D-true-assignment
                                    (cdr literals) cur fail succeed))
           succeed)))
-> (define find-cnf-true-assignment (disjunctions cur fail succeed)
     (if (null? disjunctions)
        (succeed cur fail)
        (find-D-true-assignment (car disjunctions) cur fail
           (lambda (cur' resume)
              (find-cnf-true-assignment
                 (cdr disjunctions) cur' resume succeed)))))
```

Figure 2.5: The three solver functions

There are 9 distinct solutions, which is too many to show.

143b. ⟨*transcript* 95a⟩+≡ ◁142e 143c▷

```
-> (val answers (all-solutions sample-formula))
-> (length answers)
9
```

Is there a solution in which x and y are both false? Both true?

143c. ⟨*transcript* 95a⟩+≡ ◁143b 143d▷

```
-> (exists?
       (lambda (cur) (and (= #f (find 'x cur)) (= #f (find 'y cur))))
       answers)
#f
-> (exists?
       (lambda (cur) (and (= #t (find 'x cur)) (= #t (find 'y cur))))
       answers)
#t
```

It appears that x and y can be true at the same time, but not false at the same time.

Not all formulas have solutions. Most obviously, formula $x \wedge \neg x$ has no solution.

143d. ⟨*transcript* 95a⟩+≡ ◁143c 164c▷

```
-> (one-solution '((x) ((not x))))
no-solution
```

Both the solver and `find-c` demonstrate that a function written in continuation-passing style can often be used in different ways, simply by passing it different continuations with different answer types.

al-add-element	135a
and	$\mathcal{B}$
bind	$\mathcal{B}$ 106
car	$\mathcal{P}$ 162a
cdr	$\mathcal{P}$ 162a
emptyset	105a
exists?	$\mathcal{B}$ 130
find	$\mathcal{B}$ 106
find-c	136
length	98
null?	$\mathcal{P}$ 162a
satisfies?	141b
satisfying-value	141a
variable-of	141a

The operational semantics of μScheme resembles the operational semantics of Impcore. And it uses the same techniques—an abstract machine, a big-step evaluation judgment, inference rules, and so on. But Impcore and μScheme treat environments differently:

- Impcore uses three environments, which bind functions, global variables, and formal parameters, respectively. μScheme uses a single environment ρ, which binds all names.

- In Impcore, environments bind names to values. In μScheme, environments bind names to *mutable locations*, and SET changes the contents of a location, not a binding in an environment. The contents of locations are modeled by an explicit store σ, which is a function from locations to values; think of it as the machine's memory.

- In Impcore, environments are never copied, so when the semantics says a name is rebound, the implementation can mutate the relevant environment data structure. In μScheme, an environment is copied every time a `lambda` is evaluated, so it isn't safe to mutate an environment data structure. Instead, the implementation builds an extended environment with a new binding.

μScheme's semantics assumes there is an infinite supply of fresh locations; a fresh location ℓ is allocated by writing $\ell \notin \operatorname{dom} \sigma$. In Section 2.12, this allocation judgment is implemented using `malloc`, which has only a finite supply of locations. In Chapter 4, the allocation judgment is implemented using a more sophisticated allocator, which creates the illusion of an infinite supply by reusing old locations.

In μScheme, an abstract machine evaluating an expression e in environment ρ is in state $\langle e, \rho, \sigma \rangle$. The evaluation judgment takes the form $\langle e, \rho, \sigma \rangle \Downarrow \langle v, \sigma' \rangle$. This judgment says two things:

- The result of evaluating expression e in environment ρ, when the state of the store is σ, is the value v.

- The evaluation may update the store to produce a new store σ'.

Evaluating an expression never changes an environment; at most, evaluating an expression can change the store. Therefore, the right-hand side of an evaluation judgment does not need a new environment ρ'.

Evaluation never copies a store σ, and when a rule makes a new store σ', it discards the old store. Therefore each store is used exactly once; such a store is called *single-threaded* or *linear*. The store is *designed* that way because a single-threaded store can be implemented efficiently: when a rule calls for a new store, the implementation does not have to build one; instead, it mutates the previous store.

2.11.1 *Abstract syntax and values*

μScheme's abstract syntax is straightforward. It has the definitions and expressions of Impcore, plus LETX and LAMBDAX expressions. And APPLY can apply arbitrary expressions, not just names.

144. ⟨*ast.t* 144⟩≡ 145a ▷

```
Def*  = VAL    (Name name, Exp exp)
      | EXP    (Exp)
      | DEFINE (Name name, Lambda lambda)
```

145a. ⟨*ast.t* 144⟩+≡ ◁144

```
Exp*  = LITERAL (Value)
      | VAR     (Name)
      | SET     (Name name, Exp exp)
      | IFX     (Exp cond, Exp truex, Exp falsex)
      | WHILEX  (Exp cond, Exp body)
      | BEGIN   (Explist)
      | APPLY   (Exp fn, Explist actuals)
      | LETX    (Letkeyword let, Namelist xs, Explist es, Exp body)
      | LAMBDAX (Lambda)
```


Definitions of `Value` and `Lambda` are shown with the interpreter (Section 2.12); type `Letkeyword` is defined here.

145b. ⟨*type definitions for μScheme* 145b⟩≡ (S318a) 152b▷

```
typedef enum Letkeyword { LET, LETSTAR, LETREC } Letkeyword;
```

A μScheme value is a symbol, number, Boolean, empty list, cons cell, closure, or primitive function. These values are written SYMBOL(s), NUMBER(n), BOOLV(b), NIL, PAIR$\langle \ell_1, \ell_2 \rangle$, $(\!|$LAMBDA$(\langle x_1, \ldots, x_n \rangle, e), \rho |\!)$, and PRIMITIVE$(p)$. The corresponding data definition is shown with the interpreter (Section 2.12).

2.11.2 *Variables and functions*

The most interesting parts of the semantics are the rules for `lambda`, `let`, and function application. The key ideas involve mutable locations:

- Each variable refers to a location. To examine or change a variable, we must first look up its name in ρ (to find its location), then look at or change the contents of the location (which means looking at σ or producing a new σ').[12]
- Let-bindings allocate fresh locations, bind them to variables, and initialize them.
- Function application also allocates fresh locations, which hold the values of actual parameters. These locations are then bound to the names of the formal parameters of the function being applied.

Variables

The single environment makes it easy to look up the value of a variable. Lookup requires two steps: $\rho(x)$ to find the location in which x is stored, and $\sigma(\rho(x))$ to fetch its value. In a compiled system, these two steps are implemented at different times. At compile time, the compiler decides in what location to keep x. At run time, a machine instruction fetches a value from that location.

Looking up a variable doesn't change the store σ.

$$\frac{x \in \operatorname{dom} \rho \qquad \rho(x) \in \operatorname{dom} \sigma}{\langle \text{VAR}(x), \rho, \sigma \rangle \Downarrow \langle \sigma(\rho(x)), \sigma \rangle} \quad (\text{VAR})$$

Assignment translates the name into a location, then changes the value in that location, producing a new store. The evaluation of the right-hand side may also change the store, from σ to σ'.

$$\frac{x \in \operatorname{dom} \rho \qquad \rho(x) = \ell \qquad \langle e, \rho, \sigma \rangle \Downarrow \langle v, \sigma' \rangle}{\langle \text{SET}(x, e), \rho, \sigma \rangle \Downarrow \langle v, \sigma'\{\ell \mapsto v\} \rangle} \quad (\text{ASSIGN})$$

[12] In μScheme, two variables never refer to the same location. If x and y did refer to the same location, then when x was mutated, y would change. This behavior is called "aliasing," and it makes compiler writers miserable. μScheme variables cannot alias (Exercise 51).

The threading of the store is subtle; the conclusion must extend σ', not σ. If the conclusion were to extend σ, the semantics would be saying that changes made by e should be undone. This behavior would surprise the programmer, and it would force the implementor to save a copy of the old σ and then reinstate it after the evaluation of e. At considerable expense.

Let, let, and letrec*

A LET expression evaluates all the right-hand sides, then binds the names to the resulting values, and finally evaluates its body in the resulting environment. Nothing is added to the environment ρ until all the right-hand sides have been evaluated.

$$\frac{\begin{array}{c} x_1,\ldots,x_n \text{ all distinct}\\ \ell_1,\ldots,\ell_n \notin \operatorname{dom}\sigma_n \text{ (and all distinct)}\\ \sigma_0=\sigma \\ \langle e_1,\rho,\sigma_0\rangle \Downarrow \langle v_1,\sigma_1\rangle \\ \vdots \\ \langle e_n,\rho,\sigma_{n-1}\rangle \Downarrow \langle v_n,\sigma_n\rangle \\ \langle e, \rho\{x_1\mapsto \ell_1,\ldots,x_n\mapsto\ell_n\}, \sigma_n\{\ell_1\mapsto v_1,\ldots,\ell_n\mapsto v_n\}\rangle \Downarrow \langle v,\sigma'\rangle\end{array}}{\langle \text{LET}(\langle x_1,e_1,\ldots,x_n,e_n\rangle, e),\rho,\sigma\rangle \Downarrow\langle v,\sigma'\rangle} \qquad (\text{LET})$$

Locations $\ell_1,\ldots,\ell_n$ are not only fresh but also mutually distinct.

By contrast, a LETSTAR expression binds the result of each evaluation into the environment immediately. The action is revealed by the subscripts on ρ.

$$\frac{\begin{array}{llll} & & \rho_0=\rho & \sigma_0=\sigma \\ \langle e_1,\rho_0,\sigma_0\rangle \Downarrow \langle v_1,\sigma_0'\rangle & \ell_1\notin\operatorname{dom}\sigma_0' & \rho_1=\rho_0\{x_1\mapsto\ell_1\} & \sigma_1=\sigma_0'\{\ell_1\mapsto v_1\} \\ & & \vdots & \\ \langle e_n,\rho_{n-1},\sigma_{n-1}\rangle \Downarrow \langle v_n,\sigma_{n-1}'\rangle & & & \\ & \ell_n\notin\operatorname{dom}\sigma_{n-1}' & \rho_n=\rho_{n-1}\{x_n\mapsto\ell_n\} & \sigma_n=\sigma_{n-1}'\{\ell_n\mapsto v_n\} \\ \langle e,\rho_n,\sigma_n\rangle \Downarrow \langle v,\sigma'\rangle & & & \end{array}}{\langle \text{LETSTAR}(\langle x_1,e_1,\ldots,x_n,e_n\rangle, e),\rho,\sigma\rangle \Downarrow\langle v,\sigma'\rangle}$$

(LETSTAR)

Finally, LETREC binds the locations into the environment *before* evaluating the expressions, so that references to the new names are valid in every right-hand side, and the names stand for the new locations, not for any old ones.

$$\frac{\begin{array}{c} \ell_1,\ldots,\ell_n \notin \operatorname{dom}\sigma \text{ (and all distinct)}\\ x_1,\ldots,x_n \text{ all distinct}\\ e_i \text{ has the form LAMBDA}(\cdots),\ 1\le i\le n \\ \rho'=\rho\{x_1\mapsto\ell_1,\ldots,x_n\mapsto\ell_n\} \\ \sigma_0=\sigma\{\ell_1\mapsto\text{unspecified},\ldots,\ell_n\mapsto\text{unspecified}\} \\ \langle e_1,\rho',\sigma_0\rangle \Downarrow \langle v_1,\sigma_1\rangle \\ \vdots \\ \langle e_n,\rho',\sigma_{n-1}\rangle \Downarrow \langle v_n,\sigma_n\rangle \\ \langle e,\rho',\sigma_n\{\ell_1\mapsto v_1,\ldots,\ell_n\mapsto v_n\}\rangle \Downarrow \langle v,\sigma'\rangle \end{array}}{\langle \text{LETREC}(\langle x_1,e_1,\ldots,x_n,e_n\rangle, e),\rho,\sigma\rangle \Downarrow\langle v,\sigma'\rangle} \qquad (\text{LETREC})$$

The contents of $\ell_1,\ldots,\ell_n$ are not specified until *after* all the $e_1,\ldots,e_n$ have been evaluated; informally, the e_i's are evaluated with the x_i's bound to new, uninitialized locations. Until the locations are initialized, using them is unsafe; using a location that contains "unspecified" is an *unchecked* run-time error. For safety, as in full Scheme, the evaluation of every e_i must be independent of the value of any x_j, and it also must not mutate any x_j. In other words, evaluating e_i must neither read nor write the contents of any location ℓ_j. To guarantee that evaluating e_i does not read or write *any* locations, μScheme insists that each e_i be a LAMBDA expression.

Function abstraction; function application; statically scoped closures

Functional abstraction wraps the current environment, along with a lambda expression, in a closure. LAMBDA *copies* the current environment. It is because environments can be copied that they map names to locations, not values; otherwise different closures could not share a mutable location. (One example of such sharing is the "resettable counter" in Section 2.7.1.)

$$\frac{x_1, \ldots, x_n \text{ all distinct}}{\langle \text{LAMBDA}(\langle x_1, \ldots, x_n \rangle, e), \rho, \sigma \rangle \Downarrow \langle (\!|\text{LAMBDA}(\langle x_1, \ldots, x_n \rangle, e), \rho |\!), \sigma \rangle} \quad (\text{MkClosure})$$

When a closure $(\!|\text{LAMBDA}(\langle x_1, \ldots, x_n \rangle, e_c), \rho_c |\!)$ is applied, the body of the function, e_c, is evaluated using the environment in the *closure*, ρ_c, which is extended by binding the formal parameters to *fresh* locations $\ell_1, \ldots, \ell_n$. These locations are initialized with the values of the actual parameters; afterward, the body can change them.

$$\frac{\begin{array}{c} \ell_1, \ldots, \ell_n \notin \text{dom}\, \sigma_n \text{ (and all distinct)} \\ \langle e, \rho, \sigma \rangle \Downarrow \langle (\!|\text{LAMBDA}(\langle x_1, \ldots, x_n \rangle, e_c), \rho_c |\!), \sigma_0 \rangle \\ \langle e_1, \rho, \sigma_0 \rangle \Downarrow \langle v_1, \sigma_1 \rangle \\ \vdots \\ \langle e_n, \rho, \sigma_{n-1} \rangle \Downarrow \langle v_n, \sigma_n \rangle \\ \langle e_c, \rho_c\{x_1 \mapsto \ell_1, \ldots, x_n \mapsto \ell_n\}, \sigma_n\{\ell_1 \mapsto v_1, \ldots, \ell_n \mapsto v_n\} \rangle \Downarrow \langle v, \sigma' \rangle \end{array}}{\langle \text{APPLY}(e, e_1, \ldots, e_n), \rho, \sigma \rangle \Downarrow \langle v, \sigma' \rangle} \quad (\text{ApplyClosure})$$

The ApplyClosure rule closely resembles the ApplyUser rule used in Impcore. The crucial differences are as follows:

- In μScheme, the function to be applied is designated by an arbitrary expression, which must evaluate to a closure. In Impcore, the function is designated by a name, which is looked up in ϕ to find a user-defined function. Both a μScheme closure and an Impcore user-defined function contain formal parameters and a function body, but only the closure contains the all-important environment ρ_c, which stores the locations of the variables mentioned in the body.[13] In Impcore, no such environment is needed; every function is defined at top level, so every variable is either a formal parameter or can be found in the global environment ξ.

- In μScheme, the parameters are added not to the empty environment but to the environment ρ_c stored in the closure. And like `let`-bound names, the formal parameters are bound to fresh locations, not directly to values.

As in Impcore, the evaluation of e_c is independent of the environment ρ of the calling function, so a μScheme function behaves the same way no matter where it is called from. (Also as in Impcore, the evaluation is *not* independent of the store σ at the point of the call, so when mutable state is involved, a μScheme function may

[13] In my implementation, the environment binds all variables that are in scope, not just those that are mentioned in the body of the `lambda` expression. Such promiscuous binding could use memory unnecessarily, and it could add to the expense of applying the closure. For details, see Exercise 19 on page 299 in Chapter 4 and Exercise 10 on page 325 in Chapter 5.

behave differently when called at different *times,* even when called from the same *place* in the source code. A good example is the counter-stepping function from Section 2.7.1.)

The APPLYCLOSURE rule describes an implementation of first-class, nested functions called *statically scoped closures.* The "closure" part you know about; "statically scoped" means that the meanings of the variables (scope) are determined by the compile-time (static) context in which the code appears—those variables are either bound in the global environment or are bound by statically enclosing `let`s and `lambda`s. Because static scoping is determined by properties of the text, it is sometimes also called *lexical scoping.* As an example of local reasoning about a static context, a programmer (or an implementation of Scheme) who encounters an expression like `(lambda (x) (+ x y))` can discover what `y` is simply by searching "outward" for a `let` or `lambda` that binds `y`. The search stops at the enclosing definition, which is at top level; if the search reaches top level without finding a `let` binding or `lambda` binding for `y`, then `y` must be bound in the global environment by a `val` or `define`.

Dynamic scoping: An alternative to static scoping Closures are an innovation of Scheme; they were not part of original Lisp. Original Lisp represented every function as a bare LAMBDA expression with formal parameters and a body, in much the same way as Impcore represents a user-defined function. This representation admits of a very simple implementation, which never has to copy an environment. Original Lisp treated LAMBDA as a value, using the following rule for function abstraction.

$$\frac{}{\langle \text{LAMBDA}(\langle x_1, \ldots, x_n \rangle, e), \rho, \sigma \rangle \Downarrow \langle \text{LAMBDA}(\langle x_1, \ldots, x_n \rangle, e), \sigma \rangle}$$

(LAMBDA for original Lisp)

Original Lisp applied a function by evaluating its body in the environment of its *caller,* extended with bindings of formal parameters:

$$\frac{\begin{array}{c} \ell_1, \ldots, \ell_n \notin \text{dom}\, \sigma_n \text{ (and all distinct)} \\ \langle e, \rho, \sigma \rangle \Downarrow \langle \text{LAMBDA}(\langle x_1, \ldots, x_n \rangle, e_c), \sigma_0 \rangle \\ \langle e_1, \rho, \sigma_0 \rangle \Downarrow \langle v_1, \sigma_1 \rangle \\ \vdots \\ \langle e_n, \rho, \sigma_{n-1} \rangle \Downarrow \langle v_n, \sigma_n \rangle \\ \langle e_c, \rho\{x_1 \mapsto \ell_1, \ldots, x_n \mapsto \ell_n\}, \sigma_n\{\ell_1 \mapsto v_1, \ldots, \ell_n \mapsto v_n\} \rangle \Downarrow \langle v, \sigma' \rangle \end{array}}{\langle \text{APPLY}(e, e_1, \ldots, e_n), \rho, \sigma \rangle \Downarrow \langle v, \sigma' \rangle}.$$

(APPLYLAMBDA for original Lisp)

This rule is much easier to implement than Scheme's rule, but it makes `lambda` much less useful; in original Lisp, higher-order functions that contain inner `lambda`s, like `o` and `curry`, don't work as expected.

To find the location of a free variable, an implementation of original Lisp looks at the calling function, and its caller, and so on. The context in which a function is called is a dynamic property, and the original rule is a form of *dynamic scoping.* Dynamic scoping came about because McCarthy didn't realize that closures were needed; when the original behavior was called to his attention, he characterized the semantics as a bug in the Lisp interpreter. Scheme's static scoping was widely seen as an improvement, and in the 1980s, static scoping was adopted in Common Lisp. If you want to experiment with a language that has dynamic scoping, try Emacs Lisp. Some interesting examples are presented by Abelson and Sussman (1985, pp. 321–325).

Formal parameters in an independent environment

Function application takes the environment in a closure and extends it with bindings for formal parameters:

$$\rho_c\{x_1 \mapsto v_1, \ldots, x_n \mapsto v_n\}.$$

The idea is that formal parameters hide outer variables of the same name. To express that idea formally, formal parameters can be placed in an environment of their own: $\rho_f = \{x_1 \mapsto v_1, \ldots, x_n \mapsto v_n\}$. The two environments can then be combined using a $+$ symbol: $\rho_c + \rho_f$. The combined environment, in which the body of the function is evaluated, obeys the following laws:

$$\begin{aligned} \mathrm{dom}(\rho_c + \rho_f) &= \mathrm{dom}\,\rho_c \cup \mathrm{dom}\,\rho_f, \\ (\rho_c + \rho_f)(x) &= \begin{cases} \rho_f(x), & \text{when } x \in \mathrm{dom}\,\rho_f \\ \rho_c(x), & \text{when } x \notin \mathrm{dom}\,\rho_f. \end{cases} \end{aligned}$$

To look for x in a combined environment, we look first in ρ_f, and only if we don't find it do we look in ρ_c. That is, ρ_f hides ρ_c. Combined environments start to shine when there are more of them; for example, in Smalltalk-80, the body of a method is evaluated in an environment that combines class variables, instance variables, formal parameters, and local variables.

2.11.3 *Rules for other expressions*

The rules for evaluating the other expressions of μScheme are very similar to the corresponding rules of Impcore.

As in Impcore, a literal value evaluates to itself without changing the store.

$$\frac{}{\langle \text{LITERAL}(v), \rho, \sigma\rangle \Downarrow \langle v, \sigma\rangle} \quad \text{(LITERAL)}$$

Conditionals, loops, and sequences are evaluated as in Impcore, except that falsehood is represented by BOOLV(#f), not 0.

$$\frac{\langle e_1, \rho, \sigma\rangle \Downarrow \langle v_1, \sigma'\rangle \qquad v_1 \neq \text{BOOLV}(\texttt{\#f}) \qquad \langle e_2, \rho, \sigma'\rangle \Downarrow \langle v_2, \sigma''\rangle}{\langle \text{IF}(e_1, e_2, e_3), \rho, \sigma\rangle \Downarrow \langle v_2, \sigma''\rangle} \quad \text{(IFTRUE)}$$

$$\frac{\langle e_1, \rho, \sigma\rangle \Downarrow \langle v_1, \sigma'\rangle \qquad v_1 = \text{BOOLV}(\texttt{\#f}) \qquad \langle e_3, \rho, \sigma'\rangle \Downarrow \langle v_3, \sigma''\rangle}{\langle \text{IF}(e_1, e_2, e_3), \rho, \sigma\rangle \Downarrow \langle v_3, \sigma''\rangle} \quad \text{(IFFALSE)}$$

$$\frac{\begin{array}{c}\langle e_1, \rho, \sigma\rangle \Downarrow \langle v_1, \sigma'\rangle \qquad v_1 \neq \text{BOOLV}(\texttt{\#f}) \\ \langle e_2, \rho, \sigma'\rangle \Downarrow \langle v_2, \sigma''\rangle \qquad \langle \text{WHILE}(e_1, e_2), \rho, \sigma''\rangle \Downarrow \langle v_3, \sigma'''\rangle\end{array}}{\langle \text{WHILE}(e_1, e_2), \rho, \sigma\rangle \Downarrow \langle v_3, \sigma'''\rangle} \quad \text{(WHILEITERATE)}$$

$$\frac{\langle e_1, \rho, \sigma\rangle \Downarrow \langle v_1, \sigma'\rangle \qquad v_1 = \text{BOOLV}(\texttt{\#f})}{\langle \text{WHILE}(e_1, e_2), \rho, \sigma\rangle \Downarrow \langle \text{BOOLV}(\texttt{\#f}), \sigma'\rangle} \quad \text{(WHILEEND)}$$

$$\frac{}{\langle \text{BEGIN}(), \rho, \sigma\rangle \Downarrow \langle \text{BOOLV}(\texttt{\#f}), \sigma\rangle} \quad \text{(EMPTYBEGIN)}$$

$$\frac{\begin{array}{c}\langle e_1, \rho, \sigma_0\rangle \Downarrow \langle v_1, \sigma_1\rangle \\ \langle e_2, \rho, \sigma_1\rangle \Downarrow \langle v_2, \sigma_2\rangle \\ \vdots \\ \langle e_n, \rho, \sigma_{n-1}\rangle \Downarrow \langle v_n, \sigma_n\rangle\end{array}}{\langle \text{BEGIN}(e_1, e_2, \ldots, e_n), \rho, \sigma_0\rangle \Downarrow \langle v_n, \sigma_n\rangle} \quad \text{(BEGIN)}$$

Primitives

Of μScheme's many primitives, only a few are presented here.

Arithmetic Primitive arithmetic operations obey the same rules as in Impcore, but they have to be notated differently: in Impcore, every value is a number, but in μScheme, only a value of the form $\text{NUMBER}(n)$ is a number. As in Chapter 1, addition serves as a model for all the arithmetic primitives.

$$\frac{\begin{array}{c}\langle e, \rho, \sigma_0\rangle \Downarrow \langle \text{PRIMITIVE}(\texttt{+}), \sigma_1\rangle \\ \langle e_1, \rho, \sigma_1\rangle \Downarrow \langle \text{NUMBER}(n), \sigma_2\rangle \\ \langle e_2, \rho, \sigma_2\rangle \Downarrow \langle \text{NUMBER}(m), \sigma_3\rangle\end{array}}{\langle \text{APPLY}(e, e_1, e_2), \rho, \sigma_0\rangle \Downarrow \langle \text{NUMBER}(n+m), \sigma_3\rangle} \quad (\text{APPLYADD})$$

Equality Testing for equality is a bit tricky. Primitive function `=` implements a relation $v \equiv v'$, which is defined by these rules:

$$\frac{m = n \text{ (identity of numbers)}}{\text{NUMBER}(n) \equiv \text{NUMBER}(m)} \quad (\text{EQNUMBER})$$

$$\frac{s = s' \text{ (identity of symbols)}}{\text{SYMBOL}(s) \equiv \text{SYMBOL}(s')} \quad (\text{EQSYMBOL})$$

$$\frac{b = b' \text{ (identity of Booleans)}}{\text{BOOLV}(b) \equiv \text{BOOLV}(b')} \quad (\text{EQBOOL})$$

$$\frac{}{\text{NIL} \equiv \text{NIL}}. \quad (\text{EQNIL})$$

The complementary relation is written $v \not\equiv v'$; it holds if and only if there is no proof of $v \equiv v'$. It is worth noting that $\text{PAIR}\langle \ell_1, \ell_2\rangle \not\equiv \text{PAIR}\langle \ell_1, \ell_2\rangle$. That is, cons cells never compare equal, even when they are identical.

The behavior of primitive equality is defined using relations $\equiv$ and $\not\equiv$.

$$\frac{\begin{array}{c}\langle e, \rho, \sigma_0\rangle \Downarrow \langle \text{PRIMITIVE}(\texttt{=}), \sigma_1\rangle \\ \langle e_1, \rho, \sigma_1\rangle \Downarrow \langle v_1, \sigma_2\rangle \\ \langle e_2, \rho, \sigma_2\rangle \Downarrow \langle v_2, \sigma_3\rangle \\ v_1 \equiv v_2\end{array}}{\langle \text{APPLY}(e, e_1, e_2), \rho, \sigma_0\rangle \Downarrow \langle \text{BOOLV}(\texttt{\#t}), \sigma_3\rangle} \quad (\text{APPLYEQTRUE})$$

$$\frac{\begin{array}{c}\langle e, \rho, \sigma_0\rangle \Downarrow \langle \text{PRIMITIVE}(\texttt{=}), \sigma_1\rangle \\ \langle e_1, \rho, \sigma_1\rangle \Downarrow \langle v_1, \sigma_2\rangle \\ \langle e_2, \rho, \sigma_2\rangle \Downarrow \langle v_2, \sigma_3\rangle \\ v_1 \not\equiv v_2 \text{ (i.e., no proof of } v_1 \equiv v_2)\end{array}}{\langle \text{APPLY}(e, e_1, e_2), \rho, \sigma_0\rangle \Downarrow \langle \text{BOOLV}(\texttt{\#f}), \sigma_3\rangle} \quad (\text{APPLYEQFALSE})$$

Printing As in Impcore, the operational semantics takes no formal notice of printing, so the semantics of `println` are those of the identity function.

$$\frac{\begin{array}{c}\langle e, \rho, \sigma_0\rangle \Downarrow \langle \text{PRIMITIVE}(\texttt{println}), \sigma_1\rangle \\ \langle e_1, \rho, \sigma_1\rangle \Downarrow \langle v, \sigma_2\rangle\end{array}}{\langle \text{APPLY}(e, e_1), \rho, \sigma_0\rangle \Downarrow \langle v, \sigma_2\rangle \qquad \text{while printing } v} \quad (\text{APPLYPRINTLN})$$

Primitive `println` has the same semantics as `print`, but `printu` has a more restrictive semantics: it is defined only when the code point is a suitable number.

$$\frac{\begin{array}{c}\langle e, \rho, \sigma_0\rangle \Downarrow \langle \text{PRIMITIVE}(\texttt{printu}), \sigma_1\rangle \\ \langle e_1, \rho, \sigma_1\rangle \Downarrow \langle \text{NUMBER}(n), \sigma_2\rangle \\ 0 \leq n < 2^{16}\end{array}}{\langle \text{APPLY}(e, e_1), \rho, \sigma_0\rangle \Downarrow \langle \text{NUMBER}(n), \sigma_2\rangle \qquad \text{while printing the UTF-8 coding of } n} \quad (\text{APPLYPRINTU})$$

List operations The primitive CONS builds a new cons cell. The cons cell is a pair of *locations* that hold the values of the car and cdr.

$$\frac{\begin{array}{c}\langle e,\rho,\sigma_0\rangle \Downarrow \langle \text{PRIMITIVE}(\texttt{cons}),\sigma_1\rangle \\ \langle e_1,\rho,\sigma_1\rangle \Downarrow \langle v_1,\sigma_2\rangle \\ \langle e_2,\rho,\sigma_2\rangle \Downarrow \langle v_2,\sigma_3\rangle \\ \ell_1 \notin \operatorname{dom}\sigma_3 \qquad \ell_2 \notin \operatorname{dom}\sigma_3 \qquad \ell_1 \neq \ell_2\end{array}}{\langle \text{APPLY}(e,e_1,e_2),\rho,\sigma_0\rangle \Downarrow \langle \text{PAIR}\langle \ell_1,\ell_2\rangle, \sigma_3\{\ell_1 \mapsto v_1, \ell_2 \mapsto v_2\}\rangle} \quad (\text{CONS})$$

Primitives car and cdr observe cons cells.

$$\frac{\begin{array}{c}\langle e,\rho,\sigma_0\rangle \Downarrow \langle \text{PRIMITIVE}(\texttt{car}),\sigma_1\rangle \\ \langle e_1,\rho,\sigma_1\rangle \Downarrow \langle \text{PAIR}\langle \ell_1,\ell_2\rangle,\sigma_2\rangle\end{array}}{\langle \text{APPLY}(e,e_1),\rho,\sigma_0\rangle \Downarrow \langle \sigma_2(\ell_1),\sigma_2\rangle} \quad (\text{CAR})$$

$$\frac{\begin{array}{c}\langle e,\rho,\sigma_0\rangle \Downarrow \langle \text{PRIMITIVE}(\texttt{cdr}),\sigma_1\rangle \\ \langle e_1,\rho,\sigma_1\rangle \Downarrow \langle \text{PAIR}\langle \ell_1,\ell_2\rangle,\sigma_2\rangle\end{array}}{\langle \text{APPLY}(e,e_1),\rho,\sigma_0\rangle \Downarrow \langle \sigma_2(\ell_2),\sigma_2\rangle} \quad (\text{CDR})$$

If the result of evaluating e_1 is not a PAIR, rules CAR and CDR do not apply, and the abstract machine gets stuck. In such a case, my interpreter issues a run-time error message.

2.11.4 *Rules for evaluating definitions*

A definition typically adds a new binding to the environment and changes the store. Its evaluation judgment is $\langle d,\rho,\sigma\rangle \rightarrow \langle \rho',\sigma'\rangle$, which says that evaluating definition d in environment ρ with store σ produces a new environment ρ' and a new store σ'.

Global variables

When a global variable x is bound to an expression, what happens depends on whether x is already bound in ρ. If x is bound, then VAL is equivalent to SET: the environment is unchanged, but the store is updated.

$$\frac{\begin{array}{c}x \in \operatorname{dom}\rho \\ \langle e,\rho,\sigma\rangle \Downarrow \langle v,\sigma'\rangle\end{array}}{\langle \text{VAL}(x,e),\rho,\sigma\rangle \rightarrow \langle \rho, \sigma'\{\rho(x) \mapsto v\}\rangle} \quad (\text{DEFINEOLDGLOBAL})$$

If x is *not* already bound, VAL allocates a fresh location ℓ, extends the environment to bind x to ℓ, evaluates the expression in the new environment, and stores the result in ℓ:

$$\frac{\begin{array}{c}x \notin \operatorname{dom}\rho \qquad \ell \notin \operatorname{dom}\sigma \\ \langle e,\rho\{x \mapsto \ell\},\sigma\{\ell \mapsto \text{unspecified}\}\rangle \Downarrow \langle v,\sigma'\rangle\end{array}}{\langle \text{VAL}(x,e),\rho,\sigma\rangle \rightarrow \langle \rho\{x \mapsto \ell\}, \sigma'\{\ell \mapsto v\}\rangle}. \quad (\text{DEFINENEWGLOBAL})$$

The "unspecified" value stored in ℓ effectively means that an adversary gets to look at your code and choose the least convenient value. Code that depends on an unspecified value invites disaster, or at least an unchecked run-time error.

Why does VAL add the binding to ρ before a value is available to store in ℓ? To enable a recursive function to refer to itself. To see the need, consider what would happen in the following definition of factorial if the binding were not added until after the lambda expression was evaluated:

```
(val fact
  (lambda (n)
    (if (= n 0)
      1
      (* n (fact (- n 1))))))
```

If the binding isn't added before the closure is created, then when the body of the lambda expression is evaluated, it won't be able to call fact—because the environment saved in the closure won't contain a binding for fact. That's why the semantics for VAL in μScheme is different from the semantics for VAL in Impcore.

Top-level functions

DEFINE is syntactic sugar for a VAL binding to a LAMBDA expression.

$$\frac{\langle \text{VAL}(f, \text{LAMBDA}(\langle x_1, \ldots, x_n \rangle, e)), \rho, \sigma \rangle \to \langle \rho', \sigma' \rangle}{\langle \text{DEFINE}(f, \langle x_1, \ldots, x_n \rangle, e), \rho, \sigma \rangle \to \langle \rho', \sigma' \rangle} \qquad \text{(DEFINEFUNCTION)}$$

Top-level expressions

A top-level expression is syntactic sugar for a binding to the global variable it.

$$\frac{\langle \text{VAL}(\texttt{it}, e), \rho, \sigma \rangle \to \langle \rho', \sigma' \rangle}{\langle \text{EXP}(e), \rho, \sigma \rangle \to \langle \rho', \sigma' \rangle} \qquad \text{(EVALEXP)}$$

2.12 THE INTERPRETER

μScheme's interpreter, like Impcore's interpreter, is decomposed into modules that have well-defined interfaces. Modules for names and printing are reused from Chapter 1, as is. Because Scheme's environments and values are different from Impcore's, environment and value modules are new. And the abstract-syntax module is generated automatically; its representations and code are derived from the data definition shown in Section 2.11.1.

2.12.1 *Representation of values*

The representation of values is generated from the data definition shown here. The empty list is called NIL, which is its name in Common Lisp. A function is represented by a CLOSURE, which is a Lambda with an environment; the Lambda structure contains the function's formal-parameter names and body.

152a. ⟨*value.t* 152a⟩≡

```
Lambda  = (Namelist formals, Exp body)
Value   = SYM   (Name)
        | NUM   (int32_t)
        | BOOLV (bool)
        | NIL
        | PAIR      (Value *car, Value *cdr)
        | CLOSURE   (Lambda lambda, Env env)
        | PRIMITIVE (int tag, Primitive *function)
```

152b. ⟨*type definitions for μScheme* 145b⟩+≡ (S318a) ◁145b 153a▷

```
typedef Value (Primitive)(Exp e, int tag, Valuelist vs);
```

Table 2.6: Correspondence between μScheme semantics and code

Semantics	Concept	Interpreter
d	Definition	Def (page 144)
e	Expression	Exp (page 144)
ℓ	Location	Value *
x	Name	Name (page 43)
v	Value	Value (page 152)
ρ	Environment	Env (page 153)
σ	Store	Machine memory (the C heap)
$\langle e, \rho, \sigma \rangle \Downarrow \langle v, \sigma' \rangle$	Expression evaluation	eval(e, ρ) $= v$, with σ updated to σ' (page 155)
$\langle d, \rho, \sigma \rangle \to \langle \rho', \sigma' \rangle$	Definition evaluation	evaldef(d, ρ, echo) $= \rho'$, with σ updated to σ' (page 159)
$x \in \operatorname{dom} \rho$	Definedness	find(x, ρ) != NULL (page 153)
$\rho(x)$	Location lookup	find(x, ρ) (page 153)
$\sigma(\rho(x))$	Value lookup	*find(x, ρ) (page 153)
$\rho\{x \mapsto \ell\}$	Binding	bindalloc (page 153)
$\ell \notin \operatorname{dom} \sigma$	Allocation	bindalloc (page 153)
$\sigma\{\ell \mapsto v\}$	Store update	*ℓ = v

Why does a Primitive take so many arguments? Shouldn't a primitive function just take a Valuelist and return a Value? No. If a primitive fails, it needs to show where the failure occurred; that's the Exp e. And by using an integer tag, a single Primitive function can implement multiple μScheme primitives. The C function that implements μScheme's arithmetic primitives, for example, makes it easy for those primitives to share the code that ensures both arguments are numbers. Implementations of the primitives appear in Section 2.12.5 and in Appendix L.

2.12.2 Interfaces

The Environment and the Store

In the operational semantics, the store σ models the memory of the abstract machine. In the implementation, the store is represented by the memory of the real machine; a location is represented by a C pointer of type Value *. An environment Env maps names to pointers; find(x, ρ) returns $\rho(x)$ whenever $x \in \operatorname{dom} \rho$; when $x \notin \operatorname{dom} \rho$, it returns NULL.

type Exp $\mathcal{A}$
type Name 43a
type Namelist 43a
type Value $\mathcal{A}$
type Valuelist S309c

153a. ⟨*type definitions for μScheme* 145b⟩+≡ (S318a) ◁152b
```
typedef struct Env *Env;
```

153b. ⟨*function prototypes for μScheme* 153b⟩≡ (S318a) 153c▷
```
Value *find(Name name, Env env);
```

A location is allocated, initialized, and bound to a name in one step, by function bindalloc. Formally, when called with store σ, bindalloc(x, v, ρ) chooses an $\ell \notin \operatorname{dom} \sigma$, updates the store to be $\sigma\{\ell \mapsto v\}$, and returns the extended environment $\rho\{x \mapsto \ell\}$.

153c. ⟨*function prototypes for μScheme* 153b⟩+≡ (S318a) ◁153b 154a▷
```
Env bindalloc     (Name name,    Value v,      Env env);
Env bindallocList(Namelist xs, Valuelist vs, Env env);
```

Calling bindalloclist($\langle x_1, \ldots, x_n \rangle, \langle v_1, \ldots, v_n \rangle, \rho$) does the same job for a list of values, returning $\rho\{x_1 \mapsto \ell_1, \ldots, x_n \mapsto \ell_n\}$, where $\ell_1, \ldots, \ell_n$ are fresh locations, which bindalloclist initializes to values $v_1, \ldots, v_n$.

Although environments use a different interface from Impcore, their representation is unchanged. In both interpreters, an environment is represented using mutable state; that is, the environment associates each name with a pointer to a location that can be assigned to. Impcore's interface hides the use of locations, but μScheme's interface exposes them. As a result, find can do the work of both isvalbound and fetchval.

Impcore	*μScheme*
isvalbound(x, ρ)	find(x, ρ) $\neq$ NULL
fetchval(x, ρ)	$*$find(x, ρ)

Using this interface, a μScheme variable can be mutated without using a function like Impcore's bindval; code just assigns to the location returned by find. As long as $x \in \operatorname{dom} \rho$, bindval($x, v, \rho$) is replaced by $*$find(x, ρ) = v. Leveraging C pointers and mutable locations makes μScheme's interface simpler than Impcore's.

Allocation

The fresh locations created by bindalloc and bindalloclist come from allocate. Calling allocate(v) finds a location $\ell \notin \operatorname{dom} \sigma$, stores v in ℓ (thereby updating σ), and returns ℓ.

154a. ⟨*function prototypes for μScheme* 153b⟩+≡ (S318a) ◁ 153c 154b ▷

```
Value *allocate(Value v);
```

Allocation is described in great detail in Chapter 4.

Values

Values are represented as specified by the data definition in chunk 152a. For convenience, values #t and #f are always available in C variables truev and falsev.

154b. ⟨*function prototypes for μScheme* 153b⟩+≡ (S318a) ◁ 154a 154c ▷

```
extern Value truev, falsev;
```

Values can be tested for truth or falsehood by function istrue; any value different from #f is regarded as true.

154c. ⟨*function prototypes for μScheme* 153b⟩+≡ (S318a) ◁ 154b 154d ▷

```
bool istrue(Value v);
```

When an unspecified value is called for by the semantics, one can be obtained by calling function unspecified.

154d. ⟨*function prototypes for μScheme* 153b⟩+≡ (S318a) ◁ 154c 155a ▷

```
Value unspecified(void);
```

If you get the μScheme interpreter to crash, your μScheme code is probably looking at a value returned by unspecified. That's an unchecked run-time error.

Evaluation

As in Impcore, the $\to$ relation in the operational semantics is implemented by evaldef, and the $\Downarrow$ relation is implemented by eval. The store σ is not passed or returned explicitly; it is represented by the C store, i.e., by the contents of memory. Because σ is *single-threaded*—every store is used exactly once and then discarded—the semantics can be implemented by updating memory in place.

Table 2.7: Specifications used in print and fprint

%%	Print a percent sign
%d	Print an integer in decimal
%e	Print an Exp
%E	Print an Explist (list of Exp)
%\	Print a Lambda (in ASCII, the \ character is a common proxy for λ)
%n	Print a Name
%N	Print a Namelist (list of Name)
%p	Print a Par
%P	Print a Parlist (list of Par)
%r	Print an Env
%s	Print a char* (string)
%t	Print a Def
%v	Print a Value
%V	Print a Valuelist (list of Value)

For example, eval(e, ρ), when evaluated with store σ, finds a v and a σ' such that $\langle e, \rho, \sigma\rangle \Downarrow \langle v, \sigma'\rangle$, updates the store to be σ', and returns v.

155a. ⟨*function prototypes for μScheme* 153b⟩+≡ (S318a) ◁ 154d

```
Value eval    (Exp e, Env rho);
Env   evaldef(Def d, Env rho, Echo echo);
```

Similarly, evaldef(e, ρ, echo), when evaluated with store σ, finds a ρ' and a σ' such that $\langle e, \rho, \sigma\rangle \rightarrow \langle \rho', \sigma'\rangle$, updates the store to be σ', and returns ρ'. If echo is ECHOING, evaldef also prints the name or value of whatever expression is evaluated or added to ρ.

Printing

Just like the Impcore interpreter, the μScheme interpreter uses functions print and fprint, but the μScheme interpreter knows how to print more kinds of things. The alternatives are shown in Table 2.7. Most of these specifications are used only to debug the interpreter.

2.12.3 *Implementation of the evaluator*

As in Impcore, the evaluator starts with switch, which chooses how to evaluate e based on its syntactic form:

155b. ⟨*eval.c* 155b⟩≡ 157c ▷

```
Value eval(Exp e, Env env) {
    switch (e->alt) {
    case LITERAL: ⟨evaluate e->literal and return the result 156a⟩
    case VAR:     ⟨evaluate e->var and return the result 156b⟩
    case SET:     ⟨evaluate e->set and return the result 156c⟩
    case IFX:     ⟨evaluate e->ifx and return the result 159b⟩
    case WHILEX:  ⟨evaluate e->whilex and return the result 159c⟩
    case BEGIN:   ⟨evaluate e->begin and return the result 159d⟩
    case APPLY:   ⟨evaluate e->apply and return the result 156e⟩
    case LETX:    ⟨evaluate e->letx and return the result 157d⟩
    case LAMBDAX: ⟨evaluate e->lambdax and return the result 156d⟩
    }
    assert(0);
}
```

type Def	$\mathcal{A}$
type Echo	S293f
type Env	153a
type Exp	$\mathcal{A}$
type Value	$\mathcal{A}$

Literals

As in Impcore, a literal evaluates to itself.

156a. ⟨*evaluate* `e->literal` *and return the result* 156a⟩≡ (155b 48b)

```
return e->literal;
```

Variables and assignment

Variable lookup and assignment are simpler than in Impcore, because μScheme has only one rule for each form.

$$\frac{x \in \operatorname{dom} \rho \qquad \rho(x) \in \operatorname{dom} \sigma}{\langle \text{VAR}(x), \rho, \sigma \rangle \Downarrow \langle \sigma(\rho(x)), \sigma \rangle} \qquad \text{(VAR)}$$

$$\frac{x \in \operatorname{dom} \rho \qquad \rho(x) = \ell \qquad \langle e, \rho, \sigma \rangle \Downarrow \langle v, \sigma' \rangle}{\langle \text{SET}(x, e), \rho, \sigma \rangle \Downarrow \langle v, \sigma'\{\ell \mapsto v\} \rangle} \qquad \text{(ASSIGN)}$$

In the code, $\rho(x)$ is implemented by find(x, ρ), and $\sigma(\ell)$ is implemented by $*\ell$.

156b. ⟨*evaluate* `e->var` *and return the result* 156b⟩≡ (155b 48b)

```
if (find(e->var, env) == NULL)
    runerror("name %n not found", e->var);
return *find(e->var, env);
```

In an assignment, the store is set to $\sigma'\{\ell \mapsto v\}$ by assigning to $*\ell$.

156c. ⟨*evaluate* `e->set` *and return the result* 156c⟩≡ (155b 48b)

```
if (find(e->set.name, env) == NULL)
    runerror("set unbound variable %n in %e", e->set.name, e);
return *find(e->set.name, env) = eval(e->set.exp, env);
```

Closures and function application

Wrapping a closure is simple:

$$\frac{x_1, \ldots, x_n \text{ all distinct}}{\langle \text{LAMBDA}(\langle x_1, \ldots, x_n \rangle, e), \rho, \sigma \rangle \Downarrow \langle (\!| \text{LAMBDA}(\langle x_1, \ldots, x_n \rangle, e), \rho |\!), \sigma \rangle}. \qquad \text{(MKCLOSURE)}$$

156d. ⟨*evaluate* `e->lambdax` *and return the result* 156d⟩≡ (155b)

```
return mkClosure(e->lambdax, env);
```

Formal parameters $x_1, \ldots, x_n$ are confirmed to be distinct when e is parsed, by function `check_exp_duplicates` in chunk S336c. Checking at parse time exposes problems right away, without waiting for bad code to be evaluated.

When a function is applied, its actual parameters are evaluated and stored in `vs`. The next step depends on whether the function is a primitive or a closure.

156e. ⟨*evaluate* `e->apply` *and return the result* 156e⟩≡ (155b 48b)

```
{
    Value     f  = eval     (e->apply.fn,      env);
    Valuelist vs = evallist(e->apply.actuals, env);

    switch (f.alt) {
    case PRIMITIVE:
        ⟨apply f.primitive to vs and return the result 157a⟩
    case CLOSURE:
        ⟨apply f.closure to vs and return the result 157b⟩
    default:
        runerror("%e evaluates to non-function %v in %e",
                 e->apply.fn, f, e);
    }
}
```

Because a primitive is represented by a pair containing a function pointer and a tag, its application is simpler than in Impcore. Function `f.primitive.function` gets the tag, the arguments `vs`, and the abstract syntax `e`. (The syntax is used in error messages.)

157a. ⟨*apply* `f.primitive` *to* `vs` *and return the result* 157a⟩≡ (156e)

```
return f.primitive.function(e, f.primitive.tag, vs);
```

A closure is applied by extending its stored environment (ρ_c in the operational semantics) with the bindings for the formal variables, then evaluating the body in that environment.

$$\frac{\begin{array}{c}\ell_1, \ldots, \ell_n \notin \operatorname{dom} \sigma_n \text{ (and all distinct)} \\ \langle e, \rho, \sigma \rangle \Downarrow \langle (\!| \text{LAMBDA}(\langle x_1, \ldots, x_n \rangle, e_c), \rho_c |\!), \sigma_0 \rangle \\ \langle e_1, \rho, \sigma_0 \rangle \Downarrow \langle v_1, \sigma_1 \rangle \\ \vdots \\ \langle e_n, \rho, \sigma_{n-1} \rangle \Downarrow \langle v_n, \sigma_n \rangle \\ \langle e_c, \rho_c\{x_1 \mapsto \ell_1, \ldots, x_n \mapsto \ell_n\}, \sigma_n\{\ell_1 \mapsto v_1, \ldots, \ell_n \mapsto v_n\} \rangle \Downarrow \langle v, \sigma' \rangle\end{array}}{\langle \text{APPLY}(e, e_1, \ldots, e_n), \rho, \sigma \rangle \Downarrow \langle v, \sigma' \rangle} \quad (\text{APPLYCLOSURE})$$

157b. ⟨*apply* `f.closure` *to* `vs` *and return the result* 157b⟩≡ (156e)

```
{
    Namelist xs = f.closure.lambda.formals;
    checkargc(e, lengthNL(xs), lengthVL(vs));
    return eval(f.closure.lambda.body,
                bindalloclist(xs, vs, f.closure.env));
}
```

As in Impcore's interpreter, `evallist` evaluates a list of arguments in turn, returning a list of values.

157c. ⟨*eval.c* 155b⟩+≡ ◁155b

```
static Valuelist evallist(Explist es, Env env) {
    if (es == NULL) {
        return NULL;
    } else {
        Value v = eval(es->hd, env);    // enforce uScheme's order of evaluation
        return mkVL(v, evallist(es->tl, env));
    }
}
```

`bindalloclist`	153c
`checkargc`	47c
type `Env`	153a
`env`	155b
`eval`	155a
`evallist`	S310b
type `Explist`	S309b
`find`	153b
`lengthNL`	$\mathcal{A}$
`lengthVL`	$\mathcal{A}$
`mkClosure`	$\mathcal{A}$
`mkVL`	$\mathcal{A}$
type `Namelist`	43a
`runerror`	47a
type `Value`	$\mathcal{A}$
type `Valuelist`	S309c

Let, let, and letrec*

Each expression in the `let` family uses its internal name-expression pairs to create a new environment, then evaluates the body in that environment. Each form creates the new environment in a different way.

157d. ⟨*evaluate* `e->letx` *and return the result* 157d⟩≡ (155b)

```
switch (e->letx.let) {
case LET:      ⟨extend env by simultaneously binding es to xs 158a⟩
               break;
case LETSTAR:  ⟨extend env by sequentially binding es to xs 158b⟩
               break;
case LETREC:   ⟨extend env by recursively binding es to xs 159a⟩
               break;
default:       assert(0);
}
return eval(e->letx.body, env);
```

As with `lambda`, all names are confirmed to be distinct at parse time.

A LET expression evaluates its right-hand sides, then binds them all at once. All the work is done by functions `evallist` and `bindalloclist`.

$$\frac{\begin{array}{c} x_1,\ldots,x_n \text{ all distinct} \\ \ell_1,\ldots,\ell_n \notin \operatorname{dom}\sigma_n \text{ (and all distinct)} \\ \sigma_0 = \sigma \\ \langle e_1,\rho,\sigma_0\rangle \Downarrow \langle v_1,\sigma_1\rangle \\ \vdots \\ \langle e_n,\rho,\sigma_{n-1}\rangle \Downarrow \langle v_n,\sigma_n\rangle \\ \langle e,\rho\{x_1\mapsto\ell_1,\ldots,x_n\mapsto\ell_n\},\sigma_n\{\ell_1\mapsto v_1,\ldots,\ell_n\mapsto v_n\}\rangle \Downarrow \langle v,\sigma'\rangle \end{array}}{\langle \text{LET}(\langle x_1,e_1,\ldots,x_n,e_n\rangle,e),\rho,\sigma\rangle \Downarrow \langle v,\sigma'\rangle} \quad \text{(LET)}$$

158a. ⟨*extend* `env` *by simultaneously binding* `es` *to* `xs` 158a⟩≡ (157d)

```
env = bindalloclist(e->letx.xs, evallist(e->letx.es, env), env);
```

A LETSTAR expression binds a new name as each expression is evaluated.

$$\frac{\begin{array}{lll} & \rho_0 = \rho & \sigma_0 = \sigma \\ \langle e_1,\rho_0,\sigma_0\rangle \Downarrow \langle v_1,\sigma_0'\rangle \;\; \ell_1 \notin \operatorname{dom}\sigma_0' & \rho_1 = \rho_0\{x_1\mapsto\ell_1\} & \sigma_1 = \sigma_0'\{\ell_1\mapsto v_1\} \\ & \vdots & \\ \langle e_n,\rho_{n-1},\sigma_{n-1}\rangle \Downarrow \langle v_n,\sigma_{n-1}'\rangle & & \\ \qquad \ell_n \notin \operatorname{dom}\sigma_{n-1}' & \rho_n = \rho_{n-1}\{x_n\mapsto\ell_n\} & \sigma_n = \sigma_{n-1}'\{\ell_n\mapsto v_n\} \\ \langle e,\rho_n,\sigma_n\rangle \Downarrow \langle v,\sigma'\rangle & & \end{array}}{\langle \text{LETSTAR}(\langle x_1,e_1,\ldots,x_n,e_n\rangle,e),\rho,\sigma\rangle \Downarrow \langle v,\sigma'\rangle} \quad \text{(LETSTAR)}$$

158b. ⟨*extend* `env` *by sequentially binding* `es` *to* `xs` 158b⟩≡ (157d)

```
{
    Namelist xs;
    Explist es;

    for (xs = e->letx.xs, es = e->letx.es;
         xs && es;
         xs = xs->tl, es = es->tl)
        env = bindalloc(xs->hd, eval(es->hd, env), env);
    assert(xs == NULL && es == NULL);
}
```

Finally, before evaluating any expressions, LETREC binds each name to a fresh location.

$$\frac{\begin{array}{c} \ell_1,\ldots,\ell_n \notin \operatorname{dom}\sigma \text{ (and all distinct)} \\ x_1,\ldots,x_n \text{ all distinct} \\ e_i \text{ has the form LAMBDA}(\cdots),\ 1\le i\le n \\ \rho' = \rho\{x_1\mapsto\ell_1,\ldots,x_n\mapsto\ell_n\} \\ \sigma_0 = \sigma\{\ell_1\mapsto \text{unspecified},\ldots,\ell_n\mapsto \text{unspecified}\} \\ \langle e_1,\rho',\sigma_0\rangle \Downarrow \langle v_1,\sigma_1\rangle \\ \vdots \\ \langle e_n,\rho',\sigma_{n-1}\rangle \Downarrow \langle v_n,\sigma_n\rangle \\ \langle e,\rho',\sigma_n\{\ell_1\mapsto v_1,\ldots,\ell_n\mapsto v_n\}\rangle \Downarrow \langle v,\sigma'\rangle \end{array}}{\langle \text{LETREC}(\langle x_1,e_1,\ldots,x_n,e_n\rangle,e),\rho,\sigma\rangle \Downarrow \langle v,\sigma'\rangle} \quad \text{(LETREC)}$$

The locations' initial contents are unspecified, and they remain unspecified until all the values are computed. The right-hand sides are confirmed to be LAMBDAs at parse time, by the same function that confirms the x_i's are distinct, so they needn't be checked here.

159a. ⟨*extend* env *by recursively binding* es *to* xs 159a⟩≡ (157d)
```
{
    Namelist xs;

    for (xs = e->letx.xs; xs; xs = xs->tl)
        env = bindalloc(xs->hd, unspecified(), env);
    Valuelist vs = evallist(e->letx.es, env);
    for (xs = e->letx.xs;
         xs && vs;
         xs = xs->tl, vs = vs->tl)
        *find(xs->hd, env) = vs->hd;
    assert(xs == NULL && vs == NULL);
}
```


Conditional, iteration, and sequence

The control-flow operations are implemented much as they are in Impcore. The semantic rules are not worth repeating.

159b. ⟨*evaluate* e->ifx *and return the result* 159b⟩≡ (155b 48b)
```
if (istrue(eval(e->ifx.cond, env)))
    return eval(e->ifx.truex, env);
else
    return eval(e->ifx.falsex, env);
```

159c. ⟨*evaluate* e->whilex *and return the result* 159c⟩≡ (155b 48b)
```
while (istrue(eval(e->whilex.cond, env)))
    eval(e->whilex.body, env);
return falsev;
```

159d. ⟨*evaluate* e->begin *and return the result* 159d⟩≡ (155b 48b)
```
{
    Value lastval = falsev;
    for (Explist es = e->begin; es; es = es->tl)
        lastval = eval(es->hd, env);
    return lastval;
}
```


2.12.4 *Evaluating true definitions*

Each true definition is evaluated by function evaldef, which updates the store and returns a new environment. If echo is ECHOES, evaldef also prints. Function evaldef doesn't handle record definitions; the record form is syntactic sugar, not a true definition.

159e. ⟨*evaldef.c* 159e⟩≡
```
Env evaldef(Def d, Env env, Echo echo) {
    switch (d->alt) {
    case VAL:     ⟨evaluate val binding and return new environment 160a⟩
    case EXP:     ⟨evaluate expression, assign to it, and return new environment 160b⟩
    case DEFINE: ⟨evaluate function definition and return new environment 160c⟩
    }
    assert(0);
}
```

According to the operational semantics, the right-hand side of a val binding must be evaluated in an environment in which the name d->val.name is bound.

If no binding is present, one is added, with an unspecified value.

$$\frac{x \in \operatorname{dom} \rho \qquad \langle e, \rho, \sigma \rangle \Downarrow \langle v, \sigma' \rangle}{\langle \text{VAL}(x, e), \rho, \sigma \rangle \to \langle \rho, \sigma'\{\rho(x) \mapsto v\} \rangle} \quad \text{(DEFINEOLDGLOBAL)}$$

$$\frac{x \notin \operatorname{dom} \rho \qquad \ell \notin \operatorname{dom} \sigma \qquad \langle e, \rho\{x \mapsto \ell\}, \sigma\{\ell \mapsto \text{unspecified}\} \rangle \Downarrow \langle v, \sigma' \rangle}{\langle \text{VAL}(x, e), \rho, \sigma \rangle \to \langle \rho\{x \mapsto \ell\}, \sigma'\{\ell \mapsto v\} \rangle} \quad \text{(DEFINENEWGLOBAL)}$$

160a. ⟨*evaluate* `val` *binding and return new environment* 160a⟩≡ (159e)

```
{
    if (find(d->val.name, env) == NULL)
        env = bindalloc(d->val.name, unspecified(), env);
    Value v = eval(d->val.exp, env);
    *find(d->val.name, env) = v;
    ⟨if echo calls for printing, print either v or the bound name S311e⟩
    return env;
}
```

As in Impcore, evaluating a top-level expression has the same effect on the environment as evaluating a definition of `it`, except that the interpreter always prints the value, never the name "`it`."

160b. ⟨*evaluate expression, assign to* `it`*, and return new environment* 160b⟩≡ (159e)

```
{
    Value v = eval(d->exp, env);
    Value *itloc = find(strtoname("it"), env);
    ⟨if echo calls for printing, print v S312a⟩
    if (itloc == NULL) {
        return bindalloc(strtoname("it"), v, env);
    } else {
        *itloc = v;
        return env;
    }
}
```

A DEFINE is rewritten to VAL.

160c. ⟨*evaluate function definition and return new environment* 160c⟩≡ (159e)

```
return evaldef(mkVal(d->define.name, mkLambdax(d->define.lambda)),
               env, echo);
```

2.12.5 Implementations of primitives

Each primitive is associated with a unique tag, which identifies the primitive, and with a function, which implements the primitive. The tags enable one function to implement multiple primitives, which makes it easy for similar primitives to share code. The primitives are implemented by these functions:

`arith`	Arithmetic primitives, which expect integers as arguments
`binary`	Non-arithmetic primitives that expect two arguments
`unary`	Primitives that expect one argument

Arithmetic primitives

Each arithmetic primitive expects two integer arguments, which are obtained by *projecting* μScheme values. The projection function projectint32 takes not only a value but also an expression, so if its argument is not an integer, it can issue an informative error message.

161a. ⟨*prim.c* 161a⟩≡ 161b ▷

```
static int32_t projectint32(Exp e, Value v) {
    if (v.alt != NUM)
        runerror("in %e, expected an integer, but got %v", e, v);
    return v.num;
}
```

Function arith first converts its arguments to integers, then consults the tag to decide what to do. In each case, it computes a number or a Boolean, which is converted a μScheme value by either mkNum or mkBool, both of which are generated automatically from the definition of Value in code chunk 152a. Checks for arithmetic overflow are not shown.

161b. ⟨*prim.c* 161a⟩+≡ ◁ 161a 161c ▷

```
Value arith(Exp e, int tag, Valuelist args) {
    checkargc(e, 2, lengthVL(args));
    int32_t n = projectint32(e, nthVL(args, 0));
    int32_t m = projectint32(e, nthVL(args, 1));

    switch (tag) {
    case PLUS:  return mkNum(n + m);
    case MINUS: return mkNum(n - m);
    case TIMES: return mkNum(n * m);
    case DIV:   if (m==0) runerror("division by zero");
                else return mkNum(divide(n, m));  // round to minus infinity
    case LT:    return mkBoolv(n < m);
    case GT:    return mkBoolv(n > m);
    default:    assert(0);
    }
}
```

Other binary primitives

μScheme has two other binary primitives, which don't require integer arguments: cons and =. The implementation of = is relegated to the Supplement, but the implementation of cons is shown here. Because S-expressions are a recursive type, a cons cell must contain pointers to S-expressions, not S-expressions themselves. Every cons must therefore allocate fresh locations for the pointers. This behavior makes cons a major source of allocation in μScheme programs.[14]

161c. ⟨*prim.c* 161a⟩+≡ ◁ 161b 162a ▷

```
Value cons(Value v, Value w) {
    return mkPair(allocate(v), allocate(w));
}
```


[14]In full Scheme, a cons cell is typically represented by a pointer to an object allocated on the heap, so cons requires only one allocation, not two.

Unary primitives

Unary primitives are implemented here. Most of the cases are relegated to the Supplement.

162a. ⟨*prim.c* 161a⟩+≡ ◁161c

```
Value unary(Exp e, int tag, Valuelist args) {
    checkargc(e, 1, lengthVL(args));
    Value v = nthVL(args, 0);
    switch (tag) {
    case NULLP:
        return mkBoolv(v.alt == NIL);
    case CAR:
        if (v.alt == NIL)
            runerror("in %e, car applied to empty list", e);
        else if (v.alt != PAIR)
            runerror("car applied to non-pair %v in %e", v, e);
        return *v.pair.car;
    case PRINTU:
        if (v.alt != NUM)
            runerror("printu applied to non-number %v in %e", v, e);
        print_utf8(v.num);
        return v;
    case ERROR:
        runerror("%v", v);
        return v;
    ⟨other cases for unary primitives S314c⟩
    default:
        assert(0);
    }
}
```

2.12.6 *Memory allocation*

In this chapter, a new location is allocated with `malloc`.

162b. ⟨*loc.c* 162b⟩≡

```
Value* allocate(Value v) {
    Value *loc = malloc(sizeof(*loc));
    assert(loc != NULL);
    *loc = v;
    return loc;
}
```

A much more interesting and efficient allocator is described in Chapter 4.

2.13 EXTENDING μSCHEME WITH SYNTACTIC SUGAR

Like Impcore, μScheme is stratified into two layers: a *core language* and *syntactic sugar* (page 68). The core language is defined by the operational semantics and is implemented by functions `eval` and `evaldef`. The syntactic sugar is defined and implemented by translating it into the core language. In Scheme, the core language can be very small indeed: even the LET and BEGIN forms can be implemented as syntactic sugar. (But in μScheme, they are part of the core.) The translations of LET and BEGIN are shown below, as are the translations used to implement short-circuit conditionals, `cond`, and the `record` form. These translations introduce two key programming-language concepts: *capture-avoiding substitution* and *hygiene*.

2.13.1 *Syntactic sugar for* LET *forms*

A `let` expression can be desugared into an application of a `lambda`:

$$\texttt{(let ([}x_1\ e_1\texttt{]}\cdots\texttt{[}x_n\ e_n\texttt{])}\ e\texttt{)} \triangleq \texttt{((lambda (}x_1\ \cdots\ x_n\texttt{) e)}\ e_1\ \cdots\ e_n\texttt{)}.$$

A `let*` expression can be desugared into a sequence of nested `let` expressions. The desugaring is defined by structural induction on the list of bindings in the `let*`, which calls for two equations: one for the base case (no bindings) and one for the induction step (a nonempty sequence of bindings). An empty `let*` is desugared into its body. A nonempty `let*` is desugared into a nested sequence of `let` expressions: a `let` expression for the first binding, followed by the desugaring of the `let*` expression for the remaining bindings.

$$\begin{aligned}&\texttt{(let* ()}\ e\texttt{)} \triangleq e\\ &\texttt{(let* ([}x_1\ e_1\texttt{]}\cdots\texttt{[}x_n\ e_n\texttt{])}\ e\texttt{)} \triangleq\\ &\qquad\texttt{(let ([}x_1\ e_1\texttt{]) (let* ([}x_2\ e_2\texttt{]}\cdots\texttt{[}x_n\ e_n\texttt{])}\ e\texttt{))}\end{aligned}$$

This translation works just like any other recursive function—but the recursive function is applied to *syntax*, not to values. It looks like this:

163. ⟨*parse.c* 163⟩≡

```
Exp desugarLetStar(Namelist xs, Explist es, Exp body) {
    if (xs == NULL || es == NULL) {
        assert(xs == NULL && es == NULL);
        return body;
    } else {
        return desugarLet(mkNL(xs->hd, NULL), mkEL(es->hd, NULL),
                          desugarLetStar(xs->tl, es->tl, body));
    }
}
```

The desugared code works just as well as μScheme's core code—and you can prove it (Exercises 44 and 45).

Finally, a `letrec` can be desugared into a `let` expression that introduces all the variables, which is followed by a sequence of assignments:

$$\begin{aligned}&\texttt{(letrec ([}x_1\ e_1\texttt{]}\ \cdots\ \texttt{[}x_n\ e_n\texttt{])}\ e\texttt{)} \triangleq\\ &\qquad\texttt{(let ([}x_1\ \text{unspecified}\texttt{]}\cdots\texttt{[}x_n\ \text{unspecified}\texttt{])}\\ &\qquad\quad\texttt{(begin (set}\ x_1\ e_1\texttt{)}\cdots\texttt{(set}\ x_n\ e_n\texttt{)}\\ &\qquad\qquad e\texttt{))}.\end{aligned}$$

This translation works only when each e_i is a `lambda` expression, as required by the operational semantics.

`checkargc`	47c
`type Exp`	$\mathcal{A}$
`type Explist`	S309b
`lengthVL`	$\mathcal{A}$
`mkBoolv`	$\mathcal{A}$
`mkEL`	$\mathcal{A}$
`mkNL`	$\mathcal{A}$
`type Namelist`	43a
`nthVL`	$\mathcal{A}$
`print_utf8`	S188a
`runerror`	47a
`type Value`	$\mathcal{A}$
`type Valuelist`	S309c

2.13.2 *Syntactic sugar for* `cond` *(Lisp's original conditional form)*

μScheme's conditional expression, written using `if`, allows for only two alternatives. But real programs often choose among three or more alternatives. For some such choices, C and the Algol-like languages offer a `switch` statement, but it can choose only among integer values that are known at compile time—typically enumeration literals. A more flexible multi-way choice is offered by a syntactic form from McCarthy's original Lisp: the `cond` expression. A `cond` expression contains an arbitrarily long sequence of *question-answer pairs*: one for each choice. I like `cond` more than `if` because `cond` makes it obvious how many alternatives there are and what each one is doing.

164a. ⟨*transcript for extended μScheme* 164a⟩≡ 164b ▷

```
-> (define compare-numbers (n m)
     (cond
        [(< n m)    'less]
        [(= n m)    'equal]
        [(> n m)    'greater]))
-> (compare-numbers 3 2)
greater
-> (compare-numbers 3 3)
equal
-> (compare-numbers 3 4)
less
```


As another example, `cond` can be used to implement `remove-multiples`, from chunk 102b:

164b. ⟨*transcript for extended μScheme* 164a⟩+≡ ◁ 164a 167a ▷

```
-> (define divides? (p n) (= (mod n p) 0))
-> (define remove-multiples (p ns)
     (cond [(null? ns)              '()]
           [(divides? p (car ns))   (remove-multiples p (cdr ns))]
           [#t                      (cons (car ns)
                                          (remove-multiples p (cdr ns)))]))
-> (remove-multiples 3 '(1 2 3 4 5 6))
(1 2 4 5)
```

Although `cond` is superior, it is found in very few languages—almost exclusively the Lisp-like languages—and `if` is found everywhere. For μScheme, therefore, I chose the familiar `if` over the superior `cond`. Fortunately, now that you know about `cond`, you can use it—it's syntactic sugar:

$$\texttt{(cond)} \triangleq \texttt{(error 'cond:-all-question-results-were-false)}$$
$$\texttt{(cond [}e_q\ e_a\texttt{]}\cdots \triangleq \texttt{(if } e_q\ e_a \texttt{ (cond}\cdots\texttt{))}$$

2.13.3 Syntactic sugar for conditionals: Avoiding variable capture

As a replacement for the primitive function `and`, which can be called only after both its arguments are evaluated, μScheme provides a syntactic form `&&`, which evaluates its second argument only when necessary. And actually, `&&` can accept more than two arguments; it is desugared to `if` expressions as follows:

$$\texttt{(\&\& } e\texttt{)} \triangleq e$$
$$\texttt{(\&\& } e_1 \cdots e_n\texttt{)} \triangleq \texttt{(if } e_1 \texttt{ (\&\& } e_2 \cdots e_n\texttt{) \#f)}$$

μScheme also provides a `||` form, which is also desugared into `if` expressions, but there's a challenge. The following desugaring doesn't always work:

$$\texttt{(|| } e_1\ e_2\texttt{)} \not\triangleq \texttt{(if } e_1 \texttt{ \#t } e_2\texttt{)}$$

The problem with that right-hand side is that if e_1 is not `#f`, `(||` e_1 e_2`)` should return the value of e_1, just as the predefined function `or` does. But the desugaring into `if` returns `#t`:

164c. ⟨*transcript* 95a⟩+≡ ◁ 143d 165a ▷

```
-> (or 7 'seven)
7
-> (if 7 #t 'seven)
#t
```

When e_1 is not #f, a desugaring could return e_1, but this desugaring doesn't always work either:

$$(\texttt{||}\ e_1\ e_2) \not\triangleq (\texttt{if}\ e_1\ e_1\ e_2)$$

This one fails because it could evaluate e_1 twice. And if e_1 has a side effect, the desugaring performs the side effect twice, leading to wrong answers.

165a. ⟨*transcript* 95a⟩+≡ ◁164c 165b▷

```
-> (val n 2)
-> (or (< 0 (set n (- n 1))) 'finished)
#t
-> (val n 2)
-> (if (< 0 (set n (- n 1))) (< 0 (set n (- n 1))) 'finished)
#f
```

The or function works because it is a function call: both e_1 and e_2 are evaluated, and their results are bound to the formal parameters of the or function. A desugaring could achieve the almost same effect with a let binding:

$$(\texttt{||}\ e_1\ e_2) \text{ is almost } (\texttt{let}\ (\texttt{[x}\ e_1\texttt{]})\ (\texttt{if x x}\ e_2)).$$

This one works with the examples given so far:

165b. ⟨*transcript* 95a⟩+≡ ◁165a 165c▷

```
-> (val n 2)
-> (or (< 0 (set n (- n 1))) 'finished)
#t
-> (val n 2)
-> (let ([x (< 0 (set n (- n 1)))]) (if x x 'finished))
#t
```

But binding x doesn't always work; if x is used in e_2, the desugaring can fail:

165c. ⟨*transcript* 95a⟩+≡ ◁165b 185b▷

```
-> (val n 0)
-> (val x 'finished)
-> (or (< 0 n) x)
finished
-> (val n 0)
-> (val x 'finished)
-> (let ([x (< 0 n)]) (if x x x))
#f
```

This failure has a name: the global variable x is said to be *captured* by the desugaring. To avoid capturing x, it is sufficient to choose *some* name x that doesn't appear in e_2. Such an x is called *fresh*. So finally, the following desugaring always works:

$$(\texttt{||}\ e_1\ e_2) \triangleq (\texttt{let}\ (\texttt{[}x\ e_1\texttt{]})\ (\texttt{if}\ x\ x\ e_2)), \text{ provided } x \text{ does not appear in } e_2.$$

car	$\mathcal{P}$ 162a
cdr	$\mathcal{P}$ 162a
cons	$\mathcal{P}$ S313d
mod	$\mathcal{B}$
null?	$\mathcal{P}$ 162a
or	$\mathcal{B}$

Using this idea, the general rules for desugaring || are as follows:

$$(\texttt{||}\ e) \triangleq e$$
$$(\texttt{||}\ e_1\ \cdots\ e_n) \triangleq (\texttt{let}\ (\texttt{[}x\ e_1\texttt{]})\ (\texttt{if}\ x\ x\ (\texttt{||}\ e_2\ \cdots\ e_n))), \quad \text{where } x \text{ does not appear in any } e_i.$$

Variable capture and fresh names are perennial issues in programming languages.

2.13.4 *Hygienic substitution: Making syntactic sugar precise*

Desugaring replaces one expression with another. To define replacement precisely, programming-language theorists have developed the concept of *substitution*.

- Substitution is the computational engine driving the simplest, most foundational accounts of what it means to evaluate expressions (or run programs). If you ever study the lambda calculus, you'll see that substitution is its only computational mechanism.

- Substitution is used to check the types of polymorphic functions. μScheme's functions aren't typechecked, and C's functions aren't polymorphic, but many programming languages do support both polymorphism and type checking (Chapter 6). And when a polymorphic function is used, the correctness of the use is checked using substitution. Such substitutions must avoid capturing *type variables* (Section 6.6.7). Even when types are inferred, as in ML and Haskell they are inferred using substitution (Chapter 7).

- In Prolog, when the system is trying to answer a query or prove a goal, subgoals are spawned using substitution.

Substitution algorithms that avoid variable capture are called *hygienic*. They are hard to get right. But if you are interested in programming-language foundations, you need to understand them. And if you are interested in language design, you need to understand that using a language based on substitution is not fun. (As examples, I submit TeX and Tcl.) The more different contexts in which you see substitution, the better you will understand it.

Let's use substitution to take a second look at μScheme's conditional expressions. The expression `(&&` e_1 e_2`)` is desugared into an `if` expression in three steps:

1. The replacement will be derived from the *template expression* `(if` $\square_1$ $\square_2$ `#f)`. Mathematically, the symbols $\square_1$ and $\square_2$ are ordinary program variables; the $\square$ notation telegraphs an intention to substitute for them.

2. Subexpressions e_1 and e_2 are extracted from the `&&` expression.

3. In the template, e_1 is substituted for $\square_1$ and e_2 is substituted for $\square_2$, simultaneously. The resulting expression is an *instance* of the template—"instance" being the word for a thing obtained by substitution. The original `&&` expression is replaced by the instance of the template, which is `(if` e_1 e_2 `#f)`.

The original expression and its replacement have the same semantics:

- If the original `&&` expression is evaluated in environment ρ, both e_1 and e_2 are supposed to be evaluated in environment ρ. In addition, expression e_2 is supposed to be evaluated only if e_1 evaluates to `#f`.

- If the instantiated template (the `if` expression) is evaluated in environment ρ, the semantics confirms that both e_1 and e_2 are evaluated in environment ρ. In addition, expression e_2 is evaluated only if e_1 evaluates to `#f`.

The `||` expression can't be desugared so easily.

- If the original `||` expression is evaluated in environment ρ, both e_1 and e_2 are supposed to be evaluated in environment ρ.

- If the template for `||` is

  ```
  (let ([x □1]) (if x x □2))
  ```

  and the instance is evaluated in environment ρ, then e_1 is evaluated in environment ρ, but if e_2 is evaluated, it is evaluated in environment $\rho\{\mathtt{x} \mapsto v_1\}$, where v_1 is the value of e_1.

Using this template, e_2 is evaluated in an extended environment, and variable x can be captured. For example, if $\langle e_1, \rho, \sigma\rangle \Downarrow \langle \text{BOOLV}(\texttt{\#f}), \sigma'\rangle$ and if e_2 is x, the value of the || expression should be $\sigma'(\rho(\texttt{x}))$. But the value of the instantiated template is always BOOLV(#f). If, however, x is not mentioned in e_2, then x is not captured by the substitution, and it is a theorem that

> If $\langle e, \rho, \sigma\rangle \Downarrow \langle v, \sigma\rangle$, if x is not mentioned in e, and if $\ell \notin \text{dom}\,\sigma$, then $\langle e, \rho\{x \mapsto \ell\}, \sigma\{\ell \mapsto v'\}\rangle \Downarrow \langle v, \sigma\rangle$.

This theorem follows either from Exercise 52 in this chapter or from Exercise 9 in Chapter 5.

Therefore, || can be desugared correctly if we choose a good x. Instead of a single template for ||, think of a whole *family* of templates

$$\{\texttt{(let ([}x\,\square_1\texttt{]) (if }x\;x\,\square_2\texttt{))} \mid x \text{ is a variable}\}.$$

Every choice of x determines a template, and any given e_1 and e_2 can be desugared using any template in which x does not appear in e_2.

2.13.5 *Syntactic sugar for* BEGIN

The same idea of hygiene—choosing a variable in a template that does not interfere with what is substituted—is used in the rules for desugaring BEGIN:

$$\begin{aligned}
\texttt{(begin } e\texttt{)} &\triangleq e\\
\texttt{(begin } e_1 \cdots e_n\texttt{)} &\triangleq \texttt{(let ([}x\; e_1\texttt{]) (begin } e_2 \cdots e_n\texttt{))},\\
&\quad \text{where } x \text{ does not appear in any } e_i.
\end{aligned}$$

2.13.6 *Syntactic sugar for records*

A Scheme record contains a fixed collection of named fields. In modern implementations of full Scheme, records are provided natively, as a primitive data structure. In μScheme, records are simulated using cons cells. The record-definition form in Section 2.4.1 is desugared into a sequence of function definitions:

167a. ⟨*transcript for extended μScheme* 164a⟩+≡ ◁164b 167b▷

```
-> (record frozen-dinner [protein starch vegetable dessert])
make-frozen-dinner
frozen-dinner?
frozen-dinner-protein
frozen-dinner-starch
frozen-dinner-vegetable
frozen-dinner-dessert
```

A `frozen-dinner` is represented by a list with five elements: the symbol `make-frozen-dinner`, followed by the values of the fields. This representation, when printed, resembles code that might be executed to reconstruct the record.

167b. ⟨*transcript for extended μScheme* 164a⟩+≡ ◁167a

```
-> (make-frozen-dinner 'steak 'potato 'green-beans 'pie)
(make-frozen-dinner steak potato green-beans pie)
```

Using this representation, the `record` definition is desugared into a sequence of definitions, the first of which looks something like this:

167c. ⟨*selected equivalent definitions for record* `frozen-dinner` 167c⟩≡ 168▷

```
(define make-frozen-dinner (x y z w)
  (cons 'make-frozen-dinner (cons x (cons y (cons z (cons w '()))))))
```

(The remaining definitions follow.)

And the remaining definitions:

168. ⟨*selected equivalent definitions for record* `frozen-dinner` 167c⟩+≡ ◁167c

```
(define frozen-dinner? (v)
  (&& (pair? v)
      (= 'make-frozen-dinner (car v))
      (pair? (cdr v))
      (pair? (cddr v))
      (pair? (cdddr v))
      (pair? (cdr  (cdddr v)))
      (null? (cddr (cdddr v)))))
(define frozen-dinner-protein (r)
  (if (frozen-dinner? r)
      (car (cdr r))
      (error (list2 r 'is-not-a-frozen-dinner-record))))
(define frozen-dinner-starch (r)
  (if (frozen-dinner? r)
      (car (cdr (cdr r)))
      (error (list2 r 'is-not-a-frozen-dinner-record))))
```

In general, a `record` definition with record name r and field names $f_1, \ldots, f_n$ is desugared as follows:[15]

```
(record r (f1 ··· fn)) ≜
  (define make-r (x1 ··· xn)
       (cons 'make-r (cons x1 (cons ··· (cons xn '())))))
  (define r? (x) (&& (pair? x) (= (car x) 'make-r) ···))
  (define r-f1 (x) (if (r? x) (car (cdr x)) (error ···)))
  (define r-f2 (x) (if (r? x) (car (cdr (cdr x))) (error ···)))
     ⋮
  (define r-fn (x) (if (r? x)
                        (car (cdr (cdr ··· (cdr x))))
                        (error ···)))
```

In `make-`r, hygiene requires that $x_1, \ldots, x_n$ be mutually distinct and different from `cons`; otherwise `cons` could mistakenly refer to one of the arguments. Hygiene is discussed more deeply in Section 2.14.4.

2.14 SCHEME AS IT REALLY IS

Like Lisp before it, Scheme has split into dialects. The model for μScheme is the 1998 R^{5}RS standard, which embodies the minimalist design philosophy of the original Scheme. The 2007 R^{6}RS standard defines a bigger, more complicated Scheme, which most R^{5}RS implementations chose not to adopt. The subsequent R^{7}RS standard splits Scheme into two languages: a small one, finalized in 2013, that more closely resembles the original, and a big one, still incomplete as of 2022, that is believed to be better suited to mainstream software development. And while standards have their advantages, many Schemers prefer Racket, a nonstandard dialect that benefits from a talented team of developers and contributors. But most dialects share aspects that I consider interesting, impressive, or relevant for someone making a transition from μScheme—which is the topic of this section.

2.14.1 Language differences

Let's begin with some minor lexical and syntactic differences. Through 2007, identifiers and symbols in full Scheme were not case-sensitive; for example, `'Foo` was

---

[15] The real story is more complicated: instead of using *names* `cons`, `pair?`, `car`, and so on, the desugaring creates *literals* that refer directly to those primitives.

the same as 'foo. But as of the 2007 R⁶RS standard—to give it its full name, the Revised⁶ Report on Scheme (Sperber et al. 2009)—identifiers and symbols are case-sensitive, as in μScheme.

Full Scheme uses define to introduce all top-level bindings, with slightly different concrete syntax from μScheme:

```
(define var exp)
(define (fun args) exp)
```


The define form can also be used within the body of a let or a lambda. Using definition forms within let and lambda makes programs easier to read and refactor than in μScheme, and it's cheap: these forms are desugared to a new letrec* form, which uses a single environment like letrec but is evaluated sequentially like let*.

Full Scheme operates on association lists with a function called assoc, not with find and bind. (In full Scheme, find is a function that takes a predicate and a list and returns the first element of the list that satisfies the predicate.) Calling (assoc obj alist) finds the first pair in alist whose car field is equal? to obj, and it returns that pair. If no pair in alist has obj as its car, assoc returns #f.

169a. ⟨*R⁶RS Scheme transcript* 169a⟩≡ 169b ▷

```
> (define e '((a 1) (b 2) (c 3)))  ;; r6rs Scheme implemented in Racket,
> (assoc 'a e)                     ;; not μScheme!
'(a 1)
> (assoc 'b e)
'(b 2)
> (assoc 'd e)
#f
> (assoc (list 'a) '(((a)) ((b)) ((c))))
'((a))
```

A result from assoc can be tested directly in an if expression, and if not #f, it can be updated in place by primitive function set-cdr!.

Full Scheme includes the other list functions found in μScheme, but often under slightly different names, such as for-all, exists, fold-left, and fold-right. And the full Scheme functions are more general: they can operate on any number of lists simultaneously.

Full Scheme has an additional quoting mechanism: using *quasiquotation*, you can splice computed values or lists into quoted S-expressions (Exercise 55).

In full Scheme, a function can take a variable number of arguments. Either the function takes one formal parameter, which is the whole list of arguments, or a formal parameter separated by a trailing period is bound to any "extra" arguments:

169b. ⟨*R⁶RS Scheme transcript* 169a⟩+≡ ◁ 169a

```
> ((lambda (x y . zs) zs) 3 4 5 6)    ;; Racket's r6rs Scheme
'(5 6)
> ((lambda xs xs)         3 4 5 6)
'(3 4 5 6)
```

In addition, many primitive functions and macros, such as +, <, and, max, etc., accept an arbitrary number of arguments—even zero.

In full Scheme, the syntactic form set is called set!. And full Scheme can mutate the contents of cons cells, not just variables, using primitive functions set-car! and set-cdr! (Exercises 50 and 58).

Finally, in full Scheme, the order in which expressions are evaluated is usually unspecified. To enforce a particular order of evaluation, use let* or letrec*.

2.14.2 Proper tail calls (upcoming in Chapter 3)

Implementations of full Scheme must be *properly tail-recursive*. Informally, an implementation is properly tail-recursive if every *tail call* is optimized to act as a "goto with arguments," that is, it does not push anything on the call stack (Steele 1977). An arbitrarily long sequence of tail calls takes no more space than one ordinary call.

Intuitively, a call is a tail call if it is the last thing a function does, i.e., the result of the tail call is also the result of the calling function. As an important special case, proper tail recursion requires that if the last thing a full Scheme function does is make a recursive call to itself, the implementation makes that recursive call as efficient as a `goto`.

Many tail calls are easy to identify; for example, in a C program, the last call before a `return` or before the end of a function is a tail call. And in a C statement `return f(`*args*`)`, the call to `f` is a tail call. To identify all tail calls, however, we need a more precise definition.

In Scheme, a tail call is a function call that occurs in a *tail context*. Tail contexts are defined by induction over abstract syntax. The full story is told by in Kelsey, Clinger, and Rees (1998, Section 3.5), from whom I have adapted this account, but the key rules look like this:

- The body of a `lambda` occurs in a tail context.
- When `(if` e_1 e_2 e_3`)` occurs in a tail context, e_2 and e_3 occur in a tail context.
- When `(begin` e_1 e_2 `...` e_n`)` occurs in a tail context, e_n occurs in a tail context.
- When a `let`, `let*`, or `letrec` occurs in a tail context, the body of the let occurs in a tail context.

The following example shows one tail call, to `f`. The calls to `g` and `h` are not tail calls. The reference to `x` is in a tail context, but it is not a call and so is not a tail call.

```
(lambda ()
  (if (g)
      (let ([x (h)])
        x)
      (if (g) (f) #f)))
```

The definition of tail context gives us a precise way to identify a function in continuation-passing style (Section 2.10.1): a function is written in continuation-passing style if and only if every expression in a tail context is either a call to a parameter or is a call to a function that is written in continuation-passing style.

The interpreter in this chapter does not optimize tail calls. But the interpreter in Chapter 3 does, and Chapter 3's exercises can help you understand how proper tail calls work and how they affect the use of stack space.

2.14.3 Data types

Full Scheme has more primitive data types and functions than μScheme. These types include mutable vectors (arrays), which can be written literally using the #(...) notation, as well as characters, mutable strings, and "I/O ports." And the R^6RS and R^7RS standards include records with named fields; μScheme's `record` form (Section 2.13.6) is a scaled-down version of R^6RS records.

Full Scheme supports lazy computations with `delay` and `force`.

Full Scheme provides many types of numbers, the meanings and representations of which are carefully specified in the standard. Numeric types can be arranged in a tower, in which each level contains all the levels below it:

number
complex
real
rational
integer

Numbers may also be *exact* or *inexact*. Most Scheme implementations, for example, automatically do exact arithmetic on arbitrarily large integers ("bignums"). If you are curious about bignums, you can implement them yourself; do Exercises 49 and 50 in Chapter 9 or Exercises 37 to 39 in Chapter 10.

2.14.4 From syntactic sugar to syntactic abstraction: Macros

Full Scheme includes not only the syntactic sugar described in Section 2.13 but also the ability for programmers to define new forms of syntactic sugar, called *macros* (or *syntactic abstractions*). Macros have the same status as any other Scheme code: they can be included in user code and in libraries, and anybody can define one by writing a *macro transformer*. And Scheme's macros are *hygienic*:

- If a macro transformer inserts a binding for an identifier (variable or keyword) not appearing in the macro use, the identifier is in effect renamed throughout its scope to avoid conflicts with other identifiers. For example, just as prescribed by the rules in Section 2.13.3, if a macro transformer expands `(||` e_1 e_2`)` into `(let ([`t e_1`]) (if` t t e_2`))`, then t is automatically renamed to avoid conflicting with identifiers in e_1 and e_2. Standard Scheme does something similar with `or`; the expression `(or` e_1 e_2`)` is defined to expand to `(let ([x` e_1`]) (if x x` e_2`))`. Scheme's macro facility renames `x` as needed to avoid capture.

- Hygiene also protects each macro's unbound names. For example, μScheme's `record` definition desugars into definitions that use `cons`, `car`, `cdr`, and `pair?` (Section 2.13.6). These names must not take their meanings from the context in which the `record` definition appears, as shown by this contrived example, which mixes μScheme with full Scheme:

```
(let ([z 5])
   (define (cons y ys) 'you-lose)
   (define (pair? x)  #f)
   (record point (x y))
   (assert (point? (make-point 3 4))))
```

  If `record` were desugared naïvely, the code for `point?` would use the version of `pair?` that's in scope, and the assertion would fail. But the assertion `(point? (make-point` e_1 e_2`))` should always succeed. And in a truly hygienic macro system, it does: the hygienic macro system guarantees that when a macro is desugared, its free names refer to the bindings visible where the macro was defined, regardless of how those names may be bound where the macro is used.

Hygiene makes Scheme macros remarkably powerful. Macro transformers can define new language features that in most settings that would require new abstract syntax. A good implementation of Scheme is more than just a programming language; it is a system for crafting programming languages. Details, examples, and ideas can be found in some of the readings mentioned in Section 2.15.2.

2.14.5 `call/cc` *(also upcoming in Chapter 3)*

Full Scheme includes a primitive function which can capture continuations that are defined implicitly within the interpreter, as if a program had been written in continuation-passing style. Primitive `call-with-current-continuation`, also called `call/cc`, can help you implement a staggering variety of control structures, including backtracking, multiple threads, exceptions, and more. Such *control operators* are a major topic of Chapter 3.

2.15 SUMMARY

Functional programming is a style of programming that relies on first-class, nested functions—in other words, on `lambda`. Functional programmers compose functions aggressively; they use functions to make other functions. Typical patterns of composition and computation are embodied in standard higher-order functions like maps, filters, and folds, where they can easily be reused. Such compositions emphasize "wholemeal programming": code is composed of operations on whole lists or whole S-expressions, not of operations on one element at a time. Functional programming also emphasizes the use of immutable data: rather than mutate a variable, the experienced functional programmer usually binds a new one, as discussed on page 119. Immutability simplifies unit testing and enables more function composition. And thanks to very fast allocators (Chapter 4), immutability can be implemented efficiently.

2.15.1 *Key words and phrases*

ATOM A Scheme value that can be compared for equality in constant time: a symbol, a number, a Boolean, or the empty list. Atoms are the base case in the definition of S-EXPRESSIONS.

CLOSURE The run-time representation of a function, produced by evaluating a LAMBDA ABSTRACTION. Includes a representation of the function's code and references to its FREE VARIABLES—or their locations. Closures are the simplest way to implement FIRST-CLASS, NESTED functions. A closure can be optimized to refer only to those free variables that are not also global variables—that is, the LET-bound and LAMBDA-bound variables of enclosing functions.

CONS, CAR, CDR The basic primitives that operate on lists, or more generally, S-EXPRESSIONS. By rights, `null?` should have equal status with `cons`, `car`, and `cdr`, but for some reason it is rarely mentioned in the same breath.

FILTER A HIGHER-ORDER FUNCTION that selects just some elements from a container structure—usually a list—according to a predicate function that is passed in.

FIRST-CLASS FUNCTION A function value that enjoys the same privileges as simple scalar values like machine integers: it may be passed to other functions, returned from other functions, stored in local and global variables, and stored in objects allocated on the heap, such as CONS CELLS. Most useful when NESTED. Functions in Scheme, Icon, and C are first-class values, but functions in Impcore are not.

FIRST-ORDER FUNCTION A function whose arguments and results are not functions and do not contain functions. Compare with HIGHER-ORDER FUNCTION.

FOLD A HIGHER-ORDER form of "reduction" that uses a given function to combine all elements of a container structure—usually a list. Folds can be used to implement sum, product, map, filter, and a zillion other functions that combine information two elements at a time. Like MAPS, folds can be found on lists, strings, mutable and immutable arrays, sets, trees, and so on.

FREE VARIABLE A name appearing in the body of a function that is bound neither by the LAMBDA ABSTRACTION that introduces the function nor by any LET BINDING within the body of the function. Names that refer to primitives like `+` and `cons` are typically free variables. LOCATIONS of free variables are captured in CLOSURES.

HIGHER-ORDER FUNCTION A function that either takes one or more functions as arguments, or more interestingly, that returns one or more functions as results. Classic examples include MAP, FILTER, and FOLD. More interesting higher-order functions can be defined only in a language in which functions are both FIRST-CLASS and NESTED. Compare with FIRST-ORDER FUNCTION.

LAMBDA ABSTRACTION The syntactic form by which a function is introduced. Scheme functions need not be named.

LOCATION A reference to MUTABLE storage. In both the semantics and implementation of Scheme, a variable stands for a MUTABLE location, not for a value, and what is captured in a CLOSURE are the *locations* of the FREE VARIABLES.

LOCATION SEMANTICS A semantics in which a variable stands for a mutable LOCATION in a store, not for a value. Describes languages like C and Scheme. Contrast with VALUE SEMANTICS.

MAP Any of a family of HIGHER-ORDER FUNCTIONS that operate on a container—like a list—and apply a function to each value contained. μScheme provides maps only on lists, but functional languages that provide more data structures provide more maps. For example, ML compilers typically ship with maps on lists, strings, mutable and immutable arrays, optional values, sets, and trees.

MONOMORPHIC A property of a function or value that may be used only with values of a single type. The word is Greek for "one shape." As an example, the `+` primitive is monomorphic because it works only with integers. By contrast, the `car` primitive, because it works with lists whose elements are of any type, is POLYMORPHIC .

MUTABLE Said of an entity whose state can change during the execution of a program, like a μScheme variable. The very word "variable" suggests that the value can vary, which is to say it is mutable. Mutability is ultimately implemented by reference to a machine LOCATION. In μScheme, variables are mutable but values are immutable. In full Scheme, records and CONS cells are mutable, using functions like `set-car!` and `set-cdr!`.

NESTED FUNCTION A function defined within another function. Using STATIC SCOPING, a nested function has access to the formal parameters and local variables of the enclosing function. Most useful when FIRST CLASS (and implemented by CLOSURES). Functions in Scheme and Lua may nest and are first-class; functions in Pascal and Ada may nest but are not first-class.

POLYMORPHIC A property of a function or value that may be used with more than one set of values. The word is Greek for "many shapes." As an example, the `length` function is polymorphic because it works with any list, regardless of what sorts of values are stored in the list. By contrast, the sum function (Exercise 29), because it works only on lists of integers, is MONOMORPHIC.

S-EXPRESSION The basic datatype of Scheme. Also, the concrete, parenthesized-prefix syntax used to write Scheme. A fully general S-expression is either an ATOM or a CONS cell containing two S-expressions. An "ordinary" S-expression is either an atom or a list of ordinary S-expressions.

SHARED MUTABLE STATE A means of communication at a distance, not evident in a function's arguments and results. In Scheme, any variable is mutable and any variable can be captured in a CLOSURE, so any variable can contain shared mutable state. In C, only global variables can contain shared mutable state—and they can be shared by any two functions, which is why your instructors may have warned you against them. Mutable state can be protected from over-sharing by hiding it under a LAMBDA ABSTRACTION, as in the example of the resettable counter or the random-number seed (Section 2.7.1, page 124). When a function relies on mutable state, its abilities to be unit tested or to be composed with other functions may be compromised.

SHORT-CIRCUIT EVALUATION Describes a syntactic form that looks like an ordinary function call or operator, but that does not evaluate all of its operations. Short-circuit evaluation is common for conjunction and disjunction (Boolean "and" and "or"), which in C and μScheme are written && and ||.

STORE In semantics, the set of meaningful LOCATIONS. Typically implemented by a combination of machine memory and machine registers. May include memory locations on the call stack as well as on the managed heap.

SYNTACTIC SUGAR Concrete syntax that extends a language by being translated into existing syntax. Examples in μScheme include SHORT-CIRCUIT conditionals and record definitions, among other forms (Section 2.13).

VALUE SEMANTICS A semantics in which a variable stands for a value, not a mutable LOCATION. Describes languages like Impcore, ML, and Haskell. Contrast with LOCATION SEMANTICS.

2.15.2 Further reading

For insight into how a language is born, John McCarthy's original paper (1960) and book (1962) about Lisp are well worth reading. But some later treatments of Lisp are clearer and more complete; these include books by Touretzky (1984), Wilensky (1986), Winston and Horn (1984), Graham (1993), and Friedman and Felleisen (1996). For the serious Lisper, the Common Lisp manual (Steele 1984) is an invaluable reference.

For Scheme, the closest analog is the "Lambda: The Ultimate —" series by Steele and Sussman (Sussman and Steele 1975; Steele and Sussman 1976, 1978); I especially recommend the 1978 article. For reference, Dybvig's (1987) book is clear and well organized, and there are always the official standards (Kelsey, Clinger, and Rees 1998; Sperber et al. 2009; Shinn, Cowan, and Gleckler 2013).

Recursion isn't just for functional programmers; it is also highly regarded in procedural languages, as taught by Rohl (1984), Roberts (1986), and Reingold and Reingold (1988). Proper tail recursion is precisely defined by Clinger (1998), who also explores some of the implications.

To argue that functional programming matters, Hughes (1989) shows that it provides superior ways of putting together code: tools like `map`, `filter`, and `foldr` enable us to combine small, simple functions into big, powerful functions. By Hughes's standard, μScheme is only half a functional language: although μScheme provides higher-order functions, it does not provide *lazy evaluation*, a technique now strongly associated with Haskell.

Algebraic laws are explored in depth by Bird and Wadler (1988), who include many more list laws than I present. Algebraic laws are also a great tool for specifying the behavior of abstract data types (Liskov and Guttag 1986). The algebraic approach can also be used on procedural programs, albeit with some difficulty (Hoare et al. 1987). And algebraic laws support a systematic, effective, *property-based* approach to software testing (Claessen and Hughes 2000).

Full Scheme can express a shocking range of programming idioms, algorithms, data structures, and other computer-science ideas; the demonstration by Abelson and Sussman (1985) is likely to impress you. Beginners will get more out of Harvey and Wright (1994), who aim at students with little programming experience. Another approach for beginners uses five subsets of Scheme, which are carefully crafted to help raw beginners evolve into successful Schemers (Felleisen et al. 2018).

The idea of using statically scoped closures to implement first-class, nested functions did not originate with Scheme. The idea had been developed in a number of earlier languages, mostly in Europe. Examples include Iswim (Landin 1966), Pop-2 (Burstall, Collins, and Popplestone 1971), and Hope (Burstall, MacQueen, and Sannella 1980). The book by Henderson (1980) is from this school. Also highly recommended is the short, but very interesting, book by Burge (1975).

Continuation-passing style was used by Reynolds (1972) to make the meanings of "definitional" interpreters independent of their implementation language. The continuation-passing backtracking search in Section 2.10 is based on a "Byrd box," which was used to understand Prolog programs (Byrd 1980); my terminology is that of Proebsting (1997), who describes an implementation of Icon, which has backtracking built in (Griswold and Griswold 1996).

Macros are nicely demonstrated by Flatt (2012), who creates new languages using Scheme's syntactic abstraction together with other tools unique to Racket. If you like the ideas and you want to define your own macros, continue with Hendershott's (2020) tutorial.

Macros have a long history. Kohlbecker et al. (1986) first addressed the problem of variable capture; they introduce a *hygiene condition* sufficient to avoid variable capture, and they define a hygienic macro expander. Dybvig, Hieb, and Bruggeman (1992) build on this work, reducing the cost of macro expansion and enabling macros to track source-code locations; a key element of their macro expander is the *syntax object*, which encapsulates not only a fragment of abstract-syntax tree but also some information about its environment, so that variable capture can be avoided. Moving from full Scheme to Racket, Flatt et al. (2012) further increase the power of the macro system by enabling macro expanders to share information. But the complexity of the system is acknowledged as a drawback; in particular, it is no longer so obvious that variable capture is always avoided. Flatt (2016) proposes a new, simpler model wherein a fragment of syntax is associated with a *set* of environments, which together determine the meaning of each name mentioned within the fragment.

2.16 EXERCISES

The exercises are summarized in Table 2.8. Some of the highlights are as follows:

- Exercise 13 guides you to an *efficient*, purely functional representation of queues, without using mutation.
- Exercises 22 and 24 ask you to prove some classic algebraic laws of pure functional programming: append is associative, and the composition of maps is the map of the composition. The laws can be used to improve programs, sometimes even by optimizing compilers. The proofs combine equational reasoning with induction.
- Exercise 38 asks you to implement a "data structure" whose values are represented as functions.
- Exercise 41 invites you to work toward mastery of continuation-passing style by implementing a solver for general Boolean formulas.
- Exercise 60 on page 198 asks you to add a trace facility to the μScheme interpreter; it will help you master the C code for the evaluator.

As you tackle the exercises, you can refer to Table 2.3 on page 97, which lists all the functions in μScheme's initial basis.

2.16.1 *Retrieval practice and other short questions*

A. What laws relate primitives `car`, `cdr`, `null?`, and `cons`?

B. What laws describe the behavior of the `map` function?

C. Given the definition `(record sundae [ice-cream sauce topping])`, what code do you write to find out if a sundae is topped with `'cherry`?

D. Given the same definition of `sundae`, how do you make an ice-cream sundae with vanilla ice cream, chocolate sauce, topped with sprinkles?

E. Given a food value that might be a `frozen-dinner` or a `sundae`, how do you interrogate it to find out which one it is?

F. To select all even numbers from a list of numbers, do you use `map`, `filter`, or a fold?

G. To double all the numbers in a list of numbers, do you use `map`, `filter`, or a fold?

H. To find the largest of a nonempty list of numbers, do you use `map`, `filter`, or a fold?

I. What's the cost of a naïve list reversal?

J. What's the cost of a list reversal that uses accumulating parameters?

K. According to function `equal?`, when are two S-expressions considered equal?

L. According to primitive function `=`, when are two S-expressions considered equal?

M. If you want to write procedural code in μScheme, are you better off using `let` or `let*`?

Table 2.8: Synopsis of all the exercises, with most relevant sections

Exercises	*Section*	*Notes*
1 to 5	2.3.4	Functions that consume lists, including lists that represent sets (§2.3.7).
6 and 7	2.3.2	Functions that take accumulating parameters.
8 and 9	2.2, 2.3.5	Lists all the way down—that is, S-expressions. A little coding and one proof (see §2.5.8).
10 to 12	2.4	Functions involving records and trees.
13 to 15	2.3, 2.5	Implement and specify purely functional data structures. I recommend using `let` to define local variables (§2.6).
16 to 23	2.5	Equational reasoning with first-order functions.
24 to 26	2.5	Equational reasoning with higher-order functions.
27 to 30	2.8	Standard higher-order functions on lists.
31 to 36	2.7, 2.8	Functions that take other functions as arguments.
37 to 40	2.7	Functions that return new functions made with `lambda`.
41	2.10	Continuations.
42 to 45	2.11	Using the operational semantics to reason about algebraic laws (§2.5) and syntactic sugar (§2.13).
46 to 50	2.11	Using the operational semantics to explore alternatives to the existing design and the semantics of possible new features.
51 and 52	2.11, 1.7.3	Metatheory: absence of aliasing, safety of extended environments.
53 to 55	2.12, 2.13	Implementing syntactic sugar, and adding *quasiquotation* syntax for writing S-expressions.
56 to 59	2.12.5	New primitives: `list`, `apply`, `set-car!`, `set-cdr!`, and `read`.
60	2.12	Enhancement to the interpreter: tracing calls.

N. What test is performed by the function `(o not ((curry =) 0))`?

O. Which of the following list functions are naturally polymorphic in the list element? `length`, `sum`, `reverse`, `append`, `minimum`, `member?`, `sort`

P. Which of the following list functions are not naturally polymorphic but can be made so by passing an additional (function-valued) parameter? `length`, `sum`, `reverse`, `append`, `minimum`, `member?`, `sort`

Q. A search function takes two continuations: one for success and one for failure. Which continuation expects a parameter? Why?

R. In Impcore, a variable stands for a value v, but in μScheme, a variable stands for a location ℓ. What example in the chapter exploits this aspect of μScheme's semantics?

S. The equation `(||` e_1 e_2`)` $=$ `(if` e_1 e_1 e_2`)` is not quite a valid algebraic law. What could go wrong?

T. The equation `(||` e_1 e_2`)` $=$ `(let ([x` e_1`]) (if x x` e_2`))` is not quite a valid algebraic law. What could go wrong?

2.16.2 *Functions that consume lists*

1. *Comparing elements of two lists.* Implement both of the following functions:

   (a) When both xs and ys are in set $LIST(ATOM)$, contig-sublist? determines whether the first list is a contiguous subsequence of the second. That is, (contig-sublist? xs ys) returns #t if and only if there are two other lists front and back, such that ys is equal to (append (append front xs) back).

   ⟨*exercise transcripts* 178a⟩≡

   ```
   -> (contig-sublist? '(a b c) '(x a y b z c))
   #f
   -> (contig-sublist? '(a y b) '(x a y b z c))
   #t
   -> (contig-sublist? '(x)     '(x a y b z c))
   #t
   ```

   (b) When both xs and ys are in set $LIST(ATOM)$, sublist? determines whether the first list is a mathematical subsequence of the second. That is, (sublist? xs ys) returns #t if and only if the list ys contains the elements of xs, in the same order, but possibly with other values in between.

   ⟨*exercise transcripts* 178a⟩+≡

   ```
   -> (sublist? '(a b c) '(x a y b z c))
   #t
   -> (sublist? '(a y b) '(x a y b z c))
   #t
   -> (sublist? '(a z b) '(x a y b z c))
   #f
   -> (sublist? '(x y z) '(x a y b z c))
   #t
   ```

2. *Numbers and lists of digits.* Function explode-digits converts a nonnegative number to a list of its decimal digits, and function implode-digits converts back:

   ⟨*exercise transcripts* 178a⟩+≡

   ```
   -> (explode-digits 1856)
   (1 8 5 6)
   -> (explode-digits 0)
   (0)
   -> (implode-digits '(2 4 6 8))
   2468
   ```

   Implement explode-digits and implode-digits.

   Hint: A list of digits is much easier to work with if the least significant digit is first. Work with such lists, and at need, use reverse.

3. *Sets represented as lists.* Implement the following set functions:

   (a) (remove x s) returns a set having the same elements as set s with element x removed.

   (b) (subset? s1 s2) determines if s1 is a subset of s2.

   (c) (=set? s1 s2) determines if lists s1 and s2 represent the same set.

4. *Sets as lists: Understanding equality.* Chunks 105a and 105c use lists to represent sets, and chunk 105d shows an example in which a set's *element* may also be a list. In the text, I claim that if `member?` uses = instead of `equal?`, the example in chunk 105d doesn't work.

   (a) In the example, which set functions go wrong? Is it `add-element`, `member?`, or both?

   (b) What goes wrong exactly, and why should the fault be attributed to using the = primitive instead of the `equal?` function?

5. *Synchronized access to two lists.* Implement function `dot-product`, which computes the dot product of two vectors, represented as lists. (If the vectors are $u_1, \ldots, u_n$ and $v_1, \ldots, v_n$, the dot product is $u_1 \cdot v_1 + \cdots + u_n \cdot v_n$, where $u_i \cdot v_i$ means multiplication.)

   ⟨*exercise transcripts* 178a⟩+≡

   ```
   -> (dot-product '(1 2 3) '(10 5 2))
   26
   ```

2.16.3 Accumulating parameters

6. *Accumulating parameters and reversal.* A list of things has an inductive structure; it is either empty or is a cons cell containing a thing and a list of things. A numeral has a similar inductive structure; it is either a digit or is a numeral followed by a digit. If you've done Exercise 7 in Chapter 1, you've already implemented several functions that manipulate the digits of a decimal numeral. Here's one to which you can apply the method of *accumulating parameters* described in Section 2.3.2:

   (a) Define a function `reverse-digits`, which is given a nonnegative number and returns a number whose decimal representation is the decimal representation of the original number, but with the digits reversed.

   ⟨*exercise transcripts* 178a⟩+≡

   ```
   -> (reverse-digits 123)
   321
   -> (reverse-digits 1066)
   6601
   -> (reverse-digits 100)
   1
   -> (reverse-digits 77)
   77
   ```

   Function `reverse-digits` could simply convert a number to a list of digits, call `reverse`, and convert the list back to a number. But look again at Section 2.3.2, and use similar ideas to define `reverse-digits` without ever materializing a list of digits.[16] By materializing only numbers and Booleans, you will avoid allocating space on the heap.

   (b) Is the following algebraic law valid?

   `(reverse-digits (reverse-digits n))` = `n`

   Justify your answer.

[16] To *materialize* a value is to represent it explicitly during computation. In Scheme, a materialized value is stored in a location that is either referred to by name or is part of a cons cell.

7. *Accumulating parameters and cost savings.* Function `preorder` in Section 2.4.2 may allocate unnecessary cons cells. Using the method of accumulating parameters from Section 2.3.2, rewrite `preorder` so that the number of cons cells allocated is exactly equal to the number of cons cells in the final answer.

2.16.4 *From lists to S-expressions*

8. *Inspection and manipulation of ordinary S-expressions.* As described in Section 2.5.8, an ordinary S-expression is either an atom or a list of ordinary S-expressions—and of course a list of ordinary S-expressions is either empty or formed with `cons`. Using your understanding of these possible forms, implement functions `count`, `countall`, `mirror`, and `flatten`:

   (a) When `x` is an atom and `xs` is in $LIST(SEXP_O)$, `(count x xs)` returns the number of (top-level) elements of `xs` that are equal to `x`. Assume `x` is not `'()`.

   ⟨*exercise transcripts* 178a⟩+≡

   ```
   -> (count 'a '(1 b a (c a)))
   1
   ```

   (b) When `x` is an atom and `xs` is in $LIST(SEXP_O)$, `(countall x xs)` returns the number of times `x` occurs *anywhere* in `xs`, not only at top level. Assume `x` is not `'()`.

   ⟨*exercise transcripts* 178a⟩+≡

   ```
   -> (countall 'a '(1 b a (c a)))
   2
   ```

   (c) When `xs` is a list of S-expressions, `(mirror xs)` returns a list in which every list in `xs` is recursively mirrored, and the resulting lists are in reverse order.

   ⟨*exercise transcripts* 178a⟩+≡

   ```
   -> (mirror '(1 2 3 4 5))
   (5 4 3 2 1)
   -> (mirror '((a (b 5)) (c d) e))
   (e (d c) ((5 b) a))
   ```

   Informally, `mirror` returns the S-expression you would get if you looked at its argument in a vertically oriented mirror, except that the individual atoms are not reversed. (Try putting a mirror to the right of the example, facing left.) More precisely, `mirror` consumes an S-expression and returns the S-expression that you would get if you wrote the brackets and atoms of the original S-expression in reverse order, exchanging open brackets for close brackets and vice versa.

   (d) Function `flatten` consumes a list of S-expressions and erases internal brackets. That is, when `xs` is a list of S-expressions, `(flatten xs)` constructs a list having the same atoms as `xs` in the same order, but in a flat list. For purposes of this exercise, `'()` should be considered not as an atom but as an empty list of atoms.

   ⟨*exercise transcripts* 178a⟩+≡

   ```
   -> (flatten '((I Ching) (U Thant) (E Coli)))
   (I Ching U Thant E Coli)
   -> (flatten '(((((a))))))
   (a)
   ```

⟨*exercise transcripts* 178a⟩+≡
```
-> (flatten '())
()
-> (flatten '((a) () ((b c) d e)))
(a b c d e)
```

9. *Proof about S-expressions.* Not only is a list of ordinary S-expressions itself an ordinary S-expression, a list of fully general S-expressions is also a fully general S-expression. Prove it. That is, using the inductive definitions of $\mathit{LIST}(A)$ and SEXP_{FG} in Section 2.5.8, prove that

$$\mathit{LIST}(\mathit{SEXP}_{FG}) \subseteq \mathit{SEXP}_{FG}.$$

The theorem implies that if you are writing a recursive function that consumes a list of S-expressions, you could instead try to write a more general function that consumes any S-expression. The more general function is sometimes simpler.

2.16.5 *Records and trees*

10. *Inspecting the contents of records.*

    (a) Define a function `desserts` that takes a list of frozen dinners and returns a list of the desserts.

    (b) Using `frozen-dinner?`, define a function `#dinners` that takes a list of values and returns the number of values that are frozen dinners.

    (c) Define a function `steak-dinners` that takes a list of frozen dinners and returns a list containing only those frozen dinners that offer `'steak` as a protein.

11. *Using node records to implement tree traversals.* Using the representation defined in Section 2.4, define functions that implement `postorder` and `inorder` traversal for binary trees.

12. *Traversals of rose trees.* A *rose tree* is a tree in which each node can have arbitrarily many children. We can define an abstract rose tree as a member of the smallest set that satisfies this recursion equation:

$$\mathit{ROSE}_{\mathcal{A}}(A) = \{\, \texttt{(make-rose } a\ ts\texttt{)} \mid a \in A \wedge ts \in \mathit{LIST}(\mathit{ROSE}_{\mathcal{A}}(A))\,\}.$$

If we prefer to write rose trees as S-expression literals, we can define

$$\mathit{ROSE}(A) = A \cup \{\, \texttt{(cons } a\ ts\texttt{)} \mid a \in A \wedge ts \in \mathit{LIST}(\mathit{ROSE}(A))\,\}.$$

Extend the preorder and level-order traversals of Sections 2.4.2 and 2.6 to rose trees. Note that in the non-abstract ROSE representation, a leaf node labeled a can be represented in two ways: either as `'a` or as `'(a)`.

2.16.6 *Functional data structures*

13. *Efficient queues.* The implementation of queues in Section 2.6 (page 119) is simple but inefficient; `enqueue` can take time and space proportional to the number of elements in the queue. The problem is the representation: the queue operations have to get to both ends of the queue, and getting to the

back of a list requires linear time. A better representation uses *two* lists stored in a record:

```
(record queue [front back])
```


In this record,

- The queue-front list represents the front of the queue. It stores older elements, and they are ordered with the oldest element at the beginning, so functions front and without-front can be implemented using car and cdr.
- The queue-back list represents the back of the queue. It stores young elements, and they are ordered with the youngest element at the beginning, so function enqueue can be implemented using cons.

The only trick here is that when the queue-front elements are exhausted, the queue-back elements must somehow be transferred to the front. Using the two lists, implement value emptyqueue and functions empty?, front, without-front, and enqueue. Each operation should take constant time on average. (Proofs of average-case time over a sequence of operations use *amortized analysis.*)

14. *Algebraic laws for queues.* The inefficient queue operations in Section 2.6 and the efficient queue operations in Exercise 13 can both be described by a single set of algebraic laws. As explained in Section 2.5.2, such laws must specify the result of applying any acceptable observer to any combination of constructors. (The queues in this chapter are immutable, so mutators do not come into play.)

    - Any queue can be constructed by applying enqueue zero or more times to emptyqueue.
    - Only three operations get information from (observe) queues: empty?, front, and without-front.

    Write algebraic laws sufficient to specify the behavior of all meaningful combinations of constructors and observers. Don't try to specify erroneous combinations like (front emptyqueue).

    Hint: This exercise is harder than it may appear—if you're not careful, you may find yourself specifying a stack, not a queue. Consider turning each algebraic law into a function, so you can test it as shown in Exercise 36.

15. *Graphs represented as S-expressions: Topological sort.* Many directed graphs can be represented as ordinary S-expressions. For example, if each node is labeled with a distinct symbol, a graph can be represented as a list of edges, where each edge is a list containing the labels of that edge's source and destination. Write a function that topologically sorts a graph specified by this *edge-list* representation. The function (tsort edges) should return a list that contains the labels in edges, in topological order.

    In topological sorting, the two symbols in an edge introduce a *precedence constraint*: for example, if '(a b) is an edge, then in the final sorted list of labels, a must precede b. As an example, (tsort '((a b) (a c) (c b) (d b))) can return either '(a d c b) or '(a c d b).

Not every graph can be topologically sorted; if the graph has a cycle, function `tsort` should call `error`.

For details on topological sorting, see Sedgewick (1988, Chapter 32), or Knuth (1973, Section 2.2.3).

⟨*exercise transcripts* 178a⟩+≡
```
-> (tsort '((duke commoner) (king duke) (queen duke) (country king)))
(queen country king duke commoner)
```


2.16.7 *Equational reasoning with first-order functions*

16. Prove that `(member? x emptyset)` = `#f`.

17. Prove that for any predicate `p?`, `(exists? p? '())` = `#f`.

18. Prove that for any list of values `xs`, `(all? (lambda (_) #t) xs)` = `#t`.

19. Prove that `(member? x (add-element x s))` = `#t`.

20. Prove that `(length (reverse xs))` = `(length xs)`.

21. Prove that `(reverse (reverse xs))` = `xs`.

22. Prove that `(append (append xs ys) zs)` = `(append xs (append ys zs))`.

23. Prove that `(flatten (mirror xs))` = `(reverse (flatten xs))`, where functions `flatten` and `mirror` are defined as in Exercise 8.

2.16.8 *Equational reasoning with higher-order functions*

24. Prove that the composition of `map`s is the `map` of the composition:

    `(map f (map g xs))` = `(map (o f g) xs)`

25. Prove again that the composition of `map`s is the `map` of the composition, but this time, prove equality of two functions, not just equality of two lists:

    `(o ((curry map) f) ((curry map) g))` = `((curry map) (o f g))`

    To prove that two functions are equal, show that when applied to equal arguments, they always return equal results.

26. Prove that if `takewhile` and `dropwhile` are defined as in Exercise 31, then for any list `xs`, `(append (takewhile p? xs) (dropwhile p? xs))` = `xs`.

2.16.9 *Standard higher-order functions on lists*

27. *Select a subsequence of elements.* Define function `remove-multiples-too`, which does what `remove-multiples` does, but works by using the higher-order functions in the initial basis. Copy function `divides?` from chunk 102a, and use whatever you like from the initial basis, but do not otherwise use `lambda`, `if`, or recursion.

    ⟨*exercise transcripts* 178a⟩+≡
    ```
    -> (remove-multiples-too 2 '(2 3 4 5 6 7))
    (3 5 7)
    ```

28. *Maps and folds with scalar results.* Use `map`, `curry`, `foldl`, and `foldr` to define the following functions:

    (a) `cdr*`, which lists the `cdr`'s of each element of a list of lists:

    ⟨*exercise transcripts* 178a⟩+≡
    ```
    -> (cdr* '((a b c) (d e) (f)))
    ((b c) (e) ())
    ```

    (b) `max*`, which finds the maximum of a nonempty list of integers

    (c) `gcd*`, which finds the greatest common divisor of a nonempty list of nonnegative integers

    (d) `lcm*`, which finds the least common multiple of a nonempty list of nonnegative integers.

    (e) `sum`, which finds the sum of a nonempty list of integers

    (f) `product`, which finds the product of a nonempty list of integers

    ⟨*exercise transcripts* 178a⟩+≡
    ```
    -> (sum '(1 2 3 4))
    10
    -> (product '(1 2 3 4))
    24
    -> (max* '(1 2 3 4))
    4
    -> (lcm* '(1 2 3 4))
    12
    ```

    (g) `mkpairfn`, which when applied to an argument v, returns a function that when applied to a list of lists, places v in front of each element:

    ⟨*exercise transcripts* 178a⟩+≡
    ```
    -> ((mkpairfn 'a) '(() (b c) (d) ((e f))))
    ((a) (a b c) (a d) (a (e f)))
    ```

    All seven functions can be defined by a sequence of definitions that includes only one `define`, one `lambda`, and seven `val` bindings. Try it.

29. *Maps and folds with list results.* Use `map`, `curry`, `foldl`, and `foldr` to define the following functions:

    (a) `append`, which appends two lists

    (b) `snoc`, which is `cons` spelled backwards, and which adds an S-expression to the *end* of a list:

    ⟨*exercise transcripts* 178a⟩+≡
    ```
    -> (snoc 'a '(b c d))
    (b c d a)
    ```

    (c) `reverse`, which reverses a list

    (d) `insertion-sort`, which sorts a list of numbers

    When implementing `insertion-sort`, take `insert` as given in chunk 101a.

30. *Folds for everything.* Use `foldr` or `foldl` to implement `map`, `filter`, `exists?`, and `all?`. It is OK if some of these functions do more work than their official versions, as long as they produce the same answers.

    For the best possible solution, define functions that no civilized μScheme program can distinguish from the originals. (A civilized program may execute any code, including `set`, but it may not change the functions in the initial basis.)

31. *Selections of sublists.* Function takewhile takes a predicate and a list and returns the longest prefix of the list in which every element satisfies the predicate. Function dropwhile removes the longest prefix and returns whatever is left over.

⟨*exercise transcripts* 178a⟩+≡
```
-> (define even? (x) (= (mod x 2) 0))
-> (takewhile even? '(2 4 6 7 8 10 12))
(2 4 6)
-> (dropwhile even? '(2 4 6 7 8 10 12))
(7 8 10 12)
```

Implement takewhile and dropwhile.

(You might also look at Exercise 26, which asks you to prove a basic law about takewhile and dropwhile.)

32. *Lexicographic comparison.* All sorts of sorting operations use lexicographic orderings, which are a generalization of alphabetical order. For example, to sort dates, we might compare first months, then days:

⟨*transcript* 95a⟩+≡
```
-> (record date (month day))
-> (define date< (d1 d2)
     (if (!= (date-month d1) (date-month d2))
         (< (date-month d1) (date-month d2))
         (< (date-day d1) (date-day d2))))
-> (val dates
     (let ([date-of-pair (lambda (p) (make-date (car p) (cadr p)))])
       (map date-of-pair '((4 5) (2 9) (3 3) (8 1) (2 7)))))
-> ((mk-insertion-sort date<) dates)
((make-date 2 7) (make-date 2 9) (make-date 3 3) (make-date 4 5) (make-date 8 1))
```

Generalize the date< function by writing a higher-order function lex-<* that compares lists of differing lengths lexicographically. It should take as a parameter an ordering on the elements of the list. Avoid making any assumptions about the elements, other than that they can be ordered by the parameter.

⟨*exercise transcripts* 178a⟩+≡
```
-> (val alpha-< (lex-<* <))
-> (alpha-< '(4 15 7) '(4 15 7 13 1))
#t
-> (alpha-<  '(4 15 7) '(4 15 5))
#f
```

cadr	$\mathcal{B}$ 96
car	$\mathcal{P}$ 162a
lcm*	$\mathcal{B}$
map	$\mathcal{B}$ 130
max*	$\mathcal{B}$
mk-insertion-sort	135c
mod	$\mathcal{B}$

This particular example illustrates alphabetical ordering. To see the relationship, translate the numbers to letters: the two results above say DOG $<$ DOGMA and DOG $\not<$ DOE.

33. *Binary search trees, polymorphically.* Write a higher-order implementation of binary-search trees. Use the third style of polymorphism described in Section 2.9.1. That is, write a function specialized-search that takes a comparison function as argument and returns an association list which associates symbols lookup and insert to the corresponding functions.

34. *Generalized dot product.* Exercise 5 asks for a dot-product function. Generalize this pattern of computation into a "fold-like" function foldr-pair, which operates on two lists of the same length. (This function is primitive in APL.)

35. *Generalized preorder traversal.* Function `preorder` in Section 2.4.2 is not so useful if, for example, one wants to perform some other computation on a tree, like finding its height. By analogy with `foldl` and `foldr`, define `fold-preorder`. In addition to the tree, it should take two arguments: a function to be applied to internal nodes, and a value to be used in place of the empty tree. Function `fold-preorder` can be used to get the labels and the height of the example tree on page 109:

   ⟨*exercise transcripts* 178a⟩+≡
   ```
   -> (fold-preorder
         (lambda (tag left right) (cons tag (append left right)))
         '()
         example-sym-tree)
   (A B C D E F G H I)
   -> (define tree-height (t)
        (fold-preorder (lambda (tag left right) (+ 1 (max left right)))
                       0
                       t))
   -> (tree-height example-sym-tree)
   4
   ```

36. *Generalized* `all?`*, with predicates of two or three arguments.* In this problem you generalize function `all?` so it can work with all pairs from two lists or all triples from three lists. For example, `all-pairs?` might be used with this `length-append-law` function to confirm that the law holds for 25 combinations of inputs:

   ⟨*exercise transcripts* 178a⟩+≡
   ```
   -> (define length-append-law (xs ys)
        (= (length (append xs ys))
           (+ (length xs) (length ys))))
   -> (all-pairs? length-append-law
                  '((a b c) (singleton) () (3 1 4 1 5 9) (2 7 1 8 2 8))
                  '((1 2 3) () (elephants got big feet) (z) (w x)))
   #t
   ```

   Generalize `all?` to combinations of values drawn from two or three lists:

   (a) Define function `all-pairs?`, which tests its first argument on all pairs of values taken from its second two arguments. Here are some more example calls:

      ⟨*exercise transcripts* 178a⟩+≡
      ```
      -> (all-pairs? < '(1 2 3) '(4 5 6 7))
      #t
      -> (all-pairs? < '(1 2 3) '(4 5 6 2))
      #f
      ```

      When the second test fails, the fault could be in the implementation or the specification. To simplify diagnosis, I expand the `<` function:

      ⟨*exercise transcripts* 178a⟩+≡
      ```
      -> (all-pairs? (lambda (n m) (< m n)) '(1 2 3) '(4 5 6 2))
      #f
      ```

      It is definitely *not* an algebraic law that for all m and n, $m < n$, so the fault here lies in the specification, not in the implementation of `<`.

   (b) Define function `all-triples?`, which works like `all-pairs?` but can test laws like the associativity of `append`.

⟨*exercise transcripts* 178a⟩+≡
```
-> (define a-a-law (xs ys zs)     ;; append/append law
      (equal? (append xs (append ys zs))
              (append (append xs ys) zs)))
-> (all-triples? a-a-law '((a) () (b c)) '((1 2) (3)) '((4 5 6)))
#t
```


2.16.11 *Functions as results*

37. *Using* `lambda`*: Creation and combination of fault-detection functions.* This problem models a real-life fault detector for Web input. An *input* to a Web form is represented as an association list, and a *detector* is a function that takes an input as argument, then returns a (possibly empty) list of *faults*. A fault is represented as a symbol—typically the name of an input field that is unacceptable.

    Define the following functions, each of which is either a detector or a detector builder:

    (a) Function `faults/none` is a detector that always returns the empty list of faults.

    (b) Function `faults/always` takes one argument (a fault F), and it returns a detector that finds fault F in every input.

    (c) Function `faults/equal` takes two arguments, a key k and a value v, and it returns a detector that finds fault k if the input binds k to v. Otherwise it finds no faults.

    (d) Function `faults/union` takes two detectors d_1 and d_2 as arguments. It returns a detector that, when applied to an input, returns all the faults found by detector d_1 and also all the faults found by detector d_2.

38. *Sets represented as functions.* In just about any language, sets can be represented as lists, but in Scheme, because functions are first class, a set can be represented as a function. This function, called the *characteristic function*, is the function that returns `#t` when given an element of the set and `#f` otherwise. For example, the empty set is represented by a function that always returns `#f`, and membership test is by function application:

    ⟨*exercise transcripts* 178a⟩+≡
    ```
    -> (val emptyset (lambda (x) #f))
    -> (define member? (x s) (s x))
    ```

    Representing each set by its characteristic function, solve the following problems:

    (a) Define set `evens`, which contains all the even integers.

    (b) Define set `two-digits`, which contains all two-digit (positive) numbers.

    (c) Implement `add-element`, `union`, `inter`, and `diff`. The set `(diff s1 s2)` is the set that contains every element of `s1` that is not also in `s2`.

    (d) Implement the third style of polymorphism (page 134).

`append`	$\mathcal{B}$ 99
`cons`	$\mathcal{P}$ S313d
`equal?`	$\mathcal{B}$ 104
`max`	$\mathcal{B}$

39. *Lists reimplemented using just* `lambda`. This exercise explores the power of `lambda`, which can do more than you might have expected.

    (a) I claim above that *any* implementation of `cons`, `car`, and `cdr` is acceptable provided it satisfies the list laws in Section 2.5.1. Define `cons`, `car`, cdr, and empty-list using only if, lambda, function application, the primitive =, and the literals #t and #f. Your implementations should pass this test:

⟨*exercise transcripts* 178a⟩+≡

```
-> (define nth (n xs)
      (if (= n 1)
          (car xs)
          (nth (- n 1) (cdr xs))))
nth
-> (val ordinals (cons '1st (cons '2nd (cons '3rd empty-list))))
-> (nth 2 ordinals)
2nd
-> (nth 3 ordinals)
3rd
```

(b) Under the same restrictions, define null?.

(c) Now, using only lambda and function application, define cons, car, cdr, null?, and empty-list. Don't use if, =, or any literal values.

The hard part is implementing null?, because you can't use the standard representation of Booleans. Instead, you have to invent a new representation of truth and falsehood. This new representation won't support the standard if, so you have to develop an alternative, and you have to use that alternative in place of if. For inspiration, you might look at the definition of binds? in chunk 141b, which uses find-c. If there were no such thing as a Boolean, how would you adapt the binds? function?

Equipped with your alternative to if and a new representation of Booleans, implement null? using only lambda and function application. And explain what a caller of null? should write instead of (if (null? x) e_1 e_2).

40. *Mutable reference cells implemented using* lambda. Exercise 58 invites you to add mutation to the μScheme interpreter by adding primitives set-car! and set-cdr! But if you want to program with mutation, you don't need new primitives—lambda is enough.

A mutable container that holds one value is called a *mutable reference cell*. Design a representation of mutable reference cells in μScheme, and implement in μScheme, without modifying the interpreter, these new functions:

(a) Function make-ref takes one argument v and returns a fresh, mutable reference cell that initially contains v. The mutable reference cell returned by make-ref is distinct from all other mutable locations.

(b) Function ref-get takes one argument, which is a mutable reference cell, and returns its current contents.

(c) Function ref-set! takes two arguments, a mutable reference cell and a value, and it updates the mutable reference cell so it holds the value. It also returns the value.

⟨*exercise transcripts* 178a⟩+≡

```
-> (val r (make-ref 3))
-> (ref-get r)
3
-> (ref-set! r 99)
99
-> (ref-get r)
99
```

$\langle$*exercise transcripts* 178a$\rangle$+≡

```
-> (define inc (r)
      (ref-set! r (+ 1 (ref-get r))))
-> (inc r)
100
```

2.16.12 Continuations

41. *Continuation-passing style for a Boolean-formula solver.* Generalize the solver in Section 2.10.2 to handle *any* formula, where a formula is one of the following:

    - A symbol, which stands for a variable
    - The list (not f), where f is a formula
    - The list (and f_1 ... f_n), where $f_1, \ldots, f_n$ are formulas
    - The list (or f_1 ... f_n), where $f_1, \ldots, f_n$ are formulas

    Mathematically, the set of formulas F is the smallest set satisfying this equation:

$$\begin{aligned} F = {} & \mathit{SYM} \\ & \cup \{\, \texttt{(list2 'not } f\texttt{)} \mid f \in F \,\} \\ & \cup \{\, \texttt{(cons 'and } \mathit{fs}\texttt{)} \mid \mathit{fs} \in \mathit{LIST}(F) \,\} \\ & \cup \{\, \texttt{(cons 'or } \mathit{fs}\texttt{)} \mid \mathit{fs} \in \mathit{LIST}(F) \,\}. \end{aligned}$$

    Define function `find-formula-true-asst`, which, given a satisfiable formula in this form, finds a *satisfying* assignment—that is, a mapping of variables to Booleans that makes the formula true. Remember De Morgan's laws, one of which is mentioned on page 131.

    Function `find-formula-true-asst` should expect three arguments: a formula, a failure continuation, and a success continuation. When it is called, as in `(find-formula-true-asst f fail succ)`, it should try to find a satisfying assignment for formula `f`. If it finds a satisfying assignment, it should call `succ`, passing both the satisfying assignment (as an association list) and a resume continuation. If it fails to find a satisfying assignment, it should call `(fail)`.

    You'll be able to use the ideas in Section 2.10.2, but probably not the code. Instead, try using `letrec` to define the following mutually recursive functions:

    - `(find-formula-asst formula bool cur fail succeed)` extends current assignment `cur` to find an assignment that makes the single `formula` equal to `bool`.
    - `(find-all-asst formulas bool cur fail succeed)` extends `cur` to find an assignment that makes every formula in the list `formulas` equal to `bool`.
    - `(find-any-asst formulas bool cur fail succeed)` extends `cur` to find an assignment that makes any one of the `formulas` equal to `bool`.

    In all the functions above, `bool` is `#t` or `#f`.

    Solve the problem in two parts:

    (a) Write algebraic laws for all four recommended functions.

    (b) Write the code.

car	$\mathcal{P}$ 162a
cdr	$\mathcal{P}$ 162a
cons	$\mathcal{P}$ S313d

$$\boxed{\langle e, \rho, \sigma \rangle \Downarrow \langle v, \sigma \rangle}$$

VAR
$$\frac{x \in \operatorname{dom} \rho \qquad \rho(x) \in \operatorname{dom} \sigma}{\langle \text{VAR}(x), \rho, \sigma \rangle \Downarrow \langle \sigma(\rho(x)), \sigma \rangle}$$

ASSIGN
$$\frac{x \in \operatorname{dom} \rho \qquad \rho(x) = \ell \qquad \langle e, \rho, \sigma \rangle \Downarrow \langle v, \sigma' \rangle}{\langle \text{SET}(x, e), \rho, \sigma \rangle \Downarrow \langle v, \sigma'\{\ell \mapsto v\} \rangle}$$

MKCLOSURE
$$\frac{x_1, \ldots, x_n \text{ all distinct}}{\langle \text{LAMBDA}(\langle x_1, \ldots, x_n \rangle, e), \rho, \sigma \rangle \Downarrow \langle (\!| \text{LAMBDA}(\langle x_1, \ldots, x_n \rangle, e), \rho |\!), \sigma \rangle}$$

APPLYCLOSURE
$$\frac{\begin{array}{c} \ell_1, \ldots, \ell_n \notin \operatorname{dom} \sigma_n \text{ (and all distinct)} \\ \langle e, \rho, \sigma \rangle \Downarrow \langle (\!| \text{LAMBDA}(\langle x_1, \ldots, x_n \rangle, e_c), \rho_c |\!), \sigma_0 \rangle \\ \langle e_1, \rho, \sigma_0 \rangle \Downarrow \langle v_1, \sigma_1 \rangle \\ \vdots \\ \langle e_n, \rho, \sigma_{n-1} \rangle \Downarrow \langle v_n, \sigma_n \rangle \\ \langle e_c, \rho_c\{x_1 \mapsto \ell_1, \ldots, x_n \mapsto \ell_n\}, \sigma_n\{\ell_1 \mapsto v_1, \ldots, \ell_n \mapsto v_n\} \rangle \Downarrow \langle v, \sigma' \rangle \end{array}}{\langle \text{APPLY}(e, e_1, \ldots, e_n), \rho, \sigma \rangle \Downarrow \langle v, \sigma' \rangle}$$

LITERAL
$$\frac{}{\langle \text{LITERAL}(v), \rho, \sigma \rangle \Downarrow \langle v, \sigma \rangle}$$

IFTRUE
$$\frac{\langle e_1, \rho, \sigma \rangle \Downarrow \langle v_1, \sigma' \rangle \qquad v_1 \neq \text{BOOLV(\#f)} \qquad \langle e_2, \rho, \sigma' \rangle \Downarrow \langle v_2, \sigma'' \rangle}{\langle \text{IF}(e_1, e_2, e_3), \rho, \sigma \rangle \Downarrow \langle v_2, \sigma'' \rangle}$$

IFFALSE
$$\frac{\langle e_1, \rho, \sigma \rangle \Downarrow \langle v_1, \sigma' \rangle \qquad v_1 = \text{BOOLV(\#f)} \qquad \langle e_3, \rho, \sigma' \rangle \Downarrow \langle v_3, \sigma'' \rangle}{\langle \text{IF}(e_1, e_2, e_3), \rho, \sigma \rangle \Downarrow \langle v_3, \sigma'' \rangle}$$

WHILEITERATE
$$\frac{\begin{array}{c} \langle e_1, \rho, \sigma \rangle \Downarrow \langle v_1, \sigma' \rangle \qquad v_1 \neq \text{BOOLV(\#f)} \\ \langle e_2, \rho, \sigma' \rangle \Downarrow \langle v_2, \sigma'' \rangle \qquad \langle \text{WHILE}(e_1, e_2), \rho, \sigma'' \rangle \Downarrow \langle v_3, \sigma''' \rangle \end{array}}{\langle \text{WHILE}(e_1, e_2), \rho, \sigma \rangle \Downarrow \langle v_3, \sigma''' \rangle}$$

WHILEEND
$$\frac{\langle e_1, \rho, \sigma \rangle \Downarrow \langle v_1, \sigma' \rangle \qquad v_1 = \text{BOOLV(\#f)}}{\langle \text{WHILE}(e_1, e_2), \rho, \sigma \rangle \Downarrow \langle \text{BOOLV(\#f)}, \sigma' \rangle}$$

Figure 2.9: Summary of operational semantics (expressions, except LET forms, BEGIN, and primitives)

$$\boxed{\langle e, \rho, \sigma \rangle \Downarrow \langle v, \sigma \rangle}$$

LET

$$\frac{\begin{array}{c} x_1, \ldots, x_n \text{ all distinct} \\ \ell_1, \ldots, \ell_n \notin \operatorname{dom} \sigma_n \text{ (and all distinct)} \\ \sigma_0 = \sigma \\ \langle e_1, \rho, \sigma_0 \rangle \Downarrow \langle v_1, \sigma_1 \rangle \\ \vdots \\ \langle e_n, \rho, \sigma_{n-1} \rangle \Downarrow \langle v_n, \sigma_n \rangle \\ \langle e, \rho\{x_1 \mapsto \ell_1, \ldots, x_n \mapsto \ell_n\}, \sigma_n\{\ell_1 \mapsto v_1, \ldots, \ell_n \mapsto v_n\} \rangle \Downarrow \langle v, \sigma' \rangle \end{array}}{\langle \text{LET}(\langle x_1, e_1, \ldots, x_n, e_n \rangle, e), \rho, \sigma \rangle \Downarrow \langle v, \sigma' \rangle}$$

LETSTAR

$$\frac{\begin{array}{lll} & \rho_0 = \rho & \sigma_0 = \sigma \\ \langle e_1, \rho_0, \sigma_0 \rangle \Downarrow \langle v_1, \sigma_0' \rangle \;\; \ell_1 \notin \operatorname{dom} \sigma_0' & \rho_1 = \rho_0\{x_1 \mapsto \ell_1\} & \sigma_1 = \sigma_0'\{\ell_1 \mapsto v_1\} \\ & \vdots & \\ \langle e_n, \rho_{n-1}, \sigma_{n-1} \rangle \Downarrow \langle v_n, \sigma_{n-1}' \rangle & & \\ \qquad \ell_n \notin \operatorname{dom} \sigma_{n-1}' & \rho_n = \rho_{n-1}\{x_n \mapsto \ell_n\} & \sigma_n = \sigma_{n-1}'\{\ell_n \mapsto v_n\} \\ \langle e, \rho_n, \sigma_n \rangle \Downarrow \langle v, \sigma' \rangle & & \end{array}}{\langle \text{LETSTAR}(\langle x_1, e_1, \ldots, x_n, e_n \rangle, e), \rho, \sigma \rangle \Downarrow \langle v, \sigma' \rangle}$$

LETREC

$$\frac{\begin{array}{c} \ell_1, \ldots, \ell_n \notin \operatorname{dom} \sigma \text{ (and all distinct)} \\ x_1, \ldots, x_n \text{ all distinct} \\ e_i \text{ has the form LAMBDA}(\cdots), 1 \le i \le n \\ \rho' = \rho\{x_1 \mapsto \ell_1, \ldots, x_n \mapsto \ell_n\} \\ \sigma_0 = \sigma\{\ell_1 \mapsto \text{unspecified}, \ldots, \ell_n \mapsto \text{unspecified}\} \\ \langle e_1, \rho', \sigma_0 \rangle \Downarrow \langle v_1, \sigma_1 \rangle \\ \vdots \\ \langle e_n, \rho', \sigma_{n-1} \rangle \Downarrow \langle v_n, \sigma_n \rangle \\ \langle e, \rho', \sigma_n\{\ell_1 \mapsto v_1, \ldots, \ell_n \mapsto v_n\} \rangle \Downarrow \langle v, \sigma' \rangle \end{array}}{\langle \text{LETREC}(\langle x_1, e_1, \ldots, x_n, e_n \rangle, e), \rho, \sigma \rangle \Downarrow \langle v, \sigma' \rangle}$$

EMPTYBEGIN

$$\frac{}{\langle \text{BEGIN}(), \rho, \sigma \rangle \Downarrow \langle \text{BOOLV}(\texttt{\#f}), \sigma \rangle}$$

BEGIN

$$\frac{\begin{array}{c} \langle e_1, \rho, \sigma_0 \rangle \Downarrow \langle v_1, \sigma_1 \rangle \\ \langle e_2, \rho, \sigma_1 \rangle \Downarrow \langle v_2, \sigma_2 \rangle \\ \vdots \\ \langle e_n, \rho, \sigma_{n-1} \rangle \Downarrow \langle v_n, \sigma_n \rangle \end{array}}{\langle \text{BEGIN}(e_1, e_2, \ldots, e_n), \rho, \sigma_0 \rangle \Downarrow \langle v_n, \sigma_n \rangle}$$

Figure 2.10: Summary of operational semantics (LET forms and BEGIN)

$$\boxed{\langle e, \rho, \sigma \rangle \Downarrow \langle v, \sigma \rangle}$$

ApplyAdd

$$\frac{\langle e, \rho, \sigma_0 \rangle \Downarrow \langle \text{PRIMITIVE}(\texttt{+}), \sigma_1 \rangle \quad \langle e_1, \rho, \sigma_1 \rangle \Downarrow \langle \text{NUMBER}(n), \sigma_2 \rangle \quad \langle e_2, \rho, \sigma_2 \rangle \Downarrow \langle \text{NUMBER}(m), \sigma_3 \rangle}{\langle \text{APPLY}(e, e_1, e_2), \rho, \sigma_0 \rangle \Downarrow \langle \text{NUMBER}(n+m), \sigma_3 \rangle}$$

EqNumber

$$\frac{m = n \text{ (identity of numbers)}}{\text{NUMBER}(n) \equiv \text{NUMBER}(m)}$$

EqSymbol

$$\frac{s = s' \text{ (identity of symbols)}}{\text{SYMBOL}(s) \equiv \text{SYMBOL}(s')}$$

EqBool

$$\frac{b = b' \text{ (identity of Booleans)}}{\text{BOOLV}(b) \equiv \text{BOOLV}(b')}$$

EqNil

$$\frac{}{\text{NIL} \equiv \text{NIL}}$$

ApplyEqTrue

$$\frac{\langle e, \rho, \sigma_0 \rangle \Downarrow \langle \text{PRIMITIVE}(\texttt{=}), \sigma_1 \rangle \quad \langle e_1, \rho, \sigma_1 \rangle \Downarrow \langle v_1, \sigma_2 \rangle \quad \langle e_2, \rho, \sigma_2 \rangle \Downarrow \langle v_2, \sigma_3 \rangle \quad v_1 \equiv v_2}{\langle \text{APPLY}(e, e_1, e_2), \rho, \sigma_0 \rangle \Downarrow \langle \text{BOOLV}(\texttt{\#t}), \sigma_3 \rangle}$$

ApplyEqFalse

$$\frac{\langle e, \rho, \sigma_0 \rangle \Downarrow \langle \text{PRIMITIVE}(\texttt{=}), \sigma_1 \rangle \quad \langle e_1, \rho, \sigma_1 \rangle \Downarrow \langle v_1, \sigma_2 \rangle \quad \langle e_2, \rho, \sigma_2 \rangle \Downarrow \langle v_2, \sigma_3 \rangle \quad v_1 \not\equiv v_2 \text{ (i.e., no proof of } v_1 \equiv v_2\text{)}}{\langle \text{APPLY}(e, e_1, e_2), \rho, \sigma_0 \rangle \Downarrow \langle \text{BOOLV}(\texttt{\#f}), \sigma_3 \rangle}$$

ApplyPrintln

$$\frac{\langle e, \rho, \sigma_0 \rangle \Downarrow \langle \text{PRIMITIVE}(\texttt{println}), \sigma_1 \rangle \quad \langle e_1, \rho, \sigma_1 \rangle \Downarrow \langle v, \sigma_2 \rangle}{\langle \text{APPLY}(e, e_1), \rho, \sigma_0 \rangle \Downarrow \langle v, \sigma_2 \rangle \qquad \text{while printing } v}$$

ApplyPrintu

$$\frac{\langle e, \rho, \sigma_0 \rangle \Downarrow \langle \text{PRIMITIVE}(\texttt{printu}), \sigma_1 \rangle \quad \langle e_1, \rho, \sigma_1 \rangle \Downarrow \langle \text{NUMBER}(n), \sigma_2 \rangle \quad 0 \le n < 2^{16}}{\langle \text{APPLY}(e, e_1), \rho, \sigma_0 \rangle \Downarrow \langle \text{NUMBER}(n), \sigma_2 \rangle \qquad \text{while printing the UTF-8 coding of } n}$$

Cons

$$\frac{\langle e, \rho, \sigma_0 \rangle \Downarrow \langle \text{PRIMITIVE}(\texttt{cons}), \sigma_1 \rangle \quad \langle e_1, \rho, \sigma_1 \rangle \Downarrow \langle v_1, \sigma_2 \rangle \quad \langle e_2, \rho, \sigma_2 \rangle \Downarrow \langle v_2, \sigma_3 \rangle \quad \ell_1 \notin \operatorname{dom} \sigma_3 \quad \ell_2 \notin \operatorname{dom} \sigma_3 \quad \ell_1 \neq \ell_2}{\langle \text{APPLY}(e, e_1, e_2), \rho, \sigma_0 \rangle \Downarrow \langle \text{PAIR}\langle \ell_1, \ell_2 \rangle, \sigma_3\{\ell_1 \mapsto v_1, \ell_2 \mapsto v_2\} \rangle}$$

Car

$$\frac{\langle e, \rho, \sigma_0 \rangle \Downarrow \langle \text{PRIMITIVE}(\texttt{car}), \sigma_1 \rangle \quad \langle e_1, \rho, \sigma_1 \rangle \Downarrow \langle \text{PAIR}\langle \ell_1, \ell_2 \rangle, \sigma_2 \rangle}{\langle \text{APPLY}(e, e_1), \rho, \sigma_0 \rangle \Downarrow \langle \sigma_2(\ell_1), \sigma_2 \rangle}$$

Cdr

$$\frac{\langle e, \rho, \sigma_0 \rangle \Downarrow \langle \text{PRIMITIVE}(\texttt{cdr}), \sigma_1 \rangle \quad \langle e_1, \rho, \sigma_1 \rangle \Downarrow \langle \text{PAIR}\langle \ell_1, \ell_2 \rangle, \sigma_2 \rangle}{\langle \text{APPLY}(e, e_1), \rho, \sigma_0 \rangle \Downarrow \langle \sigma_2(\ell_2), \sigma_2 \rangle}$$

Figure 2.11: Summary of operational semantics (primitives)

2.16.13 *Semantics, laws, and proof*

To help you with the operational-semantics exercises, the rules of μScheme's operational semantics are summarized in Figures 2.9 to 2.11 on pages 190 to 192.

42. *Proof or refutation of algebraic laws for* `cdr`. Algebraic laws can often be proven by appeal to other algebraic laws, but eventually some proofs have to appeal to the operational semantics. This exercise explores the algebraic law for `cdr`.

    (a) The operational semantics for μScheme includes rules for `cons`, `car`, and `cdr`. Assuming that `x` and `xs` are variables and are defined in ρ, use the operational semantics to prove that

    $$\texttt{(cdr (cons x xs))} = \texttt{xs}$$

    (b) Use the operational semantics to prove or disprove the following conjecture: if e_1 and e_2 are arbitrary expressions, then in any context in which the evaluation of e_1 terminates and the evaluation of e_2 terminates, the evaluation of `(cdr (cons` e_1 e_2`))` terminates, and

    $$\texttt{(cdr (cons } e_1\ e_2\texttt{))} = e_2$$

    The conjecture says that in any state, for any e_1 and e_2, evaluating `(cdr (cons` e_1 e_2`))` produces the same value as evaluating e_2 would have.

43. *Proof of an algebraic law for* `if`. μScheme's `if` expressions participate in many algebraic laws. Use the operational semantics to prove that

    $$\texttt{(if } e_1 \texttt{ (if } e_2\ e_3\ e_4\texttt{) (if } e_2'\ e_3\ e_4\texttt{))} = \texttt{(if (if } e_1\ e_2\ e_2'\texttt{) } e_3\ e_4\texttt{)}$$

44. *Proof of validity of desugaring for* `let`. Section 2.13.1 claims that `let` can be desugared into `lambda`:

    $$\texttt{(let ([}x_1\ e_1\texttt{]} \cdots \texttt{ [}x_n\ e_n\texttt{]) } e\texttt{)} \triangleq \texttt{((lambda (}x_1 \ \cdots\ x_n\texttt{) e) } e_1 \ \cdots\ e_n\texttt{)}.$$

    Using the operational semantics, prove that the claim is a good one for the case where $n = 1$. That is, prove that for any x_1, e_1, e, ρ, and σ, if

    $$\langle \text{LET}(\langle x_1, e_1\rangle, e), \rho, \sigma\rangle \Downarrow \langle v, \sigma'\rangle,$$

    then there exists a σ'' such that

    $$\langle \text{APPLY}(\text{LAMBDA}(\langle x_1\rangle, e), e_1), \rho, \sigma\rangle \Downarrow \langle v, \sigma''\rangle.$$

    Furthermore, show that if the choice of $\ell_1 \notin \operatorname{dom}\sigma$ is made in same way in both derivations, σ' and σ'' are the same.

45. *Proof of validity of desugaring for* `let*`. Section 2.13.1 claims that `let*` can be desugared as follows:

    $$\texttt{(let* ()} \qquad e\texttt{)} \triangleq e$$
    $$\texttt{(let* ([}x_1\ e_1\texttt{]} \cdots \texttt{ [}x_n\ e_n\texttt{]) } e\texttt{)} \triangleq$$
    $$\texttt{(let ([}x_1\ e_1\texttt{]) (let* ([}x_2\ e_2\texttt{]} \cdots \texttt{ [}x_n\ e_n\texttt{]) } e\texttt{))}$$

    Using the same technique as in Exercise 44, prove that these rules are a good desugaring of `let*` into `let`.

$$\boxed{\langle d, \rho, \sigma \rangle \rightarrow \langle \rho', \sigma' \rangle}$$

DEFINEOLDGLOBAL
$$\frac{x \in \operatorname{dom} \rho \qquad \langle e, \rho, \sigma \rangle \Downarrow \langle v, \sigma' \rangle}{\langle \text{VAL}(x, e), \rho, \sigma \rangle \rightarrow \langle \rho, \sigma'\{\rho(x) \mapsto v\} \rangle}$$

DEFINENEWGLOBAL
$$\frac{x \notin \operatorname{dom} \rho \qquad \ell \notin \operatorname{dom} \sigma \qquad \langle e, \rho\{x \mapsto \ell\}, \sigma\{\ell \mapsto \text{unspecified}\} \rangle \Downarrow \langle v, \sigma' \rangle}{\langle \text{VAL}(x, e), \rho, \sigma \rangle \rightarrow \langle \rho\{x \mapsto \ell\}, \sigma'\{\ell \mapsto v\} \rangle}$$

DEFINEFUNCTION
$$\frac{\langle \text{VAL}(f, \text{LAMBDA}(\langle x_1, \ldots, x_n \rangle, e)), \rho, \sigma \rangle \rightarrow \langle \rho', \sigma' \rangle}{\langle \text{DEFINE}(f, \langle x_1, \ldots, x_n \rangle, e), \rho, \sigma \rangle \rightarrow \langle \rho', \sigma' \rangle}$$

EVALEXP
$$\frac{\langle \text{VAL}(\texttt{it}, e), \rho, \sigma \rangle \rightarrow \langle \rho', \sigma' \rangle}{\langle \text{EXP}(e), \rho, \sigma \rangle \rightarrow \langle \rho', \sigma' \rangle}$$

Figure 2.12: Summary of operational semantics (definitions)

2.16.14 *Semantics and design: Using the operational semantics to explore language design*

46. *Alternate semantics for* `val`. In both Scheme and μScheme, when `val`'s left-hand side is already bound, `val` behaves like `set`. If `val` instead *always* created a new binding, the semantics would be simpler.

    (a) Express the operational semantics of such a `val` by writing a DEFINEGLOBAL rule.

    (b) Write a μScheme program that detects whether `val` uses the Scheme semantics or the new semantics. Explain how it works.

    (c) Compare the two ways of defining `val`. Think about how they affect code and coding style. Which design do you prefer, and why?

47. *Sensible restrictions on recursive* `val`. The behavior of the DEFINENEWGLOBAL rule may strike you as rather odd, as it permits a "definition" like

    ⟨*transcript* 95a⟩+≡
    ```
    -> (val u u)
    ```

    for a previously undefined `u`. The definition is valid, and `u` has a value, although the value is not specified. Similar behavior is typical of a number of dynamically typed languages, such as Awk, Icon, and Perl, in which a new variable—with a well-specified value, even—can be called into existence just by referring to it.

    In μScheme, the DEFINENEWGLOBAL rule makes it easy to define recursive functions, as explained on page 151. But you might prefer a semantics in which whenever `u` $\notin \operatorname{dom} \rho$, `(val u u)` is rejected.

    ⟨*imaginary transcript* 194b⟩≡
    ```
    -> (val u u)
    Run-time error: variable u not found
    ```

    Rewrite the semantics of μScheme so that `(val u u)` and similarly disturbing expressions are rejected, but it is still possible to define recursive functions.

48. *Semantics in which every variable is always defined.* μScheme's `val` definition distinguishes an undefined global variable from a global variable that is bound to the empty list. Suppose this distinction is eliminated, and that an undefined global variable behaves exactly as if it were bound to the empty list. Is it possible to write a short μScheme program that gives a different answer under the new treatment? If so, write such a program. If not, explain why not.

49. *Operational semantics for short-circuit* `&&`. Section 2.13.3 proposes syntactic sugar for short-circuit conditionals. To know if the syntactic sugar is any good, we have to have a semantics in mind. Use rules of operational semantics to specify how `&&` should behave. That is, pretending that *binary* short-circuit `&&` is actual abstract syntax and that `(&&` e_1 e_2`)` is a valid expression of μScheme, write rules for the evaluation of `&&` expressions.

50. *Operational semantics of mutation.* Write rules of operational semantics for full Scheme primitives `set-car!` and `set-cdr!`, which mutate locations in cons cells. To get started, revisit the rules for CONS, CAR, and CDR on page 151.

2.16.15 *Metatheory*

51. *Proof that variables don't alias.* Use the operational semantics to prove that variables in μScheme cannot alias. That is, prove that the evaluation of a μScheme program never constructs an environment ρ such that x and y are both defined in ρ, $x \neq y$, and $\rho(x) = \rho(y)$.

    Hint: It will help to prove that any location in the range of ρ is also in the domain of σ.

52. *Safe extension of environments.* Show that an environment can be extended with fresh variables without changing the results of evaluating an expression. In more detail,

    - You are given e and ρ such that $\langle e, \rho, \sigma \rangle \Downarrow \langle v, \sigma_1 \rangle$.
    - You are given ρ' such that $\operatorname{dom} \rho \subseteq \operatorname{dom} \rho'$, and for any x in e, $\rho'(x) = \rho(x)$.
    - You are given σ' such that $\operatorname{dom} \sigma \subseteq \operatorname{dom} \sigma'$, and for any $\ell \in \operatorname{dom} \sigma$, $\sigma'(\ell) = \sigma(\ell)$.
    - Prove that there exists a σ'_1 such that $\langle e, \rho', \sigma' \rangle \Downarrow \langle v, \sigma'_1 \rangle$, and that for any $\ell \in \operatorname{dom} \sigma$, $\sigma'_1(\ell) = \sigma_1(\ell)$.

    Use structural induction on the derivation of $\langle e, \rho, \sigma \rangle \Downarrow \langle v, \sigma_1 \rangle$.

    (This exercise is related to Exercise 9 on page 324 in Chapter 5.)

2.16.16 *Implementing new syntax and syntactic sugar*

53. *Syntactic sugar for short-circuit conditionals.* In full Scheme, `and` and `or` are macros that behave like the variadic `&&` and `||` operators defined in Section 2.13.3.

    (and) $\equiv$ #t
    (and p) $\equiv$ p
    (and p_1 p_2 ... p_n) $\equiv$ (if p_1 (and p_2 ... p_n) #f)

    Implementing `or` requires *hygiene*: you must find a fresh variable x that does not appear in any e_i.

$$\begin{aligned}
&\texttt{(or)} &&\equiv \texttt{\#f}\\
&\texttt{(or } e\texttt{)} &&\equiv e\\
&\texttt{(or } e_1 \cdots e_n\texttt{)} &&\equiv \texttt{(let ([}x\ e_1\texttt{]) (if } x\ x\ \texttt{(or } e_2 \cdots e_n\texttt{)))},\\
& && \qquad\text{where } x \text{ does not appear in any } e_i.
\end{aligned}$$

Reimplement μScheme's and and or as follows:

(a) Remove and from the initial basis of μScheme. Using the laws above, and emulating the example in Section G.7 (page S209), add a variadic, short-circuit and to μScheme as syntactic sugar.

(b) Write an auxiliary function that is given a list of expressions and returns a variable x that does not appear in any of the expressions.

(c) Remove or from the initial basis of μScheme, and using the laws above and your auxiliary function, add a variadic, short-ciruit or to μScheme as syntactic sugar.

To develop your understanding, and also to test your work, add two more parts:

(d) Write an expression of μScheme that evaluates without error using both the original and and the new and, but produces different values depending on which version of and is used.

(e) Write an expression of μScheme that evaluates without error using both the original or and the new or, but produces different values depending on which version of or is used.

54. *Syntactic sugar for records.* Implement the syntactic sugar for record described in Section 2.13.6, according to these rules:

```
(record r (f1 ··· fn)) ≜
  (define make-r (x1 ··· xn)
       (cons 'make-r (cons x1 (cons ··· (cons xn '())))))
  (define r? (x) (&& (pair? x) (= (car x) 'make-r) ···))
  (define r-f1 (x) (if (r? x) (car (cdr x)) (error ···)))
  (define r-f2 (x) (if (r? x) (car (cdr (cdr x))) (error ···)))
      ⋮
  (define r-fn (x) (if (r? x)
                          (car (cdr (cdr ··· (cdr x))))
                          (error ···)))
```

This exercise requires a lot of code. To organize it, I use these tricks:

- The record definition desugars into a *list* of definitions. It's not shown in the chapter, but μScheme has a hidden, internal mkDefs function that turns a list of definitions into a single definition. I build the list of definitions like this:

  ⟨*functions for desugaring* record *definitions* 196⟩≡
  ```
  Deflist desugarRecord(Name recname, Namelist fieldnames) {
      return mkDL(recordConstructor(recname, fieldnames),
              mkDL(recordPredicate(recname, fieldnames),
                   recordAccessors(recname, 0, fieldnames)));
  }
  ```

- I build syntax for calls to the primitives cons, car, cdr, and pair?. For each of these μScheme primitives, I define a C function, and it calls the literal primitive directly, like this:

  ⟨*functions for desugaring* record *definitions* 196⟩+≡
  ```
  static Exp carexp(Exp e) {
      return mkApply(mkLiteral(mkPrimitive(CAR, unary)), mkEL(e, NULL));
  }
  ```

- I define an auxiliary C function that generates μScheme code that applies cdr to a list a given number of times.

- My C code builds syntax for a constructor function, a type predicate, and accessor functions. For each kind of function, I first build an expression that represents the body of the function, which I put in a local variable called body. I then use body in the Def that I return.

55. *Quasiquotation.* In Section 2.7.1, I put counter operations into a record. An alternative is to put them into an association list:

    ⟨*transcript* 95a⟩+≡
    ```
    -> (val resettable-counter-from
         (lambda (x)                          ; create a counter
            (list2
              (list2 'step  (lambda () (set x (+ x 1))))
              (list2 'reset (lambda () (set x 0))))))
    ```

    Full Scheme offers a nicer way to write association lists:

    ⟨*fantasy transcript* 197c⟩≡
    ```
    -> (val resettable-counter-from
         (lambda (x)                          ; create a counter
            (quasiquote ((step  (unquote (lambda () (set x (+ x 1)))))
                         (reset (unquote (lambda () (set x 0))))))))
    ```

    The quasiquote form works like the quote form—which is normally written using the tick mark '—except that it recognizes unquote, and the unquoted expression is evaluated.

    It might not be obvious that using quasiquote and unquote is any nicer than calling list2 (or full Scheme's list). But full Scheme provides nice abbreviations: just as quote is normally written with a tick mark, quasiquote and unquote are normally written with a backtick and a comma, respectively:

    ⟨*fantasy transcript* 197c⟩+≡
    ```
    -> (val resettable-counter-from
         (lambda (x)                          ; create a counter
            `((step  ,(lambda () (set x (+ x 1))))
              (reset ,(lambda () (set x 0))))))
    ```

    list2 B 96

    (a) Look at the implementation of quote in Section L.5.1 (page S323), which relies on functions sSexp and parsesx on page S325. Emulating that code, write new functions sQuasi and parsequasi and use them to implement quasiquote and unquote.

    (b) Look at the implementation of getpar_in_context in chunk S170. Extend the function so that when read_tick_as_quote is set, it not only reads ' as quote but also reads ` as quasiquote and , as unquote.

2.16.17 *Implementing new primitives*

56. *List construction.* Add the new primitive `list`, which should accept any number of arguments.

57. *Application to a list of arguments constructed dynamically.* Add the new primitive `apply`, which takes as arguments a function and a list of values, and returns the results of applying the function to the values:

$$\frac{\begin{array}{c}\langle e, \rho, \sigma_0\rangle \Downarrow \langle \text{PRIMITIVE}(\texttt{apply}), \sigma_1\rangle \\ \langle e_1, \rho, \sigma_1\rangle \Downarrow \langle v, \sigma_2\rangle \\ \langle e_2, \rho, \sigma_2\rangle \Downarrow \langle \text{PAIR}(\ell_1, \text{PAIR}(\ell_2, \ldots, \text{PAIR}(\ell_n, \ell))), \sigma_3\rangle \\ \sigma_3(\ell) = \text{NIL} \qquad \sigma_3(\ell_i) = v_i, \quad 1 \le i \le n \\ \langle \text{APPLY}(\text{LITERAL}(v), \text{LITERAL}(v_1), \text{LITERAL}(v_2), \ldots, \text{LITERAL}(v_n)), \rho, \sigma_3\rangle \Downarrow \langle v', \sigma_4\rangle\end{array}}{\langle \text{APPLY}(e, e_1, e_2), \rho, \sigma_0\rangle \Downarrow \langle v', \sigma_4\rangle} \quad \text{(APPLY-AS-PRIMITIVE)}$$

58. *Implementation of mutation.* Add primitives `set-car!` and `set-cdr!`. Remember that `set-car!` does *not* change the value the `car` field of a cons cell; it replaces the contents of the location that the `car` field points to. You'll have it right if your mutations are visible through different variables:

⟨*mutation transcript* 198⟩≡

```
-> (val q '())
-> (val p '(a b c))
-> (set q p)
-> (set-car! p 'x)
-> (car q)
x
```

59. *Primitive to read S-expressions.* Add a `read` primitive (as in Exercise 33 of Chapter 1). You may find it helpful to call `p = getpar(...)`, followed by `mkPL(mkAtom(strtoname("quote")), mkPL(p, NULL))`.

    Use the `read` primitive to build an interactive version of the metacircular interpreter in the Supplement.

2.16.18 *Improving the interpreter*

60. *Call tracing.* Instrument the interpreter so it traces calls and returns. Whenever a traced function is called, print its name (if any) and arguments. (If the name of a function is not known, print a representation of its abstract syntax.) When a traced function returns, print the function and its result. To help users match calls with returns, indent each call and return should by an amount proportional to the number of pending calls not yet returned.

    Choose one of the following two methods to indicate which functions to trace:

    (a) Provide primitives to turn tracing of individual functions on and off.

    (b) Use variable `&trace` as a "trace count." (Simply look it up in the current environment.) While `&trace` is bound to a location containing a nonzero number, each call and return should decrement the trace count and print a line. If the trace count is negative, tracing runs indefinitely.

    Test your work by tracing `length` as shown on page 99. Also trace `sieve` and `remove-multiples`.

Printing the abstract syntax for a function provides good intuition, but it may be more helpful to print non-global functions in closure form.

(c) When calling a closure, print it in closure form instead of printing its name. Which of the two methods is better?

Chapter 3 contents

3

Control operators and a small-step semantics: μScheme+

Formalizing a system in its own terms is now a familiar occupation. . . . The formalization of a machine for evaluating expressions seems to have no precedent.

Peter Landin, *The Mechanical Evaluation of Expressions*

Chapter 2 presents applicative programming in μScheme. But μScheme doesn't just support applicative programming; it also supports the procedural programming style described in Chapter 1. In particular, it provides `while`, `set`, and `begin`. In the procedural style, `while` and `if` account for most control flow. But loops typically also use such *control operators* as `break`, `continue`, and `return`. These constructs, as well as the less canonical `try-catch` and `throw`, don't fit into the story about programming languages that we've been telling so far:

- They aren't easy to implement using a recursive `eval` function.
- They can't be formalized using a judgment of the form $\langle e, \rho, \sigma \rangle \Downarrow \langle v, \sigma' \rangle$. For example, evaluating `break` doesn't produce a value.

These troublesome constructs all involve control flow.

In early high-level languages, control flow looked a lot like hardware. Typical hardware provides a `goto` instruction, which transfers control to a particular *target* point in the code, and a *conditional* `goto`, which transfers control only if some condition is satisfied. And in the 1950s, these same instructions were what you got in high-level languages like Fortran:

`GOTO` *target-label*

or

`IF` *condition* `GOTO` *target-label*.

But a program full of `goto`s can be hard to understand: in particular, the order in which the parts are executed need not have anything to do with the order in which they are written. The `goto` statement was eventually derided as "harmful" (Dijkstra 1968), and `goto` was largely replaced with constructs like `if` and `while`. Using `if` and `while`, the order in which the parts are executed is determined by the order in which they are written, and it's easy to see. The use of `if` and `while` as primary control-flow constructs is called *structured programming*. Structured programming was the most successful programming-language revolution of all time—in today's languages, `if` and `while` are ubiquitous, and despite Donald Ervin Knuth's (1974) attempts to rehabilitate the `goto` statement, `goto` is frowned upon and is almost never used.

But Knuth had a point. Using `if` and `while` *exclusively* can lead to convoluted code, especially in loops. To express loops more clearly, structured programming languages adapted:

- Languages added more looping constructs, including constructs like `do-while`, `repeat-until`, and several kinds of `for` loop.
- Languages added *control operators* like `break`, `continue`, and `return`. Each of these operators acts like a `goto`, but a `goto` with a predetermined target: `break` goes to the point immediately after its enclosing loop; `continue` goes to the point immediately before its enclosing loop; and `return` goes to the point in the calling function from which the current function was called.

The action "go to a target" is exactly what is hard to implement in a recursive interpreter and impossible to describe using a judgment of the form $\langle e, \rho, \sigma\rangle \Downarrow \langle v, \sigma'\rangle$.

Control operators are the subject of this chapter. The chapter presents not only `break`, `continue`, and `return`, but also `try-catch` and `throw`, which model exceptional control flow between functions; and `long-label` and `long-goto`, which are low-level control operators that can implement all the others. These operators are specified and implemented using a new technique: an *explicit* representation of the *context* in which each expression is evaluated. Our representation is a *stack*. The stack is related to the C call stack of the recursive `eval` functions in Chapters 1 and 2. It is also related to the path from an evaluation judgment to the root of a derivation. In our C code, the stack is a data structure, and in our operational semantics, the stack is a part of the state of the abstract machine.

Most chapters in this book are oriented toward what you can do with new language ideas or new language features. But as you might guess from the talk about a stack, interpreters, and semantics, this chapter is oriented more toward how control operators can be specified and implemented. And in Chapter 4, the implementation is extended to show how civilized programming languages manage memory.

3.1 THE μSCHEME+ LANGUAGE

Control operators are illustrated using an extension of μScheme called μScheme+, whose concrete syntax appears in Figure 3.1. μScheme+ includes all of μScheme, plus control operators, plus syntactic sugar for procedural programming. The control operators implement new program behaviors: "go to," "throw," and "catch."

- When `(break)` is evaluated inside a `while` loop, the interpreter goes to the point right after the loop. To evaluate `(break)` outside any loop is a checked error.
- When `(continue)` is evaluated inside a `while` loop, the interpreter goes to the beginning of the loop and continues evaluating the loop (by testing its condition). To evaluate `(continue)` outside any loop is a checked error.
- When `(return` e`)` is evaluated in a function's body, the interpreter evaluates e to produce a value v, and that ends the evaluation of the function's body; the function returns v. To evaluate `(return` e`)` outside the body of any function (for example, at top level) is a checked error.
- When `(throw` L e`)` is evaluated, the interpreter evaluates e to produce a value v, and then it *throws* v to the most recently installed `try-catch` handler labeled with L. To throw a value v to L when no `try-catch` handler is installed for L is a checked run-time error.

def	::=	(val *variable-name exp*)
	|	*exp*
	|	(define *function-name* (*formals*) *exp*)
	|	(use *file-name*)
	|	*unit-test*
unit-test	::=	(check-expect *exp exp*)
	|	(check-assert *exp*)
	|	(check-error *exp*)
exp	::=	*literal*
	|	*variable-name*
	|	(set *variable-name exp*)
	|	(if *exp exp exp*)
	|	(while *exp exp*)
	|	(begin {*exp*})
	|	(*exp* {*exp*})
	|	(*let-keyword* ({[*variable-name exp*]}) *exp*)
	|	(lambda (*formals*) *exp*)
	|	*primitive*
	|	(break)
	|	(continue)
	|	(return *exp*)
	|	(try-catch *exp label-name exp*)
	|	(throw *label-name exp*)
	|	(long-label *label-name exp*)
	|	(long-goto *label-name exp*)
let-keyword	::=	let | let* | letrec
formals	::=	{*variable-name*}
literal	::=	*numeral* | #t | #f | '*S-exp* | (quote *S-exp*)
S-exp	::=	*literal* | *symbol-name* | ({*S-exp*})
primitive	::=	+ | - | * | / | = | < | > | println | print | printu | error
	|	car | cdr | cons
	|	number? | symbol? | pair? | null? | boolean? | function?
numeral	::=	token composed only of digits, possibly prefixed with a plus or minus sign
**-name*	::=	token that is not a bracket, a *numeral*, or one of the "reserved" words shown in typewriter font

Figure 3.1: Concrete syntax of μScheme+

def	⋆	::=	(define *type-exp function-name* (*formals*) {*exp*})
exp	⋆	::=	(while *exp* {*exp*})
	⋆	|	(*let-keyword* ({[*variable-name exp*]}) {*exp*})
	⋆	|	(when *exp* {*exp*})
	⋆	|	(unless *exp* {*exp*})

Figure 3.2: Syntactic sugar that supports procedural programming

`(when` $e\ e_1\ \cdots\ e_n$`)`	$\triangleq$	`(if` e `(begin` $e_1\ \cdots\ e_n$`) #f)`
`(unless` $e\ e_1\ \cdots\ e_n$`)`	$\triangleq$	`(if` e `#f (begin` $e_1\ \cdots\ e_n$`))`
`(while` $e\ e_1\ \cdots\ e_n$`)`	$\triangleq$	`(while` e `(begin` $e_1\ \cdots\ e_n$`))`
`(`*let-keyword* `(`*bindings*`)` $e_1\ \cdots\ e_n$`)`	$\triangleq$	`(`*let-keyword* `(`*bindings*`) (begin` $e_1\ \cdots\ e_n$`))`

Figure 3.3: Desugaring equations

- In `(try-catch` e_b L e_h`)`, expression e_b is the *body*, name L is the *label*, and e_h is the *handler*. When the `try-catch` is evaluated, the interpreter evaluates the handler e_h to produce a value f, which must be a function. The interpreter installs f as the most recent handler for label L, then determines the outcome of the `try-catch` expression by evaluating the body e_b:
  - If e_b evaluates normally to v, without throwing any value, the interpreter uninstalls the handler f (reverting to the previous handler, if any). The `try-catch` expression returns v.
  - If, during the evaluation of e_b, a value v is thrown to label L, and if f is the most recently installed `try-catch` handler, then the interpreter uninstalls the handler f (reverting to the previous handler, if any). This action is called *catching* v. The interpreter then applies f to v, and the `try-catch` expression does whatever the application `(`f v`)` does.
  - If expression e_b throws a value v to some label L' that is different from L, then the `try-catch` expression also throws v to L'.

  To evaluate `(try-catch` e_b L e_h`)` when e_h evaluates to a non-function value is a checked run-time error.
- When `(long-goto` L e`)` is evaluated, the interpreter evaluates e to produce a value v. Then it finds the youngest active `long-label` expression with the same label L. The interpreter goes to that `long-label` expression, which terminates immediately; it returns value v. To evaluate `(long-goto` L e`)` when no corresponding `long-label` expression is active is a checked run-time error.
- When `(long-label` L e`)` is evaluated, the interpreter starts evaluating expression e. If during that evaluation, e evaluates a `long-goto` with label L and value v, control immediately goes to the `long-label` expression, which produces value v. Otherwise, the `long-label` expression does whatever e does.

The `long-label` form is a cousin of C's `setjmp`, and the `long-goto` form is a cousin of C's `longjmp`; the label L is analogous to a `jmp_buf`. The `long-label` and `long-goto` forms can be used in your μScheme+ programs, just like labels and `goto` statements in C, but they are meant to be used to implement the other control operators, as described in Section 3.4 below.

The native forms of μScheme+ are supplemented by the syntactic sugar shown in Figure 3.2. Sugar is called for because control operators are inherently procedural: a control operator is a *command* that tells the computer to do something. And commands demand procedural programming; the very word "procedure" means a sequence of actions or commands. Using the syntactic sugar, sequences can be written without `begin`: the body of every function, loop, and let-expression is automatically a sequence. Sequences also appear as the bodies of the one-way conditional forms `when` and `unless`. These forms are desugared using the rules shown in Figure 3.3.

Armed with an informal understanding of the control operators, plus concrete syntax suitable for writing procedural code, we're ready to see how μScheme+'s control operators are used.

3.2 PROCEDURAL PROGRAMMING WITH CONTROL OPERATORS

Control operators can be studied in isolation, but in this section, procedural code that uses control operators is compared with functional code in the style of Chapter 2. I assume that you've seen procedural programming before, and I hope your experience includes `break`, `continue`, and `return`. The examples emphasize `try-catch` and `throw`; although they represent just one point in a large design space, they will help you think about design and implementation of language features for dealing with exceptional outcomes.

3.2.1 Programming with `break`, `continue`, *and* `return`

To compare procedural programming with functional programming, I use an old problem usually given to students who've studied just one semester of programming (Soloway 1986; Fisler 2014):

> Design a function called `rainfall` that computes average rainfall. The function consumes a list of numbers representing daily rainfall amounts as entered by a user. The list may contain the special number 99999, which indicates that 99999 and all numbers that follow it should be ignored. Also, only nonnegative numbers are meaningful: a negative number represents a data-collection error, not a true rainfall amount, and it should also be ignored. The `rainfall` function should produce the average of the nonnegative values in the list up to the first 99999 (if it shows up).

A functional solution to the rainfall problem

If I'm a functional programmer, I might think about the problem like this:

- Typical functional codes manipulate whole data structures: for the rainfall problem, whole lists. I care about lists like "everything up to 99999" and "all the nonnegative elements."
- A list should be consumed by a recursive function.
- I might not have to write a new recursive function—maybe I can use an existing one. Existing higher-order functions implement common recursions, and they're easy to reuse and combine. For the rainfall problem, `takewhile` can grab list elements up to 99999, and `filter` can grab the nonnegative elements. Functions like `takewhile` and `filter` make it easy to write working code quickly, although they also make it less obvious how much computer time and memory are needed.
- Functions `takewhile` and `filter` might allocate cons cells, and that's OK; a serious implementation of a functional language is designed for programs that allocate like crazy.

My design plan looks like this: grab all the numbers up to (but not including) 99999, eliminate the negative ones, and return the sum of what's left, divided by its length.

“Grab up to” is `takewhile` and “eliminate” can be done using `filter`.

206a. ⟨*transcript* 206a⟩≡ 206b ▷

```
-> (define rainfall-f (ns)
    (let* ([nonneg? (lambda (n) (>= n 0))]
           [ms (filter nonneg? (takewhile ((curry !=) 99999) ns))])
     (/ (foldl + 0 ms) (length ms))))
-> (rainfall-f '(1 2 3 99999 4 5 6))
2
-> (rainfall-f '(1 -1 2 -2 3 -3 6))
3
-> (rainfall-f '(-1 -2 -3))
Run-time error: division by zero
```


The code is good enough, but if the input list doesn’t contain any nonnegative numbers, I prefer a different error message. To avoid dividing by `(length ms)` when it might be zero, I first check if `ms` is empty. If so, I issue my own error message. My revised function looks like this:

206b. ⟨*transcript* 206a⟩+≡ ◁ 206a 207a ▷

```
-> (define rainfall-f (ns)
    (let* ([nonneg? (lambda (n) (>= n 0))]
           [ms (filter nonneg? (takewhile ((curry !=) 99999) ns))])
      (if (null? ms)
          (error 'rainfall-no-nonnegative-numbers)
          (/ (foldl + 0 ms) (length ms)))))
-> (rainfall-f '(1 2 3))
2
-> (rainfall-f '(99999 1 2 3))
Run-time error: rainfall-no-nonnegative-numbers
```

A procedural solution to the rainfall problem

If I’m a procedural programmer, I might think about the problem like this:

- Typical procedural codes manipulate lists one thing at a time.
- A list should be consumed by a loop, not by a recursive function.
- Side effects are OK. The rainfall problem calls for an average, and just as in the functional solution, I’ll need a total and a count. But in the procedural solution, the total and count can be kept in mutable variables, which can be initialized to zero and updated using `set`.
- Procedural code usually avoids allocation, and for good reason: implementations of procedural languages often assume that allocation is rare. The rainfall problem consumes a list that is allocated on the heap, but its total and count are only numbers, and it returns a number. So it has no reason to allocate.

The challenge of the rainfall problem is what to do in the loop. The loop demands a nontrivial case analysis: the sentinel value 99999, if present, marks the end of the input, and other negative values should be ignored. These special cases can be managed using `break` and `continue`. My design plan looks like this:

- Start with variables `total` and `count` set to zero.
- Loop through the inputs, updating `total` and `count` as appropriate.
- When the loop finishes, divide `total` by `count`.

One draft is enough:

207a. ⟨*transcript* 206a⟩+≡ ◁206b 207b▷

```
-> (define rainfall-p (ns)
     (let* ([count 0]   ; number of nonnegative numbers seen
               [total 0]) ; and their sum
       (while (not (null? ns))
         (let* ([n (car ns)])
           (set ns (cdr ns))
           (when (= n 99999)
             (break))
           (when (< n 0)
             (continue))
           (set count (+ count 1))
           (set total (+ total n))))
       (if (= count 0)
           (error 'rainfall-no-nonnegative-numbers)
           (/ total count))))
```


Control operators `break` and `continue` simplify the code significantly (see Exercise 2), as does the syntactic sugar. And the code works as it should:

207b. ⟨*transcript* 206a⟩+≡ ◁207a 208a▷

```
-> (rainfall-p '(1 2 3 99999 4 5 6))
2
-> (rainfall-p '(1 -1 2 -2 3 -3 6))
3
-> (rainfall-p '(-1 -2 -3))
Run-time error: rainfall-no-nonnegative-numbers
```

3.2.2 *Programming with* `try-catch` *and* `throw`

If either `rainfall` or `rainfall-p` is given a list containing no nonnegative numbers, it calls `error`, and the μScheme+ code stops running. Suppose instead that we wish it to keep going. As a model, we could look to the C code that implements Impcore and μScheme. Calling `runerror` doesn't mean that C code stops running; C code catches the error and continues (in the `readevalprint` function). How does it work? The C `runerror` function in chunk S182 calls `longjmp`, which transfers control to the `setjmp` in chunk S316c.

The C functions `setjmp` and `longjmp` are low-level mechanisms: `setjmp` initializes a `jmp_buf`, and `longjmp` transfers control to it. And `setjmp` returns a code that distinguishes initialization from transfer. These mechanisms work, but a C programmer has to think a lot about policy: how many `jmp_buf`s there should be, whether they are arranged in a stack, who is responsible for allocating and deallocating their memory, how to avoid using a stale `jmp_buf`, and so on. Many programming languages provide a mechanism that is easier to work with, usually called *exceptions*. They come with a lot of vocabulary.

- An *exception* signals that something has gone wrong or something unexpected has happened. For example, a "not found" exception might signal that an expected name is not bound in an environment.

  Depending on the language, an exception may be a value, or it may be its own unique thing, distinct from values, variables, functions, and everything else. No matter what kind of thing it is, an exception can usually carry some additional information along with it, such as a name that wasn't found.

- When the bad or unexpected thing happens, the exception is *thrown*. (Some languages say *raised* or *signaled*.)

- When an exception is thrown, control is transferred to a *handler;* the handler *catches* the exception. And unlike `break`, `continue`, or `return`, throwing an exception can transfer control to a distant function: if there's no handler in the function where the exception is thrown, the system looks for a handler in the calling function, and then the function that called the calling function, and so on. The system interrogates older and older active functions until it finds one that has an appropriate handler.

  What marks a handler as appropriate depends on the language. In some languages, exceptions have names, and a handler is appropriate if it names the exception that is thrown. In other languages, exceptions are values, a handler names a *type,* and a handler is appropriate if the value thrown is compatible with the named type. And in many languages, a handler can claim to be appropriate for *all* exceptions.

To implement exceptions, a programming language needs three mechanisms:

- A way to create or name an exception to be thrown
- A way to throw the exception
- A way to introduce one or more handlers and to evaluate an expression within the context of those handlers.

μScheme+ uses the simplest mechanisms that illustrate the ideas:

- An exception is identified by name; any name can be an exception.
- An exception is thrown using `throw`.
- A handler is introduced, and an expression is evaluated in its context, using `try-catch`.

Using `throw` and `try-catch`, we can recover from errors in the rainfall functions.

Rainfall with `try-catch` *and* `throw`

In our `rainfall-f` and `rainfall-p` functions, nothing really needs to change, except instead of calling `error`, we would like to throw an exception. I could rewrite the code, but instead I use a dirty trick, which you can use with your own μScheme code: I overwrite the global variable `error` to contain a new function that, when called, throws the exception named `:error`.[1]

208a. ⟨*transcript* 206a⟩+≡ ◁ 207b 208b ▷

```
-> (set error (lambda (msg) (throw :error msg)))
<function>
```

After this change, calling a rainfall function without any rainfalls produces a different error message.

208b. ⟨*transcript* 206a⟩+≡ ◁ 208a 209a ▷

```
-> (rainfall-p '())
Run-time error: long-goto :error with no active long-label for :error
```

This message mentions `long-goto` and `long-label` because these are the mechanisms used to implement `throw` and `try-catch` (Section 3.4); the message means there's no handler for the `:error` exception.

A handler can be provided using `try-catch`. As a vastly oversimplified example, I define a prediction function. It predicts tomorrow's rainfall by using the aver-

[1] By convention, I identify each exception using a name that begins with a colon, but you can name an exception anything you like.

age from rainfall-p, but if rainfall-p fails, it predicts a rainfall of zero. Function predicted-rainfall works even on inputs where rainfall-p fails.

209a. ⟨*transcript* 206a⟩+≡ ◁208b 209b▷

```
-> (define predicted-rainfall (data)
     (try-catch
        (rainfall-p data) ; this is evaluated in the scope of the handler
        :error            ; this is the exception that the handler catches
        (lambda (_) 0)    ; this is the handler
     ))
-> (predicted-rainfall       '(1 -1 2 -2 0 99999 6 -6))
1
-> (predicted-rainfall '(99999 1 -1 2 -2 0 99999 6 -6))
0
-> (rainfall-p         '(99999 1 -1 2 -2 0 99999 6 -6))
Run-time error: long-goto :error with no active long-label for :error
```


More throwing and catching

Exceptions are useful in many interfaces. As an example, an alternative to the search function find (Section 2.3.8, page 106) can throw the :not-found exception if a key is not found. The implementation is written in procedural style, using while and return:

209b. ⟨*transcript* 206a⟩+≡ ◁209a 209c▷

```
-> (define find-or-throw (k alist)
     (while (not (null? alist))
       (if (equal? k (alist-first-key alist))
           (return (alist-first-attribute alist))
           (set alist (cdr alist))))
     (throw :not-found k))
```

Function find-or-throw exemplifies the procedural way of consuming a list: it contains a loop but no recursion. It returns an attribute or throws the :not-found exception:

209c. ⟨*transcript* 206a⟩+≡ ◁209b 209d▷

```
-> (find-or-throw 'E '((I Ching) (E coli)))
coli
-> (find-or-throw 'X '((I Ching) (E coli)))
Run-time error: long-goto :not-found with no active long-label for :not-found
-> (try-catch (find-or-throw 'X '((I Ching) (E coli)))
              :not-found
              (lambda (exn) (list2 'not-found exn)))
(not-found X)
```

These examples might remind you of the continuation-passing function find-c (page 136). That's no accident; control operators and continuations both express non-local control flow. And each of these functions, find-or-throw and find-c, can easily be implemented in terms of the other. To implement find-or-throw using continuations, we supply a failure continuation that throws the exception. The success continuation is the identity function.

209d. ⟨*transcript* 206a⟩+≡ ◁209c 210a▷

```
-> (define alternate-find-or-throw (k alist)
      (find-c k alist (lambda (v) v) (lambda () (throw :not-found k))))
-> (alternate-find-or-throw 'E '((I Ching) (E coli)))
coli
```

210a. ⟨*transcript* 206a⟩+≡ ◁209d 210b▷

```
-> (alternate-find-or-throw 'X '((I Ching) (E coli)))
Run-time error: long-goto :not-found with no active long-label for :not-found
-> (try-catch (alternate-find-or-throw 'X '((I Ching) (E coli)))
              :not-found
              (lambda (x) (list2 'not-found x)))
(not-found X)
```

To implement `find-c` using the control operator, we install an exception handler that invokes the failure continuation.

210b. ⟨*transcript* 206a⟩+≡ ◁210a 215▷

```
-> (define alternate-find-c (k alist success-cont failure-cont)
     (try-catch (success-cont (find-or-throw k alist))
                :not-found
                (lambda (key) (failure-cont))))
-> (alternate-find-c 'Hello '((Hello Dolly) (Goodnight Irene))
                     (lambda (v) (list2 'the-answer-is v))
                     (lambda ()  'the-key-was-not-found))
(the-answer-is Dolly)
-> (alternate-find-c 'Goodbye '((Hello Dolly) (Goodnight Irene))
                     (lambda (v) (list2 'the-answer-is v))
                     (lambda ()  'the-key-was-not-found))
the-key-was-not-found
```

Continuations also turn out to be a fine way to *specify* the behavior of control operators (Stoy 1977; Allison 1986; Schmidt 1986). Sadly, continuation-based specification techniques are beyond the scope of this book.

3.3 Operational semantics: Evaluation using a stack

A control operator's behavior depends on what computations are active when it is evaluated.

- A `break` or `continue` must be evaluated inside an active `while` loop, which the control operator terminates or continues.
- A `return` must be evaluated inside an active function application, which the `return` terminates.
- A `throw` must be evaluated during the evaluation of an active `try-catch` with the same label, whose handler the `throw` starts evaluating.

In a recursive `eval` function like the ones used in Chapters 1 and 2, active computations can't easily be identified—a recursive C function cannot inspect its caller's state, so the `eval` function can't tell if a loop, function, or `try-catch` is waiting. In μScheme+, the active computations aren't hidden on the C call stack; they are maintained on an explicit *evaluation stack*, which the interpreter can inspect. The evaluation stack is demonstrated in this section with an example, then used in Section 3.5 to write the operational semantics of μScheme+.

An evaluation stack is either empty, in which case it is written $[]$, or it it is formed by pushing a *frame* F on top of another stack S, in which case it is written $F :: S$. The operator $::$ associates to the right, so for example if a stack has exactly four frames, it could be written out in full as $F_1 :: F_2 :: F_3 :: F_4 :: []$. These frames are numbered in the order in which we see them when inspecting the stack, which is the reverse of the order in which they were pushed.

Each individual frame F is an expression with a "hole" in it. The frame is "waiting" for the value of some expression, and the hole, which is written using the bullet symbol •, stands for a place where that value is expected to be plugged in. For example, the frame `(+ • 1)` is waiting for a value that it plans to add 1 to.

During computation, the evaluation stack changes, and it usually changes in the same way that the C call stack changes when the interpreter in Chapter 2 is running. For example, where Chapter 2's interpreter calls `eval`, and an activation record is pushed onto the C call stack, this chapter's interpreter pushes a frame onto the evaluation stack—and that frame is waiting for the result from `eval`. Where Chapter 2's interpreter would return from `eval`, this chapter's interpreter pops a frame off the evaluation stack, and it fills the hole in the frame with the value that Chapter 2's `eval` would have returned.[2]

The evaluation stack S is just part of an abstract machine. Like the abstract machines of Chapter 2, the abstract machine for μScheme+ also includes an environment ρ and a store σ. The μScheme+ abstract machine makes transitions between states of these two forms:

$\langle e, \rho, \sigma, S\rangle$ The machine is about to evaluate expression e; stack S is waiting for the result. The machine's next transition is determined by the syntactic form of the expression e.

$\langle v, \rho, \sigma, S\rangle$ The machine has just finished evaluating an expression to produce value v; it is about to plug v into the hole in the top frame of stack S. The machine's next transition is determined by the syntactic form of the stack S—usually by the form of the topmost frame—and possibly also by a property of v.

The state's first element, which is either e or v, is the *current item*. And an operational semantics based on transitions between states like these is an *abstract-machine semantics.*

Below, the abstract-machine transitions are illustrated by comparing a stack-based evaluation, which uses this machine, with a recursive evaluation, which gradually fills in a derivation in the style of Chapters 1 and 2. Both evaluations use the expression

`(* (+ 10 1) 9).`

Each step of evaluation is presented in a four-part template numbered N, where N is the number of steps taken since the beginning:

N | *Narrative of recursive evaluation from Chapter 2.*	*Partially traversed derivation of* $\langle e, \rho, \sigma\rangle \Downarrow \langle v, \sigma'\rangle$.
Narrative of stack-based evaluation.	*State of abstract machine with stack, either* $\langle e, \rho, \sigma, S\rangle$ *or* $\langle v, \rho, \sigma, S\rangle$.

The recursive `eval` from Chapter 2 traverses a derivation tree node by node. In a template, a partially traversed tree is indicated by the colors of the big-step judgments: a judgment whose subderivation is completely traversed is colored black, and a judgment whose subderivation is not yet traversed is colored gray. A judgment whose traversal by Chapter 2 `eval` is currently in progress is shown half and

[2]The `eval` function isn't special: *any* recursive function can be converted into a loop that uses an explicit stack. If you've seen this technique before, some of what's in this section will be old news, and you can concentrate on what's happening in the different kinds of semantics. If you haven't seen the technique before, be aware that it's good for more than just semantics: it's good for any recursive algorithm that needs very deep recursions. One of my favorite examples is depth-first search of a graph with millions of nodes.

half: black on the left and gray on the right. The colors can help you compare the progress of the two evaluations: if you follow a path from the uppermost call in progress down to the root of the derivation tree, you'll see that each judgment on the path corresponds to a frame on the stack.

In the stack-based evaluation, each state in which the current item is an expression is labeled EXP, and each state in which the current item is a value is labeled VALUE. And to make it extra easy to distinguish values from literal expressions, in this example only, values are written using an italic font, as in *99*.

Recursive evaluation starts by passing expression $e =$ `(* (+ 10 1) 9)` to `eval`. Stack-based evaluation starts in a state in which the current item is the expression e and the stack is empty:

0 | Pass the expression e to `eval`.

Make expression e the current item and make the stack empty.

$$\frac{\dfrac{\langle \texttt{10}, \rho\rangle \Downarrow \mathit{10} \qquad \langle \texttt{1}, \rho\rangle \Downarrow \mathit{1}}{\langle \texttt{(+ 10 1)}, \rho\rangle \Downarrow \mathit{11}} \qquad \langle \texttt{9}, \rho\rangle \Downarrow \mathit{9}}{\langle \texttt{(* (+ 10 1) 9)}, \rho\rangle \Downarrow \mathit{99}}$$

EXP $\langle$`(* (+ 10 1) 9)`$, \rho, \sigma, [\,]\rangle$

---

1 | Call `eval` (via `evallist`) with the first argument of `*`.

In the current expression, replace the first argument of `*` with a hole and push the resulting frame on the stack. The first argument becomes the current item.

$$\frac{\dfrac{\langle \texttt{10}, \rho\rangle \Downarrow \mathit{10} \qquad \langle \texttt{1}, \rho\rangle \Downarrow \mathit{1}}{\langle \texttt{(+ 10 1)}, \rho\rangle \Downarrow \mathit{11}} \qquad \langle \texttt{9}, \rho\rangle \Downarrow \mathit{9}}{\langle \texttt{(* (+ 10 1) 9)}, \rho\rangle \Downarrow \mathit{99}}$$

EXP $\langle$`(+ 10 1)`$, \rho, \sigma,$ `(*` $\bullet$ `9)` $:: [\,]\rangle$

---

2 | Call `eval` (via `evallist`) with the first argument of `+`.

Replace the first argument of `+` with a hole and push the resulting frame on the stack. The first argument becomes the current item.

$$\frac{\dfrac{\langle \texttt{10}, \rho\rangle \Downarrow \mathit{10} \qquad \langle \texttt{1}, \rho\rangle \Downarrow \mathit{1}}{\langle \texttt{(+ 10 1)}, \rho\rangle \Downarrow \mathit{11}} \qquad \langle \texttt{9}, \rho\rangle \Downarrow \mathit{9}}{\langle \texttt{(* (+ 10 1) 9)}, \rho\rangle \Downarrow \mathit{99}}$$

EXP $\langle$`10`$, \rho, \sigma,$ `(+` $\bullet$ `1)` $::$ `(*` $\bullet$ `9)` $:: [\,]\rangle$

---

3 | Evaluate literal `10`, returning *10* from `eval`.

Evaluate literal `10`, producing *10*. The value *10* becomes the current item; the stack is unchanged.

$$\frac{\dfrac{\langle \texttt{10}, \rho\rangle \Downarrow \mathit{10} \qquad \langle \texttt{1}, \rho\rangle \Downarrow \mathit{1}}{\langle \texttt{(+ 10 1)}, \rho\rangle \Downarrow \mathit{11}} \qquad \langle \texttt{9}, \rho\rangle \Downarrow \mathit{9}}{\langle \texttt{(* (+ 10 1) 9)}, \rho\rangle \Downarrow \mathit{99}}$$

VAL $\langle \mathit{10}, \rho, \sigma,$ `(+` $\bullet$ `1)` $::$ `(*` $\bullet$ `9)` $:: [\,]\rangle$

---

4 | Call `eval` (via `evallist`) with the second argument of `+`.

Pop the top frame off the stack; it is a call to `+` with a hole as the first argument and an expression as the second argument. Replace the hole with the current value *10*, and pull out the second argument, replacing it with a new hole. Push the modified frame back on the stack. The second argument becomes the new current item.

$$\frac{\dfrac{\langle \texttt{10}, \rho\rangle \Downarrow \mathit{10} \qquad \langle \texttt{1}, \rho\rangle \Downarrow \mathit{1}}{\langle \texttt{(+ 10 1)}, \rho\rangle \Downarrow \mathit{11}} \qquad \langle \texttt{9}, \rho\rangle \Downarrow \mathit{9}}{\langle \texttt{(* (+ 10 1) 9)}, \rho\rangle \Downarrow \mathit{99}}$$

EXP $\langle$`1`$, \rho, \sigma,$ `(+` $\mathit{10}\ \bullet$`)` $::$ `(*` $\bullet$ `9)` $:: [\,]\rangle$

5 Evaluate literal `1`, returning *1* from `eval`.

The expression `1` is evaluated to *1*, which becomes the new current item. The stack is unchanged.

$$\frac{\dfrac{\overline{\langle \texttt{10}, \rho\rangle \Downarrow 10} \qquad \overline{\langle \texttt{1}, \rho\rangle \Downarrow 1}}{\langle \texttt{(+ 10 1)}, \rho\rangle \Downarrow 11} \qquad \overline{\langle \texttt{9}, \rho\rangle \Downarrow 9}}{\langle \texttt{(* (+ 10 1) 9)}, \rho\rangle \Downarrow 99}$$

$$\textsc{val}\ \langle 1, \rho, \sigma, (\texttt{+}\ 10\ \bullet) :: (\texttt{*}\ \bullet\ \texttt{9}) :: [\,]\rangle$$

6 Function `eval` adds values *10* and *1*, returning *11*.

Pop the top frame off the stack and fill its hole with the current value *1*. The resulting expression is the complete call (+ *10 1*). Replace the call with the result *11*, which becomes the current item.

$$\frac{\dfrac{\overline{\langle \texttt{10}, \rho\rangle \Downarrow 10} \qquad \overline{\langle \texttt{1}, \rho\rangle \Downarrow 1}}{\langle \texttt{(+ 10 1)}, \rho\rangle \Downarrow 11} \qquad \overline{\langle \texttt{9}, \rho\rangle \Downarrow 9}}{\langle \texttt{(* (+ 10 1) 9)}, \rho\rangle \Downarrow 99}$$

$$\textsc{val}\ \langle 11, \rho, \sigma, (\texttt{*}\ \bullet\ \texttt{9}) :: [\,]\rangle$$

7 Call `eval` (via `evallist`) to evaluate the second argument of `*`.

Pop the top frame off the stack; it is a call with a hole as the first argument and an expression as the second argument. Replace the hole with the current value *11*, and pull out the second argument, replacing it with a new hole. Push the modified frame back on the stack, and let the second argument become the new current item.

$$\frac{\dfrac{\overline{\langle \texttt{10}, \rho\rangle \Downarrow 10} \qquad \overline{\langle \texttt{1}, \rho\rangle \Downarrow 1}}{\langle \texttt{(+ 10 1)}, \rho\rangle \Downarrow 11} \qquad \overline{\langle \texttt{9}, \rho\rangle \Downarrow 9}}{\langle \texttt{(* (+ 10 1) 9)}, \rho\rangle \Downarrow 99}$$

$$\textsc{exp}\ \langle \texttt{9}, \rho, \sigma, (\texttt{*}\ 11\ \bullet) :: [\,]\rangle$$

8 Evaluating `9` returns *9*.

The expression `9` is evaluated to *9*, which becomes the new current item. The stack is unchanged.

$$\frac{\dfrac{\overline{\langle \texttt{10}, \rho\rangle \Downarrow 10} \qquad \overline{\langle \texttt{1}, \rho\rangle \Downarrow 1}}{\langle \texttt{(+ 10 1)}, \rho\rangle \Downarrow 11} \qquad \overline{\langle \texttt{9}, \rho\rangle \Downarrow 9}}{\langle \texttt{(* (+ 10 1) 9)}, \rho\rangle \Downarrow 99}$$

$$\textsc{val}\ \langle 9, \rho, \sigma, (\texttt{*}\ 11\ \bullet) :: [\,]\rangle$$

9 Function `eval` multiplies *11* by *9*, returning *99*.

Pop the top frame off the stack and fill the hole with the current item *9*. The resulting expression is a complete call to the primitive `*`. The result of the multiplication is *99*, which becomes the current item.

$$\frac{\dfrac{\overline{\langle \texttt{10}, \rho\rangle \Downarrow 10} \qquad \overline{\langle \texttt{1}, \rho\rangle \Downarrow 1}}{\langle \texttt{(+ 10 1)}, \rho\rangle \Downarrow 11} \qquad \overline{\langle \texttt{9}, \rho\rangle \Downarrow 9}}{\langle \texttt{(* (+ 10 1) 9)}, \rho\rangle \Downarrow 99}$$

$$\textsc{val}\ \langle 99, \rho, \sigma, [\,]\rangle$$

After 9 steps, the current item is a value and the stack is empty, so $\langle 99, \rho, \sigma, [\,]\rangle$ is a valid state, and the result of evaluating the expression is *99*.

3.4 Operational semantics: Lowering to a core language

An abstract-machine semantics with an explicit evaluation stack suffers from an annoying drawback: it can require a lot of rules. Like the big-step semantics of Chapters 1 and 2, the abstract-machine semantics needs at least one rule for every form of expression. But in addition, it needs at least one rule for every form of

Table 3.4: Lowering rules

Lowering rules for control operators	
(while e_1 e_2)	$\rightsquigarrow$ (long-label :break (while* e_1 (long-label :continue e_2)))
(break)	$\rightsquigarrow$ (long-goto :break)
(continue)	$\rightsquigarrow$ (long-goto :continue)
(try-catch e_1 L e_2)	$\rightsquigarrow$ (let ([h e_2]) (long-label L (let ([x e_1]) (lambda (_) x))) h)
(throw L e)	$\rightsquigarrow$ (let ([x e]) (long-goto L (lambda (h) (h x))))
Lowering rules for lambda *and* return	
(lambda (x_1 $\cdots$ x_n) e)	$\rightsquigarrow$ (lambda* (x_1 $\cdots$ x_n) (long-label :return e))
(return)	$\rightsquigarrow$ (long-goto :return)
Lowering rules for other expression forms	
(while* e_1 e_2)	$\rightsquigarrow$ (if e_1 (begin e_2 (while* e_1 e_2)) #f)
(begin)	$\rightsquigarrow$ #f
(begin e)	$\rightsquigarrow$ e
(begin e_1 $e_2 \cdots$)	$\rightsquigarrow$ (let ([x e_1]) (begin $e_2 \cdots$))
(let* () e)	$\rightsquigarrow$ e
(let* ([x_1 e_1] $\cdots$) e)	$\rightsquigarrow$ (let ([x_1 e_1]) (let* ($\cdots$) e))

Variable h is not free in e_1, and variable x is not free in any e_i.
Form lambda* behaves like lambda, except it is not lowered.

stack frame—and there are about as many forms of stack frame as there are forms of expression. The drawback can be mitigated by reducing the number of forms of expression. To do that, some forms of expression are *lowered* to a *core language*.

A core language is a subset that is sufficient to express everything in a full language. The full language is *lowered* to a core language by a process of rewriting expressions. It works much the same way as expanding syntactic sugar, except when a full language is lowered to a core language, the original syntax is usually kept around to be used in error messages.

Core μScheme+ includes `long-label` and `long-goto` forms, but not `break`, `continue`, `try-catch`, or `throw` forms—these forms are lowered into the core. Core μScheme+ also omits `begin` and `let*` forms, which are lowered to `let` expressions. Finally, Core μScheme+ does include `return`; while `return` can be lowered using `long-goto`, lowering `return` would complicate the important tail-call optimization described on page 238. Lowering `return` is left as Exercise 23.

Expressions are lowered using the rules in Table 3.4. Each rule is written as a relation of the form $e \rightsquigarrow e'$, pronounced "expression e is lowered to expression e'." Rules in the first two groups use `long-label` and `long-goto` to implement μScheme+'s other control operators. Operators `break`, `continue`, `throw`, and `return` can be implemented using `long-goto`, for which suitable labels are introduced by the rules for `while`, `try-catch`, and `lambda`.

The only rules that demand detailed explanation are those for `try-catch` and `throw`. The `try-catch` rule sets up a `long-label` expression whose result is a function; that function takes one argument, a handler, and it returns the result of the `try-catch`. When `try-catch` terminates as the result of a `throw`, the function thrown is `(lambda (h) (h x))`, where `x` is the value thrown. This case therefore passes the value to the handler. When `try-catch` terminates as the result of its body terminating normally, the function produced is `(lambda (h) x)`, where `x` is the value of the body. This case ignores the handler.

Table 3.4 omits some important side conditions: `break` and `continue` expressions are lowered only inside a loop, and a `return` expression is lowered only inside a function. Attempts to lower these operators outside of their expected contexts result in an error message:

215. ⟨*transcript* 206a⟩+≡ ◁210b

```
-> (lambda (x) (when x (break)))
Lowering error: (break) appeared outside of any loop
```

The lowering transformation reduces the number of rules needed to express the operational semantics: all the forms that can be lowered share a single rule, and none of those forms ever goes onto the evaluation stack. The operational semantics itself is the topic of the next section.

3.5 A SEMANTICS OF CORE μSCHEME+

The example abstract-machine transitions in Section 3.3 are justified by the operational semantics of Core μScheme+. This semantics is an *abstract-machine semantics,* and it is defined by this *transition relation* between machine states:

$$\langle e/v, \rho, \sigma, S\rangle \rightarrow \langle e'/v', \rho', \sigma', S'\rangle.$$

The notation e/v stands for the current item, which may be an expression e or a value v.

An abstract-machine transition describes just one step in an evaluation, not the evaluation of an entire expression. Evaluating an entire expression usually requires multiple steps. A transition that may take multiple steps (zero or more) is written

$$\langle e/v, \rho, \sigma, S\rangle \rightarrow^* \langle e'/v', \rho', \sigma', S'\rangle.$$

The sequence of states thus passed through is often called a *reduction sequence.*

Some special states and transitions are worth looking out for; spotting them will help you understand how the machine works.

- A state of the form $\langle e, \rho, \sigma, []\rangle$ is an *initial* state, meant to evaluate e.
- A state of the form $\langle v, \rho, \sigma, []\rangle$ is a *final* state, reached after an evaluation completes. States of this form are the only acceptable final states; if the machine is in any other state and it cannot make a transition, it is considered stuck.
- In a transition of the form $\langle e, \rho, \sigma, S\rangle \rightarrow \langle e', \rho, \sigma, F :: S\rangle$, most likely e' is the first subexpression of e to be evaluated, and F is a frame formed from e by replacing e' with a hole.
- In a transition of the form $\langle v, \rho, \sigma, F :: S\rangle \rightarrow \langle e, \rho, \sigma, S\rangle$, e might be taken from F, after examining v and F.

None of these special cases describes the evaluation of a control operator, which typically inspects multiple frames on the stack.

The permissible transitions of the abstract machine are described by inference rules. These rules describe actions that differ from the actions described by big-step rules: In a big-step semantics, the action of evaluating a typical syntactic form is described by a single rule, and the evaluation of a conditional form, like `if` or `while`, is typically described by two rules: one for a true condition and one for a false condition. In an abstract-machine semantics, the action of evaluating any syntactic form is usually spread out over at least two rules, and sometimes more. One rule says what to do with the form if it appears as the current item, and one says what to do if the form appears on the stack as a frame. And the rules for stack frames tend to be less uniform big-step rules: some forms never appear on the stack, and others may appear as frames with holes in different places, requiring multiple rules per form.

Because the abstract-machine rules work so differently from the big-step rules, they are organized differently from the rules in Chapters 1 and 2. The rules for a single syntactic form still appear together, but based on how their evaluation affects the stack, the forms are organized into these groups:

- Forms that are lowered, which don't change the stack
- Other forms that don't change the stack: LITERAL, VAR, and LAMBDA
- Forms that push just one frame onto the stack: SET and IF
- Forms that evaluate subexpressions in sequence: APPLY, LET, and LETREC
- Forms that inspect the stack and jump far away: LONG-LABEL, LONG-GOTO, and RETURN

This grouping contrasts with all the other groupings in the book, which mostly show the same constructs in the same order (literal, variable, `set`, `if`, `while`, and so on).

To help you compare the small-step reduction rules with big-step natural-deduction rules, rules of μScheme+ are accompanied by corresponding rules of μScheme. If you want to leap straight to the control operators, they are described in Section 3.5.5 on page 221.

3.5.1 *Forms that are eliminated by lowering*

If expression e can be lowered, then whenever e shows up as a current item to be evaluated, it is immediately replaced by its lowered form:

$$\frac{e \rightsquigarrow e'}{\langle e, \rho, \sigma, S\rangle \to \langle e', \rho, \sigma, S\rangle}. \qquad \text{(LOWER)}$$

The stack, environment, and store aren't consulted and don't change.

While the semantics specifies that an expression be lowered only when it is about to be evaluated, the lowering relation depends only on e's syntactic form, not on any other property of the machine's state. This independence enables an optimization: all lowerable expressions can be lowered preemptively, before evaluation begins. In my implementation, no expression is lowered more than once, even if it is evaluated in a loop.

3.5.2 *Forms that don't examine or change the stack*

A literal is evaluated without looking at the stack or the store. The small-step rule looks almost exactly like the big-step rule.

$$\frac{}{\langle \text{LITERAL}(v), \rho, \sigma\rangle \Downarrow \langle v, \sigma\rangle} \qquad \text{(BIG-STEP-LITERAL)}$$

$$\frac{}{\langle \text{LITERAL}(v), \rho, \sigma, S\rangle \to \langle v, \rho, \sigma, S\rangle} \qquad \text{(SMALL-STEP-LITERAL)}$$

Likewise, a variable is evaluated in one small step. The lookup is the same as in the big-step rule, and the stack S is unexamined and unchanged.

$$\frac{x \in \operatorname{dom} \rho \qquad \rho(x) \in \operatorname{dom} \sigma}{\langle \text{VAR}(x), \rho, \sigma \rangle \Downarrow \langle \sigma(\rho(x)), \sigma \rangle} \qquad \text{(BIG-STEP-VAR)}$$

$$\frac{x \in \operatorname{dom} \rho \qquad \rho(x) \in \operatorname{dom} \sigma}{\langle \text{VAR}(x), \rho, \sigma, S \rangle \to \langle \sigma(\rho(x)), \rho, \sigma, S \rangle} \qquad \text{(SMALL-STEP-VAR)}$$

A LAMBDA expression is also evaluated in one step, as in the big-step semantics: the expression and the current environment are captured in a closure. Again, the small-step rule looks almost exactly like the big-step rule, and the stack is unexamined and unchanged.

$$\frac{x_1, \ldots, x_n \text{ all distinct}}{\langle \text{LAMBDA}(\langle x_1, \ldots, x_n \rangle, e), \rho, \sigma \rangle \Downarrow \langle (\!| \text{LAMBDA}(\langle x_1, \ldots, x_n \rangle, e), \rho |\!), \sigma \rangle}$$
(BIG-STEP-MKCLOSURE)

$$\frac{x_1, \ldots, x_n \text{ all distinct}}{\langle \text{LAMBDA}(\langle x_1, \ldots, x_n \rangle, e), \rho, \sigma, S \rangle \to \langle (\!| \text{LAMBDA}(\langle x_1, \ldots, x_n \rangle, e), \rho |\!), \rho, \sigma, S \rangle}$$
(SMALL-STEP-MKCLOSURE)

3.5.3 *Forms that push a single frame onto the stack*

If a form's semantics require it to evaluate an expression, then do something, the form must push a frame on the stack. The simplest such form is assignment. The rule for SET(x, e) first pushes a frame that says, "I must assign to x," then makes e the current item, where it will be evaluated. When e's evaluation is complete, the SET frame is popped and is used to update x. The push-evaluate-pop sequence can be derived by analyzing the big-step rule:

$$\frac{x \in \operatorname{dom} \rho \qquad \rho(x) = \ell \qquad \langle e, \rho, \sigma \rangle \Downarrow \langle v, \sigma' \rangle}{\langle \text{SET}(x, e), \rho, \sigma \rangle \Downarrow \langle v, \sigma'\{\ell \mapsto v\} \rangle}. \qquad \text{(BIG-STEP-ASSIGN)}$$

An evaluation judgment $\langle e, \rho, \sigma \rangle \Downarrow \langle v, \sigma' \rangle$ above the line is always implemented by a small step that makes e the current item and that pushes a frame that knows what to do with v. For SET, the frame is made by replacing e with a hole:

$$\frac{x \in \operatorname{dom} \rho}{\langle \text{SET}(x, e), \rho, \sigma, S \rangle \to \langle e, \rho, \sigma, \text{SET}(x, \bullet) :: S \rangle}. \qquad \text{(SMALL-STEP-ASSIGN)}$$

When e's evaluation is complete, its value v will be the current item, and the frame SET$(x, \bullet)$ will be on top of the stack. The abstract machine must pop the stack, update location $\ell = \rho(x)$, and produce v.

$$\frac{\rho(x) = \ell}{\langle v, \rho, \sigma, \text{SET}(x, \bullet) :: S \rangle \to \langle v, \rho, \sigma\{\ell \mapsto v\}, S \rangle} \qquad \text{(FINISH-ASSIGN)}$$

This rule is sound only because of a metatheoretic property of the semantics: if a machine makes a sequence of transitions from SMALL-STEP-ASSIGN to FINISH-ASSIGN, the ρ components of the two states are guaranteed to be the same. This property holds because any rule that changes the environment carefully saves the old environment on the stack.

Another expression that pushes only one frame onto the stack is the IF expression. Like an assignment, an IF is evaluated in two steps: first evaluate the condition, then continue with one of the two branches. Because there are two ways to continue, the old, big-step semantics has two rules: one for a true condition and one for a false condition.

$$\frac{\langle e_1, \rho, \sigma \rangle \Downarrow \langle v_1, \sigma' \rangle \qquad v_1 \neq \text{BOOLV}(\texttt{\#f}) \qquad \langle e_2, \rho, \sigma' \rangle \Downarrow \langle v_2, \sigma'' \rangle}{\langle \text{IF}(e_1, e_2, e_3), \rho, \sigma \rangle \Downarrow \langle v_2, \sigma'' \rangle} \quad \text{(BIG-STEP-IFTRUE)}$$

$$\frac{\langle e_1, \rho, \sigma \rangle \Downarrow \langle v_1, \sigma' \rangle \qquad v_1 = \text{BOOLV}(\texttt{\#f}) \qquad \langle e_3, \rho, \sigma' \rangle \Downarrow \langle v_3, \sigma'' \rangle}{\langle \text{IF}(e_1, e_2, e_3), \rho, \sigma \rangle \Downarrow \langle v_3, \sigma'' \rangle} \quad \text{(BIG-STEP-IFFALSE)}$$

Look at both rules above the line. Each one begins with the same judgment, $\langle e_1, \rho, \sigma \rangle \Downarrow \langle v_1, \sigma' \rangle$. Therefore, the small-step semantics can begin with the evaluation of e_1, and it can push a frame that waits for value v_1. Again, that frame is made by replacing e_1 with a hole. The frame $\text{IF}(\bullet, e_2, e_3)$ saves both e_2 and e_3 on the stack, so no matter what v_1 is, the machine knows how to continue:

$$\frac{}{\langle \text{IF}(e_1, e_2, e_3), \rho, \sigma, S \rangle \to \langle e_1, \rho, \sigma, \text{IF}(\bullet, e_2, e_3) :: S \rangle}. \quad \text{(SMALL-STEP-IF)}$$

When $\text{IF}(\bullet, e_2, e_3)$ is on the stack and v is the current item, the machine continues by evaluating either e_2 or e_3—whichever would be dictated by the big-step rules:

$$\frac{v \neq \text{BOOLV}(\texttt{\#f})}{\langle v, \rho, \sigma, \text{IF}(\bullet, e_2, e_3) :: S \rangle \to \langle e_2, \rho, \sigma, S \rangle}, \quad \text{(SMALL-STEP-IF-TRUE)}$$

$$\frac{v = \text{BOOLV}(\texttt{\#f})}{\langle v, \rho, \sigma, \text{IF}(\bullet, e_2, e_3) :: S \rangle \to \langle e_3, \rho, \sigma, S \rangle}. \quad \text{(SMALL-STEP-IF-FALSE)}$$

3.5.4 *Forms that evaluate expressions in sequence*

The forms that evaluate sequences of expressions (APPLY, LET, and LETREC) use the same idea as SET and IF—push a frame where a hole marks what the machine is waiting for—but because values in the sequence are delivered one at a time, the rules are more complicated. Each of these forms uses at least three kinds of rule:

- Every form has a rule for when the form is encountered as the current item. That rule turns the form into a frame by putting a hole in the first position.
- Every form has a rule for a hole in the middle of the sequence. The rule fills the hole with a value and moves the hole to the next position in sequence.
- Every form has a rule for a hole in the last position in the sequence. That rule captures the entire sequence and continues.

In addition, the APPLY form has a special rule for a hole in the first position, because that's the function position, not an argument position, and the function is treated specially.

Function application

Function application has a lot going on. Here's the big-step rule:

$$\frac{\begin{array}{c}\ell_1, \ldots, \ell_n \notin \operatorname{dom} \sigma \text{ (and all distinct)} \\ \langle e, \rho, \sigma \rangle \Downarrow \langle (\!|\text{LAMBDA}(\langle x_1, \ldots, x_n \rangle, e_c), \rho_c |\!), \sigma_0 \rangle \\ \langle e_1, \rho, \sigma_0 \rangle \Downarrow \langle v_1, \sigma_1 \rangle \\ \vdots \\ \langle e_n, \rho, \sigma_{n-1} \rangle \Downarrow \langle v_n, \sigma_n \rangle \\ \langle e_c, \rho_c\{x_1 \mapsto \ell_1, \ldots, x_n \mapsto \ell_n\}, \sigma_n\{\ell_1 \mapsto v_1, \ldots, \ell_n \mapsto v_n\} \rangle \Downarrow \langle v, \sigma' \rangle\end{array}}{\langle \text{APPLY}(e, e_1, \ldots, e_n), \rho, \sigma \rangle \Downarrow \langle v, \sigma' \rangle} \quad \text{(BIG-STEP-APPLYCLOSURE)}$$

Interpreted as "capture sequence and continue," the rule works like this:

- Expressions $e, e_1, \ldots, e_n$ are evaluated in sequence.
- Once e evaluates to a closure v_f and the arguments evaluate to $v_1, \ldots, v_n$, v_f's body is evaluated in a new environment built by extending ρ_c.

The small-step rules evaluate the sequence using an invariant: when $e, e_1, \ldots, e_{i-1}$ have been evaluated and it's time to start evaluating e_i, the current item is e_i, and the top of the stack holds the frame $\text{APPLY}(v_f, v_1, \ldots, v_{i-1}, \bullet, e_{i+1}, \ldots, e_n)$. Here v_f is the value of the function expression e (expected to be a closure or a primitive function), and $v_1, \ldots, v_{i-1}$ are the results of evaluating the first $i - 1$ arguments. When evaluation of e_i finishes, leaving v_i as the current item, the hole is shifted one space to the right, leaving the frame $\text{APPLY}(v_f, v_1, \ldots, v_i, \bullet, e_{i+2}, \ldots, e_n)$ on top of the stack:

$$\frac{}{\begin{array}{l}\langle v, \rho, \sigma, \text{APPLY}(v_f, v_1, \ldots, v_{i-1}, \bullet, e_{i+1}, \ldots, e_n) :: S \rangle \to \\ \quad \langle e_{i+1}, \rho, \sigma, \text{APPLY}(v_f, v_1, \ldots, v_{i-1}, v, \bullet, e_{i+2}, \ldots, e_n) :: S \rangle\end{array}} \quad \text{(SMALL-STEP-APPLY-NEXT-ARG)}$$

This rule corresponds to the transition that finishes the right-hand side of big-step judgment $\langle e_i, \rho, \sigma_{i-1} \rangle \Downarrow \langle v_i, \sigma_i \rangle$ (where $v = v_i$) and starts the next judgment $\langle e_{i+1}, \rho, \sigma_i \rangle \Downarrow \langle v_{i+1}, \sigma_{i+1} \rangle$. If the hole is in the first (function) position, a very similar rule applies:

$$\frac{}{\langle v, \rho, \sigma, \text{APPLY}(\bullet, e_1, \ldots, e_n) :: S \rangle \to \langle e_1, \rho, \sigma, \text{APPLY}(v, \bullet, e_2, \ldots, e_n) :: S \rangle} \quad \text{(SMALL-STEP-APPLY-FIRST-ARG)}$$

The $\text{APPLY}(v, e_1, \ldots, e_n)$ frame is first pushed onto the stack when a function application appears as the current expression. The expression e in the function position becomes the new current item, i.e., the next thing to be evaluated.

$$\frac{}{\langle \text{APPLY}(e, e_1, \ldots, e_n), \rho, \sigma, S \rangle \to \langle e, \rho, \sigma, \text{APPLY}(\bullet, e_1, \ldots, e_n) :: S \rangle} \quad \text{(SMALL-STEP-APPLY)}$$

Finally, when all arguments have been evaluated, the top of the stack holds an APPLY frame in which the hole has the rightmost position; the state of the machine is $\langle v_n, \rho, \sigma, \text{APPLY}(v_f, v_1, \ldots, v_{n-1}, \bullet) :: S \rangle$. What happens now? Looking back at the big-step rule, the last small-step rule has to implement the big-step judgment $\langle e_c, \rho_c\{x_1 \mapsto \ell_1, \ldots, x_n \mapsto \ell_n\}, \sigma_n\{\ell_1 \mapsto v_1, \ldots, \ell_n \mapsto v_n\} \rangle \Downarrow \langle v, \sigma' \rangle$. Making e_c the current item is no problem, but the environment is another story. After expression e_c is evaluated in the new environment, the machine has to revert the environment back to ρ. To save ρ while e_c executes, the abstract machine pushes it onto the stack in the form of a new frame $\text{ENV}(\rho, \text{CALL})$. The ρ is the saved environment, and the tag CALL says why the environment was saved.

$$\frac{\begin{array}{c} v_f = (\!|\text{LAMBDA}(\langle x_1, \ldots, x_n \rangle, e_c), \rho_c |\!) \\ \ell_1, \ldots, \ell_n \notin \operatorname{dom} \sigma \text{ (and all distinct)} \end{array}}{\begin{array}{c} \langle v_n, \rho, \sigma, \text{APPLY}(v_f, v_1, \ldots, v_{n-1}, \bullet) :: S \rangle \rightarrow \\ \langle e_c, \rho_c\{x_1 \mapsto \ell_1, \ldots, x_n \mapsto \ell_n\}, \sigma_n\{\ell_1 \mapsto v_1, \ldots, \ell_n \mapsto v_n\}, \text{ENV}(\rho, \text{CALL}) :: S \rangle \end{array}}$$

(SMALL-STEP-APPLY-LAST-ARG)

After e_c's evaluation is finished, encountering $\text{ENV}(\rho, \text{CALL})$ on the stack restores ρ:

$$\overline{\langle v, \rho', \sigma, \text{ENV}(\rho, tag) :: S \rangle \rightarrow \langle v, \rho, \sigma, S \rangle}.$$

(SMALL-STEP-RESTORE-ENVIRONMENT)

In informal English, the environment is pushed onto the stack just before a call, and when the call finishes, it is popped back off. This part of the semantics models real implementations of real languages: environment ρ holds machine registers and local variables, and $\text{ENV}(\rho, \text{CALL})$ is called a "stack frame" (or sometimes "activation record.").

Rule SMALL-STEP-APPLY-LAST-ARG applies only when v_f is a closure. When v_f is a primitive function, other rules apply, like this one:

$$\frac{v_1 = \text{NUMBER}(n) \qquad v_2 = \text{NUMBER}(m) \qquad v = \text{NUMBER}(n + m)}{\langle v_2, \rho, \sigma, \text{APPLY}(\text{PRIMITIVE}(+), v_1, \bullet) :: S \rangle \rightarrow \langle v, \rho, \sigma, S \rangle}.$$

(SMALL-STEP-APPLYADD)

The LET *expressions*

Sequences of expressions also occur in LET forms. In μScheme+, only LET and LETREC are part of the core; LETSTAR is lowered. Like APPLY, LET evaluates expressions in sequence and builds a new environment in which to evaluate a body.

$$\frac{\begin{array}{c} \ell_1, \ldots, \ell_n \notin \operatorname{dom} \sigma \text{ (and all distinct)} \\ x_1, \ldots, x_n \text{ all distinct} \\ \langle e_1, \rho, \sigma_0 \rangle \Downarrow \langle v_1, \sigma_1 \rangle \\ \vdots \\ \langle e_n, \rho, \sigma_{n-1} \rangle \Downarrow \langle v_n, \sigma_n \rangle \\ \langle e, \rho\{x_1 \mapsto \ell_1, \ldots, x_n \mapsto \ell_n\}, \sigma_n\{\ell_1 \mapsto v_1, \ldots, \ell_n \mapsto v_n\} \rangle \Downarrow \langle v, \sigma' \rangle \end{array}}{\langle \text{LET}(\langle x_1, e_1, \ldots, x_n, e_n \rangle, e), \rho, \sigma \rangle \Downarrow \langle v, \sigma' \rangle} \quad \text{(LET)}$$

LET is implemented by these small-step rules:

$$\frac{}{\begin{array}{l} \langle v, \rho, \sigma, \text{LET}(\langle x_1, v_1, \ldots, x_i, \bullet, x_{i+1}, e_{i+1}, \ldots, x_n, e_n \rangle, e) :: S \rangle \rightarrow \\ \qquad \langle e_{i+1}, \rho, \sigma, \text{LET}(\langle x_1, v_1, \ldots, x_i, v, x_{i+1}, \bullet, \ldots, e_n \rangle, e) :: S \rangle \end{array}},$$

(SMALL-STEP-NEXT-LET-EXP)

$$\frac{x_1, \ldots, x_n \text{ all distinct}}{\begin{array}{l} \langle \text{LET}(\langle x_1, e_1, \ldots, x_n, e_n \rangle, e), \rho, \sigma, S \rangle \rightarrow \\ \qquad \langle e_1, \rho, \sigma, \text{LET}(\langle x_1, \bullet, x_2, e_2, \ldots, x_n, e_n \rangle, e) :: S \rangle \end{array}}, \quad \text{(SMALL-STEP-LET)}$$

$$\frac{\ell_1, \ldots, \ell_n \notin \operatorname{dom} \sigma \text{ (and all distinct)}}{\begin{array}{l} \langle v, \rho, \sigma, \text{LET}(\langle x_1, v_1, \ldots, x_n, \bullet \rangle, e) :: S \rangle \rightarrow \\ \qquad \langle e, \rho\{x_1 \mapsto \ell_1, \ldots, x_n \mapsto \ell_n\}, \sigma_n\{\ell_1 \mapsto v_1, \ldots, \ell_n \mapsto v_n\}, \text{ENV}(\rho, \text{NONCALL}) :: S \rangle \end{array}},$$

(SMALL-STEP-LET-BODY)

$$\overline{\langle v, \rho', \sigma, \text{ENV}(\rho, \text{NONCALL}) :: S \rangle \rightarrow \langle v, \rho, \sigma, S \rangle}.$$

(SMALL-STEP-RESTORE-LET-ENVIRONMENT)

The frame $\text{ENV}(\rho, \text{NONCALL})$ behaves the same way as $\text{ENV}(\rho, \text{CALL})$—except, as shown on page 222, when viewed by the control operator `return`.

The LETREC expression is quite similar to the LET expression, except it binds fresh locations into the environment *before* evaluating expressions $e_1, \ldots, e_n$.

$$\frac{\begin{array}{c} \ell_1, \ldots, \ell_n \notin \operatorname{dom} \sigma \text{ (and all distinct)} \\ x_1, \ldots, x_n \text{ all distinct} \\ e_i \text{ has the form } \text{LAMBDA}(\cdots), 1 \le i \le n \\ \rho' = \rho\{x_1 \mapsto \ell_1, \ldots, x_n \mapsto \ell_n\} \\ \sigma_0 = \sigma\{\ell_1 \mapsto \text{unspecified}, \ldots, \ell_n \mapsto \text{unspecified}\} \\ \langle e_1, \rho', \sigma_0 \rangle \Downarrow \langle v_1, \sigma_1 \rangle \\ \vdots \\ \langle e_n, \rho', \sigma_{n-1} \rangle \Downarrow \langle v_n, \sigma_n \rangle \\ \langle e, \rho', \sigma_n\{\ell_1 \mapsto v_1, \ldots, \ell_n \mapsto v_n\} \rangle \Downarrow \langle v, \sigma' \rangle \end{array}}{\langle \text{LETREC}(\langle x_1, e_1, \ldots, x_n, e_n \rangle, e), \rho, \sigma \rangle \Downarrow \langle v, \sigma' \rangle} \quad \text{(LETREC)}$$

LETREC is implemented by similar small-step rules, starting with this one:

$$\frac{}{\begin{array}{l} \langle v, \rho, \sigma, \text{LETREC}(\langle x_1, v_1, \ldots, x_i, \bullet, x_{i+1}, e_{i+1}, \ldots, x_n, e_n \rangle, e) :: S \rangle \to \\ \qquad \langle e_{i+1}, \rho, \sigma, \text{LETREC}(\langle x_1, v_1, \ldots, x_i, v, x_{i+1}, \bullet, \ldots, e_n \rangle, e) :: S \rangle \end{array}}.$$

(SMALL-STEP-NEXT-LETREC-EXP)

Again, the old environment is saved in the transition that introduces the new environment ρ'. In LETREC, that means saving when control enters the LETREC itself, not the body:

$$\frac{\begin{array}{c} x_1, \ldots, x_n \text{ all distinct} \\ e_i \text{ has the form } \text{LAMBDA}(\cdots), 1 \le i \le n \\ \ell_1, \ldots, \ell_n \notin \operatorname{dom} \sigma \text{ (and all distinct)} \\ \rho' = \rho\{x_1 \mapsto \ell_1, \ldots, x_n \mapsto \ell_n\} \\ \sigma_0 = \sigma\{\ell_1 \mapsto \text{unspecified}, \ldots, \ell_n \mapsto \text{unspecified}\} \end{array}}{\begin{array}{l} \langle \text{LETREC}(\langle x_1, e_1, \ldots, x_n, e_n \rangle, e), \rho, \sigma, S \rangle \to \\ \qquad \langle e_1, \rho', \sigma_0, \text{LETREC}(\langle x_1, \bullet, x_2, e_2, \ldots, x_n, e_n \rangle, e) :: \text{ENV}(\rho, \text{NONCALL}) :: S \rangle \end{array}},$$

(SMALL-STEP-LETREC)

$$\frac{\ell_i = \rho(x_i), 1 \le i \le n}{\begin{array}{l} \langle v, \rho, \sigma, \text{LETREC}(\langle x_1, v_1, \ldots, x_n, \bullet \rangle, e) :: S \rangle \to \\ \qquad \langle e, \rho, \sigma\{\ell_1 \mapsto v_1, \ldots, \ell_{n-1} \mapsto v_{n-1}, \ell_n \mapsto v\}, S \rangle \end{array}}.$$

(SMALL-STEP-LETREC-BODY)

3.5.5 *Forms that inspect the stack:* LONG-LABEL, LONG-GOTO, *and* RETURN

Finally, the control operators! These operators can't easily be described using big-step semantics. Each operator carries one expression, and each operator begins by pushing itself on the stack with a hole in place of its expression. The expression becomes the current item, and when it is reduced to a value, the fun begins:

1. If $\text{LONG-LABEL}(L, \bullet)$ is on top of the stack, it doesn't do anything—it's there just to mark a destination for LONG-GOTO. The frame is popped and evaluation continues.

2. If $\text{LONG-GOTO}(L, \bullet)$ is on top of the stack, it looks at the next older frame on the stack. If that frame is $\text{LONG-LABEL}(L, \bullet)$, then the LONG-GOTO has arrived at its destination. Both frames are popped. Otherwise, the next frame is discarded, and evaluation continues by inspecting the next older frame after that.

3. RETURN works like LONG-GOTO, except its destination is not a LONG-LABEL frame; it's a frame of the form ENV(ρ, CALL).

Discarding part of the stack is called *unwinding*.

A LONG-LABEL expression pushes its label onto the stack and evaluates its body. It also saves the current environment just below the label, so that after a control transfer, the environment is properly restored.

$$\frac{}{\langle \text{LONG-LABEL}(L, e), \rho, \sigma, S\rangle \to \langle e, \rho, \sigma, \text{LONG-LABEL}(L, \bullet) :: \text{ENV}(\rho, \text{NONCALL}) :: S\rangle} \quad (\text{LABEL})$$

If control is never transferred, eventually the LONG-LABEL frame is found on top of the stack, where it is ignored.

$$\frac{}{\langle v, \rho, \sigma, \text{LONG-LABEL}(L, \bullet) :: S\rangle \to \langle v, \rho, \sigma, S\rangle} \quad (\text{LABEL-UNUSED})$$

The LONG-LABEL frame is actually used as a target for LONG-GOTO, which begins by evaluating its expression:

$$\frac{}{\langle \text{LONG-GOTO}(L, e), \rho, \sigma, S\rangle \to \langle e, \rho, \sigma, \text{LONG-GOTO}(L, \bullet) :: S\rangle}. \quad (\text{GOTO})$$

Once the expression is evaluated, the LONG-GOTO continues by looking for its matching label.

$$\frac{}{\langle v, \rho, \sigma, \text{LONG-GOTO}(L, \bullet) :: \text{LONG-LABEL}(L, \bullet) :: S\rangle \to \langle v, \rho, \sigma, S\rangle} \quad (\text{GOTO-TRANSFER})$$

If the next older frame isn't label L, LONG-GOTO unwinds it:

$$\frac{F \neq \text{LONG-LABEL}(L, \bullet)}{\langle v, \rho, \sigma, \text{LONG-GOTO}(L, \bullet) :: F :: S\rangle \to \langle v, \rho, \sigma, \text{LONG-GOTO}(L, \bullet) :: S\rangle}. \quad (\text{GOTO-UNWIND})$$

A RETURN works like a LONG-GOTO, except instead of looking for a corresponding LONG-LABEL, it looks for a frame of the form ENV(ρ', CALL).

$$\frac{}{\langle \text{RETURN}(e), \rho, \sigma, S\rangle \to \langle e, \rho, \sigma, \text{RETURN}(\bullet) :: S\rangle} \quad (\text{RETURN})$$

$$\frac{}{\langle v, \rho, \sigma, \text{RETURN}(\bullet) :: \text{ENV}(\rho', \text{CALL}) :: S\rangle \to \langle v, \rho', \sigma, S\rangle} \quad (\text{RETURN-TRANSFER})$$

$$\frac{F \text{ does not have the form ENV}(\rho', \text{CALL})}{\langle v, \rho, \sigma, \text{RETURN}(\bullet) :: F :: S\rangle \to \langle v, \rho, \sigma, \text{RETURN}(\bullet) :: S\rangle} \quad (\text{RETURN-UNWIND})$$

3.5.6 *Rules for evaluating definitions*

As in Chapter 2, the judgment form $\langle d, \rho, \sigma\rangle \to \langle \rho', \sigma'\rangle$ says that the result of evaluating definition d in environment ρ with store σ is a new environment ρ' and a new store σ'. This judgment is a big-step judgment, just as in Chapter 2. And as in Chapter 2, DEFINE is syntactic sugar for a VAL binding to a LAMBDA expression, and a top-level expression is syntactic sugar for a binding to the global variable `it`, so the rules for DEFINE and EXP are the same as in Chapter 2. But because the evaluation judgment for expressions is different, the rules for evaluating VAL bindings are also different: they use the small-step evaluation relation presented in this chapter.

A VAL form is treated differently depending on whether its variable is already bound in the environment.

$$\frac{x \in \operatorname{dom} \rho \qquad \langle e, \rho, \sigma \rangle \Downarrow \langle v, \sigma' \rangle}{\langle \text{VAL}(x, e), \rho, \sigma \rangle \rightarrow \langle \rho, \sigma'\{\rho(x) \mapsto v\} \rangle} \quad \text{(BIG-STEP-DEFINEOLDGLOBAL)}$$

$$\frac{x \notin \operatorname{dom} \rho \qquad \ell \notin \operatorname{dom} \sigma \qquad \langle \text{SET}(x, e), \rho\{x \mapsto \ell\}, \sigma\{\ell \mapsto \text{unspecified}\} \rangle \Downarrow \langle v, \sigma' \rangle}{\langle \text{VAL}(x, e), \rho, \sigma \rangle \rightarrow \langle \rho\{x \mapsto \ell\}, \sigma' \rangle} \quad \text{(BIG-STEP-DEFINENEWGLOBAL)}$$

The small-step versions of these rules are nearly identical, except that above the line, the big-step judgment $\langle e, \rho, \sigma \rangle \Downarrow \langle v, \sigma' \rangle$ is replaced by the transitive closure of the small step evaluation relation: $\langle e, \rho, \sigma, [] \rangle \rightarrow^* \langle v, \rho', \sigma', [] \rangle$. The final value v and store σ' are used below the line, and the final environment ρ' is thrown away. (It is a metatheorem of this semantics that ρ' is the same as ρ.)

$$\frac{x \in \operatorname{dom} \rho \qquad \langle e, \rho, \sigma, [] \rangle \rightarrow^* \langle v, \rho, \sigma', [] \rangle}{\langle \text{VAL}(x, e), \rho, \sigma \rangle \rightarrow \langle \rho, \sigma'\{\rho(x) \mapsto v\} \rangle} \quad \text{(SMALL-STEP-DEFINEOLDGLOBAL)}$$

$$\frac{x \notin \operatorname{dom} \rho \qquad \ell \notin \operatorname{dom} \sigma \qquad \langle \text{SET}(x, e), \rho\{x \mapsto \ell\}, \sigma\{\ell \mapsto \text{unspecified}\}, [] \rangle \rightarrow^* \langle v, \rho, \sigma', [] \rangle}{\langle \text{VAL}(x, e), \rho, \sigma \rangle \rightarrow \langle \rho\{x \mapsto \ell\}, \sigma' \rangle} \quad \text{(SMALL-STEP-DEFINENEWGLOBAL)}$$

3.6 THE INTERPRETER

The evaluator for μScheme+, which uses the stack described in the operational semantics, is presented below. The stack itself is a standard data structure, so its implementation is relegated to Appendix M, as are functions for debugging, memory management, and parsing control operators. The rest of the interpreter, including the μScheme parser, initial basis, primitives, and so on, is shared with the μScheme interpreter described in Chapter 2.

Of all the interpreters in this book, the μScheme+ interpreter least resembles a real-life interpreter. The stack inspection for `long-goto` is good, and using a stack to help evaluate expressions is common, but using a stack to implement `break` and `continue` is bizarre; sensible implementors use a stack to manage control transfers between procedures, not within a single procedure.

3.6.1 *Interfaces and instrumentation*

The evaluation stack

The evaluation stack is a sequence of frames, each of type `Frame`.

223. ⟨*type definitions for μScheme+* 223⟩≡ (S358) 226b ▷
```
typedef struct Stack *Stack;
typedef struct Frame Frame;
```

The representation of `Frame` is exposed. A frame is represented by its *form,* which is typically an expression with a hole in it. And if the expression is a function application, then the frame also stores its original syntax. That syntax is used in error messages when, e.g., a program tries to apply a value that is not a function.

224a. ⟨*structure definitions for μScheme+* 224a⟩≡ (S358)
```
struct Frame {
    struct Exp form;       // mutated in place during evaluation
    Exp syntax;            // when not NULL, kept pristine for error messages
};
```

A Stack is a mutable datatype. A Stack is created by emptystack, and it is mutated by pushframe, popframe, and clearstack (which pops all the remaining frames).

224b. ⟨*function prototypes for μScheme+* 224b⟩≡ (S358) 224c ▷
```
Stack  emptystack(void);
Exp    pushframe (struct Exp e, Stack s);
void   popframe  (Stack s);
void   clearstack(Stack s);
```

Function pushframe pushes a frame in which syntax is NULL.

Function topframe returns a pointer to the frame on the top of a stack—the youngest, most recently pushed frame—or if the stack is empty, it returns NULL. A stack s can safely be mutated by writing through topframe(s).

224c. ⟨*function prototypes for μScheme+* 224b⟩+≡ (S358) ◁ 224b 224d ▷
```
Frame *topframe(Stack s);  // NULL if empty
```

A frame may hold a saved environment, and such frames are pushed by the special function pushenv_opt, which can optimize tail calls (Section 3.6.11).

224d. ⟨*function prototypes for μScheme+* 224b⟩+≡ (S358) ◁ 224c 225a ▷
```
void pushenv_opt(Env env, SavedEnvTag tag, Stack s);  // may optimize
```

Finally, the maximum size of the stack, in a single evaluation, is tracked in global variable high_stack_mark.

224e. ⟨*global variables for μScheme+* 224e⟩≡ (S358) 224f ▷
```
extern int high_stack_mark;  // maximum number of frames
```

Except for pushenv_opt, which is described in Section 3.6.11 on page 238, the implementations of the stack functions are relegated to Appendix M.

Instrumentation

To help you understand what happens on the evaluation stack, the μScheme+ interpreter is instrumented with three *options*. Each option is a μScheme+ variable whose value can influence the behavior of the interpreter.

- Option &optimize-tail-calls, if set to #f, prevents the interpreter from optimizing tail calls.
- Option &show-high-stack-mark, if set to a non-#f value, prints the maximum size of the stack after each definition is evaluated.
- Option &trace-stack, if set to a nonnegative number n, shows the abstract-machine state for n steps. If &trace-stack is negative, all steps are shown. To change &trace-stack from a number to a non-number is an unchecked run-time error.

Options &optimize-tail-calls and &show-high-stack-mark are used to set two global variables inside the interpreter:

224f. ⟨*global variables for μScheme+* 224e⟩+≡ (S358) ◁ 224e
```
extern bool optimize_tail_calls;
extern bool show_high_stack_mark;
```

Option &trace-stack triggers calls to these functions:

225a. ⟨*function prototypes for μScheme+ 224b*⟩+≡ (S358) ◁224d 225b▷

```
void stack_trace_init(int *countp);   // how many steps to show
void stack_trace_current_expression(Exp e,   Env rho, Stack s);
void stack_trace_current_value     (Value v, Env rho, Stack s);
```

To determine the value of an option, the interpreter calls getoption. If the option is not set, getoption returns defaultval.

225b. ⟨*function prototypes for μScheme+ 224b*⟩+≡ (S358) ◁225a 225c▷

```
Value getoption(Name name, Env env, Value defaultval);
```

The instrumentation functions are implemented in Appendix M.

Diagnostic code for Chapter 4

The μScheme+ interpreter is used not only in this chapter but also in Chapter 4, which focuses on garbage collection. To help debug the garbage collectors, the interpreter frequently calls the validate function; provided the argument v represents a valid value, validate(v) returns v.

225c. ⟨*function prototypes for μScheme+ 224b*⟩+≡ (S358) ◁225b 231b▷

```
Value validate(Value v);
```

3.6.2 *Abstract syntax*

Definitions look exactly as they do in μScheme.

225d. ⟨*ast.t 225d*⟩≡ 225e▷

```
Def*   = VAL    (Name name, Exp exp)
       | EXP    (Exp)
       | DEFINE (Name name, Lambda lambda)

XDef* = DEF     (Def)
      | USE     (Name)
      | TEST    (UnitTest)

UnitTest* = CHECK_EXPECT (Exp check, Exp expect)
          | CHECK_ASSERT (Exp)
          | CHECK_ERROR  (Exp)
```

Expressions are divided into four groups. The first group contains the forms that are found in μScheme:

225e. ⟨*ast.t 225d*⟩+≡ ◁225d 225f▷

```
Exp* = LITERAL (Value)
     | VAR     (Name)
     | SET     (Name name, Exp exp)
     | IFX     (Exp cond, Exp truex, Exp falsex)
     | WHILEX  (Exp cond, Exp body)
     | BEGIN   (Explist)
     | LETX    (Letkeyword let, Namelist xs, Explist es, Exp body)
     | LAMBDAX (Lambda)
     | APPLY   (Exp fn, Explist actuals)
```

The second group contains the new forms, all of which relate to control:

225f. ⟨*ast.t 225d*⟩+≡ ◁225e 226a▷

```
     | BREAKX
     | CONTINUEX
     | RETURNX    (Exp)
     | THROW      (Name label, Exp exp)
     | TRY_CATCH  (Exp body, Name label, Exp handler)
     | LONG_LABEL (Name label, Exp body)
     | LONG_GOTO  (Name label, Exp exp)
```


type Env	153a
type Exp	$\mathcal{A}$
type Frame	223
type Name	43a
type SavedEnvTag	226b
type Stack	223
type Value	$\mathcal{A}$

The third group contains two forms that are used only in frames: the saved-environment frame and the hole.

226a. ⟨*ast.t* 225d⟩+≡ ◁225f 226c▷

```
    | ENV (Env contents, SavedEnvTag tag)
    | HOLE
```

226b. ⟨*type definitions for μScheme+* 223⟩+≡ (S358) ◁223 226d▷

```
typedef enum { CALL, NONCALL } SavedEnvTag;
```

The last two forms mark lowered expressions. A `LOWERED` form is printed as its `before` component, but evaluated as its `after` component. A `LOOPBACK` form flags an expression for the garbage collector in Chapter 4; the evaluator evaluates whatever is inside.

226c. ⟨*ast.t* 225d⟩+≡ ◁226a

```
    | LOWERED (Exp before, Exp after)
    | LOOPBACK (Exp)
```

3.6.3 *Lowering*

The lowering transformation defined in Table 3.4 (page 214) takes an additional "lowering context" parameter that is not shown in the table. That parameter tells the transformation whether an expression appears inside a loop, inside the body of a function, or both. Operators `break`, `continue`, and `return` are lowered only when they appear in an appropriate context.

226d. ⟨*type definitions for μScheme+* 223⟩+≡ (S358) ◁226b

```
typedef enum { LOOPCONTEXT = 0x01, FUNCONTEXT = 0x02 } LoweringContext;
```

A lowering function is defined for every kind of syntactic form that can contain an expression: true definitions, tests, extended definitions, and so on. All these functions call `lower`, which lowers an expression. Calling `lower(`*context*`,` *e*`)` recursively lowers every subexpression of *e*. And if the form of *e* calls for it to be lowered, `lower` returns *e*'s `LOWERED` form; otherwise it returns *e*. The code is repetitive, and it just implements the rules shown in Table 3.4, so only two cases are shown here. The rest are relegated to Appendix M.

226e. ⟨*definition of private function* `lower` 226e⟩≡ (S350g)

```
static Exp lower(LoweringContext c, Exp e) {
    switch (e->alt) {
    case SET:
        e->set.exp = lower(c, e->set.exp);
        return e;
    case BREAKX:
        if (c & LOOPCONTEXT)
            return mkLowered(e, mkLongGoto(strtoname(":break"),
                                     mkLiteral(falsev)));
        else
            othererror("Lowering error: %e appeared outside of any loop", e);
    ⟨other cases for lowering expression e S351f⟩
    }
}
```

3.6.4 *Structure and invariants of the evaluator*

As in Chapters 1 and 2, the main judgment of the operational semantics—the state transition $\langle e/v, \rho, \sigma, S\rangle \rightarrow \langle e'/v', \rho', \sigma', S'\rangle$—is implemented by function `eval`. This function starts with an expression e and an empty stack S, and it repeats the transition until the current item is a value v and the stack is once again empty. Then it returns v. Function `eval`'s essential invariants are as follows:

- The environment ρ is always in `env` and the stack is always in `evalstack`. As part of the state transition, these variables are mutated in place to hold ρ' and S', respectively.
- When the stack is not empty, the youngest frame (the "top") is pointed to by local variable `fr` (for "frame").
- When the current item is an expression e, that expression is stored in argument `e`, and the state transition begins at label `exp`.
- When the current item is a value v, that value is stored in local variable `v`, and the state transition begins at label `value`.
- Each state transition ends with `goto exp` or `goto value`. Before the goto, either `e` or `v` is set to the current item for the next state. Variables `env` and `evalstack` are also set.

227a. ⟨*eval-stack.c* 227a⟩≡ 238 ▷

```
Value eval(Exp e, Env env) {
    Value v;
    Frame *fr;
    ⟨definition of static Exp hole, which always has a hole S357c⟩
    static Stack evalstack;

    ⟨ensure that evalstack is initialized and empty S344b⟩
    ⟨use the options in env to initialize the instrumentation S346e⟩

    exp:
        stack_trace_current_expression(e, env, evalstack);
        ⟨take a step from state ⟨e, ρ, σ, S⟩ 228a⟩
        assert(0);
    value:
        stack_trace_current_value(v, env, evalstack);
        v = validate(v);
        ⟨if evalstack is empty, return v; otherwise step from state ⟨v, ρ, σ, fr :: S⟩ 227b⟩
        assert(0);
}
```

type Env	153a
type Exp	$\mathcal{A}$
falsev	S327b
type Frame	223
lower	S350e
mkLiteral	$\mathcal{A}$
mkLongGoto	$\mathcal{A}$
mkLowered	$\mathcal{A}$
othererror	S184a
type Stack	223
stack_trace_current_expression	225a
stack_trace_current_value	225a
strtoname	43b
topframe	224c
validate	225c
type Value	$\mathcal{A}$

227b. ⟨*if* `evalstack` *is empty, return* `v`; *otherwise step from state* $\langle v, \rho, \sigma,$ `fr` $:: S\rangle$ 227b⟩≡ (227a)

```
fr = topframe(evalstack);
if (fr == NULL) {
    ⟨if show_high_stack_mark is set, show maximum stack size S346g⟩
    return v;
} else {
    ⟨take a step from state ⟨v, ρ, σ, fr :: S⟩ 228b⟩
}
```

When the current item is an expression e, 13 of the 22 expression forms in μScheme+ are legitimate.

228a. ⟨*take a step from state* $\langle e, \rho, \sigma, S\rangle$ 228a⟩≡ (227a)

```
switch (e->alt) {
case LITERAL: ⟨start e->literal and step to the next state 229c⟩
case VAR:     ⟨start e->var and step to the next state 229d⟩
case SET:     ⟨start e->set and step to the next state 230a⟩
case IFX:     ⟨start e->ifx and step to the next state 230c⟩
case LETX:
    if (⟨e->letx contains no bindings 234b⟩) {
         ⟨continue by evaluating the body of the let or letrec 234c⟩
    } else {
        switch (e->letx.let) {
          case LET:      ⟨start LET e->letx and step to the next state 234d⟩
          case LETSTAR: goto want_lowered;
          case LETREC:   ⟨start LETREC e->letx and step to the next state 235a⟩
          default: assert(0);
        }
    }
case LAMBDAX:     ⟨start e->lambdax and step to the next state 229e⟩
case APPLY:       ⟨start e->apply and step to the next state 232c⟩
case RETURNX:     ⟨start e->returnx and step to the next state 237c⟩
case LONG_LABEL: ⟨start e->long_label and step to the next state 236d⟩
case LONG_GOTO:  ⟨start e->long_goto and step to the next state 237a⟩
case LOWERED:     ⟨replace e with its lowered form and continue in this state 229a⟩
case LOOPBACK:    ⟨look inside LOOPBACK and continue in this state 229b⟩
case WHILEX: case BEGIN: case BREAKX: case CONTINUEX:
case THROW: case TRY_CATCH:
want_lowered:   runerror("internal error: expression %e not lowered", e);
⟨expression-evaluation cases for forms that appear only as frames S357a⟩
}
```

An empty `LETX` form has no place for a hole, so that case is handled separately.

When the current item is a value v, 9 of the 22 expression forms in μScheme+ may legitimately appear as the youngest (top) frame on the stack, `fr`.

228b. ⟨*take a step from state* $\langle v, \rho, \sigma, \texttt{fr} :: S\rangle$ 228b⟩≡ (227b)

```
switch (fr->form.alt) {
case SET:    ⟨fill hole in fr->form.set and step to the next state 230b⟩
case IFX:    ⟨fill hole in fr->form.ifx and step to the next state 231a⟩
case APPLY: ⟨fill hole in fr->form.apply and step to the next state 233a⟩
case LETX:
    switch (fr->form.letx.let) {
      case LET:      ⟨continue with let frame fr->form.letx 235b⟩
      case LETSTAR: goto want_lowered;
      case LETREC:   ⟨continue with letrec frame fr->form.letx 236a⟩
      default:       assert(0);
    }
case ENV:     ⟨restore env from fr->form.env, pop the stack, and step 236c⟩
case RETURNX:      ⟨return v from the current function (left as exercise)⟩
case LONG_GOTO:   ⟨unwind v to the nearest matching long-label 237b⟩
case LONG_LABEL: ⟨pop the stack and step to the next state 236e⟩
⟨cases for forms that never appear as frames S357b⟩
}
```

The actions in each state are implemented below, starting with the simplest forms—the ones that don't look at the stack.

3.6.5 *Interpreting forms that don't change the stack*

To evalute an expression that has been lowered, replace it with its lowered form. Don't change the stack.

$$\frac{e \leadsto e'}{\langle e, \rho, \sigma, S\rangle \to \langle e', \rho, \sigma, S\rangle} \qquad \text{(LOWER)}$$

229a. ⟨*replace* `e` *with its lowered form and continue in this state* 229a⟩≡ (228a)

```
e = e->lowered.after;
goto exp;
```


To evaluate an expression tagged with `LOOPBACK`, replace the tagged form with the untagged form. Don't change the stack. (The `LOOPBACK` tag is used only by the garbage collector in Chapter 4.)

229b. ⟨*look inside* `LOOPBACK` *and continue in this state* 229b⟩≡ (228a)

```
e = e->loopback;
goto exp;
```

To evaluate a literal expression, take v out of the expression and make it the current item. Don't change the stack.

$$\frac{}{\langle \text{LITERAL}(v), \rho, \sigma, S\rangle \to \langle v, \rho, \sigma, S\rangle} \qquad \text{(SMALL-STEP-LITERAL)}$$

The machine must step to a state of the form $\langle v, \rho, \sigma, S\rangle$. Environment ρ and store σ are unchanged, so the machine needs only to update `v` and to go to `value`.

229c. ⟨*start* `e->literal` *and step to the next state* 229c⟩≡ (228a)

```
v = e->literal;
goto value;
```

To evaluate a variable, look up its value and make that the current item. Don't change the stack.

$$\frac{x \in \operatorname{dom} \rho \qquad \rho(x) \in \operatorname{dom} \sigma}{\langle \text{VAR}(x), \rho, \sigma, S\rangle \to \langle \sigma(\rho(x)), \rho, \sigma, S\rangle} \qquad \text{(SMALL-STEP-VAR)}$$

229d. ⟨*start* `e->var` *and step to the next state* 229d⟩≡ (228a)

```
if (find(e->var, env) == NULL)
    runerror("variable %n not found", e->var);
v = *find(e->var, env);
goto value;
```

To evaluate a LAMBDA, allocate a closure and make it the current item. Don't change the stack.

$$\frac{x_1, \ldots, x_n \text{ all distinct}}{\langle \text{LAMBDA}(\langle x_1, \ldots, x_n\rangle, e), \rho, \sigma, S\rangle \to \langle (\!|\text{LAMBDA}(\langle x_1, \ldots, x_n\rangle, e), \rho\,|\!), \rho, \sigma, S\rangle}$$
(SMALL-STEP-MKCLOSURE)

Formal parameters $x_1, \ldots, x_n$ are confirmed to be distinct when `e` is parsed.

229e. ⟨*start* `e->lambdax` *and step to the next state* 229e⟩≡ (228a)

```
v = mkClosure(e->lambdax, env);
goto value;
```

env	227a
find	153b
fr	227a
mkClosure	$\mathcal{A}$
runerror	47a

3.6.6 *Memory management for evaluation stacks*

Unlike the rules above, most small-step rules show transition from one stack to a different stack. The implementation keeps just one stack, which it updates in place. Because the stack contains frames, and a frame can be formed from an expression in the program, frames need to be updated in a way that does not overwrite the syntax of the program. And frames' memory needs to be allocated, preferably in a way that is more efficient than calling `malloc` before every push.

Both needs are met by the `Stack` abstraction, which allocates memory for a large block of frames at once. A frame is represented as described by `struct Frame` in chunk 224a. Its `form` field is not a pointer; it is a `struct Exp` whose memory is part of the `Frame`. And `pushframe` (chunk 224b) pushes a `struct Exp`, not a pointer to one. So for example, to push a frame like IF$(\bullet, e_2, e_3)$, the interpreter builds the new frame using `mkIfStruct`, not `mkIf`:

```
pushframe(mkIfStruct(hole, e2, e3), evalstack).
```

Neither `mkIfStruct` nor `pushframe` allocates; this code builds a frame in memory that is owned by `evalstack`. So any field of any frame can be overwritten without affecting the expression from which that frame was built. This technique is all that is needed to implement SET and IF.

3.6.7 *Interpreting forms that push a single frame*

To evaluate SET, push a frame on the stack, then evaluate the right-hand side.

$$\frac{x \in \operatorname{dom} \rho}{\langle \text{SET}(x, e), \rho, \sigma, S\rangle \rightarrow \langle e, \rho, \sigma, \text{SET}(x, \bullet) :: S\rangle} \quad \text{(SMALL-STEP-ASSIGN)}$$

To implement the transition, the machine pushes the frame SET$(x, \bullet)$, updates `e`, and goes to `exp`. Environment and store are unchanged.

230a. ⟨*start* `e->set` *and step to the next state* 230a⟩≡ (228a)
```
if (find(e->set.name, env) == NULL)
    runerror("set unbound variable %n", e->set.name);
pushframe(mkSetStruct(e->set.name, hole), evalstack);
e = e->set.exp;
goto exp;
```

The SET is completed by the FINISH-ASSIGN rule. When the youngest frame on the stack is a SET$(x, \bullet)$ frame, the machine completes the SET by assigning v to x, then pops the frame.

$$\frac{\rho(x) = \ell}{\langle v, \rho, \sigma, \text{SET}(x, \bullet) :: S\rangle \rightarrow \langle v, \rho, \sigma\{\ell \mapsto v\}, S\rangle} \quad \text{(FINISH-ASSIGN)}$$

230b. ⟨*fill hole in* `fr->form.set` *and step to the next state* 230b⟩≡ (228b)
```
assert(fr->form.set.exp->alt == HOLE);
assert(find(fr->form.set.name, env) != NULL);
*find(fr->form.set.name, env) = validate(v);
popframe(evalstack);
goto value;
```

Because `pushframe` does not allocate, `popframe` need not deallocate.

IF is implemented just like SET: to evaluate IF(e_1, e_2, e_3), push the frame IF$(\bullet, e_2, e_3)$, then evaluate the condition e_1.

$$\frac{}{\langle \text{IF}(e_1, e_2, e_3), \rho, \sigma, S\rangle \rightarrow \langle e_1, \rho, \sigma, \text{IF}(\bullet, e_2, e_3) :: S\rangle} \quad \text{(SMALL-STEP-IF)}$$

230c. ⟨*start* `e->ifx` *and step to the next state* 230c⟩≡ (228a)
```
pushframe(mkIfxStruct(hole, e->ifx.truex, e->ifx.falsex), evalstack);
e = e->ifx.cond;
goto exp;
```

When the youngest frame on the stack is an $\text{IF}(\bullet, e_2, e_3)$ frame, the machine continues with e_2 or e_3, as determined by v.

$$\frac{v \neq \text{BOOLV(\#f)}}{\langle v, \rho, \sigma, \text{IF}(\bullet, e_2, e_3) :: S\rangle \to \langle e_2, \rho, \sigma, S\rangle} \quad \text{(SMALL-STEP-IF-TRUE)}$$

$$\frac{v = \text{BOOLV(\#f)}}{\langle v, \rho, \sigma, \text{IF}(\bullet, e_2, e_3) :: S\rangle \to \langle e_3, \rho, \sigma, S\rangle} \quad \text{(SMALL-STEP-IF-FALSE)}$$

231a. ⟨*fill hole in* `fr->form.ifx` *and step to the next state* 231a⟩≡ (228b)

```
assert(fr->form.ifx.cond->alt == HOLE);
e = istrue(v) ? fr->form.ifx.truex : fr->form.ifx.falsex;
popframe(evalstack);
goto exp;
```


Next up is function application, which calls for infrastructure that can update a list of expressions within a frame.

3.6.8 *Updating lists of expressions within frames*

APPLY and LET expressions evaluate expressions in sequence. Values are accumulated by repeating a transition like the one in the SMALL-STEP-APPLY-NEXT-ARG rule on page 219, which takes a frame like $\text{APPLY}(v_f, v_1, \ldots, v_{i-1}, \bullet, e_{i+1}, \ldots, e_n)$ to one like $\text{APPLY}(v_f, v_1, \ldots, v_{i-1}, v, \bullet, e_{i+2}, \ldots, e_n)$. In the originating frame, the sequence $v_1, \ldots, v_{i-1}, \bullet, e_{i+1}, \ldots, e_n$ can be represented as a value of type `Explist`, where expressions $e_{i+1} \ldots e_n$ come from the original syntax, and values $v_1, \ldots, v_{i-1}$ are represented as LITERAL expressions. The transition is made by function `transition_explist`, which overwrites the hole with `v`, writes a new hole one position to the right, and returns the expression that was overwritten by the new hole. That expression is stored in static memory, so subsequent calls to `transition_explist` overwrite previous results.

231b. ⟨*function prototypes for μScheme+* 224b⟩+≡ (S358) ◁225c 231c▷

```
Exp transition_explist(Explist es, Value v); // pointer to static memory
```

When the hole is in the rightmost position, `transition_explist` overwrites the hole with `v` and then returns `NULL`.

What about initializing a frame by putting a hole in the first position? Function `head_replaced_with_hole` works much like `transition_explist`: it puts a hole in the initial position and returns a pointer to the expression that was there. If the list is empty, so there is no initial position, it returns `NULL`.

231c. ⟨*function prototypes for μScheme+* 224b⟩+≡ (S358) ◁231b 231d▷

```
Exp head_replaced_with_hole(Explist es); // shares memory
                                         // with transition_explist
```

A function like `transition_explist` helps implement APPLY, LET, and LETREC, but it has to be used carefully: if an `Explist` is overwritten, it can't be the original `Explist` from the syntax—it has to be a copy. The copy should be made when the frame containing the `Explist` is first pushed. For example, when the interpreter pushes a frame like $\text{APPLY}(\bullet, e_1, \ldots, e_n)$, it copies the list of expressions using function `copyEL`:

`pushframe(mkApplyStruct(mkHole(), copyEL(`$e_1, \ldots, e_n$`)), evalstack).`

Function `copyEL` copies a list of expressions, and when the interpreter is finished with the copy, `freeEL` recovers the memory.

231d. ⟨*function prototypes for μScheme+* 224b⟩+≡ (S358) ◁231c 232a▷

```
Explist copyEL(Explist es);
void    freeEL(Explist es);
```

The interpreter calls `freeEL` when popping a frame that contains a copied `Explist`.

env	227a
evalstack	227a
type Exp	$\mathcal{A}$
type Explist	S309b
find	153b
fr	227a
hole	S357c
istrue	154c
mkIfxStruct	$\mathcal{A}$
mkSetStruct	$\mathcal{A}$
popframe	224b
pushframe	224b
runerror	47a
validate	225c
type Value	$\mathcal{A}$

When an Explist appears in an APPLY, LET, or LETREC frame, each element goes through three states:

1. Initially it points to fresh memory that contains a copy of syntax from the original expression.
2. At some point the syntax is copied into static memory and the element's own memory is overwritten to contain a hole.
3. Finally the element's own memory is overwritten with the value that results from evaluating the original expression.

Once every element has reached its final state, the Explist contains only literals, and it can be converted to a list of values:

232a. ⟨*function prototypes for μScheme+ 224b*⟩+≡ (S358) ◁231d 232b▷
```
Valuelist asLiterals(Explist es);
Value     asLiteral (Exp e);
```

Function asLiteral implements the same conversion, but for a single Exp. And because function asLiterals has to allocate, I provide freeVL, which frees the memory allocated by asLiterals.

232b. ⟨*function prototypes for μScheme+ 224b*⟩+≡ (S358) ◁232a
```
void freeVL(Valuelist vs);
```

These tools enable us to interpret forms that evaluate expressions in sequence.

3.6.9 *Interpreting forms that evaluate expressions in sequence*

Function application

To evaluate an application, push an APPLY frame in which the function is replaced with a hole, and start evaluating the function.

$$\frac{}{\langle \text{APPLY}(e, e_1, \ldots, e_n), \rho, \sigma, S\rangle \rightarrow \langle e, \rho, \sigma, \text{APPLY}(\bullet, e_1, \ldots, e_n) :: S\rangle}$$
(SMALL-STEP-APPLY)

As explained in the previous section, the list of actuals in the frame must be a copy of the list in the syntax.

232c. ⟨*start* e->apply *and step to the next state 232c*⟩≡ (228a)
```
pushframe(mkApplyStruct(mkHole(), copyEL(e->apply.actuals)), evalstack);
topframe(evalstack)->syntax = e;
e = e->apply.fn;
goto exp;
```

When the youngest frame on the stack is an APPLY frame, the next state transition is dictated by one of these three rules:

$$\frac{}{\langle v, \rho, \sigma, \text{APPLY}(\bullet, e_1, \ldots, e_n) :: S\rangle \rightarrow \langle e_1, \rho, \sigma, \text{APPLY}(v, \bullet, e_2, \ldots, e_n) :: S\rangle},$$
(SMALL-STEP-APPLY-FIRST-ARG)

$$\frac{}{\begin{array}{l}\langle v, \rho, \sigma, \text{APPLY}(v_f, v_1, \ldots, v_{i-1}, \bullet, e_{i+1}, \ldots, e_n) :: S\rangle \rightarrow \\ \quad \langle e_{i+1}, \rho, \sigma, \text{APPLY}(v_f, v_1, \ldots, v_{i-1}, v, \bullet, e_{i+2}, \ldots, e_n) :: S\rangle\end{array}},$$
(SMALL-STEP-APPLY-NEXT-ARG)

$$\frac{\begin{array}{c}v_f = (\!|\text{LAMBDA}(\langle x_1, \ldots, x_n\rangle, e_c), \rho_c|\!) \\ \ell_1, \ldots, \ell_n \notin \text{dom}\,\sigma \text{ (and all distinct)}\end{array}}{\begin{array}{c}\langle v_n, \rho, \sigma, \text{APPLY}(v_f, v_1, \ldots, v_{n-1}, \bullet) :: S\rangle \rightarrow \\ \langle e_c, \rho_c\{x_1 \mapsto \ell_1, \ldots, x_n \mapsto \ell_n\}, \sigma_n\{\ell_1 \mapsto v_1, \ldots, \ell_n \mapsto v_n\}, \text{ENV}(\rho, \text{CALL}) :: S\rangle\end{array}}.$$
(SMALL-STEP-APPLY-LAST-ARG)

Which rule does the dictating depends how the hole appears: as the function, as an argument, or as the last argument. There is also a case not given in the semantics: the list of arguments might be empty.

233a. ⟨*fill hole in* `fr->form.apply` *and step to the next state* 233a⟩≡ (228b)

```
if (fr->form.apply.fn->alt == HOLE) {  // Small-Step-Apply-First-Arg
    *fr->form.apply.fn = mkLiteralStruct(v);
    e = head_replaced_with_hole(fr->form.apply.actuals);
    if (e)
        goto exp;                          // Small-Step-Apply-First-Arg
    else
        goto apply_last_arg;               // empty list of arguments
} else {
    e = transition_explist(fr->form.apply.actuals, v);
    if (e)
        goto exp;                          // Small-Step-Apply-Next-Arg
    else goto
        apply_last_arg;                    // Small-Step-Apply-Last-Arg
}
apply_last_arg:    // Small-Step-Apply-Last-Arg (or no arguments)
    ⟨apply fr->form's fn to its actuals; free memory; step to next state 233b⟩
```


Once the overwritten `fr->form.apply.actuals` and `fr->form.apply.fn` are converted to values, their memory is freed. The frame is popped, and the function is applied.

233b. ⟨*apply* `fr->form`*'s* `fn` *to its* `actuals`*; free memory; step to next state* 233b⟩≡ (233a)

```
{
    Value     fn = asLiteral (fr->form.apply.fn);
    Valuelist vs = asLiterals(fr->form.apply.actuals);
    free  (fr->form.apply.fn);
    freeEL(fr->form.apply.actuals);

    popframe(evalstack);

    switch (fn.alt) {
    case PRIMITIVE:
        ⟨apply fn.primitive to vs and step to the next state 233c⟩
    case CLOSURE:
        ⟨save env; bind vs to fn.closure's formals; step to evaluation of fn's body 234a⟩
    default:
        runerror("%e evaluates to non-function %v in %e",
                 fr->syntax->apply.fn, fn, fr->syntax);
    }
}
```

`copyEL`	231d
`evalstack`	227a
type `Exp`	$\mathcal{A}$
type `Explist`	S309b
`fr`	227a
`freeEL`	231d
`head_replaced_with_hole`	231c
`mkApplyStruct`	$\mathcal{A}$
`mkHole`	$\mathcal{A}$
`mkLiteralStruct`	$\mathcal{A}$
`popframe`	224b
`pushframe`	224b
`runerror`	47a
`topframe`	224c
`transition_explist`	231b
type `Value`	$\mathcal{A}$
type `Valuelist`	S309c

A primitive is applied in the standard way.

233c. ⟨*apply* `fn.primitive` *to* `vs` *and step to the next state* 233c⟩≡ (233b)

```
v = fn.primitive.function(fr->syntax, fn.primitive.tag, vs);
freeVL(vs);
goto value;
```

A closure is also applied in the standard way, according to this rule:

$$\frac{v_f = (\!|\text{LAMBDA}(\langle x_1, \ldots, x_n\rangle, e_c), \rho_c|\!) \qquad \ell_1, \ldots, \ell_n \notin \operatorname{dom} \sigma \text{ (and all distinct)}}{\langle v_n, \rho, \sigma, \text{APPLY}(v_f, v_1, \ldots, v_{n-1}, \bullet) :: S\rangle \to \langle e_c, \rho_c\{x_1 \mapsto \ell_1, \ldots, x_n \mapsto \ell_n\}, \sigma_n\{\ell_1 \mapsto v_1, \ldots, \ell_n \mapsto v_n\}, \text{ENV}(\rho, \text{CALL}) :: S\rangle}$$

(SMALL-STEP-APPLY-LAST-ARG)

Before the body of the closure is evaluated, the environment is saved on the stack.

234a. ⟨*save* `env`*; bind* `vs` *to* `fn.closure`*'s formals; step to evaluation of* `fn`*'s body* 234a⟩≡ (233b)

```
{
    Namelist xs = fn.closure.lambda.formals;

    checkargc(e, lengthNL(xs), lengthVL(vs));
    pushenv_opt(env, CALL, evalstack);
    env = bindalloclist(xs, vs, fn.closure.env);
    e   = fn.closure.lambda.body;
    freeVL(vs);
    goto exp;
}
```

Interpreting LET *and* LETREC

To evaluate a LET or LETREC that has no bindings, evaluate its body in environment ρ.

$$\frac{}{\langle \text{LET}(\langle\rangle, e), \rho, \sigma\rangle \Downarrow \langle e, \rho, \sigma\rangle} \qquad \text{(EMPTY-LET)}$$

234b. ⟨`e->letx` *contains no bindings* 234b⟩≡ (228a)

```
e->letx.xs == NULL && e->letx.es == NULL
```

234c. ⟨*continue by evaluating the body of the* `let` *or* `letrec` 234c⟩≡ (228a)

```
e = e->letx.body;
goto exp;
```

To evaluate a nonempty LET expression, push a frame in which the first right-hand side e_1 is replaced by a hole, and start evaluating e_1.

$$\frac{x_1, \ldots, x_n \text{ all distinct}}{\begin{array}{l}\langle \text{LET}(\langle x_1, e_1, \ldots, x_n, e_n\rangle, e), \rho, \sigma, S\rangle \rightarrow \\ \qquad \langle e_1, \rho, \sigma, \text{LET}(\langle x_1, \bullet, x_2, e_2, \ldots, x_n, e_n\rangle, e) :: S\rangle\end{array}} \qquad \text{(SMALL-STEP-LET)}$$

The frame is built using a copy of `e->letx.es`, and the hole is inserted into the copy by calling `head_replaced_with_hole`.

234d. ⟨*start* LET `e->letx` *and step to the next state* 234d⟩≡ (228a)

```
pushframe(mkLetxStruct(e->letx.let, e->letx.xs,
                       copyEL(e->letx.es), e->letx.body),
          evalstack);
fr = topframe(evalstack);
e  = head_replaced_with_hole(fr->form.letx.es);
assert(e);
goto exp;
```

LETREC is almost like LET:

$$\frac{\begin{array}{c} x_1, \ldots, x_n \text{ all distinct} \\ e_i \text{ has the form LAMBDA}(\cdots), 1 \le i \le n \\ \ell_1, \ldots, \ell_n \notin \operatorname{dom} \sigma \text{ (and all distinct)} \\ \rho' = \rho\{x_1 \mapsto \ell_1, \ldots, x_n \mapsto \ell_n\} \\ \sigma_0 = \sigma\{\ell_1 \mapsto \text{unspecified}, \ldots, \ell_n \mapsto \text{unspecified}\}\end{array}}{\begin{array}{l}\langle \text{LETREC}(\langle x_1, e_1, \ldots, x_n, e_n\rangle, e), \rho, \sigma, S\rangle \rightarrow \\ \qquad \langle e_1, \rho', \sigma_0, \text{LETREC}(\langle x_1, \bullet, x_2, e_2, \ldots, x_n, e_n\rangle, e) :: \text{ENV}(\rho, \text{NONCALL}) :: S\rangle\end{array}}.$$

(SMALL-STEP-LETREC)

To evaluate LETREC, save the environment on the stack, then extend it with fresh locations that are given unspecified values. Then, as for LET, push a LETREC frame, replace the first right-hand side with a hole, and start evaluating it. As in Chapter 2, the right-hand sides are confirmed to be LAMBDAs at parse time.

235a. ⟨*start* LETREC `e->letx` *and step to the next state* 235a⟩≡ (228a)

```
pushenv_opt(env, NONCALL, evalstack);
⟨bind every name in e->letx.xs to an unspecified value in env S357d⟩
pushframe(mkLetxStruct(e->letx.let, e->letx.xs,
                       copyEL(e->letx.es), e->letx.body),
          evalstack);
fr = topframe(evalstack);
e  = head_replaced_with_hole(fr->form.letx.es);
assert(e);
goto exp;
```


A LET expression in progress is governed by these rules:

$$\frac{}{\langle v, \rho, \sigma, \text{LET}(\langle x_1, v_1, \ldots, x_i, \bullet, x_{i+1}, e_{i+1}, \ldots, x_n, e_n\rangle, e) :: S\rangle \to \langle e_{i+1}, \rho, \sigma, \text{LET}(\langle x_1, v_1, \ldots, x_i, v, x_{i+1}, \bullet, \ldots, e_n\rangle, e) :: S\rangle},$$

(SMALL-STEP-NEXT-LET-EXP)

$$\frac{\ell_1, \ldots, \ell_n \notin \operatorname{dom} \sigma \text{ (and all distinct)}}{\langle v, \rho, \sigma, \text{LET}(\langle x_1, v_1, \ldots, x_n, \bullet\rangle, e) :: S\rangle \to \langle e, \rho\{x_1 \mapsto \ell_1, \ldots, x_n \mapsto \ell_n\}, \sigma_n\{\ell_1 \mapsto v_1, \ldots, \ell_n \mapsto v_n\}, \text{ENV}(\rho, \text{NONCALL}) :: S\rangle}.$$

(SMALL-STEP-LET-BODY)

Both rules are implemented by function `transition_explist`, which puts v in the hole and moves the hole. But if the hole is in last position, implementing the SMALL-STEP-LET-BODY rule is tricky. Before the frame $\text{LET}(\langle x_1, v_1, \ldots, x_n, \bullet\rangle, e)$ is popped, names $x_1, \ldots, x_n$ are used to update the environment ρ, but after the LET frame is popped, the *original* ρ needs to be saved on the stack. The steps are shown by numbered comments in the code.

235b. ⟨*continue with* `let` *frame* `fr->form.letx` 235b⟩≡ (228b)

```
e = transition_explist(fr->form.letx.es, v);
if (e) {            // Small-Step-Next-Let-Exp
    goto exp;
} else {            // Small-Step-Let-Body
    Namelist xs  = fr->form.letx.xs;        // 1. Remember x's and v's
    Explist  es  = fr->form.letx.es;
    Valuelist vs = asLiterals(es);
    e = fr->form.letx.body;                 // 2. Update e
    popframe(evalstack);                    // 3. Pop the LET frame
    pushenv_opt(env, NONCALL, evalstack);   // 4. Push env
    env = bindalloclist(xs, vs, env);       // 5. Make new env
    freeEL(es);                             // 6. Recover memory
    freeVL(vs);
    goto exp;                               // 7. Step to next state
}
```

asLiterals	232a
bindalloclist	153c
checkargc	47c
copyEL	231d
env	227a
evalstack	227a
type Explist	S309b
fn	233b
fr	227a
freeEL	231d
freeVL	232b
head_replaced_with_hole	231c
lengthNL	$\mathcal{A}$
lengthVL	$\mathcal{A}$
mkLetxStruct	$\mathcal{A}$
type Namelist	43a
popframe	224b
pushenv_opt	224d
pushframe	224b
topframe	224c
transition_explist	231b
type Valuelist	S309c

The expressions in a LETREC are already evaluated in an extended environment, so when the last expression is evaluated, the only step needed before evaluating the body is to update the store.

$$\frac{}{\langle v, \rho, \sigma, \text{LETREC}(\langle x_1, v_1, \ldots, x_i, \bullet, x_{i+1}, e_{i+1}, \ldots, x_n, e_n\rangle, e) :: S\rangle \to \langle e_{i+1}, \rho, \sigma, \text{LETREC}(\langle x_1, v_1, \ldots, x_i, v, x_{i+1}, \bullet, \ldots, e_n\rangle, e) :: S\rangle}$$

(SMALL-STEP-NEXT-LETREC-EXP)

$$\frac{\ell_i = \rho(x_i), 1 \le i \le n}{\langle v, \rho, \sigma, \text{LETREC}(\langle x_1, v_1, \ldots, x_n, \bullet\rangle, e) :: S\rangle \to \langle e, \rho, \sigma\{\ell_1 \mapsto v_1, \ldots, \ell_{n-1} \mapsto v_{n-1}, \ell_n \mapsto v\}, S\rangle}$$

(SMALL-STEP-LETREC-BODY)

236a. ⟨*continue with* `letrec` *frame* `fr->form.letx` 236a⟩≡ (228b)

```
e = transition_explist(fr->form.letx.es, v);
if (e) {  // Small-Step-Next-Letrec-Exp
    goto exp;
} else {  // Small-Step-Letrec-Body
    ⟨put values in fr->form.letx.es in locations bound to fr->form.letx.xs 236b⟩;
    freeEL(fr->form.letx.es);
    e = fr->form.letx.body;
    popframe(evalstack);
    goto exp;
}
```

236b. ⟨*put values in* `fr->form.letx.es` *in locations bound to* `fr->form.letx.xs` 236b⟩≡ (236a)

```
{
    Namelist xs = fr->form.letx.xs;
    Explist  es = fr->form.letx.es;
    while (es || xs) {
        assert(es && xs);
        assert(find(xs->hd, env));
        *find(xs->hd, env) = asLiteral(es->hd);
        es = es->tl;
        xs = xs->tl;
    }
}
```

The LET and APPLY forms both save environments on the stack. When the youngest frame on the stack is an ENV frame, the saved environment is restored by assigning it to env. In this context, the tag is ignored.

$$\frac{}{\langle v, \rho', \sigma, \text{ENV}(\rho, \mathit{tag}) :: S\rangle \rightarrow \langle v, \rho, \sigma, S\rangle}$$

(SMALL-STEP-RESTORE-ENVIRONMENT)

236c. ⟨*restore* `env` *from* `fr->form.env`*, pop the stack, and step* 236c⟩≡ (228b)

```
env = fr->form.env.contents;
popframe(evalstack);
goto value;
```

3.6.10 *Interpreting control operators*

Only the `long-label`, `long-goto`, and `return` forms are interpreted in `eval`. The other control operators are implemented by lowering.

To evaluate a label, save the current environment and the label on the stack, then evaluate the body.

$$\frac{}{\langle \text{LONG-LABEL}(L, e), \rho, \sigma, S\rangle \rightarrow \langle e, \rho, \sigma, \text{LONG-LABEL}(L, \bullet) :: \text{ENV}(\rho, \text{NONCALL}) :: S\rangle}$$

(LABEL)

236d. ⟨*start* `e->long_label` *and step to the next state* 236d⟩≡ (228a)

```
pushenv_opt(env, NONCALL, evalstack);
pushframe(mkLongLabelStruct(e->long_label.label, hole), evalstack);
e = e->long_label.body;
goto exp;
```

When the youngest frame on the stack is a LONG-LABEL frame, it is simply popped.

$$\frac{}{\langle v, \rho, \sigma, \text{LONG-LABEL}(L, \bullet) :: S\rangle \rightarrow \langle v, \rho, \sigma, S\rangle}$$

(LABEL-UNUSED)

236e. ⟨*pop the stack and step to the next state* 236e⟩≡ (228b)

```
popframe(evalstack);
goto value;
```

The label's purpose is to serve as a target for LONG-GOTO. To evaluate a LONG-GOTO, push a LONG-GOTO frame, then evaluate the body. (For an alternative semantics, see Exercise 12.)

$$\frac{}{\langle \text{LONG-GOTO}(L, e), \rho, \sigma, S\rangle \to \langle e, \rho, \sigma, \text{LONG-GOTO}(L, \bullet) :: S\rangle} \qquad \text{(GOTO)}$$

237a. ⟨*start* `e->long_goto` *and step to the next state* 237a⟩≡ (228a)

```
pushframe(mkLongGotoStruct(e->long_goto.label, hole), evalstack);
e = e->long_goto.exp;
goto exp;
```


Once the body of the LONG-GOTO has been evaluated and the youngest frame on the stack is LONG-GOTO$(L, \bullet)$, the machine starts looking for a target label. It uses these two rules:

$$\frac{F \neq \text{LONG-LABEL}(L, \bullet)}{\langle v, \rho, \sigma, \text{LONG-GOTO}(L, \bullet) :: F :: S\rangle \to \langle v, \rho, \sigma, \text{LONG-GOTO}(L, \bullet) :: S\rangle}, \qquad \text{(GOTO-UNWIND)}$$

$$\frac{}{\langle v, \rho, \sigma, \text{LONG-GOTO}(L, \bullet) :: \text{LONG-LABEL}(L, \bullet) :: S\rangle \to \langle v, \rho, \sigma, S\rangle}. \qquad \text{(GOTO-TRANSFER)}$$

To implement the rules, the interpreter pops the stack, setting `fr` to the *next* youngest frame. If `fr` points to the label L, it too is popped, and the transfer is complete. Otherwise, `*fr` is overwritten with LONG-GOTO$(L, \bullet)$, effectively unwinding one frame from the stack, and evaluation continues.

237b. ⟨*unwind* `v` *to the nearest matching* `long-label` 237b⟩≡ (228b)

```
{ Name label = fr->form.long_goto.label;
  popframe(evalstack);          // remove the LONG_GOTO frame
  fr = topframe(evalstack);     // fr now points to the next youngest frame
  if (fr == NULL) {
      runerror("long-goto %n with no active long-label for %n",
               label, label);
  } else if (fr->form.alt == LONG_LABEL &&
             fr->form.long_label.label == label) {
      popframe(evalstack);
      goto value;
  } else {
      fr->form = mkLongGotoStruct(label, hole);
      goto value;
  }
}
```

Like a `long-goto`, a `return` pushes a frame, then evaluates its expression.

$$\frac{}{\langle \text{RETURN}(e), \rho, \sigma, S\rangle \to \langle e, \rho, \sigma, \text{RETURN}(\bullet) :: S\rangle} \qquad \text{(RETURN)}$$

237c. ⟨*start* `e->returnx` *and step to the next state* 237c⟩≡ (228a)

```
pushframe(mkReturnxStruct(hole), evalstack);
e = e->returnx;
goto exp;
```

Once a `return`'s expression has been evaluated and the youngest frame on the stack is RETURN$(\bullet)$, the machine unwinds the stack until it finds an ENV frame with a CALL tag. The implementation is left for you, as Exercise 20.

237d. ⟨*return* `v` *from the current function* **⟦prototype⟧** 237d⟩≡

```
runerror("Implementation of (return e) is left as an exercise");
```

3.6.11 Implementing proper tail calls

Environment frames are tagged so that *tail calls* can be optimized (Section 2.14.2, page 170). The optimization ensures that a function called in a *tail context* reuses the stack space of its caller. Tail contexts are determined by the syntactic structure of a function's body, but an expression evaluated in a tail context is evaluated in a *dynamic* context—that is, a run-time machine state—in which the top of the stack holds one or more ENV frames, at least one of which has a CALL tag (Exercise 16).

Using the semantics in this chapter, tail-call optimization is easy to express; tail calls are optimized if the evaluation stack never holds consecutive ENV frames. For example, any evaluation stack of the form $\text{ENV}(\rho_2, \text{CALL}) :: \text{ENV}(\rho_1, \text{CALL}) :: S$ should be optimized to $\text{ENV}(\rho_1, \text{CALL}) :: S$. (The environments ρ_1 and ρ_2 are numbered in the order in which they are pushed on the stack.) So if the youngest frame on the stack is an $\text{ENV}(\rho_1, \text{CALL})$, the interpreter does not push $\text{ENV}(\rho_2, \text{CALL})$.

This optimization is justified by two metatheoretic claims:

$$\langle v, \rho, \sigma, \text{ENV}(\rho_2, \text{CALL}) :: \text{ENV}(\rho_1, \text{CALL}) :: S \rangle \to^* \langle v', \rho', \sigma', [] \rangle$$

if and only if

$$\langle v, \rho, \sigma, \text{ENV}(\rho_1, \text{CALL}) :: S \rangle \to^* \langle v', \rho', \sigma', [] \rangle,$$

and

$$\langle e, \rho, \sigma, \text{ENV}(\rho_2, \text{CALL}) :: \text{ENV}(\rho_1, \text{CALL}) :: S \rangle \to^* \langle v', \rho', \sigma', [] \rangle$$

if and only if

$$\langle e, \rho, \sigma, \text{ENV}(\rho_1, \text{CALL}) :: S \rangle \to^* \langle v', \rho', \sigma', [] \rangle.$$

These claims can be proved in Exercise 13, and the ideas of the proof are worth examining here. First, when the current item is a v, the first claim is easily and directly verified by appealing to the operational semantics. When the current item is an e, there are three possibilities:

- If e evaluates to v, then for any stack S', $\langle e, \rho, \sigma, S' \rangle \to^* \langle v, \rho', \sigma', S' \rangle$, and from there the v cases apply.
- If the evaluation of e gets stuck or keeps transitioning forever, it doesn't matter what's on the stack.
- If e tries to unwind the stack, a `long-goto` unwinds two call frames as easily as one. A `return` behaves a little more differently in the two cases, but they wind up in the same state.

In the examples above, every ENV frame has a CALL tag, but to get true, proper tail calls in all circumstances, stacks involving any mix of tags must also be optimized. Working out the semantics is Exercise 14; the code looks like this:

238. ⟨*eval-stack.c* 227a⟩+≡ ◁227a

```
void pushenv_opt(Env env, SavedEnvTag tag, Stack s) {
    assert(s);
    Frame *f = optimize_tail_calls ? topframe(s) : NULL;
    if (f && f->form.alt == ENV) {    // don't push a new frame
        if (tag == CALL && f->form.env.tag == NONCALL)
            f->form.env.tag = CALL;
    } else {
        pushframe(mkEnvStruct(env, tag), s);
    }
}
```

3.7 STACKS, CONTROL, AND SEMANTICS AS THEY REALLY ARE

3.7.1 *Stacks in programming languages*

The evaluation stack used in μScheme+'s semantics and interpreter is closely related to stacks used in real languages. The key difference lies in the representation of intraprocedural control. In real languages, control information is stored in a sequence of instructions for a real or virtual machine, and control transfer is implemented by conditional or unconditional branch instructions. In μScheme+, by contrast, control information is stored on the evaluation stack, and control transfer is implemented by popping a frame off the stack. For example, a real `if` expression is implemented by testing a condition register and using its state to transfer control to a labeled instruction sequence for expression e_2 or e_3, using a conditional branch instruction. In μScheme+, v acts like a condition register, but the destination of the control transfer (e_2 or e_3) is taken off the evaluation stack.

Although real languages handle intraprocedural control in different ways from μScheme+, real implementations do use stacks that look like special cases of our evaluation stack. For example, a language that supports recursive procedures uses a *call stack*. A call stack saves the locations and/or values of local variables, just like the ENV frames in our evaluation stack. A call stack *also* saves control information *between* procedures—at compile time, a procedure doesn't know who its caller is, so that information can't be compiled in. Control information on a call stack usually takes the form of a *return address*, which points into the instruction sequence of a calling procedure.

Real tail-call optimization works just like our model: when f calls g and g makes an optimized tail call to h, g doesn't push a new frame on the call stack. Instead, g arranges for h to see f's frame, and when h returns, it returns directly to f.

Some real implementations use a stack to evaluate function applications and similar expressions. Such an implementation includes an operation like "evaluate e and push its value on the stack." Using this operation, an application like (+ e_1 e_2) would be implemented by first pushing the value of e_1, then pushing the value of e_2, then adding the top two values on the stack. This technique is used in the Java Virtual Machine as well as in common microcontroller hardware. And in some languages, such stack-based computation is exposed directly to programmers; my two favorites are PostScript and Forth.

3.7.2 *Control operators*

The control operators `break`, `continue`, and `return`, as depicted in this chapter, are provided by many languages. Sometimes `break` is extended so it can exit a nest of several loops. For example, in the POSIX shell language, `break` may take a numeric argument that says how many nested loops to exit; in Ada, a loop can be *named* with a label, and a `break` statement can use that label.

Although `break`, `continue`, and `return` are often used in the same way as in μScheme+, they are not implemented in the same way. Any compiler, and most interpreters, will use a *static analysis*—which means "looking at the code"—based on a proof system like the one you can create in Exercise 18. The static analysis keeps track of the possible evaluation contexts at every position in the source code, and it uses this information to lower `break`, `continue`, and `return` into simple, "short" `goto` instructions, instead of our "long" ones. Such instructions don't inspect the stack at run time.

type Env 153a
type Frame 223
mkEnvStruct $\mathcal{A}$
optimize_tail_calls 224f
pushframe 224b
type SavedEnvTag 226b
type Stack 223
topframe 224c

Forms like `try-catch` and `throw` are found in dozens of real languages, usually under the name *exceptions*. There are many refinements.

- A `try-catch` can be associated with "cleanup" code that executes once the body and/or the handler have finished, regardless of whether an exception is raised. Cleanup code is usually marked by a `finally` keyword, but not always: Common Lisp provides a separate `unwind-protect` form (Exercise 21).
- In JavaScript, `try`, `catch`, and `throw` work much as they do in μScheme+, except that the control operators are unlabeled, so `throw` always transfers control to the youngest active `catch`.
- In Java, exceptions are specified using Java's *class* system, which somewhat resembles the class system of μSmalltalk (Chapter 10). A Java exception is an object of the special class `Throwable`, or of a class that inherits from `Throwable`. A `catch` handler names one of these classes instead of a label, and it catches objects of the named class and of classes that inherit from it.
- In Modula-3, exceptions are distinct from values, variables, and functions; new exceptions are defined by a special definition form. Each exception is named, and a `throw` (called `RAISE` in Modula-3) names the exception it throws. The exception's definition also specifies the type of values that may be thrown, if any. A handler may name the exceptions it handles or may offer to handle all exceptions.

  Exceptions can interact with other control operators, and in Modula-3, the interaction is explained in an unusually elegant way: both `break` and `return` are lowered into `throw`/`RAISE` operators that use special exceptions, which no program can name. This explanation is consistent with the lowering transformation used in μScheme+.

The implementation of `long-goto` used in this chapter, which involves inspecting the stack and unwinding it to reach a handler, models the widely used "zero overhead" technique of implementing exceptions. The "zero overhead" technique associates handlers and return addresses at compile time, so at run time, a `try-catch` can be entered without incurring any run-time cost. All the overhead is incurred by `throw` (modeled by `long-goto`), which visits every frame on the call stack and looks up each return address to see if it lies within the scope of a handler. A `try-catch` is therefore "free," but `throw` may be moderately expensive.

A popular alternative technique pays a small cost to enter a `try-catch`—typically just a few instructions, which push the handler's address on a stack—but makes it possible to implement `throw` in constant time. This technique can be implemented efficiently if the handler stack shares memory with the call stack; the only additional datum needed is a pointer to the top of the handler stack, which may be kept in a global variable or a machine register. This technique is used in the functional language OCaml, for example.

3.7.3 Small-step semantics

Small-step semantics are widely used. One reason is they enable a powerful proof technique: if a property holds of every initial state, and if that property is *preserved* by every state transition permitted under the semantics, then that property holds of every reachable state. This proof technique is quite good at proving *safety* properties, which say that good programs don't do bad things. One example is *memory safety*; in a memory-safe program, the condition $\ell \in \operatorname{dom} \sigma$ is always satisfied. Examples of languages that are memory-safe include full Scheme and Standard ML.

Examples of languages that are *not* memory-safe include C and C++. Unsafe access to memory can lead to bugs, blue-screen crashes, and security exploits.

Small-step semantics are also widely used because they can easily be extended to talk about *actions* taken by programs, such as I/O and communication. For example, the state-transition arrow can be *labeled*. Labels can say things like this:

- The transition causes the abstract machine to write a character to standard output.
- The transition causes the abstract machine to send a message.
- The transition causes the abstract machine to consume a character from standard input; the value of the character is bound to the name `c`.
- The transition happens only when the abstract machine receives a message, and the contents of the message are bound to the name `m`.

Small-step semantics come in many forms—not all state machines use semantic objects as part of their states. If the components of a state machine are purely syntactic, its semantics is a *reduction semantics*. In the most extreme form, the entire state is an expression or other syntactic *term* in some programming language; the language described by such a semantics is usually called a *calculus*. In a calculus, each transition rewrites one syntactic form into another syntactic form; such a transition is usually called a *reduction*. Calculi worth knowing about include Church's λ-calculus, which models functional programming, and Milner's π-calculus, which models mobility and communication (Rojas 2015; Milner 1999).

Calculi often have *nondeterministic* semantics: a machine might have a choice about which state it can transition to. For example, Church's λ-calculus has an important choice when a lambda abstraction is applied: the abstract machine can try to reduce the function's argument or it can substitute the argument into the function's body. Church and Rosser proved that either choice can lead to the same final result: no matter what reduction the machine chooses, it can choose future reductions such that from any reachable state, there are sequences of reductions that eventually arrive at the same state. But the choice makes a big difference in the way implementations perform and behave: a machine that reduces the function's argument first corresponds to a *strict* or *eager* evaluation strategy, as in ML or Scheme, and a machine that substitutes into the function's body first corresponds to a *lazy* evaluation strategy, as in Haskell.

The semantics of Core μScheme+ is intended to be *deterministic*. That is, in any given state, the next state is completely determined—unless the abstract machine is stuck or in a final state, it transitions to exactly one next state. A deterministic semantics determines an evaluation strategy, which, in a calculus, can be specified using an *evaluation context*. This is a data structure or a chunk of syntax that locates a currently evaluated expression in a larger syntactic context. For example, evaluation contexts for Core μScheme+ can be described by this (partial) grammar; a context is C, a value is v, an expression is e, and a name is x or L:

$$
\begin{array}{rcl}
C & ::= & \bullet \\
 & | & \texttt{(set}\ x\ C\texttt{)} \\
 & | & \texttt{(if}\ C\ e_2\ e_3\texttt{)} \\
 & | & \texttt{(}C\ e_1\ \cdots\ e_n\texttt{)} \\
 & | & \texttt{(}v\ v_1\ \cdots\ v_{i-1}\ C\ e_{i+1}\ \cdots\ e_n\texttt{)} \\
 & | & \texttt{(let ([}x_1\ v_1\texttt{]}\cdots\texttt{[}x_{i-1}\ v_{i-1}\texttt{] [}x_i\ C\texttt{] [}x_{i+1}\ e_{i+1}\texttt{]}\cdots\texttt{[}x_n\ e_n\texttt{])}\ e\texttt{)} \\
 & | & \texttt{(return}\ C\texttt{)} \\
 & | & \texttt{(long-label}\ L\ C\texttt{)} \\
 & | & \texttt{(long-goto}\ L\ C\texttt{)}
\end{array}
$$

The evaluation contexts specified by this grammar enforce not only an eager evaluation strategy but also an evaluation *order*: in the evaluation context for function application, everything to the left of the hole is guaranteed to be a value; only things to the right of the hole can be expressions. The context for `let` is similar. The evaluation contexts ensure that actual parameters and right-hand sides are evaluated from left to right.

Evaluation contexts are closely related to evaluation stacks. And the grammar of contexts can be converted to a grammar of *frames*; simply replace each nested context with a hole:

$$
\begin{aligned}
F ::= {} & \texttt{(set}\ x \bullet\texttt{)} \\
\mid {} & \texttt{(if}\bullet e_2\ e_3\texttt{)} \\
\mid {} & \texttt{(}\bullet e_1\ \cdots\ e_n\texttt{)} \\
\mid {} & \texttt{(}v\ v_1\ \cdots\ v_{i-1}\ \bullet\ e_{i+1}\ \cdots\ e_n\texttt{)} \\
\mid {} & \texttt{(let ([}x_1\ v_1\texttt{]}\cdots\ \texttt{[}x_{i-1}\ v_{i-1}\texttt{]}\ \texttt{[}x_i \bullet\texttt{]}\ \texttt{[}x_{i+1}\ e_{i+1}\texttt{]}\cdots\ \texttt{[}x_n\ e_n\texttt{])}\ e\texttt{)} \\
\mid {} & \texttt{(return}\bullet\texttt{)} \\
\mid {} & \texttt{(long-label}\ L \bullet\texttt{)} \\
\mid {} & \texttt{(long-goto}\ L \bullet\texttt{)}
\end{aligned}
$$

Each *stack* of frames corresponds to a unique evaluation context, and vice versa. As described in Exercise 15, the correspondences can be implemented as a pair of functions.

3.7.4 Continuations

An evaluation context C (or equivalently, a stack S) can represent a function: the function that takes one argument v, plugs v into the hole in C, then evaluates the resulting expression. This is the same function that performs the computation you get when executing the abstract machine in the state $\langle v, \rho, \sigma, S\rangle$, where S is the stack that corresponds to C. And in some languages, the stack or context in which an expression is evaluated can be captured as a function, which is called the expression's *continuation*. Such a language is said to provide *first-class continuations*; it enables code both to capture an evaluation context as a value and to use such a value as an evaluation context.

The idea of continuations is the same as the one embodied by success and failure continuations in Chapter 2; to make continuations first class, a language needs a mechanism that turns a point in the program into a continuation. The most famous mechanism is probably *call with current continuation,* usually abbreviated `call/cc`, which is part of full Scheme. It works like this:

- The language is extended with a new *value* form CONTINUATION(S). Like a closure $(\!|\lambda(\langle x\rangle, e), \rho|\!)$ or a PRIMITIVE value, a CONTINUATION(S) represents a function—in this case, a function of a single argument.

- When a continuation CONTINUATION(S') is called, the stored context S' *replaces* the current evaluation context. This operation is sometimes called *entering* the continuation. It is described by this rule:

  $$\frac{v_f = \text{CONTINUATION}(S')}{\langle v_1, \rho, \sigma, \text{APPLY}(v_f, \bullet) :: S\rangle \to \langle v_1, \rho, \sigma, S'\rangle}.$$

  (APPLY-UNDELIMITED-CONTINUATION)

  The "undelimited" part of the name is explained at the end of this section.

- The current continuation is *captured* by a new primitive, `call/cc`. "Capture" means "make a copy of."

$$\frac{}{\langle v_1, \rho, \sigma, \text{APPLY}(\text{PRIMITIVE}(\texttt{call/cc}), \bullet) :: S\rangle \rightarrow \langle \text{APPLY}(v_1, \text{CONTINUATION}(S)), \rho, \sigma, S\rangle} \quad \text{(CALL-WITH-CURRENT-CONTINUATION)}$$

As an example, suppose `f` is the function `(lambda (k) (k 5))`. Then the expression `(+ (call/cc f) 4)` evaluates to 9. That's because the continuation captured by `call/cc` is roughly APPLY(PRIMITIVE(+), •, LITERAL(4)), and it behaves like the function `(lambda (x) (+ x 4))`. So `(call/cc f)` behaves like the expression `(f (lambda (x) (+ x 4)))`, which evaluates to 9.

In theory, `call/cc` is a magnificent operation because it can be used to implement a remarkable range of control operators: coroutines, backtracking, Icon-style generators, nondeterministic choice, `setjmp`/`longjmp`, and more. (Think of `call/cc` as `setjmp` enhanced with mutant superpowers.) As just one example, my personal favorite, `call/cc` can be used to implement concurrent processes with message passing (Haynes, Friedman, and Wand 1984; Ramsey 1990). Using `call/cc` appeals to theorists and other minimalists because `call/cc` is all you need; a ton of other language features and control operators can simply be lowered into `call/cc`. And `call/cc` can be fun to program with. But in practice, `call/cc` is not so great. It's not widely implemented—copying an entire stack is expensive, and that expense can be avoided only if your implementation is really clever. Moreover, many features that might be lowered into `call/cc` don't actually use its full power, which includes the power to enter a single continuation multiple times.

And the implementation problems pale beside the modularity problems: A continuation might look like a function, but it doesn't *behave* like a function. In particular, it doesn't *compose* with other functions: The composition $f \circ g$ makes it look like f will be applied to whatever result g returns, but if g is a captured continuation, the application of f is part of the context S that is destroyed when g is applied.

Continuations that are captured with `call/cc` are called *undelimited.* A `call/cc` can grab an unbounded amount of context, and when the resulting continuation is entered, it can discard an unbounded amount of context. An interesting alternative, which addresses some of the modularity problems, is a *delimited* continuation; for example, a delimited continuation might capture just a portion of the evaluation stack, up to a *delimiter* that works a bit like `long-label`, and turn it into a function. Delimited continuations are mentioned below as possible further reading.

3.8 SUMMARY

Control operators can be awkward to handle with a big-step semantics. And big-step semantics cannot describe a computation that continues forever, like an operating system or a web server. These situations call for a small-step semantics, in which each step "reduces" a term or the state of a machine, and a sequence of reductions may end or may continue forever.

A small-step semantics for a functional language with imperative features, like μScheme or μScheme+, can use an abstract machine with four components: a control component e or v, an environment ρ, a store σ, and a continuation S. Such a machine is called a *CESK machine.* In our machine, the continuation S is represented as a stack of frames; a frame is (usually) an expression with a hole in it. Control operators are implemented by inspecting the evaluation stack and discarding or copying some of the frames found there. And at any point during evaluation, the stack can be used to convert the machine's state into an incompletely evaluated expression: use e or v to fill the youngest hole in S, then use the result to fill the next youngest hole, and so on.

Although the details are beyond the scope of this book, small-step semantics can simplify proofs of metatheoretical results, like "well-typed programs don't go wrong." Small-step proofs can be simpler than big-step proofs, because a small-step proof usually reasons about the effects of a single step, whereas a big-step proof uses an induction hypothesis to reason about entire derivations.

3.8.1 *Key words and phrases*

ABSTRACT-MACHINE SEMANTICS A SMALL-STEP SEMANTICS in which transitions go between states that include some non-syntactic, machine-like element, like a store, an environment, a stack, or a similar data structure.

`call/cc` A primitive in full Scheme that takes a function f as argument, captures the UNDELIMITED CONTINUATION of the `call/cc`, and applies f to that continuation. Its full name is `call-with-current-continuation`.

CALL STACK In a real or virtual machine, a stack of *activations* of procedures that are waiting for younger activations to return. On that call stack, an activation typically holds a return address, which tells where to resume execution upon returning to the calling procedure. An activation also holds values of formal parameters and local variables, or at least that subset of formals and locals that don't fit in machine registers. An activation may also hold saved values of machine registers. A call stack may be considered a special case of an EVALUATION STACK.

CONTINUATION In semantics, a representation of the context in which a syntactic form is evaluated. A continuation expresses "how the computation continues" when the current evaluation is complete. In μScheme+, a continuation is represented by an EVALUATION STACK S. In CONTINUATION SEMANTICS, a continuation is typically represented by a mathematical function.

In code, a representation of computational context to which control can be transferred. A continuation may be represented as a function or as a value of an abstract type.

CONTROL OPERATOR A syntactic form that transfers control outside its immediate context—that is, away from its parent in the abstract-syntax tree. Control operators that transfer control within a procedure, including `break`, `continue`, and `return`, are easily dealt with by a compiler. Control operators that transfer control between procedures—like `throw`, `longjmp`, or raising an exception—require run-time support, sometimes involving inspection of the CALL STACK. Control operators that capture a continuation, including `call/cc` and CONTROL, typically require the implementation to turn the call stack into a data structure. All control operators can be specified using a SMALL-STEP SEMANTICS. Control operators in the first two categories can be specified by extending a BIG-STEP SEMANTICS with *behaviors,* as done in Chapter 10.

DELIMITED CONTINUATION A CONTINUATION that represents a computation from a point to a *delimiter.* A delimited continuation behaves like an ordinary function: transfer of control to a delimited continuation evaluates the computation up to the point where it reaches a delimiter, then returns. Like functions, delimited continuations may be composed.

DIVERGENCE Evaluation that doesn't terminate.

EVALUATION CONTEXT A syntactic form or data structure commonly used to make a REDUCTION SEMANTICS deterministic. An expression to be reduced is decomposed into an evaluation context and a REDEX; the context tells where the semantics is "looking" to perform the next step of computation.

EVALUATION STACK The representation of an EVALUATION CONTEXT in the semantics and implementation of μScheme+. Not to be confused with the stack used for evaluation in PostScript or in the Java Virtual Machine. Contains all the information found in a CALL STACK, and more.

HOLE A technical device used to represent an EVALUATION CONTEXT: an evaluation context is represented by a program in which a single subexpression is replaced by a *hole*. Evaluating an expression e in that context is equivalent to evaluating the original program in which the expression is replaced by e.

REDEX Short for "reducible expression," a redex is a form that appears on the left-hand side of a reduction rule in a REDUCTION SEMANTICS.

REDUCTION SEMANTICS A SMALL-STEP SEMANTICS that operates entirely on syntax. That is, the transitions of the semantics are transitions between syntactic elements. A typical reduction semantics might simply specify transitions between terms, or it might use a term and evaluation context, where the context is also expressed syntactically. The evaluation of an expression e is defined by *reduction* to a value or a normal form, where reduction comprises a sequence of zero or more transitions.

SMALL-STEP SEMANTICS A species of semantics in which the primary judgment form captures a single *step* of computation, where a step, which is the atomic unit of computation, is modeled by a transition of a formal system. One advantage over a BIG-STEP SEMANTICS is the ability to express a computation that loops forever (DIVERGES), like an operating system. Small-step semantics can also easily express computations that communicate with the outside world, and they can easily specify CONTROL OPERATORS. The primary disadvantage of a small-step semantics is its complexity: A small-step semantics is usually harder to understand than a big-step semantics; it has a more complex abstract machine than a big-step semantics; and it usually has about twice as many rules as a big-step semantics.

STRUCTURED OPERATIONAL SEMANTICS A syntactic approach to SMALL-STEP SEMANTICS in which the context for REDUCTION is defined inductively via inference rules, not by an explicit data structure representing the EVALUATION CONTEXT (Plotkin 1981).

UNDELIMITED CONTINUATION A CONTINUATION that represents "the rest of the computation," that is, the entire EVALUATION STACK at the point where the continuation is *captured*. An undelimited continuation represents what is to be evaluated from a point to the end of the program. Transfer of control to an undelimited continuation never returns; the undelimited continuation takes over. In full Scheme, an undelimited continuation is captured by primitive `call-with-current-continuation`, usually abbreviated `call/cc`.

3.8.2 *Further reading*

The most influential complaint ever made about control operators was a note written by Edsger Dijkstra and published in *Communications of the ACM* as a "letter to the editor" entitled "Go To Statement Considered Harmful" (Dijkstra 1968). Dijkstra advocated for structured programming, and his later monograph on the topic was collected in book form along with monographs by Ole-Johan Dahl and Tony Hoare (Dahl, Dijkstra, and Hoare 1972). Dijkstra eventually supplemented his ideas about program structure with deep, powerful ideas about semantics and proofs of programs using *weakest preconditions*, a form of *predicate transformer* that relies on the absence of control operators, even such well-behaved ones as `break` and `continue` (Dijkstra 1976). Weakest preconditions, which Dijkstra uses to *define* his language, still offer a powerful technique for creating correct procedural programs. Many examples can be found in Dijkstra's (1976) book, which shows polished gems created by a master programmer. While the gems are worth marveling at, if you want to learn to apply the techniques yourself, you might start with Bentley (1983) and Gries (1981).

In modern programming, the essential control operators are the ones involving exceptions. Exceptions can be implemented with acceptably low overhead; the techniques are well known and are described by Drew, Gough, and Ledermann (1995). Exceptions can also be implemented, with greater overhead, using `setjmp` and `longjmp`; two good examples are presented by Roberts (1989) and Hanson (1996, chapter 4).

Continuations and ideas related to continuations can be found in much of the research of the late 1960s and early 1970s (Reynolds 1993). But continuations became widely known in a form developed by Christopher Wadsworth under the supervision of Christopher Strachey (Strachey and Wadsworth 2000). Using continuations, Wadsworth and Strachey found a clean way to give semantics to `goto` statements. This work fit into a larger program, led by Strachey and by Dana Scott, on what is now called *denotational semantics*. The results combined Scott's mathematical insights, which identified a well-behaved lattice of mathematical functions that could be used to explain recursion, with Strachey's method of defining the denotation of an expression (that is, what mathematical object the expression stands for) by composing the denotations of its subexpressions. Continuations have since been the method of choice for explaining many computational ideas connected to control. The work is definitively described by Stoy (1977), an excellent book for the mathematically inclined. The less mathematically inclined may prefer textbooks written by Allison (1986) or Schmidt (1986).

"Proper tail calls" are usually defined informally, but a precise, careful definition is presented by Clinger (1998)—using a semantics very similar to the one in this chapter.

Abstract machines are not just a semantic technique; they are commonly used in programming-language implementation. An implementor designs a machine that can be implemented relatively efficiently, then builds a compiler that translates source programs into code for that machine. Machines that have been used in this way are surveyed by Diehl, Hartel, and Sestoft (2000).

Small-step semantics are explained in depth by Felleisen, Findler, and Flatt (2009), who present major varieties of reduction semantics, including the *CESK machine* on which the semantics of μScheme+ is based. They also present standard theoretical results, of which the most important—the Church-Rosser theorem—says essentially that in standard reduction semantics, nondeterminism in the reduction relation is harmless. Finally, they present Redex, a tool for experimenting with reduction semantics.

Reduction semantics, abstract machines, and interpreters for big-step semantics are more closely related than you might think—so closely that an interpreter in the style of Chapter 2 (or more likely, Chapter 5) can be transformed automatically into an abstract-machine semantics. These relationships have been eluci-

Table 3.5: Synopsis of all the exercises, with most relevant sections

Exercises	*Section*	*Notes*
1 to 4	3.2	Programming with and without control operators; interactions among control operators.
5 to 7	3.4	Analysis and transformation of code with control operators.
8 to 10	3.3, 3.6.1, 3.6.11	Consumption of stack space.
11 to 14	3.5, 3.6.11	The evaluation stack in the semantics; optimized tail calls.
15	3.5, 3.7.3	The evaluation stack and evaluation contexts.
16 to 19	3.5	What source code can tell us about the evaluation stack.
20 to 23	3.6	Implementing control operators in the interpreter.
24 and 25	3.6	Implementing debugging aids.
26 and 27	3.7.4	Call with current continuation (`call/cc`).

dated most deeply by Olivier Danvy, his students, and his collaborators; one point of entry is Danvy's (2006) DSc thesis.

Delimited continuations and a rationale for their design are described by Felleisen (1988), who presents the control operators $\#$ and $\mathcal{F}$ (now called `prompt` and `control`). The closely related operators `shift` and `reset` are described by Danvy and Filinski (1990), who include several programming examples. The `shift` and `reset` operators have engendered significant interest, including a nice tutorial with many exercises (Asai and Kiselyov 2011).

Many examples of programming with undelimited continuations are given by Friedman, Haynes, and Kohlbecker (1984), who use `call/cc` as the main control primitive. The expressive power of `call/cc` is demonstrated by Filinski (1994), who shows that a wide variety of abstractions, including `shift` and `reset`, can be implemented using `call/cc` and a single mutable storage cell. Unfortunately, Filinski's insight is more mathematical than practical; great care is required with assumptions and corner cases (Ariola, Herbelin, and Herman 2011). A case against `call/cc` is presented by Kiselyov (2012), who argues that Filinski's techniques are brittle because their assumptions are rarely satisfied by large, practical systems.

Unless you build your entire compiler around continuations, like Appel (1992), `call/cc` is challenging to implement. The challenges are described and met by Bruggeman, Waddell, and Dybvig (1996) and by Hieb, Dybvig, and Bruggeman (1990). Even though they omit lots of details, these papers are really good. A broader view of implementation techniques is provided by Clinger, Hartheimer, and Ost (1999).

Delimited continuations are also challenging; an implementation of `shift` and `reset` in the Scheme48 virtual machine is nicely described by Gasbichler and Sperber (2002). The `shift` and `reset` operators have also been implemented in a native-code compiler for MinCaml (Masuko and Asai 2009).

If you want a feel for calculi, I recommend Milner's (1999) monograph on the π-calculus; it combines readily accessible examples of concurrent and communicating systems with the mathematical foundations needed to prove interesting properties. Parts of the book are heavily mathematical, but on a first reading, you can skip the theory chapters.

3.9 Exercises

The exercises are arranged mostly by the skill they call on (Table 3.5). The best exercises involve implementing control operators and reasoning about tail calls.

- In Exercises 13, 14, and 16, you use the operational semantics to justify tail-call optimization and to explain how to optimize evaluation stacks.
- In Exercises 20 and 21, you implement `return` and you extend μScheme+ with `unwind-protect`.

3.9.1 *Retrieval practice and other short questions*

A. In C you can write an `if` statement with no `else`. When you want to write the same kind of control structure in μScheme+, what form of expression do you use?

B. If a `throw` is evaluated inside a `try-catch` and the labels match, what happens?

C. If a `throw` is evaluated inside a function with no `try-catch`, what happens?

D. If a `throw` is evaluated inside a `try-catch` but the labels don't match, what happens?

E. What judgment or judgments of small-step semantics correspond to a single judgment of big-step semantics?

F. How many rules of small-step semantics are needed to specify what a `set` expression does? What does each rule do?

G. When the current item of the abstract machine is a value, most rules inspect only the topmost (youngest) frame on the evaluation stack. What forms of youngest frame trigger the inspection of older frames?

H. What is the name of the optimization implemented by `pushenv_opt`? What does the optimization accomplish?

I. When a frame on the evaluation stack holds an expression with a hole in it, where is the memory allocated for the `struct Exp`?

J. When you want to tell the interpreter to show you how the stack changes as an expression is evaluated, what do you do?

3.9.2 *Programming with and without control operators*

1. *Iteration over lists with early exit.* Many recursive functions that consume lists can also be implemented using loops and control operators. Use loops and control operators, but no recursion, to implement functions `exists?`, `all?`, and `member?` from Chapter 2.

2. *Early exit without control operators.* Procedural code can be written in the style of "structured programming," that is, using loops but no control operators.

   (a) Reimplement the `rainfall` function using procedural programming but without using `break`, `continue`, or `return`.

   (b) Likewise, reimplement functions `all?` and `member?` using while loops instead of recursion, but without using `break`, `continue`, or `return`.

   (c) Compare your results with the `rainfall-p` in chunk 207a and with your results from Exercise 1. In what ways are you handicapped if you don't have `break` or `continue`? How do you compensate?

3. *Nested control operators.* Control operators are an imperative feature; the order in which they are evaluated makes a difference. And many combinations of control operators can be simplified. Analyze these combinations:

   (a) Is there a simpler expression that behaves like `(return (return 1))` in every context?

   (b) Is there a simpler expression that behaves like `(return (continue))` in every context?

   (c) Is there a simpler expression that behaves like `(return (break))` in every context?

   (d) Is there a simpler expression that behaves like `(throw :L (return 3))` in every context?

   (e) Is there a simpler expression that behaves like `(return (throw :L 4))` in every context?

   (f) Can expression `(begin` e_1 e_2 $\cdots$ `(throw` L exn`)` $\cdots$ e_n`)` be replaced by `(begin` e_1 e_2 $\cdots$ `(throw` L exn`))` without changing the behavior of the program?

   (g) Can the function application `(`e e_1 e_2 $\cdots$ `(throw` L exn`)` $\cdots$ e_n`)` be simplified without changing the behavior of the program? If so, what is the simpler version? If not, why not?

4. *Nested* `try-catch` *handlers.* Combinations of `try-catch` with `throw` are less tricky. What outcome do you expect from these expressions, and why?

   (a)
```
(try-catch
    (try-catch (throw :h 'inner)
               :h
               (lambda (exn) (list2 'caught exn)))
    :h
    (lambda (exn) (list2 'outer-caught exn)))
```

   (b)
```
(try-catch
    (throw :h (try-catch 'terminated :h
                         (lambda (exn) (list2 'inner exn))))
    :h
    (lambda (exn) (list2 'outer exn)))
```

3.9.3 *Analysis and transformation of loops and control operators*

5. *Eliminating* `break` *from μScheme code.* A control operator like `break` can be eliminated by a program transformation. (Eliminating unloved control constructs by translating them to `while` loops and conditions was a nerdy pastime of the 1960s.) Generalize your knowledge from Exercise 2 by defining a program transformation that takes as input a μScheme program that uses `break` and produces as output an equivalent μScheme program that does not use `break`.

   Define your program transformation as a μScheme function that takes two inputs: a μScheme expression to be transformed, represented as an S-expression, and a list of names that are guaranteed not to appear in the program to be transformed (and can therefore safely be used as variables). To represent a μScheme expression as an S-expression, simply put a quote mark in front of its source code.

6. *Context for lowering* `break` *and* `continue`. If a `break` or `continue` appears outside any loop, my interpreter reports a "lowering error."

   (a) Write a proof system for the judgment "e is inside a loop." The body of a `lambda` expression is not considered to be inside a loop, even if the `lambda` expression itself is inside a loop.

   (b) As noted above, a μScheme+ expression can be represented as an S-expression by putting a quote mark in front of its source code. Using the proof system from part (a), define a function `loops-ok?` that examines any μScheme+ definition and returns `#f` if and `break` or `continue` occurs outside a loop, and that returns `#f` otherwise.

7. *Lowering with condition outside the loop.* The lowering transformation defined by Table 3.4 treats `break` in such a way that when `(while` e_1 e_2`)` is evaluated, executing a `break` within e_1 terminates the loop. In other words, the lowering rules treat e_1 as if it were *inside* the loop.

   These rules offend me. I think a `break` within e_1 should terminate the *enclosing* loop, if any. Define a new lowering transformation that fixes the problem. I recommend passing this transformation a long list of labels that are all distinct from one another and distinct from the labels `:continue` and `:return`.

   Test your transformation either by implementing it in μScheme or by modifying the C code in Section M.3.

3.9.4 *Understanding stack consumption*

8. *Stack requirements for* `foldl` *and* `foldr`. A list of 10 numbers can be summed using either `foldl` or `foldr`.

   (a) Using the option `&show-high-stack-mark`, measure the amount of stack space consumed by `foldl` and `foldr`.

   (b) Look at the source code for `foldl` and `foldr`. Using the definition in Figure 3.6, identify exactly which calls occur in tail position.

   (c) Use the `&trace-stack` facility to observe exactly what the stack looks like when `foldl` and `foldr` are executing. Based on your observations,

      - Write a formula that correctly predicts the high stack mark for summing n numbers using `foldl`, as a function of n.
      - Write a formula that correctly predicts the high stack mark for summing n numbers using `foldr`, as a function of n.

   (d) Based on your observations and on your analysis of the source code for `foldl` and `foldr`, justify your formulas.

9. *Implement* `map` *using constant stack space.* Implement a new version of `map` with the following property:

   > If `(`f x`)` uses constant stack space for any x, then `(map` f xs`)` uses constant stack space, no matter how many elements are in xs.

   You will have to make sure that every *recursive* call occurs in tail position, and you may have to use accumulating parameters.

10. *Compare stack consumption in μScheme and μScheme+.* Write a μScheme function and call that make the μScheme interpreter halt with a "recursion too deep" error, but which the μScheme+ interpreter runs just fine.

11. *Distinguishing saved-environment frames.* A frame formed with ENV always restores the environment, independent of its tag (CALL or NONCALL). So what does the tag do, and in which states is it possible to distinguish different tags? Considering machine states with one of these frames on top of the evaluation stack, answer these two questions:

    (a) Can you choose an environment ρ, a store σ, a stack S, a value v, and a saved environment ρ' such that $\langle v, \rho, \sigma, \text{ENV}(\rho', \text{NONCALL}) :: S\rangle$ reduces to a different final state than $\langle v, \rho, \sigma, \text{ENV}(\rho', \text{CALL}) :: S\rangle$?

    (b) Can you choose an environment ρ, a store σ, a stack S, an expression e, and a saved environment ρ' such that $\langle e, \rho, \sigma, \text{ENV}(\rho', \text{NONCALL}) :: S\rangle$ reduces to a different final state than $\langle e, \rho, \sigma, \text{ENV}(\rho', \text{CALL}) :: S\rangle$?

12. *Alternative semantics for* `long-goto`. The semantics of `long-goto` would be far more pleasant if it weren't necessary to push its frame onto the stack. A pleasant alternative might look like this:

$$\frac{F \text{ is not LONG-LABEL}(L, \bullet)}{\langle \text{LONG-GOTO}(L, e), \rho, \sigma, F :: S\rangle \to \langle \text{LONG-GOTO}(L, e), \rho, \sigma, S\rangle}, \qquad \text{(ALTERNATIVE-GOTO-UNWIND)}$$

$$\frac{F = \text{LONG-LABEL}(L, \bullet)}{\langle \text{LONG-GOTO}(L, e), \rho, \sigma, F :: S\rangle \to \langle e, \rho, \sigma, S\rangle}. \qquad \text{(ALTERNATIVE-GOTO-TRANSFER)}$$

    Write an expression of Core μScheme+ that evaluates to `#t` under the alternative semantics and to `#f` under the original semantics. Explain how it works.

13. *Prove that optimizing tail calls is safe.* Tail-call optimization is sound only if for arbitrary e, v, ρ, σ, ρ_1, ρ_2, and S, any unoptimized stack of the form $\text{ENV}(\rho_2, \text{CALL}) :: \text{ENV}(\rho_1, \text{CALL}) :: S$ can be replaced with the optimized form $\text{ENV}(\rho_1, \text{CALL}) :: S$.

    (a) Prove that when the optimized and unoptimized forms are on the top of the stack and the current item is a value, the two stacks are indistinguishable. To do so, prove that

$$\langle v, \rho, \sigma, \text{ENV}(\rho_2, \text{CALL}) :: \text{ENV}(\rho_1, \text{CALL}) :: S\rangle \to^* \langle v, \rho_1, \sigma, S\rangle$$

    and

$$\langle v, \rho, \sigma, \text{ENV}(\rho_1, \text{CALL}) :: S\rangle \to^* \langle v, \rho_1, \sigma, S\rangle$$

    (b) If e can be evaluated without control operators, so there exist a σ' and v such that $\langle e, \rho, \sigma\rangle \Downarrow \langle v, \sigma'\rangle$, we can assume (Exercise 26) that there is a ρ' such that for any stack S', $\langle e, \rho, \sigma, S'\rangle \to^* \langle v, \rho', \sigma', S'\rangle$. Using this assumption, prove that when the current item is such an expression, the optimized and unoptimized forms are indistinguishable. That is, prove that

$$\langle e, \rho, \sigma, \text{ENV}(\rho_2, \text{CALL}) :: \text{ENV}(\rho_1, \text{CALL}) :: S\rangle \to^* \langle v, \rho_1, \sigma', S\rangle$$

    and

$$\langle e, \rho, \sigma, \text{ENV}(\rho_1, \text{CALL}) :: S\rangle \to^* \langle v, \rho_1, \sigma', S\rangle.$$

(c) To prepare for cases where the optimized and unoptimized stacks have other frames pushed on top of them, prove that if the evaluation of $\langle e, \rho, \sigma, S\rangle$ does not get stuck or loop forever, then exactly one of the following holds:

- $\langle e, \rho, \sigma, S\rangle \to^* \langle v, \rho', \sigma', S\rangle$
- $\langle e, \rho, \sigma, S\rangle \to^* \langle v, \rho', \sigma', \text{RETURN}(\bullet) :: F_1 :: F_2 :: \cdots :: F_n :: S\rangle$ for some (possibly empty) sequence of frames $F_1 :: F_2 :: \cdots :: F_n$.
- $\langle e, \rho, \sigma, S\rangle \to^* \langle v, \rho', \sigma', \text{LONG-GOTO}(L, \bullet) :: F_1 :: F_2 :: \cdots :: F_n :: S\rangle$ for some (possibly empty) sequence of frames $F_1 :: F_2 :: \cdots :: F_n$.

(d) Prove that if none of $F_1 :: F_2 :: \cdots :: F_n$ has the form $\text{ENV}(\rho', \text{CALL})$, then

$$\langle v, \rho, \sigma, \text{RETURN}(\bullet) :: F_1 :: F_2 :: \cdots :: F_n :: \text{ENV}(\rho_2, \text{CALL}) :: \text{ENV}(\rho_1, \text{CALL}) :: S\rangle \to^* \langle v, \rho_1, \sigma, S\rangle$$

and

$$\langle v, \rho, \sigma, \text{RETURN}(\bullet) :: F_1 :: F_2 :: \cdots :: F_n :: \text{ENV}(\rho_1, \text{CALL}) :: S\rangle \to^* \langle v, \rho_1, \sigma, S\rangle.$$

14. *More cases for optimizing tail calls.* To implement truly proper tail calls, the interpreter must simplify every stack that contains consecutive ENV frames, regardless of tag.

(a) In state $\langle e/v, \rho, \sigma, \text{ENV}(\rho_2, \text{NONCALL}) :: \text{ENV}(\rho_1, \text{CALL}) :: S\rangle$, how can the stack be simplified?

(b) In state $\langle e/v, \rho, \sigma, \text{ENV}(\rho_2, \text{CALL}) :: \text{ENV}(\rho_1, \text{NONCALL}) :: S\rangle$, how can the stack be simplified?

(c) In state $\langle e/v, \rho, \sigma, \text{ENV}(\rho_2, \text{NONCALL}) :: \text{ENV}(\rho_1, \text{NONCALL}) :: S\rangle$, how can the stack be simplified?

(d) ENV frames on the evaluation stack are inspected by rules SMALL-STEP-RESTORE-ENVIRONMENT, GOTO-UNWIND, GOTO-TRANSFER, RETURN-UNWIND, and RETURN-TRANSFER. For each previous part of this problem, justify your answer and list the rules you appeal to.

15. *The evaluation stack as evaluation context.* Grammars for evaluation contexts and stack frames are given in Section 3.7.3. If a hole is represented by the μScheme symbol <*>, then both evaluation contexts and stack frames can be represented as S-expressions.

(a) Write a μScheme function that converts an evaluation context to a list of frames.

I would write an auxiliary, recursive function that expects an expression, which might or might not be an evaluation context, plus success and failure continuations. If the expression turned out to be a context, my function would pass the resulting list of frames to the success continuation. Otherwise it would call the failure continuation. The base case of the recursion would be a hole (success) or some other name or literal (failure). The induction step might require a search of several subexpressions to see which one represents an evaluation context.

(b) Write a μScheme function that converts a list of frames to an evaluation context.

This is the easier of the two problems. I would start by defining an auxiliary function that fills the hole in a frame.

$$\frac{\texttt{(lambda (}x_1, \ldots, x_n\texttt{)}\ e\texttt{)}\text{ is in the code}}{e \text{ is in tail position}}$$

$$\frac{\texttt{(if }e_1\ e_2\ e_3\texttt{)}\text{ is in tail position}}{e_2 \text{ is in tail position}} \qquad \frac{\texttt{(if }e_1\ e_2\ e_3\texttt{)}\text{ is in tail position}}{e_3 \text{ is in tail position}}$$

$$\frac{\texttt{(let ([}x_1\ e_1\texttt{]} \cdots \texttt{[}x_n\ e_n\texttt{])}\ e\texttt{)}\text{ is in tail position}}{e \text{ is in tail position}}$$

$$\frac{\texttt{(letrec ([}x_1\ e_1\texttt{]} \cdots \texttt{[}x_n\ e_n\texttt{])}\ e\texttt{)}\text{ is in tail position}}{e \text{ is in tail position}}$$

Figure 3.6: Partial proof system for tail position (Core μScheme+)

3.9.6 *What source code tells us about the evaluation stack*

16. *Dynamic context of an expression in tail position.* A simple proof system that says when an expression "is in tail position" is shown in Figure 3.6. Using metatheoretic reasoning about this proof system, prove that if an expression is in tail position, then when that expression is evaluated, the top of the stack contains a sequence of zero or more frames of the form $\text{ENV}(\rho, \text{NONCALL})$ followed by a frame of the form $\text{ENV}(\rho, \text{CALL})$. Try proof by induction over a derivation that uses the rules in Figure 3.6.

17. *Expressions returned and tail position.* It's tempting to say that the e in `(return` e`)` occurs in tail position. But when e is evaluated, the top of the stack does not necessarily contain a sequence of zero or more frames of the form $\text{ENV}(\rho, \text{NONCALL})$ followed by a frame of the form $\text{ENV}(\rho, \text{CALL})$. It could be made so, however, by these rules:

$$\frac{F \text{ does not have the form } \text{ENV}(\rho, \text{CALL})}{\langle \text{RETURN}(e), \rho, \sigma, F :: S\rangle \to \langle \text{RETURN}(e), \rho, \sigma, S\rangle}, \quad (\text{ALTERNATIVE-RETURN-UNWIND})$$

$$\frac{}{\langle \text{RETURN}(e), \rho, \sigma, \text{ENV}(\rho', \text{CALL}) :: S\rangle \to \langle e, \rho, \sigma, \text{ENV}(\rho', \text{CALL}) :: S\rangle}. \quad (\text{ALTERNATIVE-RETURN})$$

Solve exactly one of the following two problems:

(a) Prove that the alternative RETURN rules produce the same results as the original rules.

(b) Define a function that uses `return` in such a way that the original rules produce one result but the alternative rules produce a different result.

18. *Occurrence inside a* `long-label`. Look at Figure 3.6, which defines a little proof system to say exactly when an expression occurs "in tail position." Create a similar proof system to say exactly when an expression occurs "inside a long label L." Start with these rules:

$$\frac{\texttt{(long-label }L\ e\texttt{)}\text{ is in the code}}{e \text{ is inside long label } L} \qquad \frac{\texttt{(if }e_1\ e_2\ e_3\texttt{)}\text{ is inside long label } L}{e_1 \text{ is inside long label } L}.$$

19. *Dynamic context of a labeled expression.* In Exercise 18, you create a simple proof system that says when an expression is inside a long label.

    (a) Using metatheoretic reasoning about this proof system, prove that if expression e is inside a long label L, then when e is evaluated, the top of the stack contains a sequence of zero or more frames, none of which has the form ENV(ρ, CALL), followed by a frame LONG-LABEL($L, \bullet$). Try proof by induction over a derivation that uses the rules in your proof system.

    (b) Prove that if an expression (`long-goto` L e) occurs inside a `long-label` with label L, and if expression e evaluates to value v without an error, then the `long-goto` is also evaluated without an error. That is, from a state of the form $\langle v, \rho, \sigma, \text{LONG-GOTO}(L, \bullet) :: S\rangle$, the abstract machine makes one successful state transition after another until the LONG-GOTO frame is replaced by something else.

    The proof in part (b) guarantees that when `break` and `continue` are lowered to `long-goto` expressions, those expressions are evaluated without error.

3.9.7 *Implementing control operators*

20. *Implementing* `return`. My interpreter implements `long-goto` but not `return`. Implement `return`.

21. *Finalization.* When you're writing procedural code, sometimes you want to define cleanup code that executes no matter what. The classic example is that when you open a file, you want to be sure to close it. In many languages, cleanup code is attached to a `try-catch` using the keyword `finally`. But we'll put cleanup code inside a form called `unwind-protect`, which comes from Common Lisp:

    > Evaluating (`unwind-protect` e_b e_f) evaluates the body e_b. When e_b is finished evaluating, whether the result is a value or a control operation, the machine evaluates the *finalizer* e_f before continuing as e would have.

    The semantics can be expressed in a handful of rules. The rules code "evaluate finalizer e_f and then proceed as you would have" by synthesizing a little BEGIN expression.

$$\frac{}{\langle \text{UNWIND-PROTECT}(e_b, e_f), \rho, \sigma, S\rangle \rightarrow \langle e_b, \rho, \sigma, \text{UNWIND-PROTECT}(\bullet, e_f) :: S\rangle} \quad \text{(UNWIND-PROTECT)}$$

$$\frac{}{\langle v, \rho, \sigma, \text{UNWIND-PROTECT}(\bullet, e_f)\rangle \rightarrow \langle \text{BEGIN}(e_f, v), \rho, \sigma, S\rangle} \quad \text{(UNWIND-PROTECT-VALUE)}$$

$$\frac{}{\langle v, \rho, \sigma, \text{RETURN}(\bullet) :: \text{UNWIND-PROTECT}(\bullet, e_f) :: S\rangle \rightarrow \langle \text{BEGIN}(e_f, \text{RETURN}(v)), \rho, \sigma, S\rangle} \quad \text{(UNWIND-PROTECT-RETURN)}$$

$$\frac{}{\langle v, \rho, \sigma, \text{LONG-GOTO}(L, \bullet) :: \text{UNWIND-PROTECT}(\bullet, e_f) :: S\rangle \rightarrow \langle \text{BEGIN}(e_f, \text{LONG-GOTO}(L, v)), \rho, \sigma, S\rangle} \quad \text{(UNWIND-PROTECT-GOTO)}$$

    Implement `unwind-protect`. Because BEGIN is not part of Core μScheme+, you will need to lower it using function `lowerSequence` from Appendix M.

22. *Unwinding many frames at once.* The rules of the operational semantics say that `break`, `continue`, `return`, and `throw` remove frames from the stack one at a time. At each step the abstract machine re-examines the current item or topmost frame, even though they won't have changed. Speed things up: implement these operators by writing an inner loop that unwinds the stack.

    (a) Can you find a μScheme+ program for which this change results in a measurable difference in performance?

    (b) Is the new code simpler or more complicated than the original code?

    (c) Which version do you like better and why?

23. *Tail-call optimization in the presence of lowered* `return`. Control operators `break` and `continue` are implemented by lowering to `long-goto`, but `return` is not lowered. It could be lowered (Table 3.4), but lowering `return` would complicate tail-call optimization. Confirm this assessment: Implement `return` by lowering it, *with* proper tail calls.

    (a) Enable lowering of `return` (define `LOWER_RETURN` as `true` in file `lower.c`).

    (b) As in Exercise 8, 9, or 10, confirm that tail calls are not optimized.

    (c) Update `pushenv_opt` so that if the top of the stack contains zero or more labels followed by another environment frame, no new frame is pushed. Inspect the stack using function `topnonlabel`.

    (d) Update the `eval` case for (`long-label` L e) so that if the top of the stack contains zero or more labels followed by a LONG-LABEL$(L, \bullet)$ frame (with the same L), no LONG-LABEL frame is pushed.

    (e) Confirm that tail calls are optimized again.

The optimizations of Exercises 22 and 23 can be proven correct using the same techniques that are used in Exercise 13.

3.9.8 Debugging aids

24. *Visualizing just the call stack.* To diagnose a fault, a visualization of the stack ("stack trace") can be very helpful. But an evaluation stack includes so much information that a complete visualization can be hard to digest. Implement a visualization that shows just the active function calls.

    - Enhance the implementation of the SMALL-STEP-APPLY-LAST-ARG rule so that it copies the `syntax` field of the APPLY frame into the `syntax` field of the ENV frame.
    - Write a C function that takes a `Stack` and shows the `syntax` fields of the ENV frames that have CALL tags. Arrange for μScheme's `error` primitive to call that function.

25. *Diagnosing a* `long-goto` *with no target.* If `long-goto` is evaluated without a corresponding `long-label`, the interpreter doesn't discover the error until the context is lost. We can do better. Change the interpreter so that if it evaluates `long-goto`, it first checks to make sure that the stack contains a LONG-LABEL frame with a matching label. If not, `long-goto` should show what is on the stack, preferably using the function from Exercise 24.

3.9.9 Continuations

26. *Continuation capture.* Using the rules in Section 3.7.4, implement `call/cc`.

27. *Using captured continuations.* Implement `try-catch` and `throw` using `call/cc` and possibly an additional data structure.

CHAPTER 4 CONTENTS

Automatic memory management

4

No Scheme object is ever destroyed. The reason that implementations of Scheme do not (usually!) run out of storage is that they are permitted to reclaim the storage occupied by an object if they can prove that the object cannot possibly matter to any future computation.

Kelsey, Clinger, and Rees (1998, page 3)

A running μScheme program continually allocates fresh locations. How are they supplied? Memory is limited, and `malloc` will eventually run out. Memory can be recovered using `free`, but if a programmer must call `free`, as in C and C++, they risk memory errors: leaks, locations that are freed multiple times, and misuse of freed locations (so-called dangling-pointer errors). Memory errors can make a program crash—or, worse, silently produce wrong answers. But in languages like μScheme, full Scheme, Java, and JavaScript, which are *memory-safe*, such errors are impossible. The errors are prevented because the *implementation* of μScheme, not the μScheme programmer, figures out when it is safe to reuse a location. The techniques used to reuse locations safely are demonstrated in this chapter.

Memory-management techniques might seem like matters for implementors, but automatic memory management enables all kinds of designers to keep things simple. Language designers can include features that create closures, cons cells, and other objects without having to say when the memory they occupy must be reclaimed. Software designers can define interfaces that focus on the needs of the client; when memory management is automatic, it is not necessary to clutter an interface with extra functions and/or parameters that address such issues as where memory is allocated, who owns it, when it is freed, and how a client can make a private copy. Without automatic memory management, interfaces would be more complex, programming with higher-order functions would be nearly impossible, and object-oriented systems like Smalltalk (Chapter 10) would be much more complex. Safety guarantees, like those that Java provides, would be impossible. Automatic memory management underlies all civilized programming languages.

Automatic memory management is explained in this chapter. The chapter emphasizes *garbage collection,* the most widely used method of memory management, and its implementation in μScheme. (The name "μScheme" is used generically; the language that is actually implemented is μScheme+.) Reference counting, an alternative method, is discussed only briefly (Section 4.8).

The μScheme interpreter uses `Value` objects in two ways. Temporary values, like values `v` and `w` computed by the implementation of `cons` on page 161c, are stored in local variables, i.e., locations on the C stack. In `cons`, for example, local variables `v` and `w` hold values until they are passed to `allocate`, and afterward, those variables are not used again. But some `Value` objects are stored in locations allocated on the C heap, with `malloc`, because we can't predict how long they will live. In particular, every `car` and `cdr` of every `cons` cell is allocated on the C heap, using function `allocate`. Why? Because if a μScheme function returns a cons cell, there's no general way to decide whether that cons cell's `car` or `cdr` will be needed in a future computation. For the same reason, every location in every environment in every closure is allocated on the C heap. In C, of course, a programmer would have to call `free` at an appropriate moment. In Scheme, memory is freed and reused by the system.

How can the system know if an object can be reused? At any given time, a `Value` object may have become *unreachable,* which is to say there is no way to get to it. Objects become unreachable when pointers change, as in these examples:

- Evaluating the definition `(val x '(a b))` makes `x` point to a newly allocated location. In practice, the system allocates many locations: five hold `Value` objects,[1] and one holds an `Env` link for the top-level environment. In this picture, the `Env` object is labelled `env`; the unlabelled objects are `Values`.

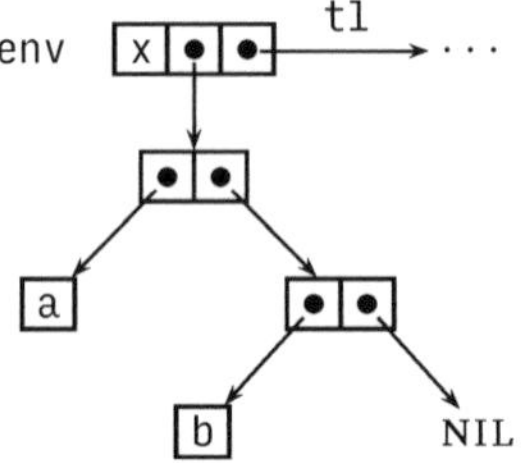

If the next definition evaluated is `(set x '())`, memory now looks like this:

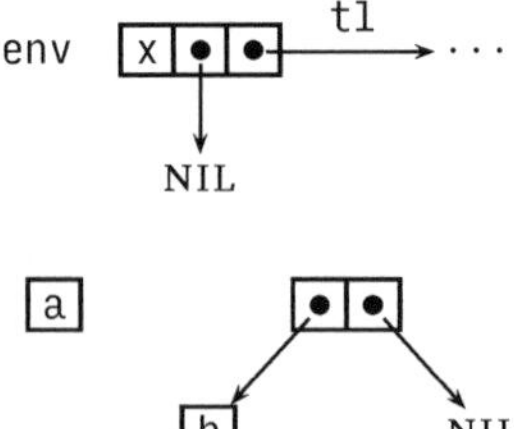

The location associated with `x` is overwritten, so the four locations holding the atom `a`, the cons cell `(b)`, the atom `b`, and NIL are now unreachable, and they cannot affect any future computation. They can be reused to satisfy future allocation requests.

- Suppose the next definition instead sets `x` to `(cdr x)`.

258. ⟨*transcript* 258⟩≡ 283▷

```
-> (val x '(a b))
-> (set x (cdr x))
```

[1] In order, they are `'b`, `'()`, `'a`, a `cons` cell, and an unspecified value associated with `x`, which is later overwritten to hold a second `cons` cell.

The second cons cell is copied over the location containing the first. Now the picture is

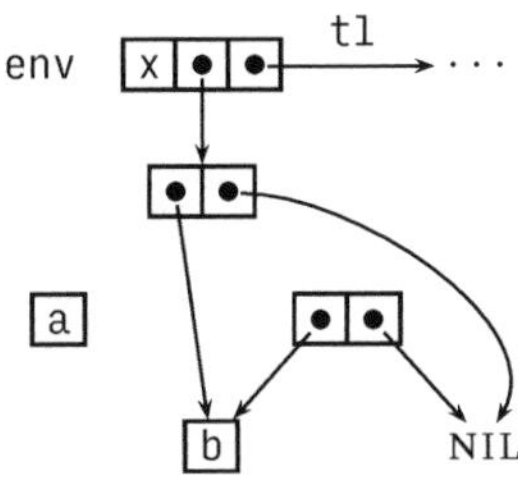

The locations containing the atom a and the original copy of the second cell of (a b) are now unreachable.

Locations holding unreachable objects are *garbage*. In a *garbage-collected* system, objects are allocated from a *managed heap*: a collection of memory blocks and metadata structures whose mission is to satisfy allocation requests. When the heap runs out of memory and so can no longer satisfy allocation requests, the computation is halted while a *garbage collector* reclaims unreachable objects, making them available to satisfy future requests.

Like all forms of memory management, garbage collection has overhead costs. The overhead on allocation is bursty: most allocations are fast, but an allocation that triggers the garbage collector makes the program pause, at least a little. To keep the pauses short, a sophisticated collector runs frequently, in short spurts, or even concurrently with the program that is allocating. And total overhead can be reduced by making the heap bigger—each collection does about the same amount of work as before, but the collector runs less often.

Garbage collection also imposes memory overhead, but here the story is more complicated. A collector requires enough memory to hold all *reachable* objects, plus an additional factor of "headroom," so the collector doesn't have to run too often. How this requirement compares with manual memory management depends on how good the manual manager is at freeing objects that are no longer needed—a property that varies from program to program.

Garbage collection has another pleasant property—as we see in this chapter, a garbage-collected heap can easily be integrated into existing code; one simply replaces `malloc` with a new allocator, them implements `free` as a no-op.

A garbage collector scans the *roots* of a system and uses these roots to find reachable objects. There are many variations, but they all draw from the two methods presented in this chapter: *mark-and-sweep* and *copying* collection.

An alternative not based on reachability is *reference counting*. In reference counting, each object stores a count of the number of pointers to that object; when the count goes to zero, the object can be put on a list of available objects. Reference counting cannot easily reclaim cyclic garbage: an unreachable circular list has no objects with zero counts, so it never gets reclaimed. For this reason and others, garbage collection is normally preferable to reference counting (Section 4.8).

4.2 Garbage-collection basics

A managed heap has at least two components: a garbage collector and an *allocator*. The garbage collector gets all the attention, but the allocator shouldn't be overlooked; the two work as a team. The team serves a third actor: in the perverse jargon of garbage collection, the client code that allocates objects and does useful work with them is called the *mutator*.

The best managed heaps use multiple processor cores and multiple threads of control to supply the mutator with new objects while disrupting its work as little as possible (Section 4.9). But to make the basic ideas concrete, the examples in this chapter use a much simpler model, called *stop the world*. The mutator runs in a single thread, and it periodically allocates a new object or changes (mutates) a pointer in an old object. (It is the accumulation of mutations that eventually makes objects unreachable.) The allocator satisfies a typical request quickly, but when it cannot do so, it suspends execution of the mutator entirely—"stopping the world"—and runs the garbage collector in that same thread.

The system in this chapter makes one other simplifying assumption: that every object allocated on the heap is the same size.

4.2.1 Performance

The performance of a managed heap can be measured along several dimensions. I focus on these three:

- *Allocation cost.* How long does it take to allocate an object?
- *Collector overhead.* How much additional work, per object allocated, does it take to run the garbage collector?
- *Memory overhead.* How much additional memory, per object, does it take to hold the data structures that support the managed heap?

The first two measures combine to give the cost per allocation, measured in time. The third measure gives the space overhead of garbage collection, e.g., the ratio of the size of the whole heap to the size of the program's data. In garbage-collected systems, space can be traded for time by adjusting the size of the heap: Provided there's enough physical memory, enlarging the heap lowers the cost per allocation. The size of the heap is written H.

A fourth measure is also worth keeping in mind:

- *Pause time.* How long does the program pause while the garbage collector is running?

This measure matters most in programs that must interact with users or on servers that must answer requests promptly. And it can be improved by another trade-off: pause times can be decreased by spending more overhead per allocation. The state of the art keeps improving; at one time, a collector with a 50-millisecond pause time could claim to be "real-time." As I write, general-purpose implementations of Go and OCaml get pause times under 10 milliseconds, and "real-time" means under 1 millisecond, if not better. Human reaction time is only about 100 milliseconds, so 10-millisecond pause times make garbage collection very effective in interactive applications.

4.2.2 Reachability and roots

As shown in the examples above, heap-allocated objects can become irrelevant as a program runs. And they can do so in an unpredictable manner and at unpredictable times. A heap object may be used immediately and never needed again, or it may be bound into a global environment and live for the rest of the session. Whether any particular heap object is relevant to any future computation is undecidable in general. Luckily, the set of relevant heap objects can be approximated.

The approximation is reasonably good, reasonably cheap to compute, and reasonably easy to implement.

The approximation is defined by observing that the interpreter's state includes pointers to data structures, which themselves include pointers, and so on. If, by following such pointers, the interpreter can reach an object allocated on the heap, then that object is *reachable*. Because any reachable object might be used in a future computation, a reachable object is considered *live data*. Any object that cannot be reached is *unreachable* and can safely be reclaimed.

Live data is defined by induction. The base case is given by a set of *roots*, which are enumerated below; roots are live by definition. The induction step says that any object pointed to by a live object is itself live. All live data can therefore be found by starting at the roots and tracing pointers. The amount of live data is written L.

In compiled code, roots are found in three places:

- Global variables from which heap-allocated objects might be reachable
- Local variables and formal parameters, anywhere on the call stack, from which heap-allocated objects might be reachable
- Hardware registers from which heap-allocated objects might be reachable

In our μScheme+ interpreter, roots are found in the same three places:

- Global variables are stored in a data structure `roots.globals` which has type `Env`. (μScheme+ also has a species of "hidden" global variable: the list of pending unit tests. Each list of pending unit tests is associated with a source of definitions, and a list is stored in data structure `roots.sources` of type `Sourcelist`.)
- Local variables and formal parameters are stored in ENV frames on the evaluation stack (Chapter 3), a data structure `roots.stack` of type `Stack`.
- The closest thing to a "hardware register" is a local variable in C code. Their addresses are recorded in a data structure `roots.registers` of type `Registerlist`.

Tricolor marking

The allocated objects, together with the pointers between them, form a graph. Following pointers amounts to tracing the edges of this graph. Tracing algorithms are modeled using an abstraction called *tricolor marking*. In the model, each object is colored as follows:

- A *white* object has not been visited by the garbage collector.
- A *gray* object has been visited, but not all of its successors have been visited.
- A *black* object has been visited, and so have all of its successors.

The colors are *abstractions*; even in the simple collectors we build in this chapter, nodes aren't colored white, gray, or black directly. Instead, an object's color is identified by looking at other properties. Abstracting over the representation in this way requires extra thinking, but it pays off because tricolor marking can guide the implementation of many different kinds of collectors.

The easiest payoff comes from the *coloring invariant*: no black object ever points to a white object; black objects point only to gray objects or to other black objects. Another payoff comes from an abstract description of how a collector works; mark-

and-sweep and copying collectors use different algorithms to traverse the graph of objects, but abstractly, both algorithms fit this description:

> color all the roots gray
> **while** there is a gray object remaining
>   choose a gray object
>   **if** the object has a white successor
>   color that successor gray
>   **else**
>   color the gray object black

This algorithm maintains the coloring invariant. Moreover, it terminates: there are finitely many objects; every gray object eventually becomes black; and no black object changes color. When the algorithm terminates, the heap contains only black and white objects. The black objects are exactly those reachable from the roots: the live data. The white objects are unreachable, and they can be reused.

The coloring abstraction does not fully specify an algorithm: it does not say which gray object to pick next or which white successor to color gray. Most modern collectors choose objects in depth-first order. Our simple, stop-the-world copying collector, however, chooses objects in breadth-first order.

4.2.3 Heap growth

In addition to recovering and reusing unreachable objects, the garbage collector manages the size of the heap. At minimum, the collector must ensure that the heap is large enough to hold all the program's live data. For example, if the mutator computes a list of all permutations of a list of length n, just holding the answer requires $n!$ lists of n elements. If there are not enough objects available on the heap, the program is doomed to fail.

Older collectors didn't worry about the size of the heap: in the very first garbage-collected systems, the computer ran one program at a time, and that program ran in all of physical memory. The collector's big challenge was to get reasonable performance when the heap was almost full. For example, if $H - L = 1$, then there is just one free location, and the garbage collector has to run after every allocation. Very expensive.

Now most garbage collectors run in virtual memory. A collector must keep the heap small enough so that virtual memory performs well, while keeping it large enough so that overhead is not too high. A collector might start with a fairly small heap, then enlarge it in response to the growth of live data. To amortize the costs of enlarging the heap, the collector may enlarge it in fairly big chunks, e.g., many virtual-memory pages.

How should the heap grow? That is a hard question to answer well. This book uses a simple rule of thumb: maintain a roughly constant *ratio of heap size to live data*, which we write $\gamma = \frac{H}{L}$. The inverse, $\frac{L}{H} = \frac{1}{\gamma}$, measures the fraction of heap memory that is used to hold the program's data. As we see below, γ bounds the fraction of memory that holds no data, and it also is a good predictor of the overhead of garbage collection. Changing γ can adjust space-time trade-offs. When γ is too small, there are too few allocations between collections, and the overhead of collection gets high. When γ is at least 2, mark-and-sweep collectors perform very well. For a copying collector, γ of at least 3 is needed (Hertz and Berger 2005). By comparison, γ in the range of 1.1 to 1.4 appears to be enough for standard implementations of `malloc` and `free` (Wilson et al. 1995; Johnstone and Wilson 1998).

Pushing γ up to 5 or 7 can reduce garbage-collection overhead substantially. The larger γ requires a larger heap, which means that more memory holds no data, but the memory is not wasted. The memory is used to reduce time: time spent allocating, time spent collecting, time spent worrying whether objects in a program need to be freed explicitly, or time spent tracking down memory leaks, double frees, and dangling-pointer errors. Space is traded for time in other dynamic-allocation systems as well; for example, fast implementations of `malloc` may require heaps 1.4 to 2 times larger than a simple first-fit implementation (Grunwald and Zorn 1993).

4.3 THE MANAGED HEAP IN μSCHEME+

In a real Scheme system, all dynamically allocated objects are allocated on the managed heap. In μScheme+, only objects of type `Value` are allocated on the managed heap. This design is not realistic, but it keeps the interpreter simple enough to study and modify. And the `Value` objects account for most memory use; objects of types `Exp`, `Explist`, and `Namelist` are allocated only by the μScheme parser, so their allocation is bounded by the amount of source code. In a real garbage collector, the techniques we use for `Value`s would be used for objects of all types.

4.3.1 *Where are* `Value` *objects stored?*

Not all `Value` objects are allocated on the heap. In particular, intermediate values computed by `eval` are either stored in the C local variable `v` or are stored in evaluation contexts on the μScheme+ stack (Chapter 3). As far as the garbage collector is concerned, these objects act as roots—values reachable from the stack could be used in future computations.

Allocating most intermediate values on the stack reduces heap allocation to just three situations:

- When the primitive `cons` is applied, the locations needed to hold the `car` and `cdr` are allocated on the managed heap, with `allocate`.
- When an environment is extended—whether it is by a function call, a `LET` form, or a definition—it is extended using the C function `bindalloc` or `bindalloclist`, both of which call `allocate`. The allocation is specified in the operational semantics: In the rules for these forms, allocation is specified by premises of the form $\ell_1, \ldots, \ell_n \notin \operatorname{dom} \sigma$. Such a premise means "call `allocate` for fresh locations $\ell_1, \ldots, \ell_n$."
- When source code is parsed, if it contains a quoted S-expression, space for that S-expression is allocated with `allocate`.

Objects allocated on the heap can be identified by this invariant: if a *pointer* to a `Value` exists in another data structure, such as another `Value`, an `Exp`, or an `Env`, the pointer points to a location allocated on the heap.

4.3.2 *Reachability of locations*

Any pointer to a `Value` allocated on the heap has to be findable during garbage collection. Such a pointer might be embedded into other data. These data are potential roots.

A. Any structure or pointer that might contain a pointer to a `Value` allocated on the heap is a potential root of category A. Their types are:

    - `Value*`, which points directly to a heap-allocated object

- Value, through pair.car and pair.cdr
- Env, through loc

B. Any structure or pointer that might contain or point to a potential root of category A is itself a potential root of category B. To avoid infinite regress, any structure or pointer that might contain or point to a potential root of category B is also a potential root of category B. Their types are:

- Valuelist, because the hd field contains a Value
- Exp, because literal is a Value
- Lambda, because body is an Exp
- Value again, through closure
- Exp again, through lambda or the many Exp*s it contains
- Env, through tl
- Explist, because the hd field contains an Exp
- Valuelist again, because the tl field points to a Valuelist
- Frame, because the context and syntax fields contain or point to Exps
- Stack, because its frames points to an array of Frames
- Def, because it can point to Exps
- UnitTest, because it contains Exps
- UnitTestlist, because it contains UnitTests
- XDef, because it can contain a Def or a UnitTest
- Source, because tests is a UnitTestlist (see Appendix N)
- Sourcelist, because the hd field contains a Source (also in Appendix N)

The list above shows not only from which types of value a heap object might be reachable but also which pointers to follow from such a value to reach the heap object. Accordingly, for each type above, I have written a procedure that follows pointers and marks heap-allocated values. These procedures appear in Sections 4.4.2 and N.1.1.

4.3.3 *Interface to the managed heap: Roots, allocator, initialization*

The managed heap offers this contract to the mutator:

- The mutator can get a fresh location by calling allocate.
- When it calls allocate, the mutator must tell the garbage collector about any previously allocated location that it might still care about.
- To improve performance, the garbage collector might move heap objects. If so, it faithfully updates every pointer to every moved object.

To enable the managed heap to fulfill this contract, the mutator and the heap share information:

- They agree on a representation of roots. Ours is shown below.
- The garbage collector knows enough about the mutator's internal data structures so it can find pointers. In our case, the garbage collector knows *everything* about the mutator's data structures—the information about pointers is summarized in the previous section.

The roots are

1. The global variables, which include both the user program's variables (the μScheme+ global environment) and any global variables internal to the mutator (the pending unit tests)

2. Local variables and actual parameters of any μScheme+ function, all of which are found on the stack of evaluation contexts

3. Local variables and actual parameters of any C function that calls `allocate` or a function that could allocate (such as `bindalloc` or `bindalloclist`)

The roots are represented as follows:

265a. ⟨*structure definitions used in garbage collection* 265a⟩≡ (S377c)

```
struct Roots {
    struct {
        Env *user;              // global variables from the user's program
        struct {
            UnitTestlistlist pending_tests; // unit tests waiting to be run
        } internal;             // the mutator's internal variables
    } globals;                  // all the global variables
    Stack stack;                // the uscheme+ stack,
                                // with all parameters and locals
    Registerlist registers;     // pointers to "machine registers"
};
```

This `struct` is the data structure that is shared between the mutator and the garbage collector, as a global variable:

265b. ⟨*global variables used in garbage collection* 265b⟩≡ (S377d)

```
extern struct Roots roots;
```

The mutator makes sure that before any call to `allocate`, `roots` is up to date and contains pointers to all locations that could affect the rest of the computation. The garbage collector inspects the roots and also updates pointers to objects that it moves. Register roots are added and removed in last-in, first-out order using functions `pushreg` and `popreg`.

265c. ⟨*function prototypes for μScheme+* 265c⟩≡ (S358) 265d ▷

```
void pushreg(Value *reg);
void popreg (Value *reg);
```

If the pointer passed to `popreg` is not equal to the pointer passed to the matching `pushreg`, it is a checked run-time error.

The mutator may also need to push or pop all the registers on a *list* of values.

265d. ⟨*function prototypes for μScheme+* 265c⟩+≡ (S358) ◁ 265c 281a ▷

```
void pushregs(Valuelist regs);
void popregs (Valuelist regs);
```

The rest of the interface supports allocation. The managed-heap function `allocloc` provides an *uninitialized* location; in chunk 266b, it is used to implement `allocate`.

265e. ⟨*function prototypes for μScheme* 265e⟩≡ (S318a S358) 266a ▷

```
Value *allocloc(void);
```

The allocator and `roots` structure are related by this precondition: clients may call `allocloc` only when *all objects that could lead to live values appear in* `roots`. The copying collector's implementation of `allocloc` also requires that, when called, *all pointers to allocated values must be reachable from* `roots`, so that they can be updated when the values move.

type `Env` 153a
type `Registerlist` S377b
type `Stack` 223
type `UnitTestlistlist` S377b
type `Value` 𝒜
type `Valuelist` S309c

The mutator has one more obligation: before calling `allocloc`, it must call `initallocate`, passing a pointer to the environment that holds the global variables.

266a. ⟨*function prototypes for μScheme* 265e⟩+≡ (S318a S358) ◁265e

```
void initallocate(Env *globals);
```

The managed-heap interface is implemented in Appendix N.

4.3.4 *Using the heap interface: μScheme allocation*

Functions `pushreg`, `popreg`, and `allocloc` are used to implement the `allocate` function of Chapter 2.

266b. ⟨*loc.c* 266b⟩≡

```
Value* allocate(Value v) {
    pushreg(&v);
    Value *loc = allocloc();
    popreg(&v);
    assert(loc != NULL);
    *loc = v;
    return loc;
}
```

What's new here are the calls to `pushreg` and `popreg`. When `v` is a `cons` cell and `allocloc` happens to call the garbage collector, `pushreg` and `popreg` prevent the garbage collector from reclaiming the locations pointed to by `v.pair.car` and `v.pair.cdr`. The call to `pushreg` makes `v` a "machine register" and ensures that the collector treats it as a root. And if the collector happens to move `v`'s `car` and `cdr`, it updates `v`'s internal pointers to point to the new locations.

4.4 Mark-and-sweep collection

The original garbage-collection technique, invented by McCarthy (1960) for Lisp, is called *mark-and-sweep*. It allocates available objects from a data structure called the *free list*. To track when objects become available, it uses an extra bit for each object, called the *mark bit*. These data structures support conceptually simple algorithms for allocating and recovering objects:

1. When an object is requested, look for a suitable object is on the free list. If there isn't one, ask the collector to recover some objects.

2. Remove an object from the free list and return it.

The collector recovers objects in two phases:

1. Mark (i.e., set the mark bit associated with) every reachable object. This phase traverses the heap starting from the roots.

2. Sweep every object in the heap. Unmarked objects are unreachable. Place each unreachable object on the free list, and clear the mark bit associated with each reachable object.

If these algorithms are implemented naïvely, the sweep phase visits the entire heap. That's a lot of objects, and they probably don't all fit in the cache. The mutator might pause for a long time. Or the *allocator* could do the sweeping. It too must visit the entire heap, but the visit is spread out over many allocation requests. Since the collector only has to mark, its running time drops. In this variant, called *lazy sweeping*, the allocator keeps a pointer into the managed heap, advancing the pointer one or more objects until it encounters one that can be reused. Such an allocator is sketched below; in Exercise 8, you complete the sketch.

4.4.1 *Prototype mark-and-sweep allocator for μScheme*

A mark-and-sweep system associates a mark bit with each heap location. To keep things simple, I don't try to pack mark bits densely; I just wrap each `Value` in another structure, which holds a single mark bit, `live`. By placing the `Value` at the beginning, I ensure that it is safe to cast between values of type `Value*` and type `Mvalue*`.

267a. ⟨*private declarations for mark-and-sweep collection* 267a⟩≡ 267c ▷
```
typedef struct Mvalue Mvalue;
struct Mvalue {
    Value v;
    unsigned live:1;
};
```

The use of mark bits has to be announced to my debugging interface (Section 4.6.1).

267b. ⟨*ms.c* 267b⟩≡ 267e ▷
```
bool gc_uses_mark_bits = true;
```

The `MValue` structures are grouped into *pages*. A single page holds a contiguous array of objects; pages are linked together into a list, which forms the heap. The page is the unit of heap growth; when the heap is too small, the collector calls `malloc` to add one or more pages to the heap.

267c. ⟨*private declarations for mark-and-sweep collection* 267a⟩+≡ ◁ 267a 267d ▷
```
#define GROWTH_UNIT 24 /* increment in which the heap grows, in objects */
typedef struct Page Page;
struct Page {
    Mvalue pool[GROWTH_UNIT];
    Page *tl;
};
```

The `tl` field links pages into a list that is referred to by multiple pointers. Pointer `pagelist` points to the head of the list, that is, the entire heap. The "heap pointer" `hp` points to the next `Mvalue` to be allocated. And `heaplimit` points to the first `Mvalue` *after* the current page, `curpage`.

267d. ⟨*private declarations for mark-and-sweep collection* 267a⟩+≡ ◁ 267c 268c ▷
```
Page *pagelist, *curpage;
Mvalue *hp, *heaplimit;
```

The pointers and page list look like this:

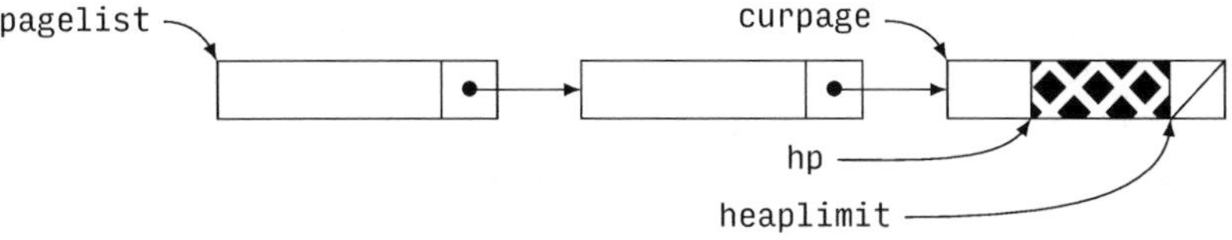

allocloc	265e
type Env	153a
popreg	265c
pushreg	265c
type Value	𝒜

White areas have been allocated; areas marked in gray diamonds are available for allocation. Pages except the current one are entirely used. The number of unallocated cells in the current page is `heaplimit - hp`.

A fresh page is made current by `makecurrent`.

267e. ⟨*ms.c* 267b⟩+≡ ◁ 267b 268a ▷
```
static void makecurrent(Page *page) {
    assert(page != NULL);
    curpage = page;
    hp = &page->pool[0];
    heaplimit = &page->pool[GROWTH_UNIT];
}
```

When the heap grows, it grows by one page at a time. Each new page is allocated with `calloc`, so its mark bits are zeroed.

268a. ⟨*ms.c* 267b⟩+≡ ◁267e 269b▷

```
static void addpage(void) {
    Page *page = calloc(1, sizeof(*page));
    assert(page != NULL);
    ⟨tell the debugging interface that each object on page has been acquired 282d⟩

    if (pagelist == NULL) {
        pagelist = page;
    } else {
        assert(curpage != NULL && curpage->tl == NULL);
        curpage->tl = page;
    }
    makecurrent(page);
}
```

It is a checked run-time error to call `addpage` except when `pagelist` is `NULL` or when `curpage` points to the last page in the list.

Writing the allocator is your job (Exercise 8). But I provide a prototype that does not collect garbage; when it runs out of space, it adds a new page.

268b. ⟨*ms.c* **[[prototype]]** 268b⟩≡ 269c▷

```
Value* allocloc(void) {
    if (hp == heaplimit)
        addpage();
    assert(hp < heaplimit);
    ⟨tell the debugging interface that &hp->v is about to be allocated 282e⟩
    return &(hp++)->v;
}
```

4.4.2 Marking heap objects in μScheme

If the heap is a directed graph containing objects of different types, the collector's marking phase is a depth-first search. Starting at the roots, for each object, the collector visits the objects it points to. When the collector visits a `Value` allocated on the heap, it sets the mark bit. If it visits such a `Value` and the mark is already set, it returns immediately; this test guarantees that the mark phase terminates even if there is a cycle on the heap.

The search itself is straightforward; it uses one procedure for each type of object to be visited. Not every type in Section 4.3.2 requires a visiting procedure, because not every type of object is reachable. For example, an object of type `Valuelist` cannot be reached by following pointers from roots.

268c. ⟨*private declarations for mark-and-sweep collection* 267a⟩+≡ ◁267d

```
static void visitloc              (Value *loc);
static void visitvalue            (Value v);
static void visitenv              (Env env);
static void visitexp              (Exp exp);
static void visitexplist          (Explist es);
static void visitframe            (Frame *fr);
static void visitstack            (Stack s);
static void visittest             (UnitTest t);
static void visittestlists        (UnitTestlistlist uss);
static void visitregister         (Register reg);
static void visitregisterlist     (Registerlist regs);
static void visitroots            (void);
```

To make visitenv work, I must expose the representation of environments. (In Chapter 2, this representation is private.)

269a. ⟨*structure definitions for μScheme+* 269a⟩≡ (S358)
```
struct Env {
    Name name;
    Value *loc;
    Env tl;
};
```


Most "visit" procedures are easy to write. As an example, the visit procedure for an environment visits all of its loc pointers.

269b. ⟨*ms.c* 267b⟩+≡ ◁268a 269d▷
```
static void visitenv(Env env) {
    for (; env; env = env->tl)
        visitloc(env->loc);
}
```

The most important such procedure visits a location and sets its mark bit. Unless the location has been visited already, its value is also visited.

269c. ⟨*ms.c* **[[prototype]]** 268b⟩+≡ ◁268b
```
static void visitloc(Value *loc) {
    Mvalue *m = (Mvalue*) loc;
    if (!m->live) {
        m->live = 1;
        visitvalue(m->v);
    }
}
```

In the tricolor-marking story, if m->live is not set, then m is white. Setting m->live makes m gray, and after m->v is visited, m is black.

A register is different from a heap location: a register has no mark bit.

269d. ⟨*ms.c* 267b⟩+≡ ◁269b 269e▷
```
static void visitregister(Value *reg) {
    visitvalue(*reg);
}
```

Function visitvalue visits a value's components of type Value *, Exp, and Env.

269e. ⟨*ms.c* 267b⟩+≡ ◁269d
```
static void visitvalue(Value v) {
    switch (v.alt) {
    case NIL:
    case BOOLV:
    case NUM:
    case SYM:
    case PRIMITIVE:
        return;
    case PAIR:
        visitloc(v.pair.car);
        visitloc(v.pair.cdr);
        return;
    case CLOSURE:
        visitexp(v.closure.lambda.body);
        visitenv(v.closure.env);
        return;
    default:
        assert(0);
        return;
    }
    assert(0);
}
```

The remaining visit procedures appear in the Supplement (Section N.1.1).

4.4.3 *Performance*

The cost of any single allocation can't easily be predicted—from the source code, you can't tell which allocation might trigger a garbage collection or how much data might be live at that time. Proper cost accounting requires an *amortized* analysis, which considers a sequence of allocations: an entire garbage-collection cycle. In that cycle, the garbage collector runs once, and the allocator is called N times, right up to just before the next time the collector runs. In a cycle, the allocator sweeps all H cells, of which L are marked live, so $N = H - L$.

As a simplifying assumption, suppose that the heap is in "steady state," i.e., H, L, and γ do not change from one cycle to the next. Because real heaps often grow and shrink wildly, this assumption seldom holds in practice, but it still helps predict and compare the costs of different garbage-collection techniques.

- *Allocation cost.* For mark-and-sweep, the cost per allocation is a constant (for finding and returning an unmarked cell), plus some fraction of the sweeping cost for the whole heap. On average, sweeping imposes a small cost per object (Exercise 14). And with high probability, the cost per object is bounded by a small constant (Exercise 16).

- *Collector overhead.* The garbage collector does work proportional to the size of the live data, not the size of the entire heap. Work per allocation is this work divided by the number of allocations, so proportional to $\frac{L}{N}$. The work itself is depth-first search and setting mark bits. Setting a mark bit seems relatively inexpensive, but the pattern of accesses to mark bits in memory can be very irregular—so unlike sweeping, marking is not cache-friendly.

- *Memory overhead.* A mark-and-sweep system pays up to five memory overheads:

  - Every object needs a mark bit. If there is not already a bit available in the object header, the mark bits can be pushed off into a separate bitmap—although a bitmap militates against parallel garbage collection.

  - The mark phase must know where to find pointers in heap objects. Ours uses the same `alt` field that is used to identify the type of a value, paying no additional overhead. In real systems, the overhead is kept low using a variety of tricks.

  - A mark-and-sweep system requires $\gamma > 1$ to perform well. While γ can be adjusted through a wide range, letting γ get too close to 1 results in poor performance. The necessary headroom may be considered a memory overhead.

  - When used to allocate objects of different sizes, a mark-and-sweep system may suffer from *fragmentation*. That is, it may have chunks of free memory that are too small to satisfy allocation requests. Classic analyses of fragmentation in dynamic memory allocators (Knuth 1973; Wilson et al. 1995) also apply to mark-and-sweep allocators.

  - The mark phase needs a place to store gray objects. Because our mark phase uses recursive visiting procedures, it stores gray objects in local variables on the C call stack. This technique is OK if the graph of heap objects does not contain very long paths, but a data structure, often called a *work list,* stores gray objects more compactly. A work list is usually a stack or a queue.

- *Pause time.* On average, allocation is fast, even when the allocator has to sweep past marked objects. But when an allocation triggers a garbage collection, our whole system pauses long enough for the collector to mark live data. If there is a lot of live data, such a pause may be too long for real-time response, but it is still better than the naïve version, which waits for the collector to sweep the entire heap. Collectors that run in time proportional to the amount of live data are effective for many applications.

4.5 Copying collection

The copying method of garbage collection, also called *stop-and-copy,* trades space for time. A copying system uses roughly twice as much heap as a mark-and-sweep system, and while the mutator is running, it leaves half the heap idle. The idle half eventually supplies *contiguous* free space that can be used to satisfy future allocation requests, making allocation blindingly fast. It works like this:

- The heap is divided into two equal *semispaces,* only one of which is normally in use. That semispace, called *from-space,* is itself divided into two *unequal* parts: The first part contains objects that have been allocated, and the second contains memory that is available for allocation. The boundary between them is marked by the *heap pointer* `hp`. Available memory is contiguous, not fragmented into objects on a free list. Each new object is allocated from the beginning of the available memory, by advancing the heap pointer. The heap looks like this:

  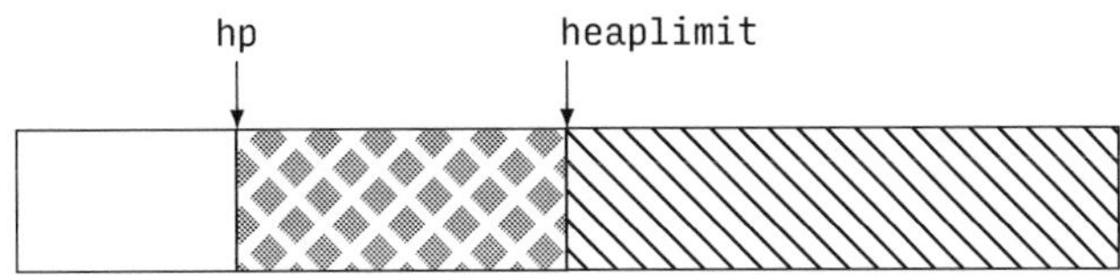

  Within from-space, on the left, the white area holds allocated objects, and the area filled with gray diamonds is unallocated. The end of the unallocated area (and the semispace) is marked by the limit pointer `heaplimit`. The striped area is not used during allocation.

  Memory is allocated by incrementing `hp`. The white area grows and the gray-diamond area shrinks until all of *from-space* contains allocated objects, and there is not enough gray-diamond area to satisfy an allocation request:

  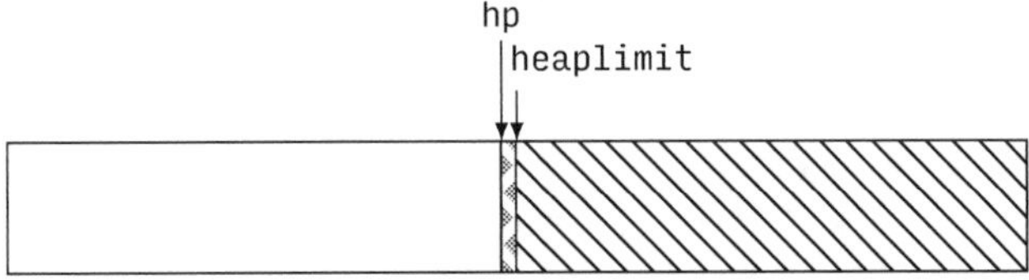

- When the unallocated area is used up, the system switches to the other semispace, called *to-space.* Before the switch, the garbage collector *copies* all the reachable objects from from-space into to-space. Because not all objects are reachable, there is room left over in to-space to satisfy future allocation requests. The system then "flips" the two spaces, and it continues executing in to-space; the allocator starts taking new memory from the first location above the copied objects.

After a flip, the heap might look like this:

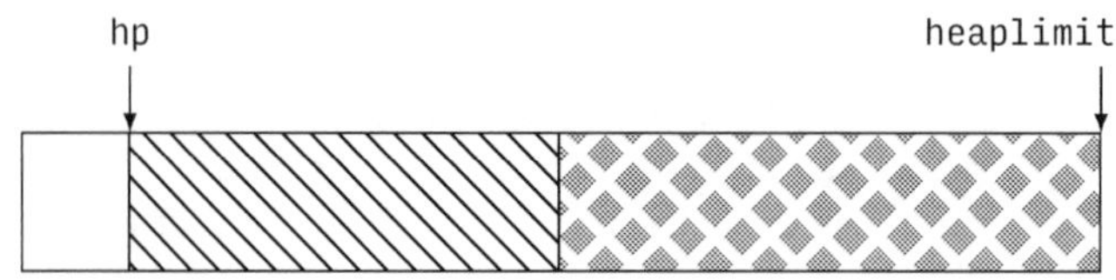

About 20% of objects have survived the collection, and 20% of a semispace is 10% of the heap, so γ is about 10. In this example, because so few objects have been copied relative to the number of past allocations, the copying system performs very well indeed.

4.5.1 *How copying collection works*

A copying collector has something in common with the "marshallers" used to send structured data in distributed systems; both components move data from one place to another.[2] To preserve sharing and cycles, a copying collector must copy each live object exactly once—and once the object has been copied, the collector must keep track of where the copy is. Luckily, the collector has a handy place to store the information: the vacated spot from which the object was copied. The collector uses that space to store a *forwarding pointer*. A forwarding pointer indicates that an object has already been copied, and it points to the location of the copy in to-space. In our μScheme system, a forwarding pointer is represented by a new form of value, with tag `FORWARD`.[3] A second new form, `INVALID`, is used for debugging; dead cells can be marked `INVALID`.

272a. ⟨*value.t* 272a⟩≡

```
Lambda  = (Namelist formals, Exp body)
Value   = NIL
        | BOOLV     (bool)
        | NUM       (int)
        | SYM       (Name)
        | PAIR      (Value *car, Value *cdr)
        | CLOSURE   (Lambda lambda, Env env)
        | PRIMITIVE (int tag, Primitive *function)
        | FORWARD   (Value *)
        | INVALID   (const char *)
```

A copying collection adjusts every pointer to every live object so that it points into to-space; the adjustment is called *forwarding* the pointer. When `p` points to an object in from-space and `*p` has not yet been copied, the collector copies `*p` to `*hp`. When `*p` has already been copied, tag `p->alt` identifies `p->forward` as a forwarding pointer, which the collector returns without copying `*p` a second time.

272b. ⟨*forward pointer* `p` *and return the result* 272b⟩≡ (278a)

```
if (p->alt == FORWARD) {
    return p->forward;
} else {
    ⟨tell the debugging interface that hp is about to be allocated 282f⟩
    *hp = *p;
    *p  = mkForward(hp);   /* overwrite *p with a new forwarding pointer */
    return hp++;
}
```

[2]The copying component of a garbage collector has sometimes been used as a marshaller.

[3]The `FORWARD` tag is not strictly necessary; a forwarding pointer can be identified simply by its value. A pointer is a forwarding pointer if and only if it points into to-space.

The copy operation never runs out of space because while pointers are being forwarded, hp points into to-space at the boundary between allocated and unallocated locations. Because to-space is as big as from-space, and because no object is copied more than once, to-space always has room for all the live objects.

The pointers that need to be forwarded and the objects that need to be copied can be explained by the tricolor marking scheme.

- An object is white if it is sitting in from-space. If it is reachable, it will need to be copied.
- An object is gray if it has been copied into to-space, but the pointers it contains have not been forwarded. The objects it points to may not have been copied.
- An object is black if it has been copied into to-space, and the pointers it contains have been forwarded. This implies that the objects it points to have also been copied into to-space.

The boundary between black objects and gray objects is marked by an additional pointer, scanp. An object's color is determined by its address a. White objects satisfy fromspace $\leq a <$ fromspace + semispacesize. Black objects satisfy tospace $\leq a <$ scanp. And gray objects satisfy scanp $\leq a <$ hp.

All four pointers are shown in this picture:

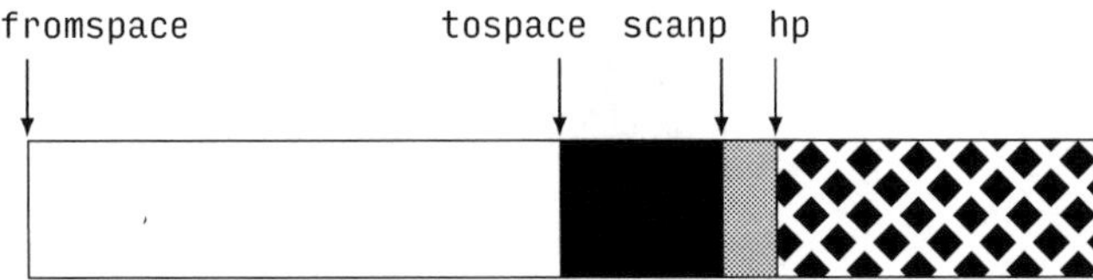

Black objects point to to-space; gray objects point to from-space.

As always, collection begins with the roots, making the objects they point to gray. The collector then turns gray objects black until there aren't any more gray objects. In concrete terms, it first forwards all the pointers that are in roots, then forwards pointers in gray objects until there are no more.

273. ⟨*copy all reachable objects into to-space* 273⟩≡

```
{
    Value *scanp = hp = tospace;    /* no black or gray objects yet */
    scanenv(*roots.globals.user);
    for (Frame *fr = roots.stack->frames; fr < roots.stack->sp; fr++)
        ⟨scan frame *fr, forwarding all internal pointers S366b⟩
    for ( UnitTestlistlist testss = roots.globals.internal.pending_tests
        ; testss
        ; testss = testss->tl
        )
        ⟨scan list of unit tests testss->hd, forwarding all internal pointers S366c⟩
    for (Registerlist regs = roots.registers; regs != NULL; regs = regs->tl)
        ⟨scan register regs->hd, forwarding all internal pointers S366d⟩

    /* all pointers in roots have now been forwarded */
    for (; scanp < hp; scanp++)
        ⟨scan object *scanp, forwarding all internal pointers S366e⟩
}
```

hp	276b
mkForward	$\mathcal{A}$

Further details are left for Exercise 1 and Appendix N.

4.5.2 *A brief example*

I illustrate copying collection using a heap of size 20. Suppose there are three roots, and the heap looks like this:

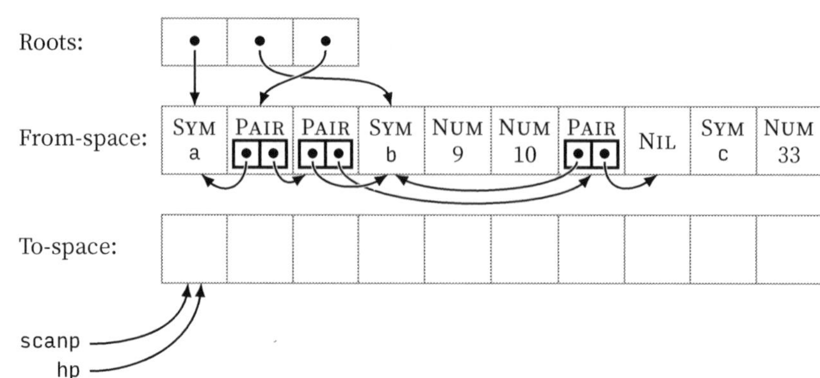

The reachable S-expressions are all part of one list; two cons cells point to the same symbol `b`:

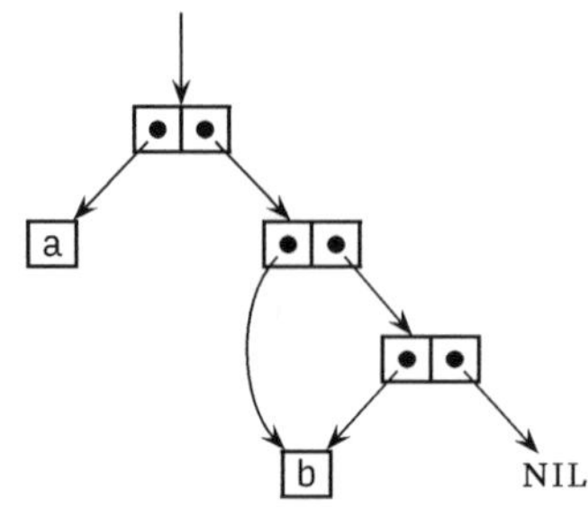

The collector begins by forwarding the roots. After the first root is forwarded, the heap looks like this:

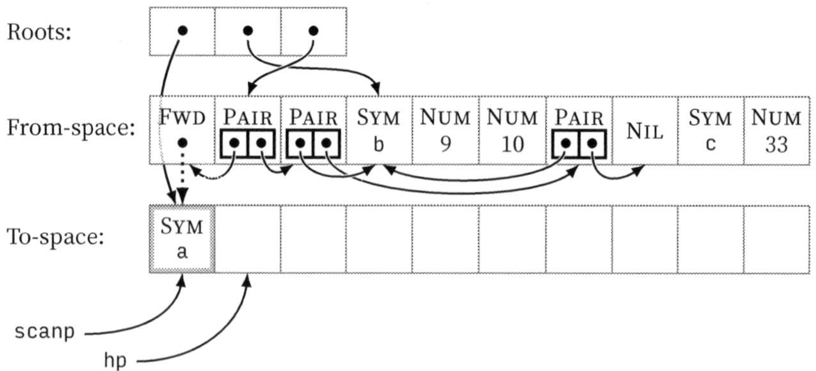

The first object in from-space has been copied into to-space and replaced with a forwarding pointer, which is shown with a dotted line. The root now points to the copy, with the pointer passing "behind" from-space so as not to clutter the diagram. The copied object, as shown by its thick border, is now gray. (Objects in the top row are white.)

After all three roots have been forwarded, that is, after the execution of the first loop in ⟨*copy all reachable objects into to-space* 273⟩, the heap looks like this:

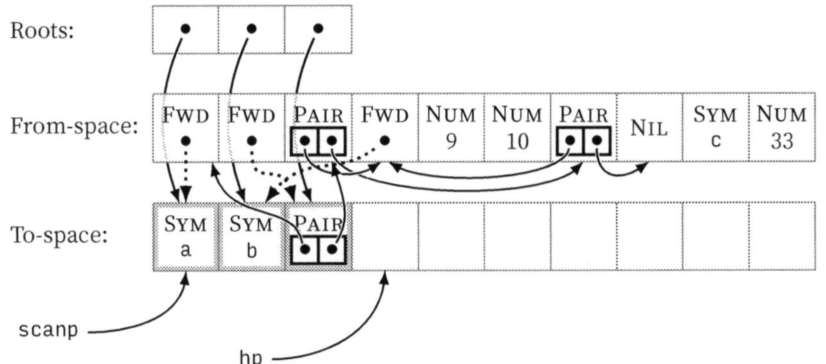

Now the collector starts scanning the gray objects located between `scanp` and `hp`. Gray objects point to white objects, which in a copying collector means that the internal pointers in these objects point back to from-space.

Scanning the first two gray objects does not change the heap, because these objects have no internal pointers. (But once `scanp` moves past them, the first two gray objects are considered black.) Scanning the third gray object (the pair) forwards its two internal pointers. The symbol `'a` has *already* been copied into to-space, so forwarding the `car` doesn't copy any data; it just adjusts a pointer:

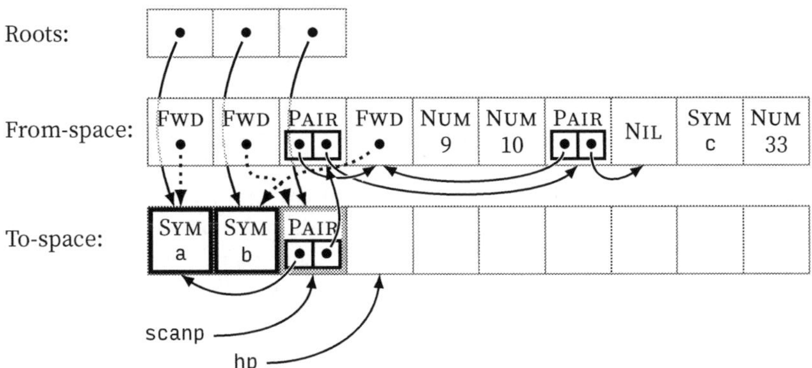

Forwarding the `cdr` requires copying another pair into to-space, however. After this copy, the collector increments `scanp`, and the newly copied pair is now the only gray object—the first three objects in to-space are black.

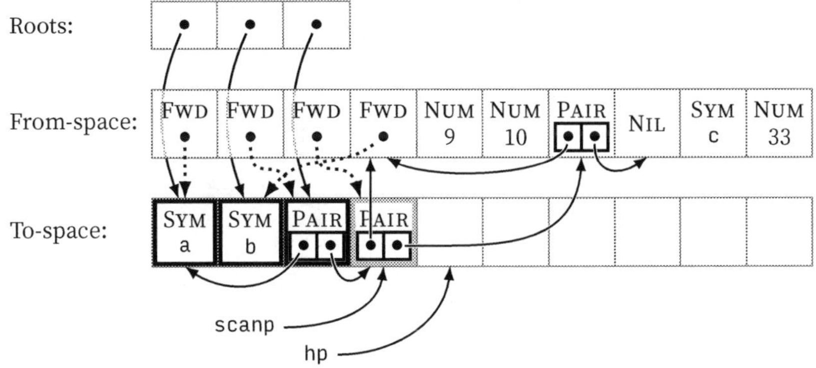

The collector continues copying objects pointed to by `*scanp` until eventually `scanp` catches up with `hp`. Now to-space holds only black objects and from-space holds only white objects. From-space can be discarded, and the mutator can resume execution. Its next allocation requests will be satisfied using the four locations recovered in to-space.

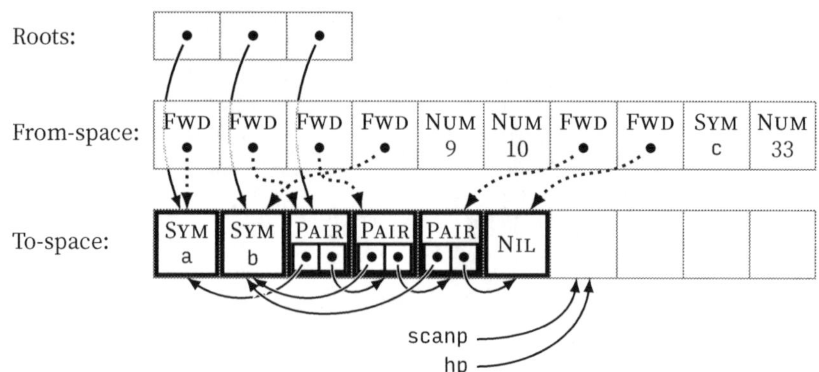

By using forwarding pointers, the collector has preserved the sharing of the symbol b by two pairs. The same technique also preserves cycles.

4.5.3 *Prototype of a copying system for μScheme*

Although conceptually more elaborate than a mark-and-sweep system, a copying system is easier to build. You'll build one (Exercises 1 to 6) based on the data structures and supporting functions described in this section.

The semispaces `fromspace` and `tospace` each have size `semispacesize`.

276a. ⟨*private declarations for copying collection* 276a⟩≡ 276b ▷

```
static Value *fromspace, *tospace; // used only at GC time
static int semispacesize;          // # of objects in fromspace or tospace
```

The system always allocates from `fromspace`. The next location available to be allocated is at the heap pointer `hp`, and the end of the available space is marked by `heaplimit`. The number of locations that can be allocated before the next collection is `heaplimit - hp`.

276b. ⟨*private declarations for copying collection* 276a⟩+≡ ◁ 276a 277a ▷

```
static Value *hp, *heaplimit;      // used for every allocation
```

Allocation

The allocator tests for heap exhaustion, increments `hp`, and returns the prior value of `hp`. In real systems, `hp` is kept in a register and `allocloc` is inlined.

276c. ⟨*copy.c* 276c⟩≡ 277b ▷

```
Value* allocloc(void) {
    if (hp == heaplimit)
        collect();
    assert(hp < heaplimit);
    ⟨tell the debugging interface that hp is about to be allocated 282f⟩
    return hp++;
}
```

The assertion can help detect bugs in a heap-growth algorithm.

Tracing roots

Just as the mark-and-sweep system has a visiting procedure for each type of potential root, the copying system has a scanning procedure for each type of potential root. These procedures implement the chunks of the form ⟨*scan..., forwarding all internal pointers*⟩ in chunk 273.

277a. ⟨*private declarations for copying collection* 276a⟩+≡ ◁276b 278b▷

```
static void scanenv      (Env env);
static void scanexp      (Exp exp);
static void scanexplist  (Explist es);
static void scanframe    (Frame *fr);
static void scantest     (UnitTest t);
static void scantests    (UnitTestlist ts);
static void scanloc      (Value *vp);
```


The implementations of the scanning procedures are more complicated than they would be in a real system. In a real system, scanning procedures would simply forward internal pointers. In our system, because only `Value` objects are allocated on the heap, scanning procedures forward pointers to `Value` objects but traverse pointers to other types of objects. For example, to scan an environment, the collector forwards the `loc` pointer and traverses the `tl` pointer (by advancing `env`).

277b. ⟨*copy.c* 276c⟩+≡ ◁276c 277c▷

```
static void scanenv(Env env) {
    for (; env; env = env->tl)
        env->loc = forward(env->loc);
}
```

The code that scans an object forwards the pointers of type `Value *` but traverses the pointers of types `Exp` and `Env`.

277c. ⟨*copy.c* 276c⟩+≡ ◁277b 278a▷

```
static void scanloc(Value *vp) {
    switch (vp->alt) {
    case NIL:
    case BOOLV:
    case NUM:
    case SYM:
        return;
    case PAIR:
        vp->pair.car = forward(vp->pair.car);
        vp->pair.cdr = forward(vp->pair.cdr);
        return;
    case CLOSURE:
        scanexp(vp->closure.lambda.body);
        scanenv(vp->closure.env);
        return;
    case PRIMITIVE:
        return;
    default:
        assert(0);
        return;
    }
}
```

`collect`	S377e
type `Env`	153a
type `Exp`	$\mathcal{A}$
type `Explist`	S309b
`forward`	278b
type `Frame`	223
type `UnitTest`	$\mathcal{A}$
type `UnitTestlist`	S309b
type `Value`	$\mathcal{A}$

The remaining scanning procedures appear in Section N.1.2.

Forwarding

The scanning procedures above closely resemble the visiting procedures used by a mark-and sweep collector (Sections 4.4.2 and N.1.1). One difference is that the `forward` operation, as shown in chunk ⟨*forward pointer* `p` *and return the result* 272b⟩, never makes a recursive call.

The complete implementation of forward suffers from one more subtlety, which arises because a root can appear on the context stack more than once. For example, an evaluation stack might contain two ENV frames whose environments share a Value * pointer associated with the name foldr. When the second such frame is scanned, the loc field associated with foldr already points into to-space. Such a pointer must not be forwarded.

278a. ⟨*copy.c* 276c⟩+≡ ◁277c

```
static Value* forward(Value *p) {
    if (isinspace(p, tospace)) {
        /* already in to space; must belong to scanned root */
        return p;
    } else {
        assert(isinspace(p, fromspace));
        ⟨forward pointer p and return the result 272b⟩
    }
}
```

The isinspace test contributes significantly to garbage-collection time, and inlining it results in a measurable improvement.

278b. ⟨*private declarations for copying collection* 276a⟩+≡ ◁277a

```
static inline bool isinspace(Value *loc, Value *space) {
    return space <= loc && loc < space + semispacesize;
}
static Value *forward(Value *p);
```

Heap growth

In a mark-and-sweep collector, a heap can be enlarged simply by adding more pages. In our simple copying system, enlarging the heap is more complicated, because semispaces are expected to be contiguous. In general, a contiguous block of memory can't be enlarged without moving it, so the semispaces have to be copied. A collector can proceed as follows:

1. Allocate a new, larger, to-space.
2. Copy the live data from from-space into to-space.
3. Flip from-space and to-space.
4. Allocate a new, larger, to-space.

If implemented carelessly, this strategy would copy the live data twice when the heap grows. A careful implementation delays the growth of the heap until the *next* collection (Exercise 4). Or the issue can be eliminated entirely by splitting each semispace into pages (Exercise 5).

4.5.4 *Performance*

As with the mark-and-sweep system, a performance analysis considers a full garbage-collection cycle with $N = \frac{H}{2} - L$ allocations. I again assume the heap is in steady state.

- *Allocation cost.* In a copying system, each allocation takes constant work: it tests for heap exhaustion and increments the heap pointer. If the heap pointer is kept in a machine register and the allocator is inlined, allocation takes just a few instructions, making it very fast indeed. Fast allocation is a principal advantage of a copying system.

For example, a compiler might generate code for cons that is analogous to this C code:

279. ⟨*untested sample C code* 279⟩≡

```
register unsigned *hp;
unsigned *heaplimit;

unsigned *cons(unsigned car, unsigned cdr) {
    if (hp+3 > heaplimit)
        gc();
    hp[0] = PAIR;
    hp[1] = car;
    hp[2] = cdr;
    hp += 3;
    return hp-3;
}
```


A cons cell is allocated *and initialized* using just a load, a test, three stores, a move, and an add.

When a system must support objects of varying sizes, a copying allocator performs well without any additional data structures or adaptations. Unlike a mark-and-sweep allocator, a copying allocator works the same way regardless of how many bytes are requested. It does not need multiple free lists, first-fit search, or any other strategy to find a chunk of free memory of an appropriate size. It simply tests and increments.

- *Collector overhead.* A copying garbage collector does work proportional to the size of the live data. The work itself is more expensive than for the mark-and-sweep system, since the collector must copy objects, not just set mark bits. But copying also produces a benefit: it "compacts" the live objects, putting them in adjacent locations in memory. Compaction improves the performance of the machine's cache and virtual memory, but more importantly, it enables fast allocation.

- *Memory overhead.* Our copying system pays only two memory overheads:

    - Because one semispace is always empty, a copying system requires at least $\gamma \geq 2$. The "headroom" needed to get adequate performance is much larger than in a mark-and-sweep system. As γ gets large, however, this difference between copying and mark-and-sweep disappears, and the most significant cost is the cost of allocation.

    - Like the mark-and-sweep collector, the copying collector must know where to find pointers in heap objects. The knowledge is implied by the alt field.

  A copying system has no memory overhead for mark bits. And because our system stores the gray objects on the heap itself, in the style of Cheney (1970), it requires no stack or work list.

- *Pause time.* Copying allocation always takes constant time; the only pauses are at collections. These pauses take time proportional to the amount of live data.

4.6 Debugging a collector

A garbage-collected system can exhibit two kinds of faults:

- *The system can fail to recycle an unreachable object.* Such a fault is a *memory leak.* A memory leak does not affect correctness, only performance: it makes the garbage collector run more often than it should, and it makes the heap grow faster than it should. Since we rarely know how often a collector "should" run or how fast a heap "should" grow, these symptoms are hard to spot—a slow memory leak may go unnoticed for a long time. A memory leak is easiest to spot when it makes the heap grow so fast that memory is exhausted.

- *The system can recycle an object that is still reachable.* When such an object is reused, its contents change. From the perspective of an old pointer to the object, the change happens for no reason, at an unpredictable time. Such a fault, which could occur if a root is overlooked or if a tracing procedure fails to follow a pointer, can be difficult to detect.

Memory leaks aren't catastrophic. You can detect them with a tool like Valgrind or Pin (Section 4.10.2), which instruments the code and looks for "lost" memory. If you don't have such a tool, you might still find a leak by observing that the garbage collector is retaining too much live data. To know how much is too much, you might rely on regression testing or on careful analysis. Once you're sure there's a leak, you (or a tool) can examine the heap to find out exactly which objects are not being recycled and by what combination of pointers those objects are reachable.

Premature recycling is harder to detect. It usually occurs because the mutator has kept a root (a pointer to a heap object) and hasn't told garbage collector. You might detect such a problem by means of aggressive assertions, also using a tool like Valgrind or Pin—this time to flag reads from or writes to an object that has been reclaimed but not yet reused—or by one of the techniques below. That said, you probably won't have such problems while working the Exercises, because the code that keeps `roots` up to date has been tested extensively.

4.6.1 An interface for debugging

If you need to find memory errors, use my debugging code. As described below, it tracks the three states shown in Figure 4.1.

- Memory that is owned by the operating system shouldn't be touched. Neither the collector nor the mutator should read or write it.

- Memory that is owned by the collector should be read or written only by collector code.

- Memory that is owned by the mutator may be read or written freely. The collector should read or write it only during a call to `allocloc`.

Memory changes ownership by means of the labeled transitions in Figure 4.1 on the facing page. Memory is *acquired* in large blocks using `malloc`; those blocks are *released* using `free`. A single object is *allocated* by calling `allocloc`; if `allocloc` calls the garbage collector, the collector will *reclaim* unreachable objects. To enable debugging, each of these transitions should be announced by calling the debugging functions declared below. These functions mark collector-owned ob-

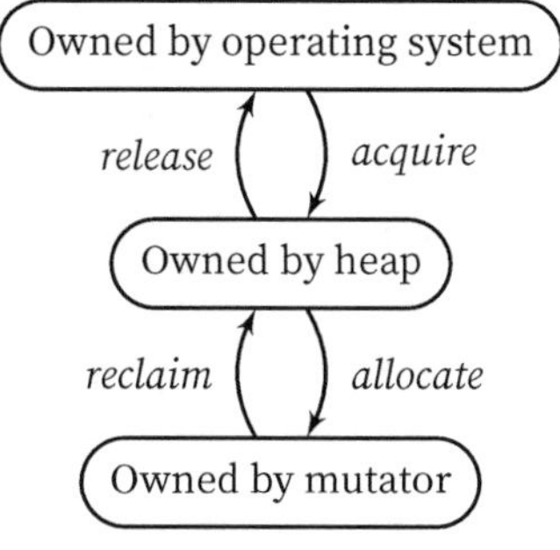

Figure 4.1: States of memory

jects as INVALID, and when Valgrind is available, they get it to enforce these rules:

- No code should read or write any object owned by the collector. If the collector mistakenly reclaims a reachable object, then the next time any code reads or writes that object, Valgrind will complain.
- A newly allocated object must be initialized before it is read. If the mutator tries to read a newly allocated object, perhaps through a stale pointer, Valgrind will complain.

The debugging functions are implemented in Section N.2, and their interfaces are described below.

After a block of memory has been acquired (via `malloc` or `calloc`) to hold heap objects, but before any object has been delivered to the mutator via `allocloc`, the collector should call `gc_debug_post_acquire`.

281a. ⟨*function prototypes for μScheme+* 265c⟩+≡ (S358) ◁265d 281b▷

```
void gc_debug_post_acquire(Value *mem, unsigned nvalues);
```

This function must be used carefully; the copying collector can announce the acquisition of an entire block at once, but because the mark-and-sweep collector wraps each `Value` in an `Mvalue`, it must call `gc_debug_post_acquire` on one object at a time.

When a block of memory that belongs to the collector is no longer needed and is about to be released, the collector should call `gc_debug_pre_release` just before calling `free`. As with acquisition, the mark-and-sweep collector must release one object at a time.

281b. ⟨*function prototypes for μScheme+* 265c⟩+≡ (S358) ◁281a 281c▷

```
void gc_debug_pre_release(Value *mem, unsigned nvalues);
```

Just before the allocator delivers a heap object to the mutator, it should call `gc_debug_pre_allocate`.

281c. ⟨*function prototypes for μScheme+* 265c⟩+≡ (S358) ◁281b 281d▷

```
void gc_debug_pre_allocate(Value *mem);
```

type `Value` $\mathcal{A}$

When the garbage collector decides an object is unreachable, it should call function `gc_debug_post_reclaim`. This function should be called *after* the collector has finished writing to any part of the object. The function will mark the object INVALID, and then it will tell Valgrind to complain about any accesses to it. Even without Valgrind, the function can help find bugs; for example, if the last cons cell in `'(a b c)` is reclaimed prematurely, you'll see the list turn into `'(a b . <invalid>)`, making the fault easy to observe.

281d. ⟨*function prototypes for μScheme+* 265c⟩+≡ (S358) ◁281c 282a▷

```
void gc_debug_post_reclaim(Value *mem);
```

To reclaim an entire semispace at once, the copying collector may call function gc_debug_post_reclaim_block. When the heap grows, the collector must pass the old, smaller size, not the new, larger size.

282a. ⟨*function prototypes for μScheme+ 265c*⟩+≡ (S358) ◁281d 282b▷
```
void gc_debug_post_reclaim_block(Value *mem, unsigned nvalues);
```

Whenever the mutator uses a value that is obtained by dereferencing a pointer into the heap, it should wrap that value in validate (chunk 225c). If the alt field of v is INVALID, validate(v) halts the program with an error message. Otherwise it returns v. The evaluator in Chapter 3 calls validate, and your own code should also call validate whenever it reads a value that you believe should be good.

If the tools above aren't enough, use functions gcprint and gcprintf to write whatever you like to standard error. Function gcprint works like print, and gcprintf works like printf, but they work only when the environment variable GCVERBOSE is set. If GCVERBOSE is not set, gcprint and gcprintf do nothing.

282b. ⟨*function prototypes for μScheme+ 265c*⟩+≡ (S358) ◁282a 282c▷
```
void gcprint (const char *fmt, ...);  /* print GC debugging info */
void gcprintf(const char *fmt, ...);
```

The debug code is initialized by initallocate in Appendix N, which calls gc_debug_init.

282c. ⟨*function prototypes for μScheme+ 265c*⟩+≡ (S358) ◁282b
```
void gc_debug_init(void);
```

Some of the debugging functions are used in some of the prototype code above:

282d. ⟨*tell the debugging interface that each object on* page *has been acquired 282d*⟩≡ (268a)
```
{   unsigned i;
    for (i = 0; i < sizeof(page->pool)/sizeof(page->pool[0]); i++)
        gc_debug_post_acquire(&page->pool[i].v, 1);
}
```

282e. ⟨*tell the debugging interface that* &hp->v *is about to be allocated 282e*⟩≡ (268b)
```
gc_debug_pre_allocate(&hp->v);
```

282f. ⟨*tell the debugging interface that* hp *is about to be allocated 282f*⟩≡ (272b 276c)
```
gc_debug_pre_allocate(hp);
```

4.6.2 Debugging techniques

Because garbage collections and allocations can happen at unpredictable times, a bug in a garbage collector often appears only intermittently. Worse, it can fail to appear until long after the initial fault. Bugs can be found sooner when every read and write is monitored by a tool like Valgrind. And you can give Valgrind more leverage—or if necessary, debug without Valgrind—by looking for faults early. Try these tricks:

- Trigger a garbage collection before *every* allocation request. This trick may slow your program by many orders of magnitude, but it gives you a chance of detecting a missing root as soon as it disappears.
- After each collection, check that every pointer points to a valid object in the right space.
- After each collection, take a snapshot of the heap and run the collector again—once for mark-and-sweep, twice for copying. If the new heap is not identical to the snapshot, there is a bug in the collector. (This technique will not detect a missing root.)

To debug a mark-and-sweep collector, try the following:

- After marking the live objects, sweep the entire heap, making unmarked objects `INVALID`.
- If you are worried about memory corruption in your mark bits, use a whole word instead of a single bit. Instead of `0` and `1`, use a pair of unusual values like `0xdeadbeef` and `0xbadface`. If you ever see a different value, something is stomping on your mark bits.

To debug a copying collector, try the following:

- When you "free" old spaces, don't actually call `free`. Invalidate them, and let `validate` flag stale pointers to those spaces.
- When you copy live data into to-space, use `gc_debug_post_reclaim_block` to make the from-space inaccessible. Then, before the flip, allocate a new from-space. If you have mistakenly failed to forward some pointer, the next access through that pointer will make Valgrind complain. (If you don't have Valgrind, the next read will find an `INVALID` value, which will make `validate` complain.)

4.7 Mark-compact collection

The great advantage of copying collection is that by moving live objects into to-space, it creates contiguous free space for allocation. Contiguous free space is also created by *mark-compact* collection. Like a mark-sweep collector, a mark-compact collector marks live objects, but instead of sweeping reclaimed objects onto a free list, it moves the live objects to eliminate the gaps between them, leaving free space contiguous. Live objects are often moved using a "sliding" algorithm, which preserves the order of live objects in memory. This algorithm maintains locality properties that can affect the performance of the mutator.

Mark-compact collection offers the same benefits for allocation as a copying collector: fast allocation from a contiguous block of memory. And it takes less space. But because it may touch every live object twice—once to mark it and once to compact it, it takes more time than either copying or mark-sweep collection.

4.8 Reference counting

Tracking roots appears to require support from the compiler or some run-time overhead.[4] If you can't get support from the compiler and you don't want to pay run-time overhead, you might look for other ideas. Because an object is definitely unreachable if there are no references to it, one idea is to reuse an object once it is no longer referred to by any other object.

To make the idea work, a system needs to track not simply *whether* an object is referred to, but *how many times*. For example, after the following definitions are evaluated, the `Value` object for `'a` is referred to twice, from both `x` and `y`:

283. ⟨*transcript* 258⟩+≡ ◁258

```
-> (set x '(a b))
-> (set y (car x))
```

If `x` were reassigned, it would remove a reference to `'a`'s object. But deallocating `'a`'s object would be unsafe, because `y` still points to it. If `'a`'s object were deallo-

[4] I say "appears to" because the ingenious *conservative* garbage-collection technique developed by Boehm and Weiser (1988) works without either one.

cated and then reused to hold a new value, say v, then y's value would suddenly be v, for no obvious reason.

References are tracked by reserving a field on each object for its *reference count*. An object's reference count is incremented when a new reference is made to it, and the count is decremented when a reference is removed. When its reference count becomes zero, the object is eligible to be reused, and it can be placed on a free list.

Reference counts can require a lot of maintenance. For example, a hypothetical μScheme interpreter would maintain reference counts as follows:

- Whenever an object was bound into to an environment, e.g., to be passed as a parameter or let-bound to a local variable, the interpreter would increment its reference count.
- When a μScheme procedure exited, the interpreter would decrement the reference counts of the procedure's formal parameters—even if the exit were caused by a run-time error.
- When the interpreter left the body of a let expression, it would decrement the reference counts of let-bound objects.
- When the interpreter evaluated a `set`, it would increment the reference count of the newly assigned value, and it would decrement the reference count of the previous value of the set variable.
- When the interpreter allocated a new cell is created, it would increment the reference counts of the car and cdr.
- When a decrement made the reference count of a cons cell go to zero, the interpreter would put the cons cell on a free list.
- When the interpreter took a cons cell off the free list, it would decrement the counts of the car and cdr.

In short, when pointers are manipulated, reference counts need to be adjusted. This adjustment creates complexity in the interpreter and inefficiency in its run time. In a reference-counted system, *work per assignment* can outweigh work per allocation. And although reference counting is conceptually simple, it can be expensive to retrofit to existing code: *any* code that moves pointers has to be modified to adjust reference counts.

Although its overhead can be high, a reference-counting system never has to pause the mutator for a long time. By delaying the decrement of a car and cdr until a cons cell is reused, the system can guarantee that every allocation and assignment requires at most a constant amount of memory-management work.

The overhead of reference counting can be reduced by static analysis and other tricks, and it can sometimes be offloaded onto a parallel processor or processor core. But unlike the overhead in a garbage-collected system, which can be reduced by enlarging the heap, the overhead of reference counting cannot easily be adjusted: the cost of each assignment and allocation is independent of the size of the heap. Because shrinking the heap does not change the overheads, reference counting easily outperforms garbage collection when heap space is tightly constrained.

Reference counting cannot reclaim "cyclic garbage"; in a circular data structure, no count ever goes to zero. Circular structures may be created by programmers using `set-car!` and `set-cdr!`, but they may also be created simply by allocating closures. (In a naïve implementation of closures, a closure contains an environment which contains a binding to a location containing the original closure.) Issues with cyclic garbage can be worked around by various clever techniques, but these techniques work only in limited domains. Reference counting seems most successful in languages that don't create cycles.

Reference counting seems to be most effective when it does "double duty," i.e., when the reference counts are used not only to reclaim memory, but also to implement some other feature. One such feature is timely *finalization,* which is to perform some user-level task when an object is reclaimed. Such tasks may include closing open file descriptors or removing windows from a graphical user interface. Garbage-collected systems can also provide finalization, but it is not always guaranteed, and it is seldom timely: the time at which a garbage collector reclaims a dead object can't easily be predicted.

Another feature for which reference counting can be useful is the *copy-on-write* optimization. This optimization applies to computations in which it is unsafe to mutate shared objects, so to play it safe, the program has to make a private copy, then mutate the copy. But if the reference count says there is only one reference to the object, then it isn't shared, and it can be mutated without making a copy. This technique is used in the Newsqueak language to make array updates efficient in the common case (Pike 1990).

Reference counting also shines in distributed systems, where costs of local computation are almost irrelevant; what counts is minimizing the number of messages sent between machines. If a garbage collector has to follow pointers across machine boundaries, that can require a lot of messages. Adjusting reference counts also requires messages, but these messages can often be combined with the messages used to refer to or assign values, so in terms of message traffic, reference counting comes essentially for free. For this reason, distributed architectures such as Java's Jini use reference counting.

4.9 GARBAGE COLLECTION AS IT REALLY IS

In most garbage-collected systems, the collector relies on a compiler to help it identify roots and distinguish pointers from non-pointers.

- The compiler and collector agree on a calling convention for procedures, so the collector can find the activations of all the procedures on the call stack. For each source procedure, the compiler provides a map of the stack frame, which tells the collector where the roots are, i.e., which machine registers and stack variables point to heap objects. A good compiler is sophisticated enough to omit dead variables (i.e., variables the compiler knows will not be used again) from the stack map.

- The compiler identifies the global variables that point to heap objects.

- The compiler identifies the size and layout of each heap object, so the collector will know how big the object is and what parts of it point to other heap objects. Most compilers put one or more *header words* before the heap object. A header word might point to a map that shows where the pointers are in the object, or it might point to a snippet of bytecode that the collector can interpret to find pointers within the object.

  In some systems, the header simply tells how many words there are in the object, and the compiler uses the low bit of each word as a marker to distinguish pointers from integers. Such systems are easy to identify, as they provide, e.g., only 63 bits of integer precision on a 64-bit machine.

State-of-the art systems reduce overheads by using *concurrent, generational,* and sometimes *parallel* garbage collection.

- Pause times can be reduced if the collector does just part of its work and then yields the processor back to the mutator; such a collector is called *incremental*. Or the collector can run concurrently with the mutator, on another processor; such a collector is called *concurrent*. Incremental and concurrent techniques can also be combined. In all cases, the shorter pause times are paid for by some additional overhead, which is required to synchronize the actions of the collector and the mutator.

- Elapsed time can be reduced if the collector does some work, like marking or copying objects, in parallel on multiple processor cores. Such a collector is called *parallel*. Parallel garbage-collection threads may require synchronization overhead, but if the relevant processor cores would otherwise be idle, net overhead drops. To balance the load among threads, a system may copy objects depth-first, using an auxiliary stack, then allow idle garbage-collection threads to "steal" work from this stack—a standard technique in parallel systems.

- Overall overhead can be reduced by arranging for most garbage collections to reclaim a higher *percentage* of objects. Collectors that do this are usually *generational*. A generational collector divides the heap into two or more *generations*. The youngest generation, or *nursery*, is where objects are allocated. When it fills, it is collected by a *minor collection*. According to the *generational hypothesis*, most objects die young and so don't survive a minor collection; the rare survivors are *promoted* into an older generation. Older generations are collected rarely, by *major collections*.

  In a generational system, the nursery is large compared to the number of objects that survive a minor collection, and older generations are relatively smaller. This arrangement achieves most of the performance benefit of large γ at a fraction of the memory cost. Some generational systems use a hybrid collector; objects are copied out of the nursery, keeping free space contiguous, but older generations are collected using mark-and-sweep techniques. This trick cuts γ in half for the older generations.

Concurrent collection and generational collection involve substantial interaction with the mutator. If the mutator runs concurrently, or if it mutates objects in an old generation, it could violate the collector's invariant that black objects point only to other black objects.

- The mutator could update a pointer inside a black object, which by definition has already been marked live or copied and is not slated to be revisited.

- During a minor collection, objects in older generations are not traced, so they are effectively black objects. If the mutator has updated such an object since the previous collection, the invariant may be violated again.

This issue is resolved by a *write barrier*. A write barrier forces the mutator to notify the collector when it writes a pointer into an object allocated on the heap. When the collector learns that a black object has been mutated to contain a pointer to a white or gray object, it has a choice: it may follow the new pointer right away, making it point to a gray object, or it may recolor the black object gray, scheduling it to be traced again before collection completes.

When notified by a write barrier, the garbage collector saves the location that is written to, in a data structure called a *remembered set*. A remembered set may or may not be precise; precision can be expensive. For example, the collector might choose to log every pointer that is updated via a write barrier, giving it very precise information—but the log may take significant space. Or at another extreme, the collector might simply mark a page containing the object written to, costing only one bit of space overhead—but it may eventually need to scan the entire page for interesting pointers.

Beyond generational, concurrent, and parallel collection, many other techniques are available to deploy.

- Many systems, especially those based on copying collectors, place sufficiently large objects in separate areas of memory. These large-object areas are treated specially, and they are not copied, even by a copying collector. A large-object area is especially useful for storing large strings or bitmaps, which do not contain pointers and so need not be scanned. Such objects can be added to the live data of an advanced system without increasing garbage-collection times proportionally.
- Modern collectors can work even without support from the compiler. The mark-and-sweep collector developed by Boehm and Weiser (1988) works without any compiler support. It finds roots by examining every word on the call stack, plus the program segments that hold initialized and uninitialized data. It finds pointers by examining every word in every heap-allocated object. In both cases, if a word appears to point to a heap-allocated object, the collector conservatively assumes that it *is* a pointer, and therefore that the object pointed to is live. (Because it is in cahoots with the allocator, the garbage collector knows the addresses of all the heap-allocated objects.) This collector has achieved remarkable results with C and C++ programs, sometimes outperforming `malloc` and `free`.

4.10 Summary

Automatic memory management recycles unneeded memory so programmers don't have to. Unless they need more live data than the machine can hold, programmers can pretend that memory is infinite—they can allocate arbitrarily many objects without ever having to free one.

In a garbage-collected system, *the collector and allocator work as a team,* and they must be analyzed as a team. The metric that should be analyzed is usually *work per allocation.*

Mark-and-sweep systems perform well when allocation rates are low, so the cost of allocation is not a bottleneck. They require just a bit more memory than is needed to hold the live data. And with little difficulty, a mark-and-sweep system can run legacy code that was written for `malloc` and `free`: the user's `free` does nothing, and the real `free` is called only by the garbage collector.

Copying systems provide very fast allocation, but objects in the heap move. These properties are related: allocation is fast because free space is contiguous, and free space is made contiguous by moving objects. Moving objects, also called *compaction,* also eliminates fragmentation and can improve locality. Copying systems perform very well when allocation rates are high, because allocation is so fast. But copying requires more memory than mark-and-sweep systems. And copying collection requires care to implement; because compaction moves objects, the compiler must be aware that objects move, and it must tell the collector exactly where to find all the pointers.

In both copying and mark-and-sweep systems, garbage-collection overhead can be reduced by making the heap larger. When there is enough memory to make γ large, allocation cost dominates, and copying collection usually wins.

The real cost of automatic memory management depends not just on the collection technique but on the program. Simple programs that don't allocate much may spend only a few percent of their time in garbage collection. Programs that allocate heavily may spend up to 20 percent of their time in garbage collection—more if the collector is badly tuned. Garbage collection can be *faster* than `malloc` and `free`, even on programs that aren't designed to exploit a garbage collector (Zorn 1993). But a garbage-collected system needs more memory, perhaps up to twice as much.

Allocation is usually perceived as expensive; using `cons` in Scheme or `new` in Smalltalk costs allocation time, initialization time, and a share of garbage-collection time. And reducing allocation *can* improve performance. But don't go too far. If you replace clean allocation code with code that works by mutating and reusing objects, say by using `set-car!` and `set-cdr!` to avoid `cons`, you risk a great loss in robustness and reliability in exchange for a small gain in performance. Since the 1990s, such tricks have been largely unnecessary. While it is never wise to allocate gratuitously, garbage-collected systems perform well enough that programmers need not use mutation merely for performance reasons. In fact, mutation makes some modern generational collectors perform *worse* than they would otherwise.

4.10.1 Key words and phrases

ALLOCATION POINTER In a COPYING COLLECTOR, a pointer to the beginning of the contiguous free space. Usually stored in a dedicated machine register.

AUTOMATIC MEMORY MANAGEMENT A memory-management technique in which the HEAP OBJECTS are allocated on a MANAGED HEAP and are recovered and reused by a language's implementation or run-time system. MEMORY SAFETY is guaranteed by the system. The most common method is GARBAGE COLLECTION, but REFERENCE COUNTING is sometimes used. Compare EXPLICIT MEMORY MANAGEMENT.

CALL STACK A stack of procedure activations, each of which is something like an ENV frame on the evaluation stack of Chapter 3. Each activation may include a return address, formal parameters, local variables, and saved registers. A call pushes an activation onto the stack; a return pops the stack.

COMPACTING COLLECTOR A GARBAGE COLLECTOR that moves or copies LIVE OBJECTS into compact, contiguous space, leaving free space also contiguous. Making free space contiguous enables fast allocation, and making live objects contiguous may improve locality. COPYING COLLECTORS are automatically compacting collectors. A MARK-AND-SWEEP collector can be made to compact by adding a compaction step.

CONSERVATIVE COLLECTOR A GARBAGE COLLECTOR that works without having precise information about where ROOTS are located, where pointers are located inside objects, or both. A conservative MARK-AND-SWEEP COLLECTOR developed by Boehm, Weiser, Demers, and others has been widely used under the name `libgc`.

COPYING COLLECTOR A GARBAGE COLLECTOR that traces pointers and copies every LIVE OBJECT to a fresh, empty region of memory. Whatever fresh memory is left over is used to satisfy future requests for HEAP ALLOCATION. Unlike a MARK-AND-SWEEP collector, a copying collector recovers *contiguous* free space, so allocation can be very efficient.

DEAD OBJECT A HEAP OBJECT whose value is guaranteed not to affect any future computation. Compare LIVE OBJECT.

DEAD VARIABLE A formal parameter or local variable whose value is guaranteed not to affect any future computation.

EVALUATION STACK In μScheme+, the stack S that holds all the information in a CALL STACK, plus additional information about what computation takes place after the current expression is evaluated.

EXPLICIT MEMORY MANAGEMENT A memory-management technique in which the HEAP OBJECTS must be recovered and reused by the programmer, using explicit primitives to allocate and deallocate objects. MEMORY SAFETY is the programmer's problem. Compare AUTOMATIC MEMORY MANAGEMENT.

FORWARDING POINTER A value left behind after a HEAP OBJECT has been copied by a COPYING COLLECTOR, so that the object won't be copied a second time.

FREE LIST In a MARK-AND-SWEEP collector, a list of reclaimed objects that can be used to satisfy future requests for HEAP ALLOCATION.

GARBAGE COLLECTION An algorithm that examines the HEAP, finds the LIVE DATA, recovers all HEAP OBJECTS that are *not* live data, and uses their memory to satisfy future requests for HEAP ALLOCATION. Garbage collection may be done while the rest of the program is stopped, as in this chapter. It may be done incrementally, so that garbage collection is interleaved with other computation. And it may be done concurrently, with both collector and MUTATOR doing work at the same time. Typical methods include MARK-AND-SWEEP COLLECTION and COPYING COLLECTION.

GENERATIONAL COLLECTOR A collector that divides HEAP OBJECTS into different groups, called *generations*, according to the number of collections they have survived. Objects that have survived more collections are collected less frequently.

GENERATIONAL HYPOTHESIS The hypothesis that most objects die young. (In the literature, this hypothesis is called the *weak* generational hypothesis.)

HEAP Memory area used for objects that may outlive the activation of the function that allocates them. In languages with EXPLICIT MEMORY MANAGEMENT, the heap is managed by the programmer using primitives like C's `malloc` and `free` or C++'s `new` and `delete`. "Heap" also means the set of all objects allocated in the heap, which is modeled by the HEAP GRAPH.

HEAP ALLOCATION Allocation of an object on the HEAP.

HEAP OBJECT An object allocated on the HEAP.

LIVE DATA The set of all LIVE OBJECTS.

LIVE OBJECT A HEAP OBJECT whose contents might affect a future computation. Liveness is an undecidable property, so it is approximated by REACHABILITY: an object that is REACHABLE from a ROOT is deemed live. Compare DEAD OBJECT.

MANAGED HEAP A HEAP under the control of AUTOMATIC MEMORY MANAGEMENT, in which MEMORY SAFETY is guaranteed.

MARK-AND-SWEEP COLLECTOR A GARBAGE COLLECTOR that traces pointers and marks every LIVE OBJECT, then reclaims DEAD OBJECTS and uses their space to satisfy future requests for HEAP ALLOCATION. Unlike a COPYING COLLECTOR, it does not move or copy objects.

MARK BIT A bit used by a MARK-AND-SWEEP COLLECTOR to tell whether a HEAP OBJECT is LIVE. May be stored with the object, or if the collector is not parallel, mark bits may be grouped and stored away from their objects, so that the hardware cache works better.

MEMORY SAFETY A property of a language which guarantees that at all times, every pointer points to valid data, every cons cell holds valid data, and so on.

MUTATOR A program doing useful work, which the GARBAGE COLLECTOR is intended to serve. So called because it may inconveniently mutate pointers inside the objects that the garbage collector is trying to manage.

REACHABILITY An analysis that finds locations that can be reached by following pointers from a ROOT.

REFERENCE COUNTING A form of AUTOMATIC MEMORY MANAGEMENT in which every HEAP OBJECT is associated with a *reference count*, which tracks the number of pointers to the object. When the reference count goes to zero, the object can be reclaimed. Useful primarily in specialized situations: when memory is nearly exhausted, or when it is difficult or impossible to find or follow pointers inside objects, or perhaps most of the overhead can be offloaded to another processor.

ROOT A global variable, formal parameter, local variable, or machine register whose contents are presumed capable of affecting the outcome of future computation.

STACK ALLOCATION Allocation on the CALL STACK. Used for variables and objects that are guaranteed to be DEAD when a function returns. In Impcore and C, formal parameters and local variables die on return and so can be allocated on the stack. In Scheme, a formal parameter or local variable can live on in a closure; if it is not captured in any closure, it can be allocated on the stack. Formals and locals that are captured in a closure are usually allocated on the HEAP, unless a sophisticated analysis shows that stack allocation is safe.

TRICOLOR MARKING An abstract model that describes the process of discovering live data by following pointers from ROOTS. The model can describe both COPYING and MARK-AND-SWEEP COLLECTION. Tricolor marking is especially useful for explaining the invariants used by incremental or concurrent collectors.

UNREACHABLE Describes an object whose contents cannot be obtained by following pointers from any root. Every unreachable object is DEAD, but not every dead object is unreachable. In GARBAGE COLLECTION, however, we approximate: unreachable objects are considered dead and reachable objects are considered LIVE.

WORK PER ALLOCATION A suitable measure of the cost of a MANAGED HEAP.

4.10.2 *Further reading*

Wilson (1992) surveys well-established garbage-collection techniques for single-processor machines; although dated, the survey is excellent and is easy to obtain. Jones, Hosking, and Moss (2011) survey more recent techniques; for a gentler introduction, see Jones and Lins (1996). All have extensive lists of references.

If you are interested in original work, McCarthy (1960) outlines the mark-and-sweep method, and Minsky (1963) describes a compacting collector that copies live data to tape, then back into main memory. Minsky points out that copying has the added benefits of linearizing `cdr` chains and compacting both the entire heap and individual objects (like lists). Fenichel and Yochelson (1969) describe copying collection that uses only machine memory, without any external storage; Cheney (1970) shows how to use to-space as a queue of gray objects. Baker (1978) describes a variant that collects garbage without stopping the computation. Dijkstra et al. (1978) analyze concurrent garbage collection; they introduce the term "mutator" and the tricolor abstraction. Lieberman and Hewitt (1983) describe real-time collection, and Ungar (1984) introduces generational collection.

Boehm and Weiser (1988) introduce a *conservative* collector; Boehm and his colleagues developed this collector into a sophisticated component that can easily be added to almost any C program. Zorn (1993) reports on experiments with Boehm's collector, adding garbage collection to programs written for manual memory management. Even without compiler support, garbage collection is competitive with `malloc` and `free`, and sometimes faster. Bartlett (1988) shows how conservative techniques can be used even in a copying system. Smith and Morrisett (1999) compare the two styles of conservative collection.

Hertz and Berger (2005) describe an experiment that explores whether and how perfect manual memory management can outperform garbage collection. A program written for garbage collection is run with instrumentation that records when every object becomes unreachable. Calls to `free` are then inserted into the program at exactly the right places, and the program is re-run with `malloc` and `free`. The resulting perfect manual management can be matched by a garbage collector, but at the cost of five times as much memory. Blackburn, Cheng, and McKinley (2004) use other experiments to elucidate connections between design choices and performance.

Heap growth is a subtle topic that I cannot do justice to, but a good place to start is with the "ergonomic" algorithm of Vengerov (2009).

Mature garbage collectors support parallel and concurrent collection. Marlow et al. (2008) describe a page-based copying collector that runs in parallel on multiple CPU cores.

The performance of reference counting can be improved by many tricks, most of which involve allowing reference counts to get out of data temporarily, to be implied by other information (like the program counter), or both. Deutsch and Bobrow (1976) describe an influential early system. Bacon et al. (2001) describe an aggressive, parallel, purely reference-counting system that achieves pause times measured in milliseconds (on year 2000 hardware!).

Tools like Valgrind have revolutionized the detection of memory errors, including errors in garbage collectors. Nethercote and Seward (2007a,b) describe Valgrind's memory-checking tool and overall instrumentation framework. Luk et al. (2005) describe Pin, a similar tool that is less widely deployed but often faster than Valgrind.

Table 4.2: Synopsis of all the exercises, with most relevant sections

Exercises	*Section*	*Notes*
1	4.5	Complete the copying collector.
2 to 6	4.5	Measure, analyze, or extend your completed copying collector.
7 and 8	4.4	Complete the mark-and-sweep collector.
9 to 11	4.4	Measure, analyze, or extend your completed mark-and-sweep collector.
12	4.4	Prove that lazy sweeping works.
13	4.5	Analyze costs of copying collection.
14 to 16	4.4	Analyze costs of mark-and-sweep collection.
17 to 19	4.4 or 4.5	Experimental study of object lifetimes. Requires a collector.

All exercises require Sections 4.1 to 4.3.

As I write, tools for analyzing and understanding the performance of managed heaps are not widely deployed. Runciman and Wakeling (1993) describe one of the first experiments with "heap profiling." Serrano and Boehm (2000) describe other tools used to understand the performance of a managed heap.

4.11 Exercises

The exercises are summarized in Table 4.2. As highlights, I recommend that you undertake these exercises:

- Build a copying collector (Exercise 1).
- Instrument your collector to gather statistics, and measure work per allocation as a function of the ratio of heap size to live data (Exercises 2 and 3).
- Derive a formula for the amount of work per allocation involved in copying collection, again as a function of the ratio of heap size to live data. Then compare the results from your measurements with the results predicted by your formula (Exercise 13). Once you understand the algorithms, you can predict costs very accurately.
- Do it all again for the mark-and-sweep collector (Exercises 7 and 14).

The copying collector is a little easier to build, and the mark-and-sweep collector is a little easier to analyze.

4.11.1 *Retrieval practice and other short questions*

A. After the expression `(set xs (cdr xs))` is evaluated, what object or objects are likely to become garbage, and why?

B. Conceptually, what is a root?

C. What are the three categories of root?

D. What is the mutator?

E. Copying an object seems like it would always be more expensive than marking. But the copying collector has a compensating performance benefit. What is it?

F. If a managed heap is just barely larger than the amount of live data, what goes wrong?

G. If all the objects we are trying to reclaim have type `Value`, what is the point in looking at objects of type `Env`?

H. The mark phase is complete and an object is unmarked. What color is it: black, white, or gray?

I. The mark phase is complete and an object is marked. What color is it: black, white, or gray?

J. The mark phase is in progress, and an object is marked. What two colors might it be?

K. In copying collection, what is a forwarding pointer?

L. During copying collection, an object has been copied into to-space, but objects that it points to are still in from-space. What color is it: black, white, or gray?

M. During copying collection, what color are the objects in from-space?

4.11.2 Build, measure, and extend the copying collector

The first four exercises are cumulative; each builds on the ones before it. The last two exercises build on just the first.

1. *Complete the copying garbage collector.*

   (a) Write a `copy` procedure that copies all live objects into to-space and leaves `hp` and `heaplimit` pointing to appropriate locations in to-space.

   (b) Write a function `collect` to be called from `allocloc` in chunk 276c. This function should call `copy`, flip the semispaces, and possibly enlarge the heap.

2. *Gather statistics.* Instrument your collector to gather statistics about memory usage and live data in the μScheme heap.

   (a) During every collection, record the number of live objects copied. After the collection, have your `copy` procedure print the total number of locations on the μScheme heap (the heap size), the number that hold live objects at the given collection (the live data), and the ratio of the heap size to live data.

   (b) Gather and print statistics about total memory usage: after every 10th garbage collection, and also when your interpreter exits, print the total number of cells allocated and the current size of the heap. This information will give you a feel for the power of reuse; with garbage collection, some of the programs in this book can run in 60 times less memory than without garbage collection.

   (c) When your interpreter exits, print the total number of collections and the number of objects copied during those collections.

3. *Implement a γ-based policy for heap growth.* The performance of a garbage collector is affected by the size of the heap, which should be controllable by the programmer. My function `gammadesired`, which is defined in chunk S369a, makes it possible to use the μScheme variable `&gamma-desired` to control the

size of the heap. Because μScheme doesn't have floating-point support, the integer `&gamma-desired` represents 100 times the desired ratio of heap size to live data. Using `gammadesired`, modify `collect` so that after each collection it enlarges the heap until the actual γ is at least $\frac{1}{100}$`&gamma-desired`.

(a) Measure the amount of work done *by the collector* for different values of `&gamma-desired` and for different programs. Think carefully about the *units* in which work is measured.

(b) Plot a graph that shows *collector work per allocation* as a function of the value of `&gamma-desired`.

(c) Using your measurements from part (a), choose a sensible default value for γ. Use that default when the μScheme code has not set `&gamma-desired`.

Remember that γ is the ratio of the *total heap size* to the amount of live data, *not* the ratio of the size of a semi-space to the amount of live data.

4. *Reduce total work by delaying heap growth.* Enlarging the heap immediately after a `copy` operation requires a *second* `copy` operation to get the live data into the new heap. This second `copy` costs work without recovering new memory; it is pure overhead. Change `collect` so that if the heap needs to be enlarged, it delays the job until just before the *next* collection. Measure the difference in GC work per allocation for both short-running and long-running programs.

5. *Implement copying collection with non-contiguous semispaces.* A heap can be grown with less overhead if each semispace is represented as a list of pages. A whole semispace is no longer contiguous, but within the semispace, each page is contiguous. Allocating from a contiguous page costs the same as allocating from a contiguous semispace, and when the allocator exhausts one empty page, it moves to the next. Over an entire garbage-collection cycle, allocation incurs only a small additional overhead per page. As long as there are enough objects per page, that overhead won't be noticed.

   (a) Modify your copying collector to represent each semispace as a linked list of pages.

   (b) Implement a heap-growth algorithm that simply adds pages to both semispaces, without copying.

   You can read more about such a system in the paper by Marlow et al. (2008).

6. *Implement a simple generational collector.* Appel (1989) describes generational collection in a very clear, simple setting. Using his technique, modify your copying collector so it uses two generations. Measure work per allocation as a function of γ.

4.11.3 *Build, measure, and extend the mark-and-sweep collector*

The first four exercises are cumulative; each builds on the ones before it.

7. *Implement a `mark` procedure.* Write a procedure `mark` that implements the mark phase of a mark-and-sweep garbage collector. At each collection, traverse the root set and mark each reachable `Mvalue` as live. Use the visiting procedures in Sections 4.4.2 and N.1.1. Your `mark` procedure should call the appropriate visiting procedure for each of the roots.

8. *Implement a mark-and-sweep allocator.* Create an allocator that, together with your `mark` procedure from Exercise 9, forms a complete mark-and-sweep system.

    - The allocator must implement not only allocation but also the unmark and sweep phases of collection. It will sweep through the heap from the first page to the last page. Instead of just taking the location pointed to by `hp`, as in chunk 268b, the allocator must check to see if the location is marked `live`. If marked, it was live at the last collection, so it cannot be used to satisfy the allocation request. Skip past it and mark it not live.

      When the allocator finds an unmarked object, it sweeps past the object and returns it to satisfy the allocation request, just as in chunk 268b. If the allocator reaches the end of the heap without finding an unmarked object, it calls `mark`.

    - In the new system, end-of-page is not the same as end-of-heap. For example, after some allocation requests, the heap might look like this:

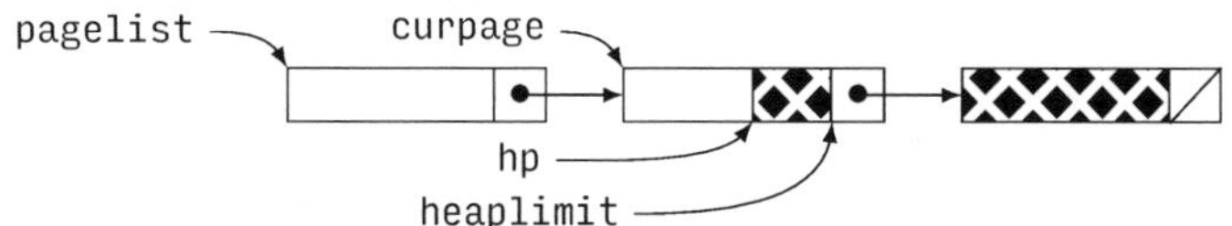

      White areas, to the left of the heap pointer, have been used to satisfy previous allocation requests. Areas marked with gray diamonds, to the right of the heap pointer, are potentially available to satisfy future allocation requests.[5] When `hp` reaches `heaplimit`, the allocator must look at the next page; modify the code in chunk 268b to make it so. Only after there are no more pages may the allocator call `mark`.

    - After your allocator calls `mark`, have it call `makecurrent(pagelist)`, which will reset `hp`, `heaplimit`, and `curpage` to point into the first page.

    - The allocator now guarantees that when `mark` is called, the entire heap is unmarked (Exercise 12). But `mark` cannot guarantee to recover anything; every cell on the heap might be live. The allocator may have to enlarge the heap by adding a new page. Write a procedure `growheap` for this purpose.

    You may find it helpful to split `allocloc` into two functions: one that attempts to allocate without calling `mark`, but sometimes fails, and another that may call the first function, `mark`, and `growheap`.

    You will have an easier time with your implementation if you work Exercise 12 first—a thorough understanding of the invariants makes the implementation relatively easy.

9. *Gather statistics.* After completing Exercise 7, instrument your collector to gather statistics about memory usage and live data in the μScheme heap. (The μScheme heap, i.e., the collection of all pages, is not the C heap. The μScheme heap is managed with `allocloc` and `mark`; the C heap is managed with `malloc` and `free`.)

    (a) During every collection, record the number of objects marked. After the collection, have your `mark` procedure print the total number of lo-

[5]They are only "potentially" available because if they are marked, they were live at the last collection and must be assumed to be live now. The allocator must unmark and skip over such cells.

cations on the μScheme heap (the heap size), the number that hold live objects at the given collection (the live data), and the ratio of the heap size to live data.

(b) Gather and print statistics about total memory usage: after every 10th garbage collection, and also when your interpreter exits, print the total number of cells allocated and the current size of the heap. This information will give you a feel for the power of reuse; with garbage collection, some of the programs in this book can run in 60 times less memory than without garbage collection.

(c) When your interpreter exits, print the total number of collections and the number of objects marked during those collections.

10. *Implement a γ-based policy for heap growth.* The performance of a garbage collector is affected by the size of the heap, which should be controllable by the programmer. My function `gammadesired`, which is defined in chunk S369a, makes it possible to use the μScheme variable `&gamma-desired` to control the size of the heap. Because μScheme doesn't have floating-point support, the integer `&gamma-desired` represents 100 times the desired ratio of heap size to live data.

    (a) Modify your collector so that after each collection it enlarges the heap, possibly by adding more than one page, until the measured γ is as close as possible to $\frac{1}{100}$`&gamma-desired`, without going under. For example, executing `(set &gamma-desired 175)` should cause your collector to increase the heap size to make γ about 1.75. (If γ is too big, do not try to make the heap smaller; see Exercise 15.)

    (b) Measure the amount of work done *by the collector* for different values of `&gamma-desired` and for different programs. Think carefully about the *units* in which work is measured.

    (c) Plot a graph that shows *collector work per allocation* as a function of the value of `&gamma-desired`.

    (d) Using your measurements from part (b), choose a sensible default value for γ. Use that default when the μScheme code has not set `&gamma-desired`.

11. *Placement of mark bits.* Our system puts mark bits in the object headers even though there's no spare bit and we therefore have to allocate an extra word per object.

    (a) Rewrite the allocator and collector to pack the mark bits into one or more words in the page. You will need to be able to map the address of an object to the address of the page containing that object. If you arrange for the addresses of pages to fall on k-bit boundaries, where `GROWTH_UNIT` $< 2^k$, you can find the address of the page simply by masking out the least significant k bits of the address of the object.

    (b) Using the new representation, how many more objects can fit into an page of the same size? What does this result imply about choosing γ?

    (c) Will this representation work well for a parallel collector? Why or why not?

12. *Correctness of lazy sweeping.* Prove that in the scheme outlined in Exercise 8, `mark` is called only when no S-expression is marked `live`.

    (a) Find an invariant for the current page pointed to by `curpage`. When `&curpage->pool[i]` < `hp`, you'll need a property for `curpage->pool[i]`; when `&curpage->pool[i]` >= `hp`, you'll need a different property. Your `growheap` procedure will have to establish the invariant for every new page.

    (b) Extend the invariant to include pages before and after `curpage`. The invariants for these two kinds of pages should look an awful lot like the invariants for `curpage->pool[i]` where `&curpage->pool[i]` < `hp` and `&curpage->pool[i]` >= `hp`. Together, these invariants describe the white and gray-diamond areas in the picture of the heap.

    (c) Show that `growheap`, `allocloc`, and `mark` all maintain this invariant.

    (d) Show that conditions when `mark` is called, together with the invariant, imply that `mark` is called only when no S-expression is marked `live`.

4.11.4 *Analyze costs of collection*

13. *Cost of copying collection as a function of* γ. Even a simple analysis can enable you to predict the cost of garbage collection.

    (a) Derive a formula to express the cost of copying garbage collection as a function of γ. Measure cost in units of *GC work per allocation.* Assume a fixed percentage of whatever is allocated becomes garbage by the next collection.

    You needn't assume that you know anything else about the heap besides γ.

    (b) If you have done Exercise 3, discuss how your formula compares with your measurements. Explain any inconsistencies.

14. *Cost of mark-and-sweep collection as a function of* γ.

    (a) Derive a formula to express the cost of mark-and-sweep garbage collection as a function of γ. Measure cost in units of *GC work per allocation*—in a mark-and-sweep system, this cost is often called the *mark/cons ratio.* Assume a fixed percentage of whatever is allocated becomes garbage by the next collection.

    You needn't assume that you know anything else about the heap besides γ.

    (b) If you have done Exercise 10, discuss how your formula compares with your measurements. Explain any inconsistencies.

15. *Probability of an empty page.* Because objects in our mark-and-sweep collector don't move, it can shrink the heap only if it finds a completely empty page. Assume that $\gamma = 10$, so the heap is 90% empty, and that `GROWTH_UNIT` is chosen so that one page just fits on a virtual-memory page (about 4KB to 8KB). Assuming that objects die independently of their locations, what is the probability that an page chosen at random has no live objects in it and can be removed from the heap? (The assumption is not borne out in practice—real objects tend to die in clumps.)

16. *Expected number of cells swept in an allocation.* The mark-and-sweep allocator skips marked cells until it finds an unmarked cell. Assume that the marked cells are distributed independently, so that the probability of any particular cell being marked is $\frac{1}{\gamma}$. (Just as in the previous problem, this assumption is not borne out in practice.)

    (a) Derive a formula giving, as a function of γ, the expected number of marked cells the allocator must skip before finding an unmarked cell. Calculate this number for some interesting values of γ, e.g., 1, 1.1, 1.2, 1.5, 2, 3, and 5.

    (b) Derive a formula giving, as a function of γ, the probability that the allocator skips at most 3 cells. Calculate this probability for some interesting values of γ.

4.11.5 *Deeper experimental study*

17. *Distribution of objects' lifetimes.* Pick a collector and measure the distributions of objects' lifetimes for several programs. Measure lifetimes in units of *number of objects allocated.* You will need to add a field to each object that tells when it was allocated, and at each collection you will be able to estimate the lifetimes of the objects that died at that collection. The fewer objects that are allocated between collections, the more accurate your estimate will be.

    (a) For several programs, approximately what is the distribution of objects' lifetimes?

    (b) Does the distribution of lifetimes depend on γ? Why or why not?

    (c) Does the distribution of lifetimes tell you anything about the generational hypothesis? If so, what?

18. *Measuring space lost to drag.* An object may becomes unreachable only some times after it is last used. This time, called the *drag time* of the object, contributes to excess space usage in garbage-collected systems. Drag time should be measured in units of *number of objects allocated.* Measure drag times in your own system:

    (a) Keep count of the total number of objects ever allocated. This count will act as a clock.

    (b) Add a field to each object that tells when it was last used. Every time an object is used, its field should be set to the current time. An object might be considered "used" when it is looked up in an environment or is obtained by a `car` or `cdr` operation.

    (c) Add another field to each object that tells when it was last known to be reachable. This field can be updated by the garbage collector, or for more accurate measurements, you can create a checking function that will run more frequently and will update the fields. Such a checking function would look a lot like `mark`.

    (d) When an unreachable object is garbage-collected, log the two times (time of last use and time of unreachability) to a file. When the program ends, log the same information for the remaining objects.

    (e) Write a program to read the log and compute two curves. The *in-use curve* records the number of objects in use as a function of time. The *reachable curve* records the number of objects that are reachable, also as a function of time.

(f) The area under each curve is a good measure of space usage. The ratio of in-use space to reachable space can measure the degree to which reachability overestimates the lifetimes of objects. Compute this ratio for several executions of several programs.

19. *Measuring performance costs of overaggressive closures.* My implementation of `lambda` captures the entire current environment, including all live variables. As long as the closure is live, those variables and all the heap objects they point to, transitively, are live. But the only variables a closure really needs are the ones that appear free in the body of its `lambda`. The other variables may unnecessarily cause objects to be retained.

   (a) Re-implement `lambda` to build a new environment containing only the variables that are actually needed. You might use function `freevars` from Appendix L.

   (b) Measure how this change affects the performance of the garbage-collected heap. You might measure the number of collections, equilibrium heap size, average lifetime of objects, or drag time. Drag time is probably the most interesting measure, since my implementation "drags" these unneeded variables along for the ride.

Chapter 5 contents

Interlude: μScheme in ML

5

STUDENT: *You and Chris have spent ten years working on your compiler, and now you have this highly polished literate program, published as a book. What did you learn?*

HANSON: *C is a lousy language to write a compiler in.*

Conversation with David R. Hanson, coauthor of *A Retargetable C Compiler: Design and Implementation* (Fraser and Hanson 1995).

The interpreters in Chapters 1 to 4 are written in C, which has much to recommend it: C is relatively small and simple; it is widely known and widely supported; its perspicuous cost model makes it is easy to discover what is happening at the machine level; and it provides pointer arithmetic, which makes it a fine language in which to write a garbage collector. But for implementing more complicated or ambitious languages, C is less than ideal. In this and succeeding chapters, I therefore present interpreters written in the functional language Standard ML.

Standard ML is particularly well suited to symbolic computing, especially functions that operate on abstract-syntax trees; some advantages are detailed in the sidebar on the next page. And an ML program can illustrate connections between language design, formal semantics, and implementations more clearly than a C program can. Infrastructure suitable for writing interpreters in ML is presented in this chapter and in Appendices H and I. That infrastructure is introduced by using it to implement a language that is now familiar: μScheme.

The μScheme interpreter in this chapter is structured in the same way as the interpreter in Chapter 2. Like that interpreter, it has environments, abstract syntax, primitives, an evaluator for expressions, and an evaluator for definitions. Many details are as similar as I can make them, but many are not: I want the interpreters to look similar, but even more, I want my ML code to look like ML and my C code to look like C.

The ML code will be easier to read if you know my programming conventions.

- My naming conventions are the ones recommended by the SML'97 Standard Basis Library (Gansner and Reppy 2002). Names of types are written in lowercase letters with words separated by underscores, like `exp`, `def`, or `unit_test`. Names of functions and variables begin with lowercase letters, like `eval` or `evaldef`, but long names may be written in "camel case" with a mix of uppercase and lowercase letters, like `processTests` instead of the C-style `process_tests`. (Rarely, I may use an underscore in the name of a local variable.)

Helpful properties of the ML family of languages

- ML is *safe*: there are no unchecked run-time errors, which means there are no faults that are entirely up to the programmer to avoid.
- Like Scheme, ML is naturally *polymorphic*. Polymorphism simplifies everything. For example, unlike the C code in Chapters 1 to 4, the ML code in Chapters 5 to 10 uses just one representation of lists and one length function. As another example, where the C code in Appendix F defines three different types of streams, each with its own `get` function, the ML code in Appendix H defines one type of stream and one `streamGet` function. And when a job is done by just one polymorphic function, not a group of similar functions, you know that the one function always does the same thing.
- Unlike Scheme, ML uses a static type system, and this system guarantees that data structures are internally consistent. For example, if one element of a list is a function, every element of that list is a function. This happens without requiring variable declarations or type annotations to be written in the code.

  If talk of polymorphism mystifies you, don't worry; polymorphism in programming languages is an important topic in its own right. Polymorphism is formally introduced and defined in Chapter 6, and the algorithms that ML uses to provide polymorphism without type annotations are described in Chapter 7.
- Like Scheme, ML provides first-class, nested functions, and its initial basis contains useful higher-order functions. These functions help simplify and clarify code. For example, they can eliminate the special-purpose functions that the C code uses to run a list of unit tests from back to front; the ML code just uses `foldr`.
- To detect and signal errors, ML provides *exception handlers* and *exceptions*, which are more flexible and easier to use then C's `setjmp` and `longjmp`.
- Finally, least familiar but most important, ML provides native support for *algebraic data types*, which I use to represent both abstract syntax and values. These types provide *value constructors* like the `IFX` or `APPLY` used in previous chapters, but instead of `switch` statements, ML provides *pattern matching*. Pattern matching enables ML programmers to write function definitions that look like algebraic laws; such definitions are easier to follow than C code. The technique is demonstrated in the definition of function `valueString` on page 307. For a deeper dive into algebraic data types, jump ahead to Chapter 8 and read through Section 8.1.

Names of exceptions are capitalized, like `NotFound` or `RuntimeError`, and they use camel case. Names of *value constructors*, which identify alternatives in algebraic data types, are written in all capitals, possibly with underscores, like `IFX`, `APPLY`, or `CHECK_EXPECT`—just like enumeration literals in C.

- If you happen to be a seasoned ML programmer, you'll notice something missing: the interpreter is not decomposed into modules. Modules get a book chapter of their own (Chapter 9), but compared to what's in Chapter 9, Standard ML's module system is complicated and hard to understand. To avoid explaining it, I define no modules—although I do use "dot notation" to select functions that are defined in Standard ML's predefined modules. By avoiding module definitions, I enable you to digest this chapter even if your only previous functional-programming experience is with μScheme.

Because I don't use ML modules, I cannot easily write interfaces or distinguish them from implementations. Instead, I use a literate-programming trick: I put the types of functions and values, which is mostly what ML interfaces describe, in boxes preceding the implementations. These types are checked by the ML compiler, and the trick makes it possible to present a function's interface just before its implementation.

My code is also affected by two limitations of ML: ML is persnickety about the order in which definitions appear, and it has miserable support for mutually recursive data definitions. These limitations arise because unlike C, which has syntactic forms for both declarations and definitions, ML has only definition forms.

In C, as long as declarations precede definitions, you can be careless about the order in which both appear. Declare all your structures (probably in `typedef`s) in any order you like, and you can define them in just about any order you like. Then declare all your functions in any order you like, and you can define them in any order you like—even if your data structures and functions are mutually recursive. Of course there are drawbacks: not all variables are guaranteed to be initialized, and global variables can be initialized only in limited ways. And you can easily define mutually recursive data structures that allow you to chase pointers forever.

In ML, there are no declarations, and you may write a definition only *after* the definitions of the things it refers to. Of course there are benefits: every definition initializes its name, and initialization may use any valid expression, including `let` expressions, which in ML can contain nested definitions. And unless your code assigns to mutable reference cells, you cannot define circular data structures that allow you to chase pointers forever. As a consequence, unless a structurally recursive function fetches the contents of mutable reference cells, it is guaranteed to terminate. ML's designers thought this guarantee was more important than the convenience of writing data definitions in many orders. (And to be fair, using ML modules makes it relatively convenient to get things in the right order.)

What about mutually recursive data? Suppose for example, that type `exp` refers to `value` and type `value` refers to `exp`? Mutually recursive definitions like `exp` and `value` must be written together, adjacent in the source code, connected with the keyword `and`. (You won't see `and` often, but when you do, please remember this: it means mutual recursion, never a Boolean operation.)

Mutually recursive function definitions provide more options: they can be joined with `and`, but it is usually more convenient and more idiomatic to nest one inside the other using a `let` binding. You would use `and` only when both mutually recursive functions need to be called by some third, client function. When I use mutual recursion, I identify the technique I use. Now, on to the code!

5.1 NAMES AND ENVIRONMENTS, WITH INTRODUCTION TO ML

In my C code, `Name` is an abstract type, and by design, two values of type `Name` can be compared using C's built-in == operator. In my ML code, because ML strings are immutable and can be meaningfully compared using ML's built-in = operator, names are represented as strings.

303. ⟨*support for names and environments* 303⟩≡ (S213a) 304 ▷
```
type name = string
```

ML's `type` syntax is like C's `typedef`; it defines a type by *type abbreviation*.

Each μScheme name is bound to a location that contains a value. In C, such a location is represented by a pointer of C type `Value *`. In ML, such a pointer has type `value ref`. Like a C pointer, an ML `ref` can be read from and written to, but unlike a C pointer, it can't be added to or subtracted from.

Table 5.1: Correspondence between μScheme semantics and ML code

Semantics	*Concept*	*Interpreter*
d	Definition	`def` (page 307)
e	Expression	`exp` (page 306)
x	Name	`name` (page 303)
v	Value	`value` (page 306)
ℓ	Location	`value ref` (`ref` is built into ML)
ρ	Environment	`value ref env` (page 304)
σ	Store	Machine memory (the ML heap)
$\langle e, \rho, \sigma \rangle \Downarrow \langle v, \sigma' \rangle$	Expression evaluation	`eval(`e`, `ρ`)` $= v$, with σ updated to σ' (page 309)
$\langle d, \rho, \sigma \rangle \rightarrow \langle \rho', \sigma' \rangle$	Definition evaluation	`evaldef(`d`, `ρ`)` $= (\rho', s)$, with σ updated to σ' (page 311)
$x \in \operatorname{dom} \rho$	Definedness	`find (`x`, `ρ`)` terminates without raising an exception (page 305)
$\rho(x)$	Location lookup	`find (`x`, `ρ`)` (page 305)
$\sigma(\rho(x))$	Value lookup	`!(find (`x`, `ρ`))` (page 305)
$\rho\{x \mapsto \ell\}$	Binding	`bind (`x`, `ℓ`, `ρ`)` (page 305)
$\sigma\{\ell \mapsto v\}$, where $\ell \notin \operatorname{dom} \sigma$	Allocation	call `ref` v; the result is ℓ
$\sigma\{\ell \mapsto v\}$, where $\ell \in \operatorname{dom} \sigma$	Store update	ℓ `:=` v

In C, the code that looks up or binds a name has to know what kind of thing a name stands for; that's why the Impcore interpreter uses one set of environment functions for value environments ξ and ρ and another set for a function environment ϕ. In ML, the code that looks up or binds a name is independent of what a name stands for; it is naturally *polymorphic*. *One* set of polymorphic functions suffices to implement environments that hold locations, values, or types.

ML has a static type system, and polymorphism is reflected in the types. An environment has type `'a env`; such an environment binds each name in its domain to a value of type `'a`. The `'a` is called a *type parameter* or *type variable*; it stands for an unknown type. (Type parameters are explained in detail in Section 6.6, where they have an entire language devoted to them.) Type `'a env`, like any type that takes a type parameter, can be *instantiated* at any type; instantiation *substitutes* a known type for every occurrence of `'a`. μScheme's environment binds each name to a mutable location, and it is obtained by instantiating type `'a env` using `'a` = `value ref`; the resulting type is `value ref env`.

My environments are implemented using ML's native support for lists and pairs. Although my C code represents an environment as a pair of lists, in ML, it's easier and simpler to use a list of pairs. The type of the list is `(name * 'a) list`; the type of a single pair is `name * 'a`. A pair is created by an ML expression of the form `(`e_1`, `e_2`)`; this pair contains the value of e_1 and the value of e_2. The pair `(`e_1`, `e_2`)` has type `name * 'a` if e_1 has type `name` and e_2 has type `'a`.

304. ⟨*support for names and environments* 303⟩+≡ (S213a) ◁303 305a▷

```
type 'a env = (name * 'a) list
```

The representation guarantees that there is an `'a` for every `name`.

The empty environment is represented by the empty list. In ML, that's written using square brackets. The `val` form is like μScheme's `val` form.

305a. ⟨*support for names and environments* 303⟩+≡ (S213a) ◁304 305b▷

```
val emptyEnv = []
```

`emptyEnv : 'a env`

(The phrase in the box is like a declaration that could appear in an interface to an ML module; through some Noweb hackery, it is checked by the ML compiler.)

A name is looked up by function `find`, which is closely related to the `find` from Chapter 2: it returns whatever is in the environment, which has type `'a`. If the name is unbound, `find` *raises* an *exception*. Raising an exception is a lot like the `throw` operator in Chapter 3; it is roughly analogous to `longjmp`. The exceptions I use are listed in Table 5.2 on the following page.

305b. ⟨*support for names and environments* 303⟩+≡ (S213a) ◁305a 305c▷

`find : name * 'a env -> 'a`

```
exception NotFound of name
fun find (name, []) = raise NotFound name
  | find (name, (x, v)::tail) = if name = x then v else find (name, tail)
```

The `fun` definition form is ML's analog to `define`, but unlike μScheme's `define`, it uses multiple clauses with *pattern matching*. Each clause is like an algebraic law. The first clause says that calling `find` with an empty environment raises an exception; the second clause handles a nonempty environment. The infix `::` is ML's way of writing `cons`, and it is pronounced "cons."

To check $x \in \operatorname{dom} \rho$, the ML code uses function `isbound`.

305c. ⟨*support for names and environments* 303⟩+≡ (S213a) ◁305b 305d▷

```
fun isbound (name, []) = false
  | isbound (name, (x, v)::tail) = name = x orelse isbound (name, tail)
```

Again using `::`, function `bind` adds a new binding to an existing environment. Unlike Chapter 2's `bind`, it does not allocate a mutable reference cell.

305d. ⟨*support for names and environments* 303⟩+≡ (S213a) ◁305c 305e▷

`bind : name * 'a * 'a env -> 'a env`

```
fun bind (name, v, rho) =
  (name, v) :: rho
```

Even though an `'a env` is a list of pairs, functions that operate on two lists, like those in Chapters 1 and 2, are still useful. Function `bindList` adds a sequence of bindings to an environment; it is used to implement μScheme's `let` and `lambda`. If the lists aren't the same length, it raises another exception. Function `bindList` resembles Chapter 2's `bindalloclist`, but it does not allocate. Related function `mkEnv` manufactures a new environment given just a list of names and `'a`'s.

305e. ⟨*support for names and environments* 303⟩+≡ (S213a) ◁305d 305f▷

```
bindList : name list * 'a list * 'a env -> 'a env
mkEnv    : name list * 'a list -> 'a env
```

```
exception BindListLength
fun bindList (x::vars, v::vals, rho) = bindList (vars, vals, bind (x, v, rho))
  | bindList ([], [], rho) = rho
  | bindList _ = raise BindListLength

fun mkEnv (xs, vs) = bindList (xs, vs, emptyEnv)
```

type name 303

Finally, environments can be composed using the $+$ operator. In my ML code, this operator is implemented by function `<+>`, which I declare to be `infix`. It uses the predefined infix function `@`, which is ML's way of writing `append`.

305f. ⟨*support for names and environments* 303⟩+≡ (S213a) ◁305e

`<+> : 'a env * 'a env -> 'a env`

```
(* composition *)
infix 6 <+>
fun pairs <+> pairs' = pairs' @ pairs
```

Function `<+>` obeys the algebraic law `bindList(`xs`, `vs`, `ρ`)` $=$ ρ `<+> mkEnv(`xs`, `vs`)`. Later chapters use `<+>` and `mkEnv` instead of `bindList`.

Table 5.2: Exceptions defined for my interpreters

Exceptions raised at run time	
NotFound	A name was looked up in an environment but not found there.
BindListLength	A call to bindList tried to extend an environment, but it passed two lists (names and values) of different lengths (also raised by mkEnv).
RuntimeError	Something else went wrong during evaluation, i.e., during the execution of eval.

5.2 ABSTRACT SYNTAX AND VALUES

An abstract-syntax tree can contain a literal value. A value, if it is a closure, can contain an abstract-syntax tree. These two types are therefore mutually recursive, so they must be defined together, using and.

These particular types use as complicated a nest of definitions as you'll ever see. The keyword datatype defines a new algebraic datatype; the keyword withtype introduces a new type abbreviation that is mutually recursive with the datatype. The first two and keywords define additional algebraic datatypes, and the third and keyword defines an additional type abbreviation. Everything in the whole nest is mutually recursive.

306. ⟨*definitions of* exp *and* value *for μScheme* 306⟩≡ (S380a)

```
datatype exp   = LITERAL of value
               | VAR     of name
               | SET     of name * exp
               | IFX     of exp * exp * exp
               | WHILEX  of exp * exp
               | BEGIN   of exp list
               | APPLY   of exp * exp list
               | LETX    of let_flavor * (name * exp) list * exp
               | LAMBDA  of lambda
and let_flavor = LET | LETREC | LETSTAR
and      value = SYM       of name
               | NUM       of int
               | BOOLV     of bool
               | NIL
               | PAIR      of value * value
               | CLOSURE   of lambda * value ref env
               | PRIMITIVE of primitive
withtype primitive = exp * value list -> value (* raises RuntimeError *)
     and lambda    = name list * exp
```

The representations are the same as in C, with these exceptions:

- In a LETX expression, the bindings are represented by a list of pairs, not a pair of lists—just like environments.
- In the representation of a primitive function, there's no need for an integer tag. As shown in Section 5.4 below, ML's higher-order functions makes it easy to create groups of primitives that share code. Tags would be useful only if we wanted to distinguish one primitive from another when printing.
- None of the fields of exp, value, or lambda is named. Instead of being referred to by name, these fields are referred to by pattern matching.

A primitive function that goes wrong raises the RuntimeError exception, which is the ML equivalent of calling runerror.

True definitions are as in the C code, except again, fields are not named.

307a. ⟨*definition of* def *for μScheme* 307a⟩≡ (S380a)

```
datatype def  = VAL    of name * exp
              | EXP    of exp
              | DEFINE of name * lambda
```

Unit tests and other extended definitions are relegated to Appendix O.

The rest of this section defines utility functions on values.

String conversion

Instead of printf, ML provides functions that can create, manipulate, and combine strings. So instead using something like Chapter 1's extensible print function, this chapter builds strings using string-conversion functions. One example, valueString, which converts an ML value to a string, is shown here. The other string-conversion functions are relegated to the Supplement.

Function valueString is primarily concerned with S-expressions. An atom is easily converted, but a list made up of cons cells (PAIRs) requires care; the cdr is converted by a recursive function, tail, which implements the same list-printing algorithm as the C code. (The algorithm, which goes back to McCarthy, is implemented by C function printtail on page S332.) Function tail is defined inside valueString, with which it is mutually recursive.

307b. ⟨*definition of* valueString *for μScheme, Typed μScheme, and nano-ML* 307b⟩≡ (S380a)

```
                                              valueString : value -> string
fun valueString (SYM v)    = v
  | valueString (NUM n)    = intString n
  | valueString (BOOLV b) = if b then "#t" else "#f"
  | valueString (NIL)      = "()"
  | valueString (PAIR (car, cdr))  =
      let fun tail (PAIR (car, cdr)) = " " ^ valueString car ^ tail cdr
            | tail NIL = ")"
            | tail v = " . " ^ valueString v ^ ")"
      in  "(" ^ valueString car ^ tail cdr
      end
  | valueString (CLOSURE   _) = "<function>"
  | valueString (PRIMITIVE _) = "<function>"
```

Function valueString demonstrates pattern matching. It takes one argument and does a case analysis on its form. Each case corresponds to a clause in the definition of valueString; there is one clause for each datatype constructor of the value type. On the left of the =, each clause contains a *pattern* that applies a datatype constructor to a variable, to a pair of variables, or to the special "wildcard" pattern _ (the underscore). Each variable, but not the wildcard, is introduced into the environment and is available for use on the right-hand side of the clause, just as if it had been bound by a μScheme let or ML val.

type env	304
intString	S214c
type name	303

From the point of view of a C programmer, a pattern match combines a switch statement with assignment to local variables. The notation is sweet; for example, in the matches for BOOLV and PAIR, I like b and car much better than the v.u.boolv and v.u.pair.car that I have to write in C. And I really like that the variables b and car can be used only where they are meaningful—in C, v.u.pair.car is accepted whenever v has type Value, but if v isn't a pair, the reference to its car is meaningless (and to evaluate it is an *unchecked* run-time error). In ML, only meaningful references are accepted.

Embedding and projection

Inside the interpreter, μScheme values sometimes need to be converted to or from ML values of other types.

- When it sees a quote mark and brackets, the parser defined in the Supplement produces a native ML list of S-expressions represented by a combination of `[]` and `::`. But the evaluator needs a μScheme list represented by a combination of `NIL` and `PAIR`.
- When it evaluates a condition in a μScheme `if` expression, the evaluator produces a μScheme value. But to test that value with a native ML `if` expression, the evaluator needs a native ML Boolean.

Such needs are met by using functions that convert values from one language to another. Similar needs arise whenever one language is used to implement or describe another, and to keep two such languages straight, we typically resort to jargon:

- The language being implemented or described—in our case, μScheme—is called the *object language*.
- The language doing the describing or implementation—in our case, ML—is called the *metalanguage*. (The name ML actually stands for "metalanguage.")

To convert, say, an integer between object language and metalanguage, we use a pair of functions called *embedding* and *projection*. The embedding puts a metalanguage integer into the object language, converting an `int` into a `value`. The projection extracts a metalanguage integer from the object language, converting a `value` into an `int`. If the `value` can't be interpreted as an integer, the projection fails.[1] The embedding/projection pair for integers is defined as follows:

308a. ⟨*utility functions on values (μScheme, Typed μScheme, nano-ML)* 308a⟩≡ (S379) 308b ▷

```
fun embedInt n = NUM n
fun projectInt (NUM n) = n
  | projectInt v =
      raise RuntimeError ("value " ^ valueString v ^ " is not an integer")
```

```
embedInt   : int   -> value
projectInt : value -> int
```

Embedding and projection for Booleans is a little different; unlike some projection functions, `projectBool` is *total*: it always succeeds. Function `projectBool` reflects the operational semantics of μScheme, which treats any value other than `#f` as a true value.[2]

308b. ⟨*utility functions on values (μScheme, Typed μScheme, nano-ML)* 308a⟩+≡ (S379) ◁ 308a 308c ▷

```
fun embedBool b = BOOLV b
fun projectBool (BOOLV false) = false
  | projectBool _             = true
```

```
embedBool   : bool  -> value
projectBool : value -> bool
```

The same Boolean projection function is used in Chapter 2, but without the jargon; there, the projection function is called `istrue`.

A list of values can be embedded as a single value by converting ML's `::` and `[]` to μScheme's `PAIR` and `NIL`. The corresponding projection is left as Exercise 4.

308c. ⟨*utility functions on values (μScheme, Typed μScheme, nano-ML)* 308a⟩+≡ (S379) ◁ 308b

```
fun embedList []     = NIL
  | embedList (h::t) = PAIR (h, embedList t)
```

```
embedList : value list -> value
```

[1] In general, we embed a smaller set into a larger set. Embeddings don't fail, but projections might. A mathematician would say that an embedding e of S into S' is an injection from $S \to S'$. The corresponding projection π_e is a left inverse of the embedding; that is $\pi_e \circ e$ is the identity function on S. There is no corresponding guarantee for $e \circ \pi_e$; for example, π_e may be undefined ($\bot$) on some elements of S', or $e(\pi_e(x))$ may not equal x.

[2] A Boolean projection function formalizes the concepts of "truthy" and "falsy" found in languages like JavaScript: a value is truthy if it projects to `true` and falsy if it projects to `false`.

The machinery above is enough to write an evaluator, which takes an expression and an environment and produces a value. Because the environment rarely changes, my evaluator is structured as a nested pair of mutually recursive functions. The outer function, `eval`, takes both expression `e` and environment `rho` as arguments. The inner function, `ev`, takes only an expression as argument; it uses the `rho` from the outer function.

Function `ev` begins with a clause that evaluates a `LITERAL` form, which evaluates to the carried value `v`.

309a. ⟨*definitions of* `eval` *and* `evaldef` *for μScheme* 309a⟩≡ 311b ▷

```
eval : exp * value ref env -> value
ev   : exp                 -> value
```

```
fun eval (e, rho) =
  let fun ev (LITERAL v) = v
        ⟨more alternatives for ev for μScheme 309b⟩
  in  ev e
  end
```

A `VAR` or `SET` form looks up a name `x` in `rho`. The name is expected to be bound to a mutable reference cell, which is ML's version of a pointer to a location allocated on the heap. Such locations are read and written not by using special syntax like C's `*`, but by using functions `!` and `:=`, which are in the initial basis of Standard ML. (The `:=` symbol, like the `+` symbol, is an ordinary ML function that is declared to be *infix*.)

309b. ⟨*more alternatives for* `ev` *for μScheme* 309b⟩≡ (309a) 309c ▷

```
| ev (VAR x) = !(find (x, rho))
| ev (SET (x, e)) =
    let val v = ev e
    in  find (x, rho) := v;
        v
    end
```

Because the right-hand side of `SET`, here called `e`, is evaluated in the same environment as the `SET`, it can be evaluated using `ev`.

An `IF` or `WHILE` form must interpret a μScheme value as a Boolean. Both forms use the projection function `projectBool`.

309c. ⟨*more alternatives for* `ev` *for μScheme* 309b⟩+≡ (309a) ◁ 309b 309d ▷

```
| ev (IFX (e1, e2, e3)) = ev (if projectBool (ev e1) then e2 else e3)
| ev (WHILEX (guard, body)) =
    if projectBool (ev guard) then
      (ev body; ev (WHILEX (guard, body)))
    else
      BOOLV false
```

The code used to evaluate a `while` loop is nearly identical to the rule for lowering `while` loops in Chapter 3 (page 214).

A `BEGIN` form is evaluated by evaluating its subexpressions in order, retaining the value of the last one. The subexpressions are evaluated by auxiliary function `b`, which remembers the value of the last expression in an accumulating parameter `lastval`. To ensure that an empty `BEGIN` is evaluated correctly, `lastval` is initially a μScheme `#f`.

309d. ⟨*more alternatives for* `ev` *for μScheme* 309b⟩+≡ (309a) ◁ 309c 310a ▷

```
| ev (BEGIN es) =
    let fun b (e::es, lastval) = b (es, ev e)
          | b (   [], lastval) = lastval
    in  b (es, BOOLV false)
    end
```

A LAMBDA form captures a closure, which is as simple as in C.

310a. ⟨*more alternatives for* ev *for μScheme* 309b⟩+≡ (309a) ◁309d 310b▷

```
| ev (LAMBDA (xs, e)) = CLOSURE ((xs, e), rho)
```

An application is evaluated by first evaluating the expression f that appears in the function position. How the result is applied depends on whether f evaluates to a primitive or a closure. As in C, a primitive is applied by applying it to the syntax e and to the values of the arguments.

310b. ⟨*more alternatives for* ev *for μScheme* 309b⟩+≡ (309a) ◁310a 310d▷

```
| ev (e as APPLY (f, args)) =
       (case ev f
          of PRIMITIVE prim => prim (e, map ev args)
           | CLOSURE clo    => ⟨apply closure clo to args 310c⟩
           | v => raise RuntimeError
                            ("Applied non-function " ^ valueString v)
       )
```

The pattern e as APPLY (f, args) matches an APPLY node. On the right-hand side, e stands for the entire node, and f and args stand for the children.

A closure is applied by first creating fresh locations to hold the values of the actual parameters. In Chapter 2, the locations are allocated by function allocate; here, they are allocated by the built-in function ref. Calling ref v allocates a new location and initializes it to v. The ML expression map ref actuals does half the work of Chapter 2's bindalloclist; the other half is done by bindList.

310c. ⟨*apply closure* clo *to* args 310c⟩≡ (310b)

```
let val ((formals, body), savedrho) = clo
    val actuals = map ev args
in  eval (body, bindList (formals, map ref actuals, savedrho))
    handle BindListLength =>
        raise RuntimeError ("Wrong number of arguments to closure; " ^
                            "expected (" ^ spaceSep formals ^ ")")
end
```

If the number of actual parameters doesn't match the number of formal parameters, bindList raises the BindListLength exception, which eval catches using handle. The handler then raises RuntimeError.

A LET form is most easily evaluated by first unzipping the list of pairs bs into a pair of lists (names, rightSides); function ListPair.unzip is from the ListPair module in ML's Standard Basis Library. Each right-hand side is then evaluated with ev and stored in a fresh location by ref. To do the whole list at once, I use map with the function composition ref o ev. Finally, the body of the LET is evaluated in a new environment built by bindList; since ev works only with the current rho, the body must be evaluated by eval.

310d. ⟨*more alternatives for* ev *for μScheme* 309b⟩+≡ (309a) ◁310b 310e▷

```
ListPair.unzip : ('a * 'b) list -> 'a list * 'b list
```

```
| ev (LETX (LET, bs, body)) =
    let val (names, rightSides) = ListPair.unzip bs
    in  eval (body, bindList (names, map (ref o ev) rightSides, rho))
    end
```

A LETSTAR form, by contrast, is more easily evaluated by walking the bindings one pair at a time.

310e. ⟨*more alternatives for* ev *for μScheme* 309b⟩+≡ (309a) ◁310d 311a▷

```
| ev (LETX (LETSTAR, bs, body)) =
    let fun step ((x, e), rho) = bind (x, ref (eval (e, rho)), rho)
    in  eval (body, foldl step rho bs)
    end
```

As in Chapter 2, a LETREC form is evaluated by first building a new environment rho' that binds each name to a fresh location, then evaluating each right-hand side in the new environment, updating the fresh locations, and finally evaluating the body. The updates are performed by List.app, which, just like μScheme's app, applies a function to every element of a list, just for its side effect. Functions List.app and map are used here with anonymous functions, each of which is written with fn—which is ML's way of writing lambda.

311a. ⟨*more alternatives for* ev *for μScheme* 309b⟩+≡ (309a) ◁ 310e

List.app : ('a -> unit) -> 'a list -> unit

```
| ev (LETX (LETREC, bs, body)) =
    let val (names, rightSides) = ListPair.unzip bs
        val rho' =
          bindList (names, map (fn _ => ref (unspecified())) rightSides, rho)
        val updates = map (fn (x, rightSide) => (x, eval (rightSide, rho'))) bs
    in  List.app (fn (x, v) => find (x, rho') := v) updates;
        eval (body, rho')
    end
```

5.3.1 *Evaluating definitions*

As in Chapter 2, true definitions are evaluated by evaldef. This function takes a definition and an environment, and it returns a new environment and the interpreter's (string) response. (The C versions of evaldef in Chapters 1 and 2 *print* the response, but the ML code in this chapter is used not only for μScheme, but also for statically typed languages in Chapters 6 to 8. For those languages, it is better to *return* a response from evaluation, so the response from evaluation can be combined with a response from type checking.)

When a definition introduces a new name, that definition is evaluated in an environment that *already* includes the name being defined. If the name x is not already bound, the NotFound exception is handled, and x is bound to a fresh location that is initialized with an unspecified value.

311b. ⟨*definitions of* eval *and* evaldef *for μScheme* 309a⟩+≡ ◁ 309a 311c ▷

withNameBound : name * value ref env -> value ref env

```
fun withNameBound (x, rho) =
  (find (x, rho); rho)
  handle NotFound _ => bind (x, ref (unspecified ()), rho)
```

Given a VAL form with binding to name x and right-hand side e, evaldef first uses withNameBound to make sure x is bound to a location in the environment. It then evaluates e and stores its value in x's location. It also computes a response, which is usually the value. But if the definition binds a lambda expression, the response is instead the name x.

311c. ⟨*definitions of* eval *and* evaldef *for μScheme* 309a⟩+≡ ◁ 311b 312a ▷

evaldef : def * value ref env -> value ref env * string

```
fun evaldef (VAL (x, e), rho) =
      let val rho = withNameBound (x, rho)
          val v   = eval (e, rho)
          val _   = find (x, rho) := v
          val response = case e of LAMBDA _ => x
                                 | _ => valueString v
      in  (rho, response)
      end
```

As in Chapter 2, define is syntactic sugar for val with lambda.

312a. ⟨*definitions of* eval *and* evaldef *for μScheme* 309a⟩+≡ ◁311c 312b▷

```
  | evaldef (DEFINE (f, lambda), rho) =
      let val (xs, e) = lambda
      in  evaldef (VAL (f, LAMBDA lambda), rho)
      end
```


The EXP form doesn't bind a name; evaldef just evaluates the expression, binds the result to it, and responds with the value.

312b. ⟨*definitions of* eval *and* evaldef *for μScheme* 309a⟩+≡ ◁312a

```
  | evaldef (EXP e, rho) =
      let val v   = eval (e, rho)
          val rho = withNameBound ("it", rho)
          val _   = find ("it", rho) := v
      in  (rho, valueString v)
      end
```

The differences between VAL and EXP are subtle: for VAL, the semantics demands that the name be added to environment rho *before* evaluating expression e. For EXP, the name it isn't bound until *after* evaluating the first EXP form.

5.4 Defining and embedding primitives

μScheme primitives like + and cons have ML counterparts like + and PAIR. But the ML counterparts operate on ML values, and the μScheme versions must operate on μScheme values. Each μScheme primitive is implemented just as in Chapter 2 (chunk 161b): take μScheme values as arguments, project them to ML values, apply an ML primitive, and embed the ML result into μScheme. But the code is structured differently: instead of projecting arguments and embedding a result, I embed the *function*. Each primitive function is written with its own most natural ML type, then is embedded into the type of μScheme primitives: exp * value list -> value. The embedding takes care of the function's arguments and results. (Because no μScheme function ever acts as an ML function, a corresponding projection is not needed.)

The embedding for a function depends on the function's type. Each embedding is composed of other functions, which gradually "lift" a primitive function from its native ML type to type exp * value list -> value. For example, the primitive function + passes through these types:

- ML primitive + has type int * int -> int.
- The primitive is embedded into a function that operates on μScheme values; its type is now lifted to value * value -> value.
- The lifted function is embedded into a function that can be applied to a list of values; after this second lifing, its type is now value list -> value.
- Finally, the twice-lifted function is embedded into a function that is given not just a list of values but also the syntax of the expression in which the μScheme primitive appears; its final type is exp * value list -> value, which is the type of the primitive used in the evaluator.

Let's look at these lifting steps in reverse order, from last to first.

The final lifting step is given a function `f` of type `value list -> value`, and it produces a new function `inExp f` of type `exp * value list -> value`. The new function applies `f`, and if applying `f` raises the `RuntimeError` exception, it handles the exception, adds to the error message, and re-raises the exception.

313a. ⟨*utility functions for building primitives in μScheme* 313a⟩≡ (S382a) 313b ▷

```
fun inExp f =   inExp : (value list -> value) -> (exp * value list -> value)
  fn (e, vs) => f vs
                handle RuntimeError msg =>
                  raise RuntimeError ("in " ^ expString e ^ ", " ^ msg)
```


The middle lifting step is given a function `f` that takes one or two arguments of type `value` and returns a result of type `value`, and it produces a new function `unaryOp f` or `binaryOp f` of type `value list -> value`. The new function uses pattern matching to extract the expected number of arguments and pass them to `f`. If the number of arguments is unexpected, function `arityError` raises `RuntimeError`.

313b. ⟨*utility functions for building primitives in μScheme* 313a⟩+≡ (S382a) ◁ 313a 313c ▷

```
                unaryOp  : (value         -> value) -> (value list -> value)
                binaryOp : (value * value -> value) -> (value list -> value)
fun arityError n args =
  raise RuntimeError ("expected " ^ intString n ^
                      " but got " ^ intString (length args) ^ " arguments")
fun unaryOp  f = (fn [a]    => f a      | args => arityError 1 args)
fun binaryOp f = (fn [a, b] => f (a, b) | args => arityError 2 args)
```

Functions `unaryOp` and `binaryOp` help implement any μScheme primitive that is a "unary operator" or "binary operator."

The first lifting step is given a function like `+` that expects and returns ML integers, and it produces a new function `arithOp +` of type `value list -> value`. The anonymous function passed to `binaryOp` has type `value * value -> value`.

313c. ⟨*utility functions for building primitives in μScheme* 313a⟩+≡ (S382a) ◁ 313b 314a ▷

```
                              arithOp: (int * int -> int) -> (value list -> value)
fun arithOp f = binaryOp (fn (NUM n1, NUM n2) => NUM (f (n1, n2))
                           | (NUM n, v) => ⟨report v is not an integer 314b⟩
                           | (v, _)     => ⟨report v is not an integer 314b⟩
                         )
```

Now μScheme primitives like `+` and `*` can be defined by applying first `arithOp` and then `inExp` to their ML counterparts.

The μScheme primitives are organized into a list of (name, function) pairs, in Noweb code chunk ⟨*primitives for μScheme* `::` 313d⟩. Each primitive on the list has type `value list -> value`. In chunk S382a, each primitive is passed to `inExp`, and the results are used build μScheme's initial environment.[3] The list of primitives begins with these four elements:

313d. ⟨*primitives for μScheme* `::` 313d⟩≡ (S382a) 314c ▷

```
("+", arithOp op +  ) ::
("-", arithOp op -  ) ::
("*", arithOp op *  ) ::
("/", arithOp op div) ::
```

The ML keyword `op` converts an infix identifier to an ordinary value, so `arithOp op +` passes the value `+` (a binary function) to the function `arithOp`.

DEFINE	307a
eval	309a
evaldef	311c
EXP	307a
type exp	306
expString	S383b
find	305b
intString	S214c
LAMBDA	306
NUM	306
RuntimeError	S213b
VAL	307a
type value	306
valueString	307b
withNameBound	311b

[3] Actually, the list contains all the primitives except one: the `error` primitive, which must not be wrapped in `inExp`.

Primitives like < and null? return Booleans, so they can't be lifted by arithOp. For primitives like these, the first and middle lifting steps are performed by functions predOp, comparison, and intcompare.

314a. ⟨*utility functions for building primitives in μScheme* 313a⟩+≡ (S382a) ◁ 313c

```
predOp     : (value          -> bool) -> (value list -> value)
comparison : (value * value  -> bool) -> (value list -> value)
intcompare : (int   * int    -> bool) -> (value list -> value)
```

```
fun predOp f     = unaryOp  (embedBool o f)
fun comparison f = binaryOp (embedBool o f)
fun intcompare f = comparison (fn (NUM n1, NUM n2) => f (n1, n2)
                                | (NUM n, v) => ⟨report v is not an integer 314b⟩
                                | (v, _)     => ⟨report v is not an integer 314b⟩
                              )
```

314b. ⟨*report* v *is not an integer* 314b⟩≡ (313c 314a)

```
raise RuntimeError ("expected an integer, but got " ^ valueString v)
```

μScheme's primitive predicates are implemented by ML primitives (< and >), by function equalatoms (defined in Appendix O), and by anonymous functions.

314c. ⟨*primitives for μScheme* :: 313d⟩+≡ (S382a) ◁ 313d

```
("<", intcompare op <) ::
(">", intcompare op >) ::
("=", comparison equalatoms) ::
("null?",    predOp (fn (NIL     ) => true | _ => false)) ::
("boolean?", predOp (fn (BOOLV _) => true | _ => false)) ::
```

The remaining type predicates, the list primitives, and the printing primitives are defined in Appendix O.

5.5 Notable differences between ML and C

The ML interpreter presented in Sections 5.3 and 5.4 uses the same overall design as the C interpreters of Chapters 1 and 2. But the many small differences in the two languages add up to a different programming experience; the ML version is more compact and more reliable. The two experiences compare as follows:

- Both interpreters allocate mutable locations on the heap, which they operate on with C pointer syntax (*) or ML primitive functions (! and :=). The C code leaks memory like crazy; plugging *all* the leaks would require a garbage collector considerably more elaborate than the one in Chapter 4. ML ships with a comprehensive garbage collector built in.

- Both interpreters use the same abstraction to represent abstract syntax trees: a tagged sum of products. Thanks to the little data-description language of Chapter 1, the representations are even specified similarly. But C's unions are unsafe: making the alt tag consistent with the payload is up to the programmer. ML's algebraic data types guarantee consistency. The C code does offer one advantage, however: in the source code, the definitions of struct Value and struct Exp can appear separately. In the ML code, the definitions value and exp, because they are mutually recursive, must appear adjacent in the source code so they can be connected with and.

- Both interpreters manage run-time errors in the same way. An error may be detected and signaled anywhere; C code uses runerror, which calls longjmp (in C), and ML code uses raise. And in both interpreters, an error once detected is handled in a central place, using setjmp or handle, as described in the Supplement.

- Both interpreters use functions, like "length of a list" and "find a name in an environment," that could in principle be polymorphic. But only ML code can define a function that is actually polymorphic. The C code in Chapters 1 and 2 must define a new length function for every type of list and a new find function for every type of environment.

- C code can use `printf`, and it can even define new functions that resemble `printf`, like `print`. ML code has nothing comparable: because the ML type checker won't check the types of the arguments based on a format string, ML code can only print strings—so it must use string-conversion functions.

- To define primitives, both interpreters use first-order embedding and projection functions to embed and project numbers (`projectint32` and `mkNum` or `projectInt` and `embedInt`) and Booleans. But only the ML code can embed *functions*, using `binaryOp`, `intcompare`, and so on. And in ML, operations like / and `div` are functions, not syntax, so they can be embedded into μScheme directly. Their counterparts in C require significant "glue code."

5.6 FREE AND BOUND VARIABLES: DEEPER INTO μSCHEME

The ML implementation of μScheme is easier to modify than the C version. And no matter what mistakes you make, the ML code cannot dump core or fail with inexplicable pointer errors. These properties make ML a good vehicle for exploring techniques that are actually used to implement functional languages (Exercises 9 and 10, pages 324 and 325). These techniques rely on a crucial concept in programming languages: the distinction between *free* and *bound* variables.

When an expression e refers to a name y that is introduced outside of e, we say that y is *free* in e. Such names are called "free variables," even though "free names" would be more accurate. A variable in e that is introduced within e is a *bound* variable. For example, in the expression

```
(lambda (n) (+ 1 n))
```

the name `+` is a free variable, but `n` is a bound variable. Every variable that appears in an expression is either free or bound.

Each variable that appears in a definition is also free or bound. For example, in

```
(define map (f xs)
  (if (null? xs)
    '()
    (cons (f (car xs)) (map f (cdr xs)))))
```

the names `null?`, `cons`, `car`, and `cdr` are free, and the names `map`, `f`, and `xs` are bound. (And `if` is not a name; it is a *reserved word* that, like `if` in ML or C, marks a syntactic form.)

Free variables enable compilers to represent closures efficiently. According to the operational semantics, evaluating a `lambda` expression captures the *entire* environment ρ_c:

$$\frac{x_1, \ldots, x_n \text{ all distinct}}{\langle \text{LAMBDA}(\langle x_1, \ldots, x_n \rangle, e), \rho_c, \sigma \rangle \Downarrow \langle (\!| \text{LAMBDA}(\langle x_1, \ldots, x_n \rangle, e), \rho_c |\!), \sigma \rangle}. \qquad \text{(MKCLOSURE)}$$

Does the closure really need *all* the information in ρ_c? How is ρ_c used?

$$\frac{\begin{array}{c}\ell_1,\ldots,\ell_n \notin \operatorname{dom}\sigma_n \text{ (and all distinct)}\\ \langle e,\rho,\sigma\rangle \Downarrow \langle (\!|\text{LAMBDA}(\langle x_1,\ldots,x_n\rangle,e_c),\rho_c|\!),\sigma_0\rangle\\ \langle e_1,\rho,\sigma_0\rangle \Downarrow \langle v_1,\sigma_1\rangle\\ \vdots\\ \langle e_n,\rho,\sigma_{n-1}\rangle \Downarrow \langle v_n,\sigma_n\rangle\\ \langle e_c,\rho_c\{x_1\mapsto\ell_1,\ldots,x_n\mapsto\ell_n\},\sigma_n\{\ell_1\mapsto v_1,\ldots,\ell_n\mapsto v_n\}\rangle \Downarrow \langle v,\sigma'\rangle\end{array}}{\langle \text{APPLY}(e,e_1,\ldots,e_n),\rho,\sigma\rangle \Downarrow \langle v,\sigma'\rangle} \quad (\text{APPLYCLOSURE})$$

Environment ρ_c is used only to evaluate the body of the LAMBDA. So the MKCLOSURE rule need not store all of ρ_c—it needs only those bindings that refer to variables that are free in the LAMBDA expression (Exercise 9). You can use this fact to make the interpreter faster (Exercise 10).

To do Exercises 9 and 10, you need a precise definition of what a free variable is. And precision calls for formal judgments and proofs. The judgment form for identifying free variables in an expression is $\boxed{y \in \text{fv}(e)}$. The notation $\text{fv}(e)$ refers to the set of all variables that appear free in e, but constructing the set is not necessary, and the judgment $y \in \text{fv}(e)$ should be pronounced as "y appears free in e." The judgment may be provable in different ways for each syntactic form.

A literal expression has no free variables. Formally speaking, no judgment of the form $y \in \text{fv}(\text{LITERAL}(v))$ can ever be proved, so there is no rule for literals.

A lone variable x is always free.

$$\frac{}{x \in \text{fv}(\text{VAR}(x))}$$

A variable is free in a SET expression if it is assigned to or if it is free in the right-hand side. So a SET expression has two proof rules:

$$\frac{}{x \in \text{fv}(\text{SET}(x,e))} \qquad \frac{y \in \text{fv}(e)}{y \in \text{fv}(\text{SET}(x,e))}.$$

A variable is free in an IF expression if and only if it is free in one of the subexpressions:

$$\frac{y \in \text{fv}(e_1)}{y \in \text{fv}(\text{IF}(e_1,e_2,e_3))} \qquad \frac{y \in \text{fv}(e_2)}{y \in \text{fv}(\text{IF}(e_1,e_2,e_3))} \qquad \frac{y \in \text{fv}(e_3)}{y \in \text{fv}(\text{IF}(e_1,e_2,e_3))}.$$

A variable is also free in a WHILE expression if and only if it is free in one of the subexpressions:

$$\frac{y \in \text{fv}(e_1)}{y \in \text{fv}(\text{WHILE}(e_1,e_2))} \qquad \frac{y \in \text{fv}(e_2)}{y \in \text{fv}(\text{WHILE}(e_1,e_2))}.$$

And the same for BEGIN:

$$\frac{y \in \text{fv}(e_i)}{y \in \text{fv}(\text{BEGIN}(e_1,\ldots,e_n))}.$$

A variable is free in an application if and only if it is free in the function or in one of the arguments:

$$\frac{y \in \text{fv}(e)}{y \in \text{fv}(\text{APPLY}(e,e_1,\ldots,e_n))} \qquad \frac{y \in \text{fv}(e_i)}{y \in \text{fv}(\text{APPLY}(e,e_1,\ldots,e_n))}.$$

Finally, an interesting case! A variable is free in a LAMBDA expression if it is free in the body and it is *not* one of the arguments:

$$\frac{y \in \text{fv}(e) \qquad y \notin \{x_1, \ldots, x_n\}}{y \in \text{fv}(\text{LAMBDA}(\langle x_1, \ldots, x_n \rangle, e))}.$$

The various LET forms require care. A variable is free in an ordinary LET if it is free in the right-hand side of any binding, or if it is both free in the body and not bound by the LET.

$$\frac{y \in \text{fv}(e_i)}{y \in \text{fv}(\text{LET}(\langle x_1, e_1, \ldots, x_n, e_n \rangle, e))} \qquad \frac{y \in \text{fv}(e) \qquad y \notin \{x_1, \ldots, x_n\}}{y \in \text{fv}(\text{LET}(\langle x_1, e_1, \ldots, x_n, e_n \rangle, e))}$$

The similarity between the second LET rule and the LAMBDA rule shows a kinship between LET and LAMBDA.

The rules for LETREC are almost identical to the rules for LET, except that in a LETREC, the bound names x_i are never free:

$$\frac{y \in \text{fv}(e_i) \qquad y \notin \{x_1, \ldots, x_n\}}{y \in \text{fv}(\text{LETREC}(\langle x_1, e_1, \ldots, x_n, e_n \rangle, e))},$$

$$\frac{y \in \text{fv}(e) \qquad y \notin \{x_1, \ldots, x_n\}}{y \in \text{fv}(\text{LETREC}(\langle x_1, e_1, \ldots, x_n, e_n \rangle, e))}.$$

As usual, a LETSTAR rule would be a nuisance to write directly. Instead, I treat a LETSTAR expression as a set of nested LET expressions, each containing just one binding. And an empty LETSTAR behaves just like its body.

$$\frac{y \in \text{fv}(\text{LET}(\langle x_1, e_1 \rangle, \text{LETSTAR}(\langle x_2, e_2, \ldots, x_n, e_n \rangle, e)))}{y \in \text{fv}(\text{LETSTAR}(\langle x_1, e_1, \ldots, x_n, e_n \rangle, e))}$$

$$\frac{y \in \text{fv}(e)}{y \in \text{fv}(\text{LETSTAR}(\langle\rangle, e))}$$

5.7 SUMMARY

By exploiting algebraic data types, pattern matching, higher-order functions, and exceptions, we can make interpreters that are simpler, smaller, easier to read, more reliable, and more flexible than interpreters we can write in C.

5.7.1 *Key words and phrases*

ALGEBRAIC DATA TYPE A representation defined by a set of VALUE CONSTRUCTORS. Every value of the type is made by using or applying one of the type's value constructors. An algebraic data type is defined with the keyword `datatype`. Mutually recursive algebraic data types are defined with an initial `datatype`, and individual definitions are separated by keyword `and`.

BOUND VARIABLE A variable introduced by a function definition or other construct and whose meaning is independent of any appearance of its name outside the construct. Formal parameters of functions are bound variables, as are variables introduced by `let` forms. Variables that aren't bound are FREE. The name of a bound variable can be changed without changing the meaning of the program, provided the new name does not conflict with any variable that is free in the scope of the binding.

CLAUSAL DEFINITION A syntactic form of definition that combines a function definition and a PATTERN MATCH. It is introduced with the keyword `fun`, and arms of the pattern are separated by vertical bars. Unlike an ordinary pattern match that is used with `case` or `handle`, the pattern match in a clausal definition begins with the name of the function being defined.

A clausal definition is the idiomatic way to define an ML function that begins with a pattern match. It is preferred over a function whose body is a `case` expression.

EMBEDDING A mapping from METALANGUAGE values to OBJECT-LANGUAGE values. The mapping always succeeds. For example, any ML `int` can be mapped to a μScheme value. An embedded value can be mapped back to the metalanguage by a PROJECTION.

EXCEPTION A way of signaling a named error condition. Exceptions replace C's `longjmp`. An exception acts like a VALUE CONSTRUCTOR: it can stand by itself, or it can carry one or more values. In ML, evaluating an expression may *raise* an exception, produce a value, or cause a checked run-time error.

EXCEPTION HANDLER Code that is executed when an exception is raised. Exception handlers replace C's `setjmp`. An exception handler may include a PATTERN MATCH that determines which exceptions are handled. Our interpreter's primary exception handlers are associated with the GENERIC READ-EVAL-PRINT LOOP.

EXHAUSTIVE PATTERN MATCH A pattern match that is guaranteed to match every possible value. Pattern matches should be exhaustive. If you write one that is not exhaustive, the ML compiler is required to warn you. You should deploy compiler options which turn that warning into an error.

FREE VARIABLE A variable that is defined outside the function in which it appears. The meaning of a free variable depends on context. The idea of free variable generalizes beyond function definitions to include any language construct that introduces new variables, like a `let` expression. Variables that aren't free are BOUND.

INTERACTIVITY A term I coined to describe the behavior of the READ-EVAL-PRINT LOOP. Interactivity determines whether the loop *prompts* the user before reading input, and whether it *prints* after evaluating a definition.

LIST CONSTRUCTOR Special syntax for writing lists and list patterns in ML. Instead of using cons (written `::`) and `nil`, a list constructor uses square brackets containing zero or more elements separated by commas. If the list constructor appears as an expression, each element is an expression. If the list constructor appears as a PATTERN, each element is a pattern.

METALANGUAGE In an interpreter, the language in which the interpreter is implemented. In a semantics, the language used for semantic description. A metalanguage describes an OBJECT LANGUAGE. In this chapter, the metalanguage is Standard ML. (The ML in Standard ML stands for "metalanguage.")

MUTABLE REFERENCE CELL A location allocated on the heap. In ML, variables stand for values, not for locations, so the only way to get a location is to allocate a mutable reference cell. A reference cell containing a value of type τ has type τ `ref`. It is created by primitive function `ref`, which acts like μScheme's `allocate` function (page 154). It is dereferenced by primitive function `!`, which acts like C's dereferencing operator `*`. It is mutated by the infix primitive function `:=`; the ML expression p `:=` e is equivalent to the C expression `*`p = e.

MUTUAL RECURSION (CODE) Two or more functions, each of which can call the other. In ML, many mutually recursive functions are defined by nesting the definition of one inside the definition of the other. When both have to be called from outside, they can be defined at the same level using keywords `fun` and `and`. Mutually recursive functions can also be defined in C style, using mutable reference cells.

MUTUAL RECURSION (DATA) Two or more ALGEBRAIC DATA TYPES, each of which can contain a value of another. Defined using `datatype` and keyword `and`; in ML, the `and` always signifies mutual recursion. In most languages in this book, types `exp` and `value` are mutually recursive: an `exp` can contain a literal `value`, and a value might be a closure, which contains an `exp`.

OBJECT LANGUAGE In an interpreter, the language being implemented. In a semantics, the language being described. An object language is described by a METALANGUAGE. In this chapter, the object language is μScheme.

PATTERN A variable, which matches anything, or a VALUE CONSTRUCTOR applied to zero or more patterns, which matches only a value created with that constructor. Or a tuple of patterns.

PATTERN MATCHING The computational process by which a value of ALGEBRAIC DATA TYPE is observed. A pattern match comprises an expression being observed, called the SCRUTINEE, and a list of *arms*, each of which has a PATTERN on the left and an expression on the right. The *first* pattern that matches the scrutinee is chosen, and the corresponding right-hand side is evaluated. Pattern matching may be used in a `case` expression, in an EXCEPTION HANDLER, or in a CLAUSAL DEFINITION. Pattern matching is explained at length in Chapter 8.

POLYMORPHIC TYPE A type with one or more TYPE VARIABLES. A value or function with a polymorphic type may be used with any type replacing the type variable. For example in type `'a env`, the `'a` may stand for `value ref`, which gives us environments that store MUTABLE REFERENCE CELLS.

PROJECTION A mapping from OBJECT-LANGUAGE values to METALANGUAGE values. The mapping might fail. For example, the μScheme value `3` cannot meaningfully be projected into an ML function. A projection is the inverse of an EMBEDDING; an attempt to project an embedded value should recover the original value. And some projections, like `bool` in chunk 308b, always succeed—in a Boolean context, every μScheme value is meaningful.

READ-EVAL-PRINT LOOP The control center of an interactive interpreter. It *reads* concrete syntax and parses it into abstract syntax, it *evaluates* the abstract syntax, and it *prints* the result. If an EXCEPTION is raised during evaluation, the exception is handled in the read-eval-print loop, and looping continues. The read-eval-print loop in Appendix O is reused throughout this book; in every language, it handles extended definitions. True definitions are handled by function `processDef`, which is different in each interpreter.

REDUNDANT PATTERN An arm in a PATTERN MATCH that is guaranteed never to be evaluated, because any values it might match are matched by preceding patterns. A redundant pattern match is a sign of a bug in your code—perhaps a misspelling of a VALUE CONSTRUCTOR. Most ML compilers warn you of redundant patterns. You should deploy compiler options which turn that warning into an error.

SHORT-CIRCUIT CONDITIONAL A conditional operator that evaluates its second operand only when necessary. In Standard ML, the short-circuit conditionals are `andalso` and `orelse`. Keyword `and`, which looks like it should be a conditional, actually means mutual recursion. Thanks, Professor Milner.

TYPE ABBREVIATION An abbreviation for a type, defined with keyword `type`. May take one or more TYPE VARIABLES as parameters. When there are no type parameters, a type abbreviation acts just like C's `typedef`.

TYPE VARIABLE In ML, a name that begins with a quote mark, like `'a`. Stands for an unknown type. When used in an ML type, a type variable makes the type POLYMORPHIC.

VALUE CONSTRUCTOR A name that either constitutes a value of ALGEBRAIC DATA TYPE, like `nil` or `NONE`, or that produces a value of algebraic data type when applied to a value or a tuple of values, like `::` or `SOME`.

5.7.2 *Further reading*

To learn Standard ML, you have several good choices. The most comprehensive published book is by Paulson (1996), but it may be more than you need. The much shorter book by Felleisen and Friedman (1997) introduces ML using an idiosyncratic, dialectical style. If you can learn from that style, the information is good. If you are a proficient C programmer, you might like the book by Ullman (1997). This book has helped many C programmers make a transition to ML, but it also has a problem: the ML that it teaches is far from idiomatic.

There are also several good unpublished resources. Harper's (1986) introduction is short, sweet, and easy to follow, but it is for an older version of Standard ML. More recently, Harper (2011) has released an unfinished textbook on programming in Standard ML; it is up to date with the language, but the style is less congenial to beginners. Tofte (2009) presents "tips" on Standard ML, which I characterize as a 20-page quick-reference card. You probably can't get by on the "tips" alone, but when you are working at the computer, they are useful.

5.8 EXERCISES

The exercises are summarized in Table 5.3 on page 321. The highlights encourage you to extend or improve μScheme:

- In Exercise 2, you extend μScheme so a function can take an unbounded number of arguments.
- In Exercise 6, you develop a different technique for using ML functions as μScheme primitives: instead of applying functions to the ML functions, you *compose* each ML function with an embedding function and a projection function. It's a very type-oriented way of building an interpreter.
- In Exercise 10, you use facts about free variables to change the representation of closures, and you measure to see if the change matters.

Exercises 2 and 10 are very satisfying.

Table 5.3: Synopsis of all the exercises, with most relevant sections

Exercises	*Sections*	*Notes*
1 and 2	5.2, 5.3	Working with syntax and semantics: add `cond`, support variadic functions.
3 to 6	5.3, 5.4	μScheme closures represented as ML functions; embedding and projection functions.
7 and 8	1.7, 5.2	Derivations of operational semantics represented as ML data structures.
9 and 10	5.6	Prove that closures use only free variables, and use that proof to improve the implementation (§5.3).

5.8.1 *Retrieval practice and other short questions*

A. What's one way to produce an ML value of type `name * int`?

B. What ML values inhabit the type `(name * int) list`?

C. In type `'a env`, what can the `'a` stand for?

D. What are `[]` and `::`? How are they pronounced?

E. In ML, any two-argument function can be defined as `infix`. Functions `+` and `*` you know. What do functions `@` and `^` do?

F. From function `bind`, what species of value is produced by the ML expression `(name, v) :: rho`?

G. What μScheme definition form corresponds to ML's `fun`?

H. Why is ML's definition of `find` split into two clauses? How does the ML evaluator decide which clause to execute? What does each clause do?

I. During evaluation, what would cause exception `BindListLength` to be raised?

J. In this chapter, what's the object language and what's the metalanguage?

K. Can an ML value of type `int` always be embedded into a μScheme `value`? If so, how? If not, why not?

L. Can a μScheme `value` always be projected into an ML value of type `int`? If so, how? If not, why not?

M. Can an ML function of type `int * int -> int` always be embedded into a μScheme primitive of type `exp * value list -> value`? If so, how? If not, why not?

N. Suppose you want to change the semantics of μScheme so that in `if` expressions and `while` loops, the number zero is treated as falsehood, as in JavaScript. What interpreter code do you change and how?

O. In chunk ⟨*apply closure* `clo` *to* `args` 310c⟩, explain what `bindList` constructs and why.

P. In expression `(lambda (n) (+ 1 n))`, what names are free?

Q. In expression `(lambda (x) (f (g x)))`, what names are free?

R. In expression `(lambda (f g) (lambda (x) (f (g x))))`, what names are free?

S. Besides `lambda`, what other syntactic form of expression can introduce new names that are bound in that expression?

5.8.2 *Working with syntax and semantics*

1. *Syntactic sugar for* `cond`. Section 2.13.2 (page 163) describes syntactic sugar for Lisp's original conditional expression: the `cond` form. Add a `cond` form to μScheme. Start with this code:

   322. ⟨*rows added to ML μScheme's* `exptable` *in exercises* **⟦prototype⟧** 322⟩≡

   ```
   desugarCond : (exp * exp) list -> exp
   ```

   ```
   , ("(cond ([q a] ...))",
      let fun desugarCond qas = raise LeftAsExercise "desugar cond"
          val qa = bracket ("[question answer]", pair <$> exp <*> exp)
      in  desugarCond <$> many qa
      end
     )
   ```

2. *Variadic functions.* Extend μScheme to support functions with a variable number of arguments. Do so by giving the name `...` (three dots) special significance when it appears as the last formal parameter in a lambda. For example:

   ```
   -> (val f (lambda (x y ...)) (+ x (+ y (foldl + 0 ...)))
   -> (f 1 2 3 4 5) ; in f, rho = { x |-> 1, y |-> 2, ... |-> '(3 4 5) }
   15
   ```

   In this example, if `f` gets fewer than two arguments, it is a checked run-time error. If `f` gets at least two arguments, any additional arguments are placed into an ordinary list, and the list is used to initialize the location of the formal parameteter associated with `...`.

   (a) Implement this new feature. Begin by changing the definition of `lambda` on page 306 to

   ```
   and lambda = name list * { varargs : bool } * exp
   ```

   Now recompile; type-error messages will tell you what other code you have to change.

   For the parser, you may find the following function useful:

   ```
   fun newLambda (formals, body) =
      case reverse formals
        of "..." :: fs' => LAMBDA (reverse fs', {varargs=true},
                                   body)
         | _            => LAMBDA (formals, {varargs=false}, body)
   ```

   This function has type

   ```
   name list * exp -> name list * { varargs : bool } * exp,
   ```

   and it is designed for you to adapt old syntax to new syntax; just drop it into the parser wherever `LAMBDA` is used.

   (b) As a complement to the varargs lambda, write a new `apply` primitive such that

   ```
   (apply f '(1 2 3))
   ```

   is equivalent to

   ```
   (f 1 2 3)
   ```

   Sadly, you can't use `PRIMITIVE` for this; you'll have to invent a new kind of thing that has access to the internal `eval`.

(c) Demonstrate these utilities by writing a higher-order μScheme function cons-logger that counts cons calls in a private variable. It should operate as follows:

```
-> (val cl (cons-logger))
-> (val log-cons (car cl))
-> (val conses-logged (cdr cl))
-> (conses-logged)
0
-> (log-cons f e1 e2 ... en) ; returns (f e1 e2 ... en),
                             ; incrementing private counter
                             ; whenever cons is called
-> (conses-logged)
99  ; or whatever else is the number of times cons is called
    ; during the call to log-cons
```


(d) Rewrite the APPLYCLOSURE rule (page 316) to account for the new abstract syntax and behavior.

5.8.3 *Higher-order functions, embedding, and projection*

3. *μScheme closures represented as ML functions.* Change the evaluation of lambda expressions so that evaluating a `LAMBDA` produces an ML function of type `exp * value list -> value`. (The `exp` parameter should be ignored.) That's the same type as a primitive function, so with this change, evaluating a `LAMBDA` can produce a `PRIMITIVE`, not a `CLOSURE`. On the strength of this trick, rename `PRIMITIVE` to `FUNCTION`, and eliminate `CLOSURE` from the interpreter.

   Identify the advantages of this simplification. Identify the drawbacks.

4. *Embedding and projection for lists.*

   (a) Define function `projectList` of type `value -> value list`. If projection fails, `projectList` should raise the `RuntimeError` exception.

   (b) Rewrite function `embedList` to use `foldr`.

5. *Reusable embedding for integer functions.* In Section 5.4, functions `arithOp` and `comparison` use the same code fragment for embedding functions that consume integers. Break this embedding out into its own function, `intBinary` of type `(int * int -> 'a) -> (value * value -> 'a)`. Rewrite `arithOp` and `comparison` to use `intBinary`.

<$>	S249a
<*>	S247b
bracket	S264a
type exp	306
exp	S387b
LeftAsExercise	S213b
many	S253a
pair	S249b

6. *Embedding by composing first-order functions.* In Section 5.4 (page 312), the primitive functions are defined by applying higher-order embedding functions to ML primitives. In this exercise, you instead compose the ML primitives on the right with first-order projection functions and on the left with first-order embedding functions. Embedding functions should be total; that is, application of an embedding function should always succeed. But projection functions can be partial; application of a projection function can fail, in which case it should raise `RuntimeError`.

   (a) Define a projection function of type `value list -> value * value` and another of type `value list -> value`.

   (b) Define a projection function of type `value * value -> int * int`

   (c) Find an embedding function of type `int -> value`, or if you can't find one, define one.

(d) Find an embedding function of type `bool -> value`, or if you can't find one, define one.

(e) Using your embedding and projection functions, redefine the μScheme primitives using function composition. For example, define μScheme's `cons` by composing ML's `PAIR` on the right with projection functions and on the left with embedding functions.

For any primitive, the projections used on its right should depend only on its argument type, and the embeddings used on its left should depend only on its result type.

Continue to use `inExp` to build `initialBasis`.

5.8.4 *Proofs as data*

7. *Representation of judgments and derivations in ML.*

   (a) Devise a representation, in Standard ML, of the judgments of the operational semantics for μScheme.

   (b) Devise a representation, in Standard ML, of derivations that use the operational semantics of μScheme.

   (c) Change the `eval` function of the μScheme interpreter to return a *derivation* instead of a value.

   You may wish to revisit the material on proofs and derivations in Section 1.7 (page 55).

8. *Validity of derivations.* Using the representation of derivations in item 7(b), write a *proof checker* that tells whether a given tree represents a valid derivation.

5.8.5 *Free variables*

9. *Proof: A closure needs only the free variables of its code part.* In this exercise, you prove that the evaluation of an expression doesn't depend on arbitrary bindings in the environment, but only on the bindings of the expression's free variables.

   If X is a set of variables, we can ask what happens to an environment ρ if we remove the bindings of all the names that are *not* in the set X. The modified environment is written $\rho|_X$, and it is called the *restriction* of ρ to X. You will prove, by structural induction on derivations, that if $\langle e, \rho, \sigma \rangle \Downarrow \langle v, \sigma \rangle$, then $\langle e, \rho|_{\mathrm{fv}(e)}, \sigma \rangle \Downarrow \langle v, \sigma \rangle$. (This theorem also justifies the syntactic sugar for short-circuit `||` described in Section 2.13.3 on page 164. And it is related to a similar theorem from Exercise 52 on page 195 in Chapter 2.)

   To structure the proof, I recommend you introduce a definition and a lemma.

   - To account of the idea of "extra" or "unneeded" variables, define the relation $\rho \sqsubseteq \rho'$ (pronounced "ρ' *extends* ρ" or "ρ' *refines* ρ"). It means that the domain of ρ' contains the domain of ρ, and on their common domain, they agree: $\operatorname{dom} \rho \subseteq \operatorname{dom} \rho'$ and $\forall x \in \operatorname{dom} \rho : \rho(x) = \rho'(x)$.
   - Prove this lemma: If $X \subseteq X' \subseteq \operatorname{dom} \rho$, then $\rho|_X \sqsubseteq \rho|_{X'} \sqsubseteq \rho$.

These tools are useful because except for LET forms and LAMBDA expressions, if an expression e has a subexpression e_i, then $\text{fv}(e_i) \subseteq \text{fv}(e)$.

Now prove, by structural induction on derivations, that if $\langle e, \rho, \sigma \rangle \Downarrow \langle v, \sigma \rangle$, then $\langle e, \rho|_{\text{fv}(e)}, \sigma \rangle \Downarrow \langle v, \sigma \rangle$. A reasonable induction hypothesis might be that if that if $\langle e, \rho, \sigma \rangle \Downarrow \langle v, \sigma \rangle$, and if $\rho|_{\text{fv}(e)} \sqsubseteq \rho'$, then $\langle e, \rho', \sigma \rangle \Downarrow \langle v, \sigma \rangle$.

10. *Smaller closures and their performance.* The result proved in Exercise 9 can be used to optimize code. In chunk 310a, a LAMBDA expression is evaluated by capturing a full environment ρ.

    (a) Modify the code to capture a restricted environment that contains only the free variables of the LAMBDA expression. That is, instead of allocating the closure $(\!| \text{LAMBDA}(\langle x_1, \ldots, x_n \rangle, e), \rho |\!)$, allocate the smaller closure $(\!| \text{LAMBDA}(\langle x_1, \ldots, x_n \rangle, e), \rho|_X |\!)$, where the set X is defined by $X = \text{fv}(\text{LAMBDA}(\langle x_1, \ldots, x_n \rangle, e))$.

    (b) Measure the modified interpreter to see if the optimization makes a difference. As a sufficiently long-running computation, you could try a quadratic sort of a very long list, or an exponential count of the number of distinct subsequences of an integer sequence that sum to zero. Or you could run a computation using the metacircular evaluator in Section E.1.

Chapter 6 contents

Type systems for Impcore and μScheme

6

But in a typed language a separate sort function must be defined for each type, while in a typeless language syntactic checking is lost. We suggest that a solution to this problem is to permit types themselves to be passed as a special kind of parameter, whose usage is restricted in a way which permits the syntactic checking of type correctness.

John Reynolds, *Towards a Theory of Type Structure*

The real success of a formal technique is when it is used ubiquitously without the designer being aware of it (e.g., type systems).

Arvind, IFIP Working Group 2.8, June 17, 2008

The languages of the preceding chapters, Impcore and μScheme, are *dynamically typed*, which is to say that many faults, such as applying a function to the wrong number of arguments, adding non-numbers, or applying `car` to a symbol, are not detected until run time. Dynamically typed languages are very flexible, but on any given execution, a fault might surprise you; even a simple mistake like typing `cdr` when you meant `car` might not have been detected on previous runs. And using `cdr` instead of `car` doesn't cause a fault right away: `cdr` simply returns a list in a context where you were expecting an element. But if, for example, you then try to add 1 to the result of applying `cdr`, that is a *checked run-time error*: adding 1 to a list instead of a number. To rule out such errors at compile time, without having to run the faulty code, a programming language can use *static typing*.

Static typing is implemented by a compile-time analysis, which decides if the analyzed code is OK to run. All such analyses build on the same two approaches: *type checking* and *type inference*. In type checking, every variable and formal parameter is annotated with a type, which restricts the values that the variable or parameter may have at run time. Type checking is used in such languages as Ada, Algol, C, C++, Go, Java, Modula-3, Pascal, and Rust. In type inference, also called type reconstruction, variables and parameters need not be annotated; instead, each variable or parameter is given a type by an algorithm, which looks at how the variable or parameter is used—the types are reconstructed from the code. Type inference is used in such languages as Haskell, Hope, Miranda, OCaml, Standard ML, and TypeScript. In both approaches, the decision about whether it is OK to run a program is made according to the rules of a language-dependent *type system*.

Effective types do much more than just rule out programs that might commit run-time errors; types also act as documentation—the more expressive the type system, the better the documentation. In a truly expressive system, the name and type of a function often suffice to show what the function is supposed to do.

Type systems, type checking, and type inference can be used in many ways. One of the most effective uses is to help guarantee *safety*. In a safe language, meaningless operations (adding non-numbers, dereferencing a null pointer, and so on) are either ruled out or are detected and reported. Although safety can be guaranteed by checking every operation at run time—as in Impcore, μScheme, and full Scheme—a good static type system performs most checks at compile time. A simple static type system can guarantee properties like these:

- Numbers are added only to numbers.
- Every function receives the correct number of arguments.
- Only Booleans are used in `if` expressions.
- Primitives `car` and `cdr` are applied only to lists.

When these properties are guaranteed, potentially meaningless operations are reported to the programmer right away, before a program is shipped to its users. And the implementations of addition, function call, and `if` don't have to check their operands at run time.

To guarantee safety, a type system must be crafted such that if it accepts a program, its rules guarantee that no meaningless operations can be executed. The guarantee is established by a *type-soundness theorem*, an idea so popular that it has its own slogan: "well-typed programs don't go wrong." The slogan is lovely, but not a cure-all; "going wrong" has a precise, technical meaning, which is usually narrow. For example, "going wrong" does not typically include unwanted behaviors like these:

- A number is divided by zero.
- The `car` or `cdr` primitive is applied to an *empty* list.
- A reference to an element of an array falls outside the bounds of that array.

These misbehaviors *can* be ruled out by a static type analysis, but the types get complicated, so they often aren't. Most general-purpose languages keep their types simple, and they guarantee safety by supplementing the static type system with run-time checks for errors like division by zero or array access out of bounds.

A safe language shouldn't put the programmer in a straitjacket. When a type system is overly restrictive, programmers complain, often using slang terms like "strong typing." And restrictive type systems can make it hard to reuse code. For example, Pascal's type system notoriously made it impossible to write a function capable of sorting arrays of different *lengths*. As another example, in Chapters 1 and 2, C's type system requires a distinct set of list functions for each possible list type, even though the functions defined on different types have identical bodies. Such duplication can be avoided, while maintaining safety and type checking, by using a *polymorphic* type system, like the one described in Section 6.6 of this chapter. Polymorphic type systems provide abstractions that can be parameterized by types; one example of such an abstraction is the C++ template.

Or restrictions can be dodged by using *unsafe* language features, like casts to and from `void *` in C. Unsafe features are useful in situations like these:

- You want to write a program that manipulates memory directly, like a device driver or a garbage collector. Such a program would ideally be safe, but how best to make such a thing safe—say, by combining a sophisticated type system with a formal proof of correctness—is a topic of ongoing research.

- You want a relatively simple type system and you don't want to pay overhead for run-time checks. For example, you like the simplicity of C, and you love that casting a pointer from one type to another costs nothing. And although casts are unsafe in general, you've convinced yourself that *yours* are safe.

Even in a language with unsafe features, static typing is useful: types document the code, and they can prevent many run-time errors, even if a few slip through. The ones that slip through are called *unchecked* run-time errors—it's those errors that make a language unsafe. The best designs allow unsafe features only in limited contexts; to see this done well, study Modula-3 (Nelson 1991).

Type systems are highly developed, and in the next four chapters you will learn how they work and how to use them effectively. In this chapter, you will learn about type systems and type checking. You will study not one language but two: Typed Impcore and Typed μScheme. Typed Impcore is straightforward; it models the restrictive type systems of such languages as Pascal and C. Typed Impcore introduces type systems and serves as an uncomfortably restrictive example. Typed μScheme is more ambitious; although its design starts from μScheme, it ends up requiring so many type annotations it feels very different. Typed μScheme introduces polymorphism and serves as an eye-opening example.

Typed μScheme is powerful, but its explicit annotations make it unpleasant to write. This unpleasantness is relieved by the more advanced type systems described in Chapters 7 to 9. Chapter 7 describes nano-ML. Nano-ML eliminates annotations, and yet it provides most of the polymorphism that Typed μScheme enjoys. It does so by using the *Hindley-Milner type system*, which defines a form of polymorphism that can be inferred. The Hindley-Milner type system forms the core of many of today's innovative, statically typed languages, including Standard ML, Haskell, OCaml, Agda, Idris, and many others. It works most effectively when coupled with user-defined algebraic data types, which are the main idea of Chapter 8.

Chapter 9 presents a different alternative to Typed μScheme: Molecule. Like Typed μScheme, Molecule uses annotations, but the annotations that direct polymorphism are applied to entire modules, not to individual functions. The resulting language provides the explicit control you get with Typed μScheme, without the notational burden.

6.1 TYPED IMPCORE: A STATICALLY TYPED IMPERATIVE CORE

A type system finds errors that might otherwise be hard to detect. (A type system may also help determine how values are represented and where variables can be stored, but such topics are beyond the scope of this book.) A type system worth studying should therefore be coupled with a language that provides ample opportunities to commit detectable errors—and that is simple enough to learn easily. Impcore is suitably simple, but the only readily detectable error is to pass the wrong number of arguments to a function. To create a few more opportunities for detectable errors, I have designed *Typed Impcore*:

- A value may be an *integer*, a *Boolean*, an *array* of values, or *unit* (page 334). Now you can try to use the wrong species of value.
- Every variable and expression must have a *type* that is known at compile time. The types of some variables, such as the formal parameters of functions, are written down explicitly, much as they are in C and Java. Precise, formal rules determine whether an expression has a type and what the type is.
- The typing rules are implemented by a *type checker*. The type checker permits a definition to be evaluated only if all its expressions have types. The type checker I present in this chapter checks only integer and Boolean types; extending it to check arrays is left to you (Exercise 18).

```
def       ::= exp
            | (use file-name)
            | (val variable-name exp)
            | (define type function-name (formals) exp)
            | unit-test

unit-test ::= (check-expect exp exp)
            | (check-assert exp)
            | (check-error exp)
            | (check-type-error def)
            | (check-function-type function ({type} -> type))

exp       ::= literal
            | variable-name
            | (set variable-name exp)
            | (if exp exp exp)
            | (while exp exp)
            | (begin {exp})
            | (function-name {exp})

formals   ::= {[variable-name : type]}

type      ::= int | bool | unit | (array type)

literal   ::= numeral
```

Figure 6.1: Concrete syntax of Typed Impcore

- Impcore's type system is *sound* (Exercise 26), which means informally that in *every* execution, at *every* point in the program, when an expression produces a value, that value is consistent with the expression's type. Type soundness ensures that if a program passes the type checker, it does not suffer from type errors at run time.

Typed Impcore is presented in two stages: first the integer and Boolean parts, then (Section 6.3) arrays.

6.1.1 *Concrete syntax of Typed Impcore*

Typed Impcore has the concrete syntax shown in Figure 6.1. Unlike untyped Impcore, Typed Impcore requires that the argument and result types of functions be declared explicitly. Types are written using new syntax; in addition to Impcore's definitions (*def*) and expressions (*exp*), Typed Impcore includes a syntactic category of types (*type*).

Explicit types are needed only in function definitions:

330. ⟨*transcript* 330⟩≡ 331a ▷

```
-> (define int add1 ([n : int]) (+ n 1))
add1 : (int -> int)
-> (add1 4)
5 : int
-> (define int double ([n : int]) (+ n n))
double : (int -> int)
-> (double 4)
8 : int
```

Types provide good documentation, and to document a function's type in a testable way, Typed Impcore adds a new unit-test form, check-function-type:

331a. ⟨*transcript* 330⟩+≡ ◁330 331b▷

```
-> (check-function-type add1   (int -> int))
-> (check-function-type double (int -> int))
```

Because unit tests are not run until the end of a file, a function's type test can—and should—be placed *before* its definition.

331b. ⟨*transcript* 330⟩+≡ ◁331a 331c▷

```
-> (check-function-type positive? (int -> bool))
-> (define bool positive? ([n : int]) (> n 0))
```

Unlike C, Typed Impcore accepts only Boolean conditions:

331c. ⟨*transcript* 330⟩+≡ ◁331b 344a▷

```
-> (if 1 77 88)
type error: Condition in if expression has type int, which should be bool
-> (if (positive? 1) 77 99)
77 : int
```

6.1.2 *Predefined functions of Typed Impcore*

The predefined functions of Typed Impcore do the same work at run time as their counterparts in Chapter 1, but because they include explicit types for arguments and results, their definitions look different. And because Typed Impcore has no Boolean literals, falsehood is written as (= 1 0), and truth as (= 0 0).

331d. ⟨*predefined Typed Impcore functions* 331d⟩≡ 331e▷

```
(define bool and ([b : bool] [c : bool]) (if b c b))
(define bool or  ([b : bool] [c : bool]) (if b b c))
(define bool not ([b : bool])            (if b (= 1 0) (= 0 0)))
```

The comparison functions accept integers and return Booleans.

331e. ⟨*predefined Typed Impcore functions* 331d⟩+≡ ◁331d

```
(define bool <= ([m : int] [n : int]) (not (> m n)))
(define bool >= ([m : int] [n : int]) (not (< m n)))
(define bool != ([m : int] [n : int]) (not (= m n)))
```

Functions mod and negated are defined in the Supplement.

6.1.3 *Types, values, and abstract syntax of Typed Impcore*

As in Chapter 5, the abstract syntax of Typed Impcore is defined by the representation used in the implementation. The abstract syntax for a type (ty) is also the internal representation of a type. The internal representation of a function type (funty) is also the abstract syntax used in check-function-type.

331f. ⟨*types for Typed Impcore* 331f⟩≡ (S391a) 332a▷

```
datatype ty    = INTTY | BOOLTY | UNITTY | ARRAYTY of ty
datatype funty = FUNTY of ty list * ty
```

A funty describes just one type; for example, FUNTY ([INTTY, INTTY], BOOLTY) describes the type of a function that takes two integer arguments and returns a Boolean result. In Typed Impcore, a function or variable has at most one type, which makes Typed Impcore *monomorphic*.

Types are printed with the help of functions typeString and funtyString, which are defined in Appendix P.

Types are checked for equality by mutually recursive functions eqType and eqTypes:

332a. ⟨*types for Typed Impcore* 331f⟩+≡ (S391a) ◁331f 332b▷

```
eqType  : ty      * ty      -> bool
eqTypes : ty list * ty list -> bool
```

```
fun eqType (INTTY,      INTTY)      = true
  | eqType (BOOLTY,     BOOLTY)     = true
  | eqType (UNITTY,     UNITTY)     = true
  | eqType (ARRAYTY t1, ARRAYTY t2) = eqType (t1, t2)
  | eqType (_,          _)          = false
and eqTypes (ts1, ts2) = ListPair.allEq eqType (ts1, ts2)
```

Types should always be checked for equality using eqType, not the built-in = operator. As shown in Section 6.6.6 below, a single type can sometimes have multiple representations, which = reports as different but should actually be considered the same. Using eqType gets these cases right; if you use =, you risk introducing bugs that will be hard to find.

Function types are checked for equality using function eqFunty.

332b. ⟨*types for Typed Impcore* 331f⟩+≡ (S391a) ◁332a

```
eqFunty  : funty * funty -> bool
```

```
fun eqFunty (FUNTY (args, result), FUNTY (args', result')) =
  eqTypes (args, args') andalso eqType (result, result')
```

Moving to run time, there are only two forms of value. Values of integer, Boolean, or unit type are represented using the NUM form; values of array types are represented using the ARRAY form.

332c. ⟨*definitions of* exp *and* value *for Typed Impcore* 332c⟩≡ (S391b) 332d▷

```
datatype value = NUM   of int
               | ARRAY of value array
```

And finally the syntax. Typed Impcore includes every form of expression found in untyped Impcore, plus new forms for equality, printing, and array operations.

332d. ⟨*definitions of* exp *and* value *for Typed Impcore* 332c⟩+≡ (S391b) ◁332c

```
datatype exp  = LITERAL of value
              | VAR     of name
              | SET     of name * exp
              | IFX     of exp * exp * exp
              | WHILEX  of exp * exp
              | BEGIN   of exp list
              | APPLY   of name * exp list
              ⟨Typed Impcore syntax for equality and printing 332e⟩
              ⟨array extensions to Typed Impcore's abstract syntax 344d⟩
```

In Typed Impcore, the =, print, and println operations cannot be implemented by primitive functions, because they operate on values of more than one type: they are *polymorphic*. In a monomorphic language like Typed Impcore or C, each polymorphic primitive needs its own syntax.

332e. ⟨*Typed Impcore syntax for equality and printing* 332e⟩≡ (332d)

```
| EQ      of exp * exp
| PRINTLN of exp
| PRINT   of exp
```

Similarly, as described in Section 6.3.2 below, Typed Impcore's array operations also need special-purpose syntax. Such special-purpose syntax is typical; in many languages, array syntax is written using square brackets. As another example, a pointer in C is dereferenced by a syntactic form written with * or ->.

In Typed Impcore, the syntax for a function definition includes explicit parameter types and an explicit result type. As is customary in formal semantics and in Pascal-like and ML-like languages, but not in C, the syntax places a formal parameter's type to the right of its name.

333a. ⟨*definition of* `def` *for Typed Impcore* 333a⟩≡ (S391b)

```
type userfun = { formals : (name * ty) list, body : exp, returns : ty }
datatype def = VAL    of name * exp
             | EXP    of exp
             | DEFINE of name * userfun
```


Typed Impcore's unit tests include `check-expect` and `check-error` from untyped Impcore and μScheme, plus two new unit tests related to types:

333b. ⟨*definition of* `unit_test` *for Typed Impcore* 333b⟩≡ (S391b)

```
datatype unit_test = CHECK_EXPECT        of exp * exp
                   | CHECK_ASSERT        of exp
                   | CHECK_ERROR         of exp
                   | CHECK_TYPE_ERROR    of def
                   | CHECK_FUNCTION_TYPE of name * funty
```

In Typed Impcore, as in Impcore, a function is not an ordinary value. A function takes one of two forms: `USERDEF`, which represents a user-defined function, and `PRIMITIVE`, which represents a primitive function. Because the type system rules out most errors in primitive operations, primitive functions are represented more simply than in Chapter 5: in Typed Impcore, a primitive function is represented by an ML function of type `value list -> value`; there is no parameter of type `exp`.

333c. ⟨*definition of type* `func`*, to represent a Typed Impcore function* 333c⟩≡ (S391b)

```
datatype func = USERDEF   of name list * exp
              | PRIMITIVE of value list -> value
```

A `func` contains no types; types are needed only during type checking, and the `func` representation is used at run time, after all types have been checked.

6.1.4 *Type system for Typed Impcore*

By design, Typed Impcore's static type system is more restrictive than Impcore's dynamic type system. For example, because the static type system distinguishes integers from Booleans, it prevents you from using an integer to control an `if` expression. This restriction should not burden you overmuch; if you have an integer `i` that you wish to treat as a Boolean, simply write `(!= i 0)`. Similarly, if you have a Boolean `b` that you wish to treat as an integer, write `(if b 1 0)`. Typed Impcore also prevents you from assigning the result of a `while` loop to an integer variable—which there is no good reason to do, because the result is always zero.

Typed Impcore accepts a definition only if its expressions, also called *terms*, have types. Which terms have types is determined by a formal proof system (the type system), which is related to the formal proof system that determines which terms have values (the operational semantics). To refer to a type, the type system uses a metavariable formed with the Greek letter τ (pronounced "tau," which rhymes with "wow"). And to remember the type of a variable or function, the type system uses a metavariable formed with the Greek letter Γ (pronounced "gamma").

Typed Impcore's type system relates these elements: *simple types*, which are written τ; three *base types*, which are written INT, BOOL, and UNIT; one *type constructor*, which is written ARRAY; many *function types*, which are written τ_f; and three *type environments*, which are written Γ_ξ, Γ_ϕ, and Γ_ρ. The type environments give the types of global variables, functions, and formal parameters, respectively.

`ARRAYTY`	331f
`BOOLTY`	331f
`FUNTY`	331f
type `funty`	331f
`INTTY`	331f
type `name`	303
type `ty`	331f
`UNITTY`	331f

A simple type is a base type or the array constructor applied to a simple type.[1] Because each type in Typed Impcore requires its own special-purpose abstract syntax, I write the names using the SMALL CAPS font, which I conventionally use for abstract syntax.

$$\tau ::= \text{INT} \mid \text{BOOL} \mid \text{UNIT} \mid \text{ARRAY}(\tau)$$

The type of a function is formed from argument types τ_1 to τ_n and result type τ.

$$\tau_f ::= \tau_1 \times \cdots \times \tau_n \to \tau$$

Just as functions are not values, function types are not value types.

The integer, Boolean, and array types describe values that represent integers, Booleans, and arrays. The unit type plays a more subtle role; its purpose is to be different from the others. It is the type we give to an expression that is executed purely for its side effect and does not produce an interesting value—like a `while` loop or `println` expression. In most typed languages, an operation that is executed only for side effects is described by a special type. In C, C++, and Java, this type is called `void`, because the type is *uninhabited*, i.e., there are no values of type `void`. In the functional language ML, the special type is called `unit`, because the `unit` type has exactly one inhabitant. For Typed Impcore, the `unit` type is more appropriate than `void`, because in Typed Impcore, every terminating evaluation produces a value.

In ML, the inhabitant of the unit type is the empty tuple, which is written `()`. Its value is uninteresting: every expression of type `unit` produces the same empty tuple, unless its evaluation fails to terminate or raises an exception. In Typed Impcore, the inhabitant of the unit type is the value 0—but as long as the type system is designed and implemented correctly, no Typed Impcore program can tell what the inhabitant is.

6.1.5 *Typing rules for Typed Impcore*

A type system is written using the same kind of formal rules we use to write operational semantics; only the forms of the judgments are different. Where the judgments in an operational semantics determine when an expression is evaluated to produce a value, the judgments in a type system determine when an expression has a type. The judgments of a type system and the judgments of the corresponding operational semantics are closely related (Exercise 26).

Type-formation rules

A type system usually begins with rules that say what is and isn't a type. Typed Impcore's types are so simple that rules aren't really necessary; the tiny grammar for τ above tells the story. But the judgment form for Typed Impcore is $\boxed{\tau \text{ is a type}}$, and the rules are as follows:

$$\text{(UNITTYPE)}\quad \frac{}{\text{UNIT is a type}} \qquad \text{(INTTYPE)}\quad \frac{}{\text{INT is a type}} \qquad \text{(BOOLTYPE)}\quad \frac{}{\text{BOOL is a type}},$$

$$\frac{\tau \text{ is a type}}{\text{ARRAY}(\tau) \text{ is a type}}. \qquad \text{(ARRAYTYPE)}$$

In the interpreter, every value of type `ty` (chunk 331f) is a type.

[1] In other words, types are defined by induction, and the base types are the base cases. In Typed Impcore, the type of an array does not include the array's size.

Typing judgment for expressions

The typing judgment for expressions is $\boxed{\Gamma_\xi, \Gamma_\phi, \Gamma_\rho \vdash e : \tau}$, meaning that given type environments $\Gamma_\xi, \Gamma_\phi, \Gamma_\rho$, expression e has type τ. Judgments of this form are proved by the rules of Typed Impcore's type system. These rules are deterministic, and in a well-typed Typed Impcore program, every expression has exactly one type. In other words, given the environments $\Gamma_\xi, \Gamma_\phi, \Gamma_\rho$ and the abstract-syntax tree e, there is at most one τ such that $\Gamma_\xi, \Gamma_\phi, \Gamma_\rho \vdash e : \tau$ (Exercise 20). To find this τ, or to report an error if no such τ exists, is the job of a *type checker*.

Typing rules for expressions

All literals are integers. This rule is sound because there are no Boolean literals in Typed Impcore: the parser creates only integer literals.

$$\frac{}{\Gamma_\xi, \Gamma_\phi, \Gamma_\rho \vdash \text{LITERAL}(v) : \text{INT}} \qquad \text{(LITERAL)}$$

A use of a variable is well typed if the variable is bound in the environment. As in Chapter 1, formals hide globals.

$$\frac{x \in \operatorname{dom} \Gamma_\rho}{\Gamma_\xi, \Gamma_\phi, \Gamma_\rho \vdash \text{VAR}(x) : \Gamma_\rho(x)} \qquad \text{(FORMALVAR)}$$

$$\frac{x \notin \operatorname{dom} \Gamma_\rho \qquad x \in \operatorname{dom} \Gamma_\xi}{\Gamma_\xi, \Gamma_\phi, \Gamma_\rho \vdash \text{VAR}(x) : \Gamma_\xi(x)} \qquad \text{(GLOBALVAR)}$$

An assignment is well typed if the type of the right-hand side matches the type of the variable being assigned to. In other words, assigning to a variable mustn't change its type. And just as in the operational semantics, the rules consult two environments.

$$\frac{x \in \operatorname{dom} \Gamma_\rho \qquad \Gamma_\rho(x) = \tau \qquad \Gamma_\xi, \Gamma_\phi, \Gamma_\rho \vdash e : \tau}{\Gamma_\xi, \Gamma_\phi, \Gamma_\rho \vdash \text{SET}(x, e) : \tau} \qquad \text{(FORMALASSIGN)}$$

$$\frac{x \notin \operatorname{dom} \Gamma_\rho \qquad x \in \operatorname{dom} \Gamma_\xi \qquad \Gamma_\xi(x) = \tau \qquad \Gamma_\xi, \Gamma_\phi, \Gamma_\rho \vdash e : \tau}{\Gamma_\xi, \Gamma_\phi, \Gamma_\rho \vdash \text{SET}(x, e) : \tau} \qquad \text{(GLOBALASSIGN)}$$

If the assignment is well typed, its type is the type of the variable and of the value assigned to it. An assignment could instead be given type `unit`, but this choice would rule out such expressions as `(set x (set y 0))`. In Typed Impcore, as in C, such expressions are permitted.

A conditional expression is well typed if the condition is Boolean and the two branches have the same type. In that case, the type of the conditional expression is the type shared by the branches.

$$\frac{\Gamma_\xi, \Gamma_\phi, \Gamma_\rho \vdash e_1 : \text{BOOL} \qquad \Gamma_\xi, \Gamma_\phi, \Gamma_\rho \vdash e_2 : \tau \qquad \Gamma_\xi, \Gamma_\phi, \Gamma_\rho \vdash e_3 : \tau}{\Gamma_\xi, \Gamma_\phi, \Gamma_\rho \vdash \text{IF}(e_1, e_2, e_3) : \tau} \qquad \text{(IF)}$$

Unlike the rules for literals, variables, and assignment, the IF rule is structured differently from the IF rules in the operational semantics. The operational semantics has two rules: one corresponds to $e_1 \Downarrow \text{BOOLV}(\texttt{\#t})$ and evaluates e_2, and one corresponds to $e_1 \Downarrow \text{BOOLV}(\texttt{\#f})$ and evaluates e_3. Each rule evaluates just two of the three subexpressions. The type system, which cares only about the *type* of e_1, not its value, needs only one rule, which checks the types of all three subexpressions.

A WHILE loop is well typed if the condition is Boolean and the body is well typed. The τ that is the type of the body e_2 is not used in the conclusion of the rule, because it matters only that type τ exists, not what it is.

$$\frac{\Gamma_\xi, \Gamma_\phi, \Gamma_\rho \vdash e_1 : \text{BOOL} \qquad \Gamma_\xi, \Gamma_\phi, \Gamma_\rho \vdash e_2 : \tau}{\Gamma_\xi, \Gamma_\phi, \Gamma_\rho \vdash \text{WHILE}(e_1, e_2) : \text{UNIT}} \qquad \text{(WHILE)}$$

As explained above, because a WHILE loop is executed for its side effect and does not produce a useful result, it is given the unit type.

Like the IF rule, the WHILE rule is structured differently from the WHILE rules in the operational semantics. The operational semantics has two rules: one corresponds to $e_1 \Downarrow \text{BOOLV}(\texttt{\#t})$ and iterates the loop, and one corresponds to $e_1 \Downarrow \text{BOOLV}(\texttt{\#f})$ and terminates the loop. The type system needs only one rule, which checks both types.

A BEGIN expression is well typed if all of its subexpressions are well typed. Because every subexpression except the last is executed only for its side effect, it could legitimately be required to have type UNIT. But I want to allow SET expressions inside BEGIN expressions, so I permit a subexpression in a BEGIN sequence to have any type.

$$\frac{\Gamma_\xi, \Gamma_\phi, \Gamma_\rho \vdash e_1 : \tau_1 \qquad \cdots \qquad \Gamma_\xi, \Gamma_\phi, \Gamma_\rho \vdash e_n : \tau_n}{\Gamma_\xi, \Gamma_\phi, \Gamma_\rho \vdash \text{BEGIN}(e_1, \ldots, e_n) : \tau_n} \qquad \text{(BEGIN)}$$

The premises mentioning $e_1, \ldots, e_{n-1}$ are necessary because although it doesn't matter what the types of $e_1, \ldots, e_{n-1}$ are, it does matter that they have types.

An empty BEGIN is always well typed and has type UNIT.

$$\frac{}{\Gamma_\xi, \Gamma_\phi, \Gamma_\rho \vdash \text{BEGIN}() : \text{UNIT}} \qquad \text{(EMPTYBEGIN)}$$

A function application is well typed if the function is applied to the right number and types of arguments. A function's type is looked up in the function-type environment Γ_ϕ. The type of the application is the result type of the function.

$$\frac{\Gamma_\phi(f) = \tau_1 \times \cdots \times \tau_n \to \tau \qquad \Gamma_\xi, \Gamma_\phi, \Gamma_\rho \vdash e_i : \tau_i, \quad 1 \le i \le n}{\Gamma_\xi, \Gamma_\phi, \Gamma_\rho \vdash \text{APPLY}(f, e_1, \ldots, e_n) : \tau} \qquad \text{(APPLY)}$$

As is typical for a monomorphic language, each polymorphic operation has its own syntactic form and its own typing rule. An equality test is well typed if it tests two values of the same type.

$$\frac{\Gamma_\xi, \Gamma_\phi, \Gamma_\rho \vdash e_1 : \tau \qquad \Gamma_\xi, \Gamma_\phi, \Gamma_\rho \vdash e_2 : \tau}{\Gamma_\xi, \Gamma_\phi, \Gamma_\rho \vdash \text{EQ}(e_1, e_2) : \text{BOOL}} \qquad \text{(EQ)}$$

A `print` or `println` expression is well typed if its subexpression is well typed.

$$\frac{\Gamma_\xi, \Gamma_\phi, \Gamma_\rho \vdash e : \tau}{\Gamma_\xi, \Gamma_\phi, \Gamma_\rho \vdash \text{PRINTLN}(e) : \text{UNIT}} \qquad \text{(PRINTLN)}$$

Typing judgment and typing rules for definitions

Like the corresponding rules of operational semantics, the typing rule for a definition may produce type environments with new bindings. The judgment has the form $\boxed{\langle d, \Gamma_\xi, \Gamma_\phi \rangle \to \langle \Gamma'_\xi, \Gamma'_\phi \rangle}$, which says that when definition d is typed given type environments Γ_ξ and Γ_ϕ, the new environments are Γ'_ξ and Γ'_ϕ.

If a variable x has not been bound before, its VAL binding requires only that the right-hand side be well typed. The newly bound x takes the type of its right-hand side.

$$\frac{\Gamma_\xi, \Gamma_\phi, \{\} \vdash e : \tau \qquad x \notin \operatorname{dom} \Gamma_\xi}{\langle \text{VAL}(x, e), \Gamma_\xi, \Gamma_\phi \rangle \to \langle \Gamma_\xi\{x \mapsto \tau\}, \Gamma_\phi \rangle} \quad (\text{NEWVAL})$$

If x is already bound, the VAL binding acts like a SET. And just like a SET, the VAL must not change x's type (Exercise 29).

$$\frac{\Gamma_\xi, \Gamma_\phi, \{\} \vdash e : \tau \qquad \Gamma_\xi(x) = \tau}{\langle \text{VAL}(x, e), \Gamma_\xi, \Gamma_\phi \rangle \to \langle \Gamma_\xi, \Gamma_\phi \rangle} \quad (\text{OLDVAL})$$

A top-level expression is checked, but it doesn't change the type environments. (In untyped Impcore, the value of a top-level expression is bound to global variable `it`. But in Typed Impcore, the type of `it` can't be allowed to change, lest the type system become unsound. So a top-level expression doesn't create a binding.)

$$\frac{\Gamma_\xi, \Gamma_\phi, \{\} \vdash e : \tau}{\langle \text{EXP}(e), \Gamma_\xi, \Gamma_\phi \rangle \to \langle \Gamma_\xi, \Gamma_\phi \rangle} \quad (\text{EXP})$$

A function definition updates the function environment. The definition gives the type τ_i of each formal parameter x_i, and the type τ of the result. In an environment where each x_i has type τ_i, the function's body e must be well typed and have type τ. In that case, function f is added to the type environment Γ_ϕ with function type $\tau_1 \times \cdots \times \tau_n \to \tau$. Because f could be called recursively from e, f also goes into the type environment used to typecheck e.

$$\frac{\begin{array}{c}\tau_1, \ldots, \tau_n \text{ are types} \\ \tau_f = \tau_1 \times \cdots \times \tau_n \to \tau \\ f \notin \operatorname{dom} \Gamma_\phi \\ \Gamma_\xi, \Gamma_\phi\{f \mapsto \tau_f\}, \{x_1 \mapsto \tau_1, \ldots, x_n \mapsto \tau_n\} \vdash e : \tau\end{array}}{\langle \text{DEFINE}(f, (\langle x_1 : \tau_1, \ldots, x_n : \tau_n \rangle, e : \tau)), \Gamma_\xi, \Gamma_\phi \rangle \to \langle \Gamma_\xi, \Gamma_\phi\{f \mapsto \tau_f\} \rangle} \quad (\text{DEFINE})$$

In addition to the typing judgment for e, the body of the function, this rule also uses well-formedness judgments for types τ_1 to τ_n. In general, when a type appears in syntax, the rule for that syntax may need a premise saying the type is well formed. (The result type τ here does not need such a premise, because when the judgment form $\cdots \vdash e : \tau$ is derivable, τ is guaranteed to be well formed; see Exercise 22.)

A function can be redefined, but the redefinition may not change its type (Exercise 29).

$$\frac{\begin{array}{c}\tau_1, \ldots, \tau_n \text{ are types} \\ \Gamma_\phi(f) = \tau_1 \times \cdots \times \tau_n \to \tau \\ \Gamma_\xi, \Gamma_\phi\{f \mapsto \tau_1 \times \cdots \times \tau_n \to \tau\}, \{x_1 \mapsto \tau_1, \ldots, x_n \mapsto \tau_n\} \vdash e : \tau\end{array}}{\langle \text{DEFINE}(f, (\langle x_1 : \tau_1, \ldots, x_n : \tau_n \rangle, e : \tau)), \Gamma_\xi, \Gamma_\phi \rangle \to \langle \Gamma_\xi, \Gamma_\phi \rangle} \quad (\text{REDEFINE})$$

6.2 A TYPE-CHECKING INTERPRETER FOR TYPED IMPCORE

Typed Impcore is interpreted using the techniques used to interpret μScheme in Chapter 5, plus support for types: in addition to abstract syntax for expressions and definitions, I define abstract syntax for types, which is shown in the code chunk ⟨*types for Typed Impcore* 331f⟩. Because the type system is so simple, the abstract syntax can also serve as the internal representation of types.

Types are checked by new functions `typeof` and `typdef`, which are invoked by the read-eval-print loop. The type checker I present handles only integer, Boolean, and unit types; array types are left for the exercises.

Table 6.2: Correspondence between Typed Impcore's type system and code

Type system	*Concept*	*Interpreter*
d	Definition	`def`, `xdef`, or `unit_test` (pages 333, S214 and 333)
e	Expression	`exp` (page 332)
x, f	Name	`name` (page 303)
τ	Type	`ty` (page 331)
Γ_ξ, Γ_ρ	Type environment	`ty env` (pages 304 and 331)
Γ_ϕ	Function-type environment	`funty env` (pages 304 and 331)
$\Gamma_\xi, \Gamma_\phi, \Gamma_\rho \vdash e : \tau$	Typecheck e	`typeof(`e`, `Γ_ξ`, `Γ_ϕ`, `Γ_ρ`)` $=$ τ, and often `ty` $e = \tau$ (page 338)
$\langle d, \Gamma_\xi, \Gamma_\phi \rangle \to \langle \Gamma'_\xi, \Gamma'_\phi \rangle$	Typecheck d	`typdef(`d`, `Γ_ξ`, `Γ_ϕ`)` $=$ `(`Γ_ξ`', `Γ_ϕ`', `s`)` (page 341)
$x \in \operatorname{dom} \Gamma$	Definedness	`find (`x`, `Γ`)` terminates without raising an exception (page 305)
$\Gamma(x)$	Type lookup	`find (`x`, `Γ`)` (page 305)
$\Gamma\{x \mapsto \tau\}$	Binding	`bind (`x`, `τ`, `Γ`)` (page 305)
$\Gamma\{x_1 \mapsto \tau_1, \ldots, x_n \mapsto \tau_n\}$	Binding	`bindlist (`$[x_1, \ldots, x_n]$`, `$[\tau_1, \ldots, \tau_n]$`, `Γ`)` (page 305)

6.2.1 *Type checking*

Given an expression e and a collection of type environments Γ_ξ, Γ_ϕ, and Γ_ρ, calling `typeof`$(e, \Gamma_\xi, \Gamma_\phi, \Gamma_\rho)$ returns a type τ such that $\Gamma_\xi, \Gamma_\phi, \Gamma_\rho \vdash e : \tau$. If no such type exists, `typeof` raises the `TypeError` exception (or possibly `NotFound`). Internal function `ty` computes the type of e using the environments passed to `typeof`.

338a. ⟨*type checking for Typed Impcore* 338a⟩≡ (S391a) 341b ▷

```
typeof  : exp * ty env * funty env * ty env -> ty
ty      : exp -> ty
```

```
fun typeof (e, globals, functions, formals) =
  let ⟨function ty, checks type of expression given Γξ, Γφ, Γρ 338b⟩
  in  ty e
  end
```

Just as `eval` implements the rules of operational semantics, `ty` implements the rules of the type system. Each rule is shown before the code that implements it.

Every literal has type `int`.

$$\frac{}{\Gamma_\xi, \Gamma_\phi, \Gamma_\rho \vdash \text{LITERAL}(v) : \text{INT}} \quad \text{(LITERAL)}$$

338b. ⟨*function* `ty`*, checks type of expression given* $\Gamma_\xi, \Gamma_\phi, \Gamma_\rho$ 338b⟩≡ (338a) 339a ▷

```
fun ty (LITERAL v) = INTTY
```

A variable x has a type if it is defined in environment Γ_ρ or Γ_ξ.

$$\frac{x \in \operatorname{dom} \Gamma_\rho}{\Gamma_\xi, \Gamma_\phi, \Gamma_\rho \vdash \text{VAR}(x) : \Gamma_\rho(x)} \quad \text{(FORMALVAR)}$$

$$\frac{x \notin \operatorname{dom}\Gamma_\rho \qquad x \in \operatorname{dom}\Gamma_\xi}{\Gamma_\xi, \Gamma_\phi, \Gamma_\rho \vdash \text{VAR}(x) : \Gamma_\xi(x)} \qquad \text{(GLOBALVAR)}$$

If x is not found in either Γ_ρ or Γ_ξ, the type checker raises the NotFound exception.

339a. ⟨*function* ty, *checks type of expression given* $\Gamma_\xi, \Gamma_\phi, \Gamma_\rho$ 338b⟩+≡ (338a) ◁338b 339b▷

```
| ty (VAR x) = (find (x, formals) handle NotFound _ => find (x, globals))
```

An assignment (set x e) has a type if both x and e have the same type, in which case the assignment has that type.

$$\frac{x \in \operatorname{dom}\Gamma_\rho \qquad \Gamma_\rho(x) = \tau \qquad \Gamma_\xi, \Gamma_\phi, \Gamma_\rho \vdash e : \tau}{\Gamma_\xi, \Gamma_\phi, \Gamma_\rho \vdash \text{SET}(x, e) : \tau} \qquad \text{(FORMALASSIGN)}$$

$$\frac{x \notin \operatorname{dom}\Gamma_\rho \qquad x \in \operatorname{dom}\Gamma_\xi \qquad \Gamma_\xi(x) = \tau \qquad \Gamma_\xi, \Gamma_\phi, \Gamma_\rho \vdash e : \tau}{\Gamma_\xi, \Gamma_\phi, \Gamma_\rho \vdash \text{SET}(x, e) : \tau} \qquad \text{(GLOBALASSIGN)}$$

The types of both x and e are found by recursive calls to ty.

339b. ⟨*function* ty, *checks type of expression given* $\Gamma_\xi, \Gamma_\phi, \Gamma_\rho$ 338b⟩+≡ (338a) ◁339a 339d▷

```
| ty (SET (x, e)) =
        let val tau_x = ty (VAR x)
            val tau_e = ty e
        in  if eqType (tau_x, tau_e) then tau_x
            else ⟨raise TypeError for an assignment 339c⟩
        end
```

When x and e have different types—a case not covered by the specification—ty issues an explanatory error message. Creating this message takes more work than checking the types.

339c. ⟨*raise* TypeError *for an assignment* 339c⟩≡ (339b)

```
raise TypeError ("Set variable " ^ x ^ " of type " ^ typeString tau_x ^
                 " to value of type " ^ typeString tau_e)
```

A conditional has a type if its condition is Boolean and if both branches have the same type—in which case the conditional has that type.

$$\frac{\Gamma_\xi, \Gamma_\phi, \Gamma_\rho \vdash e_1 : \text{BOOL} \qquad \Gamma_\xi, \Gamma_\phi, \Gamma_\rho \vdash e_2 : \tau \qquad \Gamma_\xi, \Gamma_\phi, \Gamma_\rho \vdash e_3 : \tau}{\Gamma_\xi, \Gamma_\phi, \Gamma_\rho \vdash \text{IF}(e_1, e_2, e_3) : \tau} \qquad \text{(IF)}$$

Again, most of the code is devoted to error messages.

339d. ⟨*function* ty, *checks type of expression given* $\Gamma_\xi, \Gamma_\phi, \Gamma_\rho$ 338b⟩+≡ (338a) ◁339b 340a▷

```
| ty (IFX (e1, e2, e3)) =
     let val tau1 = ty e1
         val tau2 = ty e2
         val tau3 = ty e3
     in  if eqType (tau1, BOOLTY) then
           if eqType (tau2, tau3) then
             tau2
           else
             raise TypeError
               ("In if expression, true branch has type " ^
                typeString tau2 ^ " but false branch has type " ^
                typeString tau3)
         else
           raise TypeError
             ("Condition in if expression has type " ^ typeString tau1 ^
              ", which should be " ^ typeString BOOLTY)
     end
```


BOOLTY	331f
type env	304
eqType	332a
type exp	332d
find	305b
type funty	331f
IFX	332d
INTTY	331f
LITERAL	332d
NotFound	305b
SET	332d
type ty	331f
TypeError	S213c
typeString	S398e
VAR	332d

A `while` loop has a type if its condition is Boolean and if its body has a type—we don't care what type. In that case the `while` loop has type `unit`.

$$\frac{\Gamma_\xi, \Gamma_\phi, \Gamma_\rho \vdash e_1 : \text{BOOL} \qquad \Gamma_\xi, \Gamma_\phi, \Gamma_\rho \vdash e_2 : \tau}{\Gamma_\xi, \Gamma_\phi, \Gamma_\rho \vdash \text{WHILE}(e_1, e_2) : \text{UNIT}} \qquad (\text{WHILE})$$

340a. ⟨*function* `ty`*, checks type of expression given* $\Gamma_\xi, \Gamma_\phi, \Gamma_\rho$ 338b⟩+≡ (338a) ◁339d 340b▷

```
| ty (WHILEX (e1, e2)) =
    let val tau1 = ty e1
        val tau2 = ty e2
    in  if eqType (tau1, BOOLTY) then
          UNITTY
        else
          raise TypeError ("Condition in while expression has type " ^
                           typeString tau1 ^ ", which should be " ^
                           typeString BOOLTY)
    end
```

A `begin` has a type if all its subexpressions have types, in which case the `begin` has the type of its *last* subexpression. Or if there are no subexpressions, type `unit`.

$$\frac{\Gamma_\xi, \Gamma_\phi, \Gamma_\rho \vdash e_1 : \tau_1 \qquad \cdots \qquad \Gamma_\xi, \Gamma_\phi, \Gamma_\rho \vdash e_n : \tau_n}{\Gamma_\xi, \Gamma_\phi, \Gamma_\rho \vdash \text{BEGIN}(e_1, \ldots, e_n) : \tau_n} \qquad (\text{BEGIN})$$

$$\frac{}{\Gamma_\xi, \Gamma_\phi, \Gamma_\rho \vdash \text{BEGIN}() : \text{UNIT}} \qquad (\text{EMPTYBEGIN})$$

The implementation uses Standard ML basis function `List.last`.

340b. ⟨*function* `ty`*, checks type of expression given* $\Gamma_\xi, \Gamma_\phi, \Gamma_\rho$ 338b⟩+≡ (338a) ◁340a 340c▷

```
| ty (BEGIN es) =
     let val bodytypes = map ty es
     in  List.last bodytypes handle Empty => UNITTY
     end
```

An equality test (`=` e_1 e_2) has a type if e_1 and e_2 have the same type, in which case the equality test has type `bool`.

$$\frac{\Gamma_\xi, \Gamma_\phi, \Gamma_\rho \vdash e_1 : \tau \qquad \Gamma_\xi, \Gamma_\phi, \Gamma_\rho \vdash e_2 : \tau}{\Gamma_\xi, \Gamma_\phi, \Gamma_\rho \vdash \text{EQ}(e_1, e_2) : \text{BOOL}} \qquad (\text{EQ})$$

The types of e_1 and e_2 are computed using an ML trick: `val` binds the pair of names `(tau1, tau2)` to a pair of ML values. This trick has the same effect as the separate computations of `tau1` and `tau2` in the `WHILEX` case above, but it highlights the similarity of the two computations, and it uses scarce vertical space more effectively.

340c. ⟨*function* `ty`*, checks type of expression given* $\Gamma_\xi, \Gamma_\phi, \Gamma_\rho$ 338b⟩+≡ (338a) ◁340b 340d▷

```
| ty (EQ (e1, e2)) =
     let val (tau1, tau2) = (ty e1, ty e2)
     in  if eqType (tau1, tau2) then
           BOOLTY
         else
           raise TypeError ("Equality sees values of different types " ^
                            typeString tau1 ^ " and " ^ typeString tau2)
     end
```

A print expression has a type if its subexpression is well typed, in which case its type is `unit`.

$$\frac{\Gamma_\xi, \Gamma_\phi, \Gamma_\rho \vdash e : \tau}{\Gamma_\xi, \Gamma_\phi, \Gamma_\rho \vdash \text{PRINTLN}(e) : \text{UNIT}} \qquad (\text{PRINTLN})$$

340d. ⟨*function* `ty`*, checks type of expression given* $\Gamma_\xi, \Gamma_\phi, \Gamma_\rho$ 338b⟩+≡ (338a) ◁340c 341a▷

```
| ty (PRINTLN e) = (ty e; UNITTY)
| ty (PRINT   e) = (ty e; UNITTY)
```

A function application has a type if its function is defined in environment Γ_ϕ, and if the function is applied to the right number and types of arguments. In that case, the type of the application is the result type of the function type found in Γ_ϕ.

$$\frac{\Gamma_\phi(f) = \tau_1 \times \cdots \times \tau_n \to \tau \qquad \Gamma_\xi, \Gamma_\phi, \Gamma_\rho \vdash e_i : \tau_i, \quad 1 \le i \le n}{\Gamma_\xi, \Gamma_\phi, \Gamma_\rho \vdash \text{APPLY}(f, e_1, \ldots, e_n) : \tau} \qquad \text{(APPLY)}$$

If the function is applied to the wrong number or types of arguments, function `badParameter`, which is defined in the Supplement, finds one bad parameter and builds an error message.

341a. ⟨*function* `ty`*, checks type of expression given* $\Gamma_\xi, \Gamma_\phi, \Gamma_\rho$ 338b⟩+≡ (338a) ◁ 340d

```
| ty (APPLY (f, actuals)) =        badParameter : int * ty list * ty list -> 'a
    let val actualtypes                    = map ty actuals
        val FUNTY (formaltypes, resulttype) = find (f, functions)
        ⟨definition of badParameter S392b⟩
    in  if eqTypes (actualtypes, formaltypes) then
          resulttype
        else
          badParameter (1, actualtypes, formaltypes)
    end
```

6.2.2 *Typechecking definitions*

The typing judgment for a definition d has the form $\langle d, \Gamma_\xi, \Gamma_\phi \rangle \to \langle \Gamma'_\phi, \Gamma'_\xi \rangle$. This judgment is implemented by a static analysis that I call *typing* the definition. Calling `typdef` $(d, \Gamma_\xi, \Gamma_\phi)$ returns a triple $(\Gamma'_\xi, \Gamma'_\phi, s)$, where s is a string describing a type.

341b. ⟨*type checking for Typed Impcore* 338a⟩+≡ (S391a) ◁ 338a

```
                    typdef : def * ty env * funty env -> ty env * funty env * string
fun typdef (d, globals, functions) =
    case d
      of ⟨cases for typing definitions in Typed Impcore 341c⟩
```

Each case of `typdef` implements one syntactic form of definition d. The first form is a variable definition, which may change a variable's value but not its type. Depending on whether the variable is already defined, there are two rules.

$$\frac{\Gamma_\xi, \Gamma_\phi, \{\} \vdash e : \tau \qquad x \notin \operatorname{dom} \Gamma_\xi}{\langle \text{VAL}(x, e), \Gamma_\xi, \Gamma_\phi \rangle \to \langle \Gamma_\xi\{x \mapsto \tau\}, \Gamma_\phi \rangle} \qquad \text{(NEWVAL)}$$

$$\frac{\Gamma_\xi, \Gamma_\phi, \{\} \vdash e : \tau \qquad \Gamma_\xi(x) = \tau}{\langle \text{VAL}(x, e), \Gamma_\xi, \Gamma_\phi \rangle \to \langle \Gamma_\xi, \Gamma_\phi \rangle} \qquad \text{(OLDVAL)}$$

Which rule applies depends on whether x is already defined.

341c. ⟨*cases for typing definitions in Typed Impcore* 341c⟩≡ (341b) 342b ▷

```
VAL (x, e) =>
  if not (isbound (x, globals)) then
    let val tau  = typeof (e, globals, functions, emptyEnv)
    in  (bind (x, tau, globals), functions, typeString tau)
    end
  else
    let val tau' = find (x, globals)
        val tau  = typeof (e, globals, functions, emptyEnv)
    in  if eqType (tau, tau') then
          (globals, functions, typeString tau)
        else
          ⟨raise TypeError with message about redefinition 342a⟩
    end
```

342a. ⟨*raise* `TypeError` *with message about redefinition* 342a⟩≡ (341c)

```
raise TypeError ("Global variable " ^ x ^ " of type " ^ typeString tau' ^
                 " may not be redefined with type " ^ typeString tau)
```

A top-level expression must have a type, and it leaves the environments unchanged.

$$\frac{\Gamma_\xi, \Gamma_\phi, \{\} \vdash e : \tau}{\langle \text{EXP}(e), \Gamma_\xi, \Gamma_\phi \rangle \to \langle \Gamma_\xi, \Gamma_\phi \rangle} \quad (\text{EXP})$$

342b. ⟨*cases for typing definitions in Typed Impcore* 341c⟩+≡ (341b) ◁341c 342c▷

```
| EXP e =>
    let val tau = typeof (e, globals, functions, emptyEnv)
    in  (globals, functions, typeString tau)
    end
```

Like a variable definition, a function definition has two rules, depending on whether the function is already defined.

$$\frac{\begin{array}{c}\tau_1, \ldots, \tau_n \text{ are types} \\ \tau_f = \tau_1 \times \cdots \times \tau_n \to \tau \\ f \notin \operatorname{dom} \Gamma_\phi \\ \Gamma_\xi, \Gamma_\phi\{f \mapsto \tau_f\}, \{x_1 \mapsto \tau_1, \ldots, x_n \mapsto \tau_n\} \vdash e : \tau\end{array}}{\langle \text{DEFINE}(f, (\langle x_1 : \tau_1, \ldots, x_n : \tau_n \rangle, e : \tau)), \Gamma_\xi, \Gamma_\phi \rangle \to \langle \Gamma_\xi, \Gamma_\phi\{f \mapsto \tau_f\} \rangle} \quad (\text{DEFINE})$$

$$\frac{\begin{array}{c}\tau_1, \ldots, \tau_n \text{ are types} \\ \Gamma_\phi(f) = \tau_1 \times \cdots \times \tau_n \to \tau \\ \Gamma_\xi, \Gamma_\phi\{f \mapsto \tau_1 \times \cdots \times \tau_n \to \tau\}, \{x_1 \mapsto \tau_1, \ldots, x_n \mapsto \tau_n\} \vdash e : \tau\end{array}}{\langle \text{DEFINE}(f, (\langle x_1 : \tau_1, \ldots, x_n : \tau_n \rangle, e : \tau)), \Gamma_\xi, \Gamma_\phi \rangle \to \langle \Gamma_\xi, \Gamma_\phi \rangle} \quad (\text{REDEFINE})$$

The common parts of these rules are implemented first: build the function type, get the type of the body (τ), and confirm that τ is equal to the `returns` type in the syntax. Only then does the code check $f \in \operatorname{dom} \Gamma_\phi$ and finish accordingly.

342c. ⟨*cases for typing definitions in Typed Impcore* 341c⟩+≡ (341b) ◁342b

```
| DEFINE (f, {returns, formals, body}) =>
    let val (fnames, ftys) = ListPair.unzip formals
        val def's_type     = FUNTY (ftys, returns)
        val functions'     = bind (f, def's_type, functions)
        val formals        = mkEnv (fnames, ftys)
        val tau            = typeof (body, globals, functions', formals)
    in  if eqType (tau, returns) then
          if not (isbound (f, functions)) then
             (globals, functions', funtyString def's_type)
          else
            let val env's_type = find (f, functions)
            in  if eqFunty (env's_type, def's_type) then
                  (globals, functions, funtyString def's_type)
                else
                  raise TypeError
                    ("Function " ^ f ^ " of type " ^ funtyString env's_type
                     ^ " may not be redefined with type " ^
                     funtyString def's_type)
            end
        else
          raise TypeError ("Body of function has type " ^ typeString tau ^
                           ", which does not match declared result type " ^
                           "of " ^ typeString returns)
    end
```

6.3 Extending Typed Impcore with arrays

Types are associated with data, and a designer who adds a new data structure must often add a new type. The process is shown here by adding arrays to Typed Impcore. As shown below, arrays require new types, new concrete syntax, new abstract syntax, new evaluation code, and new typing rules.

6.3.1 *Types for arrays*

The array type is a different *kind* of thing from the integer, Boolean, and UNIT types. Properly speaking, "array" is not a "type" at all: it is a *type constructor,* i.e., a thing you use to build types. To name just a few possibilities, you can build arrays of integers, arrays of Booleans, and arrays of arrays of integers. In general, given any type τ, you can build the type "array of τ." In our abstract syntax, the array type constructor is represented by ARRAY, and in the ML code, by `ARRAYTY` (chunk 331f). In the concrete syntax, it is represented by `(array` *type*`)` (page 330). So for example, the type of arrays of Booleans is `(array bool)`, and the type of arrays of arrays of integers is `(array (array int))`.

"Type constructor" is such a useful idea that even INT, UNIT, and BOOL are often treated as type constructors, even though they take no arguments and so can be used to build only one type apiece. Such nullary type constructors are usually called *base types,* because the set of all types is defined by induction and the nullary type constructors are the base cases.

Whenever you add a new type to a language, whether it is a base type or a more interesting type constructor, you also add operations for values of that type. Let's look at operations for arrays.

6.3.2 *New syntax for arrays*

Like Typed Impcore's equality and printing operations, each of its array operations gets its own syntactic form.

- To evaluate an expression of the form `(make-array` e_1 e_2`)`, we evaluate e_1 to get an integer size n and e_2 to get a value v. We then allocate and return a new array containing n elements, each initialized to v; if n is negative, the evaluation results in a checked run-time error. A `make-array` expression is analogous to a creator (Section 2.5.2) for the array type.
- To evaluate an expression of the form `(array-at` e_1 e_2`)`, we evaluate e_1 to get an array a and e_2 to get an integer index i. We then return the ith element of a, where the first element is element number 0; if i is out of bounds, the evaluation results in a checked run-time error. An `array-at` expression is analogous to an observer for the array type.
- To evaluate an expression of the form `(array-put` e_1 e_2 e_3`)`, we evaluate e_1 to get an array a, e_2 to get an integer index i, and e_3 to get a value v. We then modify a by storing v as its ith element; if i is out of bounds, the evaluation results in a checked run-time error. An `array-put` expression is analogous to a mutator for the array type.
- To evaluate an expression of the form `(array-size e)`, we evaluate e to get an array a. We then return the number of elements in a. An `array-size` expression is analogous to an observer for the array type.

These operations can be illustrated with an array of Booleans.

344a. ⟨*transcript* 330⟩+≡ ◁331c 344b▷

```
-> (val truth-vector (make-array 3 (= 0 1)))
[0 0 0] : (array bool)
-> (array-put truth-vector 1 (= 0 0))
1 : bool
-> truth-vector
[0 1 0] : (array bool)
```


As another example, array operators work on arrays that contain other arrays. Such an array can represent a matrix:

344b. ⟨*transcript* 330⟩+≡ ◁344a 344c▷

```
-> (define (array (array int)) matrix-using-a-and-i
      ; return square matrix of side length; a and i are for local use only
      ([length : int] [a : (array (array int))] [i : int])
     (begin
       (set a (make-array length (make-array 0 0)))
       (set i 0)
       (while (< i length)
          (begin
            (array-put a i (make-array length 0))
            (set i (+ i 1))))
       a))
-> (define (array (array int)) matrix ([length : int])
     (matrix-using-a-and-i length (make-array 0 (make-array 0 0)) 0))
```

Function `matrix` fills a matrix with zeros; the matrix is updated using syntactic forms `array-put` and `array-at`.

344c. ⟨*transcript* 330⟩+≡ ◁344b

```
-> (val a (matrix 3))
[[0 0 0] [0 0 0] [0 0 0]] : (array (array int))
-> (val i 0)
-> (val j 0)
-> (while (< i 3) (begin
      (set j 0)
      (while (< j 3) (begin
         (array-put (array-at a i) j (+ i j))
         (set j (+ j 1))))
      (set i (+ i 1))))
-> a
[[0 1 2] [1 2 3] [2 3 4]] : (array (array int))
-> (val a.1 (array-at a 1))
[1 2 3] : (array int)
-> (val a.1.1 (array-at a.1 1))
2 : int
```

The `array-at` form operates on arrays of any type. As shown, it can index into an array of type `(array int)` and return a result of type `int`. It can also index into an array of type `(array (array int))` and return a result of type `(array int)`. Such behavior is *polymorphic*. Typed Impcore is *monomorphic*, which means that a function can be used for arguments and results of one and only one type. So like = and `println`, `array-at` can't be implemented as a primitive function; it must be a syntactic form. In fact, *every* array operation is a syntactic form, defined as follows:

344d. ⟨*array extensions to Typed Impcore's abstract syntax* 344d⟩≡ (332d)

```
| AMAKE of exp * exp
| AAT   of exp * exp
| APUT  of exp * exp * exp
| ASIZE of exp
```

This example illustrates a general principle: *in a monomorphic language, polymorphic primitives require special-purpose abstract syntax.* This principle also applies to C and C++, for example, which denote array operations with syntax involving square brackets.

Each array operation is governed by rules that say how it is typechecked and evaluated. Type checking is presented in the next section; evaluation is presented here. Because the evaluation *rules* are not particularly interesting, they are omitted from this book; only the code is shown.

Array operations expect arrays and integers, which are obtained from Typed Impcore `values` by projection (Section 5.2). The projections are implemented by functions `toArray` and `toInt`. If a program type checks, its projections should always succeed; if a projection fails, there is a bug in the type checker.

345a. ⟨*definitions of functions* `toArray` *and* `toInt` *for Typed Impcore* 345a⟩≡ (S391b)

```
toArray : value -> value array
toInt   : value -> int
```

```
fun toArray (ARRAY a) = a
  | toArray _         = raise BugInTypeChecking "non-array value"
fun toInt   (NUM n)   = n
  | toInt _           = raise BugInTypeChecking "non-integer value"
```

Given `toArray` and `toInt`, the array operations are implemented using the `Array` module from ML's Standard Basis Library. The library includes run-time checks for bad subscripts or array sizes; these checks are needed because Typed Impcore's type system is not powerful enough to preclude such errors.

345b. ⟨*more alternatives for* `ev` *for Typed Impcore* 345b⟩≡ (S397b)

```
ev : exp -> value
```

```
  | ev (AAT (a, i)) =
      Array.sub (toArray (ev a), toInt (ev i))
  | ev (APUT (e1, e2, e3)) =
      let val (a, i, v) = (ev e1, ev e2, ev e3)
      in  Array.update (toArray a, toInt i, v);
          v
      end
  | ev (AMAKE (len, init)) =
      ARRAY (Array.array (toInt (ev len), ev init))
  | ev (ASIZE a) =
      NUM   (Array.length (toArray (ev a)))
```

6.3.3 *Rules for type constructors: Formation, introduction, and elimination*

In a monomorphic language, a new type constructor needs new syntax, and new syntactic forms need new typing rules. Like the operations described in Section 2.5.2, syntax should include forms that create and observe, as well as forms that produce or mutate, or both. Rules have similar requirements.

ARRAY 332c
BugInTypeChecking S213c
ev S397b
type exp 332d
NUM 332c
type value 332c

Rules should say how to use the new type constructor to make new types. Such rules are called *formation rules*. Rules should also say what syntactic forms *create new values* that are described by the new type constructor. Such rules are called *introduction rules*; an introduction rule describes a syntactic form that is analogous to a *creator* function as described in Section 2.5.2. Finally, rules should say what syntactic forms *use the values* that are described by the new type constructor. Such rules are called *elimination rules*; an elimination rule describes a syntactic form that may be analogous to a mutator or observer function as described in Section 2.5.2.

A rule can be recognized as a formation, introduction, or elimination rule by first drawing a box around the type of interest, then seeing if the rule matches any of these templates:

- A formation rule answers the question, "what types can I make?" Below the line, it has the judgment "$\square$ is a type," where $\square$ is a type of interest:

$$\frac{\cdots}{\square \text{ is a type}}. \qquad \text{(FORMATION TEMPLATE)}$$

- An introduction rule answers the question, "how do I *make* a value of the interesting type?" Below the line, it has a typing judgment that ascribes the type of interest to an expression whose form is somehow related to the type. To write that expression, I use a ? mark:

$$\frac{\cdots}{\Gamma \vdash ? : \square}. \qquad \text{(INTRODUCTION TEMPLATE)}$$

- An elimination rule answers the question, "what can I *do* with a value of the interesting type?" Above the line, it has a typing judgment that ascribes the type of interest to an expression whose form is unknown. Such an expression will be written as e, e_1, e', or something similar:

$$\frac{\cdots \qquad \Gamma \vdash e : \square \qquad \cdots}{\cdots}. \qquad \text{(ELIMINATION TEMPLATE)}$$

These templates work perfectly with the formation, introduction, and elimination rules for arrays. To start, an array type is formed by supplying the type of its elements. In Typed Impcore, the length of an array is not part of its type.[2]

$$\frac{\tau \text{ is a type}}{\text{ARRAY}(\tau) \text{ is a type}} \qquad \text{(ARRAYFORMATION)}$$

An array is made using `make-array`, which is described by an introduction rule.

$$\frac{\Gamma_\xi, \Gamma_\phi, \Gamma_\rho \vdash e_1 : \text{INT} \qquad \Gamma_\xi, \Gamma_\phi, \Gamma_\rho \vdash e_2 : \tau}{\Gamma_\xi, \Gamma_\phi, \Gamma_\rho \vdash \text{MAKE-ARRAY}(e_1, e_2) : \text{ARRAY}(\tau)} \qquad \text{(MAKEARRAY)}$$

The MAKE-ARRAY form is definitely related to the array type, and this rule matches the introduction template.

An array is used by indexing it, updating it, or taking its length. Each operation is described by an elimination rule.

$$\frac{\Gamma_\xi, \Gamma_\phi, \Gamma_\rho \vdash e_1 : \text{ARRAY}(\tau) \qquad \Gamma_\xi, \Gamma_\phi, \Gamma_\rho \vdash e_2 : \text{INT}}{\Gamma_\xi, \Gamma_\phi, \Gamma_\rho \vdash \text{ARRAY-AT}(e_1, e_2) : \tau} \qquad \text{(ARRAYAT)}$$

$$\frac{\Gamma_\xi, \Gamma_\phi, \Gamma_\rho \vdash e_1 : \text{ARRAY}(\tau) \qquad \Gamma_\xi, \Gamma_\phi, \Gamma_\rho \vdash e_2 : \text{INT} \qquad \Gamma_\xi, \Gamma_\phi, \Gamma_\rho \vdash e_3 : \tau}{\Gamma_\xi, \Gamma_\phi, \Gamma_\rho \vdash \text{ARRAY-PUT}(e_1, e_2, e_3) : \tau} \qquad \text{(ARRAYPUT)}$$

$$\frac{\Gamma_\xi, \Gamma_\phi, \Gamma_\rho \vdash e : \text{ARRAY}(\tau)}{\Gamma_\xi, \Gamma_\phi, \Gamma_\rho \vdash \text{ARRAY-SIZE}(e) : \text{INT}} \qquad \text{(ARRAYSIZE)}$$

[2] Because the length of an array is not part of its type, Typed Impcore requires a run-time safety check for every array access. Such checks can be eliminated by a type system in which the length of an array *is* part of its type (Xi and Pfenning 1998), but these sorts of type systems are beyond the scope of this book.

Understanding formation, introduction, and elimination

Not all syntactically correct types and expressions are acceptable in programs; acceptability is determined by formation, introduction, and elimination rules. Formation rules tell us what types are acceptable; for example, in Typed Impcore, `int`, `bool`, and `(array int)` are acceptable types, but `(int bool)`, `array`, and `(array array)` are not. In C, `unsigned` and `unsigned*` are acceptable, but `*` and `*unsigned` are not. Type-formation rules are usually easy to write.

Introduction and elimination rules tell us what terms (expressions) are acceptable. The words "introduction" and "elimination" come from formal logic; the ideas they represent have been adopted into programming languages via the principle of *propositions as types*. This principle says that a type constructor corresponds to a logical connective, a type corresponds to a proposition, and a term of the given type corresponds to a proof of the proposition. For example, logical implication corresponds to the function arrow; if type τ corresponds to proposition P, then the type $\tau \to \tau$ corresponds to the proposition "P implies P"; and the identity function of type $\tau \to \tau$ corresponds to a proof of "P implies P."

A term may inhabit a particular type "directly" or "indirectly." Which is which depends on how the term relates to the type constructor used to make the type. For example, a term of type `(array bool)` might refer to the variable `truth-vector`, might evaluate a conditional that returns an array, or might apply a function that returns an array. All these forms are *indirect*: variable reference, conditionals, and function application can produce results of any type and are not specific to arrays. But if the term has the `make-array` form, it builds an array *directly*; a `make-array` term always produces an array. Similar direct and indirect options are available in proofs.

In both type theory and logic, the direct forms are the *introduction* forms, and their acceptable usage is described by introduction rules. The indirect forms are typically *elimination* forms, described by elimination rules. For example, the conditional is an elimination form for Booleans, and function application is an elimination form for functions. In general, an introduction form puts new information into a proof or a term, whereas an elimination form extracts information that was put there by an introduction form. For example, if I get a Boolean using `array-at`, I'm getting information that was in the array, so I'm using an elimination form for arrays, not an introduction form for Booleans.

An introduction or elimination form is a syntactic form of *expression*, and it is associated with a *type* (or type constructor) that appears in its typing rule. An introduction form for a type constructor μ will have a typing rule that has a μ type in the conclusion; types in premises are often arbitrary types τ. An elimination form for the same μ will have a typing rule that has a μ type in a premise; the type in the conclusion is often an arbitrary type τ, or sometimes a fixed type like `bool`. Identifying introduction and elimination forms is the topic of Exercise 2 (page 388).

In a good design, information created by any introduction form can be extracted by an elimination form, and vice versa. A design that has all the forms and rules it needs resembles as design that has all the algebraic laws it needs, as discussed in Section 2.5.2 (page 111). Introduction forms relate to algebraic laws' *creators* and *producers*, and elimination forms relate to *observers*.

In each of these rules, an expression of array type (e_1 or e) has an arbitrary syntactic form, which need not be related to arrays. These rules match the elimination template.

These rules can be turned into code for the type checker, which you can fill in (Exercise 18):

348. ⟨*function* ty, *checks type of expression given* $\Gamma_\xi, \Gamma_\phi, \Gamma_\rho$ **[[prototype]]** 348⟩≡

```
| ty (AAT (a, i))           = raise LeftAsExercise "AAT"
| ty (APUT (a, i, e))       = raise LeftAsExercise "APUT"
| ty (AMAKE (len, init)) = raise LeftAsExercise "AMAKE"
| ty (ASIZE a)              = raise LeftAsExercise "ASIZE"
```

6.4 Common type constructors

Arrays are just one type of data. Others include functions, products, sums, and mutable references. All these types have proven their worth in many languages, and they all have standard typing rules, which are described in this section. The rules use a single type environment Γ, which replaces the triple $\Gamma_\xi, \Gamma_\phi, \Gamma_\rho$ used in Typed Impcore.

Functions If functions are first-class values, they should have first-class types. The function type constructor, which takes two arguments, is written using an infix $\rightarrow$. Functions are introduced by λ-abstraction and eliminated by function application. The λ-abstraction I show here makes the types of the formal parameters explicit, like a function definition in Typed Impcore. And for simplicity, it takes just one parameter.

$$\frac{\tau_1 \text{ and } \tau_2 \text{ are types}}{\tau_1 \rightarrow \tau_2 \text{ is a type}} \qquad \text{(ArrowFormation)}$$

$$\frac{\Gamma\{x \mapsto \tau\} \vdash e : \tau'}{\Gamma \vdash \text{LAMBDA}(x : \tau, e) : \tau \rightarrow \tau'} \qquad \text{(ArrowIntro)}$$

$$\frac{\Gamma \vdash e_1 : \tau \rightarrow \tau' \qquad \Gamma \vdash e_2 : \tau}{\Gamma \vdash \text{APPLY}(e_1, e_2) : \tau'} \qquad \text{(ArrowElim)}$$

Products A *product,* often called a *pair* or *tuple,* groups together values of different types. It corresponds to ML's "tuple" type, to C's "struct," to Pascal's "record," and to the "Cartesian product" you may remember from math class. It is written using an infix $\times$. (To motivate the word "product," think about counting inhabitants: if two values inhabit type `bool` and five values inhabit type `lettergrade`, how many values inhabit product type `bool` $\times$ `lettergrade`?)

In addition to a formation rule, product types are supported by one introduction form, PAIR, and two elimination forms, FST and SND.

$$\frac{\tau_1 \text{ and } \tau_2 \text{ are types}}{\tau_1 \times \tau_2 \text{ is a type}} \qquad \text{(PairFormation)}$$

$$\frac{\Gamma \vdash e_1 : \tau_1 \qquad \Gamma \vdash e_2 : \tau_2}{\Gamma \vdash \text{PAIR}(e_1, e_2) : \tau_1 \times \tau_2} \qquad \text{(PairIntro)}$$

$$\frac{\Gamma \vdash e : \tau_1 \times \tau_2}{\Gamma \vdash \text{FST}(e) : \tau_1} \qquad \text{(Fst)}$$

$$\frac{\Gamma \vdash e : \tau_1 \times \tau_2}{\Gamma \vdash \text{SND}(e) : \tau_2} \qquad \text{(Snd)}$$

Like array operations, the pair operations are polymorphic, i.e., they can work with pairs of any types. And the pair operations are familiar: they appear in Chapter 2 under the names cons, car, and cdr. As noted in that chapter, their dynamic semantics is given by these algebraic laws:

$$\text{FST}(\text{PAIR}(v_1, v_2)) = v_1$$
$$\text{SND}(\text{PAIR}(v_1, v_2)) = v_2$$

Pair operations can be written using other notations. Often $\text{PAIR}(e_1, e_2)$ is written in concrete syntax as (e_1, e_2). Syntactic forms FST and SND may be written to look like functions fst and snd. In ML, these forms are written #1 and #2; in mathematical notation, they are sometimes written π_1 and π_2. Or they may be written using postfix notation; for example, $\text{FST}(e)$ might be written as $e.1$.

Using FST and SND to get the elements of a pair can be awkward. In ML code, there is a better idiom: pattern matching, which is combines elimination and binding. The ML pattern match `let val (`x`, `y`) = `e'` in `e` end` can be given a type as follows:

$$\frac{\Gamma \vdash e' : \tau_1 \times \tau_2 \qquad \Gamma\{x \mapsto \tau_1, y \mapsto \tau_2\} \vdash e : \tau}{\Gamma \vdash \texttt{let val (}x\texttt{, }y\texttt{) = }e'\texttt{ in }e\texttt{ end} : \tau}. \quad \text{(LETPAIR)}$$

The pair rules can be generalized to give types to tuples with any number of elements—even zero! The type of tuples with zero elements can serve as a UNIT type, since it is inhabited by only one value: the empty tuple. The tuple rules can be further generalized to give a name to each element of a tuple, so elements can be referred to by name instead of by position, something like a C `struct` (Exercise 5).

Sums Where a product provides an ordered collection of values of different types, a sum provides a *choice* among values of different types. And where products are supported in similar, obvious ways in almost every language, sums are supported in more diverse ways, some of which are hard to recognize. Easily recognizable examples include C's "union" types and Pascal's "variant records." ML's `datatype` is also a form of sum type.

In type theory, a sum type is written $\tau_1 + \tau_2$. A value of type $\tau_1 + \tau_2$ is either a value of type τ_1 or a value of type τ_2, tagged or labeled in a way that lets you tell which is which. (To motivate the word "sum," count the inhabitants of type `bool` $+$ `lettergrade`. If you're not sure about counting inhabitants, do Exercise 3.) In addition to a formation rule, sum types are supported by two introduction forms:

$$\frac{\tau_1 \text{ and } \tau_2 \text{ are types}}{\tau_1 + \tau_2 \text{ is a type}}, \quad \text{(SUMFORMATION)}$$

$$\frac{\Gamma \vdash e : \tau_1 \qquad \tau_2 \text{ is a type}}{\Gamma \vdash \text{LEFT}_{\tau_2}(e) : \tau_1 + \tau_2}, \quad \text{(LEFT)}$$

$$\frac{\Gamma \vdash e : \tau_2 \qquad \tau_1 \text{ is a type}}{\Gamma \vdash \text{RIGHT}_{\tau_1}(e) : \tau_1 + \tau_2}. \quad \text{(RIGHT)}$$

AAT	344d
AMAKE	344d
APUT	344d
ASIZE	344d
LeftAsExercise	S213b

Sum types are supported by a single elimination form: case, which in some languages is called switch. Let the let pattern match above, a case expression has too many parts to be understood when written in abstract-syntax notation; the rule uses ML-like concrete syntax.

$$\frac{\Gamma \vdash e : \tau_1 + \tau_2 \qquad \Gamma\{x_1 \mapsto \tau_1\} \vdash e_1 : \tau \qquad \Gamma\{x_2 \mapsto \tau_2\} \vdash e_2 : \tau}{\Gamma \vdash \textbf{case } e \textbf{ of } \text{LEFT}(x_1) \Rightarrow e_1 \mid \text{RIGHT}(x_2) \Rightarrow e_2 : \tau} \quad \text{(SUMELIMCASE)}$$

Sums and case expressions behave as described by these rules of operational semantics, which use (unsubscripted) value forms $\text{LEFT}(v)$ and $\text{RIGHT}(v)$:

$$\frac{\langle e, \rho, \sigma \rangle \Downarrow \langle v, \sigma' \rangle}{\langle \text{LEFT}_\tau(e), \rho, \sigma \rangle \Downarrow \langle \text{LEFT}(v), \sigma' \rangle} \;\text{(LEFT)} \qquad \frac{\langle e, \rho, \sigma \rangle \Downarrow \langle v, \sigma' \rangle}{\langle \text{RIGHT}_\tau(e), \rho, \sigma \rangle \Downarrow \langle \text{RIGHT}(v), \sigma' \rangle} \;\text{(RIGHT)},$$

$$\frac{\begin{array}{c}\langle e, \rho, \sigma \rangle \Downarrow \langle \text{LEFT}(v_1), \sigma' \rangle \\ \ell_1 \notin \operatorname{dom} \sigma' \\ \langle e_1, \rho\{x_1 \mapsto \ell_1\}, \sigma'\{\ell_1 \mapsto v_1\} \rangle \Downarrow \langle v, \sigma'' \rangle\end{array}}{\langle \textbf{case } e \textbf{ of } \text{LEFT}(x_1) \Rightarrow e_1 \mid \text{RIGHT}(x_2) \Rightarrow e_2, \rho, \sigma \rangle \Downarrow \langle v, \sigma'' \rangle}, \qquad \text{(CASELEFT)}$$

$$\frac{\begin{array}{c}\langle e, \rho, \sigma \rangle \Downarrow \langle \text{RIGHT}(v_2), \sigma' \rangle \\ \ell_2 \notin \operatorname{dom} \sigma' \\ \langle e_2, \rho\{x_2 \mapsto \ell_2\}, \sigma'\{\ell_2 \mapsto v_2\} \rangle \Downarrow \langle v, \sigma'' \rangle\end{array}}{\langle \textbf{case } e \textbf{ of } \text{LEFT}(x_1) \Rightarrow e_1 \mid \text{RIGHT}(x_2) \Rightarrow e_2, \rho, \sigma \rangle \Downarrow \langle v, \sigma'' \rangle}. \qquad \text{(CASERIGHT)}$$

If a language has first-class functions, the `case` expression can be replaced with a simpler form, `either`. The expression `(either` $e\ f\ g$`)`, which is equivalent to the case expression $\textbf{case } e \textbf{ of } \text{LEFT}(x_1) \Rightarrow f(x_1) \mid \text{RIGHT}(x_2) \Rightarrow g(x_2)$, applies either f or g to the value "carried" inside e.

Just like products, sums can be generalized so that each alternative has a name (Exercise 6).

Mutable cells The types shown above are all *immutable*, meaning that once created, a value can't be changed. Since mutation is a useful programming technique, essential for both procedural and object-oriented programming, type systems should support mutability—for example, with a type for "mutable cell containing value of type τ" (Exercise 7).

6.5 TYPE SOUNDNESS

If a program is well typed, what does that imply? It depends on the type system. A static type system should guarantee some properties about programs—usually safety properties. In other words, if a program type checks at compile time, that should tell you something about the program's behavior at run time.

A serious type system is designed around a safety property and supported by a proof that "well-typed programs don't go wrong," i.e., that well-typed programs satisfy the safety property. The type systems in this book can guarantee such properties as "the program never attempts to take `car` of an integer" or "a function is always called with the correct number of arguments." More advanced type systems can guarantee such properties as "no array access is ever out of bounds," "no pointer ever refers to memory that has been deallocated," or "no private information is ever stored in a public variable." Whatever the property of interest, the proof that a type system guarantees it is a *soundness* result.

A precise claim about soundness might refer to the intended meaning of each type. One common meaning is that a type τ prescribes a set of values $[\![\tau]\!]$. For example,

$$\begin{array}{lcl}
[\![\texttt{int}]\!] & = & \{\text{NUMBER}(n) \mid n \text{ is an integer}\} \\
[\![\texttt{bool}]\!] & = & \{\text{BOOLV}(\texttt{\#t}), \text{BOOLV}(\texttt{\#f})\} \\
[\![\texttt{sym}]\!] & = & \{\text{SYMBOL}(s) \mid s \text{ is a string}\} \\
[\![\tau \to \tau']\!] & = & \text{a set of functions taking values in } [\![\tau]\!] \text{ to values in } [\![\tau']\!].
\end{array}$$

A simple soundness claim might say that an expression of type τ evaluates to a value in the set $[\![\tau]\!]$. The claim is subject to conditions: evaluation must terminate, and evaluation and type checking must be done in compatible environments. A properly phrased claim might read like this:

> If for any x in $\operatorname{dom}\Gamma$, $x \in \operatorname{dom}\rho \wedge \rho(x) \in [\![\Gamma(x)]\!]$, and if $\Gamma \vdash e : \tau$, and if $\langle \rho, e \rangle \Downarrow v$, then $v \in [\![\tau]\!]$.

That is, if the environments make sense, and if expression e has type τ, and if evaluating e produces a value, then evaluation produces a value in $[\![\tau]\!]$. (To simplify the statement of the claim, I've used the simplest possible operational semantics, which uses no store.) A claim like this could be proved by simultaneous induction on the structure of the proof of $\Gamma \vdash e : \tau$ and the proof of $\langle \rho, e \rangle \Downarrow v$.

An even stronger soundness claim might add that unless a primitive like `/` or `car` fails, or unless e loops forever, that the evaluation of e does indeed produce a value. Using a small-step semantics like the one described in Chapter 3, such a claim might say that when all the expressions in an abstract machine are well typed, the machine has either terminated with a value and an empty stack, or it can step to a new state in which all its expressions are still well typed.

A type system with a strong soundness claim rules out most run-time errors. For example, in a sound, typed, Scheme-like language, then if evaluating e does not attempt to divide by zero or take `car` or `cdr` of the empty list, and if evaluating e doesn't get into an infinite loop, then the evaluation of e completes successfully.

6.6 Polymorphic type systems and Typed μScheme

The full benefits of types aren't provided by Typed Impcore, which is both too complicated and not powerful enough. Typed Impcore is too complicated because of its multiple type environments Γ_ξ, Γ_ϕ, and Γ_ρ. It is not powerful enough because each operation that works with values of more than one type, like `=` or `println`, has to be built into its abstract syntax. A function defined by a user can operate only on values of a single type, which is to say it is *monomorphic*. For example, a user can't define a reusable array-reversal function that could operate on both an array of Booleans and an array of integers. This limitation is shared by such languages as C and Pascal.

Monomorphism handicaps programmers. Many primitive structures, including arrays, lists, tables, pointers, products, sums, and objects, inherently work with multiple types: they are *polymorphic*. But when user-defined functions are monomorphic, a computation like the length of a list has to be coded anew for each type of list element, as in Chapter 1.

And monomorphic languages are hard to extend with new type constructors. A language designer can do it, provided they are willing to add new rules to a type system and to revisit its proof of type soundness. But a programmer can't; unless there is some sort of template or macro system, no programmer can add a user-defined, polymorphic type *constructor* such as the `env` type constructor used for environments in Chapters 5 to 10. At best, a programmer can add a new base type, not a new type constructor.

These problems are solved by *polymorphic type systems*. Such type systems enable a programmer to write polymorphic functions and to add new type constructors. Our first polymorphic type system is part of a language called *Typed micro-Scheme*, or Typed μScheme for short. Typed μScheme is patterned after μScheme: it uses the same *values* as μScheme and similar abstract syntax.

Our study of Typed μScheme begins with concrete syntax. It continues with *kinds* and *quantified types*; these are the two ideas at the core of the type system. Kinds are used to ensure that every type written in the source code is well formed and meaningful; kinds classify types in much the same way that types classify terms. Quantified types express polymorphism; they make it possible to implement polymorphic operations using ordinary functions instead of special-purpose abstract syntax. Building on these ideas, the rest of the chapter presents technical details needed to make a polymorphic type system work: *type equivalence* and *substitution*. Type equivalence is a relation that shows when two types cannot be distinguished by any program, even if they don't look identical. And substitution is the mechanism by which a polymorphic value is *instantiated* so it can be used.

6.6.1 Concrete syntax of Typed μScheme

Typed μScheme is much like μScheme, except as follows:

- Function definitions and `lambda` abstractions require type annotations for parameters.
- Function definitions require explicit result types.
- All `letrec` expressions require type annotations for bound names—and each name may be bound only to a `lambda` abstraction.
- Instead of μScheme's single `val` form, Typed μScheme provides two forms: `val-rec`, which is recursive and defines only functions, and `val`, which is non-recursive and can define any type of value. Only the `val-rec` form requires a type annotation. Typed μScheme's `val` and `val-rec` forms resemble the corresponding forms in Standard ML.

The type system of Typed μScheme is more powerful than that of Typed Impcore:

- Typed μScheme adds quantified types, which are written with `forall`. Values of quantified type are introduced by a new syntactic form of expression: `type-lambda`. They are eliminated by the new syntactic form `@`.
- Syntactically, Typed μScheme does not distinguish a "type" from a "type constructor"; both can be called "types," and both are in the syntactic category *type-exp*. The category, which is called "type-level expression," also includes ill-formed nonsense that is neither type nor type constructor, like `(int int)`.
- In Typed μScheme, only the type constructor for functions requires special-purpose syntax; a function is introduced by `lambda` and eliminated by function application. Other type constructors, like pairs and arrays, require no new syntax or new typing rules. They go into the initial basis, where their operations are implemented as ordinary (primitive) functions.

The syntax of Typed μScheme is shown in Figure 6.3 on the next page.

6.6.2 A replacement for type-formation rules: Kinds

Types in source code are written by programmers, and they can't be trusted. "Types" like `(int int)` are ill formed and must be rejected. In Typed Impcore, types are determined to be well formed or ill formed by type-formation rules. And for a language with a fixed set of types and type constructors, that's fine. But in Typed μScheme, we want to be able to add new type constructors without adding new rules. So Typed μScheme uses just a few rules to encompass arbitrarily many type constructors. The rules rely on each type constructor having a *kind*.

Kinds classify types (and type constructors) in much the same way that types classify terms. A kind shows how a type constructor may be used. For example,

def	::=	`(val` *variable-name exp*`)`
	|	`(val-rec [`*variable-name* `:` *type-exp*`]` *exp*`)`
	|	`(define` *type-exp function-name* `(`*formals*`)` *exp*`)`
	|	*exp*
	|	`(use` *file-name*`)`
	|	*unit-test*
unit-test	::=	`(check-expect` *exp exp*`)`
	|	`(check-assert` *exp*`)`
	|	`(check-error` *exp*`)`
	|	`(check-type` *exp type-exp*`)`
	|	`(check-type-error` *def*`)`
exp	::=	*literal*
	|	*variable-name*
	|	`(set` *variable-name exp*`)`
	|	`(if` *exp exp exp*`)`
	|	`(while` *exp exp*`)`
	|	`(begin` {*exp*}`)`
	|	`(`*exp* {*exp*}`)`
	|	`(`*let-keyword* `(`{`[`*variable-name exp*`]`}`)` *exp*`)`
	|	`(letrec [`{`([`*variable-name* `:` *type-exp*`]` *exp*`)`}`]` *exp*`)`
	|	`(lambda (`*formals*`)` *exp*`)`
	|	`(type-lambda [`*type-formals*`]` *exp*`)`
	|	`[@` *exp* {*type-exp*}`]`
let-keyword	::=	`let` | `let*`
formals	::=	{`[`*variable-name* `:` *type-exp*`]`}
type-formals	::=	{`'`*type-variable-name*}
type-exp	::=	*type-constructor-name*
	|	`'`*type-variable-name*
	|	`(forall (`{`'`*type-variable-name*}`)` *type-exp*`)`
	|	`(`{*type-exp*} `->` *type-exp*`)`
	|	`(`*type-exp* {*type-exp*}`)`
literal	::=	*numeral* | `#t` | `#f` | `'`*S-exp* | `(quote` *S-exp*`)`
S-exp	::=	*literal* | *symbol-name* | `(`{*S-exp*}`)`
numeral	::=	token composed only of digits, possibly prefixed with a plus or minus sign
**-name*	::=	token that is not a bracket, a *numeral*, or one of the "reserved" words shown in `typewriter font`

Figure 6.3: Concrete syntax of Typed μScheme

both int and array are type constructors of Typed μScheme, but they must be used differently. The int constructor is a kind of constructor that is a type all by itself; the array constructor is a kind of constructor that has to be applied to an element type in order to make another type. The first kind is written $*$ and pronounced "type"; the second kind is written $* \Rightarrow *$ and pronounced "type arrow type." A kind is attributed to a type by a formal judgment: $\tau :: \kappa$ says that type constructor τ has kind κ. As a special case, the judgment "$\tau :: *$" is equivalent to the judgment "τ is a type" used in Typed Impcore.

Like types, kinds are defined inductively: there is one base kind, "type" ($*$), and other kinds are made using arrows ($\Rightarrow$). As concrete notation, we write

$$\kappa ::= * \mid \kappa_1 \times \cdots \times \kappa_n \Rightarrow \kappa.$$

Types that are inhabited by values, like int or (list bool), have kind $*$. Types of other kinds, like list and array, are ultimately used to make types of kind $*$.

Some common kinds, with example type constructors of those kinds, are as follows:

$*$	int, bool, unit
$* \Rightarrow *$	list, array, option
$* \times * \Rightarrow *$	pair, sum, Standard ML's ->

More exotic kinds can be found in languages like Haskell, which includes not only "monads," which are all types of kind $* \Rightarrow *$, but also "monad transformers," which are types of kind $(* \Rightarrow *) \Rightarrow (* \Rightarrow *)$.

Every syntactically expressible kind κ is well formed:

$$\frac{}{* \text{ is a kind}}, \qquad \text{(KINDFORMATIONTYPE)}$$

$$\frac{\kappa_1, \ldots, \kappa_n \text{ are kinds} \qquad \kappa \text{ is a kind}}{\kappa_1 \times \cdots \times \kappa_n \Rightarrow \kappa \text{ is a kind}}. \qquad \text{(KINDFORMATIONARROW)}$$

How do we know which type constructors have which kinds? The kind of each type constructor is stored in a *kind environment*, written Δ. The example environment Δ_0 below shows the kinds of the primitive type constructors of Typed μScheme. Each binding is written using the :: symbol, which is used instead of $\mapsto$; it is pronounced "has kind."

$$\Delta_0 = \{\texttt{int} :: *,\ \texttt{bool} :: *,\ \texttt{unit} :: *,\ \texttt{pair} :: * \times * \Rightarrow *,\ \texttt{sum} :: * \times * \Rightarrow *,\ \texttt{array} :: * \Rightarrow *,\ \texttt{list} :: * \Rightarrow *\}$$

The kind environment determines how both int and array may be used. New type constructors can be added to Typed μScheme just by adding them to Δ_0 (Exercises 10 to 13).

A kind environment is used to tell what *types* are well formed. No matter how many type constructors are defined, they are handled using just three type-formation rules:

- A type can be formed by writing a type constructor. In abstract syntax, a type constructor is written TYCON(μ), where μ is the name of the constructor. In concrete syntax it is written just using its name, like int or list. A type constructor is well formed if and only if it is bound in Δ.
- A type can be formed by applying a type to other types. In abstract syntax, type application is written CONAPP($\tau, [\tau_1, \ldots, \tau_n]$), where τ and $\tau_1, \ldots, \tau_n$

are type-level expressions. In concrete syntax, application of a type constructor is written using the same concrete syntax as application of a function. For example, (list int) is the type "list of integer." A constructor application is well formed if its arguments have the kinds it expects, as formalized in the KINDAPP rule below.

- A type can be a function type. In abstract syntax, it is $\tau_1 \times \cdots \times \tau_n \to \tau$, where $\tau_1, \ldots, \tau_n$ are the argument types and τ is the result type. In concrete syntax, a function type is (τ_1 $\cdots$ τ_n -> τ).[3] A function type is well formed if and only if types τ_1 to τ_n and τ all have kind $*$.

These rules are formalized using the *kinding judgment* $\Delta \vdash \tau :: \kappa$. This judgment says that in kind environment Δ, type-level expression τ has kind κ. Kinds classify types in much the same way that types classify expressions.

$$\frac{\mu \in \operatorname{dom} \Delta}{\Delta \vdash \text{TYCON}(\mu) :: \Delta(\mu)} \quad \text{(KINDINTROCON)}$$

$$\frac{\Delta \vdash \tau :: \kappa_1 \times \cdots \times \kappa_n \Rightarrow \kappa \qquad \Delta \vdash \tau_i :: \kappa_i,\ 1 \le i \le n}{\Delta \vdash \text{CONAPP}(\tau, [\tau_1, \ldots, \tau_n]) :: \kappa} \quad \text{(KINDAPP)}$$

$$\frac{\Delta \vdash \tau_i :: *,\ 1 \le i \le n \qquad \Delta \vdash \tau :: *}{\Delta \vdash \tau_1 \times \cdots \times \tau_n \to \tau :: *} \quad \text{(KINDFUNCTION)}$$

No matter how many type constructors we may add to Typed μScheme, these kinding rules tell us everything we will ever need to know about the formation of types. Compare this situation with the situation in Typed Impcore. In Typed Impcore, we need the BASETYPES rule for int and bool. To add arrays we need the ARRAYFORMATION rule. To add lists we would need a list-formation rule (Exercise 4, page 389). And so on. Unlike Typed Impcore's type system, Typed μScheme's type system can easily be extended with new type constructors (Exercises 10 to 13). Similar ideas are used in languages in which *programmers* can define new type constructors, including μML and Molecule (Chapters 8 and 9).

Implementing kinds

A kind is represented using the datatype kind.

355a. ⟨*kinds for typed languages* 355a⟩≡ (S405a) 355b▷

```
datatype kind = TYPE                          (* kind of all types *)
              | ARROW of kind list * kind     (* kind of many constructors *)
```

Kinds are equal if and only if they are identical.

355b. ⟨*kinds for typed languages* 355a⟩+≡ (S405a) ◁355a

```
                                   eqKind  : kind      * kind      -> bool
                                   eqKinds : kind list * kind list -> bool
fun eqKind (TYPE, TYPE) = true
  | eqKind (ARROW (args, result), ARROW (args', result')) =
      eqKinds (args, args') andalso eqKind (result, result')
  | eqKind (_, _) = false
and eqKinds (ks, ks') = ListPair.allEq eqKind (ks, ks')
```

[3] The arrow that signifies a function occurs in the *middle* of the parentheses, between types. In other words, the function arrow -> is an *infix* operator. This infix syntax violates Lisp's *prefix* convention, in which keywords, type constructors, and operators always come first, immediately after an open parenthesis. Prefix syntax might look like "(function (τ_1 ... τ_n) τ)." But when functions take or return other functions, prefix syntax is too hard to read.

The kinds of the primitive type constructors, which populate the initial kind environment Δ_0, are represented as follows.

356. ⟨*primitive type constructors for Typed μScheme* **::** 356⟩≡ (382c)

```
("int",  TYPE) ::
("bool", TYPE) ::
("sym",  TYPE) ::
("unit", TYPE) ::
("list", ARROW ([TYPE], TYPE)) ::
```

The kind system and the type-formation rules shown above replace the type-formation rules of Typed Impcore. To get polymorphism, however, we need something more: quantified types.

6.6.3 *The heart of polymorphism: Quantified types*

Polymorphic functions aplenty can be found in Chapter 2; one of the simplest is `length`. As defined in (untyped) μScheme, `length` can be applied to any list of values, no matter what the types of its elements:

```
(define length (xs)
  (if (null? xs) 0 (+ 1 (length (cdr xs)))))
```

Suppose `length` could be defined in Typed Impcore; what would its type be? In a monomorphic language like Typed Impcore or C, a function can have at most one type, so the definition would have to designate an element type. To use `length` with different types of lists would require different versions:

```
(define int lengthI ([xs : (list int)])
   (if (null? xs) 0 (+ 1 (lengthI (cdr xs)))))
(define int lengthB ([xs : (list bool)])
   (if (null? xs) 0 (+ 1 (lengthB (cdr xs)))))
(define int lengthS ([xs : (list sym)])
   (if (null? xs) 0 (+ 1 (lengthS (cdr xs)))))
```

Such duplication wastes effort; except for the types, the functions are identical. but Typed Impcore's type system cannot express the idea that `length` works with any list, independent of the element type. To express the idea that `length` could work with any element type, we need *type variables* and *quantified types.*

A type variable stands for an unknown type; a quantified type grants permission to *substitute* any type for a type variable. In this book, type variables are written using the Greek letters α, β, and γ; quantified types are written using $\forall$. For example, the type of a polymorphic `length` function is $\forall\alpha\,.\,\alpha$ `list` $\rightarrow$ `int`. Greek letters and math symbols can be awkward in code, so in Typed μScheme this type is written `(forall ['a] ((list 'a) -> int))`.

A `forall` type is not a function type; the `length` function can't be used on a list of Booleans, for example, until it is *instantiated.* The instantiation `(@ length bool)` strips "$\forall\alpha$." from the front of `length`'s type, and in what remains, substitutes `bool` for α. The type of the resulting *instance* is `bool list` $\rightarrow$ `bool`, or in Typed μScheme, `((list bool) -> int)`. This instance can be applied to a list of Booleans.

Like `lambda`, $\forall$ is a *binding* construct, and the variable α is sometimes called a *type parameter*. Like the name of a formal parameter, the name of a type parameter doesn't matter; for example, the type of the `length` function could also be written $\forall\beta\,.\,\beta$ `list` $\rightarrow$ `int`, and its meaning would be unchanged. That's because the meaning of a quantified type is determined by how it behaves when we strip the quantifier and substitute for the bound type variable.

In abstract syntax, type variables and quantified types are written using TYVAR and FORALL. And like TYCON and CONAPP, TYVAR and FORALL are governed by kinding rules. (The kind system replaces the type-formation rules used in Typed Impcore; remember the slogan "just as types classify terms, kinds classify types.")

The kind of a type variable, like the kind of a type constructor, is looked up in the environment Δ.

$$\frac{\alpha \in \operatorname{dom} \Delta}{\Delta \vdash \text{TYVAR}(\alpha) :: \Delta(\alpha)} \qquad \text{(KINDINTROVAR)}$$

The kind of a quantified type is always $*$, and the FORALL quantifier may be used only over types of kind $*$. Within the body of the FORALL, the quantified variables stand for types. So above the line, they are introduced into the kind environment with kind $*$.

$$\frac{\Delta\{\alpha_1 :: *, \ldots, \alpha_n :: *\} \vdash \tau :: *}{\Delta \vdash \text{FORALL}(\langle \alpha_1, \ldots, \alpha_n \rangle, \tau) :: *} \qquad \text{(KINDALL)}$$

In some polymorphic type systems, including the functional language Haskell, type variables may have other kinds.

In Typed μScheme, every type is written using a type-level expression (nonterminal *type-exp* in Figure 6.3, page 353). In the interpreter, a type-level expression is represented by a value of the ML type `tyex`; its forms include not only TYVAR and FORALL but also TYCON, CONAPP, and a function-type form.

357a. ⟨*types for Typed μScheme* 357a⟩≡ (S405a) 381a ▷

```
datatype tyex = TYCON  of name                (* type constructor *)
              | CONAPP of tyex * tyex list    (* type-level application *)
              | FUNTY  of tyex list * tyex    (* function type *)
              | FORALL of name list * tyex    (* quantified type *)
              | TYVAR  of name                (* type variable *)
```

Even though not every `tyex` represents a well-formed type, it's easier to call them all "types"—except when we have to be careful.

Examples of well-formed types, written using concrete syntax, include the types of the following polymorphic functions and values related to lists:

357b. ⟨*transcript* 357b⟩≡ 358a ▷

```
-> length
<function> : (forall ['a] ((list 'a) -> int))
-> cons
<function> : (forall ['a] ('a (list 'a) -> (list 'a)))
-> car
<function> : (forall ['a] ((list 'a) -> 'a))
-> cdr
<function> : (forall ['a] ((list 'a) -> (list 'a)))
-> '()
() : (forall ['a] (list 'a))
```


Polymorphism is not restricted to functions: even though it is not a function, the empty list has a quantified type.

The parenthesized-prefix syntax above is easy to parse and easy to understand, but not so easy to read. So I also use an algebraic notation in which type constructors are μ, type variables are α, and types are τ. I follow the ML postfix convention for application of type constructors, and I use special notation for the function constructor:

$$\tau ::= \mu \mid \alpha \mid (\tau_1, \ldots, \tau_n)\, \tau \mid \forall \alpha_1, \ldots, \alpha_n \,.\, \tau \mid \tau_1 \times \cdots \times \tau_n \to \tau.$$

Using this special notation, the types of `length`, `cons`, `car`, `cdr`, and `'()` are written as follows:

$$\begin{aligned}
&\texttt{length} : \forall\alpha\,.\,\alpha\,\texttt{list} \to \texttt{int}\\
&\texttt{cons} \;\;: \forall\alpha\,.\,\alpha \times \alpha\,\texttt{list} \to \alpha\,\texttt{list}\\
&\texttt{car} \;\;\;: \forall\alpha\,.\,\alpha\,\texttt{list} \to \alpha\\
&\texttt{cdr} \;\;\;: \forall\alpha\,.\,\alpha\,\texttt{list} \to \alpha\,\texttt{list}\\
&\texttt{'()} \;\;\;: \forall\alpha\,.\,\alpha\,\texttt{list}
\end{aligned}$$

A function (or other value) with a quantified type can't be used until it is *instantiated.* Instantiation determines what type each bound type variable stands for. A polymorphic expression is instantiated by a syntactic form, written with `@` symbol, which gives the expression to be instantiated plus a type to be substituted for each bound type variable. Instantiation produces an *instance.* Both the instantiation and the instance may be pronounced with the word "at," as in "`length` at integer," which would be appropriate in these examples:[4]

358a. ⟨*transcript* 357b⟩+≡ ◁357b 358b▷

```
-> (val length-at-int [@ length int])
length-at-int : ((list int) -> int)
-> (val cons-at-bool [@ cons bool])
cons-at-bool : (bool (list bool) -> (list bool))
-> pair
<function> : (forall ['a 'b] ('a 'b -> (pair 'a 'b)))
-> (val car-at-pair [@ car (pair sym int)])
car-at-pair : ((list (pair sym int)) -> (pair sym int))
-> (val cdr-at-sym [@ cdr sym])
cdr-at-sym : ((list sym) -> (list sym))
-> (val empty-at-int [@ '() int])
() : (list int)
```

In each case, the type of the instance is obtained by *substituting* each type parameter for the corresponding type variable in the `forall`. Each instance is monomorphic, and if it has an arrow type, it can be applied to values.

358b. ⟨*transcript* 357b⟩+≡ ◁358a 358c▷

```
-> (length-at-int '(1 4 9 16 25))
5 : int
-> (cons-at-bool #t '(#f #f))
(#t #f #f) : (list bool)
-> (car-at-pair ([@ cons (pair sym int)]
                 ([@ pair sym int] 'Office 231)
                 [@ '() (pair sym int)]))
(Office . 231) : (pair sym int)
-> (cdr-at-sym '(a b c d))
(b c d) : (list sym)
```

Getting the instances you want takes thought and practice. A common mistake is to instantiate by substituting the type you want the instance to have. If you want a function of type `((list bool) -> int)`, instantiate `length` at `bool`. If instead you instantiate `length` at the desired type `((list bool) -> int)`, the instance won't have the type you hoped for:

358c. ⟨*transcript* 357b⟩+≡ ◁358b 359a▷

```
-> (val useless-length [@ length ((list bool) -> int)])
useless-length : ((list ((list bool) -> int)) -> int)
```

[4] Instantiation is also called *type application.* It is deeply related to function application. Instantiation is defined by substituting for type variables bound by ∀. And in Alonzo Church's fundamental theory of programming languages, the lambda calculus, function application is defined by substituting for term variables bound by λ.

A function like `useless-length` has a good type but can't be used to take the length of a list of Booleans.

359a. ⟨*transcript* 357b⟩+≡ ◁358c 362▷

```
-> (useless-length '(#t #f #f))
type error: function useless-length of type ...
-> [@ length bool]
<function> : ((list bool) -> int)
-> ([@ length bool] '(#t #f #f))
3 : int
```


As the `car-at-pair` example and the final two `length` examples show, an instance doesn't have to be named; instances can be used directly.

The instantiation form `@` lets you *use* a polymorphic value; it is the elimination form for quantified types. To *create* a polymorphic value you need an introduction form. In Typed μScheme, the introduction form is written using `type-lambda`; it is sometimes called *type abstraction*. As an example, I use `type-lambda` to define the polymorphic functions `list1`, `list2`, and `list3`.

359b. ⟨*predefined Typed μScheme functions* 359b⟩≡ 359c▷

```
(val list1 (type-lambda ['a] (lambda ([x : 'a])
                               ([@ cons 'a] x [@ '() 'a]))))
(val list2 (type-lambda ['a] (lambda ([x : 'a] [y : 'a])
                               ([@ cons 'a] x ([@ list1 'a] y)))))
(val list3 (type-lambda ['a] (lambda ([x : 'a] [y : 'a] [z : 'a])
                               ([@ cons 'a] x ([@ list2 'a] y z)))))
```

As another example, `type-lambda` is used to define some of the higher-order functions in Chapter 2. Their types are as follows:

$$
\begin{array}{ll}
\texttt{o} & : \forall \alpha, \beta, \gamma \,.\, (\beta \to \gamma) \times (\alpha \to \beta) \to (\alpha \to \gamma) \\
\texttt{curry} & : \forall \alpha, \beta, \gamma \,.\, (\alpha \times \beta \to \gamma) \to (\alpha \to (\beta \to \gamma)) \\
\texttt{uncurry} & : \forall \alpha, \beta, \gamma \,.\, (\alpha \to (\beta \to \gamma)) \to (\alpha \times \beta \to \gamma)
\end{array}
$$

Their implementations use only `type-lambda`, `lambda`, and function application:

359c. ⟨*predefined Typed μScheme functions* 359b⟩+≡ ◁359b 359d▷

```
(val o (type-lambda ['a 'b 'c]
  (lambda ([f : ('b -> 'c)] [g : ('a -> 'b)])
     (lambda ([x : 'a]) (f (g x))))))

(val curry (type-lambda ['a 'b 'c]
   (lambda ([f : ('a 'b -> 'c)])
      (lambda ([x : 'a]) (lambda ([y : 'b]) (f x y))))))

(val uncurry (type-lambda ['a 'b 'c]
   (lambda ([f : ('a -> ('b -> 'c))])
      (lambda ([x : 'a] [y : 'b]) ((f x) y)))))
```

Other higher-order functions are not only polymorphic but also recursive. Such functions are defined by nesting `letrec` (for recursion) inside `type-lambda` (for polymorphism).

359d. ⟨*predefined Typed μScheme functions* 359b⟩+≡ ◁359c 360a▷

```
(val length
  (type-lambda ['a]
    (letrec
       [([length-mono : ((list 'a) -> int)]
             (lambda ([xs : (list 'a)])
               (if ([@ null? 'a] xs)
                   0
                   (+ 1 (length-mono ([@ cdr 'a] xs))))))]
       length-mono)))
```

The inner function is called `length-mono` because it—like any value introduced with `lambda`—is monomorphic, operating only on lists of the given element type `'a`: the recursive call to `length-mono` does *not* require an instantiation.

Every polymorphic, recursive function is defined using the same pattern: `val` to `type-lambda` to `letrec`. Another example is an explicitly typed version of the reverse-append function:

360a. ⟨*predefined Typed μScheme functions* 359b⟩+≡ ◁359d 360b▷

```
(val revapp
  (type-lambda ['a]
    (letrec [([revapp-mono : ((list 'a) (list 'a) -> (list 'a))]
                (lambda ([xs : (list 'a)] [ys : (list 'a)])
                  (if ([@ null? 'a] xs)
                    ys
                    (revapp-mono ([@ cdr 'a] xs)
                                 ([@ cons 'a] ([@ car 'a] xs) ys)))))]
      revapp-mono)))
```

As another example, `filter` is defined as follows:

360b. ⟨*predefined Typed μScheme functions* 359b⟩+≡ ◁360a 360c▷

```
(val filter
  (type-lambda ('a)
    (letrec
      [([filter-mono : (('a -> bool) (list 'a) -> (list 'a))]
          (lambda ([p? : ('a -> bool)] [xs : (list 'a)])
            (if ([@ null? 'a] xs)
                [@ '() 'a]
                (if (p? ([@ car 'a] xs))
                    ([@ cons 'a] ([@ car 'a] xs)
                                 (filter-mono p? ([@ cdr 'a] xs)))
                    (filter-mono p? ([@ cdr 'a] xs))))))]
      filter-mono)))
```

And likewise `map`:

360c. ⟨*predefined Typed μScheme functions* 359b⟩+≡ ◁360b

```
(val map
  (type-lambda ('a 'b)
    (letrec
      [([map-mono : (('a -> 'b) (list 'a) -> (list 'b))]
          (lambda ([f : ('a -> 'b)] [xs : (list 'a)])
            (if ([@ null? 'a] xs)
                [@ '() 'b]
                ([@ cons 'b] (f ([@ car 'a] xs))
                             (map-mono f ([@ cdr 'a] xs))))))]
      map-mono)))
```

As shown by these examples, explicit types and polymorphism impose a notational burden. At the cost of a little expressive power, that burden can be lifted by *type inference*, as in nano-ML (Chapter 7). Or the burden can be lightened by instantiating an entire module at once, as in Molecule (Chapter 9).

To summarize this section, the essential new idea in a polymorphic type system is the *quantified type*. It comes with its own special-purpose syntax: `forall` to form a quantified type, `type-lambda` to introduce a quantified type, and `@` to eliminate a quantified type. The rest of this chapter shows how quantified types are combined with μScheme to produce Typed μScheme.

6.6.4 *Abstract syntax, values, and evaluation of Typed μScheme*

Like the concrete syntax, the abstract syntax of Typed μScheme resembles the abstract syntax of μScheme. Typed μScheme adds two new expressions, TYLAMBDA and TYAPPLY, which introduce and eliminate quantified types. And it requires that names bound by `letrec` or `lambda` (internal recursive functions and the parameters of every function) be annotated with explicit types.

361a. ⟨*definitions of* `exp` *and* `value` *for Typed μScheme* 361a⟩≡ (S405b) 361b ▷

```
datatype exp    = LITERAL  of value
                | VAR      of name
                | SET      of name * exp
                | IFX      of exp * exp * exp
                | WHILEX   of exp * exp
                | BEGIN    of exp list
                | APPLY    of exp * exp list
                | LETX     of let_flavor * (name * exp) list * exp
                | LETRECX  of ((name * tyex) * exp) list * exp
                | LAMBDA   of lambda_exp
                | TYLAMBDA of name list * exp
                | TYAPPLY  of exp * tyex list
and let_flavor = LET | LETSTAR
```

The values of Typed μScheme are the same as the values of μScheme; adding a type system doesn't change the representation used at run time.

361b. ⟨*definitions of* `exp` *and* `value` *for Typed μScheme* 361a⟩+≡ (S405b) ◁ 361a

```
and     value = NIL
              | BOOLV     of bool
              | NUM       of int
              | SYM       of name
              | PAIR      of value * value
              | CLOSURE   of lambda_value * value ref env
              | PRIMITIVE of primitive
withtype primitive    = value list -> value (* raises RuntimeError *)
     and lambda_exp   = (name * tyex) list * exp
     and lambda_value = name          list * exp
```

The definitions of Typed μScheme are like those of Typed Impcore, plus the recursive binding form VALREC (see sidebar on the following page).

361c. ⟨*definition of* `def` *for Typed μScheme* 361c⟩≡ (S405b)

```
datatype def  = VAL    of name * exp
              | VALREC of name * tyex * exp
              | EXP    of exp
              | DEFINE of name * tyex * lambda_exp
```

6.6.5 *Typing rules for Typed μScheme*

type env	304
type name	303
type tyex	357a

The typing rules for Typed μScheme are very like the rules for Typed Impcore. The important differences are these:

- There is only one type environment, Γ. It maps values to types.
- There is a kind environment, Δ, which keeps track of the kinds of type variables and type constructors.
- There are no special-purpose typing rules associated with individual type constructors. Type formation is handled by the general-purpose kinding

Language design: True definitions in a typed language with `lambda`

Like μScheme, Typed μScheme has more definition forms that it really needs: given its `lambda` and `letrec` expressions, the only definition form it really needs is `val` (Exercise 21). But Typed μScheme is not meant to be as small as possible; it's meant to convey understanding and to facilitate comparisons. So it includes `define`.

In untyped μScheme, `define` is just syntactic sugar for a `val` binding to a `lambda` (page 120). Because a μScheme `val` makes its bound name visible on the right-hand side, such functions can even be recursive. μScheme's operational semantics initializes the name to an unspecified value, then overwrites the name with a closure. This semantics extends to *all* `val` bindings; for example, in untyped μScheme you can write `(val n (+ n 1))`, and on the right-hand side, the value of `n` is unspecified. But in Typed μScheme, we can't afford to compute with unspecified values; if an expression like `(+ n 1)` typechecks, we have to *know* that `n` has an integer value.

Typed μScheme works around this problem by changing the operational semantics of `val` back to the semantics used in Impcore: in Typed μScheme, as in Impcore, a `val` binding is not recursive, and the name being defined is not visible on the right-hand side.

362. ⟨*transcript* 357b⟩+≡ ◁359a 368a▷

```
-> (val n (+ n 1))
Name n not found
```

For recursive bindings, Typed μScheme introduces the new form `val-rec`, which has the same operational semantics as μScheme's `val` form. To ensure that the right-hand side does not evaluate the name before it is initialized, Typed μScheme restricts the right-hand side to be a `lambda` form. And to make it possible to typecheck recursive calls, Typed μScheme requires a type annotation that gives the type of the bound name. Using `val-rec` and `lambda`, `define` can easily be expressed as syntactic sugar.

The distinction between `val` and `val-rec` can be found in other languages. Look for it! For example, in C, type definitions act like `val`, but in Modula-3, they act like `val-rec`. And in Haskell, *every* definition form acts like `val-rec`! (Haskell gets away with this because no definition form evaluates its right-hand side.)

rules; introduction and elimination are handled by the general-purpose typing rules for type abstraction, instantiation, `lambda` abstraction, and application.

Two technical details should not be overlooked:

- In a `forall` type, the names of quantified type variables are not supposed to matter. This detail affects any decision about whether two types are the same.
- Type application using `@` works by substituting a type for a type variable. And when `forall` types are nested, substitution is easy to get wrong.

As I present the rules, I take it for granted that the names of quantified type variables don't matter and that substitution is implemented correctly. To enable you to implement the rules, I then present detailed implementations of type-equivalence testing and substitution (Sections 6.6.6 and 6.6.7).

Typing rules for expressions

The typing judgment for an expression is $\boxed{\Delta, \Gamma \vdash e : \tau}$, meaning that given kind environment Δ and type environment Γ, expression e has type τ. Each form of e has its own rule or rules, starting with literal expressions.

The type of a literal depends only on its value; different forms of value have different rules. The rules force lists to be homogeneous, with one fine point: empty lists are polymorphic, but nonempty lists are monomorphic.

$$\frac{}{\Delta, \Gamma \vdash \text{LITERAL}(\text{NUM}(n)) : \texttt{int}} \qquad \frac{}{\Delta, \Gamma \vdash \text{LITERAL}(\text{BOOLV}(n)) : \texttt{bool}}$$

(LITERALS1)

(LITERALS2)

$$\frac{}{\Delta, \Gamma \vdash \text{LITERAL}(\text{SYM}(n)) : \texttt{sym}}$$

$$\frac{}{\Delta, \Gamma \vdash \text{LITERAL}(\text{NIL}) : \forall \alpha \,.\, \alpha\ \texttt{list}} \qquad \frac{\Delta, \Gamma \vdash \text{LITERAL}(v) : \tau}{\Delta, \Gamma \vdash \text{LITERAL}(\text{PAIR}(v, \text{NIL})) : \tau\ \texttt{list}}$$

(LISTLITERALS1)

$$\frac{\Delta, \Gamma \vdash \text{LITERAL}(v) : \tau \qquad \Delta, \Gamma \vdash \text{LITERAL}(v') : \tau\ \texttt{list}}{\Delta, \Gamma \vdash \text{LITERAL}(\text{PAIR}(v, v')) : \tau\ \texttt{list}} \quad \text{(LISTLITERALS2)}$$

A use of a variable x is well typed if x is bound in the type environment Γ. The variable x may also be assigned to, provided the type of the right-hand side is also the type of x.

$$\frac{x \in \operatorname{dom} \Gamma \qquad \Gamma(x) = \tau}{\Delta, \Gamma \vdash \text{VAR}(x) : \tau} \quad \text{(VAR)}$$

$$\frac{\Delta, \Gamma \vdash e : \tau \qquad x \in \operatorname{dom} \Gamma \qquad \Gamma(x) = \tau}{\Delta, \Gamma \vdash \text{SET}(x, e) : \tau} \quad \text{(SET)}$$

As in Typed Impcore, a `while` loop is well typed if the condition is Boolean and the body is well typed. The result has type `unit`.

$$\frac{\Delta, \Gamma \vdash e_1 : \texttt{bool} \qquad \Delta, \Gamma \vdash e_2 : \tau}{\Delta, \Gamma \vdash \text{WHILE}(e_1, e_2) : \texttt{unit}} \quad \text{(WHILE)}$$

Also as in Typed Impcore, a conditional expression is well typed if the condition is Boolean and the two branches have the same type τ. In that case, the type of the conditional expression is also τ.

$$\frac{\Delta, \Gamma \vdash e_1 : \texttt{bool} \qquad \Delta, \Gamma \vdash e_2 : \tau \qquad \Delta, \Gamma \vdash e_3 : \tau}{\Delta, \Gamma \vdash \text{IF}(e_1, e_2, e_3) : \tau} \quad \text{(IF)}$$

As in Typed Impcore, a sequence is well typed if its subexpressions are well typed.

$$\frac{\Delta, \Gamma \vdash e_i : \tau_i, \quad 1 \le i \le n}{\Delta, \Gamma \vdash \text{BEGIN}(e_1, \ldots, e_n) : \tau_n} \quad \text{(BEGIN)}$$

Also as in Typed Impcore, the empty BEGIN has type `unit`.

$$\frac{}{\Delta, \Gamma \vdash \text{BEGIN}() : \texttt{unit}} \quad \text{(EMPTYBEGIN)}$$

A LET expression is well typed if all of the right-hand sides are well typed, and if in an environment extended with the types of the bound names, the body is well typed. The type of the LET expression is the type of the body.

$$\frac{\Delta, \Gamma \vdash e_i : \tau_i, \quad 1 \le i \le n \qquad \Delta, \Gamma\{x_1 \mapsto \tau_1, \ldots, x_n \mapsto \tau_n\} \vdash e : \tau}{\Delta, \Gamma \vdash \text{LET}(\langle x_1, e_1, \ldots, x_n, e_n \rangle, e) : \tau} \quad \text{(LET)}$$

The rule applies equally well to the empty LET.

Recursive `letrec` *bindings in a typed language*

The `letrec` form is intended for recursive functions. In a form like

```
(letrec [([f1 : τ1] e1)
         ([f2 : τ2] e2)]
  e),
```

each bound name f_i is visible during the evaluation of each right-hand side e_i. But at run time, f_1 and f_2 don't get their values until *after* e_1 and e_2 have been evaluated. The operational semantics leaves their initial values unspecified:

$$\frac{\begin{array}{c}\ell_1, \ell_2 \notin \operatorname{dom} \sigma \text{ (and all distinct)} \\ \rho' = \rho\{f_1 \mapsto \ell_1, f_2 \mapsto \ell_2\} \\ \sigma_0 = \sigma\{\ell_1 \mapsto \text{unspecified}, \ell_2 \mapsto \text{unspecified}\} \\ \langle e_1, \rho', \sigma_0 \rangle \Downarrow \langle v_1, \sigma_1 \rangle \\ \langle e_2, \rho', \sigma_1 \rangle \Downarrow \langle v_2, \sigma_2 \rangle \\ \langle e, \rho', \sigma_2\{\ell_1 \mapsto v_1, \ell_2 \mapsto v_2\} \rangle \Downarrow \langle v, \sigma' \rangle\end{array}}{\langle \text{LETREC}(\langle f_1 : \tau_1, e_1, f_2 : \tau_2, e_2 \rangle, e), \rho, \sigma \rangle \Downarrow \langle v, \sigma' \rangle} \quad \text{(LETREC2)}$$

While e_1 and e_2 are being evaluated, the contents of ℓ_1 and ℓ_2 are unspecified, and therefore untrustworthy. In particular, the contents of ℓ_1 and ℓ_2 are independent of the *types* τ_1 and τ_2. While e is being evaluated, by contrast, the contents of ℓ_1 and ℓ_2 do respect types τ_1 and τ_2, and so f_1 and f_2 can be evaluated safely. To preserve type safety, then, Typed μScheme's type system must prevent f_1 and f_2 from being evaluated until after ℓ_1 and ℓ_2 have been updated to hold values v_1 and v_2. And in μScheme, the way to keep something from being evaluated is to protect it under a LAMBDA. (In a lazy language like Haskell, a right-hand side is never evaluated until its value is needed, so Haskell's `letrec` is not restricted in this way.) Typed μScheme uses the same tactic as the ML family of languages: it requires that the right-hand sides e_1 and e_2 be LAMBDA forms. So `letrec` is useful only for defining recursive functions, including mutually recursive functions.

A LETREC is well typed when the corresponding LET is well typed, except that each right-hand side e_i can refer to any of the bound names x_j. So the right-hand sides are typechecked in the extended environment $\Gamma\{x_1 \mapsto \tau_1, \ldots, x_n \mapsto \tau_n\}$. Types τ_1 to τ_n, which are written in the syntax, must all have kind $*$.

$$\frac{\begin{array}{c}\Delta \vdash \tau_i :: *, \quad 1 \leq i \leq n \\ \Delta, \Gamma\{x_1 \mapsto \tau_1, \ldots, x_n \mapsto \tau_n\} \vdash e_i : \tau_i, \quad 1 \leq i \leq n \\ \Delta, \Gamma\{x_1 \mapsto \tau_1, \ldots, x_n \mapsto \tau_n\} \vdash e : \tau\end{array}}{\Delta, \Gamma \vdash \text{LETREC}(\langle x_1 : \tau_1, e_1, \ldots, x_n : \tau_n, e_n \rangle, e) : \tau} \quad \text{(LETREC)}$$

As in untyped μScheme, the parser ensures that every e_i has the form of a LAMBDA. This requirement prevents any e_i from evaluating an uninitialized x_j (see sidebar above).

A rule for LETSTAR would be annoying to write down directly—it would require a lot of bookkeeping for environments. Instead, I use syntactic sugar. A LETSTAR is well typed if the corresponding nest of LETs is well typed.

$$\frac{\Delta, \Gamma \vdash \text{LET}(\langle x_1, e_1 \rangle, \text{LETSTAR}(\langle x_2, e_2, \ldots, x_n, e_n \rangle, e)) : \tau \qquad n > 0}{\Delta, \Gamma \vdash \text{LETSTAR}(\langle x_1, e_1, \ldots, x_n, e_n \rangle, e) : \tau} \quad (\text{LETSTAR})$$

$$\frac{\Delta, \Gamma \vdash e : \tau}{\Delta, \Gamma \vdash \text{LETSTAR}(\langle\rangle, e) : \tau} \quad (\text{EMPTYLETSTAR})$$

A function is well typed if its body is well typed, in an environment that gives the types of the arguments. These types must be well formed and have kind $*$. The type of the body is the result type of the function.

$$\frac{\Delta \vdash \tau_i :: *, \ 1 \leq i \leq n \qquad \Delta, \Gamma\{x_1 \mapsto \tau_1, \ldots, x_n \mapsto \tau_n\} \vdash e : \tau}{\Delta, \Gamma \vdash \text{LAMBDA}(\langle x_1 : \tau_1, \ldots, x_n : \tau_n \rangle, e) : \tau_1 \times \cdots \times \tau_n \to \tau} \quad (\text{LAMBDA})$$

An application is well typed if the term being applied has an arrow type, and if the types and number of actual parameters match the types and number of formal parameters on the left of the arrow. The type of the application is the type to the right of the arrow (the result type).

$$\frac{\Delta, \Gamma \vdash e : \tau_1 \times \cdots \times \tau_n \to \tau \qquad \Delta, \Gamma \vdash e_i : \tau_i, \ 1 \leq i \leq n}{\Delta, \Gamma \vdash \text{APPLY}(e, e_1, \ldots, e_n) : \tau} \quad (\text{APPLY})$$

The most interesting rules, which have no counterpart in Typed Impcore, are for type abstraction and application, which introduce and eliminate polymorphism. The elimination form is simpler. To use ("eliminate") a polymorphic value, one chooses the types with which to instantiate the type variables. A type application is well typed if the instantiated term has a quantified type with the expected number of bound type variables, and if every actual type parameter (τ_1 to τ_n) has kind $*$. The notation $[\alpha_1 \mapsto \tau_1, \ldots, \alpha_n \mapsto \tau_n]$ indicates the *simultaneous, capture-avoiding substitution* of τ_1 for α_1, τ_2 for α_2, and so on.

$$\frac{\Delta, \Gamma \vdash e : \forall \alpha_1, \ldots, \alpha_n \,.\, \tau \qquad \Delta \vdash \tau_i :: *, \ 1 \leq i \leq n}{\Delta, \Gamma \vdash \text{TYAPPLY}(e, \tau_1, \ldots, \tau_n) : \tau[\alpha_1 \mapsto \tau_1, \ldots, \alpha_n \mapsto \tau_n]} \quad (\text{TYAPPLY})$$

Simultaneous means "substitute for all the α_i's at once," not one at a time. Simultaneous substitution can differ from sequential substitution if some τ_i contains an α_j. *Capture-avoiding* means that the substitution doesn't inadvertently change the meaning of a type variable; the details are explored at length in Section 6.6.7 (page 371).

The TYAPPLY rule justifies my informal claim that the names of quantified type variables don't matter. All you can do with a value of quantified type is substitute for its type variables, and once you substitute for them, they are gone. The names exist only to mark the correct locations for substitution—no more, and no less.

The introduction form for a quantified type is type abstraction. To create ("introduce") a polymorphic value, one abstracts over new type variables using TYLAMBDA. The type variables go into the kind environment Δ. In Typed μScheme, type variables always stand for types, so they have kind $*$. (In related, more ambitious languages like Haskell or F_ω, a type variable may have any kind.) A type abstraction is well typed if its body is well typed—and the body may refer to the newly bound type variables.

$$\frac{\alpha_i \notin \text{ftv}(\Gamma), \ 1 \leq i \leq n \qquad \Delta\{\alpha_1 :: *, \ldots \alpha_n :: *\}, \Gamma \vdash e : \tau}{\Delta, \Gamma \vdash \text{TYLAMBDA}(\alpha_1, \ldots, \alpha_n, e) : \forall \alpha_1, \ldots, \alpha_n \,.\, \tau} \quad (\text{TYLAMBDA})$$

A type abstraction must also satisfy the side condition $\alpha_i \notin \text{ftv}(\Gamma)$. Why? The set $\text{ftv}(\Gamma)$ contains the *free type variables* of Γ (page 372), and the side condition is needed to avoid changing the meaning of α_i in e. This need is illustrated in Section 6.6.9 (page 377).

Typing rules for definitions

Just as in the operational semantics, a definition can produce a new environment. The new environment is a type environment, not a value environment: it contains the types of the names introduced by the definition. As in Typed Impcore, the new environment is produced by *typing* the definition. The relevant judgment has the form $\boxed{\langle d, \Delta, \Gamma\rangle \to \Gamma'}$, which says that when definition d is typed in kind environment Δ and type environment Γ, the new type environment is Γ'. In Typed μScheme, a definition does not introduce any new types, so typing a definition leaves Δ unchanged.

A VAL binding is not recursive, so the name being bound is not visible to the right-hand side.

$$\frac{\Delta, \Gamma \vdash e : \tau}{\langle \text{VAL}(x, e), \Delta, \Gamma\rangle \to \Gamma\{x \mapsto \tau\}} \quad (\text{VAL})$$

A VAL-REC binding, by contrast, is recursive, and it requires an explicit type τ. Type τ must be well formed and have kind $*$, and it must be the type of the right-hand side.

$$\frac{\Delta \vdash \tau :: * \qquad \Delta, \Gamma\{x \mapsto \tau\} \vdash e : \tau \qquad e \text{ has the form LAMBDA}(\cdots)}{\langle \text{VAL-REC}(x, \tau, e), \Delta, \Gamma\rangle \to \Gamma\{x \mapsto \tau\}} \quad (\text{VALREC})$$

The bound name x is visible during the typechecking of the right-hand side e, but for safety, x must not be *evaluated* within e until *after* e's value has been stored in x. Restricting e to have the form of a LAMBDA prevents e from evaluating x, even if the body of the LAMBDA mentions x.[5]

A top-level expression is syntactic sugar for a binding to `it`.

$$\frac{\langle \text{VAL}(\texttt{it}, e), \Delta, \Gamma\rangle \to \Gamma'}{\langle \text{EXP}(e), \Delta, \Gamma\rangle \to \Gamma'} \quad (\text{EXP})$$

A DEFINE is syntactic sugar for a suitable VAL-REC. Indeed, Typed μScheme has VAL-REC only because it is easier to typecheck VAL-REC and LAMBDA independently than to typecheck DEFINE directly.

$$\frac{\langle \text{VAL-REC}(f, \tau_1 \times \cdots \times \tau_n \to \tau, \text{LAMBDA}(\langle x_1 : \tau_1, \ldots, x_n : \tau_n\rangle, e)), \Delta, \Gamma\rangle \to \Gamma'}{\langle \text{DEFINE}(f, \tau, \langle x_1 : \tau_1, \ldots, x_n : \tau_n\rangle, e), \Delta, \Gamma\rangle \to \Gamma'} \quad (\text{DEFINE})$$

Type checking

The rules above are to be implemented by a type checker, which I hope you will write (Exercise 19). Type checking requires an expression or definition, a type environment, and a kind environment. Calling `typeof`(e, Δ, Γ) should return a τ such that $\Gamma \vdash e : \tau$, or if no such τ exists, it should raise the exception `TypeError`. Calling `typdef`(d, Δ, Γ) should return a pair (Γ', s), where $\langle d, \Delta, \Gamma\rangle \to \Gamma'$ and s is a string that represents the type of the thing defined.

366. ⟨*type checking for Typed μScheme* **[[prototype]]** 366⟩≡

```
typeof : exp * kind env * tyex env -> tyex
typdef : def * kind env * tyex env -> tyex env * string
```

```
fun typeof _ = raise LeftAsExercise "typeof"
fun typdef _ = raise LeftAsExercise "typdef"
```

[5] In a lazy language like Haskell, a right-hand side is not evaluated until its value is needed, so a definition like `(val-rec [x : int] x)` is legal, but evaluating `x` produces an infinite loop (sometimes called a "black hole.")

Table 6.4: Correspondence between Typed μScheme's type system and code

Type system	*Concept*	*Interpreter*
d	Definition	`def` (page 361)
e	Expression	`exp` (page 361)
x	Name	`name` (page 303)
α	Type variable	`name` (page 303)
τ	Type	`tyex` (page 357)
κ	Kind	`kind` (page 355)
Γ	Type environment	`tyex env` (pages 304 and 357)
Δ	Kind environment	`kind env` (pages 304 and 355)
$\Delta \vdash \tau :: \kappa$	Kind checking	`kindof(`τ`, `Δ`)` $= \kappa$, also `kind` $\tau = \kappa$ (page 378)
τ where $\Delta \vdash \tau :: *$	Kind checking	`asType(`τ`, `Δ`)` (page 380)
$\Delta, \Gamma \vdash e : \tau$	Typecheck e	`typeof(`e`, `Δ`, `Γ`)` $= \tau$, and often `ty` $e = \tau$ (left as an exercise, page 366)
$\langle d, \Delta, \Gamma \rangle \to \Gamma'$	Typecheck d	`typdef(`d`, `Δ`, `Γ`)` $=$ `(`Γ'`, `s`)` (left as an exercise, page 366)
$\text{ftv}(\tau)$	Free type variables	`freetyvars` τ (page 371)
$\text{ftv}(\Gamma)$	Free type variables	`freetyvarsGamma` Γ (page 372)
$\tau[\alpha \mapsto \tau']$	Capture-avoiding substitution	`tysubst(`τ`, `$\{\alpha \mapsto \tau'\}$`)` (page 374)
$\forall \alpha \,.\, \tau$ becomes $\tau[\alpha \mapsto \tau']$	Instantiation	`instantiate(`$\forall \alpha \,.\, \tau$`, [`$\tau'$`], `$\Delta$`)` (page 376)
$\tau \equiv \tau'$	Type equivalence	`eqType(`τ`, `τ'`)` (page 370)
$x \in \text{dom}\, \Gamma$	Definedness	`find (`x`, `Γ`)` terminates without raising an exception (page 305)
$\Gamma(x)$	Type lookup	`find (`x`, `Γ`)` (page 305)
$\Gamma\{x \mapsto \tau\}$	Binding	`bind (`x`, `τ`, `Γ`)` (page 305)
$\Gamma\{x_1 \mapsto \tau_1, \ldots, x_n \mapsto \tau_n\}$	Binding	Γ `<+> mkEnv (`$x_1, \ldots, x_n$`, `$\tau_1, \ldots, \tau_n$`)` (page 305)
`int`, `bool`, ...	Base types	`inttype`, `booltype`, ... (page 381)
$\tau_1 \times \cdots \times \tau_n \to \tau$	Function type	`FUNTY([`$\tau_1, \ldots, \tau_n$`], `τ`)` (page 357)

To implement these functions, you need function `eqType`, which tells when two types are equivalent, and function `instantiate`, which instantiates polymorphic types. Equivalence and instantiation are the topics of the next two sections.

6.6.6 *Type equivalence and type-variable renaming*

Many typing rules require that two types be the same. For example, in an `if` expression, the types of the two branches have to be the same. And in Typed μScheme, two types may be considered the same even if they are not identical. For example, types $\forall \alpha \,.\, \alpha$ `list` $\to$ `int` and $\forall \beta \,.\, \beta$ `list` $\to$ `int` are considered to be the same—the *names* of bound type variables α and β are irrelevant. The names are irrelevant because the only thing we can do with a quantified type is substitute for its

type def 361c
type env 304
type exp 361a
type kind 355a
LeftAsExercise S213b
type tyex 357a

bound type variables, and once we have substituted, the names are gone. In general, type $\forall\alpha_1 \,.\, \tau_1$ is equivalent to $\forall\alpha_2 \,.\, \tau_2$ if for every possible τ, $\tau_1[\alpha_1 \mapsto \tau]$ is equivalent to $\tau_2[\alpha_2 \mapsto \tau]$. When two types are equivalent, we write $\tau \equiv \tau'$.

A type-equivalence relation must preserve type soundness. Soundness says that well-typed programs don't go wrong; in particular, if a well-typed program has a subterm e of type τ, a type-soundness theorem allows us to change the program by substituting any other term e' of the *same* type τ. While the changed program might produce a different answer, it's still guaranteed not to go wrong. And if there is an equivalent type, say $\tau' \equiv \tau$, we must also be allowed to substitute any term e'' of type τ', and the program must still not go wrong.

The names of parameters are irrelevant

In Typed μScheme, two types are equivalent if one can be obtained from the other by renaming bound type variables. And a bound type variable originates as a type parameter in a `type-lambda`. Bound type variables and `type-lambda`s may seem new and mysterious, but just like the parameters in an ordinary `lambda`, the parameters in a `type-lambda` can be renamed without changing the meaning of the code. Let's look at examples of each.

In `(lambda (x) (+ x n))`, renaming `x` to `y` doesn't change the meaning of the code:

```
(lambda (x) (+ x n))    ; two equivalent μScheme functions
(lambda (y) (+ y n))
```

And in a `(type-lambda ['a] ···)`, similarly renaming `'a` to `'b` doesn't change the meaning of the code:

368a. ⟨*transcript* 357b⟩+≡ ◁362 368c▷

```
-> (val id1 (type-lambda ['a] (lambda ([x : 'a]) x)))
id1 : (forall ['a] ('a -> 'a))
-> (val id2 (type-lambda ['b] (lambda ([x : 'b]) x)))
id2 : (forall ['b] ('b -> 'b))
```

The renaming gives functions `id1` and `id2` types that are syntactically different, but still equivalent: one type is obtained from the other by renaming `'a` to `'b`. In fact, function `id1` has *every* type that can be obtained from `(forall ['a] ('a -> 'a))` by renaming `'a`. Here is some evidence:

368b. ⟨*type-tests-id.tus* 368b⟩≡

```
(check-type id1 (forall ['a] ('a -> 'a)))
(check-type id1 (forall ['b] ('b -> 'b)))
(check-type id1 (forall ['c] ('c -> 'c)))
```

368c. ⟨*transcript* 357b⟩+≡ ◁368a 373a▷

```
-> (use type-tests-id.tus)
All 3 tests passed.
```

When *can't* we rename a bound type variable? Imagine a function that takes a value of any type and returns a value of type `'c`; that is, imagine a function of type `(forall ['a] ('a -> 'c))`. Renaming `'a` to `'b` doesn't change the type:

```
(forall ['a] ('a -> 'c)) ; equivalent types
(forall ['b] ('b -> 'c))
```

But renaming `'a` to `'c` *does* change the type:

```
(forall ['c] ('c -> 'c)) ; not equivalent to the first two
```

As illustrated above, type `(forall ['c] ('c -> 'c))` is the type of the identity function, and it's not the same as `(forall ['a] ('a -> 'c))`. Functions of these types have to behave differently: a function of type `(forall ['a] ('a -> 'c))` *ignores* its argument, and a function of type `(forall ['c] ('c -> 'c))` *returns* its argument.

That last renaming is invalid because it *captures* type variable `'c`: `'c` is free in the original type but bound in the new type, so its meaning has been changed. Whenever we rename a bound type variable, whether it is bound by `forall` or `type-lambda`, we must not capture any free type variables. (The same restriction applies to the formal parameters of a `lambda` expression; for example, `x` can be renamed to `y` in `(lambda (x) (+ x n))`, but `x` can't be renamed to `n`; `(lambda (n) (+ n n))` is not the same function!) Also, when we substitute a type τ for a free type variable, we must not capture any free type variables of τ.

Soundness of type equivalence in Typed μScheme

Why is it sound to consider types equivalent if one can be obtained from the other by renaming bound type variables? Because if two types differ only in the names of their bound type variables, no combination of instantiations and substitutions can distinguish them. To show what it means to distinguish types by instantiation and substitution, let's compare the three types above. First I instantiate each type at τ_1, then I substitute τ_2 for free occurrences of `'c`:

Original type	*After instantiation*	*After substitution*
`(forall ['a] ('a -> 'c))`	$(\tau_1$ `->` `'c`$)$	$(\tau_1$ `->` $\tau_2)$
`(forall ['b] ('b -> 'c))`	$(\tau_1$ `->` `'c`$)$	$(\tau_1$ `->` $\tau_2)$
`(forall ['c] ('c -> 'c))`	$(\tau_1$ `->` $\tau_1)$	$(\tau_1$ `->` $\tau_1)$

No matter how τ_1 and τ_2 are chosen, the first two `forall` types produce identical results. But when τ_1 and τ_2 are chosen intelligently—`int` and `bool` will do—the first two `forall` types become `(int -> bool)`, but the third one becomes `(int -> int)`, which is different.

Rules and code for type equivalence

Typed μScheme's type equivalence $\tau \equiv \tau'$ is defined by a proof system. A type variable or type constructor is equivalent to itself, and type equivalence is structural through function types, constructor applications and quantifications.

EQUALVARIABLES

$$\frac{}{\alpha \equiv \alpha}$$

EQUALCONSTRUCTORS

$$\frac{}{\mu \equiv \mu}$$

EQUIVFUNS

$$\frac{\tau_i \equiv \tau_i',\ 1 \le i \le n \qquad \tau \equiv \tau'}{\tau_1 \times \cdots \times \tau_n \to \tau \equiv \tau_1' \times \cdots \times \tau_n' \to \tau'}$$

EQUIVAPPLICATIONS

$$\frac{\tau_i \equiv \tau_i',\ 1 \le i \le n \qquad \tau \equiv \tau'}{(\tau_1, \ldots, \tau_n)\ \tau \equiv (\tau_1', \ldots, \tau_n')\ \tau'}$$

EQUIVQUANTIFIEDS

$$\frac{\tau \equiv \tau'}{\forall \alpha_1, \ldots, \alpha_n \,.\, \tau \equiv \forall \alpha_1, \ldots, \alpha_n \,.\, \tau'}$$

These five rules make syntactically identical types equivalent. The next rule makes two types equivalent if one is obtained from the other by renaming a bound type variable. Provided new type variable β is not free in τ, any α_i can be renamed to β:

$$\frac{\beta \notin \mathrm{ftv}(\tau) \qquad \beta \notin \{\alpha_1, \ldots, \alpha_n\}}{\forall \alpha_1, \ldots, \alpha_n \,.\, \tau \equiv \forall \alpha, \ldots, \alpha_{i-1}, \beta, \alpha_{i+1}, \alpha_1, \ldots, \alpha_n \,.\, \tau[\alpha_i \mapsto \beta]}.$$

(EQUIVRENAMED)

The second premise $\beta \notin \{\alpha_1, \ldots, \alpha_n\}$ ensures that even after the renaming, the bound type variables are all distinct.

Like any equivalence relation, type equivalence is symmetric. (Symmetry permits variables to be renamed on the left side of the $\equiv$ sign, for example.)

$$\frac{\tau \equiv \tau'}{\tau' \equiv \tau} \qquad \text{(SYMMETRY)}$$

Type equivalence is also reflexive and transitive (Exercise 24).

Typed μScheme's type-equivalence relation is implemented by function eqType. Given types formed with TYVAR, TYCON, CONAPP, or FUNTY, function eqType implements the unique rule that applies to the form.

370a. ⟨*type equivalence for Typed μScheme* 370a⟩≡ (S405a)

```
eqType  : tyex      * tyex      -> bool
eqTypes : tyex list * tyex list -> bool
```

```
⟨infinite supply of type variables S417e⟩
fun eqType (TYVAR a, TYVAR a') = a = a'
  | eqType (TYCON c, TYCON c') = c = c'
  | eqType (CONAPP (tau, taus), CONAPP (tau', taus')) =
      eqType (tau, tau') andalso eqTypes (taus, taus')
  | eqType (FUNTY (taus, tau), FUNTY (taus', tau')) =
      eqType (tau, tau') andalso eqTypes (taus, taus')
  | eqType (FORALL (alphas, tau), FORALL (alphas', tau')) =
      ⟨Boolean saying if FORALL (alphas, tau) ≡ FORALL (alphas', tau') 370b⟩
  | eqType _ = false
and eqTypes (taus, taus') = ListPair.allEq eqType (taus, taus')
```

Given types formed with FORALL, say $\forall \alpha_1, \ldots, \alpha_n \,.\, \tau$ and $\forall {\alpha'}_1, \ldots, {\alpha'}_n \,.\, \tau'$, eqType first renames the bound type variables on *both* sides to $\beta_1, \ldots, \beta_n$. It then compares the renamed types:

$$\forall \beta_1, \ldots, \beta_n \,.\, \tau[\alpha_1 \mapsto \beta_1, \ldots, \alpha_n \mapsto \beta_n] \text{ and}$$
$$\forall \beta_1, \ldots, \beta_n \,.\, \tau'[\alpha'_1 \mapsto \beta_1, \ldots, \alpha'_n \mapsto \beta_n].$$

According to rule EQUIVQUANTIFIEDS, the comparison succeeds if the first body type, $\tau[\alpha_1 \mapsto \beta_1, \ldots, \alpha_n \mapsto \beta_n]$, is equivalent to $\tau'[\alpha'_1 \mapsto \beta_1, \ldots, \alpha'_n \mapsto \beta_n]$.

Because *all* the α_i's and α'_i's are renamed, no β_j can collide with an existing α_i or α'_i.

370b. ⟨*Boolean saying if* FORALL (alphas, tau) ≡ FORALL (alphas', tau') 370b⟩≡ (370a)

```
let fun ok a  =
      not (member a (freetyvars tau) orelse member a (freetyvars tau'))
    val betas = streamTake (length alphas, streamFilter ok infiniteTyvars)
in  length alphas = length alphas' andalso
    eqType (rename (alphas, betas, tau), rename (alphas', betas, tau'))
end
```

Type variables $\beta_1, \ldots, \beta_n$ (betas) are drawn from an infinite *stream*. Streams and stream operators, as well as the particular stream infiniteTyvars, are defined in the Supplement. Because the stream contains infinitely many type variables, of which only finitely many can be free in τ or τ', it is guaranteed to hold n good ones.

Function rename is implemented using substitution; both rename and tysubst are defined in the next section.

Function eqType can be used in the implementation of any typing rule that requires two types to be the same. To formalize the use of equivalence instead of identity, I extend the type system with the following rule, which says that if e has a type, it also has any equivalent type.

$$\frac{\Delta, \Gamma \vdash e : \tau \qquad \tau \equiv \tau'}{\Delta, \Gamma \vdash e : \tau'} \qquad \text{(EQUIV)}$$

6.6.7 *Instantiation and renaming by capture-avoiding substitution*

Capture-avoiding substitution is tricky—even eminent professors sometimes get it wrong. To study it, we first need to get precise about free and bound type variables.

Free and bound type variables

Type variables may occur *free* or *bound*, and we substitute only for *free* occurrences. A free type variable acts like a global variable; a bound type variable acts like a formal parameter. And a *binding occurrence* is an appearance next to a `forall`. All three kinds of occurrences are shown in this example type:

Example type A	`('c -> (forall ['a] ('a -> 'c)))`
Free occurrence of `'c` in A	`('c -> (forall ['a] ('a -> 'c)))`
Binding occurrence of `'a` in A	`('c -> (forall ('a) ('a -> 'c)))`
Bound occurrence of `'a` in A	`('c -> (forall ('a) ('a -> 'c)))`
Free occurrence of `'c` in A	`('c -> (forall ('a) ('a -> 'c)))`

As the wording suggests, "free" and "bound" are not absolute properties; they are relative to a particular type. For example, type variable `'a` occurs bound in type `(forall ['a] ('a -> 'c))`, but it occurs free in type `('a -> 'c)`.

Free type variables can be specified by a proof system. The judgment of the system is $\boxed{\alpha \in \text{ftv}(\tau)}$, which means "$\alpha$ is free in τ."[6] The proof system resembles the proof system for free *term* variables in Section 5.6 (page 316):

$$\frac{}{\alpha \in \text{ftv}(\alpha)} \qquad \frac{\alpha \in \text{ftv}(\tau_i)}{\alpha \in \text{ftv}((\tau_1, \ldots, \tau_n)\ \tau)} \qquad \frac{\alpha \in \text{ftv}(\tau)}{\alpha \in \text{ftv}((\tau_1, \ldots, \tau_n)\ \tau)},$$

$$\frac{\alpha \in \text{ftv}(\tau_i)}{\alpha \in \text{ftv}(\tau_1 \times \cdots \times \tau_n \to \tau)} \qquad \frac{\alpha \in \text{ftv}(\tau)}{\alpha \in \text{ftv}(\tau_1 \times \cdots \times \tau_n \to \tau)},$$

$$\frac{\alpha \in \text{ftv}(\tau) \qquad \alpha \neq \alpha_i,\ \ 1 \leq i \leq n}{\alpha \in \text{ftv}(\forall \alpha_1, \ldots, \alpha_n \,.\, \tau)}.$$

Also, if $\alpha_i \in \text{ftv}(\tau)$, then α_i is *bound* in $\forall \alpha_1, \ldots, \alpha_n \,.\, \tau$.

The free type variables of a type are computed by function `freetyvars`. Bound type variables are removed using `diff`. Using `foldl`, `union`, `diff`, and `reverse` puts type variables in the set in the order of their first appearance.

371. ⟨*sets of free type variables in Typed μScheme* 371⟩≡ (S405a) 372 ▷

`freetyvars : tyex -> name set`

```
fun freetyvars t =
  let fun free (TYVAR v,           ftvs) = insert (v, ftvs)
        | free (TYCON _,           ftvs) = ftvs
        | free (CONAPP (ty, tys), ftvs) = foldl free (free (ty, ftvs)) tys
        | free (FUNTY  (tys, ty), ftvs) = foldl free (free (ty, ftvs)) tys
        | free (FORALL (alphas, tau), ftvs) =
               union (diff (free (tau, emptyset), alphas), ftvs)
  in  reverse (free (t, emptyset))
  end
```

CONAPP	357a
diff	S217b
emptyset	S217b
FORALL	357a
FUNTY	357a
infiniteTyvars	S417e
insert	S217b
member	S217b
type name	303
rename	375c
reverse	S219b
streamFilter	S231d
streamTake	S232d
TYCON	357a
type tyex	357a
TYVAR	357a
union	S217b

[6] "Binding occurrence" doesn't need a proof system; binding occurrences are those introduced by ∀.

The free type variables of a type environment, which are needed to enforce the side condition in rule TYLAMBDA page 365, are computed by calling function freetyvarsGamma.

372. ⟨*sets of free type variables in Typed μScheme* 371⟩+≡ (S405a) ◁ 371

```
fun freetyvarsGamma Gamma =        freetyvarsGamma : tyex env -> name set
  foldl (fn ((x, tau), ftvs) => union (ftvs, freetyvars tau)) emptyset Gamma
```

Substitution is for free variables only

Free occurrences govern the behaviors of both renaming and substitution. When we rename a bound type variable in a `forall`, we rename only the free occurrences in the body of the `forall`. And when we substitute for a type variable is substituted for, we substitute only for free occurrences. Restricting substitution to free variables may seem arbitrary, but it is motivated by a principle of observational equivalence: If types τ_1 and τ_2 are equivalent, and if τ is substituted for α in both types, then the resulting types $\tau_1[\alpha \mapsto \tau]$ and $\tau_2[\alpha \mapsto \tau]$ should still be equivalent. For example, here are two equivalent types:

```
('c -> (forall ['a] ('a -> 'c)))    ; example A
('c -> (forall ['b] ('b -> 'c)))    ; example B
```

Suppose I wish to substitute `'c` for `'b`. In example A, there are no occurrences of `'b`, and nothing happens. What about example B? There are no *free* occurrences of `'b`, just one binding occurrence and one bound occurrence. So also, nothing happens! And when nothing happens to two equivalent types, the results are still equivalent.

If I mistakenly substitute for the binding occurrence of `'b` or for the bound occurrence of `'b`, or for both, the resulting types are no longer be equivalent to example type A.

```
('c -> (forall ['c] ('b -> 'c)))  ;; WRONG B1
('c -> (forall ['b] ('c -> 'c)))  ;; WRONG B2
('c -> (forall ['c] ('c -> 'c)))  ;; WRONG B3
```

Each mistake goes wrong in a different way:

B1. I substitute for the binding occurrence of `'b` but not for the bound occurrence in the body. If I now rename the bound type variable `'c` to `'a`, I get the type `('c -> (forall ['a] ('b -> 'a)))`. The outer part now matches example A, but the but inner function type `('b -> 'a)` is not equivalent to example A's `('a -> 'c)`.

B2. I substitute for the bound occurrence of `'b` in the body but not for the binding occurrence in the `forall`. If I now rename the bound type variable `'b` to `'a`, I get `('c -> (forall ['a] ('c -> 'a)))`, and again, inner function type `('c -> 'c)` is not equivalent to example A's `('a -> 'c)`.

B3. I substitute for both binding and bound occurrences of `'b`. If I now rename the bound type variable `'c` to `'a`, I get `('c -> (forall ['a] ('a -> 'a)))`, and again, inner function type `('a -> 'a)` is not equivalent to example A's `('a -> 'c)`.

When I'm substituting for `'b` and I hit a `forall` that binds `'b`, I must leave it alone. If that thought makes you uneasy, imagine "leave it alone" as a three-step procedure:

1. First rename the bound `'b` to `'z`, which preserves equivalence.

2. Now substitute `'c` for `'b`. But there are no `'b`'s—it's just like example A!

3. Finally rename the bound `'z` back to `'b`, which again preserves equivalence.

Here's one more example of not substituting for a bound type variable. I define a polymorphic value `strange` of type $\forall\alpha\,.\,\forall\alpha\,.\,\alpha \to \alpha$:

373a. ⟨*transcript* 357b⟩+≡ ◁368c 373b▷

```
-> (val strange
       (type-lambda ['a]
          (type-lambda ['a]
              (lambda ([x : 'a]) x))))
strange : (forall ['a] (forall ['a] ('a -> 'a)))
```

To instantiate `strange` at `int`, I strip the outer $\forall\alpha.$, and I substitute `int` for free occurrences of α in $\forall\alpha\,.\,\alpha \to \alpha$. But there are no free occurrences! Type variable α is bound in $\forall\alpha\,.\,\alpha \to \alpha$, and substituting `int` yields $\forall\alpha\,.\,\alpha \to \alpha$:

373b. ⟨*transcript* 357b⟩+≡ ◁373a

```
-> [@ strange int]
<function> : (forall ['a] ('a -> 'a))
```

It's strange but true.

Substitution avoids capturing variables

Substitution must not only avoid substituting for bound occurrences; it must also avoid changing a free occurrence to a bound occurrence. That is, supposing τ is substituted for `'c`, every type variable that is free in τ must also be free in the result. As an example, let us substitute `(list 'b)` for `'c` in example types A and B:

```
('c -> (forall ['a] ('a -> 'c)))               ; example A
('c -> (forall ['b] ('b -> 'c)))               ; example B
((list 'b) -> (forall ['a] ('a -> (list 'b)))) ; A substituted
((list 'b) -> (forall ['b] ('b -> (list 'b)))) ; B substituted WRONG
```

In both examples, we substitute for two free occurrences of `'c`. The type we substitute has one free occurrence of `'b`. In example A, the result has, as expected, two free occurrences of `'b`, But in example B, the second free occurrence of `'b` has become a *bound* occurrence. We say variable `'b` is *captured.*

Capture is a problem in any computation that involves substitutions—think *macros*—and the problem is one we have solved before: it's the problem of the faulty `let` sugar for `||` in Section 2.13.3 (page 165). The faulty sugar suggests that `(||` e_1 e_2`)` be implemented by substituting for e_1 and e_2 in this template:

`(let ([x` e_1`]) (if x x` e_2`))`.

emptyset	S217b
type env	304
freetyvars	371
type name	303
type tyex	357a
union	S217b

The substitution fails if `x` appears as a free variable in e_2—when e_2 is substituted into the template for `||`, variable `x` is *captured* and its meaning is changed. Capture is avoided by renaming the bound variable `x` to something that is not free in e_2.

A polymorphic type system avoids capture in the same way: by renaming a bound type variable. And in the type system, renaming is easy to justify: when we rename, instead of substituting into example type B, we are substituting into an equivalent type. In the example above, the only type variable bound in B is `'b`, and we rename it to `'z`:

```
('c -> (forall ('z) ('z -> 'c)))               ; equivalent to B
((list 'b) -> (forall ('z) ('z -> (list 'b)))) ; and now substituted
```

Now the substitution is correct, and the result is equivalent to A substituted.

Specifying and implementing substitution

Let's generalize from the example to a specification. To substitute one type τ for free occurrences of type variable α, without allowing any variable to be captured, the judgment form is $\boxed{\tau'[\alpha \mapsto \tau] \equiv \tau''}$. It is pronounced "$\tau'$ with α going to τ is equivalent to τ''."

Substitution for α changes only α. And it preserves the structure of constructors, constructor applications, and function types.

$$\frac{}{\alpha[\alpha \mapsto \tau] \equiv \tau} \qquad \frac{\alpha \neq \alpha'}{\alpha'[\alpha \mapsto \tau] \equiv \alpha'} \qquad \frac{}{\mu[\alpha \mapsto \tau] \equiv \mu}$$

$$\frac{\tau'[\alpha \mapsto \tau] \equiv \tau''}{((\tau_1', \ldots, \tau_n')\ \tau')[\alpha \mapsto \tau] \equiv (\tau_1'[\alpha \mapsto \tau], \ldots, \tau_n'[\alpha \mapsto \tau])\ \tau''}$$

$$\frac{}{(\tau_1' \times \cdots \times \tau_n' \to \tau')[\alpha \mapsto \tau] \equiv \tau_1'[\alpha \mapsto \tau] \times \cdots \times \tau_n'[\alpha \mapsto \tau] \to \tau'[\alpha \mapsto \tau]}$$

Substitution into a quantified type may substitute for free variables only, and it may not capture a free type variable of τ:

$$\frac{\alpha \notin \{\alpha_1, \ldots, \alpha_n\} \qquad \mathrm{ftv}(\tau) \cap \{\alpha_1, \ldots, \alpha_n\} = \emptyset}{(\forall \alpha_1, \ldots, \alpha_n \,.\, \tau')[\alpha \mapsto \tau] \equiv \forall \alpha_1, \ldots, \alpha_n \,.\, (\tau'[\alpha \mapsto \tau])}.$$

The second premise prevents variable capture. Substitution can proceed without capture by substituting into an equivalent type:

$$\frac{\tau' \equiv \tau''}{\tau'[\alpha \mapsto \tau] \equiv \tau''[\alpha \mapsto \tau]}.$$

Substitution for a bound variable has no effect:

$$\frac{}{(\forall \alpha_1, \ldots, \alpha_n \,.\, \tau')[\alpha_i \mapsto \tau] \equiv (\forall \alpha_1, \ldots, \alpha_n \,.\, \tau')}.$$

In Typed μScheme, substituting for a single type variable isn't enough; instantiation substitutes for multiple type variables simultaneously. A substitution is represented by an environment of type `tyex env`, which is passed to function `tysubst` as parameter `varenv`. This environment maps each type variable to the type that should be substituted for it. If a type variable is not mapped, substitution leaves it unchanged.

374. ⟨*capture-avoiding substitution for Typed μScheme* 374⟩≡ (S405a) 375c ▷

```
                                          tysubst : tyex * tyex env -> tyex
                                          subst   : tyex            -> tyex
  fun tysubst (tau, varenv) =
    let ⟨definition of renameForallAvoiding for Typed μScheme (left as an exercise)⟩
        fun subst (TYVAR a) = (find (a, varenv) handle NotFound _ => TYVAR a)
          | subst (TYCON c) = (TYCON c)
          | subst (CONAPP (tau, taus)) = CONAPP (subst tau, map subst taus)
          | subst (FUNTY  (taus, tau)) = FUNTY  (map subst taus, subst tau)
          | subst (FORALL (alphas, tau)) =
              ⟨use varenv to substitute in tau; don't capture or substitute for any alphas 375b⟩
    in  subst tau
    end
```

Substitution into a quantified type must not substitute for a bound variable and must avoid capturing any variables. Postponing for the moment the issue of capture, tysubst prevents substitution for a bound type variable by extending varenv so that each bound type variable is mapped to itself:

375a. ⟨*substitute* varenv *in* FORALL (alphas, tau) *(OK only if there is no capture)* 375a⟩≡ (375b)

```
let val varenv' = varenv <+> mkEnv (alphas, map TYVAR alphas)
in  FORALL (alphas, tysubst (tau, varenv'))
end
```


To avoid capture, tysubst identifies and renames bindings that might capture a variable. The scenario has three parts:

- A type τ_{new} is substituted for a variable that appears free in $\forall\alpha_1, \ldots, \alpha_n . \tau$.
- Among the free variables of type τ_{new} is one of the very type variables α_i that appears under the $\forall$.
- To avoid capturing α_i, the bound α_i has to be renamed.

Below, α_i's that have to be renamed are put in a set called actual_captures. If the set is empty, the code above works. Otherwise, the variables in actual_captures are renamed by function renameForallAvoiding.

375b. ⟨*use* varenv *to substitute in* tau*; don't capture or substitute for any* alphas 375b⟩≡ (374)

```
let val free                = freetyvars (FORALL (alphas, tau))
    val new_taus            = map (subst o TYVAR) free
    val potential_captures = foldl union emptyset (map freetyvars new_taus)
    val actual_captures    = inter (potential_captures, alphas)
in  if null actual_captures then
      ⟨substitute varenv in FORALL (alphas, tau) (OK only if there is no capture) 375a⟩
    else
      subst (renameForallAvoiding (alphas, tau, potential_captures))
end
```

When capture may occur, function renameForallAvoiding renames the alphas to avoid potentially captured variables. It must return a type that is equivalent to FORALL (alphas, tau) but that does not result in variable capture. In detail, renameForallAvoiding($[\alpha_1, \ldots, \alpha_n], \tau, C$) returns a type $\forall\beta_1, \ldots, \beta_n . \tau'$ that has these properties:

$$\forall\beta_1, \ldots, \beta_n . \tau' \equiv \forall\alpha_1, \ldots, \alpha_n . \tau,$$
$$\{\beta_1, \ldots, \beta_n\} \cap C = \emptyset.$$

The implementation of renameForallAvoiding is left to you (Exercise 28).

<+>	305f
CONAPP	357a
emptyset	S217b
find	305b
FORALL	357a
freetyvars	371
FUNTY	357a
inter	S217b
mkEnv	305e
type name	303
NotFound	305b
renameForall-Avoiding	397
TYCON	357a
type tyex	357a
TYVAR	357a
union	S217b

Renaming and instantiation

Renaming is a special case of substitution. It substitutes one set of variables for another.

375c. ⟨*capture-avoiding substitution for Typed μScheme* 374⟩+≡ (S405a) ◁374 376a▷

```
rename : name list * name list * tyex -> tyex
```

```
fun rename (alphas, betas, tau) =
  tysubst (tau, mkEnv (alphas, map TYVAR betas))
```

Instantiation is also implemented by substitution. It builds a type environment that maps formal type parameters to actual type parameters. Most of the code enforces restrictions: only quantified types may be instantiated, only at actual types of kind TYPE, and only with the right number of types.

376a. ⟨*capture-avoiding substitution for Typed μScheme* 374⟩+≡ (S405a) ◁ 375c

```
instantiate : tyex * tyex list * kind env -> tyex
List.find : ('a -> bool) -> 'a list -> 'a option
```

```
fun instantiate (FORALL (formals, tau), actuals, Delta) =
      (case List.find (fn t => not (eqKind (kindof (t, Delta), TYPE)))
                      actuals
         of SOME t => raise TypeError
                              ("instantiated at type constructor `" ^
                               typeString t ^ "', which is not a type")
          | NONE =>
              (tysubst (tau, mkEnv (formals, actuals))
               handle BindListLength =>
                 raise TypeError
                   "instantiated polymorphic term at wrong number of types"))
  | instantiate (tau, _, _) =
       raise TypeError ("tried to instantiate term " ^
                        "of non-quantified type " ^ typeString tau)
```

The Standard ML function `List.find` takes a predicate and searches a list for an element satisfying that predicate.

6.6.8 *Subverting the type system through variable capture*

We avoid variable capture because if capture were permitted, the type system could be subverted: a value of any type could be cast to a value of any other type.

In a world where capture isn't avoided, subverting the type system requires just two `type-lambda`s and two type variables. We first define a Curried function that takes an argument, takes a function to apply to the argument, then returns the application. In untyped μScheme, the code might look like this:

376b. ⟨*μScheme transcript* 376b⟩≡

```
-> (val flip-apply (lambda (x) (lambda (f) (f x))))
-> ((flip-apply '(a b c)) reverse)
(c b a)
-> (val apply-to-symbols (flip-apply '(a b c)))
-> (apply-to-symbols reverse)
(c b a)
-> (apply-to-symbols cdr)
(b c)
```

To add types, we give `x` type β and `f` type $\beta \to \alpha$, so `flip-apply` has type

$$\texttt{flip-apply} : \forall\beta\,.\,\beta \to (\forall\alpha\,.\,(\beta \to \alpha) \to \alpha).$$

This perfectly reasonable type implies that if we supply a value of type β and a function of type $\beta \to \alpha$, we can get a value of type α. Function `flip-apply` can be defined with this type without any variable capture (Exercise 33).

376c. ⟨*variable-capture transcript* 376c⟩≡ 376d ▷

```
-> (val flip-apply ⟨typed version of flip-apply (left as an exercise)⟩)
flip-apply : (forall ['b] ('b -> (forall ['a] (('b -> 'a) -> 'a))))
```

Given `flip-apply`, I poke at the hole in the type system: I try to substitute `'a` for `'b` and then `'b` for `'a`. If the first substitution is done incorrectly, `'a` is captured, and I can define a polymorphic function with a senseless type:

376d. ⟨*variable-capture transcript* 376c⟩+≡ ◁ 376c 377a ▷

```
-> (type-lambda ['a] [@ flip-apply 'a])  ; variable 'a is captured!
<function> : (forall ['a] ('a -> (forall ['a] (('a -> 'a) -> 'a))))
```

This anonymous function, after it is instantiated and applied, will return a result of type $\forall\alpha\,.\,(\alpha \to \alpha) \to \alpha$. That result can be instantiated at any type τ. If I then supply an identity function of type $\tau \to \tau$, I get back a value of type τ. Which is nonsense! A single polymorphic function cannot manufacture a value of an arbitrary type τ, for any τ.

Having captured `'a`, I make the nonsense more obvious by instantiating the problematic result type at `'b`:

377a. ⟨*variable-capture transcript* 376c⟩+≡ ◁376d 377b▷

```
-> (val pre-cast
     (type-lambda ['a 'b]
       (lambda ([x : 'a])
          [@ ([@ flip-apply 'a] x) 'b])))
pre-cast : (forall ['a 'b] ('a -> (('b -> 'b) -> 'b)))
```

Now you modify `pre-cast` by supplying an identity function in the right place (Exercise 33 again). Use `flip-apply` to define a function `cast` of type $\forall\alpha,\beta\,.\,\alpha \to \beta$:

377b. ⟨*variable-capture transcript* 376c⟩+≡ ◁377a 377c▷

```
-> (val cast ⟨definition of cast (left as an exercise)⟩)
cast : (forall ['a 'b] ('a -> 'b))
```

Function `cast` can be used to change a value of any type to any other type. For example, we can "make a function" out of the number 42. doesn't work. When we apply the supposed function, the evaluator reports a bug in the type checker.

377c. ⟨*variable-capture transcript* 376c⟩+≡ ◁377b

```
-> ([@ cast int (int -> int)] 42)
42 : (int -> int)
-> (([@ cast int (int -> int)] 42) 0)
bug in type checking: applied non-function
```

6.6.9 *Preventing capture with* `type-lambda`

To make the type system sound, it's not enough to substitute correctly into quantified types; we must also take care when introducing them. A quantified type is introduced by `type-lambda`, and to ensure soundness, `type-lambda` restricts the names of its formal (type) parameters:

$$\frac{\alpha_i \notin \mathrm{ftv}(\Gamma),\ 1 \le i \le n \qquad \Delta\{\alpha_1 :: *, \ldots \alpha_n :: *\}, \Gamma \vdash e : \tau}{\Delta, \Gamma \vdash \textsc{tylambda}(\alpha_1, \ldots, \alpha_n, e) : \forall\alpha_1, \ldots, \alpha_n\,.\,\tau}. \qquad (\textsc{TyLambda})$$

The restriction $\alpha_i \notin \mathrm{ftv}(\Gamma)$ prevents a form of variable capture.

The restriction is necessary because a polymorphic term $\textsc{tylambda}(\alpha, e)$ can be instantiated by substituting any type τ for α. And if α already stands for something else, there's trouble. As a first example, I can make α already stand for the type of a term variable `x`; I wrap a `type-lambda` around a `lambda`:

```
(type-lambda ['a] (lambda ([x : 'a]) ...))
```

Within the `...`, the typing environment binds `x` to `'a`, so `'a` is a free type variable of Γ. Suppose an *inner* `type-lambda` were permitted to bind `'a` for a second time:

```
(type-lambda ['a] (lambda ([x : 'a])
   (type-lambda ['a] (lambda ([y : 'a]) ...))))
```

In the position of the `...` in the new example, it looks like `x` and `y` both have the same type, but they can be given different types. That puts a hole in the type system.

`BindListLength`	305e
`cdr`	$\mathcal{P}$ 162a
type `env`	304
`eqKind`	355b
`FORALL`	357a
type `kind`	355a
`kindof`	378b
`mkEnv`	305e
`reverse`	$\mathcal{B}$
type `tyex`	357a
`TYPE`	355a
`TypeError`	S213c
`typeString`	S410a
`tysubst`	374

For example, two values can be compared for equality regardless of their types:

378a. ⟨*transcript with no restriction on* `type-lambda` 378a⟩≡

```
-> (val bad= (type-lambda ['a] (lambda ([x : 'a])
                (type-lambda ['a] (lambda ([y : 'a])
                  ([@ = 'a] x y))))))
bad= : (forall ['a] ('a -> (forall ['a] ('a -> bool))))
-> (val worse= (type-lambda ['a 'b]
                 (lambda ([x : 'a] [y : 'b])
                   ([@ ([@ bad= 'a] x) 'b] y))))
worse= : (forall ['a 'b] ('a 'b -> bool))
```


By using a similar trick, you can make a value of any type masquerade as a value of any other type (Exercises 31 and 32).

6.6.10 *Other building blocks of a type checker*

The functions for equivalence, substitution, and instantiation, which are presented above, are all key elements of a type checker, which I hope you will write (Exercise 19). When you do, you can take advantage of some more useful functions, which are presented below.

Ensuring well-formed types: Kind checking

A type in the syntax, like the type of a parameter in a `lambda` abstraction, can't be trusted—it has to be checked to make sure it is well formed. In Typed μScheme, a `tyex` is well formed if it has a *kind* (Section 6.6.2, page 355). The kind is computed by function `kindof`, which implements the kinding judgment $\Delta \vdash \tau :: \kappa$. This judgment says that given kind environment Δ, type-level expression τ is well formed and has kind κ. Given Δ and τ, `kindof(`τ`, `Δ`)` returns a κ such that $\Delta \vdash \tau :: \kappa$, or if no such kind exists, it raises the exception `TypeError`.

378b. ⟨*kind checking for Typed μScheme* 378b⟩≡ (S405a) 380a ▷

```
fun kindof (tau, Delta) =
  let ⟨definition of internal function kind 378c⟩
  in  kind tau
  end
```

```
kindof : tyex * kind env -> kind
kind   : tyex            -> kind
```

The internal function `kind` computes the kind of `tau`; the environment `Delta` is assumed. Function `kind` implements the kinding rules in the same way that `typeof` implements the typing rules and `eval` implements the operational semantics.

The kind of a type variable is looked up in the environment.

$$\frac{\alpha \in \operatorname{dom} \Delta}{\Delta \vdash \text{TYVAR}(\alpha) :: \Delta(\alpha)} \qquad \text{(KINDINTROVAR)}$$

Thanks to the parser in Section Q.6, the name of a type variable always begins with a quote mark, so it is distinct from any type constructor.

378c. ⟨*definition of internal function* `kind` 378c⟩≡ (378b) 378d ▷

```
fun kind (TYVAR a) =
      (find (a, Delta)
       handle NotFound _ => raise TypeError ("unknown type variable " ^ a))
```

The kind of a type constructor is also looked up.

$$\frac{\mu \in \operatorname{dom} \Delta}{\Delta \vdash \text{TYCON}(\mu) :: \Delta(\mu)} \qquad \text{(KINDINTROCON)}$$

378d. ⟨*definition of internal function* `kind` 378c⟩+≡ (378b) ◁ 378c 379a ▷

```
  | kind (TYCON c) =
      (find (c, Delta)
       handle NotFound _ => raise TypeError ("unknown type constructor " ^ c))
```

The kind of a function type is $*$, provided that the argument types and result type also have kind $*$.

$$\frac{\Delta \vdash \tau_i :: *, \quad 1 \leq i \leq n \qquad \Delta \vdash \tau :: *}{\Delta \vdash \tau_1 \times \cdots \times \tau_n \rightarrow \tau :: *} \qquad \text{(KINDFUNCTION)}$$

379a. ⟨*definition of internal function* `kind` 378c⟩+≡ (378b) ◁378d 379b▷

```
  | kind (FUNTY (args, result)) =
      let fun badKind tau = not (eqKind (kind tau, TYPE))
      in  if badKind result then
            raise TypeError "function result is not a type"
          else if List.exists badKind args then
            raise TypeError "argument list includes a non-type"
          else
            TYPE
      end
```

The argument types are inspected using Standard ML function `List.exists`, which corresponds to the μScheme function `exists?`.

Provided that an applied constructor has an arrow kind, the kind of its application is the arrow's result kind. The kinds of the argument types must be what is expected from the arrow's arguments.

$$\frac{\Delta \vdash \tau :: \kappa_1 \times \cdots \times \kappa_n \Rightarrow \kappa \qquad \Delta \vdash \tau_i :: \kappa_i, \quad 1 \leq i \leq n}{\Delta \vdash \text{CONAPP}(\tau, [\tau_1, \ldots, \tau_n]) :: \kappa} \qquad \text{(KINDAPP)}$$

379b. ⟨*definition of internal function* `kind` 378c⟩+≡ (378b) ◁379a 379c▷

```
  | kind (CONAPP (tau, actuals)) =
      (case kind tau
         of ARROW (formal_kinds, result_kind) =>
              if eqKinds (formal_kinds, map kind actuals) then
                  result_kind
              else
                  raise TypeError ("type constructor " ^ typeString tau ^
                                   " applied to the wrong arguments")
          | TYPE =>
              raise TypeError ("tried to apply type " ^ typeString tau ^
                               " as type constructor"))
```

The kind of a quantified type is always $*$, provided its body also has kind $*$.

$$\frac{\Delta\{\alpha_1 :: *, \ldots, \alpha_n :: *\} \vdash \tau :: *}{\Delta \vdash \text{FORALL}(\langle \alpha_1, \ldots, \alpha_n \rangle, \tau) :: *} \qquad \text{(KINDALL)}$$

The quantified variables $\alpha_1, \ldots, \alpha_n$ may be used in τ, so they are added to Δ before the kind of τ is computed.

379c. ⟨*definition of internal function* `kind` 378c⟩+≡ (378b) ◁379b

```
  | kind (FORALL (alphas, tau)) =
      let val Delta' =
            foldl (fn (a, Delta) => bind (a, TYPE, Delta)) Delta alphas
      in  case kindof (tau, Delta')
            of TYPE    => TYPE
             | ARROW _ =>
                 raise TypeError "quantifed a non-nullary type constructor"
      end
```

Variables and parameters must have kind TYPE

A tyex used to describe a variable or parameter must have kind TYPE. Function asType ensures it.

380a. ⟨*kind checking for Typed μScheme* 378b⟩+≡ (S405a) ◁378b

```
fun asType (ty, Delta) =                     asType : tyex * kind env -> tyex
  case kindof (ty, Delta)
    of TYPE    => ty
     | ARROW _ => raise TypeError ("used type constructor `" ^
                                    typeString ty ^ "' as a type")
```

Evaluation in the presence of polymorphism

This chapter is about types, but the code does eventually have to be evaluated. In Typed μScheme, types have no effect at run time; expressions are therefore evaluated using the same rules as for untyped μScheme. And there are new rules for evaluating type abstraction and application. These rules specify that the evaluator behaves as if these type abstraction and application aren't there.

$$\frac{\langle e, \rho, \sigma\rangle \Downarrow \langle v, \sigma'\rangle}{\langle \text{TYAPPLY}(e, \tau_1, \ldots, \tau_n), \rho, \sigma\rangle \Downarrow \langle v, \sigma'\rangle} \quad (\text{TYAPPLY})$$

$$\frac{\langle e, \rho, \sigma\rangle \Downarrow \langle v, \sigma'\rangle}{\langle \text{TYLAMBDA}(\langle \alpha_1, \ldots, \alpha_n\rangle, e), \rho, \sigma\rangle \Downarrow \langle v, \sigma'\rangle} \quad (\text{TYLAMBDA})$$

This semantics is related to a program transformation called *type erasure*: if you start with a program written in Typed μScheme, and you remove all the TYAPPLYs and the TYLAMBDAs, and you remove the types from the LAMBDAs and the definitions, and you rewrite VALREC to VAL, then what's left is a μScheme program.

The evaluator for Typed μScheme resembles the evaluator for μScheme in Chapter 5. The code for the new forms acts as if TYAPPLY and TYLAMBDA aren't there.

380b. ⟨*alternatives for* ev *for* TYAPPLY *and* TYLAMBDA 380b⟩≡ (S411b)

```
| ev (TYAPPLY  (e, _)) = ev e
| ev (TYLAMBDA (_, e)) = ev e
```

The rest of the evaluator can be found in Appendix Q.

Definitions are evaluated slightly differently than in untyped μScheme. As in Typed Impcore, the type system and operational semantics cooperate to ensure that no definition ever changes the type of an existing name. In Typed Impcore, the assurance is provided by the type system: it permits a name to be redefined only when the existing type is preserved. In Typed μScheme, the assurance is provided by the operational semantics: as in Exercise 46 from Chapter 2, evaluating a definition always creates a new binding. In a VAL binding, the right-hand side is evaluated in the old environment; in a VAL-REC binding, the right-hand side is evaluated in the new environment. The type system guarantees that the result of evaluation does not depend on the unspecified value with which ℓ is initialized.

$$\frac{\ell \notin \operatorname{dom} \sigma \qquad \langle e, \rho, \sigma\rangle \Downarrow \langle v, \sigma'\rangle}{\langle \text{VAL}(x, e), \rho, \sigma\rangle \to \langle \rho\{x \mapsto \ell\}, \sigma'\{\ell \mapsto v\}\rangle} \quad (\text{VAL})$$

$$\frac{\ell \notin \operatorname{dom} \sigma \qquad \langle e, \rho\{x \mapsto \ell\}, \sigma\{\ell \mapsto \text{unspecified}\}\rangle \Downarrow \langle v, \sigma'\rangle}{\langle \text{VAL-REC}(x, \tau, e), \rho, \sigma\rangle \to \langle \rho\{x \mapsto \ell\}, \sigma'\{\ell \mapsto v\}\rangle} \quad (\text{VAL-REC})$$

These rules are implemented in Appendix Q.

Primitive type constructors of Typed μScheme

The types of the primitive functions have to be written using ML code inside the interpreter, but the raw representation isn't easy to write. For example, the type of cons is represented by this enormous constructed value:

```
FORALL (["'a"],
          FUNTY ([TYVAR "'a", CONAPP (TYCON "list", [TYVAR "'a"])]),
                 CONAPP (TYCON "list", [TYVAR "'a"])))
```


To make such values easier to construct, I provide these representations:

381a. ⟨*types for Typed μScheme* 357a⟩+≡ (S405a) ◁ 357a

```
val inttype  = TYCON "int"
val booltype = TYCON "bool"
val symtype  = TYCON "sym"
val unittype = TYCON "unit"
val tvA      = TYVAR "'a"
fun listtype ty = CONAPP (TYCON "list",[ty])
```

```
inttype   : tyex
booltype  : tyex
symtype   : tyex
unittype  : tyex
tvA       : tyex
listtype  : tyex -> tyex
```

Each of these type constructors creates a type or types that are inhabited by certain forms of value. For example, types int and bool are inhabited by values of the form NUM *n* and BOOLV *b*; that's what eval returns when interpreting an expression of type int or bool. What about type unit? That type also needs an inhabitant, which is defined here:

381b. ⟨*utility functions on values (μScheme, Typed μScheme, nano-ML)* 381b⟩≡ (S379 S405a)

```
val unitVal = NIL
```

```
unitVal : value
```

This conventional inhabitant is used to represent every value of type unit, which ensures that when comparing two unit values, the primitive = function always returns #t.

Selected primitive functions of Typed μScheme

Each primitive function has a name, a value, and a type. Most of them appear in the Supplement, but to show you how primitives are defined, a few appear here.

As in Chapter 5, primitive values are made using functions unaryOp, binaryOp, and arithOp. But if something goes wrong at run time, the Typed μScheme versions don't raise the RuntimeError exception; they raise BugInTypeChecking. And Typed μScheme's primitives need types! As the type of the arithmetic primitives, I define arithtype.

381c. ⟨*utility functions and types for making Typed μScheme primitives* 381c⟩≡ (S406d)

```
unaryOp   : (value         -> value) -> (value list -> value)
binaryOp  : (value * value -> value) -> (value list -> value)
arithOp   : (int * int -> int)       -> (value list -> value)
arithtype : tyex
```

```
val arithtype =
  FUNTY ([inttype, inttype], inttype)
```

As in Chapter 5, the names, values, and types of the primitives are written in one long list in chunk ⟨*primitive functions for Typed μScheme* :: 381d⟩. That list is used to build the initial basis.

381d. ⟨*primitive functions for Typed μScheme* :: 381d⟩≡ (382c) 382a ▷

```
("+", arithOp op +,   arithtype) ::
("-", arithOp op -,   arithtype) ::
("*", arithOp op *,   arithtype) ::
("/", arithOp op div, arithtype) ::
```

arithOp	S393b
ARROW	355a
binaryOp	S393a
CONAPP	357a
type env	304
ev	S411b
FUNTY	357a
type kind	355a
kindof	378b
NIL	361b
TYAPPLY	361a
TYCON	357a
type tyex	357a
TYLAMBDA	361a
TYPE	355a
TypeError	S213c
typeString	S410a
TYVAR	357a
unaryOp	S393a
type value	361b

The list primitives have polymorphic types.

382a. ⟨*primitive functions for Typed μScheme* :: 381d⟩+≡ (382c) ◁381d

```
("null?", unaryOp (BOOLV o (fn (NIL    ) => true | _ => false))
        , FORALL (["'a"], FUNTY ([listtype tvA], booltype))) ::
("cons", binaryOp (fn (a, b) => PAIR (a, b))
       , FORALL (["'a"], FUNTY ([tvA, listtype tvA], listtype tvA))) ::
("car",  unaryOp  (fn (PAIR (car, _)) => car
                    | v => raise RuntimeError
                               ("car applied to non-list " ^ valueString v))
       , FORALL (["'a"], FUNTY ([listtype tvA], tvA))) ::
("cdr",  unaryOp  (fn (PAIR (_, cdr)) => cdr
                    | v => raise RuntimeError
                               ("cdr applied to non-list " ^ valueString v))
       , FORALL (["'a"], FUNTY ([listtype tvA], listtype tvA))) ::
```

Other primitives are relegated to the Supplement.

Typed μScheme's basis

In Typed μScheme, a basis comprises a kind environment, a type environment, and a value environment.

382b. ⟨*definition of* `basis` *for Typed μScheme* 382b⟩≡ (S406c)

```
type basis = kind env * tyex env * value ref env
```

The initial basis starts with the kinds of the primitive type constructors, plus the types and values of the primitive functions and values.

382c. ⟨*definition of* `primBasis` *for Typed μScheme* 382c⟩≡ (S406d)

```
kinds     : kind       env
types     : tyex       env
values    : value ref  env
primBasis : basis
```

```
val primBasis =
  let fun addKind ((name, kind), kinds) =
            bind (name, kind, kinds)
      val kinds   = foldl addKind emptyEnv
                      (⟨primitive type constructors for Typed μScheme :: 356⟩ [])
      fun addPrim ((name, prim, funty), (types, values)) =
        ( bind (name, funty, types)
        , bind (name, ref (PRIMITIVE prim), values)
        )
      val (types, values) = foldl addPrim (emptyEnv, emptyEnv)
                              (⟨primitive functions for Typed μScheme :: 381d⟩ [])
      fun addVal ((name, v, ty), (types, values)) =
        ( bind (name, ty, types)
        , bind (name, ref v, values)
        )
      val (types, values) =
        foldl addVal (types, values)
        (⟨primitives that aren't functions, for Typed μScheme :: S407d⟩ [])
  in  (kinds, types, values)
  end
```

With the primitives in place, the basis is completed by reading and evaluating the predefined functions. That code is relegated to the Supplement.

6.7 TYPE SYSTEMS AS THEY REALLY ARE

Typed Impcore is a good model of a monomorphic language, but real languages are more complicated. As one example, most programming languages, especially monomorphic ones, use product types with named fields. These types are often called "record" or "struct" types. Their typing rules are mostly straightforward; the type of each component is associated with the component's name, not its position.

Typed μScheme is not a good model for any widely used language, because the annotations are too heavy: no programmer should have to code the instantiation of every use of every polymorphic value. Typed μScheme is, however, a good model for an intermediate language to which a real polymorphic source language could be translated. It becomes an even better, more powerful model, if `type-lambda` can quantify over a type variable of *any* kind, not just of kind $*$. Such quantification is permitted in some versions of the functional language Haskell.

Real type equality is more complicated than what you see in this chapter. Here, two types are equal if and only if they apply equal constructors to equal arguments. Quantified types are considered equal up to renaming of bound type variables, but that is a minor matter. In real languages, type equality is complicated by *generativity*, among other issues. A syntactic form is *generative* if every appearance creates a distinct type, different from any other type. As an example, the product-type constructor in C, called `struct`, is generative. Standard ML's sum-type definition form, called `datatype`, is also generative. Languages without generativity are sometimes said to compare types using *structural equivalence*; languages with generativity are said to use *name equivalence* or *occurrence equivalence*. Generativity is explained in detail in Chapter 8.

The types of names are often more complicated than what you see in this chapter. In particular, many languages permit a name to be used at more than one type, but not at infinitely many types. For example, the + function in ML may be used at two types: `int * int -> int` and `real * real -> real`. Such a function is not parametrically polymorphic; instead, it is said to be *overloaded*. The + operator in C is even more heavily overloaded; because of implicit type conversions, it may be used at many types. In some languages, including Ada, C++, and Haskell, programmers can define new overloaded operators or functions. Overloading can complicate a type system, but it can also be done simply (Chapter 9).

Type systems used for research go far beyond what is presented in this book. In systems based on *dependent* types, for example, type checking can be undecidable while still giving useful results in practice!

6.8 SUMMARY

Type systems are the world's most successful formal method. Types guide the construction of programs: for example, throughout Chapter 2, if you are writing a function that consumes a value of type τ, most likely the body of your function is the elimination form for τ. (And if you are trying to produce a value of type τ', the body of your function might include the introduction form for τ'.) Types also provide a relatively painless way of documenting code, and they rule out many silly programming errors.

If types are good, polymorphic types are better. Polymorphic types help make code reusable, robustly. The polymorphism in Typed μScheme is easy to implement, but unpleasant to use—it should be hidden inside a compiler. But similar forms of polymorphism can be easy to use, and sometimes a great pleasure. These are found in Chapters 7 to 9.

A type discipline is usually enforced by a type checker. Most type checkers are easy to implement because most type systems have one rule for each syntactic form. But if you add sophisticated features, parts of a type checker can become more challenging. In Typed μScheme, these parts include type equivalence, which is an interesting aspect of many experimental type systems, and substitution, which is a ubiquitous, annoying problem.

6.8.1 *Key words and phrases*

ELIMINATION FORM A syntactic form used to observe a value of a given TYPE. For example, the elimination form for a function type is function application. An elimination form "takes information out" that was put in using an an INTRODUCTION FORM. The typing rule for an elimination form can be called an ELIMINATION RULE.

FORMATION RULE A rule that says how to make a well-formed type. For example, `(array int)` is a well-formed type.

GENERATIVITY If a language construct always creates a new type distinct from any other type, that construct is called *generative*. Examples of generative constructs include C's `struct` and ML's `datatype`.

INSTANTIATION The process of determining at what type a polymorphic value is used. In Typed μScheme, a polymorphic value is instantiated explicitly using the TYPE-APPLICATION form `@`. In ML, instantiation is implicit and is handled automatically by the language implementation.

INTRODUCTION FORM A syntactic form used to create a value of a given TYPE. For example, the introduction form for a function type is `lambda`. An introduction form "puts information in" to the value. The information can be recovered using an ELIMINATION FORM. The typing rule for an introduction form can be called an INTRODUCTION RULE.

KIND A means of classifying TYPE CONSTRUCTORS and TYPES. Using kinds makes it possible to handle an unbounded number of TYPE CONSTRUCTORS using finitely many FORMATION RULES.

MONOMORPHIC TYPE SYSTEM If every TERM, variable, and function in a language has at most one TYPE, that language uses a *monomorphic* type system. For example, Pascal's type system is monomorphic. A type system may also be POLYMORPHIC.

MONOTYPE A type that cannot be instantiated. For example, the function type `int list` $\rightarrow$ `int` is a monotype. (As contrasted with a POLYTYPE.)

PARAMETRIC POLYMORPHISM The form of POLYMORPHISM that uses type parameters and INSTANTIATION.

POLYMORPHIC TYPE SYSTEM If a TERM, variable, or function in a language may be used at more than one TYPE, that language uses a *polymorphic* type system. For example, ML's type system is polymorphic. A type system may also be MONOMORPHIC.

POLYMORPHISM A language is polymorphic if it is possible to write programs that operate on values of more than one type. For example, Scheme and ML are polymorphic languages. A value is polymorphic if it can be used at more than one type; for example, the list `length` function is polymorphic because it can operate on many types of lists.

POLYTYPE A type that can be instantiated in more than one way. In Typed μScheme, a polytype has the form $\forall\alpha_1, \ldots, \alpha_n \,.\, \tau$. (As contrasted with a MONOTYPE.)

QUANTIFIED TYPE A type formed with the universal quantifier $\forall$. Also called a POLYTYPE.

TERM The pointy-headed theory word for "expression." More generally, a syntactic form that is computed with at run time and that may have a TYPE.

TYPE A specification for a TERM. Or a means of classifying terms. Or a collection of values, called the INHABITANTS.

TYPE ABSTRACTION In PARAMETRIC POLYMORPHISM, the INTRODUCTION FORM for a polymorphic type. In Typed μScheme, written `type-lambda`.

TYPE APPLICATION In PARAMETRIC POLYMORPHISM, the ELIMINATION FORM for a polymorphic type. It substitutes actual type parameters for quantified type variables. It is a form of INSTANTIATION.

TYPE CHECKER A part of a language's implementation that enforces the rules of the TYPE SYSTEM, by checking code before it is run.

TYPE CONSTRUCTOR The fundamental unit from which TYPES are built. Type constructors come in various KINDS. Nullary type constructors such as `int` and `bool` are types all by themselves; they have kind $*$. Other type constructors, such as `list` and `array`, are applied to types to make more types.

TYPE SYSTEM A language's *type system* encompasses both the set of TYPES that can be expressed in the language and the rules that say what TERMS have what types. A type system may be MONOMORPHIC or POLYMORPHIC.

6.8.2 *Further reading*

Pierce (2002) has written a wonderful textbook covering many aspects of typed programming languages. Cardelli (1997) presents an alternative view of type systems; his tutorial inspired some of the material in this chapter.

Reynolds (1974) presents the polymorphic, typed lambda calculus now known as System F, which is the basis of Typed μScheme. Reynolds says,

> Although this language is hardly an adequate vehicle for programming, it seems to pose the essence of the type structure problem, and it is simple enough to permit a brief but rigorous exposition of its semantics.

I hope you agree.

Using types to guide the construction of programs is a key part of the "design recipe" method of Felleisen et al. (2018). Because the language used by Felleisen et al. does not have a static type checker, the types are written only in comments—but they are there. Crestani and Sperber (2010) describe an extension in which type "signatures" are used to check types at run time.

Perhaps suprisingly, type systems can be used to guarantee safety even in C programs, although at a significant run-time penalty. Systems such as CCured (Necula, McPeak, and Weimer 2002) run C programs at about half the speed of unsafe compilers, but their error-detection power is comparable to that of tools such as Purify and Valgrind, which may slow down a program by a factor of 5 to 10.

Table 6.5: Synopsis of all the exercises, with most relevant sections

Exercises	*Sections*	*Notes*
1 to 3	6.1	Type-system fundamentals: type errors vs run-time errors; introduction forms vs elimination forms (§6.3.1); inhabitants of sum and product types (§6.4).
4 to 7	6.3.1, 6.4	Extending a monomorphic language with lists, records, sums, or mutable references.
8 and 9	6.6.3	Coding in a polymorphic language
10 to 15	6.4, 6.6.2, 6.6.3, 6.6.5	Extending a polymorphic language with queues, pairs, sums, polymorphic references, or records.
16 and 17	6.1.5, 6.6.5, 1.7	Writing typing derivations.
18 and 19	6.2, 6.3, 6.6.5	Type checking: add arrays to Typed Impcore's type checker, implement a type checker for Typed μScheme.
20 to 24	6.1, 6.6.5	Metatheory: types are unique, expressions have well-formed types, syntactic sugar preserves typing, $\equiv$ is an equivalence relation (§6.6.6).
25 and 26	6.1.5, 6.5	Metatheory about implementation: type checking terminates and prevents bugs.
27 and 28	6.6.7	Capture-avoiding substitution: rename variables to avoid capture; prove that substitution terminates.
29 to 33	6.1.5, 6.6.5, 6.6.7	Holes in type systems: what goes wrong when restrictions are lifted.

6.9 EXERCISES

The exercises are summarized in Table 6.5. This chapter's exercises are unusually diverse; they include programming, adding new typing rules, proving things about type systems, extending interpreters, and subverting type systems. They include these favorites:

- Nothing solidifies your understanding of type systems like writing a type checker. You should write one for Typed μScheme, using the typing rules as your specification (Exercise 19; use Figures 6.9 to 6.12, which appear on pages 394 to 396). If you want your type checker to be sound, you will also want to complete the implementation of capture-avoiding substitution (Exercise 28). An easier alternative, or a warmup, would be to extend the type checker for Typed Impcore so it supports arrays (Exercise 18; use Figures 6.6 to 6.8, which appear on pages 391 and 392).

- Another way to develop understanding is to write typing rules for familiar language constructs (Exercises 4 to 7). The easiest and more familiar constructs are for lists (Exercise 4).

- To understand both the power and the agony of programming with explicit polymorphism, implement `exists?` or `all?` in Typed μScheme (Exercise 9).

- To understand how explicit polymorphism benefits implementors and language designers, extend Typed μScheme with new type constructors (Exercises 10 to 13). You won't have to change any infrastructure. The easiest, most familiar new type constructor is the `pair` type constructor (Exercise 11).

- Type systems lend themselves well to metatheory. My favorite metatheoretic exercise is to show that in Typed μScheme, any type that classifies a term is well formed and has kind $*$ (Exercise 23). Exercise 20 calls for similar reasoning but has a more familiar conclusion: type checking is deterministic.

6.9.1 *Retrieval practice and other short questions*

A. What's an example of a checked run-time error in Impcore that is guaranteed to be prevented by the type system of Typed Impcore?

B. What's an example of a checked run-time error in Impcore that is *not* guaranteed to be prevented by the type system of Typed Impcore?

C. How many *values* inhabit the type `bool`?

D. How many *terms* have type `bool`?

E. In Typed Impcore, a global variable may have an array type. How many distinct array types are possible?

F. When you look up a name x in environment Γ_ξ, what information about x do you get back?

G. How do you pronounce the judgment form $\Gamma_\xi, \Gamma_\phi, \Gamma_\rho \vdash e : \tau$?

H. How do you pronounce the judgment form $\Delta, \Gamma \vdash e : \tau$?

I. When the Typed Impcore interpreter checks the type of a WHILE loop, is the type checking guaranteed to terminate? Why or why not?

J. When the Typed Impcore interpreter checks the type of a WHILE loop, how does the type of the loop's body affect the type of the loop?

K. If the body of a WHILE loop doesn't have a type, what happens?

L. In Typed Impcore, what syntactic form is the introduction form for array types?

M. In Typed μScheme, what syntactic form is the introduction form for function types?

N. In Typed μScheme, what syntactic form is the elimination form for function types?

O. In Typed μScheme, what syntactic form is the introduction form for polymorphic types?

P. In Typed μScheme, what syntactic form is the elimination form for polymorphic types?

Q. In Typed μScheme, what is the type of the primitive function "`null?`"?

R. In Typed μScheme, the primitive function `cons` does not have a function type—it has a polymorphic type. How do you get it to act as a function?

S. In both Typed Impcore and Typed μScheme, what types have to be checked to make sure they are well formed? Where would an ill-formed type come from?

T. In Typed μScheme, why aren't there type-formation rules for list types? How does the type checker know if a list type is well formed?

U. In Typed μScheme, what's the relationship between instantiation and substitution?

V. Why does Typed μScheme need a complicated $\equiv$ relation? Why doesn't Typed Impcore need such a thing?

6.9.2 *Type-system fundamentals*

1. *Differences between type errors and run-time errors.* Programming-language people get good at thinking about *phases* of computation. A type-checking phase, which happens before the evaluation phase, is introduced in this chapter. And in different phases, different things can go wrong; a type error is not the same as a run-time error. To convince yourself that you understand what can go wrong in each phase, create unit tests using both `check-type-error` and `check-error`.

   (a) Using the `array-at` primitive, create one test for each phase.

   (b) Using an integer-arithmetic primitive, create one test for each phase.

   All four tests should pass.

2. *Introduction forms and elimination forms.* In this exercise, you identify syntactic forms (and their associated rules) as introduction forms or elimination forms. The exercise is modeled on communication techniques found in languages like PML/Pegasus, Concurrent ML, and Haskell.

   A expression of type $\mathrm{PROTO}(\tau)$ is a set of instructions, or *protocol*, for communicating with a remote server. Such an expression can be *run* by a special syntactic form, which communicates with the server. When a communication is run, the local interpreter gets an *outcome* of type τ. Here is a grammar, with informal explanations:

exp ::= `send` *exp*	Send a value to the server
| `receive`	Receive a value from the server
| `do` $x \leftarrow exp_1$ `in` exp_2	Protocol exp_1, whose outcome is x, followed by exp_2
| `locally` *exp*	Produce result *exp* locally, without communicating
| `run` *exp*	Run a protocol

   An *exp* is given a type by these rules:

$$\textsc{Proto}\ \frac{\tau \text{ is a type}}{\mathrm{PROTO}(\tau) \text{ is a type}} \qquad \textsc{Send}\ \frac{\Gamma \vdash e : \tau}{\Gamma \vdash \texttt{send}\ e : \mathrm{PROTO}(\mathrm{UNIT})},$$

$$\textsc{Receive}\ \frac{\tau \text{ is a type}}{\Gamma \vdash \texttt{receive} : \mathrm{PROTO}(\tau)} \qquad \textsc{Do}\ \frac{\Gamma \vdash e_1 : \mathrm{PROTO}(\tau) \qquad \Gamma, x : \tau \vdash e_2 : \mathrm{PROTO}(\tau')}{\Gamma \vdash \texttt{do}\ x \leftarrow e_1\ \texttt{in}\ e_2 : \mathrm{PROTO}(\tau')},$$

$$\textsc{Locally}\ \frac{\Gamma \vdash e : \tau}{\Gamma \vdash \texttt{locally}\ e : \mathrm{PROTO}(\tau)} \qquad \textsc{Run}\ \frac{\Gamma \vdash e : \mathrm{PROTO}(\tau)}{\Gamma \vdash \texttt{run}\ e : \tau}.$$

   Classify each rule as a formation rule, an introduction rule, or an elimination rule. Justify your answers.

3. *Counting inhabitants.* Type `bool` is inhabited by the two values `#t` and `#f`. Let's say type `lettergrade` is inhabited by values A, B, C, D, and F.

   (a) List all the values inhabited by product type `bool` $\times$ `lettergrade`.

   (b) List all the values inhabited by sum type `bool` $+$ `lettergrade`.

   (c) Are your results consistent with the words "sum" and "product"? Justify your answer.

6.9.3 *Extending a monomorphic language*

4. *Rules for lists in Typed Impcore.* In this exercise, you add lists to Typed Impcore. Use the same technique we use for arrays: devise new abstract syntax to support lists, and write appropriate type-formation, type-introduction, and type-elimination rules. The rules should resemble the rules shown in Section 6.4.

   Review the discussion of rules in the sidebar on page 347, and make it obvious which rules are formation rules, which rules are introduction rules, and which rules are elimination rules: Divide your rules into three groups and label each group.

   - Some rules can be classified just by looking to see where list types appear. For example, a rule for `null?` should have a list type in the premise but not in the conclusion, so `null?` has to be an elimination form. Similarly, a `car` rule should have a list type in the premise but not necessarily in the conclusion, so it too has to be an elimination form.
   - Other rules have list types in both premises and conclusion. When you have forms like `cons` and `cdr`, which both take and produce lists, you have to fall back on thinking about information. Does a form put new information into a value, which can later be extracted by another form? Then it is an introduction form. Does a form put in no new information, but only extract information that is already present? Then it is an elimination form.

   Your abstract syntax should cover all the list primitives defined in Chapter 2: the empty list, test to see if a list is empty, `cons`, `car`, and `cdr`. Your abstract syntax may differ from the abstract syntax used in μScheme.

   Be sure your rules are deterministic: it should be possible to compute the type of an expression given only the syntax of the expression and the current type environment.

5. *Rules for records in Typed Impcore.* Following the same directions as in Exercise 4, give typing rules for records with named fields.

6. *Rules for sums in Typed Impcore.* Following the same directions as in Exercise 4, give typing rules for sums with named variants.

7. *Rules for mutable references in Typed Impcore.* Mutable cells can be represented by a type constructor `ref`. The appropriate operations are `ref`, `!`, and `:=`. The function `ref` is like the function `allocate` in Chapter 2; applying `ref` to a value v allocates a new mutable cell and initializes it to hold v. Applying `!` to a mutable cell returns the value contained in that cell. Applying `:=` to a mutable cell and a value replaces the contents of the cell with the value. (These functions are also part of Standard ML.)

   Give typing rules for a type constructor for mutable cells. (See also Exercise 13.)

6.9.4 *Coding in a polymorphic language*

8. *Folds.* Implement `foldl` and `foldr` in Typed μScheme.

   (a) Both functions should have the same polymorphic type. Give it.

   (b) Write an implementation of each function.

9. *Higher-order, polymorphic linear search.* Implement `exists?` and `all?` in Typed μScheme.

   (a) Both functions should have the same polymorphic type. Give it.

   (b) Write an implementation of `exists?` using recursion.

   (c) Write an implementation of `all?` using your implementation of `exists?` and De Morgan's laws.

6.9.5 *Extending a polymorphic language*

10. *Add queues to Typed μScheme.* A great advantage of a polymorphic type system is that a language can be extended without touching the abstract syntax, the values, the type checker, or the evaluator. Without changing any of these parts of Typed μScheme, extend Typed μScheme with a `queue` type constructor and the polymorphic values `empty-queue`, `empty?`, `put`, `get-first`, and `get-rest`. (A more typical functional queue provides a single `get` operation which returns a pair containing both the first element in the queue and any remaining elements. By instead providing `get-first` and `get-rest`, you avoid fooling with pair types.)

    (a) What is the kind of the type constructor `queue`? Add it to the initial Δ.

    (b) What are the types of `empty-queue`, `empty?`, `get-first`, `get-rest`, and `put`?

    (c) Add the new primitive functions to the initial Γ and ρ. You will need to write implementations in Standard ML.

11. *Add pairs to Typed μScheme. Without* changing the abstract syntax, values, type checker, or evaluator of Typed μScheme, extend Typed μScheme with the `pair` type constructor and the polymorphic functions `pair`, `fst`, and `snd`.

    (a) What is the kind of the type constructor `pair`? Add it to the initial Δ.

    (b) What are the types of `pair`, `fst`, and `snd`?

    (c) Add the new primitive functions to the initial Γ and ρ. As you add them to ρ, you can use the same implementations that we use for `cons`, `car`, and `cdr`.

12. *Add sums to Typed μScheme. Without* changing the abstract syntax, values, type checker, or evaluator of Typed μScheme, extend Typed μScheme with the `sum` type constructor and the polymorphic functions `left`, `right`, and `either`.

    (a) What is the kind of the type constructor `sum`? Add it to the initial Δ.

    (b) What are the types of `left`, `right`, and `either`?

    (c) Page 349 gives algebraic laws for *pair* primitives in a monomorphic language. If the *sum* primitives were added to a monomorphic language, what would be the laws relating LEFT, RIGHT, and EITHER?

    (d) Since `left`, `right`, and `either` have the polymorphic types in part 12(b), what are the laws relating them?

    (e) Add `left`, `right`, and `either` to the initial Γ and ρ of Typed μScheme. Try representing a value of sum type as a `PAIR` containing a tag and a value.

$\boxed{\tau \text{ is a type}}$

$$\textsc{UnitType}\quad \frac{}{\textsc{unit} \text{ is a type}} \qquad \textsc{IntType}\quad \frac{}{\textsc{int} \text{ is a type}} \qquad \textsc{BoolType}\quad \frac{}{\textsc{bool} \text{ is a type}}$$

$$\textsc{ArrayType}\quad \frac{\tau \text{ is a type}}{\textsc{array}(\tau) \text{ is a type}}$$

Figure 6.6: Type-formation rules for Typed Impcore

$\boxed{\Gamma_\xi, \Gamma_\phi, \Gamma_\rho \vdash e : \tau}$

$$\textsc{Literal}\quad \frac{}{\Gamma_\xi, \Gamma_\phi, \Gamma_\rho \vdash \textsc{literal}(v) : \textsc{int}}$$

$$\textsc{FormalVar}\quad \frac{x \in \operatorname{dom} \Gamma_\rho}{\Gamma_\xi, \Gamma_\phi, \Gamma_\rho \vdash \textsc{var}(x) : \Gamma_\rho(x)}$$

$$\textsc{GlobalVar}\quad \frac{x \notin \operatorname{dom} \Gamma_\rho \qquad x \in \operatorname{dom} \Gamma_\xi}{\Gamma_\xi, \Gamma_\phi, \Gamma_\rho \vdash \textsc{var}(x) : \Gamma_\xi(x)}$$

$$\textsc{FormalAssign}\quad \frac{x \in \operatorname{dom} \Gamma_\rho \qquad \Gamma_\rho(x) = \tau \qquad \Gamma_\xi, \Gamma_\phi, \Gamma_\rho \vdash e : \tau}{\Gamma_\xi, \Gamma_\phi, \Gamma_\rho \vdash \textsc{set}(x, e) : \tau}$$

$$\textsc{GlobalAssign}\quad \frac{x \notin \operatorname{dom} \Gamma_\rho \qquad x \in \operatorname{dom} \Gamma_\xi \qquad \Gamma_\xi(x) = \tau \qquad \Gamma_\xi, \Gamma_\phi, \Gamma_\rho \vdash e : \tau}{\Gamma_\xi, \Gamma_\phi, \Gamma_\rho \vdash \textsc{set}(x, e) : \tau}$$

$$\textsc{If}\quad \frac{\Gamma_\xi, \Gamma_\phi, \Gamma_\rho \vdash e_1 : \textsc{bool} \qquad \Gamma_\xi, \Gamma_\phi, \Gamma_\rho \vdash e_2 : \tau \qquad \Gamma_\xi, \Gamma_\phi, \Gamma_\rho \vdash e_3 : \tau}{\Gamma_\xi, \Gamma_\phi, \Gamma_\rho \vdash \textsc{if}(e_1, e_2, e_3) : \tau}$$

$$\textsc{While}\quad \frac{\Gamma_\xi, \Gamma_\phi, \Gamma_\rho \vdash e_1 : \textsc{bool} \qquad \Gamma_\xi, \Gamma_\phi, \Gamma_\rho \vdash e_2 : \tau}{\Gamma_\xi, \Gamma_\phi, \Gamma_\rho \vdash \textsc{while}(e_1, e_2) : \textsc{unit}}$$

$$\textsc{Begin}\quad \frac{\Gamma_\xi, \Gamma_\phi, \Gamma_\rho \vdash e_1 : \tau_1 \qquad \cdots \qquad \Gamma_\xi, \Gamma_\phi, \Gamma_\rho \vdash e_n : \tau_n}{\Gamma_\xi, \Gamma_\phi, \Gamma_\rho \vdash \textsc{begin}(e_1, \ldots, e_n) : \tau_n}$$

$$\textsc{EmptyBegin}\quad \frac{}{\Gamma_\xi, \Gamma_\phi, \Gamma_\rho \vdash \textsc{begin}() : \textsc{unit}}$$

$$\textsc{Apply}\quad \frac{\Gamma_\phi(f) = \tau_1 \times \cdots \times \tau_n \to \tau \qquad \Gamma_\xi, \Gamma_\phi, \Gamma_\rho \vdash e_i : \tau_i, \quad 1 \le i \le n}{\Gamma_\xi, \Gamma_\phi, \Gamma_\rho \vdash \textsc{apply}(f, e_1, \ldots, e_n) : \tau}$$

$$\textsc{Eq}\quad \frac{\Gamma_\xi, \Gamma_\phi, \Gamma_\rho \vdash e_1 : \tau \qquad \Gamma_\xi, \Gamma_\phi, \Gamma_\rho \vdash e_2 : \tau}{\Gamma_\xi, \Gamma_\phi, \Gamma_\rho \vdash \textsc{eq}(e_1, e_2) : \textsc{bool}}$$

$$\textsc{Println}\quad \frac{\Gamma_\xi, \Gamma_\phi, \Gamma_\rho \vdash e : \tau}{\Gamma_\xi, \Gamma_\phi, \Gamma_\rho \vdash \textsc{println}(e) : \textsc{unit}}$$

Figure 6.7: Typing rules for Typed Impcore expressions

$$\boxed{\langle t, \Gamma_\xi, \Gamma_\phi \rangle \to \langle \Gamma'_\xi, \Gamma'_\phi \rangle}$$

NEWVAL
$$\frac{\Gamma_\xi, \Gamma_\phi, \{\} \vdash e : \tau \qquad x \notin \operatorname{dom} \Gamma_\xi}{\langle \text{VAL}(x, e), \Gamma_\xi, \Gamma_\phi \rangle \to \langle \Gamma_\xi\{x \mapsto \tau\}, \Gamma_\phi \rangle}$$

OLDVAL
$$\frac{\Gamma_\xi, \Gamma_\phi, \{\} \vdash e : \tau \qquad \Gamma_\xi(x) = \tau}{\langle \text{VAL}(x, e), \Gamma_\xi, \Gamma_\phi \rangle \to \langle \Gamma_\xi, \Gamma_\phi \rangle}$$

EXP
$$\frac{\Gamma_\xi, \Gamma_\phi, \{\} \vdash e : \tau}{\langle \text{EXP}(e), \Gamma_\xi, \Gamma_\phi \rangle \to \langle \Gamma_\xi, \Gamma_\phi \rangle}$$

DEFINE
$$\frac{\begin{array}{c}\tau_1, \ldots, \tau_n \text{ are types} \\ \tau_f = \tau_1 \times \cdots \times \tau_n \to \tau \\ f \notin \operatorname{dom} \Gamma_\phi \\ \Gamma_\xi, \Gamma_\phi\{f \mapsto \tau_f\}, \{x_1 \mapsto \tau_1, \ldots, x_n \mapsto \tau_n\} \vdash e : \tau\end{array}}{\langle \text{DEFINE}(f, (\langle x_1 : \tau_1, \ldots, x_n : \tau_n \rangle, e : \tau)), \Gamma_\xi, \Gamma_\phi \rangle \to \langle \Gamma_\xi, \Gamma_\phi\{f \mapsto \tau_f\} \rangle}$$

REDEFINE
$$\frac{\begin{array}{c}\tau_1, \ldots, \tau_n \text{ are types} \\ \Gamma_\phi(f) = \tau_1 \times \cdots \times \tau_n \to \tau \\ \Gamma_\xi, \Gamma_\phi\{f \mapsto \tau_1 \times \cdots \times \tau_n \to \tau\}, \{x_1 \mapsto \tau_1, \ldots, x_n \mapsto \tau_n\} \vdash e : \tau\end{array}}{\langle \text{DEFINE}(f, (\langle x_1 : \tau_1, \ldots, x_n : \tau_n \rangle, e : \tau)), \Gamma_\xi, \Gamma_\phi \rangle \to \langle \Gamma_\xi, \Gamma_\phi \rangle}$$

Figure 6.8: Typing rules for Typed Impcore definitions

13. *Add references to Typed μScheme.* In Typed μScheme, it is not necessary to add any special abstract syntax to support mutable cells as in Exercise 7. Give the kind of the `ref` constructor and the types of the operations `ref`, `!`, and `:=`.

14. *Add simple polymorphic records to Typed μScheme.* Extend Typed μScheme by adding polymorphic records with named fields. Types of fields are not specified; instead, the extension creates functions that work like the `record` functions in Chapter 2, except these functions are polymorphic.

    (a) Add a new form of definition. It should have this concrete syntax:

    def ::= `(record` *record-name* `(`{*field-name*}`))`

    The abstract syntax can be this:

    ```
    RECORD of name * name list
    ```

    (b) Modify `typdef` so that it returns a new kind environment Δ' as well as a new type environment Γ'.

    (c) A `record` definition should extend Δ by adding a new type constructor *record-name* with kind $*_1 \times \cdots \times *_n \Rightarrow *$, where n is the number of *field-names*.

    (d) The `record` definition should add a new function `make-`*record-name*. This function should take one argument for each field and build a record value.

    (e) For each field, the `record` definition should add a function named by joining the *record-name* and *field-name* with a dash. This function should extract the named field from the structure and return its value.

As an example, I define an assoc record with fields key and value:

393a. ⟨*exercise transcript* 393a⟩≡ 393b ▷

```
-> (record assoc key value)
-> (val p ((@ make-assoc sym int) 'class 152))
p : (assoc sym int)
-> ((@ assoc-key sym int) p)
class : sym
-> ((@ assoc-value sym int) p)
152 : int
```


15. *Add more expressive records to Typed μScheme.* Extend Typed μScheme by adding records with fields that are named and typed. This extension creates record functions whose types are determined by the types in the record specification.

   (a) Add a new kind of definition. It should have this concrete syntax:

   def ::= (typed-record (*record-name* {'*type-variable-name*})
   ({[*field-name* : *type*]}))

   This sort of record is also polymorphic, but under more control: type parameters are listed explicitly, and the type of each field is declared. The abstract syntax can be this:

   ```
   TYPED_RECORD of name * name list * (name * tyex) list
   ```

   (b) Modify typdef so that it returns a new kind environment Δ' as well as a new type environment Γ'.

   (c) The typed-record definition should extend Δ by adding a new type constructor *record-name* with kind $*_1 \times \cdots \times *_n \Rightarrow *$, where n is the number of *type-variable-name*s in the definition.

   (d) The typed-record definition should add a new function make-*record-name*. This function should take one argument for each field and build a record value.

   (e) For each field, the typed-record definition should add a function named by joining the *record-name* and *field-name* with a dash. This function should extract the named field from the structure and return its value.

Here is an example.

393b. ⟨*exercise transcript* 393a⟩+≡ ◁ 393a

```
-> (typed-record (assoc 'a) ([key : sym] [value : 'a]))
-> (val p ((@ make-assoc int) 'class 152))
p : (assoc int)
-> ((@ assoc-key int) p)
class : sym
-> ((@ assoc-value int) p)
152 : int
```

$$\boxed{\kappa \text{ is a kind}} \qquad \frac{\textsc{KindFormationType}}{* \text{ is a kind}} \qquad \textsc{KindFormationArrow}\ \frac{\kappa_1, \ldots, \kappa_n \text{ are kinds} \qquad \kappa \text{ is a kind}}{\kappa_1 \times \cdots \times \kappa_n \Rightarrow \kappa \text{ is a kind}}$$

Figure 6.9: Kind-formation rules for Typed μScheme

$$\boxed{\Delta \vdash \tau :: \kappa} \qquad \textsc{KindIntroCon}\ \frac{\mu \in \text{dom}\,\Delta}{\Delta \vdash \text{TYCON}(\mu) :: \Delta(\mu)} \qquad \textsc{KindIntroVar}\ \frac{\alpha \in \text{dom}\,\Delta}{\Delta \vdash \text{TYVAR}(\alpha) :: \Delta(\alpha)}$$

$$\textsc{KindApp}\ \frac{\Delta \vdash \tau :: \kappa_1 \times \cdots \times \kappa_n \Rightarrow \kappa \qquad \Delta \vdash \tau_i :: \kappa_i,\ 1 \le i \le n}{\Delta \vdash \text{CONAPP}(\tau, [\tau_1, \ldots, \tau_n]) :: \kappa}$$

$$\textsc{KindFunction}\ \frac{\Delta \vdash \tau_i :: *,\ 1 \le i \le n \qquad \Delta \vdash \tau :: *}{\Delta \vdash \tau_1 \times \cdots \times \tau_n \rightarrow \tau :: *} \qquad \textsc{KindAll}\ \frac{\Delta\{\alpha_1 :: *, \ldots, \alpha_n :: *\} \vdash \tau :: *}{\Delta \vdash \text{FORALL}(\langle \alpha_1, \ldots, \alpha_n \rangle, \tau) :: *}$$

Figure 6.10: Kinding rules for Typed μScheme types

6.9.6 *Typing derivations*

16. *The type of a polymorphic function in Typed μScheme.*

    (a) What is the type of the following function?

    ```
    (type-lambda ('a) (type-lambda ('b)
       (lambda ([f : ('a -> 'b)] [x : 'a]) (f x))))
    ```

    (b) Using the typing rules from the chapter, give a derivation tree proving the correctness of your answer to part (a).

17. *The type of a polymorphic function in* extended *Typed μScheme.* Suppose we get tired of writing @ signs everywhere, so we extend Typed μScheme by making PAIR, FST, and SND abstract syntax instead of functions.

    (a) What is the type of the following function?

    ```
    (type-lambda ('a) (type-lambda ('b)
       (lambda ([p : (pair 'a 'b)]) (pair (snd p) (fst p)))))
    ```

    (b) Using the typing rules from the chapter, give a derivation tree proving the correctness of your answer to part (a).

6.9.7 *Implementing type checking*

18. *Type checking for arrays.* Finish the type checker for Typed Impcore so that it handles arrays. It is sufficient to implement the four cases in code chunk 348.

19. *Type checking for Typed μScheme.* Write a type checker for Typed μScheme. That is, implement `typdef` in code chunk 366. Although you could write this checker by cloning and modifying the type checker for Typed Impcore, you

$$\boxed{\Delta, \Gamma \vdash e : \tau}$$

$$\textsc{Var}\quad \frac{x \in \operatorname{dom} \Gamma \qquad \Gamma(x) = \tau}{\Delta, \Gamma \vdash \textsc{var}(x) : \tau}$$

$$\textsc{Set}\quad \frac{\Delta, \Gamma \vdash e : \tau \qquad x \in \operatorname{dom} \Gamma \qquad \Gamma(x) = \tau}{\Delta, \Gamma \vdash \textsc{set}(x, e) : \tau}$$

$$\textsc{While}\quad \frac{\Delta, \Gamma \vdash e_1 : \texttt{bool} \qquad \Delta, \Gamma \vdash e_2 : \tau}{\Delta, \Gamma \vdash \textsc{while}(e_1, e_2) : \texttt{unit}}$$

$$\textsc{If}\quad \frac{\Delta, \Gamma \vdash e_1 : \texttt{bool} \qquad \Delta, \Gamma \vdash e_2 : \tau \qquad \Delta, \Gamma \vdash e_3 : \tau}{\Delta, \Gamma \vdash \textsc{if}(e_1, e_2, e_3) : \tau}$$

$$\textsc{Begin}\quad \frac{\Delta, \Gamma \vdash e_i : \tau_i, \;\; 1 \le i \le n}{\Delta, \Gamma \vdash \textsc{begin}(e_1, \ldots, e_n) : \tau_n}$$

$$\textsc{EmptyBegin}\quad \frac{}{\Delta, \Gamma \vdash \textsc{begin}() : \texttt{unit}}$$

$$\textsc{Let}\quad \frac{\Delta, \Gamma \vdash e_i : \tau_i, \;\; 1 \le i \le n \qquad \Delta, \Gamma\{x_1 \mapsto \tau_1, \ldots, x_n \mapsto \tau_n\} \vdash e : \tau}{\Delta, \Gamma \vdash \textsc{let}(\langle x_1, e_1, \ldots, x_n, e_n \rangle, e) : \tau}$$

$$\textsc{LetStar}\quad \frac{\Delta, \Gamma \vdash \textsc{let}(\langle x_1, e_1 \rangle, \textsc{letstar}(\langle x_2, e_2, \ldots, x_n, e_n \rangle, e)) : \tau \qquad n > 0}{\Delta, \Gamma \vdash \textsc{letstar}(\langle x_1, e_1, \ldots, x_n, e_n \rangle, e) : \tau}$$

$$\textsc{EmptyLetstar}\quad \frac{\Delta, \Gamma \vdash e : \tau}{\Delta, \Gamma \vdash \textsc{letstar}(\langle\rangle, e) : \tau}$$

$$\textsc{Letrec}\quad \frac{\begin{array}{c} \Delta \vdash \tau_i :: *, \;\; 1 \le i \le n \\ \Delta, \Gamma\{x_1 \mapsto \tau_1, \ldots, x_n \mapsto \tau_n\} \vdash e_i : \tau_i, \;\; 1 \le i \le n \\ \Delta, \Gamma\{x_1 \mapsto \tau_1, \ldots, x_n \mapsto \tau_n\} \vdash e : \tau \end{array}}{\Delta, \Gamma \vdash \textsc{letrec}(\langle x_1 : \tau_1, e_1, \ldots, x_n : \tau_n, e_n \rangle, e) : \tau}$$

$$\textsc{Lambda}\quad \frac{\Delta \vdash \tau_i :: *, \;\; 1 \le i \le n \qquad \Delta, \Gamma\{x_1 \mapsto \tau_1, \ldots, x_n \mapsto \tau_n\} \vdash e : \tau}{\Delta, \Gamma \vdash \textsc{lambda}(\langle x_1 : \tau_1, \ldots, x_n : \tau_n \rangle, e) : \tau_1 \times \cdots \times \tau_n \to \tau}$$

$$\textsc{Apply}\quad \frac{\Delta, \Gamma \vdash e : \tau_1 \times \cdots \times \tau_n \to \tau \qquad \Delta, \Gamma \vdash e_i : \tau_i, \;\; 1 \le i \le n}{\Delta, \Gamma \vdash \textsc{apply}(e, e_1, \ldots, e_n) : \tau}$$

$$\textsc{TyLambda}\quad \frac{\alpha_i \notin \operatorname{ftv}(\Gamma), \;\; 1 \le i \le n \qquad \Delta\{\alpha_1 :: *, \ldots \alpha_n :: *\}, \Gamma \vdash e : \tau}{\Delta, \Gamma \vdash \textsc{tylambda}(\alpha_1, \ldots, \alpha_n, e) : \forall \alpha_1, \ldots, \alpha_n \,.\, \tau}$$

$$\textsc{TyApply}\quad \frac{\Delta, \Gamma \vdash e : \forall \alpha_1, \ldots, \alpha_n \,.\, \tau \qquad \Delta \vdash \tau_i :: *, \;\; 1 \le i \le n}{\Delta, \Gamma \vdash \textsc{tyapply}(e, \tau_1, \ldots, \tau_n) : \tau[\alpha_1 \mapsto \tau_1, \ldots, \alpha_n \mapsto \tau_n]}$$

Figure 6.11: Typing rules for Typed μScheme expressions

$\boxed{\langle d, \Delta, \Gamma\rangle \to \Gamma'}$

VAL
$$\frac{\Delta, \Gamma \vdash e : \tau}{\langle \text{VAL}(x, e), \Delta, \Gamma\rangle \to \Gamma\{x \mapsto \tau\}}$$

VALREC
$$\frac{\begin{array}{c}\Delta \vdash \tau :: * \\ \Delta, \Gamma\{x \mapsto \tau\} \vdash e : \tau \\ e \text{ has the form } \text{LAMBDA}(\cdots)\end{array}}{\langle \text{VAL-REC}(x, \tau, e), \Delta, \Gamma\rangle \to \Gamma\{x \mapsto \tau\}}$$

EXP
$$\frac{\langle \text{VAL}(\texttt{it}, e), \Delta, \Gamma\rangle \to \Gamma'}{\langle \text{EXP}(e), \Delta, \Gamma\rangle \to \Gamma'}$$

DEFINE
$$\frac{\langle \text{VAL-REC}(f, \tau_1 \times \cdots \times \tau_n \to \tau, \text{LAMBDA}(\langle x_1 : \tau_1, \ldots, x_n : \tau_n\rangle, e)), \Delta, \Gamma\rangle \to \Gamma'}{\langle \text{DEFINE}(f, \tau, \langle x_1 : \tau_1, \ldots, x_n : \tau_n\rangle, e), \Delta, \Gamma\rangle \to \Gamma'}$$

Figure 6.12: Typing rules for Typed μScheme definitions

will get better results if you build a checker from scratch by following the typing rules for Typed μScheme, which are shown in Figure 6.11 on the previous page and in Figure 6.12 above.

- When a type in a program is supposed to be the type of a variable, the rules require that type to have kind $*$. You will find such types in the syntax of a `define`, `val-rec`, and `lambda`. The requirement that such types have kind $*$ can be enforced by the function `asType` on page 380.
- When you typecheck literals, use the rules on page 363. Although these rules are incomplete, they should suffice for anything the parser can produce. If a literal `PRIMITIVE` or `CLOSURE` reaches your type checker, the impossible has happened, and your code should raise an appropriate exception.

6.9.8 *Metatheory*

20. *Types are unique.* Prove that an expression in Typed Impcore has at most one type. That is, prove that given environments $\Gamma_\xi, \Gamma_\phi, \Gamma_\rho$ and abstract-syntax tree e, there is at most one τ such that $\Gamma_\xi, \Gamma_\phi, \Gamma_\rho \vdash e : \tau$.

21. *Desugaring preserves types.* The sidebar on page 362 notes that the only definition form we really need is `val`; `define` and `val-rec` can be expressed as syntactic sugar. The desugaring of `define` is given in the text; in this exercise, you desugar `val-rec`.

    (a) Express VAL-REC as syntactic sugar. That is, specify a translation from an arbitrary VAL-REC form into a combination of VAL and LETREC forms.

    (b) Prove that your translation preserves typing. That is, prove that a VAL-REC form is well typed if and only if its desugaring is well typed. And prove that when both are well typed, the final type environments on the right-hand side of the $\to$ judgment are equal.

22. *The type of a Typed Impcore expression is well formed.* Using a metatheoretic argument about typing derivations in Typed Impcore, prove that if there is a derivation of a typing judgment $\Gamma_\xi, \Gamma_\phi, \Gamma_\rho \vdash e : \tau$, there is also a derivation

of the judgment "τ is a type." Use structural induction on the derivation of the typing judgment.

23. *The type of a Typed μScheme expression is well formed.* In Typed μScheme, types like `list` and `pair` are well formed, with kinds $* \Rightarrow *$ and $* \times * \rightarrow *$, respectively, but they are not the types of any term: no expression can have type `list` or `pair`. The type of a term must have kind $*$. Using a metatheoretic argument about typing derivations in Typed μScheme, prove that if there is a derivation of a typing judgment $\Delta, \Gamma \vdash e : \tau$, there is also a derivation of the judgment $\Delta \vdash \tau :: *$. Use structural induction on the derivation of the typing judgment.

24. *"Type equivalence" is an equivalence.* Prove that $\equiv$, as defined in Section 6.6.6 (page 367), is an equivalence relation:

    (a) For any τ, $\tau \equiv \tau$.

    (b) For any τ and τ', if $\tau \equiv \tau'$, then $\tau' \equiv \tau$.

    (c) For any τ_1, τ_2, and τ_3, if $\tau_1 \equiv \tau_2$ and $\tau_2 \equiv \tau_3$, then $\tau_1 \equiv \tau_3$.

    In each case, structure your proof by assuming you have a derivation of the fact or facts assumed, and construct a derivation of the conclusion.

6.9.9 *Metatheory about implementation*

25. *Type checking terminates.* Using an argument about the rules in the type system, prove that type checking for Typed Impcore always terminates.

26. *Type checking is sound.* Show that if an expression in Typed Impcore has a type, and if the values stored in the value environments ξ, ϕ, and ρ inhabit the types in the corresponding type environments, then the `eval` function never raises the exception `BugInTypeChecking`.

6.9.10 *Capture-avoiding substitution*

27. *Proof that substitution terminates.* Function `tysubst` on page 374 works by defining and calling an inner recursive function `subst`, with which `tysubst` is mutually recursive. We need to know that no matter what Typed μScheme code a programmer writes, `tysubst` and `subst` terminate. Of particular concern is the recursive call in chunk 375b: given a `FORALL` type, the code makes a recursive call on a similar `FORALL` type. Could this process repeat forever?

    Prove that `tysubst` terminates by showing that at every recursive call something is getting smaller. You might consider assigning each type a pair of numbers and show that the pair shrinks lexicographically. One number worth considering is the number of bound type variables that are in the range of the substitution.

`LeftAsExercise`	S213b
`type name`	303
`type tyex`	357a

28. *Renaming type variables.* In substitution, rename type variables to avoid capture: Given a type $\forall \alpha_1, \ldots, \alpha_n \,.\, \tau$ and a set C of captured type variables, rename as many α_i's as necessary to avoid conflicts with variables in C and with free variables of τ. Do so in the body of function `renameForallAvoiding`, which is nested within function `tysubst` on page 374:

    397. ⟨*definition of* `renameForallAvoiding` *for Typed μScheme* **[[prototype]]** 397⟩≡

```
                     renameForallAvoiding : name list * tyex * name set -> tyex
fun renameForallAvoiding (alphas, tau, captured) =
  raise LeftAsExercise "renameForallAvoiding"
```

Calling renameForallAvoiding($[\alpha_1, \ldots, \alpha_n], \tau, C$) must choose variables β_i not in C and return a type $\forall \beta_1, \ldots, \beta_n \,.\, \tau'$ with these properties:

$$\forall \beta_1, \ldots, \beta_n \,.\, \tau' \equiv \forall \alpha_1, \ldots, \alpha_n \,.\, \tau,$$
$$\{\beta_1, \ldots, \beta_n\} \cap C = \emptyset.$$

For each α_i, there are two cases:

- If $\alpha_i \notin C$, then it doesn't need to be renamed, and to maximize readability of the resulting type, let $\beta_i = \alpha_i$.
- If $\alpha_i \in C$, then β_i must be a new variable that does not appear in C, is not free in τ, and is different from every α_i.

To find a β_i, use function freshName, which returns a name based on α but not in a given set of type variables.

398. ⟨*shared utility functions on sets of type variables* 398⟩≡ (S405a)

```
fun freshName (alpha, avoid) =        freshName : name * name set -> name
  let val basename = stripNumericSuffix alpha
      val candidates =
        streamMap (fn n => basename ^ "-" ^ intString n) naturals
      fun ok beta = not (member beta avoid)
  in  case streamGet (streamFilter ok candidates)
        of SOME (beta, _) => beta
         | NONE => raise InternalError "ran out of natural numbers"
  end
```

6.9.11 *Loopholes in type systems*

29. *Changing a thing's type can break the type system.* If a global variable or function is already defined, Typed Impcore doesn't let you write a new definition at a different type. To show why such definitions aren't permitted, complete this exercise:

    (a) Remove the restriction that a `val` binding may not change the type of the value bound. (An easy way to do this is to change the condition in chunk 341c so that it says "`if true`.")

    (b) With the restriction removed, create a Typed Impcore program whose evaluation raises `BugInTypeChecking`, e.g., by adding 1 to an array.

    (c) Restore the restriction on `val`, and remove the restriction that a `define` binding may not change the type of a function.

    (d) With the restriction removed, create a Typed Impcore program whose evaluation raises `BugInTypeChecking`, e.g., by doing an array lookup on an integer.

30. *Polymorphic mutable reference cells are unsound.* In a polymorphic system, the `ref` constructor (Exercise 13) leads to unsoundness: it can be used to subvert the type system. You can wrap `ref` in a `type-lambda` in a way that allows you instantiate a polymorphic, mutable data structure at any type you want. You can then instantiate it at one type with `:=` and at another type with `!`, enabling you to write a function that, for example, converts a Boolean to an integer.

    (a) Using polymorphism and references, trigger the `BugInTypeChecking` exception in Typed μScheme by adding 1 to `#t`.

(b) Write an *identity* function of type `bool` $\to$ `int`

(c) Write a polymorphic function of type $\forall\alpha, \beta \,.\, \alpha \to \beta$.

(d) Close this dreadful loophole in the system by making `ref` abstract syntax and permitting it to be instantiated only at a type that has no free type variables.

31. *A* `type-lambda` *may not abstract over a variable in the environment.* In Typed μScheme, remove the restriction that a `type-lambda` may not abstract over a type variable that's free in the type environment. Now

    (a) Write the `const` function of type $\forall\alpha \,.\, \alpha \to \forall\beta \,.\, \beta \to \alpha$.

    (b) Write a similar function `unsafe-const` that uses α in both places, instead of the two distinct α and β. (Change the inner β to an α.)

    (c) Use `unsafe-const` to define a variable that has type `int` but value `#t`.

    (d) Trigger `BugInTypeChecking` by adding one to this variable.

32. *Misuse of* `type-lambda` *can give any term any type.* The discussion of Typed μScheme rule TYLAMBDA on page 365 observes that if the side conditions are not enforced, then

$$\{\alpha :: *\}, \{x : \alpha\} \vdash \text{TYLAMBDA}(\alpha, x) : \forall\alpha \,.\, \alpha.$$

    This observation suggests that by wrapping TYLAMBDA(α, x) in code that introduces both α and β into the kind environment and x into the type environment, then instantiating TYLAMBDA(α, x) at β, one might well be able to define a function of type $\forall\alpha, \beta \,.\, \alpha \to \beta$.

    (a) Define such a function. Call it `cast`, or perhaps `Obj.magic`.

    (b) To enable `cast` to be accepted by the interpreter, remove the restriction that a `type-lambda` may not abstract over a type variable that's free in the type environment.

    (c) Use `cast` to trigger `BugInTypeChecking`.

33. *Variable capture can break the type system.* In Typed μScheme, change the code in chunk 375b so that substitution is always done naïvely, in a way that allows the capture of a $\forall$-bound variable. (It suffices to write `if true` instead of `if null actual_captures`.)

    (a) Define a typed, polymorphic version of function `flip-apply` from page 376, which should have type $\forall\beta \,.\, \beta \to (\forall\alpha \,.\, (\beta \to \alpha) \to \alpha)$.

    (b) Using `type-lambda` and suitable instantiations of `flip-apply`, define a function `cast` that behaves like the identity function but has type $\forall\alpha, \beta \,.\, \alpha \to \beta$. This function is *not* acceptable; in a correct version of Typed μScheme, it doesn't typecheck. But if you allow variable capture, you can write it.

    (c) Use `cast` to introduce a variable that has type `int` but value `#t`.

    (d) Trigger `BugInTypeChecking` by adding one to this variable.

`InternalError` S219e
`intString` S214c
`member` S217b
type `name` 303
`naturals` S230c
`streamFilter` S231d
`streamGet` S229a
`streamMap` S231c
`stripNumericSuffix` S217a

CHAPTER 7 CONTENTS

ML and type inference

7

It soon appeared intolerable to have to declare—for example— a new maplist function for mapping a function over a list, every time a new type of list is to be treated. Even if the maplist function could possess what Strachey called "parametric polymorphism," it also appeared intolerable to have to supply an appropriate type explicitly as a parameter, for each use of this function.

Robin Milner, *How ML Evolved*

Typed Impcore and Typed μScheme represent two extremes. Typed Impcore is easy to program in and easy to write a type checker for, but because it is monomorphic, it cannot accept polymorphic functions, and it can accommodate new type constructors and polymorphic operations only if its syntax and type checker are extended. Typed μScheme is also easy to write a type checker for, and as a polymorphic language, it can accept polymorphic functions, and it can accommodate new type constructors and polymorphic functions with no change to its syntax or its type checker. But Typed μScheme is difficult to program in: as Milner observed, supplying a type parameter at every use of every polymorphic value soon becomes intolerable. To combine the expressive power of polymorphism with great ease of programming, this chapter presents a third point in the design space: nano-ML. Nano-ML is expressive, easy to extend, and also easy to program in. This ease of use is delivered by a new typing algorithm: instead of type checking, nano-ML uses *type inference*.

A language with type inference doesn't require explicit type annotations; the types of variables and parameters are discovered by an algorithm. Type inference is used in such languages as Haskell, Miranda, OCaml, Standard ML, and TypeScript. Type inference works with a limited form of polymorphism: typically the *Hindley-Milner type system*. In this type system, a quantified $\forall$ type may appear only at top level; a $\forall$ type may *not* be passed to a type constructor. In particular, a $\forall$ type may not appear as an argument in a function type. This restriction makes type inference decidable.

In this chapter, the Hindley-Milner type system and its type inference are illustrated by nano-ML, a language that is closely related to Typed μScheme.

- Like Typed μScheme, nano-ML has first-class, higher-order functions, and its values are S-expressions.
- Like Typed μScheme, nano-ML has polymorphic types that are checked at compile time.

- Unlike Typed μScheme, nano-ML has *implicit* types. In nano-ML, the programmer never writes a type or a type constructor.
- Unlike Typed μScheme, nano-ML has no mutation. Nano-ML lacks `set`, and its names stand for values, not for mutable locations. Because there is no mutation, nano-ML programs are nearly always written in *applicative* style. Imperative actions are limited to printing and error primitives.
- Unlike Typed μScheme, nano-ML restricts polymorphism: quantified types may appear only at top level. This restriction enables nano-ML to instantiate polymorphic values automatically and also to introduce polymorphic types automatically. Explicit `@` and `type-lambda` are not needed.

Nano-ML, Typed μScheme, and μScheme are closely related. If the types are erased from a Typed μScheme program, the result is a valid μScheme program. And if the program does not use `set` or `while`, and if it uses `type-lambda` appropriately, it is also a valid nano-ML program.

Like the interpreter for Typed μScheme, nano-ML's interpreter is based on the μScheme interpreter from Chapter 5. And as with the type checker from Chapter 6, substantial parts of the implementation are left as exercises.

7.1 Nano-ML: A nearly applicative language

Aside from its type system, nano-ML differs from μScheme by forbidding mutation.[1] Mutation is the archetypal example of an *imperative feature*. Although nano-ML does not have mutation, it does have other imperative features: printing primitives, `error`, and `begin` (see sidebar).

Nano-ML and μScheme have subtly different definition forms. In μScheme, a `val` definition can mutate an existing binding, but in nano-ML, `val` always creates a new binding. To define a recursive function, nano-ML uses a `val-rec` definition form like Typed μScheme's `val-rec`. And like Typed μScheme, nano-ML uses `define` as syntactic sugar for a combination of `val-rec` and `lambda`.

Nano-ML needs fewer primitives than μScheme. Because nano-ML has a type system, every symbol, number, Boolean, and function is identified as such at compile time—so nano-ML doesn't need type predicates `symbol?`, `number?`, `boolean?`, or `function?`. Nano-ML does need the `null?` predicate, which is used to tell the difference between empty and nonempty lists, but it does not also need `pair?`.

Except for the addition of `val-rec`, the concrete syntax of nano-ML, which is shown in Figure 7.1 on page 404, is mostly a subset of that of μScheme. But nano-ML's syntax also includes forms for type-related unit tests: `check-type`, `check-type-error`, and `check-principal-type`.

The `check-type` test serves the same role as the corresponding test in Typed μScheme, but as explained in Section 7.4.6, it is more permissive. To test for type equivalence in nano-ML, use `check-principal-type`.

402. ⟨*transcript* 402⟩≡ 409b ▷

```
-> (check-principal-type revapp
                         (forall ['a] ((list 'a) (list 'a) -> (list 'a))))
-> (define revapp (xs ys)
     (if (null? xs)
         ys
         (revapp (cdr xs) (cons (car xs) ys))))
```

Function `revapp` is written exactly as we wrote it in μScheme.

[1] To add mutation soundly requires some subtlety in the type system, and in this chapter we are going for simplicity. Mutation is relegated to Exercise 23.

Imperative features

Despite the fact the Impcore is a procedural language and the dialects of μScheme are functional languages, all three share syntactic forms devoted to imperative features: `set`, `while`, and `begin`. These forms are used more heavily in procedural languages; functional languages emphasize `let` binding, function application, and recursion. In nano-ML, imperative features are so little emphasized that `set` and `while` are entirely absent, and `begin` is used rarely—primarily for `printf`-style debugging.

What are imperative features, and why do we care? A feature is imperative if *when the feature is used, different orders of evaluation can produce different results.*[a]

- The `set` form, also called assignment or mutation, is an imperative feature: if two expressions assign to the same mutable location, the order of evaluation matters. In particular, after two assignments, the second assignment determines what value the location holds.
- Input and output are imperative features. For example, if different `print` expressions are evaluated in different orders, the program's output is different. Similarly, if a program reads x and y from its input, it may produce different results depending on the order in which the variables are read.
- Exceptions are an imperative feature: if different expressions raise different exceptions, order matters. Which exception is raised depends on which expression is evaluated first. In μScheme and nano-ML, `error` is a similar imperative feature, because the error message depends on the order of evaluation.

In the presence of imperative features, order of evaluation is controlled by sequencing and looping constructs, like `begin` and `while`.

- Sequencing is fundamental to procedural programming. In languages such as C, C++, and OCaml, which have imperative features but do not say in what order a function's arguments are evaluated, sequencing is essential; without it, some programs' behavior would be impossible to predict.
- Loops are useful only in the presence of imperative features. Without imperative features, for example, a `while` expression has only uninteresting outcomes: nontermination, immediate termination, or a run-time error.

Limiting imperative features, as in nano-ML, has two benefits:

- When imperative features are absent, we can reason about programs more easily, especially using algebraic laws. We can more easily build correct programs, and we can more easily transform programs to make them more efficient.
- When imperative features are absent or restricted, a compiler can often produce better code. In ML-like languages, restrictions on mutation have been used to reduce memory requirements, improve instruction scheduling, and reduce the overhead of garbage collection.

A language containing no imperative features may be called *pure*; a language containing imperative features may be called *impure*.

[a] For purposes of deciding whether a feature is imperative, we don't consider nontermination to be a "different result." (A reordering that makes a program terminate more often is typically benign.)

`car` $\mathcal{P}$ 440a
`cdr` $\mathcal{P}$ 440a
`cons` $\mathcal{P}$ 440a
`null?` $\mathcal{P}$ 440a

def	::=	`(val` *variable-name exp*`)`
	|	`(val-rec` *variable-name exp*`)`
	|	*exp*
	|	`(define` *function-name* `(`*formals*`)` *exp*`)`
	|	`(use` *file-name*`)`
	|	*unit-test*
unit-test	::=	`(check-expect` *exp exp*`)`
	|	`(check-assert` *exp*`)`
	|	`(check-error` *exp*`)`
	|	`(check-type` *exp type-exp*`)`
	|	`(check-principal-type` *exp type-exp*`)`
	|	`(check-type-error` *exp*`)`
exp	::=	*literal*
	|	*variable-name*
	|	`(if` *exp exp exp*`)`
	|	`(begin` {*exp*}`)`
	|	`(`*exp* {*exp*}`)`
	|	`(`*let-keyword* `(`{`(`*variable-name exp*`)`}`)` *exp*`)`
	|	`(lambda` `(`*formals*`)` *exp*`)`
let-keyword	::=	`let` | `let*` | `letrec`
type-exp	::=	*type-constructor-name*
	|	`'`*type-variable-name*
	|	`(forall [`{`'`*type-variable-name*}`]` *type-exp*`)`
	|	`(`{*type-exp*} `->` *type-exp*`)`
	|	`(`*type-exp* {*type-exp*}`)`
formals	::=	{*variable-name*}
literal	::=	*numeral* | `#t` | `#f` | `'`*S-exp* | `(quote` *S-exp*`)`
S-exp	::=	*literal* | *symbol-name* | `(`{*S-exp*}`)`
numeral	::=	token composed only of digits, possibly prefixed with a plus or minus sign
**-name*	::=	token that is not a bracket, a *numeral*, or one of the "reserved" words shown in `typewriter font`

Figure 7.1: The concrete syntax of nano-ML

7.2 ABSTRACT SYNTAX AND VALUES OF NANO-ML

Nano-ML's abstract syntax is the same as μScheme's, minus `WHILEX` and `SET`.

404. ⟨*definitions of* `exp` *and* `value` *for nano-ML* 404⟩≡ (S419b)

```
datatype exp = LITERAL of value
             | VAR     of name
             | IFX     of exp * exp * exp
             | BEGIN   of exp list
             | APPLY   of exp * exp list
             | LETX    of let_flavor * (name * exp) list * exp
             | LAMBDA  of name list * exp
and let_flavor = LET | LETREC | LETSTAR
and ⟨definition of value for nano-ML 405b⟩
```

The `BEGIN` form is intended for use with primitive functions `println` and `print`.

Except for VALREC, definitions are as in μScheme.

405a. ⟨*definition of* `def` *for nano-ML* 405a⟩≡ (S419b)

```
datatype def  = VAL    of name * exp
              | VALREC of name * exp
              | EXP    of exp
              | DEFINE of name * (name list * exp)
```

In the operational semantics, nano-ML and μScheme have the same values, and their representations are similar enough that I can reuse the projection, embedding, and printing functions from Chapter 5.

405b. ⟨*definition of* `value` *for nano-ML* 405b⟩≡ (404)

```
value = SYM       of name
      | NUM       of int
      | BOOLV     of bool
      | NIL
      | PAIR      of value * value
      | CLOSURE   of lambda * value env ref
      | PRIMITIVE of primop
withtype primop = value list -> value (* raises RuntimeError *)
     and lambda = name list * exp
```

Only one thing is different: the representation of closures.

A closure includes an environment, and if the closure represents a recursive function, the closure's environment includes a reference to the closure itself. Such self-reference is implemented using mutation. In μScheme, the environment maps every name to a mutable reference cell. Recursion is implemented by first putting an unspecified value in the function's cell, then updating the cell once the closure is created. In nano-ML, an environment maps each name to a value—the mutable cell is part of the closure, not the environment. Recursion is implemented by first putting an unspecified environment in the closure's cell, then building a new environment, and finally updating the cell to hold that environment. Therefore the closure stores a `value env ref`, not a `value ref env` as in μScheme.

7.3 Operational semantics

Because nano-ML doesn't have mutation and because the effects of its imperative primitives aren't specified formally, its operational semantics is simple. Its abstract machine has no locations and no store; evaluating an expression just produces a value. The judgment is $\langle e, \rho\rangle \Downarrow v$. The environment ρ maps a name to a value, not to a mutable location as in μScheme. And evaluating a definition produces a new environment; the form of that judgment is $\langle d, \rho\rangle \to \rho'$.

7.3.1 *Rules for expressions*

Most of the rules should be self-explanatory.

type env	304
type name	303

$$\frac{}{\langle \text{LITERAL}(v), \rho\rangle \Downarrow v} \qquad \text{(LITERAL)}$$

$$\frac{x \in \operatorname{dom} \rho}{\langle \text{VAR}(x), \rho\rangle \Downarrow \rho(x)} \qquad \text{(VAR)}$$

$$\frac{\langle e_1, \rho\rangle \Downarrow v_1 \qquad v_1 \neq \text{BOOLV}(\texttt{\#f}) \qquad \langle e_2, \rho\rangle \Downarrow v_2}{\langle \text{IF}(e_1, e_2, e_3), \rho\rangle \Downarrow v_2} \qquad \text{(IFTRUE)}$$

$$\frac{\langle e_1, \rho\rangle \Downarrow v_1 \qquad v_1 = \text{BOOLV}(\texttt{\#f}) \qquad \langle e_3, \rho\rangle \Downarrow v_3}{\langle \text{IF}(e_1, e_2, e_3), \rho\rangle \Downarrow v_3} \qquad \text{(IFFALSE)}$$

The rules for BEGIN are a cheat; the purpose of BEGIN is to force order of evaluation, but these rules are so simplified that they don't enforce an order of evaluation.

$$\frac{}{\langle \text{BEGIN}(), \rho \rangle \Downarrow \text{NIL}} \qquad \text{(EMPTYBEGIN)}$$

$$\frac{\langle e_1, \rho \rangle \Downarrow v_1 \qquad \langle e_2, \rho \rangle \Downarrow v_2 \qquad \cdots \qquad \langle e_n, \rho \rangle \Downarrow v_n}{\langle \text{BEGIN}(e_1, e_2, \ldots, e_n), \rho \rangle \Downarrow v_n} \qquad \text{(BEGIN)}$$

Just as in μScheme, LAMBDA captures an environment in a closure, and APPLY uses the captured environment. Because nano-ML does not store actual parameters in mutable locations, its rules are simpler than μScheme's rules.

$$\frac{}{\langle \text{LAMBDA}(\langle x_1, \ldots, x_n \rangle, e), \rho \rangle \Downarrow (\!| \text{LAMBDA}(\langle x_1, \ldots, x_n \rangle, e), \rho |\!)} \qquad \text{(MKCLOSURE)}$$

$$\frac{\begin{array}{c}\langle e, \rho \rangle \Downarrow (\!| \text{LAMBDA}(\langle x_1, \ldots, x_n \rangle, e_c), \rho_c |\!) \\ \langle e_i, \rho \rangle \Downarrow v_i, \quad 1 \le i \le n \\ \langle e_c, \rho_c\{x_1 \mapsto v_1, \ldots, x_n \mapsto v_n\} \rangle \Downarrow v\end{array}}{\langle \text{APPLY}(e, e_1, \ldots, e_n), \rho \rangle \Downarrow v} \qquad \text{(APPLYCLOSURE)}$$

The semantic rule for applying a nano-ML primitive is to apply the function attached to that primitive. The implementation is equally simple.

$$\frac{\begin{array}{c}\langle e, \rho \rangle \Downarrow \text{PRIMITIVE}(f) \\ \langle e_i, \rho \rangle \Downarrow v_i, \quad 1 \le i \le n \\ f(v_1, \ldots, v_n) = v\end{array}}{\langle \text{APPLY}(e, e_1, \ldots, e_n), \rho \rangle \Downarrow v} \qquad \text{(APPLYPRIMITIVE)}$$

Because a LET-bound name stands for a value, not a location, rules for LET forms are also simplified.

$$\frac{\begin{array}{c}\langle e_i, \rho \rangle \Downarrow v_i, \quad 1 \le i \le n \\ \langle e, \rho\{x_1 \mapsto v_1, \ldots, x_n \mapsto v_n\} \rangle \Downarrow v\end{array}}{\langle \text{LET}(\langle x_1, e_1, \ldots, x_n, e_n \rangle, e), \rho \rangle \Downarrow v} \qquad \text{(LET)}$$

As in μScheme, a LETSTAR expression requires a sequence of environments.

$$\frac{\begin{array}{c}\langle e_1, \rho_0 \rangle \Downarrow v_1 \qquad \rho_1 = \rho_0\{x_1 \mapsto v_1\} \\ \vdots \\ \langle e, \rho_{n-1} \rangle \Downarrow v_n \qquad \rho_n = \rho_{n-1}\{x_n \mapsto v_n\} \\ \langle e, \rho_n \rangle \Downarrow v\end{array}}{\langle \text{LETSTAR}(\langle x_1, e_1, \ldots, x_n, e_n \rangle, e), \rho_0 \rangle \Downarrow v} \qquad \text{(LETSTAR)}$$

LETREC is the tricky one. The expressions are evaluated in an environment ρ' in which their names are already bound to the resulting values. In other words, to evaluate each e_i, we have to have ρ', but to build ρ', we have to know all the v_i's. It seems like it should be impossible to make progress, but because the expressions are all `lambda` abstractions, we can pull it off.

$$\frac{\begin{array}{c}\rho' = \rho\{x_1 \mapsto v_1, \ldots, x_n \mapsto v_n\} \\ \langle e_1, \rho' \rangle \Downarrow v_1 \qquad \cdots \qquad \langle e_n, \rho' \rangle \Downarrow v_n \\ \langle e, \rho' \rangle \Downarrow v\end{array}}{\langle \text{LETREC}(\langle x_1, e_1, \ldots, x_n, e_n \rangle, e), \rho \rangle \Downarrow v} \qquad \text{(LETREC)}$$

Because each e_i is a LAMBDA, evaluating it is going to produce a closure that captures ρ' and the body of the LAMBDA. And in `eval`, that makes it possible to build ρ' without calling `eval` recursively (chunk S430a). The resulting ρ' satisfies the equations in the premises, and the implementation closes the loop by stuffing ρ' into the mutable cell contained in each closure.

7.3.2 *Rules for evaluating definitions*

In μScheme or Typed μScheme, evaluating a definition produces a new environment and a new store. In nano-ML, because there is no mutation, evaluating a definition produces only a new environment. (It may also print.) The judgment has the form $\langle d, \rho \rangle \to \rho'$.

Nano-ML's definitions differ from μScheme's in several significant ways:

- In nano-ML, as in full ML and in Typed μScheme, a VAL definition never mutates a previous binding; it always adds a new binding. (See Exercise 46 on page 194 of Chapter 2.) If the old binding was used to create a function or other value, that function still refers to the old binding, not the new one. In an interactive interpreter, this behavior can be baffling, particularly if you load a new definition of an old function but you don't also load the definitions of the functions that depend on it.

$$\frac{\langle e, \rho \rangle \Downarrow v}{\langle \text{VAL}(x, e), \rho \rangle \to \rho\{x \mapsto v\}} \qquad (\text{VAL})$$

- Like Typed μScheme but unlike μScheme, nano-ML has VAL-REC. The semantics requires a ρ' that binds f to a closure containing ρ'.

$$\frac{\rho' = \rho\{f \mapsto (\!| \text{LAMBDA}(\langle x_1, \ldots, x_n \rangle, e), \rho' |\!)\}}{\langle \text{VAL-REC}(f, \text{LAMBDA}(\langle x_1, \ldots, x_n \rangle, e)), \rho \rangle \to \rho'} \qquad (\text{VALREC})$$

  This self-reference is implemented using the same mutable-cell trick used to implement LETREC.

- In nano-ML, as in Typed μScheme, $\text{DEFINE}(f, a, e)$ is syntactic sugar for $\text{VAL-REC}(f, \text{LAMBDA}(a, e))$.

$$\frac{\langle \text{VAL-REC}(f, \text{LAMBDA}(\langle x_1, \ldots, x_n \rangle, e)), \rho \rangle \to \rho'}{\langle \text{DEFINE}(f, \langle x_1, \ldots, x_n \rangle, e), \rho \rangle \to \rho'} \qquad (\text{DEFINE})$$

As in μScheme, a top-level expression e is syntactic sugar for a binding to `it`.

$$\frac{\langle \text{VAL}(\texttt{it}, e), \rho \rangle \to \rho'}{\langle \text{EXP}(e), \rho \rangle \to \rho'} \qquad (\text{EXP})$$

7.4 TYPE SYSTEM FOR NANO-ML

Like other type systems, the type system of nano-ML determines which terms have types, which in turn determines what definitions are accepted by the interpreter. As before, the types of terms are specified by a formal proof system. The system uses the same elements as the type system of Typed μScheme.

7.4.1 *Types, type schemes, and type environments*

As in Typed μScheme, types are built using four elements:

- Type variables, which are written using α
- Type constructors, which are written generically using μ or specifically using a name such as `int` or `list`
- Constructor application, which is written using ML notation $(\tau_1, \ldots, \tau_n)\ \tau$
- Quantification, which is written using $\forall$

In nano-ML, unlike in Typed μScheme, quantified types are restricted: a type quantified with $\forall$ may appear only at top level, never as an argument to a type constructor. In nano-ML, this restriction is built in to the *syntax* of types:

- A type built with type variables, type constructors, and constructor application is written using the metavariable τ.

  $$\tau ::= \alpha \mid \mu \mid (\tau_1, \ldots, \tau_n)\ \tau$$

  A τ is called a *type*.

- A quantified type is written using the metavariable σ.

  $$\sigma ::= \forall \alpha_1, \ldots, \alpha_n \,.\, \tau$$

  A σ is called a *type scheme*.

In the code, a τ is represented by a `ty` and a σ by a `type_scheme`:[2]

408. ⟨*representation of Hindley-Milner types* 408⟩≡ (S420a)

```
type tyvar  = name
datatype ty = TYVAR  of tyvar                  (* type variable alpha *)
            | TYCON  of tycon                  (* type constructor mu *)
            | CONAPP of ty * ty list           (* type-level application *)

datatype type_scheme = FORALL of tyvar list * ty
```

The set of type schemes σ in which the $\alpha_1, \ldots, \alpha_n$ is empty is isomorphic to the set of types τ. The isomorphism relates each type `tau` to the type scheme `FORALL([], tau)`. A type without $\forall$ or a type scheme in which the $\alpha_1, \ldots, \alpha_n$ is empty is sometimes called a *monotype* or *ground type*. A type scheme in which the $\alpha_1, \ldots, \alpha_n$ is not empty is sometimes called a *polytype*.

When a type application appears in code, the type constructor goes *before* its arguments, as in

```
CONAPP(TYCON "list", [TYCON "int"]).
```

But in the text, the type constructor goes *after* its arguments, as in `int list`. This is the way types are written in ML source code.

In nano-ML, all type constructors are predefined; no program can add new ones. New type constructors can be added in the more advanced bridge languages μML (Chapter 8) and Molecule (Chapter 9). In nano-ML, the predefined constructors `arguments` and `function` appear in the typing rules for functions. Other constructors, like `bool`, `int`, `sym`, and so on, give types to literals or primitives.

To write types made with `arguments` and `function`, I use ML's abbreviations.

Type	*Abbreviation*
(τ_1, τ_2) `function`	$\tau_1 \to \tau_2$
$(\tau_1, \ldots, \tau_n)$ `arguments`	$\tau_1 \times \tau_2 \cdots \times \tau_n$

In nano-ML, as in Typed μScheme, a type environment is written using the Greek letter Γ. In nano-ML, a type environment Γ maps a term variable [3] to a type scheme. Type environments are used only during type inference, not at run time.

[2] Nano-ML's representation has only four of the five forms found in Typed μScheme. The fifth form, `FUNTY`, is represented in nano-ML as a nested application of type constructors `function` and `arguments` (chunk 412b). Coding function types in this way simplifies type inference.

[3] Term variables, which appear in terms (expressions) and are bound by `let` or `lambda`, stand for values. Don't confuse them with type variables, which stand for types. The name of a term variable begins with a letter or symbol; the name of a type variable begins with the ASCII quote (`'`) character.

In nano-ML, unlike in Typed μScheme, types don't appear in code. And types inferred by the system are guaranteed to be well formed, so the type system doesn't need formation rules or kinds. (An ill-formed type may appear in a unit test, but in that case the test just fails; no other checking is needed.) Kinds are used again in μML (Chapter 8) and in full ML.

7.4.2 *Simple type constructors*

Because all type constructors are predefined, a type constructor can be represented simply by its name. Because type names cannot be redefined, a name like `int` always means "integer," and two type constructors are the same if and only if they have the same name.

409a. ⟨`tycon`, `eqTycon`, *and* `tyconString` *for named type constructors* 409a⟩≡ (S420a)

```
type tycon = name
fun eqTycon (mu, mu') = mu = mu'
fun tyconString mu = mu
```

```
type tycon
eqTycon : tycon * tycon -> bool
tyconString : tycon -> string
```

7.4.3 *Substitution, instances, and instantiation*

In nano-ML, the system automatically instantiates polymorphic values. To show how this feature works, I define `empty-list` with type $\forall\alpha\,.\,\alpha$ `list`, then let the system instantiate it at types `int` and `sym list`:

409b. ⟨*transcript* 402⟩+≡ ◁402 414▷

```
-> (val empty-list '())
() : (forall ['a] (list 'a))
-> (val p (pair (cons 1 empty-list) (cons '(a b c) empty-list)))
(PAIR (1) ((a b c))) : (pair (list int) (list (list sym)))
```

In Typed μScheme, `empty-list` would have to be instantiated explicitly, using expressions `(@ empty-list int)` and `(@ empty-list (list sym))`. Likewise, primitives `pair` and `cons` would have to be instantiated explicitly. These instantiations are what Professor Milner found intolerable. In ML, no `@` form is needed; every polymorphic name is instantiated automatically by Milner's inference algorithm. The algorithm works by computing an appropriate *substitution*.

A substitution is a finite map from type variables to types; one is written using the Greek letter θ (pronounced "THAYT-uh"). A θ has many interpretations:

- As a function from type variables to types
- As a function from types to types
- As a function from type schemes to type schemes
- As a function from type environments to type environments
- As a function from type-equality constraints to type-equality constraints
- As a function from typing judgments to typing judgments
- As a function from typing derivations to typing derivations

`cons`	$\mathcal{P}$ 440a
`type name`	303
`pair`	$\mathcal{P}$

These interpretations are all related and mutually consistent. They all appear in the math, and some appear in my code. The interpretation I use most is the function from types to types. Such a function θ is a substitution if it preserves type constructors and constructor application:

- For any type constructor μ, $\theta\mu = \mu$.
- For any constructor application $\text{CONAPP}(\tau, \langle\tau_1, \ldots, \tau_n\rangle)$,

$$\theta(\text{CONAPP}(\tau, \langle\tau_1, \ldots, \tau_n\rangle)) = \text{CONAPP}(\theta\tau, \langle\theta\tau_1, \ldots, \theta\tau_n\rangle).$$

Or, using informal ML-like notation,

$$\theta((\tau_1, \ldots, \tau_n)\ \tau) = (\theta\tau_1, \ldots, \theta\tau_n)\ (\theta\tau).$$

In the common case where the τ being applied is a simple constructor μ, $\theta\mu = \mu$ and

$$\theta((\tau_1, \ldots, \tau_n)\ \mu) = (\theta\tau_1, \ldots, \theta\tau_n)\ \mu.$$

To be a substitution, a function from types to types must meet one other condition:

- The set $\{\alpha \mid \theta\alpha \neq \alpha\}$ must be *finite*. This set is the set of variables substituted for. It is called the *domain* of the substitution, and it is written $\operatorname{dom}\theta$.

Such a function is defined by `tysubst` in Chapter 6 on page 371; its inner function `subst` has all the properties claimed above (Exercise 3).

Substitution determines when τ' is an *instance* of τ: like Milner (1978), we write $\tau' \leqslant \tau$ if and only if there exists a substitution θ such that $\tau' = \theta\tau$. The instance relation $\tau' \leqslant \tau$ is pronounced in two ways: not only "τ' is an *instance* of τ" but also "τ is *at least as general* as τ'."

The instance relation is extended to type schemes: $\tau' \leqslant \forall\alpha_1, \ldots, \alpha_n \,.\, \tau$ if and only if there exists a substitution θ such that $\operatorname{dom}\theta \subseteq \{\alpha_1, \ldots, \alpha_n\}$ and $\theta\tau = \tau'$. The first condition says that the instantiating substitution θ may substitute only for type variables that are bound by the $\forall$.

To *instantiate* a type scheme $\sigma = \forall\alpha_1, \ldots, \alpha_n \,.\, \tau$ is to choose a $\tau' \leqslant \sigma$. An instance of σ is obtained by substituting for the type variables $\alpha_1, \ldots, \alpha_n$, and *only* for those type variables. It's like instantiation in Typed μScheme, except in ML, the system instantiates each σ automatically.

In my code, a substitution is represented as a finite map from type variables to types: an environment of type `ty env`. A substitution's domain is computed by function `dom`.

410a. ⟨*shared utility functions on Hindley-Milner types* 410a⟩≡ (S420a) 410b ▷

```
type subst = ty env
fun dom theta = map (fn (a, _) => a) theta
```

```
type subst
dom : subst -> name set
```

To interpret a substitution as a function from type variables to types, we apply `varsubst` to it:

410b. ⟨*shared utility functions on Hindley-Milner types* 410a⟩+≡ (S420a) ◁ 410a 410c ▷

```
varsubst : subst -> (name -> ty)
```

```
fun varsubst theta =
  (fn a => find (a, theta) handle NotFound _ => TYVAR a)
```

As the code shows, the function defined by a substitution is *total*. If type variable a is not in the domain of `theta`, then `varsubst theta` leaves a unchanged.

A substitution is most often interpreted as a function from types to types. That interpretation is provided by function `tysubst`. It is almost the same as the `tysubst` function in the interpreter for Typed μScheme (page 374), but because it has no quantified types to deal with, it is simpler.

410c. ⟨*shared utility functions on Hindley-Milner types* 410a⟩+≡ (S420a) ◁ 410b 411a ▷

```
tysubst : subst -> (ty -> ty)
subst   :           ty -> ty
```

```
fun tysubst theta =
  let fun subst (TYVAR a) = varsubst theta a
        | subst (TYCON c) = TYCON c
        | subst (CONAPP (tau, taus)) = CONAPP (subst tau, map subst taus)
  in  subst
  end
```

A function produced by `tysubst` has type `ty -> ty` and so can be composed with any other function of the same type, including all functions that correspond to substitutions. To be precise, if θ_1 and θ_2 are substitutions, then the composition `tysubst` $\theta_2 \circ$ `tysubst` θ_1 is a function from types to types (and also corresponds to a substitution). Composition is really useful, but a substitution *data structure* θ is strictly more useful than the corresponding *function* `tysubst` θ. For one thing, θ can be asked about its domain. To compose substitutions in a way that lets me ask about the domain of the composition, I define a function `compose`, which obeys these algebraic laws:

$$\mathtt{tysubst}(\mathtt{compose}(\theta_2, \theta_1)) = \mathtt{tysubst}\ \theta_2 \circ \mathtt{tysubst}\ \theta_1,$$
$$\mathtt{dom}(\mathtt{compose}(\theta_2, \theta_1)) = \mathtt{dom}\ \theta_1 \cup \mathtt{dom}\ \theta_2.$$

411a. ⟨*shared utility functions on Hindley-Milner types* 410a⟩+≡ (S420a) ◁ 410c 411b ▷

compose : subst * subst -> subst

```
fun compose (theta2, theta1) =
  let val domain  = union (dom theta2, dom theta1)
      val replace = tysubst theta2 o varsubst theta1
  in  mkEnv (domain, map replace domain)
  end
```

Instantiation is as in Chapter 6, except no kind environment is needed. Because instantiations are computed by the system, instantiating a type scheme with the wrong number of arguments indicates an internal error. Such an error is signaled by raising the exception `BugInTypeInference`, which is raised only when there is a fault in the interpreter; it should never be triggered by a faulty nano-ML program.

411b. ⟨*shared utility functions on Hindley-Milner types* 410a⟩+≡ (S420a) ◁ 411a 411c ▷

instantiate : type_scheme * ty list -> ty

```
fun instantiate (FORALL (formals, tau), actuals) =
  tysubst (mkEnv (formals, actuals)) tau
  handle BindListLength =>
    raise BugInTypeInference "number of types in instantiation"
```

All substitutions can be built with `mkEnv`, but that's not how Milner's algorithm creates them. Milner's algorithm substitutes for one type variable at a time, then composes those substitutions. To create a substitution that substitutes for a single variable, I define an infix function `|-->`. The expression `alpha |--> tau` is the substitution that substitutes `tau` for `alpha`. In math, that substitution is written $(\alpha \mapsto \tau)$.

411c. ⟨*shared utility functions on Hindley-Milner types* 410a⟩+≡ (S420a) ◁ 411b 411d ▷

|--> : name * ty -> subst

```
infix 7 |-->
fun a |--> (TYVAR a') = if a = a' then emptyEnv
                        else bind (a, TYVAR a', emptyEnv)
  | a |--> tau        = bind (a, tau, emptyEnv)
```

The `|-->` function accepts any combination of α and τ. But if α appears free in τ (for example, if $\tau = \alpha$ `list`), then the resulting substitution θ is not *idempotent*. If θ is not idempotent, then $\theta \circ \theta \neq \theta$, and moreover, $\theta\alpha \neq \theta\tau$. But type inference is all about using substitutions to guarantee equality of types, and we must be sure that every substitution we create is idempotent, so if $\theta = (\alpha \mapsto \tau)$, then $\theta\alpha = \theta\tau$. If this equality does not hold, there is a bug in type inference (Exercise 2).

A final useful substitution is the identity substitution, which is represented by an empty environment.

411d. ⟨*shared utility functions on Hindley-Milner types* 410a⟩+≡ (S420a) ◁ 411c 412a ▷

idsubst : subst

```
val idsubst = emptyEnv
```

In math, the identity substitution is written θ_I, and it is a left and right identity of composition: $\theta_I \circ \theta = \theta \circ \theta_I = \theta$.

bind	305d
BindListLength	305e
BugInType-Inference	S213d
CONAPP	408
emptyEnv	305a
type env	304
find	305b
FORALL	408
mkEnv	305e
type name	303
NotFound	305b
type ty	408
TYCON	408
type type_scheme	408
TYVAR	408
union	S217b

My representation of substitutions is simple but not efficient. Efficient implementations of type inference represent each type variable as a mutable cell, and they apply and compose substitutions by mutating those cells.

7.4.4 *Functions that compare, create, and print types*

Because a Hindley-Milner type contains no quantifiers, type equivalence is easier to define than in Typed μScheme (chunk 370a).

412a. ⟨*shared utility functions on Hindley-Milner types* 410a⟩+≡ (S420a) ◁411d 433b▷

```
fun eqType (TYVAR a, TYVAR a') = a = a'                eqType : ty * ty -> bool
  | eqType (TYCON c, TYCON c') = eqTycon (c, c')
  | eqType (CONAPP (tau, taus), CONAPP (tau', taus')) =
      eqType (tau, tau') andalso eqTypes (taus, taus')
  | eqType _ = false
and eqTypes (taus, taus') = ListPair.allEq eqType (taus, taus')
```

The types of primitive operations are written using convenience functions very much like those from Chapter 6.

412b. ⟨*creation and comparison of Hindley-Milner types with named type constructors* 412b⟩≡

```
val inttype  = TYCON "int"
val booltype = TYCON "bool"
val symtype  = TYCON "sym"
val alpha    = TYVAR "a"
val beta     = TYVAR "b"
val unittype = TYCON "unit"
fun listtype ty =
  CONAPP (TYCON "list", [ty])
fun pairtype (x, y) =
  CONAPP (TYCON "pair", [x, y])
fun funtype (args, result) =
  CONAPP (TYCON "function", [CONAPP (TYCON "arguments", args), result])
fun asFuntype (CONAPP (TYCON "function",
                      [CONAPP (TYCON "arguments", args), result])) =
      SOME (args, result)
  | asFuntype _ = NONE
```

```
inttype   : ty
booltype  : ty
symtype   : ty
alpha     : ty
beta      : ty
unittype  : ty
listtype  : ty -> ty
pairtype  : ty * ty -> ty
funtype   : ty list * ty -> ty
asFuntype : ty -> (ty list * ty) option
```

To make it possible to print types and substitutions, Appendix R defines functions `typeString`, `typeSchemeString`, and `substString`.

7.4.5 *Typing rules for nano-ML*

In Typed μScheme, you may define and use quantified types anywhere, but you must write `type-lambda` and `@` everywhere. As shown in Chapter 6, writing these type abstractions and type applications explicitly is tiresome. And in ML, type abstraction and type application are done for you; the only downside is that ML can express fewer types than Typed μScheme. In ML, the $\forall$ quantifier appears only in a type scheme, never in a type, and a function cannot expect an argument of a quantified type.

To fill in the missing type abstractions and instantiations, nano-ML's type system does more work than a type checker for Typed μScheme:

- When a value is polymorphic, the code doesn't say how to instantiate it; the type system has to figure out a type at which the value should be instantiated.
- When a function is defined, the code doesn't state the types of its arguments; the type system has to figure out a type for each argument.

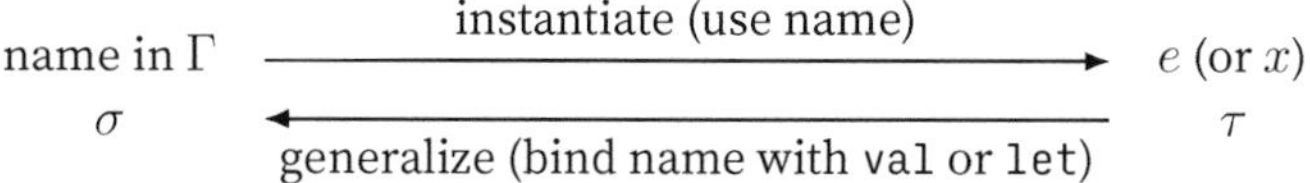

Figure 7.2: Relationship between type schemes and types

The types can be figured out because in the Hindley-Milner type system, $\forall$ cannot appear just anywhere. In particular, it cannot appear in the type of an expression: *every well-typed expression has a monotype,* although the monotype may have free type variables. *Only a name bound in the environment may have a polytype.* When a name from Γ is used as an expression, its type scheme is *instantiated* to give it a monotype. This instantiation amounts to an implicit `@` operation. When a name is bound by `val` or `let`, the type of its right-hand side is *generalized* to make a type scheme, which is then put into the environment. This generalization amounts to an implicit `type-lambda` operation. Instantiation and generalization are depicted in Figure 7.2. (There's also a sidebar on page 435.)

When a type is instantiated, what types should be substituted for the type variables? When a function's type is determined, what types should the arguments have? Luckily, these questions don't have to be answered right away. Nano-ML's type system can be described by *nondeterministic* rules that show a type τ without saying how τ is computed. Those rules take up the rest of this section. In Sections 7.5.1 and 7.5.2, the nondeterministic rules are refined into new rules that specify a deterministic type-inference algorithm.

Nondeterministic typing rules for expressions

The typing judgment for an expression has the form $\Gamma \vdash e : \tau$, meaning that given type environment Γ, expression e has type τ. An expression may have more than one type; for example, the empty list has many types, and the judgments $\Gamma \vdash \text{LITERAL}(\text{NIL}) : \texttt{int list}$ and $\Gamma \vdash \text{LITERAL}(\text{NIL}) : \texttt{bool list}$ are both valid.

A use of a variable is well typed if the variable is bound in the environment. The variable's type is not fully determined; it may have any type that is an instance of its type scheme.

$$\frac{\Gamma(x) = \sigma \qquad \tau \leqslant \sigma}{\Gamma \vdash x : \tau} \tag{\textsc{Var}}$$

Unlike our rules for operational semantics, this rule does *not* specify a deterministic algorithm. Any τ that is an instance of σ is acceptable, and the rule does not say how to find the "right" one. A τ is determined by the algorithm in Section 7.5.2, which finds a *most general* τ (Exercise 5).

A conditional expression is well typed if the condition is Boolean and the two branches have the same type τ. The conditional expression also has type τ.

$$\frac{\Gamma \vdash e_1 : \texttt{bool} \qquad \Gamma \vdash e_2 : \tau \qquad \Gamma \vdash e_3 : \tau}{\Gamma \vdash \text{IF}(e_1, e_2, e_3) : \tau} \tag{\textsc{If}}$$

A sequence is well typed if its subexpressions are well typed.

$$\frac{\Gamma \vdash e_i : \tau_i, \quad 1 \leq i \leq n}{\Gamma \vdash \text{BEGIN}(e_1, \ldots, e_n) : \tau_n} \tag{\textsc{Begin}}$$

An empty BEGIN is always well typed with type `unit`.

$$\frac{}{\Gamma \vdash \text{BEGIN}() : \texttt{unit}} \tag{\textsc{EmptyBegin}}$$

An application is well typed if the function has arrow type, and if the types and number of actual parameters match the types and number of formal parameters on the left of the arrow.

$$\frac{\Gamma \vdash e_i : \tau_i, \quad 1 \le i \le n \qquad \Gamma \vdash e : \tau_1 \times \cdots \times \tau_n \to \tau}{\Gamma \vdash \text{APPLY}(e, e_1, \ldots, e_n) : \tau} \quad \text{(APPLY)}$$

A function is well typed if, in an environment that binds each formal parameter to its type, the function's body is well typed. The type of the function is formed from the types of its formal parameters and its body.

$$\frac{\Gamma\{x_1 \mapsto \tau_1, \ldots, x_n \mapsto \tau_n\} \vdash e : \tau}{\Gamma \vdash \text{LAMBDA}(\langle x_1, \ldots, x_n \rangle, e) : \tau_1 \times \cdots \times \tau_n \to \tau} \quad \text{(LAMBDA)}$$

Like the VAR rule, the LAMBDA rule is nondeterministic; types $\tau_1, \ldots, \tau_n$ aren't in the syntax, and the rule doesn't say what they should be.

In the LAMBDA rule, the notation $\{x_i \mapsto \tau_i\}$ is shorthand for $\{x_i \mapsto \forall.\tau_i\}$; each τ_i is converted into a type scheme by wrapping it in an empty $\forall$. The type scheme $\forall.\tau_i$ has only one instance, which is τ_i itself. Therefore, when x_i is used in e, it always has the same type. This rule restricts the set of functions that can be given types: an ML programmer cannot define a function that *requires* its arguments to be polymorphic. No matter how polymorphic an *actual* parameter may be, inside the function the *formal* parameter has just one type. The restriction helps make type inference decidable.

The restriction can be illustrated by comparing two bindings. If `empty-list` is defined as a global variable and is bound to the empty list, then it has a polymorphic type scheme, and both an integer and a boolean can be consed onto it. But if `empty-list` is defined as a formal parameter, then no matter what actual parameter it is eventually bound to, it cannot be polymorphic:

414. ⟨*transcript* 402⟩+≡ ◁409b 415▷

```
-> (val empty-list '())
() : (forall ['a] (list 'a))
-> (val p (pair (cons 1 empty-list) (cons #t empty-list)))
(PAIR (1) (#t)) : (pair (list int) (list bool))
-> (val too-polymorphic
     (lambda (empty-list) (pair (cons 1 empty-list) (cons #t empty-list))))
type error: cannot make int equal to bool
```

Because the `val` definition form corresponds to a `let`, the difference shown here is usually called the difference between a lambda-bound variable and a let-bound variable. The difference can be formalized in a typing rule.

The simplest possible rule describes MLET, a restricted form of LET that binds a single variable. When x is bound in Γ, x is given a type scheme that may quantify over a nonempty set of type variables and so may be polymorphic:

$$\frac{\begin{array}{c}\Gamma \vdash e' : \tau' \qquad \text{ftv}(\tau') - \text{ftv}(\Gamma) = \{\alpha_1, \ldots, \alpha_n\} \\ \Gamma\{x \mapsto \forall \alpha_1, \ldots, \alpha_n \,.\, \tau'\} \vdash e : \tau\end{array}}{\Gamma \vdash \text{MLET}(x, e', e) : \tau} . \quad \text{(MILNER'S LET)}$$

The set $\{\alpha_1, \ldots, \alpha_n\}$ is the difference of two sets computed with ftv, a function that finds free type variables. Operationally, a type checker first finds τ', the type of e', but it doesn't simply extend Γ with $\{x \mapsto \tau'\}$. Instead, using $\forall$, it *closes* over the free type variables of τ' that are not also free type variables of types in Γ. Milner discovered that if a type variable isn't mentioned in the environment, it can be instantiated any way you want, and it can even be instantiated it *differently* at different uses of x. Closing over such type variables might give x a polymorphic type scheme. For example, in the following variation on too-poly, the let-bound variable empty-list gets a polymorphic type scheme, and when the polymorphic empty-list is used, it is instantiated once with int and once with bool.

415. ⟨*transcript* 402⟩+≡ ◁414 417a▷

```
-> (val not-too-polymorphic
      (let ([empty-list '()])
         (pair (cons 1 empty-list) (cons #t empty-list))))
(PAIR (1) (#t)) : (pair (list int) (list bool))
```


If let-bound variables might be polymorphic, why not λ-bound variables? λ-bound variables can't be made polymorphic because the type checker doesn't know what type of value a λ-bound variable might stand for—it could be any actual parameter. By contrast, the type checker knows exactly what type of value a let-bound variable stands for, because it is right there in the program: it is the type of e'. If e' could be polymorphic (because it has type variables that don't appear in the environment), that polymorphism can be made explicit in the type scheme associated with x.

The polymorphic MLET is sometimes called "Milner's let." Milner's let is type-checked with the help of a new operation on types: *generalization*. Generalization is defined by function generalize, which takes as argument a type τ and a set of constrained type variables $\mathcal{A}$:

$$\texttt{generalize}(\tau, \mathcal{A}) = \forall \alpha_1, \ldots, \alpha_n \,.\, \tau, \text{ where } \{\alpha_1, \ldots, \alpha_n\} = \text{ftv}(\tau) - \mathcal{A}.$$

Often $\mathcal{A}$ is the set of type variables that appear free in a type environment, e.g., $\mathcal{A} = \text{ftv}(\Gamma)$. As suggested in Figure 7.2 on page 413, generalization is like an inverse of instantiation: for any τ and Γ, it's true that $\tau \leqslant \texttt{generalize}(\tau, \text{ftv}(\Gamma))$. Function generalize is implemented in code chunk 434b.

Using generalize, the rule for Milner's let is written as follows:

$$\frac{\Gamma \vdash e' : \tau' \qquad \sigma = \texttt{generalize}(\tau', \text{ftv}(\Gamma)) \qquad \Gamma\{x \mapsto \sigma\} \vdash e : \tau}{\Gamma \vdash \text{MLET}(x, e', e) : \tau}. \qquad \text{(MILNER'S LET)}$$

The corresponding rule for nano-ML's LET, which simultaneously binds multiple names, has a premise that generalizes the type of each e_i, and its environment binds each x_i to its corresponding type scheme σ_i.

$$\frac{\begin{array}{c}\Gamma \vdash e_i : \tau_i, \quad 1 \le i \le n \\ \sigma_i = \texttt{generalize}(\tau_i, \text{ftv}(\Gamma)), \quad 1 \le i \le n \\ \Gamma\{x_1 \mapsto \sigma_1, \ldots, x_n \mapsto \sigma_n\} \vdash e : \tau\end{array}}{\Gamma \vdash \text{LET}(\langle x_1, e_1, \ldots, x_n, e_n \rangle, e) : \tau} \qquad \text{(LET)}$$

The typing rule for LETREC is similar, except that the e_i's are checked in type environment Γ', which itself contains the bindings for the x_i's. Environment Γ' is defined using the set $\{\tau_1, \ldots, \tau_n\}$, and each type τ_i is in turn computed using Γ'. So Γ' is defined in terms of itself, using types $\tau_1, \ldots, \tau_n$ as intermediaries:

$$\frac{\begin{array}{c}\Gamma' = \Gamma\{x_1 \mapsto \tau_1, \ldots, x_n \mapsto \tau_n\} \\ \Gamma' \vdash e_i : \tau_i, \quad 1 \le i \le n \\ \sigma_i = \texttt{generalize}(\tau_i, \text{ftv}(\Gamma)), \quad 1 \le i \le n \\ \Gamma\{x_1 \mapsto \sigma_1, \ldots, x_n \mapsto \sigma_n\} \vdash e : \tau\end{array}}{\Gamma \vdash \text{LETREC}(\langle x_1, e_1, \ldots, x_n, e_n \rangle, e) : \tau}. \qquad \text{(LETREC)}$$

cons 𝒫 440a
pair 𝒫

Within Γ', the variables x_i are *not* given polymorphic type schemes. Only once all the types of the e_i's are fixed can the types of the x_i's be generalized and used to compute the type of e. A LETREC defines a nest of mutually recursive functions, and because `generalize` is not applied until the types of all the functions are computed, these functions are not polymorphic when used in each other's definitions—they are polymorphic only when used in e. This rule can surprise even experienced ML programmers; in the presence of `letrec`, functions that look polymorphic may be less polymorphic than you expected.

A rule for LETSTAR would be annoying to write down directly: there is too much bookkeeping. Instead, LETSTAR is treated as syntactic sugar for a nest of LETs.

$$\frac{\Gamma \vdash \text{LET}(\langle x_1, e_1\rangle, \text{LETSTAR}(\langle x_2, e_2, \ldots, x_n, e_n\rangle, e)) : \tau \qquad n > 0}{\Gamma \vdash \text{LETSTAR}(\langle x_1, e_1, \ldots, x_n, e_n\rangle, e) : \tau} \quad \text{(LETSTAR)}$$

$$\frac{\Gamma \vdash e : \tau}{\Gamma \vdash \text{LETSTAR}(\langle\rangle, e) : \tau} \quad \text{(EMPTYLETSTAR)}$$

Typing rules for definitions

In the operational semantics, a definition produces a new value environment. In the type system, a definition produces a new type environment. The new environment is given by a judgment of the form $\langle d, \Gamma\rangle \rightarrow \Gamma'$, which says that when definition d is typed in environment Γ, the new environment is Γ'.

A VAL binding is just like Milner's let binding, and it has almost the same rule.

$$\frac{\Gamma \vdash e : \tau \qquad \sigma = \texttt{generalize}(\tau, \text{ftv}(\Gamma))}{\langle \text{VAL}(x, e), \Gamma\rangle \rightarrow \Gamma\{x \mapsto \sigma\}} \quad \text{(VAL)}$$

VAL-REC requires that a recursive value be defined in the environment used to find its type.

$$\frac{\Gamma\{x \mapsto \tau\} \vdash e : \tau \qquad \sigma = \texttt{generalize}(\tau, \text{ftv}(\Gamma))}{\langle \text{VAL-REC}(x, e), \Gamma\rangle \rightarrow \Gamma\{x \mapsto \sigma\}} \quad \text{(VALREC)}$$

A top-level expression is syntactic sugar for a binding to `it`.

$$\frac{\langle \text{VAL}(\texttt{it}, e), \Gamma\rangle \rightarrow \Gamma'}{\langle \text{EXP}(e), \Gamma\rangle \rightarrow \Gamma'} \quad \text{(EXP)}$$

A DEFINE is syntactic sugar for a combination of VAL-REC and LAMBDA.

$$\frac{\langle \text{VAL-REC}(f, \text{LAMBDA}(\langle x_1, \ldots, x_n\rangle, e)), \Gamma\rangle \rightarrow \Gamma'}{\langle \text{DEFINE}(f, (\langle x_1, \ldots, x_n\rangle, e)), \Gamma\rangle \rightarrow \Gamma'} \quad \text{(DEFINE)}$$

7.4.6 *Nondeterministic typing, principal types, and type testing*

Nondeterministic typing rules can't easily be used directly; the judgment $\Gamma \vdash e : \tau$ can often be proved for infinitely many types τ. Fortunately, in the Hindley-Milner type system, if there is any such τ, then there is a *principal* type τ_P, to which every other τ is related. A principal type of e is at least as general as every other type of e. That is, if τ_P is a principal type of e, and if $\Gamma \vdash e : \tau$, then $\tau \leqslant \tau_P$. Therefore every type of e can be obtained by substituting for free type variables of τ_P.

The idea of principality can be extended to type schemes. To do so, we relate two type schemes in the same way that we relate types in Typed μScheme: σ_g is at least as general as σ_i, written $\sigma_i \leqslant \sigma_g$, if σ_i can be obtained from σ_g by substitution and by *reordering* of type variables. (Because nano-ML has no explicit instantiation, the order of type variables doesn't matter, and two type schemes that differ up to permutations of type variables are equivalent.) Equivalently, $\sigma_i \leqslant \sigma_g$ if and only if σ_g has all of σ_i's instances. That is, whenever $\tau \leqslant \sigma_i$, it is also true that $\tau \leqslant \sigma_g$.

Given that relation, type scheme σ_P is a principal type scheme of e in environment Γ if there is a derivation of $\langle \text{VAL}(x, e), \Gamma \rangle \to \Gamma\{x \mapsto \sigma_P\}$, and furthermore, whenever there is a σ such that $\langle \text{VAL}(x, e), \Gamma \rangle \to \Gamma\{x \mapsto \sigma\}$, then $\sigma \leqslant \sigma_P$.

In nano-ML, generality and principality can be unit-tested. Using `check-type`, an expression's type is compared with a given type scheme. If the expression's type is at least as general as the given type scheme, the test passes. For example, the following tests both pass:

417a. ⟨*transcript* 402⟩+≡ ◁415 423▷

```
-> (define arg1 (x y) x)
-> (check-type arg1 (forall ['a 'b] ('a 'b -> 'a)))  ; the principal type
-> (check-type arg1 (forall ['a]    ('a 'a -> 'a)))  ; a less general type
```

Essentially, `(check-type` e σ`)` checks if a variable defined equal to e can be bound into the type environment with type scheme σ—that is, if there can be a derivation of $\langle \text{VAL}(x, e), \Gamma \rangle \to \Gamma\{x \mapsto \sigma\}$.

To test *exactly* what type a function has, use a `check-principal-type` test.

417b. ⟨*principal-types.nml* 417b⟩≡ 417c▷

```
(define arg1 (x y) x)
(check-principal-type arg1 (forall ['a 'b] ('a 'b -> 'a)))  ; pass
(check-principal-type arg1 (forall ['a]    ('a 'a -> 'a)))  ; FAIL
```

As another example, `length` has many types and many type schemes, but only one principal type scheme:

417c. ⟨*principal-types.nml* 417b⟩+≡ ◁417b

```
(check-type           length ((list int) -> int)) ; pass
(check-principal-type length ((list int) -> int)) ; FAIL
(check-type           length (forall ['a] ((list (list 'a)) -> int))) ; pass
(check-principal-type length (forall ['a] ((list (list 'a)) -> int))) ; FAIL
(check-type           length (forall ['a] ((list 'a) -> int))) ; pass
(check-principal-type length (forall ['a] ((list 'a) -> int))) ; pass
```

The implementations of `check-type` and `check-principal-type`, which are found in Appendix R on page S427, use the $\leqslant$ relation on type schemes.

7.5 From typing rules to type inference

The nondeterministic typing rules don't specify an algorithm that can decide if a nano-ML term has a type, let alone find a principal type. That is, given Γ and e, the rules don't say how to find a τ such that $\Gamma \vdash e : \tau$. The LAMBDA rule doesn't specify the types of the formal parameters, and the VAR rule doesn't specify *which* instance of σ to use as τ. But these rules *can* be used in an algorithm if the algorithm uses a trick: whenever a type is unknown, the algorithm identifies that type with fresh type variable. For example, when a LAMBDA takes an argument x_i, x_i's type is recorded as α_i, where α_i is a new type variable that is not used anywhere else in the program. The α_i stands for an unknown type, and the way x_i is used might tell us something about it. For example, if x_i were added to 1, that would tell us that α_i has to be equal to `int`. Eventually `int` would be *substituted* for α_i.

How does an algorithm discover what type to substitute for each fresh type variable? There are two good methods:

- The first method is the method of *explicit substitutions*. When the type checker wants two types to be equal, it calls ML function `unify`(τ_1, τ_2). A *unification* algorithm returns a θ such that $\theta(\tau_1) = \theta(\tau_2)$; substitution θ is called a *unifier* of τ_1 and τ_2. These substitutions are composed to implement *type inference*: given Γ and e, the algorithm can find θ and τ such that $\boxed{\theta\Gamma \vdash e : \tau}$.

The method of explicit substitutions is described by simple mathematics and is easy to prove correct, but it generates an awful lot of substitutions, which have to be composed in exactly the right order. And it is easy to forget to apply a substitution; in short, the implementation is hard to get right.

- The second method is the method of *type-equality constraints*. When the type checker wants two types τ_1 and τ_2 to be equal, it *doesn't* unify them right away. Instead, it remembers the *constraint* $\tau_1 \sim \tau_2$, which says that τ_1 must equal τ_2. If the type checker needs two or more such constraints, it conjoins them into a single constraint using logical *and*, as in $C_1 \wedge C_2$. The constraints are used in a judgment of the form $\boxed{C, \Gamma \vdash e : \tau}$.

  The method of explicit constraints is described by more elaborate mathematics and is not as easy to prove correct, but the composition operation $\wedge$ is associative and commutative, so unlike substitutions, constraints can be composed in any order—there's no wrong way to do it. Using constraints, most of type inference is not so hard to get right.

  In the method of explicit constraints, unification happens lazily: when it sees a LET binding or a VAL binding, the type checker calls on a *constraint solver* to produce a substitution that makes the constraints true. The constraint solver does the same job as `unify`, and solving constraints is only a little bit more complicated than unifying types. And with a constraint solver, implementing type inference itself is infinitely easier. For this reason, the method of explicit constraints is the one that I recommend.

Both methods of type inference are justified by the same principle: if in a valid derivation, we substitute for free type variables, the new derivation is also valid. That is, if $\dfrac{\mathcal{D}}{\Gamma \vdash e : \tau}$ is a valid derivation, then for all substitutions θ, $\dfrac{\theta\mathcal{D}}{\theta\Gamma \vdash \theta e : \theta\tau}$ is a valid derivation.

Which method should you study? It depends what you want to do.

- If you want to read original, primary sources, study explicit substitutions, because that's what Milner (1978) describes.
- If you want to prove that type inference is consistent with the nondeterministic type system in Section 7.4.5 (Exercise 11), study explicit substitutions—the proof is much easier.
- If you want to build something (Exercises 18 and 19), study type-equality constraints—the code is much easier.

7.5.1 *The method of explicit substitutions*

Milner's original type-inference algorithm uses explicit substitutions. To understand explicit substitutions in detail, we can start by developing a syntactic proof system for judgments of the form $\theta\Gamma \vdash e : \tau$. Such a proof system would contain this rule for IF:

$$\frac{\begin{array}{c}\theta_1\Gamma \vdash e_1 : \tau_1 \qquad \theta_2(\theta_1\Gamma) \vdash e_2 : \tau_2 \qquad \theta_3(\theta_2(\theta_1\Gamma)) \vdash e_3 : \tau_3 \\ \theta(\theta_3\tau_2) = \theta(\tau_3) = \tau \\ \theta'(\theta(\theta_3(\theta_2(\tau_1)))) = \theta'(\texttt{bool})\end{array}}{(\theta' \circ \theta \circ \theta_3 \circ \theta_2 \circ \theta_1)\,\Gamma \vdash \textsc{if}(e_1, e_2, e_3) : \theta'\tau}. \qquad \text{(IF)}$$

The rule can be interpreted operationally as part of an algorithm that takes Γ and e as inputs and produces τ and θ as outputs.

1. Infer type τ_1 for e_1, producing substitution θ_1.
2. Apply θ_1 to the environment Γ, and continue in similar fashion, inferring types and substitutions from e_2 and e_3.
3. Unify types $\theta_3\tau_2$ and τ_3, producing a new substitution θ. The resulting type τ becomes (after one more substitution) the type of the entire IF expression.
4. Unify the type of e_1 with `bool`, producing substitution θ'. Be careful to apply proper substitutions.
5. Return the composition of the substitutions, together with $\theta'\tau$.

This new rule is *sound*, which means that whenever there is a derivation using the new IF rule, there is a corresponding derivation using the original IF rule. A real proof of soundness is beyond the scope of this book (Exercise 11), but to help you understand how the system works, here is a hand-waving argument: To prove soundness, we rewrite derivations systematically so that if we are given a derivation in the new system, we can rewrite it into a derivation in the old system. In the case of the IF rule, we rewrite $(\theta' \circ \theta \circ \theta_3 \circ \theta_2 \circ \theta_1)\,\Gamma$ as $\tilde{\Gamma}$, $(\theta' \circ \theta \circ \theta_3 \circ \theta_2)\,\tau_1$ as $\tilde{\tau}_1$, and so on. For example, if $\theta_1\Gamma \vdash e_1 : \tau_1$, we apply substitution $(\theta' \circ \theta \circ \theta_3 \circ \theta_2)$ to both sides, rewrite, and the premise becomes equivalent to $\tilde{\Gamma} \vdash e_1 : \tilde{\tau}_1$. A similar rewriting of all the premises enables us to apply the original IF rule to draw the conclusion.

Although the new IF rule is sound, and it has a clear operational interpretation, it requires a *lot* of explicit substitutions; it's a bookkeeping nightmare. But the bookkeeping can be reduced by a trick: extend the typing judgment to *lists* of expressions and types. Write $\theta\Gamma \vdash e_1, \ldots, e_n : \tau_1, \ldots, \tau_n$ as an abbreviation for a set of n separate judgments: $\theta\Gamma \vdash e_1 : \tau_1,\ \ldots\ , \theta\Gamma \vdash e_n : \tau_n$. When $n = 1$, this judgment degenerates to $\theta\Gamma \vdash e_1 : \tau_1$. For $n > 1$, finding the common substitution θ requires combining substitutions from different judgments.

$$\frac{\theta\Gamma \vdash e_1 : \tau_1 \qquad \theta'(\theta\Gamma) \vdash e_2, \ldots, e_n : \tau_2, \ldots, \tau_n}{(\theta' \circ \theta)\,\Gamma \vdash e_1, \ldots, e_n : \theta'\tau_1, \tau_2, \ldots, \tau_n} \qquad (\text{TYPESOF})$$

This new judgment can be used to reduce the number of substitutions in any rule that has multiple subexpressions, like IF. For example, the application rule can be written like this:

$$\frac{\begin{array}{c}\theta\Gamma \vdash e, e_1, \ldots, e_n : \hat{\tau}, \tau_1, \ldots, \tau_n \\ \theta'(\hat{\tau}) = \theta'(\tau_1 \times \cdots \times \tau_n \to \alpha),\ \text{where } \alpha \text{ is fresh}\end{array}}{(\theta' \circ \theta)\,\Gamma \vdash \text{APPLY}(e, e_1, \ldots, e_n) : \theta'\alpha}. \qquad (\text{APPLY})$$

The most difficult rule to express using explicit substitutions is probably LETREC. The nondeterministic rule is

$$\frac{\begin{array}{c}\Gamma' = \Gamma\{x_1 \mapsto \tau_1, \ldots, x_n \mapsto \tau_n\} \\ \Gamma' \vdash e_i : \tau_i, \quad 1 \le i \le n \\ \sigma_i = \mathtt{generalize}(\tau_i, \mathrm{ftv}(\Gamma)), \quad 1 \le i \le n \\ \Gamma\{x_1 \mapsto \sigma_1, \ldots, x_n \mapsto \sigma_n\} \vdash e : \tau\end{array}}{\Gamma \vdash \text{LETREC}(\langle x_1, e_1, \ldots, x_n, e_n\rangle, e) : \tau}. \qquad (\text{LETREC})$$

The rule with explicit substitutions is

$$\frac{\begin{array}{c}\Gamma' = \Gamma\{x_1 \mapsto \alpha_1, \dots, x_n \mapsto \alpha_n\}, \text{ where all } \alpha_i\text{'s are fresh} \\ \theta\Gamma' \vdash e_1, \dots, e_n : \tau_1, \dots, \tau_n \\ \theta'\tau_i = \theta'(\theta\alpha_i), \quad 1 \le i \le n \\ \sigma_i = \texttt{generalize}(\theta'\tau_i, \text{ftv}((\theta' \circ \theta)\,\Gamma)), \quad 1 \le i \le n \\ \theta''(((\theta' \circ \theta)\,\Gamma)\{x_1 \mapsto \sigma_1, \dots, x_n \mapsto \sigma_n\}) \vdash e : \tau\end{array}}{(\theta'' \circ \theta' \circ \theta)\,\Gamma \vdash \text{LETREC}(\langle x_1, e_1, \dots, x_n, e_n\rangle, e) : \tau}. \qquad \text{(LETREC)}$$

The soundness proof must show that the substitution θ'' does not change any type variable that is *bound* in any σ_i.

Using explicit substitutions, rules like LETREC are hard to implement: not only must you compose three or more substitutions, but you must compose them in the right order, and you must apply certain substitutions or even compositions (like $\theta' \circ \theta$) to one or more arguments of other calls. In my experience, people who tackle this implementation task almost always forget a substitution somewhere, leading to an implementation of type inference that almost works, but not quite. There is a better way.

7.5.2 *The method of explicit constraints*

To find that better way, we return to the nondeterministic type system of Section 7.4.5. In a rule like

$$\frac{\Gamma \vdash e_1 : \texttt{bool} \qquad \Gamma \vdash e_2 : \tau \qquad \Gamma \vdash e_3 : \tau}{\Gamma \vdash \text{IF}(e_1, e_2, e_3) : \tau}, \qquad \text{(IF)}$$

expression e_1 angelically has the right type `bool`, and e_2 and e_3 angelically have the same type τ. Instead of requiring angels, the method of explicit constraints allows each e_i to have whatever type it wants, which I'll call τ_i. Then the type checker insists that τ_1 must equal `bool` and τ_2 must equal τ_3. Its insistence is recorded in an explicit constraint C, which is added to the typing judgment as part of the typing context. For the IF rule, the constraint C is $\tau_1 \sim \texttt{bool} \wedge \tau_2 \sim \tau_3$. Operators $\sim$ and $\wedge$ are explained below.

Using explicit constraints, a typing judgment has the form $C, \Gamma \vdash e : \tau$, which means "assuming the constraint C is satisfied, in environment Γ term e has type τ." Constraints are formed by conjoining *simple equality constraints*:

- A simple equality constraint has the form $\tau_1 \sim \tau_2$ (pronounced "τ_1 must equal τ_2"), and it is satisfied if and only if the types τ_1 and τ_2 are equal.

- A conjunction has the form $C_1 \wedge C_2$ (pronounced "C_1 and C_2"), and it is satisfied if and only if both C_1 and C_2 are satisfied. Just as in ordinary logic, conjunction of constraints is associative and commutative.

Not every judgment requires a constraint, so to keep the math and the code uniform, such a judgment uses a third form of constraint:

- The *trivial constraint* has the form $\mathbf{T}$, and it is always considered satisfied. The trivial constraint is a left and right identity of $\wedge$. The constraint may be pronounced "trivial" or "true."

Formally, constraints are described by this grammar:

$$C ::= \tau_1 \sim \tau_2 \bigm| C_1 \wedge C_2 \bigm| \mathbf{T}.$$

If the type system derives $C, \Gamma \vdash e : \tau$, the constraint captures conditions that are sufficient to ensure that term e has type τ. And if constraint C is satisfied, then erasing constraints produces a derivation of $\Gamma \vdash e : \tau$ that is valid in the original, nondeterministic type system. Operationally, constraint C, like type τ, is an output from the type checker; the inputs are term e and environment Γ.

Using constraints, we can write a deterministic IF rule. The rule not only produces new constraints $\tau_1 \sim \texttt{bool}$ and $\tau_2 \sim \tau_3$; it also remembers old constraints used to give types to the subexpressions e_1, e_2, and e_3. "Old" constraints propagate from the premises of a rule to the conclusion.

$$\frac{C_1, \Gamma \vdash e_1 : \tau_1 \qquad C_2, \Gamma \vdash e_2 : \tau_2 \qquad C_3, \Gamma \vdash e_3 : \tau_3}{C_1 \wedge C_2 \wedge C_3 \wedge \tau_1 \sim \texttt{bool} \wedge \tau_2 \sim \tau_3, \Gamma \vdash \text{IF}(e_1, e_2, e_3) : \tau_2} \qquad (\text{IF})$$

The conclusion of this rule conjoins three old constraints with two new simple equality constraints. For the IF expression to have a type, all the constraints needed to give types to e_1, e_2, and e_3 must be satisfied. And so must constraints $\tau_1 \sim \texttt{bool}$ and $\tau_2 \sim \tau_3$. If all the constraints are satisfied, which implies that $\tau_1 = \texttt{bool}$ and $\tau_2 = \tau_3$, then the rule is equivalent to the original IF rule.

Constraints require much less bookkeeping than do the substitutions in Section 7.5.1, but a typing judgment that describes lists of expressions and types is still worth defining. Judgment $C, \Gamma \vdash e_1, \ldots, e_n : \tau_1, \ldots, \tau_n$ expresses the effects of n separate judgments, where C is the conjunction of the constraints of the individual judgments:

$$\frac{C_1, \Gamma \vdash e_1 : \tau_1 \quad \cdots \quad C_n, \Gamma \vdash e_n : \tau_n}{C_1 \wedge \cdots \wedge C_n, \Gamma \vdash e_1, \ldots, e_n : \tau_1, \ldots, \tau_n}. \qquad (\text{TYPESOF})$$

This judgment can help simplify some rules, like the IF rule:

$$\frac{C, \Gamma \vdash e_1, e_2, e_3 : \tau_1, \tau_2, \tau_3}{C \wedge \tau_1 \sim \texttt{bool} \wedge \tau_2 \sim \tau_3, \Gamma \vdash \text{IF}(e_1, e_2, e_3) : \tau_2}. \qquad (\text{IF})$$

The same judgment is used in the application rule, but the application rule also does something new. In an application, the function must have an arrow type, so if an expression e of type $\hat{\tau}$ appears in the function position, $\hat{\tau}$ must be an arrow type. But what arrow type? The argument types are the types $\tau_1, \ldots, \tau_n$ of e's actual parameters, but what is the result type? Because $\hat{\tau}$ might itself be a type variable, we can't always know. So to stand in for the result type, the type checker uses a fresh type variable α, whose ultimate identity will be determined by a new constraint. The new constraint says that type $\hat{\tau}$ must be equal to $\tau_1 \times \cdots \times \tau_n \to \alpha$:

$$\frac{C, \Gamma \vdash e, e_1, \ldots, e_n : \hat{\tau}, \tau_1, \ldots, \tau_n \qquad \alpha \text{ is fresh}}{C \wedge \hat{\tau} \sim \tau_1 \times \cdots \times \tau_n \to \alpha, \Gamma \vdash \text{APPLY}(e, e_1, \ldots, e_n) : \alpha}. \qquad (\text{APPLY})$$

Again, if the constraints are satisfied, the rule is equivalent to the original.

These rules are enough to build an example derivation. The example uses a type environment Γ that contains these bindings:

$$\Gamma = \{+ : \forall.\texttt{int} \times \texttt{int} \to \texttt{int}, \texttt{cons} : \forall\alpha.\alpha \times \alpha\,\texttt{list} \to \alpha\,\texttt{list}\}.$$

This Γ has no free type variables. Derivation of a type for `(+ 1 2)` looks roughly like this, where α_{10} is a fresh type variable:

$$\frac{\dfrac{\cdots}{\mathbf{T}, \Gamma \vdash \texttt{+} : \texttt{int} \times \texttt{int} \to \texttt{int}} \qquad \dfrac{}{\mathbf{T}, \Gamma \vdash \texttt{1} : \texttt{int}} \qquad \dfrac{}{\mathbf{T}, \Gamma \vdash \texttt{2} : \texttt{int}}}{\mathbf{T} \wedge \mathbf{T} \wedge \mathbf{T} \wedge \texttt{int} \times \texttt{int} \to \texttt{int} \sim \texttt{int} \times \texttt{int} \to \alpha_{10}, \Gamma \vdash \texttt{(+ 1 2)} : \alpha_{10}}.$$

Substituting int for α_{10} yields

$$\frac{\overline{\mathbf{T}, \Gamma \vdash \texttt{+} : \texttt{int} \times \texttt{int} \to \texttt{int} \sim \texttt{int}} \qquad \overline{\mathbf{T}, \Gamma \vdash \texttt{1} : \texttt{int}} \qquad \overline{\mathbf{T}, \Gamma \vdash \texttt{2} : \texttt{int}}}{\mathbf{T} \wedge \mathbf{T} \wedge \mathbf{T} \wedge \texttt{int} \times \texttt{int} \to \texttt{int} \sim \texttt{int} \times \texttt{int} \to \texttt{int}, \Gamma \vdash \texttt{(+ 1 2)} : \texttt{int}}.$$

All the constraints are satisfied, and if they are erased, what's left is a derivation in the original, nondeterministic system.

Converting nondeterministic rules to use constraints

Every nondeterministic rule can be converted to a deterministic, constraint-based rule. Most conversions use just two techniques:

- If the original rule uses the same type τ in more than one place, give each use its own name (like τ_2 and τ_3), and introduce constraints forcing the names to be equal.
- If the original rule uses τ but does not specify what τ is, represent τ by a fresh type variable.

The first technique is illustrated by the IF rule. The second technique can be illustrated by converting the nondeterministic VAR rule to use explicit constraints. The nondeterministic rule says

$$\frac{\Gamma(x) = \sigma \qquad \tau \leqslant \sigma}{\Gamma \vdash x : \tau}. \tag{VAR}$$

By definition, $\tau' \leqslant \sigma$ when $\sigma = \forall \alpha_1, \ldots, \alpha_n . \tau$ and some (unknown) types are substituted for the $\alpha_1, \ldots, \alpha_n$. For the unknown types, the rule uses fresh type variables $\alpha'_1, \ldots, \alpha'_n$.

$$\frac{\Gamma(x) = \forall \alpha_1, \ldots, \alpha_n . \tau \qquad \alpha'_1, \ldots, \alpha'_n \text{ are fresh and distinct}}{\mathbf{T}, \Gamma \vdash x : ((\alpha_1 \mapsto \alpha'_1) \circ \cdots \circ (\alpha_n \mapsto \alpha'_n))\, \tau} \tag{VAR}$$

In τ, each α_i is replaced by the corresponding fresh α'_i, and $\alpha'_1, \ldots, \alpha'_n$ are eventually constrained by the way x is used. For example, if x is cons and it occurs in the expression (cons 1 '()), the instance of cons uses a fresh type variable, which eventually should be constrained to be equal to int. The derivation looks roughly like this:

$$\frac{\dfrac{\Gamma(\texttt{cons}) = \forall \alpha . \alpha \times \alpha\,\texttt{list} \to \alpha\,\texttt{list}}{\mathbf{T}, \Gamma \vdash \texttt{cons} : \alpha_{11} \times \alpha_{11}\,\texttt{list} \to \alpha_{11}\,\texttt{list}} \qquad \overline{\mathbf{T}, \Gamma \vdash \texttt{1} : \texttt{int}} \qquad \overline{\mathbf{T}, \Gamma \vdash \texttt{'()} : \alpha_{12}\,\texttt{list}}}{\mathbf{T} \wedge \mathbf{T} \wedge \alpha_{11} \times \alpha_{11}\,\texttt{list} \to \alpha_{11}\,\texttt{list} \sim \texttt{int} \times \alpha_{12}\,\texttt{list} \to \alpha_{13}, \Gamma \vdash \texttt{(cons 1 '())} : \alpha_{13}}.$$

That big constraint is equivalent to this simpler constraint:

$$\alpha_{11} \sim \texttt{int} \wedge \alpha_{11}\,\texttt{list} \sim \alpha_{12}\,\texttt{list} \wedge \alpha_{11}\,\texttt{list} \sim \alpha_{13}.$$

Both constraints are solved by the substitution

$$(\alpha_{11} \mapsto \texttt{int}) \circ (\alpha_{12} \mapsto \texttt{int}) \circ (\alpha_{13} \mapsto \texttt{int list}),$$

and the type of (cons 1 '()) is int list.

Inferring polytypes for bound names

In the examples above, each type variable is determined to be a completely known type, like `int` or `int list`. But when a polymorphic function or other value is defined, some free type variables will remain undetermined. The function being defined will be given a polymorphic type scheme that uses ∀ with those type variables. For example, a function that makes a singleton list has a polymorphic type:

423. ⟨*transcript* 402⟩+≡ ◁417a 425▷

```
-> (val singleton (lambda (x) (cons x '())))
singleton : (forall ['a] ('a -> (list 'a)))
```

Converting from a monotype τ with free type variables to a type scheme σ with an explicit `forall` is the most challenging part of type inference; this conversion is called *generalization*.

Generalization is at its simplest in the rule for a VAL binding:

$$\frac{\begin{array}{c} C, \Gamma \vdash e : \tau \\ \theta C \text{ is satisfied} \qquad \theta\Gamma = \Gamma \\ \sigma = \texttt{generalize}(\theta\tau, \text{ftv}(\Gamma)) \end{array}}{\langle \text{VAL}(x, e), \Gamma \rangle \to \Gamma\{x \mapsto \sigma\}}. \qquad \text{(VAL)}$$

The rule is interpreted operationally as follows:

- Typecheck e in environment Γ, getting back type τ and constraint C.
- Choose a substitution θ such that θC is satisfied, making sure that θ does not affect any free type variables of Γ. (This step is called *solving* C; it is the subject of Section 7.5.3 below.)
- Generalize the type $\theta\tau$ to form the type scheme σ, which becomes the type of x in a new environment $\Gamma\{x \mapsto \sigma\}$.

Assuming there is a valid derivation of the first premise $C, \Gamma \vdash e : \tau$, the rule works because for any θ,

- $\theta C, \theta\Gamma \vdash e : \theta\tau$ is a derivable judgment.
- Because $\theta\Gamma = \Gamma$, the judgment $\theta C, \Gamma \vdash e : \theta\tau$ is also derivable.
- Because θC is satisfied, $\Gamma \vdash e : \theta\tau$ is a derivable judgment in the original, nondeterministic system.
- If the original system can derive type $\theta\tau$ for e, that type can safely be generalized.

The VAL rule illustrates the key ideas underlying constraint-based inference of polymorphic type schemes:

cons 𝒫 440a

- Type inference requires a substitution θ that solves a constraint C but does not substitute for any free type variables of the environment Γ.
- Using substitution θ on a type τ produces a type that can be generalized.

For an example, in the definition

```
(val singleton (lambda (x) (cons x '())))
```

the body of the `lambda` is checked in type environment $\Gamma' = \Gamma\{\texttt{x} \mapsto \forall.\alpha_{14}\}$, and the derivation of the type of the `lambda` looks something like this:[4]

$$\frac{\dfrac{\dfrac{\Gamma'(\texttt{cons}) = \forall\alpha.\alpha \times \alpha\ \texttt{list} \to \alpha\ \texttt{list}}{\mathbf{T}, \Gamma \vdash \texttt{cons} : \alpha_{15} \times \alpha_{15}\ \texttt{list} \to \alpha_{15}\ \texttt{list}} \qquad \dfrac{\Gamma'(\texttt{x}) = \forall.\alpha_{14}}{\mathbf{T}, \Gamma' \vdash \texttt{x} : \alpha_{14}} \qquad \dfrac{}{\mathbf{T}, \Gamma \vdash \texttt{'()} : \alpha_{16}\ \texttt{list}}}{\alpha_{15} \times \alpha_{15}\ \texttt{list} \to \alpha_{15}\ \texttt{list} \sim \alpha_{14} \times \alpha_{16}\ \texttt{list} \to \alpha_{17}, \Gamma' \vdash \texttt{(cons x '())} : \alpha_{17}}}{\alpha_{15} \times \alpha_{15}\ \texttt{list} \to \alpha_{15}\ \texttt{list} \sim \alpha_{14} \times \alpha_{16}\ \texttt{list} \to \alpha_{17}, \Gamma \vdash \texttt{(lambda (x) (cons x '()))} : \alpha_{14} \to \alpha_{17}}.$$

The constraint can be simplified to

$$\alpha_{15} \sim \alpha_{14} \wedge \alpha_{15}\ \texttt{list} \sim \alpha_{16}\ \texttt{list} \wedge \alpha_{15}\ \texttt{list} \sim \alpha_{17}$$

and then further simplified to

$$C = \alpha_{15} \sim \alpha_{14} \wedge \alpha_{15} \sim \alpha_{16} \wedge \alpha_{15}\ \texttt{list} \sim \alpha_{17}.$$

This constraint is solved by several substitutions; for example, it is solved by the substitution $\theta = (\alpha_{14} \mapsto \alpha_{15}) \circ (\alpha_{16} \mapsto \alpha_{15}) \circ (\alpha_{17} \mapsto \alpha_{15}\ \texttt{list})$. The most interesting premises of the VAL are then

$$C, \Gamma \vdash \texttt{(lambda (x) (cons x '()))} : \tau,$$

$$\tau = \alpha_{14} \to \alpha_{17}, \qquad \theta\tau = \alpha_{15} \to \alpha_{15}\ \texttt{list}, \qquad \sigma = \forall\alpha_{15}.\alpha_{15} \to \alpha_{15}\ \texttt{list}.$$

Name `singleton` is therefore added to Γ with type scheme $\forall\alpha_{15}.\alpha_{15} \to \alpha_{15}\ \texttt{list}$, which we prefer to write in canonical form as $\forall\alpha.\alpha \to \alpha\ \texttt{list}$.

A term that has no type produces an unsolvable constraint

In the method of explicit substitutions, when a term has no type, type inference fails because the type checker calls `unify` with two types that can't be unified. In the method of explicit constraints, when a term has no type, type inference fails because the type checker produces a constraint that can't be solved. One such constraint is produced by this example:

```
(lambda (x) (cons x x))
```

Let's assume that `x` is introduced to the environment with the monotype $\forall.\alpha_{18}$, that `cons` is instantiated with type $\alpha_{19} \times \alpha_{19}\ \texttt{list} \to \alpha_{19}\ \texttt{list}$, and that the return type of the `lambda` is type variable α_{20}. Then the system derives a judgment that looks roughly like this:

$$\alpha_{19} \times \alpha_{19}\ \texttt{list} \to \alpha_{19}\ \texttt{list} \sim \alpha_{18} \times \alpha_{18} \to \alpha_{20}, \Gamma \vdash \texttt{(lambda (x) (cons x x))} : \alpha_{18} \to \alpha_{20}.$$

The constraint can be simplified to

$$\alpha_{19} \sim \alpha_{18} \wedge \alpha_{19}\ \texttt{list} \sim \alpha_{18} \wedge \alpha_{19}\ \texttt{list} \sim \alpha_{20}.$$

The third simple equality $\alpha_{19}\ \texttt{list} \sim \alpha_{20}$ can be satisfied by substituting $\alpha_{19}\ \texttt{list}$ for α_{20}. The first simple equality $\alpha_{19} \sim \alpha_{18}$ can be satisfied by substituting α_{19} for α_{18} or vice versa. So the full constraint is solvable if and only if the simple equality

$$\alpha_{19}\ \texttt{list} \sim \alpha_{19}$$

is solvable (or equivalently, if $\alpha_{18}\ \texttt{list} \sim \alpha_{18}$ is solvable). But no possible substi-

[4]Just as in the nondeterministic system, the rule for `lambda` typechecks the body in an extended environment that binds the formal parameter `x` to a monotype. If you wonder why I don't show you a rule for `lambda`, it's because I want you to develop the rule yourself; see Exercise 8 on page 446.

tution for α_{19} can make α_{19} `list` equal to α_{19}.[5] And after putting the unsolvable constraint into canonical form, that's what the interpreter reports:

425. ⟨*transcript* 402⟩+≡ ◁423 426▷

```
-> (val broken (lambda (x) (cons x x)))
type error: cannot make 'a equal to (list 'a)
```


A prequel to LETX *forms: Adding constraints is OK*

What's left are the rules for LETX forms. These forms generalize the types of multiple bound names, which gets complicated. To avoid that complexity, most presentations of this theory work with a simplified "core calculus." But if you're building an interpreter that infers types, you don't want some simplified core calculus; you want to infer types for code you actually write. To do it soundly, you'll need a rule that allows us to add a constraint:

$$\frac{C_i, \Gamma \vdash e_i : \tau_i \qquad C \text{ has a solution}}{C \wedge C_i, \Gamma \vdash e_i : \tau_i}. \qquad \text{(OVERCONSTRAINED)}$$

The idea is that although the constraint C_i is *sufficient* to give e_i a type, we may add another constraint C, provided that C has a solution. To prove this rule sound, we appeal to the substitution θ that solves C: if θ is applied to the valid derivation associated with the judgment $C_i, \Gamma \vdash e_i : \tau_i$, the result is another valid derivation.

Generalization in Milner's LET *binding*

The most difficult part of constraint-based type inference is its generalization at a LET binding. In `(let ([`x_1 e_1`])` $\cdots$`)`, the key elements are the type of e_1 and the type scheme bound to x_1. These types are determined by this sequence of operations:

- The type checker recursively checks e_1 in type environment Γ, getting back a type τ_1 and a constraint C.
- The type checker asks a constraint solver to solve C, getting substitution θ.
- Constraint C affects type variables that are free in τ or in Γ. The type variables that are free in τ can be eliminated by applying θ to τ. But free type variables of Γ can't be substituted for; that would be unsound. Instead, the effect of θ on those type variables is captured in a new constraint C'. Constraint C' is built by applying θ to the free type variables of Γ:

  $$C' = \bigwedge\{\alpha \sim \theta\alpha \mid \alpha \in \operatorname{dom}\theta \cap \operatorname{ftv}(\Gamma)\}.$$

  The notation $\bigwedge\{\ldots\}$ says to form a single constraint by conjoining the constraints in the set. If the set is empty, $\bigwedge\emptyset = \mathbf{T}$.
- Type scheme σ_1 is computed in two steps: First, apply θ to τ_1, getting the type of e_1 as refined by constraint C. Second, generalize $\theta\tau_1$ by quantifying over all of the type variables that are mentioned neither in Γ nor in C'.

[5] For a proof, consider the number of times that `list` appears on each side. No matter what you substitute for α_{19}, there will always be one more `list` constructor on the left than on the right, so the two sides can never be equal.

These operations can be formalized as an incomplete rule, which puts the type scheme of x_1 into Γ':

$$\frac{\begin{array}{c} C, \Gamma \vdash e_1 : \tau_1 \\ \theta C \text{ is satisfied} \qquad \theta \text{ is idempotent} \\ C' = \bigwedge\{\alpha \sim \theta\alpha \mid \alpha \in \operatorname{dom}\theta \cap \operatorname{ftv}(\Gamma)\} \\ \sigma_1 = \texttt{generalize}(\theta\tau_1, \operatorname{ftv}(\Gamma) \cup \operatorname{ftv}(C')) \\ \Gamma' = \Gamma\{x_1 \mapsto \sigma_1\} \end{array}}{\cdots}. \qquad \text{(INCOMPLETE SIMPLE LET)}$$

Because θ is used to form both C' and σ_1, it can eventually be used twice, so for soundness, it must be idempotent (sidebar on the facing page).

To complete the rule, tell the type checker to use new environment Γ' to infer the type of the body of the `let`. Extending the incomplete rule to work with an arbitrary number of bound variables $x_1, \ldots, x_n$ results in this rule:

$$\frac{\begin{array}{c} C, \Gamma \vdash e_1, \ldots, e_n : \tau_1, \ldots, \tau_n \\ \theta C \text{ is satisfied} \qquad \theta \text{ is idempotent} \\ C' = \bigwedge\{\alpha \sim \theta\alpha \mid \alpha \in \operatorname{dom}\theta \cap \operatorname{ftv}(\Gamma)\} \\ \sigma_i = \texttt{generalize}(\theta\tau_i, \operatorname{ftv}(\Gamma) \cup \operatorname{ftv}(C')), \quad 1 \le i \le n \\ C_b, \Gamma\{x_1 \mapsto \sigma_1, \ldots, x_n \mapsto \sigma_n\} \vdash e : \tau \end{array}}{C' \wedge C_b, \Gamma \vdash \text{LET}(\langle x_1, e_1, \ldots, x_n, e_n \rangle, e) : \tau}. \qquad \text{(LET)}$$

In LETREC, the e_i's are checked in an extended environment where each x_i is bound to a fresh type variable α_i, and *before* generalization, each type τ_i is constrained to be equal to the corresponding α_i. The rest is the same.

$$\frac{\begin{array}{c} e_1, \ldots, e_n \text{ are all LAMBDA expressions} \\ \Gamma' = \Gamma\{x_1 \mapsto \alpha_1, \ldots, x_n \mapsto \alpha_n\}, \text{ where all } \alpha_i\text{'s are distinct and fresh} \\ C_r, \Gamma' \vdash e_1, \ldots, e_n : \tau_1, \ldots, \tau_n \\ C = C_r \wedge \tau_1 \sim \alpha_1 \wedge \cdots \wedge \tau_n \sim \alpha_n \\ \theta C \text{ is satisfied} \qquad \theta \text{ is idempotent} \\ C' = \bigwedge\{\alpha \sim \theta\alpha \mid \alpha \in \operatorname{dom}\theta \cap \operatorname{ftv}(\Gamma)\} \\ \sigma_i = \texttt{generalize}(\theta\tau_i, \operatorname{ftv}(\Gamma) \cup \operatorname{ftv}(C')), \quad 1 \le i \le n \\ C_b, \Gamma\{x_1 \mapsto \sigma_1, \ldots, x_n \mapsto \sigma_n\} \vdash e : \tau \end{array}}{C' \wedge C_b, \Gamma \vdash \text{LETREC}(\langle x_1, e_1, \ldots, x_n, e_n \rangle, e) : \tau} \qquad \text{(LETREC)}$$

As an example of generalization in LET, I present a function that builds nested singleton lists:

426. ⟨*transcript* 402⟩+≡ ◁425

```
-> (val ss (lambda (y)
             (let ([single (lambda (x) (cons x '()))])
               (single (single y)))))
ss : (forall ['a] ('a -> (list (list 'a))))
```

The whole derivation won't fit on a page, so let's look at pieces. Start by assuming that the *body* of the outer `lambda` is typechecked in an environment

$$\Gamma = \{\texttt{cons} : \forall\alpha.\alpha \times \alpha\ \texttt{list} \to \alpha\ \texttt{list}, \texttt{y} : \alpha_{20}\}.$$

In a similar environment, the `singleton` example on page 423 shows a derivation for the `lambda`, so if $C = \alpha_{22} \times \alpha_{22}\ \texttt{list} \to \alpha_{22}\ \texttt{list} \sim \alpha_{21} \times \alpha_{23}\ \texttt{list} \to \alpha_{24}$, we can take it for granted that

$$C, \Gamma \vdash \texttt{(lambda (x) (cons x '()))} : \alpha_{21} \to \alpha_{24}$$

Soundness of generalization with constraints

Informally, generalization uses constraints as follows:

- The type being generalized is computed by the judgment $C, \Gamma \vdash e_1 : \tau_1$. For example,
$$\alpha \sim \texttt{int}, \Gamma \vdash \texttt{(+ x 1)} : \alpha,$$
where $\Gamma = \{\texttt{x} : \alpha\}$. Even though the type of `(+ x 1)` has a type variable, it can't be generalized: α *has* to be `int`.

- Solving constraint C produces substitution $\theta = (\alpha \mapsto \texttt{int})$. The type τ_1 is an output, so `int` can be substituted for α there, getting type $\theta\tau_1 = \texttt{int}$. But Γ is an input, so there's no way to substitute there: the constraint has to be retained.

- In the general case, the type checker takes the constraint C and its solution θ, and it splits θ into two parts, so that $\theta = \theta_g \circ \theta_l$, where
  - $\theta_l = \theta|_{\operatorname{dom}\theta \setminus \operatorname{ftv}(\Gamma)}$ is the *local* part; it substitutes for type variables that are mentioned in C (and possibly in τ) but never in Γ. Substitution θ_l can be applied to τ and then thrown away.
  - $\theta_g = \theta|_{\operatorname{ftv}(\Gamma)}$ is the *global* part; it substitutes for type variables that are mentioned in Γ. It can be applied to τ but not to Γ. Substitution θ_g can't be thrown away, so it is converted to constraint C'.

- Because σ_1 is computed by generalizing $\theta\tau_1$, none of the variables in $\operatorname{dom}\theta$ is generalized, and θ is idempotent, $\theta\sigma_1 = \sigma_1$.

From a valid derivation of $\theta C', \theta\Gamma \vdash e_1 : \theta\sigma_1$, the equalities above can be used to recover a valid derivation in the original, nondeterministic system.

is derivable. The next part of the derivation uses an instance of the LET rule with these values for its metavariables:

$$\begin{aligned}
C &= \alpha_{22} \times \alpha_{22}\ \texttt{list} \to \alpha_{22}\ \texttt{list} \sim \alpha_{21} \times \alpha_{23}\ \texttt{list} \to \alpha_{24}\\
\tau_1 &= \alpha_{21} \to \alpha_{24}\\
\theta &= (\alpha_{21} \mapsto \alpha_{22}) \circ (\alpha_{23} \mapsto \alpha_{22}) \circ (\alpha_{24} \mapsto \alpha_{22}\ \texttt{list})\\
C' &= \textstyle\bigwedge\{\,\} = \mathbf{T}\\
\operatorname{ftv}(\Gamma) &= \{\alpha_{20}\}\\
\sigma_1 &= \texttt{generalize}(\alpha_{22} \to \alpha_{22}\ \texttt{list}, \operatorname{ftv}(\Gamma)) = \forall\alpha_{22}.\alpha_{22} \to \alpha_{22}\ \texttt{list}.
\end{aligned}$$

The body of the LET, `(single (single x))`, is checked in the extended environment $\Gamma_e = \Gamma\{\texttt{single} : \forall\alpha_{22}.\alpha_{22} \to \alpha_{22}\ \texttt{list}\}$. Each instance of `single` gets its own type, and the typing derivation gets crowded. Abbreviating constraint $C_{inner} = \alpha_{25} \to \alpha_{25}\ \texttt{list} \sim \alpha_{20} \to \alpha_{26}$, we have

cons 𝒫 440a

$$\dfrac{\dfrac{\Gamma_e(\texttt{single}) = \forall\alpha_{22}.\alpha_{22} \to \alpha_{22}\ \texttt{list}}{\mathbf{T}, \Gamma_e \vdash \texttt{single} : \alpha_{27} \to \alpha_{27}\ \texttt{list}} \quad \dfrac{\dfrac{\Gamma_e(\texttt{single}) = \forall\alpha_{22}.\alpha_{22} \to \alpha_{22}\ \texttt{list}}{\mathbf{T}, \Gamma_e \vdash \texttt{single} : \alpha_{25} \to \alpha_{25}\ \texttt{list}} \quad \dfrac{\Gamma_e(\texttt{y}) = \forall.\alpha_{20}}{\mathbf{T}, \Gamma_e \vdash \texttt{y} : \alpha_{20}}}{C_{inner}, \Gamma_e \vdash \texttt{(single y)} : \alpha_{26}}}{\alpha_{27} \to \alpha_{27}\ \texttt{list} \sim \alpha_{26} \to \alpha_{28} \land C_{inner}, \Gamma_e \vdash \texttt{(single (single y))} : \alpha_{28}}.$$

The type of the outer `lambda` is therefore $\alpha_{20} \to \alpha_{28}$, with constraint $C' \land C_b$, which is

$$\mathbf{T} \land \alpha_{27} \to \alpha_{27}\ \texttt{list} \sim \alpha_{26} \to \alpha_{28} \land \alpha_{25} \to \alpha_{25}\ \texttt{list} \sim \alpha_{20} \to \alpha_{26}.$$

This constraint is equivalent to

$$\alpha_{27} \sim \alpha_{26} \wedge \alpha_{27}\ \texttt{list} \sim \alpha_{28} \wedge \alpha_{25} \sim \alpha_{20} \wedge \alpha_{25}\ \texttt{list} \sim \alpha_{26},$$

which is solved by the substitution

$$(\alpha_{27} \mapsto \alpha_{20}\ \texttt{list}) \circ (\alpha_{28} \mapsto \alpha_{27}\ \texttt{list}) \circ (\alpha_{25} \mapsto \alpha_{20}) \circ (\alpha_{26} \mapsto \alpha_{25}\ \texttt{list}),$$

which is equivalent to the substitution

$$(\alpha_{27} \mapsto \alpha_{20}\ \texttt{list}) \circ (\alpha_{28} \mapsto \alpha_{20}\ \texttt{list list}) \circ (\alpha_{25} \mapsto \alpha_{20}) \circ (\alpha_{26} \mapsto \alpha_{20}\ \texttt{list}),$$

The type of the outer `lambda` is therefore $\alpha_{20} \rightarrow \alpha_{20}$ `list list`, and at the VAL binding, this type is generalized to the type scheme $\forall\alpha_{20}.\alpha_{20} \rightarrow \alpha_{20}$ `list list`.

7.5.3 *Solving constraints*

As shown by the examples above, the method of explicit constraints reduces type inference to a constraint-solving problem. Solving a constraint tells us what, if anything, to substitute for each type variable. The substitutions are used to finalize types at LET and VAL, where potentially polymorphic names are bound. The details are all here, and you can use them to build your own constraint solver.

A constraint is *satisfied* if types that are supposed to be equal actually are equal:

$$\frac{\tau_1 = \tau_2}{\tau_1 \sim \tau_2 \text{ is satisfied}} \qquad \frac{C_1 \text{ is satisfied} \qquad C_2 \text{ is satisfied}}{C_1 \wedge C_2 \text{ is satisfied}} \qquad \frac{}{\mathbf{T} \text{ is satisfied}}.$$

Constraints, like types, can be substituted in, as specified by these laws:

$$\theta(\tau_1 \sim \tau_2) = \theta\tau_1 \sim \theta\tau_2, \qquad \theta(C_1 \wedge C_2) = \theta C_1 \wedge \theta C_2, \qquad \theta\mathbf{T} = \mathbf{T}.$$

The laws are implemented in chunk 436c, and the constraints' ML representation is shown in chunk 436a.

A constraint C is *solved* by finding a substitution θ such that θC is satisfied; we say that θ solves C. Not all constraints can be solved; for example, the constraint `int` $\sim$ `bool` is not solved by any θ, and neither is $\alpha \sim \alpha$ `list`.

If a constraint can be solved, a solution can be found by an algorithm called a constraint solver. A constraint solver has the same power as the `unify` function (page 417). Given a solver, any two types τ_1 and τ_2 can be unified by a substitution that solves the constraint $\tau_1 \sim \tau_2$. And given `unify`, any constraint can be solved by a substitution that unifies two types constructed from the constraint (Exercise 20).

Our constraint solver accumulates substitutions; this strategy works because once a constraint is satisfied, it remains satisfied even after further substitutions (Exercise 4). That is, if θC is satisfied, and if θ' is another substitution, then $\theta'(\theta C)$ is also satisfied. Equivalently, $(\theta' \circ \theta)C$ is satisfied.

Cases for constraint solving

A constraint solver is given a constraint C and returns a substitution θ such that θC is satisfied. The solver need consider only three cases:

- C is the trivial constraint $\mathbf{T}$, in which case θ_I solves C.
- C is the conjunction $C_1 \wedge C_2$, in which case both sub-constraints C_1 and C_2 must be solved.
- C is a simple equality constraint of the form $\tau_1 \sim \tau_2$.

Both conjunctions and simple equality constraints require attention to detail.

Sadly, a conjunction $C_1 \wedge C_2$ can't be solved by first solving C_1, then solving C_2, then composing the solutions. This technique works only some of the time, as expressed by the following rule:

$$\frac{\theta_1 C_1 \text{ is satisfied} \qquad \tilde{\theta}_2 C_2 \text{ is satisfied}}{(\tilde{\theta}_2 \circ \theta_1)(C_1 \wedge C_2) \text{ may or may not be satisfied}}. \qquad \text{(UNSOLVEDCONJUNCTION)}$$

Even when θ_1 solves C_1 and $\tilde{\theta}_2$ solves C_2, neither $\tilde{\theta}_2 \circ \theta_1$ nor $\theta_1 \circ \tilde{\theta}_2$ is guaranteed to solve $C_1 \wedge C_2$. The substitution $\tilde{\theta}_2$ wears a tilde because I'm going to treat it as the bad guy; looking at $\tilde{\theta}_2 \circ \theta_1$, here's what goes wrong:

- We want $(\tilde{\theta}_2 \circ \theta_1)(C_1 \wedge C_2)$ to be satisfied. According the rule for satisfying conjunctions, this means both $(\tilde{\theta}_2 \circ \theta_1)C_1$ and $(\tilde{\theta}_2 \circ \theta_1)C_2$ must be satisfied.
- By the assumption that θ_1 solves C_1, $\theta_1 C_1$ is satisfied. And because satisfaction is preserved by substitution, $(\tilde{\theta}_2 \circ \theta_1)C_1$ is satisfied. So far, so good.
- Constraint $(\tilde{\theta}_2 \circ \theta_1)C_2 = \tilde{\theta}_2(\theta_1 C_2)$ must also be satisfied. But unfortunately, although $\tilde{\theta}_2$ solves C_2, that doesn't guarantee that it also solves $\theta_1 C_2$.

This line of thinking can be carried further with a proof and some examples (Exercises 12 and 16).

The unreliable technique fails because in the last step, the constraint that must be solved is not C_2; it is $\theta_1 C_2$. This observation leads to a reliable technique, which is expressed by the following rule:

$$\frac{\theta_1 C_1 \text{ is satisfied} \qquad \theta_2(\theta_1 C_2) \text{ is satisfied}}{(\theta_2 \circ \theta_1)(C_1 \wedge C_2) \text{ is satisfied}}. \qquad \text{(SOLVEDCONJUNCTION)}$$

Substitution θ_2, which may be different from $\tilde{\theta}_2$, does what we need (Exercise 13). The rule is interpreted operationally as follows: To solve a conjunction, call the solver recursively, apply θ_1 to C_2, call the solver recursively again, and return the composition of the two substitutions.

To remember the rule and the algorithm, I think like this: if θ_1 solves C_1, then θ_1 represents the *assumptions* that I have to make for C_1 to have a solution. If those assumptions are to hold everywhere, then they must be accounted for when I look at C_2. And they are accounted for by applying θ_1.

Solving simple equality constraints

In addition to conjunctions, a constraint solver must also solve simple equality constraints of the form $\tau_1 \sim \tau_2$. Because each type may be formed in three different ways, a simple equality constraint is formed in one of *nine* different ways. Nine cases is a lot, but the code can be cut down by clever use of ML pattern matching. And in every case, the goal is the same: find a θ such that $\theta\tau_1 = \theta\tau_2$. Let's tackle the most tricky case first, the easy cases next, and the most involved case last.

The tricky case is one in which the left-hand side is a type variable, giving the constraint the form $\alpha \sim \tau_2$. This constraint can be solved by the substitution $(\alpha \mapsto \tau_2)$, but only in some cases:

- If τ_2 does not mention α, then $(\alpha \mapsto \tau_2)\tau_2 = \tau_2$, and also $(\alpha \mapsto \tau_2)\alpha = \tau_2$. Solved!
- If τ_2 is *equal* to α, then $(\alpha \mapsto \alpha)$ is the identity substitution θ_I. Also solved.
- If τ_2 *mentions* α but is *not equal* to α—for example, suppose τ_2 is α `list`—then the constraint $\alpha \sim \tau_2$ cannot be solved (Exercise 15).

Type τ_2 mentions α if and only if α *occurs free in* τ_2. This property has to be tested; the test is called the *occurs check*.

Performance of type inference

Nano-ML's type inference is designed for clarity, not performance. If you write a definition that includes hundreds of function applications, you get hundreds of constraints. Solving them may result in hundreds of *thousands* of calls to `tysubst`, which in turn may mean tens of *millions* of string comparisons in `find`—the total cost of finding out what to substitute for each type variable is quadratic in the number of variables, and type inference can take hours.

A production compiler has no such issues. Production code uses efficient representations of names and environments, and substitution is implemented in constant time by updating the contents of a mutable reference cell, much as in a union-find algorithm.

To avoid nano-ML's performance issues, avoid deeply nested calls. For example, if you want to build a list of a thousand elements, try something like this:

```
(let*
   ([ns '()]
    [ns (cons 1000 ns)]
    [ns (cons  999 ns)]
      ...
    [ns (cons    1 ns)])
  ns)
```

At every binding the constraint solver is called with a small constraint involving just a few type variables, so type inference is quick.

Alternatively, type inference of large lists can be made efficient by better language design: a *list constructor* builds a list of any length using just a single type variable, which represents the element type of the list (Exercise 22).

Suppose the left-hand side of the constraint is not a type variable, but the right-hand side is. That is, the constraint has the form $\tau_1 \sim \alpha$. This constraint has the same solutions as $\alpha \sim \tau_1$; the solver can swap the two sides and call itself recursively.

If neither side is a type variable, then each side must be a type constructor or a type application (TYCON or CONAPP). If the left is a constructor and the right is an application, or vice versa, the constraint can't be solved. And if both sides are type constructors, substitution leaves them unchanged, so a constraint of the form $\mu \sim \mu$ is solved by the identity substitution, and a constraint of the form $\mu \sim \mu'$, where $\mu \neq \mu'$, cannot be solved.

The most complicated case is a constraint in which both sides are constructor applications. Because every substitution must preserve the structure of a constructor application (see the substitution laws on page 409), such a constraint can be broken down into a conjunction of smaller constraints:

$$\frac{\theta(\tau \sim \tau' \land \tau_1 \sim \tau_1' \land \cdots \land \tau_n \sim \tau_n') \text{ is satisfied}}{\theta(\text{CONAPP}(\tau, \langle \tau_1, \ldots, \tau_n \rangle) \sim \text{CONAPP}(\tau', \langle \tau_1', \ldots, \tau_n' \rangle)) \text{ is satisfied}}. \quad \text{(SOLVECONAPPCONAPP)}$$

This rule is also sound (Exercise 14). Operationally, the solver is given the constraint on the bottom. It then builds the constraint on the top, on which it calls itself recursively. The recursion terminates because the number of CONAPPs decreases.

An example of constraint solving

Using the ideas above, let's solve the constraint from `(cons 1 '())`,

$$\mathbf{T} \wedge (\mathbf{T} \wedge \alpha_{11} \times \alpha_{11}\,\texttt{list} \to \alpha_{11}\,\texttt{list} \sim \texttt{int} \times \alpha_{12}\,\texttt{list} \to \alpha_{13}). \tag{7.1}$$

This constraint is big enough to be interesting, but for a complete, formal derivation, it's a little too big. So let's solve it informally.

The constraint is a conjunction, so we first solve the left conjunct, which is $\mathbf{T}$. This conjunct is solved by the identity substitution θ_I, which we then apply to the right conjunct

$$\mathbf{T} \wedge \alpha_{11} \times \alpha_{11}\,\texttt{list} \to \alpha_{11}\,\texttt{list} \sim \texttt{int} \times \alpha_{12}\,\texttt{list} \to \alpha_{13}. \tag{7.2}$$

The identity substitution leaves this conjunct unchanged, and we continue solving recursively. The same steps lead us to solve

$$\alpha_{11} \times \alpha_{11}\,\texttt{list} \to \alpha_{11}\,\texttt{list} \sim \texttt{int} \times \alpha_{12}\,\texttt{list} \to \alpha_{13}. \tag{7.3}$$

This simple equality constraint has CONAPP (with the $\to$ constructor) on both sides. We use the SOLVECONAPPCONAPP rule to convert this constraint to

$$(\to \sim \to) \wedge (\alpha_{11} \times \alpha_{11}\,\texttt{list} \sim \texttt{int} \times \alpha_{12}\,\texttt{list} \wedge \alpha_{11}\,\texttt{list} \sim \alpha_{13}). \tag{7.4}$$

The left conjunct, $(\to \sim \to)$, has two equal type constructors and so is solved by θ_I, which, when applied to the right conjunct, leaves it unchanged. So we solve

$$\alpha_{11} \times \alpha_{11}\,\texttt{list} \sim \texttt{int} \times \alpha_{12}\,\texttt{list} \wedge \alpha_{11}\,\texttt{list} \sim \alpha_{13}. \tag{7.5}$$

The next step is to solve the left conjunct

$$\alpha_{11} \times \alpha_{11}\,\texttt{list} \sim \texttt{int} \times \alpha_{12}\,\texttt{list}, \tag{7.6}$$

which requires another application of the SOLVECONAPPCONAPP rule, asking us to solve

$$(\times \sim \times) \wedge \alpha_{11} \sim \texttt{int} \wedge \alpha_{11}\,\texttt{list} \sim \alpha_{12}\,\texttt{list}. \tag{7.7}$$

We must next solve

$$\alpha_{11} \sim \texttt{int} \wedge \alpha_{11}\,\texttt{list} \sim \alpha_{12}\,\texttt{list}, \tag{7.8}$$

and we begin with its left conjunct

$$\alpha_{11} \sim \texttt{int}. \tag{7.9}$$

Finally we have a case with a type variable on the left, and constraint 7.9 is solved by $\theta_1 = \alpha_{11} \mapsto \texttt{int}$. We then apply θ_1 to the constraint $\alpha_{11}\,\texttt{list} \sim \alpha_{12}\,\texttt{list}$, yielding

$$\texttt{int list} \sim \alpha_{12}\,\texttt{list}. \tag{7.10}$$

Let's not go through all the steps; constraint 7.10 is solved by $\theta_2 = \alpha_{12} \mapsto \texttt{int}$. Constraints 7.6, 7.7, and 7.8 are therefore solved by the composition of θ_1 and θ_2, which is $\theta_2 \circ \theta_1 = (\alpha_{12} \mapsto \texttt{int} \circ \alpha_{11} \mapsto \texttt{int})$.

Now we can return to constraint 7.5. We apply $\theta_2 \circ \theta_1$ to the right conjunct $\alpha_{11}\,\texttt{list} \sim \alpha_{13}$, yielding

$$\texttt{int list} \sim \alpha_{13}, \tag{7.11}$$

which is solved by substitution $\theta_3 = \alpha_{13} \mapsto \texttt{int list}$. Constraint 7.5 is therefore solved by substitution $\theta_3 \circ \theta_2 \circ \theta_1$, which is

$$\theta = \theta_3 \circ \theta_2 \circ \theta_1 = \alpha_{13} \mapsto \texttt{int list} \circ \alpha_{12} \mapsto \texttt{int} \circ \alpha_{11} \mapsto \texttt{int}.$$

Substitution θ also solves constraints 7.1 to 7.4.

Table 7.3: Correspondence between nano-ML's type system and code

Type system	Concept	Interpreter
d	Definition	`def` (page 405)
e	Expression	`exp` (page 404)
x	Variable	`name` (page 303)
α	Type variable	`tyvar` (page 408)
τ	Type	`ty` (page 408)
$\sigma, \forall\alpha.\tau$	Type scheme	`type_scheme` (page 408)
$\tau \equiv \tau'$	Type equivalence	`eqType(`τ`, `τ'`)` (page 412)
Γ	Type environment	`type_env` (page 435)
$\Gamma(x) = \sigma$	Type lookup	`findtyscheme(`x`, `Γ`)` $= \sigma$ (page 435)
$\Gamma\{x \mapsto \sigma\}$	Type binding	`bindtyscheme(`x`, `σ`, `Γ`)` (page 435)
C	Constraint	`con` (page 436)
$\tau_1 \sim \tau_2$	Equality constraint	τ_1 `~` τ_2 (page 436)
$C_1 \wedge C_2$	Conjunction	C_1 `/\` C_2 (page 436)
$\mathbf{T}$	Trivial constraint	`TRIVIAL` (page 436)
$\bigwedge_i C_i$	Conjunction	`conjoinConstraints` $[C_1, \ldots, C_n]$ (page 436)
$\text{ftv}(\tau)$	Free type variables	`freetyvars` τ (page 433)
$\text{ftv}(\Gamma)$	Free type variables	`freetyvarsGamma` Γ (page 435)
$\text{ftv}(C)$	Free type variables	`freetyvarsConstraint` C (page 436)
$C, \Gamma \vdash e : \tau$	Type inference	`typeof(`e`, `Γ`)` $= (\tau, C)$, also `ty` $e = (\tau, C)$ (page 437; some parts left as an exercise)
$\langle d, \Gamma \rangle \to \Gamma'$	Type inference	`typdef(`d`, `Γ`)` = `(`Γ'`, `s`)` (page 439)
θ	A substitution	`subst` (page 410)
θ_I	Identity substitution	`idsubst` (page 411)
$[\alpha \mapsto \tau]$	Substitution for α	α `|-->` τ (page 411)
$\theta\tau$	Substitution	`tysubst` $\theta\ \tau$ (page 410)
$\theta\alpha$	Substitution	`varsubst` $\theta\ \alpha$ (page 410)
θC	Substitution	`consubst` $\theta\ C$ (page 436)
$\theta_2 \circ \theta_1$	Composition	`compose` (page 411)
$\text{dom}\,\theta$	Domain	`dom` (page 411)
$\theta C \equiv \mathbf{T}$	Constraint solving	$\theta =$ `solve` C (left as an exercise, page 437)
$C \equiv \mathbf{T}$	Solved constraint	`isSolved` C (page 437)
$\forall\alpha.\tau$ becomes $\tau[\alpha \mapsto \tau']$	Instantiation	`instantiate(`$\forall\alpha.\tau$`, [`τ'`])` (page 411)
`int`, `bool`, ...	Base types	`inttype`, `booltype`, ... (page 412)
$\tau_1 \times \cdots \times \tau_n \to \tau$	Function type	`funtype([`$\tau_1, \ldots, \tau_n$`], `τ`)` (page 412)

In most respects, the interpreter for nano-ML is the interpreter for μScheme (Chapter 5), plus type inference. Significant parts of type inference don't appear here, however, because they are meant to be exercises.

7.6.1 *Functions on types and type schemes*

This section defines functions that are used throughout type inference.

Function `freetyvars` returns a set containing the free type variables of a type. For readability, it builds the set so type variables appear in the order of their first appearance in the type, when reading from left to right.

433a. ⟨*sets of free type variables in Hindley-Milner types* 433a⟩≡ (S420a)

`freetyvars : ty -> name set`

```
fun freetyvars t =
  let fun f (TYVAR v,          ftvs) = insert (v, ftvs)
        | f (TYCON _,          ftvs) = ftvs
        | f (CONAPP (ty, tys), ftvs) = foldl f (f (ty, ftvs)) tys
  in  reverse (f (t, emptyset))
  end
```

Canonical type schemes

Type variables like `'t136` are not suitable for use in error messages. A type scheme like `(forall ['t136] ((list 't136) -> int))` is unpleasant to look at, and it is equivalent to the more readable `(forall ['a] ((list 'a) -> int))` When a type variable is $\forall$-bound, its name is irrelevant, so function `canonicalize` renames bound type variables using names `'a`, `'b`, and so on.

433b. ⟨*shared utility functions on Hindley-Milner types* 410a⟩+≡ (S420a) ◁412a 434a▷

```
canonicalize : type_scheme -> type_scheme
newBoundVars : int * name list -> name list
```

```
fun canonicalize (FORALL (bound, ty)) =
  let fun canonicalTyvarName n =
        if n < 26 then "'" ^ str (chr (ord #"a" + n))
        else "'v" ^ intString (n - 25)
      val free = diff (freetyvars ty, bound)
      fun unusedIndex n =
        if member (canonicalTyvarName n) free then unusedIndex (n+1) else n
      fun newBoundVars (index, [])                = []
        | newBoundVars (index, oldvar :: oldvars) =
            let val n = unusedIndex index
            in  canonicalTyvarName n :: newBoundVars (n+1, oldvars)
            end
      val newBound = newBoundVars (0, bound)
  in  FORALL (newBound,
              tysubst (mkEnv (bound, map TYVAR newBound)) ty)
  end
```


CONAPP	408
diff	S217b
emptyset	S217b
FORALL	408
insert	S217b
intString	S214c
member	S217b
mkEnv	305e
type name	303
reverse	S219b
type ty	408
TYCON	408
type type_scheme	408
tysubst	410c
TYVAR	408

Internal function `unusedIndex` finds a name for a single bound type variable; it ensures that the name is not the name of any free type variable.

Fresh type variables

A type variable that does not appear in any type environment or substitution is called *fresh*. When a function is introduced, fresh type variables are used as the (unknown) types of its arguments. When a polytype is instantiated, fresh type variables are used as the unknown types that are substituted for its bound type variables. And when a function is applied, a fresh type variable is used as its (unknown) result type.

Fresh type variables are created by the freshtyvar function. The function uses a private mutable counter to supply an arbitrary number of type variables of the form tn. Because a nano-ML expression or definition never contains any explicit type variables, the names don't collide with other names.

434a. ⟨*shared utility functions on Hindley-Milner types* 410a⟩+≡ (S420a) ◁ 433b 434b ▷

`freshtyvar : 'a -> ty`

```
local
  val n = ref 1
in
  fun freshtyvar _ = TYVAR ("'t" ^ intString (!n) before n := !n + 1)
end
```

Generalization and instantiation

Calling generalize$(\tau, \mathcal{A})$ generalizes type τ to a type scheme by closing over type variables not in $\mathcal{A}$. It also puts the type scheme into canonical form.

434b. ⟨*shared utility functions on Hindley-Milner types* 410a⟩+≡ (S420a) ◁ 434a 434c ▷

`generalize : ty * name set -> type_scheme`

```
fun generalize (tau, tyvars) =
  canonicalize (FORALL (diff (freetyvars tau, tyvars), tau))
```

The dual function, instantiate, is defined in chunk 411b. It requires a list of types with which to instantiate. That list is often a list of fresh type variables, as provided by function freshInstance.

434c. ⟨*shared utility functions on Hindley-Milner types* 410a⟩+≡ (S420a) ◁ 434b

`freshInstance : type_scheme -> ty`

```
fun freshInstance (FORALL (bound, tau)) =
  instantiate (FORALL (bound, tau), map freshtyvar bound)
```

7.6.2 *Type environments*

Function generalize is called with the free type variables of some type environment. And a type environment contains the type of every defined name, so it can get big. To reduce the cost of searching a large environment for free type variables, a type environment is represented in a way that enables the type checker to find free type variables in constant time.

A representation of type environments must support these functions:

- Function bindtyscheme adds a binding $x : \sigma$ to the environment Γ. It is used to implement the LAMBDA rule and the various LET rules.
- Function findtyscheme looks up a variable x to find σ such that $\Gamma(x) = \sigma$. It is used to implement the VAR rule.
- Function freetyvarsGamma finds the type variables free in Γ, i.e., the type variables free in any σ in Γ. It is used to get a set of free type variables to use in generalize; when a type scheme is assigned to a let-bound variable, only those type variables not free in Γ may be $\forall$-bound.

If freetyvarsGamma used a representation of type type_scheme env, it would visit every type scheme in every binding in the environment. Because most bindings contribute no free type variables, most visits would be unnecessary. Instead, all

Why generalize and instantiate?

We use quantified types (i.e., type schemes) so we can instantiate them when we look them up in an environment. Instantiation gives us the full effect of polymorphism. Without instantiation, we wouldn't be able to type such ML terms as `(1::nil, true::nil)`. Suppose we had an environment Γ with only types, not type schemes:

$$\Gamma = \{1 : \texttt{int}, \mathit{true} : \texttt{bool}, \mathit{nil} : \alpha\,\texttt{list}, :: : \alpha \times \alpha\,\texttt{list} \to \alpha\,\texttt{list}\}.$$

When typechecking `1::nil`, we would get the constraint $\alpha \sim \texttt{int}$. And when typechecking `true::nil`, we would get the constraint $\alpha \sim \texttt{bool}$. But the conjunction $\alpha \sim \texttt{int} \wedge \alpha \sim \texttt{bool}$ has no solution, and type checking would fail.

Instead, we use `freshInstance` to make sure that every use of a polymorphic value (here `::` and `nil`) has a type different from any other instance. In order to make that work, the environment has to contain polytypes:

$$\Gamma = \{1 : \forall.\texttt{int}, \mathit{true} : \forall.\texttt{bool}, \mathit{nil} : \forall\alpha.\alpha\,\texttt{list}, :: : \forall\alpha.\alpha \times \alpha\,\texttt{list} \to \alpha\,\texttt{list}\}.$$

Now, we can imagine our sample term like this, writing `::` as a prefix operator so as to show the types:

```
(op :: : 't121 * 't121 list -> 't121 list (1    : int,  nil : 't122 list),
 op :: : 't123 * 't123 list -> 't123 list (true : bool, nil : 't124 list))
```

The constraint `'t121` $\sim$ `int` $\wedge$ `int` $\sim$ `'t122` $\wedge$ `'t123` $\sim$ `bool` $\wedge$ `bool` $\sim$ `'t124` does have a solution, and the whole term has the type `int list * bool list`, as desired.

functions use a representation that includes a cache of the type environment's free type variables.

435a. ⟨*specialized environments for type schemes* 435a⟩≡ (S420a) 435b ▷

```
type type_env = type_scheme env * name set
```

An empty type environment binds no variables and has an empty cache. Looking up a type scheme ignores the cache.

435b. ⟨*specialized environments for type schemes* 435a⟩+≡ (S420a) ◁ 435a 435c ▷

```
val emptyTypeEnv =
      (emptyEnv, emptyset)
fun findtyscheme (x, (Gamma, free)) = find (x, Gamma)
```

```
emptyTypeEnv : type_env
findtyscheme : name * type_env -> type_scheme
```

Adding a new binding also adds to the cache. The new cache is the union of the existing cache with the free type variables of the new type scheme σ.

435c. ⟨*specialized environments for type schemes* 435a⟩+≡ (S420a) ◁ 435b 435d ▷

```
bindtyscheme : name * type_scheme * type_env -> type_env
```

```
fun bindtyscheme (x, sigma as FORALL (bound, tau), (Gamma, free)) =
  (bind (x, sigma, Gamma), union (diff (freetyvars tau, bound), free))
```

Free type variables are found in the cache in constant time.

435d. ⟨*specialized environments for type schemes* 435a⟩+≡ (S420a) ◁ 435c

```
fun freetyvarsGamma (_, free) = free
```

```
freetyvarsGamma : type_env -> name set
```

bind	305d
canonicalize	433b
diff	S217b
emptyEnv	305a
emptyset	S217b
type env	304
find	305b
FORALL	408
freetyvars	433a
instantiate	411b
intString	S214c
type name	303
type ty	408
type type_scheme	408
TYVAR	408
union	S217b

7.6.3 *Constraints and constraint solving*

In the interpreter, constraints are represented in a way that resembles the math: the $\sim$ operator is `~`; the $\wedge$ operator is `/\`; and the $\mathbf{T}$ constraint is `TRIVIAL`.

436a. ⟨*representation of type constraints* 436a⟩≡ (S420b)

```
datatype con = ~  of ty  * ty
             | /\ of con * con
             | TRIVIAL
infix 4 ~
infix 3 /\
```

(The name `~` normally stands for ML's negation function. An unqualified `~` is redefined by this `datatype` definition, but negation can still be referred to by its qualified name `Int.~`.)

Utility functions on constraints

Many of the utility functions defined on types have counterparts on constraints. For example, we can find free type variables in a constraint, and we can substitute for free type variables.

436b. ⟨*utility functions on type constraints* 436b⟩≡ (S420b) 436c ▷

```
fun freetyvarsConstraint (t ~  t') = union (freetyvars t, freetyvars t')
  | freetyvarsConstraint (c /\ c') = union (freetyvarsConstraint c,
                                            freetyvarsConstraint c')
  | freetyvarsConstraint TRIVIAL    = emptyset
```

A substitution is applied to a constraint using the following laws:

$$\theta(\tau_1 \sim \tau_2) = \theta\tau_1 \sim \theta\tau_2, \qquad \theta(C_1 \wedge C_2) = \theta C_1 \wedge \theta C_2, \qquad \theta\mathbf{T} = \mathbf{T}.$$

The code resembles the code for `tysubst` in chunk 410c.

436c. ⟨*utility functions on type constraints* 436b⟩+≡ (S420b) ◁ 436b 436d ▷

`consubst : subst -> con -> con`

```
fun consubst theta =
  let fun subst (tau1 ~ tau2) = tysubst theta tau1 ~ tysubst theta tau2
        | subst (c1 /\ c2)    = subst c1 /\ subst c2
        | subst TRIVIAL       = TRIVIAL
  in  subst
  end
```

The $\bigwedge\{\cdots\}$ notation is implemented by ML function `conjoinConstraints`. To preserve the number and order of sub-constraints, it avoids using `foldl` or `foldr`.

436d. ⟨*utility functions on type constraints* 436b⟩+≡ (S420b) ◁ 436c 437c ▷

`conjoinConstraints : con list -> con`

```
fun conjoinConstraints []      = TRIVIAL
  | conjoinConstraints [c]     = c
  | conjoinConstraints (c::cs) = c /\ conjoinConstraints cs
```

Two more utility functions are defined in Appendix R: `constraintString` can be used to print constraints, and `untriviate`, whose type is `con -> con`, removes trivial conjuncts from a constraint.

Constraint solving

If type inference is given an ill-typed program, it produces an *unsolvable* constraint. Examples of unsolvable constraints include `int` $\sim$ `bool` and α `list` $\sim \alpha$. Given an unsolvable constraint, the type checker should issue a readable error message, not one full of machine-generated type variables. To do so, function `unsatisfiableEquality` takes the pair of types that can't be made equal, puts the *pair* into canonical form, and raises the `TypeError` exception.

437a. ⟨*constraint solving* 437a⟩≡ (S420b)

```
fun unsatisfiableEquality (t1, t2) =
  let val t1_arrow_t2 = funtype ([t1], t2)
      val FORALL (_, canonical) =
            canonicalize (FORALL (freetyvars t1_arrow_t2, t1_arrow_t2))
  in  case asFuntype canonical
        of SOME ([t1'], t2') =>
             raise TypeError ("cannot make " ^ typeString t1' ^
                              " equal to " ^ typeString t2')
         | _ => raise InternalError "failed to synthesize canonical type"
  end
```


The mechanism is a little weird. To make a single type out of τ_1 and τ_2, so their variables can be canonicalized together, I make the type $\tau_1 \to \tau_2$. What's weird is that there's no function—it's just a device to make one type out of two. When I get the canonical version, I take it apart to get back canonical types `t1'` and `t2'`.

I don't provide a solver; I hope you will implement one.

437b. ⟨*constraint solving* **[[prototype]]** 437b⟩≡

```
fun solve c = raise LeftAsExercise "solve"
```

```
solve : con -> subst
```

For debugging, it can be useful to see if a substitution solves a constraint.

437c. ⟨*utility functions on type constraints* 436b⟩+≡ (S420b) ◁ 436d

```
isSolved : con -> bool
solves : subst * con -> bool
```

```
fun isSolved TRIVIAL = true
  | isSolved (tau ~ tau') = eqType (tau,tau')
  | isSolved (c /\ c') = isSolved c andalso isSolved c'
fun solves (theta, c) = isSolved (consubst theta c)
```

7.6.4 *Type inference*

Type inference builds on constraint solving. It comprises two functions: `typeof`, which implements the typing rules for expressions, and `typdef`, which implements the rules for definitions.

Type inference for expressions

Given an expression e and type environment Γ, function `typeof`(e, Γ) returns a pair (τ, C) such that $C, \Gamma \vdash e : \tau$. It uses internal functions `typesof`, `literal`, and `ty`.

437d. ⟨*definitions of* `typeof` *and* `typdef` *for nano-ML and* μ*ML* 437d⟩≡ (S420b) 439a ▷

```
typeof  : exp      * type_env -> ty      * con
typesof : exp list * type_env -> ty list * con
literal : value -> ty * con
ty      : exp   -> ty * con
```

```
fun typeof (e, Gamma) =
  let ⟨shared definition of typesof, to infer the types of a list of expressions 438a⟩
      ⟨function literal, to infer the type of a literal constant (left as an exercise)⟩
      ⟨function ty, to infer the type of a nano-ML expression, given Gamma 438c⟩
  in  ty e
  end
```

Calling `typesof`($\langle e_1, \ldots, e_n \rangle, \Gamma$) returns $(\langle \tau_1, \ldots, \tau_n \rangle, C)$ such that for every i from 1 to n, $C, \Gamma \vdash e_i : \tau_i$. The base case is trivial; the inductive case uses this rule from Section 7.5.2:

$$\frac{C_1, \Gamma \vdash e_1 : \tau_1 \quad \cdots \quad C_n, \Gamma \vdash e_n : \tau_n}{C_1 \wedge \cdots \wedge C_n, \Gamma \vdash e_1, \ldots, e_n : \tau_1, \ldots, \tau_n}. \qquad \text{(TYPESOF)}$$

Both cases are implemented by function typesof.

438a. ⟨*shared definition of* typesof*, to infer the types of a list of expressions* 438a⟩≡ (437d)

```
fun typesof ([],      Gamma) = ([], TRIVIAL)
  | typesof (e::es, Gamma) =
      let val (tau,  c)  = typeof  (e,  Gamma)
          val (taus, c') = typesof (es, Gamma)
      in  (tau :: taus, c /\ c')
      end
```


To infer the type of a literal value, we call literal, which is left as Exercise 19.

438b. ⟨*function* literal*, to infer the type of a literal constant* **[[prototype]]** 438b⟩≡

```
fun literal _ = raise LeftAsExercise "literal"
```

438c. ⟨*function* ty*, to infer the type of a nano-ML expression, given* Gamma 438c⟩≡ (437d)

```
fun ty (LITERAL n) = literal n
  ⟨more alternatives for ty 438d⟩
```

To infer the type of a variable, we use fresh type variables to create a most general instance of the variable's type scheme in Γ. No constraint is needed.

438d. ⟨*more alternatives for* ty 438d⟩≡ (438c) 438e ▷

```
  | ty (VAR x) = (freshInstance (findtyscheme (x, Gamma)), TRIVIAL)
```

To infer the type of a function application, we need a rule that uses constraints. By rewriting the nondeterministic rule as described in Section 7.5.2, we get this rule:

$$\frac{C, \Gamma \vdash e, e_1, \ldots, e_n : \hat{\tau}, \tau_1, \ldots, \tau_n \qquad \alpha \text{ is fresh}}{C \wedge \hat{\tau} \sim \tau_1 \times \cdots \times \tau_n \to \alpha, \Gamma \vdash \text{APPLY}(e, e_1, \ldots, e_n) : \alpha}. \qquad \text{(APPLY)}$$

This rule is implemented by letting funty stand for $\hat{\tau}$, actualtypes stand for $\tau_1, \ldots, \tau_n$, and rettype stand for α. The first premise is implemented by a call to typesof and the second by a call to freshtyvar. The constraint is formed just as specified in the rule.

438e. ⟨*more alternatives for* ty 438d⟩+≡ (438c) ◁ 438d 438f ▷

```
  | ty (APPLY (f, actuals)) =
       (case typesof (f :: actuals, Gamma)
          of ([], _) => raise InternalError "pattern match"
           | (funty :: actualtypes, c) =>
                let val rettype = freshtyvar ()
                in  (rettype, c /\ (funty ~ funtype (actualtypes, rettype)))
                end)
```

To infer the type of a LETSTAR form, we desugar it into nested LETs.

438f. ⟨*more alternatives for* ty 438d⟩+≡ (438c) ◁ 438e

```
  | ty (LETX (LETSTAR, [], body)) = ty body
  | ty (LETX (LETSTAR, (b :: bs), body)) =
      ty (LETX (LET, [b], LETX (LETSTAR, bs, body)))
```

Inference for the remaining expression forms is left as an exercise.

438g. ⟨*more alternatives for* ty **[[prototype]]** 438g⟩≡

```
  | ty (IFX (e1, e2, e3))        = raise LeftAsExercise "type for IFX"
  | ty (BEGIN es)                = raise LeftAsExercise "type for BEGIN"
  | ty (LAMBDA (formals, body))  = raise LeftAsExercise "type for LAMBDA"
  | ty (LETX (LET, bs, body))    = raise LeftAsExercise "type for LET"
  | ty (LETX (LETREC, bs, body)) = raise LeftAsExercise "type for LETREC"
```

Typing and type inference for definitions

A definition extends the top-level type environment. Function `typdef` infers the type of the thing defined, generalizes it to a type scheme, and adds a binding to the environment. This step *types* the definition. Function `typdef` returns the new type environment, plus a string that describes the type scheme of the new binding.

439a. ⟨*definitions of* `typeof` *and* `typdef` *for nano-ML and μML* 437d⟩+≡ (S420b) ◁ 437d

```
fun typdef (d, Gamma) =          typdef : def * type_env -> type_env * string
  case d
    of VAL    (x, e)      => ⟨infer and bind type for VAL    (x, e) for nano-ML 439b⟩
     | VALREC (x, e)      => ⟨infer and bind type for VALREC (x, e) for nano-ML 439c⟩
     | EXP e              => typdef (VAL ("it", e), Gamma)
     | DEFINE (x, lambda) => typdef (VALREC (x, LAMBDA lambda), Gamma)
    ⟨extra case for typdef used only in μML S435a⟩
```


Forms `EXP` and `DEFINE` are syntactic sugar.

The cases for `VAL` and `VALREC` resemble each other. A `VAL` computes a type and generalizes it.

$$\frac{\begin{array}{c} C, \Gamma \vdash e : \tau \\ \theta C \text{ is satisfied} \qquad \theta\Gamma = \Gamma \\ \sigma = \texttt{generalize}(\theta\tau, \text{ftv}(\Gamma)) \end{array}}{\langle \text{VAL}(x, e), \Gamma \rangle \to \Gamma\{x \mapsto \sigma\}} \qquad (\text{VAL})$$

439b. ⟨*infer and bind type for* `VAL` `(x, e)` *for nano-ML* 439b⟩≡ (439a)

```
let val (tau, c) = typeof (e, Gamma)
    val theta    = solve c
    val sigma    = generalize (tysubst theta tau, freetyvarsGamma Gamma)
in  (bindtyscheme (x, sigma, Gamma), typeSchemeString sigma)
end
```

This code takes a big shortcut: it assumes that $\theta\Gamma = \Gamma$. That assumption is sound because *a top-level* Γ *never contains a free type variable* (Exercise 10). This property guarantees that $\theta\Gamma = \Gamma$ for any θ.

A `VALREC` is a bit more complicated. The nondeterministic rule calls for an environment that binds x to τ, but τ isn't known until e is typechecked:

$$\frac{\Gamma\{x \mapsto \tau\} \vdash e : \tau \qquad \sigma = \texttt{generalize}(\tau, \text{ftv}(\Gamma))}{\langle \text{VAL-REC}(x, e), \Gamma \rangle \to \Gamma\{x \mapsto \sigma\}}. \qquad (\text{VALREC})$$

The rule is made deterministic by initially using a fresh α to stand for τ, then once τ is known, adding the constraint $\alpha \sim \tau$:

$$\frac{\begin{array}{c} C, \Gamma\{x \mapsto \alpha\} \vdash e : \tau \qquad \alpha \text{ is fresh} \\ \theta(C \wedge \alpha \sim \tau) \text{ is satisfied} \qquad \theta\Gamma = \Gamma \\ \sigma = \texttt{generalize}(\theta\alpha, \text{ftv}(\Gamma)) \end{array}}{\langle \text{VAL-REC}(x, e), \Gamma \rangle \to \Gamma\{x \mapsto \sigma\}}. \qquad (\text{VALREC with constraints})$$

439c. ⟨*infer and bind type for* `VALREC` `(x, e)` *for nano-ML* 439c⟩≡ (439a)

```
let val alpha    = freshtyvar ()
    val Gamma'   = bindtyscheme (x, FORALL ([], alpha), Gamma)
    val (tau, c) = typeof (e, Gamma')
    val theta    = solve (c /\ alpha ~ tau)
    val sigma    = generalize (tysubst theta alpha, freetyvarsGamma Gamma)
in  (bindtyscheme (x, sigma, Gamma), typeSchemeString sigma)
end
```

7.6.5 *Primitives*

As in Typed μScheme, each primitive has a value and a type. Most of nano-ML's primitives are just as in Typed μScheme; only a few are shown below. As in Chapters 5 and 6, the values are defined using higher-order functions `unaryOp`, `binaryOp`, and `arithOp`, which are defined in the Supplement. The values are unchanged, except that errors raise `BugInTypeInference`, not `BugInTypeChecking`.

A primitive may have a polymorphic type scheme, but type schemes aren't coded directly. Instead, each primitive is coded with a type that may have free type variables, and when the primitive is installed in the initial type environment, its type is generalized. Types are shorter and easier to read than type schemes.

440a. ⟨*primitives for nano-ML* :: 440a⟩≡ (S425c)

```
("null?", unaryOp  (fn NIL => BOOLV true | _ => BOOLV false),
          funtype ([listtype alpha], booltype)) ::
("cons",  binaryOp (fn (a, b) => PAIR (a, b)),
          funtype ([alpha, listtype alpha], listtype alpha)) ::
("car",   unaryOp
            (fn (PAIR (car, _)) => car
              | NIL => raise RuntimeError "car applied to empty list"
              | _   => raise BugInTypeInference "car applied to non-list"),
          funtype ([listtype alpha], alpha)) ::
("cdr",   unaryOp
            (fn (PAIR (_, cdr)) => cdr
              | NIL => raise RuntimeError "cdr applied to empty list"
              | _   => raise BugInTypeInference "cdr applied to non-list"),
          funtype ([listtype alpha], listtype alpha)) ::
```

The other primitive worth showing here is `error`. Its type, $\forall\alpha, \beta \,.\, \alpha \to \beta$, tells us something interesting about its behavior. The type suggests that `error` can produce an arbitrary β without ever consuming one. Such a miracle is impossible; what the type tells us is that the `error` function never returns normally. In nano-ML, a function of this type either halts the interpreter or fails to terminate; in full ML, a function of this type could also raise an exception.

440b. ⟨*primitives for nano-ML and* μ*ML* :: 440b⟩≡ (S425c)

```
("error", unaryOp (fn v => raise RuntimeError (valueString v)),
          funtype ([alpha], beta)) ::
```

The remaining primitives are relegated to the Supplement.

7.6.6 *Predefined functions*

Nano-ML's predefined functions are nearly identical to μScheme's predefined functions, except for association lists. In nano-ML, an association list is represented as a list of pairs, not a list of two-element lists. This representation is needed so that keys and values can have different types. And if a key in an association list is not bound, `find` can't return the empty list, because the empty list might not have the right type—instead, `find` causes a checked run-time error. To avert such errors, nano-ML defines a `bound?` function. Functions `bind`, `find`, and `bound?` are defined in the Supplement; only their types are shown here:

440c. ⟨*types of predefined nano-ML functions* 440c⟩≡

```
(check-principal-type bind
   (forall ['a 'b] ('a 'b (list (pair 'a 'b)) -> (list (pair 'a 'b)))))
(check-principal-type find
   (forall ['a 'b] ('a (list (pair 'a 'b)) -> 'b)))
(check-principal-type bound?
   (forall ['a 'b] ('a (list (pair 'a 'b)) -> bool)))
```

7.7 HINDLEY-MILNER AS IT REALLY IS

The Hindley-Milner type system has been used in many languages, but the first is the one Milner himself worked on: Standard ML. In Standard ML, as in most other languages based on Hindley-Milner, a programmer can mix inferred types with explicit types. For example, instead of `type-lambda`, Standard ML allows explicit type variables after a `val` or `fun` keyword. And instead of `@`, Standard ML offers a *type-ascription* form $(e : \tau)$. Where an `@` form gives the type at which a polymorphic value is instantiated, an ascription gives the type of the resulting instance. As an example of explicit instantiation, the following Typed μScheme code instantiates polymorphic list functions `null?`, `car`, and `cdr`:

441a. ⟨*sum function for Typed μScheme* 441a⟩≡
```
(val-rec [sum : ((list int) -> int)]
    (lambda ([ns : (list int)])
       (if ([@ null? int] ns)
           0
           (+ ([@ car int] ns) (sum ([@ cdr int] ns))))))
```

In Standard ML, type ascription can be used to give the types of the instances of the corresponding functions, `null`, `hd`, and `tl`, as well as the parameter `ns`:

441b. ⟨*sum function for Standard ML* 441b⟩≡
```
val rec sum =
  fn (ns : int list) =>
    if (null : int list -> bool) ns then 0
    else (hd : int list -> int) ns + sum ((tl : int list -> int list) ns)
```

The Hindley-Milner type system is just a starting point. A good next step is functional language Haskell, whose type system combines Hindley-Milner type inference with operator overloading. Most implementations of Haskell also support more general polymorphism; for example, the Glasgow Haskell Compiler provides an explicit `forall` that supports lambda-bound variables with polymorphic types.

7.8 SUMMARY

Type inference changed the landscape of functional languages. Milner (1978) presented his type-inference algorithm just 4 years after Reynolds (1974) described the polymorphic calculus underlying Typed μScheme. Over 40 years later, although it has been extended and elaborated in many innovative ways, Milner's type inference remains a sweet spot in the design of typed languages.

Milner's original formulation manipulates only substitutions generated by unification. From unifications to constraints is just a small step, but the constraint-based, "generate-and-solve" model of type inference has proven resilient and extensible. For type inference today, it is the model of choice.

7.8.1 *Key words and phrases*

AT LEAST AS GENERAL The relation of a TYPE or a TYPE SCHEME to its INSTANCES. For example, a `check-type` test checks if an expression's PRINCIPAL TYPE is at least as general as the type scheme written in the test.

CONSTRAINT An EQUALITY CONSTRAINT.

CONSTRAINT SOLVER An algorithm that finds a SUBSTITUTION that solves a CONSTRAINT. Constraint C is solved by θ if all the SIMPLE EQUALITY CONSTRAINTS in θC relate identical TYPES. To work in type inference, a constraint solver must find a MOST GENERAL substitution.

EQUALITY CONSTRAINT A constraint or requirement on TYPES that must be true if a program is to be well typed. Formed by writing conjunctions of SIMPLE EQUALITY CONSTRAINTS, each of which takes the form $\tau_1 \sim \tau_2$.

GENERALIZATION The process of creating a TYPE SCHEME from a TYPE by quantifying over those free type variables that are not also free in the environment, if any. In ML, when an expression is bound to a LET-BOUND VARIABLE, its type is automatically generalized.

INSTANCE A TYPE obtained from another type by SUBSTITUTING for type variables. Also, a TYPE SCHEME obtained from another type scheme by first substituting for bound type variables, then GENERALIZING over variables in the range of the substitution.

INSTANTIATION The process of creating a TYPE from a TYPE SCHEME by substituting for the quantified type variables, if any. In ML, when a variable is used, its type is automatically instantiated.

λ-BOUND VARIABLE A formal parameter to a function. Compare with LET-BOUND VARIABLE.

LET-BOUND VARIABLE A variable introduced by `let`, `let*`, `letrec`, `val`, or `val-rec`. Compare with λ-BOUND VARIABLE.

MONOTYPE A monomorphic type. May be a TYPE or may be a TYPE SCHEME that quantifies over an empty list of type variables. In ML, every λ-bound variable has a monotype. Compare with POLYTYPE.

MOST GENERAL Given a set of SUBSTITUTIONS, a substitution θ is a *most general* substitution if any other member of the set can be obtained by composing θ with another substitution. Or given a set of TYPES, a type τ is a most general type if any other member of the set can be obtained from τ by substitution.

POLYTYPE A TYPE SCHEME that may be instantiated in more than one way. That is, one that quantifies over a nonempty list of type variables. In ML, only a let-bound variable may have a polytype. Compare with MONOTYPE.

PRINCIPAL TYPE A type that can be ascribed to an expression such that any other type ascribable to the expression is an INSTANCE of the principal type. In other words, a MOST GENERAL type of an expression. Also used as shorthand for PRINCIPAL TYPE SCHEME, which is similar. In ML, principal type schemes are unique up to renaming of bound type variables.

SUBSTITUTION A finite map from type variables to TYPES. Also defines maps from types to types, CONSTRAINTS to constraints, and others.

TYPE In ML, a type formed using type constructors, type variables, and function arrows. Does not include any quantification. Compare with TYPE SCHEME.

TYPE INFERENCE An algorithm that reconstructs and checks types in a program that does not necessarily include explicit type declarations for let-bound or λ-bound variables. Also called TYPE RECONSTRUCTION.

TYPE SCHEME A quantified type with exactly one universal quantifier, which is the outermost part of the type. The set of quantified variables may be empty, in which case the type scheme is equivalent to a TYPE.

UNIFICATION An algorithm that finds a MOST GENERAL SUBSTITUTION that makes two types equal. Can be used to implement a CONSTRAINT SOLVER, or vice versa.

7.8.2 Further reading

The original work on the Hindley-Milner type system appears in two papers. Milner (1978) emphasizes the use of polymorphism in programming, and Hindley (1969) emphasizes the existence of principal types. Milner describes Algorithm W, which is the "method of explicit substitutions" in this chapter. Damas and Milner (1982) show that Algorithm W finds the most general type of every term.

Odersky, Sulzmann, and Wehr (1999) present HM(X), a general system for implementing Hindley-Milner type inference with abstract constraints. This system is considerably more ambitious than nano-ML; it allows a very broad class of constraints, and it decouples constraint solving from type inference. Pottier and Rémy (2005) use the power of HM(X) to explore a number of extensions to ML. Their tutorial includes code written in the related language OCaml.

Vytiniotis, Peyton Jones, and Schrijvers (2010) argue that as type systems grow more sophisticated, Milner's LET rule makes it harder, not easier, to work with the associated constraints. They recommend that by default, the types of LET-bound names should *not* be generalized.

In the presence of mutable reference cells, Milner's LET rule is unsound. While the unsoundness can be patched by various annotations on type variables, a better approach is to generalize the type of a LET-bound variable only if the expression to which the variable is bound is a *syntactic value*, such as a variable, a literal, or a `lambda` expression (Wright 1995).

Cardelli (1997) provides a general tutorial on type sytems. Cardelli (1987) has also written a tutorial specifically on type inference; it includes an implementation in Modula-2. The implementation represents type variables using mutable cells and does not use explicit substitutions.

Peyton Jones et al. (2007) show how by adding type annotations, one can implement type inference for types in which a $\forall$ quantifier may appear to the left of an arrow—that is, types in which functions may require callers to pass polymorphic arguments. Such types are an example of *higher-rank types*. The authors present both nondeterministic and deterministic rules. The paper is accompanied by code, and it repays careful study.

Material on Haskell can be found at `www.haskell.org`. A nice implementation of Haskell's type system, in Haskell, is presented by Jones (1999).

7.9 EXERCISES

The exercises are summarized in Table 7.4 on the next page. There are many that I like, but type inference takes center stage.

- In Exercises 18 and 19 (pages 448 and 449), you implement a constraint solver and finish the implementation of type inference. Before you tackle the constraint solver, I recommend that you do Exercises 12 and 16, which will help you solve conjunction constraints in the right way.
- Exercises 1 and 5 offer nice insights into properties of the type system.
- In Exercises 21 to 23, you extend nano-ML. Of these exercises, Exercise 21 (pair primitives) is probably the easiest, and it's useful. But Exercise 22 offers the most satisfying benefit to the nano-ML programmer.

Table 7.4: Synopsis of all the exercises, with most relevant sections

Exercises	*Section*	*Notes*
1	Ch. 5	Using type inference to get a term of an unusual type.
2 to 4	7.4.3	Substitutions: understand idempotence; confirm properties of the implementation; substitution preserves constraint satisfaction (§7.5.3).
5 to 7	7.4	Principal types: equivalence, uniqueness up to equivalence. Most general instances of type schemes.
8 to 11	7.4, 7.5	Writing constraint-based rules; consequences of the rules.
12 to 15	7.5.3	Constraints: solvability of conjunctions, soundness of rules for the solver.
16 to 20	7.5, 7.6	Implementation of constraint solving and type inference.
21 to 23	7.6	Extending nano-ML: pairs, a list constructor, mutable reference cells.
24 and 25	7.6	Improving error messages; elaborating untyped nano-ML terms into Typed μScheme terms.

7.9.1 *Retrieval practice and other short questions*

A. In lambda calculus, the type of the successor function on Church numerals is $(\forall\alpha.(\alpha \to \alpha) \to (\alpha \to \alpha)) \to (\forall\alpha.(\alpha \to \alpha) \to (\alpha \to \alpha))$. This type is valid in Typed μScheme, with kind $*$, but it is not a valid Hindley-Milner type. Why not?

B. In Typed μScheme, a programmer may instantiate any expression using the instantiation form, written with the `@` operator. In nano-ML, instantiation is performed automatically. What syntactic forms are automatically instantiated?

C. To ensure that types are well formed, Typed μScheme uses a system of kinds. Why doesn't nano-ML need such a system?

D. What kind of a thing is θ? What can a θ be applied to?

E. If θ is applied to a type constructor μ, what are the possible results?

F. What's an example of a substitution that's *not* idempotent?

G. Function type `int` $\times$ `int` $\to$ `int` is printed as `(int int -> int)`. How is it represented in the nano-ML interpreter?

H. The nondeterministic typing rule VAR includes judgment $\tau \leqslant \sigma$. What does the judgment mean? Given a particular σ, if we want a τ satisfying $\tau \leqslant \sigma$, how must such a τ be formed?

I. Suppose that Γ's only binding is $\{\texttt{f} \mapsto \forall\alpha.\alpha \to \beta\}$. What are Γ's free type variables?

J. If $\sigma = \texttt{generalize}(\tau, \mathcal{A})$ and $\mathcal{A}$ is empty, what do we know about the free type variables of σ?

K. In the nondeterministic type system, does term `(lambda (x y) x)` have type `(int int -> int)`?

L. What is the principal type (or principal type scheme) of `(lambda (x y) x)`?

M. In the initial basis, what principal type scheme should be assigned to the primitive function "`null?`"?

N. What's the difference, if any, between substitution $\theta_1 \circ \theta_2$ and substitution $\theta_2 \circ \theta_1$?

O. What's the difference, if any, between constraint $C_1 \wedge C_2$ and constraint $C_2 \wedge C_1$?

P. What's the difference, if any, between constraint $\tau_1 \sim \tau_2$ and constraint $\tau_2 \sim \tau_1$?

Q. For type inference, why do I recommend against implementing the method of explicit substitutions? What's an example of a typing rule that illustrates the difficulties of this method?

R. Can the constraint $\alpha \sim$ `bool` be satisfied? If so, by what substitution? What about constraint $\alpha \times$ `int` $\sim$ `bool` $\times \alpha$? What about constraint $\alpha \times$ `int` $\sim$ `bool` $\times \beta$?

S. If constraint $\tau \sim \tau_1 \to \tau_2$ is to be satisfied, what form must τ have?

T. If θ_1 solves C_1 and θ_2 solves C_2, does $\theta_2 \circ \theta_1$ solve $C_1 \wedge C_2$?

U. What's the algorithm for solving a constraint of the form $C_1 \wedge C_2$?

V. In the interpreter, why does Γ have a different representation than it did in Chapter 6?

W. Given a list of constraints $C_1, \ldots, C_n$, what interpreter function do you call to combine them into a single constraint $C_1 \wedge \cdots \wedge C_n$? (The combined constraint may also be written $\bigwedge\{C_1, \ldots, C_n\}$.)

X. When a constraint can't be solved, what interpreter function should you call?

Y. In chunk 438e, the combination of `f` and `actuals` into a single list is a little awkward. How does the code work? What's the alternative? Why do you think I coded it this way?

7.9.2 *Manipulating type inference*

1. *Functions with seemingly impossible types.*

   (a) Without using any primitives, and without using `letrec`, write a function in nano-ML that has type $\forall \alpha, \beta \,.\, \alpha \to \beta$.

   (b) Based on your experience, if you see a function whose result type is a quantified type variable, what should you conclude about that function?

7.9.3 *Properties of substitutions*

2. *Idempotence.* A substitution θ is *idempotent* if $\theta \circ \theta = \theta$.

   (a) Give an example of a substitution $\theta_x = (\alpha \mapsto \tau)$ that is *not* idempotent.

   (b) Prove that $\theta_x \circ \theta_x \neq \theta_x$.

   (c) Prove that if $\alpha \notin \text{ftv}(\tau)$, then $(\alpha \mapsto \tau)$ is idempotent.

   (d) Instrument the `|-->` function in the interpreter so that if $\alpha \in \text{ftv}(\tau)$, calling α `|-->` τ raises the exception `BugInTypeInference`.

3. *Code that produces substitutions.* Go back to function `tysubst` from Chapter 6 on page 371, and look at the inner function `subst`, which is a function from types to types. Given that `varenv` is finite, show that `subst` satisfies each of the properties claimed for a substitution θ on pages 409 and 410.

4. *Substitution preserves satisfaction.* Look at the definition of satisfaction in Section 7.5.3, and prove that if constraint C is satisfied and θ is a substitution, then θC is also satisfied.

7.9.4 *Properties of type schemes and principal types*

5. *Most general instances.* Prove that for any type scheme σ, there is a *most general* instance $\tau \leqslant \sigma$. An instance τ is a most general instance of σ if and only if $\forall \tau' . \tau' \leqslant \sigma \implies \tau' \leqslant \tau$.

6. *Uniqueness of principal types.* Principal types are unique up to renaming of variables.

   (a) Give an example of an environment and a term such that the term has more than one principal type. Show two different principal types.

   (b) Prove that if $\Gamma \vdash e : \tau_P$ and $\Gamma \vdash e : \tau'_P$, and both τ_P and τ'_P are principal types for e in Γ, then τ'_P can be obtained from τ_P by renaming variables. Use the definition of principal type on page 416.

7. *Equivalence of type schemes.* The implementation of `check-principal-type` takes as inputs an expression e and a type scheme σ. It infers a principal type scheme σ_P for e, then checks to see that σ_P is equivalent to σ. The two type schemes are equivalent if $\sigma_P \leqslant \sigma$ and $\sigma \leqslant \sigma_P$, which is to say that they have the same instances. But in the *Definition of Standard ML*, equivalence of type schemes is defined syntactically:

   > Two type schemes σ and σ' are considered equal if they can be obtained from each other by renaming and reordering of bound type variables, and deleting type variables from the prefix which do not occur in the body. [The *prefix* is the list of variables between the $\forall$ and the dot. —NR]

   Prove that these definitions are equivalent.

   (a) Prove that renaming a bound type variable in σ does not change its set of instances.

   (b) Prove that reordering bound type variables in σ does not change its set of instances. It suffices to prove that adjacent type variables can be swapped without changing the set of instances.

   (c) Prove that if a type variable appears in the prefix of σ but does not appear in the body, then removing that variable from the prefix does not change the set of instances.

   (d) Conclude that if type schemes σ and σ' are considered equal according to the *Definition of Standard ML*, then they have the same instances, and so they are also considered equal by `check-principal-type`.

7.9.5 *Typing rules and their properties*

8. *Adding constraints to typing rules.* Consulting the rules summary on pages 450 and 451, rewrite these rules to use explicit constraints:

   (a) The rule for BEGIN:

   $$\frac{\Gamma \vdash e_i : \tau_i, \quad 1 \leq i \leq n}{\Gamma \vdash \text{BEGIN}(e_1, \ldots, e_n) : \tau_n}. \qquad \text{(BEGIN)}$$

   (b) The rule for LAMBDA:

   $$\frac{\Gamma\{x_1 \mapsto \tau_1, \ldots, x_n \mapsto \tau_n\} \vdash e : \tau}{\Gamma \vdash \text{LAMBDA}(\langle x_1, \ldots, x_n \rangle, e) : \tau_1 \times \cdots \times \tau_n \to \tau}. \qquad \text{(LAMBDA)}$$

9. *Recursive definitions.* In nano-ML, the parser enforces the restriction that the right-hand side of a `val-rec` definition must be a `lambda`. But the typing rules permit a definition of the form `(val-rec x x)`. Given this definition, what type scheme σ do the rules say is inferred for `x`? Is that σ inhabited by any values? In other words, is there a value that could be stored in ρ that is consistent with that σ?

10. *Absence of free type variables in top-level type environments.* Prove that in nano-ML, a top-level type environment never contains a free type variable. Your proof should be by induction on the sequence of steps used to create Γ:

    (a) Prove that an empty type environment contains no free type variables.

    (b) Using the code in chunk S425c, show that if Γ contains no free type variables, then `addPrim(`(x, p, τ)`, `(Γ, ρ)`)` returns a pair in which the new Γ' also contains no free type variables.

    (c) Show that if Γ contains no free type variables, and if Γ' is specified by $\langle \text{VAL}(x, e), \Gamma \rangle \to \Gamma'$, then Γ' contains no free type variables.

    (d) Show that if Γ contains no free type variables, and if Γ' is specified by $\langle \text{VAL-REC}(x, e), \Gamma \rangle \to \Gamma'$, then Γ' contains no free type variables.

11. *Consistency of type inference with nondeterministic rules.* Prove that whenever there is a derivation of a judgment $\theta\Gamma \vdash e : \tau$ using the rules for explicit substitutions in Section 7.5.1, then if $\Gamma' = \theta\Gamma$, there is also a derivation of $\Gamma' \vdash e : \tau$ using the nondeterministic rules in Section 7.4.5.

    To prove this property for nano-ML would be tedious; nano-ML has too many syntactic forms. Instead, prove it for a subset, which I'll call "pico-ML," and which has just these forms: `lambda`, function application, variable, and `let`. Both `let` and `lambda` bind exactly one name, and a function application has exactly one argument.

    What about the other direction? If there is a derivation using the nondeterministic rules, is there a corresponding derivation using explicit substitutions? Yes, but the corresponding derivation might not derive the same type. The most we can say about a type derivable using the nondeterministic rules is that it must be an *instance* of the type derived using type inference with explicit substitutions. The type derived using type inference is special, because all other derivable types are instances of it; it is the term's principal type. Proving that a principal type exists and that the type-inference algorithm finds one are problems that are beyond the scope of this book.

7.9.6 *Properties of constraints and constraint solving*

12. *Solvability and conjunction.*

    (a) Using the proof system in Section 7.5.3, prove that if the constraint $C_1 \wedge C_2$ is solvable, then constraints C_1 and C_2 are also solvable.

    (b) Find a particular pair of constraints C_1 and C_2 such that C_1 is solvable, C_2 is solvable, but $C_1 \wedge C_2$ is *not* solvable. *Prove* that $C_1 \wedge C_2$ is not solvable.

13. *Soundness of the* SOLVEDCONJUNCTION *rule.* Using the definition of what it means for a constraint to be satisfied, prove that the SOLVEDCONJUNCTION

rule on page 429 is sound. That is, prove that whenever both premises hold, so does the conclusion. The rule is reproduced here:

$$\frac{\theta_1 C_1 \text{ is satisfied} \qquad \theta_2(\theta_1 C_2) \text{ is satisfied}}{(\theta_2 \circ \theta_1)(C_1 \wedge C_2) \text{ is satisfied}}. \qquad (\text{SOLVEDCONJUNCTION})$$

14. *Soundness of the* SOLVECONAPPCONAPP *rule.* Using the laws for applying substitutions to constraints and to types, prove that the SOLVECONAPPCONAPP rule on page 430 is sound and complete. That is, prove that a substitution θ solves the constraint

$$\text{CONAPP}(\tau, \langle \tau_1, \ldots, \tau_n \rangle) \sim \text{CONAPP}(\tau', \langle \tau_1', \ldots, \tau_n' \rangle)$$

if and only if it also solves the constraint

$$\tau \sim \tau' \wedge \tau_1 \sim \tau_1' \wedge \cdots \wedge \tau_n \sim \tau_n'.$$

15. *Need for an occurs check.* Prove that if τ_2 *mentions* α but is *not equal* to α, then there is no substitution θ such that $\theta\alpha = \theta\tau_2$. (*Hint*: Count type constructors.)

7.9.7 *Implementation of constraint solving and type inference*

16. *Practice with conjunction constraints.* The most common mistake made in constraint solving is to get conjunctions wrong (Section 7.5.3). Before you tackle a solver, this exercise asks you to develop some examples and to verify that the naïve approach works sometimes, but not always.

    (a) Find two constraints C_1 and C_2 and substitutions θ_1 and θ_2 such that
    - C_1 has a free type variable,
    - C_2 has a free type variable,
    - θ_1 solves C_1,
    - θ_2 solves C_2, and
    - $\theta_2 \circ \theta_1$ solves $C_1 \wedge C_2$.

    (b) Find two constraints C_1 and C_2 and substitutions θ_1 and θ_2 such that
    - C_1 has a free type variable,
    - C_2 has a free type variable,
    - θ_1 solves C_1,
    - θ_2 solves C_2, and
    - $\theta_2 \circ \theta_1$ does *not* solve $C_1 \wedge C_2$.

17. *Understanding a recursive solver.* Page 431 discusses the solution of constraint 7.1, which involves synthesizing and solving constraints 7.2 to 7.11. List the numbered constraints *in the order that they would be solved* by a recursive solver.

18. *Implementing a constraint solver.* Using the ideas in Section 7.5.3, implement a function `solve` which takes as argument a constraint of type `con` and returns an idempotent substitution of type `subst`. (If a substitution is created using only the value `idsubst` and the functions `|-->` and `compose`, and if `|-->` is used as described in Exercise 2, then the substitution is guaranteed to be idempotent.) The resulting substitution should solve the constraint, obeying the law

    `solves (solve` C`,` C`).`

    If the constraint has no solution, call function `unsatisfiableEquality` from chunk 437a, which raises the `TypeError` exception.

19. *Implementing type inference.* Complete the definitions of functions `ty` and `literal` so they never raise `LeftAsExercise`. If your code discovers a type error, it should raise the exception `TypeError`.

    The function `literal` must give a suitable type to integer literals, Boolean literals, symbol literals (which have type `sym`), and quoted lists in which all elements have the same type (including the empty list). For example, the value `'(1 2 3)` must have type `int list`. Values created using `CLOSURE` or `PRIMITIVE` cannot possibly appear in a `LITERAL` node, so if your `literal` function sees such a value, it can raise `BugInTypeInference`.

    You will probably find it helpful to refer to the typing rules for nano-ML, which are summarized in Figures 7.5 to 7.8 on pages 450 and 451. And don't overlook the `typesof` function.

20. *Constraint solving from unification.* Milner's original formulation of type inference relies on unification of explicit substitutions. To show that unification is as powerful as constraint solving, suppose that you have a function `unify` such that given any two types τ_1 and τ_2, `unify(`τ_1`, `τ_2`)` returns a substitution θ such that $\theta\tau_1 = \theta\tau_2$, or if no such θ exists, raises an exception. Use `unify` to implement a constraint solver.

    Hint: To help convert a constraint-solving problem into a unification problem, try using the SOLVECONAPPCONAPP rule on page 430 *in reverse.*

7.9.8 *Extending nano-ML*

21. *Pair primitives.* Extend nano-ML with primitives `pair`, `fst`, and `snd`. Give the primitives appropriate types. Function `pair` should be used to create pairs of any type, and functions `fst` and `snd` should retrieve the elements of any pair.

22. *A list constructor.* In nano-ML, the most convenient way to build a large list is by using a large expression that contains a great many applications of `cons`. But as described in the sidebar on page 430, type inference using my data structures requires time and space that is quadratic in the number of applications of `cons`. The problem can be addressed through more efficient representations, but there is a surprisingly simple fix through language design: extend nano-ML with a `LIST` form of expression, which should work the same way as Standard ML's square-bracket-and-comma syntax. The form should obey this rule of operational semantics:

$$\frac{\langle e_1, \rho\rangle \Downarrow v_1 \qquad \cdots \qquad \langle e_n, \rho\rangle \Downarrow v_n \qquad v = \text{PAIR}(v_1, \text{PAIR}(v_2, \ldots, \text{PAIR}(v_n, \text{NIL})))}{\langle \text{LIST}(e_1, \ldots, e_n), \rho\rangle \Downarrow v}. \qquad (\text{LIST})$$

   And here is a nondeterministic typing rule:

$$\frac{\Gamma \vdash e_1 : \tau \qquad \cdots \qquad \Gamma \vdash e_n : \tau}{\Gamma \vdash \text{LIST}(e_1, \ldots, e_n) : \tau\ \texttt{list}}. \qquad (\text{LIST})$$

   Implement a list constructor for nano-ML, in the following four steps:

   (a) Extend the abstract syntax for `exp` with a case `LIST of exp list`.

   (b) Extend the parser to accept `(list` $e_1\ \cdots\ e_n$`)` to create a `LIST` node. As a model, use the parser for `begin`.

   (c) Extend the evaluator to handle the `LIST` case.

   (d) Extend type inference to handle the `LIST` case.

$$\boxed{\Gamma \vdash e : \tau}$$

$$\textsc{Var}\quad \frac{\Gamma(x) = \sigma \qquad \tau \leqslant \sigma}{\Gamma \vdash x : \tau}$$

$$\textsc{If}\quad \frac{\Gamma \vdash e_1 : \texttt{bool} \qquad \Gamma \vdash e_2 : \tau \qquad \Gamma \vdash e_3 : \tau}{\Gamma \vdash \textsc{if}(e_1, e_2, e_3) : \tau}$$

$$\textsc{Apply}\quad \frac{\Gamma \vdash e_i : \tau_i, \quad 1 \le i \le n \qquad \Gamma \vdash e : \tau_1 \times \cdots \times \tau_n \to \tau}{\Gamma \vdash \textsc{apply}(e, e_1, \ldots, e_n) : \tau}$$

$$\textsc{Lambda}\quad \frac{\Gamma\{x_1 \mapsto \tau_1, \ldots, x_n \mapsto \tau_n\} \vdash e : \tau}{\Gamma \vdash \textsc{lambda}(\langle x_1, \ldots, x_n \rangle, e) : \tau_1 \times \cdots \times \tau_n \to \tau}$$

$$\textsc{Let}\quad \frac{\begin{array}{c}\Gamma \vdash e_i : \tau_i, \quad 1 \le i \le n \\ \sigma_i = \texttt{generalize}(\tau_i, \text{ftv}(\Gamma)), \quad 1 \le i \le n \\ \Gamma\{x_1 \mapsto \sigma_1, \ldots, x_n \mapsto \sigma_n\} \vdash e : \tau\end{array}}{\Gamma \vdash \textsc{let}(\langle x_1, e_1, \ldots, x_n, e_n \rangle, e) : \tau}$$

$$\textsc{Letrec}\quad \frac{\begin{array}{c}\Gamma' = \Gamma\{x_1 \mapsto \tau_1, \ldots, x_n \mapsto \tau_n\} \\ \Gamma' \vdash e_i : \tau_i, \quad 1 \le i \le n \\ \sigma_i = \texttt{generalize}(\tau_i, \text{ftv}(\Gamma)), \quad 1 \le i \le n \\ \Gamma\{x_1 \mapsto \sigma_1, \ldots, x_n \mapsto \sigma_n\} \vdash e : \tau\end{array}}{\Gamma \vdash \textsc{letrec}(\langle x_1, e_1, \ldots, x_n, e_n \rangle, e) : \tau}$$

$$\textsc{Letstar}\quad \frac{\Gamma \vdash \textsc{let}(\langle x_1, e_1 \rangle, \textsc{letstar}(\langle x_2, e_2, \ldots, x_n, e_n \rangle, e)) : \tau \qquad n > 0}{\Gamma \vdash \textsc{letstar}(\langle x_1, e_1, \ldots, x_n, e_n \rangle, e) : \tau}$$

$$\textsc{EmptyLetstar}\quad \frac{\Gamma \vdash e : \tau}{\Gamma \vdash \textsc{letstar}(\langle\rangle, e) : \tau} \qquad \textsc{Begin}\quad \frac{\Gamma \vdash e_i : \tau_i, \quad 1 \le i \le n}{\Gamma \vdash \textsc{begin}(e_1, \ldots, e_n) : \tau_n} \qquad \textsc{EmptyBegin}\quad \frac{}{\Gamma \vdash \textsc{begin}() : \texttt{unit}}$$

Figure 7.5: Nondeterministic typing rules for expressions

$$\boxed{\langle d, \Gamma \rangle \to \Gamma'}$$

$$\textsc{Val}\quad \frac{\Gamma \vdash e : \tau \qquad \sigma = \texttt{generalize}(\tau, \text{ftv}(\Gamma))}{\langle \textsc{val}(x, e), \Gamma \rangle \to \Gamma\{x \mapsto \sigma\}}$$

$$\textsc{ValRec}\quad \frac{\Gamma\{x \mapsto \tau\} \vdash e : \tau \qquad \sigma = \texttt{generalize}(\tau, \text{ftv}(\Gamma))}{\langle \textsc{val-rec}(x, e), \Gamma \rangle \to \Gamma\{x \mapsto \sigma\}} \qquad \textsc{Exp}\quad \frac{\langle \textsc{val}(\texttt{it}, e), \Gamma \rangle \to \Gamma'}{\langle \textsc{exp}(e), \Gamma \rangle \to \Gamma'}$$

$$\textsc{Define}\quad \frac{\langle \textsc{val-rec}(f, \textsc{lambda}(\langle x_1, \ldots, x_n \rangle, e)), \Gamma \rangle \to \Gamma'}{\langle \textsc{define}(f, (\langle x_1, \ldots, x_n \rangle, e)), \Gamma \rangle \to \Gamma'}$$

Figure 7.6: Nondeterministic typing rules for definitions

$$\boxed{C, \Gamma \vdash e : \tau}$$

VAR

$$\frac{\Gamma(x) = \forall \alpha_1, \ldots, \alpha_n . \tau \qquad \alpha'_1, \ldots, \alpha'_n \text{ are fresh and distinct}}{\mathbf{T}, \Gamma \vdash x : ((\alpha_1 \mapsto \alpha'_1) \circ \cdots \circ (\alpha_n \mapsto \alpha'_n))\, \tau}$$

IF

$$\frac{C, \Gamma \vdash e_1, e_2, e_3 : \tau_1, \tau_2, \tau_3}{C \wedge \tau_1 \sim \texttt{bool} \wedge \tau_2 \sim \tau_3, \Gamma \vdash \text{IF}(e_1, e_2, e_3) : \tau_2}$$

APPLY

$$\frac{C, \Gamma \vdash e, e_1, \ldots, e_n : \hat{\tau}, \tau_1, \ldots, \tau_n \qquad \alpha \text{ is fresh}}{C \wedge \hat{\tau} \sim \tau_1 \times \cdots \times \tau_n \to \alpha, \Gamma \vdash \text{APPLY}(e, e_1, \ldots, e_n) : \alpha}$$

LET

$$\frac{\begin{array}{c} C, \Gamma \vdash e_1, \ldots, e_n : \tau_1, \ldots, \tau_n \\ \theta C \text{ is satisfied} \qquad \theta \text{ is idempotent} \\ C' = \bigwedge\{\alpha \sim \theta\alpha \mid \alpha \in \operatorname{dom}\theta \cap \operatorname{ftv}(\Gamma)\} \\ \sigma_i = \texttt{generalize}(\theta\tau_i, \operatorname{ftv}(\Gamma) \cup \operatorname{ftv}(C')), \quad 1 \le i \le n \\ C_b, \Gamma\{x_1 \mapsto \sigma_1, \ldots, x_n \mapsto \sigma_n\} \vdash e : \tau \end{array}}{C' \wedge C_b, \Gamma \vdash \text{LET}(\langle x_1, e_1, \ldots, x_n, e_n \rangle, e) : \tau}$$

LETREC

$$\frac{\begin{array}{c} e_1, \ldots, e_n \text{ are all LAMBDA expressions} \\ \Gamma' = \Gamma\{x_1 \mapsto \alpha_1, \ldots, x_n \mapsto \alpha_n\}, \text{ where all } \alpha_i\text{'s are distinct and fresh} \\ C_r, \Gamma' \vdash e_1, \ldots, e_n : \tau_1, \ldots, \tau_n \\ C = C_r \wedge \tau_1 \sim \alpha_1 \wedge \cdots \wedge \tau_n \sim \alpha_n \\ \theta C \text{ is satisfied} \qquad \theta \text{ is idempotent} \\ C' = \bigwedge\{\alpha \sim \theta\alpha \mid \alpha \in \operatorname{dom}\theta \cap \operatorname{ftv}(\Gamma)\} \\ \sigma_i = \texttt{generalize}(\theta\tau_i, \operatorname{ftv}(\Gamma) \cup \operatorname{ftv}(C')), \quad 1 \le i \le n \\ C_b, \Gamma\{x_1 \mapsto \sigma_1, \ldots, x_n \mapsto \sigma_n\} \vdash e : \tau \end{array}}{C' \wedge C_b, \Gamma \vdash \text{LETREC}(\langle x_1, e_1, \ldots, x_n, e_n \rangle, e) : \tau}$$

Figure 7.7: Constraint-based typing rules for expressions

$$\boxed{\langle d, \Gamma \rangle \to \Gamma'}$$

VAL

$$\frac{\begin{array}{c} C, \Gamma \vdash e : \tau \\ \theta C \text{ is satisfied} \qquad \theta\Gamma = \Gamma \\ \sigma = \texttt{generalize}(\theta\tau, \operatorname{ftv}(\Gamma)) \end{array}}{\langle \text{VAL}(x, e), \Gamma \rangle \to \Gamma\{x \mapsto \sigma\}}$$

VALREC with constraints

$$\frac{\begin{array}{c} C, \Gamma\{x \mapsto \alpha\} \vdash e : \tau \qquad \alpha \text{ is fresh} \\ \theta(C \wedge \alpha \sim \tau) \text{ is satisfied} \qquad \theta\Gamma = \Gamma \\ \sigma = \texttt{generalize}(\theta\alpha, \operatorname{ftv}(\Gamma)) \end{array}}{\langle \text{VAL-REC}(x, e), \Gamma \rangle \to \Gamma\{x \mapsto \sigma\}}$$

Figure 7.8: Constraint-based typing rules for definitions

23. *Mutable reference cells and the value restriction.*

    (a) Add new primitives `ref`, `!`, and `:=` with the same meanings as in full ML. You will have to use ML "ref cells" to add a new form of `value`, and you will have to extend the `primitiveEquality` function to compare ref cells for equality. But you should not have to touch environments or the evaluator.

    (b) Write a program in extended nano-ML that subverts the type system, i.e., that makes the evaluator raise the exception `BugInTypeInference`. For example, try writing a program that applies `+` to a non-integer argument. (*Hint:* `(ref (lambda (x) x))`.)

    (c) Restore type safety by implementing the "value restriction" on polymorphism: the type of `val`-bound name is generalized only if the name is bound to syntactic value (a variable, a literal, or a λ-abstraction).

7.9.9 *Improving the interpreter*

24. *Improved error messages.* Improve the interpreter's error messages:

    (a) If a type error arises from a function application, show the function and show the arguments. Show what types of arguments the function expects and what the types the arguments actually have.

    (b) If a type error arises from an IF expression, show either that the type of the condition is inconsistent with `bool` or that the two branches do not have consistent types.

    (c) Highlight the differences between inconsistent types. For example, if your message says

    ```
    function cons expected int * int list, got int * int,
    ```

    this is better than saying "cannot unify `int` and `int list`," but it is not as good as showing *which* argument caused the problem, e.g.,

    ```
    function cons expected int * >>int list<<, got int * >>int<<.
    ```

    To complete this part, it would be helpful to define a more sophisticated version of `unsatisfiableEquality`, which returns strings in which types that don't match are highlighted.

    To associate a type error with a function application, look at the APPLY rule on page 421 and see whether the constraint in the premise is solvable, and if so, whether the constraint in the conclusion is solvable.

25. *Elaboration into explicitly typed terms.* Change the implementation of type inference so that instead of inferring and checking types in one step, the interpreter takes an untyped term and infers an explicitly typed term in Typed μScheme. Adding information to the original code is an example of *elaboration*. I recommend copying the syntax of Typed μScheme into a submodule of your interpreter, as in

    ```
    structure Typed = struct
      datatype exp = ...
        ⋮
    end
    ```

    You can then translate `LAMBDA` to `Typed.LAMBDA`, and so on.

Part II. Programming at Scale

Programming at scale is supported by many techniques, tools, and language features, but the key enabling idea is to hide information. The role of a programming language is to hide information about the representation of data, which is called *data abstraction*. There are two techniques: *abstract data types*, which uses a type system to limit access to representation, and *objects*, which uses environments to limit access to representation. These ideas are illustrated by the languages Molecule (Chapter 9) and μSmalltalk (Chapter 10).

To write programs at scale, particularly if you want to describe representations using a type system, you need more data types than can be found in languages like Typed Impcore, Typed μScheme, and nano-ML. To provide suitable types, this part of the book begins with μML, which extends nano-ML with user-defined types. μML's *algebraic data types* give programmers the ability to group parts together, to express choices among forms of a single representation, and to define recursive representations. They also support pattern matching.

Molecule starts with μML's data representation and with Typed μScheme's type system, adding a modules system that can describe interfaces and implementations. Like Typed μScheme, Molecule requires no type inference, only type checking.

μSmalltalk introduces a different programming paradigm: objects. Code doesn't call functions; instead, it sends *messages* to objects, and these messages are dispatched dynamically to *methods*. In μSmalltalk, methods are defined by *classes*, and classes can *inherit* methods from other classes. Dynamic dispatch and inheritance are simple mechanisms, but they have far-reaching consequences. Using them well enables new forms of reuse but requires new ways of thinking.

Molecule and μSmalltalk provide data abstraction in different ways. Both hide representations except from code that is inside the abstraction, but what's considered "inside" is different. Within a Molecule module, an operation can see the representation of any value of any abstract type defined inside the module. Within a μSmalltalk class, an operation can see the representation of just one object: the object on which the operation is defined. The representations of other objects are hidden. These different forms of information hiding lead to different kinds of flexibility. Using Molecule's abstract data types, it is easy to define operations that inspect multiple representations, like an efficient merge of leftist heaps. But it is impossible to define operations that work with new abstractions defined outside the operation's cluster: each operation works only with arguments that have the static types given in its signature. Using μSmalltalk's objects, it is possible to define operations that inspect multiple representations, but to do so requires exposing the representation, violating abstraction. But if abstraction is not violated, then it is easy to use existing operations with new representations: each operation works with any object that responds correctly to the messages in the specification's protocol. These differences in visibility and interoperability are essential differences that apply when comparing any language that uses abstract data types with any language that uses objects.

Other differences between Molecule and Smalltalk apply to a more limited set of languages. For example, Molecule provides code reuse through parametric polymorphism, and μSmalltalk provides code reuse through inheritance. But a language can have abstract data types without having parametric polymorphism, and a language can also have objects without having classes and inheritance. There are also incidental differences; for example, a Molecule module controls which operations are exported to client code, but a Smalltalk class exposes all operations to every client. In the context of its language's semantics, each decision makes good design sense.

CHAPTER 8 CONTENTS

8 User-defined, algebraic types (and pattern matching)

Representation is the essence of programming. . . .
Much more often, strategic breakthrough will come from
redoing the representation of the data or the tables.
This is where the heart of a program lies. Show me
your flowcharts and conceal your tables, and I shall
continue to be mystified. Show me your tables, and I
won't usually need your flowcharts; they'll be obvious.

Fred Brooks, *The Mythical Man-Month*, Chapter 9

Chapters 1 to 7 don't give us many ways to organize data. S-expressions are great, but you might have noticed that they serve as a kind of high-level assembly language on top of which you have to craft your own data structures. For programming at scale, that's not good enough—programmers need to define proper data structures whose shapes and contents are known. Proper data-definition mechanisms must be able to express these possibilities:

- Data can take multiple *forms*, like a C `union`.
- Data can have multiple *parts*, like a C `struct`.
- One or more parts may be like the whole, that is, data can be *recursive*.

All these possibilities can be expressed using *algebraic data types*. Algebraic data types, supplemented by the base types, function types, and array types shown in previous chapters, suffice to describe and typecheck representations of data at any scale. They are ubiquitous in the ML family and in languages derived from it, including Standard ML, OCaml, Haskell, Agda, Coq/Gallina, and Idris.

Algebraic data types can be added to any language; this chapter adds them to nano-ML, making the new language μML. To add algebraic data types requires a new species of value, a new expression form for looking at the values, and a new definition form for introducing the types and values.

The new species of value is a *constructed value*. A constructed value is made by applying some *value constructor* to zero or more other values. In the syntax, however, zero-argument value constructors aren't applied; a zero-argument value constructor is a value all by itself. For example, `'()` is a value constructor for lists, and it expects no arguments, so it is a constructed value. And `cons` is also a value constructor for lists, but it expects arguments, so to make a constructed value, `cons` must be applied to two other values: an element and a list.

A constructed value is interrogated, observed, or eliminated scrutinized by a *case expression*. A case expression provides concise, readable syntax for asking a key question about any datum: how was it formed, and from what parts? A case expression gets the answer by using *patterns*: a pattern can *match* a particular value constructor, and when it does, it can name each of the values to which the constructor was applied. For example, the pattern `(cons y ys)` matches any cons cell, and when it matches, it binds the name `y` to the `car` and `ys` to the `cdr`.

Case expressions and pattern matching eliminate the clutter associated with functions like `null?`, `car`, `cdr`, `fst`, and `snd`. Instead of using such functions, you lay out the possible forms of the data, and for each form, you name the parts directly. The resulting code is short and clear, and it operates at a higher level of abstraction than Scheme code or C code. With the right syntactic sugar, your code can look a lot like algebraic laws (Section 8.4).

A case expression inspects a *scrutinee*, and it includes a sequence of *choices*, each of which associates a pattern with a right-hand side. And if the choices don't cover all possible cases, a compiler can tell you what case you left out (Exercise 38). As an example, a case expression can be used to see if a list is empty; the scrutinee is the formal parameter `xs`, and there are two choices: one for each form of list.

458. ⟨*predefined μML functions* 458⟩≡ 464d ▷

```
(define null? (xs)
  (case xs
    [(cons y ys) #t]
    ['()         #f]))
```

```
null? : (forall ['a] ((list 'a) -> bool))
```

Each choice has a pattern on the left and a result on the right.

Patterns are formed using value constructors, and each value constructor belongs to a unique type. The type and its constructors are added to a basis (a type environment and a value environment) by a new form of definition: the *data definition*. In μML, this definition form comes in two flavors: "implicit" and "explicit." The `implicit-data` form mimics Standard ML's `datatype` form; it is simple and almost impossible to get wrong. But `implicit-data` is actually syntactic sugar for μML's explicit `data` form, which states, in full, the *kind* of the new type and the *types* of its value constructors.

A data definition can name the new type whatever it wants. For example, a new algebraic data type can be called `int`, in which case it hides the built-in `int`. In the interpreter, such type names are translated into internal types (Section 8.5).

Algebraic data types support new programming practices and also require new theoretical techniques, both of which are addressed in this chapter.

- Programming practices, which will help you learn enough Standard ML to be able to work on the interpreters that appear from Chapter 5 onward, are illustrated by programming examples (Sections 8.1 and 8.2), an informal description of evaluation (Section 8.2), and some easy exercises (Section 8.11). As in Chapter 2, programming can include equational reasoning about code that uses algebraic data types (Section 8.3), and it can be made more pleasant by syntactic sugar, which is used routinely in languages like ML and Haskell (Section 8.4).

- To know when two types are different, even when they have the same structure, requires a theory of *type generativity* (Section 8.5). Algebraic data types also require type theory and operational semantics that describe user-written type definitions (Section 8.7) and case expressions with pattern matching (Section 8.8). The theory and semantics are implemented in my interpreter.

Skills in both theory and implementation can be developed through the exercises at the end of the chapter.

8.1 CASE EXPRESSIONS AND PATTERN MATCHING

To understand what you can do with algebraic data types, study the case expression, which is described by this fragment of μML's grammar:

exp ::= (case *exp* {*choice*})

choice ::= [*pattern exp*]

pattern ::= *variable-name*
 | *value-constructor-name*
 | (*value-constructor-name* {*pattern*})
 | _

A case expression looks at a constructed value—called the *scrutinee*—and asks two questions: What value constructor was used to make it? And what values, if any, was that constructor applied to? In other words, the case expression asks how the scrutinee was formed and from what parts. Let's work some examples.

Value constructors that take no arguments

As an example, I define type traffic-light; a value of type traffic-light is made by one of the value constructors RED, GREEN, or YELLOW. The type and its value constructors are introduced by this implicit-data definition:

459a. ⟨*transcript* 459a⟩≡ 459b ▷

```
-> (implicit-data traffic-light
       RED
       GREEN
       YELLOW)
traffic-light :: *
RED : traffic-light
GREEN : traffic-light
YELLOW : traffic-light
```

The definition extends the basis with the information shown: the name and kind of the new type, traffic-light, plus the name and type of each new value constructor. These value constructors take no arguments, so the only values of the new type are RED, GREEN, and YELLOW.

Using a case expression, I can define a function to change a light.

459b. ⟨*transcript* 459a⟩+≡ ◁ 459a 460a ▷

change-light : (traffic-light -> traffic-light)

```
-> (define change-light (light)
     (case light
       [GREEN YELLOW]
       [YELLOW RED]
       [RED GREEN]))
-> (change-light GREEN)
YELLOW : traffic-light
```

When function change-light is applied, the case expression is evaluated as follows: First, expression light is evaluated to produce GREEN. Next, the value GREEN is matched to each *choice* in turn; each choice has a *pattern* on the left and an *expression* on the right. When a pattern matches the value GREEN, that choice is selected, and the expression on its right-hand side is evaluated. In this example, the very first choice is [GREEN YELLOW], GREEN matches GREEN, and so (change-light GREEN) returns the right-hand side, YELLOW.

As another example, here's a function that says what the light means:

460a. ⟨*transcript* 459a⟩+≡ ◁459b 460b▷

`light-meaning : (traffic-light -> sym)`

```
-> (define light-meaning (light)
      (case light
         [RED    'stop]
         [GREEN  'go]
         [YELLOW 'go-faster]))
-> (light-meaning GREEN)
go : sym
```

Again, `light` evaluates to `GREEN`. The first choice has pattern `RED`, which doesn't match `GREEN`. The second choice has pattern `GREEN`, which does match `GREEN`, and the result is the right-hand side: green means `'go`.

Multiple constructed values can be inspected with multiple case expressions. As an example, two traffic lights can be compared to see if one is safer to drive through. To compute that `GREEN` is safer than `YELLOW`, I use nested case expressions:

460b. ⟨*transcript* 459a⟩+≡ ◁460a 460c▷

`safer? : (traffic-light traffic-light -> bool)`

```
-> (define safer? (light1 light2)
      (case light1
         [GREEN  (case light2
                    [GREEN  #f]
                    [YELLOW #t]
                    [RED    #t])]
         [YELLOW (case light2
                    [GREEN  #f]
                    [YELLOW #f]
                    [RED    #t])]
         [RED    #f]))
safer? : (traffic-light traffic-light -> bool)
-> (safer? GREEN YELLOW)
#t : bool
```

In this example, `light1` evaluates to `GREEN`, and the first pattern matches. On the right-hand side, the inner `case` first evaluates `light2` to get `YELLOW`, then finds that the pattern in the second choice matches, and finally returns the right-hand side `#t`.

Nested patterns

Nested case expressions can be ugly and hard to read; they don't make it obvious what is being compared. A more idiomatic comparison forms a pair and scrutinizes it using *nested patterns*. In a nested pattern, a value constructor is applied to one or more patterns that are also formed using value constructors. In this example, I nest value constructors for `traffic-light` inside the predefined `PAIR` value constructor, as in the nested pattern `(PAIR GREEN YELLOW)`.

460c. ⟨*transcript* 459a⟩+≡ ◁460b 461a▷

```
-> (define safer? (light1 light2)
      (case (PAIR light1 light2)
         [(PAIR GREEN  GREEN)  #f]
         [(PAIR GREEN  YELLOW) #t]
         [(PAIR GREEN  RED)    #t]
         [(PAIR YELLOW GREEN)  #f]
         [(PAIR YELLOW YELLOW) #f]
         [(PAIR YELLOW RED)    #t]
         [(PAIR RED    GREEN)  #f]
         [(PAIR RED    YELLOW) #f]
         [(PAIR RED    RED)    #f]))
safer? : (traffic-light traffic-light -> bool)
```

This time the expression (PAIR light1 light2) is evaluated, and it produces the value (PAIR GREEN YELLOW). When this value is scrutinized in the case expression, the second choice matches it, and the result is the right-hand side #t.

461a. ⟨*transcript* 459a⟩+≡ ◁460c 461b▷

```
-> (safer? GREEN YELLOW)
#t : bool
```


Patterns with wildcards

Nested patterns make it easy to write out an entire truth table, but an entire truth table can get big. To write fewer patterns, I use the "wildcard" pattern, written with a single underscore, which means "match anything; I don't care." To test safety at traffic lights, "I don't care" can be used with every color:

- Green is no safer than itself but is safer than anything else—I don't care what.
- Yellow is safer than red but *not* safer than anything else—I don't care what.
- Red is not safer than anything—I don't care what.

These shortcuts are coded as follows:

461b. ⟨*transcript* 459a⟩+≡ ◁461a 461c▷

```
-> (define safer? (light1 light2)
      (case (PAIR light1 light2)
         [(PAIR GREEN  GREEN)  #f]
         [(PAIR GREEN  _)      #t]
         [(PAIR YELLOW RED)    #t]
         [(PAIR YELLOW _)      #f]
         [(PAIR RED    _)      #f]))
-> (safer? GREEN YELLOW)
#t : bool
-> (safer? RED GREEN)
#f : bool
-> (safer? YELLOW RED)
#t : bool
```

In many programming problems, wildcard patterns can be used to avoid enumerating all cases explicitly.

Value constructors that take arguments

From here, let's assume the lights are green, and let's ask how fast we can drive. If, like me, you drive between the U.S. and Canada, it's not always easy to know—my countrymen can't agree with the Canadians on what constitutes a speed.

- In the U.S., a speed is (MPH n), where n is a number.
- In Canada, a speed is (KPH n), where n is a number.

GREEN 459a
PAIR $\mathcal{B}$
RED 459a
type traffic-light 459a
YELLOW 459a

This sad situation can be expressed by defining an algebraic data type. Unlike RED, GREEN, and YELLOW, MPH and KPH are value constructors that take arguments:

461c. ⟨*transcript* 459a⟩+≡ ◁461b 462a▷

```
-> (implicit-data speed
      [MPH of int]
      [KPH of int])
speed :: *
MPH : (int -> speed)
KPH : (int -> speed)
```

To make a speed, apply MPH to an integer, or apply KPH to an integer.

Now I can answer questions about driving. Towns in Quebec usually have local speed limits of 50 kph. Towns in New England usually have local speed limits of 25 or 30 mph. Given that a kilometer is $5/8$ of a mile, which is faster?

462a. ⟨*transcript* 459a⟩+≡ ◁461c 462b▷

```
speed< : (speed speed -> bool)
faster : (speed speed -> speed)
```

```
-> (define speed< (speed1 speed2)
     (case (PAIR speed1 speed2)
       [(PAIR (MPH n1) (MPH n2))    (< n1 n2)]
       [(PAIR (KPH n1) (KPH n2))    (< n1 n2)]
       [(PAIR (MPH n1) (KPH n2))    (< (* 5 n1) (* 8 n2))]
       [(PAIR (KPH n1) (MPH n2))    (< (* 8 n1) (* 5 n2))]))
-> (define faster (speed1 speed2)
     (if (speed< speed1 speed2) speed2 speed1))
-> (faster (KPH 50) (MPH 30))
(KPH 50) : speed
```

Data types with polymorphic constructors

What really matters is whether I'm obeying the speed limit. In Quebec and New England, a speed limit is just a speed. But in parts of western North America and Europe, there is no speed limit. So a speed limit could be represented as one of the following:

- `(SOME` s`)`, where the posted speed limit is a speed s
- `NONE`, where there is no posted speed limit

462b. ⟨*transcript* 459a⟩+≡ ◁462a 462c▷

```
legal-speed? : (speed (option speed) -> bool)
```

```
-> (define legal-speed?
             (my-speed limit)
     (case limit
       [(SOME max) (not (speed< max my-speed))]
       [NONE #t]))
```

Can I go 65 mph in a 110 kph zone? On the autobahn, if there is no speed limit?

462c. ⟨*transcript* 459a⟩+≡ ◁462b 462d▷

```
-> (legal-speed? (MPH 65) (SOME (KPH 110)))
#t : bool
-> (legal-speed? (MPH 65) NONE)
#t : bool
```

Value constructors `SOME` and `NONE` have many more uses. For example, they can describe the result of looking up a key k in an association list:

- `(SOME` v`)`, if key k is associated with value v
- `NONE`, if key k is not present

They can also describe the result of reading a line from a file:

- `(SOME` s`)`, where s is a string representing the next line from the file
- `NONE`, if the end of the file has been reached

If `SOME` can be used with a speed, or a string, or a value of unknown type, what type must it have? A polymorphic type. Value constructors `SOME` and `NONE` belong to μML's built-in `option` type, which is copied from full Standard ML.

462d. ⟨*transcript* 459a⟩+≡ ◁462c 463c▷

```
-> SOME
<function> : (forall ['a] ('a -> (option 'a)))
-> NONE
NONE : (forall ['a] (option 'a))
```

The option type is not primitive; it is predefined using ordinary user code. Its definition uses the explicit data form, which gives the kind of the option type constructor and the full types of the SOME and NONE value constructors:

463a. ⟨*predefined μML types* 463a⟩≡ 473a ▷

```
(data (* => *) option
  [SOME : (forall ['a] ('a -> (option 'a)))]
  [NONE : (forall ['a] (option 'a))])
```

If you prefer less notation, any algebraic data type in μML can also be defined using implicit-data:

463b. ⟨*transcript of implicit definitions* 463b⟩≡

```
-> (implicit-data ['a] option
       NONE
       [SOME of 'a])
option@{2} :: (* => *)
NONE : (forall ['a] (option@{2} 'a))
SOME : (forall ['a] ('a -> (option@{2} 'a)))
```

But what is option@{2}?! It is the *print name* of the option type just defined. The suffix "@{2}" lets you know that this type is a *redefinition* of the option type built into μML. Types option and option@{2} are incompatible; a function that works with one won't work with the other. This incompatibility is a consequence of the *generativity* of datatype definitions (Section 8.5).

No matter how NONE and SOME are defined, they are polymorphic. And if they are used in a function, that function may also be polymorphic. As an example, function get-opt takes a value of type (option 'a) and a default value of type 'a, and it returns either the option value or the default:

463c. ⟨*transcript* 459a⟩+≡ ◁ 462d 463d ▷

```
get-opt : (forall ['a] ((option 'a) 'a -> 'a))
```

```
-> (define get-opt (maybe default)
     (case maybe
        [(SOME a)  a]
        [NONE      default]))
get-opt : (forall ['a] ((option 'a) 'a -> 'a))
```

Recursive data types

In a datatype definition, a value constructor can take an argument of the type being defined—which makes the data type recursive. The best simple example is a list; another good, simple example is a binary tree. At each internal node, a simple binary tree might carry one value of type 'a, plus left and right subtrees:

463d. ⟨*transcript* 459a⟩+≡ ◁ 463c 463e ▷

```
-> (data (* => *) bt
      [BTNODE  : (forall ['a] ('a (bt 'a) (bt 'a) -> (bt 'a)))]
      [BTEMPTY : (forall ['a] (bt 'a))])
bt :: (* => *)
BTNODE : (forall ['a] ('a (bt 'a) (bt 'a) -> (bt 'a)))
BTEMPTY : (forall ['a] (bt 'a))
```

Such a tree's elements can be listed in preorder (node before children):

463e. ⟨*transcript* 459a⟩+≡ ◁ 463d 464a ▷

```
preorder-elems : (forall ['a] ((bt 'a) -> (list 'a)))
```

```
-> (define preorder-elems (t)
     (case t
      [BTEMPTY '()]
      [(BTNODE a left right)
          (cons a (append (preorder-elems left) (preorder-elems right)))]))
```

And a test case:

464a. ⟨*transcript* 459a⟩+≡ ◁463e 464b▷

```
single-node : (forall ['a] ('a -> (bt 'a)))
-> (define single-node (a)
      (BTNODE a BTEMPTY BTEMPTY))
-> (val int-bt
      (BTNODE 1
         (BTNODE 2
            BTEMPTY
            (single-node 3))
         (BTNODE 4
            (BTNODE 5
                 (single-node 6)
                 (single-node 7))
            (single-node 8))))
-> (preorder-elems int-bt)
(1 2 3 4 5 6 7 8) : (list int)
```

For a binary *search* tree, which our example is not, the classic traversal is an inorder traversal: left subtree before node before right subtree.

464b. ⟨*transcript* 459a⟩+≡ ◁464a 464c▷

```
inorder-elems : (forall ['a] ((bt 'a) -> (list 'a)))
-> (define inorder-elems (t)
      (case t
         [BTEMPTY '()]
         [(BTNODE a left right)
            (append (inorder-elems left) (cons a (inorder-elems right)))]))
-> (inorder-elems int-bt)
(2 3 1 6 5 7 4 8) : (list int)
```

Like lists, binary trees support operations that map, filter, and fold.

464c. ⟨*transcript* 459a⟩+≡ ◁464b 465▷

```
bt-map : (forall ['a 'b] (('a -> 'b) (bt 'a) -> (bt 'b)))
-> (define bt-map (f t)
     (case t
        [BTEMPTY BTEMPTY]
        [(BTNODE a left right)
                 (BTNODE (f a) (bt-map f left) (bt-map f right))]))
-> (preorder-elems (bt-map (lambda (n) (* n n)) int-bt))
(1 4 9 16 25 36 49 64) : (list int)
```

A fold function for a binary search tree is part of Exercise 14.

Data types with just one value constructor each

Most often, an algebraic data type defines more than one way to form a constructed value—that is, more than one value constructor. But an algebraic datatype can usefully have just a single constructor, as shown by the `pair` type:

464d. ⟨*predefined μML functions* 458⟩+≡ ◁458 464e▷

```
(data (* * => *) pair
  [PAIR : (forall ['a 'b] ('a 'b -> (pair 'a 'b)))])
```

Using this definition, functions `pair`, `fst`, and `snd` don't have to be implemented as primitives the way they do in nano-ML; they are defined using ordinary user code:

464e. ⟨*predefined μML functions* 458⟩+≡ ◁464d 474c▷

```
(val pair PAIR)
(define fst (p)
   (case p [(PAIR x _) x]))
(define snd (p)
   (case p [(PAIR _ y) y]))
```

(Because pattern matching is more idiomatic, functions fst and snd are rarely used, but they are included for compatibility with nano-ML.)

Single-constructor types like pair are typically used in two different ways:

- When the single constructor takes multiple arguments, like PAIR, the algebraic data type acts as a record type. This usage can be supported by syntactic sugar; μML provides a record definition form, which desugars into datatype definition and a sequence of function definitions.

- When the single constructor takes a single argument, the algebraic data type acts as a renaming of some other type. The types that are most commonly renamed are types that are used with many meanings, like integers and Booleans; for example, in order to distinguish a height from a weight, we might rename int:

465. ⟨*transcript* 459a⟩+≡ ◁464c 470b▷

```
-> (data * height [HEIGHT : (int -> height)])
-> (data * weight [WEIGHT : (int -> weight)])
-> (val h (HEIGHT 196))
(HEIGHT 196) : height
-> (val w (WEIGHT 87))
(WEIGHT 87) : weight
```

In full ML, this kind of renaming has zero run-time cost; at run time, (HEIGHT 196) is represented in exactly the same way as just 196.

Sum of products: A universal representation

Algebraic data types can express all the possibilities we demand from a "proper" type-definition mechanism. These possibilities can be expressed in the language of type theory:

- A type whose values can take on multiple forms is called a *sum type*.
- A type that gathers multiple parts is called a *product type*.[1]
- A type with a part that is like the whole is called a *recursive type*.

At first glance, an algebraic data type appears to be just a sum type: each form corresponds to a value constructor. But because each value constructor may carry any number of parts, an algebraic data type is a *sum of products*. And it expresses the others as special cases: Omit carried values, as in traffic-light, and it's a pure sum. Or define a type with just one value constructor, as in pair, and it's a pure product.

append	$\mathcal{B}$
type bt	463d
BTEMPTY	463d
BTNODE	463d
preorder-elems	463e

Because algebraic data types can express sums, products, and recursion, they are technically universal. But they are also universal in a more important, less technical sense: sums of products turn out to be a great model for data structures. For example, a linked list is a sum of products. So is a binary tree. So are the abstract-syntax trees found throughout this book. A sum of products is something that every programmer must know how to code, in any language. As examples, I discuss two languages or language families: C, the language of Chapters 1 to 4 (and also of the world's computing infrastructure), and object-oriented languages, a popular and maybe even dominant language family for over 20 years.

In C, a general sum of products is awkward to code. C's union type implements a sum, but a value of union type doesn't record *which* choice is represented—that

[1]If you are wondering about the names, pick some finite types like bool and traffic-light, then count the number of values that inhabit a sum like "Boolean or light" or a product like "Boolean and light." And note that "product" is the *Cartesian* product, which you may have studied in math class.

information has to be stored in a tag off to the side. In the general case, a sum of products is therefore a struct containing both a tag and a union of structs. But there is an important and common special case: a sum with only two forms, only one of which carries a product. In that case, the sum of products can be represented by a pointer:

- The form that carries a product is represented by a pointer to a `struct` containing the product, which is usually allocated on the heap.
- The form that does not carry a product is represented by the `NULL` pointer.

This representation works nicely for lists, binary trees, and things like `option`. In particular, it supports a simple, efficient test to identify the form of the data: ask if a pointer is `NULL`.

In object-oriented languages (Chapter 10), a sum of products emerges whenever different forms of objects work together to implement the same abstraction. Each individual object is a product: the product of the values of all its *instance variables* (sometimes called *members* or *fields*). And a collection of related objects is a sum of those products, referred to by the conventions of a particular language. For example, in Smalltalk, that collection would be a set of objects that respond to the same protocol; in Java, a set of objects that implement the same interface; and in C++, a set of objects whose classes inherit from the same superclass.

With these universal ideas in mind, we're ready to study algebraic data types in the context of a complete programming language: μML. A programmer's view encompasses an informal description of type definitions, case expressions, and pattern matching, with examples; equational reasoning with algebraic data types, and the extension of pattern matching to other language constructs. A theorist's view encompasses *generativity* and its effect on type equivalence; a theory of user-defined types; and a theory of case expressions.

8.2 Algebraic data types in μML

Algebraic data types combine nicely with nano-ML; the resulting language is called μML. μML's concrete syntax is shown in Figure 8.1 on the facing page. The syntax includes not only the case-expression and data-definition forms, but also three syntactic categories not found in nano-ML: *patterns, kinds,* and *type expressions.*

- Patterns are used in case expressions. A case expression is evaluated as shown by example above, as explained informally just below, and as specified formally in Section 8.8.
- Types and kinds are used data definitions. The only truly new definition form is `data`; the `implicit-data` and `record` forms are syntactic sugar for `data`. Unlike the definition and expression forms in nano-ML, which do not mention kinds or types, the `data` definition specifies both *kind* and *type-exp*, using the same syntax as Typed μScheme.

Figure 8.1 hints at a syntactic distinction, or really a lexical distinction, that is not made in Typed μScheme or nano-ML: μML's term language uses two disjoint sets of names. One set is used for *value variables* and the other for *value constructors.* The distinction parallels a distinction made in the *type* languages for Typed μScheme, nano-ML, and now μML, in which type variables are notated differently from type constructors. (The name of a type variable begins with an ASCII quote character, and the name of a type constructor doesn't.) In the term language

def ::= (val *value-variable-name exp*)
⋆ | (val *pattern exp*)
| (val-rec *value-variable-name exp*)
| *exp*
| (define *function-name* ({*value-variable-name*}) *exp*)
⋆ | (define* {[(*function-name* {*pattern*}) *exp*]})
| (data *kind type-constructor-name* {[*value-constructor-name* : *type-exp*]})
⋆ | (implicit-data [[{'*type-variable-name*}]] *type-constructor-name*
{*value-constructor-name* | [*value-constructor-name* of *type-exp*]})
⋆ | (record [[{'*type-variable-name*}]] *record-name*({[*field-name*:*type-exp*]}))
| (use *file-name*)
| *unit-test*

type-exp ::= *type-constructor-name*
| '*type-variable-name*
| (forall [{'*type-variable-name*}] *type-exp*)
| [{*type-exp*} -> *type-exp*]
| [*type-exp* {*type-exp*}]

kind ::= * | ({*kind*} => *kind*)

unit-test ::= (check-expect *exp exp*)
| (check-assert *exp*)
| (check-error *exp*)
| (check-type *exp type-exp*)
| (check-principal-type *exp type-exp*)
| (check-type-error *exp*)

exp ::= *literal*
| *value-variable-name* | *value-constructor-name*
| (case *exp* {*choice*})
| (if *exp exp exp*)
| (begin {*exp*})
| (*exp* {*exp*})
| ((let | let* | letrec) ({[*value-variable-name exp*]}) *exp*)
| (lambda ({*value-variable-name*}) *exp*)
⋆ | ((let | let*) ({[*pattern exp*]}) *exp*)
⋆ | (lambda ({*pattern*}) *exp*)

choice ::= [*pattern exp*]

pattern ::= *value-variable-name*
| *value-constructor-name*
| (*value-constructor-name* {*pattern*})
| _

literal ::= *numeral* | '*S-exp* | (quote *S-exp*)

S-exp ::= *literal* | *symbol-name* | ({*S-exp*})

numeral ::= token composed only of digits, possibly prefixed with a plus or minus sign

value-constructor-name
::= cons | '() | a token that begins with # or with a capital letter or with make-

*-name ::= token that is not a bracket, a *numeral*, a *value-constructor-name*, or one of the "reserved" words shown in typewriter font

Figure 8.1: The concrete syntax of μML (⋆ marks syntactic sugar)

of μML, it is the value constructor that is specially marked: after any preceding fragments that are separated with dots, the name of a value constructor begins with a capital latter or the hash character, and the name of a value variable doesn't. The details are presented in Section 8.2.2.

Figure 8.1 shows only the syntax of μML, not its values. In addition to the symbols, numbers, and functions found in μScheme and nano-ML, μML provides just one other form of value: a constructed value. Constructed values represent not only values of algebraic data types defined by users, but also pairs, cons cells, `NIL`, and Booleans. By contrast, in nano-ML, pairs, lists, and Booleans each have their own special representations. The change may sound significant—and for a compiler writer, type theorist, or semanticist, it is a welcome simplification—but as a programmer, you won't notice.

The rest of this section describes the evaluation of case expressions, pattern matching, and data definitions. It also shows some of the code used to build μML's initial basis. The chapter continues with equational reasoning (Section 8.3) and with popular syntactic sugar (Section 8.4), before wrapping up with theory topics (Sections 8.5, 8.7, and 8.8).

8.2.1 *Evaluation of pattern matching*

Given an environment ρ, an expression of the form $(\texttt{case}\ e\ [p_1\ e_1] \cdots [p_n\ e_n])$ is evaluated by *pattern matching*.

1. First e is evaluated in environment ρ to produce a value v (the scrutinee).

2. Next v is checked against $p_1, \ldots, p_n$ in turn, to identify the first p_i that *matches*.[2] Matching not only selects $[p_i\ e_i]$; it also produces a set of bindings ρ' that are used to extend the environment ρ. Environment ρ' includes a binding for every variable that appears in pattern p_i.

3. Finally e_i is evaluated in an extended environment containing bindings from both ρ and ρ'. The value of e_i becomes the value of the entire case expression.

Matching is defined by induction on the structure of a pattern:

- A variable x matches any value v, and the match produces the singleton set of bindings $\{x \mapsto v\}$.

- A wildcard matches any value v, and the match produces no bindings.

- A value constructor K matches a value v if and only if $v = K$. That is, if v is the value constructor by itself, not applied to any arguments. The match produces no bindings.

- Finally, when pattern p is a value constructor K applied to one or more sub-patterns, say $p = (K\ p'_1 \cdots p'_m)$, this pattern matches value v if there are values $v_1, \ldots, v_m$ such that $v = (K\ v_1 \cdots v_m)$, and for every i from 1 to k, p'_i matches v_i. The match produces the bindings obtained by taking the union of all sets of bindings produced by each of the sub-matches of p_i to v_i. To ensure that the union is well defined, variables appearing in sub-patterns must be distinct.

[2]Compilers for languages that use algebraic data types, including ML and Haskell, don't actually try each pattern in sequence. Instead, they translate each case expression into an efficient automaton. Using such an automaton, the matching pattern is found cheaply; the cost is typically a few machine instructions times the maximum number of value constructors appearing in any one pattern.

Table 8.2: Examples of pattern matching

Pattern	*Value*	*Result*
`(cons x xs)`	`'(1 2 3)`	Succeeds, $\rho' = \{$`x` $\mapsto 1,$ `xs` $\mapsto$ `'(2 3)`$\}$
`(cons x2 xs)`	`'(b c)`	Succeeds, $\rho' = \{$`x2` $\mapsto$ `'b`, `xs` $\mapsto$ `'(c)`$\}$
`x1`	`'a`	Succeeds, $\rho' = \{$`x1` $\mapsto$ `'a`$\}$
`(cons x1 (cons x2 xs))`	`'(a b c)`	Succeeds, $\rho' = \{$`x1` $\mapsto$ `'a`, `x2` $\mapsto$ `'b`, `xs` $\mapsto$ `'(c)`$\}$
`(cons x1 (cons x2 xs))`	`'(a)`	Fails
`(cons x2 xs)`	`'()`	Fails
`(cons x '())`	`'()`	Fails
`(cons x '())`	`'(a)`	Succeeds, $\rho' = \{$`x` $\mapsto$ `'a`$\}$
`(cons x '())`	`'(a b)`	Fails
`'()`	`'(a)`	Fails
`'()`	`'()`	Succeeds, $\rho' = \{\}$

A good simple example is a non-nested pattern $(K\ x_1 \cdots x_m)$ matched against a value $(K\ v_1 \cdots v_m)$; this match succeeds, and it produces the set of bindings $\{x_1 \mapsto v_1, \ldots, x_m \mapsto v_m\}$. This kind of match corresponds to the first two example entries in Table 8.2. The fourth entry in the table uses a nested pattern: `(cons x1 (cons x2 xs))` is matched against the value `'(a b c)`. The matching of the sub-patterns is shown in the previous two entries: Sub-pattern `x1` is matched against value `'a` and succeeds, producing binding $\{$`x1` $\mapsto$ `'a`$\}$. Sub-pattern `(cons x2 xs)` is matched against value `'(b c)` and succeeds, producing bindings $\{$`x2` $\mapsto$ `'b`, `xs` $\mapsto$ `'(c)`$\}$. So the whole match succeeds, producing bindings $\{$`x1` $\mapsto$ `'a`, `x2` $\mapsto$ `'b`, `xs` $\mapsto$ `'(c)`$\}$.

In the next entry, the same pattern `(cons x1 (cons x2 xs))` is matched against value `'(a)`. The first sub-match succeeds, producing $\{$`x1` $\mapsto$ `'a`$\}$. But the sub-match of `(cons x2 xs)` against `'()` fails, because `cons` and `'()` are different value constructors. So the whole match fails.

8.2.2 *Distinguishing value constructors from variables*

As implemented in Standard ML, pattern matching has a pitfall: if you misspell the name of a value constructor, which matches only itself, Standard ML might take the misspelling for a value variable, which matches anything. If you're lucky, you'll get a warning from the compiler, but whether you are warned or not, you'll get different behavior from what you intended. For example, given a list of lights, does this Standard ML code test to see if the first one is green?

469. ⟨*pitfall in Standard ML* 469⟩≡

```
datatype traffic_light = GREEN | YELLOW | RED
val startsWithGreen : traffic_light list -> bool =
  fn lights =>
    case lights
      of GREEEN :: _ => true
       | _           => false
```

As shown on the next page, this code doesn't do what you might think.

It seems that any list starts with GREEN:

470a. ⟨*transcript of Standard ML using* startsWithGreen 470a⟩≡

```
- startsWithGreen [GREEN, YELLOW, RED];
val it = true : bool
- startsWithGreen [YELLOW, RED, GREEN];
val it = true : bool
```


In the case expression on the previous page, I misspelled GREEN. The compiler parses GREEEN as a variable, so the first choice matches any nonempty list. And the compiler gives no warning, because the second case can also match: it matches the empty list. What's called startsWithGreen is actually a "not null" function.

This problem can be mitigated by using the wildcard pattern cautiously—for example, only as an argument to a value constructor. But the problem can be avoided entirely through better language design. Languages like OCaml, Haskell, and μML mandate a spelling convention: depending on the way a name is spelled, it can stand for a variable or for a value constructor, but never both. (Standard ML uses such a convention in the type language, but not in the term language.) μML's convention, in order to preserve compatibility with nano-ML and μScheme, is more elaborate than most:

- If a name contains a dot (.), every character up to and including the last dot is removed. If what's left begins with a capital letter or with the # symbol, it's the name of a value constructor; it cannot stand for a variable or function.
- To enable us to write lists that look like μScheme and nano-ML lists, the name cons and the syntax '() are both deemed to be value constructors.
- For compatibility with the record form, any name beginning with make- is the name of a value constructor.
- Any other name is the name of a *value variable*, or simply a variable; it cannot stand for a value constructor.

In μML, the name GREEEN begins with a capital letter, so it must be the name of a value constructor. Since no value constructor by that name appears in the environment, the following starts-with-green function, which has the same bug as the version above, is rejected by the type checker:

470b. ⟨*transcript* 459a⟩+≡ ◁465 470c▷

```
-> (val starts-with-green
     (lambda (lights)
       (case lights
          [(cons GREEEN _)   #t]
          [_                 #f])))
type error: no value constructor named GREEEN
```

When the spelling is corrected, everything works as it should:

470c. ⟨*transcript* 459a⟩+≡ ◁470b 474d▷

starts-with-green : ((list traffic-light) -> bool)

```
-> (val starts-with-green
     (lambda (lights)
       (case lights
          [(cons GREEN _)   #t]
          [_                #f])))
starts-with-green : ((list traffic-light) -> bool)
-> (starts-with-green (list3 GREEN YELLOW RED))
#t : bool
-> (starts-with-green (list3 YELLOW RED GREEN))
#f : bool
```

When you're working on interpreters written in Standard ML, beware of this pitfall. If you a see a strange error message about "redundant" pattern matches, or if your code produces senseless results, look for a misspelled value constructor.

8.2.3 *Typing and evaluation of datatype definitions*

In μML, as in Haskell, an algebraic data type may be defined in two ways. The `data` form gives the kind of the type constructor and the type of each of its value constructors. The `implicit-data` form leaves the kind of the type constructor to be inferred, and it gives only the *argument* types, if any, of each value constructor. Each form has advantages and disadvantages:

- In the `data` form, all types and kinds appear explicitly in the source code, so they are crystal clear. But to use the `data` form, you have to understand and follow the rules given below for the types of value constructors; if you break the rules, your definition will be rejected by the type checker.

- In the `implicit-data` form, you have to follow only one rule: the argument type of each value constructor must be well kinded. But the types of the value constructors don't appear in the source code; if you want to know them, you have to reconstruct them mentally.

The `data` form supports some fancy extensions that are described in Appendix S, but the `implicit-data` form is easier to write, and it is isomorphic to the corresponding forms in Standard ML and OCaml. (Full Haskell supports both forms, including extensions; OCaml supports extensions by adding constraints to the `implicit-data` form.)

A `data` form that defines algebraic data type T looks like this:

(`data` κ T `[`$K_1 : t_1$`]` $\cdots$ `[`$K_n : t_n$`])`,

where κ is a kind, T is the name of the type or type constructor being defined, each K_i is the name of a value constructor, and each t_i is a type expression giving the type of that value constructor. To enable type inference to work, each t_i must obey these rules:

- Every t_i must be well kinded. Each type t_i may use type name T, but only in a way that is consistent with its kind κ: If κ is `*`, then T is a type all by itself, and it takes no parameters. If κ has the form (`*` $\cdots$ `* => *`), then T takes as many type parameters as there are stars to the left of the arrow.

- If T takes type parameters, then each value constructor must be polymorphic, and in its type t_i, the number of variables under the `forall` must be equal the to number of type parameters T is expecting. If T takes no type parameters, each value constructor must be monomorphic.

  For example, the `traffic-light` type takes no parameters, and its value constructors are monomorphic. But the `option` type takes a type parameter, so its value constructors `SOME` and `NONE` are polymorphic.

cons 𝓑
GREEN 459a
list3 𝓑
type traffic-light 459a

- Underneath the `forall`, if any, each type t_i has a *result type*, and that type must be *valid*. The result type is determined by the shape of the type under the `forall`: if it is a function type, the result type is the type to the right of the function arrow. Otherwise, the result type is whatever appears under the `forall`. Any given t_i may or may not use `forall`, and it may or may not be a function type, so there are four cases in total, as illustrated by these examples:

Type	*Result type*	*Validity*
`traffic-light`	`traffic-light`	Valid
`(forall ['a] (list 'a))`	`(list 'a)`	Valid
`(int -> speed)`	`speed`	Valid
`(forall ['a] ('a -> (option 'a)))`	`(option 'a)`	Valid

A result type is valid if and only if it is T itself or it applies T to one or more *distinct* type variables. The four examples above have valid result types; here are two examples with invalid result types:

Type	*Result type*	*Validity*
`(list int)`	`(list int)`	Invalid
`(forall ['a] ('a -> (pair 'a 'a))`	`(pair 'a 'a)`	Invalid

These rules make type inference relatively straightforward. In more ambitious languages, some of the rules can be relaxed—full languages like Haskell support not only standard algebraic data types but also *generalized* algebraic data types and *existential* algebraic data types, as described in Appendix S—but relaxing the rules makes type inference more difficult.

The rules are checked when a `data` definition is typed. If the rules are respected, type T is added to the basis, where it stands for a unique type constructor of kind κ, distinct from all other type constructors. The guarantee of distinction makes the definition *generative*. Each K_i is also added to the basis, to the type environment with type t_i, and to the value environment either as the bare constructed value K_i or as an anonymous primitive function that applies K_i to its arguments.

The `implicit-data` form is described by this EBNF:

def ::= `(implicit-data` $\big[$`[`$\{$`'`*type-variable-name*$\}$`]`$\big]$ *type-constructor-name*
$\{$*value-constructor-name* $|$ `[`*value-constructor-name* `of` $\{$*type-exp*$\}$`]`$\}$`)`

The form includes optional type parameters, the name of the type constructor being defined, and specifications of one or more value constructors. A value constructor that takes no arguments is specified by its name. A value constructor that takes arguments is specified by its name, followed by the keyword `of`, followed by the types of its arguments, all wrapped in parentheses. Using metavariables, an example of the form looks like this:

`(implicit-data` $\big[$`[`$\alpha_1 \cdots \alpha_m$`]`$\big]$ T
$K_1 \cdots K_k$ `[`K_{k+1} `of` $t \cdots t$`]` $\cdots$ `[`K_n `of` $t \cdots t$`])`

This `implicit-data` form requires less notation than the `data` form—for example, there is never an explicit `forall`—and it imposes just one rule: the t's must be well kinded. The `implicit-data` form closely resembles the `datatype` form in Standard ML, which is used to implement the interpreters in this book from Chapter 5 onwards.

When typed and evaluated, `implicit-data` does exactly what `data` does: it adds T to the basis, bound to a fresh type constructor, and it adds each K_i. Each K_i's *result type* t_r is either T alone, if there are no type parameters, or if there are type parameters, it is $(T\ \alpha_1\ \cdots\ \alpha_m)$. If K_i is specified just by its name, its type is the result type t_r; if K_i is specified using the form `[`K_i `of` $t_1\ \cdots\ t_n$`]`, then its type

```
(implicit-data T                (data * T
  K₁                              [K₁ : T]
  ⋮                               ⋮
  [Kᵢ of t₁ ··· tₙ]       ≜       [Kᵢ : (t₁ ··· tₙ -> T)]
  ⋮                               ⋮
)                               )
```

(a) Without type parameters

```
                                (data (*₁ ··· *ₘ => *) T
(implicit-data (α₁ ··· αₘ) T      [K₁ : (forall (α₁ ··· αₘ)
  K₁                                        (T α₁ ··· αₘ))]
  ⋮                               ⋮
  [Kᵢ of t₁ ··· tₙ]       ≜       [Kᵢ : (forall (α₁ ··· αₘ)
                                            (t₁ ··· tₙ ->
  ⋮                                           (T α₁ ··· αₘ)))]
)                                 ⋮
                                )
```

(b) With type parameters

Figure 8.3: Desugaring `implicit-data`

is the function type $t_1 \times \cdots \times t_n \to t_r$. In both cases, when type parameters are present, the type of each K_i is turned into a polymorphic type scheme by using `forall` to close over them.

Formally, `implicit-data` is syntactic sugar for `data`. It is desugared by one of two equations, depending on whether type parameters are present (Figure 8.3). When type parameters are absent, every value constructor gets a monomorphic type. When type parameters are present, every value constructor is polymorphic in exactly those parameters. Type name T is applied to the parameters and is given a kind consistent with them. In the interpreter, the desugaring is implemented by function `makeExplicit` (Appendix S, page S469).

8.2.4 *Predefined algebraic data types*

Many of the algebraic data types found in Standard ML are also predefined in μML. They are defined using `data` or `implicit-data`. In most cases, to make the types of the value constructors explicit, I use the `data` form.

A Boolean is either `#t` or `#f`.

473a. ⟨*predefined μML types* 463a⟩+≡ ◁463a 473b▷

```
(data * bool
  [#t : bool]
  [#f : bool])
```

A list is made using either `'()` or `cons`.

473b. ⟨*predefined μML types* 463a⟩+≡ ◁473a 474a▷

```
(data (* => *) list
  ['()  : (forall ['a] (list 'a))]
  [cons : (forall ['a] ('a (list 'a) -> (list 'a)))])
```

The unit type, which is the result type of println and print, is inhabited by the single value UNIT.

474a. ⟨*predefined μML types* 463a⟩+≡ ◁473b 474b▷
```
(data * unit [UNIT : unit])
```

Type pair is defined on page 464, with accompanying functions pair, fst, and snd. Types for triples and larger tuples are also predefined; the value constructor for type triple is TRIPLE, and the value constructors for types 4-tuple through 10-tuple are T4 to T10, respectively (Appendix S). These types are defined without any accompanying functions. If you want functions, define them using pattern matching. Or do Exercise 27 and match tuples directly in let forms.

The order type is a standard result type for comparison functions. It represents a relation between elements of a totally ordered set: one element may be less than, equal to, or greater than another.

474b. ⟨*predefined μML types* 463a⟩+≡ ◁474a
```
(implicit-data order LESS EQUAL GREATER)
```

This representation is used in the predefined function Int.compare:

474c. ⟨*predefined μML functions* 458⟩+≡ ◁464e 475a▷

`Int.compare : (int int -> order)`
```
(define Int.compare (n1 n2)
  (if (< n1 n2) LESS
      (if (< n2 n1) GREATER
          EQUAL)))
```

The order type is equally useful in user-defined functions:

474d. ⟨*transcript* 459a⟩+≡ ◁470c 474e▷

`compare-speeds : (speed speed -> order)`
```
-> (define compare-speeds (speed1 speed2)
      (if (speed< speed1 speed2)
          LESS
          (if (speed< speed2 speed1)
              GREATER
              EQUAL)))
```

Because values of order type can be can be scrutinized in case expressions, using them often results in simpler code than using Booleans, which require nested if expressions. A nested if can implement a three-way comparison:

474e. ⟨*transcript* 459a⟩+≡ ◁474d 474f▷

`speed-opinion : (speed -> sym)`
```
-> (define speed-opinion (s)
      (if (speed< s (MPH 65))
          'too-slow
          (if (speed< (MPH 65) s)
             'too-fast
             'just-right)))
-> (speed-opinion (KPH 110)) ; guide for Canadians in the US
too-fast : sym
```

But a pattern match on an order is simpler and clearer:

474f. ⟨*transcript* 459a⟩+≡ ◁474e 488a▷

`speed-opinion-too : (speed -> sym)`
```
-> (define speed-opinion-too (s)
      (case (compare-speeds s (MPH 65))
         [LESS    'too-slow]
         [GREATER 'too-fast]
         [EQUAL   'just-right]))
-> (speed-opinion-too (KPH 110))
too-fast : sym
-> (speed-opinion-too (MPH 65))
just-right : sym
```

8.2.5 *Pattern matching in predefined functions*

In μScheme and nano-ML, list values are built in, so the basic list functions must be built in as primitives. In μML, the basic list functions are user-defined.

475a. ⟨*predefined μML functions* 458⟩+≡ ◁474c 475b▷

```
null? : (forall ['a] ((list 'a) -> bool))
car   : (forall ['a] ((list 'a) -> 'a))
cdr   : (forall ['a] ((list 'a) -> (list 'a)))
```

```
(define null? (xs)
   (case xs ['()          #t]
            [(cons _ _) #f]))
(define car (xs)
   (case xs ['()          (error 'car-of-empty-list)]
            [(cons y _) y]))
(define cdr (xs)
   (case xs ['()           (error 'cdr-of-empty-list)]
            [(cons _ ys) ys]))
```

Don't get fond of `null?`, `car`, and `cdr`. These functions are rarely needed; most code uses pattern matching, as in these versions of `append` and `revapp`:

475b. ⟨*predefined μML functions* 458⟩+≡ ◁475a 475c▷

```
append : (forall ['a] ((list 'a) (list 'a) -> (list 'a)))
revapp : (forall ['a] ((list 'a) (list 'a) -> (list 'a)))
```

```
(define append (xs ys)
  (case xs
    ['()         ys]
    [(cons z zs) (cons z (append zs ys))]))

(define revapp (xs ys)
  (case xs
    ['()         ys]
    [(cons z zs) (revapp zs (cons z ys))]))
```

Function `bind` operates on association lists. The code uses only pattern matching, not `null?`, `car`, or `cdr`. I encourage you to compare it with the nano-ML version in chunk S423b.

475c. ⟨*predefined μML functions* 458⟩+≡ ◁475b 475d▷

```
bind : (forall ['a 'b] ('a 'b (list (pair 'a 'b)) -> (list (pair 'a 'b))))
```

```
(define list1 (x) (cons x '()))
(define bind (x y alist)
  (case alist
    ['() (list1 (pair x y))]
    [(cons p ps)
       (if (= x (fst p))
           (cons (pair x y) ps)
           (cons p (bind x y ps)))]))
```

Functions `find` and `bound?` also improve on their nano-ML versions. When a key is not found, `find` needn't call `error`; it can instead return a value of `option` type. Using nested patterns, `find` can be implemented without using `fst` or `snd`.

475d. ⟨*predefined μML functions* 458⟩+≡ ◁475c 476▷

```
find : (forall ['a 'b] ('a (list (pair 'a 'b)) -> (option 'b)))
```

```
(define find (x alist)
  (case alist
       ['()   NONE]
       [(cons (PAIR key value) pairs)
          (if (= x key)
              (SOME value)
              (find x pairs))]))
```


EQUAL	$\mathcal{B}$
GREATER	$\mathcal{B}$
LESS	$\mathcal{B}$
type speed	461c
speed<	462a

In nano-ML, bound? must reimplement the same search algorithm used in find. But in μML, bound? simply calls find.

476. ⟨*predefined μML functions* 458⟩+≡ ◁475d

```
bound? : (forall ['a 'b] ('a (list (pair 'a 'b)) -> bool))
```

```
(define bound? (x alist)
  (case (find x alist)
    [(SOME _) #t]
    [NONE     #f]))
```

The rest of the predefined functions are defined in Section S.2.4 (page S445).

8.3 Equational reasoning with case expressions

Like μScheme and nano-ML, μML is a functional language. As such, it supports the same equational-reasoning techniques as μScheme, and even the same algebraic laws (Section 2.5). But unlike μScheme, μMLhas algebraic data types and case expressions. And equational reasoning can be used on them, too.

- Case expressions obey several useful laws.
- Laws involving constructed data can be proved by generalizing the inductive proof techniques that are used to prove facts about lists and S-expressions.

The laws for case expressions follow from the rules for evaluating case expressions:

- If its scrutinee matches the pattern in the first choice, a case expression is equivalent to a let expression.
- If its scrutinee doesn't match the pattern in the first choice, a case expression is equivalent to the same case expression with the first choice removed.

If you can't tell whether a scrutinee matches the pattern in a first choice, then you break your proof down by cases, adding one case for each value constructor in some algebraic data type. You can make it easy to tell by eliminating nested patterns. Matching of non-nested patterns is described by simple laws.

Each law of matching applies to a case expression in which the first choice contains one particular form of pattern: variable, bare constructor, or constructor application. If its first pattern is a variable, a case expression is equivalent to a let expression.

$$\texttt{(case}\ e\ \texttt{[}x\ e'\texttt{]}\ \cdots\texttt{)} = \texttt{(let ([}x\ e\texttt{])}\ e'\texttt{)}$$

If its first pattern is a value constructor, and if the scrutinee is that same value constructor, then a case expression is equivalent to the first right-hand side.

$$\texttt{(case}\ K\ \texttt{[}K\ e'\texttt{]}\ \cdots\texttt{)} = e'$$

If the first pattern *applies* a value constructor K, and if the scrutinee is constructed by applying K, then a case expression is equivalent to a let expression.

$$\begin{array}{l}\texttt{(case (}K\ e_1\ \cdots\ e_n\texttt{)}\\ \quad\texttt{[(}K\ x_1\ \cdots\ x_n\texttt{)}\ e'\texttt{]}\ \cdots\texttt{)}\end{array} = \texttt{(let ([}x_1\ e_1\texttt{]}\ \cdots\ \texttt{[}x_n\ e_n\texttt{])}\ e'\texttt{)}$$

If the first pattern involves a value constructor, it might not match the scrutinee. In that event, the case expression is equivalent to a similar expression with the first choice removed. For example, when $K \neq K'$,

$$\begin{array}{l}\texttt{(case (}K\ e_1\ \cdots\ e_n\texttt{)} \\ \quad\texttt{[(}K'\ x_1\ \cdots\ x_m\texttt{)}\ e'\texttt{]} \\ \quad\texttt{[}p\ e''\texttt{]}\ \cdots\texttt{)}\end{array} = \begin{array}{l}\texttt{(case (}K\ e_1\ \cdots\ e_n\texttt{)} \\ \quad\texttt{[}p\ e''\texttt{]}\ \cdots\texttt{)}.\end{array}$$

Other laws you can work out for yourself.

To show some case-expression laws at work, I prove two properties of the bt-map function, which is defined on the binary trees of Section 8.1 (page 463):

```
             (bt-map f BTEMPTY) = BTEMPTY
(bt-map f (BTNODE x t1 t2)) = (BTNODE (f x) (bt-map f t1) (bt-map f t2))
```

Both properties are proved by appealing to the definition of bt-map; the proofs are shown in Figure 8.4.

The first proof uses just the one case-expression law; the second proof uses two case-expression laws, plus laws that simplify let expressions.

As these examples show, the laws for case expressions enable us to prove equalities involving particular constructed values. But to prove properties that hold for *all* values of a given type τ, we need a proof principle for τ. When τ is an algebraic data type, the proof principle requires only that we prove one case for each of τ's value constructors. And if any value constructor takes an argument of type τ, that case can use an inductive hypothesis.

As an example, I prove this "map-preorder" property:

```
(preorder-elems (bt-map f t)) = (map f (preorder-elems t))
```

A property like this is sometimes expressed using a *commutative diagram*. Assuming that f has type (τ -> τ'), the diagram looks like this:

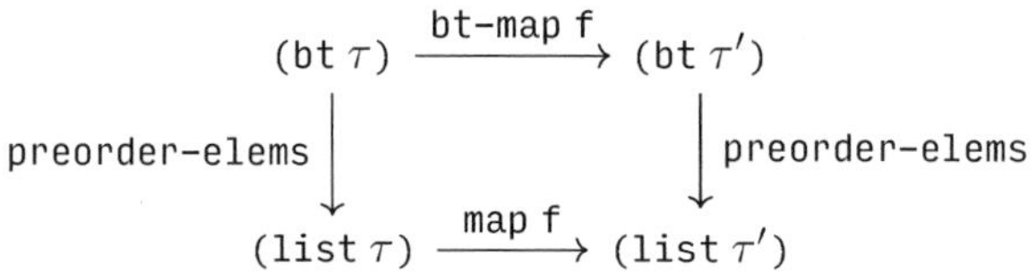

$$\begin{array}{ccc} \texttt{(bt }\tau\texttt{)} & \xrightarrow{\texttt{bt-map f}} & \texttt{(bt }\tau'\texttt{)} \\ \texttt{preorder-elems}\big\downarrow & & \big\downarrow\texttt{preorder-elems} \\ \texttt{(list }\tau\texttt{)} & \xrightarrow{\texttt{map f}} & \texttt{(list }\tau'\texttt{)} \end{array}$$

In a commutative diagram, any path between two points is supposed to be equivalent to any other path. In this case, the paths from upper left to lower right are equivalent, which is exactly the property I'm about to prove.

To show how preorder-elems commutes with the map functions, I use these laws, the proof of which is left to you (Exercise 20):

```
           (preorder-elems BTEMPTY) = '()
(preorder-elems (BTNODE x t1 t2)) = (cons x (append (preorder-elems t1)
                                                    (preorder-elems t2)))
```

```
(bt-map f BTEMPTY)
```
= {substitute actual parameters in definition of bt-map}
```
(case BTEMPTY
   [BTEMPTY BTEMPTY]
   [(BTNODE a left right) (BTNODE (f a) (bt-map f left) (bt-map f right))])
```
= {first choice matches, with no bindings}
```
BTEMPTY
```

(a) The first law: bt-map applied to an empty tree

```
(bt-map f (BTNODE x t1 t2))
```
= {substitute actual parameters in definition of bt-map}
```
(case (BTNODE x t1 t2)
   [BTEMPTY BTEMPTY]
   [(BTNODE a left right) (BTNODE (f a) (bt-map f left) (bt-map f right))])
```
= {first choice doesn't match}
```
(case (BTNODE x t1 t2)
   [(BTNODE a left right) (BTNODE (f a) (bt-map f left) (bt-map f right))])
```
= {first choice matches, with bindings}
```
(let ([a x]
      [left t1]
      [right t2])
  (BTNODE (f a) (bt-map f left) (bt-map f right)))
```
= {substitute x for a and drop binding}
```
(let ([left t1]
      [right t2])
  (BTNODE (f x) (bt-map f left) (bt-map f right)))
```
= {substitute t1 for left and drop binding}
```
(let ([right t2])
  (BTNODE (f x) (bt-map f t1) (bt-map f right)))
```
= {substitute t2 for right and drop binding}
```
(let ()
  (BTNODE (f x) (bt-map f t1) (bt-map f t2)))
```
= {simplify empty let}
```
(BTNODE (f x) (bt-map f t1) (bt-map f t2))
```

(b) The second law: bt-map applied to a nonempty tree

Figure 8.4: Proofs of the basic bt-map laws

To prove that the map-preorder property holds for any tree t, I need consider only two cases: tree t is made either with BTEMPTY or with BTNODE. The case of the empty t is easy:

```
(preorder-elems (bt-map f t))
   = {assumption that t is empty}
(preorder-elems (bt-map f BTEMPTY))
   = {first bt-map law}
(preorder-elems BTEMPTY)
   = {first preorder-elems law}
'()
   = {map-empty law}
(map f '())
   = {first preorder-elems law}
(map f (preorder-elems BTEMPTY))
   = {assumption that t is empty}
(map f (preorder-elems t))
```


The case of a nonempty t requires induction. I assume that t is (BTNODE x t1 t2), and I use the inductive hypothesis on subtrees t1 and t2:

```
(preorder-elems (bt-map f t))
   = {assumption that t is (BTNODE x t1 t2)}
(preorder-elems (bt-map f (BTNODE x t1 t2)))
   = {second bt-map law}
(preorder-elems (BTNODE (f x) (bt-map f t1) (bt-map f t2)))
   = {second preorder-elems law}
(cons (f x) (append (preorder-elems (bt-map f t1)) (preorder-elems (bt-map f t2))))
   = {inductive hypothesis applied to t1}
(cons (f x) (append (map f (preorder-elems t1)) (preorder-elems (bt-map f t2))))
   = {inductive hypothesis applied to t2}
(cons (f x) (append (map f (preorder-elems t1)) (map f (preorder-elems t2))))
   = {map-append law from Chapter 2}
(cons (f x) (map f (append (preorder-elems t1) (preorder-elems t2))))
   = {cons-map law}
(map f (cons x (append (preorder-elems t1) (preorder-elems t2))))
   = {second preorder-elems law}
(map f (preorder-elems (BTNODE x t1 t2)))
   = {assumption that t is (BTNODE x t1 t2)}
(map f (preorder-elems t))
```

More proofs can be found in the Exercises.

Officially, μML's patterns appear only in case expressions. But in real languages, patterns aren't just for case expressions; patterns are used anywhere variables are bound, including `lambda`, `let`, `let*`, `define`, and `val`. In μML, thanks to syntactic sugar, patterns can appear in all these places as well. Such patterns are rewritten into case expressions; the rewrite rules, which you can implement (Exercises 23 to 28), are described below.

A pattern may appear as the single argument to a `lambda` expression. Such a pattern is most useful when the argument is a pair or a triple or something else with just one value constructor:

480a. ⟨*patterns-everywhere transcript* 480a⟩≡ 480b ▷

```
-> (lambda ((PAIR x _)) x)
<function> : (forall ['a 'b] ((pair 'a 'b) -> 'a))
-> (lambda ((PAIR _ y)) y)
<function> : (forall ['a 'b] ((pair 'a 'b) -> 'b))
```

A single-argument `lambda` is desugared as follows:

$$\texttt{(lambda (}p\texttt{) }e\texttt{)} \triangleq \texttt{(lambda (}x\texttt{) (case }x\texttt{ [}p\ e\texttt{]))}, \text{ where } x \notin \text{fv}(e).$$

Variable x must not be a free variable of e, lest e's meaning by changed by variable capture (Section 2.13.3, page 165).

Patterns may also appear in a `lambda` abstraction that has multiple arguments. Such a `lambda` is desugared using a trick: its arguments are bundled into a tuple:

$$\begin{aligned}&\texttt{(lambda (}p_1 \cdots p_n\texttt{) }e\texttt{)} \triangleq\\ &\quad\texttt{(lambda (}x_1 \cdots x_n\texttt{) (case (T}n\ x_1 \cdots x_n\texttt{) [(T}n\ p_1 \cdots p_n\texttt{) }e\texttt{]))},\end{aligned}$$

where for $1 \le i \le n$, $x_i \notin \text{fv}(e)$. The value constructor Tn is `PAIR` when $n = 2$, `TRIPLE` when $n = 3$, and `T4` through `T10` when $4 \le n \le 10$ (chunk S441a). Value constructor Tn is used in two different syntactic forms that look identical: in the scrutinee of the case expression, (T$n\ x_1 \cdots x_n$) is an expression, but in the choice, (T$n\ p_1 \cdots p_n$) is a pattern.

The desugaring transformation for `lambda` also works for `define`:

$$\begin{aligned}&\texttt{(define }f\texttt{ (}p_1 \cdots p_n\texttt{) }e\texttt{)} \triangleq\\ &\quad\texttt{(define }f\texttt{ (}x_1 \cdots x_n\texttt{) (case (T}n\ x_1 \cdots x_n\texttt{) [(T}n\ p_1 \cdots p_n\texttt{) }e\texttt{]))}.\end{aligned}$$

But for function definitions, a far more interesting transformation is available: a function can be defined using a sequence of *clauses*, each of which resembles an equation—an algebraic law. Such a *clausal definition* is desugared into an ordinary function definition that uses a case expression.

In μML, a clausal definition begins with the keyword `define*` and continues with a sequence of clauses, each of which specifies an equation that is true of the function being defined. A clause's left-hand side applies the function to a list of patterns; its right-hand side specifies what that application is equal to. As an example, a clausal definition of the standard `length` function has two clauses:

480b. ⟨*patterns-everywhere transcript* 480a⟩+≡ ◁ 480a 481a ▷

```
-> (define*                          length : (forall ['a] ((list 'a) -> int))
       [(length '())            0]
       [(length (cons x xs))    (+ 1 (length xs))])
length : (forall ['a] ((list 'a) -> int))
-> (length '(a b c))
3 : int
```

Function change-light from the beginning of this chapter can be defined using three clauses:

481a. ⟨*patterns-everywhere transcript* 480a⟩+≡ ◁480b 481b▷

```
                              change-light : (traffic-light -> traffic-light)
-> (define*
     [(change-light GREEN)    YELLOW]
     [(change-light YELLOW)   RED]
     [(change-light RED)      GREEN])
change-light : (traffic-light -> traffic-light)
```

The define* form can also be used to define a function that takes multiple arguments, as in this clausal definition of legal-speed?.

481b. ⟨*patterns-everywhere transcript* 480a⟩+≡ ◁481a 481c▷

```
                              legal-speed? : (speed (option speed) -> bool)
-> (define*
      [(legal-speed? my-speed (SOME limit)) (not (speed< limit my-speed))]
      [(legal-speed? my-speed NONE)         #t])
legal-speed? : (speed (option speed) -> bool)
```

As another example, same-length, which compares the lengths of two lists, uses more interesting patterns:

481c. ⟨*patterns-everywhere transcript* 480a⟩+≡ ◁481b 481d▷

```
-> (define* same-length? : (forall ['a 'b] ((list 'a) (list 'b) -> bool))
      [(same-length? '()           '())         #t]
      [(same-length? (cons _ xs) (cons _ ys)) (same-length? xs ys)]
      [(same-length? _             _)           #f])
same-length? : (forall ['a 'b] ((list 'a) (list 'b) -> bool))
```

All these definitions are desugared using the same rule. A clausal definition defines function f using k clauses, and in each clause, f is applied to n patterns:

$$
\begin{array}{l}
\texttt{(define*} \\
\quad \texttt{[(}f\ p_{1,1}\ \cdots\ p_{1,n}\texttt{)}\ e_1\texttt{]} \\
\quad \texttt{[(}f\ p_{2,1}\ \cdots\ p_{2,n}\texttt{)}\ e_2\texttt{]} \\
\quad \vdots \\
\quad \texttt{[(}f\ p_{k,1}\ \cdots\ p_{k,n}\texttt{)}\ e_k\texttt{])}
\end{array}
\;\triangleq\;
\begin{array}{l}
\texttt{(define}\ f\ \texttt{(}x_1\ \cdots\ x_n\texttt{)} \\
\quad \texttt{(case (T}n\ x_1\ \cdots\ x_n\texttt{)} \\
\qquad \texttt{[(T}n\ p_{1,1}\ \cdots\ p_{1,n}\texttt{)}\ e_1\texttt{]} \\
\qquad \texttt{[(T}n\ p_{2,1}\ \cdots\ p_{2,n}\texttt{)}\ e_2\texttt{]} \\
\qquad \vdots \\
\qquad \texttt{[(T}n\ p_{k,1}\ \cdots\ p_{k,n}\texttt{)}\ e_k\texttt{])),}
\end{array}
$$

where none of $x_1, \ldots, x_n$ appears free in any expression e_i.

An anonymous function can be defined clausally using lambda*; as an example, I define a function that splits a list into two halves (Section E.2). It uses an internal function (scan $\hat{l}$ r ys), which, when possible, transfers an element from r to $\hat{l}$ and drops two elements from ys, then continues. When ys or r is exhausted, scan returns the pair (l, r). A letrec with a clausal lambda* is much simpler than nested case expressions (chunk S130a):

481d. ⟨*patterns-everywhere transcript* 480a⟩+≡ ◁481c 482a▷

```
                  halves : (forall ['a] ((list 'a) -> (pair (list 'a) (list 'a))))
-> (define halves (xs)
     (letrec
       ([scan
          (lambda*
            [(left^ (cons w ws) (cons _ (cons _ zs)))
                                 (scan (cons w left^) ws zs)]
            [(left^ right       _) (pair (reverse left^) right)])])
      (scan '() xs xs)))
```


'()	$\mathcal{B}$
cons	$\mathcal{B}$
GREEN	459a
NONE	$\mathcal{B}$
PAIR	$\mathcal{B}$
pair	$\mathcal{B}$
RED	459a
reverse	$\mathcal{B}$
SOME	$\mathcal{B}$
type speed	461c
speed<	462a
type traffic-light	459a
YELLOW	459a

The halves function does indeed split a list into two halves:

482a. ⟨*patterns-everywhere transcript* 480a⟩+≡ ◁481d 482b▷
```
-> (halves '(1 2 3 4 5))
(PAIR (1 2) (3 4 5)) : (pair (list int) (list int))
-> (halves '(1 2 3 4))
(PAIR (1 2) (3 4)) : (pair (list int) (list int))
-> (halves '())
(PAIR () ()) : (forall ['a] (pair (list 'a) (list 'a)))
```

A lambda* is desugared in the same way as a define*:

$$\begin{array}{l}\texttt{(lambda*}\\ \quad\texttt{[(}p_{1,1}\ \cdots\ p_{1,n}\texttt{)}\ e_1\texttt{]}\\ \quad\texttt{[(}p_{2,1}\ \cdots\ p_{2,n}\texttt{)}\ e_2\texttt{]}\\ \quad\vdots\\ \quad\texttt{[(}p_{k,1}\ \cdots\ p_{k,n}\texttt{)}\ e_k\texttt{])}\end{array} \triangleq \begin{array}{l}\texttt{(lambda (}x_1\ \cdots\ x_n\texttt{)}\\ \quad\texttt{(case (T}n\ x_1\ \cdots\ x_n\texttt{)}\\ \quad\quad\texttt{[(T}n\ p_{1,1}\ \cdots\ p_{1,n}\texttt{)}\ e_1\texttt{]}\\ \quad\quad\texttt{[(T}n\ p_{2,1}\ \cdots\ p_{2,n}\texttt{)}\ e_2\texttt{]}\\ \quad\quad\vdots\\ \quad\quad\texttt{[(T}n\ p_{k,1}\ \cdots\ p_{k,n}\texttt{)}\ e_k\texttt{]))}.\end{array}$$

Finally, patterns may appear in let expressions. The let expression has the most complex desugaring rule, because the desugaring must ensure that every free variable of every pattern may have its type generalized into a polymorphic type scheme. Suppose a let expression binds pattern p_1, which has free variables $y_1, \ldots, y_n$. The idea of the desugaring transformation is to move p_1 from the let into a case. A simple transformation almost works:

$$\texttt{(let ([}p_1\ e_1\texttt{] [}p_2\ e_2\texttt{]} \ldots\texttt{)}\ e\texttt{)} \not\triangleq \texttt{(let ([}x_1\ e_1\texttt{] [}p_2\ e_2\texttt{]} \ldots\texttt{) (case}\ x_1\ \texttt{[}p_1\ e\texttt{]))},$$

where $x_1 \notin \text{fv}(e)$. This transformation works whenever every free variable of pattern p_1 is used only with a monomorphic type scheme. But it fails if free variable of p_1 is used polymorphically, as f is here:

482b. ⟨*patterns-everywhere transcript* 480a⟩+≡ ◁482a 482c▷
```
-> (let ([(PAIR f n)    (pair (lambda (x) x) 73)])
      (TRIPLE (f n) (f f) (f #t)))
(TRIPLE 73 <function> #t) : (forall ['a] (triple int ('a -> 'a) bool))
```

If this code is desugared directly to a single case, the result doesn't typecheck:

482c. ⟨*patterns-everywhere transcript* 480a⟩+≡ ◁482b 482d▷
```
-> (let ([x_1  (pair (lambda (x) x) 73)])
      (case x_1 [(PAIR f n)
                  (TRIPLE (f n) (f f) (f #t))]))
type error: cannot make int equal to (int -> int)
```

For f to be used polymorphically, it must be bound by a let, not by a case. The example let should be desugared like this:

482d. ⟨*patterns-everywhere transcript* 480a⟩+≡ ◁482c 483a▷
```
-> (let ([x_1  (pair (lambda (x) x) 73)])
      (let ([f (case x_1 ((PAIR f n) f))]
            [n (case x_1 ((PAIR f n) n))])
        (TRIPLE (f n) (f f) (f #t))))
(TRIPLE 73 <function> #t) : (forall ['a] (triple int ('a -> 'a) bool))
```

In a general let expression, each pattern-expression pair $\texttt{[}p_i\ e_i\texttt{]}$ is desugared independently. If pattern p_i is a variable, it is left alone. If p_i is a wildcard, it is converted to a new variable x that is not free in e. And if p_i is a constructor application that binds variables $y_1, \ldots, y_n$, the let expression is rewritten to wrap its body e in a let expression that binds all the variables $y_1, \ldots, y_n$:

$$\begin{array}{l}\texttt{(let (}\cdots\ \texttt{[}p_i\ e_i\texttt{]}\ \cdots\texttt{)}\ e\texttt{)} \triangleq \texttt{(let (}\cdots\ \texttt{[}x_i\ e_i\texttt{]}\ \cdots\texttt{)}\\ \qquad\qquad\qquad\qquad\qquad\texttt{(let (}\cdots\ \texttt{[}y_j\ \texttt{(case}\ x_i\ \texttt{[}p_i\ y_j\texttt{])]}\ \cdots\texttt{)}\ e\texttt{))},\end{array}$$

where x_i is not free in e. This rewriting continues until all the let forms bind only variables, not other patterns.

A caution: because the desugaring transformation converts a non-nested `let` into nested `let`s, patterns p_i have to be checked for duplicate variables *before* desugaring begins, as in this example:

483a. ⟨*patterns-everywhere transcript* 480a⟩+≡ ◁482d 483b▷

```
-> (let ([(PAIR x y) (pair 3 4)] [(PAIR y z) (pair 7 8)]) (+ x (+ y z)))
syntax error: bound name y appears twice in let
```


Patterns are also useful in the `val` form. The `val` form is closely related to `let`, and if it could be desugared using the same tricks, life would be good. Unfortunately, what corresponds to "an x_i not free in e" is "an x_i not used in the rest of the program." But the desugaring transformation can't know what x_i's might be used in the rest of the program. The best it can do is just pick a name, which, once bound, sits in the basis from then on. A reasonable name is `it`:

$$\texttt{(val}\ p\ e\texttt{)} \stackrel{\triangle}{=} \texttt{(val it}\ e\texttt{)}$$

$$\vdots$$

$$\texttt{(val}\ y_i\ \texttt{(case it [}p\ y_i\texttt{]))}$$

$$\vdots$$

This expansion does evaluate e exactly once, and it does bind each y_i with the correct, generalized type scheme. But it clobbers the variable `it`.

483b. ⟨*patterns-everywhere transcript* 480a⟩+≡ ◁483a

```
-> (val (PAIR left right) (halves '(a b c d)))
(PAIR (a b) (c d)) : (pair (list sym) (list sym))
(c d) : (list sym)
(a b) : (list sym)
-> left
(a b) : (list sym)
-> right
(c d) : (list sym)
```

The syntactic sugar completes what you need to know in order to program effectively using algebraic data types. To understand more deeply how they work, consult the theory and code in the next sections: when and how a user-defined type is distinct from similar types (Section 8.5), how the relevant syntax and values are represented (Section 8.6), how type definitions are typed and evaluated (Section 8.7), and how case expressions are typechecked and evaluated (Section 8.8).

8.5 Type generativity and type equivalence

In any language that has user-defined types, a programmer has to know if and when the types they define are equivalent to anything else. That knowledge is determined by the ways the language uses three concepts: structural equivalence, generativity, and type abbreviation.

`halves`	481d
`PAIR`	$\mathcal{B}$
`pair`	$\mathcal{B}$

- *Structural equivalence* says two types are equivalent when they are applications of equivalent type constructors to equivalent type arguments, as in Typed μScheme's EquivApplications rule (page 369):

$$\frac{\tau_i \equiv \tau_i',\ 1 \le i \le n \qquad \tau \equiv \tau'}{(\tau_1, \ldots, \tau_n)\ \tau \equiv (\tau_1', \ldots, \tau_n')\ \tau'}. \qquad \text{(EquivApplications)}$$

  In μML, as in Typed μScheme and nano-ML, structural equivalence is used for list types, function types, pair types, and so on. In C, structural equivalence is used for pointer types and array types; for example, pointers to equivalent types are equivalent. And in Modula-3, for example, structural equivalence is used for record types: record types with the same fields are equivalent, provided that corresponding fields have equivalent types.

- *Generativity* is a property that a language designer can associate with any syntactic form involving types. If a syntactic form is *generative*, then a type or type constructor introduced by that form is distinct from—that is, *not* equivalent to—any other type or type constructor. In Typed μScheme and nano-ML, no forms are generative, because Typed μScheme and nano-ML have no type-definition forms. In μML, the `data` and `implicit-data` forms are generative, as are the corresponding forms in Standard ML, OCaml, and Haskell. μML's `record` form is syntactic sugar for `data`, so it is generative, but the corresponding form in Standard ML is not. In C, the `struct`, `union`, and `enum` type *definition* forms—the ones that include fields in curly braces—are generative, but the corresponding type *reference* forms, like just plain `struct Exp`, are not (Exercise 29). In Haskell, both `data` and `newtype` definition forms are generative; `newtype` introduces a new, distinct type that has the same run-time representation as an existing type.

- A *type abbreviation* introduces a new name for an existing type. A type-abbreviation form is purposefully *not* generative; the new name is equivalent to the original type. In Molecule (Chapter 9), as well as Standard ML, type abbreviations are written using the `type` keyword; the same form appears in Haskell, where it is called a *type synonym*, and in C, where it is called a "`typedef` declaration."

By design, only structural equivalence and generativity are used in μML; type abbreviations are added in Exercise 32.

Generativity is a powerful idea, but in older work, especially work oriented toward compilers, you may see the term "name equivalence" or "occurrence equivalence." These terms refer to special applications of generativity—for example, "name equivalence" may describe a language that has a syntactic form which resembles a type abbreviation but is generative. The terms "name equivalence" and "occurrence equivalence" usually describe language designs that were popular in the 1970s, but these terms are outmoded and should no longer be used. The concept of generativity is more flexible and can be applied to more designs.

Of what use is generativity? Generativity helps ensure that two types are equivalent only when you mean them to be equivalent. This issue matters most when programs are split into multiple modules (Chapter 9). For example, if two record types both have numeric fields `heading` and `distance`, but one is degrees and miles and the other is radians and kilometers, you want them not to be equivalent.

Generativity should inform our thinking about design, theory, and implementation of programming languages.

- The effect of typing a generative construct can be expressed by the idea of a "fresh" or "distinct" type constructor. To define freshness, μML's type theory remembers a set containing every type constructor ever created; a fresh constructor is one not in that set. In the implementation, there's less bookkeeping; each new type constructor is assigned an identity that is guaranteed to be unique. The techniques used are the same techniques used to allocate fresh locations in the operational semantics and implementation of μScheme.

- When definitions can be generative and type names can be redefined, a single name can stand for different types in different parts of a program. In this way, a type name is like a variable name, which can stand for different values in different parts of a program.

In the interpreter, types are represented in two ways. Type syntax, represented by ML type tyex (chunk S454c) and shown mathematically as t, appears in programs, and type syntax is built up using *type names* (ML type name). Types themselves, represented by ML types ty and type_scheme (chunk 408) and shown mathematically as τ and σ, are used by the type checker, and types are built up using *type constructors* (ML type tycon).

The internal representation of type constructors, the generation of fresh type constructors, and a type-equivalence function are presented below.

8.5.1 Representing and generating type constructors

The representation of a type constructor must solve two problems: it should be easy to create a type constructor that is distinct from all others, and it should be easy to tell if two type constructors are the same. I address both problems by assigning each type constructor an *identity,* which I represent by an integer.

485a. ⟨*foundational definitions for generated type constructors* 485a⟩≡ (S438d) 485b ▷

```
type tycon_identity = int
```

Integers are great for algorithms but not so good for talking to programmers. To make it possible to print an informative representation of any type, I represent a type constructor as a record containing not only its identity but also a name used to print it.

485b. ⟨*foundational definitions for generated type constructors* 485a⟩+≡ (S438d) ◁ 485a 485c ▷

```
type tycon = { printName : name, identity : tycon_identity }
```

Every type constructor is created by function freshTycon, which is defined in Appendix S. This function takes a type name as its argument and returns a tycon with a distinct printName and a unique identity. Type constructors are equal if and only if they have the same identity.

485c. ⟨*foundational definitions for generated type constructors* 485a⟩+≡ (S438d) ◁ 485b

eqTycon : tycon * tycon -> bool

```
fun eqTycon ( { identity = id,  printName = _ }
            , { identity = id', printName = _ }) =
  id = id'
```

With eqTycon defined, type equivalence is determined by function eqType, which is carried over unchanged from chunk 412a in Chapter 7.

Generativity is implemented by calling freshTycon whenever a generative type definition is typed. Definitions of primitive types are also considered generative, and their type constructors are also created using freshTycon.

485d. ⟨*type constructors built into μML and μHaskell* 485d⟩≡ (S438d)

```
val inttycon  = freshTycon "int"
val symtycon  = freshTycon "sym"
```

freshTycon	S449b
type name	303

8.6 ABSTRACT SYNTAX AND VALUES OF μML

User-defined, algebraic data types require new syntactic forms, which are shown in Figure 8.5:

- A DATA definition form defines a type.
- A VCONX expression form introduces constructed data, and a CASE expression observes it. (In an expression, a value constructor VCONX has the same type theory and operational semantics as a value variable VAR, but as noted in Section 8.2.2 [page 469], a VCONX and a VAR are written differently in the

486a. ⟨*definition of* def *for μML* 486a⟩≡ (S437b)

type data_def

```
datatype def = DATA of data_def
                | ⟨forms of def carried over from nano-ML S438b⟩
  withtype data_def = name * kind * (vcon * tyex) list
```

486b. ⟨*definitions of* exp *and* value *for μML* 486b⟩≡ (S437b) 486d ▷

```
type vcon = name   (* a value constructor *)
datatype exp
  = VCONX of vcon
  | CASE  of exp * (pat * exp) list
  | ⟨forms of exp carried over from nano-ML S438a⟩
```

Case expressions include patterns.

486c. ⟨*definition of* pat, *for patterns* 486c⟩≡ (S437b)

```
datatype pat = WILDCARD
             | PVAR     of name
             | CONPAT   of vcon * pat list
```

486d. ⟨*definitions of* exp *and* value *for μML* 486b⟩+≡ (S437b) ◁ 486b

```
and value
  = CONVAL of vcon * value list
  | SYM    of name
  | NUM    of int
  | CLOSURE   of lambda * value env ref
  | PRIMITIVE of primop
 withtype lambda = name list * exp
      and primop = value list -> value
```

Figure 8.5: Key elements of μML's abstract syntax and values

source code—and they play different roles in patterns. They are represented differently in expressions, as well; that way, if a name is not found, the error message can clarify what the interpreter was expecting, as shown in chunk S452c.)

Constructed data requires a representation, which in μML is formed with CONVAL (Figure 8.5, bottom).

Values formed with CONVAL replace some forms of value that are used in nano-ML. Nano-ML's BOOLV form is no longer needed; in μML, #t and #f are defined using a data definition, as value constructors of type bool. So for example, #t is represented by CONVAL ("#t", []), not by the BOOLV true used in nano-ML. Similarly, nano-ML forms NIL and PAIR are no longer needed: value constructors '() and cons are also defined using a data definition. μML's values include only constructed data, symbols, numbers, and functions—a welcome simplification.[3]

The DATA definition and the CONVAL value are explained below, in Section 8.7. The CASE expression and associated patterns are explained in Section 8.8.

8.7 Theory and implementation of user-defined types

New type constructors are created by type definitions. And in any language with user-defined types, type definitions introduce new names, which have to be ac-

[3]Nano-ML's internal language could be simplified even more by eliminating the IFX syntax; if could be syntactic sugar for case. But to enable μML's interpreter to share code with nano-ML's interpreter, I have kept both forms.

counted for in the type theory. And if type constructors and type names are distinct, type constructors must also be accounted for. In μML's type theory, the accounting works like this:

- Each type name and type variable *has* a kind and *stands for* a type. The kind and the type are associated with the name in a kind environment Δ, which is part of μML's basis. Δ is extended by each `data` definition, which adds a binding for the name of the defined type.

- μML's basis also includes a *type-constructor set* M, which contains the set of all type constructors ever created. A type constructor created by a `data` definition must not be a member of M; that requirement makes the `data` form generative. Once created, each new type constructor is added to M. In the code, set M is represented by the mutable variable `nextIdentity`, which is used by `freshTycon` to ensure that each type constructor has a unique identity (chunk S449b). M is the set given by this equation:

$$M = \{i \mid 0 \leq i < \texttt{!nextIdentity}\}.$$

In addition to Δ and M, the basis of μML also includes a type environment Γ. As in nano-ML, Γ gives a type scheme for each value, and Γ is extended by `val`, `val-rec`, and `define`. In μML, Γ is also extended by `data`: a `data` definition adds one value binding for each value constructor.

When a μML definition is typed, any part of the basis may change. The judgment form is therefore $\boxed{\langle d, \Gamma, \Delta, M\rangle \to \langle \Gamma', \Delta', M'\rangle}$. Rules for this judgment form rely on the following other judgment forms:

Form	*Informal meaning*
$\langle d, \Gamma\rangle \to \Gamma'$	Nano-ML definition d is typed (new value)
$\langle d, \Gamma, \Delta, M\rangle \to \langle \Gamma', \Delta', M'\rangle$	μML definition d is typed (new value/type)
$\sigma \preccurlyeq \mu :: \kappa$	Type scheme σ works for a value constructor of type μ
$\Delta \vdash t \rightsquigarrow \sigma :: *$	Type syntax t is translated to type scheme σ

The third judgment is a *compatibility* judgment $\sigma \preccurlyeq \mu :: \kappa$; it says "type scheme σ can be the type of a value constructor for algebraic data type μ, which has kind κ." It is discussed in detail below.

8.7.1 *Typing datatype definitions using type compatibility*

In μML's `data` form, the type of every value constructor is explicit in the syntax. The type of each value constructor must be compatible with the new type that is being defined; for example, a value constructor of type `int` is not compatible with a definition of type `bool`. Compatibility is enforced by the $\sigma_i \preccurlyeq \mu :: \kappa$ premises in this rule:

type env 304
type kind 355a
type name 303
type tyex S454c

$$\frac{\begin{array}{c}\mu \notin M \qquad M' = M \cup \{\mu\} \\ \Delta' = \Delta\{T \mapsto (\mu, \kappa)\} \\ \Delta' \vdash t_i \rightsquigarrow \sigma_i :: *,\ 1 \leq i \leq n \\ \sigma_i \preccurlyeq \mu :: \kappa,\ 1 \leq i \leq n \\ \Gamma' = \Gamma\{K_1 : \sigma_1, \ldots, K_n : \sigma_n\}\end{array}}{\langle \text{DATA}(T :: \kappa, K_1 : t_1, \ldots, K_n : t_n), \Gamma, \Delta, M\rangle \to \langle \Gamma', \Delta', M'\rangle}. \qquad (\text{DATA})$$

The DATA rule is interpreted operationally as follows:

1. Create a fresh type constructor μ, and record in the kind environment that type name T stands for type μ with kind κ.

2. For each value constructor K_i with given type t_i, confirm that type t_i has kind $*$, and translate it into an internal type scheme σ_i. This operation, expressed by judgment $\Delta' \vdash t_i \rightsquigarrow \sigma_i :: *$, extends Typed μScheme's judgment $\Delta' \vdash t_i :: *$, which merely checks that the programmer's type syntax is well kinded. It is described below.

3. Also for each value constructor, check that its type scheme is compatible with the new type being defined ($\sigma_i \preccurlyeq \mu :: \kappa$).

4. Finally, assuming that all the types are compatible, enter the types of the value constructors into the type environment.

The compatibility judgment $\sigma \preccurlyeq \mu :: \kappa$ says that a value constructor for type μ had better *be* a μ or *return* a μ. As an example, I define type `fish` with two compatible value constructors and one incompatible one:

488a. ⟨*transcript* 459a⟩+≡ ◁ 474f 488b ▷

```
-> (data * fish
      [BLUEGILL : fish]                ; OK, you're a fish
      [BASS     : (sym -> fish)]       ; OK, you return a fish
      [PISCES   : sym]                 ; No good!  A symbol is not a fish
   )
type error: value constructor PISCES should have type fish, but it has type sym
```

Since `PISCES` has an incompatible type, the definition is rejected. Eliminate `PISCES` and the definition is good:[4]

488b. ⟨*transcript* 459a⟩+≡ ◁ 488a 493c ▷

```
-> (data * fish
      [BLUEGILL : fish]                ; OK, you're a fish
      [BASS     : (sym -> fish)]       ; OK, you return a fish
   )
-> BLUEGILL
BLUEGILL : fish@{2}
-> (BASS 'largemouth)
(BASS largemouth) : fish@{2}
-> (BASS 'striped)
(BASS striped) : fish@{2}
```

A monomorphic value constructor is compatible if it *is* a fish or it *returns* a fish. A polymorphic constructor is the same, but with more fiddly detail:

$\boxed{\sigma \preccurlyeq \mu :: \kappa}$

MONOISCOMPAT
$$\frac{}{\mu \preccurlyeq \mu :: *}$$

MONORETURNSCOMPAT
$$\frac{}{\tau_1 \times \cdots \times \tau_n \to \mu \preccurlyeq \mu :: *}$$

POLYISCOMPAT
$$\frac{\alpha'_1, \ldots, \alpha'_k \text{ all distinct}}{\forall \alpha_1, \ldots, \alpha_k . (\alpha'_1, \ldots, \alpha'_k)\ \mu \preccurlyeq \mu :: *_1 \cdots *_k \Rightarrow *}$$

POLYRETURNSCOMPAT
$$\frac{\alpha'_1, \ldots, \alpha'_k \text{ all distinct}}{\forall \alpha_1, \ldots, \alpha_k . \tau_1 \times \cdots \times \tau_n \to (\alpha'_1, \ldots, \alpha'_k)\ \mu \preccurlyeq \mu :: *_1 \cdots *_k \Rightarrow *}$$

[4] Because every `data` generates a fresh type contructor, the new type prints as `fish@{2}`, which distinguishes it from the original, bad `fish`.

$$\boxed{\Delta \vdash t \rightsquigarrow \tau :: \kappa}$$

KINDINTROCON
$$\frac{T \in \operatorname{dom} \Delta \qquad \Delta(T) = (\tau, \kappa)}{\Delta \vdash T \rightsquigarrow \tau :: \kappa}$$

KINDINTROVAR
$$\frac{\alpha \in \operatorname{dom} \Delta \qquad \Delta(\alpha) = (\tau, \kappa)}{\Delta \vdash \alpha \rightsquigarrow \tau :: \kappa}$$

KINDAPP
$$\frac{\Delta \vdash t \rightsquigarrow \tau :: \kappa_1 \times \cdots \times \kappa_n \Rightarrow \kappa \qquad \Delta \vdash t_i \rightsquigarrow \tau_i :: \kappa_i,\ 1 \le i \le n}{\Delta \vdash (t\ \ t_1\ \cdots\ t_n) \rightsquigarrow (\tau_1, \ldots, \tau_n)\ \tau :: \kappa}$$

KINDFUNCTION
$$\frac{\Delta \vdash t_i \rightsquigarrow \tau_i :: *,\ 1 \le i \le n \qquad \Delta \vdash t \rightsquigarrow \tau :: *}{\Delta \vdash (t_1\ \cdots\ t_n\ \texttt{->}\ t) \rightsquigarrow \tau_1 \times \cdots \times \tau_n \rightarrow \tau :: *}$$

$$\boxed{\Delta \vdash t \rightsquigarrow \sigma :: *}$$

SCHEMEKINDALL
$$\frac{\alpha_1, \ldots, \alpha_n \text{ are all distinct} \qquad \Delta\{\alpha_1 \mapsto (\alpha_1, *), \ldots, \alpha_n \mapsto (\alpha_n, *)\} \vdash t \rightsquigarrow \tau :: *}{\Delta \vdash (\texttt{forall}\ (\alpha_1\ \cdots\ \alpha_n)\ t) \rightsquigarrow \forall \alpha_1, \ldots, \alpha_n . \tau :: *}$$

SCHEMEKINDMONOTYPE
$$\frac{\Delta \vdash t \rightsquigarrow \tau :: *}{\Delta \vdash t \rightsquigarrow \forall . \tau :: *}$$

Figure 8.6: Translation of μML's type syntax, with kinds

The type variables $\alpha'_1, \ldots, \alpha'_k$, which are the parameters to μ, are actually a permutation of the quantified type variables $\alpha_1, \ldots, \alpha_k$. But in the compatibility judgment, it's enough for the α'_i's to be distinct. If they are, the translation judgment $\Delta' \vdash t_i \rightsquigarrow \sigma_i :: *$ (below) ensures that they are a permutation of the α_i's.

The compatibility rules are implemented by function `validate` in Appendix S. Using that function, and using function `txTyScheme` to implement the translation judgment described below, function `typeDataDef` types a `data` definition. It returns Γ', Δ', and a list of strings: the name T followed by names $[K_1, \ldots, K_n]$.

489. ⟨*typing and evaluation of* `data` *definitions* 489⟩≡ (S437a) 490 ▷

```
                        typeDataDef : data_def * type_env * (ty * kind) env
                                    -> type_env * (ty * kind) env * string list
fun typeDataDef ((T, kind, vcons), Gamma, Delta) =
  let ⟨definition of validate, for the types of the value constructors of T S450a⟩
      val mu      = freshTycon T
      val Delta'  = bind (T, (TYCON mu, kind), Delta)
      fun translateVcon (K, tx) = (K, txTyScheme (tx, Delta'))
      val Ksigmas = map translateVcon vcons
      val ()      = app (fn (K, sigma) => validate (K, sigma, mu, kind))
                        Ksigmas
      val Gamma'  = extendTypeEnv (Gamma, Ksigmas)
      val strings = kindString kind :: map (typeSchemeString o snd) Ksigmas
  in  (Gamma', Delta', strings)
  end
```

bind 305d
type env 304
extendTypeEnv S453c
freshTycon S449b
type kind 355a
kindString S462d
snd S249b
txTyScheme S456c
type ty 408
TYCON 408
type type_env 435a
typeSchemeString S431d
validate S450a

8.7.2 Translating type syntax into types

Just as in Typed μScheme, type syntax written by a programmer isn't trusted; nonsense like `(int int)` and `(list -> list)` is rejected by the type system. In Typed μScheme, it suffices to check the kind of each type, then pass the syntax on to the type checker. But in μML, the syntax of types is different from the internal representation used for type inference, so the syntax can't be passed on. Instead, it is translated.

The translation is expressed using two judgment forms, $\boxed{\Delta \vdash t \rightsquigarrow \tau :: \kappa}$ and $\boxed{\Delta \vdash t \rightsquigarrow \sigma :: *}$, which translate μML type syntax into either a Hindley-Milner type or a type scheme, respectively. The rules are shown in Figure 8.6. The implementation is so similar to Typed μScheme's kind checking that I doubt you need to see it. But if you do, you will find functions `txType` and `txTyScheme` in Appendix S.

8.7.3 *Run-time representation of value constructors*

Datatype definitions are not only typed; they are also evaluated. Evaluating a datatype definition introduces a function or value for every value constructor. A value constructor with a function type gets a function; a value constructor with a non-function type is a value by itself. To tell which is which, function `isPolymorphicFuntyex` looks at the type syntax. As with nano-ML, evaluation isn't formalized.

490. ⟨*typing and evaluation of* `data` *definitions* 489⟩+≡ (S437a) ◁ 489

```
evalDataDef : data_def * value env -> value env * string list
isPolymorphicFuntyex : tyex -> bool
```

```
fun evalDataDef ((_, _, typed_vcons), rho) =
  let fun valFor (K, t) = if isPolymorphicFuntyex t then
                            PRIMITIVE (fn vs => CONVAL (K, vs))
                          else
                            CONVAL (K, [])
      fun addVcon ((K, t), rho) = bind (K, valFor (K, t), rho)
  in  (foldl addVcon rho typed_vcons, map fst typed_vcons)
  end
```

8.8 THEORY AND IMPLEMENTATION OF CASE EXPRESSIONS

The operational semantics and type theory of pattern matching apply to any language with pattern-matching case expressions.

8.8.1 *Evaluation of case expressions and pattern matching*

As illustrated in Section 8.2.1, a case expression is evaluated by trying one choice after another, selecting the first choice whose pattern matches the scrutinee. If an attempt at pattern matching *succeeds*, it produces an environment ρ', which binds the variables that appear in the pattern. If the attempt at pattern matching *fails*, I say it produces † (pronounced "failure," but think of a dagger in the heart). The † is not an environment or a value or an expression or anything we have encountered before; it is a new symbol that means pattern-match failure. To stand for the result of a pattern match, which is either an environment ρ' or †, I use the metavariable r. The matching judgment therefore takes the form $\boxed{\langle p, v\rangle \rightarrowtail r}$:

$\langle p, v\rangle \rightarrowtail \rho'$	Pattern p matches value v, producing bindings ρ';
$\langle p, v\rangle \rightarrowtail \dagger$	Pattern p does not match value v.

Since patterns are matched only in the context of a case expression, understanding of pattern matching begins with case expressions.

A case expression is evaluated by first evaluating the scrutinee e, which involves no pattern matching. Once e is evaluated to produce a value v, the operational semantics puts v back into the scrutinee position as a literal expression. This trick

Table 8.7: Correspondence between μML's type system and code
(See also Table 7.3, page 432)

Type system	Concept	Interpreter
d	Definition	`def` (page 486)
e	Expression	`exp` (page 486)
t	Type syntax	`tyex` (page 486)
x	Variable	`name` (page 303)
K	Value constructor	`vcon` (page 486)
p	Pattern	`pat` (page 486)
T	Syntactic type name	
α	Type variable	`tyvar` (page 408)
μ	Type constructor	`tycon` (page 485)
M	Set of type constructors	Hidden inside `freshTycon` (page S449)
τ	Type	`ty` (page 408)
$\sigma, \forall\alpha.\tau$	Type scheme	`type_scheme` (page 408)
Γ	Type environment	`type_env` (page 435)
$\Gamma_1 \uplus \Gamma_2$	Disjoint union	`disjointUnion` (page 497)
$\Gamma + \Gamma'$	Extension	`<+>` (page 305)
C	Constraint	`con` (page 436)
$\tau_1 \sim \tau_2$	Equality constraint	τ_1 `~` τ_2 (page 436)
$C_1 \wedge C_2$	Conjunction	C_1 `/\` C_2 (page 436)
$\mathbf{T}$	Trivial constraint	`TRIVIAL` (page 436)
$\bigwedge_i C_i$	Conjunction	`conjoinConstraints` $[C_1, \ldots, C_n]$ (page 436)
$\Delta \vdash t \rightsquigarrow \tau :: \kappa$	Type elaboration	`txType` (page S455)
$\sigma \preccurlyeq \mu :: \kappa$	Type compatibility	`validate` (page S450)
$C, \Gamma \vdash e : \tau$	Type inference	`ty` $e = (\tau, C)$ (chunk 497a)
$C, \Gamma \vdash$ `[`p e`]` $: \tau \to \tau'$	Type inference	`choicetype(`(p, e)`,` Γ`)` $= (\tau \to \tau', C)$ (page 497)
$C, \Gamma, \Gamma' \vdash p : \tau$	Type inference	`pattype(`p`,` Γ`)` $= (\Gamma', \tau, C)$ (page 498)
$\langle d, \Gamma, \Delta, M\rangle \to \Gamma'$	Type inference	`typdef(`d`,` Γ`)` $=$ `(`Γ'`,` s`)` (page 439) and also `typeDataDef` (page 489)

avoids the need for a special form of judgment that would otherwise try to match v with each choice in turn. The trick is implemented by this rule:

$$\frac{\langle e, \rho, \sigma\rangle \Downarrow v \qquad \langle \text{CASE}(\text{LITERAL}(v), \texttt{[}p_1\ e_1\texttt{]}, \ldots, \texttt{[}p_n\ e_n\texttt{]}), \rho, \sigma\rangle \Downarrow v'}{\langle \text{CASE}(e, \texttt{[}p_1\ e_1\texttt{]}, \ldots, \texttt{[}p_n\ e_n\texttt{]}), \rho, \sigma\rangle \Downarrow v'}. \qquad (\text{CASESCRUTINEE})$$

Once the scrutinee is a literal v, pattern matching can begin.

The value of the scrutinee is always matched against the first pattern p_1. If that match succeeds, producing environment ρ', the value of the case expression is the

Table 8.8: Correspondence between μML's operational semantics and code

Semantics	Concept	Interpreter
e	Expression	`exp` (page 486)
x	Variable	`name` (page 303)
K	Value constructor	`vcon` (page 486)
p	Pattern	`pat` (page 486)
v	Value	`value` (page 486)
$\rho + \rho'$	Extension	`<+>` (page 305)
$\rho_1 \uplus \rho_2$	Disjoint union	`disjointUnion` (page 497)
$\langle p, v \rangle \rightarrowtail \rho'$	Pattern matches	`match`$(p, v) = \rho'$ (page 494)
$\langle p, v \rangle \rightarrowtail \dagger$	Pattern match fails	`match`(p, v) raises `Doesn'tMatch`

value produced by evaluating the corresponding right-hand side e_1 in the extended environment $\rho + \rho'$.

$$\frac{\langle p_1, v \rangle \rightarrowtail \rho' \qquad \langle e_1, \rho, \sigma + \rho' \rangle \Downarrow v'}{\langle \text{CASE}(\text{LITERAL}(v), [p_1\ e_1], \ldots, [p_n\ e_n]), \rho, \sigma \rangle \Downarrow v'} \qquad (\text{CASEMATCH})$$

The extension $\rho + \rho'$ is defined for any two environments ρ and ρ'; environment ρ is extended by adding ρ''s bindings to it.

$$\text{dom}(\rho + \rho') = \text{dom}\,\rho \cup \text{dom}\,\rho'$$

$$(\rho + \rho')(x) = \begin{cases} \rho'(x), \text{if } x \in \text{dom}\,\rho' \\ \rho(x), \text{if } x \notin \text{dom}\,\rho' \end{cases}$$

The $+$ operation can also express an environment extended with bindings:

$$\rho\{x_1 \mapsto v_1, \ldots, x_n \mapsto v_n\} = \rho + \{x_1 \mapsto v_1, \ldots, x_n \mapsto v_n\}.$$

Back to the case expression: what if the first pattern *doesn't* match? Evaluation continues with the next pattern. The operational semantics drops choice $[p_1\ e_1]$ from the case expression, and it evaluates a new case expression whose first choice is $[p_2\ e_2]$:

$$\frac{\langle p_1, v \rangle \rightarrowtail \dagger \qquad \langle \text{CASE}(\text{LITERAL}(v), [p_2\ e_2], \ldots, [p_n\ e_n]), \rho, \sigma \rangle \Downarrow v'}{\langle \text{CASE}(\text{LITERAL}(v), [p_1\ e_1], \ldots, [p_n\ e_n]), \rho, \sigma \rangle \Downarrow v'}. \qquad (\text{CASEFAIL})$$

What if there are no more choices—that is, what if $n = 1$? Then no rule applies. The operational semantics gets stuck, and the interpreter raises the `RuntimeError` exception.

Each rule is implemented as a clause for function `ev`. To avoid an infinite loop, the clauses for $\text{CASE}(\text{LITERAL}(v), cs)$ must precede the clause for $\text{CASE}(e, cs)$. The matching judgment is implemented by function `match`: if matching succeeds, it returns ρ', and if not, it raises the exception `Doesn'tMatch`. In that case it's time to try the remaining choices.

492. ⟨*more alternatives for* `ev` *for nano-ML and* μ*ML* 492⟩≡ (S429a) 493a ▷

```
match : pat * value -> value env
<+>   : 'a env * 'a env -> 'a env
```

```
  | ev (CASE (LITERAL v,
              (p, e) :: choices)) =
      (let val rho' = match (p, v)
       in  eval (e, rho <+> rho')
       end
       handle Doesn'tMatch => ev (CASE (LITERAL v, choices)))
```

If no choices match a `LITERAL` form, then the case expression does not match.

493a. ⟨*more alternatives for* `ev` *for nano-ML and μML* 492⟩+≡ (S429a) ◁492 493b▷

```
| ev (CASE (LITERAL v, [])) =
    raise RuntimeError ("'case' does not match " ^ valueString v)
```

If the scrutinee `e` hasn't yet been evaluated, `ev` calls itself recursively to evaluate `e`, places the resulting value into a `LITERAL` expression, then tail-calls itself to select a choice.

493b. ⟨*more alternatives for* `ev` *for nano-ML and μML* 492⟩+≡ (S429a) ◁493a

```
| ev (CASE (e, choices)) =
    ev (CASE (LITERAL (ev e), choices))
```


Now that we know how matching is used, we can examine in detail, formally, how it works. We start with a simple but common special case: a value constructor applied to a list of variables. A pattern of the form $(K\ x_1\ \cdots\ x_m)$ matches values of the form $\text{VCON}(K, [v_1, \ldots, v_m])$. This case can be described by a specialized rule:

$$\frac{\begin{array}{c} x_1, \ldots, x_m \text{ all distinct} \\ \rho = \{x_1 \mapsto v_1, \ldots, x_m \mapsto v_m\} \end{array}}{\langle (K\ x_1\ \cdots\ x_m), \text{VCON}(K, [v_1, \ldots, v_m])\rangle \rightarrowtail \rho}. \qquad \text{(SPECIALIZED MATCH RULE)}$$

And the case is illustrated by this example:

493c. ⟨*transcript* 459a⟩+≡ ◁488b 494a▷

```
-> (case '(1 2 3 4 5) [(cons x xs) (cons x (reverse xs))])
(1 5 4 3 2) : (list int)
```

The simple case is easy: bind each variable to the corresponding value. But it's *too* simple; in real code, patterns can be nested to arbitrary depth. Nesting complicates the theory, but, as you can see in some of the traffic-light examples in Section 8.1 and in Standard ML code throughout this book, nesting simplifies code. If you want to understand why programmers like algebraic data types, experiment with nested patterns. Once you're convinced they are worth having, you'll have an easier time with the theory.

In general, when a value constructor K appears in a pattern p, K is applied not to a list of variables but to a list of sub-patterns: $p = (K\ p_1\ \cdots\ p_m)$. *Each* sub-pattern p_i can introduce new variables, and bindings for all those variables have to be combined. When combining bindings, the operational semantics avoids the ambiguity that would arise if the same variable appeared in more than one binding: it combines bindings using a new operation, *disjoint union.*

The disjoint union of environments ρ_1 and ρ_2 is written $\rho_1 \uplus \rho_2$, and it is defined if and only if $\text{dom}\,\rho_1 \cap \text{dom}\,\rho_2 = \emptyset$:

$$\text{dom}(\rho_1 \uplus \rho_2) = \text{dom}\,\rho_1 \cup \text{dom}\,\rho_2,$$

$$(\rho_1 \uplus \rho_2)(x) = \begin{cases} \rho_1(x), \text{if } x \in \text{dom}\,\rho_1 \\ \rho_2(x), \text{if } x \in \text{dom}\,\rho_2. \end{cases}$$

What if pattern-matching fails, so there is no environment? Disjoint union can be extended to *all* pattern matching results; disjoint union of failure with any result is still failure:

$$\dagger \uplus \rho = \dagger \qquad \rho \uplus \dagger = \dagger \qquad \dagger \uplus \dagger = \dagger.$$

This extended definition is implemented by function `disjointUnion` in Appendix S. Using it, a constructor application is matched by combining the results of matching

`<+>`	305f
`CASE`	486b
`cons`	$\mathcal{B}$
`Doesn'tMatch`	494b
`type env`	304
`ev`	S429a
`eval`	S429a
`LITERAL`	S438a
`match`	494b
`type pat`	486c
`reverse`	$\mathcal{B}$
`rho`	S429a
`RuntimeError`	S213b
`type value`	486d
`valueString`	S461b

its argument patterns:

$$\frac{\langle p_i, v_i\rangle \rightarrowtail r_i, \quad 1 \le i \le m \qquad r = r_1 \uplus \cdots \uplus r_m}{\langle (K\ p_1\ \cdots\ p_m), \text{VCON}(K, [v_1, \ldots, v_m])\rangle \rightarrowtail r}. \qquad \text{(MATCHVCON)}$$

Because disjoint union is associative and commutative, results r_i can be combined in any order. And if any sub-pattern fails to match, the whole pattern fails to match.

A constructor pattern also fails to match when value v is not made with K.

$$\frac{v \text{ does not have the form VCON}(K, [v_1, \ldots, v_m])}{\langle (K\ p_1\ \cdots\ p_m), v\rangle \rightarrowtail \dagger} \qquad \text{(FAILVCON)}$$

Other patterns match using much simpler rules. A bare value constructor matches only itself, and it produces no bindings.

$$\frac{}{\langle K, \text{VCON}(K, [\,])\rangle \rightarrowtail \{\}} \qquad \text{(MATCHBAREVCON)}$$

$$\frac{v \neq \text{VCON}(K, [\,])}{\langle K, v\rangle \rightarrowtail \dagger} \qquad \text{(FAILBAREVCON)}$$

A wildcard matches any value, and it produces no bindings.

$$\frac{}{\langle \text{WILDCARD}, v\rangle \rightarrowtail \{\}} \qquad \text{(MATCHWILDCARD)}$$

A variable matches any value v, and it produces a binding of itself to v.

$$\frac{}{\langle x, v\rangle \rightarrowtail \{x \mapsto v\}} \qquad \text{(MATCHVAR)}$$

The result of matching any pattern to any value is determined by the six rules above. Let's look at an example and a derivation, this time with a nested pattern:

494a. ⟨*transcript* 459a⟩+≡ ◁493c 499▷

```
-> (case '(1 2 3 4 5) [(cons x1 (cons x2 xs))   (cons x2 (cons x1 xs))])
(2 1 3 4 5) : (list int)
```

The derivation tree, which applies rule MATCHVAR at each leaf and MATCHVCON at each internal node, looks like this:

$$\frac{\frac{}{\langle \texttt{x1}, 1\rangle \rightarrowtail \{\texttt{x1} \mapsto 1\}} \qquad \frac{\frac{}{\langle \texttt{x2}, 2\rangle \rightarrowtail \{\texttt{x2} \mapsto 2\}} \qquad \frac{}{\langle \texttt{xs}, \texttt{'(3 4 5)}\rangle \rightarrowtail \{\texttt{xs} \mapsto \texttt{'(3 4 5)}\}}}{\langle (\texttt{cons x2 xs}), \text{VCON}(\texttt{cons}, [2, \texttt{'(3 4 5)}])\rangle \rightarrowtail \{\texttt{x2} \mapsto 2, \texttt{xs} \mapsto \texttt{'(3 4 5)}\}}}{\langle (\texttt{cons x1 (cons x2 xs)}), \text{VCON}(\texttt{cons}, [1, \text{VCON}(\texttt{cons}, [2, \texttt{'(3 4 5)}])])\rangle \rightarrowtail \{\texttt{x1} \mapsto 1, \texttt{x2} \mapsto 2, \texttt{xs} \mapsto \texttt{'(3 4 5)}\}}.$$

The rules are implemented by function `match`, which implements judgment $\langle p, v\rangle \rightarrowtail \rho'$ by returning ρ'. And it implements judgment $\langle p, v\rangle \rightarrowtail \dagger$ by raising the ML exception `Doesn'tMatch`.

494b. ⟨*definitions of* `match` *and* `Doesn'tMatch` 494b⟩≡ (S438e)

```
match         : pat * value -> value env (* or raises Doesn'tMatch *)
disjointUnion : 'a env list -> 'a env
```

```
exception Doesn'tMatch    (* pattern-match failure *)
fun match (CONPAT (k, ps), CONVAL (k', vs)) =
     if k = k' then
       disjointUnion (ListPair.mapEq match (ps, vs))
     else
       raise Doesn'tMatch
  | match (CONPAT _, _) = raise Doesn'tMatch
  | match (WILDCARD, _) = emptyEnv
  | match (PVAR x,   v) = bind (x, v, emptyEnv)
```

If patterns `ps` and values `vs` were lists of different lengths, function `ListPair.mapEq` would raise an exception, but μML's type system ensures that this can't happen.

8.8.2 *Type inference for case expressions and pattern matching*

Like any other type system, μML's type system guarantees that run-time computations do not "go wrong." μML's type system extends nano-ML's type system to provide these guarantees:

- When a value is constructed using CONVAL, the value constructor in question is applied to an appropriate number of values of appropriate types.
- In every pattern, every value constructor is applied to an appropriate number of sub-patterns of appropriate types.
- In every case expression, every pattern in every choice has a type consistent with the type of the scrutinee. And every variable in every pattern is bound to a value that is consistent with the type and value of the scrutinee.
- In every case expression, the right-hand sides all have the same type, which is the type of the case expression.

As in any type system, these guarantees are provided by a combination of type-formation rules, introduction rules, and elimination rules. μML uses all of the rules used in nano-ML, plus rules for constructed data.

- As in other languages that support algebraic data types, type formation is governed by a kinding system like the one used in Typed μScheme; both `implicit-data` and `data` definition forms specify the kind of each new type.
- The introduction form for constructed data is the named value constructor. Its typing rule is just like the typing rule for a named variable: look up the type in Γ.
- The elimination form is the case expression, which includes patterns. The typing rules for case expressions and patterns are the subject of this section.

Like nano-ML, μML has two sets of typing rules: nondeterministic rules and constraint-based rules.

Nondeterministic typing rules for case expressions, choices, and patterns

μML inherits all the judgment forms and rules from nano-ML. Its basic nondeterministic judgment form is still $\boxed{\Gamma \vdash e : \tau}$. But case expressions and pattern matching call for new judgment forms. The easiest form to explain is the one that deals with a *choice* within a case expression; the form of the judgment is $\boxed{\Gamma \vdash [p\ e] : \tau \to \tau'}$. In this form, type τ is the type of pattern p and type τ' is the type of expression e. Informally, the judgment says that if a case expression is scrutinizing an expression of type τ, and if pattern p matches the value of that expression, then in the context of that match, expression e has type τ'. The judgment is used in the nondeterministic typing rule for a case expression:

bind	305d
CONPAT	486c
cons	*B*
CONVAL	486d
disjointUnion	S453b
emptyEnv	305a
PVAR	486c
WILDCARD	486c

$$\frac{\Gamma \vdash e : \tau \qquad \Gamma \vdash [p_i\ e_i] : \tau \to \tau', \quad 1 \le i \le n}{\Gamma \vdash \text{CASE}(e, [p_1\ e_1], \ldots, [p_n\ e_n]) : \tau'}. \tag{CASE}$$

Every pattern p_i has the same type as the scrutinee e, and every right-hand side e_i has type τ', which is the type of the whole case expression.

As in the dynamic semantics, the key judgment is a pattern-matching judgment. And also as in the dynamic semantics, pattern matching produces an environment—a type environment, not a value environment. But compared with the dynamic semantics, the type system is more complicated:

- Type inference produces not only an output environment Γ', which gives the types of the variables that appear in the pattern, but also a type τ, which is the type of the whole pattern.
- As inputs, the dynamic semantics requires only the pattern and the value to be matched. In particular, the dynamic semantics requires no environment. But type inference requires an input environment, which tells the system the type of every value constructor that appears in the pattern.

The typing judgment for pattern matching therefore requires inputs p and Γ and produces outputs τ and Γ'. This two-input, two-output judgment form is written $\boxed{\Gamma, \Gamma' \vdash p : \tau}$. The notation is inspired by the notation for typechecking an expression (Exercise 33).

When p is a bare value constructor, it has the type it is given in the input environment, and it produces an empty output environment.

$$\frac{\Gamma \vdash K : \tau}{\Gamma, \{\} \vdash K : \tau} \qquad \text{(PATBAREVCON)}$$

The premise is a typing judgment for the expression K, which is a value constructor. Just like a value variable, a value constructor is looked up and instantiated:

$$\frac{\Gamma(K) = \sigma \qquad \tau' \leqslant \sigma}{\Gamma \vdash K : \tau'}. \qquad \text{(VCON)}$$

A wildcard pattern has any type and produces the empty output environment.

$$\frac{}{\Gamma, \{\} \vdash \text{WILDCARD} : \tau} \qquad \text{(PATWILDCARD)}$$

A variable pattern also has any type, and it produces an output environment that binds itself to its type.

$$\frac{}{\Gamma, \{x \mapsto \tau\} \vdash x : \tau} \qquad \text{(PATVAR)}$$

The most important pattern is one that applies a value constructor K to a list of sub-patterns: $p = (K\ p_1\ \cdots\ p_m)$. The types of the sub-patterns must be the argument types of the value constructor, and the type of the whole pattern is the result type of the value constructor. Each sub-pattern p_i can introduce new variables; the environment produced by the whole pattern is the disjoint union of the environments produced by the sub-patterns (page 493). If the disjoint union isn't defined, the pattern doesn't typecheck.

$$\frac{\begin{array}{c}\Gamma \vdash K : \tau_1 \times \cdots \times \tau_m \to \tau \\ \Gamma, \Gamma'_i \vdash p_i : \tau_i, \quad 1 \le i \le m \\ \Gamma' = \Gamma'_1 \uplus \cdots \uplus \Gamma'_m\end{array}}{\Gamma, \Gamma' \vdash (K\ p_1\ \cdots\ p_m) : \tau} \qquad \text{(PATVCON)}$$

The judgment for patterns is used in the rule for a choice $[p\ e]$. Typing pattern p produces a set of variable bindings Γ', and the right-hand side e is checked in a context formed by extending Γ with Γ', which holds p's bindings:

$$\frac{\Gamma, \Gamma' \vdash p : \tau \qquad \Gamma + \Gamma' \vdash e : \tau'}{\Gamma \vdash [p\ e] : \tau \to \tau'}. \qquad \text{(CHOICE)}$$

The CHOICE rule concludes the nondeterministic type theory of case expressions.

Constraint-based type inference for case expressions, choices, and patterns

To turn the nondeterministic rules into an inference algorithm, I introduce constraints. Just as in Chapter 7, each occurrence of an unknown type is represented by a fresh type variable, and within each rule, multiple occurrences are constrained to be equal. The rules are shown in Figure 8.9 on the following page. They are implemented using the same ty representation used in nano-ML.

The CASE rule checks the scrutinee and each choice.

$$\frac{\begin{array}{c} C_e, \Gamma \vdash e : \tau \\ C_i, \Gamma \vdash \texttt{[}p_i\ e_i\texttt{]} : \tau_i, \quad 1 \le i \le n \\ C' = \bigwedge_i \{\tau_i \sim (\tau \to \alpha)\}, \text{where } \alpha \text{ is fresh} \\ C = C_e \wedge C' \wedge C_1 \wedge \cdots \wedge C_n \end{array}}{C, \Gamma \vdash \text{CASE}(e, \texttt{[}p_1\ e_1\texttt{]}, \ldots, \texttt{[}p_n\ e_n\texttt{]}) : \alpha} \qquad \text{(CASE)}$$

The scrutinee judgment $C_e, \Gamma \vdash e : \tau$ is implemented by function typeof (Chapter 7), and the choice judgment $C_i, \Gamma \vdash \texttt{[}p_i\ e_i\texttt{]} : \tau_i$ is implemented by function choicetype (bottom of this page). Each constraint in the set $\{\tau_i \sim (\tau \to \alpha)\}$ is built by applying internal function constrainArrow to τ_i.

497a. ⟨*more alternatives for* ty 497a⟩≡ (438c)

```
ty          : exp                      -> ty * con
typeof      : exp          * type_env -> ty * con
choicetype  : (pat * exp) * type_env -> ty * con
```

```
  | ty (CASE (e, choices)) =
      let val (tau, c_e) =
                 typeof (e, Gamma)
          val (tau_i's, c_i's) =
                 ListPair.unzip (map (fn ch => choicetype (ch,Gamma)) choices)
          val alpha = freshtyvar ()
          fun constrainArrow tau_i = tau_i ~ funtype ([tau], alpha)
          val c' = conjoinConstraints (map constrainArrow tau_i's)
          val c = c_e /\ c' /\ conjoinConstraints c_i's
      in  (alpha, c)
      end
```

Function ListPair.unzip converts a list of pairs to a pair of lists.

The rule for a choice infers a type for the pattern and the expression:

$$\frac{C, \Gamma, \Gamma' \vdash p : \tau \qquad C', \Gamma + \Gamma' \vdash e : \tau'}{C \wedge C', \Gamma \vdash \texttt{[}p\ e\texttt{]} : \tau \to \tau'}. \qquad \text{(CHOICE)}$$

Function choicetype returns a pair containing the arrow type $\tau \to \tau'$ and the conjoined constraint $C \wedge C'$.

497b. ⟨*definition of function* choicetype 497b⟩≡ (S453a)

```
choicetype : (pat * exp) * type_env -> ty * con
```

```
  fun choicetype ((p, e), Gamma) =
        let val (Gamma', tau, c) = pattype (p, Gamma)
            val (tau', c') = typeof (e, extendTypeEnv (Gamma, Gamma'))
            val (ty,  con) = (funtype ([tau], tau'), c /\ c')
            val _ = ⟨check p, e, Gamma', Gamma, ty, and con for escaping skolem types S460f⟩
        in  (ty, con)
        end
```

The combination $\Gamma + \Gamma'$ is implemented by function extendTypeEnv, which is defined in the Supplement. (Because Γ is a type_env, not a ty env, it can't be extended using the <+> function.)

$\boxed{C, \Gamma \vdash e : \tau}$

CASE

$$\frac{\begin{array}{c} C_e, \Gamma \vdash e : \tau \\ C_i, \Gamma \vdash [p_i \ e_i] : \tau_i, \quad 1 \le i \le n \\ C' = \bigwedge_i \{\tau_i \sim (\tau \to \alpha)\}, \text{where } \alpha \text{ is fresh} \\ C = C_e \wedge C' \wedge C_1 \wedge \cdots \wedge C_n \end{array}}{C, \Gamma \vdash \text{CASE}(e, [p_1 \ e_1], \ldots, [p_n \ e_n]) : \alpha}$$

VCON

$$\frac{\begin{array}{c} \Gamma(K) = \forall \alpha_1, \ldots, \alpha_n . \tau \\ \alpha'_1, \ldots, \alpha'_n \text{ are fresh and distinct} \end{array}}{\mathbf{T}, \Gamma \vdash K : ((\alpha_1 \mapsto \alpha'_1) \circ \cdots \circ (\alpha_n \mapsto \alpha'_n))\,\tau}$$

$\boxed{C, \Gamma \vdash [p \ e] : \tau \to \tau'}$

CHOICE

$$\frac{C, \Gamma, \Gamma' \vdash p : \tau \qquad C', \Gamma + \Gamma' \vdash e : \tau'}{C \wedge C', \Gamma \vdash [p \ e] : \tau \to \tau'}$$

$\boxed{C, \Gamma, \Gamma' \vdash p : \tau}$

PATVCON

$$\frac{\begin{array}{c} \mathbf{T}, \Gamma \vdash K : \tau_K \\ C_i, \Gamma, \Gamma'_i \vdash p_i : \tau_i, \quad 1 \le i \le m \\ C = \tau_K \sim \tau_1 \times \cdots \times \tau_m \to \alpha, \text{ where } \alpha \text{ is fresh} \\ C' = C_1 \wedge \cdots \wedge C_m \qquad \Gamma' = \Gamma'_1 \uplus \cdots \uplus \Gamma'_m \end{array}}{C \wedge C', \Gamma, \Gamma' \vdash (K \ p_1 \ \cdots \ p_m) : \alpha}$$

PATBAREVCON

$$\frac{\mathbf{T}, \Gamma \vdash K : \tau}{\mathbf{T}, \Gamma, \{\} \vdash K : \tau}$$

PATWILDCARD

$$\frac{\alpha \text{ is fresh}}{\mathbf{T}, \Gamma, \{\} \vdash \text{WILDCARD} : \alpha}$$

PATVAR

$$\frac{\alpha \text{ is fresh}}{\mathbf{T}, \Gamma, \{x \mapsto \alpha\} \vdash x : \alpha}$$

Figure 8.9: Constraint-based rules for case expressions, choices, and patterns

Function pattype has four cases: one for each rule.

498. ⟨*definition of function* pattype 498⟩≡ (S453a)

```
                        pattype : pat * type_env -> type_scheme env * ty * con
fun pattype (p as CONPAT (vcon, pats as _ :: _), Gamma) =
      let val vcon_tau = pvconType (vcon, Gamma)
          val (Gamma'_is, tau_is, c_is) = pattypes (pats, Gamma)
          val alpha  = freshtyvar ()
          val c      = vcon_tau ~ funtype (tau_is, alpha)
          val c'     = conjoinConstraints c_is
          val Gamma' = disjointUnion Gamma'_is
                       handle DisjointUnionFailed x =>
                         raise TypeError ("name " ^ x ^ " is bound multiple " ^
                                          "times in pattern " ^ patString p)
      in  (Gamma', alpha, c /\ c')
      end
  | pattype (CONPAT (K, []), Gamma) =
      (emptyEnv, pvconType (K, Gamma), TRIVIAL)
  | pattype (WILDCARD, _) =
      (emptyEnv, freshtyvar(), TRIVIAL)
  | pattype (PVAR x, _) =
      let val alpha = freshtyvar ()
      in  (bind (x, FORALL ([], alpha), emptyEnv), alpha, TRIVIAL)
      end
and pattypes (ps, Gamma) = unzip3 (map (fn p => pattype (p, Gamma)) ps)
```

The type of a value constructor vcon (K) comes from pvconType (chunk S452d), which instantiates vcon's type scheme with fresh type variables.

The implementations of pattype and pattypes complete type inference for case expressions. Inference code for the other expressions, except for value constructors, is shared with nano-ML. Type inference for a value constructor instantiates its type scheme with fresh variables; the code appears in the Supplement.

8.9 ALGEBRAIC DATA TYPES AS THEY REALLY ARE

Algebraic data types and pattern matching are found primarily in the ML family of languages and in languages descended from them, including Standard ML, OCaml, Haskell, Clean, Coq/Gallina, Agda, Idris, and more. All support algebraic data types as presented in this chapter, but some offer extended or restricted versions.

8.9.1 Syntax

Syntax varies. The implicit-data form is used in Standard ML, OCaml, standard Haskell, and Clean; the data form is used in Agda and Coq/Gallina. Both forms are used in Idris and by the Glasgow Haskell Compiler. Spelling of value constructors also varies; in Standard ML, value constructors are typically written in all capital letters; elsewhere, they are typically written with a single, initial capital letter.

Examples of concrete syntax, including datatype definitions, case expressions, and clausal definitions, can be found in any of the interpreters in this book from Chapter 5 onward. As is typical, pattern matching and decision making are done primarily by means of clausal definitions, not by case expressions. Because clausal definitions look so much like algebraic laws, they are preferred.

Pattern matching is used in Erlang, even though Erlang does not have algebraic data types (or even a type system). Erlang's pattern matching is defined over *terms*; the role of value constructors is played by *atoms*. Erlang includes both case expressions and clausal function definitions.

Pattern matching is so popular that it is sometimes used in other contexts. For example, in the multiparadigm language Scala, algebraic data types are encoded using objects and classes, but the language also includes a case expression written using the keyword match. As a more whimsical example, Nigel Horspool has used Java exception handlers to implement pattern matching.

8.9.2 Additional checking: Exhaustiveness and redundancy

An algebraic data type is *closed*: once it is defined, new value constructors can't be added. Because each type is closed, a compiler can analyze each case expression and see if at run time, every possible value is guaranteed to be matched by some pattern. The analysis is called the *exhaustiveness check*. An exhaustiveness check is mandated by the *Definition of Standard ML* (Milner et al. 1997), but the *Definition* also requires that inexhaustive matches be let off with a mere warning. No such latitude is extended to my students.

When a case expression's patterns are not exhaustive, evaluating the expression can cause a run-time error. Here's an example:

499. ⟨*transcript* 459a⟩+≡ ◁494a

```
-> (define last (xs)                    last : (forall ['a] ((list 'a) -> 'a))
     (case xs
        [(cons y '()) y]
        [(cons _ ys)  (last ys)]))
-> (last '(1 2 3))
3 : int
-> (last '())
Run-time error: 'case' does not match ()
```

When checking for exhaustiveness, a compiler may discover a pattern that can never match. Such a pattern is often called *redundant*. (It's redundant because it can be removed without changing the behavior of the program.) Most compilers warn of redundant patterns; confusingly, the Glasgow Haskell Compiler refers to such patterns as "overlapped" or "overlapping."

"Overlapping" is also used to describe a pair of patterns that match one or more values in common. When patterns overlap, the first matching pattern is always chosen. Overlapping patterns are useful; for example, if just one case needs special handling, you can put a very specific pattern like `(cons _ (cons _ zs))` before a general pattern like the wildcard, even though the specific pattern and the wildcard overlap. Non-overlapping patterns are also useful; if no patterns overlap, then patterns in a case expression or clauses in a definition can be written in any order, without changing the meaning of the program. But non-overlapping patterns are primarily a conceptual tool: they simplify equational reasoning. If you cared whether patterns overlapped, your compiler could easily tell you, but no compiler I know of actually does.

8.9.3 *Efficient implementation*

In modern compilers, constructed values are represented efficiently. A value constructor that takes no arguments is typically represented by a small integer that fits in a machine register. A value constructor that has been applied to arguments is typically represented by a pointer to an object allocated on the heap; the object holds the arguments as well as a small-integer *tag* that identifies the value constructor. In some important special cases, such as `list` and `option`, where only one value constructor takes any arguments, the tag can be omitted.

Pattern matching is also compiled efficiently. Each case expression is translated by a *match compiler*, which produces a finite-state automaton. In the automaton, each initial or intermediate state examines the small-integer tag associated with one value constructor, then makes a transition to another state. Each final state knows which pattern matches, where all the bound variables are located, and how to transfer control to the corresponding right-hand side. At run time, an initial or intermediate state is typically implemented by a load instruction and an indirect branch; a final state is implemented by a direct branch. Pattern-matching automata come in two flavors: a *backtracking automaton* has compact code, but it may examine some tags more than once; a *decision tree* examines each tag at most once, but in pathological cases it may require space exponential in the size of the source code.

In strict languages like Standard ML and OCaml, pattern matching causes no side effects, and the match compiler may examine the arguments of any value constructor in whatever order it thinks best. Finding the best order is an NP-complete problem, so most compilers resort to heuristics; if you want to know more, consult the Further Reading section. In a lazy language like Haskell or Clean, however, pattern matching *can* have a side effect: it can trigger the evaluation of an expression that would otherwise go unevaluated. To make such evaluations predictable, the order in which arguments must be examined is dictated by the language definition, and the match compiler must obey.

In general, pattern matching is cheap, and in an important special case, it has no run-time cost at all: when an algebraic data type has only one value constructor, and when that value constructor takes exactly one argument, applying or matching on that value constructor should cost nothing. There's an example in Section H.2.4:

```
datatype 'a collection = C of 'a set
```

At run time, a `collection` has the same representation as a `set`, which happens to be the same representation as a `list`. But to the type system, they are different—I use a `collection` in circumstances where I have both collections and lists and I want to avoid confusing the two (Exercise 38).

8.10 SUMMARY

Case expressions and pattern matching not only simplify conditional logic but also reduce the amount of boilerplate needed to get at parts of product values (records). And clausal definitions, which use pattern matching, make it possible for the definition of a function to look an awful lot like the function's algebraic laws. The succinctness and readability of pattern matching is highly valued by many programmers—sometimes even more than type inference.

8.10.1 Key words and phrases

ALGEBRAIC DATA TYPE A data type whose values may be one of a set of enumerated alternatives, in which each alternative is a CONSTRUCTED VALUE created by a unique VALUE CONSTRUCTOR. Each of a type's value constructors may be applied to other values of given types, making the entire algebraic data type a SUM OF PRODUCTS.

CASE EXPRESSION The core-language elimination form for an ALGEBRAIC DATA TYPE. It examines a CONSTRUCTED VALUE, called the SCRUTINEE, and it provides a sequence of choices, each of which has a PATTERN on the left and an expression on the right. When the case expression is evaluated, the result is determined by the first choice whose pattern matches the scrutinee.

CLAUSAL DEFINITION A definition form for functions. A clausal definition is written as a sequence of clauses, each of which applies the function to a PATTERN and equates that application to an expression on the right-hand side. When the function is applied, it executes the first clause whose pattern matches. A clausal definition desugars to an ordinary definition whose body is a CASE EXPRESSION.

CONSTRUCTED VALUE A value created by applying a VALUE CONSTRUCTOR to one or more values. Or a value constructor that does not expect any arguments.

GENERATIVITY A definition form is generative when the thing it defines is distinct from all other things, even when the other things' definitions look identical. The definition of an ALGEBRAIC DATA TYPE is typically generative, which implies that the type and its value constructors are distinct from types and value constructors introduced by other definitions—even if the other definitions use the same type name and the same constructor names.

PATTERN A syntactic form that is unique to CASE EXPRESSIONS. A pattern is a literal, a variable, or a VALUE CONSTRUCTOR applied to patterns. A pattern matches any CONSTRUCTED VALUE that can be obtained by replacing each variable in the pattern with some actual value.

PATTERN MATCHING The algorithm by which a choice is selected in a CASE EXPRESSION. In industrial compilers an interpreters, pattern matching is implemented by an efficient automaton that is compiled from the patterns in the case expression.

SCRUTINEE A value of algebraic data type that is examined in a CASE EXPRESSION.

SUM OF PRODUCTS Describes a set of structured values that is a discriminated union (sum), in which each element of the sum may carry a record-like collection (product) of other values. In general, an ALGEBRAIC DATA TYPE is a sum of products. In object-oriented language, a set of subclasses of a given class can also form a sum of products.

TYPE ABBREVIATION A definition form that enables a programmer to add a new name to the environment, where the new name refers to a type that is already present in the program. In some languages, a type abbreviation may take parameters, just like a type constructor. Compare with USER-DEFINED TYPE.

USER-DEFINED TYPE A definition form that enables a programmer to add a new, named *type* to the environment. Typically the new type is distinct from any existing type, making the type-definition form GENERATIVE. Compare with TYPE ABBREVIATION.

VALUE CONSTRUCTOR The name of an alternative in an ALGEBRAIC DATA TYPE. A value constructor is either a CONSTRUCTED VALUE by itself or may be applied to arguments to make a constructed value. Value constructors are also used to form PATTERNS for use in case expressions. Except in very old programming languages, a value constructor can usually be distinguished from a variable by looking at its lexical form. For example, value constructors may be capitalized and variables may not.

8.10.2 Further reading

Algebraic data types were first explored in the experimental language HOPE, described by Burstall, MacQueen, and Sannella (1980). Among other concerns, Burstall and his colleagues wanted to support user-defined types, to help programmers avoid forgetting cases, and to avoid cluttering the environment with names for functions like `null?`, `car`, and `cdr`, which they replaced with pattern matching.

Algebraic data types don't have to be closed: Millstein, Bleckner, and Chambers (2004) present a design that makes them extensible. Sadly, the design has not caught on.

The type theory and operational semantics in this chapter draw heavily on the *Definition of Standard ML* (Milner et al. 1997). The *Definition* is worth reading, but it presents two challenges: First, it describes a whole language, the complexity of which can't be avoided. Second, its notation can be hard to follow: the rules rely not only on subtle differences between forms of judgment but also on implicit premises that are mentioned only briefly at the beginning of some sections. But the truth is all there, and while I could not call the *Definition* elegant, I admire its parsimony. Anyone reading the *Definition* is advised also to have the *Commentary* (Milner and Tofte 1991), which contains not only discussion but also many worked examples of problems similar to those in this book.

If you want to tackle the *Definition of Standard ML*, I owe you two additional cautions. First, I find the terminology challenging. For example, I believe that the *Definition* uses the words "type name" and "type constructor" the way I use the words "type constructor" and "type name." (I stand by my guns.) Second, the treatment of generativity in the *Definition* is now widely believed to be inferior—it is too much a description of an implementation, it has too much mechanism, and it may be too difficult to reason about. A surprising alternative is to treat generative `data` definitions as a special case of generative *modules* (Harper and Stone 2000). The idea

Table 8.10: Synopsis of all the exercises, with most relevant sections

Exercises	*Sections*	*Notes*
1	8.1, 8.2	Check your understanding of pattern matching.
2 to 4	8.1, 8.2	Pattern matching on lists and pairs.
5 to 7	8.1, 8.2	Higher-order functions on lists.
8 and 9	8.2	Using `option`.
10 to 12	8.2	Using `order`: Comparisons and sorts.
13 to 19	8.2	Tree structures: join lists, binary trees, tries, and ternary search trees.
20 and 21	8.3	Equational reasoning.
22 to 28	8.4	Using and implementing syntactic sugar.
29 and 30	8.5	Type generativity.
31 and 32	8.7	Kinds; type abbreviations; type constraints.
33 to 38	8.8	Properties of pattern matching; extensions; finding non-exhaustive patterns.

is further developed in a very nice if very technical paper by Dreyer, Crary, and Harper (2003).

Algebraic data types lend themselves to some nice extensions. In Appendix S, you can read about existentially quantified value constructors and generalized algebraic data types (GADTs). Existential quantification is suggested by Mitchell and Plotkin (1988) as a way of coding abstract types; its use with value constructors was first suggested by Perry (1991). GADTs are beautifully introduced by Hinze (2003), and some nice applications are presented by Pottier and Régis-Gianas (2006) and by Ramsey, Dias, and Peyton Jones (2010).

The compilation of ML pattern matching into decision trees was first described by Baudinet and MacQueen (1985), who claim NP-completeness and present a number of heuristics. Scott and Ramsey (2000) present preliminary experiments suggesting that in practice, choice of heuristics may not matter; they also present pseudocode for a match compiler. But the definitive work in this area is by Maranget (2008), who carefully compares decision trees with backtracking automata. Maranget also develops new heuristics and also a fine methodology for experimental evaluation. In a separate paper, Maranget (2007) describes checks for exhaustiveness and redundancy.

8.11 Exercises

The exercises are summarized in Table 8.10. The highlights include some nice data structures:

- The "zipper" (Exercise 16) is a purely functional data structure whose operations have an imperative feel. It's a classic. If you're a beginner, the zipper is a good challenge problem. If you have more experience and you have not yet seen the zipper, you will find it very satisfying.

- Binary tries (Exercises 17 and 18) connect tries with binary representations of integers in a way that has a nice theory and a nice implementation. And ternary search trees (Exercise 19) show how case expressions and pattern matching make it easy to code tree algorithms.

The remaining highlights explore the theory and implementation of μML.

- The concrete syntax of patterns resembles the concrete syntax of a subset of expressions (those formed from value variables, value constructors, and function application). You can confirm this resemblance by showing that a pattern and its corresponding expression have the same type (Exercise 33).

- Pattern matches should be checked to make sure they are exhaustive and no patterns are redundant. You can implement this check and simultaneously get a feel for how pattern matches can be compiled into efficient code (Exercise 38).

8.11.1 *Retrieval practice and other short questions*

A. What are some examples of value constructors?

B. What are some examples of algebraic data types?

C. Is constructed data always made with a value constructor? If not, when is it not?

D. Is a value constructor always constructed data? If not, when is it not?

E. What's the idiomatic way to compare two values when both are constructed data, like the color of a traffic light?

F. What is the `option` type and how is it used? What are its value constructors?

G. What are the possible forms of a pattern?

H. When does matching a pattern add new bindings to the environment?

I. How can you tell the difference between a value constructor and a variable?

J. If K is a value constructor defined with algebraic type T, what do the typing rules tell us about the type of K?

K. In μML, how often should you expect to use predefined functions `null?`, `car`, and `cdr`?

L. In μML, what is the result type of the predefined function `find`? Why does the μML version return something different from the μScheme version?

M. What other expression form is `(case` e `[`x e'`]` $\cdots$`)` equivalent to?

N. What is a clausal definition and why would you want one?

O. What's the most important difference between a generative type definition and a type abbreviation?

P. What is the judgment form $\Delta \vdash t \rightsquigarrow \tau :: *$ and what problems does it solve?

Q. What are the meanings of the two judgments $\langle p, v \rangle \rightarrowtail \rho'$ and $\langle p, v \rangle \rightarrowtail \dagger$? What's an example of each?

R. The typing rules for `case` expressions include a specialized judgment that takes the form $\Gamma \vdash$ `[`p e`]` $: \tau \rightarrow \tau'$. In this form, what are the types τ and τ'?

S. If the patterns in a `case` expression are exhaustive, what does that tell us about the evaluation of the `case` expression?

8.11.2 *Understanding pattern matching*

1. *Identify matching values.* Test your understanding of pattern matching by seeing which values are matched by the pattern `(PAIR (cons x (cons y zs)) w)`. For each of the following expressions, tell whether the pattern matches the value denoted. If the pattern matches, say what value is bound to each of the four variables `x`, `y`, `zs`, and `w`. If it does not match, explain why not.

   505a. ⟨*sample expressions* 505a⟩≡
   ```
   (PAIR '(1 2 3) (PAIR 'Fisher 105))
   (PAIR (PAIR 'Fisher 105) '(1 2 3))
   (PAIR '(#t #f) 314159)
   (PAIR '(a) '(b c d))
   (PAIR '(a b) '(c d))
   (PAIR '(a b c) '(d))
   ```


8.11.3 *Pattern matching: Lists and pairs*

If you can, write the functions in this section using `define*`. You can implement it yourself (Exercise 26), or if you are using this book for a class, your instructor may have my implementation.

2. *Match a list of pairs of integers.* Define a function `consecutive-pair` that takes a list of integers and returns, as a pair, the first two consecutive integers in the given list that are also consecutive in the list of all integers. If there is no such pair, `consecutive-pair` should return `NONE`. Use only two patterns: the wildcard pattern and the nested pattern `(cons n (cons m ms))`.

   505b. ⟨*exercise transcripts* 505b⟩≡ 505c ▷
   ```
   -> consecutive-pair
   <function> : ((list int) -> (option (pair int int)))
   -> (consecutive-pair '(6 1 7))
   NONE : (option (pair int int))
   -> (consecutive-pair '(7 8 1))
   (SOME (PAIR 7 8)) : (option (pair int int))
   -> (consecutive-pair '(4 3 3 4))
   (SOME (PAIR 3 4)) : (option (pair int int))
   ```

3. *Create a list of pairs.* Define a function `zip` that takes a pair of lists (of equal length) and returns the list of pairs containing the same elements in the same order. If the lengths don't match, pass the symbol `'length-mismatch` to the `error` primitive. Do not use `if`, `null?`, `car`, or `cdr`.

   505c. ⟨*exercise transcripts* 505b⟩+≡ ◁ 505b 506a ▷
   ```
   -> zip
   <function> : (forall ['a 'b] ((list 'a) (list 'b) -> (list (pair 'a 'b))))
   -> (zip '(a b c) '(1 2 3))
   ((PAIR a 1) (PAIR b 2) (PAIR c 3)) : (list (pair sym int))
   -> (zip '(a b c) '())
   Run-time error: length-mismatch
   ```

4. *Nested patterns.* If your `zip` from Exercise 3 includes more than one case expression, reimplement it using a single case expression, while still adhering to all the restrictions in Exercise 3.

8.11.4 Higher-order functions on lists and `option`

5. *Using* `option` *values.* Define a function `List.find` which generalizes function `exists?` by producing a *witness* (if one exists). Given a predicate `p?` and a list `xs`, `List.find` returns (`SOME` v) if `xs` contains a value v satisfying `p?`, and `NONE` otherwise.

506a. ⟨*exercise transcripts* 505b⟩+≡ ◁505c 506b▷

```
-> List.find
<function> : (forall ['a] (('a -> bool) (list 'a) -> (option 'a)))
-> (define positive? (n) (> n 0))
-> (List.find positive? '(-3 -2 -1 0 1 2 3))
(SOME 1) : (option int)
-> (List.find (lambda (n) (> n 100)) '(-3 -2 -1 0 1 2 3))
NONE : (option int)
```

6. *Consuming* `option` *values.* A partial function from τ to τ' can be represented by a total function of type $\tau \rightarrow \tau'$ `option`. Such a function can be mapped over a list, keeping only the `SOME` results. In this example I map the `consecutive-pair` function from Exercise 2.

506b. ⟨*exercise transcripts* 505b⟩+≡ ◁506a 506c▷

```
-> map-partial
<function> : (forall ['a 'b] (('a -> (option 'b)) (list 'a) -> (list 'b)))
-> (map         consecutive-pair (list6 '(1 2 3)   '(4 5 6)
                                        '(1 9 7 6) '(2 0 1 4)
                                        '(7 7 4 2) '(4 3 3 4)))
((SOME (PAIR 1 2)) (SOME (PAIR 4 5)) NONE (SOME (PAIR 0 1)) ...
-> (map-partial consecutive-pair (list6 '(1 2 3)   '(4 5 6)
                                        '(1 9 7 6) '(2 0 1 4)
                                        '(7 7 4 2) '(4 3 3 4)))
((PAIR 1 2) (PAIR 4 5) (PAIR 0 1) (PAIR 3 4)) : (list (pair int int))
```

Without using `if`, `null?`, `car`, or `cdr`, implement `map-partial`.

7. *Removing* `option` *values.* Define function `keep-somes`, which takes a list of option values and returns only the `SOME` values, with `SOME` stripped off.

506c. ⟨*exercise transcripts* 505b⟩+≡ ◁506b 506d▷

```
-> keep-somes
<function> : (forall ['a] ((list (option 'a)) -> (list 'a)))
-> (keep-somes
     (list6 NONE (SOME 'freedom) NONE NONE (SOME 'is) (SOME 'slavery)))
(freedom is slavery) : (list sym)
```

8.11.5 Functions on `option` alone

8. *Maps over* `option`. Define function `Option.map`, which acts like `map` but works on `option` values, not `list` values.

506d. ⟨*exercise transcripts* 505b⟩+≡ ◁506c 507a▷

```
-> Option.map
<function> : (forall ['a 'b] (('a -> 'b) (option 'a) -> (option 'b)))
-> (Option.map positive? NONE)
NONE : (option bool)
-> (Option.map positive? (SOME 4))
(SOME #t) : (option bool)
-> (Option.map reverse NONE)
NONE : (forall ['a] (option (list 'a)))
-> (Option.map reverse (SOME '(1 2 3)))
(SOME (3 2 1)) : (option (list int))
```

9. *Nested* option. Define function Option.join, which takes an "option of option" and returns a single option that is SOME whenever possible:

507a. ⟨*exercise transcripts* 505b⟩+≡ ◁506d 507b▷

```
-> Option.join
<function> : (forall ['a] ((option (option 'a)) -> (option 'a)))
-> (Option.join (SOME NONE))
NONE : (forall ['a] (option 'a))
-> (Option.join (SOME (SOME 4)))
(SOME 4) : (option int)
```


8.11.6 *Functions that use* order

10. *Comparison using* order. Define a higher-order sort function mk-sort of type (forall ['a] (('a 'a -> order) -> ((list 'a) -> (list 'a)))). Avoid using if, null?, car, and cdr.

507b. ⟨*exercise transcripts* 505b⟩+≡ ◁507a 507c▷

```
-> mk-sort
<function> : (forall ['a] (('a 'a -> order) -> ((list 'a) -> (list 'a))))
-> (mk-sort Int.compare)
<function> : ((list int) -> (list int))
-> (it '(0 2 1 5 5))
(0 1 2 5 5) : (list int)
-> (val sort-down (mk-sort (lambda (n m) (Int.compare m n))))
-> (sort-down '(0 2 1 5 5))
(5 5 2 1 0) : (list int)
```

11. *Merge sort via pattern matching.* Without using if, null?, car, or cdr, define a higher-order mergesort function, which should have the same type as above: (forall ['a] (('a 'a -> order) -> ((list 'a) -> (list 'a)))). I recommend defining a top-level mergesort that takes compare as an argument, and which contains a letrec that defines split, merge, and sort.

    Unlike most sorting algorithms, mergesort requires two base cases: not only is a list matching '() considered sorted, but so is a list matching (cons x '()). Your sort function should therefore discriminate among three cases—the two base cases and one inductive case. The inductive case splits the list into two *smaller* lists, sorts each, and merges the results.

12. *Higher-order functions with* order. Comparison is useful not just on individual values but on pairs, triples, lists, and so on. Such comparisons are typically *lexicographic*: you compare the first elements, and if they are unequal, that's the result of the comparison. But if the first elements are equal, you compare the remaining elements lexicographically. Try your hand at the higher-order functions below. Use case expressions, and look for opportunities to use the wildcard pattern.

Int.compare	$\mathcal{B}$
list6	$\mathcal{B}$
map	$\mathcal{B}$
reverse	$\mathcal{B}$

    (a) Without using if, define function compare-like-pairs, which is given a comparison function for values of type τ and returns a comparison function for values of type $\tau \times \tau$.

    507c. ⟨*exercise transcripts* 505b⟩+≡ ◁507b 508a▷

```
-> (check-type compare-like-pairs
       (forall ['a] (('a 'a -> order) ->
                         ((pair 'a 'a) (pair 'a 'a) -> order))))
```

    (Test cases appear on the next page.)

Your implementation of compare-like-pairs should pass these tests:

508a. ⟨*exercise transcripts* 505b⟩+≡ ◁507c 508b▷

```
-> (val compare-NxN (compare-like-pairs Int.compare))
-> (check-expect (compare-NxN (pair 1 2) (pair 3 4)) LESS)
-> (check-expect (compare-NxN (pair 7 2) (pair 3 4)) GREATER)
-> (check-expect (compare-NxN (pair 3 2) (pair 3 4)) LESS)
-> (check-expect (compare-NxN (pair 3 4) (pair 3 4)) EQUAL)
-> (check-expect (compare-NxN (pair 3 5) (pair 3 4)) GREATER)
```

(b) Define function compare-pairs, which is given two comparison functions, one for values of type τ and one for values of type τ', and returns a comparison function for values of type $\tau \times \tau'$.

508b. ⟨*exercise transcripts* 505b⟩+≡ ◁508a 508c▷

```
-> (check-type compare-pairs
        (forall ['a 'b] (('a 'a -> order) ('b 'b -> order) ->
                          ((pair 'a 'b) (pair 'a 'b) -> order))))
```

(c) Use compare-pairs to implement compare-like-pairs.

(d) Define function compare-lists, which is given a comparison function for values of type τ and returns a comparison function for values of type τ list. Lists should be ordered lexicographically (dictionary order), and the empty list should be considered smaller than any nonempty list. The function should pass these tests:

508c. ⟨*exercise transcripts* 505b⟩+≡ ◁508b 514a▷

```
-> (val compare-Ns (compare-lists Int.compare))
-> (check-expect (compare-Ns '(2 1 3 4) '(2 1 4 8)) LESS)
-> (check-expect (compare-Ns '(2 1 5 5) '(2 1 4 8)) GREATER)
-> (check-expect (compare-Ns '(2 1 5 5) '(2 1 5 5)) EQUAL)
-> (check-expect (compare-Ns '(2 1 5 5) '(2 1))      GREATER)
-> (check-expect (compare-Ns '(2 1 5 5) '(2 1 4 8 1)) GREATER)
-> (check-expect (compare-Ns '(2 1 4 8) '(2 1 4 8 1)) LESS)
```

(e) Use compare-pairs to implement compare-lists without matching a value of type order directly.

8.11.7 *Tree structures*

An algebraic data type defines a set of trees, and pattern matching is exceptionally good for writing recursive functions on trees.

13. *Binary trees.* Implement a function bt-depth that gives the depth of a binary tree from Section 8.1 (page 463). An empty tree has depth zero; a nonempty tree has depth 1 more than the maximum depth of its subtrees.

14. *Binary search trees.* A *binary search tree* can represent a finite map, which is to say a set of key-value pairs in which each key appears at most once. A binary search tree is one of the following:

    - The empty tree, which represents the empty set of key-value pairs
    - An internal node, which has a key, a value, a left subtree, and a right subtree, and which represents the singleton set containing the given key and value, unioned with the sets represented by the left and right subtrees

Every binary search tree satisfies an *order invariant.* The empty tree satisfies the order invariant by definition. An internal node satisfies the order invariant if it has all of these properties:

- The left subtree satisfies the order invariant.
- The right subtree satisfies the order invariant.
- Every key in the left subtree is smaller than the key in the internal node.
- Every key in the right subtree is greater than the key in the internal node.

Using an algebraic data type, implement a binary search tree. Use pattern matching, not `if`. Ideally your tree will be polymorphic in both keys and values, but if it simplifies things sufficiently, you could use integer keys.

(a) Define an algebraic data type that represents binary search trees. I recommend that your algebraic data type include a value constructor that takes no arguments and that represents an empty tree.

(b) Define an `insert` function that takes a key, a value, and a tree, and returns a new tree that is like the original tree, but binding the given key to the given value. (In particular, if the given key is present in the old tree, the new tree should associate that key with the new value.)

(c) Define a `lookup` function that takes a key and a tree. If the tree associates the key with a value v, the function should return (`SOME` v). If not, the function should return `NONE`.

(d) Define a `delete` function that takes a tree and a key, and returns a tree that is equivalent to the original, except that the key is not associated with any value. If you are not familiar with deletion in binary search trees, the usual heuristic is to reduce every case to the problem of deleting the key-value pair from a given internal node. This problem divides into three overlapping cases:

- If the left subtree is empty, the internal node can be replaced by the right subtree.
- If the right subtree is empty, the internal node can be replaced by the left subtree.
- If neither subtree is empty, delete the largest key-value pair from the left subtree. Form a new internal node using that key-value pair along with the modified left subtree and the original right subtree.

(e) Define a record type that holds `insert`, `lookup`, and `delete` functions. Define a polymorphic function that takes a `compare` function and returns such a record.

`Int.compare` $\mathcal{B}$

(f) Define a function `treefoldr` that does an inorder traversal of a binary search tree. For example, given tree `t`,

```
(treefoldr (lambda (key value answer) (cons key answer)) '() t)
```

will return a *sorted* list of the keys in the tree.

15. *Sequences with fast append.* List `append` takes time and space proportional to the length of the left-hand argument. In this problem, you define a new representation of sequences that supports append in constant time.

Informally, a sequence of τ's is either empty, or it is a single value of type τ, or it is a sequence of τ's followed by another sequence of τ's.

(a) Use this informal definition to define an algebraic datatype `seq` of kind `(* => *)`. As with any abstraction that is defined by choices, your definition should contain one value constructor for each choice.

(b) Define `s-cons`, with type `(forall ['a] ('a (seq 'a) -> (seq 'a)))`, to add a single element to the front of a sequence, *using constant time and space.*

(c) Define `s-snoc`, with type `(forall ['a] ('a (seq 'a) -> (seq 'a)))`, to add a single element to the *back* of a sequence, *using constant time and space.* (As always, `snoc` is `cons` spelled backward.)

Here the order of arguments is the *opposite* of the order in which the results go in the data structure. That is, in `(s-snoc x xs)`, `x` *follows* `xs`. The arguments are the way they are so that `s-snoc` can be used with `foldl` and `foldr`.

(d) Define `s-append`, type `(forall ['a] ((seq 'a) (seq 'a) -> (seq 'a)))`, to append two sequences, *using constant time and space.*

(e) Define `list-of-seq`, with type `(forall ['a] ((seq 'a) -> (list 'a)))`, to convert a sequence into a list containing the same elements in the same order. Function `list-of-seq` should allocate only as much space as is needed to hold the result.

(f) Without using explicit recursion, define function `seq-of-list`, with type `(forall ['a] ((list 'a) -> (seq 'a)))`, which converts an ordinary list to a sequence containing the same elements in the same order.

(g) Ideally, function `list-of-seq` would take time proportional to the number of elements in the sequence. But when a sequence contains many empty-sequence constructors, it can take longer. Prevent this outcome by altering your solutions to maintain the invariant that the empty-sequence value constructor never follows or is followed by another sequence.

16. *Emulating mutable lists.* When lists are immutable, as they are in μScheme and in the ML family, they appear not to support typical imperative operations, like inserting or deleting a node at a point. But these operations *can* be implemented on purely functional data structures, efficiently, in ways that look imperative. The implementation uses a technique called *the zipper.*

    You will learn the zipper by implementing a *list with indicator.* A list with indicator is a *nonempty* sequence of values, together with an "indicator" that points at one value in the sequence. Elements can be inserted or deleted at the indicator, in constant time.

    (a) Define a representation for type `ilist` of kind `(* => *)`. Document your representation by saying, in a short comment, what sequence is meant by any value of type `'a ilist`.

    Given a good representation, the code is easy: almost every function can be implemented as a case expression with one or two choices, each of which has a simple right-hand side. But a good representation might be challenging to design.

    (b) Support the documentation in part (a) by writing `list-of-ilist`:

    510. ⟨*list-with-indicator functions* 510⟩≡ 511a ▷

```
(check-type list-of-ilist
            (forall ['a] ((ilist 'a) -> (list 'a))))
```

(c) Define function singleton-ilist, which takes a single value and returns a list whose indicator points at that value.

511a. ⟨*list-with-indicator functions* 510⟩+≡ ◁510 511b▷

```
(check-type singleton-ilist (forall ['a] ('a -> (ilist 'a))))
```

(d) Define function at-indicator, which returns the value the indicator points at.

511b. ⟨*list-with-indicator functions* 510⟩+≡ ◁511a 511c▷

```
(check-type at-indicator (forall ['a] ((ilist 'a) -> 'a)))
```


(e) To move the indicator, define indicator-left and indicator-right, with these types:

511c. ⟨*list-with-indicator functions* 510⟩+≡ ◁511b 511d▷

```
(check-type indicator-left
            (forall ['a] ((ilist 'a) -> (option (ilist 'a)))))
(check-type indicator-right
            (forall ['a] ((ilist 'a) -> (option (ilist 'a)))))
```

Calling (indicator-left xs) creates a new list ys that is like xs, except the indicator is moved one position to the left. And it returns (SOME ys). But if the indicator belonging to xs already points to the leftmost position, then (indicator-left xs) returns NONE. Function indicator-right is similar. Both functions must run in *constant time and space*.

These functions "move the indicator," but no mutation is involved. Instead of mutating an existing list, each function creates a new list.

(f) To remove an element, define delete-left and delete-right, with these types:

511d. ⟨*list-with-indicator functions* 510⟩+≡ ◁511c 511e▷

```
(check-type delete-left
            (forall ['a] ((ilist 'a) -> (option (ilist 'a)))))
(check-type delete-right
            (forall ['a] ((ilist 'a) -> (option (ilist 'a)))))
```

Calling (delete-left xs) creates a new list ys that is like xs, except the element to the left of the indicator has been removed. And it returns (SOME ys). If the indicator points to the leftmost position, then delete-left returns NONE. Function delete-right is similar. Both functions must run in constant time and space, and as before, no mutation is involved.

(g) To insert an element, define insert-left and insert-right, with these types:

511e. ⟨*list-with-indicator functions* 510⟩+≡ ◁511d 512a▷

```
(check-type insert-left
            (forall ['a] ('a (ilist 'a) -> (ilist 'a))))
(check-type insert-right
            (forall ['a] ('a (ilist 'a) -> (ilist 'a))))
```

Calling (insert-left x xs) returns a new list that is like xs, except the value x is inserted to the left of the indicator. Function insert-right is similar. Both functions must run in constant time and space. As before, no mutation is involved.

(h) Define functions `ffoldl` and `ffoldr`, with these types:

512a. ⟨*list-with-indicator functions* 510⟩+≡ ◁511e

```
(check-type ffoldl
          (forall ['a 'b] (('a 'b -> 'b) 'b (ilist 'a) -> 'b)))
(check-type ffoldr
          (forall ['a 'b] (('a 'b -> 'b) 'b (ilist 'a) -> 'b)))
```

These functions do the same thing as `foldl` and `foldr`, but on lists with indicators. They ignore the position of the indicator.

To test these functions, start with the list `test-ilist` defined below. The list is created by a sequence of insertions, plus a movement. To emphasize the imperative feel of the abstraction, `test-ilist` is created by using `let*` to rebind the name `xs` repeatedly. The code should remind you of a sequence of assignment statements.

512b. ⟨*list-with-indicator test cases* 512b⟩≡ 512c ▷

```
(val test-ilist
  (let* ((xs (singleton-ilist 3))
         (xs (insert-left 1 xs))
         (xs (insert-left 2 xs))
         (xs (insert-right 4 xs))
         (xs (case (indicator-right xs) ((SOME ys) ys)))
         (xs (insert-right 5 xs)))
    xs))
```

The resulting `test-ilist` should be the list `'(1 2 3 4 5)`, with the indicator pointing at 4. It should pass these tests:

512c. ⟨*list-with-indicator test cases* 512b⟩+≡ ◁512b

```
(check-expect (list-of-ilist test-ilist) '(1 2 3 4 5))
(check-expect (at-indicator  test-ilist) 4)
(check-expect (Option.map list-of-ilist (delete-left test-ilist))
              (SOME '(1 2 4 5)))
```

17. *Tries as sets.* A *binary trie* searches by looking at bits of an integer. A binary trie can represent a set of integers, and set union, intersection, and difference are easy to implement efficiently. You'll implement a *little-endian* binary trie, which looks at the least-significant bits first.

    A binary trie has three kinds of nodes: empty, singleton, and union.

    - The empty trie represents the empty set of integers.
    - The singleton trie contains a single integer n, and it represents the singleton set $\{n\}$.
    - The union trie contains two subtries e and o (for "even" and "odd"), which represent sets $[\![e]\!]$ and $[\![o]\!]$, respectively. In the little-endian form, the union trie represents the set

      $$\{2 \cdot k \mid k \in [\![e]\!]\} \cup \{2 \cdot k + 1 \mid k \in [\![o]\!]\},$$

      where $2 \cdot k$ means twice k. As a consequence of this definition, when you are looking for an element n in a union trie, you look in e if n is even and in o if n is odd—and either way, in the sub-trie you look for n div 2.

Implement a little-endian binary trie as follows:

(a) Define an algebraic data type `ints` that represents a binary trie, which in turn represents a set of integers.

(b) Define function `ints-member?`, which tells whether an integer is in the set.

(c) Define function `ints-insert`, which inserts an integer into the set.

(d) Define function `ints-delete`, which removes an integer from the set, if present.

(e) Define function `ints-union`, which takes the union of two sets. Find an implementation that allocates fewer `CONVAL`s than simply union by repeated insertion.

(f) Define function `ints-inter`, which takes the intersection of two sets.

(g) Define function `ints-diff`, which takes the intersection of two sets.

(h) Define function `ints-fold`, which folds over all the integers in a trie. Give it type `(forall ['a] ((int 'a -> 'a) 'a ints -> 'a))`.

As a representation of sets, the binary trie has some redundancy:

- The empty set can be represented not only as an empty trie, but also as the union of two empty tries—or the union of any two tries that each represent the empty set. The empty set is represented most efficiently as the empty trie.
- A singleton set can be represented not only as a singleton trie, but also as the union of a singleton trie and an empty trie—or the union of any two tries that respectively represent the appropriate singleton set and the empty set. A singleton set is represented most efficiently as a singleton trie.

The potential redundancy can be eliminated by wrapping the value constructor for union in a "smart constructor":

(i) Revisit the functions you have implemented above, and identify which functions can create a union node of which one child is empty and the other is either empty or singleton.

(j) Rewrite the functions you have implemented above so that no function ever creates a union node of which one child is empty and the other is either empty or singleton. The standard technique is not to use the value constructor for union directly, but to define a *smart constructor*: A smart constructor is a function that, at the abstract level, has the same specification as a value constructor, but at the representation level, can may be more efficient. For the binary trie, the smart constructor should recognize two special cases: union of empty and empty should return empty, and union of singleton n and empty should return either singleton $2 \cdot n$ or singleton $2 \cdot n + 1$. In other cases, the smart constructor should behave like the value constructor for a union trie.

18. *Tries as finite maps.* Generalize your results from Exercise 17 to implement a finite map with integer keys.

    (a) To represent a finite map with integer keys, define an algebraic data type `intmap` of kind `(* => *)`.

(b) Define values and functions with these types:

514a. ⟨*exercise transcripts* 505b⟩+≡ ◁508c 514b▷

```
-> (check-type empty-intmap
               (forall ['a] (intmap 'a)))
-> (check-type intmap-insert
               (forall ['a] (int 'a (intmap 'a) -> (intmap 'a))))
-> (check-type intmap-find
               (forall ['a] (int (intmap 'a) -> (option 'a))))
-> (check-type intmap-delete
               (forall ['a] (int (intmap 'a) -> (intmap 'a))))
-> (check-type intmap-fold
               (forall ['a 'b]
                       ((int 'a 'b -> 'b) 'b (intmap 'a) -> 'b)))
```

19. *Search trees with lists as keys.* A *ternary search tree* combines aspects of a trie and of a binary search tree. The original ternary search tree is specialized to null-terminated C strings (Bentley and Sedgewick 1997, 1998). The ternary search tree that you will implement is polymorphic: it works with any type of list.

A tree of type `(ternary` τ_a τ_b`)` represents a finite map whose *keys* have type `(list` τ_a`)` and whose *values* have type τ_b. A ternary search tree has two species of nodes: a *decision* node and a *final* node.

- A *decision* node contains a *decision element* d of type `'a`, and it has three children, each of which is also a ternary search tree:
  - The *left* subtree stores all key-value pairs whose keys are lists that begin with an element that is *smaller* than d.
  - The *right* subtree stores all key-value pairs whose keys are lists that begin with an element that is *larger* than d.
  - The *middle* subtree stores all the key-value pairs whose keys have the form `(cons` d xs`)`. However, in the middle subtree, only the xs part of the key is used—the d part is implicit in the position of the middle subtree directly under a decision node.

  In addition to its three subtrees, the decision node also stores the value whose key is the empty list (if any).
- A *final* node stores only the value whose key is the empty list, if any. It has no children.

This exercise has three parts:

(a) Using an algebraic data type, define a representation of ternary search trees.

(b) Define function `ternary-insert`, to insert a key-value pair into a ternary search tree.

(c) Define function `ternary-find`, to look up a key in a ternary search tree.

Your functions should be higher-order and should have these types:

514b. ⟨*exercise transcripts* 505b⟩+≡ ◁514a 522b▷

```
-> (check-type ternary-find
     (forall ['a 'b] (('a 'a -> order) ->
                          ((list 'a) (ternary 'a 'b) -> (option 'b)))))
-> (check-type ternary-insert
     (forall ['a 'b]
         (('a 'a -> order) ->
          ((list 'a) 'b (ternary 'a 'b) -> (ternary 'a 'b)))))
```

Hint: The case that's easy to get wrong is the one in which the key is an empty list. If you can associate a value with the empty list and look it up successfully, you're on your way.

8.11.8 *Equational reasoning*

20. *Laws of tree traversal.* Using equational reasoning, prove two laws about function `preorder-elems`, which is defined on page 463.

```
          (preorder-elems BTEMPTY) = '()
(preorder-elems (BTNODE x t1 t2)) = (cons x (append (preorder-elems t1)
                                                     (preorder-elems t2)))
```

21. *Laws of case expressions.* In all functional languages, one of the most important compiler optimizations is function inlining. Inlining sometimes results in expressions that have a "case-of-case" structure:

$$\texttt{(case}\;\;\texttt{(case}\; e\; \texttt{[}p_1\; e_1\texttt{]} \cdots \texttt{[}p_k\; e_k\texttt{])}\;\; \texttt{[}p'_1\; e'_1\texttt{]} \;\vdots\; \texttt{[}p'_m\; e'_m\texttt{])}.$$

Write an algebraic law that will enable a compiler to rewrite such an expression so that the scrutinee is not a case expression. Assume that all the expressions are evaluated without side effects, so duplicating code is OK. (With luck, any duplicate code will be eliminated by applications of laws described in Section 8.3.)

8.11.9 *Syntactic sugar*

In the exercises below, you implement the "patterns everywhere" syntactic sugar described in Section 8.4. This sugar makes μML almost as expressive as core ML. ("Almost" because μML does not support exceptions.) By and large, the exercises don't touch code related to evaluation or type checking; all they do is extend the μML parser (Appendix S, page S462). The parsers in the appendix contain some "hooks" and extra code that should make things easier—you can focus on the desugaring functions.

22. *Benefits of clausal definitions.* Using `define*` as described in Section 8.4 (page 481), rewrite the implementation of `preorder-elems` to make the laws in Exercise 20 blindingly obvious.

23. *Patterns for* `lambda` *parameters.* Using syntactic sugar, extend μML's `lambda` expression so that each formal parameter is a pattern, not just a variable (Section 8.4, page 480).

    - In the `exptable` function of Appendix S, change the `lambda` case to use parser `patFormals` instead of `formals`; `patFormals` parses a list of patterns in brackets.
    - Redefine function `lambda` to rewrite a list of patterns as a list of variables, adding a case expression. If the list of patterns is empty, the

`LAMBDA` takes no arguments, and it need not be transformed. Otherwise, where `lambda` takes one or more patterns as arguments, implement the desugaring with the help of functions `freshVars` to get new names for the arguments, `tupleexp` to form a scrutinee, and `tuplepat` to build the single pattern that goes in the case expression.

Even with this extension, many `lambda` expressions use only `PVAR` patterns. These `lambda` expressions can be transformed using `case`, but if you instead convert them to ordinary `lambda` expressions without `case`, your code will be easier to debug.

24. *Patterns for* `define` *parameters.* Using syntactic sugar, extend μML's `define` form so the formal-parameter list is a list of patterns, not just a list of variables (Section 8.4, page 480). Replace the `formals` parser with `patFormals`, and rewrite the `define` function. As in Exercise 23, use `freshVars`, `tupleexp`, and `tuplepat`—if you've done Exercise 23, you may be able to reuse code. And as in Exercise 23, if all the patterns are `PVAR` patterns, it's better not to introduce a case expression.

25. *Clausal* `lambda` *expressions.* Using syntactic sugar, implement the `lambda*` expression (Section 8.4, page 482). Don't change any parsers; just update the ML code in Appendix S to replace the `lambdastar` function with one that returns `OK` e, where e is a lambda expression. As above, use `freshVars`, `tupleexp`, and `tuplepat` to good advantage. And your `lambdastar` function should check that each list of patterns has the same length (shown as n on page 482). The check isn't strictly necessary, but if it is omitted and the lengths aren't equal, the error messages are baffling.

26. *Clausal definitions.* Using syntactic sugar, implement clausal definitions. That is, implement the `define*` form (Section 8.4, page 481). Don't change any parsers; just update the ML code in Appendix S to replace the `definestar` function with one that returns `OK` d, where d is a definition. If you have done Exercise 25, use ML function `lambdastar` to implement `definestar`.

27. *Pattern binding in* `let` *expressions.* Using syntactic sugar, implement the transformation that enables `let` expressions to bind patterns, not just variables (Section 8.4, page 482). Rewrite the `letx` expression-builder function in Appendix S, which should now take a `(pat * exp) list` instead of a `(name * exp) list`. Your new `letx` function must handle three cases:

    - If the parser is configured correctly, a `LETREC` uses only `PVAR` patterns, and it can be converted to an ordinary `LETREC`. If your `LETREC` case encounters a pattern that is not a `PVAR`, your interpreter should halt with a fatal error message.
    - A `LETSTAR` should be desugared into nested `LET`s in the standard way.
    - A `LET` should be desugared as shown on page 482. The desugaring must be applied to *each* pattern/expression pair.

    You will also need to replace these parsers in the `exptable` function:

Original μML	*μML with patterns everywhere*
`letBs`	`patBs`
`letstarBs`	`patBs`
`letrecBs`	`patLetrecBs`

28. *Pattern binding in* `val` *definitions.* Using syntactic sugar, extend `val` so it can bind to a pattern (Section 8.4, page 483). Add a new row to μML's `xdeftable`, with the usage string `"(val pat e)"` and parser `valpat <$> pattern <*> exp`. The `valpat` function is a new definition builder that you need to write. It should build one `val` binding for each free variable of the given pattern; free variables can be found using function `freePatVars`. Once built, the bindings are combined with a binding to `it`, and the list of bindings is wrapped in the secret `DEFS` constructor.

    Perform the full desugaring only if the pattern in the `val` is in `CONPAT` form. If the pattern is a variable or a wildcard, turn it into a variable and move on.

8.11.10 *Type generativity*

29. *Generativity in C.* In C, a `struct` *definition* is generative. A struct definition is any occurrence of `struct` that is followed by a list of fields in curly braces. For example, the definition

    517a. ⟨*generativity.c* 517a⟩≡ 517b ▷
    ```
    typedef struct point *Point;
    ```

    does *not* include a `struct` definition, because no fields are given. But the declaration

    517b. ⟨*generativity.c* 517a⟩+≡ ◁ 517a
    ```
    double distance_from_origin(struct point {double x; double y; });
    ```

    does include a `struct` definition, because fields are given—even though those fields are in unusual places.

    This exercise will help you discover how generativity works in C and how your favorite C compiler deals with it.

    (a) Write a C program that contains at least two distinct `struct` definitions, both of `struct point`, and both containing two `double` fields `x` and `y`.

    (b) Extend your C program so that you try to use one `struct point` where the other one is expected, causing a compile-time error.

    (c) Find a C compiler that complains about your program of part (b), saying that it expected `struct point` but found `struct point` instead—or something similar.

30. *Generativity in Modula-3.* In most statically typed languages, generativity is associated with a particular syntactic form: in the ML family, the definition of an algebraic data type; in C, the definition of a `struct` or `union`. Such languages give programmers no choices: if you define a particular species of type, the definition is generative.

    Modula-3, by contrast, lets you choose which types are generative (Cardelli et al. 1992). No type is generative by default, but any pointer type can be made generative by *branding* it, using the `BRANDED` keyword. (Pointer types are called "references," and the corresponding type constructor is written `REF`.)

    (a) Consult the language definition for Modula-3—try not to distract yourself with subtyping—and design a similar `branded` mechanism for μML. Update the formal system to account for brands, and give additional rules for the translation of type syntax into types.

    (b) Write rules for type equivalence that account for brands.

(c) Write introduction and elimination rules for expressions that have branded types. This part of the exercise may suggest to you why the designers of Modula-3 limited branding to reference types.

8.11.11 *User-defined types*

31. *Kinds.* Show that μML's kind system is a conservative extension of Typed μScheme's kind system. Start with a definition of *erasure*:

    - The erasure of the empty environment is the empty environment.
    - If $\hat{\Delta}$ is the erasure of environment Δ, then the erasure of environment $\Delta' = \Delta\{T \mapsto (\tau, \kappa)\}$ is $\hat{\Delta}\{T \mapsto \kappa\}$.
    - The erasure of judgment $\Delta \vdash t \leadsto \tau :: \kappa$ is judgment $\Delta \vdash \tau :: \kappa$.

    Prove both of the following claims:

    (a) If there is a derivation of $\Delta \vdash t \leadsto \tau :: \kappa$, then there is a derivation of $\hat{\Delta} \vdash \tau :: \kappa$.

    (b) If there is a derivation of $\Delta_0 \vdash \tau :: \kappa$, then there exist a t and a Δ such that $\Delta_0 = \hat{\Delta}$ and there is a derivation of $\Delta \vdash t \leadsto \tau :: \kappa$.

32. *Type abbreviations.* As your programs get more sophisticated and types get bigger, you will wish for type abbreviations. In this exercise, you get them. You will change the rules and the code for the type translation on page S455.

    (a) Change environment Δ so that a type name T may stand for one of two things:

    - A type
    - A function from a list of types to a type

    (b) To keep things simple, change the KINDAPP rule so that only a type name T can be applied. The rule will then work as long as T stands for a type.

    (c) When T stands for the function $\lambda\alpha_1, \ldots, \alpha_n.\tau$, use this new rule:

$$\frac{\begin{array}{c}\Delta(t) = (\lambda\alpha_1, \ldots, \alpha_n.\tau, *_1 \times \cdots \times *_n \Rightarrow \kappa)\\ \Delta \vdash t_i \leadsto \tau_i :: \kappa_i, \quad 1 \le i \le n\end{array}}{\Delta \vdash (\mathtt{t}\ \ t_1\ \ \cdots\ \ t_n) \leadsto \tau[\alpha_1 \mapsto \tau_1, \ldots, \alpha_n \mapsto \tau_n] :: \kappa}. \qquad (\textsc{KindAppAbbrev})$$

    (d) Implement the new semantics in function `txType`.

    (e) Add a new definition form `(type` $[$`[`$\alpha_1\ \cdots\ \alpha_n$`]`$]$ T `t)`, which enters T into Δ as the appropriate function on types.

8.11.12 *Theory and implementation of pattern matching*

33. *Types of patterns and expressions.* A pattern is a variable, a wildcard, or a constructor application. Except for the wildcard, each of these syntactic elements can also be used to form an expression. Put patterns into one-to-one correspondence with a subset of expressions and show that this correspondence preserves types:

(a) For each form of pattern p *except* the wildcard, show the corresponding expression form $[\![p]\!]$. For clarity, you may wish to express the correspondence as an ML function of type `(pat -> exp)`.

(b) Use metatheory to prove that if p has no wildcard, and if $\Gamma, \Gamma' \vdash p : \tau$, then $\Gamma + \Gamma' \vdash [\![p]\!] : \tau$.

(c) Extend the expression syntax with a new form `HOLE`, written in the concrete syntax as `_`. A hole behaves like a name with type scheme $\forall \alpha . \alpha$.

$$\textsc{Hole}\ \frac{}{\Gamma \vdash \textsc{Hole} : \tau} \qquad \frac{\alpha \notin \text{ftv}(\Gamma)}{\mathbf{T}, \Gamma \vdash \textsc{Hole} : \alpha}\ \textsc{Hole, with constraints}$$

(d) Given the extension in part (c), use metatheory to prove that regardless of whether p has a wildcard, if $\Gamma, \Gamma' \vdash p : \tau$, then $\Gamma + \Gamma' \vdash [\![p]\!] : \tau$.

34. *Pattern-match failures.* Using the operational semantics, prove that if there is a derivation of the judgment $\langle p, v \rangle \rightarrowtail \dagger$, then the derivation contains an instance of either the FAILVCON rule or the FAILBAREVCON rule.

35. *Type inference for patterns.* The constraint-based rules for typechecking patterns (Figure 8.9, page 498) do more bookkeeping than they have to. The constraint can be eliminated: instead of judgment $C, \Gamma, \Gamma' \vdash p : \tau$, new rules can use the simpler judgment $\Gamma, \Gamma' \vdash p : \tau$. Constraint C is eliminated by finding a substitution θ that solves C and whose domain is the free variables of C. The original derivation is transformed by applying θ to it. The resulting judgment about p is $\theta C, \Gamma, \theta\Gamma' \vdash p : \theta\tau$, and since $\theta C = \mathbf{T}$ by definition, this transformation leads to the simpler judgment form.

    The hard part of the exercise is to show that applying θ doesn't affect the type that is inferred in the rest of the derivation.

    (a) Prove that in any derivation of the judgment $\mathbf{T}, \Gamma \vdash K : \tau$, the free variables of τ are distinct from the free variables of Γ.

    (b) By induction over derivations of judgments of the form $C, \Gamma, \Gamma' \vdash p : \tau$, prove that the free type variables of C are distinct from the free type variables of Γ.

    (c) By induction over derivations of judgments of the form $C, \Gamma, \Gamma' \vdash p : \tau$, prove that the free type variables of Γ' are distinct from the free type variables of Γ.

    (d) Prove that in a valid derivation of $C, \Gamma \vdash e : \tau$, if there is a subderivation of $C', \Gamma, \Gamma' \vdash p : \tau'$, and if θ is a substitution whose domain is contained in $\text{fv}(C')$, and if $\theta C' \equiv \mathbf{T}$, then

        i. Substitution θ can affect only the types of the new bindings Γ' and the type τ' of pattern p.
        ii. Applying θ to the entire derivation results in a valid derivation.
        iii. Applying θ does not change τ, that is, $\theta\tau = \tau$.

    The preceding results imply that constraint C can be eliminated by solving it eagerly at each application of the PATVCON rule.

    (e) Write new rules for the judgment form $\Gamma, \Gamma' \vdash p : \tau$. Except for choice of fresh type variables, your rules should be deterministic. Rules PATBAREVCON, PATWILDCARD, and PATVAR can be rewritten simply by removing the trivial output constraint. The PATVCON rule needs to solve constraint C and apply the resulting substitution to Γ' and α. (Constraints $C_1, \ldots, C_m$ are all trivial, and therefore so is constraint C'.)

(f) Simplify the CHOICE rule.
(g) Rewrite the code to reflect your new, simpler rules.

36. *Matching integer literals.* Extend pattern matching so it is possible to match on an integer literal. An integer-literal pattern has type `int`, introduces no bindings, and matches only the corresponding integer value.

    (a) Extend the parser, type checker, and evaluator of μML to support integer-literal patterns.

    (b) Using patterns, write a recursive Fibonacci function that does not use `if`.

37. *Matching quoted symbols.* Extend pattern matching so it is possible to match a quoted symbol. A quoted-symbol pattern has type `sym`, introduces no bindings, and matches only the corresponding symbol. Extend the parser, type checker, and evaluator of μML to support quoted-symbol patterns.

38. *Exhaustive or redundant patterns.* Section 8.9.2 on page 499 describes checks for exhaustive and redundant patterns. Given a scrutinee of type τ, a set of patterns is exhaustive if every value that inhabits type τ is matched by some pattern. In this exercise you write an analysis that prints a warning message when it finds a non-exhaustive or redundant pattern match.

    The idea is this: Suppose you have the set of all possible values of type τ. And suppose that, for each member of this set, you can tell if it does or does not match a particular pattern p. Then you can check for both exhaustiveness and redundancy using an iterative algorithm that maintains a set of all values not yet matched.

    - The set is initially the set of all values of type τ.
    - At each step of the iteration, the set is split into two subsets: those that do and do not match pattern p.
    - The set that matches p must not be empty; otherwise pattern p is redundant.
    - The set that does not match p is passed on to the next pattern.
    - At the end of the iteration, if the set of values not yet matched is non-empty, the pattern match is not exhaustive.

    There's only one snag: for interesting types, the sets are infinite. To represent such sets, I define a "simple value set" to be one of two choices:

    - All values of type τ, for a given τ
    - A given value constructor K, applied to a list of zero or more simple value sets

    A full set of values is a *collection* of simple sets, using the collections defined in Section H.2.4 (page S218).

    520. ⟨*exhaustiveness analysis for μML* 520⟩≡ (S420b) 521b ▷

    ```
    datatype simple_vset = ALL of ty
                         | ONE of vcon * simple_vset list
    type vset = simple_vset collection
    ```

In the analysis, each set of values is *classified* according to whether it does or does not match a pattern. Full sets can be classified, simple sets can be classified, and even lists of sets can be classified. Start with this code:

521a. ⟨*exhaustiveness analysis for μML* **⟦prototype⟧** 521a⟩≡ 522a ▷

```
classifyVset    : pat -> vset        -> (bool * simple_vset) collection
classifySimple : pat -> simple_vset -> (bool * simple_vset) collection
```

```
fun classifyVset   p vs = joinC (mapC (classifySimple p) vs)
and classifySimple p vs = raise LeftAsExercise "match classification"
```


Classification takes a single value set as input and produces a collection as output. A simple value set vs is classified by a pattern p as follows:

- If p is a wildcard or a variable, it always matches, and the result is a singleton collection containing (true, vs).
- If p is $(K\ p_1\ \cdots\ p_n)$ and vs is the application of a different constructor K', then vs doesn't match, and the result is a singleton collection containing (false, vs).
- If p is $(K\ p_1\ \cdots\ p_n)$ and vs is $(K\ v_1\ \cdots\ v_n)$, then the value-set list $v_1\ \cdots\ v_n$ is classified against the pattern list $p_1\ \cdots\ p_n$. Do this using a third function, classifyList. The empty value-set list always matches the empty pattern list, and the subset of $v_1\ \cdots\ v_n$ matching $p_1\ \cdots\ p_n$ is the subset of v_1 matching p_1 combined with the subset of $v_2 \cdots v_n$ matching $p_2 \cdots p_n$. To implement classifyList, use recursion, use classifySimple, and use the collection function map2C.
- Finally, if p is $(K\ p_1\ \cdots\ p_n)$ and vs is ALL τ, change ALL τ to unroll τ and try again. When τ is an algebraic data type, unroll τ returns a vset that is equivalent to ALL τ but that does not use ALL at top level.

521b. ⟨*exhaustiveness analysis for μML* 520⟩+≡ (S420b) ◁ 520

```
fun unroll tau =                                    unroll : ty -> vset
  let val mu = case tau of TYCON mu => mu
                         | CONAPP (TYCON mu, _) => mu
                         | _ => raise BugInTypeInference "not ADT"
      fun ofVcon (name, sigma) =
        let val tau'   = freshInstance sigma
            val argTys = case asFuntype tau'
                           of SOME (args, res) =>
                                let val theta = solve (res ∼ tau)
                                in  map (tysubst theta) args
                                end
                            | NONE => []
        in  ONE (name, map ALL argTys) : simple_vset
        end
  in  C (map ofVcon (vconsOf mu))
  end
```

asFuntype	S440e
BugInType-Inference	S213d
CONAPP	408
freshInstance	434c
joinC	S218b
LeftAsExercise	S213b
mapC	S218b
solve	437b
type ty	408
TYCON	408
tysubst	410c
type vcon	486b

Function call vconsOf mu returns the name and type scheme of each value constructor associated with mu. Function vconsOf is omitted from this book.

Using this classification, the exhaustiveness check can be implemented in three stages, as described on the next page.

Implement the exhaustiveness check in three stages:

(a) Implement `classifySimple`, but leave out the case of matching value constructors.

(b) Implement `classifyList`, which has type

```
pat list * simple_vset list -> (bool * simple_vset list) collection,
```

and use it to complete the implementation of `classifySimple`. Classify lists using these rules:

- The empty list of values always matches the empty list of patterns.
- A list of values v `::` vs matches a list of patterns p `::` ps if and only if v matches p and also vs matches ps.

(c) Implement `exhaustivenessCheck`, replacing this placeholder:

522a. ⟨*exhaustiveness analysis for μML* **[[prototype]]** 521a⟩+≡ ◁521a

```
exhaustivenessCheck : pat list * ty -> unit
```

```
fun exhaustivenessCheck (ps, tau) =
  eprintln "(Case expression not checked for exhaustiveness.)"
```

The replacement should compute successive value sets that are as yet unmatched. Start with the value-set collection `singleC (ALL tau)`, and classify value sets using each pattern from `ps` in turn. Issue a warning message for each redundant pattern, and if the list of patterns is not exhaustive, issue a warning for that too.

You can test your code on these examples:

522b. ⟨*exercise transcripts* 505b⟩+≡ ◁514b

```
-> (lambda (z) (case z [(SOME _) #t] [_ #f] [NONE #f] [_ #f]))
Warning: in choice 3, pattern NONE cannot match
Warning: in choice 4, pattern _ cannot match
<function> : (forall ['a] ((option 'a) -> bool))
-> (lambda (z) (case z [(SOME _) #t] [NONE #f] [_ #f]))
Warning: in choice 3, pattern _ cannot match
<function> : (forall ['a] ((option 'a) -> bool))
-> (lambda (z) (case z [(SOME _) #t] [NONE #f]))
<function> : (forall ['a] ((option 'a) -> bool))
-> (lambda (z) (case z [(SOME (PAIR '() _)) #t] [NONE #f]))
Warning: case expression does not match values of this form:
  (SOME (PAIR (cons _ _) _))
<function> : (forall ['a 'b] ((option (pair (list 'a) 'b)) -> bool))
```

Chapter 9 contents

9 Molecule, abstract data types, and modules

[The programmer] is concerned with the way his program makes use of the abstractions, but not with any details of how those abstractions may be realized. . . . A structured programming language must provide a mechanism whereby the language can be extended to contain the abstractions which the user requires.

Barbara Liskov and Stephen Zilles,
Programming with Abstract Data Types

In the languages we've examined so far, when we have a high-level problem like "see if a list contains an interesting element," we can define a high-level, problem-specific function like `exists?`. But we can't yet define problem-specific *data*; no matter what problem we're working on, our code is written in terms of *representations* like numbers, symbols, Booleans, lists, S-expressions, and constructed data. We should hope for better; if we're implementing high-level actions like "find the rule in the table," "multiply two 50-digit numbers," or "stop recording when the event is over," then our code should be written in terms of *abstractions* like tables, large numbers, and events. Such abstractions can be defined by the language features described in the last two chapters of this book.

The ability to define a new form of data, hiding its true representation from most code, is called *data abstraction*. Data abstraction is typically supported by *abstract data types, objects*, or a combination thereof. Using abstract data types, code is organized into *modules*, and only a function that is inside a module has access to the representation of values of that module's abstract types. Using objects, code is organized into *methods*, and only a method that is defined on an object has access to the representation of that object. Abstract data types and modules are described in this chapter, which also describes some proven strategies for designing programs that use data abstraction. Objects and methods are described in Chapter 10.

Why use data abstraction? It enables us to replace a representation with a new one, without breaking code; it helps limit the effects of future changes; and it protects vulnerable representations from most careless or faulty code. For example,

- The Linux kernel (and much else besides) is built by a program called Make. Make works by composing *rules*, which say how to build the components of a system. In Make's initial implementation, rules were kept on an association list, which was fine, because Makefiles started out small: a Makefile contained at most one or two dozen rules. But Make's author, Stuart Feldman, decided that for the first public version, craftsmanship demanded a hash table. Because the representation was hidden, it was easy to replace.

  Did it matter? When Feldman was asked to help debug a Makefile, he found *thousands* of rules. Luckily, the hash table performed well—far better than the association list would have. Data abstraction enabled Feldman to *replace one representation with another,* without breaking code.

- My digital video recorder is programmed to record a ball game. Thanks to real-time game information, it records until the game is actually over, not just until the end of the game's scheduled time slot. But real-time game information often changes format; first it's HTML, next it's XML, now it's JSON. Its content changes, too. These changes break my code, but I *limit their effects* by defining an abstraction that tells me only who's playing, whether the game has started, and whether it's over. Only the abstraction knows the ever-changing representation of game information, and when the representation changes again, I can update my code quickly—without missing any games.

- In Chapters 1 to 3, two `Names` with different pointer values are guaranteed to point to different strings. This property is an *invariant* property of the data structure defined in file `name.c`. It is guaranteed only because the representation of `struct Name` is hidden. Because the representation is hidden, code outside of `name.c` can create a `Name` only by calling `strtoname`, which guarantees that each such name respects the invariant. Data abstraction *protects the invariant,* so faulty outside code can't invalidate it. (Malicious code could invalidate the invariant by using `memcpy` or similar skullduggery.)

Abstractions and invariants are the key elements in a proven strategy for designing with data abstraction, which is sketched in Section 9.6.

Data abstraction can be accomplished using abstract types, objects, or both, but because abstract types are easier to learn, they are where we begin. Every abstract type is defined in some module, and its representation is exposed only to functions that are defined in that same module. Functions defined outside the module, which are called *client* functions, know only the name of the abstract type, not its representation. When a client function wants to create, observe, or mutate a value of abstract type, it must call a function defined inside the module. Types and functions defined in a module are visible to client code only if they are named in the module's *interface*; such types and functions are said to be *exported.*

Abstract data types militate toward a particular programming style, which you already have some experience with: in the C interpreters in Chapters 1 to 4, you have seen abstract types `Name` and `Env`, as well as C's built-in `FILE *`. Primitive types, such as Typed μScheme's `int` or C's `float` and `double`, also behave like abstract types—that is, all we know about these primitive types are their names. To work with primitive types, we must use primitive functions, which have privileged access to the representations.

In this book, abstract data types are illustrated by the programming language *Molecule,* which borrows from the Modula, ML, and CLU families of languages. Molecule's key feature is abstract data types, but to enable you to program interesting examples, Molecule provides two other notable features. First, it supports polymorphism through *generic modules.* Second, to enable `check-expect` testing and a read-eval-print loop without violating abstraction, Molecule *overloads* names like `=` and `print`, among others.

A caution: When programs are built from modules and are full of abstractions, programming feels different. Molecule emulates languages like Ada, CLU, and Modula-3, and unlike Scheme, ML, and Smalltalk, these languages don't help you knock out small, interesting programs quickly—they help you build large systems that can *evolve.* But in one chapter of a survey book, we can't build a large system, and we can't realistically show how software evolves. To appreciate the software-engineering benefits that modules provide, you must use your imagination.

Language design for modules

A language for learning about modules should include distinct syntax for interfaces and implementations, a clean type theory, a relatively simple core layer, and support for generic (parameterized) modules. Unfortunately, no single language found in the wild meets all three criteria. To create a language for learning about modules, I borrowed from the *Mo*dula family, which pioneered separately compiled interfaces and implementations, from Xavier *Le*roy's formulation of ML modules, which exemplifies simple, clean generic modules with modular type checking, and from *CLU*, which demonstrated the benefits of abstract types. Because the name "Moleclu" would be hard to pronounce, the resulting language is called *Molecule*.

9.1 THE VOCABULARY OF DATA ABSTRACTION

To program with data abstraction, we must understand our programs at two levels: the concrete level, which explains details that appear in the code, and the abstract level, which explains the ideas that drive the code's design. Relating these levels requires some vocabulary.

The key word is *abstraction*. An abstraction is the thing that we want to write most of our code in terms of: a ball game, a large number, a table, or what have you. Narrowly, "an abstraction" is the thing that a value of abstract type stands for. An abstraction isn't code; it's an *idea* that tells us what code is doing. An abstraction might be described using mathematics or metaphor.

Representation describes the data in the code. For example, a ball game in my video recorder is represented by a JSON object of unholy complexity.

Access to representation determines whether code operates at an abstract level or a concrete level. Code that can see only an abstraction is abstract; it is called *client* code. Code that can see the representation of an abstraction is concrete; it is part of the abstraction's *implementation*.

When using abstract data types, an implementation is called a *module*. Or it should be—in practice, modules are called different things in different languages. For example, in the Modula family a module is an "implementation module," in Ada it's a "package body," and in Standard ML it's a "structure." In Molecule, it's a *module*.

A module grants access to its clients through an *interface*. An interface describes the abstractions implemented by a module and the *operations* on the abstractions. In the world of abstract data types, operations are functions; in the world of objects, operations are methods. Either way, operations described in an interface are said to be *exported* or *public*. For example, the operations exported by the ball-game module are to get a list of games from the Internet and to ask a single game who is the home team, who is the away team, if the game has started, or if it is over.

The word "interface" always means "what you need to know to use a module." But what you truly need to know depends on what you want to do. If you want to write client code, you need to understand the abstraction, and you need to know the complete specification of every operation: its name, its type, and how it is supposed to behave. This information is an "application program interface" (API). Behavioral specifications are usually written informally, in natural language; they might be found on a web page of developer documentation, or for an older interface, on a Unix `man` page. When I want to emphasize this meaning of "interface," I use "API" or "complete API."

Table 9.1: Examples of qualified names

Name	*Component*
`IntArray.t`	The type of an array of integers
`IntArray.size`	Function that gives the size of an array of integers
`IntArray.new`	Function that creates a new array of integers
`Int.t`	The type of an integer
`Int.<`	Function that compares two integers
`Bool.t`	The type of a Boolean

If you just want code to compile, then all you need to know are the names and types of the operations. This information is usually written formally, in a programming language, where it can be checked by an interpreter or compiler; the language construct used to express it is also called an "interface." Or it should be—in practice, interfaces, which are bit like C's `.h` files, are called different things in different languages. For example, in the Modula family an interface is a "definition module," in Ada it's a "package specification," in Standard ML it's a "signature," and in Java it's an "interface." In Molecule, it's a *module type*. When I want to emphasize this meaning of "interface," I use "module type."

Finally, "abstraction" often refers not just to what a value of abstract type stands for, but also to the things around it. When a programmer says, "I'm going to design an abstraction," they mean at least the abstraction and its complete API, and maybe also an implementation.

9.2 Introduction to Molecule, part I: Writing client code

To introduce Molecule, I present an example of client code—code that *uses* an abstraction. The abstraction, which is implemented by a module and specified by an interface, is "array of integers." The client code finds the smallest integer in such an array.

Modules, components, and qualified names

Client code refers to types and operations that are defined in a module. Each such defined thing is called a *component*. Client code may refer to any component that is exported by a module's module type. Every component has a name, and every module also has a name, and the two together are used to form the component's *qualified name*. The qualified name is the name of the module, followed by a dot, followed by the name of the component, as in `IntArray.new`, which is an operation that creates a new array. If you are used to dot notation for the members of a `struct` or `record`, as in C, you may think of a module as a sort of glorified record, which includes not only value components but also type and module components.

Some examples of qualified names appear in Table 9.1. The `t` in `Int.t` is conventional: when a module exports one, primary abstract type—like an array, a list, or a hash table, for example—the abstract-type component is conventionally called `t`. For example, `Int.t` is the type of integers, `IntArray.t` is the type of arrays of integers, `IntList.t` is the type of lists of integers, and so on. This convention is borrowed from Modula-3 (Nelson 1991; Horning et al. 1993; Hanson 1996).

The `.t` convention is useful, but for continuity, you can continue to refer to primitive types using the unqualified names that are used in other chapters: `int`, bool, sym, and unit. In Molecule, these names are defined as *type abbreviations*:

529a. ⟨*predefined Molecule types, functions, and modules* 529a⟩≡ 529b ▷

```
(type int  Int.t)
(type bool Bool.t)
(type unit Unit.t)
(type sym  Sym.t)
```


What any client must know: An example interface

Client code depends on a complete API, including a description of the abstraction, a module type, and a behavioral specification of every exported operation. The example client below depends on the IntArray module, whose abstraction is an array of integers. The abstraction, which I hope is familiar, can be described using this metaphor: A value of type IntArray.t (or just "an array") is a sequence of boxes, each of which holds a value of type int.

The IntArray module implements the ARRAY module type, which is part of the initial basis of Molecule and is defined here:

529b. ⟨*predefined Molecule types, functions, and modules* 529a⟩+≡ ◁ 529a 540a ▷

```
(module-type ARRAY
 (exports [abstype t]    ;; an array
          [abstype elem] ;; one element of the array
          [new    : (int elem -> t)]
          [empty  : (          -> t)]
          [size   : (t -> int)]
          [at     : (t int -> elem)]
          [at-put : (t int elem -> unit)]))
```

The complete API for arrays specifies not just the type but also the behavior of each exported operation. Crucially, the specifications are written in terms of the abstraction (the box metaphor).

- Calling (new n v) creates an array of n boxes, numbered from 0 to $n - 1$. Each box holds the value v.
- Calling (empty) creates a new, empty array with no boxes in it.
- Calling (size A) tells us how many boxes are in array A.
- Calling (at A i) tells us what value is in box i of array A.
- Calling (at-put A i v) puts value v into box i of array A.

The meaning of a module type

In Molecule, as in OCaml and Standard ML, a module type has its own identity, independent of any module that might implement it. And the ARRAY module type may be implemented by many modules: array of integers, array of Booleans, array of symbols, and so on. A module type is a species of promise, which any implementation must redeem. The promise is to provide each of the exported components listed in the module type. Therefore, a module can implement the ARRAY module type if it provides two types t and elem, plus the five functions new, empty, size, at, and at-put—all with the correct types.

In Molecule, a module can implement more than one module type. The most specific module type that a module can implement is specified when the module is defined. For IntArray, the module type ARRAY is not quite specific enough: it doesn't say what elem is. To write a client that finds the smallest integer in an array, we need to know not only that IntArray.at returns a value of type IntArray.elem; we also need to know that type IntArray.elem is the same as type int. In Molecule, elem's identity is *revealed* by a *manifest-type declaration*:

```
[type elem int]
```


The IntArray module implements *both* the ARRAY module type and a module type that reveals elem, as confirmed by these unit tests:

530a. ⟨*interface checks of predefined modules* 530a⟩≡ 540b ▷

```
(check-module-type IntArray ARRAY)
(check-module-type IntArray (exports [type elem Int.t]))
```

Example client code

Knowing that IntArray implements module type ARRAY with type elem equal to int, client code can use the exported operations, referring to them by their qualified names. As an example, I use IntArray.new to make an array:

530b. ⟨*transcript* 530b⟩≡ 530c ▷

```
-> (val a (IntArray.new 4 99))
[99 99 99 99] : IntArray.t
```

To find the smallest element in a nonempty array of integers, I define function smallest-int, which uses exported operations IntArray.at and IntArray.size:

530c. ⟨*transcript* 530b⟩+≡ ◁ 530b 530d ▷

```
-> (define int smallest-int ([a : IntArray.t])
     (let ([smallest (IntArray.at a 0)]
           [i 1]
           [n (IntArray.size a)])
       (while (Int.< i n)
          (when (Int.< (IntArray.at a i) smallest)
            (set smallest (IntArray.at a i)))
          (set i (Int.+ i 1)))
       smallest))
smallest-int : (IntArray.t -> Int.t)
```

Molecule code is quite similar to Typed μScheme code, but as illustrated here, Molecule has some additional features that simplify procedural programming. One is the when form, which is "an if with no else"; its body is executed only when the condition holds. Another is that the body of a let expression, a while loop, or a function definition may be a *sequence* of expressions. At parse time, each such sequence is wrapped in an implicit (begin · · ·).

The smallest-int function can be used with our example array a. And mutating a can change the outcome:

530d. ⟨*transcript* 530b⟩+≡ ◁ 530c 542 ▷

```
-> a
[99 99 99 99] : IntArray.t
-> (smallest-int a)
99 : Int.t
-> (IntArray.at-put a 1 55)
-> (IntArray.at-put a 2 33)
-> (smallest-int a)
33 : Int.t
```

For more examples of array computations, see Exercises 1 and 2.

9.3 Introduction, part II: Implementing an abstraction

The hard part of programming with data abstraction is thinking up good abstractions and their specifications—once an abstraction is specified, implementing it is comparatively easy. I would love to demonstrate using IntArray, but IntArray is not actually implemented in Molecule; the array operations are implemented by primitive functions, which are implemented using ML code in the interpreter. Instead, I demonstrate with a module that implements a new, less useful abstraction: a point in the two-dimensional plane.

Interface and client code for a point abstraction

A complete API for two-dimensional points includes a module type that lists the exported operations. Each operation's behavior is specified in a comment.

531a. ⟨*2dpoint.mcl* 531a⟩≡ 532b ▷

```
(module-type 2DPOINT
  [exports
    [abstype t]  ;; a point on the plane
    [new      : (int int -> t)] ; takes (X, Y) coordinates and
                                ;     returns a new point

    [get-x    : (t -> int)]     ; return x coordinate
    [get-y    : (t -> int)]     ; return y coordinate
    [quadrant : (t -> sym)]     ; return 'upper-right, 'upper-left,
                                ;    'lower-right, or 'lower-left
    [print    : (t -> unit)]    ; print characters representing the point

    [reflect  : (t -> unit)]    ; reflect the point through the origin
    [rotate+  : (t -> unit)]])  ; rotate point 90 degrees CCW about origin
```

As seen by the types and the comments, the abstraction is mutable: reflection and rotation change the state of an existing point.

The API can be illustrated by some simple examples. First, some bureaucracy: load the code from file 2dpoint.mcl, then use overload to tell the interpreter to print points using function 2Dpoint.print:

531b. ⟨*2Dpoint transcript* 531b⟩≡ 531c ▷

```
-> (use 2dpoint.mcl)
module type 2DPOINT = ...
  ...
-> (overload 2Dpoint.print) ;; tell the interpreter how to print a 2Dpoint.t
overloaded print : (2Dpoint.t -> Unit.t)
```

The overload directive is described in Section 9.4.3 below.

For our example, I create a point p and then change its state twice. All three states are depicted in Figure 9.2. Initially, p has coordinates $(3, 4)$, which puts it in the upper-right quadrant of the plane.

531c. ⟨*2Dpoint transcript* 531b⟩+≡ ◁ 531b 531d ▷

```
-> (val p (2Dpoint.new 3 4))
(3, 4) : 2Dpoint.t
-> (2Dpoint.quadrant p)
upper-right : Sym.t
```

When I rotate p about the origin, it moves to the upper-left quadrant.

531d. ⟨*2Dpoint transcript* 531b⟩+≡ ◁ 531c 532a ▷

```
-> (2Dpoint.rotate+ p)
-> (2Dpoint.quadrant p)
upper-left : Sym.t
-> p
(-4, 3) : 2Dpoint.t
```

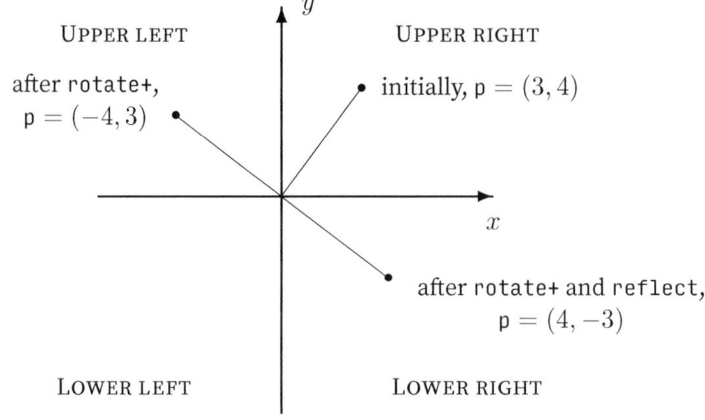

Figure 9.2: Three states of a mutable `2Dpoint`

Reflecting `p` through the origin negates both coordinates, leaving `p` in the lower-right quadrant.

532a. ⟨*2Dpoint transcript* 531b⟩+≡ ◁531d

```
-> (2Dpoint.reflect p)
-> p
(4, -3) : 2Dpoint.t
-> (2Dpoint.quadrant p)
lower-right : Sym.t
```

Implementation of the point abstraction

To implement the point abstraction, I define a new module named `2Dpoint`. The definition identifies `2DPOINT` as the interface that `2Dpoint` is supposed to implement:

532b. ⟨*2dpoint.mcl* 531a⟩+≡ ◁531a

```
(module [2Dpoint : 2DPOINT]
  ⟨definition of type t inside module 2Dpoint 533a⟩
  ⟨definitions of functions inside module 2Dpoint 533b⟩
)
```

The use of `2DPOINT` here does more than just say, "module `2Dpoint` implements the `2DPOINT` interface." It also *seals* the module. Sealing prevents information from escaping; only what's exposed in the module type is visible.

- The representation of the abstract type `2Dpoint.t` is hidden.
- Components that are not exported are hidden.

The sealing is checked by the Molecule interpreter, which confirms that the `2Dpoint` module redeems the promises made by the `2DPOINT` module type. Each promise made by a module type is redeemed as follows:

- Every abstract type is given a defined representation.
- Every manifest type is defined to be equal to the type specified.
- Every exported variable, function, or value constructor is defined with the type specified.

The body of a module is a sequence of definitions. In our example, the first definition is the definition of type t. I've chosen an algebraic data type (Chapter 8).

533a. ⟨*definition of type* t *inside module* 2Dpoint 533a⟩≡ (532b)

```
(data t [XY : (int int -> t)])
```

This definition says that a value of type 2Dpoint.t is constructed by applying *value constructor* XY to two values of type int. In Molecule, by contrast with μML, constructed values are mutable; the value constructor allocates two fresh, mutable locations and stores an argument in each one. These locations become accessible through pattern matching in a case expression.

Value constructor XY is used in function 2Dpoint.new to create a new point from the given coordinates x and y.

533b. ⟨*definitions of functions inside module* 2Dpoint 533b⟩≡ (532b) 533c ▷

```
(define t new ([x : int] [y : int])
  (XY x y))
```

Because this code is *inside* the 2Dpoint module, it can use constructor XY. Because the constructor is not exported by the interface, client code can't use it.

Inside the module, value constructor XY can also be used for pattern matching, as it is in functions get-x and get-y.

533c. ⟨*definitions of functions inside module* 2Dpoint 533b⟩+≡ (532b) ◁ 533b 533d ▷

```
(define int get-x ([p : t])
  (case p [(XY x y) x]))


(define int get-y ([p : t])
  (case p [(XY x y) y]))
```

Now let's see how a point is mutated. To reflect a point through the origin, I negate both x and y coordinates, using function Int.negated from Molecule's predefined Int module. The pattern matching on point p makes names x and y refer to the mutable locations holding p's coordinates. Like the locations named by other variables, these locations can be set.

533d. ⟨*definitions of functions inside module* 2Dpoint 533b⟩+≡ (532b) ◁ 533c 533e ▷

```
(define unit reflect ([p : t])
  (case p [(XY x y)  (begin
                       (set x (Int.negated x))
                       (set y (Int.negated y)))]))
```

The rotate+ operation also mutates a point, replacing x with $-y$ and y with x. To calculate new values of x and y before any location is mutated, I use a let form:

533e. ⟨*definitions of functions inside module* 2Dpoint 533b⟩+≡ (532b) ◁ 533d 533f ▷

```
(define unit rotate+ ([p : t])
  (case p [(XY x y)  (let ([new-x (Int.negated y)]
                           [new-y x])
                        (set x new-x)
                        (set y new-y))]))
```

I print a point using Descartes's classic notation. To print parentheses and whitespace, I use values and the print operation from the predefined module Char.

533f. ⟨*definitions of functions inside module* 2Dpoint 533b⟩+≡ (532b) ◁ 533e 534 ▷

```
(define unit print ([p : t])
   (Char.print Char.left-round)
   (Int.print (get-x p))
   (Sym.print ',)
   (Char.print Char.space)
   (Int.print (get-y p))
   (Char.print Char.right-round)
)
```

The code uses a little syntactic sugar: the body of a define may be a sequence of expressions, which are implicitly wrapped in a begin.

I complete the implementation with the quadrant operation. A point on a boundary between quadrants is considered to be in the quadrant on the positive side of the boundary.

534. ⟨*definitions of functions inside module* 2Dpoint 533b⟩+≡ (532b) ◁533f

```
(define sym quadrant ([p : t])
   (case p [(XY x y)  (if (>= x 0)
                          (if (>= y 0) 'upper-right 'lower-right)
                          (if (>= y 0) 'upper-left  'lower-left))]))
```

9.4 THE MOLECULE LANGUAGE

The examples above illustrate Molecule's key mechanisms: each abstraction is specified by a *module type* (the interface), which is implemented by a *module* (the implementation). A module type specifies the names, natures, and types of a module's *components*; a module defines those same components. In the syntax, modules and module types account for the forms in Molecule's *module layer*; the remaining forms, which express types, expressions, and definitions, make up Molecule's *core layer*. Organizing the language in two layers has significant benefits:

- The core layer is stuff you already know from Chapters 6 and 8: it's Typed μScheme plus algebraic data types from μML. And the core-layer part of the type system is a lot like Typed Impcore's type system; there's nothing fancy.

- Only the module layer has to worry about enforcing data abstraction. And it's reusable: the module layer, which is based on the work of Leroy (2000), could be grafted onto a different core layer and it still do its job.

To keep the type system as simple as possible, both layers share a single name space (environment), which is used for everything: values, types, and modules. A name that originates in the core layer may stand for a mutable location holding a value, as in Typed Impcore or Typed μScheme, or it may stand for a type; type names are not relegated to a separate environment as they are in Typed μScheme. A name that originates in the module layer may stand for a module or a module type. Finally, a name may be *overloaded* (Section 9.4.3), standing for a set of values of different types.

9.4.1 Molecule's core layer

Molecule's core layer is very much like Typed μScheme (Chapter 6). The core layer combines familiar elements (Chapters 6 and 8) in new ways:

- The core layer uses a monomorphic type system—polymorphism is implemented in the module layer, using generic modules.

- Like Typed μScheme, Molecule provides atomic data (symbols, numbers, and Booleans) and first-class functions. Like Typed Impcore, Molecule provides primitive arrays. Like μML (Chapter 8), Molecule provides constructed data using algebraic data types, which, in one tidy package, support "struct/union," "record/variant," and "sum of products" programming. And in Molecule, constructed data can be mutated.

- Molecule's core layer includes the familiar syntactic forms from Impcore and μScheme: set, if, while, begin, function application, let forms, and `lambda`. For deconstructing constructed data, it also includes the `case` form from μML. And to better support procedural programming, it provides syntactic sugar for sequencing and conditionals.

Each of these aspects is presented in more detail below.

Core-layer types

Molecule's support for polymorphism resides in the module layer; the core layer is monomorphic. A core-layer type is either a type constructor or a function type—there are no type parameters, no type variables, and no polymorphic types. The typing rules are exactly what you would expect from Typed μScheme, and they are very close to Typed Impcore.

Molecule's core layer includes algebraic data types like those in μML (Chapter 8), but as in the rest of the core layer, there are no type parameters. Every algebraic data type has kind $*$.

Like μML but unlike Typed μScheme and Typed Impcore, Molecule enables programmers to create new type constructors. A new type constructor can be created by a `data` form, as in μML. And, uniquely to Molecule, a new type constructor can be created by sealing a module (typing rules in Section 9.8).

Core-layer values

Molecule has all the values found in μScheme, plus a form of constructed data. Unlike in μML, where a value constructor carries other *values*, in Molecule, a value constructor carries mutable *locations*. A constructed value is introduced either by using a value constructor alone, like `#f`, or by applying a value constructor to arguments, as in `(XY 3 4)`. When a value constructor is applied, a fresh, mutable location is allocated for each argument.

A constructed value is eliminated via pattern matching in a `case` expression. When a pattern names the argument of a value constructor, that name refers to the mutable location that is carried with the value constructor. Such a location can be mutated using `set`, as in the implementation of `rotate+` in Section 9.3.

Core-layer syntax and syntactic sugar

The core layer's concrete syntax is shown in Figure 9.3 on the next page. It is the same as the syntax for Typed μScheme (Figure 6.3, page 353), except for these changes:

- The *exp* form that names a variable or function may use a qualified name, not only a simple name. Similarly, the *type-exp* form that names a type constructor may use a qualified name.

- To support algebraic data types, Molecule includes the `data` definition form, the `case` expression form, and the *pattern* syntactic category from μML (Figure 8.1, page 467).

- To support operator overloading, Molecule includes an `overload` definition form (Section 9.4.3, page 543).

- Because its core layer is monomorphic, Molecule does not have Typed μScheme's `type-lambda` or `@` expression forms. And Molecule does not have Typed μScheme's type variables or `forall` types.

- A literal S-expression evaluates to an array, not to a list.

```
def ::= (val variable-name exp)
      | (val-rec [variable-name : type-exp] exp)
      | (define type-exp function-name ({[variable-name : type-exp]}) exp)
      | (data type-name {[value-constructor-name : type-exp]})    (from μML)
      | exp
      | (overload {qualified-name})
      | (use file-name)
      | unit-test

unit-test ::= (check-expect exp exp)
            | (check-assert exp)
            | (check-error exp)
            | (check-type exp type-exp)
            | (check-type-error def)

exp     ::= literal
          | qualified-name                    (replaces variable-name form)
          | (set variable-name exp)
          | (if exp exp exp)
          | (while exp exp)
          | (begin {exp})
          | (exp {exp})
          | (let-keyword ({[variable-name exp]}) {exp})
          | (letrec [{([variable-name : type-exp] exp)}] {exp})
          | (lambda ({[variable-name : type-exp]}) exp)
          | (case exp {[pattern exp]})        (from μML)

let-keyword    ::= let | let*

qualified-name ::= name | qualified-name.name  (names module, type, or variable)
                 | (@m qualified-name {qualified-name})

pattern        ::= variable-name
                 | value-constructor-name
                 | (value-constructor-name {pattern})
                 | _

type-exp       ::= qualified-name              (replaces type-constructor-name)
                 | ({type-exp} -> type-exp)

literal        ::= numeral | #t | #f | 'S-exp | (quote S-exp)

S-exp          ::= literal | symbol-name | ({S-exp})

numeral        ::= token composed only of digits, possibly prefixed with a plus
                   or minus sign

value-constructor-name
               ::= cons | '() | a token that begins with # or with a capital letter
                   or with make-

*-name         ::= a token that is not a bracket, a dot, a numeral, a value-
                   constructor-name, or one of the "reserved" words shown in
                   typewriter font
```

(Compare it with Typed μScheme; see Figure 6.3, page 353.)

Figure 9.3: Molecule's core layer

```
modtype ::= modtype-name
          | (exports {dec})
          | (allof {modtype})
          | ({[module-name : modtype]} --m-> modtype)

dec     ::= [abstype type-name]
          | [type type-name type-exp)
          | [name : type-exp]
          | [module [module-name : modtype]]

def     ::= (module-type modtype-name modtype)
          | (module [module-name : modtype] {def})
          | (generic-module [module-name : modtype] {def})
          | (module [module-name : modtype] qualified-name)   (sealing)
          | (module module-name qualified-name)               (abbreviation)
          | (type type-name type-exp)

unit-test ::= (check-module-type qualified-name modtype)
```

Figure 9.4: Molecule's module layer

```
modtype ⋆::= (exports-record-ops type-name ({[variable-name : type-exp]}))

def ⋆::= (record-module module-name type-name
                        ({[variable-name : type-exp]}))
    ⋆ | (define type-exp function-name ({[variable-name : type-exp]}) {exp})

exp ⋆::= (assert exp)
    ⋆ | (&& {exp})
    ⋆ | (|| {exp})
    ⋆ | (when exp {exp})
    ⋆ | (unless exp {exp})
    ⋆ | (while exp {exp})
    ⋆ | ((let|let*|letrec) (...) {exp})
```

Figure 9.5: Syntactic sugar

- In addition to familiar syntactic sugar for `&&` and `||`, Molecule provides syntactic sugar that helps with procedural programming (Figure 9.5). Forms `when` and `unless` implement one-way conditionals, and each of these forms, as well as the `while`, `let`, and `define` forms, supports a body that is a sequence of expressions, not just a single expression.

The core-layer definition forms shown in Figure 9.3 are supplemented by module-layer definition forms, which appear in Figure 9.4 and are described below.

Core-layer evaluation

The core-layer forms are evaluated as in μScheme or μML, with extra support for overloading (Section 9.4.3). The new forms, which are syntactic sugar, are evaluated as follows:

- The `assert` form evaluates its *exp*, and if the *exp* is not true, halts the program with a checked run-time error.

- The when form evaluates its condition, and if the condition is true, evaluates every expression in the body, in sequence. The unless form is similar, except the body is evaluated only if the condition is false.
- The body of an extended while, let, or define form is evaluated as if wrapped in begin.

9.4.2 *Molecule's module layer*

Molecule's module layer expresses both *module types* and *modules* (Figure 9.4). The sheer number of *modtype* and *def* forms looks intimidating, but most code needs only the exports form of *modtype* and the first three forms of *def*: one form to define a module type, one to define an ordinary module, and one to define a generic module. The complete list of module-related forms, which is summarized in Table 9.6, is best examined through the type-theoretic lens of formation, introduction, and elimination.

Formation of module types

A module type both controls access to a module and makes promises on the module's behalf. A module type can be referred to by name, but its ultimate definition takes one of three forms:

- An *export list,* written using exports, which lists the module's *components,* to which it promises access
- A *module-arrow type,* written using the module arrow --m->, which describes the parameters and the result type of a generic module
- An *intersection type,* written using allof, which promises every component that is listed in any of the intersected module types

Each of these forms is described in detail below.

Export lists

An export list specifies the components exported by a module. Each component is specified by a *declaration.* Like a field of a record, a component of a module has a name, but unlike a field of a record, a component may be not just a value but also a type or another module.

- A *value component* is a variable or a function, and it is declared by giving its name and type, using the same syntax we use to give the name and type of a formal parameter to a function. For example,

  538a. ⟨*example module components* 538a⟩≡ 538b ▷
  ```
  [size : (t -> int)]
  [at   : (t int -> elem)]
  ```

- A *type component* may be either *abstract* or *manifest*. An abstract type has a definition, but its definition is hidden; only its qualified name is known. An abstract type is unique and is distinct from any other type, even if the other type happens to have the same definition (like Int.t and Char.t). A manifest type exposes its definition, so clients know not only that the type component exists but also how it is defined. The qualified name of a manifest type is treated as an abbreviation for its definition. For example,

  538b. ⟨*example module components* 538a⟩+≡ ◁ 538a 539a ▷
  ```
  [abstype t]          ; abstract type
  [type elem Elem.t]   ; manifest type (abbreviation for Elem.t)
  ```

Table 9.6: Some syntactic forms of Molecule

	Definition form	Declaration form	Expression form
Module	`module`	`(module [`M `:` $\mathcal{T}$`])`	none! (2nd class)
Generic module	`generic-module`	none (not a component)	none! (2nd class)
Module type	`module-type`	none (not a component)	`(exports` $\cdots$`)`
Type	`type`, `data`	`[abstype` t`]`, `[type` t τ`]`	(as in μML)
Value	`val`, `define`	`[`x `:` τ`]`	(as in μML)

- A *module component* is a nested module. Like a value component, it is declared with its name and its module type, but the declaration uses the keyword `module`. For example,

  539a. ⟨*example module components* 538a⟩+≡ ◁538b

```
(module [Move : (exports [type t]
                         [to-string : (t -> String.t)]
                         [of-string : (String.t -> t)])])
```

To contrast it with a generic module, a module that exports components can be called an *exporting module.*

A module type is well formed if every type that is used is defined and if every component is uniquely defined. In detail,

- In an export list, before a type component can be used to give the type of a value component, the type component must be declared.
- Within a single export list, no component may be declared more than once.
- The types used in every declaration must be well formed.

The formalities appear in Section 9.8.6.

A module type can be named using a `module-type` form (Figure 9.4):

539b. ⟨*example module-layer definitions* 539b⟩≡

```
(module-type EXPORTS-T (exports [abstype t]))
```

Module introduction: Definition forms for exporting modules

A module type only makes promises—it doesn't deliver any values, types, or modules. To deliver on the promises requires a module, which is defined using one of the `module` forms from Figure 9.4. An exporting module is typically defined by giving its name M, its module type $\mathcal{T}$, and a sequence of definitions, like so: `(module [`M `:` $\mathcal{T}$`]` $d_1 \cdots d_n$`)`. The definition of M is well typed only if all the d_i's are well typed and if M provides all the components listed in $\mathcal{T}$. And the definition *seals* module M with type $\mathcal{T}$. Sealing limits access to the components defined by definitions $d_1 \cdots d_n$: outside of M, the only components that can be named are those mentioned in $\mathcal{T}$. And if any of the type components is declared as an *abstract* type, its definition is hidden.

Exporting modules can also be defined using two other forms. First, an existing module M' may be sealed using the form `(module [`M `:` $\mathcal{T}$`]` M'`)`. New module M has the same components as existing module M', but only components exported by module type $\mathcal{T}$ are visible. And if any type component t is declared as abstract in $\mathcal{T}$, then sealing gives type $M.t$ a new identity that is distinct from $M'.t$. (In the language of Chapter 8, sealing is *generative.*) Second, an existing module may be abbreviated, without sealing, using the form `(module` M M'`)`, as in `(module IR (@m Ref Int))`. Such abbreviations are used primarily for instances of generic modules, which are discussed below.

Module elimination: Qualified names

Client code can observe or interrogate a module in only one way: it can name a component. The component's *qualified name* is formed by concatenating the name of the module, a dot, and the name of the component. Qualified names are used in many languages, including Ada, CLU, Haskell, Java, OCaml, Modula-3, and Standard ML. In Molecule, as in most of these languages, a qualified name like `IntArray.at` selects a component from a module. Qualified names can also instantiate *generic* modules, as described below.

Generic modules

A good module can embody a lot of craft—think about the engineering that goes into a balanced search tree or a good hash table. Such engineering should be reusable, and you already know a suitable mechanism: higher-order, polymorphic functions. But at this scale, `lambda` and `type-lambda` are awkward; they work with individual values and types, and the unit of reuse should be the module. To support polymorphism with modules, Molecule provides *generic modules*.

A generic module takes one or more other modules as formal parameters, and it produces a module as its result. By taking *modules* as parameters, generic modules provide, in one mechanism, the capabilities of higher-order functions (functions as parameters, as with `lambda`) and parametric polymorphism (types as parameters, as with `type-lambda`).

A parameter of a generic module may not itself be generic. This sort of restriction, which says that the parameter to a polymorphic thing may not itself be polymorphic, makes the polymorphism *predicative*. Predicativity can simplify a type theory considerably, so predicative polymorphism is common. For example, the Hindley-Milner type system used in core ML is predicative, and so are systems for other languages that support generic modules, including CLU, Ada, and Modula-3. Type systems in which type parameters are not restricted, like Typed μScheme, are called *impredicative*.

In Molecule, the type of a generic module is written like a function type, except that each formal parameter gets a name (so that later parameters and the result type may refer to it), and the parameters are separated from the result type by the module arrow `--m->`. For example, the type of Molecule's predefined, generic `Array` module is as follows:

540a. ⟨*predefined Molecule types, functions, and modules* 529a⟩+≡ ◁529b 541b▷

```
(module-type GENERIC-ARRAY
 ([Elem : (exports [abstype t])] --m->
     (exports [abstype t]        ;; an array
              [type elem Elem.t] ;; one element of the array
              [new    : (int elem -> t)]
              [empty  : (          -> t)]
              [size   : (t -> int)]
              [at     : (t int -> elem)]
              [at-put : (t int elem -> unit)])))
```

The `elem` type in the result module is known to be equal to the type `t` in the parameter module, `Elem`. That crucial identity can be expressed only because the formal parameter is named.

Module type `GENERIC-ARRAY` is the type of the primitive module `Array`:

540b. ⟨*interface checks of predefined modules* 530a⟩+≡ ◁530a

```
(check-module-type Array GENERIC-ARRAY)
```

A module-arrow type is well formed only if the module type of each formal parameter describes an exporting module, not a generic module—that's the predicative polymorphism. The module type of each parameter must be well formed, and the module type of the result must also be well formed. The module type of the result may refer to formal parameters, like `Elem` in the example above. And the module types of later parameters may refer to earlier parameters.[1]

A generic module is introduced using the same definition form as an exporting module, except that it uses the keyword `generic-module`, and the module type used to seal it must be a module-arrow type. For an example, see the definition of generic module `ArrayHeap` in chunk 552a.

A generic module is eliminated by *instantiating* it. Instantiation creates an exporting instance of a generic module. The concrete syntax resembles the instantiation of a polymorphic value in Typed μScheme, but to remind us of the distinction between a generic module in Molecule and a polymorphic value in Typed μScheme, a generic instantiation is written using keyword `@m`. For example, the predefined module `String` is an instance of the generic `Array` module:

541a. ⟨*definition of module* `String` 541a⟩≡
```
(module String (@m Array Char))
```

The instance is pronounced "`Array` at `Char`."

An instance of a generic module also plays a second role: an instance of a generic module counts as a qualified name. This quirk of Molecule's type system, which is explained in depth in Section 9.8.7, supports a simple algorithm for type checking with abstract types. To get the right intuition, think of the instance as being like the application of a type constructor, like `(array char)` in Typed Impcore.

Intersection types

An intersection type combines multiple export-list module types, forming a refined export-list module type. The term "intersection" can be confusing because if you focus on the components, it looks like an intersection type takes their *union*. Intersection is happening to the *inhabitants*; a module inhabits the intersection type if and only if it inhabits *all* of the intersected module types.

An intersection type is well formed if all of its constituent module types are well formed. The constituent module types need not be compatible; the intersection of incompatible module types is well formed but uninhabited.

Intersection types are most often used to intersect a named module type with an `exports` module type that reveals the identity of an abstract type. For example, an intersection type is used to seal the `IntArray` module:

541b. ⟨*predefined Molecule types, functions, and modules* 529a⟩+≡ ◁ 540a 543a ▷
```
(module [IntArray : (allof ARRAY (exports [type elem Int.t]))]
   (@m Array Int))
```

Module values and evaluation

Every module has a run-time representation as a value. An exporting module is represented as a record with named fields: one field for each value component and each module component. Type components are used only for type checking and are not present at run time. A generic module is represented as a function from modules to modules.

When a `module` definition form is evaluated, it produces a record containing the value and module components. When a qualified name (with a dot) is evaluated,

[1] A function type with these kinds of references is called a *dependent function type*; in type theory, it is often written with a Π symbol, as in $\Pi x{:}\tau\,.\,\tau'$, where τ' may mention x.

```
+   <    =        negated
-   >    !=
*   <=   print
/   >=   println
```

Figure 9.7: Names that are overloaded in Molecule's initial basis

it selects a named component from a module record. When a `generic-module` definition form is evaluated, it produces a function whose arguments are module records and whose result is a module record. When a generic module is instantiated, the function is applied.

A pitfall

In Molecule, the function that a generic module evaluates to can be impure. For example, if a generic module includes mutable state—say it mutates a private variable defined with `val`—each instance gets fresh mutable state, which isn't shared with other instances. This behavior might cause confusing results, especially if a generic module is instantiated by the type checker during the resolution of an overloaded operator. So don't mutate variables that are defined inside generic modules.

Syntactic sugar for records

By analogy with μScheme's `record` definition, Molecule provides syntactic sugar for modules that behave as records do. A record module is specified by naming the type of the record and listing the names and types of its fields. The module exports a getter function and a setter function for each field, plus a constructor function called `make`. A record module's type can also be written using syntactic sugar. For example, the module type

```
(exports-record-ops t ([n : Int.t] [b : Bool.t]))
```

expands to

```
(exports [abstype t]
         [make : (Int.t Bool.t -> t)]
         [n : (t -> Int.t)]
         [b : (t -> Bool.t)]
         [set-n! : (t Int.t -> Unit.t)]
         [set-b! : (t Bool.t -> Unit.t)])
```

A module with this type can be defined using `record-module`:

542. ⟨*transcript* 530b⟩+≡ ◁530d 543b▷

```
-> (record-module MyPair t ([n : Int.t] [b : Bool.t]))
module MyPair :
  (exports
    [abstype t]
    [make : (Int.t Bool.t -> MyPair.t)]
    [n : (MyPair.t -> Int.t)]
    [b : (MyPair.t -> Bool.t)]
    [set-n! : (MyPair.t Int.t -> Unit.t)]
    [set-b! : (MyPair.t Bool.t -> Unit.t)])
```

9.4.3 *Overloading*

When every operation needs a qualified name, code can feel bloated and tedious; unqualified names like +, `print`, and = are easier on the eyes. To enable unqualified names to be used in more contexts, Molecule allows the name of a function to be *overloaded*. An overloaded name may stand for more than one value or function; to determine which function is meant, Molecule looks at the type of its first argument.

Overloading helps answer three questions that the designers of any statically typed programming language ought to address:

1. Programmers like to use + for both integer addition and floating-point addition. How is the language to know which is meant, when?

2. Programmers like to use = for equality. How is equality supposed to be decided for values of different types? Especially abstract types? After all, equality for something like association lists is not always obvious (page 132). And anything like `check-expect` has to use the right equality for each test.

3. Interpreters and debuggers need to be able to print values. How does an interpreter know what to print? In some languages, printing the representation might be good enough, but if representation is supposed to be hidden, perhaps a `print` operation shouldn't reveal it.

Each of these questions is addressed by overloading: arithmetic, equality, and printing use conventional, overloaded names, and by overloading these names, programmers can specify how arithmetic, equality, and printing should behave.

In Molecule, you overload a name by putting a function's *qualified* name in an `overload` definition. Molecule's initial basis overloads arithmetic, comparisons, and printing (Figure 9.7 on the facing page):

543a. ⟨*predefined Molecule types, functions, and modules* 529a⟩+≡ ◁541b

```
(overload Int.+ Int.-  Int.* Int./ Int.negated
          Int.= Int.!= Int.< Int.> Int.<= Int.>=
          Int.print Int.println)
(overload Bool.= Bool.!= Bool.print Bool.println)
(overload Sym.=  Sym.!=  Sym.print  Sym.println)
(overload Char.= Char.!= Char.print Char.println)
```

After these definitions, the *unqualified* form of each function name is now overloaded. To see what an unqualified name might stand for, ask the interpreter:

543b. ⟨*transcript* 530b⟩+≡ ◁542 543c▷

```
-> =
overloaded = : (Char.t Char.t -> Bool.t)
           = : (Sym.t Sym.t -> Bool.t)
           = : (Bool.t Bool.t -> Bool.t)
           = : (Int.t Int.t -> Bool.t)
```

Each of the types given is a type at which = can be used:

543c. ⟨*transcript* 530b⟩+≡ ◁543b 558b▷

```
-> (= 'yes 'yes)
#t : Bool.t
-> (= #f #f)
#t : Bool.t
-> (= 3 3)
#t : Bool.t
-> (= Char.newline Char.space)
#f : Bool.t
```

User-defined functions can also be overloaded. For example, printing can be overloaded to work with user-defined complex numbers (Exercise 8):

544a. ⟨*complex-number transcript* 544a⟩≡ 544b ▷

```
-> (overload Complex.print Complex.* Complex.+)
-> (val i (Complex.new 0 1))
i : Complex.t
```


Arithmetic can also be overloaded:

544b. ⟨*complex-number transcript* 544a⟩+≡ ◁ 544a

```
-> (+ (Complex.new 1 2) (Complex.new 3 -4))
4-2i : Complex.t
-> (* i i)
-1+0i : Complex.t
```

Each use of an overloaded name is associated with a single function during type checking; the process is called *overload resolution*. In Molecule, overload resolution uses the simplest algorithm that I could find, which is based on CLU: an overloaded name may be used only as a function that is applied to one or more arguments, and the meaning of the overloaded name is resolved by looking at the type of the first argument. The formalities appear in Section 9.8.8.

Overloading is sometimes called *ad hoc polymorphism*. I don't care for this term; overloading resembles parametric polymorphism and other forms of polymorphism a little too superficially for my taste. But the term is used in some other books and in some important and interesting papers.

9.5 Molecule's initial basis

Interesting abstract types require the tools needed to define interesting representations. In addition to algebraic data types and record modules, Molecule provides our customary primitive representations, plus several array modules.

Primitive types are defined in modules `Int`, `Bool`, `Unit`, and `Sym`. Their main types are abbreviated `int`, `bool`, `unit`, and `sym`. They are supplemented by predefined functions `and`, `or`, `not`, and `mod`, by value constructors `#t`, `#f`, and `unit`, and by the overloaded names listed in Figure 9.7 on page 542.

Molecule includes a predefined `Char` module, which is not primitive; a value of type `Char.t` is represented by its Unicode code point (an integer), and module `Char` is a client of module `Int`. In addition to function `new`, which takes an integer designating a Unicode code point and returns the corresponding character, module `Char` exports characters `left-curly`, `right-curly`, `left-round`, `right-round`, `left-square`, `right-square`, `newline`, `space`, `semicolon`, and `quote`.

To enable a compact way of implementing comparisons, Molecule includes a predefined module `Order`, whose exported type `Order.t` has value constructors `LESS`, `EQUAL`, and `GREATER`.

Molecule provides several array abstractions, including `ArrayList`, which can grow and shrink at either end. All array abstractions provide constant-time access to elements. Arrays are supported by modules `UnsafeArray`, `ArrayCore`, `Array`, `IntArray`, and `ArrayList`.

Predefined module types include `ARRAY`, `GENERIC-ARRAY`, and `ARRAYLIST`.

Molecule also provides a generic `Ref` module, with operations `new`, `!`, and `:=`. References work as they do in ML.

9.6 Program design: Abstractions

Because programming at scale is challenging, learning to use abstract data types and modules can also be challenging. But you can get started with just a few techniques:

- When designing an interface, you must say what an abstraction is, whether it is mutable, what operations are supported, and what they cost. And you must plan for a representation that can do the job.

  Once an interface is designed, you can classify each operation as a *creator, producer, mutator,* or *observer* (page 111). The classification can help you confirm that the interface is not missing anything obvious and that its operations will work well together.

- To specify the behaviors of an interface's operations, you use the metaphorical or mathematical language of the interface's abstractions, perhaps with some algebraic laws (Chapter 2).

- To relate an abstraction to its implementation, you can use two powerful tools: an *abstraction function* and a *representation invariant.*

These techniques apply equally well to program design with objects (Chapter 10), but in this chapter they are illustrated with modules and abstract data types. Description and classification are illustrated with array lists and sets; abstraction functions are illustrated with multiple examples, and representation invariants are illustrated with priority queues, both here and in Section 9.7.

9.6.1 *Interface-design choices*

Every designer must decide whether an abstraction will be mutable, what operations an interface will provide, and what those operations might cost. All three considerations influence (and are influenced by) the intended representation.

If an abstraction has a *state* that can change over time, it's *mutable.* Otherwise, it's *immutable.* A mutable abstraction has a mutable representation. An immutable abstraction usually has an immutable representation, but it can have a mutable representation—a classic example is an immutable data structure with a mutable cache.

Mutability isn't arbitrary; for example, atomic values—like integers, Booleans, characters, and enumeration literals—are expected to be immutable. Aggregate values like strings, arrays, and records, which store other values inside, are often mutable—though in functional languages, strings and records are typically immutable, while arrays typically appear in both mutable and immutable forms.

Mutable representations normally require less allocation than immutable representations and so can be less expensive; for example, a mutable binary search tree can be updated with at most constant allocation. But a mutable representation demands a mutable abstraction, and compared with immutable abstractions, mutable abstractions are harder to test and can lead to more bugs. In particular, when mutable data is shared among different parts of a program, one part can make a change that another wasn't expecting. ("Not found? But that key was in the table!") With *immutable* abstractions, these sorts of bugs can't happen.

General-purpose abstractions should often be designed in *both* mutable and immutable forms. For example, if I'm using an association list to represent an environment in an interpreter, I want an *immutable* `alist`—that's going to make it easy to implement `let` expressions and closures. But if I'm using an association list to implement a sparse array, I want a *mutable* `alist`—that's going to reduce the allocation cost of an update from linear to constant. If you design mutable and immutable abstractions in tandem, you'll always have the one you want when you want it.

Abstractions can be designed in tandem in part because mutability is surprisingly independent of the designer's other big choice: what operations to provide. Mutability rarely affects what operations are implemented; for example, whether it is mutable or immutable, a dictionary abstraction needs to implement the same operations: insert, lookup, update, and delete. The same is true of a stack, a priority queue, an array, and many other abstractions. Mutability *does* affect costs; the cost of each operation, called the *cost model*, often depends both on mutability and on the representation the designer has in mind.

A cost model determines what operations will be cheap, what operations will be expensive, and what operations won't be implemented at all. Identifying the right operations at the right cost calls for techniques from beyond the world of programming languages. But once you have a set of operations, programming-language techniques can help you see if it's a good one: You can analyze the operations according to their classification (Chapter 2, page 111), which is closely related to classification of rules in type theory (sidebar, page 347).

- Every interface needs an operation that creates a new value of abstract type: a *creator*.
- Most interfaces need operations that can take an existing value of abstract type and do something with it. An operation that updates a value in place is a *mutator*; one that uses an existing value to make a new value is a *producer*. One example is insertion into a dictionary: a mutable dictionary would implement insertion as a mutator, and an immutable dictionary would implement it as a producer.
- Every interface needs operations that get information out of a value of abstract type: *observers*. As examples, observers in my digital video recorder tell me whether a game has started, whether it's over, and who's playing.

A classification of operations can be used to ask if a design is complete:

- Can every part of the abstraction be observed?
- Can every mutation be observed?
- Can the effect of every producer be observed?
- Can every observable be mutated (or changed by a producer)?

A design with these properties probably meets clients' needs—and can be tested without having to violate abstraction.

9.6.2 *Case study in design and specification: The array list*

Once you've chosen your abstraction and its operations, it's time to write the complete API. The abstraction is central: it dictates the language you use to specify the behavior of each operation. When precision is important, the abstraction and the language should be mathematical, so operations can be described with mathematical precision. As an example, I present what Java calls an `ArrayList`: a mutable sequence that provides constant-time indexing but can also grow and shrink.

The abstraction is a sequence of elements, each of type `elem`. The elements are numbered sequentially, and the number of the first element is part of the abstraction. I write the abstraction as $\langle k, vs \rangle$, where vs is a sequence of values and k is the index of the first value.

The abstraction looks like an array, but it can grow or shrink at either end, in constant amortized time. I plan a single creator, operation `from`, which takes one argument k and returns $\langle k, [\,]\rangle$, the empty array starting at k. I don't plan any producers; rather than produce a new array from an existing array, I plan to update arrays in place.

Update is implemented by mutator `at-put`. Growth and shrinkage are implemented by mutators `addlo`, `addhi`, `remlo`, and `remhi`. Individual elements are observed by `at`, and the size and bounds of the array are observed by `size`, `lo`, and `nexthi`.

547. ⟨*arraylist.mcl* 547⟩≡ (S486d)

```
(module-type ARRAYLIST
  (exports [abstype t]
           [abstype elem]
           [from   : (int -> t)]          ; creator (from initial index)
           [size   : (t -> int)]          ; observer
           [at     : (t int -> elem)]     ; observer
           [at-put : (t int elem -> unit)] ; mutator

           [lo     : (t -> int)]       ; observer
           [nexthi : (t -> int)]       ; observer
           [addlo  : (t elem -> unit)] ; mutator
           [addhi  : (t elem -> unit)] ; mutator
           [remlo  : (t -> elem)]      ; mutator
           [remhi  : (t -> elem)]))    ; mutator
```

The behavior of each operation is specified mathematically, using algebraic laws with the abstraction $\langle k, vs\rangle$. For example,

$$\begin{aligned}
\texttt{size}(\langle k, vs\rangle) &= \mathit{length}(vs)\\
\texttt{lo}(\langle k, vs\rangle) &= k\\
\texttt{nexthi}(\langle k, vs\rangle) &= k + \mathit{length}(vs)\\
\texttt{at}(\langle k, v :: vs\rangle, k) &= v\\
\texttt{at}(\langle k, v :: vs\rangle, k') &= \texttt{at}(\langle k+1, vs\rangle, k'), \text{ when } k' \neq k.
\end{aligned}$$

Such laws can easily specify the behavior or creators, producers, and observers. Specifying mutators requires more work. The best simple specification relates the two states of the abstraction before and after the mutation; an array A would have states A_{pre} and A_{post}. For example,

- If $A_{pre} = \langle k, vs\rangle$, then after `(addlo` $A\ v$`)`, $A_{post} = \langle k-1, v :: vs\rangle$.
- If $A_{pre} = \langle k, v :: vs\rangle$, then `(remlo` A`)` $= v$, and $A_{post} = \langle k+1, vs\rangle$.
- After `(at-put` $A\ i\ v$`)`, $A_{post} = \mathit{update}(A_{pre}, i, v)$, where

$$\begin{aligned}
&\mathit{update}(\langle k, v :: vs\rangle, k, v') = \langle k, v' :: vs\rangle\\
&\mathit{update}(\langle k, v :: vs\rangle, k', v') = \langle k, vs'\rangle,\\
&\qquad \text{where } k \neq k' \text{ and } \mathit{update}(\langle k+1, vs\rangle, k', v') = \langle k+1, vs'\rangle.
\end{aligned}$$

This design is complete: Index k can be observed using `lo`, and all of vs can be observed by using `at` with an index i in the range `lo` $\leq i <$ `nexthi`. Every `at-put` can be observed by an `at`. Effects of `addlo` and `remlo` can be observed by `lo`, `size`, and `at`. Similarly for `addhi` and `remhi`.

The design is implemented in the Supplement, as module `ArrayList`.

Abstraction	*Operations*
Set	At least `empty`/`new`, `insert`, `delete`, `member?`; possibly also `empty?`, `size`, `union`, `inter`, `diff`
Representation	*Invariant*
Array	No element is repeated.
List	No element is repeated.
Sorted list	No element is repeated; elements are sorted.
Binary search tree	No element is repeated; smaller elements are in left subtrees; larger elements are in right subtrees; perhaps some sort of balance invariant.
Abstraction functions	
The abstraction function combines all elements of the representation. A function for a binary search tree is specified in the text on the facing page; for a list, the laws of the abstraction function are $\mathcal{A}($`'()`$) = \{\,\}$ and $\mathcal{A}($`cons` $v\ vs) = \{v\} \cup \mathcal{A}(vs)$.	

Figure 9.8: Possible representations of a set

9.6.3 *Case study in specification using only algebraic laws: An immutable set*

Operations can be specified precisely without attributing any mathematical structure to their abstraction: only the result of observing the abstraction is specified. If the abstraction is immutable, it's enough to specify the result of each observer applied to the result of each creator or producer, as in Section 2.5. As an example, I present an abstraction of an immutable set, each element of which has type `elem`:

548. ⟨*set.mcl* 548⟩≡

```
(module-type SET
  (exports [abstype t]     ;; a set
           [abstype elem] ;; an element of the set
           [empty   : t]                      ; creator
           [empty?  : (t -> bool)]            ; observer
           [delete  : (elem t -> t)]          ; producer
           [insert  : (elem t -> t)]          ; producer
           [member? : (elem t -> bool)]))     ; observer
```

The interface is completely specified by these laws:

`(member?` v `empty)`	$=$ `#f`
`(member?` v `(insert` $v\ s$`))`	$=$ `#t`
`(member?` v' `(insert` $v\ s$`))`	$=$ `(member?` $v'\ s$`)`, where $v \neq v'$
`(empty? empty)`	$=$ `#t`
`(empty? (insert` $v\ s$`))`	$=$ `#f`
`(delete` v `empty)`	$=$ `empty`
`(delete` v `(insert` $v\ s$`))`	$=$ `(delete` $v\ s$`)`
`(delete` v `(insert` $v'\ s$`))`	$=$ `(insert` v' `(delete` $v\ s$`))`, where $v \neq v'$

Observers `member?` and `empty?` are applied to sets made with `empty` and `insert`. Results from `delete` are specified by rewriting `delete` away: by applying the `delete` laws repeatedly from left to right, every set made using `delete` is eventually shown to be equal to a set made with only `empty` and `insert`.

These algebraic laws are so simple that I feel no need to specify the operations informally. Try writing such laws for yourself (Exercise 15)!

Abstraction	*Operations*
Dictionary	At least `empty/new`, `insert/bind`, `delete`, `lookup` or `find`; possibly also `empty?`, `size`, and others
Representation	*Invariant*
Association list	Every key is paired with the value it maps to.
Hash table	Every key-value pair is stored in a bucket in an array, the index of which is a function of the array's size and the element's integer hash.
Binary search tree	Pairs with smaller keys are in left subtrees; pairs with larger keys are in right subtrees.

Abstraction functions

To specify an abstraction function, treat the dictionary abstraction as an environment (a set of key-value pairs), and use the $+$ operation defined on page 149. For example, the abstraction function for an association list is defined by these laws:

$$\mathcal{A}(\texttt{'()}) = \{\}$$
$$\mathcal{A}(\texttt{(cons (pair } k\ v\texttt{) } ps\texttt{)}) = \mathcal{A}(ps) + \{k \mapsto v\}$$

Figure 9.9: Possible representations of a dictionary

9.6.4 *Representations, abstraction functions, and invariants: Getting code right*

Interface design is followed by implementation. The key choice is the representation of each abstract type; just as an abstraction dictates the language you use to write the API, a representation dictates the code that you use to implement the module.

A representation is chosen based on the abstraction the designer is trying to implement, its mutability, and the expected cost model. To choose well requires an understanding of data structures. Depending on circumstances, even a simple abstraction like a set might be represented as an array, a list, a sorted list, a move-to-front list, a binary search tree, a red-black tree, an AVL tree, or a hash table. If the set's elements have a suitable structure, it might also be represented by a trie, a Patricia tree, or a bit vector.

In this book, I can't help you choose a data structure—or any other representation. But once you have a representation in mind, I can show you how to get code right. To start, since your code operates on values of the representation, you had better know what those values represent. That's the job of an *abstraction function.* Given any acceptable value of the representation type, the abstraction function says *what* abstraction the value stands for. For example, if your abstraction is a set and your representation is a binary search tree, your abstraction function might say that "a tree represents the set that contains all the elements stored at the nodes."

When code has to be right, its abstraction function should be written precisely—likely using algebraic laws. (Because an abstraction is just an idea, many abstraction functions can't easily be written as code.) As an example, suppose a set is represented as a binary search tree. A binary tree is either `Empty` or is `(Node` $l\ v\ r$`)`, where v is a value and l and r are binary trees. The abstraction function $\mathcal{A}$ can be written with just two laws:

$$\begin{aligned}\mathcal{A}(\texttt{Empty}) &= \{\},\\ \mathcal{A}(\texttt{Node } l\ v\ r) &= \mathcal{A}(l) \cup \mathcal{A}(r) \cup \{v\}.\end{aligned}$$

Abstraction	*Operations*
Priority queue	At least `empty/new`, `insert`, `empty?`, and `delete-min`; possibly also `size`, `find-min`, `merge`
Representation	*Invariant*
List	List is sorted with the smallest element at the front (inefficient unless small).
Array	Element at index i is not larger than the elements at indices $2i$ and $2i + 1$, if any.
Binary tree	Element at node is not larger than elements at left and right child, if any.
Leftist heap	Binary tree, with the additional invariant that every left subtree is at least as high as the corresponding right subtree.
Abstraction functions	
The abstraction function for a priority queue has the same structure as the abstraction function for a set. For example, the abstraction function for a leftist heap says $\mathcal{A}$(`Empty`) $= \wr\, \wr$ and $\mathcal{A}$(`Node` $l\ v\ r$) $= \mathcal{A}(l) \cup \mathcal{A}(r) \cup \wr v \wr$.	

Figure 9.10: Possible representations of a priority queue

For a simple implementation like a linked list, an abstraction function may be all you need. But many implementations work correctly only with well-behaved representations. For example, a binary *search* tree works only when values in the left tree are smaller than the value at the root, and similarly for the right subtree. This property, which is usually called the "order invariant," is an example of a *representation invariant*. The order invariant guarantees that `member?` can find an object, if present, without having to look at every node of the tree.

Interesting data structures often satisfy multiple representation invariants. These may be referred to individually, and they may also be collectively called "the invariant." For example, a sophisticated binary search tree also has a *balance invariant*. Balance invariants come in many forms, but they all guarantee that `member?` takes time at most logarithmic in the size of the tree.

Example abstraction functions and representation invariants for sets, dictionaries, priority queues, and complex numbers are sketched in Figures 9.8 to 9.12. Each figure presents an abstraction, some reasonable operations, some suggested representations, the invariants of each representation, and something about an abstraction function.

A *set* (Figure 9.8) is defined by the elements it contains.

A *dictionary* (Figure 9.9), which is also called a "table," "associative array," "environment," or "finite map," is defined by a mapping from keys to values.

A *priority queue* (Figure 9.10) is a "bag" or "multiset" of values. (For another view, see Exercise 10.) A bag is notated just like a set—elements are separated by commas and wrapped in brackets—but where set brackets look like $\{\cdots\}$, bag brackets look like $\wr \cdots \wr$. A priority queue provides fast insertion and fast access to the smallest value in the bag. The best representation depends on what other operations you want to perform at what costs. If you're willing to mutate, an array is very effective (Section 9.6.5). If you want an efficient `merge` operation, I recommend an immutable priority queue represented as a leftist heap (Section 9.7.1).

Abstraction	*Operations*
2D point	Constructor, vector addition, distance from origin, scaling by a number, translation, rotation, ...
Representation	*Invariant*
Cartesian coordinates (x, y)	None
Polar coordinates (r, θ)	$r \geq 0$, possibly $-\pi \leq \theta < \pi$
Quadrant-magnitude $(Q, \lvert x\rvert, \lvert y\rvert)$	$\lvert x\rvert \geq 0, \lvert y\rvert \geq 0, 0 \leq Q < 4$
Abstraction functions	
For the Cartesian representation, the abstraction function is the identity function. For the polar representation, it is $\mathcal{A}(r, \theta) = (r \cos \theta, r \sin \theta)$.	

Figure 9.11: Possible representations of a point in two dimensions

Abstraction	*Operations*
Complex number	Constructor, +, -, *, /, `negated`
Representation	*Invariant*
Cartesian coordinates (x, y)	None
Polar coordinates (r, θ)	$r \geq 0$, possibly $-\pi \leq \theta < \pi$

Figure 9.12: Possible representations of a complex number

A *two-dimensional point* on the plane (Figure 9.11) is defined by its x and y coordinates. If all you have is integers, Cartesian coordinates are the only game in town—though Exercise 6 invites you to play with a representation that stores a point's quadrant and the magnitudes of the x and y coordinates. But if you have floating-point numbers, and if you plan lots of rotations or magnitude tests, polar coordinates could be a good choice.

A *complex number* (Figure 9.12) is defined by its real and imaginary parts. The set of all complex numbers is isomorphic to the set of all two-dimensional points, but their operations are different. For example, two complex numbers can be multiplied to form a third complex number, which is not true of two-dimensional points.

9.6.5 *Case study: Using invariants to code a priority queue*

To demonstrate representation invariants at work, I implement a priority queue. The abstraction is a bag of elements, and I implement a mutable version, as described by this interface:

551. ⟨*pq.mcl* 551⟩≡ 552a ▷

```
(module-type MUTABLE-PQ
   (exports [abstype t]
            [abstype elem]
            [new    : ( -> t)]           ; creator
            [insert : (elem t -> unit)]  ; mutator
            [empty? : (t -> bool)]       ; observer
            [delete-min : (t -> elem)])) ; mutator *and* observer
```

Calling `insert` or `delete-min` mutates the queue that is passed in, and calling `new` creates a fresh, empty queue that is distinct from all other queues. Both `insert` and `delete-min` run in time logarithmic in the size of the queue, and the other operations run in constant time.

My implementation is generic: it works with any type of element, provided only that the smaller of any two elements can be identified. My generic module `ArrayHeap` therefore takes one argument, module `Elem`, which exports type `Elem.t` and function `Elem.<=`. Function `Elem.<=` must behave like a total order: it must be reflexive, transitive, and antisymmetric. To use `ArrayHeap` with any other `<=` function is an *unchecked* run-time error.

552a. ⟨*pq.mcl* 551⟩+≡ ◁551

```
(generic-module
  [ArrayHeap : ([Elem : (exports [abstype t]
                                 [<= : (t t -> bool)])] --m->
                (allof MUTABLE-PQ
                       (exports [type elem Elem.t])))]
  ⟨representation of a priority queue 552b⟩
  ⟨definitions of operations on priority queues 553a⟩
)
```

The result type of generic module `ArrayHeap` uses `allof` in the same way as `IntArray` (chunk 541b), for the same reason: it needs to let client code know that in any instance of `ArrayHeap`, type `elem` is the same as type `Elem.t`.

My implementation uses the classic representation of a mutable heap: an array.

552b. ⟨*representation of a priority queue* 552b⟩≡ (552a)

```
(module EA (@m ArrayList Elem))    ; EA stands for "element array"
(type t EA.t)
(type elem Elem.t)
```

The array represents a complete binary tree in which the root is stored at index 1 and the two children of the node at index i are the nodes at indices $2 \cdot i$ and $2 \cdot i + 1$. My array A is actually the "array list" whose interface is described in Section 9.6.2, so in addition to its elements, it has integers lo and $nexthi$, which mark the extreme indices of the array. A representation A represents the bag containing all the elements of A:

$$\mathcal{A}(A) = \wr A[i] \mid 1 \leq i < nexthi \wr.$$

A good representation satisfies these invariants:

$$lo = 1 \qquad \begin{array}{l} \forall i : lo \leq i < nexthi : \text{if } 2 \cdot i \quad\;\;\; < nexthi \text{ then } A[i] \leq A[2 \cdot i] \\ \forall i : lo \leq i < nexthi : \text{if } 2 \cdot i + 1 < nexthi \text{ then } A[i] \leq A[2 \cdot i + 1]. \end{array}$$

These invariants say that the value of every node is no greater than the values of its children, if any.

In the invariants, the universal quantifier $\forall i$ applies to all *nodes*. The invariant can be simplified by writing the quantifier in a way that applies to all *children*: each child must be at least as great as its parent:

$$lo = 1 \qquad\qquad \forall i : 2 \leq i < nexthi : A[i \operatorname{div} 2] \leq A[i].$$

These invariants help me guarantee that both `insert` and `delete-min` execute in time proportional to the logarithm of the number of elements in A.

To ensure that the invariants hold, I use the classic method of *rely-guarantee reasoning*:

- At the start of every operation, my code *relies* on every value of abstract type having a representation that satisfies the invariants.
- At the end of every operation, my code *guarantees* that the representation of every value of abstract type satisfies the invariants.

If your invariants keep airplanes from falling out of the sky or keep nuclear power plants from venting radioactive gas, you *prove* that they hold, using *program verification*. But program-verification techniques are beyond the scope of this book. A "cheap and cheerful" alternative is to check invariants at run time. (Dynamic checking is cheap only in programming effort; it can be expensive in run-time cost.) In Molecule, dynamic checking uses an `assert` form. Assertions can invalidate an interface's cost model, do not actually prove anything, and do not even catch all invariant violations. But assertions do catch some bugs, which can be a fine thing.

To use the invariant in an assertion, I need to express it in code. I use the version that quantifies over children, and to check a single child, I define an auxiliary function `good-child?`, to which I pass $2 \cdot i$ or $2 \cdot i + 1$.

553a. ⟨*definitions of operations on priority queues* 553a⟩≡ (552a) 553b ▷

```
(define bool good-child? ([a : t] [child-index : int])
  (let ([parent-index (/ child-index 2)])
    (Elem.<= (EA.at a parent-index) (EA.at a child-index))))
```

The invariant is satisfied if $lo = 1$ and all children are good. To test it, I define higher-order function `all-in-range?`, which tests all integers in a given range.

553b. ⟨*definitions of operations on priority queues* 553a⟩+≡ (552a) ◁ 553a 553c ▷

```
(define bool all-in-range? ([i : int] [limit : int] [p? : (int -> bool)])
  ;; true iff for every k such that i <= k < limit, k satisfies p?
  (|| (>= i limit)
      (&& (p? i) (all-in-range? (+ i 1) limit p?))))

(define bool invariant? ([a : t])
  (&& (= (EA.lo a) 1)
      (all-in-range? 2 (EA.nexthi a) (lambda ([i : int]) (good-child? a i)))))
```

Using function `invariant?`, I define a validator for representations. An invalid representation triggers an assertion failure.

553c. ⟨*definitions of operations on priority queues* 553a⟩+≡ (552a) ◁ 553b 553d ▷

```
(define t validate ([a : t])
  (assert (invariant? a))
  a)
```

The invariant is exploited for both insertion and deletion, and insertion is a little easier to understand. Function `insert` adds a new element at the high end of the array, in position n. Now every position i satisfies the invariant, except possibly position n. If $A[n \operatorname{div} 2] \le A[n]$, then position n satisfies the invariant. Otherwise `insert` swaps $A[n]$ with $A[n \operatorname{div} 2]$, then tries again with a new value of n. Eventually either $A[n \operatorname{div} 2] \le A[n]$ or else $n = 1$, and either way the invariant is eventually satisfied.

553d. ⟨*definitions of operations on priority queues* 553a⟩+≡ (552a) ◁ 553c 554a ▷

```
(define unit insert ([v : Elem.t] [q : t])
  (let ([n (EA.nexthi (validate q))])
    (EA.addhi q v)
    ; loop invariant: (EA.at q n) == v
    (while (&& (> n 1) (not (Elem.<= (EA.at q (/ n 2)) v)))
      (EA.at-put q n (EA.at q (/ n 2)))
      (EA.at-put q (/ n 2) v)
      (set n (/ n 2)))
    (assert (invariant? q))))
```

Deletion is a little more complicated. The invariant ensures that the smallest element is always stored in $A[1]$, so function `delete-min` removes $A[1]$, then moves in the last element of A, if any. At that point the invariant could be violated in this way: $A[1]$ could be larger than its children, $A[2]$ and $A[3]$. To restore the invariant, `delete-min` swaps $A[1]$ with the *smaller* of $A[2]$ and $A[3]$. Now $A[1]$ satisfies the invariant, but the child that was swapped may not. That child is at index 2 or 3, but the computation generalizes to $A[i]$, $A[2 \cdot i]$, and $A[2 \cdot i + 1]$. Function `delete-min` keeps swapping, and i keeps growing, and this computation continues until either the relations are satisfied or $A[i]$ has no children.

554a. ⟨*definitions of operations on priority queues* 553a⟩+≡ (552a) ◁553d 554d▷

```
⟨definition of internal operation swap 554c⟩
(define Elem.t delete-min ([a : t])
  (let* ([a   (validate a)]
         [min (EA.at a 1)]   ; to be returned
         [v   (EA.remhi a)]) ; to move into position 1
    (when (> (EA.size a) 0)
      (let* ([i 1]
             [_ (EA.at-put a i v)]
             [left-index  (* i 2)]
             [right-index (+ 1 left-index)]
             [limit       (EA.nexthi a)]
             [in-array?   (lambda ([j : int]) (< j limit))]
             [bad?        (lambda ([j : int])
                             (&& (in-array? j) (not (good-child? a j))))])
        ; loop invariant: left-index  == 2 * i
        ;                 right-index == 2 * i + 1
        (while (|| (bad? left-index) (bad? right-index))
          ⟨swap A[i] with the smaller of A[right-index] and A[left-index] 554b⟩)))
    (assert (invariant? a))
    min))
```

The swap is a little more complicated than I make it sound. If `right-index` is beyond the bounds of A, the only choice is to swap with the left child.

554b. ⟨*swap* A[i] *with the smaller of* A[right-index] *and* A[left-index] 554b⟩≡ (554a)

```
(let* ([hasn't-right (>= right-index (EA.nexthi a))]
       [to-swap (if hasn't-right
                    left-index
                    (if (Elem.<= (EA.at a left-index) (EA.at a right-index))
                        left-index
                        right-index))])
  (swap a i to-swap)
  (set i to-swap)
  (set left-index  (* 2 i))
  (set right-index (+ left-index 1)))
```

The swap function uses a `let` expression:

554c. ⟨*definition of internal operation* swap 554c⟩≡ (554a)

```
(define unit swap ([a : t] [i : int] [j : int])
  (let ([x (EA.at a i)]
        [y (EA.at a j)])
    (EA.at-put a i y)
    (EA.at-put a j x)))
```

To wrap up, a priority queue is empty if its representation has no elements.

554d. ⟨*definitions of operations on priority queues* 553a⟩+≡ (552a) ◁554a 554e▷

```
(define bool empty? ([q : t])
  (= 0 (EA.size (validate q))))
```

And a new priority queue is empty and satisfies $lo = 1$.

554e. ⟨*definitions of operations on priority queues* 553a⟩+≡ (552a) ◁554d

```
(define t new ()
  (validate (EA.from 1)))
```

The priority queue can be used, among other things, for sorting (Exercise 40).

As noted at the beginning of this chapter, a programming language may support data abstraction through one or both of two mechanisms: abstract data types or objects. Both mechanisms work equally well with the design techniques in the previous section, but they aren't equally good at everything. Each mechanism can do things that the other cannot, and one of the most important differences is illustrated in this section: A function defined in a module can see the representations of all its arguments of any abstract type defined in that module; a method defined on an object can see only the representation of that object, not the representations of other objects of the same class. (Objects' limitations are also a strength: *because* a method sees only the representation of its own object, it can easily interoperate with other objects of different classes. This is a benefit that can't be achieved using abstract data types—see Section 10.8.) To show the power of being able to see representations of multiple arguments, I present an example using priority queues; examples involving arbitrary-precision arithmetic and sets of integers are left as exercises.

9.7.1 *Priority queues optimized for merging: Leftist heaps*

The priority queue in the previous section—a complete binary tree represented by an array—provides insertion and removal in $O(\log N)$ time, but it does not provide a merge operation. To merge two priority queues you would have to remove all the elements from one and add them to the other, which would cost $O(N \log N)$. In this section, I present an immutable priority-queue abstraction with an efficient merge operation: the *leftist heap*. The merge operation can be implemented efficiently *only* because it can inspect the representation of both heaps.

An immutable priority queue exports roughly the same operations as a mutable priority queue, but the operations have different types:

555a. ⟨*leftist.mcl* 555a⟩≡ 555b ▷

```
(module-type IMMUTABLE-PQ
  [exports [abstype elem]
           [abstype t]
           [empty      : t]                  ; creator
           [insert     : (elem t -> t)]      ; producer
           [merge      : (t t -> t)]         ; producer
           [empty?     : (t -> bool)]        ; observer
           [module [Pair : (exports-record-ops pair
                                    ([min : elem] [others : t]))]]
           [delete-min : (t -> Pair.pair)]]) ; observer/producer
```

Operation `delete-min` returns a pair holding `min`, the smallest element, and the `others`; the pair type is defined internally in nested module `Pair`.

Module `Leftist` uses `allof` in the same way as `IntArray` and `ArrayHeap`.

555b. ⟨*leftist.mcl* 555a⟩+≡ ◁ 555a

```
(generic-module
  [Leftist : ([Elem : (exports [abstype t]
                               [<= : (t t -> bool)])] --m->
               (allof IMMUTABLE-PQ
                      (exports [type elem Elem.t])))]
  ⟨representation of a priority queue as a leftist heap 556a⟩
  ⟨definitions of operations on leftist heaps 556b⟩
)
```

The representation and operations are shown on the next couple of pages.

A leftist heap is a binary tree in which every node satisfies two invariants:

- The *heap invariant* says that the value stored at the node is no greater than any value stored in either of its subtrees.
- The *path-length invariant* says that if path lengths are measured from the node to the leaves, the shortest path is on the right.

The path-length invariant needs to be made precise, but the imprecise version explains why the representation is called "leftist": longer paths are on the left, so the left subtree tends to have more nodes.

To make the path-length invariant precise, I define the *rank* of a tree as the length of the shortest path from the root to a leaf. Rank is defined inductively: the empty tree has rank zero, and a nonempty tree has rank one more than the minimum rank of both subtrees. The path-length invariant says that in any nonempty node of a leftist representation, the rank of the left subtree is at least as great as the rank of the right subtree. To maintain the invariant, when I make a new node I put the higher-rank subtree on the left.

Rank can be computed by visiting every node, but that's costly. Instead, each node's rank is cached in the node itself, making the rank available in constant time. Because the representation is immutable, rank needs to be computed only once, when the node is built—afterward, the cached rank is always up to date. The binary tree is represented using an algebraic data type; rank is cached only in a nonempty tree.

556a. ⟨*representation of a priority queue as a leftist heap* 556a⟩≡ (555b)

```
(type elem Elem.t)
(data t
  [LEAF : t]
  [NODE : (Elem.t t t int -> t)])  ; value, left and right subheaps, rank
```

Thanks to the cache, the rank of any tree is available in constant time:

556b. ⟨*definitions of operations on leftist heaps* 556b⟩≡ (555b) 556c ▷

```
(define int rank ([heap : t])
  (case heap
     [LEAF             0]
     [(NODE _ _ _ n)    n]))
```

A new node is built by unexported operation `make-node-heap`, which takes an element `x` and two subheaps `h1` and `h2`. The function uses ranks to maintain the path-length invariant of the data structure: it puts the higher-rank subheap on the left. The caller must ensure that `x` is no greater than any element of `h1` or `h2`.

556c. ⟨*definitions of operations on leftist heaps* 556b⟩+≡ (555b) ◁ 556b 557 ▷

```
(define t make-node-heap ([x : Elem.t] [h1 : t] [h2 : t])
  ;; return a node containing the given element and subheaps
  (let* ([rank1 (rank h1)]
         [rank2 (rank h2)])
    (if (> rank1 rank2)
        (NODE x h1 h2 (+ 1 rank2))
        (NODE x h2 h1 (+ 1 rank1)))))
```

Function `make-node-heap` is used in the efficient merge operation. Function `merge` takes two arguments and so must handle four cases, but three of those cases are uninteresting: when an empty heap `LEAF` is merged with any other heap h, the result is just h. When two nonempty `NODE` heaps are merged, the smaller of the two root values is chosen to be the root value of the new heap, and from among its left and right subheaps, plus the heap not chosen, `merge` has to make two subtrees for the new node. Because the left subheap of the chosen heap has higher rank, it is left alone, and the right subheap is merged with the not-chosen heap. Using the lower-rank subheap in the recursive merge guarantees good performance.

557. ⟨*definitions of operations on leftist heaps* 556b⟩+≡ (555b) ◁ 556c

```
(define t merge ([h1 : t] [h2 : t])
  (case h1
    [LEAF   h2]
    [(NODE x1 left1 right1 rank1)
      (case h2
        [LEAF     h1]
        [(NODE x2 left2 right2 rank2)
            (if (Elem.<= x1 x2)
                (make-node-heap x1 left1 (merge right1 h2))
                (make-node-heap x2 left2 (merge right2 h1)))])]))
```


This optimized merge is possible only because `merge` can inspect the representations of both arguments, `h1` and `h2`.

The other operations are left to you (Exercise 33).

9.7.2 In-depth case study: Arithmetic

To get experience writing functions that can inspect all of their arguments, try implementing arithmetic. A function that adds two numbers, for example, needs access to every digit of both numbers. By implementing arithmetic on so-called *large integers*, where there is no *a priori* limit to the number of digits, you can compare the abstract-type approach to data abstraction (this chapter) with the object-oriented approach (Chapter 10). Arithmetic was once every schoolchild's introduction to algorithms, but if you have forgotten the classic algorithms used to add, subtract, and multiply numbers of many digits, they are explained in detail in Appendix B.

Implementing arithmetic will give you insight into similarities and differences between abstract data types and objects. Abstract data types and objects use the same representation ("sequence of digits"), and they use data abstraction to protect the same invariants ("the leading digit of a nonzero number is never zero"), but from there, they diverge:

- In Exercise 49 in this chapter, you can define a function that adds two natural numbers. Because it is defined in the same module as the representation of natural numbers, this function can simply look at the digits of both representations, add them pairwise, and return a result. But this function is limited to the type on which it is defined; it cannot dream of, for example, adding a natural number to a machine integer to get a natural-number result. If client code wants to add a natural number and a machine integer, it must first *coerce* the machine integer to a natural number. (Such a coercion is a key step in the algorithm for multiplying two natural numbers.)

- By contrast, an addition method defined on an object can see only the digits of the addend on which it is defined; it must treat the other addend as an abstraction. To make addition possible requires changing the abstraction's API, so it can include operations like "tell me your least-significant digit." But *because* the other addend is an abstraction, it doesn't have to have the same representation as the first addend—and in Exercises 37 to 39 in Chapter 10, you can build an object-oriented implementation of arithmetic that can seamlessly add machine integers and large integers. Using objects, client code can simply add numbers and not worry about their types.

Large integers make a great case study for comparing abstract data types with objects, but they are also a vital abstraction in their own right—integers of practically unlimited size are supported natively in many programming languages, including Icon, Haskell, Python, and full Scheme.

9.8 Molecule's type system: Enforcing abstraction

Access to information about abstract types is controlled by a type system. Molecule's type system supports data abstraction with abstract types and modules, including generic modules and nested modules, in much the same way as other languages that provide these features. Molecule's type system also supports function overloading, but Molecule's overloading is just a convenience, not a good model of overloading as it is found elsewhere. Regardless, Molecule's type system is more ambitious than the type systems in Chapters 6 to 8. What the type system does and how it works are explained in this section. The section begins informally, goes deep into formal details, and concludes with some comparisons.

9.8.1 *What the type system does and how*

The type system's main job is to make modules and abstract types work:

- When a module is sealed, the type system hides the representations of its abstract types, and it gives each abstract type a new identity.
- When a module is copied or is passed as a parameter to instantiate a generic module, the type system preserves the identities of its abstract types.
- When a module type is ascribed to a module, whether by sealing or by instantiation, the type system ensures that the module implements the module type ascribed to it.
- When a generic module is defined, the type system checks it right away, assuming that each parameter has the module type claimed for it. When the module is instantiated, the type system checks that each actual parameter implements the corresponding module type, but it needn't check the generic code again—if the actual parameters are OK, the instance is guaranteed to be well typed. This ability to check a generic module once, rather than have to check each instance, is an example of *modular type checking*.

Each aspect of the job is illustrated below with an example.

As an example of sealing, module `Char` is sealed with a signature that declares `[abstype t]`. Inside `Char`, type `Char.t` is defined as type `int`, and the values exported from module `Char` are just integers:

558a. ⟨*definitions inside module* `Char` 558a⟩≡ (S484b)

```
(type t int)
(val space        32)
(val right-curly 125)
```

Although type `Char.t` is defined as `int`, this identity is known only inside the `Char` module. On the outside, type `Char.t` has a new identity that is distinct from `int`, and it is known only by that identity. So a value of type `Char.t` won't work with integer operations:

558b. ⟨*transcript* 530b⟩+≡ ◁543c 559a▷

```
-> (+ 1 Char.right-curly)
type error: function + expects second argument of type Int.t, but got Char.t
-> (= 125 Char.right-curly)
type error: function = expects second argument of type Int.t, but got Char.t
```

`Char.right-curly` does not work with operations exported from `Int`; it works only with the operations exported from `Char` (`print` and `println`).

As an example of identity preservation, I copy module Char into module C. Because copying the module doesn't change its types, type C.t is the same type as Char.t. And the right-curly value from module Char *does* work with the println operation from module C:

559a. ⟨*transcript* 530b⟩+≡ ◁558b 559b▷

```
-> (module C Char)
-> (C.println Char.right-curly)
}
unit : Unit.t
```

The identity of type Char.t is preserved by a transformation called *strengthening*: when Char is used on the right-hand side, all uses of its abstract type t are replaced with the fully qualified name Char.t. In addition, the module type is changed so that type t is no longer abstract; instead, t is made manifestly equal to itself:

559b. ⟨*transcript* 530b⟩+≡ ◁559a 559c▷

```
-> (module C Char)
module C :
  (exports
    [type t Char.t]
    [new : (Int.t -> Char.t)]
    ...
```

Both representation hiding and identity preservation rely on a single mechanism: each abstract type is identified with a fully qualified name, which is called its *absolute access path*. The absolute access path is the path you would use at top level to refer to the type; such a path begins with the name of a module or with an instance of a generic module. As examples, the type "integer" is identified with absolute access path Int.t, and the type of "array of Booleans" is identified with the absolute access path (@m Array Bool).t.

Every absolute access path begins with a *root*, which identifies the top-level definition in which the path is located. A root is one of the following:

- An exporting module defined at top level
- A formal parameter to a generic module
- A definition of a module type (the special "placeholder" root •)
- The result type of a generic-module type (another placeholder)

A new, unique root is created for every new module, regardless of what the module is named—that is, module-definition forms are *generative* (Sections 8.5 and 9.8.9). Because every root is unique, or has a unique root substituted for it when used, every absolute access path is also unique.

Giving every type a unique absolute access path is the key to the type system: in Molecule, *two types are equal if and only if they are identified with the same path* (or if they are function types mapping equal argument types to equal result types). Type equality is used to ensure that each component of a module meets its specification—that is, if a module type includes a value component, the module must define that component, and the component must have the expected type.

When sealed, an entire module is also checked to see if it meets its specification. For example, module IntArray cannot be sealed with a module type that specifies "array of Booleans":

559c. ⟨*transcript* 530b⟩+≡ ◁559b 560a▷

```
-> (module-type BOOLARRAY (allof ARRAY (exports [type elem Bool.t])))
-> (module [MyArray : BOOLARRAY] IntArray)
type error: interface calls for type elem to manifestly equal Bool.t,
            but it is Int.t
```

Because IntArray does not implement BOOLARRAY—the element type is wrong—this sealing doesn't typecheck. But sealing IntArray with a module type that specifies "array of integers" is just fine:

560a. ⟨*transcript* 530b⟩+≡ ◁559c 560b▷

```
-> (module-type INTARRAY (allof ARRAY (exports [type elem Int.t])))
-> (module [MyArray : INTARRAY] IntArray)
module MyArray :
  (exports
    [abstype t]
    [type elem Int.t]
    [new : (Int.t Int.t -> MyArray.t)]
    [empty : ( -> MyArray.t)]
    [size : (MyArray.t -> Int.t)]
    [at : (MyArray.t Int.t -> Int.t)]
    [at-put : (MyArray.t Int.t Int.t -> Unit.t)])
```

The type system checks that IntArray implements INTARRAY, and this sealing is accepted.

As another example, even though an integer heap made with ArrayHeap has an array representation, it cannot be sealed with an ARRAY specification:

560b. ⟨*transcript* 530b⟩+≡ ◁560a 560c▷

```
-> (module [IntHeap : ARRAY] (@m ArrayHeap Int))
type error: interface calls for value new to have type ...
            but it has type (-> (@m ArrayHeap Int).t)
```

The check fails because the integer heap's new operation has a type that is different from what the ARRAY interface specifies. The types of all the operations can be seen by giving the instance a name (IntHeap) without any sealing:

560c. ⟨*transcript* 530b⟩+≡ ◁560b 560d▷

```
-> (module IntHeap (@m ArrayHeap Int))
module IntHeap :
  (exports
    [type t (@m ArrayHeap Int).t]
    [type elem Int.t]
    [new : ( -> (@m ArrayHeap Int).t)]
    [insert : (Int.t (@m ArrayHeap Int).t -> Unit.t)]
    [empty? : ((@m ArrayHeap Int).t -> Bool.t)]
    [delete-min : ((@m ArrayHeap Int).t -> Int.t)])
```

When a module is sealed, the type system checks that the module implements the interface used to seal it. And similarly, when a generic module is instantiated, the type system checks that each module argument implements the interface of the corresponding formal parameter. For example, the ArrayHeap module requires a formal parameter whose interface exports a type t and a <= operation. Module Int implements that interface, but Bool doesn't, so ArrayHeap can't be instantiated with Bool:

560d. ⟨*transcript* 530b⟩+≡ ◁560c 560e▷

```
-> (module BoolHeap (@m ArrayHeap Bool))
type error: module Bool cannot be used as argument Elem to generic module ...
```

To create a Boolean heap, I must define a module that implements an order operation on Booleans:

560e. ⟨*transcript* 530b⟩+≡ ◁560d 561▷

```
-> (module [OrderedBool : (exports [type t Bool.t]
                                   [<= : (Bool.t Bool.t -> Bool.t)])]
      (type t Bool.t)
      (define t <= ([p : t] [q : t])
         (or (not p) q)))
```

> *Subtype and supertype: Which way?*
>
> The *directions* of "subtype" and "supertype" always confuse me. I think of the "sub" in "subtype" and think it means "fewer," but actually a subtype has *more* components. I correct my thinking by asking how many *inhabitants* a module type has. A subtype has fewer inhabitants—that is, there are fewer modules that redeem the promise made by the type. In fact the inhabitants of a subtype are a subset of the inhabitants of the supertype—which is why an inhabitant of the subtype may be used anywhere an inhabitant of the supertype is expected.

Now module `OrderedBool` can be used to instantiate `ArrayHeap`:

561. ⟨*transcript* 530b⟩+≡ ◁560e 566▷

```
-> (module BoolHeap (@m ArrayHeap OrderedBool))
module BoolHeap :
  (exports
    [type t (@m ArrayHeap OrderedBool).t]
    [type elem Bool.t]
    ...
```

To check whether a module implements an interface, Molecule's type system uses two ideas: *subtyping* and *principal module types*. One module type is a subtype of another, written $\mathcal{T}_{sub} <: \mathcal{T}_{super}$, if a module of type $\mathcal{T}_{sub}$ can be used anywhere that a module of type $\mathcal{T}_{super}$ is expected. (This idea generalizes to other languages, including languages without modules, in which subtyping is defined only on core-layer types.) For modules, subtyping is determined by a module's components: A subtype has to include every component called for in the supertype, and every component has to meet the supertype's specification. A subtype could also include extra components not called for in the supertype (sidebar on the current page).

The principal module type of a module is the one that reveals as much information as possible about the module's component definitions. Each definition may contribute one or more declarations to the principal module type: A `val` or `define` definition contributes a `val` declaration, a `type` definition contributes a manifest-type declaration, and a `module` definition contributes a `module` declaration. A `data` definition contributes one declaration for the type and one for each value constructor, and an `overload` definition doesn't contribute any declarations.

9.8.2 *Introducing the formalism*

Molecule's type system uses techniques that should be familiar from Chapters 6 and 8, but at a larger scale. Its elements are shown in Figure 9.13 on the following page, which depicts the major metavariables, the syntax, and the environment.

The type system is organized around access paths; a path is written π. A path may be a bare module name M, or it may be formed by selecting a value, type, or module component from a shorter path. Or a path may be an instance of a generic module, or finally, a path may be just $\bullet$, which is a placeholder used to describe a module type that is not yet part of a module definition, like the module type `ARRAY`.

The typing rules are written using a compact representation of syntax (Figure 9.13e). Because the type system is so large and because declarations and components are so similar, the metavariable D stands not only for a declaration as written externally in the source code but also for a component of a module used internally.

(a) Names

t	Name of a type
T	Name of a module type
x or f	Name of a variable (or function)
M	Name of a module
K	Name of a value constructor

(b) Syntax, environments

π	Access path
e	Expression
d	Definition
ds	List of definitions
τ	Type
$\mathcal{T}$	Module type
D	Declaration or component
Ds	List of declarations or components
C	Context of a definition
E	Static (typechecking) environment
ρ	Dynamic (evaluation) environment

(c) Declarations: Syntax and theory

`[abstype` t`]`	$t :: *$ or $t :: \lfloor * \rfloor_\pi$
`[type` $t\ \tau$`]`	$t = \tau$
`[`x `:` τ`]`	$x : \tau$
`[module [`M `:` $\mathcal{T}$`]]`	$M : \mathcal{T}$

(d) Bindings in the typechecking environment

$t = \tau$	Name t is an abbreviation for type τ
$T = \mathcal{T}$	Name T is an abbreviation for module type $\mathcal{T}$
$x : \tau$	Variable x is defined with type τ
$M : \lfloor \mathcal{T} \rfloor_\pi$	Module M is defined at absolute path π with module type $\mathcal{T}$
$x \in [\tau_1, \ldots, \tau_n]$	Name x is overloaded at types τ_1 to τ_n

(e) Grammars for syntax, environments, paths, and contexts

$$\pi \ ::= M \mid \pi.x \mid \pi.t \mid \pi.M \mid (\texttt{@m}\ \pi\ \pi_1\ \cdots\ \pi_n) \mid \bullet$$

$$\mathcal{T} ::= \text{EXPORTS}(Ds) \mid \mathcal{T}_1 \wedge \mathcal{T}_2 \mid (M_1 : \mathcal{T}_1) \times \cdots \times (M_n : \mathcal{T}_n) \to \mathcal{T}$$

$$D ::= t = \tau \mid t :: * \mid x : \tau \mid M : \mathcal{T}$$

$$C ::= [] \mid \pi.[]$$

$$\tau \ ::= \pi \mid \tau_1 \times \cdots \times \tau_n \to \tau$$

$$E ::= [] \mid E, t = \tau \mid E, x : \tau \mid E, M : \lfloor \mathcal{T} \rfloor_\pi \mid E, T = \mathcal{T} \mid E, x \in [\tau_1, \ldots, \tau_n]$$

$$\begin{aligned} d \ ::= &\ \text{VAL}(x, e) \mid \text{VAL-REC}(x : \tau, e) \mid \text{TYPE}(t, \tau) \mid \text{OVERLOAD}(\pi) \mid \text{DATA}(\cdots) \\ \mid &\ \text{MODULE-TYPE}(T, \mathcal{T}) \\ \mid &\ \text{MODULE}([M : \mathcal{T}], ds) \mid \text{MODULE}([M : \mathcal{T}], \pi) \mid \text{MODULE}(M, \pi) \end{aligned}$$

Figure 9.13: Metavariables, syntax, and the type-checking environment

Figure 9.13c clarifies the meaning of the declaration forms by relating concrete syntax to theory notation. Each form of theory notation expresses a type-theoretic idea: abstract type t has kind $*$; manifest type t is equal to τ; and so on. As shown in the figure, abstract-type declarations have two theory forms: The external form simply identifies an abstract type t, and it is notated $t :: *$. The internal form is decorated with its absolute access path π, and it is notated $t :: \lfloor * \rfloor_\pi$.

To compute the absolute access path of each type and module, the type system tracks the *context* of each declaration and definition. The form of a context C is shown in Figure 9.13e. A context has a hole $[\,]$, which is filled in with a name, like the name of a defined module. Filling the hole turns the context into a path. Each top-level definition is elaborated in the context $[\,]$, which is just a hole. The name used to fill it is the name of the module being defined.

A type τ is either an absolute access path or a function type.

Abstract syntax includes lists of definitions ds and of declarations Ds. In this chapter, lists are written differently than in other chapters: a nonempty list is formed using an infix comma, which can mean not only cons but also append or snoc (which adds a single element to the end of a list). The comma is also used to pattern match on nonempty lists. This notation simplifies the typing rules.

Compared with type systems that appear in earlier chapters, Molecule's differs most in its type-checking environment. Molecule's type-checking environment does the same work as Typed μScheme's Γ and Δ environments combined: it tracks the type of each value and the kind of each type constructor.[2] But it also tracks the type that each type abbreviation stands for, the module type of each module, the module type that each module-type abbreviation stands for, and the possible types of each overloaded name. This information could conceivably be distributed over multiple different environments, much as types and kinds are distributed over environments Γ and Δ in Typed μScheme, but putting it all into a single environment E simplifies the forms of many judgments. One consequence is that Molecule cannot simultaneously have both a value and a type of the same name, but this restriction is one I can live with.

A type-checking environment E is written as a sequence of *bindings*. A binding resembles a declaration, and both bindings and declarations are notated with metavariable D. But a binding differs from a declaration in the following ways:

- A type binding in an environment always contains a manifest type; no type is ever bound into an environment as abstract. If an abstract type is entered into an environment, it is entered as manifestly equal to itself. This trick is analogous to strengthening.

- When a binding associates a module's name M with its module type $\mathcal{T}$, the module type is *rooted* in path π; the binding is written $M : \lfloor \mathcal{T} \rfloor_\pi$, where π is M's absolute access path. Both type and path are needed because M can be used in two ways: When M is used to define another module or as an actual parameter to a generic module, its type $\mathcal{T}$ is needed for type checking. And when M is used to form a path—that is, when code names a type component like $M.t$—M's absolute path π is used to form path $\pi.t$, which determines the identity of the type.

- A binding of the form $T = \mathcal{T}$ can associate module type $\mathcal{T}$ with name T. Because a module type cannot be a component, such a binding has no corresponding declaration form.

- The binding of an overloaded name, which is written $x \in [\tau_1, \ldots, \tau_n]$, tracks all the types at which name x may be used. Such a binding has no corresponding declaration form.

Even though an environment is written as a sequence of bindings, it still has a domain; $\text{dom}(E)$ is a set of names, each of the form t, x, M, or T. An environment E can even be applied, like a function, to a name in its domain, but Molecule's typing rules use a different notation. The typing rules look names up using the relation $E \ni D$, pronounced "E has D," where D is a binding. This notation has the advantage that it can be extended to suggest that E binds *paths* (Figure 9.22, page 574), which provides a compact way to associate types with quali-

[2] In Molecule, that kind is always $*$.

fied names. For example, if E_0 is Molecule's initial environment, then judgment $E_0 \ni$ `Int.negated` : (`Int.t` $\rightarrow$ `Int.t`) is derivable.

An environment may bind relative paths as well as absolute ones. As an example, in module `OrderedBool`, the relative path `t` is bound to type `Bool.t`. As another example, in the definition of module type `IMMUTABLE-PQ` (chunk 555a), the relative path `Pair.t` is bound to the absolute path •`.Pair.t`.

One last preliminary: To avoid dealing with too many lists, the type theory simplifies the syntax in two ways. First, the `allof` form is expressed using an $\wedge$ operator, according to these equations:

$$\begin{aligned}\text{ALLOF}([]) &= \text{EXPORTS}()\\ \text{ALLOF}([\mathcal{T}]) &= \mathcal{T}\\ \text{ALLOF}([\mathcal{T}_1, \mathcal{T}_2, \ldots, \mathcal{T}_n]) &= \mathcal{T}_1 \wedge \text{ALLOF}([\mathcal{T}_2, \ldots, \mathcal{T}_n]).\end{aligned}$$

Like an `allof` type, a type of the form $\mathcal{T}_1 \wedge \mathcal{T}_2$ is an *intersection type*; the $\wedge$ symbol can be pronounced "and also."

The second simplification is for `overload`: although the concrete syntax may list as many paths as you like, the type theory overloads one path at a time.

An overview of the entire type system is shown in Figure 9.14 on the next page. While the figure shows a lot of judgments, only three things are really going on: elaboration, principal types, and subtyping. In this order,

- Types and module types are *elaborated*, which replaces each type abbreviation with its referent. Elaboration also replaces relative paths with absolute paths as needed. And although it is mostly glossed over, elaboration decorates the application of every overloaded function name, so the evaluator knows which overloaded function is meant.

- The principal type of each module is computed. The key judgment is $E \vdash \lfloor d \rfloor_C : Ds$, which checks a definition d and produces bindings Ds. The bindings are added to the environment and may also become components of a principal module type.

- *Ascriptions* are checked using subtyping. A module type may be ascribed to a module in two ways: the module is sealed with a module type, in which case the sealing module type is ascribed to the module, or the module is used to instantiate a generic module, in which case the type of the formal parameter is ascribed to the module. In both cases, the module's principal type is checked to be sure it is a subtype of the module type ascribed to it.

Checking ascriptions is the ultimate goal, so we begin our study with subtyping, then work through principal module types and elaboration.

9.8.3 *Subtyping and intersection types*

Module type $\mathcal{T}$ is a subtype of $\mathcal{T}'$ if $\mathcal{T}$ provides everything that $\mathcal{T}'$ is expecting. The judgment is written $\mathcal{T} <: \mathcal{T}'$, and it is sound if every inhabitant of $\mathcal{T}$ is also an inhabitant of $\mathcal{T}'$. Relevant rules are shown in Figure 9.15 on page 566.

In Molecule, only the types of exporting modules are related by subtyping.[3] The judgment form $\mathcal{T} <: \mathcal{T}'$ needs only two rules: one when the supertype $\mathcal{T}'$ is an intersection type, and one when it is a list of exported components. The rule for

[3]Subtyping of intersection types *or* module-arrow types is relatively easy, but combining them can be gnarly.

Elaboration	Replaces type abbreviations with their referents; converts relative paths to absolute paths; resolves applications of overloaded names.
$E \vdash \tau \rightsquigarrow \tau'$	Type τ is well formed (with kind $*$) and stands for τ'.
$E \vdash \lfloor \mathcal{T} \rfloor_\pi \rightsquigarrow \mathcal{T}'$	At path π, module type $\mathcal{T}$ is well formed and elaborates to $\mathcal{T}'$ (`elabmt`).
$E \vdash \lfloor Ds \rfloor_\pi \rightsquigarrow Ds'$	Declarations within `exports` elaborate.
$E \vdash \lfloor D \rfloor_\pi \rightsquigarrow D'$	A single declaration elaborates.
$E \vdash e \rightsquigarrow e' : \tau$	Expression e has type τ and elaborates to e' (which is e decorated with the resolution of overloaded functions).
$E \vdash e : \tau$	Expression e is elaborated, but we ignore the elaboration and look only at the type τ.
Principal Types	Checks that a module is well formed and computes its principal type.
$E \vdash \lfloor ds \rfloor_\pi : \mathcal{T}$	At path π, a module with definitions ds is well formed and has principal module type $\mathcal{T}$.
$E \vdash \lfloor ds \rfloor_\pi : Ds$	At path π, definitions ds are described by declarations Ds.
$E \vdash \lfloor d \rfloor_C : Ds$	In context C and environment E, definition d is well formed and adds bindings Ds to the environment.
$E \vdash \pi : \mathcal{T}$	The module defined at path π has type $\mathcal{T}$.
Subtyping	Tests if a module or component meets a specification.
$\mathcal{T} <: \mathcal{T}'$	Module type $\mathcal{T}$ is a subtype of module type $\mathcal{T}'$.
$D <: D'$	A component described by D matches the specification D'.
$Ds <: Ds'$	A sequence of components described by Ds matches specification Ds'.
Lookup	Looks up a name or a path, including instances of generic modules.
$E \ni D$	Environment E binds a name or path as described in binding D.

Figure 9.14: Judgments of the type system

subtypes of intersection types gets at the very idea of subtyping and intersection: a module inhabits type $\mathcal{T}_1' \wedge \mathcal{T}_2'$ if and only if it inhabits both $\mathcal{T}_1'$ and $\mathcal{T}_2'$. The rule for subtypes of an intersection type is therefore sound and complete. (If you like math, subtyping is a partial order, and the $\wedge$ operator finds a greatest lower bound.)

The rule for a subtype of an export list checks that every component of the supertype is present in the subtype. The components of the subtype are calculated by this function:

$$\begin{aligned} \texttt{comps}(\text{EXPORTS}(Ds)) &= Ds \\ \texttt{comps}(\mathcal{T}_1 \wedge \mathcal{T}_2) &= \texttt{comps}(\mathcal{T}_1), \texttt{comps}(\mathcal{T}_2) \\ \texttt{comps}((M_1 : \mathcal{T}_1) \times \cdots \times (M_n : \mathcal{T}_n) \xrightarrow{m} \mathcal{T}) &= []. \end{aligned}$$

The result of applying `comps` to an intersection type might not be a well-formed export list. That's because intersected module types may have repeated components or may even be inconsistent. It turns out, however, that an inconsistent module type can be accepted by the type system without causing a problem. For example,

$$\boxed{\mathcal{T} <: \mathcal{T}'} \qquad \frac{\mathcal{T} <: \mathcal{T}_1' \qquad \mathcal{T} <: \mathcal{T}_2'}{\mathcal{T} <: \mathcal{T}_1' \wedge \mathcal{T}_2'} \qquad \frac{\texttt{comps}(\mathcal{T}) <: Ds'}{\mathcal{T} <: \text{EXPORTS}(Ds')}$$

$$\boxed{Ds <: Ds'} \qquad \frac{}{Ds <: [\,]}$$

$$\frac{Ds = Ds_{pre}, D, Ds_{post} \qquad D <: D'' \qquad Ds <: Ds''}{Ds <: (D'', Ds'')}$$

$$\boxed{D <: D'} \qquad \frac{}{t :: \lfloor * \rfloor_\pi <: t :: \lfloor * \rfloor_{\pi'}} \qquad \frac{}{t = \tau <: t :: \lfloor * \rfloor_{\pi'}} \qquad \frac{}{t = \tau <: t = \tau}$$

$$\frac{}{t :: \lfloor * \rfloor_\pi <: t = \pi} \qquad \frac{}{x : \tau <: x : \tau} \qquad \frac{\mathcal{T} <: \mathcal{T}'}{M : \mathcal{T} <: M : \mathcal{T}'}$$

Figure 9.15: Subtyping

a module type might be inconsistent because it claims two different identities for a type t:

566. ⟨*transcript* 530b⟩+≡ ◁561 567▷

```
-> (module-type INCONSISTENT
                (allof (exports [type t Bool.t]) (exports [type t Int.t])))
module type INCONSISTENT =
  (allof (exports [type t Bool.t]) (exports [type t Int.t]))
```

Because this module type has no inhabitants, it's harmless. In particular, because module type INCONSISTENT is uninhabited, proving a judgment of the form INCONSISTENT $<: \mathcal{T}'$ causes no issues. Because INCONSISTENT has no inhabitants, every inhabitant of INCONSISTENT is also an inhabitant of $\mathcal{T}'$, so the judgment is sound. And if you try to seal a module with type INCONSISTENT, you'll find that you can't—although you might be frustrated by the error messages.

Once function comps produces components, they are checked using judgment $Ds <: Ds'$. If Ds' is empty, it is supplied by *any* sequence of components. If Ds' is nonempty, then it has the form (D'', Ds''), which is supplied if both D'' and Ds'' are supplied. Components may be supplied in any order.

A single supplied component is checked using judgment $D <: D'$. An abstract type may be supplied by another abstract type or by any manifest type—to have an abstract type supplied by a manifest type is the essence of sealing. A manifest type may be supplied either by an identical manifest type or by an abstract type that is demonstrably equal to it. A value may be supplied only by a value of the same type, and a module of type $\mathcal{T}'$ may be supplied by a module of the same name whose type $\mathcal{T}$ is a subtype of $\mathcal{T}'$.

9.8.4 *Principal module types, sealing, and realization*

A module can be sealed with any module type whose promises are redeemed by the module. Gloriously, every well-typed module has a *principal module type* that is at least as good as any module type whose promises are redeemed by the module. For modules, "at least as good" means "a subtype of"—and, if you study the subtype relation, you'll see that it also means "provides at least as much information as." A principal module type (henceforth, "principal type") provides as much information as possible; it hides nothing.

$$
\begin{aligned}
\mathtt{msubsn}(\lfloor \mathrm{EXPORTS}(Ds) \rfloor_\pi) &= \mathtt{msubsn}(\lfloor Ds \rfloor_\pi)\\
\mathtt{msubsn}(\lfloor \mathcal{T}_1 \wedge \mathcal{T}_2 \rfloor_\pi) &= \mathtt{msubsn}(\lfloor \mathcal{T}_1 \rfloor_\pi) \circ \mathtt{msubsn}(\lfloor \mathcal{T}_2 \rfloor_\pi)\\
\mathtt{msubsn}(\lfloor\, \rfloor_\pi) &= \theta_I\\
\mathtt{msubsn}(\lfloor t = \tau, Ds \rfloor_\pi) &= \mathtt{msubsn}(\lfloor Ds \rfloor_\pi) \circ (\pi.t \mapsto \tau)\\
\mathtt{msubsn}(\lfloor t :: \lfloor * \rfloor_{\pi'}, Ds \rfloor_\pi) &= \mathtt{msubsn}(\lfloor Ds \rfloor_\pi)\\
\mathtt{msubsn}(\lfloor x : \tau, Ds \rfloor_\pi) &= \mathtt{msubsn}(\lfloor Ds \rfloor_\pi)\\
\mathtt{msubsn}(\lfloor M : \lfloor \mathcal{T} \rfloor_{\pi'}, Ds \rfloor_\pi) &= \mathtt{msubsn}(\lfloor Ds \rfloor_\pi) \circ \mathtt{msubsn}(\lfloor \mathcal{T} \rfloor_{\pi'})\\
\theta_I &= \text{the identity substitution}
\end{aligned}
$$

Figure 9.16: Substitution from manifest types

A module's principal type is also intersection of all the types that could be ascribed to it. In Molecule, a module's principal type is unique up to reordering of components. The existence of unique principal types is the result of careful design, which I have borrowed from the ML family of languages.

Principal module types are used primarily for sealing. The module being sealed is the *implementation*, and its type is the *implementation type*. The module type doing the sealing is the *interface type* or just the *interface*. Before the two can be compared, the interface type has to be *realized*. To see that the interface type can't always be compared directly, consider the example below: module `R` has principal module type `(exports [type t Int.t] [x : Int.t])`, and it is sealed with an interface in which not only is `t` abstract, but `x` is given the *abstract* type `R.t`, not type `Int.t`.

567. ⟨*transcript* 530b⟩+≡ ◁566 570▷

```
-> (module [R : (exports [abstype t] [x : t])]
     (type t Int.t)
     (val x 1983))
module R : (exports [abstype t] [x : R.t])
```

As illustrated by the `Char` example at the start of this section, types `R.t` and `Int.t` are different, but we want the example to be accepted anyway. After all, the interface places no constraints on type `t`, and the `t` and `x` components demanded by the interface are provided by the implementation.

The type component `t` is easy to accept; the interface demands an abstract-type component `t` $::$ $\lfloor * \rfloor_{\mathtt{R}}$, and the module's principal type has component `t` $=$ `Int.t`. According to Figure 9.15, any manifest type `t` is a subtype of abstract type `t`. All good.

What about `x`? The interface demands value component `x` : `R.t`, and the implementation's principal type has component `x` : `Int.t`. Just like types `Char.t` and `Int.t`, types `R.t` and `Int.t` are different, and according to Figure 9.15, one value component is a subtype of another only if their types are the same. But inside module `R`, they *are* the same—the question is, how does the type system know? Molecule uses a technique that is borrowed from Standard ML, called *realization*.

An interface is realized by replacing each abstract type with its representation, which comes from the implementation. Realization also transforms each abstract-type component into a manifest-type component. The type definitions in the implementation are converted to a substitution by function `msubsn` (Figure 9.16), which is applied to the principal type of the implementation. In the example of module `R` above, `msubsn` returns the substitution that replaces type `R.t` with type `Int.t`.

$$
\begin{aligned}
\theta(\textsc{exports}(D_1, \ldots, D_n) &= \textsc{exports}(\theta(D_1), \ldots, \theta(D_n)) \\
\theta(\mathcal{T}_1 \wedge \mathcal{T}_2) &= \theta(\mathcal{T}_1) \wedge \theta(\mathcal{T}_2) \\
\theta((M_1 : \mathcal{T}_1) \times \cdots \times (M_n : \mathcal{T}_n) \xrightarrow{m} \mathcal{T}) &= (M_1 : \theta(\mathcal{T}_1)) \times \cdots \times (M_n : \theta(\mathcal{T}_n)) \xrightarrow{m} \theta(\mathcal{T}) \\
\theta(t = \tau) &= t = \theta(\tau) \\
\theta(t :: \lfloor * \rfloor_\pi) &= t :: \lfloor * \rfloor_\pi, \text{when } \pi \notin \operatorname{dom} \theta \\
\theta(t :: \lfloor * \rfloor_\pi) &= t = \theta(\pi), \text{when } \pi \in \operatorname{dom} \theta \qquad (\star) \\
\theta(x : \tau) &= x : \theta(\tau) \\
\theta(M : \mathcal{T}) &= M : \theta(\mathcal{T})
\end{aligned}
$$

Figure 9.17: Module-type realization

The substitution is used to realize the interface by applying it to the interface type as shown in Figure 9.17. The equation marked with a star replaces every abstract type in the interface with its manifest definition from the implementation (assuming the type is defined). The other equations are structural.

Realization and subtyping work together to determine when a module type can be used to seal a module; an implementation of principal type $\mathcal{T}$ defined at path π can be sealed with interface type $\mathcal{T}'$ if and only if the implementation type is a subtype of the *realized* interface:

$$\mathcal{T} <: \texttt{msubsn}(\lfloor \mathcal{T} \rfloor_\pi)(\mathcal{T}').$$

9.8.5 *Computing principal module types*

A module's principal type is computed by a process that resembles the typechecking of definitions in Typed Impcore and Typed μScheme. But in Typed Impcore and Typed μScheme, typechecking a definition produces only a new environment. In Molecule, typechecking a definition also produces bindings. These bindings are added to the environment, and they can also become components of a principal module type. Typically one definition produces one binding; for example, a definition of the form `(val` x e`)` produces a binding of the form $x : \tau$, where τ is the type of e. But a `data` definition produces multiple bindings: one for the type and one for each value constructor. And typically the bindings produced by a definition also declare components in a principal module type, but the binding produced by an `overload` definition doesn't declare any components.

The judgment form for checking a definition is $\boxed{E \vdash \lfloor d \rfloor_C : Ds}$, where the metavariables stand for the following:

d	The definition
C	The context in which it appears
E	The environment in which it is checked
Ds	The bindings or components that it contributes

The context is used to generate an absolute access path for every defined module and every new type defined by `data`. For example, in module `Intlist` below, the module definition is checked in the empty context, but the `data` definition is

$$\boxed{E \vdash \lfloor d \rfloor_C : Ds}$$

(DefVal)
$$\frac{E \vdash e : \tau}{E \vdash \lfloor \textsc{val}(x, e) \rfloor_C : [x : \tau]}$$

(DefValRec)
$$\frac{E \vdash \tau \rightsquigarrow \tau' \qquad E, x : \tau' \vdash e : \tau'}{E \vdash \lfloor \textsc{val-rec}(x : \tau, e) \rfloor_C : [x : \tau']}$$

(DefType)
$$\frac{E \vdash \tau \rightsquigarrow \tau'}{E \vdash \lfloor \textsc{type}(t, \tau) \rfloor_C : [t = \tau']}$$

(a) Core-layer definition forms

$$\boxed{E \vdash \lfloor d \rfloor_C : Ds}$$

(DefModType)
$$\frac{E \vdash \lfloor \mathcal{T} \rfloor_{\bullet} \rightsquigarrow \mathcal{T}'}{E \vdash \lfloor \textsc{module-type}(T, \mathcal{T}) \rfloor_{[]} : [T = \mathcal{T}']}$$

(DefSealedModule)
$$\frac{\begin{array}{c} E \vdash \lfloor ds \rfloor_{C[M]} : \mathcal{T}_{sub} \\ E \vdash \lfloor \mathcal{T} \rfloor_{C[M]} \rightsquigarrow \mathcal{T}_{super} \qquad \theta = \mathtt{msubsn}(\mathcal{T}_{sub}) \qquad \mathcal{T}_{sub} <: \theta\mathcal{T}_{super} \end{array}}{E \vdash \lfloor \textsc{module}(\texttt{[}M : \mathcal{T}\texttt{]}, ds) \rfloor_C : [M : \mathcal{T}_{super}]}$$

(DefCopyModule)
$$\frac{E \vdash \pi : \mathcal{T}}{E \vdash \lfloor \textsc{module}(M, \pi) \rfloor_C : [M : \mathcal{T}]}$$

(DefResealModule)
$$\frac{\begin{array}{c} E \vdash \pi : \mathcal{T}_{sub} \\ E \vdash \lfloor \mathcal{T} \rfloor_{C[M]} \rightsquigarrow \mathcal{T}_{super} \qquad \theta = \mathtt{msubsn}(\mathcal{T}_{sub}) \qquad \mathcal{T}_{sub} <: \theta\mathcal{T}_{super} \end{array}}{E \vdash \lfloor \textsc{module}(\texttt{[}M : \mathcal{T}\texttt{]}, \pi) \rfloor_C : [M : \mathcal{T}_{super}]}$$

(DefGenericModule)
$$\frac{\begin{array}{c} \mathcal{T}_g = \texttt{[}M_1 : \mathcal{T}_1\texttt{]} \times \cdots \times \texttt{[}M_k : \mathcal{T}_k\texttt{]} \xrightarrow{m} \mathcal{T} \\ E \vdash \lfloor \mathcal{T}_g \rfloor_{[]} \rightsquigarrow \mathcal{T}_g' \\ \mathcal{T}_g' = \texttt{[}M_1 : \mathcal{T}_1'\texttt{]} \times \cdots \times \texttt{[}M_k : \mathcal{T}_k'\texttt{]} \xrightarrow{m} \mathcal{T}' \\ \pi_b = (\texttt{@m}\ C[M]\ M_1\ \cdots\ M_k) \\ E, M_1 : \mathcal{T}_1', \ldots, M_k : \mathcal{T}_k' \vdash \lfloor ds \rfloor_{\pi_b} : \mathcal{T}_b \\ \theta = \mathtt{msubsn}(\mathcal{T}_b) \qquad \mathcal{T}_b <: \theta\mathcal{T}' \end{array}}{E \vdash \lfloor \textsc{generic-module}(\texttt{[}M : \mathcal{T}_g\texttt{]}, ds) \rfloor_C : [M : \mathcal{T}_g']}$$

(b) Module-layer definition forms

$$\boxed{E \vdash \lfloor ds \rfloor_\pi : \mathcal{T}}$$

$$\frac{E \vdash \lfloor ds \rfloor_\pi : Ds}{E \vdash \lfloor ds \rfloor_\pi : \textsc{exports}(Ds)}$$

$$\boxed{E \vdash \lfloor ds \rfloor_\pi : Ds}$$

$$\frac{}{E \vdash \lfloor\,\rfloor_\pi : [\,]}$$

(NonemptyDefs)
$$\frac{\begin{array}{c} E \vdash \lfloor d \rfloor_{\pi.[]} : Ds' \\ E, Ds' \vdash \lfloor ds \rfloor_\pi : Ds'' \\ \mathrm{dom}(\mathcal{C}(Ds)) \cap \mathrm{dom}(Ds'') = \emptyset \end{array}}{E \vdash \lfloor d, ds \rfloor_\pi : \mathcal{C}(Ds), Ds''}$$

(c) Sequences of definitions

Figure 9.18: Typing rules for definitions

$$\boxed{E \vdash \pi : \mathcal{T}} \qquad \frac{E \ni \pi : \lfloor \mathcal{T}' \rfloor_{\pi'}}{E \vdash \pi : \mathcal{T}'/\pi'}$$

$$\begin{aligned}(\mathcal{T}_1 \wedge \mathcal{T}_2)/\pi &= \mathcal{T}_1/\pi \wedge \mathcal{T}_2/\pi \\ \text{EXPORTS}(Ds)/\pi &= \text{EXPORTS}(Ds/\pi) \\ []/\pi &= [] \\ (D, Ds)/\pi &= D/\pi, Ds/\pi\end{aligned} \qquad \begin{aligned}(t = \tau)/\pi &= (t = \tau) \\ (t :: \lfloor * \rfloor_{\pi'})/\pi &= (t = \pi.t) \\ (x : \tau)/\pi &= x : \tau \\ (M : \mathcal{T})/\pi &= x : \mathcal{T}/\pi.M\end{aligned}$$

Figure 9.19: Strengthening module types and components

checked in the context Intlist.[ ]. That context makes the type's absolute access path Intlist.t.

570. ⟨*transcript* 530b⟩+≡ ◁567 593▷

```
-> (module [Intlist : (exports [abstype t] [Nil : t] [Cons : (int t -> t)])]
      (data t
         [Nil : t]
         [Cons : (int t -> t)]))
module Intlist :
  (exports
    [abstype t]
    [Nil : Intlist.t]
    [Cons : (Int.t Intlist.t -> Intlist.t)])
```

Definitions are checked by the rules shown in Figure 9.18. Because there are a lot of definition forms, there are a lot of rules; part (a) shows rules for just the core-layer forms. Rule DEFVAL resembles the VAL rule for Typed μScheme; expression e is typechecked to have type τ, and the result binding list Ds is the singleton list $[x : \tau]$. In other words, $x : \tau$ is produced as a binding (and a component).

Unlike VAL forms, VAL-REC and TYPE forms include types in the syntax, and those types have to be checked. A type is checked by a judgment of the form $E \vdash \tau \rightsquigarrow \tau'$, where type τ is the type written in the syntax and τ' is the internal representation used in the type checker. The judgment, pronounced "τ elaborates to τ'," produces τ' by expanding all the type abbreviations found in τ, and it also checks that τ is well formed. Elaboration, which is presented in the next section, subsumes the kind checking used in Typed μScheme (judgment $\Delta \vdash \tau :: *$).

With the understanding that types have to be elaborated, rules DEFVALREC and DEFTYPE are otherwise similar to DEFVAL: each rule produces one binding.

In part (b), on module-layer definition forms, the DEFMODTYPE rule resembles the DEFTYPE rule. The elaboration of a module type is more involved than the elaboration of a type, and it too is discussed in the next section. And there's one more subtlety: a MODULE-TYPE definition typechecks only when evaluated in the empty context [ ]. That requirement ensures that module types may be defined only at top level.

The remaining rules typecheck module definitions. The main rule is DEF-SEALEDMODULE: a module M is sealed with interface $\mathcal{T}$ and defined by a sequence of definitions ds. Above the line, the first judgment $E \vdash \lfloor ds \rfloor_{C[M]} : \mathcal{T}_{sub}$ says that the principal type of the implementation is $\mathcal{T}_{sub}$. Next, the interface type is elaborated to produce internal representation $\mathcal{T}_{super}$. Then, as described in the previous section, the interface type is *realized* by substituting for every manifest type in $\mathcal{T}_{sub}$. Provided the principal type is a subtype of the realized interface type, the module definition is well typed, and a binding is produced that associates the module with its (unrealized) interface type, *not* with its principal type. This step, in this rule, is where a manifest type inside M is converted to an abstract type outside—it's where data abstraction happens.

Rules DEFCOPYMODULE and DEFRESEALMODULE are similar, except the module's body is obtained not from a sequence of definitions but from another module named at path π. Judgment $E \vdash \pi : \mathcal{T}_{sub}$ says that the module at π has principal type $\mathcal{T}_{sub}$, and that type is obtained in two steps: first the path π is looked up in the environment, and then the type of the module at that path is *strengthened.* Strengthening converts every abstract type into a type that is manifestly equal to itself (Figure 9.19, on the facing page). The strengthening transformation is used in the single rule for judgment $E \vdash \pi : \mathcal{T}$; both are shown in Figure 9.19.

Rule DEFGENERICMODULE looks complicated, but it's more of the same. A generic module has to have a module-arrow type, and that type is elaborated to produce the internal representations of the argument types $\mathcal{T}'_1, \ldots, \mathcal{T}'_k$ and the result type $\mathcal{T}'$. The body of the module ds is checked at path π_b, which is the path formed by instantiating the module at its formal parameters. (When the module is instantiated, the formal parameters are replaced by the absolute access paths of the actual parameters.) And the body is checked in an extended environment, which has access to the formal parameters. Finally, in the usual way, the body's principal type $\mathcal{T}_b$ is checked to make sure it delivers everything demanded by interface type $\mathcal{T}'$. If all is well, the generic module typechecks with the module type claimed for it, and a binding is produced with that type. Because a generic module appears only at top level, this binding won't ever be converted to a component.

Figure 9.18c shows how to check a sequence of definitions in the body of a module. The principal type of a sequence of a definitions is always an EXPORTS type, and definitions are checked one at a time. The key rule is rule NONEMPTYDEFS, which checks definitions $\lfloor d, ds \rfloor_\pi$ at path π. Definition d is checked first, and the resulting bindings Ds' are added to the environment that is used to check the remaining definitions ds. But not everything in Ds' necessarily contributes a component. The sequence of bindings Ds' is converted into a sequence of components by function $\mathcal{C}$, which is defined as follows:

$$\begin{aligned}
\mathcal{C}([\,]) &= [\,] \\
\mathcal{C}(t = \tau, Ds) &= t = \tau, \mathcal{C}(Ds) \\
\mathcal{C}(x : \tau, Ds) &= x : \tau, \mathcal{C}(Ds) \\
\mathcal{C}(M : \lfloor \mathcal{T} \rfloor_\pi, Ds) &= M : \mathcal{T}, \mathcal{C}(Ds) \\
\mathcal{C}(x \in [\tau_1, \ldots, \tau_n], Ds) &= \mathcal{C}(Ds).
\end{aligned}$$

The rule has a side condition: a module may not have duplicate components. This condition is enforced by the premise $\mathrm{dom}(\mathcal{C}(Ds')) \cap \mathrm{dom}(Ds'') = \emptyset$. In my implementation, this condition is relaxed: a value component—and only a value component—may be redefined. Redefining a function can be useful when debugging.

9.8.6 *Elaborating types and module types*

As in Typed μScheme and μML, type syntax written in a program must be validated. Because every type in Molecule has kind $*$, validation is less involved than in Typed μScheme or μML: it suffices if every path is well formed and refers to a type. And if such a path begins with an instance of a generic module, the module must be instantiated correctly. Molecule's type checker not only validates syntax but also translates it into internal form: it replaces each type abbreviation with its

$$\boxed{E \vdash \tau \rightsquigarrow \tau'} \qquad \frac{E \vdash \tau_i \rightsquigarrow \tau_i', \quad 1 \le i \le n \qquad E \vdash \tau \rightsquigarrow \tau'}{E \vdash \tau_1 \times \cdots \times \tau_n \to \tau \rightsquigarrow \tau_1' \times \cdots \times \tau_n' \to \tau'}$$

$$\frac{E \ni t = \tau}{E \vdash t \rightsquigarrow \tau} \qquad \frac{E \ni \pi.t = \tau}{E \vdash \pi.t \rightsquigarrow \tau}$$

(a) Elaboration of types

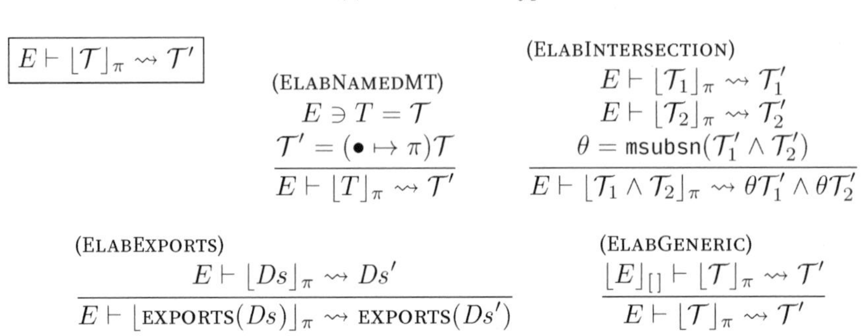

$$\boxed{E \vdash \lfloor \mathcal{T} \rfloor_\pi \rightsquigarrow \mathcal{T}'}$$

$$\text{(ElabNamedMT)}\ \frac{E \ni T = \mathcal{T} \quad \mathcal{T}' = (\bullet \mapsto \pi)\mathcal{T}}{E \vdash \lfloor T \rfloor_\pi \rightsquigarrow \mathcal{T}'} \qquad \text{(ElabIntersection)}\ \frac{E \vdash \lfloor \mathcal{T}_1 \rfloor_\pi \rightsquigarrow \mathcal{T}_1' \quad E \vdash \lfloor \mathcal{T}_2 \rfloor_\pi \rightsquigarrow \mathcal{T}_2' \quad \theta = \texttt{msubsn}(\mathcal{T}_1' \wedge \mathcal{T}_2')}{E \vdash \lfloor \mathcal{T}_1 \wedge \mathcal{T}_2 \rfloor_\pi \rightsquigarrow \theta\mathcal{T}_1' \wedge \theta\mathcal{T}_2'}$$

$$\text{(ElabExports)}\ \frac{E \vdash \lfloor Ds \rfloor_\pi \rightsquigarrow Ds'}{E \vdash \lfloor \text{EXPORTS}(Ds) \rfloor_\pi \rightsquigarrow \text{EXPORTS}(Ds')} \qquad \text{(ElabGeneric)}\ \frac{\lfloor E \rfloor_{[]} \vdash \lfloor \mathcal{T} \rfloor_\pi \rightsquigarrow \mathcal{T}'}{E \vdash \lfloor \mathcal{T} \rfloor_\pi \rightsquigarrow \mathcal{T}'}$$

(b) Elaboration of module types

$$\boxed{E \vdash \lfloor Ds \rfloor_\pi \rightsquigarrow Ds'} \qquad \frac{}{E \vdash \lfloor\, \rfloor_\pi \rightsquigarrow []} \qquad \frac{E \vdash \lfloor D \rfloor_\pi \rightsquigarrow D' \quad E, \mathcal{B}(\lfloor D' \rfloor_\pi) \vdash \lfloor Ds \rfloor_\pi \rightsquigarrow Ds' \quad \mathrm{dom}(D) \cap \mathrm{dom}(Ds) = \emptyset}{E \vdash \lfloor D, Ds \rfloor_\pi \rightsquigarrow D', Ds'}$$

$$\boxed{E \vdash \lfloor D \rfloor_\pi \rightsquigarrow D'} \qquad \frac{}{E \vdash \lfloor t :: * \rfloor_\pi \rightsquigarrow t :: \lfloor * \rfloor_{\pi.t}} \qquad \frac{E \vdash \tau \rightsquigarrow \tau'}{E \vdash \lfloor t = \tau \rfloor_\pi \rightsquigarrow t = \tau'}$$

$$\frac{E \vdash \tau \rightsquigarrow \tau'}{E \vdash \lfloor x : \tau \rfloor_\pi \rightsquigarrow x : \tau'} \qquad \text{(ElabSubmodule)}\ \frac{E \vdash \lfloor \mathcal{T} \rfloor_{\pi.M} \rightsquigarrow \mathcal{T}'}{E \vdash \lfloor M : \mathcal{T} \rfloor_\pi \rightsquigarrow M : \mathcal{T}'}$$

(c) Elaboration of declarations

$$\boxed{\lfloor E \rfloor_{\pi s} \vdash \lfloor \mathcal{T} \rfloor_\pi \rightsquigarrow \mathcal{T}'}$$

(ElabGenericArg)

$$\frac{\begin{array}{c} n > 0 \qquad E \vdash \lfloor \mathcal{T}_1 \rfloor_\pi \rightsquigarrow \mathcal{T}_1' \\ \lfloor E, \pi.M_1 : \mathcal{T}_1' \rfloor_{\pi s, M_1} \vdash \lfloor (M_2 : \mathcal{T}_2) \times \cdots \times (M_n : \mathcal{T}_n) \xrightarrow{m} \mathcal{T} \rfloor_\pi \rightsquigarrow \\ (M_2 : \mathcal{T}_2') \times \cdots \times (M_n : \mathcal{T}_n') \xrightarrow{m} \mathcal{T}' \end{array}}{\begin{array}{c} \lfloor E \rfloor_{\pi s} \vdash \lfloor (M_1 : \mathcal{T}_1) \times \cdots \times (M_n : \mathcal{T}_n) \xrightarrow{m} \mathcal{T} \rfloor_\pi \rightsquigarrow \\ (M_1 : \mathcal{T}_1') \times \cdots \times (M_n : \mathcal{T}_n') \xrightarrow{m} \mathcal{T}' \end{array}}$$

$$\text{(ElabGenericResult)}\ \frac{E \vdash \lfloor \mathcal{T} \rfloor_{(\texttt{@m}\ \pi\ \pi s)} \rightsquigarrow \mathcal{T}'}{\lfloor E \rfloor_{\pi s} \vdash \lfloor \xrightarrow{m} \mathcal{T} \rfloor_\pi \rightsquigarrow \xrightarrow{m} \mathcal{T}'}$$

(d) Elaboration of generic module types

Figure 9.20: Elaboration

$\boxed{\mathcal{B}(\lfloor D \rfloor_\pi) = D'}$

$$\mathcal{B}(\lfloor t = \tau \rfloor_\pi) = t = \tau$$
$$\mathcal{B}(\lfloor t :: \lfloor * \rfloor_{\pi'} \rfloor_\pi) = t = \pi'$$
$$\mathcal{B}(\lfloor x : \tau \rfloor_\pi) = x : \tau$$
$$\mathcal{B}(\lfloor x : \mathcal{T} \rfloor_\pi) = x : \lfloor \mathcal{T} \rfloor_\pi$$

(abstract component becomes manifest)

Figure 9.21: Conversion of component to binding

referent and each relative access path with the corresponding absolute access path. This kind of translation is called *elaboration*. If a module type is elaborated successfully, it is well formed.

Types are elaborated by the rules shown in Figure 9.20a (on the facing page). A function type is elaborated structurally, and a path is elaborated by looking it up in the environment. Lookup, whose judgment form is $E \ni D$, is specified in Figure 9.22 (page 574).

Module types, in Figure 9.20b, are more involved. They are elaborated by judgment form $\boxed{E \vdash \lfloor \mathcal{T} \rfloor_\pi \rightsquigarrow \mathcal{T}'}$, which requires an absolute path π as a context. In rule ELABNAMEDMT, this path is used to "re-root" module types and abstract types that aren't yet associated with any absolute path. Such types come from module-type abbreviations $T = \mathcal{T}$. The other rules are primarily structural, but some rules have fine points or entail additional transformations:

- When an intersection type $\mathcal{T}_1 \wedge \mathcal{T}_2$ is elaborated, any exported type that is manifest in *either* module type is made manifest in *both* types, using `msubsn`. Intersection is typically used to refine the result type of a generic module; for example, in the definition of the `ArrayHeap` module in chunk 552a, the elaboration of the intersection type converts the result's abstract type `elem` into a type that is manifestly equal to `Elem.t`.

- When the structural elaboration works its way down to an EXPORTS type (rule ELABEXPORTS), the exported declarations are elaborated one by one in sequence (Figure 9.20c). Once a declaration is elaborated, it is also added to the environment, for which purpose it is converted to a binding. Each definition is converted by function $\mathcal{B}$, which treats every abstract type as an abbreviation for its absolute access path (Figure 9.21). For example, when module type `2DPOINT` is elaborated (chunk 531a), the abstract type `t` is first added to the environment as an abbreviation for its absolute access path `•.t`. Next, when declaration for `new` is elaborated, it gets type `(Int.t Int.t -> •.t)`.

- A sequence of declarations elaborates successfully only if it contains no duplicates. This condition is enforced in Figure 9.20c by the condition $\mathrm{dom}(D) \cap \mathrm{dom}(Ds) = \emptyset$.

- When the declaration of a nested module M is elaborated, the type system tracks the absolute access path of its type $\mathcal{T}$ by extending the context to $\pi.M$ (rule ELABSUBMODULE).

Elaborating a module-arrow type requires some extra context. In judgments of the form $\boxed{\lfloor E \rfloor_{\pi s} \vdash \lfloor \mathcal{T} \rfloor_\pi \rightsquigarrow \mathcal{T}'}$, the list of paths πs names the formal parameters. This list is accumulated in rule ELABGENERICARG, and in rule ELABGENERICRESULT, the qualified name (`@m` π `πs`) is used to re-root the result type.

$\boxed{E \ni D}$

$$\frac{\text{dom}(E') \cap \text{dom}(D) = \emptyset}{E, D, E' \ni D} \quad \text{(LOOKUPBINDING)}$$

$$\frac{E \ni \pi : \lfloor \mathcal{T} \rfloor_{\pi'} \qquad t = \tau \in \texttt{comps}(\mathcal{T})}{E \ni \pi.t = \tau} \quad \text{(LOOKUPMANIFESTTYPECOMPONENT)}$$

$$\frac{E \ni \pi : \lfloor \mathcal{T} \rfloor_{\pi'} \qquad t :: \lfloor * \rfloor_{\pi''} \in \texttt{comps}(\mathcal{T})}{E \ni \pi.t = \pi''} \quad \text{(LOOKUPABSTRACTTYPECOMPONENT)}$$

$$\frac{E \ni \pi : \lfloor \mathcal{T} \rfloor_{\pi'} \qquad x : \tau \in \texttt{comps}(\mathcal{T})}{E \ni \pi.x : \tau} \quad \text{(LOOKUPVALUECOMPONENT)}$$

$$\frac{E \ni \pi : \lfloor \mathcal{T} \rfloor_{\pi'} \qquad M : \lfloor \mathcal{T}' \rfloor_{\pi''} \in \texttt{comps}(\mathcal{T})}{E \ni \pi.M : \lfloor \mathcal{T}' \rfloor_{\pi''}} \quad \text{(LOOKUPMODULECOMPONENT)}$$

(LOOKUPINSTANCE)

$$\frac{\begin{array}{c} E \ni \pi : (M_1 : \mathcal{T}_1') \times \cdots \times (M_n : \mathcal{T}_n') \xrightarrow{m} \mathcal{T}' \\ E \vdash \pi_i : \mathcal{T}_i, \quad 1 \leq i \leq n \\ ((M_1 : \mathcal{T}_1') \times \cdots \times (M_n : \mathcal{T}_n') \xrightarrow{m} \mathcal{T}')@(\pi_1 : \mathcal{T}_1 \cdots \pi_n : \mathcal{T}_n) : \mathcal{T}'' \end{array}}{E \ni (\texttt{@m}\ \pi\ \pi_1\ \cdots\ \pi_n) : \lfloor \mathcal{T}'' \rfloor_{(\texttt{@m}\ \pi\ \pi_1\ \cdots\ \pi_n)}}$$

$$\boxed{((M_1 : \mathcal{T}_1') \times \cdots \times (M_n : \mathcal{T}_n') \xrightarrow{m} \mathcal{T}')@(\pi_1 : \mathcal{T}_1 \cdots \pi_n : \mathcal{T}_n) : \mathcal{T}''}$$

(INSTANTIATE)

$$\frac{\begin{array}{c} \theta_m = \texttt{msubsn}(\mathcal{T}_1) \qquad \theta_r = (M_1 \mapsto \pi_1) \qquad \mathcal{T}_1 <: \theta_m(\theta_r \mathcal{T}_1') \\ ((M_2 : \theta_r \mathcal{T}_2') \times \cdots \times (M_n : \theta_r \mathcal{T}_n') \xrightarrow{m} \theta_m(\theta_r \mathcal{T}'))@(\pi_2 : \mathcal{T}_2 \cdots \pi_n : \mathcal{T}_n) : \mathcal{T}'' \end{array}}{((M_1 : \mathcal{T}_1') \times \cdots \times (M_n : \mathcal{T}_n') \xrightarrow{m} \mathcal{T}')@(\pi_1 : \mathcal{T}_1 \cdots \pi_n : \mathcal{T}_n) : \mathcal{T}''}$$

$$\frac{}{(\xrightarrow{m} \mathcal{T}'')@() : \mathcal{T}''}$$

Figure 9.22: Path lookup in the environment (D stands for a binding)

And when a module-arrow type is elaborated, the first formal parameter M_1 may be referred to in the types of any of the subsequent formal parameters or in the type of the result. In rule ELABGENERICMT, after $\mathcal{T}_1$ is elaborated to $\mathcal{T}_1'$, the arrow type is elaborated in an environment extended with the binding $\pi.M_1 : \mathcal{T}_1'$.

9.8.7 *Environment lookup and instantiation of generic modules*

As shown in Figure 9.13 (page 562), a name in an environment may be bound to a type abbreviation, a value, a module, a module type, or a set of overloaded types. A name is looked up just as in any other chapter: lookup finds the most recent binding in the environment. But in this chapter, lookup isn't written $E(t) = \tau$ or $E(x) = \tau$; such notation would make it hard to distinguish a type binding from a value binding. Instead, lookup is written using a containment relation like $E \ni t = \tau$ or $E \ni x : \tau$, or in the general case $E \ni D$.[4] The $\ni$ notation has another advantage: it can be extended to describe the result of looking up an access path in the current environment—which is what is meant by a *relative* access path. Environment lookup is described by the rules in Figure 9.22 (on the facing page). Rule LOOKUPBINDING describes standard environment lookup: any binding D can be looked up by name, but it may not be superseded by a binding to its right (in E'). The next four rules describe lookup of a module component using its path, which may refer to a manifest type, an abstract type, a value, or a module. At lookup time, each abstract type is converted to a manifest type by making it manifestly equal to itself. (As noted in Figure 9.13, an abstract type may be a component but not a binding.)

Paths also include instances of generic modules, which are governed by the INSTANTIATE rule. When the generic module expects multiple parameters, the rule uses a crazy amount of substitution, but in the special case where the generic module expects just one parameter, the rule is simpler:

$$\text{(INSTANTIATEWITHONEPARAMETER)}\quad \frac{\begin{array}{cc} E \ni \pi : (M_1 : \mathcal{T}_1') \xrightarrow{m} \mathcal{T}' & E \vdash \pi_1 : \mathcal{T}_1 \\ \theta_r = (M_1 \mapsto \pi_1) & \theta_m = \mathtt{msubsn}(\mathcal{T}_1) \\ \mathcal{T}_1 <: \theta_m(\theta_r \mathcal{T}_1') & \mathcal{T}'' = \theta_m(\theta_r \mathcal{T}') \end{array}}{E \ni \mathtt{(@m}\ \pi\ \pi_1\mathtt{)} : \lfloor \mathcal{T}'' \rfloor_{\mathtt{(@m}\ \pi\ \pi_1\mathtt{)}}}.$$

The specialized rule works like this:

- The module being instantiated is π, and it has a module-arrow type with one formal parameter M_1 of type $\mathcal{T}_1'$. The actual parameter π_1 has type $\mathcal{T}_1$.

- The module type of the formal parameter, $\mathcal{T}_1'$, can include references to type components of that parameter. For example, in the generic module `ArrayHeap` defined in chunk 552a, the formal parameter is `Elem`, and type $\mathcal{T}_1'$ declares a value `<=` of type `(Elem.t Elem.t -> Bool.t)`. Module `ArrayHeap` can be instantiated with actual parameter `Int` only because `Int.t` and `Elem.t` are the same. The identity is demonstrated by "re-rooting" module type $\mathcal{T}_1'$ using substitution θ_r, which maps M_1 to π_1. In the example, it maps `Elem` to `Int`.

- Once the module type of the formal parameter is re-rooted, the actual parameter is checked using subtyping, just as when sealing. And as when sealing, θ_m substitutes for every manifest type in $\mathcal{T}_1$. In the example, the module type of the actual parameter, `Int`, doesn't have any manifest types, so θ_m is the identity substitution.

- Provided the subtyping test passes, the instantiated module has type $\mathcal{T}''$. Type $\mathcal{T}''$ is obtained by taking the result type $\mathcal{T}'$ from the module-arrow type, then substituting both for M_1 and for any manifest types that occur in $\mathcal{T}_1$. The substitution says, for example, that in module `(@m ArrayHeap Int)`, type `elem` is an abbreviation for type `Int.t`.

If the types of generic modules were curried, so that a generic module always took exactly one parameter, the special-case rule would be enough. Multi-parameter modules require more bureaucracy. Actual parameters $\pi_1, \ldots, \pi_n$ are checked one at a time against formal parameters $M_1, \ldots, M_n$. And the type components of actual parameter π_1 can be referred to not only in the result type $\mathcal{T}'$, but

[4] Here D stands for a binding, which resembles a declaration or component.

$\boxed{E \vdash \lfloor d \rfloor_C : Ds}$

$$\frac{E \vdash \pi.x : \tau \qquad E \text{ does not overload } x}{E \vdash \lfloor \text{OVERLOAD}(\pi.x) \rfloor_C : x \in [\tau]}$$

$$\frac{E \vdash \pi.x : \tau \qquad E \ni x \in [\tau_1, \ldots, \tau_k]}{E \vdash \lfloor \text{OVERLOAD}(\pi.x) \rfloor_C : x \in [\tau, \tau_1, \ldots, \tau_k]}$$

(a) Typing rules for `overload` definition

$\boxed{E \vdash e \rightsquigarrow e' : \tau}$

$$\frac{E \vdash e_i \rightsquigarrow e_i' : \tau_i, \ \ 1 \le i \le n \qquad E \ni x \in [\tau_1', \ldots, \tau_k'] \qquad \tau_j' = \tau_1 \times \cdots \times \tau_n \to \tau \qquad \nexists k : k < j \wedge \tau_k' = \tau_1 \times \cdots \times \tau'' \to \tau'''}{E \vdash \text{APPLY}(x, e_1, \ldots, e_n) \rightsquigarrow \text{APPLY}(x, e_1', \ldots, e_n')_j : \tau}$$

$$\frac{E \vdash e_i \rightsquigarrow e_i' : \tau_i, \ \ 1 \le i \le n \qquad E \ni x : \tau_1 \times \cdots \times \tau_n \to \tau}{E \vdash \text{APPLY}(e, e_1, \ldots, e_n) \rightsquigarrow \text{APPLY}(e, e_1', \ldots, e_n') : \tau}$$

(b) Elaboration of function application, with overloading

$\boxed{\langle e, \rho, \sigma \rangle \Downarrow \langle v, \sigma' \rangle}$

$$\frac{\begin{array}{c}\langle x, \rho, \sigma \rangle \Downarrow \langle [v_1, \ldots, v_k], \sigma \rangle \\ v_j = (\!|\text{LAMBDA}(\langle x_1, \ldots, x_n \rangle, e_c), \rho_c|\!) \\ \langle e_1, \rho, \sigma_0 \rangle \Downarrow \langle v_1, \sigma_1 \rangle \quad \cdots \quad \langle e_n, \rho, \sigma_{n-1} \rangle \Downarrow \langle v_n, \sigma_n \rangle \\ \ell_1, \ldots, \ell_n \notin \text{dom}\, \sigma_n \text{ (and all distinct)} \\ \langle e_c, \rho_c\{x_1 \mapsto \ell_1, \ldots, x_n \mapsto \ell_n\}, \sigma_n\{\ell_1 \mapsto v_1, \ldots, \ell_n \mapsto v_n\} \rangle \Downarrow \langle v, \sigma' \rangle\end{array}}{\langle \text{APPLY}(x, e_1, \ldots, e_n)_j, \rho, \sigma \rangle \Downarrow \langle v, \sigma' \rangle}$$

(c) Evaluation of overloaded application

Figure 9.23: Overloading

also in the types of later formal parameters M_2 to M_n. So after each actual parameter, substitutions θ_r and θ_m have to be applied not only to the result module type, but also to the remaining formal parameters. To apply those substitutions correctly requires an auxiliary judgment, which takes up the last two rules in Figure 9.22.

9.8.8 *Overloading*

Molecule's overloading is just a quick hack. In any given typing environment E, each overloaded name is associated with a sequence of types. In the evaluation environment ρ, that same name is associated with a sequence of values—one for each corresponding type. The associations are made, respectively, during the elaboration of and during the evaluation of an OVERLOAD definition. Elaboration is shown at the top of Figure 9.23: if name x is not already overloaded, the elaborator associates it with the singleton sequence τ. If x is already overloaded, the elaborator adds type τ to the existing sequence. Evaluation, which is not shown, works similarly.

At run time, an overloaded name is evaluated with the help of bread crumbs left by the type checker. Molecule's type checker checks expressions using rules that are essentially identical to the rules for Typed μScheme, and in addition, it decorates every application of an overloaded name. Decorations are added during elaboration, which is described by judgment $E \vdash e \rightsquigarrow e' : \tau$, pronounced "$e$ elaborates to e' and has type τ." If an overloaded name x is the function in an APPLY expression, the expression is decorated with an index j, which shows which overloaded type is selected for x.

A decoration is added to an APPLY node by the first rule in Figure 9.23b. Each actual parameter e_i is typechecked and decorated, and the possible types of x are enumerated as $[\tau'_1, \dots, \tau'_k]$. One of those types, τ'_j, is a function type whose first argument has type τ_1, which is the type of e_1. And the other e_i's have the types of the other arguments in type τ'_j. The final premise takes the *first* τ'_j whose first argument has type τ_1. This premise, or something like it, is needed to make the semantics deterministic. (For a better algorithm, see Exercise 51.)

If x is not overloaded, or if a function is applied that is not a simple name, then the second rule applies. This rule is like the rule for typechecking an application in Typed μScheme, except that each argument may be decorated.

When an APPLY expression is decorated with an index j, it is evaluated specially (Figure 9.23c). The overloaded name x evaluates to a *sequence* of values $[v_1, \dots, v_k]$: one for each type at which x was overloaded during the typechecking phase. The correct value v_j is selected by the decoration on the APPLY node. Assuming that v_j is a closure, as shown in the rule, evaluation proceeds as in Scheme or Typed μScheme.

The elaboration of expressions and definitions is ignored by the typing rules that appear earlier in this section. Those rules pretend that expressions and definitions need only to be typechecked, not decorated. The pretense amounts to the assumption of a rule like

$$\frac{E \vdash e \rightsquigarrow e' : \tau}{E \vdash e : \tau}.$$

But when a definition of the form $\text{VAL}(x, e)$ is typechecked in the interpreter, every expression is elaborated.

9.8.9 *Analysis of the design*

Molecule's type system works can usefully be compared with other type systems along three dimensions: polymorphism, generativity, and substitution.

How polymorphism works: Molecule and Typed μScheme compared

Typed μScheme, nano-ML, and Molecule demonstrate three approaches to statically typed polymorphism:

- In Typed μScheme, every type abstraction and instantiation is explicit. The resulting language is very expressive—polymorphism is *impredicative,* which means that a type variable can be instantiated with a polymorphic value. But the language is painful to use. It's especially painful to have to instantiate every polymorphic function before it can be used.

- In nano-ML, polymorphism is *predicative,* which means that a type variable may not be instantiated with a polymorphic value. Moreover, the argument to a function may not be polymorphic. The resulting language, while less expressive than Typed μScheme, is plenty expressive enough for many purposes. And it is a joy to use: the type checker automatically instantiates every polymorphic function at its point of use, and it even infers polymorphic types where possible.

- In Molecule, type abstraction is replaced by *module* abstraction (generic modules). And instantiation is done one module at a time, not one value at a time. Polymorphism is predicative, meaning that the argument to a generic module may not itself be generic. And the language is pleasant enough to use: once a generic module is instantiated, its functions can be used arbitrarily many times without further bureaucracy.

The relationship between Typed μScheme and Molecule warrants a more technical comparison.

- Both type systems have a function type (in the interpreters, `FUNTY`).
- Both type systems have type constructors of kind $*$. In Typed μScheme, a type constructor is represented by its name. In Molecule, a type constructor is represented by its absolute access path.
- Both type systems have abstract "type formers" of higher kinds, like "list" or "array." Such an abstraction is not a type by itself, but once supplied with actual parameters, it can produce a type. In Typed μScheme, the abstraction is a type constructor of kind $* \Rightarrow *$, or of any other kind with an arrow in it. In Molecule, the abstraction is a generic module—that is, a module whose module type has an arrow in it. In Typed μScheme, a type constructor produces a type when it is applied. In Molecule, a generic module produces a type when it is instantiated and a type component is selected from the instance. These constructions are analogous; for example, the Typed μScheme type `(array bool)` is analogous to the Molecule type `(@m Array Bool).t`.
- Both type systems can create a polymorphic value by abstracting over unknown types, and both enable code to refer to an unknown type by name. In Typed μScheme, a polymorphic value is introduced by a `type-lambda`, and the unknown type is named by a type variable written in the `type-lambda`. In Molecule, a polymorphic value is not introduced directly; instead, Molecule code introduces a generic module, then selects a value component. The unknown type is a type component of an unknown module, which is named by a formal module parameter in the generic module.

In effect, except for impredicative polymorphism, Molecule can do everything that Typed μScheme can do. And impredicative polymorphism is relatively easy to add, provided you avoid trying to intersect the types of generic modules (Leroy 2000).

Generativity

Molecule's module definitions are *generative*, in the sense explained in Section 8.5 (page 483): every module definition introduces new types, even if the module is defined with the same name as a previous module. Generativity is *not* expressed in Molecule's type system as it is presented in this section—to track it would require so much bookkeeping that the main ideas would be hard to follow. For that reason, the type system as presented is sound only under the assumption that every module has a distinct absolute access path. Under the covers, my implementation makes it so:

- A path may begin with a *module identifier* Y, which cannot be written in the syntax.
- The elaboration of a module definition introduces a fresh module identifier. A fresh module identifier is also introduced for each formal parameter of a generic module.
- During elaboration, every path that appears in the syntax is elaborated into an absolute path, which begins with a module identifier.

The uniqueness of the module identifiers ensures the uniqueness of every absolute access path, which makes module definitions generative and helps guarantee soundness.

An alternative design: Type checking without substitutions

Molecule enforces type abstraction by making sure that outside a module, an abstract type looks different from its definition—and types that look different always are different. When types look different but actually are the same, like `int` and `Int.t`. Molecule makes them the same via elaboration and substitution: `int` is replaced by `Int.t`; references to manifest types are replaced by their definitions; and when a generic module is instantiated, the formal parameters are replaced by the actual parameters. But substitution is nobody's favorite mechanism: it can be hard to get right, and when substitution is used in an inference rule, what it's doing is not always obvious. Substitution is a good choice for this chapter because it keeps the type system consistent with the type systems presented in Chapters 6 and 7, but a nice alternative is to define type equality and subtyping in a way that is not consistent with Chapters 6 and 7: they can depend on context.

This alternative, designed by Leroy (2000), extends the core-layer type system with a contextual type-equality judgment $E \vdash \tau \approx \tau'$, and it replaces the module-layer subtyping judgment with the judgment $E \vdash \mathcal{T} <: \mathcal{T}'$. These judgments have access to all the type equalities in environment E; for example, Molecule's initial environment E_0 supports the judgment $E_0 \vdash$ `int` $\approx$ `Int.t`. Making these judgments contextual enables Leroy's system to check ascriptions without substituting; for example, instead of extracting a substitution from the manifest-type declarations of a module, his system puts those declarations into E. The system is elegant, but its test for type equality is so different from the tests in Chapters 6 and 7 that it is a poor fit here.

9.9 Notes on the interpreter

As you might guess from the size of the type system, Molecule's interpreter is a beast; it's about the size of the interpreters for Typed μScheme and μML combined. But the type checker uses the same techniques that are used in Typed μScheme, and the evaluator uses the same techniques that are used in μML, so the code doesn't have much to teach you. The interpreter is therefore relegated to the Supplement. Should you choose to study it, its most salient aspects are as follows:

- Many syntactic forms have two representations: one for the form as it appears in the source code and one for the form as it appears after elaboration. They are, for example, `pathex` and `path`, `tyex` and `ty`, `modtyex` and `modty`, and so on.

- Expressions have only one representation; in that representation, the `APPLY` node includes a mutable cell. This cell holds the decoration, if any, that identifies the resolution of an overloaded name. Elaboration is implemented not by translating from one representation to another but by updating that cell.

- The implementation includes a type not shown in Section 9.8: type `ANYTYPE` is the type assigned to an `error` expression. Type `ANYTYPE` is uninhabited, so it is compatible with any type.

- In the implementation, unlike the type theory, declarations, components, and bindings have different representations: `decl`, `component`, and `binding`. In the theory, blurring the distinction simplifies the notation and makes the ideas easier to follow. In the code, enforcing the distinction helps me get the invariants right.

9.10 Abstract data types, modules, and overloading as they really are

Different languages provide abstract data types and modules in very different ways. To add to the potential confusion, many languages, including Java, C++, Modula-3, and Ada 95, combine abstract data types with objects. In this section, I stick to abstract data types: I enumerate some major design choices, I describe what I consider the best choices, and I describe a key mechanism that's not included in Molecule: exceptions. I also say a few words about overloading.

Major design choices

Designs for abstract types and modules vary along many dimensions. The important variations can be identified by a litany of questions. When you encounter a new language, the questions will help you understand what you're dealing with.

- *Can an interface be written (and compiled) separately from any implementation?* In the Modula family, Ada, Java, the ML family, and Molecule, yes. In CLU, Oberon, and Haskell, no. (This is the key question, about which I rant below.)

- *Can modules be generic?* In Modula-3, Ada, and the ML family, yes. In Modula-2, Oberon, and Haskell, no. (In C++, Java, and CLU, you will find some form of generics, but not exactly modules.)

- *Do generic modules support modular typechecking?* That is, can you typecheck a generic module and its arguments separately, then combine them? (If not, only instances can be typechecked.) In the ML family, Java, and Molecule, yes. In Modula-3 and Ada, no. And in C++, templates don't support modular typechecking.

- *Is instantiation generative?* That is, if a generic module is instantiated with the same arguments, in two different places, are the resulting instances different? In Ada, Modula-3, and Standard ML, yes. In OCaml and Molecule, no.

- *Can a module be defined without being sealed by an interface or an export list?* In Ada, CLU, the Modula family, Oberon, and Molecule, no. In Haskell and in the ML family, yes.

- *Can a module export manifest types as well as abstract types?* In CLU, no. In all subsequent languages, yes. (Modula-3 has an especially nifty mechanism, the *partial revelation*, which can expose *selected* information about a type.)

- *Does every module have a name?* In CLU, Ada, the Modula family, Oberon, Haskell, and Molecule, yes. In the ML family, no—modules can be anonymous.

- *Can modules nest?* In CLU, Ada, the Modula family, and Oberon, no. In the ML family and Molecule, yes. And in Haskell, a module cannot nest inside another module, but the name space of modules is hierarchical, which gives the appearance of nesting—and some of the same benefits. (When a system grows large, nested modules help programmers avoid naming conflicts.)

- *What are things called?* An interface has been called a "signature" (Standard ML and OCaml), a "module type" (Molecule and OCaml), a "definition module" (Modula family), a "package specification" (Ada), an "interface" (Java), and who knows what else. An implementation has been called a "structure" (Standard ML and OCaml), a "module" (Molecule and Haskell), an "implementation module" (Modula family), a "package body," (Ada), and who knows what else. A generic module has been called "generic" (Molecule, Modula–3, Ada) and a "functor" (Standard ML and OCaml).

In any given language, many of these questions will be answered differently than they are in Molecule, but experience with Molecule will still give you a feel for consequences. However, that experience won't teach you just how good generic modules are when they are paired with a polymorphic core layer, as in Standard ML and OCaml.

Choices to look for

The design choices that matter most are those that determine how you express or discover what operations a module exports. Can you work with a separately compiled interface, or do you have only the implementation? Ideally, you can write client code based only on an interface, and you don't need to look at an implementation. But there are trade-offs:

- When names, types, and other information are explicit in the interface, all the information needed to write client code is gathered in one place, and the cognitive load involved in understanding the interface is independent of the size of the implementation. I claim that when interfaces are defined in this style, you can work with larger systems than you could otherwise. Other designers agree; for example, the designers of Modula-3 write, "To keep large programs well structured, you either need super-human will power, or proper language support for interfaces" (Nelson 1991, §1.4.1).

- When there is no interface, only an implementation, there might still be a tool that extracts types from the implementation, perhaps even putting the results on Web pages; if you use C++ or Java, you may know Doxygen and Javadoc. Such tools help limit cognitive load, but I claim that they are still inferior to designs that enable programmers to *write* and *typecheck* interfaces separately. System design is interface design, and if you can't write an interface and have it checked by the compiler, you're missing a valuable design tool.

- While I favor separately compiled interfaces, I acknowledge that they come at a cost. The primary cost is that type information in the interface is often repeated in the implementation. Sometimes it is even repeated verbatim. I find this cost acceptable, but reasonable designers disagree.

Designers of popular languages are found in both camps—sometimes even a *single* designer is in both camps. For example, Java has had separately compiled interfaces from the beginning, but for many years C++ had only `.h` files, which mix details of interface and implementation. Twenty-five years after its introduction, however, C++ acquired "concepts," which constrain uses of C++ templates in somewhat the same way that module types constrain the instantiation of generic modules. (The template is a C++ mechanism that supports polymorphism—and much else besides.)

As another example, Niklaus Wirth, designer of Pascal, Modula-2, and Oberon, has made different choices at different times: standard Pascal has no modules or interfaces; Modula-2 has separately compiled interfaces; and Oberon has no interfaces, not even an export list. (In Oberon, exported names are those marked with a * in the implementation.)

The programming language Go makes a similar choice to Oberon: names beginning with capital letters are exported—but in Go it is also possible to declare an *interface type*, which enumerates operations associated with an abstract type.

Among popular functional languages, languages in the ML family work both ways: you can write interfaces if you want to, and where you don't, the compiler infers them. By contrast, Haskell works like CLU: exported names are listed, but information about their types must be gleaned from the implementation. Some of Haskell's designers regret this choice:

> Haskell 1.4 completely abandoned interfaces as a formal part of the language; instead, interface files were regarded as a possible artifact of separate compilation. As a result, Haskell sadly lacks a formally checked language in which a programmer can advertise the interface that the module supports (Hudak et al. 2007, §8.2).

Distinct, separate interfaces are a great starting point for any design. But I hope for more:

- In a good design, any implementation can be typechecked given only the interface it implements and the interfaces it depends on—without needing other implementations. This feature enables abstractions to be implemented from the top down. For example, if I am designing a Web application to search the text of this book, I should be able to describe the index using only an interface, then write the search module that uses the index, and finally the build module that creates the index. I should be able to refine my design without being required to implement the index abstraction. Why? Because if there is no implementation, I can change the interface at almost no cost—for example, if I decide that the search module needs to be able to ask the index about fragments of words, not just whole words, I just change the index interface. If an implementation were required, then every time I changed the interface, I might have to change the implementation to match.

  Independent typechecking is key, but an implementation doesn't have to be *compiled* independently of all the others. While independent compilation sounds nice, performance is often better when the compiler can look across module boundaries—to inline small functions, for example.

- If all implementations typecheck, it should be possible to compile and link them without any chance of a type error or other compile-time error.

- A single interface should admit of more than one implementation, and when I put together a program, I should be able to choose which implementation of each interface I wish to use.

These criteria are most likely to be met by a language that offers generic modules with modular type checking, like Molecule. And in practice, most statically typed languages intended for large-scale use meet most of these criteria—but I'm not aware of any language that does it all *well*. In most cases, meeting the criteria requires mechanisms that lie outside the programming language; for example, interfaces and implementations may be required to be stored in files with conventional names. Or as another example, a separate language may be required just to explain how modules should be linked together to form a program.

When computation can't continue: Exceptions

In one way, Molecule illustrates modules and abstract data types badly: it lacks *exceptions*. Exceptions give an operation a way to respond when it can't return a result. For example, if asked to look up a key in an empty dictionary or to produce the smallest element in an empty priority queue, an implementation can *raise* an exception. Molecule is limited to other responses: An operation can return a value of sum type, like the `option` type; it can halt with a checked run-time error; or it can invoke a failure continuation. Each of these alternatives causes problems for client code:

- If an operation returns a value of sum type, every client has to deconstruct it with `case`. That's a lot of `case` expressions. Plus, nothing inherent in a sum type suggests that one of the cases represents an important error, or that perhaps a special action is called for.

- If an operation halts, every client has to protect against the possibility. For example, every call to `delete-min` must be protected by a call to `empty?`.

- If an operation invokes a failure continuation, every client has to be written, at least a little, in continuation-passing style. Nobody wants to read that.

All three alternatives lead to annoying code, especially in a language without first-class, nested functions.[5]

Languages like C, C++, Java, and Modula-3 offer another alternative: because abstractions are represented by pointers, an operation with no other recourse can often return a null pointer. In Molecule, CLU, Haskell, and ML, by contrast, there is no such thing as a null pointer. We should be grateful; Tony Hoare, the inventor of the null pointer, called it a "billion-dollar mistake" (Hoare 2009). Exceptions are better.

Exceptions appear in many major languages, including Ada, C++, Haskell, Java, ML, and Modula-3. Exceptions are typically supported by two syntactic forms, variously called `raise` and `handle`, `signal` and `except`, `throw` and `try-catch` (Section 3.2.2, page 207), or similar names. The `handle`/`except`/`try-catch` form defines a *handler*, inside of which code is evaluated. When a `raise` is evaluated, it terminates the evaluation of an expression, statement, or code block, and it transfers control to the nearest enclosing handler. If the `raise` is not enclosed in a handler in its own function, then it terminates the evaluation of its function and looks for a handler in the caller. If the call site isn't enclosed in a suitable handler, then the caller is terminated as well, and this computation—*unwinding* the call stack—continues until it reaches a call site that is enclosed in a suitable handler.

As an example, interpreters from Chapter 5 onward raise the `RuntimeError` exception in many places, and in each case, the call stack is unwound until control

[5]If you have true higher-order functions, you can design a lot of code around a polymorphic `error` type like the one in Appendix H, and some of the suffering caused by working with sum types can be mitigated by higher-order functions like >>= and >>=+, which are defined there.

reaches the handler in the read-eval-print loop. At that point, the read-eval-print loop prints an error message, and evaluation continues with the next definition.

Exceptions have been used in different ways at different times. Exceptions as we know them originated with CLU, but CLU imposed two restrictions that we would find severe today: in CLU, the set of exceptions a function can raise must be enumerated in that function's type, and every exception that a function might raise must be handled by its caller. These restrictions enabled a remarkably efficient implementation: Adding a handler to a statement entailed no cost at run time, and raising an exception, at least on machines of the day, cost barely more than using `return`. In particular, an exception could be raised without having to allocate anything on the heap.

CLU's exceptions were intended for more than just errors; they were recommended to be used to ensure that every operation does something well-defined on every argument in its domain. For example, exceptions were used to indicate such ordinary, non-error situations as hitting end of file on input, not finding a name in an environment, or trying to choose a value from an empty set.

Things have changed. While in some languages the exceptions a function can raise are still part of its type, we no longer require every caller to handle every possible exception. And raising an exception has gotten more expensive—for example, the designers of Modula-3 recommend to spend a thousand instructions per exception raised if that expenditure will save one instruction per procedure call (Nelson 1991). Moreover, *attitudes* have changed. Many respected programmers believe that exceptions should be reserved for truly exceptional events. I personally find that routine use of exceptions leads to cleaner interfaces, but I know that the cost models aren't what they were in CLU. If I intend to use exceptions routinely, I pay close attention to costs.

Overloading as it really is

From the time there has been floating-point arithmetic, language designers have wanted operators like + to mean *either* integer or floating-point arithmetic, depending on the types of arguments. Early designs were *ad hoc* and often unsatisfying; for examples, look no further than the two implementation languages of this book: C and Standard ML.

In the 1970s, CLU took a nice step forward: CLU uses overloading to *define* a whole bunch of syntactic forms—including not only infix operators but also dot notation and assignment statements—as notations for function application. CLU's notations work equally well with both built-in types and user-defined types; CLU overloads a fixed set of syntactic forms, each of which takes a fixed number of arguments, by dispatching each one to a well-known qualified name, as determined by the type of the first argument. For example, an expression of the form e_1 + e_2 is rewritten to function call M.add(e_1, e_2), where M is the module that defines the type of e_1. CLU's mechanism inspired the algorithm I use in Molecule.

In 1981, Ada extended overloading to include not just a fixed set of syntactic forms (often called "operator overloading") but also user-defined functions (often called "function overloading," or in Ada jargon, "subprogram overloading"). Ada's overloading was notable for two innovations: first, user-defined functions could be overloaded not just based on the *types* of the arguments but also on the *number* of arguments—something not necessary when overloading a syntactic form like *exp* + *exp*, which always has exactly two subexpressions. Second, and more startling, functions could be overloaded based on their *result types*, enabling the context in which a call appears to influence what function is called. Ada's ideas for overloading were adapted for use in both C++ and Java, although neither C++ nor Java supports overloading based on a result type.

In the 1990s, Haskell adopted a mechanism proposed by Wadler and Blott (1989): functions are overloaded using *type classes*. A type class can be used to overload any name; because a Haskell "operator" is just an ordinary function name written in infix notation, type classes provide both operator overloading and function overloading. Type classes defy simple description, but their most important element is a relation that says "this type implements this operation using this function." The relation is established using an *instance declaration*; for example, an instance declaration can be used to establish that machine integers implement + using a primitive function, while complex numbers implement + using a function that independently adds the real and imaginary parts. Crucially, an instance declaration takes the form of an inference rule; for example, Haskell includes a rule that says, in effect, that if τ is a type that implements `print`, then "list of τ" is also a type that implements `print`. The rule also says how to construct the `print` function for a list of τ. Type classes are worth mastering; the ability to tell the compiler to construct new functions by combining inference rules has had implications far beyond the original goals of overloading. For a nice example, see Claessen and Hughes (2000).

9.11 SUMMARY

Abstract data types as we know them are descended from CLU, whose designers' goal was "to provide programmers with a tool that would enhance their effectiveness in constructing programs of high quality—programs that are reliable and reasonably easy to understand, modify, and maintain" (Liskov et al. 1977). Abstract data types and modules separate concerns and hide information, limiting the scope of modifications.

By focusing attention on abstractions and their operations, not representations, abstract data types and modules make programs relatively easy to understand. Ideally, focus can be directed by an explicit interface, like a module type, which can be written, read, and typechecked independently of any implementation that it describes.

Any form of abstract data type has a public name but a private representation. Access to the representation is limited to operations defined inside some sort of syntactic "capsule," like a module. But within the capsule, each operation can inspect the representation of every argument of the abstract type. And because access is granted by type, defining an operation that takes multiple abstract arguments—like the sum of two arbitrary-precision integers or the merge of two leftist heaps—is easy.

The major limitation of abstract data types is that every access is controlled by a static type, and every representation is fixed by a static type. Strict access control means that different implementations of similar abstractions do not interoperate; for example, a machine integer cannot be added to an arbitrary-precision integer. Interoperation is possible only if a programmer inserts explicit coercions. And a new representation can be added to an existing abstraction only by modifying the source code, which may change the cost model or even the interface.

9.11.1 *Key words and phrases*

ABSTRACT DATA TYPE A form of DATA ABSTRACTION that operates using a static type system. An abstract data type has a public name and a private REPRESENTATION. The representation is visible only inside a syntactic "capsule," like a MODULE. Operations defined within the capsule have access to the representation of *any* value of the abstract type.

ABSTRACTION A thing in the world of ideas, or its realization in the computer as a value of ABSTRACT DATA TYPE. An abstraction is often specified by appeal to mathematical objects like sets, sequences, and finite maps, but it can also be specified by axioms or by algebraic laws, or even informal English.

ABSTRACTION FUNCTION A map from a REPRESENTATION to the ABSTRACTION it is supposed to represent. The abstraction function is defined only on values that satisfy the REPRESENTATION INVARIANT. Explicit thinking about abstractions and abstraction functions helps programmers get their code right. An abstraction function can also be used to help prove code correct.

API All the information needed to write CLIENT code that uses an ABSTRACTION. Not just a list of exported operations and their types, an API also says how each operation behaves and when it is permissible to use it. Also called a COMPLETE API.

CLIENT Code that uses the operations of an ABSTRACTION and does not have access to the abstraction's REPRESENTATION.

DATA ABSTRACTION The practice of characterizing data by its operations and their specifications, not by its REPRESENTATION.

ENCAPSULATION A term with disputed meaning. Variously used to mean "information hiding," "data abstraction," or "programming-language mechanism for enforcing information hiding or data abstraction." Useful primarily because it includes the idea of a syntactic CAPSULE within which a representation is exposed. Capsules are provided in various languages by constructs called `cluster` (CLU), `class` (Simula 67, Smalltalk), `module` (Modula-2, Modula-3, OCaml), `form` (Alphard), and `package` (Ada).

GENERIC MODULE A polymorphic MODULE that can be specialized or instantiated by providing one or more argument modules. Especially useful for general-purpose, reusable data structures.

IMPLEMENTATION Code that implements the operations of an ABSTRACTION and has access to the abstraction's REPRESENTATION.

INFORMATION HIDING A principle that encourages designers to build systems from parts whose awareness of each other is limited. Limiting awareness limits dependencies and makes systems easier to change. Awareness of REPRESENTATION is limited by DATA ABSTRACTION.

INTERFACE The primary unit of design: Separately compiled syntax that specifies whatever properties of an ABSTRACTION are needed to get CLIENT code to typecheck. In Molecule, an interface is a MODULE TYPE, which gives names and types of the exported operations, plus the types of any nested modules. "Interface" is also used to mean a complete API.

INVARIANT A REPRESENTATION INVARIANT or a LOOP INVARIANT.

LOOP INVARIANT A property of program state—typically the states of program variables and of mutable abstractions—that is true on every iteration of a loop. The loop's body guarantees that if the invariant holds at the beginning of the body's execution, the invariant continues to hold at the end of the body's execution. The guarantee can rely on the truth of the loop's guard.

MODULE The primary unit of implementation: A container that can ENCAPSULATE auxiliary definitions and knowledge of REPRESENTATION, hiding them from CLIENT code.

MODULE TYPE The formal construct that describes an INTERFACE in Molecule or OCaml. Analogous constructs in other languages include Java interfaces, Modula definition modules, Ada package specifications, and Standard ML signatures.

OBJECT-ORIENTATION A form of DATA ABSTRACTION that operates by bundling operations with shared state, which is usually mutable (Chapter 10).

RELY-GUARANTEE REASONING A method of ensuring that a REPRESENTATION INVARIANT holds. Each operation relies on the property that when the operation starts, the invariant holds true of every value of the type. And each operation guarantees that on exit from the operation, the property holds once again. But during the execution of an operation, a representation invariant may be *temporarily* invalidated.

REPRESENTATION How an ABSTRACTION is realized or represented on a computer. In Molecule, as well as in other statically typed languages, a representation is specified by a type. A representation may be constrained by a REPRESENTATION INVARIANT.

REPRESENTATION INVARIANT A property that is true of the REPRESENTATION of every value of an abstract type. The representation invariant refers to properties that are not inherent in the representation but that must be guaranteed by the operations that have access to the representation. One example is that in a heap, the smallest element is at the root. Another is that in a binary search tree, smaller elements are in the left subtree and larger elements are in the right subtree. A third example is that when a list is used to represent a set, the list contains no duplicate elements. Some representations satisfy only trivial invariants, but in most interesting implementations, a representation invariant is needed to make the code work.

SUBTYPING A relation $\mathcal{T} <: \mathcal{T}'$ which says that any MODULE of type $\mathcal{T}$ also has type $\mathcal{T}'$—and therefore can be used wherever a module of type $\mathcal{T}'$ is expected. A programming language may also offer a subtype relation on the types of expressions.

9.11.2 Further reading

Data abstraction is a form of information hiding, for which best practices were developed in the 1970s. Parnas (1972) argues that an effective module hides a design decision that is likely to change. Such decisions include input formats, output formats, and algorithms, as well as the decisions emphasized in this chapter: the representations of abstractions. Parnas is sometimes paraphrased as saying "every module hides a secret." Wirth (1971) describes top-down development of programs by "stepwise refinement" of high-level specifications into working code. He emphasizes that decisions about representation should be delayed as long as possible (and thereby hidden from one another). Dahl and Hoare (1972) say that "good decomposition means that each component may be programmed independently and revised with no, or reasonably few, implications for the rest of the system." They argue for a language mechanism based on the *objects* and *classes* of the Simula 67 programming language; the realization of those ideas in Smalltalk is the subject of Chapter 10 of this book.

The implementation of an abstract data type can be proved correct using a method developed by Hoare (1972). Hoare's paper introduces the ideas of abstraction function and representation invariant, and it argues that the method is essential for succinct specifications. If you like math with your code, read it.

Languages that support abstract data types owe a great deal to CLU. CLU's initial ideas are described by Liskov and Zilles (1974). At that point compile-time type checking was just a glimmer on the horizon; the paper emphasizes a deep philosophical difference between CLU and its predecessor Simula 67—Simula 67 was designed to expose details of representation, and CLU was designed to hide them. A fully developed CLU, complete with compile-time type checking, is described by Liskov et al. (1977). The context in which CLU was developed—including the state of programming languages before CLU, the connections between CLU and programming methodology, the major principles underlying CLU's design, and CLU's history—is the subject of a later retrospective (Liskov 1996). And if you are interested in an innovative aspect of the implementation, CLU's exception mechanism is described in a more technical paper (Liskov and Snyder 1979).

Beyond CLU, data abstraction plays an important or even central role in Simula 67 (Dahl and Hoare 1972; Birtwistle et al. 1973), Alphard (Wulf, London, and Shaw 1976), Modula-2 (Wirth 1982), and Ada. Data abstraction can also be achieved using `lambda` in Scheme, as described by Abelson and Sussman (1985, Chapter 2).

Abstract data types work very well for data structures; some classic, well-engineered examples are presented by Hanson (1996). Hanson's implementations are written in C, so he's working with stone knives and bearskins, but the results are both informative and useful. For more depth in the use of abstract types, and to delve into the relationship between software development and software specification, consult the excellent book on programming by Liskov and Guttag (1986). And for an example of pushing generic modules beyond reasonable bounds, I recommend my own work on building a type-safe, separately compiled, extensible interpreter (Ramsey 2005).

Modules and modular type checking are beautifully explained by Leroy (1994), who opens with two pages that explain what we ought to expect from modules and interfaces, and why. I cannot recommend this work highly enough. The technical part of the paper is equally strong, showing how to accommodate a mix of abstract and exposed types in one interface; this problem was solved independently by Harper and Lillibridge (1994). Leroy (2000) follows up with a longer paper that implements his ideas in a way that enables a compiler or interpreter to easily add modules to an existing language. This work directly inspired Molecule's type system—Molecule's module layer includes just one feature not taken from Leroy: the intersection type, as proposed by Ramsey, Fisher, and Govereau (2005).

Modules are not normally recursive or mutually recursive, and yet much ink and even more thought have been expended on making them so. This work has yet to find its way into wide use, but my favorite proposal replaces "modules" with "units"; a "unit" is a syntactic capsule that puts imports and exports on equal footing. Units are linked into larger units by a separate linking language (Flatt and Felleisen 1998).

Modules are often viewed as competing with classes. In a talk by Leroy (1999), the two are compared from both theoretical and practical perspectives. Leroy argues that modules are most effective in situations where the set of kinds of things (data) is likely to remain stable, but the set of operations performed on things is fluid. Classes are most effective in situations where the set of operations performed on things is stable, but the set of kinds of things is fluid. In a more technical comparison, Cook (2009) focuses on fundamental semantic differences between

Table 9.24: Synopsis of all the exercises, with most relevant sections

Exercises	*Section*	*Notes*
1 and 2	9.2	"Finger exercises" on writing client code using qualified names: simple client functions of the `IntArray` module, comparable to what is in Section 9.2.
3 to 5	9.3	Opportunities to modify an existing abstraction (the `2Dpoint` abstraction).
6	9.4	Changing representation without affecting client code.
7 and 8	9.4, 9.5	Defining simple abstractions from scratch.
9 to 13	9.6.1, 9.6.4	*Reasoning* about abstractions: abstraction functions, invariants, specification, and proof.
14 to 18	9.6	Interface design for common data structures, including careful specification of operations. Focus on mutability and immutability. A couple of small implementations.
19 to 28	9.6	Using module types to express common properties of data, like "comparable for equality" or "totally ordered." Interface design, some intersection types, and a touch of implementation.
29 to 36	9.6.5, 9.7.1	Reusable data structures using generic modules: lists, trees, heaps, and a hash table. Substantial implementation.
37 to 40	9.6.5	Less demanding applications of generic modules: algorithms like sorting and tree traversal.
41 to 45	9.6.1	Performance and cost analysis, building primarily on the generic-module exercises. Experimental work and substantial implementation.
46 to 50	9.7	Operations that inspect representations of multiple arguments: linear-time set union, followed by increasingly ambitious forms of arithmetic, culminating in arbitrary-precision signed-integer arithmetic.
51 to 55	9.8	Extensions to Molecule's type system.

abstract data types and objects and on the relationship between them. Cook also discusses how both mechanisms are used in Java, Haskell, and Smalltalk.

In Haskell, names are overloaded using the *type classes* proposed by Wadler and Blott (1989). Depth in the underlying theory is provided by Jones (1993). Type classes are related to modules and module types by Dreyer et al. (2007). And they are very cleverly applied by Claessen and Hughes (2000).

Syntactic forms `raise` and `handle` are not actually very good at expressing the ways we usually use exceptions. For a lovely alternative, see the proposal by Benton and Kennedy (2001).

9.12 Exercises

Exercises are arranged mostly by the skill they call on (Table 9.24). Some of my favorites, from least difficult to most difficult, are as follows:

- A circularly linked list with constant-time append demonstrates a simple, clever use of a mutable representation (Exercise 30).

- A hash table, which is a client of an association list, showcases separation of concerns (Exercise 34).
- True integers, as opposed to machine integers, have unbounded magnitude (Exercises 49 and 50). Thanks to Molecule's operator overloading, they are relatively easy to use as a replacement for `int`. True-integer exercises also appear in Chapter 10, to be done in μSmalltalk. The version in Molecule does somewhat less and is somewhat easier to implement—but it is not easy. The exercises illustrate differences between abstract data types and objects.
- The order invariant of a binary search tree can be stated simply, precisely, and formally—but discovering such a statement is surprisingly difficult (Exercise 9).

9.12.1 *Retrieval practice and other short questions*

A. What kinds of components can a module have?

B. What is a qualified name? What are some examples?

C. How is it that the = function can be called without qualification, but the `new` function has to be called by a qualified name?

D. What is a client?

E. By what syntactic form is a generic module instantiated?

F. In Molecule, how do we write the type of an array of Booleans?

G. When a `case` expression matches on a pattern like `(XY x y)`, what kind of thing do `x` and `y` stand for? Is this semantics more like the semantics of μScheme or more like the semantics of μML?

H. What is an abstraction function? What is a representation invariant?

I. Pick your favorite data structure and state the representation invariant.

J. What's the domain of an abstraction function?

K. What representation invariant enables an array to represent a priority queue (that is, a heap)?

L. What's the cost of removing the smallest element from a heap?

M. What is a creator? A producer? A mutator? An observer?

N. What does an operation's type tell you about whether it is a creator, producer, mutator, or observer?

O. Just by analyzing its module type, how can you tell the difference between a mutable abstraction and an immutable abstraction?

P. When you want to reveal the representation of the `elem` type in an `ARRAY` abstraction, what keyword do you use to write the module type?

Q. If the representation of a natural number is changed from a list of digits to an array of digits, can client code tell the difference? If so, how? If not, what prevents it?

R. How is the judgment $E \vdash \tau \rightsquigarrow \tau'$ pronounced, and what does it do?

S. If $\mathcal{T}$ is a subtype of $\mathcal{T}'$, can $\mathcal{T}$ have fewer components than $\mathcal{T}'$? How about more?

T. What sub*set* relation corresponds to the sub*type* relation?

U. What is an intersection type? What subtypes does an intersection type have?

9.12.2 *Using abstractions; programming with qualified names*

1. *Integer-array operations.* Study the implementation of the `smallest-int` function in chunk 530c, then implement these operations on integer arrays:

   (a) Define a function `index-of-smallest` which finds the *index* of the smallest element in an array of integers.

   (b) Define a function `smallest-to-front` that moves an array's smallest element to the front, without changing the order of other elements.

   (c) Define a function `partition` that finds an array's kth smallest element and partitions the array around it. The function should permute the array's elements and should leave it with this postcondition (for an array of size N):

   $$a[i] \le a[k], \text{for each } i \text{ in the range } 0 \le i < k,$$
   $$a[k] \le a[j], \text{for each } j \text{ in the range } k \le j < N.$$

   (This function resembles the partition step in Tony Hoare's Quicksort algorithm, and you may want to implement it recursively.)

2. *Iteration.* Because Molecule's core layer is not polymorphic, a function like `foldr` is not terribly useful. The monomorphism of the core layer militates toward a function like μScheme's `app`, which applies a function to every element of a list (for side effects).

   (a) Define a similar function `foreach`, which takes a function of type `(int -> unit)` and applies it to every element of an integer array.

   (b) Use `foreach` to compute the sum of elements in an integer array.

9.12.3 *Changing existing abstractions*

3. *New operation: clockwise rotation.* Extend the `2Dpoint` module with a `rotate-` operation, which rotates a point 90 degrees clockwise.

4. *New operations: equality and inequality.* Add operations `=` and `!=` to module `2Dpoint`. Seal your module with this module type:

```
(allof 2DPOINT (exports [abstype t]
                        [=  : (t t -> bool)]
                        [!= : (t t -> bool)]))
```

5. *Change of abstraction.* In the `2Dpoint` example of Section 9.3, function `quadrant` returns a value of type `sym`, but only four quadrants are possible (chunk 534). Alter the module so that the limitation of four quadrants is reflected in the types.

   (a) Change the `2DPOINT` module type to include an abstract type `quadrant` and four values of that type, with names `UPPER-LEFT`, `UPPER-RIGHT`, and so on. (Because these names begin with uppercase letters, they must be value constructors.) Replace operation `quadrant` with a new operation `get-quadrant` of type `(t -> quadrant)`.

   (b) Change the implementation of the `2Dpoint` module to conform to the new interface. To define type `quadrant` and its value constructors, use a `data` definition.

9.12.4 *Change of representation*

6. *Quadrant-magnitude points.* In the `2Dpoint` example of Section 9.3, client code can't depend on your representation, which leaves you free to change it. As a contrived example, change the representation of a `2Dpoint` to use only nonnegative integers in what I call "quadrant-magnitude" representation. This representation is analogous to the sign-magnitude representation used by floating-point hardware.

   Change the representation used in `2Dpoint` so that a point is represented by the result of applying a value constructor to three values:

   - The magnitude `x-mag` of the x coordinate
   - The magnitude `y-mag` of the y coordinate
   - The quadrant in which the point lies

   Represent a quadrant in whatever way you like; a small integer will do, but you might prefer a symbol or the constructed data of Exercise 5.

   (a) Define an internal `invariant` function that expresses all the invariants of your representation. At minimum, magnitudes `x-mag` and `y-mag` must be nonnegative.

   (b) The representation stands for that unique point that is located an absolute distance of `x-mag` from the y axis, `y-mag` from the x axis, and that is located in the given quadrant. Make this idea precise by defining an abstraction function that maps your representation to a pair of Cartesian coordinates (x, y). The abstraction function is to be applied only to representations that satisfy the invariant; if applied to any other representation, it can fail, or it can even give wrong answers.

   (c) Update the operations so they work correctly with your new representation. When you finish, the new version should be observationally equivalent to the original: it should be impossible for any program to tell which version of `2Dpoint` it is using. Take special care with points whose x or y magnitudes are zero.

9.12.5 *New, simple abstractions*

7. *User-interface window.* In the world of graphical user interfaces, a *window* is a rectangle in the plane whose sides are parallel to the x and y coordinate axes.

   (a) Using your preferred abstraction for 2-dimensional points, define a `Window` module that supports the operations shown in Figure 9.25 on the next page.

   (b) Make the abstraction mutable, and add two mutators: `+x`, which shifts the window in a positive x direction, and `+y`, which shifts the window in a positive y direction.

8. *Complex numbers.* A complex-number abstraction should export functions `+`, `-`, `*`, `/`, `negated`, `=`, `!=`, and `print`. In addition, it should export function `new`, which creates a complex number given its (integer) real and imaginary parts, and functions `re` and `im`, which observe the real and imaginary parts of a complex number.

Creator	
`new`	Is given opposite corners (either upper-left/lower-right or lower-left/upper-right) and returns a new window with those corners.
Observers	
`get-ll`, `get-ur`	Returns a two-dimensional point that represents either the lower-left or the upper-right corner of a given window.
`intersect?`	Tells if two windows overlap.
Producer	
`intersection`	Is given two windows that overlap, and returns a new window that represents the overlapping region.

Figure 9.25: Operations on user-interface windows (Exercise 7)

An integer complex number can be represented by constructed data containing its real and imaginary parts:

```
(data t [C : (int int -> t)])
```

This representation need not satisfy any invariants; all pairs of real and imaginary parts are meaningful.

Using this representation, define a module `Complex` that implements integer complex numbers.

9.12.6 *Abstraction functions, invariants, specification, and proof*

Assuming types `key` and `value` are defined, a binary search tree can be represented as constructed data of type `bst`:

593. ⟨*transcript* 530b⟩+≡ ◁570 598▷

```
-> (data bst [EMPTY : bst] [NODE : (bst key value bst -> bst)])
bst :: *
EMPTY : bst
NODE : (bst key value bst -> bst)
```

Use this representation in Exercises 9 and 32.

9. *Order invariant on a binary search tree.* Algebraic data type `bst` defines a binary tree in which each node carries two values, one of type `key` and one of type `value`. But not every value of this type is a binary *search* tree: a search tree must obey an order invariant.

   (a) Using the inductive structure of binary trees, write a proof system for the judgment "tree T satisfies the order invariant." Take advantage of nondeterminism.

   (b) Using your proof system, define a recursive function `order-invariant?` that checks if a value of type `bst` tree satisfies the order invariant.

   Hint: As in many proofs by induction, it helps to strengthen the induction hypothesis. In your proof system, find another, stronger judgment that is easier to prove inductively, and then add a rule that uses the stronger judgment to prove the order invariant. In your code, define a recursive function that checks something stronger than your order invariant, and check the order invariant by calling that function.

10. *Priority queue as a sorted list.* Section 9.6.4 describes a priority queue as a bag of values. But a priority queue can also be specified as a *sorted list* of values. Using sorted lists as the abstraction,

    (a) Write algebraic laws to specify the abstraction function for a representation of type `(@m ArrayList Elem).t`, as in Section 9.6.5.

    (b) Write algebraic laws to specify the abstraction function for a representation as a binary tree. Use the representation given by the type `t` in my implementation of leftist heaps (chunk 556a).

    (c) Write algebraic laws to specify the `insert`, `empty?`, and `delete-min` operations on the immutable abstraction described by module type `IMMUTABLE-PQ` (chunk 555a).

The next three exercises build on the discussion of arithmetic in Appendix B.

11. *Specifications for natural-number arithmetic.* Using the representation of a natural number as a list, complete the mathematical development for addition and subtraction of natural numbers, from Appendix B (page S13):

    (a) Give equations for computing $X + c$, where X is a natural number and c is a carry bit.

    (b) Give equations for computing $X - 1$, where X is a natural number.

12. *Algorithmic invariants of addition.* Prove that when large natural numbers X and Y are added, the following invariants hold:

    (a) Every carry bit c_i is either 0 or 1.

    (b) Every z_i is in the range $0 \leq z_i < b$.

    Also prove that addition is correct, that is

    (c) Using equational reasoning, prove that

$$\left(\sum_i x_i \cdot b^i\right) + \left(\sum_i y_i \cdot b^i\right) = \left(\sum_i z_i \cdot b^i\right).$$

13. *Proof of correctness of short division.* Using the definitions of X, Q, and r from Table B.2 in Appendix B, prove that

$$Q \cdot d + r = X.$$

    Use equational reasoning.

9.12.7 *Design, specification, and mutability*

14. *Interfaces for sets.*

    (a) Define a module type `ISET` which describes immutable sets. It should export types `t` and `elem`, and it should export values `emptyset`, `member?`, `add-element`, `union`, `inter`, and `diff`.

(b) Define a module type `MSET` which describes mutable sets. It should export types `t` and `elem`, and it should export values `emptyset`, `member?`, and `add-element`, as well as functions that compute union, intersection, and difference of two sets. Each two-set function should mutate its first argument, and those functions should be called `add-set`, `intersect`, and `remove-set`.

You may wish to revisit the "third approach" to polymorphism described in Chapter 2 (page 134).

15. *Association lists.* Define a module type `ALIST` for association lists (Section 2.3.8, page 105). It should export types `t`, `key`, and `value` and values `empty`, `find`, and `bind`. Using that module type, write two specifications:

    (a) The abstraction represented by an association list is a set of key-value pairs in which no key appears more than once. Using the notation of this abstraction, as in Section 9.6.2, write specifications for `empty`, `find`, and `bind`. Notate each key-value pair in the form $x \mapsto v$.

    (b) Using algebraic laws, as in Section 9.6.3, relate the `empty`, `find`, and `bind` operations. You might want to revisit the algebraic laws for sets (page 548) or laws in general (Section 2.5, page 110).

16. *Specification for removal from association lists.* Add a `remove` operation to your module type for association lists (Exercise 15). The operation could work in either of two ways:

    (a) Calling `(remove k ps)` could return an association list that has no binding for `k`. In other words, `(remove k ps)` could remove *all* bindings for `k`. Write algebraic laws for this version of `remove`.

    (b) Calling `(remove k ps)` could remove only the *most recent* binding for `k`. (This is how association lists and hash tables work in OCaml.) This version of `remove` cannot be specified using the abstraction of a set of key-value pairs as in Exercise 15a, but it is easy to specify using algebraic laws. Write algebraic laws for this version of `remove`.

17. *Mutable association lists.* In Molecule, a linked list represented as constructed data is mutable.

    (a) Design a mutable association-list abstraction and call the resulting module type `MUTABLE-ALIST`. The module type should export a creator `new`, and `bind` should be a mutator, not a producer.

    (b) A mutable association list can implement `bind` using fewer allocations than an immutable one: Even in the worst case, a mutable association list should be able to implement `bind` by allocating at most one new record. Including such a version of `bind`, implement your abstraction.

18. *Mutability via reference.* Module `(@m Ref M)` exports a type `t` which is a mutable reference cell containing one value of type `M.t`. Such a cell is created using function `new`, read using function `!`, and written using function `:=`. A reference cell can be used to create a mutable abstraction from an immutable one. Demonstrate this trick by defining a generic module `MutablePQ`, which should take one argument of type `IMMUTABLE-PQ`, and which, when instantiated, should have type `MUTABLE-PQ`. (This trick provides a mutable abstraction without providing the cost benefit usually associated with mutable abstractions.)

9.12.8 *Design with module types*

By intersecting module types using `allof`, many specifications can be written compositionally—common properties of abstractions can be specified using module types, then combined using `allof`. In the exercises below, you define several such module types. The exercises are inspired by the standard *type classes* in the programming language Haskell. (Type classes are another way, related to modules and module types, of describing an abstraction.) In most of the exercises, module types can be verified using a `check-module-type` unit test.

19. *Equality.* Define a module type `EQ`, which specifies an abstraction whose values of type `t` are comparable for equality and inequality. Verify that built-in modules `Int`, `Bool`, `Sym`, and `Char` have module type `EQ`.

20. *Total order via relational operators.* Define a module type `ORD`, which specifies an abstraction whose values of type `t` are totally ordered, supporting the classic four inequality operators. Your definition of `ORD` should refer to `EQ`. Verify that primitive module `Int` has module type `ORD`.

21. *Total order via comparison function.* Define a module type `COMPARE`, which specifies an abstraction whose values of type `t` can be compared using a `compare` function, which returns a value of type `Order.t`.

22. *Interconvertible total orders.* Convert between order abstractions:

    (a) Define a generic module `MkCompare`, which takes as a parameter a module that has both type `ORD` and type `EQ`; an instance of `MkCompare` should have module type `COMPARE`, operating on the type `t` from its parameter.

    (b) Define a generic module `MkOrd`, which takes as a parameter a module of type `COMPARE`. An instance should have both type `ORD` and type `EQ`, operating on the type `t` from `MkOrd`'s parameter.

23. *Numbers.* Define a module type `NUM`, which specifies an abstraction that supports addition, subtraction, negation, multiplication, and division, plus a conversion function `of-int`, which takes an argument of type `Int.t` and returns a value of the abstraction. Verify that module `Int` has module type `NUM`.

24. *Printability.* Define a module type `PRINT`, which specifies an abstraction that exports functions `print` and `println`. Verify that modules `Int`, `Sym`, and so on have module type `PRINT`.

25. *Collection.* Define a module type `COLLECTION`, which should describe a mutable collection of elements. It should export types `t` and `elem`, plus three operations:

    - Function `add` should add an element to the collection.
    - Function `remove-cps` should remove an element from the collection, or if the element is not present, call a failure continuation.
    - Function `app` should take a function as an argument and should apply that function to every element of the collection.

26. *Types of module* `Int`. Verify, using a *single* `check-module-type` test, that module `Int` has module types `EQ`, `ORD`, `NUM`, and `PRINT`.

27. *Types of module* `Complex`. Verify that the complex-number abstraction from Exercise 8 has module types `EQ`, `NUM` and `PRINT`. And use `check-type-error` to verify that it does *not* have type `ORD`.

28. *Generic complex numbers via* `NUM` *and* `PRINT`. Using an argument module that has module types `NUM` and `PRINT`, define a generic module `MkComplex`, which should be a generic version of the complex-number module described in Exercise 8.

9.12.9 *Data structures as generic modules*

Classic data structures—of the kind that are agnostic to the data they structure—are perfect candidates for generic modules. While comparable to the core-layer polymorphism used to implement sets in μScheme and to the explicit polymorphism of Typed μScheme, generic modules make polymorphism easier to use in two ways: First, a generic module can depend on an operation as easily as it can depend on a type. Second, instantiating a generic module specializes a whole group of operations *and types* at once. These benefits are demonstrated in the exercises below.

29. *Immutable list.* A module type for Scheme-like lists might look like this:

    597. ⟨*list.mcl* 597⟩≡
    ```
    (module-type LIST
       (exports
          [abstype elem]
          [abstype t]
          [empty : t]
          [null? : (t -> bool)]
          [cons  : (elem t -> t)]
          [car   : (t -> elem)]
          [cdr   : (t -> t)]
          [app   : ((elem -> unit) t -> unit)]
          ))
    ```

    Implement a generic module `List` that takes one parameter, a module `Elem`, and returns a module that implements `LIST` and also has the following module type:

    ```
    (exports [type elem Elem.t])
    ```

30. *Mutable list.* Design and implement two variations of mutable list:

    (a) A simple variation exposes the representation: client code can mutate any `car` or `cdr`. This variation corresponds to a "linked list" that is often taught to beginning programmers.

    (b) A more sophisticated variation can provide some abstraction and a representation invariant. Design and implement a mutable list abstraction in which the representation points to the *last* element of a *circularly linked* list. For the representation, you can use your solution to part (a). Such a representation enables you to implement a variety of observers and mutators in constant space and time:

    - Find first element or last element.
    - Remove first element or last element.
    - Add element at head or tail.
    - Append two lists, mutating both (the first is left with the results of the append and the second is left empty).

    This representation is used to implement the `List` class that is built in to μSmalltalk (Chapter 10).

31. *Immutable association list.* Using the interface from Exercise 15, implement an immutable association list Alist with exported values empty, find, and bind. Make it generic, taking key and value modules as parameters.

32. *Binary search tree.* Exercise 15 defines the interface not just for an association list, but for any immutable finite map. Implement this abstraction, just as in the previous exercise, but as the representation, use the binary search tree bst defined in chunk 593.

33. *Leftist heap.* Finish the implementation of the leftist heap whose merge operation is given in Section 9.7.1 (page 555). That is, implement operations new, empty?, insert, and delete-min. Do not write any new *recursive* functions—any operation that involves more than one node should call merge.

34. *Hash table.* A generic hash table might have this module type:

598. ⟨*transcript* 530b⟩+≡ ◁593 599a▷

```
-> (module-type GENERIC-HASH
      ([Key : (exports [abstype t]
                       [hash : (t -> int)]
                       [= : (t t -> bool)])]
       [Value : (exports [abstype t])]
          --m->
            (exports
              [abstype t]

              [abstype maybe-value] ; result of lookup
              [Not-Found : maybe-value]
              [Found     : (Value.t -> maybe-value)]

              [new    : ( -> t)]
              [insert : (Key.t Value.t t -> unit)]
              [delete : (Key.t t -> unit)]
              [lookup : (Key.t t -> maybe-value)])))
module type GENERIC-HASH = ...
  ...
```

Exported type t is a mutable finite map.

A simple hash table can keep an array of *buckets*, where a bucket holds an association list mapping keys to values. Every key on the list must hash to that bucket. To support dynamic growth, I recommend augmenting a buckets array with an integer population and an integer grow-at, with these invariants:

- If a key-value pair (k, v) is stored in the hash table, it is stored in the association list stored in buckets$[i]$, where $i =$ (Key.hash k) $\bmod n$, where n is the size of buckets.
- The total number of key-value pairs stored in the hash table is equal to population.
- The value of population is less than the value of grow-at.
- The number of buckets n is at least 1.3 times the value of grow-at.

To maintain these invariants as key-value pairs are added, the hash table has to grow. In particular, it has to grow whenever an insert operation makes population equal to grow-at. Growth is easy to get wrong; I have used a production system in which the hash table grew too slowly, the association lists got too long, and eventually operations that should have taken constant time took linear time instead. For ideas about monitoring the internal state of the hash table, see Exercise 35.

I recommend initializing a hash table with $n = 17$ buckets, then growing n using the following sequence of prime numbers:

599a. ⟨*transcript* 530b⟩+≡ ◁598

```
-> (val prime-sizes
        '(17 23 31 41 59 79 103 137 179 233 307 401 523 683 907 1181
          1543 2011 2617 3407 4441 5779 7517 9781 12721 16547 21517
          27983 36383 47303 61507 79967 103963 135173 175727 228451
          296987 386093 501931 652541 848321 1102823 1433681 1863787
          2422939 3149821 4094791 5323229 6920201 8996303 11695231
          15203803 19764947 25694447 33402793))
```


A prime size uses of all the bits in the hash value effectively, and each of these primes is at least 1.3 times larger than the one the precedes it.

Using these guidelines, implement a generic hash table Hash that grows as needed, on demand. Keep your code simple by relying on the association-list interface to find a key in a given bucket.

35. *Hash-table diagnosis.* A hash table is efficient only when its lists are short. But if we want to confirm efficiency experimentally, the lengths of the lists are hidden by the abstraction! To study a hash table's performance, we have to open up the abstraction barrier. In this exercise, I recommend exposing a *histogram* of the lengths. For example, the histogram below depicts the state of a hash table built by inserting the names of 10 Turing laureates into an empty hash table:

```
0 |*********
1 |******
2 |**
```

The hash table has 17 buckets in all; 9 are empty, 6 have exactly one element, and just 2 buckets have more than one element. The table contains 10 key-value pairs and so is about 60% full. The expected cost of a successful lookup is determined by the average number of pairs in a nonempty bucket, which is 1.25.

The next insertion brings the population to 11, triggering the grow operation. The number of buckets increases to 23:

```
0 |**************
1 |*******
2 |**
```

Histograms can be obtained by extending the hash-table interface with an operation histogram of type (t -> Histogram.t), where module Histogram implements this interface:

599b. ⟨*histogram.mcl* 599b⟩≡

```
(module-type HISTOGRAM
   [exports
      [abstype t] ;; finite map int -> int (key to count)
      [new       : ( -> t)]           ; every int maps to zero
      [inc       : (int t -> unit)]   ; increment count of given int
      [inc-by    : (int int t -> unit )]  ; increment by more than 1
      [count-of  : (int t -> int)]    ; fetch count of given int
      [visualize : (t -> unit)]])     ; visualize the whole thing
```

Source code for Histogram can be found in the Supplement.

Add the histogram operation to your hash table from the previous exercise, and use it to diagnose performance.

36. *Mutable and immutable sets.* Using the data structure and invariants of your choice, implement the set abstractions from Exercise 14.

    (a) Implement the mutable set abstraction MSET.

    (b) Implement the immutable set abstraction ISET.

9.12.10 *Algorithms as generic modules*

Like a polymorphic data structure, a polymorphic algorithm can be written as a generic module.

37. *Generic array functions.* Revisit Exercise 1, and reimplement its functions to work generically on any array whose elements are totally ordered. (If you have completed Exercise 20, use module type ORD.)

38. *Abstract tree traversals.* Define a generic module Traversals, which should export functions for traversing binary trees. It should take one parameter Tree of this type:

    600. ⟨*exercises.mcl* 600⟩≡ 602 ▷

```
(module-type BINARY-TREE
  (exports [abstype t]
           [abstype value]
           [empty? : (t -> bool)]       ; observer
           [the-value : (t -> value)]   ; observe only nonempty tree
           [left  : (t -> t)]           ; subtree of nonempty tree
           [right : (t -> t)]))         ; subtree of nonempty tree
```

    Module Traversals should export the following functions, each of which takes an argument of type Tree.t and another of type (Tree.value -> unit):

    (a) Function preorder should implement a preorder traversal.

    (b) Function inorder should implement an inorder traversal.

    (c) Function postorder should implement a postorder traversal.

    (d) Function levelorder should implement a level-order traversal.

39. *Sorting.* Define a generic module Sort that takes as parameters an ARRAY abstraction whose elements satisfy the ORD module type from Exercise 20. The module should export one function sort, which sorts an array in place (by mutating it).

40. *Heapsort.* Define a generic module Heapsort that takes as parameters an Elem abstraction and exports a function sort, which sorts an array of type (@m Array Elem).t in place. Sort the array by inserting every element into a priority queue, then using the priority queue to order the elements.

9.12.11 *Performance and cost models*

41. *Comparing heap performance.* The chapter describes two representations of a heap: a mutable array representation and an immutable leftist heap.

    (a) For various sizes of array, measure the cost of building a mutable heap from an array in the style of the Heapsort module (Exercise 40), which calls insert repeatedly.

(b) For various sizes of array, measure the cost of building a leftist heap from an array, in a different style, by calling `merge` repeatedly: start by making one-element heaps, then merge pairs to make two-element heaps, then merge pairs to make four-element heaps, and so on until you have a single heap. This algorithm can be implemented fairly easily by using an `ArrayList` as a queue.

(c) How large an array do you need before the repeated-merge algorithm beats the repeated-insert algorithm?

(d) Revisit Exercise 40 (Heapsort), and implement two versions: one that uses the priority queue based on a mutable array, and one that uses the priority queue based on an immutable leftist heap. Measure which heap provides a faster sort as the array to be sorted gets large.

42. *Cost model of a hash table.* An abstraction has both a semantics and a cost model. For a hash table, the cost model includes constant-time insertion. Since an insertion can make the hash table grow, the appropriate bound is not worst-case cost; it is *amortized* cost: as N gets large, a sequence of N insertions must have a cost proportional to N.

    This aspect of hash-table implementation can be hard to get right. A mistake can change the cost of N insertions to $O(N \log N)$ or even $O(N^2)$. In Exercise 34, all elements are reinserted every time the hash table grows, and it grows $O(\log N)$ times in total. But nevertheless, the total work is not $O(N \log N)$; it is $O(N)$.

    (a) Suppose that at each growth step, N doubles. Some elements will be reinserted for the $\log_2 N$th time, but half of the elements are reinserted for the first time. Prove that the *average* number of reinsertions is at most 2.

    (b) Now suppose that at each growth step, N increases by a factor of 1.3. Prove that the *average* number of reinsertions is bounded by a constant, and find the constant.

    (c) Demonstrate experimentally that as N gets large, the cost of inserting N elements into the hash table is proportional to N. A plot of CPU time versus N should resemble a straight line, but because the costs of garbage collection may vary with N, your plot may have some jitter.

    To make your experiments as painless as possible, I recommend compiling the Molecule interpreter with MLton or some other Standard ML compiler that generates native machine code.

43. *Refinements to a hash table.* To find a key in a given bucket, the hash table in Exercise 34 uses an association list. This convenience keeps the hash-table code simple: the hash table manages the array of buckets, and in any bucket, it lets the association list search for the right key. But the convenience may cost something at run time, especially if comparing keys for equality is expensive. A production hash table might include these refinements:

    - Along with each key-value pair, a production hash table can store the *hash* of each key, so it never needs to be recomputed.
    - In `lookup`, `insert`, and `delete`, a production hash table can avoid comparing keys except when they have the same hash. Hashes are small integers and can be compared very quickly, whereas keys might be long arrays (strings) or large data structures whose comparison takes much

longer. When there are multiple keys in a bucket, saving comparisons might matter.

How and when these refinements actually improve things is an experimental question.

(a) Which do you expect to be faster: the original hash table, or one with the refinements? On what grounds? Justify your answer.

(b) Compared with the size of the `Hash` module, how much additional code do you expect a refined version to require?

(c) Create a new module `RefinedHash` that implements the same interface as `Hash` but incorporates the refinements listed above.

(d) Construct, if you can, a test program that exposes a performance difference between the two different implementations of the hash table. Explain your results.

44. *Hybrid structures.* Hash tables and arrays provide similar abstractions, but with different cost models. But why should picking the right cost model be up to the poor programmer? In this exercise, you make the computer do the work. In the following abstraction, integers can index into a hash table *or* an array, whichever seems better:

602. ⟨*exercises.mcl* 600⟩+≡ ◁600

```
(module-type HYBRID-ARRAY
 (exports [abstype t]     ;; an array
          [abstype elem] ;; one element of the array
          [new    : ( -> t)]                ; creator
          [at     : (t int -> elem)]        ; observer
          [at-put : (t int elem -> unit)]   ; mutator
          [foreach-at : (t (int elem -> unit) -> unit)])) ; observer
```

Design and implement a generic module `HybridArray`, which takes one parameter: a module `Elem` that exports a type `t`, a value `default` of type `t`, a `hash` function, and an `=` function. An instance should have module type `HYBRID-ARRAY`, and your implementation should have these properties:

- Function `new` should return an array that maps every index to the `default` element from the `Elem` parameter.
- Function `foreach-at` should apply its function parameter to every *non-default* element in the array, with index.
- The representation should include an array part and a hash part. The implementation should identify an interval of integer keys that is dense with non-default values; it should store these values in the array part, and it should place the remaining key-value pairs in the hash part. As an invariant, the implementation might require that the array part either be of size 8 or hold at least 70% non-default values.

This sort of hybrid array provides the best of both worlds, but the implementation may occasionally have to migrate keys from the hash table to the internal array, or vice versa.

A design like this is used to implement the *table* abstraction in the programming language Lua.

45. *Influence of base on natural-number performance.* After completing the implementation of natural numbers described in Exercise 49, experiment with different values of the base b:

    (a) Implement large natural numbers using base $b = 10$.

    (b) Implement large natural numbers using the largest possible base that is a power of 10 (so that `print` can be implemented without implementing short division). It must be possible to compute `(* (-` b `1) (-` b `1))` without causing arithmetic overflow; to find the largest such b, experiment with your version of Molecule.

    (c) Create a benchmark that exposes a performance difference between these two implementations of large natural numbers. Explain the difference. Make your explanation quantitative!

    (d) Implement large natural numbers using the largest possible b, not necessarily a power of 10, such that `(* (-` b `1) (-` b `1))` can be computed without causing arithmetic overflow. In order to print your natural numbers, you will have to implement short division.

    (e) Create a benchmark that exposes a performance difference between the bases used in parts (c) and (d). Under what circumstances does the performance improvement of part (d) justify the effort of implementing short division?

    (f) Change b to be as small as possible without breaking the code. Explain why this value of b can be expected to work, and measure the cost in performance relative to a more efficient b.

9.12.12 *Inspecting multiple representations*

Compared with objects, abstract data types offer one great strength: a function can easily inspect the representations of multiple arguments. This strength is demonstrated in the exercises below, starting with a simple set-union problem and continuing through progressively more ambitious forms of arithmetic.

46. *Linear-time set union.* Define an integer-set abstraction whose representation is a *sorted* list without duplicates. Use the invariant to implement a `union` operation that takes time proportional to the sum of the lengths of the operands.

47. *Rational-number arithmetic.* Design and implement module `Fraction`, which does arithmetic on rational numbers. Rational numbers should be immutable, and at minimum, your module should implement operations `new` (to create a rational number from an integer), `+`, `-`, `*`, `/`, `negated`, `=`, `!=`, `<`, `<=`, `>`, `>=`, and `print`. A rational number should be printed in lowest terms; that is, the greatest common divisor of the numerator and denominator should be 1.

    Reduce code bloat by keeping in mind such algebraic laws as $(x > y) = (y < x)$ and $(x \leq y) = \neg(x > y)$.

    For some ideas, look to the implementation of class `Fraction` in Chapter 10 (page 664).

48. *Floating-point arithmetic.* Design and implement module `Float`, which does arithmetic on floating-point numbers. Your module should implement operations `new` (to create a floating-point number from an integer), `+`, `-`, `*`, `/`, `negated`, `=`, `!=`, `<`, `<=`, `>`, `>=`, and `print`. Floating-point numbers are immutable.

    A floating-point number approximates a real number by a rational number of the form $m \cdot b^e$, where m is the *mantissa*, b is the *base*, and e is the *exponent*. For ease of printing, I recommend using $b = 10$, and to prevent arithmetic overflow, I recommend maintaining the representation invariant $-32767 \leq m \leq 32767$.

    For some ideas, look to the implementation of class `Float` in Appendix U (page S567). The class uses these tricks:

    - During computation, the invariant that restricts the size of m might be violated temporarily. The invariant is restored in this way: While m is too big, divide m by b and add 1 to e. Each division may lose precision, introducing *floating-point rounding error*, but restoring the invariant protects against future overflow.
    - The abstraction is immutable, but an implementation may benefit from using a mutable representation—as long as no mutation has an effect that can be observed by client code.
    - Two floating-point numbers can be added if they have equal exponents: $m_1 \cdot b^e + m_2 \cdot b^e = (m_1 + m_2) \cdot b^e$. To make exponents equal, find the number with the smaller exponent, and keep dividing m by b and adding 1 to e until the exponents are equal. Then add the mantissas, and if $m_1 + m_2$ violates the representation invariant, restore it.
    - Any two floating-point numbers can be multiplied using the algebraic law $m_1 \cdot b^{e_1} \cdot m_2 \cdot b^{e_2} = (m_1 \cdot m_2) \cdot b^{e_1+e_2}$: multiply the mantissas and add the exponents. And if $m_1 \cdot m_2$ violates the representation invariant, restore it.
    - Not every operation has to be implemented from scratch. If you have `+` and `negated`, you have `-`. And for comparisons, $x < y$ if and only if $y - x > 0$.

49. *Arbitrary-precision natural-number arithmetic.* Read about natural-number arithmetic in Appendix B. Following the guidelines there, design and build a module `Natural` that implements the `NATURAL` abstraction. Supplement Appendix B with this advice:

    - Implement `print` using short division. To print a nonzero number X in decimal format, use short division to compute quotient $Q = X \text{ div } 10$ and remainder $r = X \bmod 10$. First print Q, then print r.
    - If you represent a natural number as an array of digits, define a non-exported operation `digit` that will help you pretend that X and Y are the same size: asking for a digit beyond the bounds of an array should return 0. And you may benefit from using `ArrayList`, which can grow or shrink at need.
    - When testing, bear in mind that `check-expect` relies on your implementation of `=`, which might have a bug. You might want to extend your module with an operation called `decimals`, which returns an array of decimal digits with the most significant digit first. That array can

then be given to check-expect, to be compared with an array written by hand.

50. *Arbitrary-precision signed-integer arithmetic.* Read about signed-integer arithmetic in Appendix B. Following the guidelines there, design and implement a generic module Bignum that implements *large signed integers.* This abstraction of the integers is not limited by the size of a machine word—a large integer can be any integer whose representation fits in your machine's memory. Large integers, like machine integers, are immutable.

A useful implementation of signed integers will provide everything in the INT interface in Appendix B, plus short division, plus a way to create a large integer from a small one.

605a. ⟨*bignum.mcl* 605a⟩≡ 605b ▷

```
(module-type BIGNUM
  (allof
    INT
    (exports
      [abstype t]
      [module [QR : (exports-record-ops pair ([quotient : t]
                                               [remainder : int]))]]
      [sdiv : (t int -> QR.pair)]
      [of-int : (Int.t -> t)])))
```

Your Bignum module should take a module Natural of type NATURAL as a parameter, and it should return a module that implements BIGNUM, like this:

605b. ⟨*bignum.mcl* 605a⟩+≡ ◁ 605a

```
(generic-module [Bignum : ([Natural : NATURAL] --m-> BIGNUM)]
  ⟨implementation of signed integers (left as an exercise)⟩ )
```

To represent the magnitude of an integer, use a value of type Natural.t (Exercise 49). To couple the magnitude with a sign, you might choose any of the representations suggested in Appendix B.

Because long division is tiresome, I recommend that your / operation simply evaluate an error expression, but if you want to implement long division, read Brinch Hansen (1994) or Hanson (1996, Chapters 17 and 18).

9.12.13 Molecule's type system

51. *Better overloading.* Molecule's function overloading chooses the most recently overloaded type whose first argument matches the type of the function's first actual parameter. But Molecule could instead choose a function based on the types *and number* of *all* the actual parameters.

    (a) Update the function-application rule to make it so.

    (b) Venture into the interpreter and implement your new rule. (The main challenge will involve error messages.)

52. *Principal type of a generic module.* When an exporting module is sealed, it is checked by confirming that its principal type is a subtype of the (realized) module type used to seal it. Perhaps generic modules could be checked the same way. Supposing that we extend Molecule with a one-argument generic-module form MODULE-LAMBDA(M : $\mathcal{T}$, ds), write typing rules to give the principal type of such a form.

53. *Module-arrow subtyping.* Following up on the previous exercise, when both subtype and supertype are arrow types, the result part of the subtype must provide at least as many components as the supertype's result is expecting. But the *argument* part works the other way: the subtype must ask for *at most* as much from its argument as the supertype argument is capable of providing. This reversal of direction is called *contravariance,* and it is part of any sound type system that supports subtyping with arrow types. Extend the rules for the subtyping judgment so that it works on module-arrow types.

54. *Contextual type equality.* Type equality can be made contextual, with a judgment of the form $E \vdash \tau_1 \approx \tau_2$, which means that under the assumptions explicit in environment E, types τ_1 and τ_2 are equivalent.

    (a) Write rules for this judgment.

    (b) Implement this judgment.

    For part (b), I wouldn't try to compute a substitution—I would use a union-find algorithm.

55. *Subtyping in the core layer.* In Standard ML or OCaml, subtyping of module types is complicated by the presence of polymorphism in the core layer. For example, if a supertype demands a `length` component of type `((list int) -> int)`, that demand could be satisfied by a `length` definition with the more polymorphic type `(forall ['a] ((list 'a) -> int))`.

    (a) In ML, type τ is a subtype of τ' if τ is "at least as polymorphic" as τ'—in other words, if τ is more general than τ'. Write rules for this subtype relation on core-layer types.

    (b) Assuming that there is a subtype relation $\tau <: \tau'$ on core-layer types, update the rules for subtyping on module types.

Chapter 10 contents

Smalltalk and object-orientation

10

Smalltalk's design—and existence—is due to the insight that everything we can describe can be represented by the recursive composition of a single kind of behavioral building block that hides its combination of state and process inside itself and can be dealt with only through the exchange of messages.

Alan Kay, *The Early History of Smalltalk*

Data and operations belong together, and most useful program constructs contain both.

Ole-Johan Dahl and Kristen Nygaard,
The Development of the SIMULA Languages

An abstract data type is not the only way to hide the representation of data: a representation can also be hidden in an *object*. An object is a bundle of operations—often called *methods*—that may share hidden state. An object interacts with other objects by sending *messages*; each message activates a method on the receiving object. An object's methods can see the representation of the object's own state, but not the representations of the states of other objects.

Grouping state with methods turns out to be unreasonably powerful. Perhaps as a result, object-oriented languages—or more precisely, procedural languages infused with object-oriented ideas—have been popular since the 1990s. The popular languages draw from ideas originally developed in Simula 67, Smalltalk-80, and Self, which collectively represent three decades of language design. Simula 67 (Nygaard and Dahl 1981) introduced objects and classes, which it layered on top of Algol 60, a procedural language. Smalltalk-80 simplified Nygaard and Dahl's design by eliminating the underlying procedural language; Smalltalk is purely object-oriented. Self (Ungar and Smith 1987) simplified Smalltalk's design still further, eliminating classes. For learning, the best of these languages is Smalltalk: Because it is not layered on top of a procedural language, it won't distract you with superfluous features. And because it does have classes, it is easy to relate to such successor languages as Objective C, C++, Modula-3, Ruby, Java, Ada 95, and Swift—even though most of these successors are actually procedural languages with object-oriented features.

Smalltalk is designed around one idea, simplified as much as possible, and pushed to a logical extreme: everything is an object. In Smalltalk-80, every value is an object: for example, the number 12 is an object; every class is an object; the program is an object; the compiler is an object; every activation on the call stack is an object; the programming environment is an object; every window is an object; and even most parts of the hardware (display, keyboard, mouse) are modeled by objects. Furthermore, conditionals and loops are implemented not by evaluating special syntactic forms like `if` and `while` but by sending continuations to objects. While μSmalltalk does not treat the interpreter and the hardware as objects, it does ensure that every value and class is an object, and it does implement conditionals and loops by sending continuations.

10.1 OBJECT-ORIENTED PROGRAMMING BY EXAMPLE

In Smalltalk, a computation proceeds as a sequence of actions, each of which typically mutates a variable or sends a message to an object. (An action may also allocate a closure or terminate the execution[1] of a method.) When a message is sent to an object, which is called the *receiver,* that message is *dispatched* to a *method.* Like a function in full Scheme, a Smalltalk method binds *arguments* to formal parameters, then evaluates a sequence of expressions. The method to which a message is dispatched is determined by the *class* of the object receiving the message. A class defines methods, but it also *inherits* methods from a designated *superclass.* And a class defines the representation of each of its objects, which are called *instances* of the class.

While method dispatch and inheritance are important, the heart of object-oriented programming is exchanging messages: "You don't send messages because you have objects; you have objects because you send messages" (Metz 2013, page 67). In the examples below, messages are exchanged among four sorts of objects:

- Coordinate pairs, which represent locations and which can be added and subtracted as vectors
- Shapes, which can be asked about their locations, moved to given locations, and drawn on canvases
- Pictures, which collect shapes
- Canvases, on which shapes and pictures can be drawn

The examples below begin by sending messages that draw a picture.

10.1.1 *Objects and messages*

The object that receives a message is called the message's *receiver.* On receiving a message, an object activates the execution of a *method;* the method does some internal computation and eventually replies with an *answer.* A method is a bit like a function, and an object is a lot like a bundle of functions that share state—typically mutable state. But in Smalltalk, unlike a procedural or functional programming language, the caller cannot choose what function is called—a caller chooses only what message to send. When the message is received, the method that is executed is determined by the *class* of the receiver.

Syntactically, a message send has three parts: an expression that evaluates to the receiver, the name of the message, and zero or more *arguments*:

$$exp ::= (exp\ message\text{-}name\ \{exp\})$$

[1] For Smalltalk, I say "execute" instead of "evaluate." They mean the same thing, but "execute" carries connotations of imperative features and mutable state, which are typical of Smalltalk.

In this syntax, as in Impcore's function-call syntax "(*function-name* {*exp*})," the operation that is intended is *named*. But the name means something different, and it is therefore written in a different place:

- In a procedural language like Impcore, the caller determines the code that is executed and identifies it by naming the procedure, which is written first.
- In an object-oriented language like Smalltalk, the caller picks the *name* of the message sent, and a method with that name is eventually executed, but the receiver determines which one. That's why the receiver is written first.
- In a functional language like μScheme, the caller doesn't have to *name* the code that is executed, but the semantics and syntax are like procedural semantics and syntax: the caller determines what function is executed, and the function is written first.

Receiver-first syntax is found not only in Smalltalk but also in C++, Java, JavaScript, Ruby, Modula–3, Lua, Swift, and essentially all languages that emphasize object-oriented features. Most typically, the receiver is followed by a dot, the name of the message, and arguments in parentheses.

Message sends by themselves are enough to write some interesting computations, provided some interesting objects are available to send messages to. To illustrate, I send messages that draw the picture "○□△." The messages are sent to objects that represent classes, shapes, the picture, and a "canvas" on which the picture is drawn. To start, I send the new message to the Circle class, which creates a circle object.

611a. ⟨*transcript* 611a⟩≡ 611b ▷

```
-> (use shapes.smt)      ; load shape classes defined in this section
-> (val c (Circle new))
<Circle>
```

The Circle class, like every Smalltalk class, is also an object, and by default, sending new to a class object creates a new instance of that class. The word new does not signal a special syntactic form the way it does in Java or C++; it's a message name like any other.

Next I send new to the Square class, creating a new square:

611b. ⟨*transcript* 611a⟩+≡ ◁ 611a 611c ▷

```
-> (val s (Square new))
<Square>
```

By default, a new shape has radius 1 and is located at the coordinate origin. So both s and c are initially at the origin—and s needs to be moved to the right of c. I send two messages:

- Ask circle c for the location of its East "control point."
- Tell square s to adjust its position to put its West control point at that same location.

adjustPoint:to: 621a
Circle 620
location: 621a
Square 621b

A "control point" is a point on a square in which a shape is inscribed (page 619). Control points are labeled with symbols 'North, 'South, and so on. Using control points, I tell the square, "adjust yourself to place your West control point at the same location as the circle's East control point":

611c. ⟨*transcript* 611a⟩+≡ ◁ 611b 612a ▷

```
-> (s adjustPoint:to: 'West (c location: 'East))
<Square>
```

Both `adjustPoint:to:` and `location:` are *message names*, also called *message selectors*; `s` and `c` are *receivers*; `'West`, `'East`, and `(c location: 'East)` are *arguments*. The combination of message name and arguments forms a *message*. Each message name has a number of colons equal to the number of arguments in the message.

I create a new triangle and adjust it immediately, without first placing it in a variable. The `adjustPoint:to:` message answers the triangle (its receiver).[2]

612a. ⟨*transcript* 611a⟩+≡ ◁611c 612b▷

```
-> (val t ((Triangle new) adjustPoint:to: 'Southwest (s location: 'East)))
<Triangle>
```

The expression reads almost like pidgin English: "hey new triangle, adjust your southwest control point to the location of s's east point."

I now put all three shapes into a picture.

612b. ⟨*transcript* 611a⟩+≡ ◁612a 612c▷

```
-> (val pic (Picture empty))
<Picture>
-> (pic add: c)
<Picture>
-> (pic add: s)
<Picture>
-> (pic add: t)
<Picture>
```

Message `empty` is sent to the `Picture` class, which answers a new object that represents an empty picture. Message `add:` is then sent to that object, `pic`, with different arguments. Each `add:` message answers the (modified) picture.

The picture is rendered using a *canvas*, which is created by sending the `new` message to class `TikzCanvas`.

612c. ⟨*transcript* 611a⟩+≡ ◁612b 622b▷

```
-> (val canvas (TikzCanvas new))
<TikzCanvas>
-> (pic renderUsing: canvas)
\begin{tikzpicture}[x=4pt,y=4pt]
\draw (0,0)ellipse(1 and 1);
\draw (3,1)--(1,1)--(1,-1)--(3,-1)--cycle;
\draw (4,2)--(3,0)--(5,0)--cycle;
\end{tikzpicture}
<Picture>
```

The arcane output is a program written for the TikZ package of the LaTeX typesetting system, which produces "○□△."

The examples above send `new` to several class objects, send `location:` and `adjustPoint:to:` to objects that represent shapes, send `empty` to the `Picture` class, and send `add:` and `renderUsing:` to the resulting instance of `Picture`. How did I know what messages to send? And how do the receiving objects know what to do with them? Messages and their associated behaviors are determined by *protocols* and *class definitions*, which are the subject of the next section.

10.1.2 Protocols, methods, classes, and inheritance

In Impcore, we can call any function named in the function environment ϕ. In Scheme, we can call any function we can compute, even if it has no name.

[2]Smalltalk uses the verb "to answer" in a nonstandard way. In standard English, when you answer something, the thing answered is a request: you might "answer" an email or "answer" your phone. But in Smalltalk jargon, "answer" means "to send as the answer." A method might "answer a new object" or "answer a number." This usage should grate on your ear, but like any other jargon, it soon seems normal.

withX:y: aNumber aNumber	Answer a new instance of class CoordPair with the given arguments as its (x, y) coordinates.

(a) Class protocol for CoordPair

x	Answer the x coordinate of the receiver.
y	Answer the y coordinate of the receiver.
* aNumber	Answer a new instance of class CoordPair whose (x, y) coordinates are the coordinates of the receiver, multiplied by the given number.
+ aCoordPair	Answer a new instance of class CoordPair whose (x, y) coordinates are the vector sum of the receiver and the argument.
- aCoordPair	Answer a new instance of class CoordPair whose (x, y) coordinates are the vector difference of the receiver and the argument.
print	Print the receiver in the form (x,y).

(b) Instance protocol for CoordPair

Figure 10.1: Protocols for CoordPair

In Smalltalk, we can send any message that the receiver understands. The message name is not looked up in an environment, as in Impcore, and it does not evaluate to a value, as in Scheme. Instead, it is used by the receiver to determine what code should be executed in response to the message, using the *dynamic dispatch* algorithm described in Section 10.3.4 (page 631).

The messages that an object understands form the object's *protocol*. Like a Molecule interface, a Smalltalk protocol describes an abstraction by saying what we can do with it: what messages an object understands, what arguments are sent with that message, and how the object responds.

Our first example protocols (Figure 10.1) are associated with class CoordPair, which defines an abstraction of (x, y) coordinate pairs, or equivalently, two-dimensional vectors. In the pictures, these pairs represent locations.

- The first protocol is the *class protocol* for CoordPair. This protocol specifies messages that can be sent to the CoordPair class, which is represented by an object named CoordPair. Sending withX:y: to the class results in a new object that is an *instance* of the class.

- The second protocol is the *instance protocol* for CoordPair. This protocol specifies messages that can be sent to any instance of the class. Sending * multiplies the receiving vector by a scalar, while sending + or - does vector arithmetic. Sending print prints a textual representation of the instance.

  The methods in the instance protocol are divided into three groups: access to coordinates, arithmetic, and printing. In Smalltalk-80, such groups were called "message categories," but today they are just "protocols"—so a class's instance protocol is a collection of smaller protocols.

add:,
@Collection $\mathcal{B}$ 644
@Picture 617
adjustPoint:to: 621a
location: 621a
Picture 617
renderUsing: 617
TikzCanvas 619

The CoordPair abstraction is immutable, as we can tell from its protocol: no message mutates its receiver. In general, messages can be classified using the ideas and terminology introduced in Section 2.5.2 (page 111), which are also used to classify operations in a Molecule interface. In the class protocol, message withX:y: is a *creator*. In the instance protocol, messages `*`, `-`, and `+` are *producers*. The abstraction is immutable, so the protocols include no *mutators*. Messages `x`, `y`, and `print` are *observers*.

The protocols for a class and its instances are determined by a *class definition*. A class definition associates each message name (the interface) with a method (the implementation). In μSmalltalk, a class definition is written with this syntax:

```
def ::= (class class-name
            [subclass-of superclass-name]
            [[ivars {instance-variable-name} ]]
            {method-definition} )

method-definition ::=
      (class-method method-name (formals) [[locals locals]] {exp} )
    | (method       method-name (formals) [[locals locals]] {exp} )
```

From the top down,

- A class definition names the new class and identifies its *superclass*.
- A class definition determines how every instance of the class is represented. Except for a few kinds of primitive objects, the representation is a set of named variables called *instance variables*. Each instance variable stands for a mutable location, which may contain any object.[3] The names of a class's instance variables, if any, are listed just after its superclass. And in addition to the names listed, an instance *inherits* instance-variable names from the superclass.
- A `method` definition determines how an *instance* of the class responds to the corresponding message; the message becomes part of the instance protocol.
- A `class-method` definition determines how the *class itself* responds to the corresponding message; the message becomes part of the class protocol. Both instance methods and class methods may declare local variables.

Like instance variables, the instance methods and class methods of a superclass are inherited by subclasses.

Our first class definition defines `CoordPair`, which implements the `CoordPair` protocols (Figure 10.2, on the next page).

- Every new class has to have a superclass. Unless there is a reason to choose something else, the superclass should be class `Object`. Class `Object` defines and implements a protocol useful for all objects, including such operations as printing, checking for equality, and several others. Class `CoordPair` inherits this protocol and the corresponding methods, with two exceptions: the inherited `=` and `print` methods are redefined, or, in object-oriented terminology, *overridden*.
- An instance of class `CoordPair` is represented by the *instance variables* `x` and `y`. As noted in the comment, both `x` and `y` are numbers—this is the representation invariant of the abstraction.

[3]In this book, "variable" means the name you look up in an environment to find a mutable location. But in the literature on Smalltalk-80, "variable" means the mutable location. Alas, terminology is hard to agree on.

615. ⟨*shape classes* 615⟩≡ 617 ▷

```
(class CoordPair
   [subclass-of Object]
   [ivars x y] ; two numbers          ;;;;;; Representation,
                                      ;;;;;; as instance variables

   (class-method withX:y: (anX aY)    ;;;;;; Initialization
      ((self new) initializeX:andY: anX aY))
   (method initializeX:andY: (anX aY) ;; private
      (set x anX)
      (set y aY)
      self)

   (method x () x)                    ;;;;;; Observation of coordinates
   (method y () y)

   (method = (coordPair)              ;;;;;; Equivalence
      ((x = (coordPair x)) & (y = (coordPair y))))

   (method print ()                   ;;;;;; Printing
      (left-round print) (x print) (', print) (y print) (right-round print))

   (method * (k)                      ;;;;;; Scaling and translation
      (CoordPair withX:y: (x * k) (y * k)))

   (method + (coordPair)
      (CoordPair withX:y: (x + (coordPair x)) (y + (coordPair y))))
   (method - (coordPair)
      (CoordPair withX:y: (x - (coordPair x)) (y - (coordPair y))))
)
```

Figure 10.2: Definition of class CoordPair

The method definitions can be understood only once we understand the meanings of the names they use. In Smalltalk, unlike in Molecule, access to information is controlled by controlling the environment in which each method body is evaluated; a method can access only what it can name.

Every method has access to global variables and to its named parameters, as in Scheme or Molecule, plus any local variables that might be declared with `locals`. And every method can use the special name `self`, which refers to the object receiving the message.[4] (The name `self` cannot be assigned to; a method's receiver is mutated by mutating its instance variables.) Finally, every method has access to the instance variables of the receiver, which are referred to directly by name. For example, in Figure 10.2, method `initializeX:andY:` mentions names `x` and `y`.

left-round *B* 641
Object *B* 637
print *B* 637
right-round *B* 641

Unlike a function in a Molecule module, which has access to the representation of every argument whose type is defined in that module, a Smalltalk method has access *only* to the representation of the receiver; arguments are *encapsulated.* A method has no access to the representation of any argument; all it can do with an argument is send messages to it.

In Figure 10.2, the method definitions of class `CoordPair` are organized into three groups.

[4]Because the receiver does not appear on the list of a method's formal parameters, referring to it requires a special name. Some object-oriented languages use `this` instead of `self`; others provide syntax by which the programmer can choose a name.

- Instances of class CoordPair are created by class method withX:y:, then initialized by instance method initializeX:andY:. In the class method, the self in (self new) refers to the *class* object, not to any instance. The class, like all classes, inherits the new method from class Class; the new method creates and answers a new, uninitialized object that is an instance of class CoordPair. After sending new, class method withX:y: finishes by sending the message initializeX:andY: to the new object. Method initializeX:andY: initializes instance variables x and y, then answers self—when message withX:y: is sent to the CoordPair class object, the final answer is the newly allocated, correctly initialized instance. This idiom is common: a Smalltalk object is created by sending some message to its class, and because the corresponding class method has no access to the instance variables of the new object, it initializes the object using an instance method. (The class object has no access to the instance variables of any other object, not even one of its own instances.)

  Method initializeX:andY: is commented as *private*, which means that it is intended to be used only by other methods of the class, or of its subclasses. Private methods are an essential part of object-oriented programming, and in different object-oriented languages "private" is interpreted in slightly different ways. In Smalltalk, private methods are purely a programming convention, which is not enforced by the language. Methods that initialize instance variables are often private.

- An instance of class CoordPair is printed by the print method, in the form "(x,y)." The method's body is a sequence of message sends. The print message may be sent to *any* object; it is part of the protocol for all objects (Section 10.4.1, page 636). Names x and y refer to instance variables; left-round and right-round refer to predefined objects stored in global variables, and ', is a literal symbol.

- Every instance of class CoordPair provides two methods, x and y, which answer the values of the corresponding instance variables x and y.

- Instances of class CoordPair are operated on as vectors by methods *, +, and -. The * method takes a scalar argument k and multiplies the receiver by k. Because the CoordPair abstraction is immutable, the method does not mutate any instance variables; instead, it multiplies each instance variable by k, then uses the resulting products to create a new object of class CoordPair.

  The + and - methods implement vector sum and difference. To compute the sum of the receiver vector self and the argument vector coordPair, the methods need access not only to the instance variables x and y of the receiver, but also to the x and y coordinates of the argument coordPair. They get that access by sending messages x and y to coordPair.

The definition of class CoordPair illustrates basic Smalltalk. For more advanced techniques, we examine the definitions of classes Picture and TikzCanvas, which illustrate looping over lists, then the shape classes, which illustrate inheritance.

10.1.3 Pictures: Programming with lists and blocks

Class Picture provides an abstraction of a list of shapes. Shapes can be added to the picture, and the shapes can be drawn on a *canvas*.

empty	The class answers a new instance of itself, which contains no shapes.

(a) Class protocol for pictures

add: aShape	The shape is added to those remembered by the receiver.
renderUsing: aCanvas	The receiver sends messages to aCanvas, drawing all of its remembered shapes, then answers itself.

(b) Instance protocol for pictures

Figure 10.3: Protocols for pictures

617. ⟨*shape classes* 615⟩+≡ ◁615 619▷

```
(class Picture
    [subclass-of Object]
    [ivars shapes] ; the representation: a list of shapes

    (class-method empty ()       ;;;;;;;;;;;; Initialization
        ((self new) init))
    (method init () ; private
        (set shapes (List new))
        self)

    (method add: (aShape)        ;;;;;;;;;;;; Add a shape,
        (shapes add: aShape)     ;;;;;;;;;;;; reply with the picture
        self)

    (method renderUsing: (aCanvas)
        (aCanvas startDrawing)
        (shapes do:              ;; draw each shape
           [block (shape) (shape drawOn: aCanvas)])
        (aCanvas stopDrawing)
        self)
)
```

Figure 10.4: Definition of class Picture

add: $\mathcal{B}$ 644
do: $\mathcal{B}$ 644
drawOn:,
@Circle 620
@Shape 621a
@Square 621b
Object $\mathcal{B}$ 637
startDrawing 619
stopDrawing 619

The protocols for pictures are shown in Figure 10.3. The class protocol includes just one message: sending empty to the class creates an empty picture. The instance protocol includes messages add:, which adds a shape to a picture, and renderUsing:, which asks a picture to draw itself on a canvas. The protocols are implemented by the class definition in Figure 10.4. A picture is represented by the single instance variable shapes, which is a list of shapes. An empty picture is initialized using the same idiom as in class CoordPair: class method empty calls private initialization method init, which initializes shapes with an empty list. (Class List is predefined.)

To add a shape to a picture, method add: adds the shape to the shapes list. To render a picture on a canvas, method renderUsing: prepares the canvas, draws each shape, then notifies the canvas that drawing is complete.

Shapes are drawn by a loop, which is implemented using only message passing; unlike Impcore or μScheme, Smalltalk does not have looping syntax. The loop is

new	Answer a new instance of itself, which is not yet prepared for drawing.

(a) Class protocol for canvases

`startDrawing`	Prepare the receiver for drawing.
`stopDrawing`	Tell the receiver that drawing is complete.
`drawEllipseAt:width:height: aCoordPair aNumber aNumber`	The receiver issues drawing commands for an ellipse centered at the point with the given coordinates and with the given width and height.
`drawPolygon: aList`	The receiver issues drawing commands for a polygon whose vertices are specified by the given list, which is a list of `CoordPair`s.

(b) Instance protocol for canvases

Figure 10.5: Protocols for canvases, including `TikzCanvas`

implemented by sending the `do:` message to the list of shapes. The argument to the `do:` message is a *block*, which is created by evaluating the special syntactic form

exp ::= `[block (`$\{$*argument-name*$\}$`)` $\{exp\}$`]`

Just like a `lambda` expression in Scheme, a `block` expression evaluates to a closure. But a block is not a function; it is an object, and it is activated when it receives the right sort of message.

In the `renderUsing:` method of class `Picture`, the block is activated once for each shape in the list `shapes`. That's accomplished by sending the `do:` message to the list, with the block as an argument. Sending `do:` is a lot like applying μScheme's `app` function; when passed the block shown in the figure, the `do:` method ends up sending the `drawOn:` message to each shape in `shapes`, with the canvas as the argument. This is higher-order imperative programming at its finest: without any special-purpose syntax, we achieve the effect of a `for` loop.[5]

10.1.4 A canvas, on which pictures can be drawn

A canvas object hides a secret: how to draw ellipses and polygons, and how to surround them with the bureaucracy that the rendering engine requires. A simple canvas protocol is shown in Figure 10.5, and class `TikzCanvas`, shown in Figure 10.6 on the facing page, encapsulates what I know about drawing simple pictures with LaTeX's TikZ package. Like all good encapsulation, the design makes the code easy to change: to switch to a different drawing language, like PostScript, I could simply define a new class using the same protocol (Exercise 5).

The methods of class `TikzCanvas` are ugly—because μSmalltalk does not have strings, the TikZ syntax can be emitted only by a sequence of `print` messages, which are sent both to literal symbols and to predefined Unicode characters like `left-curly`.

Like the `renderUsing:` method of class `Picture`, the `drawPolygon:` method iterates over a list, but here it is a list containing the vertices of the polygon. The block—which is effectively the body of the loop—prints the coordinates of a vertex, followed by the `--` symbol.

[5]The `drawOn:` message is part of the protocol for shapes; it is defined below.

619. ⟨*shape classes* 615⟩+≡ ◁617 620▷

```
(class TikzCanvas
    ;;;;;;;;;;;; Encapsulates TikZ syntax
    [subclass-of Object]
    (method startDrawing ()
        ('\begin print)
        (left-curly print) ('tikzpicture print) (right-curly print)
        (left-square print) ('x=4pt,y=4pt print) (right-square println))

    (method stopDrawing ()
        ('\end print)
        (left-curly print) ('tikzpicture print) (right-curly println))

    (method drawPolygon: (coord-list)
        ('\draw print) (space print)
        (coord-list do: [block (pt) (pt print) ('-- print)])
        ('cycle print)
        (semicolon println))

    (method drawEllipseAt:width:height: (center w h)
        ('\draw print) (space print) (center print) ('ellipse print)
        (left-round print)
          ((w div: 2) print) (space print) ('and print) (space print)
          ((h div: 2) print)
        (right-round print)
        (semicolon println))
)
```


Figure 10.6: Definition of class `TikzCanvas`

The `drawEllipseAt:width:height:` method requires no iteration. It converts width and height to radii, which are what TikZ wants, and then it prints.

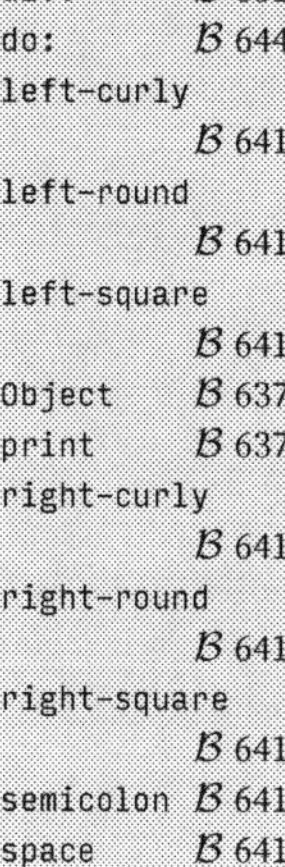

`div:`	*B* 651
`do:`	*B* 644
`left-curly`	*B* 641
`left-round`	*B* 641
`left-square`	*B* 641
`Object`	*B* 637
`print`	*B* 637
`right-curly`	*B* 641
`right-round`	*B* 641
`right-square`	*B* 641
`semicolon`	*B* 641
`space`	*B* 641

10.1.5 Shapes: Taking inheritance seriously

The `CoordPair` class illustrates arithmetic and printing, which are found in all languages. The `Picture` and `TikzCanvas` classes illustrate two of Smalltalk's built-in abstractions: lists and blocks, which are similar to abstractions found in μScheme (lists and closures). Our final example—shapes—illustrates inheritance, which is found only in object-oriented languages. Inheritance is used to create related abstractions that share functionality.

Notionally, every shape is inscribed in a square. The square is specified by its location and its *radius*, which is half its side. A square also has nine "control points," each of which is named with a symbol:

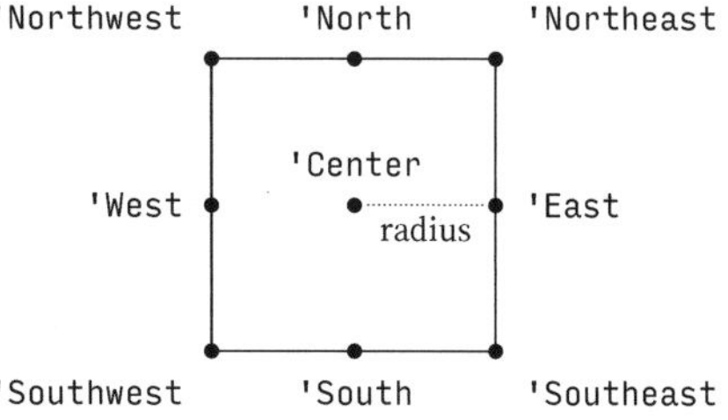

Our example picture includes three different shapes. And although each shape draws itself differently, each shape handles the circumscribing square and its con-

`new`	The class answers a new instance of itself, whose radius is 1 and whose center control point is at the coordinate origin.

(a) Class protocol for shapes

`location: aSymbol`	Answers the location of the receiver's control point that is named by the given symbol (`'North`, `'South`, ...). If the given symbol does not name a control point, the result is a checked run-time error.
`locations: symbols`	Given a list or array `symbols`, each of which names a control point, return the list of the corresponding locations. If any symbol in `symbols` does not name a control point, the result is a checked run-time error.
`adjustPoint:to: aSymbol aCoordPair`	Changes the location of the receiver so that the control point named by the given symbol is located at the given coordinate pair. Answers the receiver. If the given symbol does not name a control point, the result is a checked run-time error.
`scale: aNumber`	Multiply the size (radius) of the receiver by the given number.
`drawOn: aCanvas`	The receiver draws itself on the given canvas.

(b) Instance protocol for shapes

Figure 10.7: Protocols for shapes

trol points in the same way. For that reason, all shapes can share an implementation of the first part of the shape protocol: messages `location:`, `locations:`, `adjustPoint:to:`, and `scale:` (Figure 10.7). Each shape needs its own implementation of only one method: `drawOn:`. This kind of "sharing with a difference" is exactly what inheritance is designed to provide.

- Shared methods `location:`, `locations:`, `adjustPoint:to:`, and `scale:` are defined in a common *superclass*, which I call `Shape`. Class `Shape` (Figure 10.8, on the next page) also defines instance variables `center` and `radius`, which specify the square in which the shape is inscribed.

- Each `drawOn:` method is defined in a unique *subclass*, which inherits the representation and the other methods of class `Shape`.

My design separates concerns: the superclass knows only how to use control points to move and resize shapes, and a subclass knows only how to draw a shape.

Because each subclass defines only the `drawOn:` method, the subclass definitions are tiny, requiring little programming effort. For example, a circle is drawn by drawing an ellipse whose width and height are both twice the radius of the circumscribing square:

620. ⟨*shape classes* 615⟩+≡ ◁619 621b▷

```
(class Circle
   [subclass-of Shape]
   ;; no additional representation
   (method drawOn: (canvas)
      (canvas drawEllipseAt:width:height: center (2 * radius) (2 * radius)))
)
```

621a. ⟨*definition of class* Shape 621a⟩≡
```
(class Shape
   [subclass-of Object]
   [ivars center radius] ;; CoordPair and number

   (class-method new ()
       ((super new) center:radius: (CoordPair withX:y: 0 0) 1))
   (method center:radius: (c r) ;; private
       (set center c)
       (set radius r)
       self)

   (method location: (point-name)
       (center + ((point-vectors at: point-name) * radius)))

   (method locations: (point-names) [locals locs]
       (set locs (List new))
       (point-names do: [block (pname) (locs add: (self location: pname))])
       locs)

   (method adjustPoint:to: (point-name location)
       (set center (center + (location - (self location: point-name))))
       self)

   (method scale: (k)
       (set radius (radius * k))
       self)

   (method drawOn: (canvas)
      (self subclassResponsibility))
)
```

Figure 10.8: Definition of class Shape

What's new here is in the subclass-of form: class Circle inherits from Shape, not from Object. So it gets the representation and methods of Shape.

As another example, class Square also inherits from Shape. Its drawOn: method draws the polygon whose vertices are the four corners of the square:

621b. ⟨*shape classes* 615⟩+≡ ◁620 622a▷
```
(class Square
   [subclass-of Shape]
   ;; no additional representation
   (method drawOn: (canvas)
      (canvas drawPolygon:
              (self locations: '(Northeast Northwest Southwest Southeast))))
)
```

add:,
@Collection *B* 644
@Picture 617
at: *B* 647
CoordPair 615
do: *B* 644
drawEllipse-At:width:height: 619
drawPolygon: 619
Object *B* 637

The locations: method converts the list of control-point names into a list of coordinate pairs, which is then sent with drawPolygon:. Other shapes, including Triangle, can be defined in the Exercises.

Both Circle and Square inherit from the superclass, Shape (Figure 10.8).

- A shape is created by sending message new to its class. Class method new uses the now-familiar pattern of creating a new object, then using a private method to initialize it. But there is something different here: to allocate the new object, the class method sends the new message to super, not to self. Sending a message to super is a language feature that is described in detail in

Section 10.3.4 (page 632); for now, accept that sending new to super sends the new message to class Shape, but in a way that dispatches to the new method inherited from class Class. Sending new to self would dispatch to the redefined new method, which would cause infinite recursion.

- The location associated with a control point is computed by the location: method, which finds a vector associated with the control point, multiplies that vector by the radius, and adds the resulting vector to the center. To associate a vector with each control point, I define a global variable point-vectors of class Dictionary (page 646).

622a. ⟨*shape classes* 615⟩+≡ ◁621b

```
(val point-vectors (Dictionary new))
(point-vectors at:put: 'Center    (CoordPair withX:y: 0 0))
(point-vectors at:put: 'East      (CoordPair withX:y: 1 0))
(point-vectors at:put: 'Northeast (CoordPair withX:y: 1 1))
; ... six more definitions follow ...
```

Sending at:put: to a dictionary stores a key-value pair. Sending at: to the dictionary, as in method location: of class Shape, answers the value stored with the given key.

- A list of locations is computed by the locations: method, which uses the same do: as the renderUsing: method of the Picture class. In locations:, the do: loop adds each location to a list locs, which is stored in a local variable of the method.

- A shape is moved by adjusting a given control point to a given location. The adjustPoint:to: method updates the center of the shape, computing a new center by sending + and - messages to objects of class CoordPair. This arithmetic is hidden from clients that send messages to shapes; such clients know only about the names of control points, not about vector arithmetic.

- A shape is changed in size by changing its instance variable radius, which is done in the scale: method.

- A shape is drawn by sending it the drawOn: message, but if drawOn: is sent to an instance of class Shape, the message send fails with a special run-time error:

622b. ⟨*transcript* 611a⟩+≡ ◁612c 632a▷

```
-> ((Shape new) drawOn: canvas)
Run-time error: subclass failed to implement a method it was responsible for
Method-stack traceback:
  In shapes.smt, line 105, sent `subclassResponsibility' to an object of class Shape
  In standard input, line 45, sent `drawOn:' to an object of class Shape
```

Sending drawOn: to an instance of class Shape causes an error because class Shape is not meant to be instantiated—only *subclasses* like Circle, Square, and Triangle are meant to be instantiated. A class like Shape, which is meant to collect reusable methods but not to be instantiated, is called an *abstract class*. Subclasses then inherit from the abstract class. A subclass that is meant to be instantiated may inherit as many methods as it likes, except those that send subclassResponsibility—those methods must be redefined.

In Smalltalk, the "abstract class," like the "private method," is a programming convention, not a language feature. Client code should never create an instance of an abstract class; it should instead create instances of concrete subclasses.

10.1.6 *Object-orientation means dynamic dispatch*

The shapes examples uncover some of the essence of Smalltalk. In some ways, Smalltalk resembles Impcore:

- Smalltalk has no static types.
- Idiomatic code is imperative: it uses `set` and it evaluates expressions in sequence.
- A message send, like an Impcore function call, always uses a name.

In Impcore, calling a function requires you to name the function, and in Smalltalk, sending a message requires you to name the message. But in Impcore, a function name always refers to the same function, no matter what arguments are passed; the code that is executed is determined by the caller. Whereas in Smalltalk, a message name may be implemented by any number of methods, and the code that is executed—the method that a message is *dispatched* to—is determined by the receiver. For example whenever a `+` or `-` message is sent to an instance of class `CoordPair`, the message dispatches to the `+` or `-` method defined in class `CoordPair`. But in the body of those methods, the `+` and `-` messages are sent to instances of numeric classes, and those messages dispatch to different methods.

Even a single message send from a single place in the source code can be dispatched to different methods on different evaluations. For example, in the `renderUsing:` method of class `Picture`, the `drawOn:` message is sent to each of a list of shapes. But depending on whether a shape is a `Circle`, `Square`, or `Triangle`, that message dispatches to a different method—even though the source code being evaluated is the same each time. When a message is sent, it dispatches to a method that is selected by an algorithm called *dynamic dispatch*. Dynamic dispatch is the essence of object-oriented programming; Smalltalk's version is explained in Section 10.3.4 (page 631).

10.1.7 *Review and analysis*

The shapes examples illustrate message sends, method dispatch, protocols, representation, object creation, and inheritance.

- A computation is implemented by a small army of objects that exchange *messages*. Each message is dispatched to a *method*, which is chosen at run time based on the class of the *receiver*. As often as not, a method is executed for its side effects, like updating instance variables, or printing.
- A method may be designated *private*, which means that its use should be limited to certain senders. For example, a message designated as private might be sent only by an object to itself, or by a class to its instances. In Smalltalk, the designation is purely advisory: it records a programmer's intent, but it is not enforced. In practice, "private" may also designate a message that is intended to be sent by instances of a class to other objects that are believed to be of the same class.
- The set of messages an object understands, together with the behavior that is expected in response to those message, is the object's *protocol*. Because Smalltalk does not have a static type system, protocols are specified informally. An object's protocol is determined by the class of which the object is an *instance*. The same protocol can be implemented by many different classes, which are often related by *inheritance*. But they don't have to be

related: an existing protocol can be implemented by an entirely new class that does not inherit from any existing implementation, like `PSCanvas` (Exercise 5).

Although Smalltalk does not have a static type system, it does have a way to ensure that a message is accompanied by the correct number of arguments: the number of arguments is determined by the name of the message. If the name begins with a letter, like `drawOn:`, the message expects a number of arguments equal to the number of colons in the name. If the name begins with a nonletter, like `+`, the message expects exactly one argument. Ensuring that the number of arguments matches the number expected by the name costs almost nothing, but like a type, it serves as documentation that is checked by the compiler. And it catches mistakes at compile time. In proper Smalltalk-80 syntax, colons break the name into parts, which are *interleaved* among the arguments. This concrete syntax, while unusual, leads to code that I enjoy reading (Section 10.12).

- An object is represented by a fixed set of named *instance variables*. An object's instance variables are visible only to the object's own methods; they are hidden from all other objects, even from other instances of the same class. And an object's instance variables form the product in the *sum of products* representation mentioned in Chapters 8 and 9, which is so useful for representing linked data structures.

- A new object is created by sending a message to its class, often the `new` message. The message dispatches to a class method, which allocates a new object and may also invoke an instance method to initialize the new object's instance variables. Occasionally a new object is created by evaluating some other syntactic form, like a `block` expression, a literal integer, a literal symbol, or a class definition.

- Every class definition specifies a *superclass*, from which the new class inherits both methods and instance variables. A class can be defined whose sole purpose is to be inherited from, like the `Shape` class. Such a class, which is not intended for instantiation, is called an *abstract class*. A class whose methods send the `subclassResponsibility` message is always abstract.

Although Smalltalk shares ideas with procedural and functional languages, it does many things in its own way.

- A method resembles a function or a procedure, and an object resembles a bundle of functions that share mutable state. And since objects themselves are sent with messages and are returned as answers, object-oriented programming resembles programming with higher-order functions, only more so: any time an object is sent with a message, the message may set off a higher-order computation. This is why we study functions before objects.

- In Impcore, Scheme, and ML, conditional expressions are a normal way to make decisions. A conditional expression might ask, "Are you a circle or a triangle or a square?" and then draw the shape accordingly. Not in Smalltalk! Instead, decisions are made via dynamic dispatch: code just sends the `drawOn:` message, and based on the class of the receiver, method dispatch decides how to draw it.

  Multiple classes that all respond to `drawOn:` form a sum in the sum of products mentioned above and in Chapters 8 and 9. And because `drawOn:` is dispatched dynamically, new elements (new shapes) can easily be added to the sum without touching any existing code. This open extensibility, which can't be replicated using standard algebraic data types, is characteristic of object-oriented programming.

- Making decisions via dynamic dispatch influences the structure of programs: compared with the number of function definitions and function calls in a functional program, a similar object-oriented program likely has more method definitions and more message sends. For example, to draw a picture, we send messages to shapes, which send messages back to the picture object. For a programmer who is used to procedural or functional programming, distributing a computation over multiple methods defined on multiple classes may make it hard to identify the algorithm: the "procedure," meaning the sequence of steps being performed, is not written in one place.

  Moving from procedural programming to object-oriented programming requires a change in mindset. If you are used to seeing the steps of an algorithm laid out in sequence in a single block of code, you are going to be frustrated by object-oriented programming: what the procedural programmer thinks of as a simple sequence of commands is usually distributed over many methods defined on many classes, and it may be hard to identify. The object-oriented programmer focuses on the protocols. If the protocols are well designed and each object does one job, each individual method becomes much easier to understand than a typical procedure full of conditionals and `while` loops. Moreover, although a conceptual procedure may be hard to identify, the individual commands become easy to reuse: for example, a class that inherits from `Shape` reuses everything except the `drawOn:` method. Learning to design with protocols and message passing—though difficult—is the key to becoming a productive object-oriented programmer.

- In Smalltalk, the initial basis plays a greater role than in Impcore, Scheme, or ML. Even basic control structures and data structures, like conditionals, loops, and lists, are coded in the initial basis; they are not part of the language proper. To program effectively in Smalltalk, you must learn about the predefined classes, like the lists and dictionaries used in the pictures example.

10.2 DATA ABSTRACTION ALL OVER AGAIN

A Smalltalk class defines an abstraction. And as an abstraction, a Smalltalk class is subject to the same design criteria that apply to an abstract data type in a Molecule module (Section 9.6). In a good design, the abstractions are well thought out and are specified using mathematics or metaphor. The operations on the abstraction—the methods defined on the class—have costs that are clearly stated. And to be sure the code is right, the implementation of the abstraction is accompanied by a representation invariant and an abstraction function.

Although object fits within the same data-abstraction framework as abstract types, objects are not abstract types and Smalltalk is not Molecule; they have different capabilities, and they are customarily used in different ways.

- An object-oriented abstraction, like any other abstraction, is either mutable or immutable. But the choice is influenced by the surroundings. Smalltalk, which is built on `set` expressions, favors mutable abstractions, while Molecule, which is built on `case` expressions, favors immutable abstractions. And in Smalltalk, as in other object-oriented languages, the customary, predefined abstractions tend to be mutable.

Data abstraction for "open" and "closed" systems

Systems based on abstract data types are "closed," and can thereby be made reliable. Systems based on objects and protocols are "open," and can thereby be made extensible.

Using abstract data types, as in Molecule, a representation is hidden in a module, and access is mediated by a module type that exports an abstract type T. The line between "visible" and "hidden" is fixed:

- Only operations inside the module can see the representation of values of type T.
- An operation inside the module can see the representation of *any* value of type T, no matter where it comes from.

Once the module is sealed, the representation of T can't be seen by new modules. And new abstractions can't be made compatible with T: a new module's abstract types, even if defined identically to T, cannot be used in a context that expects T. New, compatible code can be added only by opening up an existing module and editing it; the interface used to seal the module might also need editing. Code added outside the module can't extend its capabilities but also can't make it fail.

Using objects, as in Smalltalk, a representation is hidden inside an object, and access is mediated by a protocol. The line between "visible" and "hidden" is drawn differently:

- Only methods defined on an object can see that object's representation.
- A method defined on an object can see *only* that object's representation, not the representation of any other object. This principle, which Cook (2009) calls the *autognostic principle,* is a defining characteristic of object-oriented programming.

The representation of an object can be seen by new code, provided that code appears in methods that are defined in a new subclass. And new abstractions can be made compatible with old ones: if a new object implements an old protocol, then it can be used in any context that expects the old protocol. An object-oriented system can be extended without editing existing code.

- Like Molecule functions, Smalltalk methods can be classified as creators, producers, observers, or mutators. But in Molecule, all the functions are specified in a single module type. In Smalltalk, the methods are part of *two* protocols. The instance protocol specifies only mutators, producers, and observers, but not creators. By definition, a creation message is sent in order to create an instance where none yet exists, so it can't be sent to an instance. A creation message is sent to an object's class, and an object's creators are therefore part of a class protocol.

Objects and abstract data types support data abstraction in different ways, and these differences lead to differences in client code.

- In Molecule, an abstraction is specified by a named abstract data type, and operations of the abstraction work only with values of that type. In Smalltalk, an abstraction is specified by a protocol, and operations of the abstraction work with objects of any class that implements the protocol. If an object implements the fraction protocol, then it walks like a fraction, talks like a fraction, and exchanges messages in the protocol for fractions—so even if its definition doesn't inherit from class `Fraction`, for programming purposes it's a fraction. Because an object's behavior is what matters, this property is called *behavioral subtyping*, or by Ruby programmers, "duck typing."

- In a Smalltalk method, `self` is the only object whose representation is accessible. Objects sent as arguments must implement the expected protocols, but a method defined on the receiver cannot see their representations. Methods that wish they could see arguments' representations, like `+` and `-` on class `CoordPair`, have to send messages to those arguments instead—usually messages like `x` and `y`. In Molecule, the analogous operations get to see all relevant representations directly.

- A Smalltalk class can specify not a single abstraction, but a family of related abstractions. Members of the family are implemented by subclasses. Examples shown in this chapter include shapes, numbers, and "collections." Additional examples found only in full Smalltalk include input streams and user-interface widgets.

Compared with Molecule modules, Smalltalk classes are more flexible and easier to reuse, but operations that wish to see multiple representations are harder to implement. And unlike Molecule, Smalltalk does not have a type checker, so it cannot guarantee that every operation is given abstractions that it knows how to work with. To understand how these trade-offs work, study the design and implementation of the `Collection` hierarchy, shown in Sections 10.4.5, 10.7.1, 10.7.2, and 10.9.

10.3 THE μSMALLTALK LANGUAGE

10.3.1 Concrete syntax and its evaluation

The concrete syntax of μSmalltalk is shown in Figure 10.9 on the next page. Three of the first four expression forms are shared with Impcore and μScheme: variables, `set`, and `begin`. All three languages also have literal expressions, but each one has a different set—μSmalltalk has integer literals and symbol literals as in μScheme, but in place of list literals, μSmalltalk has array literals, and it has no Boolean literals.

μSmalltalk's remaining expression forms are found neither in Impcore nor in μScheme. Most important, instead of function application μSmalltalk has message send. In a send, the message, like an Impcore function, is identified by name.[6] Every message name has an *arity*, which is the number of arguments that the message expects. If the *message-name* begins with a nonletter, its arity is 1. If the *message-name* begins with a letter, its arity is the number of colons in the name.

In addition to message send and to the shared forms, a μSmalltalk expression can be a *block*, which is like a `lambda` abstraction in Scheme. A block specifies

[6] Impcore's functions are not values, but μScheme's functions *are* values. Are μSmalltalk's functions values? It depends what you mean by "function." If you mean "block," then yes, blocks are values. If you mean "message name," then no, message names are not values. (In Smalltalk-80, the message name is called a *message selector*, and it can be given as a value with the `perform:` message.)

```
exp       ::= literal
            | variable-name
            | (set variable-name exp)
            | (begin {exp})
            | (exp message-name {exp})
            | [block ({argument-name}) {exp}]
            | {{exp}}
            | (return exp)
            | (primitive primitive-name {exp})
            | (compiled-method (formals) [[locals locals]] {exp})

literal   ::= integer-literal
            | 'symbol-name
            | '({array-element})

array-element
          ::= integer-literal
            | symbol-name
            | ({array-element})

formals   ::= {formal-parameter-name}

locals    ::= {local-variable-name}


def       ::= (val variable-name exp)
            | exp
            | (define block-name (formals) exp)
            | (class subclass-name
                 [subclass-of superclass-name]
                 [[ivars {instance-variable-name}]]
                 {method-definition})
            | (use file-name)
            | unit-test

unit-test ::= (check-expect exp exp)
            | (check-assert exp)
            | (check-error exp)
            | (check-print exp name)

method-definition
          ::= (method        method-name (formals) [[locals locals]] {exp})
            | (class-method  method-name (formals) [[locals locals]] {exp})


numeral   ::= token composed only of digits, possibly prefixed with a plus
              or minus sign

any *-name
          ::= token that is not a bracket, a numeral, or one of the "re-
              served" words shown in typewriter font
```

Figure 10.9: Concrete syntax of μSmalltalk

zero or more formal parameters and a body. The body contains a sequence of expressions, which are executed in, well, sequence. Because parameterless blocks are used often to implement control flow, they are supported with some syntactic sugar: the μSmalltalk expression `{`$e_1 \cdots e_n$`}` stands for `[block ()` $e_1 \cdots e_n$`]`. This syntax is borrowed from Ruby, a descendant of Smalltalk-80.[7]

Expression forms for literals, variables, `set`, and `begin` are evaluated as in Impcore or μScheme—though it may be worth noting that the evaluation of a literal expression allocates a new object. But message send, although it may look like a function call, is its own beast; it is discussed in Section 10.3.4 (page 631). And a block, whether it is written using the `block` keyword or the curly braces, is evaluated very much like μScheme's `lambda`: it captures an environment and forms a closure.

The last three expression forms in Figure 10.9 are not related to anything in Impcore or μScheme. The `return` form is a control operator that is subtly different from the control operators in Chapter 3: a `return` is evaluated by terminating the *method* in which it appears. A `primitive` expression is evaluated almost like a call to a primitive function in Impcore: the primitive is named, it takes arguments, and it returns one object as a result. And a `compiled-method` expression is evaluated a little bit like a block, except it does not capture an environment; a `compiled-method` evaluates to an object that contains only code, which can be added to an existing class as a new method.

The definition forms of μSmalltalk include the usual `val`, *exp*, `define`, `use` forms found in Impcore and μScheme, as well as a `class` definition. The familiar forms are evaluated as expected, except that in μSmalltalk, `define` defines a block, not a function. Class definitions are unique to μSmalltalk; evaluating a class definition adds a new *class object* to the global environment. Class objects and their creation are discussed in detail in Section 10.11.4 (page 694).

μSmalltalk also has the same unit-test forms as Impcore and μScheme, plus an additional `check-print` form: provided an object prints as a single token, the `check-print` form can be used to test its `print` method.

To understand how message sends and class objects work, we should first study μSmalltalk's values.

10.3.2 Values

In μSmalltalk, every value is an object. An object's properties are determined by its class, so working with objects requires knowledge of the predefined classes and their protocols. The protocols are described in detail below (Section 10.4), but there are a lot of them, and a preview will help.

Properties shared by all objects

Every object is an instance of some class, which eventually inherits from class `Object`. Therefore every object responds to the messages in `Object`'s protocol. These messages include `=`, `==`, `println`, `class`, and many others. They are a bit like predefined functions in other languages, with an important difference: they can be redefined.

[7] Smalltalk-80 writes blocks in square brackets, but in this book, square brackets work just like round brackets—you mix square and round brackets in whatever way you find easiest to read.

The undefined object, `nil`

The object `nil` is the sole instance of class `UndefinedObject`. It conventionally represents a bad, missing, undefined, or uninitialized value. Smalltalk's `nil` is quite different from the `nil` used in some dialects of Lisp, Scheme, Prolog, and ML, which represents the empty list.

Other predefined objects

A literal symbol, written `'`*name*, is an object of class `Symbol`. Like all objects, symbols can usefully be printed and compared for equality. A symbol also understands a `hash` message, to which it responds with an integer.

The Boolean objects `true` and `false` are predefined. A Boolean object responds to the message `ifTrue:ifFalse:`, whose arguments are two *blocks*. Depending on the value of the receiver, `ifTrue:ifFalse:` evaluates one block or the other. Boolean objects also respond to many other messages, including `and:`, `or:`, and `not`.

A block is an object that understands messages `value`, `value:`, `value:value:`, and so on. A block behaves just like a `lambda` abstraction, except that it is activated by sending it one of these messages, not by applying it—Smalltalk does not have function application. A block also responds to the message `whileTrue:`, whose argument is a block; the method keeps sending `value` to `self`, and as long the receiver answers `true`, the argument block is executed.

Class objects

Every class definition creates a class object, which itself has a class that inherits (through intermediaries) from class `Class`. The class object can respond to `new` and possibly to other class-dependent initialization messages. And the class object is an instance of another class: The object representing class `C` is an instance of `C`'s *metaclass*. (It is the *only* instance of `C`'s metaclass.) The metaclass holds `C`'s class methods. In more detail, if an object `c` is an instance of class `C`, the messages that `c` can respond to are those defined on `C`'s class object. Similarly, the messages that class `C` can respond to are those defined on `C`'s metaclass. Because every metaclass inherits from class `Class`, which defines `new`, every class object can respond to a `new` message.

In addition to `new`, class `Class` defines other methods that enable client code to interrogate or alter a class. For example, `printProtocol` prints all the messages that a class and its instances know how to respond to; `superclass` answers the class object of the receiver's superclass, if any; `compiledMethodAt:` answers a method; and `addSelector:withMethod:` can add a new method or change an existing one. Such *reflective* facilities, which enable the language to manipulate itself, are even more numerous in full Smalltalk-80, in which you can learn the names of methods and instance variables, execute methods by name, create new subclasses, and much more, all by sending messages. The reflection methods are so powerful that Smalltalk-80's class browsers and debuggers are implemented in Smalltalk itself.

10.3.3 Names

Just as Impcore has distinct name spaces for functions and values, μSmalltalk has distinct name spaces for message names and variables. The name of a message is resolved *dynamically*: until a message is sent, we can't tell what method will be executed to respond to it. The name of a variable is resolved *statically*; that is, we can tell by looking at a class definition what each variable name in each method must stand for. In particular, the name of a variable stands for one of the following possibilities:

1. A formal parameter of a block
2. A local variable of a method
3. A formal parameter of a method
4. An instance variable of an object
5. A global variable

A name stands for the first possibility that is consistent with the source code where the name appears. For example, if a name appears in a block, is not a formal parameter of that block, but is a local variable of the method in which the block appears, then it's a local variable (possibility 2). In the implementation, each possibility is represented by an environment, and the environments are combined into a single environment using the <+> function (chunks 690a and 691c). Not all possibilities apply in all contexts; for example, a name in a top-level expression doesn't appear inside a method or a class definition, so it must stand either for a parameter of a block or for a global variable.

In possibility 4, a name x appearing in a method of class C can stand for an instance variable if x is declared as an instance variable in class C *or in any of C's ancestors.* (To avoid confusion, if x is declared as an instance variable of an ancestor, it may not also be declared as an instance variable of class C.)

The environment in which a name is looked up enforces a form of encapsulation: *the instance variables of an object are visible only to a method executed on that object.* This encapsulation of the instance variables hides them from all other objects, even other objects of the same class. This encapsulation mechanism differs from Molecule's mechanism: in Molecule, if an operation is located inside a module that defines an abstract type, it automatically has access to the representation of *any* value of that type. A Smalltalk method, by contrast, has access only to the representation of its receiver. To an object, all *other* objects are abstract.

The names `self` and `super` are not, properly speaking, variables; for one thing, `self` and `super` cannot be mutated with `set`. Within a method, `self` stands for the object that received the message which caused the method to be executed. The name `super` stands for the same object, but with different rules for method dispatch, which are described in the next section.

Unlike the name of a variable, the name of a message—called a *message selector* —does not by itself determine what method will be executed when the message is sent. Instead, the method is determined at run time by a process called *dynamic dispatch.* Dynamic dispatch determines a method based on the *combination* of the message selector and the class of the object to which the message is sent. This object, the receiver, may be different on different executions, even on different iterations of the same loop—and so may be the method.

10.3.4 Message sends, inheritance, and dynamic dispatch

Except when a message is sent to `super`, an object of class C responds to any message for which a method is defined in C—or in any of C's ancestors. When an object of class C receives a message with selector m, it looks in C's definition for a method named m. If that fails, it looks in the definition of C's superclass, and so on. When it finds a definition of a method for m, it executes that method. If it reaches the top of the hierarchy without finding a definition of m, an error has occurred: the message is *not understood.*

For example, when `location:` is sent to an object of class `Circle`, class `Circle` does not define a `location:` method, but `Circle`'s superclass, class `Shape`, *does* define a `location:` method, so the message is dispatched to the `location:` method defined on class `Shape`. On the other hand, if `drawOn:` is sent to an object of class `Circle`, it is immediately dispatched to the `drawOn:` method defined on class `Circle`—class `Shape` is not consulted.

Unlike an ancestor's instance variable, an ancestor's method can be redefined. When a method is defined in C and also in an ancestor, and the relevant message is sent to an object of class C, it is C's definition of the method that is executed. This method-dispatch rule produces outcomes that might surprise you, so let's look at a contrived example.

Suppose classes `B` (the superclass or ancestor) and `C` (the subclass) are defined as follows:

632a. ⟨*transcript* 611a⟩+≡ ◁622b 632b▷

```
-> (class B [subclass-of Object]
     (method m1 () (self m2))
     (method m2 () 'B))
-> (class C [subclass-of B]
     (method m2 () 'C))
```

Method `m2`, which is defined in superclass `B`, is also defined in subclass `C`. Method `m2` is said to be *overridden* by class `C`.

When message `m1` or `m2` is sent to an instance of class `B` or `C`, what happens? When `m1` or `m2` is sent to an instance of class `B`, the instance answers the symbol `B`. And when `m2` is sent to an instance of class `C`, method dispatch finds the definition of `m2` within `C`, and the instance answers the symbol `C`. But when `m1` is sent to an instance of class `C`, the instance's answer might surprise you:

632b. ⟨*transcript* 611a⟩+≡ ◁632a 635b▷

```
-> (val x (C new))
-> (x m1)
C
```

The answer `C` is delivered by the following computation:

1. When `m1` is sent to `x`, `x` is an instance of class `C`, and class `C` does not define method `m1`. But `C`'s superclass, class `B`, *does* define `m1`. So the message is dispatched to `B`'s `m1` method, which executes.

2. `B`'s `m1` method sends message `m2` to `self`—which is to say, to `x`. The search for method `m2` begins in `x`'s class, namely `C`.

3. Class `C` defines `m2`, so the message send dispatches to that definition. And class `C`'s `m2` method answers the symbol `C`.

This example illustrates a crucial fact about Smalltalk: *the search for a method begins in the class of the receiver.* Many more examples of method dispatch appear throughout the chapter.

Does method dispatch *always* begin in the class of the receiver? Almost always. A message sent to `super` is dispatched in a special way. The message is sent to `self`, but the method search begins *in the superclass of the class in which the message to* `super` *appears.* That is, unlike the starting place for a normal message send, the starting place for a message to `super` is *statically determined,* independent of the class of the receiver `self`. This behavior guarantees that a particular method from the superclass will be executed.

We typically send to `super` when we wish to *add* to the behavior of an inherited method, not simply replace it. The most common examples are class methods that initialize objects, like method `new` in class `Shape`. A `new` method is defined on every class, and a properly designed `new` method not only allocates a new object but also establishes the private invariants of its class. Simply sending `new` to `self` executes only the `new` method defined on the class of the object being created. But if there are invariants associated with the superclass, those invariants need to be established too. *All* the invariants can be established by the following idiom: each subclass sends `new` to `super`, establishing the superclass invariants, then executes whatever additional code is needed to establish subclass invariants. And when a subclass has no invariants of its own, it can take a shortcut and simply inherit `new`.

10.3.5 Equality: Identity and equivalence

Below, Section 10.4 dives into Smalltalk's initial basis, starting with the messages that every object understands. But some of those messages implement equality tests, which deserve a section of their own.

The issue of when two objects should be considered equal is one we have danced around since Chapter 2. Equality is so central, and yet so seldom addressed well, that when you encounter a new programming language, it is one of the first things you should look at. This section will tell you what to look for.

Almost all languages support constant-time equality tests on simple, scalar values like integers and Booleans. But equality tests on more structured data, like records, sums, and arrays, can be done in more than one way—and there is no single right way (Noble et al. 2016). Moreover, when a language supports data abstraction, it is all too easy to test equality in the wrong way, by violating abstraction. To expose some of the issues, let's review some designs you've already seen.

- C has only one form of equality, and it applies only to scalar data (integers, Booleans, floating-point numbers, and similar) and to pointers. Two pointers are equal if and only if they point to the same memory; viewed at a higher level of abstraction, C's == operator tests for *object identity*. (A well-known beginner's mistake is to use == to compare strings for equality; that comparison demands `strcmp`.) Structured data like `struct`s and `union`s cannot be compared for equality, and C famously does not have arrays—only pointers and memory.[8]

- μScheme has two forms of equality, written `=` and `equal?`. The `=` operator works only on scalar data; given two pairs, it always returns `#f`—according to μScheme's `=`, a cons cell is not even equal to itself. The `equal?` predicate, on the other hand, provides *structural similarity*; it returns `#t` whenever two values have the same structure, even if the structure is arbitrarily large.

  Full Scheme, in which cons cells are mutable, has a more principled design. Function `equal?` acts as in μScheme, providing structural similarity. Function `eqv?` provides object identity, and it compares not only scalar data but also cons cells, vectors, and procedures. And function `eq?` provides object identity on structured data, but on numeric data and character data it is more efficient if less predictable than `eqv?`.

`Object` *B* 637

- Standard ML has "polymorphic equality" comparison on integers, Booleans, strings, and mutable reference cells, but not on functions or floating-point numbers. Polymorphic equality can compare values of any type that "admits equality"; such types include the ones listed above, plus any constructed data

[8]"Does not have arrays" stretches the truth. In initialized data, array notation and pointer notation mean different things (Van der Linden 1994, chapter 4).

(tuple type, record type, or algebraic data type) whose components all admit equality. There are even special type variables that admit equality and that instantiated only with types that admit equality. Polymorphic equality hacks together object identity (for arrays and references) with structural similarity (for constructed data) in a hybrid that gets common cases right.

OCaml, like Scheme, has two forms of equality; the = sign means structural similarity, and the == sign means object identity (and is fully defined for mutable types only).

All these designs get abstract data wrong. For evidence, review the association lists in Section 2.9 (page 132). Two association lists should be considered equal if and only if each contains all the key-value pairs found in the other. This equivalence relation, which is the correct one, is coarser than equivalence of representation. If two association lists have the same representation, they definitely represent the same associations, and therefore if two association lists represent different associations, they definitely have different representations. But two association lists may have different representations and yet represent the same associations. Given such lists, Scheme's `equal?` and ML's polymorphic equality produce wrong answers. Smalltalk's *built-in* = and == messages, which correspond roughly to μScheme's `equal?` and =, pose the same risk. To produce right answers, the built-in = method may have to be overridden. And overriding it correctly requires deep understanding of what it could mean to consider two objects equivalent.

Notions of equivalence

To get equality right, Smalltalk uses the same methodology as Molecule. The methodology is based on a central idea of programming-language theory, called *observational equivalence.* A pointy-headed theorist would say that two things are observationally equivalent if there is no computational context that can distinguish them. For a programmer who doesn't normally talk about computational contexts, the idea makes more sense as a programming principle:

> *Two values should be considered equal if no program can tell them apart.*

The principle has immediate consequences:

- A mutable abstraction, like a dictionary, should compare equal only with itself. That's because two different mutable objects can be told apart by mutating one and seeing that the other doesn't change. Therefore, on mutable data, equality must be implemented as *object identity.*
- Structurally similar representations of immutable, non-atomic abstractions, like large integers, should be considered equal.

In Smalltalk, object identity is implemented by the == method, which is defined on class `Object`:

634. ⟨*methods of class* `Object` 634⟩≡ 635a ▷

```
(method ==  (anObject) (primitive sameObject self anObject))
(method !== (anObject) ((self == anObject) not))
```

The = method, by contrast, should implement observational equivalence. But "any program" shouldn't be allowed to observe a representation; programs are just too powerful. Like object identity and ML's polymorphic equality, an unrestricted program can observe differences between objects even when the objects really should be considered the same. It's better to restrict programs by ruling out some observations.

- *Abstractions* should be considered equivalent when no *client* code can tell them apart. For example, if finite maps are represented as association lists, and if no combination of `find` and `bind` operations can tell two maps apart, then they should be considered equivalent even if they are represented differently (page 132).

- If an abstraction is mutable, you might want to rule out *mutation* as a way of observing differences. For example, perhaps lists `ns` and `ms` have the same elements right now, so you'd like to consider them equivalent, even if adding number 80 to list `ns` (but not `ms`) would enable you to tell them apart.

- Finally, in a language like Smalltalk, even though reflection can breach the abstraction barrier it should not be used to distinguish objects that would otherwise be indistinguishable.

All these restrictions apply to μSmalltalk's notion of equivalence:

> *Two objects are considered equivalent if, without mutating either object or using reflection, client code cannot tell them apart.*

In other words, two objects are considered equivalent if at this moment they represent the same abstraction. This is the equivalence that is used by μSmalltalk's `check-expect` and implemented by the = method.

To implement = correctly on each class requires an understanding of the class's representation invariant and abstraction function (Section 9.6, page 545). But as a default, a conservative approximation is defined on all objects:

635a. ⟨*methods of class* `Object` 634⟩+≡ ◁634 655a▷

```
(method =  (anObject) (self == anObject))
(method != (anObject) ((self = anObject) not))
```

This default is conservative in the sense that if it says two objects are equivalent, they really are. If two objects are equivalent but not identical, however, the default = will report, incorrectly, that they are different.

Identity versus equivalence: An example

To illustrate the distinction between identity and equivalence, the following example uses lists. The two lists `ns` and `ms` are built differently:

635b. ⟨*transcript* 611a⟩+≡ ◁632b 636▷

```
-> (val ns (List new))
List( )
-> (ns addFirst: 3)
-> (ns addFirst: 2)
-> (ns addFirst: 1)
-> ns
List( 1 2 3 )
-> (val ms (List new))
List( )
-> (ms addLast: 1)
-> (ms addLast: 2)
-> (ms addLast: 3)
-> ms
List( 1 2 3 )
```

`addFirst:` *B* 649
`addLast:` *B* 649
`List` *B* 649

> *Why no mutation?*
>
> If object-orientation is all about data abstraction, then of course objects should be considered different only if *client* code can tell them apart. But why shouldn't the client code be allowed to mutate? In isolation, this restriction makes little sense. But in the context of a whole language design, the restriction makes pragmatic sense: if you already have object identity, and if you permit client code to mutate objects, then client-code observation gives you nothing new. A second form of observational equivalence is useful only if it gives different results.

Lists `ns` and `ms` aren't the same object, but because they represent the same sequence of values, they are equivalent:

636. ⟨*transcript* 611a⟩+≡ ◁635b 637▷

```
-> (ns == ms)
<False>
-> (ns = ms)
<True>
```

10.4 THE INITIAL BASIS OF μSMALLTALK

Much of Smalltalk's power comes from its impressive predefined classes; using and inheriting from these classes is an essential part of effective Smalltalk programming. By the standards of Smalltalk-80, μSmalltalk's hierarchy of predefined classes is small, but by the standards of this book, it is large—sufficient to help you learn what Smalltalk programming is like, but too large to digest all at once. So you'll start by digesting just the abstractions that the predefined classes represent and the protocols they understand (this section, 10.4). That will be enough so that you can use the classes. Then to develop good μSmalltalk skills, you can go on to study key techniques as illustrated by *implementations* of some predefined classes (Sections 10.6 to 10.9).

10.4.1 Protocol for all objects

Every μSmalltalk object responds to the messages in Figure 10.10 (on the next page), which are defined on the primitive class `Object`. Messages `=` and `!=` test for equivalence, while `==` and `!==` test for identity. Messages `isNil` and `notNil` test for "definedness."

The `print` message is used by the μSmalltalk interpreter itself to print the values of objects; `println` follows with a newline.

The `error:` message is used to report errors. The `subclassResponsibility` message, which also reports an error when sent, is used to mark a class as abstract (page 622); a method that sends `subclassResponsibility` is sometimes called a "marker method." Finally, the `leftAsExercise` message is sent by methods that are meant for you to implement, as exercises.

The three messages `class`, `isKindOf:`, and `isMemberOf:` enable introspection into objects. Message `class` gives the class of a receiver, and messages `isKindOf:` and `isMemberOf:` test properties of that class. For example, the literal integer 3 is

`== anObject`	Answer whether the argument is the same object as the receiver.
`!== anObject`	Answer whether the argument is not the same object as the receiver.
`= anObject`	Answer whether the argument should be considered equal to the the receiver, even if they are not identical.
`!= anObject`	Answer whether the argument should be considered different from the receiver.
`isNil`	Answer whether the receiver is `nil`.
`notNil`	Answer whether the receiver is not `nil`.
`print`	Print the receiver on standard output.
`println`	Print the receiver, then a newline, on standard output.
`error: aSymbol`	Issue a run-time error message which includes `aSymbol`.
`subclassResponsibility`	Report to the user that a method specified in the superclass of the receiver should have been implemented in the receiver's class.
`leftAsExercise`	Report to the user that a method should have been implemented as an exercise.
`class`	Answer the class of the receiver.
`isKindOf: aClass`	Answer whether the receiver's class is the argument or a subclass of the argument, `aClass`. Use only at the read-eval-print loop.
`isMemberOf: aClass`	Answer whether the receiver's class is exactly the argument, `aClass`. Use only at the read-eval-print loop.

Figure 10.10: Protocol for all objects

an object from some proper subclass of `Number`, and the literal symbol `'3` is not a number at all:

637. ⟨*transcript* 611a⟩+≡ ◁636 639a▷

```
-> (3 isKindOf: Number)
<True>
-> (3 isMemberOf: Number)
<False>
-> ('3 isKindOf: Number)
<False>
```

`Number` *B* 663

These messages can sometimes distinguish objects that should be considered equivalent. They are suitable for building system infrastructure or for exploring how Smalltalk works, interactively; except possibly for `class`, they shouldn't find their way into your code. If you're tempted use `isKindOf:` or `isMemberOf:` in definitions of other methods, don't. Decisions should never be made by using `isKindOf:` or `isMemberOf:`; they should be made by dispatching to a method that already knows what class it's defined on, as in the definitions of `isNil` and `notNil` methods on classes `Object` and `UndefinedObject` or any method on class `True` (Section 10.6, pages 654 and 655).

`new`	The receiver is a class; answer a new instance of that class. A class may override `new`, e.g., if it needs arguments to initialize a newly created instance.
`name`	The receiver is a class; answer its name.
`superclass`	The receiver is a class; answer its superclass, or if it has no superclass, answer `nil`.
`printProtocol`	The receiver is a class; print the names of all the messages it knows how to respond to, plus the names of the messages its instances know how to respond to.
`printLocalProtocol`	The receiver is a class; print the names of the class and instance methods that are defined by this class, not those that are inherited from its superclass.
`methodNames`	The receiver is a class; answer an array containing the name of every method defined on the class.
`compiledMethodAt: aSymbol`	The receiver is a class; answer the compiled method with the given name defined on that class. (If no method with that name exists, cause a checked run-time error.)
`removeSelector: aSymbol`	The receiver is a class; if the receiver defines a method with the given name, remove it.
`addSelector:withMethod: aSymbol aCompiledMethod`	The receiver is a class; update the receiver's internal state to associate the given compiled method with the given name. The argument method may replace an existing method or may be entirely new. The name must be consistent with the arity of the method.

Figure 10.11: Protocol for classes

10.4.2 *Protocol for classes*

Because every class is also an object, a class can answer messages. Every class object inherits from `Class`, and it responds to the protocol in Figure 10.11 (as well as to every message in the `Object` protocol). Parts of the protocol approximate capabilities that a full Smalltalk system provides in a graphical user interface: messages `printProtocol` and `printLocalProtocol` are meant for interactive exploration, and message `addSelector:withMethod` enables you to modify or extend built-in classes.

10.4.3 *Blocks and Booleans*

A block is a Smalltalk object that corresponds to a Scheme closure. A block that expects no arguments is conventionally written in curly brackets (Smalltalk-80 uses square brackets). A bracketed expression of the form {*exp*} evaluates to a block

`ifTrue:ifFalse: trueBlock falseBlock`	If the receiver is true, evaluate `trueBlock`, otherwise evaluate `falseBlock`.
`ifTrue: trueBlock`	If the receiver is true, evaluate `trueBlock`, otherwise answer `nil`.
`ifFalse: falseBlock`	If the receiver is false, evaluate `falseBlock`, otherwise answer `nil`.
`and: alternativeBlock`	If the receiver is `true`, answer the value of the argument; otherwise, answer `false` (short-circuit conjunction).
`or: alternativeBlock`	If the receiver is `false`, answer the value of the argument; otherwise, answer `true` (short-circuit disjunction).
`& aBoolean`	Answer the conjunction of the receiver and the argument.
`| aBoolean`	Answer the disjunction of the receiver and the argument.
`not`	Answer the complement of the receiver.
`eqv: aBoolean`	Answer `true` if the receiver is equivalent to the argument.
`xor: aBoolean`	Answer `true` if the receiver is different from the argument (exclusive or).

Figure 10.12: Protocol for Booleans

object; the expression inside the brackets is not evaluated until the block is sent the `value` message.

639a. ⟨*transcript* 611a⟩+≡ ◁637 639b▷

```
-> (val index 0)
-> {(set index (index + 1))}
<Block>
-> index
0
-> ({(set index (index + 1))} value)
1
-> index
1
```

Just like any object, a block can be assigned to a variable and used later.

639b. ⟨*transcript* 611a⟩+≡ ◁639a 640a▷

```
-> (val incrementBlock {(set index (index + 1))})
<Block>
-> (val sumPlusIndexSquaredBlock {(sum + (index * index))})
<Block>
-> (val sum 0)
0
-> (set sum (sumPlusIndexSquaredBlock value))
1
-> (incrementBlock value)
2
-> (set sum (sumPlusIndexSquaredBlock value))
5
```

`value` *B* 641

Parameterless blocks are used primarily as continuations, to implement loop bodies, exception handlers, or conditional expressions, for example. In other languages, including Scheme, a conditional expression requires a special syntactic form, like (`if` e_1 e_2 e_3). This form is evaluated specially by the interpreter, which first evaluates e_1, then evaluates *either* e_2 or e_3, as needed. In μSmalltalk, as in full Smalltalk-80, `if` does not have its own syntactic form; it is coded using message passing and continuations.[9] In μSmalltalk, writing (e_1 `ifTrue:ifFalse:` e_2 e_3) asks the interpreter to evaluate *all three* expressions e_1, e_2, and e_3 before dispatching to method `ifTrue:ifFalse:` on the object that e_1 evaluates to. If e_2 and e_3 are meant to be evaluated conditionally, their evaluation must be *delayed* by putting them in blocks: (e_1 `ifTrue:ifFalse:` {e_2} {e_3}). The effect of the delay is illustrated by this transcript:

640a. ⟨*transcript* 611a⟩+≡ ◁639b 640b▷

```
-> ((sum < 0) ifTrue:ifFalse: {'negative} {'nonnegative})
nonnegative
-> ((sum < 0) ifTrue:ifFalse:  'negative   'nonnegative )
Run-time error: Symbol does not understand message value
Method-stack traceback:
  In predefined classes, line 37, sent `value' to an object of class Symbol
  In standard input, line 154, sent `ifTrue:ifFalse:' to an object of class False
```

On the first line, `(sum < 0)` produces the Boolean object `false`. Sending message `ifTrue:ifFalse:` to `false` causes `false` to send `value` to the block `{'nonnegative}`, which answers the symbol `'nonnegative`, which is the result of the entire expression. On the second line, `false` sends `value` to the *symbol* `'nonnegative`, which results in an error message and a stack trace.

The `ifTrue:ifFalse:` message is an example of *continuation-passing style* (Section 2.10, page 136). Two blocks—the continuations—are passed to a Boolean. The `true` object continues by executing the first block; `false` continues by executing the second. Message `ifTrue:ifFalse:` and the other continuation-passing messages of the Booleans are shown in the top half of Figure 10.12 (on the previous page). In addition to classic conditionals, these messages also include short-circuit `and:` and `or:`. The bottom half of the figure shows messages that implement simple Boolean operations.

Like conditionals, loops are implemented in continuation-passing style. But a loop is implemented not by sending a message to a Boolean, but by sending a message to a block, which holds the condition. The condition must be a block because it must be re-evaluated on each iteration of the loop.

640b. ⟨*transcript* 611a⟩+≡ ◁640a 645a▷

```
-> ({(sum < 10000)} whileTrue: {(set sum (5 * sum)) (sum println)})
25
125
625
3125
15625
nil
```

When the loop terminates, the `whileTrue:` method answers `nil`, which the interpreter prints.

A parameterless block also understands the `messageTrace` message, which tells the interpreter to show every message send and response during the evaluation of

[9]In fact, implementations of Smalltalk-80 have traditionally “open coded” conditionals, preventing user-defined classes from usefully defining method `ifTrue:ifFalse:` (ANSI 1998). The Self language manages efficiency without such hacks (Chambers and Ungar 1989; Chambers 1992).

`value`	Evaluate the receiver and answer its value.
`value: anArgument`	Allocate a fresh location to hold the argument, bind that location to the receiver's formal parameter, evaluate the body of the receiver, and answer the result.

`value:value: arg1 arg2`
`value:value:value: arg1 arg2 arg3`
`value:value:value:value: arg1 arg2 arg3 arg4`
	Like `value:`, but with two, three, or four arguments.

`whileTrue: bodyBlock`	Send `value` to the receiver, and if the response is true, send `value` to `bodyBlock` and repeat. When the receiver responds `false`, answer `nil`.
`whileFalse: bodyBlock`	Send `value` to the receiver, and if the response is false, send `value` to `bodyBlock` and repeat. When the receiver responds `true`, answer `nil`.
`messageTrace`	Send `value` to the receiver, and print a trace of every message send and reply until the receiver answers.
`messageTraceFor: anInteger`	Send `value` to the receiver, and print a trace of the first `anInteger` message sends and replies.

Figure 10.13: Protocol for blocks

the block's body. The number of sends shown can be capped by instead sending `messageTraceFor:` (Figure 10.13).

A block may also take parameters. Such a block must be written using the `block` keyword, like this block from the `drawPolygon:` method of class `TikzCanvas`:

```
(coord-list do: [block (pt) (pt print) ('-- print)])
```

A block that expects one parameter is activated by sending it the `value:` message with one argument. A block that expects two parameters is activated by `value:value:` with two arguments, and so on up to four parameters.

10.4.4 *Unicode characters*

ifTrue:ifFalse: *B* 639
sum 639b

μSmalltalk doesn't support strings, but most output can be emitted by printing symbols. To emit something that can't be written as a symbol, like a newline or a left parenthesis, μSmalltalk code can print a Unicode character, which is typically specified by an integer "code point" of 16 or more bits. And because nobody wants to read code points, μSmalltalk defines the following objects of class `Char`, which can be printed by sending them the `print` message:

```
newline   semicolon   left-round    left-square    left-curly
space     quotemark   right-round   right-square   right-curly
```

More characters can be created by using `new:`, as in `(Char new: 955)`.

10.4.5 Collections

All languages need ways of grouping individual data elements into larger collections. Some form of collection is usually found in a language's initial basis; for example, Scheme has lists and Molecule has arrays. μSmalltalk predefines four useful collections: sets, lists, arrays, and dictionaries. And defining new collections is exceptionally easy, because any new collection can inherit most of its code from class `Collection` or from one of its subclasses.

Collections are also found in Smalltalk-80, whose collection classes are similar to μSmalltalk's classes but are structured somewhat differently (Section 10.12.3, page 705). μSmalltalk's collection hierarchy is inspired by Budd (1987).

A collection is an abstraction, like the abstractions written in Molecule in Chapter 9. But a collection isn't a type or a type constructor; Smalltalk provides data abstractions using objects, not abstract data types, and object-oriented abstractions work differently. In Smalltalk, a collection is an object that responds to the *collection protocol* (Figure 10.15, page 644); whether it has anything to do with the `Collection` class is a matter of convenience. The protocol's core operations are iteration, addition, and removal:

- A collection must respond to the `do:` message by iterating over its contents. When a message of the form (*collection* `do: [block (x)` *body*`])` is sent, the receiver must respond by evaluating *body* once for each item `x` that it contains. A `do:` method acts like the μScheme `app` function, but it works on any collection, not just on a list.

- Collections are mutable; a typical collection object should respond to message `add:` by adding the argument to itself, and it should respond to `remove:` by removing the argument from itself. Some collections, like `Arrays`, have a fixed number of elements; when receiving `add:` or `remove:` messages, such collections report errors.

The collection protocol is specified and is partially implemented by class `Collection`, which is an abstract class: like class `Shape` (Section 10.1), it defines many useful methods but is intended to be inherited from, not instantiated. The full implementation is spread out over three abstract classes and four concrete classes:

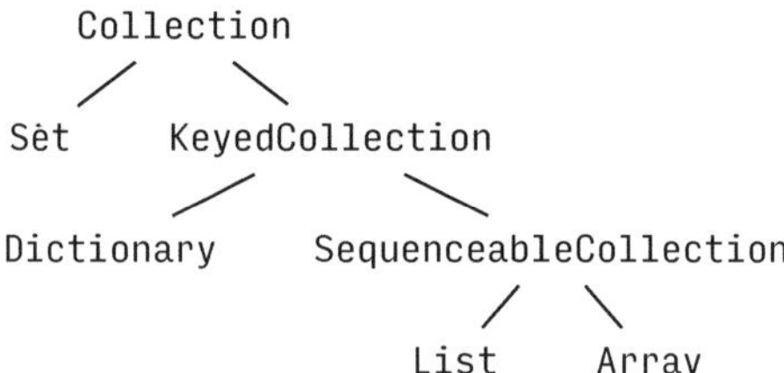

Each class has its own role.

- Class `Collection` defines an abstraction that contains objects. It is an abstract class that implements all but four of the methods in the collection protocol. The remaining four methods are implemented by subclasses.

- Class `Set` implements a set. A set contains objects in no particular order, with no duplicates (as decided by `=`). Class `Set` implements the four crucial methods missing from the `Collection` class, and it can be used to instantiate objects—it is a concrete subclass.

`with: anObject`	Create and answer a singleton collection holding the given object.
`withAll: aCollection`	Create and answer a collection that holds all the elements of the argument.

Figure 10.14: Class protocol for `Collection`

- Class `KeyedCollection` refines the `Collection` abstraction to associate each object with a key—or equivalently, it defines a collection of key-value pairs. A keyed collection shares a lot of protocol with an ordinary collection, and its protocol includes additional messages that can add, retrieve, and mutate objects by using a key. `KeyedCollection` is an abstract class.

- Class `Dictionary` implements a finite map. Class `Dictionary` is a concrete subclass of `KeyedCollection`; it is used to instantiate objects. It assumes as little as possible about keys: in a dictionary, keys need only to be comparable for equality.

- Class `SequenceableCollection` defines a sequence abstraction, which the designers of Smalltalk view as a keyed collection whose keys are consecutive integers. Class `SequenceableCollection` is another abstract class that adds yet more protocol to `KeyedCollection`.

- Class `List` implements a list, which is a sequence that can grow or shrink. Unlike a list in Scheme or ML, a Smalltalk list is *mutable,* and it can add or remove elements at either its beginning or its end, in constant time. Class `List` is a concrete subclass that can be used to instantiate lists.

- Class `Array` implements an array, which is a sequence whose elements can be accessed in constant time—but which cannot grow or shrink. Although class `Array` inherits from `SequenceableCollection` and therefore indirectly from `Collection`, it does not implement the full collection protocol: it implements only those methods that can be implemented without growing or shrinking. Class `Array` is a concrete subclass that can be used to instantiate arrays.

The collection protocols are described in detail in Figures 10.14 (class protocol) and 10.15 (instance protocol).

- Each collection *class* responds to a `with:` message, which creates a collection containing a single element, and to a `withAll:` message, which creates a collection that contains all the elements from another collection.

- The instance methods in the first group are *mutators;* they define ways of adding and removing elements. In μSmalltalk, a mutator typically answers the receiver, which makes it easy to send several mutation messages to the same object in sequence.

- The instance methods in the second group are *observers;* they define ways of finding out about the elements in a collection. The `includes:` and `occurrencesOf:` observers ask about elements directly; the `detect:` and `detect:ifNone:` observers ask for *any* element satisfying a given predicate, which is typically represented as a block. The = observer asks if two collections contain the same objects (according to =).

`add: newObject`	Include the argument, `newObject`, as one of the elements of the receiver. Answer the receiver.
`addAll: aCollection`	Add every element of the argument to the receiver; answer the receiver.
`remove: oldObject`	Remove the argument, `oldObject`, from the receiver. If no element is equal to `oldObject`, report an error; otherwise, answer the receiver.
`remove:ifAbsent: oldObject exnBlock`	Remove the argument, `oldObject`, from the receiver. If no element is equal to `oldObject`, answer the result of evaluating `exnBlock`; otherwise, answer the receiver.
`removeAll: aCollection`	Remove every element of the argument from the receiver; answer the receiver or report an error.
`isEmpty`	Answer whether the receiver has any elements.
`size`	Answer how many elements the receiver has.
`includes: anObject`	Answer whether the receiver has `anObject`.
`occurrencesOf: anObject`	Answer how many of the receiver's elements are equal to `anObject`.
`detect: aBlock`	Answer the first element `x` in the receiver for which `(aBlock value: x)` is true, or report an error if none.
`detect:ifNone: aBlock exnBlock`	Answer the first element `x` in the receiver for which `(aBlock value: x)` is true, or answer `(exnBlock value)` if none.
`= aCollection`	Answer whether the contents of the receiver are equivalent to the contents of the argument.
`do: aBlock`	For each element `x` of the collection, evaluate `(aBlock value: x)`.
`inject:into: aValue binaryBlock`	Evaluate `binaryBlock` once for each element in the receiver. The first argument of the block is an element from the receiver; the second argument is the result of the previous evaluation of the block, starting with `aValue`. Answer the final value of the block.
`select: aBlock`	Answer a new collection like the receiver, containing every element `x` of the receiver for which `(aBlock value: x)` is true.
`reject: aBlock`	Answer a new collection like the receiver, containing every element `x` of the receiver for which `(aBlock value: x)` is false.
`collect: aBlock`	Answer a new collection like the receiver, containing `(aBlock value: x)` for every element `x` of the receiver.

Figure 10.15: Public instance protocol for `Collection`

- The instance methods do: and inject:into: are *iterators*. An iterator is a special kind of observer that repeats a computation once for every element in a collection. The do: method performs a computation only for side effect, while inject:into: accumulates and answers a value. These two methods correspond to the μScheme functions app and foldl, but they are defined on *all* collections, not only on lists.

- The instance methods in the final group are *producers*; given a collection, a producer makes a new collection without mutating the original. Methods select: and collect: correspond to the μScheme functions filter and map, which are also defined in ML.

Collection is an abstract class, so a client should not send a new, with:, or withAll: message directly to Collection—only to one of its concrete subclasses.

The simplest subclass of Collection is Set; to get a feel for sets and for the Collection protocol, look at this transcript:

645a. ⟨*transcript* 611a⟩+≡ ◁ 640b 645b ▷

```
-> (val s (Set new))
Set( )
-> (s size)
0
-> (s add: 2)
Set( 2 )
-> (s add: 'abc)
Set( 2 abc )
-> (s includes: 2)
<True>
-> (s add: 2)
Set( 2 abc )
```

Remember that when a message is sent to a receiver, the method has access not only to the values of the arguments but also to the receiver. For example, the add: method takes only one argument, the item to be added, but it also has access to the collection to which the item is added.

Collection methods can operate on collections of mixed kinds. For example, I build a set s from an array, and then I use the set's addAll: method to add the elements of another array.

645b. ⟨*transcript* 611a⟩+≡ ◁ 645a 645c ▷

```
-> (set s (Set withAll: '(1 2 3 1 2 3)))
Set( 1 2 3 )
-> (s addAll: '(1 2 3 a b c d e f))
Set( 1 2 3 a b c d e f )
-> (s includes: 'b)
<True>
```

This kind of mixed computation, where I pass an array as an argument to a set operation, is not possible using abstract data types. But using objects, it's easy: the addAll: method treats the argument object abstractly. As long as the argument responds to the Collection protocol, addAll: doesn't care what class it's an instance of. The addAll: method interacts with the argument only by sending it the do: message.

Number 𝓑 663
Set 𝓑 S563

Other messages that work with any collection include removeAll: and reject:.

645c. ⟨*transcript* 611a⟩+≡ ◁ 645b 648 ▷

```
-> (s removeAll: '(e f))
Set( 1 2 3 a b c d )
-> (val s2 (s reject: [block (x) (x isKindOf: Number)]))
Set( a b c d )
```

Object-orientation also provides an effortless form of polymorphism. In the example, set `s` is initialized by sending `Set` the `withAll:` message with array argument `'(1 2 3 1 2 3)`, which contains duplicate elements. The implementation of `withAll:`, which is shared by multiple collection classes, eliminates the duplicates. It identifies duplicates by sending the `=` message to individual elements. Because the `=` message is dispatched dynamically, it automatically has the right semantics for comparing elements, no matter what classes the elements are instances of. In Scheme, by contrast, getting equality right requires either passing an equality function as a parameter, storing it in a data structure, or capturing it in a closure (Section 2.9, page 131). But in Smalltalk, as in every object-oriented language, an object already acts like a closure—it is data bundled with code—and the bundle includes the right version of `=`. No additional coding is required.

Keyed collections and class `Dictionary`

`KeyedCollection` is another abstract class; the abstraction is a set of key-value pairs in which no key occurs more than once. This abstraction is one of the most frequently used abstractions in computing, and it has many names: depending on context, it may be called an "associative array," a "dictionary," a "finite map," or a "table." In Smalltalk, "keyed collections" include not only general-purpose key-value data structures but also special-purpose structures, including lists and arrays.

An object of class `KeyedCollection` responds to the `Collection` protocol as if it were a simple collection of values, with no keys. But `KeyedCollection` adds new messages that can present a key and use it to look up, change, or remove the corresponding value (Figure 10.16, on the next page).

- The `at:put:` message updates the receiver; `(kc at:put: key value)` modifies collection `kc` by associating `value` with `key`.

- The observers `at:` and `keyAtValue:` answer the value associated with a key or the key associated with a value. The observer `at:ifAbsent:` can be used to learn whether a given key is in the collection. (To learn whether a given *value* is in a collection, use the observer `includes:` from the `Collection` protocol.) Each of these observers works with a key that is *equivalent* to the key originally used with `at:put:`—identical keys are not needed.

- The observer `associationAt:` and the iterator `associationsDo:` provide access to the key-value pairs directly, in the form of `Association` objects (Figure 10.17).

- Mutators `removeKey:` and `removeKey:ifAbsent:` can remove a key-value pair by presenting an equivalent key.

Observer `at:` and mutator `at:put:` are the most frequently used of the new messages. Old messages `size`, `isEmpty`, and `includes:` are also used frequently.

`KeyedCollection` is an abstract class; a client should create instances of subclasses only. Its simplest subclass is `Dictionary`, which represents a collection as a list of associations. Class `Dictionary` assumes only that its keys respond correctly to the `=` message. A more efficient subclass might assume that keys respond to a hash message or a comparison message, which would enable it to use a hash table or a search tree (Exercises 28 and 29).

Message	Description
`at:put: key value`	Modify the receiver by associating `key` with `value`. (May add a new value or replace an existing value.) Answer the receiver.
`removeKey: key`	Modify the receiver by removing `key` and its associated value. If `key` is not in the receiver, report an error; otherwise, answer the value associated with `key`.
`removeKey:ifAbsent: key aBlock`	Modify the receiver by removing `key` and its associated value. If `key` is not in the receiver, answer the result of sending `value` to `aBlock`; otherwise, answer the value associated with `key`.
`at: key`	Answer the value associated with `key`, or if there is no such value, report an error.
`at:ifAbsent: key aBlock`	Answer the value associated with `key`, or the result of evaluating `aBlock` if there is no such value.
`includesKey: key`	Answer `true` if there is some value associated with `key`, or `false` otherwise.
`keyAtValue: value`	Answer the key associated with `value`, or if there is no such value, report an error.
`keyAtValue:ifAbsent: value aBlock`	Answer the key associated with `value`, or if there is no such value, answer the result of evaluating `aBlock`.
`associationAt: key`	Answer the `Association` in the collection with key `key`, or if there is no such `Association`, report an error.
`associationAt:ifAbsent: key exnBlock`	Answer the `Association` in the collection with key `key`, or if there is no such `Association`, answer the result of evaluating `exnBlock`.
`associationsDo: aBlock`	Iterate over all `Associations` in the collection, evaluating `aBlock` with each one.

Figure 10.16: New instance protocol for keyed collections (`KeyedCollection`)

`withKey:value: key value`	Create a new association with the given key and value.

(a) Class protocol for `Association`

`key`	Answer the receiver's key.
`value`	Answer the receiver's value.
`setKey: key`	Set the receiver's key to `key`.
`setValue: value`	Set the receiver's value to `value`.

(b) Instance protocol for `Association`

Figure 10.17: Protocols for associations

`first`	Answer the first element of the receiver.
`firstKey`	Answer the integer key that is associated with the first value of the receiver.
`last`	Answer the last element of the receiver.
`lastKey`	Answer the integer key that is associated with the last value of the receiver.

Figure 10.18: New instance protocol for sequenceable collections

Sequenceable collections

The abstract class `SequenceableCollection` represents a keyed collection whose keys are consecutive integers—in other words, a sequence. Such a collection understands additional messages: `firstKey` and `lastKey` answer the first and last keys, and `first` and `last` answer the first and last values (Figure 10.18).

Lists A `List` is a sequence that can change size: an element can be added or removed at either end (Figure 10.19, on the next page). Unlike a Scheme list, a Smalltalk list is *mutable*: adding or removing an element mutates the original list, rather than creating a new one. The `add:` message is a synonym for `addLast:`.

Lists are illustrated by this transcript:

648. ⟨*transcript* 611a⟩+≡ ◁ 645c 652a ▷

```
-> (val xs (List new))
List( )
-> (xs addLast: 'a)
List( a )
-> (xs add: 'b)
List( a b )
-> (xs addFirst: 'z)
List( z a b )
-> (xs first)
z
-> (xs addFirst: 'y)
List( y z a b )
-> (xs at: 2)
a
-> (xs removeFirst)
y
-> xs
List( z a b )
```

`addLast: anObject`	Add `anObject` to the end of the receiver and answer the receiver.
`addFirst: anObject`	Add `anObject` to the beginning of the receiver and answer the receiver.
`removeFirst`	Remove the first object from the receiver and answer that object. Causes an error if the receiver is empty.
`removeLast`	Remove the last object from the receiver and answer that object. Causes an error if the receiver is empty.

Figure 10.19: New instance protocol for lists (`List`)

Arrays An array is a sequence that cannot change size, but that implements `at:` and `at:put:` in constant time. Arrays are found in many programming languages; in μSmalltalk, every array is one-dimensional, and the first element's key is 0. (In Smalltalk-80, the first element's key is 1.)

An instance of `Array` responds to the messages of the `SequenceableCollection` protocol. (Because an array cannot change size, it responds to `add:` and `remove:` with errors.) The `Array` *class* responds to the messages of the `SequenceableCollection` *class* protocol, and also to message `new:`, which expects a size:

`new: anInteger`	Create and answer an array of size `anInteger` in which each element is `nil`.

Inheriting from `Collection`

To define a new subclass of `Collection` might seem like an enormous job; after all, Figure 10.15 shows a great many messages, an instance of any subclass must understand. But the `Collection` class is carefully structured so that a subclass need implement only *four* of the methods in Figure 10.15: `do:`, to iterate over elements, `add:`, to add an element, `remove:ifAbsent:`, to remove an element, and `=`, to compare contents. The details appear in Section 10.7.1.

10.4.6 Magnitudes and numbers

Collections make up a large part of μSmalltalk's initial basis. Much of the rest of the basis deals with numbers. The numeric classes illustrate the same inheritance techniques as the collection classes: each concrete subclass defines a minimal set of representation-specific methods like `+`, `*`, and `negated`, and they all share inherited implementations of generic methods like `-`, `isNegative`, and `abs`. The most important numeric classes fit into this hierarchy:

`add:`	*B* 644
`at:`	*B* 647

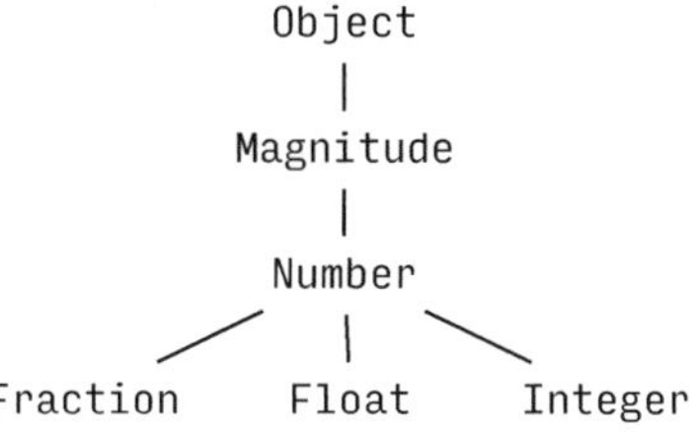

On page 651, this hierarchy is extended with large integers.

Class `Magnitude` supports comparisons, as well as `min:` and `max:` operations. The `Magnitude` protocol can be implemented by any totally ordered abstraction, like a number, a date, or a time. Magnitudes can be used in the implementations

`= aMagnitude`	Answer whether the receiver equals the argument.
`< aMagnitude`	Answer whether the receiver is less than the argument.
`> aMagnitude`	Answer whether the receiver is greater than the argument.
`<= aMagnitude`	Answer whether the receiver is no greater than the argument.
`>= aMagnitude`	Answer whether the receiver is no less than the argument.
`min: aMagnitude`	Answer the lesser of the receiver and `aMagnitude`.
`max: aMagnitude`	Answer the greater of the receiver and `aMagnitude`.

(a) Instance protocol for `Magnitude`

`negated`	Answer the negation of the receiver ("unary minus").
`reciprocal`	Answer the reciprocal of the receiver.
`abs`	Answer the absolute value of the receiver.
`+ aNumber`	Answer the sum of the receiver and the argument.
`- aNumber`	Answer the difference of the receiver and the argument.
`* aNumber`	Answer the product of the receiver and the argument.
`/ aNumber`	Answer the quotient of the receiver and the argument. The quotient is *not* rounded to the nearest integer, so the quotient of two integers may be a fraction.
`isNegative`	Answer whether the receiver is negative.
`isNonnegative`	Answer whether the receiver is nonnegative.
`isStrictlyPositive`	Answer whether the receiver is positive (> 0). (The "strictly" is from Smalltalk-80, which inexplicably uses "positive" to mean ≥ 0.)
`isZero`	Answer whether the receiver is zero.
`raisedToInteger: anInteger`	Answer the receiver, raised to the integer power `anInteger`.
`squared`	Answer the receiver squared.
`sqrtWithin: eps`	Answer a number that is within eps of the square root of the receiver.
`sqrt`	Answer the square root of the receiver, to within some eps defined by the implementation.
`coerce: aNumber`	Answer a `Number` that is of the same *kind* as the receiver, but represents the same *value* as the argument.
`asInteger`	Answer the integer nearest to the value of the receiver.
`asFraction`	Answer the fraction nearest to the value of the receiver.
`asFloat`	Answer the floating-point number nearest to the value of the receiver.

(b) Instance protocol for `Number`

Figure 10.20: Protocols for magnitudes and numbers

`div: anInteger`	Answer the integer quotient of the receiver and the argument, rounding towards $-\infty$.
`mod: anInteger`	Answer the modulus of the receiver and the argument, with division rounding towards $-\infty$.
`gcd: anInteger`	Answer the greatest common denominator of the receiver and the argument.
`lcm: anInteger`	Answer the least common multiple of the receiver and the argument.
`timesRepeat: aBlock`	If the receiver is the integer n, send `value` to `aBlock` n times.

Figure 10.21: New instance protocol for integers

of search trees, sorted collections, and so on. Class `Number` supports not only comparisons but also arithmetic, plus other operations that can be performed only on numbers: a `Number` can be asked about its sign; it can be asked for a power, square, or square root; and it can be *coerced* (converted) to be an integer, a fraction, or a floating-point number. Protocols for both `Magnitude` and `Number` are shown in Figure 10.20 (on the facing page).

In Smalltalk-80, the predefined magnitudes include dates, times, and characters; in μSmalltalk, the predefined magnitudes include only natural numbers and the `Number` classes. Other magnitudes can be defined (Exercise 33). μSmalltalk's predefined numbers are more interesting: objects of class `Integer` represent integers, and instances of `Fraction` and `Float` represent rational numbers. A `Fraction` represents a rational number as the ratio of numerator n to denominator d. A `Float` represents a rational number of the form $m \cdot 10^e$, where m is an integer mantissa and e is an integer exponent.

These predefined numeric classes support all of the arithmetic and comparison operations in the `Magnitude` and `Number` protocols, but they support only *homogeneous* operations: for example, integers can be compared only with integers, fractions only with fractions, and floating-point numbers only with floating-point numbers. The same goes for addition, subtraction, multiplication, and so on. For example, the fraction $3/4$ can't be asked if it is less than the integer 1—and yet, such questions are both convenient and in the spirit of object-oriented programming. Fortunately, *mixed* comparisons and arithmetic are not hard to implement (Exercise 36).

Integers Integers provide not just the standard arithmetic operations expected of all numbers, but also `div:`, `mod:`, `gcd:`, and `lcm:`, which are defined only on integers. And an integer n can be told to evaluate a block n times. In μSmalltalk, integers come in two forms: small integers, which I implement, and large integers, which I invite you to implement (Exercise 38). The integer subhierarchy looks like this:

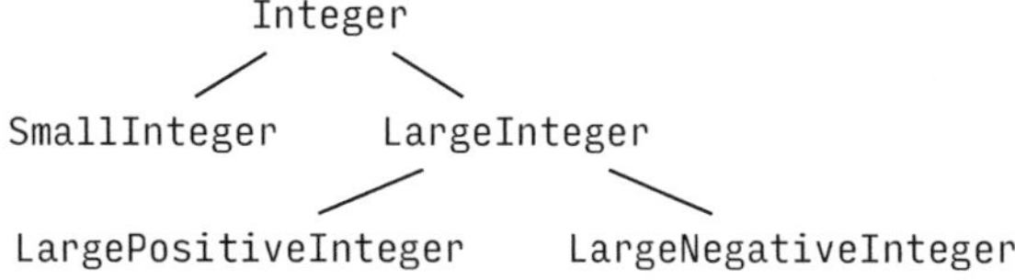

These classes are discussed in Section 10.8.3 (page 667), and they all answer the protocol shown in Figure 10.21.

Fractions A `Fraction` represents a rational number as a fraction. For example, in the session below, sending `(two sqrtWithin: epsilon)` answers $\frac{17}{12}$, which approximates $\sqrt{2}$ to within `epsilon` ($\frac{1}{10}$). The approximation, $1.41\bar{6}$, is quite close to the actual value of $1.4142+$.

652a. ⟨*transcript* 611a⟩+≡ ◁648 652b▷

```
-> (val two (Fraction num:den: 2 1))
-> (val epsilon (Fraction num:den: 1 10))
1/10
-> (val root2 (two sqrtWithin: epsilon))
17/12
```

Better precision can be had by decreasing `epsilon`. And fractions can be computed conveniently and idiomatically by dividing integers or by using `asFraction`.

652b. ⟨*transcript* 611a⟩+≡ ◁652a 652c▷

```
-> (val epsilon (1 / 100))
1/100
-> (val root2 ((2 asFraction) sqrtWithin: epsilon))
577/408
```

The square root of n is computed by using the Newton-Raphson technique for finding a zero of the function $x^2 - n$. Newton-Raphson produces accurate results quickly; the approximation $\frac{577}{408}$ is accurate to five decimal places.

Floating-point numbers A number in floating-point form is represented by a mantissa m and exponent e, which stand for the number $m \cdot 10^e$. Both m and e can be negative. A `Float` satisfies the representation invariant that $|m| \leq 32767$; this restriction, which provides about 15 bits of precision, ensures that two mantissas can be multiplied without arithmetic overflow.

Class `Float` can be used as follows:

652c. ⟨*transcript* 611a⟩+≡ ◁652b

```
-> (val epsilon ((1 / 100) asFloat))
1x10^-2
-> ((2 asFloat) sqrtWithin: epsilon)
14142x10^-4
```

The result is good to five decimal places.

10.4.7 *Natural numbers*

A natural number is more than a magnitude but less than a full `Number`: μSmalltalk's class `Natural` supports limited arithmetic and a couple of new observers. A natural number is a form of magnitude, and class `Natural` is a subclass of `Magnitude`. In addition to the protocol for `Magnitude`, including comparisons, class `Natural` and its instances respond to the protocol in Figure 10.22 on the next page.

Natural numbers may be added and multiplied without fear of overflow—the size of a natural number is limited only by the amount of memory available. Natural numbers may also be subtracted, provided that the argument is no greater than the receiver. And a natural number may be divided by a small, positive integer; the `s` in `sdiv:` and `smod:` stands for "short." (As noted on page S19, long division is beyond the scope of this book.)

The protocol for instances of `Natural` includes an observer `decimal`, which converts the receiver to a list of decimal digits. (For efficiency, the receiver is expected to use an internal representation with a base much larger than 10.)

`fromSmall: anInteger`	Answer a natural-number object whose value is equal to the value of the argument, which must be a *nonnegative* integer.

(a) Class protocol for `Natural`

`+ aNatural`	Answer the sum of the receiver and the argument.
`* aNatural`	Answer the product of the receiver and the argument.
`- aNatural`	Answer the difference of the receiver and the argument, or if this difference is not a natural number, fail with a run-time error.
`sdiv: aSmallInteger`	Answer the largest natural number whose value is at most the quotient of the receiver and the argument.
`smod: aSmallInteger`	Answer a small integer that is the remainder when the receiver is divided by the argument.
`decimal`	Answer a `List` containing the *decimal* digits of the receiver, most significant digit first.
`sdivmod:with: aSmallInteger aBlock`	An object n receiving (`n sdivmod:with: d b`) answers the result of sending (`b value:value: Q r`), where Q is n div d and r is $n \bmod d$.
`subtract:withDifference:ifNegative: aNatural diffBlock negBlock`	Subtract `aNatural` from the receiver to obtain difference d. If the difference is a natural number, answer (`diffBlock value:` d). If the difference is negative, answer (`negBlock value`).
`isZero`	If the receiver is zero, answer `true`; otherwise answer `false`.

(b) Instance protocol for natural numbers

Figure 10.22: Protocols for natural numbers

Finally, the `Natural` protocol includes three methods that are intended to promote efficiency:

- Method `sdivmod:with:` computes *both* quotient and remainder in a single operation. It is necessary in order to implement division in linear time. If a division operation were to send both `sdiv:` and `smod:`, division could take time exponential in the number of digits, which is not acceptable.
- Method `subtract:withDifference:ifNegative:` combines comparison and subtraction into a single operation. Implemented independently, each of these operations could take linear time, and comparison comes "for free" with a subtraction.
- Method `isZero` can sometimes be implemented more efficiently than `=`.

asFloat 𝓑 650
asFraction 𝓑 650
Fraction 𝓑 664
sqrtWithin: 𝓑 650

The implementation of class `Natural` is left to you (Exercise 37). Ideas are presented on page 669.

10.5 OBJECT-ORIENTED PROGRAMMING TECHNIQUES

To get started programming in μSmalltalk, you can focus on the examples from Section 10.1 and on the protocols and informal descriptions of the predefined classes in Section 10.4. But to internalize object-oriented ways of thinking and programming, you need to study more deeply. Four increasingly deep techniques are presented in the next four sections:

- Section 10.6 shows how to make decisions by dispatching messages to the right methods, not by evaluating conditionals. The technique is illustrated with example methods defined on classes `Object`, `UndefinedObject`, and `Boolean`.
- Section 10.7 shows how to reuse code by building abstract classes that provide many useful methods on top of just a few subclass responsibilities. The technique is illustrated with example methods defined on collection classes.
- Section 10.8 shows how to define methods that want to look at representations of more than one object, even though a method defined on an object has access only to its own instance variables. The technique is illustrated with example methods defined on numeric classes.
- Section 10.9 shows how to integrate ideas from Sections 10.6 and 10.7 with program-design ideas from Chapter 9, including an abstraction function and representation invariant. The techniques are illustrated with a complete implementation of class `List`.

10.6 TECHNIQUE I: METHOD DISPATCH REPLACES CONDITIONALS

An object-oriented program differs most from a functional or procedural program in the way it makes decisions. An object-oriented program doesn't ask an object, "How were you formed?" Instead, it sends a message that asks a different question or makes a request. The form of the receiver becomes known not by evaluating an expression but by dispatching to a method. For example, we can ask any object, "Are you `nil`?" by sending it message `isNil` or `notNil`. Methods `isNil` and `notNil` are defined in ordinary μSmalltalk, on classes `Object` and `UndefinedObject`. Before we study the definitions, here's how *not* to do it—two ways to test for `nil` by evaluating an expression:

```
(method isNil () (self == nil))                        ; embarrassing
(method isNil () (self isMemberOf: UndefinedObject))  ; more embarrassing
```

This code makes a real Smalltalk programmer cringe. In Smalltalk, case analysis should be implemented by method dispatch. For `isNil` there are only two possible cases: an object is `nil` or it isn't. I arrange that on the `nil` object, the `isNil` method answers `true`, and that on all other objects, it answers `false`. I need only two method definitions: one on class `UndefinedObject`, which is used only to answer messages sent to `nil`, and one on class `Object`, which all other classes inherit. I implement `notNil` the same way. The definitions on class `UndefinedObject` are

654. ⟨*methods of class* `UndefinedObject` 654⟩≡ S559d ▷

```
(method isNil  () true)    ;; definitions on UndefinedObject
(method notNil () false)
```

On class Object, they are

655a. ⟨*methods of class* Object 634⟩+≡ ◁635a S558c▷

```
(method isNil  () false)  ;; definitions on Object
(method notNil () true)
```

The definitions contain no conditionals; decisions are made entirely by method dispatch. For example, when isNil is sent to nil, nil is an instance of class UndefinedObject, so the message dispatches to UndefinedObject's isNil method, which answers true. But when isNil is sent to any other object, method search starts in the class of that object and eventually reaches class Object, where it dispatches to Object's isNil method, which answers false. A notNil message works the same way.

If you take object-oriented programming seriously, you will *never use an explicit conditional if you can achieve the same effect using method dispatch*. Method dispatch is preferred because it is *extensible*: to add new cases, you just add new classes—think, for example, about adding new kinds of shapes to the pictures in Section 10.1. To add new cases to a conditional, you would have to edit the code—at every location where a similar conditional decision is made. Method dispatch makes it easier to evolve the code. And in many implementations, it is also more efficient.

Some conditionals can't be avoided. For example, to know if a number n is at least 10, we must send a conditional message like ifTrue: to the Boolean object produced by (n >= 10). But ifTrue: is itself implemented using method dispatch! Smalltalk's conditionals and loops aren't written using syntactic forms like μScheme's if and while, because Smalltalk has no such forms—it has only message passing and return. Conditionals are implemented by sending continuations to Boolean objects, and loops are implemented by sending continuations to block objects.[10]

A conditional method like ifTrue: is implemented in both of the subclasses of Boolean: True and False. By the time a method is activated, the conditional decision has already been made by method dispatch; the method has only to take the action appropriate to the subclass it is defined on. Each subclass defines methods according to what its instance represents; for example, class True has one instance, true, which represents truth, and its methods are defined accordingly:

655b. ⟨*predefined μSmalltalk classes and values* 655b⟩≡ S548d▷

```
(class True
  [subclass-of Boolean]
  (method ifTrue:         (trueBlock)            (trueBlock value))
  (method ifFalse:        (falseBlock)           nil)
  (method ifTrue:ifFalse: (trueBlock falseBlock) (trueBlock value))
  (method ifFalse:ifTrue: (falseBlock trueBlock) (trueBlock value))

  (method not ()                    false)
  (method & (aBoolean)              aBoolean)
  (method | (aBoolean)              self)
  (method eqv: (aBoolean)           aBoolean)
  (method xor: (aBoolean)           (aBoolean not))

  (method and: (alternativeBlock) (alternativeBlock value))
  (method or:  (alternativeBlock) self)
)
```

The implementation of class False, which is similar, is left as Exercise 16. The ingenious division of class Boolean into subclasses True and False is owed to Dan Ingalls (2020).

[10] This implementation of conditionals is the same one used in the *Church encoding* of Booleans in the *lambda calculus*—a tool used in the theoretical study of programming languages.

10.7 TECHNIQUE II: ABSTRACT CLASSES

Object-oriented code can achieve a form of polymorphism not readily available in languages like Scheme and ML: By relying on subclass responsibilities, methods like `min:` and `max:` (for magnitudes) or `detect:` and `select:` (for collections) can be implemented once and reused by many different subclasses. Such reuse is illustrated below with examples from magnitudes and collections. The collection example is then developed further by showing how subclasses for keyed and sequenceable collections refine and extend the `Collection` protocol. This is a great technique to emulate in your own designs.

10.7.1 Implementing wide protocols: Magnitudes and collections

The `Magnitude` protocol suits any abstraction that is totally ordered, even those that do not support arithmetic: numbers, dates, times, and so on. A subclass of `Magnitude` has only two responsibilities: comparisons = and <.[11]

656a. ⟨*numeric classes* 656a⟩≡ (S548d) 664a ▷

```
(class Magnitude
    [subclass-of Object] ; abstract class
    (method = (x) (self subclassResponsibility)) ; may not inherit
    (method < (x) (self subclassResponsibility))
    ⟨other methods of class Magnitude 656b⟩
)
```

The other comparisons, as well as `min:` and `max:`, are implemented using <, and they can be reused in every subclass.

656b. ⟨*other methods of class* `Magnitude` 656b⟩≡ (656a)

```
(method >  (y) (y < self))
(method <= (x) ((self > x) not))
(method >= (x) ((self < x) not))
(method min: (aMagnitude)
   ((self < aMagnitude) ifTrue:ifFalse: {self} {aMagnitude}))
(method max: (aMagnitude)
   ((self > aMagnitude) ifTrue:ifFalse: {self} {aMagnitude}))
```

Another big protocol that relies on just a few subclass responsibilities is the `Collection` protocol. This protocol is a joy to work with; it includes not only object-oriented analogs to functions like `exists?`, `map`, `filter`, and `foldl`, but also many other methods, which do things like add, remove, find, and count elements (Figure 10.15, page 644). And unlike their Scheme analogs, these operations support not only lists but also several other forms of collection. All this functionality is provided using just four subclass responsibilities: a collection class must define methods `do:`, `add:`, `remove:ifAbsent:`, and =.

656c. ⟨*collection classes* 656c⟩≡ (S548d) 659a ▷

```
(class Collection
  [subclass-of Object] ; abstract
  (method do:       (aBlock)       (self subclassResponsibility))
  (method add:      (newObject)    (self subclassResponsibility))
  (method remove:ifAbsent: (oldObject exnBlock)
                                   (self subclassResponsibility))
  (method =         (aCollection)  (self subclassResponsibility))
  ⟨other methods of class Collection 657a⟩
)
```

To see how these subclass responsibilities are implemented, look at class `Set` (Appendix U, page S562). To see how the subclass responsibilities are used, look below.

[11]According to the rules of Smalltalk, a magnitude may not inherit the default implementation of = from class `Object`, which is object identity. That's why method = is redefined as a subclass responsibility.

To create a singleton collection, we send add: to a new instance; to create a collection holding all of an argument's elements, we send addAll: to a new instance.

657a. ⟨*other methods of class* Collection 657a⟩≡ (656c) 657b ▷

```
(class-method with: (anObject)
    ((self new) add: anObject))
(class-method withAll: (aCollection)
    ((self new) addAll: aCollection))
```


When addAll: is sent to an object of a subclass, the message dispatches to the method shown here, which is defined on class Collection. It is implemented using do: and add:.

657b. ⟨*other methods of class* Collection 657a⟩+≡ (656c) ◁ 657a 657c ▷

```
(method addAll: (aCollection)
    (aCollection do: [block (x) (self add: x)])
    self)
```

When method addAll: sends do: and add:, they dispatch to the methods defined on the subclass.

Removal works in the same way, building on do: and remove:ifAbsent:.

657c. ⟨*other methods of class* Collection 657a⟩+≡ (656c) ◁ 657b 657d ▷

```
(method remove: (oldObject)
    (self remove:ifAbsent: oldObject {(self error: 'remove-was-absent)}))
(method removeAll: (aCollection)
    (aCollection do: [block (x) (self remove: x)])
    self)
```

In addition to these mutators, the Collection protocol defines a host of observers, including isEmpty and size, among others (page 644). The default implementations given here iterate through the elements of the collection using do:.

657d. ⟨*other methods of class* Collection 657a⟩+≡ (656c) ◁ 657c 657e ▷

```
(method size () [locals n]
    (set n 0)
    (self do: [block (_) (set n (n + 1))])
    n)
(method occurrencesOf: (anObject) [locals n]
    (set n 0)
    (self do: [block (x) ((x = anObject) ifTrue: {(set n (n + 1))})])
    n)
```

Using a linear search to compute size, for example, may seem inefficient, but if a subclass knows a more efficient way to compute the number of elements, it redefines the size method. And for some collections, like List, there is no more efficient way to compute size or count occurrences.

An iteration that uses do: can be cut short by a return expression, as in methods isEmpty, includes:, and detect:ifNone: below. And again, if the collection is a linked list, no more efficient implementation is possible.

657e. ⟨*other methods of class* Collection 657a⟩+≡ (656c) ◁ 657d 658a ▷

```
(method isEmpty ()
    (self do: [block (_) (return false)])
    true)
(method includes: (anObject)
    (self do: [block (x) ((x = anObject) ifTrue: {(return true)})])
    false)
(method detect:ifNone: (aBlock exnBlock)
    (self do: [block (x) ((aBlock value: x) ifTrue: {(return x)})])
    (exnBlock value))
(method detect: (aBlock)
    (self detect:ifNone: aBlock {(self error: 'no-object-detected)}))
```

species	Answer a class that should be used to create new instances of collections like the receiver, to help with the implementation of select:, collect:, and similar methods.
printName	Print the name of the object's class, to help with the implementation of print. (Almost all Collection objects print as the name of the class, followed by the list of elements in parentheses. Array objects omit the name of the class.)

Figure 10.23: Private methods internal to Collection classes.

In addition to mutators and observers, the Collection protocol also provides iterators. These iterators are akin to μScheme's higher-order functions on lists. For example, do: resembles μScheme's app, and inject:into: resembles μScheme's foldl. But as before, objects offer this advantage: unlike μScheme's foldl, inject:into: works on *any* collection, not just on lists.

658a. ⟨*other methods of class* Collection 657a⟩+≡ (656c) ◁657e 658b▷

```
(method inject:into: (aValue binaryBlock)
   (self do: [block (x) (set aValue (binaryBlock value:value: x aValue))])
   aValue)
```

The methods select:, reject:, and collect: resemble μScheme's filter and map functions. Like inject:into:, they work on all collections, not just on lists. The implementations use species, which is a private message used to create "a new collection like the receiver" (Figure 10.23).

658b. ⟨*other methods of class* Collection 657a⟩+≡ (656c) ◁658a 658c▷

```
(method select: (aBlock) [locals temp]
   (set temp ((self species) new))
   (self do: [block (x) ((aBlock value: x) ifTrue: {(temp add: x)})])
   temp)
(method reject: (aBlock)
   (self select: [block (x) ((aBlock value: x) not)]))
(method collect: (aBlock) [locals temp]
   (set temp ((self species) new))
   (self do: [block (x) (temp add: (aBlock value: x))])
   temp)
```

A species defaults to the class of the receiver.

658c. ⟨*other methods of class* Collection 657a⟩+≡ (656c) ◁658b 658d▷

```
(method species () (self class))
```

Finally, Collection defines its own print method. By default, a collection prints as the name of its class, followed by a parenthesized list of its elements.

658d. ⟨*other methods of class* Collection 657a⟩+≡ (656c) ◁658c

```
(method print ()
    (self printName)
    (left-round print)
    (self do: [block (x) (space print) (x print)])
    (space print)
    (right-round print)
    self)
(method printName () (((self class) name) print))
```

Both methods may be overridden by subclasses.

Table 10.24: How protocols are refined for keyed and sequenceable collections

	Implements	Passes on	Adds	Overrides
Keyed	`do:`, `=`	`add`, `remove:ifAbsent`	`at:put`, `associationsDo:`, `removeKey:ifAbsent:`	—
Seq.	`associationsDo:`	`add`, `at:put`, `remove:ifAbsent`, `removeKey:ifAbsent`, `species`	`firstKey`, `lastKey`	`at:IfAbsent:`

10.7.2 Widening a protocol: Keyed and sequenceable collections

`Collection` isn't just an abstract class with multiple implementations. It's an abstraction that is refined into more abstractions:

- Keyed collections, which collect key-value pairs and can be indexed by key
- Sequenceable collections, which are keyed by consecutive integers

Each of these collections refines the protocol defined by its superclass. To study such refinement, we ask the same questions about each subclass:

- Which of the subclass responsibilities inherited from the superclass does it *implement*?
- What subclass responsibilities inherited from the superclass does it *pass on* to its own subclasses?
- What new subclass responsibilities does it *add*?
- What methods inherited from the superclass does it *override*? On what grounds?

For keyed and sequenceable collections, the answers are shown in Table 10.24.

Implementation of `KeyedCollection`

A keyed collection provides access to key-value pairs. It must define method `associationsDo:`, which replaces `do:`, method `removeKey:ifAbsent:`, which replaces `remove:ifAbsent:`, and method `at:put:`, which sometimes replaces `add:`. The key-value pairs answer the `Association` protocol.

659a. ⟨*collection classes* 656c⟩+≡ (S548d) ◁656c 661a▷

```
(class KeyedCollection
    [subclass-of Collection]  ; abstract class
    (method associationsDo: (aBlock)          (self subclassResponsibility))
    (method removeKey:ifAbsent: (key exnBlock) (self subclassResponsibility))
    (method at:put: (key value)               (self subclassResponsibility))
    ⟨other methods of class KeyedCollection 659b⟩
)
```

The `associationsDo:` method is used to implement the `do:` method required by the superclass:

659b. ⟨*other methods of class* `KeyedCollection` 659b⟩≡ (659a) 660a▷

```
(method do: (aBlock)
    (self associationsDo: [block (anAssoc) (aBlock value: (anAssoc value))]))
```

Every method in the "at" family, as well as includesKey:, is ultimately implemented on top of associationAt:ifAbsent:, which uses associationsDo:.

660a. ⟨*other methods of class* KeyedCollection 659b⟩+≡ (659a) ◁659b 660b▷

```
(method at: (key)
   (self at:ifAbsent: key {(self error: 'key-not-found)}))
(method at:ifAbsent: (key exnBlock)
   ((self associationAt:ifAbsent: key {(return (exnBlock value))}) value))
(method includesKey: (key)
   ((self associationAt:ifAbsent: key {}) notNil))
(method associationAt: (key)
   (self associationAt:ifAbsent: key {(self error: 'key-not-found)}))
(method associationAt:ifAbsent: (key exnBlock)
   (self associationsDo: [block (x) (((x key) = key) ifTrue: {(return x)})])
   (exnBlock value))
```

When a key is found, method associationAt:ifAbsent: terminates the search immediately by evaluating a return expression. This efficiency benefits all the other methods. And if a subclass implements associationAt:ifAbsent: in a more efficient way, the other methods benefit from that, too.

The key associated with a value is found in the same way as the value associated with a key.

660b. ⟨*other methods of class* KeyedCollection 659b⟩+≡ (659a) ◁660a 660c▷

```
(method keyAtValue: (value)
   (self keyAtValue:ifAbsent: value {(self error: 'value-not-found)}))
(method keyAtValue:ifAbsent: (value exnBlock)
   (self associationsDo: [block (x)
       (((x value) = value) ifTrue: {(return (x key))})])
   (exnBlock value))
```

A key is removed by removeAt:ifAbsent.

660c. ⟨*other methods of class* KeyedCollection 659b⟩+≡ (659a) ◁660b 660d▷

```
(method removeKey: (key)
   (self removeKey:ifAbsent: key {(self error: 'key-not-found)}))
```

The = method can be implemented once on class KeyedCollection, instead of separately for dictionaries, lists, and arrays. Two keyed collections are equivalent if they have equivalent associations. For efficiency, the code looks first for an association that's in the receiver but not in the argument. If it finds one, the collections are not equivalent, and it returns false immediately. Otherwise, it just has to confirm that both receiver and argument have the same number of associations—then and only then are they equivalent.

660d. ⟨*other methods of class* KeyedCollection 659b⟩+≡ (659a) ◁660c

```
(method = (collection)
   (self associationsDo:    ; look for `anAssoc' not in `collection'
       [block (anAssoc)
          (((anAssoc value) !=
                (collection at:ifAbsent: (anAssoc key) {(return false)}))
           ifTrue:
           {(return false)})])
   ((self size) = (collection size)))
```

The classic keyed collection is Dictionary. My implementation, which appears in Appendix U (page S564), is a simple list of key-value pairs, just like the env type in Chapter 5. Implementations using hash tables or search trees can be explored in Exercises 28 and 29.

Implementation of SequenceableCollection

The abstract class SequenceableCollection defines methods used by keyed collections whose keys are consecutive integers. Its concrete, predefined subclasses are List and Array.

661a. ⟨*collection classes* 656c⟩+≡ (S548d) ◁659a 674a▷

```
(class SequenceableCollection
    [subclass-of KeyedCollection] ; abstract class
    (method firstKey () (self subclassResponsibility))
    (method lastKey  () (self subclassResponsibility))
    (method last     () (self at: (self  lastKey)))
    (method first    () (self at: (self firstKey)))
    (method at:ifAbsent: (index exnBlock) [locals current]
        (set current (self firstKey))
        (self do: [block (v)
            ((current = index) ifTrue: {(return v)})
            (set current (current + 1))])
        (exnBlock value))
    ⟨other methods of class SequenceableCollection 661b⟩
)
```


Because keys are consecutive integers, method at:ifAbsent: can track the value of the key inside a do: loop, without ever allocating an Association. This implementation is more efficient than the generic implementation inherited from class KeyedCollection.

Method associationsDo: also loops over consecutive keys.

661b. ⟨*other methods of class* SequenceableCollection 661b⟩≡ (661a)

```
(method associationsDo: (bodyBlock) [locals i last]
    (set i    (self firstKey))
    (set last (self lastKey))
    ({(i <= last)} whileTrue:
        {(bodyBlock value: (Association withKey:value: i (self at: i)))
         (set i (i + 1))}))
```

The implementation of concrete class List is described in detail in Section 10.9.

10.7.3 Compromising on protocol: Class Array

Classes KeyedCollection and SequenceableCollection refine the Collection protocol, adding new operations. Sometimes, however, a class may want to *remove* operations from a protocol; it wants to reuse methods defined in a superclass while implementing only some of its subclass responsibilities. A classic example is a fixed-size array: it is a sequenceable collection, and at: and at:put: take only constant time, but after it is allocated, a fixed-size array cannot grow or shrink. As a result, it does not implement subclass responsibilities add:, remove:ifAbsent, or removeKey:ifAbsent; sending any of those messages results in a checked run-time error.

661c. ⟨*other methods of class* Array 661c⟩≡ (S565e) 662▷

```
(method add:                (x)   (self fixedSizeError))
(method remove:ifAbsent:    (x b) (self fixedSizeError))
(method removeKey:ifAbsent: (x b) (self fixedSizeError))
(method fixedSizeError      ()    (self error: 'arrays-have-fixed-size))
```

Because class Array exists to promote efficiency, it overrides many inherited methods; in particular, it uses primitives to implement methods size, at:, and at:put:. These methods are then used to implement firstKey, lastKey, and do:.

662. ⟨*other methods of class* Array 661c⟩+≡ (S565e) ◁ 661c

```
(method firstKey () 0)
(method lastKey  () ((self size) - 1))
(method do: (aBlock) [locals index]
    (set index (self firstKey))
    ((self size) timesRepeat:
       {(aBlock value: (self at: index))
        (set index (index + 1))}))
```

Instance methods select: and collect: and class method withAll: are left as Exercises 20 and 21, and the rest of Array is relegated to Appendix U.

10.8 Technique III: Multiple representations the object-oriented way

Smalltalk's collection abstractions are relatively easy to implement, in part because a typical operation involves only one collection: the receiver. And even an operation that takes a collection as argument doesn't have to look at the argument's representation; for example, methods addAll: and removeAll: simply use do: to iterate over the argument's elements. But in some other abstractions, like the leftist heap from Chapter 9 (page 555), an operation like heap merge does have to look at the representation of an argument. Such an operation is called *complex* (Cook 2009). And in a pure object-oriented language like Smalltalk, complex operations are not so easy to implement.

We'll study complex operations on numbers (page 650), which have to look at the representations of two numbers. For example,

- Operation < on fractions needs to look at the numerators and denominators of both fractions.
- Operation * on floating-point numbers needs to look at the mantissas and exponents of both numbers.

In a language that uses abstract data types, like Molecule, complex operations like these are easy to implement: if an operation can see the definition of a type, it can see the representation of every argument of that type. But in a pure object-oriented language, like Smalltalk, a complex method isn't so easy to implement: it can see only the representation of the receiver, and all it can do with an argument is send messages to it. To figure out what messages to send, we have several options:

- We can extend the argument's protocol with new messages that provide access to its representation. This technique is illustrated using classes Number, Integer, and especially Fraction (Sections 10.8.1 and 10.8.2).
- If we don't know the argument's representation, we might not know what new messages it can respond to. In such a case, we can have the *receiver* send a message to the *argument* telling the argument what new messages the receiver can respond to. This technique, called *double dispatch*, is illustrated using the integer classes (Section 10.8.3).
- We can *coerce* one object to have the same representation as another. For example, to add aNumber to a fraction, we can coerce aNumber to a fraction.

This technique is illustrated using the Fraction and Integer classes (Section 10.8.4).

All three techniques can work with any representation. To help you integrate them into your own programming, I recommend a case study for which there is more than one reasonable representation: arithmetic on natural numbers. A natural number should be represented as a sequence of digits, and every representation of that sequence suggests its own set of new messages that are analogous to the new messages defined on class Fraction (Section 10.8.5).

10.8.1 *A context for complex operations: Abstract classes* Number *and* Integer

Before studying complex operations on fractions, we look at the context in which fractions are defined. A fraction is a number, and abstract class Number (Figure 10.20 on page 650) defines two groups of subclass responsibilities: arithmetic methods (+, *, negated, and reciprocal) and coercion methods (asInteger, asFraction, asFloat, and coerce:).

663a. ⟨*definition of class* Number 663a⟩≡

```
(class Number
    [subclass-of Magnitude]  ; abstract class
    ;;;;;;; arithmetic
    (method +    (aNumber)      (self subclassResponsibility))
    (method *    (aNumber)      (self subclassResponsibility))
    (method negated     ()      (self subclassResponsibility))
    (method reciprocal ()       (self subclassResponsibility))

    ;;;;;;; coercion
    (method asInteger   ()      (self subclassResponsibility))
    (method asFraction ()       (self subclassResponsibility))
    (method asFloat     ()      (self subclassResponsibility))
    (method coerce: (aNumber) (self subclassResponsibility))
    ⟨other methods of class Number 663b⟩
)
```

Subclasses of Number must also implement subclass responsibilities for magnitudes: methods = and <. Methods =, <, +, *, and coerce: take another Number as argument, and all except coerce: turn out to be complex.

To get a feel for the class, let's see how subclass responsibilities are used to implement other parts of the Number protocol (page 650). Arithmetic methods are implemented on top of subclass arithmetic methods, and sign tests are implemented on top of comparison and coercion:

663b. ⟨*other methods of class* Number 663b⟩≡ (663a) S566b ▷

```
(method -   (y) (self + (y  negated)))
(method abs () ((self isNegative) ifTrue:ifFalse: {(self negated)} {self}))
(method /   (y) (self * (y reciprocal)))

(method isZero             () (self  = (self coerce: 0)))
(method isNegative         () (self  < (self coerce: 0)))
(method isNonnegative      () (self >= (self coerce: 0)))
(method isStrictlyPositive () (self  > (self coerce: 0)))
```

The Number protocol also requires methods squared, sqrt, sqrtWithin:, and raisedToInteger:, which are relegated to the Supplement.

Before we get to class Fraction, we should also sketch class Integer, which provides the gcd: operation needed to put a fraction in lowest terms. The gcd: method is one of the four division-related methods gcd:, lcm:, div:, and mod:. Only div: has to be implemented in subclasses.

664a. ⟨*numeric classes* 656a⟩+≡ (S548d) ◁656a 664c▷

```
(class Integer
    [subclass-of Number] ; abstract class
    (method div: (n) (self subclassResponsibility))
    (method mod: (n) (self - (n * (self div: n))))
    (method gcd: (n) ((n = (self coerce: 0))
                       ifTrue:ifFalse: {self} {(n gcd: (self mod: n))}))
    (method lcm: (n) (self * (n div: (self gcd: n))))
    ⟨other methods of class Integer 664b⟩
)
```

Class Integer typically has three concrete subclasses: SmallInteger, for integers that fit in a machine word (Appendix U); LargePositiveInteger, for arbitrarily large positive integers; and LargeNegativeInteger, for arbitrarily large negative integers (Section 10.8.3). In μSmalltalk, only SmallInteger is defined; the other two are meant to be added by you (Exercise 38).

Class Integer implements the subclass responsibility reciprocal, and it also overrides the default / method. Both methods answer fractions, not integers.

664b. ⟨*other methods of class* Integer 664b⟩≡ (664a) 669b▷

```
(method reciprocal () (Fraction num:den: 1 self))
(method / (aNumber) ((self asFraction) / aNumber))
```

10.8.2 *Implementing complex operations: Class* Fraction

A method is *complex* when it needs to inspect the representation of an argument. I introduce complex methods using class Fraction, whose representation includes a numerator num and denominator den, both of which are integer instance variables.

664c. ⟨*numeric classes* 656a⟩+≡ (S548d) ◁664a 670▷

```
(class Fraction
    [subclass-of Number]
    [ivars num den]
    (method print () (num print) ('/ print) (den print) self)
    ⟨other methods of class Fraction 664d⟩
)
```

This representation stands for the ratio $\frac{\texttt{num}}{\texttt{den}}$. Such ratios can be compared, added, and multiplied only if each method has access to the numerator and denominator of its argument, not just its receiver—that is, if the methods are complex. The access is provided by private methods num and den, each of which answers the value of the instance variable with which it shares a name.

664d. ⟨*other methods of class* Fraction 664d⟩≡ (664c) 665a▷

```
(method num () num)  ; private
(method den () den)  ; private
```

Methods num and den are used to implement the four complex operations =, <, *, and +. Each operation relies on and guarantees these representation invariants:

1. The denominator is positive.
2. If the numerator is zero, the denominator is 1.

3. The numerator and denominator are reduced to lowest terms, that is, their only common divisor is 1.

These invariants imply that two `Fraction` objects represent the same fraction if and only if they have the same numerator and denominator, and they enable the following implementations of the comparison methods from class `Magnitude`:

665a. ⟨*other methods of class* `Fraction` 664d⟩+≡ (664c) ◁ 664d 665b ▷

```
(method = (f) ((num = (f num)) and: {(den = (f den))}))
(method < (f) ((num * (f den)) < ((f num) * den)))
```

The < method uses the law that $\frac{n}{d} < \frac{n'}{d'}$ if and only if $n \cdot d' < n' \cdot d$, which holds only because d and d' are positive. And argument `f` doesn't have to be an instance of class `Fraction`; it's enough if `f` is a number and if it responds sensibly to messages `num` and `den`.

Methods = and < rely on the representation invariants. The invariants for any given fraction are established by two private methods: method `signReduce` establishes invariant 1, and method `divReduce` establishes invariants 2 and 3.

665b. ⟨*other methods of class* `Fraction` 664d⟩+≡ (664c) ◁ 665a 665c ▷

```
(method signReduce () ; private
    ((den isZero) ifTrue: {(self error: 'ZeroDivide)})
    ((den isNegative) ifTrue:
        {(set num (num negated)) (set den (den negated))})
    self)
(method divReduce () [locals temp] ; private
    ((num = 0) ifTrue:ifFalse:
        {(set den 1)}
        {(set temp ((num abs) gcd: den))
         (set num  (num div: temp))
         (set den  (den div: temp))})
    self)
```

When a new `Fraction` is created by public class method `num:den:`, all three invariants are established by private method `initNum:den:`.

665c. ⟨*other methods of class* `Fraction` 664d⟩+≡ (664c) ◁ 665b 665d ▷

```
(class-method num:den: (a b) ((self new) initNum:den: a b))
(method setNum:den: (a b) (set num a) (set den b) self) ; private
(method initNum:den: (a b) ; private
    (self setNum:den: a b)
    (self signReduce)
    (self divReduce))
```

Private method `setNum:den:` sets the numerator and denominator of a fraction, but it does not establish the invariants. It is used in multiplication and addition.

Multiplication is specified by the law $\frac{n}{d} \cdot \frac{n'}{d'} = \frac{n \cdot n'}{d \cdot d'}$, but the right-hand side could violate invariant 2 or 3. (Numerator $n \cdot n'$ and denominator $d \cdot d'$ can have common factors, but $d \cdot d'$ cannot be negative.) The multiplication method therefore sends `divReduce` to the naïve result.

665d. ⟨*other methods of class* `Fraction` 664d⟩+≡ (664c) ◁ 665c 666a ▷

```
(method * (f)
  (((Fraction new) setNum:den: (num * (f num)) (den * (f den))) divReduce))
```

Addition is specified by the law $\frac{n}{d} + \frac{n'}{d'} = \frac{n \cdot d' + n' \cdot d}{d \cdot d'}$. The resulting numerator and denominator may have common factors, violating invariant 3, but such factors are eliminated by `divReduce`, as in the example $\frac{1}{2} + \frac{1}{2} = \frac{4}{4} = \frac{1}{1}$. Method `divReduce` also restores invariant 2. In addition, the computation of denominator $d \cdot d'$ might overflow. To make overflow less likely, my code defines `temp` $= \mathrm{lcm}(d, d')$, puts temp in the denominator, and uses $\frac{\texttt{temp}}{d}$ and $\frac{\texttt{temp}}{d'}$ as needed. Without this tweak, the square-root computations in Section 10.4.6 would overflow.

666a. ⟨*other methods of class* Fraction 664d⟩+≡ (664c) ◁665d 666b▷

```
(method + (f) [locals temp]
    (set temp (den lcm: (f den)))
    (((Fraction new) setNum:den:
                     ((num     * (temp div: den)) +
                      ((f num) * (temp div: (f den))))
                     temp)
        divReduce))
```

Method + is the last of the complex methods. But it's not the last of the methods that rely on or guarantee invariants. For example, reciprocal must not leave a negative fraction with a negative denominator. The denominator is given the correct sign by sending signReduce to the inverted fraction. (The reciprocal of zero cannot be put into reduced form. Nothing can be done about it.)

666b. ⟨*other methods of class* Fraction 664d⟩+≡ (664c) ◁666a 666c▷

```
(method reciprocal ()
   (((Fraction new) setNum:den: den num) signReduce))
```

Negation negates the numerator; the invariants are guaranteed to be maintained.

666c. ⟨*other methods of class* Fraction 664d⟩+≡ (664c) ◁666b 666d▷

```
(method negated () ((Fraction new) setNum:den: (num negated) den))
```

The invariants enable the sign tests to inspect only the receiver's numerator. These tests are much more efficient than the versions inherited from Number.

666d. ⟨*other methods of class* Fraction 664d⟩+≡ (664c) ◁666c 668a▷

```
(method isZero             () (num isZero))
(method isNegative         () (num isNegative))
(method isNonnegative      () (num isNonnegative))
(method isStrictlyPositive () (num isStrictlyPositive))
```

Class Fraction must also fulfill subclass responsibilities involving coercion, which is the topic of Section 10.8.4 (page 667).

10.8.3 *Interoperation with more than one representation: Double dispatch*

Given methods num and den, fractions can be compared with fractions, added to fractions, and so on. Comparison and arithmetic methods can't see the representations of their arguments, but they don't have to: it's enough to know that each argument responds to messages num and den. But comparison and arithmetic on integers are not so easy.

The difficulty with integers is that Smalltalk supports two forms of integer: small and large. A small integer must fit in a machine word; a large integer may be arbitrarily large. Both forms must respond to a + message, but the algorithm used to implement + depends on what is being added:

- If two small integers are being added, the algorithm uses primitive addition, which ultimately executes a hardware addition instruction.
- If two large integers are being added, the algorithm adds the digits pairwise, with carry digits, as described in Appendix B.
- If a large integer and a small integer are being added, the algorithm coerces the small integer to a large integer, then adds the resulting large integers.

The appropriate algorithm depends on more than just the class of the receiver.

To select the appropriate algorithm, the + method doesn't interrogate objects to ask about their classes. (The object-oriented motto is, "Don't ask; tell.") Instead, when a small integer receives a + message, its + method sends another message to its *argument*, saying, "I'm a small integer; add me to yourself."

667. ⟨SmallInteger *methods revised to use double dispatch* 667⟩≡

```
(method + (anInteger) (anInteger addSmallIntegerTo: self))
```


The addSmallIntegerTo: method knows that its argument is a small integer, and like all methods, it knows what class it's defined on. This is enough information to choose the right algorithm:

- On a small integer, the addSmallIntegerTo: method uses a machine primitive to add self to the argument.
- On a large integer, the addSmallIntegerTo: method coerces its argument to a large integer, then sends the receiver a + message.

This technique, by which a complex binary operation is implemented in two message sends instead of one, is called *double dispatch.*

The story above glosses over an important fact about large-integer operations: a large integer has both a sign and a magnitude, and the algorithm for adding large integers depends on the sign. If two integers have the same sign, their magnitudes are added, but if they have different signs, their magnitudes are subtracted. As always, the + method doesn't interrogate an integer about its sign; instead, positive and negative large integers are instances of different classes, and the + method on each class dispatches depending on the sign of the receiver. That means that an integer class must support *three* double-dispatch methods for addition: it can be told to add a *small* integer to itself, to add a large *positive* integer to itself, or to add a large *negative* integer to itself (Figure 10.25, on the next page).

Methods + and * invoke the double-dispatch method appropriate to the operation wanted and the class of the receiver. For example, method + on class LargePositiveInteger is defined as follows:

```
(method + (anInteger) (anInteger addLargePositiveIntegerTo: self))
```

The rest of Figure 10.25 describes the other methods needed to implement arithmetic on large integers. Method magnitude plays the same role for large integers that methods num and den play for fractions. And methods sdiv: and smod: provide a protocol for dividing a large integer by a small integer. (Division of a large integer by another large integer requires long division. Long division is fascinating algorithmically, but it's too hairy to make a good exercise.)

A starter kit for class LargeInteger is shown in Figure 10.26 (page 669). The LargeInteger class is meant to be abstract; do not instantiate it. Instead, define subclasses LargePositiveInteger and LargeNegativeInteger, which you can then instantiate (Exercise 38).

10.8.4 *Coercion between abstractions in* Fraction *and* Integer

A binary message like < or + should be sent only when the receiver and the argument are compatible. If numbers aren't compatible, they can be made so using *coercion.* In Smalltalk, coercion is part of the Number protocol; every number must be able to coerce itself to an integer, a floating-point number, or a fraction. A coercion

`addSmallIntegerTo: aSmallInteger`	Answer the sum of the argument and the receiver.
`addLargePositiveIntegerTo: aLargePositiveInteger`	Answer the sum of the argument and the receiver.
`addLargeNegativeIntegerTo: aLargeNegativeInteger`	Answer the sum of the argument and the receiver.
`multiplyBySmallInteger: aSmallInteger`	Answer the product of the argument and the receiver.
`multiplyByLargePositiveInteger: aLargePositiveInteger`	Answer the product of the argument and the receiver.
`multiplyByLargeNegativeInteger: aLargeNegativeInteger`	Answer the product of the argument and the receiver.

(a) Private instance protocol for both large and small integers

`fromSmall: aSmallInteger`	Answer a large integer whose value is equal to the value of the argument.
`withMagnitude: aNatural`	Answer an instance of the receiver whose magnitude is the given magnitude.

(b) Class protocol for `LargeInteger`

`magnitude`	Answer an object of class `Natural` that represents the absolute value of the receiver.
`sdiv: aSmallInteger`	Answer the large integer closest to but not greater than the quotient of the receiver and the argument.
`smod: aSmallInteger`	Answer the small integer that is the remainder when the receiver is divided by the argument.

(c) Private instance protocol for large integers only

Figure 10.25: Private protocols for integers

method typically uses the public protocol of the classes it is coercing its receiver to, like these methods defined on class `Fraction`:

668a. ⟨*other methods of class* `Fraction` 664d⟩+≡ (664c) ◁666d 668b▷

```
(method asInteger  () (num div: den))
(method asFloat    () ((num asFloat) / (den asFloat)))
(method asFraction () self)
```

To coerce itself to an integer or a floating-point number, a fraction divides `num` by `den`. Division may be implemented by the integer-division message `div:` or (after coercing `num` and `den` to floating point) by the floating-point division message `/`. To coerce itself to a fraction, a fraction needn't divide at all.

When their classes aren't known, numbers can still be made compatible by sending the `coerce:` message, which tells the receiver to coerce its argument to be like itself. For example, a fraction coerces its argument to a fraction.

668b. ⟨*other methods of class* `Fraction` 664d⟩+≡ (664c) ◁668a

```
(method coerce: (aNumber) (aNumber asFraction))
```

669a. ⟨*large integers* 669a⟩≡
```
(class LargeInteger
  [subclass-of Integer]
  [ivars magnitude]

  (class-method withMagnitude: (aNatural)
      ((self new) magnitude: aNatural))
  (method magnitude: (aNatural) ; private, for initialization
      (set magnitude aNatural)
      self)

  (method magnitude () magnitude)

  (class-method fromSmall: (anInteger)
     ((anInteger isNegative) ifTrue:ifFalse:
        {(((self fromSmall: 1) + (self fromSmall: ((anInteger + 1) negated)))
          negated)}
        {((LargePositiveInteger new) magnitude: (Natural fromSmall: anInteger))}))
  (method asLargeInteger () self)
  (method isZero () (magnitude isZero))
  (method = (anInteger) ((self - anInteger)     isZero))
  (method < (anInteger) ((self - anInteger) isNegative))

  (method div: (_) (self error: 'long-division-not-supported))
  (method mod: (_) (self error: 'long-division-not-supported))

  (method sdiv: (aSmallInteger) (self leftAsExercise))
  (method smod: (aSmallInteger) (self leftAsExercise))
)
```

Figure 10.26: Abstract class `LargeInteger`

The coercion methods on classes `Float` and `Integer` follow the same structure. Class `Float` is relegated to Appendix U, but the `Integer` methods are shown here. Just as a fraction must know what integer or floating-point operations to use to divide its numerator by its denominator, an integer must know what fractional or floating-point operations to use to represent an integer. In this case, it's `self` divided by 1 and `self` times a base to the power 0, respectively.

669b. ⟨*other methods of class* `Integer` 664b⟩+≡ (664a) ◁664b 669c▷
```
(method asFraction () (Fraction num:den:  self 1))
(method asFloat     () (Float    mant:exp: self 0))
```

Just as in class `Fraction`, the other two methods simply exploit the knowledge that the receiver is an integer:

669c. ⟨*other methods of class* `Integer` 664b⟩+≡ (664a) ◁669b S567a▷
```
(method asInteger () self)
(method coerce: (aNumber) (aNumber asInteger))
```

10.8.5 Choice of representation: Natural numbers

Using representations that I have defined, the examples above demonstrate techniques used to implement complex methods like `+` and `<`. The same techniques can be applied to a representation that you can define: a representation of natural numbers (Exercise 37). To get started, follow the guidance below, which presents hints, ideas, and private protocols for two possible representations.

670. ⟨*numeric classes* 656a⟩+≡ (S548d) ◁ 664c S567b ▷

```
(class Natural
   [subclass-of Magnitude]
   ; instance variables left as an exercise

   (class-method fromSmall: (anInteger) (self leftAsExercise))

   (method = (aNatural) (self leftAsExercise))
   (method < (aNatural) (self leftAsExercise))

   (method + (aNatural) (self leftAsExercise))
   (method * (aNatural) (self leftAsExercise))
   (method - (aNatural)
      (self subtract:withDifference:ifNegative:
            aNatural
            [block (x) x]
            {(self error: 'Natural-subtraction-went-negative)}))
   (method subtract:withDifference:ifNegative: (aNatural diffBlock exnBlock)
      (self leftAsExercise))

   (method sdiv: (n) (self sdivmod:with: n [block (q r) q]))
   (method smod: (n) (self sdivmod:with: n [block (q r) r]))
   (method sdivmod:with: (n aBlock) (self leftAsExercise))

   (method decimal () (self leftAsExercise))
   (method isZero  () (self leftAsExercise))

   (method print   () ((self decimal) do: [block (x) (x print)]))
)
```

Figure 10.27: Template for a definition of class `Natural`

For efficiency, a natural number should be represented as a sequence of digits in some base b (Appendix B). The sequence may reasonably be represented as an array or as a list. μSmalltalk's `Array` class works fine here, but the predefined `List` class does not; you are better off defining empty and nonempty lists of digits as subclasses of class `Natural`. For this reason, I refer to the two representations as the "array representation" and the "subclass representation." Each representation calls for its own private protocol to be used to implement the complex methods. And both can start with the template in Figure 10.27.

Natural numbers: The array representation

If a natural number is represented using an array of digits, I recommend giving it two instance variables: `degree` and `digits`. The representation invariant should be as follows: `digits` should be an array containing at least `degree` $+ 1$ integers, each of which lies in the range $0 \leq x_i < b$, where b is the base. If `digits` contains coefficients x_i, where $0 \leq i \leq$ `degree`, then the abstraction function says that the object represents natural number X, where

$$X = \sum_{i=0}^{\texttt{degree}} x_i \cdot b^i.$$

With this array representation, I recommend the private protocol shown in Figure 10.28 on the next page.

`base`	Answers b.

(a) Private class method for class `Natural`

`digit: anIndex`	Upon receiving `digit:` i, answer x_i. Should work for any nonnegative i, no matter how large.
`digit:put: anIndex aDigit`	On receiving `digit:put:` i y, mutate the receiver, making $x_i = y$. Although `Natural` is not a mutable type (and therefore this method should never be called by clients), it can be quite useful to mutate individual digits while you are constructing a new instance.
`digits: aSequence`	Take a sequence of x_i and use it to initialize `digits` and `degree`.
`doDigitIndices: aBlock`	For i from zero to `degree`, send `value` i to `aBlock`.
`trim`	Set `degree` on the receiver as small as possible, and answer the receiver.
`degree`	Answer the `degree` of the receiver.
`makeEmpty: aDegree`	Set `digits` to an array suitable for representing natural numbers of the specified degree. (Also change the `degree` of the receiver to `aDegree`.)

(b) Private instance methods for class `Natural`

Figure 10.28: Suggested private methods for class `Natural`, array representation

- The `base` method on the class provides a single point of truth about b, which you choose.
- The digit-related methods are used to read, write, and iterate over digits.
- Methods `trim` and `degree` are used to keep the arrays as small as possible, so leading zeroes don't accumulate.
- Method `makeEmpty:` is used to initialize newly allocated instances.

The array representation offers these trade-offs: Because it provides easy access to any digit you like, it enables you to treat Smalltalk as if it were a procedural language, like C. In particular, you can get away without thinking too hard about dynamic dispatch, because a lot of decisions can be made by looking at digits and at `degree`. But the individual methods are a little complicated, and you may not learn a whole lot—my array-based code uses objects only to hide information from client code, and it doesn't exploit dynamic dispatch or inheritance.

Natural numbers: The subclass representation

If a natural number is represented as a list of digits, I recommend defining two additional classes that inherit from `Natural`: `NatZero` and `NatNonzero`. An instance of class `NatZero` represents zero, and it doesn't need any instance variables. An instance of class `NatNonzero` represents the natural number $x_0 + X' \cdot b$, where

`base`	Answers b, the base of `Natural` numbers.
`first:rest: anInteger aNatural`	Answers a `Natural` number representing `anInteger` $+$ `aNatural` $\cdot\, b$.

(a) Private class methods for class `Natural`

`modBase`	Answers a small integer whose value is the receiver modulo b.
`divBase`	Answers a `Natural` whose value is the receiver divided by b.
`timesBase`	Answers a `Natural` whose value is the receiver multiplied by b.
`compare:withLt:withEq:withGt: aNatural ltBlock eqBlock gtBlock`	Compares `self` with `aNatural`. If `self` is smaller than `aNatural`, evaluate `ltBlock`. If they are equal, evaluate `eqBlock`. If `self` is greater, evaluate `gtBlock`.
`plus:carry: aNatural c`	Answer the sum `self` $+$ `aNatural` $+$ `c`, where `c` is a carry bit (either 0 or 1).
`minus:borrow: aNatural c`	Compute the difference `self` $-$ (`aNatural` $+$ `c`), where `c` is a borrow bit (either 0 or 1). If the difference is nonnegative, answer the difference; otherwise, halt the program with a checked run-time error.

(b) Private instance methods for class `Natural`

Figure 10.29: Suggested private methods for class `Natural`, subclass representation

x_0 is a digit (a small integer), X' is a natural number, and b is the base. Class `NatNonzero` needs instance variables for x_0 and X'; these might be called `x-0` and `other-digits`. The representation invariants are that x_0 and X' are not both zero, and $0 \leq x_0 < b$.

With the subclass representation, I recommend the private protocol in Figure 10.29.

- As with arrays, class method `base` provides a single point of truth about b.
- Class method `first:rest:` creates a new instance of one of the two subclasses. If both arguments are zero, it answers an instance of class `NatZero`. Otherwise, it answers an instance of class `NatNonzero`.
- Private methods `modBase`, `divBase`, and `timesBase`, together with public method `isZero` (Figure 10.22), are the protocol that allows a method to inspect its argument. If a natural number X is $x_0 + X' \cdot b$, then `modBase` answers x_0 and `divBase` answers X'. (If a natural number is zero, it answers all of these messages with zero.)
- The comparison method simplifies the implementations of methods `<` and `=`, which are subclass responsibilities of class `Natural` (from the `Magnitude` protocol).
- Methods `plus:carry:` and `minus:borrow:` implement functions adc and sbb, which are explained in Appendix B.

The subclass representation offers these trade-offs: Because it provides easy access only to the least significant digit of a natural number (using modBase), it forces you to treat the other digits abstractly. The abstraction implies that many decisions about what to do next and when algorithms should terminate are made implicitly by dynamic dispatch: in each method, the action is determined by the class on which the method is defined. And each individual method is therefore simpler than corresponding methods that use the array representation; for example, the + method defined on class NatZero simply answers its argument, and the * method simply answers zero. No conditionals, no scrutiny, end of story. But although the individual methods are simple, the overall algorithm makes sense only once you understand dynamic dispatch.

10.9 Technique IV: Invariants in object-oriented programming

Object-oriented programmers use the same program-design techniques that are described in Chapter 9 in the context of abstract data types—especially abstraction functions and invariants. In this section, an abstraction function and representation invariant are used to implement a mutable linked list with an appealing cost model: linear-time traversal and constant-time access to first and last elements.

As in μScheme, the representation uses cons cells. But unlike μScheme code, μSmalltalk code never asks a list if it is empty or nonempty. Instead, empty and nonempty lists are represented by objects of different classes, and decisions are made by dispatching to the right method.

To support efficient insertion and deletion at either end of a list, I represent it using a *circular* list of cons cells. This representation relies on a sophisticated invariant: both the beginning and end of the list are marked by a special cons cell, which is called a *sentinel*. A sentinel is a standard technique that often simplifies the implementation of a data structure (Sedgewick 1988). And in Smalltalk, the sentinel can handle all the special cases normally associated with the end of a list, just by defining appropriate methods. As a result, the list code does not contain even one conditional that checks if a list is empty.

Just as in μScheme, a cons cell holds two values: a car and a cdr. Unlike in μScheme, the cdr *always* points to another cons cell. This invariant holds because every list is circularly linked—the other cons cell might be a sentinel. For example, a list containing the elements 1, 2, and 3 (plus a sentinel) is structured as follows:

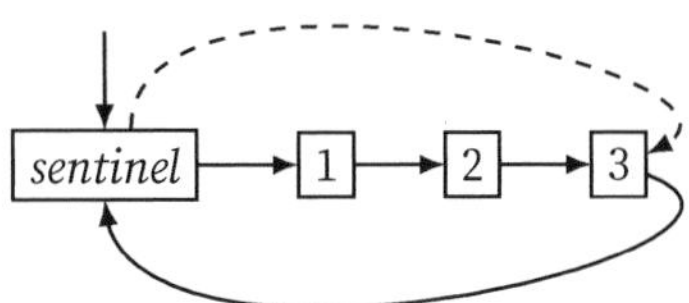

The sentinel contains *two* pointers: the cdr (solid line), which it inherits from class Cons, points to the elements of the list, if any; the pred (dashed line), which is found only on objects of class ListSentinel, points to the sentinel's *predecessor*.

A sentinel's predecessor is normally the last element of its list, but when a list is empty, both fields of its sentinel point to the sentinel itself:

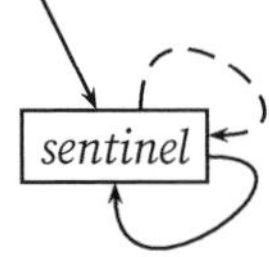

When the cdr points to the sentinel itself, the abstraction function maps the representation to the empty sequence. When the cdr points to another object, that object is a cons cell, and the abstraction function maps the representation to the sequence of objects stored in the cons cells pointed to by the cdr of the sentinel.

Each cons cell, including the sentinel, responds to the protocol shown in Figure 10.30 (on the next page).

A List object has only one instance variable: a pointer to the sentinel.

674a. ⟨*collection classes* 656c⟩+≡ (S548d) ◁661a S563▷

```
⟨classes that define cons cells and sentinels 675b⟩
(class List
   [subclass-of SequenceableCollection]
   [ivars sentinel]
   (class-method new ()        ((super new) sentinel: (ListSentinel new)))
   (method sentinel: (s)       (set sentinel s) self) ; private
   (method isEmpty   ()        (sentinel == (sentinel cdr)))
   (method last      ()        ((sentinel pred) car))
   (method do:       (aBlock)  ((sentinel cdr) do: aBlock))
   ⟨other methods of class List 674b⟩
)
```

The method addLast: mutates a list by adding an element to the end. This means inserting an element just after the predecessor of the sentinel. Similarly, addFirst: inserts an element just after the sentinel. Having a sentinel means there is no special-case code for an empty list.

674b. ⟨*other methods of class* List 674b⟩≡ (674a) 674c▷

```
(method addLast:  (item)   ((sentinel pred) insertAfter: item) self)
(method addFirst: (item)   (sentinel insertAfter: item)        self)
(method add:      (item)   (self addLast: item))
```

Method removeFirst removes the element after the sentinel; removeLast is left as Exercise 25.

674c. ⟨*other methods of class* List 674b⟩+≡ (674a) ◁674b 674d▷

```
(method removeFirst ()     (sentinel deleteAfter))
(method removeLast  ()     (self leftAsExercise))
```

Method remove:ifAbsent:, which removes an element holding a given object, uses the private cons-cell protocol described in Figure 10.30; the private method rejectOne:ifAbsent:withPred: is modeled on the more general reject: method defined on all collections.

674d. ⟨*other methods of class* List 674b⟩+≡ (674a) ◁674c 674e▷

```
(method remove:ifAbsent: (oldObject exnBlock)
    ((sentinel cdr)
        rejectOne:ifAbsent:withPred:
        [block (x) (oldObject = (x car))]
        exnBlock
        sentinel))
```

Method removeKey:ifAbsent: is left as an exercise.

674e. ⟨*other methods of class* List 674b⟩+≡ (674a) ◁674d 674f▷

```
(method removeKey:ifAbsent: (n exnBlock) (self leftAsExercise))
```

List is a subclass of SequenceableCollection, so it must answer messages involving integer keys. The first key in a List is always 0.

674f. ⟨*other methods of class* List 674b⟩+≡ (674a) ◁674e 675a▷

```
(method firstKey () 0)
(method lastKey  () ((self size) - 1))
```

car	Answer the car of the receiver.
cdr	Answer the cdr of the receiver.
car: anObject	Set the receiver's car and answer the receiver.
cdr: anObject	Set the receiver's cdr and answer the receiver.
pred: aCons	Notify the receiver that its predecessor is the cons cell aCons.
deleteAfter	Delete the cons cell that the receiver's cdr points to. Answer the car of that cons cell.
insertAfter: anObject	Insert a new cons cell after the receiver, letting the new cons cell's car point to anObject. Answer anObject.
do: aBlock	For each cons cell c in the receiver, excluding the sentinel, use a value: message to send (c car) to aBlock.
rejectOne:ifAbsent:withPred: aBlock exnBlock aCons	Starting at the receiver, search the list for a cons cell c such that (aBlock value: c) is true. If such a cell is found, remove it. Otherwise, answer (exnBlock value). As a precondition, the argument aCons *must* be the predecessor of the receiver.

(a) Instance protocol for all cons cells

pred	Answer the predecessor of the receiver.

(b) Instance protocol for sentinels only

Figure 10.30: Protocols for cons cells

List element n is updated by skipping n cons cells and then sending the next cons call the car: message.

675a. ⟨*other methods of class* List 674b⟩+≡ (674a) ◁674f

```
(method at:put: (n value) [locals tmp]
    (set tmp (sentinel cdr))
    ({(n isZero)} whileFalse:
       {(set n (n - 1))
        (set tmp (tmp cdr))})
    (tmp car: value)
    self)
```

If n is out of range, the method can produce wrong answers—which can be made right (Exercise 26).

The low-level work of manipulating pointers is done by the methods in the cons-cell protocol (Figure 10.30).

675b. ⟨*classes that define cons cells and sentinels* 675b⟩≡ (674a) 677▷

```
(class Cons
    [subclass-of Object]
    [ivars car cdr]
    ⟨methods of class Cons 676a⟩
)
```

The first four methods of class Cons expose the representation as a pair of car and cdr. And the pred: method makes it possible to tell *any* cons cell what its predecessor is—information that is used only by the sentinel. (A sentinel is an instance of a subclass of Cons.)

676a. ⟨*methods of class* Cons 676a⟩≡ (675b) 676b ▷

```
(method car ()           car)
(method cdr ()           cdr)
(method car: (anObject)  (set car anObject) self)
(method cdr: (anObject)  (set cdr anObject) self)
(method pred: (aCons)    nil)
```

Methods deleteAfter and insertAfter: implement the standard pointer manipulations for a circularly linked list. Circularity comes into play when a node is deleted or inserted; sending pred: notifies the node's successor of its new predecessor.

676b. ⟨*methods of class* Cons 676a⟩+≡ (675b) ◁ 676a 676c ▷

```
(method deleteAfter () [locals answer]
    (set answer (cdr car))
    (set cdr    (cdr cdr))
    (cdr pred: self)
    answer)
(method insertAfter: (anObject)
    (set cdr (((Cons new) cdr: cdr) car: anObject))
    ((cdr cdr) pred: cdr)
    anObject)
```

The iteration and removal methods take full advantage of object-oriented programming. By defining do: differently on classes and ListSentinel, I create code that iterates over a list without ever using an explicit if or while—all it does is method dispatch. To make the computation a little clearer, I present some of the methods of class Cons right next to the corresponding methods of class ListSentinel.

The do: method iterates over a list of cons cells by first doing the car, then continuing with a tail call to the do: method of the cdr. The iteration terminates in the sentinel, whose do: method does nothing.

676c. ⟨*methods of class* Cons 676a⟩+≡ (675b) ◁ 676b 676e ▷

```
(method do: (aBlock)       ; defined on an ordinary cons cell
    (aBlock value: car)
    (cdr do: aBlock))
```

676d. ⟨*iterating methods of class* ListSentinel 676d⟩≡ (677) 676f ▷

```
(method do: (aBlock) nil)  ; defined on a sentinel
```

Similarly, method rejectOne:ifAbsent:withPred: checks the current cons cell to see if it should be removed, and if so, sends deleteAfter to its predecessor, which is passed as parameter pred. Otherwise, the method tries the next cons cell. If the method reaches the sentinel, it hasn't found what it's looking for, and it terminates the loop by sending the value message to the exception block.

676e. ⟨*methods of class* Cons 676a⟩+≡ (675b) ◁ 676c

```
(method rejectOne:ifAbsent:withPred: (aBlock exnBlock pred)
    ((aBlock value: self) ifTrue:ifFalse:
        {(pred deleteAfter)}
        {(cdr rejectOne:ifAbsent:withPred: aBlock exnBlock self)}))
```

676f. ⟨*iterating methods of class* ListSentinel 676d⟩+≡ (677) ◁ 676d

```
(method rejectOne:ifAbsent:withPred: (aBlock exnBlock pred)
    (exnBlock value))
```

The final instance methods of class ListSentinel expose the pred pointer. And class method new allocates a new sentinel, whose pred and cdr both point to itself. Such a sentinel represents an empty list.

677. ⟨*classes that define cons cells and sentinels* 675b⟩+≡ (674a) ◁675b

```
(class ListSentinel
    [subclass-of Cons]
    [ivars pred]
    (method pred: (aCons)   (set pred aCons))
    (method pred  ()        pred)
    (class-method new ()
        [locals tmp]
        (set tmp (super new))
        (tmp pred: tmp)
        (tmp  cdr: tmp)
        tmp)
    ⟨iterating methods of class ListSentinel 676d⟩)
```


10.10 Operational semantics

The operational semantics of μSmalltalk is in the same family as the operational semantics of μScheme: it's a big-step semantics in which each variable name stands for a mutable location. And like μScheme's semantics, μSmalltalk's semantics uses closures; a block in μSmalltalk works about the same way as a lambda expression in μScheme. But in several other ways, μSmalltalk's semantics works quite differently.

- Unlike a block, a μSmalltalk method does not evaluate to a closure; a method is represented as code plus a static superclass, with no other environment. When a message is dispatched to a method, the method's body is evaluated in an environment built from global variables, instance variables, message arguments, and local variables. Like arguments and local variables, the instance variables and global variables are not known until the message is sent. Because methods send messages that activate other methods, global variables must be available separately, to help build the environment of the next method. The globals' locations are therefore stored in their own environment ξ. All other variables' locations are stored in environment ρ.

- The semantics of return, which terminates the method in which it appears, cannot be expressed using the same judgment as the evaluation of an expression. The return expression is a "control operator" like those described in Chapter 3, and like those other control operators, it could be described using a small-step semantics with an explicit stack. But this would be a bad idea: unless you already understand how a language works, that kind of semantics is hard to follow. Instead, the return operator is described by a new big-step judgment form; with some parts omitted, the judgment looks like $\langle e, \cdots\rangle \uparrow \langle v, F; \cdots\rangle$, and it means that evaluating e causes stack frame F to return value v.

- Every value is an object, and every object has both a *class* and a *representation*. When necessary, a value v is written in the form $v = \langle\!| \mathit{class}, \mathit{rep} |\!\rangle$.

- The behaviors of literal integers, symbols, and arrays are defined by classes, and if class SmallInteger, Symbol, or Array is redefined, the behaviors of the associated literals change. For example, if you complete Exercises 36, 38, and 39, you will change the behavior of integer literals to provide a seamless,

Table 10.31: Components of an initial state

Metavariable		*What it stands for*
e	Expression	Expression being evaluated
ρ	Environment	Instance variables, arguments, and local variables
$c_{\texttt{super}}$	Class	Destination for messages to `super`
F	Stack frame	Method activation that is terminated by `return`
ξ	Environment	Global variables
σ	Store	Current values of all variables
$\mathcal{F}$	Frame set	Every activation of every method ever

transparent blend of small- and large-integer arithmetic, all without touching the μSmalltalk interpreter. The power comes at a price: if you make a mistake redefining `SmallInteger`, for example, you could render your interpreter unusable. The dependence of behavior on the current definitions of classes like `SmallInteger` is reflected in the semantics.

μSmalltalk's semantics requires a more elaborate abstract-machine state than is needed for μScheme. μScheme's state, $\langle e, \rho, \sigma \rangle$, has only three components: the syntax being evaluated, the locations of all the variables, and the contents of all the locations. To specify message send, sending to `super`, and `return`, μSmalltalk's abstract-machine state needs four more components (Table 10.31):

- Environment ξ holds the locations of the global variables. It's needed because unlike a μScheme function, a method is given access to the global variables defined at the time it receives a message, not at the time it is defined.

- Class $c_{\texttt{super}}$ tracks the *static* superclass of the method definition within which an expression is evaluated. This class, which is not the same as the superclass of the object that received the message (Exercise 9), is the class at which method search begins when a message is sent to `super`. A static superclass is associated with every method and every block, and for all the expressions and blocks of a single method, it remains unchanged.

- Stack frame F tracks the method activation that `return` should cause to return. Like a static superclass, an active frame is associated with every method and every block, and for all the expressions and blocks of a single activation of a single method, it remains unchanged.

- Set $\mathcal{F}$ records all the stack frames that have ever been used. It is used to ensure that every time a method is activated, the activation is uniquely identified with a new stack frame F. That device ensures in turn that if a `return` escapes its original activation, any attempt to evaluate that `return` results in a checked run-time error. The frame set $\mathcal{F}$ is threaded throughout the entire computation, in much the same way as the store σ.

Each individual component is used in a straightforward way, but the sheer number can be intimidating. No wonder most theorists prefer to work with functional languages!

The seven components listed in Table 10.31 form the initial state of an abstract machine for evaluating μSmalltalk: $\langle e, \rho, c_{\texttt{super}}, F, \xi, \sigma, \mathcal{F} \rangle$. If expression e is evaluated successfully, the machine transitions, expressing one of two *behaviors*:

- If an expression terminates normally and produces a value v, this behavior is represented by a judgment of the form $\boxed{\langle e, \rho, c_{\mathsf{super}}, F, \xi, \sigma, \mathcal{F}\rangle \Downarrow \langle v; \sigma', \mathcal{F}'\rangle}$. As usual for a language with imperative features, evaluating e can change the values of variables, so evaluation results in a new store σ'. And evaluation may send messages and allocate new stack frames, so evaluation also produces a new used-frame set $\mathcal{F}'$. But the main result of evaluation is the value v; σ' and $\mathcal{F}'$ just capture *effects*. To make the judgment a little easier to read, v is separated from the effects using a semicolon, not a comma.

- If an expression evaluates a `return`, it immediately terminates an activation of the method in which the `return` appears. I say it "returns v to frame F'," and the behavior is represented by a judgment of the form $\boxed{\langle e, \rho, c_{\mathsf{super}}, F, \xi, \sigma, \mathcal{F}\rangle \uparrow \langle v, F'; \sigma', \mathcal{F}'\rangle}$, with an arrow pointing up. Again, the main results are separated from the effects by a semicolon.

If a syntactic form contains an expression, its evaluation can end in `return` behavior. But while we are learning the main part of the language, `return` behaviors are distracting. For that reason, the semantics of `return` are presented in their own section.

Another complication of `return` is that its evaluation can terminate the evaluation of a list of expressions. To express this behavior precisely, the semantics uses new judgment forms that describe the possible outcomes of evaluating a list of expressions.

- $\boxed{\langle [e_1, \ldots, e_n], \rho, c_{\mathsf{super}}, F, \xi, \sigma, \mathcal{F}\rangle \Downarrow \langle [v_1, \ldots, v_n]; \sigma', \mathcal{F}'\rangle}$
  Evaluating a list of expressions produces a list of values $[v_1, \ldots, v_n]$.

- $\boxed{\langle [e_1, \ldots, e_n], \rho, c_{\mathsf{super}}, F, \xi, \sigma, \mathcal{F}\rangle \uparrow \langle v, F'; \sigma', \mathcal{F}'\rangle}$
  Evaluating a list of expressions returns v to F'.

The first judgment describes evaluation as it would happen in a language like μScheme, and its rules are worth giving right away. Formally, a list of expressions $[e_1, \ldots, e_n]$ has one of two forms: it is $[\,]$ or it has the form $e :: es$. The corresponding result of its evaluation also has two forms: it is $[\,]$ or it has the form $v :: vs$. Each form has its own rule for evaluation.

$$\frac{}{\langle [\,], \rho, c_{\mathsf{super}}, F, \xi, \sigma, \mathcal{F}\rangle \Downarrow \langle [\,]; \sigma, \mathcal{F}\rangle} \quad \text{(EMPTYLIST)}$$

$$\frac{\begin{array}{c}\langle e, \rho, c_{\mathsf{super}}, F, \xi, \sigma, \mathcal{F}\rangle \Downarrow \langle v; \sigma', \mathcal{F}'\rangle \\ \langle es, \rho, c_{\mathsf{super}}, F, \xi, \sigma', \mathcal{F}'\rangle \Downarrow \langle vs; \sigma'', \mathcal{F}''\rangle\end{array}}{\langle e :: es, \rho, c_{\mathsf{super}}, F, \xi, \sigma, \mathcal{F}\rangle \Downarrow \langle v :: vs; \sigma'', \mathcal{F}''\rangle} \quad \text{(NONEMPTYLIST)}$$

The rules for the second list-evaluation judgment are given with the rules for the other returns.

Finally, because the `value` primitive evaluates a block, which can contain any μSmalltalk expression, the evaluation of a primitive requires its own form. A primitive gets access to global variables through ξ; it may change values of variables in the store σ; and it may allocate new stack frames, adding to $\mathcal{F}$. When a primitive p is passed values $v_1, \ldots, v_n$, its behavior is therefore described using the judgment form $\boxed{\langle p, [v_1, \ldots, v_n], \xi, \sigma, \mathcal{F}\rangle \Downarrow_p \langle v; \sigma', \mathcal{F}'\rangle}$.

10.10.1 *Semantics of expressions without* `return`

The part of μSmalltalk's semantics that is most compatible with μScheme is the part that applies to situations in which no `return` is evaluated. Except for `return`, each syntactic form in Figure 10.9 (page 628) has a rule that describes its non-returning evaluation. (The semantics of `return` is deferred to Section 10.10.2.)

Variables and assignment As in Impcore, environments ρ and ξ track local and global variables, but as in μScheme, they bind each defined name x to a mutable location. Aside from the extra bookkeeping imposed by messages to `super` and by returns, which manifests as extra components in the abstract-machine state, nothing here is new.

$$\frac{x \in \operatorname{dom} \rho \qquad \rho(x) = \ell}{\langle \text{VAR}(x), \rho, c_{\texttt{super}}, F, \xi, \sigma, \mathcal{F} \rangle \Downarrow \langle \sigma(\ell); \sigma, \mathcal{F} \rangle} \qquad \text{(VAR)}$$

$$\frac{x \notin \operatorname{dom} \rho \qquad x \in \operatorname{dom} \xi \qquad \xi(x) = \ell}{\langle \text{VAR}(x), \rho, c_{\texttt{super}}, F, \xi, \sigma, \mathcal{F} \rangle \Downarrow \langle \sigma(\ell); \sigma, \mathcal{F} \rangle} \qquad \text{(GLOBALVAR)}$$

Assignment to x translates x into a location ℓ, then changes the value in ℓ. As in μScheme, the store is threaded. The set of allocated stack frames is threaded in the same way; evaluating expression e transitions that set from $\mathcal{F}$ to $\mathcal{F}'$.

$$\frac{x \in \operatorname{dom} \rho \qquad \rho(x) = \ell \qquad \langle e, \rho, c_{\texttt{super}}, F, \xi, \sigma, \mathcal{F} \rangle \Downarrow \langle v; \sigma', \mathcal{F}' \rangle}{\langle \text{SET}(x, e), \rho, c_{\texttt{super}}, F, \xi, \sigma, \mathcal{F} \rangle \Downarrow \langle v; \sigma'\{\ell \mapsto v\}, \mathcal{F}' \rangle} \qquad \text{(ASSIGN)}$$

$$\frac{x \notin \operatorname{dom} \rho \qquad x \in \operatorname{dom} \xi \qquad \xi(x) = \ell \qquad \langle e, \rho, c_{\texttt{super}}, F, \xi, \sigma, \mathcal{F} \rangle \Downarrow \langle v; \sigma', \mathcal{F}' \rangle}{\langle \text{SET}(x, e), \rho, c_{\texttt{super}}, F, \xi, \sigma, \mathcal{F} \rangle \Downarrow \langle v; \sigma'\{\ell \mapsto v\}, \mathcal{F}' \rangle}$$
(ASSIGNGLOBAL)

Assignment to names `self`, `super`, `true`, `false`, and `nil` is not permitted, but this restriction is enforced in the parser, so it need not be mentioned here.

Self and super In μSmalltalk's syntax, `self` is treated as an ordinary variable, but `super` is a distinct syntactic form. In most contexts, `super` is evaluated like `self`.

$$\frac{\langle \text{VAR}(\texttt{self}), \rho, c_{\texttt{super}}, F, \xi, \sigma, \mathcal{F} \rangle \Downarrow \langle v; \sigma, \mathcal{F} \rangle}{\langle \text{SUPER}, \rho, c_{\texttt{super}}, F, \xi, \sigma, \mathcal{F} \rangle \Downarrow \langle v; \sigma, \mathcal{F} \rangle} \qquad \text{(SUPER)}$$

When `super` identifies the recipient of a message, however, it behaves differently from `self`; to account for the difference in behavior, message send requires a special rule for messages sent to `super` (page 682).

Values As in Impcore, a VALUE form evaluates to itself without changing the store.

$$\frac{}{\langle \text{VALUE}(v), \rho, c_{\texttt{super}}, F, \xi, \sigma, \mathcal{F} \rangle \Downarrow \langle v; \sigma, \mathcal{F} \rangle} \qquad \text{(VALUE)}$$

Literals A literal evaluates to an instance of `SmallInteger`, `Symbol`, or `Array`. Only integer and symbol literals are formalized here.

$$\frac{}{\langle \text{LITERAL}(\text{NUM}(n)), \rho, c_{\texttt{super}}, F, \xi, \sigma, \mathcal{F} \rangle \Downarrow \langle \langle\!| \sigma(\xi(\texttt{SmallInteger})), \text{NUM}(n) |\!\rangle; \sigma, \mathcal{F} \rangle}$$
(LITERALNUMBER)

$$\frac{}{\langle \text{LITERAL}(\text{SYM}(s)), \rho, c_{\texttt{super}}, F, \xi, \sigma, \mathcal{F} \rangle \Downarrow \langle \langle\!| \sigma(\xi(\texttt{Symbol})), \text{SYM}(s) |\!\rangle; \sigma, \mathcal{F} \rangle}$$
(LITERALSYMBOL)

The class of a literal number or a literal symbol is taken from the current global environment ξ, which means that a literal's behavior can be changed by changing class `SmallInteger` or `Symbol`.

Blocks A block is much like a `lambda` abstraction, except that its body es is a sequence of expressions, not a single expression. Evaluating a block creates a closure, which captures the current environment ρ, the static superclass c_{super}, and the current stack frame F. If the block is sent somewhere else and is evaluated inside another method, as in the `isEmpty` method on class `Collection` (chunk 657e), for example, its `return` still terminates frame F.

$$\frac{v = \langle\!|\sigma(\xi(\texttt{Block})), \text{CLOSURE}(\langle x_1, \ldots, x_n\rangle, es, \rho, c_{\mathsf{super}}, F)|\!\rangle}{\langle \text{BLOCK}(\langle x_1, \ldots, x_n\rangle, es), \rho, c_{\mathsf{super}}, F, \xi, \sigma, \mathcal{F}\rangle \Downarrow \langle v; \sigma, \mathcal{F}\rangle} \quad \text{(MKCLOSURE)}$$

Sequential execution BEGIN expressions are evaluated as in μScheme: evaluate the expressions in sequence and produce the last value.

$$\frac{}{\langle \text{BEGIN}(), \rho, c_{\mathsf{super}}, F, \xi, \sigma, \mathcal{F}\rangle \Downarrow \langle nil; \sigma, \mathcal{F}\rangle} \quad \text{(EMPTYBEGIN)}$$

$$\frac{\langle [e_1, \ldots, e_n], \rho, c_{\mathsf{super}}, F, \xi, \sigma, \mathcal{F}\rangle \Downarrow \langle [v_1, \ldots, v_n]; \sigma', \mathcal{F}'\rangle}{\langle \text{BEGIN}(e_1, e_2, \ldots, e_n), \rho, c_{\mathsf{super}}, F, \xi, \sigma, \mathcal{F}\rangle \Downarrow \langle v_n; \sigma', \mathcal{F}'\rangle} \quad \text{(BEGIN)}$$

Message send A message send takes place in four stages: evaluate the receiver and the arguments, find the method to dispatch to, set up a new environment and frame, and evaluate the method's body. The dispatch algorithm is expressed using the judgment form $\boxed{m \rhd c \mathbin{@} imp}$, which should be pronounced "sending m to c is answered by imp." The judgment means that sending a message m to an object of class c dispatches to the implementation imp. Judgment $m \rhd c \mathbin{@} imp$ is provable if and only if imp is the *first* method named m defined either on class c or on one of c's superclasses (Exercise 40).

An ordinary message send tries $m \rhd c \mathbin{@} imp$ on the class of the receiver:

$$\frac{\begin{array}{c} e \neq \text{SUPER} \\ \langle e, \rho, c_{\mathsf{super}}, F, \xi, \sigma, \mathcal{F}\rangle \Downarrow \langle \langle\!| c, r|\!\rangle; \sigma_0, \mathcal{F}_0\rangle \\ \langle [e_1, \ldots, e_n], \rho, c_{\mathsf{super}}, F, \xi, \sigma_0, \mathcal{F}_0\rangle \Downarrow \langle [v_1, \ldots, v_n]; \sigma_n, \mathcal{F}_n\rangle \\ m \rhd c \mathbin{@} \text{METHOD}(\_, \langle x_1, \ldots, x_n\rangle, \langle y_1, \ldots, y_k\rangle, e_m, \mathsf{s}) \\ \hat{F} \notin \mathcal{F}_n \\ \ell_1, \ldots, \ell_n \notin \operatorname{dom} \sigma_n \qquad \ell'_1, \ldots, \ell'_k \notin \operatorname{dom} \sigma_n \\ \ell_1, \ldots, \ell_n, \ell'_1, \ldots, \ell'_k \text{ all distinct} \\ \rho_i = \texttt{instanceVars}(\langle\!| c, r|\!\rangle) \\ \rho_a = \{x_1 \mapsto \ell_1, \ldots, x_n \mapsto \ell_n\} \\ \rho_l = \{y_1 \mapsto \ell'_1, \ldots, y_k \mapsto \ell'_k\} \\ \hat{\sigma} = \sigma_n\{\ell_1 \mapsto v_1, \ldots \ell_n \mapsto v_n, \ell'_1 \mapsto nil, \ldots \ell'_k \mapsto nil\} \\ \langle e_m, \rho_i + \rho_a + \rho_l, \mathsf{s}, \hat{F}, \xi, \hat{\sigma}, \mathcal{F}_n \cup \{\hat{F}\}\rangle \Downarrow \langle v; \sigma', \mathcal{F}'\rangle \end{array}}{\langle \text{SEND}(m, e, e_1, \ldots, e_n), \rho, c_{\mathsf{super}}, F, \xi, \sigma, \mathcal{F}\rangle \Downarrow \langle v; \sigma', \mathcal{F}'\rangle}. \quad \text{(SEND)}$$

The premise on the first line shows that this is a rule for an ordinary send, not a send to SUPER. The rest of the rule has much in common with the closure rule for μScheme:

- The premises on the next two lines show the evaluation of the receiver e and of the arguments $e_1, \ldots, e_n$. After these evaluations, we know we are sending message m to receiver r of class c with actual parameters $v_1, \ldots, v_n$, and the store is σ_n.
- The premise $m \rhd c \mathbin{@} \text{METHOD}(\_, \langle x_1, \ldots, x_n\rangle, \langle y_1, \ldots, y_k\rangle, e_m, \mathsf{s})$ shows that this send executes a method with formal parameters $x_1, \ldots, x_n$, local variables $y_1, \ldots, y_k$, body e_m, and static superclass s.

- The next three lines show the allocation of a fresh stack frame and of fresh locations to hold the message arguments and the local variables of the method.
- The equations for ρ_i, ρ_a, and ρ_l create environments for the receiver's instance variables, the method's formal parameters, and the method's local variables, respectively.
- The equation for $\hat{\sigma}$ initializes the formal parameters and the local variables.
- Finally, the last premise shows the evaluation of the body of the method e_m, in the new environment created by combining environments for instance variables, actual parameters, and local variables. Any returns go to the new stack frame $\hat{F}$.

Function `instanceVars` is not specified formally. Calling $\texttt{instanceVars}(\langle\!|c, r|\!\rangle)$, as defined in chunk 690a, takes the representation r of an object and returns an environment mapping the names of that object's instance variables to the locations containing those instance variables. The environment also maps the name `self` to a location containing the object itself.

When a message is sent to SUPER, the action is almost the same, except the method search takes place on c_{super}, the static superclass of the current method, not on the class of the receiver. The new parts of the SUPER rule are shown in black; the parts that are shared with the ordinary SEND rule appear in gray.

$$\frac{\begin{array}{c}\langle \mathrm{SUPER}, \rho, c_{\mathsf{super}}, F, \xi, \sigma, \mathcal{F}\rangle \Downarrow \langle \langle\!|c, r|\!\rangle; \sigma_0, \mathcal{F}_0\rangle \\ \langle [e_1, \ldots, e_n], \rho, c_{\mathsf{super}}, F, \xi, \sigma_0, \mathcal{F}_0\rangle \Downarrow \langle [v_1, \ldots, v_n]; \sigma_n, \mathcal{F}_n\rangle \\ m \rhd c_{\mathsf{super}} \mathbin{@} \mathrm{METHOD}(\_, \langle x_1, \ldots, x_n\rangle, \langle y_1, \ldots, y_k\rangle, e_m, \mathtt{s}) \\ F \notin \mathcal{F} \\ \ell_1, \ldots, \ell_n \notin \operatorname{dom} \sigma_n \qquad \ell'_1, \ldots, \ell'_k \notin \operatorname{dom} \sigma_n \\ \ell_1, \ldots, \ell_n, \ell'_1, \ldots, \ell'_k \text{ all distinct} \\ \rho_i = \texttt{instanceVars}(\langle\!|c, r|\!\rangle) \\ \rho_a = \{x_1 \mapsto \ell_1, \ldots, x_n \mapsto \ell_n\} \\ \rho_l = \{y_1 \mapsto \ell'_1, \ldots, y_k \mapsto \ell'_k\} \\ \hat{\sigma} = \sigma_n\{\ell_1 \mapsto v_1, \ldots \ell_n \mapsto v_n, \ell'_1 \mapsto nil, \ldots \ell'_k \mapsto nil\} \\ \langle e_m, \rho_i + \rho_a + \rho_l, \mathtt{s}, \hat{F}, \xi, \hat{\sigma}, \mathcal{F} \cup \{\hat{F}\}\rangle \Downarrow \langle v; \sigma', \mathcal{F}'\rangle \end{array}}{\langle \mathrm{SEND}(m, \mathrm{SUPER}, e_1, \ldots, e_n), \rho, c_{\mathsf{super}}, F, \xi, \sigma, \mathcal{F}\rangle \Downarrow \langle v; \sigma', \mathcal{F}'\rangle} \quad (\textsc{SendSuper})$$

Primitives When a PRIMITIVE expression is evaluated, it evaluates its arguments, then passes them to the primitive named by p.

$$\frac{\begin{array}{c}\langle [e_1, \ldots, e_n], \rho, c_{\mathsf{super}}, F, \xi, \sigma, \mathcal{F}\rangle \Downarrow \langle [v_1, \ldots, v_n]; \sigma', \mathcal{F}'\rangle \\ \langle p, [v_1, \ldots, v_n], \xi, \sigma', \mathcal{F}'\rangle \Downarrow_p \langle v; \sigma'', \mathcal{F}''\rangle \end{array}}{\langle \mathrm{PRIMITIVE}(p, e_1, \ldots, e_n), \rho, c_{\mathsf{super}}, F, \xi, \sigma, \mathcal{F}\rangle \Downarrow \langle v; \sigma'', \mathcal{F}''\rangle} \quad (\textsc{Primitive})$$

Each primitive p is described by its own rule. The most interesting one is the `value` primitive, which evaluates a block. Its rule resembles the rule for sending a message, except unlike a method, a block has no local variables or instance variables of its own. And the body of a block is evaluated using its stored `return`

$$\boxed{\langle [e_1,\ldots,e_n],\rho,c_{\mathsf{super}},F,\xi,\sigma,\mathcal{F}\rangle \uparrow \langle v,F';\sigma',\mathcal{F}'\rangle}$$

$$\frac{\langle e,\rho,c_{\mathsf{super}},F,\xi,\sigma,\mathcal{F}\rangle \uparrow \langle v,F';\sigma',\mathcal{F}'\rangle}{\langle e :: es,\rho,c_{\mathsf{super}},F,\xi,\sigma,\mathcal{F}\rangle \uparrow \langle v,F';\sigma',\mathcal{F}'\rangle}$$

$$\frac{\begin{array}{c}\langle e,\rho,c_{\mathsf{super}},F,\xi,\sigma,\mathcal{F}\rangle \Downarrow \langle v;\sigma',\mathcal{F}'\rangle\\ \langle es,\rho,c_{\mathsf{super}},F,\xi,\sigma,\mathcal{F}\rangle \uparrow \langle v,F';\sigma'',\mathcal{F}''\rangle\end{array}}{\langle e :: es,\rho,c_{\mathsf{super}},F,\xi,\sigma,\mathcal{F}\rangle \uparrow \langle v,F';\sigma'',\mathcal{F}''\rangle}$$

$$\boxed{\langle e,\rho,c_{\mathsf{super}},F,\xi,\sigma,\mathcal{F}\rangle \uparrow \langle v,F';\sigma',\mathcal{F}'\rangle}$$

$$\frac{\langle e,\rho,c_{\mathsf{super}},F,\xi,\sigma,\mathcal{F}\rangle \Downarrow \langle v;\sigma',\mathcal{F}'\rangle}{\langle \mathrm{RETURN}(e),\rho,c_{\mathsf{super}},F,\xi,\sigma,\mathcal{F}\rangle \uparrow \langle v,F;\sigma',\mathcal{F}'\rangle}$$

$$\frac{\langle e,\rho,c_{\mathsf{super}},F,\xi,\sigma,\mathcal{F}\rangle \uparrow \langle v,F';\sigma',\mathcal{F}'\rangle}{\langle \mathrm{SET}(x,e),\rho,c_{\mathsf{super}},F,\xi,\sigma,\mathcal{F}\rangle \uparrow \langle v,F';\sigma',\mathcal{F}'\rangle}$$

$$\frac{\langle [e_1,\ldots,e_n],\rho,c_{\mathsf{super}},F,\xi,\sigma,\mathcal{F}\rangle \uparrow \langle v,F';\sigma',\mathcal{F}'\rangle}{\langle \mathrm{BEGIN}(e_1,\ldots,e_n),\rho,c_{\mathsf{super}},F,\xi,\sigma,\mathcal{F}\rangle \uparrow \langle v,F';\sigma',\mathcal{F}'\rangle}$$

$$\frac{\langle e,\rho,c_{\mathsf{super}},F,\xi,\sigma,\mathcal{F}\rangle \uparrow \langle v,F';\sigma',\mathcal{F}'\rangle}{\langle \mathrm{SEND}(m,e,e_1,\ldots,e_n),\rho,c_{\mathsf{super}},F,\xi,\sigma,\mathcal{F}\rangle \uparrow \langle v,F';\sigma',\mathcal{F}'\rangle}$$

$$\frac{\begin{array}{c}\langle e,\rho,c_{\mathsf{super}},F,\xi,\sigma,\mathcal{F}\rangle \Downarrow \langle (\!| c,r |\!);\sigma_0,\mathcal{F}_0\rangle\\ \langle [e_1,\ldots,e_n],\rho,c_{\mathsf{super}},F,\xi,\sigma_0,\mathcal{F}_0\rangle \uparrow \langle v,F';\sigma',\mathcal{F}'\rangle\end{array}}{\langle \mathrm{SEND}(m,e,e_1,\ldots,e_n),\rho,c_{\mathsf{super}},F,\xi,\sigma,\mathcal{F}\rangle \uparrow \langle v,F';\sigma',\mathcal{F}'\rangle}$$

Figure 10.32: Rules for propagation of returns (other RETURN rules appear in the text)

frame F_c, not the frame of the calling context.

$$\frac{\begin{array}{c}\ell_1,\ldots,\ell_n \notin \operatorname{dom}\sigma \qquad \ell_1,\ldots,\ell_n \text{ all distinct}\\ \hat{\sigma} = \sigma\{\ell_1 \mapsto v_1,\ldots \ell_n \mapsto v_n\}\\ \langle \mathrm{BEGIN}(es),\rho_c + \{x_1 \mapsto \ell_1,\ldots,x_n \mapsto \ell_n\},\mathsf{s}_c,F_c,\xi,\hat{\sigma},\mathcal{F}\rangle \Downarrow \langle v;\sigma',\mathcal{F}'\rangle\end{array}}{\langle \mathtt{value},[(\!| c,\mathrm{CLOSURE}(\langle x_1,\ldots,x_n\rangle,es,\mathsf{s}_c,\rho_c,F_c) |\!),v_1,\ldots,v_n],\xi,\sigma,\mathcal{F}\rangle \Downarrow_p \langle v;\sigma',\mathcal{F}'\rangle}$$

(VALUEPRIMITIVE)

10.10.2 Semantics of returns

Most of the rules for `return` describe variations on one situation: during the evaluation of an expression e, one of e's subexpressions returns, and this behavior causes e also to return (Figure 10.32). But eventually the `return` terminates an activation frame of the method in which it appears. When a return to frame $\hat{F}$ reaches a method body executing in frame $\hat{F}$, the result of the return becomes the result of the SEND that activated the method. As with messages to `super`, the gray parts of the rule are the same as in SEND, and the black parts are different.

$$\frac{\begin{array}{c}\langle e, \rho, c_{\mathsf{super}}, F, \xi, \sigma, \mathcal{F}\rangle \Downarrow \langle (\!| c, r |\!); \sigma_0, \mathcal{F}_0\rangle \\ \langle [e_1, \ldots, e_n], \rho, c_{\mathsf{super}}, F, \xi, \sigma_0, \mathcal{F}_0\rangle \Downarrow \langle [v_1, \ldots, v_n]; \sigma_n, \mathcal{F}_n\rangle \\ m \rhd c \,@\, \mathrm{METHOD}(\_, \langle x_1, \ldots, x_n\rangle, \langle y_1, \ldots, y_k\rangle, e_m, \mathsf{s}) \\ \hat{F} \notin \mathcal{F} \\ \ell_1, \ldots, \ell_n \notin \mathrm{dom}\,\sigma_n \qquad \ell'_1, \ldots, \ell'_k \notin \mathrm{dom}\,\sigma_n \\ \ell_1, \ldots, \ell_n, \ell'_1, \ldots, \ell'_k \text{ all distinct} \\ \rho_i = \mathtt{instanceVars}((\!| c, r |\!)) \\ \rho_a = \{x_1 \mapsto \ell_1, \ldots, x_n \mapsto \ell_n\} \\ \rho_l = \{y_1 \mapsto \ell'_1, \ldots, y_k \mapsto \ell'_k\} \\ \hat{\sigma} = \sigma_n\{\ell_1 \mapsto v_1, \ldots \ell_n \mapsto v_n, \ell'_1 \mapsto nil, \ldots \ell'_k \mapsto nil\} \\ \langle e_m, \rho_i + \rho_a + \rho_l, \mathsf{s}, \hat{F}, \xi, \hat{\sigma}, \mathcal{F} \cup \{\hat{F}\}\rangle \uparrow \langle v, \hat{F}; \sigma', \mathcal{F}'\rangle\end{array}}{\langle \mathrm{SEND}(m, e, e_1, \ldots, e_n), \rho, c_{\mathsf{super}}, F, \xi, \sigma, \mathcal{F}\rangle \Downarrow \langle v; \sigma', \mathcal{F}'\rangle} \quad \text{(RETURNTO)}$$

If method body e_m tries to return somewhere else, to F', the whole SEND operation returns to F'.

$$\frac{\begin{array}{c}\langle e, \rho, c_{\mathsf{super}}, F, \xi, \sigma, \mathcal{F}\rangle \Downarrow \langle (\!| c, r |\!); \sigma_0, \mathcal{F}_0\rangle \\ \langle [e_1, \ldots, e_n], \rho, c_{\mathsf{super}}, F, \xi, \sigma_0, \mathcal{F}_0\rangle \Downarrow \langle [v_1, \ldots, v_n]; \sigma_n, \mathcal{F}_n\rangle \\ m \rhd c \,@\, \mathrm{METHOD}(\_, \langle x_1, \ldots, x_n\rangle, \langle y_1, \ldots, y_k\rangle, e_m, \mathsf{s}) \\ \hat{F} \notin \mathcal{F} \\ \ell_1, \ldots, \ell_n \notin \mathrm{dom}\,\sigma_n \qquad \ell'_1, \ldots, \ell'_k \notin \mathrm{dom}\,\sigma_n \\ \ell_1, \ldots, \ell_n, \ell'_1, \ldots, \ell'_k \text{ all distinct} \\ \rho_i = \mathtt{instanceVars}((\!| c, r |\!)) \\ \rho_a = \{x_1 \mapsto \ell_1, \ldots, x_n \mapsto \ell_n\} \\ \rho_l = \{y_1 \mapsto \ell'_1, \ldots, y_k \mapsto \ell'_k\} \\ \hat{\sigma} = \sigma_n\{\ell_1 \mapsto v_1, \ldots \ell_n \mapsto v_n, \ell'_1 \mapsto nil, \ldots \ell'_k \mapsto nil\} \\ \langle e_m, \rho_i + \rho_a + \rho_l, \mathsf{s}, \hat{F}, \xi, \hat{\sigma}, \mathcal{F} \cup \{\hat{F}\}\rangle \uparrow \langle v, F'; \sigma', \mathcal{F}'\rangle \qquad F' \neq \hat{F}\end{array}}{\langle \mathrm{SEND}(m, e, e_1, \ldots, e_n), \rho, c_{\mathsf{super}}, F, \xi, \sigma, \mathcal{F}\rangle \uparrow \langle v, F'; \sigma', \mathcal{F}'\rangle} \quad \text{(RETURNPAST)}$$

10.10.3 Semantics of definitions

A definition d is evaluated in the context of the top-level, persistent state of a μSmalltalk machine, which has only three of the seven components listed in Table 10.31: a global environment ξ, a store σ, and a set of used stack frames $\mathcal{F}$. Evaluating d may change all three; the judgment form is $\langle d, \xi, \sigma, \mathcal{F}\rangle \to \langle \xi', \sigma', \mathcal{F}'\rangle$.

Global variables As in μScheme, a VAL binding for an existing variable x assigns the value of a right-hand side e to x's location. Expression e is evaluated using the judgment form $\langle e, \rho, c_{\mathsf{super}}, F, \xi, \sigma, \mathcal{F}\rangle \Downarrow \langle v; \sigma', \mathcal{F}'\rangle$, so the VAL rule has to gin up an environment ρ, a class c_{super} that will receive messages sent to `super`, and a new stack frame F. Since e is evaluated outside any method, there are no instance variables and no formal parameters, and ρ is empty. To receive messages sent to `super`, the VAL rule uses the root class `Object`—the original definition of `Object` taken from the initial global environment ξ_0, not whatever definition of `Object` happens to be current. (In practice, the identity of c_{super} is irrelevant. If a message is sent to `super`, the abstract machine tries to look up `self` in the empty environment, and it gets stuck.) The new frame F is $\hat{F}$, which may be any frame not previously allocated, that is, any frame not in $\mathcal{F}$.

$$\frac{x \in \operatorname{dom} \xi \qquad \xi(x) = \ell \qquad \hat{F} \notin \mathcal{F} \qquad \langle e, \{\}, \xi_0(\texttt{Object}), \hat{F}, \xi, \sigma, \{\hat{F}\} \cup \mathcal{F}\rangle \Downarrow \langle v; \sigma', \mathcal{F}'\rangle}{\langle \text{VAL}(x, e), \xi, \sigma, \mathcal{F}\rangle \rightarrow \langle \xi, \sigma'\{\ell \mapsto v\}, \mathcal{F}'\rangle} \quad \text{(DEFINEOLDGLOBAL)}$$

$$\frac{x \notin \operatorname{dom} \xi \qquad \ell \notin \operatorname{dom} \sigma \qquad \hat{F} \notin \mathcal{F} \qquad \langle e, \{\}, \xi_0(\texttt{Object}), \hat{F}, \xi, \sigma, \{\hat{F}\} \cup \mathcal{F}\rangle \Downarrow \langle v; \sigma', \mathcal{F}'\rangle}{\langle \text{VAL}(x, e), \xi, \sigma, \mathcal{F}\rangle \rightarrow \langle \xi\{x \mapsto \ell\}, \sigma'\{\ell \mapsto v\}, \mathcal{F}'\rangle} \quad \text{(DEFINENEWGLOBAL)}$$

Top-level expressions A top-level expression is syntactic sugar for a binding to `it`.

$$\frac{\langle \text{VAL}(\texttt{it}, e), \xi, \sigma, \mathcal{F}\rangle \rightarrow \langle \xi', \sigma', \mathcal{F}'\rangle}{\langle \text{EXP}(e), \xi, \sigma, \mathcal{F}\rangle \rightarrow \langle \xi', \sigma', \mathcal{F}'\rangle} \quad \text{(EVALEXP)}$$

Block definition DEFINE is syntactic sugar for creating a block.

$$\frac{\langle \text{VAL}(f, \text{BLOCK}(\langle x_1, \ldots, x_n\rangle, e)), \xi, \sigma, \mathcal{F}\rangle \rightarrow \langle \xi', \sigma', \mathcal{F}'\rangle}{\langle \text{DEFINE}(f, \langle x_1, \ldots, x_n\rangle, e), \xi, \sigma, \mathcal{F}\rangle \rightarrow \langle \xi', \sigma', \mathcal{F}'\rangle} \quad \text{(DEFINEBLOCK)}$$

Class definition The evaluation of a class definition is rather involved; the interpreter creates an object that represents the class. The details are hidden in the function `newClassObject`, which I don't specify formally. To see how it works, consult the code in chunk 695a.

$$\frac{x \in \operatorname{dom} \xi \qquad \xi(x) = \ell \qquad v = \texttt{newClassObject}(d, \xi, \sigma)}{\langle \text{CLASSD}(d), \xi, \sigma, \mathcal{F}\rangle \rightarrow \langle \xi, \sigma\{\ell \mapsto v\}, \mathcal{F}\rangle} \quad \text{(DEFINEOLDCLASS)}$$

$$\frac{x \notin \operatorname{dom} \xi \qquad \ell \notin \operatorname{dom} \sigma \qquad v = \texttt{newClassObject}(d, \xi, \sigma)}{\langle \text{CLASSD}(d), \xi, \sigma, \mathcal{F}\rangle \rightarrow \langle \xi\{x \mapsto \ell\}, \sigma\{\ell \mapsto v\}, \mathcal{F}\rangle} \quad \text{(DEFINENEWCLASS)}$$

10.11 THE INTERPRETER

The key parts of μSmalltalk's interpreter involve the elements that make Smalltalk unique: objects and classes. An object is represented in two parts: a class and an internal representation (ML types `class` and `rep`). The class determines the object's response to messages, and the internal representation holds the object's state. And although the Smalltalk word is "object," the ML type of its representation is called `value`, just like whatever thing an expression evaluates to in every other interpreter in this book.

type class 686c
type rep 686a

685. ⟨*definitions of* `value` *and* `method` *for μSmalltalk* 685⟩≡ (S548a) 686d ▷

```
withtype value = class * rep
```

The `rep` part of an object exposes one of the biggest differences between μSmalltalk and Smalltalk-80. In Smalltalk-80, every object owns a collection of mutable locations, called "instance variables," each of which can be filled either with an ordinary object or with a sequence of bytes. But because μSmalltalk is implemented in ML, raw locations and sequences of bytes are not useful representations. In μSmalltalk, every object owns a single representation, which is defined by ML datatype rep. That representation may be a collection of named, mutable locations representing instance variables, or it may be any of half a dozen other primitive representations.

686a. ⟨*definitions of* exp, rep, *and* class *for μSmalltalk* 686a⟩≡ (S548a) 686c ▷

```
datatype rep
  = USER     of value ref env (* ordinary object *)
  | ARRAY    of value Array.array
  | NUM      of int
  | SYM      of name
  | CLOSURE  of name list * exp list * value ref env * class * frame
  | CLASSREP of class
  | METHODV  of method         (* compiled method *)
```

A primitive representation is typically created by evaluating some particular syntactic form in the source code: an array literal, a numeric literal, a literal symbol, a block, a class definition, or a compiled-method form. Several representations (arrays, numbers, classes) can also be created by primitives.

No matter what its internal representation, every object provides instance variables to its methods. A USER object provides all the instance variables dictated by its class's definition, a set that always includes self. An object with any other representation provides *only* self.

686b. ⟨*utility functions on μSmalltalk classes, methods, and values* 686b⟩≡ (S547) S587c ▷

```
fun instanceVars (_, USER rep) = rep    instanceVars : value -> value ref env
  | instanceVars self = bind ("self", ref self, emptyEnv)
```

Internally, an object's class is represented by an ML value of type class. The internal representation includes a superclass, instance-variable names, and methods. A superclass is found on every class except the distinguished root class, Object. A class's ivars and methods lists include only the instance variables and methods defined in that class, not those of its superclass.

686c. ⟨*definitions of* exp, rep, *and* class *for μSmalltalk* 686a⟩+≡ (S548a) ◁ 686a 688a ▷

```
and class
  = CLASS of { name    : name             (* name of the class *)
             , super   : class option     (* superclass, if any *)
             , ivars   : string list      (* instance variables *)
             , methods : method env ref   (* both exported and private *)
             , class   : metaclass ref    (* class of the class object *)
             }
and metaclass = PENDING | META of class
```

Every class is also an object, and as an object, it is an instance of another class—its metaclass, which is stored in field class. This field initially holds PENDING, but when the metaclass becomes available, class is updated to hold it.

A method has a name, formal parameters, local variables, and a body. A method also stores the superclass of the class in which it is defined, which it uses to interpret messages sent to super.

686d. ⟨*definitions of* value *and* method *for μSmalltalk* 685⟩+≡ (S548a) ◁ 685

```
and method = { name : name, formals : name list, locals : name list
             , body : exp, superclass : class
             }
```

The class and value representations inform the representations of the elements of the abstract-machine state (Table 10.31, page 678).

- An expression e or definition d is represented in the usual way by a constructed value from algebraic data type exp or def, as defined below.

- An environment ρ or ξ is represented in the usual way by an ML environment of type `value ref env`.

- A superclass c_{super} is represented by an ML value of type `class`.

- A stack frame F is represented by an ML value of type `frame`. The definition of `frame` isn't important; it's enough to know that a new frame can be allocated by calling `newFrame`, and that a frame is equal only to itself.

- The store σ and the set of used frames $\mathcal{F}$ are both represented by mutable state of the ML program. Just as in the other interpreters, σ and σ' never coexist; instead, the interpreter updates its state, in effect replacing σ by σ'. The set $\mathcal{F}$ is updated to $\mathcal{F}'$ in the same way.

The `value` and `frame` types are also used to represent behaviors.

- The behavior of producing a value, which is described by judgment form $\langle e, \ldots \rangle \Downarrow \langle v; \sigma', \mathcal{F}' \rangle$, is represented by an ML computation that produces a value v of ML type `value`, while writing σ' and $\mathcal{F}'$ over the previous σ and $\mathcal{F}$ as a side effect.

- The behavior of a μSmalltalk `return`, which is described by judgment form $\langle e, \ldots \rangle \uparrow \langle v, F'; \sigma', \mathcal{F}' \rangle$, is represented by an ML computation that raises the ML `Return` exception, again writing σ' and $\mathcal{F}'$ as a side effect. The `Return` exception is defined as follows:

  687a. ⟨*definition of the* `Return` *exception* 687a⟩≡ (S548c)
  ```
  exception
    Return of { value : value, to : frame, unwound : active_send list }
  ```

  Fields `value` and `to` hold v and F. And in the unhappy event that a block tries to return after its frame has died, field `unwound` is used to print diagnostics.

  Raising the `Return` exception, like any other exception, interrupts computation in exactly the same way as the propagated returns described in Figure 10.32 (page 683). That's not a coincidence; both exceptions and returns are language features that are designed to interrupt planned computations.

10.11.1 Abstract syntax

Of the two major syntactic categories, expressions and definitions, it's the definition category whose forms most resemble forms found in other languages. A definition may be one of our old friends `VAL` and `EXP`, a block definition (`DEFINE`), or a class definition (`CLASSD`). A class definition may include method definitions, which come in two flavors: instance methods and class methods.

687b. ⟨*definition of* `def` *for μSmalltalk* 687b⟩≡ (S548a)
```
datatype def = VAL    of name * exp
             | EXP    of exp
             | DEFINE of name * name list * exp
             | CLASSD of { name    : string
                         , super   : string
                         , ivars   : string list
                         , methods : method_def list
                         }
and method_flavor = IMETHOD          (* instance method *)
                  | CMETHOD          (* class method    *)
 withtype method_def = { flavor : method_flavor, name : name
                       , formals : name list, locals : name list, body : exp
                       }
```

The expression category also contains many forms that resemble forms found in other languages, but the forms that relate to literals are unique to μSmalltalk. The forms defined by VAR, SET, SEND, BEGIN, and BLOCK have analogs in μScheme, μML, and Molecule. (Even though blocks have two forms in concrete syntax, both with and without parameters, they have just one form in abstract syntax, with a list of parameters that might be empty.) Forms defined by RETURN, PRIMITIVE, and METHOD have no analogs in other interpreters, but they are also typical abstract syntax. And SUPER simply makes it easy to recognize super and give it the semantics it should have. But literal values are handled differently than in other interpreters.

A literal must ultimately evaluate to an object, whose representation has type value. That representation includes a class, but until the interpreter is bootstrapped, most classes aren't yet defined (Section 10.11.6). For example, a literal integer can't evaluate to an object until class Integer is defined. So a LITERAL expression holds only a rep; its class isn't computed until it is evaluated.

The LITERAL form is complemented by a VALUE form. This form is used internally, primarily as a way to turn an object into an expression that can receive a SEND. For example, the interpreter sends println to a VALUE form at the end of a read-eval-print loop, and it sends = to a VALUE form when testing a check-expect.

688a. ⟨*definitions of* exp, rep, *and* class *for μSmalltalk* 686a⟩+≡ (S548a) ◁686c

```
and exp = VAR       of name
        | SET       of name * exp
        | SEND      of srcloc * exp * name * exp list
        | BEGIN     of exp list
        | BLOCK     of name list * exp list
        | RETURN    of exp
        | PRIMITIVE of name * exp list
        | METHOD    of name list * name list * exp list
        | SUPER
        | LITERAL   of rep
        | VALUE     of class * rep
```

The abstract syntax for SEND includes a field that is not explicit in the concrete syntax: srcloc is the source-code location of the SEND, and it is used in diagnostic messages.

10.11.2 Evaluating expressions, including dynamic dispatch

Just as in the operational semantics, a μSmalltalk expression is evaluated in a context that tells it about environments ρ and ξ (rho and xi), a static superclass to which messages to super are sent, and the frame that is terminated if the expression is return. The states σ and σ' represent states of the underlying ML interpreter, and the used-frame set $\mathcal{F}$ is stored in a mutable variable, so they are not passed explicitly.

688b. ⟨*evaluation,* basis, *and* processDef *for μSmalltalk* 688b⟩≡ (S548c) 691c▷

```
eval: exp * value ref env * class * frame * value ref env -> value
ev  : exp -> value
```

```
fun eval (e, rho, superclass, F, xi) =
  let ⟨definition of function invokeMethod 690a⟩
      ⟨function ev, the evaluator proper 689a⟩
  in  ev e
  end
```

Internal function ev handles all the syntactic forms, the most interesting of which are RETURN and SEND.

Evaluating returns and sends A RETURN evaluates the expression to be returned, then returns to frame F by raising the Return exception.

689a. ⟨*function* ev*, the evaluator proper* 689a⟩≡ (688b) 689b ▷

```
fun ev (RETURN e) = raise Return { value = ev e, to = F, unwound = [] }
```

That Return exception is caught by the code that interprets message send. The SEND code carries a lot of freight: it implements most of rules SEND, SENDSUPER, RETURNTO, and RETURNPAST, and it also supports diagnostic tracing. The send and return rules all follow the same outline; for reference, that outline is formalized by the first, highlighted part of the SEND rule:

$$\frac{\begin{array}{c} e \neq \text{SUPER} \\ \langle e, \rho, c_{\mathsf{super}}, F, \xi, \sigma, \mathcal{F}\rangle \Downarrow \langle (\!|c, r|\!); \sigma_0, \mathcal{F}_0\rangle \\ \langle [e_1, \dots, e_n], \rho, c_{\mathsf{super}}, F, \xi, \sigma_0, \mathcal{F}_0\rangle \Downarrow \langle [v_1, \dots, v_n]; \sigma_n, \mathcal{F}_n\rangle \\ m \rhd c \mathbin{@} \text{METHOD}(\_, \langle x_1, \dots, x_n\rangle, \langle y_1, \dots, y_k\rangle, e_m, \mathsf{s}) \\ \hat{F} \notin \mathcal{F}_n \\ \ell_1, \dots, \ell_n \notin \operatorname{dom} \sigma_n \qquad \ell'_1, \dots, \ell'_k \notin \operatorname{dom} \sigma_n \\ \ell_1, \dots, \ell_n, \ell'_1, \dots, \ell'_k \text{ all distinct} \\ \rho_i = \mathtt{instanceVars}((\!|c, r|\!)) \\ \rho_a = \{x_1 \mapsto \ell_1, \dots, x_n \mapsto \ell_n\} \\ \rho_l = \{y_1 \mapsto \ell'_1, \dots, y_k \mapsto \ell'_k\} \\ \hat{\sigma} = \sigma_n\{\ell_1 \mapsto v_1, \dots \ell_n \mapsto v_n, \ell'_1 \mapsto nil, \dots \ell'_k \mapsto nil\} \\ \langle e_m, \rho_i + \rho_a + \rho_l, \mathsf{s}, \hat{F}, \xi, \hat{\sigma}, \mathcal{F}_n \cup \{\hat{F}\}\rangle \Downarrow \langle v; \sigma', \mathcal{F}'\rangle \end{array}}{\langle \text{SEND}(m, e, e_1, \dots, e_n), \rho, c_{\mathsf{super}}, F, \xi, \sigma, \mathcal{F}\rangle \Downarrow \langle v; \sigma', \mathcal{F}'\rangle}. \qquad \text{(SEND)}$$

Each SEND computation begins in the same way: evaluate the receiver and the arguments using ev, then use the syntax of the receiver to identify the class on which method search begins. Message send dispatches on the receiver, whose class is used to find the method that defines message, *except* when the message is sent to super, in which case the superclass of the currently running method is used. At that point, because of tracing and returns, things start to get complicated, so let's look at the code, then focus on the anonymous function passed to trace:

689b. ⟨*function* ev*, the evaluator proper* 689a⟩+≡ (688b) ◁ 689a 691a ▷

```
| ev (SEND (srcloc, receiver, msgname, args))  =
    let val obj as (class, rep) = ev receiver
        val vs = map ev args
        val startingClass =
              case receiver of SUPER => superclass | _ => class
        ⟨definition of function trace S583b⟩
    in  trace
        (fn () =>
           let val imp  = findMethod (msgname, startingClass)
               val Fhat = newFrame ()
           in  invokeMethod (imp, obj, vs, Fhat)
               handle Return { value = v, to = F', unwound = unwound } =>
                 if F' = Fhat then
                   v
                 else
                   ⟨reraise Return, adding msgname, class, and loc to unwound S590d⟩
           end)
    end
```

type class	686c
type env	304
findMethod	690b
type frame	S590a
invokeMethod	690a
type name	303
newFrame	S590a
type rep	686a
Return	687a
trace	S583b
type value	685

The anonymous function calls findMethod to get imp from $m \rhd c \mathbin{@}$ imp, and it allocates $\hat{F}$ as Fhat. It then delegates the second part of the SEND rules to function invokeMethod, except for the conditions in the RETURNTO and RETURNPAST rules.

Those conditions are dealt with by `handle`, which catches *every* `Return` exception. If the `Return` is meant to terminate this very `SEND`—that is, if $F' = \hat{F}$—then the anonymous function returns `v` as the result of the call to `ev`. If not, the anonymous function re-raises `Return`, adding information to the `unwound` list.

What about function `trace`? It wraps the action of the anonymous function, so if `findMethod` results in a "message not understood" error, or if `invokeMethod` results in some other run-time error, `trace` can produce a stack trace. Function `trace` is defined in Appendix U.

The second part of the SEND rule is implemented by function `invokeMethod`.

$$\frac{\begin{array}{c} e \neq \text{SUPER} \\ \langle e, \rho, c_{\text{super}}, F, \xi, \sigma, \mathcal{F}\rangle \Downarrow \langle (\!| c, r |\!); \sigma_0, \mathcal{F}_0\rangle \\ \langle [e_1, \ldots, e_n], \rho, c_{\text{super}}, F, \xi, \sigma_0, \mathcal{F}_0\rangle \Downarrow \langle [v_1, \ldots, v_n]; \sigma_n, \mathcal{F}_n\rangle \\ m \rhd c \mathbin{@} \text{METHOD}(\_, \langle x_1, \ldots, x_n\rangle, \langle y_1, \ldots, y_k\rangle, e_m, \mathtt{s}) \\ F \notin \mathcal{F}_n \\ \ell_1, \ldots, \ell_n \notin \operatorname{dom} \sigma_n \qquad \ell'_1, \ldots, \ell'_k \notin \operatorname{dom} \sigma_n \\ \ell_1, \ldots, \ell_n, \ell'_1, \ldots, \ell'_k \text{ all distinct} \\ \rho_i = \mathtt{instanceVars}((\!| c, r |\!)) \\ \rho_a = \{x_1 \mapsto \ell_1, \ldots, x_n \mapsto \ell_n\} \\ \rho_l = \{y_1 \mapsto \ell'_1, \ldots, y_k \mapsto \ell'_k\} \\ \hat{\sigma} = \sigma_n\{\ell_1 \mapsto v_1, \ldots \ell_n \mapsto v_n, \ell'_1 \mapsto nil, \ldots \ell'_k \mapsto nil\} \\ \langle e_m, \rho_i + \rho_a + \rho_l, \mathtt{s}, \hat{F}, \xi, \hat{\sigma}, \mathcal{F}_n \cup \{\hat{F}\}\rangle \Downarrow \langle v; \sigma', \mathcal{F}'\rangle \end{array}}{\langle \text{SEND}(m, e, e_1, \ldots, e_n), \rho, c_{\text{super}}, F, \xi, \sigma, \mathcal{F}\rangle \Downarrow \langle v; \sigma', \mathcal{F}'\rangle} \quad (\text{SEND})$$

Function `invokeMethod` computes ρ_i as `ivars`, ρ_a as `args`, and ρ_l as `locals`. It also allocates and initializes locations $\ell_1, \ldots, \ell_n$ and $\ell'_1, \ldots, \ell'_k$, then calls `eval`.

690a. ⟨*definition of function* `invokeMethod` 690a⟩≡ (688b)

```
invokeMethod   : method * value * value list * frame -> value
```

```
fun invokeMethod ({ name, superclass, formals, locals, body },
                  receiver, vs, Fhat) =
      let val ivars  = instanceVars receiver
          val args   = mkEnv (formals, map ref vs)
          val locals = mkEnv (locals,  map (fn _ => ref nilValue) locals)
      in  eval (body, ivars <+> args <+> locals, superclass, Fhat, xi)
      end
```

All that remains is `findMethod`. If $m \rhd c \mathbin{@} imp$, then `findMethod` (m, c) returns imp. If there is no imp such that $m \rhd c \mathbin{@} imp$, then `findMethod` raises the `RuntimeError` exception.

690b. ⟨*helper functions for evaluation* 690b⟩≡ (S548c)

```
findMethod : name * class -> method
fm         : class        -> method
```

```
fun findMethod (name, class) =
  let fun fm (subclass as CLASS { methods, super, ...}) =
        find (name, !methods)
        handle NotFound m =>
          case super
            of SOME c => fm c
             | NONE   =>
                 raise RuntimeError (className class ^
                                     " does not understand message " ^ m)
  in  fm class
  end
```

Allocating and evaluating blocks Evaluating a `BLOCK` form captures the current environment, superclass, and stack frame in a closure.

$$\frac{v = \langle\!|\sigma(\xi(\texttt{Block})), \text{CLOSURE}(\langle x_1, \ldots, x_n\rangle, es, \rho, c_{\mathsf{super}}, F)|\!\rangle}{\langle \text{BLOCK}(\langle x_1, \ldots, x_n\rangle, es), \rho, c_{\mathsf{super}}, F, \xi, \sigma, \mathcal{F}\rangle \Downarrow \langle v; \sigma, \mathcal{F}\rangle} \quad (\text{MKCLOSURE})$$

691a. ⟨*function* `ev`*, the evaluator proper* 689a⟩+≡ (688b) ◁689b 691d▷

```
| ev (BLOCK (formals, body)) = mkBlock (formals, body, rho, superclass, F)
```

Code inside a closure is evaluated by the `value` primitive. The `value` primitive is the only primitive that is mutually recursive with `eval`; it uses the function stored in `applyClosureRef`.

691b. ⟨*ML code for remaining classes' primitives* 691b⟩≡ (S550c) 699b▷

```
type closure = name list * exp list * value ref env * class * frame
val applyClosureRef : (closure * value list * value ref env -> value) ref
  = ref (fn _ => raise InternalError "applyClosureRef not set")

fun valuePrim ((_, CLOSURE clo) :: vs, xi) = !applyClosureRef (clo, vs, xi)
  | valuePrim _ = raise RuntimeError "primitive 'value' needs a closure"
```

Once `eval` is defined, `applyClosureRef` can be initialized properly, to a function that implements this rule:

$$\frac{\begin{array}{c}\ell_1, \ldots, \ell_n \notin \operatorname{dom}\sigma \qquad \ell_1, \ldots, \ell_n \text{ all distinct} \\ \hat\sigma = \sigma\{\ell_1 \mapsto v_1, \ldots \ell_n \mapsto v_n\} \\ \langle \text{BEGIN}(es), \rho_c + \{x_1 \mapsto \ell_1, \ldots, x_n \mapsto \ell_n\}, \mathsf{s}_c, F_c, \xi, \hat\sigma, \mathcal{F}\rangle \Downarrow \langle v; \sigma', \mathcal{F}'\rangle\end{array}}{\langle \texttt{value}, [\langle\!| c, \text{CLOSURE}(\langle x_1, \ldots, x_n\rangle, es, \mathsf{s}_c, \rho_c, F_c)|\!\rangle, v_1, \ldots, v_n], \xi, \sigma, \mathcal{F}\rangle \Downarrow_p \langle v; \sigma', \mathcal{F}'\rangle}. \quad (\text{VALUEPRIMITIVE})$$

691c. ⟨*evaluation,* `basis`*, and* `processDef` *for μSmalltalk* 688b⟩+≡ (S548c) ◁688b 693c▷

```
applyClosure : closure * value list * value ref env -> value
```

```
fun applyClosure ((formals, body, rho_c, superclass, frame), vs, xi) =
  eval (BEGIN body, rho_c <+> mkEnv (formals, map ref vs), superclass,
        frame, xi)
  handle BindListLength =>
    raise RuntimeError ("wrong number of arguments to block; expected " ^
                        "(<block> " ^ valueSelector formals ^ " " ^
                        spaceSep formals ^ ")")
val () = applyClosureRef := applyClosure
```

Evaluating literal and value forms A `LITERAL` form represents a literal integer or symbol, and it is evaluated by calling `mkInteger` or `mkSymbol`. These functions cannot be called safely until after the initial basis has been read and the interpreter has been bootstrapped (Section 10.11.6, page 697); for that reason, integer and symbol literals in the initial basis may appear only inside method definitions.

$$\frac{}{\langle \text{LITERAL}(\text{NUM}(n)), \rho, c_{\mathsf{super}}, F, \xi, \sigma, \mathcal{F}\rangle \Downarrow \langle\langle\!|\sigma(\xi(\texttt{SmallInteger})), \text{NUM}(n)|\!\rangle; \sigma, \mathcal{F}\rangle} \quad (\text{LITERALNUMBER})$$

$$\frac{}{\langle \text{LITERAL}(\text{SYM}(s)), \rho, c_{\mathsf{super}}, F, \xi, \sigma, \mathcal{F}\rangle \Downarrow \langle\langle\!|\sigma(\xi(\texttt{Symbol})), \text{SYM}(s)|\!\rangle; \sigma, \mathcal{F}\rangle} \quad (\text{LITERALSYMBOL})$$

691d. ⟨*function* `ev`*, the evaluator proper* 689a⟩+≡ (688b) ◁691a 692a▷

```
| ev (LITERAL c) =
    (case c of NUM n => mkInteger n
             | SYM s => mkSymbol s
             | _ => raise InternalError "unexpected literal")
```

By contrast, a VALUE form may be evaluated safely at any time; it evaluates to the value it carries.

$$\frac{}{\langle \text{VALUE}(v), \rho, c_{\mathsf{super}}, F, \xi, \sigma, \mathcal{F}\rangle \Downarrow \langle v; \sigma, \mathcal{F}\rangle} \quad \text{(VALUE)}$$

692a. ⟨*function* ev, *the evaluator proper* 689a⟩+≡ (688b) ◁691d 692b▷

```
| ev (VALUE v) = v
```

Reading and writing variables The VAR and SET forms are evaluated as we would expect; they use the local and global environments in the same way as Impcore.

$$\frac{x \in \operatorname{dom} \rho \qquad \rho(x) = \ell}{\langle \text{VAR}(x), \rho, c_{\mathsf{super}}, F, \xi, \sigma, \mathcal{F}\rangle \Downarrow \langle \sigma(\ell); \sigma, \mathcal{F}\rangle} \quad \text{(VAR)}$$

$$\frac{x \notin \operatorname{dom} \rho \qquad x \in \operatorname{dom} \xi \qquad \xi(x) = \ell}{\langle \text{VAR}(x), \rho, c_{\mathsf{super}}, F, \xi, \sigma, \mathcal{F}\rangle \Downarrow \langle \sigma(\ell); \sigma, \mathcal{F}\rangle} \quad \text{(GLOBALVAR)}$$

$$\frac{x \in \operatorname{dom} \rho \qquad \rho(x) = \ell \qquad \langle e, \rho, c_{\mathsf{super}}, F, \xi, \sigma, \mathcal{F}\rangle \Downarrow \langle v; \sigma', \mathcal{F}'\rangle}{\langle \text{SET}(x, e), \rho, c_{\mathsf{super}}, F, \xi, \sigma, \mathcal{F}\rangle \Downarrow \langle v; \sigma'\{\ell \mapsto v\}, \mathcal{F}'\rangle} \quad \text{(ASSIGN)}$$

$$\frac{x \notin \operatorname{dom} \rho \qquad x \in \operatorname{dom} \xi \qquad \xi(x) = \ell \qquad \langle e, \rho, c_{\mathsf{super}}, F, \xi, \sigma, \mathcal{F}\rangle \Downarrow \langle v; \sigma', \mathcal{F}'\rangle}{\langle \text{SET}(x, e), \rho, c_{\mathsf{super}}, F, \xi, \sigma, \mathcal{F}\rangle \Downarrow \langle v; \sigma'\{\ell \mapsto v\}, \mathcal{F}'\rangle} \quad \text{(ASSIGNGLOBAL)}$$

692b. ⟨*function* ev, *the evaluator proper* 689a⟩+≡ (688b) ◁692a 692c▷

```
| ev (VAR x) = !(find (x, rho) handle NotFound _ => find (x, xi))
| ev (SET (x, e)) =
    let val v = ev e
        val cell = find (x, rho) handle NotFound _ => find (x, xi)
    in  cell := v; v
    end
```

The SUPER form is evaluated as if it were `self`.

$$\frac{\langle \text{VAR}(\texttt{self}), \rho, c_{\mathsf{super}}, F, \xi, \sigma, \mathcal{F}\rangle \Downarrow \langle v; \sigma, \mathcal{F}\rangle}{\langle \text{SUPER}, \rho, c_{\mathsf{super}}, F, \xi, \sigma, \mathcal{F}\rangle \Downarrow \langle v; \sigma, \mathcal{F}\rangle} \quad \text{(SUPER)}$$

692c. ⟨*function* ev, *the evaluator proper* 689a⟩+≡ (688b) ◁692b 692d▷

```
| ev (SUPER) = ev (VAR "self")
```

Sequential evaluation The BEGIN form is evaluated as in Impcore and μScheme.

$$\frac{}{\langle \text{BEGIN}(), \rho, c_{\mathsf{super}}, F, \xi, \sigma, \mathcal{F}\rangle \Downarrow \langle \mathit{nil}; \sigma, \mathcal{F}\rangle} \quad \text{(EMPTYBEGIN)}$$

$$\frac{\langle [e_1, \ldots, e_n], \rho, c_{\mathsf{super}}, F, \xi, \sigma, \mathcal{F}\rangle \Downarrow \langle [v_1, \ldots, v_n]; \sigma', \mathcal{F}'\rangle}{\langle \text{BEGIN}(e_1, e_2, \ldots, e_n), \rho, c_{\mathsf{super}}, F, \xi, \sigma, \mathcal{F}\rangle \Downarrow \langle v_n; \sigma', \mathcal{F}'\rangle} \quad \text{(BEGIN)}$$

692d. ⟨*function* ev, *the evaluator proper* 689a⟩+≡ (688b) ◁692c 693a▷

```
| ev (BEGIN es) =
    let fun b (e::es, lastval) = b (es, ev e)
          | b (   [], lastval) = lastval
    in  b (es, nilValue)
    end
```

Evaluating primitives Each μSmalltalk primitive is implemented by a function that expects a list of values and a global environment ξ. (The global environment is used only by the `value` primitive, which calls `applyClosure`.) The primitives are stored on the association list primitives list (Appendix U, page S550), and a PRIMITIVE form is evaluated by looking up the associated function on the list, then applying that function to the values of the arguments.

693a. ⟨*function* ev, *the evaluator proper* 689a⟩+≡ (688b) ◁692d 693b▷

```
| ev (PRIMITIVE (p, args)) =
    let val f = find (p, primitives)
                handle NotFound n =>
                  raise RuntimeError ("There is no primitive named " ^ n)
    in  f (map ev args, xi)
    end
```


Compiled methods A compiled-method is evaluated without actual compilation; its formal parameters, local variables, body, and current superclass go into an object.

693b. ⟨*function* ev, *the evaluator proper* 689a⟩+≡ (688b) ◁693a

```
| ev (METHOD (xs, ys, es)) =
    mkCompiledMethod { name = "", formals = xs, locals = ys
                     , body = BEGIN es, superclass = objectClass }
```

Function mkCompiledMethod is defined in the Supplement (page S570).

10.11.3 *Evaluating definitions*

Most definitions are evaluated more or less as in other interpreters, but class definitions require a lot of special-purpose code for creating classes.

Function evaldef, *for evaluating definitions*

Evaluating a definition computes a new global environment, and it also has a side effect on the state of the interpreter.

693c. ⟨*evaluation,* basis, *and* processDef *for μSmalltalk* 688b⟩+≡ (S548c) ◁691c S548e▷

```
evaldef : def * value ref env -> value ref env * value
ev      : exp -> value
```

```
fun evaldef (d, xi) =
  let fun ev e = eval (e, emptyEnv, objectClass, noFrame, xi)
                 ⟨handle unexpected Return in evaldef S590e⟩
      val (x, v) =
        case d
          of VAL (name, e)             => (name, ev e)
           | EXP e                     => ("it", ev e)
           | DEFINE (name, args, body) => (name, ev (BLOCK (args, [body])))
           | CLASSD (d as {name, ...}) => (name, newClassObject d xi)
      val xi' = optimizedBind (x, v, xi)
  in  (xi', v)
  end
```


This implementation is best understood in four steps:

1. Define ev to evaluate an expression e in the context of a message sent to an instance of class Object: use an empty ρ, use Object as the superclass, and use the given xi. And because e is not in a method, there is no method invocation to which it can return, so its current frame F is given as noFrame, which is different from any allocated frame.
2. Analyze the definition d to find the name x being defined and to compute the value v that x stands for. Depending on the form of the definition, v may be the result of evaluating an expression, or it may be a new class object.
3. Compute the new environment ξ'.

```
mkClass      : name -> metaclass -> class -> name list -> method list -> class
methodDefns : class * class -> method_def list -> method list * method list
setMeta      : class * class -> unit
className    : class -> name
classId      : class -> metaclass ref
methodName   : method -> name
methodsEnv   : method list -> method env
findClassAndMeta : name * value ref env -> class * class
```

Figure 10.33: Utilities for manipulating classes (from the Supplement)

4. Return ξ' and v.

Evaluating a VAL or EXP form evaluates the given expression and binds it to a name—either the given name or "it". DEFINE is syntactic sugar for a definition of a block. And evaluating a class definition binds a new class object, as described below.

10.11.4 Class objects and metaclasses

In both concrete and abstract syntax, a class definition can define methods in two flavors: instance method or class method. But in the operational semantics and at run time, there is only one flavor: "method." What's up with that? There truly is just one mechanism for dynamic dispatch, regardless of whether a message is sent to a class or to an instance. The distinction between instance method and class method is implemented by creating an extra, hidden class for each class in the system: a *metaclass*. Metaclasses aren't needed for writing typical Smalltalk code, but if you want to know how the system implements the two flavors of methods or how it creates new objects, metaclasses are essential.

Metaclasses are governed by these invariants:

- Every object is an instance of some class.
- Every class is also an object—and is therefore an instance of some class.
- A class whose instances are classes is called a *metaclass*.
- Classes and metaclasses are one to one: every class has a unique metaclass, and every metaclass has a unique instance.
- The instance methods of a class are stored in the class object.
- The class methods of a class are stored in the metaclass object.
- Every metaclass is an instance of class Metaclass.
- If a class C has a superclass, the metaclass of its superclass is the superclass of its metaclass. This invariant can be expressed as the algebraic law ((C superclass) metaclass) $=$ ((C metaclass) superclass).
- Class Object has no superclass, and the superclass of its metaclass is class Class.

The invariants dictate that classes and metaclasses be linked in memory in circular ways: because every class points both to its superclass and to its metaclass, the graph of class and metaclass objects has a cycle. By itself, the "subclass-of" relation has no cycles, but the "instance-of" relation has a cycle, and the combined relation has an additional cycle. The cycles are implemented by using mutable state: every class object is first created with a metaclass pointer that is PENDING; then its metaclass object is created; and finally the original class is mutated to point to the new metaclass.

The representation of class objects is defined in code chunk 686c, but the large record type is awkward to manipulate directly. Instead, functions that manipulate ML values of type `class` do so using utility functions that are defined in Appendix U and are summarized in Figure 10.33 on the facing page.

A typical class object and its corresponding metaclass are both created by function `newClassObject`, which is given the definition of the class. The new class has a superclass, which is found (along with *its* metaclass) by function `findClass`, which looks up the name of the superclass in environment ξ. The method definitions are segrated into class methods and instance methods by function `methodDefns`, which also attaches the correct static superclass to each method. The new class is built by `mkClass`, its metaclass is built by `mkMeta`, and the final class object is built by `classObject`.

695a. ⟨*definition of* `newClassObject` *and supporting functions* 695a⟩≡ (S548c)

```
fun newClassObject {name, super, ivars, methods} xi =
  let val (super, superMeta) = findClassAndMeta (super, xi)
        handle NotFound s =>
          raise RuntimeError ("Superclass " ^ s ^ " not found")
      val (cmethods, imethods) = methodDefns (superMeta, super) methods
      val class = mkClass name PENDING super ivars imethods
      val ()    = setMeta (class, mkMeta class cmethods)
  in  classObject class
  end
```

Function `classObject` uses `CLASSREP` to make the class a `rep`, then pairs it with the class of which it is an instance, that is, its metaclass. Any attempt to refer to an uninitialized metaclass results in a checked run-time error.

695b. ⟨*metaclass utilities* 695b⟩≡ (S550c) S588d ▷

```
metaclass   : class -> class
classObject : class -> value
```

```
fun metaclass (CLASS { class = ref meta, ... }) =
  case meta of META c => c
             | PENDING => raise InternalError "pending class"

fun classObject c = (metaclass c, CLASSREP c)
```

When `mkMeta` creates a metaclass for class C, it gives C's metaclass a superclass, that is, it finds the class that will be `((`C` metaclass) superclass)`. C's metaclass's superclass is actually found by function `metaSuper`, and as noted above, it is normally `((`C` superclass) metaclass)`. But when C has no superclass, its metaclass's superclass is instead class `Class`. Internal representation `classClass` is defined below.

695c. ⟨*metaclasses for built-in classes* 695c⟩≡ (S550c) 695d ▷

```
metaSuper : class -> class
```

```
fun metaSuper (CLASS { super = NONE,        ... }) = classClass
  | metaSuper (CLASS { super = SOME c_sup, ... }) = metaclass c_sup
```

To make a metaclass for C, function `mkMeta` needs C's internal representation `c` and C's class methods. The new metaclass is given a name derived from C's name, and it is made an instance of class `Metaclass`. It has the superclass computed by `metaSuper`, no instance variables, and the given class methods.

695d. ⟨*metaclasses for built-in classes* 695c⟩+≡ (S550c) ◁ 695c 697c ▷

```
mkMeta : class -> method list -> class
```

```
fun mkMeta c classmethods =
  mkClass ("class " ^ className c) (META metaclassClass) (metaSuper c)
          [] classmethods
```

CLASS	686c
type class	686c
classClass	696d
className	S588a
CLASSREP	686a
findClassAndMeta	S588c
InternalError	S219e
META	686c
metaclassClass	696d
type method	686d
methodDefns	S589b
mkClass	S588e
NotFound	305b
PENDING	686c
RuntimeError	S213b
setMeta	S588d

Function newClassObject, in the previous section, is what's called when a class definition is evaluated, and it is sufficient to create almost every class in μSmalltalk. The exceptions are the four primitive classes, which are created using ML code:

- Object is primitive because it has no superclass.
- UndefinedObject is primitive because it is nil's class, and nil is primitive because a number of primitives need it, as does the evaluator.
- Class and Metaclass are primitive because they are needed to create new classes: every metaclass descends from class Class and is an instance of class Metaclass.

Every other class in the initial basis is defined by a class definition written in μSmalltalk itself.

Class Object is the ultimate superclass. To support the implementation of self, it has one instance variable, self. Defining self on class Object ensures that every user-defined object has an instance variable called self, into which, when a new object is created, function newUserObject places a pointer to the object itself (chunk 700).

696a. ⟨*built-in class* Object 696a⟩≡ (S550c)

```
val objectMethods =
  internalMethods ⟨methods of class Object, as strings (from chunk 634)⟩
val objectClass =
  CLASS { name = "Object", super = NONE, ivars = ["self"]
        , class = ref PENDING, methods = ref (methodsEnv objectMethods)
        }
```

The ⟨*methods of class* Object 634⟩ are defined throughout this chapter and in Appendix U, starting in chunk 634.

Class UndefinedObject, whose sole instance is nil, redefines isNil, notNil, and print, as shown in chunks 654 and S559d.

696b. ⟨*built-in class* UndefinedObject *and value* nilValue 696b⟩≡ (S550c) 696c ▷

```
val nilClass =
  mkClass "UndefinedObject" PENDING objectClass []
    (internalMethods ⟨methods of class UndefinedObject, as strings (from chunk 654)⟩)
```

Class UndefinedObject has a single instance, internally called nilValue. To enable it to be returned from some primitives, it is created here.

696c. ⟨*built-in class* UndefinedObject *and value* nilValue 696b⟩+≡ (S550c) ◁ 696b

```
val nilValue =
  let val nilCell  = ref (nilClass, USER []) : value ref
      val nilValue = (nilClass, USER (bind ("self", nilCell, emptyEnv)))
      val _        = nilCell := nilValue
  in  nilValue
  end
```

Class Class is in the interpreter so that metaclasses can inherit from it, and Metaclass is here so that each metaclass can be an instance of it.

696d. ⟨*built-in classes* Class *and* Metaclass 696d⟩≡ (S550c)

```
val classClass =
  mkClass "Class" PENDING objectClass []
    (internalMethods ⟨methods of class Class, as strings (from chunk 697a)⟩)

val metaclassClass =
  mkClass "Metaclass" PENDING classClass []
    (internalMethods ⟨methods of class Metaclass, as strings (from chunk 697b)⟩)
```

Most of the methods of class Class are relegated to Appendix U, but the default implementation of new is shown here:

697a. ⟨*methods of class* Class 697a⟩≡ S559b ▷
```
(method new () (primitive newUserObject self))
```

For metaclasses, this default is overridden; a metaclass may not be used to instantiate new objects.

697b. ⟨*methods of class* Metaclass 697b⟩≡
```
(method new () (self error: 'a-metaclass-may-have-only-one-instance))
```


Internal classes classClass and metaclassClass are used in the implementation of mkMeta, shown above in chunk 695d. Once mkMeta is defined, it is used to create the metaclasses of classes Object, UndefinedObject, Class, and Metaclass.

697c. ⟨*metaclasses for built-in classes* 695c⟩+≡ (S550c) ◁ 695d
```
fun patchMeta c = setMeta (c, mkMeta c [])
val () = app patchMeta [objectClass, nilClass, classClass, metaclassClass]
```

10.11.6 *Bootstrapping for literal and Boolean values*

In most languages, literal integers, Booleans, and nil would be simple atomic values. But in Smalltalk, they are objects, every object has a class, and relations among objects and classes include circular dependencies:

1. When the evaluator sees an integer literal, it must create an integer value.
2. That value must be an instance of class SmallInteger.[12]
3. Class SmallInteger is defined by μSmalltalk code.
4. That code must be interpreted by the evaluator.

Another circular dependency involves Boolean values and their classes:

1. Value true must be an instance of class Boolean.
2. Class Boolean must be a subclass of class Object.
3. Class Object has method notNil.
4. Method notNil must return true on class Object.

Each of these things depends on all the others, creating a cycle that must be broken. Value false and method isNil participate in a similar cycle.

Each cycle is broken with a well-placed ref cell. First, the ref cell is initialized with an unusable value; then the interpreter is bootstrapped by feeding it the definitions of the predefined classes; and finally the ref cell is assigned its proper value, closing the cycle. The ref cells and the functions that update them are defined in the chunk ⟨*support for bootstrapping classes/values used during parsing* 698a⟩. The ref cells are used by primitives, by built-in objects, and by the parser.

Cycles of literals When an integer literal is evaluated, the evaluator must create an object of class SmallInteger, which means that the evaluator requires a representation of SmallInteger. But that representation is created by evaluating a class definition (chunk S567b), which requires the evaluator!

I break the cycle by reserving a mutable reference cell, intClass, to hold the representation of class SmallInteger. The cell is initially empty, but after the definition of SmallInteger is read, it is updated. The cell is used every time an integer literal is read: the evaluator calls function mkInteger, which fetches the SmallInteger class out of intClass. Provided SmallInteger has been read,

[12] In full Smalltalk-80, an integer literal could also be an instance of a large-integer class.

intClass is not empty, and mkInteger creates and returns a new instance of the class. Otherwise, it crashes the interpreter by raising the InternalError exception. Similar functions and reference cells are used to create objects from symbol literals and array literals.

Because reference cells are hard to reason about, I define them inside ML's local form. This form limits the scope of code that the reference cells can affect; the reference cells are accessible only to functions defined between local and end.

698a. ⟨*support for bootstrapping classes/values used during parsing* 698a⟩≡ (S547) 698b ▷

```
mkInteger : int        -> value
mkSymbol  : string     -> value
mkArray   : value list -> value
```

```
local
  val intClass    = ref NONE : class option ref
  val symbolClass = ref NONE : class option ref
  val arrayClass  = ref NONE : class option ref
  fun badlit what =
    raise InternalError
      ("(bootstrapping) -- can't " ^ what ^ " in predefined classes")
in
  fun mkInteger n = (valOf (!intClass), NUM n)
    handle Option => badlit "evaluate integer literal or use array literal"

  fun mkSymbol s = (valOf (!symbolClass), SYM s)
    handle Option => badlit "evaluate symbol literal or use array literal"

  fun mkArray a = (valOf (!arrayClass), ARRAY (Array.fromList a))
    handle Option => badlit "use array literal"
```

Function valOf and exception Option are part of the initial basis of Standard ML.

Once the predefined class definitions have been read, the reference cells are updated by function saveLiteralClasses, which takes one parameter, the global environment xi.

698b. ⟨*support for bootstrapping classes/values used during parsing* 698a⟩+≡ (S547) ◁ 698a 699a ▷

```
findClass : string * value ref env -> class
```

```
  fun saveLiteralClasses xi =
    ( intClass    := SOME (findClass ("SmallInteger", xi))
    ; symbolClass := SOME (findClass ("Symbol",       xi))
    ; arrayClass  := SOME (findClass ("Array",        xi))
    )
  and findClass (name, xi) =
        case !(find (name, xi))
          of (_, CLASSREP c) => c
           | _ => raise InternalError ("class " ^ name ^ " isn't defined")
end
```

Cycles of blocks The same drill that applies to literal expressions also applies to blocks: Evaluating a block expression creates an object of class Block, which also is not defined until its definition is read. Blocks are supported by these functions defined in Appendix U:

```
mkBlock : name list * exp list * value ref env * class * frame -> value
saveBlockClass : value ref env -> unit
```

sameObject	className	addWithOverflow	value
class	protocol	subWithOverflow	printu
isKindOf	localProtocol	mulWithOverflow	printSymbol
isMemberOf	getMethod	+	newSymbol
error	setMethod	-	arrayNew
subclassResponsibility	removeMethod	*	arraySize
leftAsExercise	methodNames	div	arrayAt
newUserObject	newSmallInteger	<	arrayUpdate
superclass	printSmallInteger	>	

Figure 10.34: μSmalltalk's primitives

Booleans Booleans also participate in a cycle, but it's the Boolean *objects*, not the Boolean classes, that must be bootstrapped. Each Boolean object is stored in its own mutable reference cell.

699a. ⟨*support for bootstrapping classes/values used during parsing* 698a⟩+≡ (S547) ◁ 698b S561a ▷

mkBoolean : bool -> value

```
local
  val trueValue  = ref NONE : value option ref
  val falseValue = ref NONE : value option ref
in
  fun mkBoolean b = valOf (!(if b then trueValue else falseValue))
    handle Option => raise InternalError "uninitialized Booleans"
  fun saveTrueAndFalse xi =
    ( trueValue  := SOME (!(find ("true",  xi)))
    ; falseValue := SOME (!(find ("false", xi)))
    )
end
```

10.11.7 Primitives

μSmalltalk's primitives are listed in Figure 10.34. Each primitive's specification should be suggested by its name, but if you are uncertain about what a primitive does, you can study how it is used in predefined classes.

A μSmalltalk primitive is almost the same thing as a μScheme primitive function, and like a μScheme primitive function, it is represented as an ML function. For example, the value primitive is defined as function valuePrim in chunk 691b. Like μScheme's primitive functions (Chapter 5, page 312), most of μSmalltalk's primitives are defined using higher-order ML functions in the interpreter. The definitions are so similar to the examples in Chapter 5 that only a couple are worth showing here: class, which returns an object's class, and newUserObject, which creates a new object.

The class primitive takes an object as its single argument. The object is represented by a pair that includes the object's class, which is promoted to a full object by calling function classObject (chunk 695b).

ARRAY	686a
type class	686c
classObject	695b
CLASSREP	686a
find	305b
InternalError	S219e
NUM	686a
SYM	686a
unaryPrim	S551a
type value	685

699b. ⟨*ML code for remaining classes' primitives* 691b⟩+≡ (S550c) ◁ 691b 700 ▷

```
val classPrimitive = unaryPrim (fn (c, rep) => classObject c)
```

The `newUserObject` primitive allocates fresh instance variables, each containing `nilValue`. It then allocates the object, and finally it assigns `self` to point to the object itself.

700. ⟨*ML code for remaining classes' primitives* 691b⟩+≡ (S550c) ◁699b S551b▷

```
                                      mkIvars       : class -> value ref env
                                      newUserObject : class -> value
local
  fun mkIvars (CLASS { ivars, super, ... }) =
    let val supervars = case super of NONE => emptyEnv | SOME c => mkIvars c
    in  foldl (fn (x, rho) => bind (x, ref nilValue, rho)) supervars ivars
    end
  fun newUserObject c =
        let val ivars = mkIvars c
            val self = (c, USER ivars)
        in  (find ("self", ivars) := self; self)
        end
in
  val newPrimitive = classPrim (fn (meta, c) => newUserObject c)
end
```

10.12 SMALLTALK AS IT REALLY IS

The Smalltalk *language* is so small and simple that μSmalltalk can model almost all of it: assignment, message send, block creation, and nonlocal return. But Smalltalk-80 is not just a programming language. It is a programming *system*, unifying elements of programming language and operating system. And it is also an interactive programming *environment*. Neither of these aspects is captured in μSmalltalk, which is more of a Unix-style programming language: μSmalltalk programs are stored in a file system and are run by a standalone interpreter. Smalltalk-80, the programming system, is described in the first part of this section. Smalltalk-80, the programming environment, is not described here, because a book is not the right medium. (Two excellent Smalltalk environments, Squeak and Pharo, are readily available for download; I urge you to explore them.) Finally, in the rest of this section, Smalltalk-80's language and classes are compared with μSmalltalk's language and classes.

10.12.1 Programming language as operating system

Like all of the bridge languages, μSmalltalk fits comfortably into the development paradigm made popular by Unix:

- Programs are stored in files, which are managed by an underlying operating system.
- Whether a program is run by an interpreter or compiled by a compiler, it is invoked by an operating-system command, which finds the program in the file system. A program is typically invoked because a person typed something at a *shell*.
- A program's variables have to be initialized when the program is run, and when the program terminates, their values are lost. Persistent state is stored only in the file system.
- Source code is edited and organized by programs that are unrelated to the interpreter or compiler, except they share a file system.

- When code changes, programs that use the code are restarted from the beginning.

Smalltalk-80 operates on a different paradigm:

- Programs are stored in an *image* of a running Smalltalk system. Operating-system abstractions like files are mostly irrelevant.

- Persistent state is stored in Smalltalk variables, not in files. The state of the entire Smalltalk image, including the values of the variables of all the objects and classes that are defined—that is, ξ and σ—automatically persists.

- There are no programs or commands *per se*. Instead of "run a program," the paradigm of execution is "send a message to an object." Usually, the message is sent because a person interacted with a graphical user interface.

- Variables and objects don't need to be initialized before code runs; they retain their (persistent) state from the time they were first created. And when code finishes running—that is, when a message send terminates—the internal state of the relevant objects is (still) part of the image's state, so it persists; nothing is lost.

- Source code is just data, and it need not live in files. It is stored in instance variables of objects, and it is edited by sending messages to objects—usually by means of the graphical user interface.

- Unless something goes dramatically wrong, images don't terminate and aren't restarted. Sending a message to an object updates the image's state in much the same way that running a Unix command updates the file system's state. Restarting an image is a rare event, like restoring a file system from backup.

This image-based paradigm has deep consequences for language design. Most dramatically, Smalltalk-80 doesn't have definition forms! To create a new class, for example, you don't evaluate a definition form; instead, you send a message like `subclass:instanceVariableNames:` to the superclass of the class you wish to create. It responds with a class object, to which you add methods by sending `addSelector:withMethod:` or something similar. Or more likely, you manipulate a graphical user interface which sends these messages on your behalf.

10.12.2 Smalltalk-80's language

More literals and classes

Smalltalk-80 provides all the forms of data that μSmalltalk does, and more besides. And more classes, including classes for characters and strings, can be instantiated by evaluating literal expressions:

Class	**Literal**
Integer	230
Character	$a
Float	3.39e-5
Symbol	#hashnotquote
String	's p a c e s'
Array	#($a $b $c)

For symbols and arrays, Smalltalk-80 uses the hash mark, not our quote mark.

```
class name                          Shape
superclass                          Object
instance variable names             center
                                    radius

class methods
instance creation
   new
      ↑super new center: (CoordPair x: 0 y: 0) radius: 1

instance methods
observing locations
   location: pointName
      ↑center + ((pointVectors at: pointName) * radius)

   locations: pointNames
      | locs |
      pointNames do: [:point | locs add: (self location: point)].
      ↑locs

mutators
   adjustPoint: pointName to: location
      center ← center + (location - (self location: pointName))

   scale: k
      radius ← radius * k

drawing
   drawOn: picture
      self subclassResponsibility

private
   center: c radius: r
      center ← c.
      radius ← r
```

Figure 10.35: Class Shape, in Smalltalk-80 publication format

Syntax in context, with postfix, infix, and mixfix message sends

Smalltalk-80's syntax is meant to be displayed using a graphical user interface. But I'm stuck with ink on paper. I could show screen shots, but because they don't interact, they don't do justice to the experience. Instead, just to give you a feel for concrete syntax, I display code using the old "publication format" from the Smalltalk Blue Book (Goldberg and Robson 1983).

As an example, the publication format of the Shape class (Section 10.1.5) is shown in Figure 10.35. This format isn't source code; it's a display—it is tuned to printed paper in much the same way that real Smalltalk is tuned to two-dimensional graphics. Compare this display of Shape with my code from page 621. The protocols and computations are the same, but both the abstract syntax and the concrete syntax are different.

- As noted above, full Smalltalk doesn't use syntax for a class definition. The display at the top, which shows the class's name, superclass, and instance variables, could be obtained by sending messages name, superclass, and instVarNames to the class object.

- Instead of tagging each individual method as a class method or an instance method, Smalltalk-80 displays groups of methods. These displays are also computed by sending messages to the class object.

- The Smalltalk-80 display shows information about *subgroups* of methods: "instance creation," "observing locations," "mutators," and "private." These subgroups, which have no analog in μSmalltalk, serve as documentation. In Smalltalk-80 the subgroups are called *message categories*. In more modern Smalltalks, a subgroup is called a *protocol*, just like the collection of messages as a whole.

- Each method definition is introduced by a line set in bold type; this line, which is called the *message pattern*, gives the name of the method and the names of its arguments. A method that expects no arguments has a name composed of letters and numbers. A method that expects one argument has a colon after the name; the name of the method is followed by the name of the argument. When a method expects more than one argument, the name of the method is split into *keywords*: each keyword ends with a colon and is followed by the name of one argument. This concrete syntax matches the concrete syntax of message sends, as shown below.

  When a method has two or more arguments, it is named by concatenating the keywords; thus, the private message is "center:radius:," just as in μSmalltalk.

- The display indents the bodies of the methods. The body of a method contains a sequence of *statements*, which are separated by periods. To return a value from a method, Smalltalk-80 uses `return`, which is written using the up arrow ↑ or caret ^. A method that doesn't evaluate a return answers self, but such a method is likely to be evaluated only for its effects, not its answer.

- The "←" symbol is used for assignment. (Modern implementations use `:=`.)

- The most pervasive difference between Smalltalk-80 syntax and μSmalltalk syntax is that when a keyword message is sent, the message's arguments are *interleaved* with the parts of the message's name. And parentheses are used only where they are needed to disambiguate. For example, in μSmalltalk we write,

  ```
  ((Triangle new) adjustPoint:to: 'Southwest (s location: 'East))
  ```

  but in Smalltalk-80, we write,

  ```
  Triangle new adjustPoint: #Southwest :to (s location: #East)
  ```

- As in μSmalltalk, + and − are *binary messages*: a binary message is sent to a receiver and expects one argument. As with keyword messages, the send is written in receiver-message-argument form, for example, `3 + 4`. Binary messages have higher precedence than keyword messages; for example, in the location: method, to prevent `pointName` from being interpreted as the receiver of `*`, the message send pointVectors at: pointName is wrapped in parentheses.

- Blocks are written in square brackets, not in curly braces. (μSmalltalk's curly braces come from Ruby, a close relative of Smalltalk.) And when a block takes arguments, its syntax is lighter weight than what μSmalltalk uses. Formal parameters are written after the opening "[" and before a vertical bar "|"; their names are preceded by colons. Thus, the μSmalltalk block

```
[block (x) (self add: x)]
```

is written in Smalltalk-80 as

```
[:x | self add: x].
```

Smalltalk-80's keyword syntax, which interleaves keywords and arguments, has rarely been emulated, although both Objective C and Grace use it. In several other languages, however, keyword syntax can be simulated, e.g., by passing a literal dictionary as an argument.

More variables: Class instance variables and class variables

In Smalltalk-80, a class object has its own instance variables, which are distinct from the instance variables of its instances. These variables are called *class instance variables.* Class instance variables are specific to a class, and their values are not shared with subclasses—they are, quite simply, the instance variables of the metaclass. Smalltalk-80 also has *class variables,* which, unlike instance variables or class instance variables, are shared: they are accessible to all the instances of a class and its subclasses, as well as the class itself and its subclasses. Class variables can make global variables unnecessary: because *every* class inherits from Object, the class variables of class Object can play the role of global variables. So in full Smalltalk, for example, the global `point-vectors` dictionary (page 622) would instead be a class variable of class `Shape`.

Restricted primitives

In μSmalltalk, a `primitive` expression may appear anywhere within a method, with any arguments. In Smalltalk-80, primitives are numbered, not named, and a primitive may appear only at the beginning of a method, before any statements or expressions.

With these restrictions, a Smalltalk-80 method may be defined as a numbered primitive followed by one or more expressions, possibly ending in a return:

> *message-pattern*
> <primitive n>
> *expressions*

When the method is invoked, it executes the primitive numbered n. If the primitive fails, the *expressions* are executed; if the primitive succeeds, its result is returned and the *expressions* are ignored.

Primitives are not used by application programmers; as in μSmalltalk, they are used only in methods of predefined classes.

10.12.3 *Smalltalk-80's class hierarchy*

Smalltalk-80 comes with many, many class definitions. Only the Number and Collection subhierarchies are discussed here; these general-purpose classes are used by many programmers. Special-purpose hierarchies, including some that support graphics, compilation, and process scheduling, are beyond the scope of this book.

Smalltalk-80's numbers

In Smalltalk-80, the part of the class hierarchy that contains numeric classes, which is the model for μSmalltalk, looks like this:

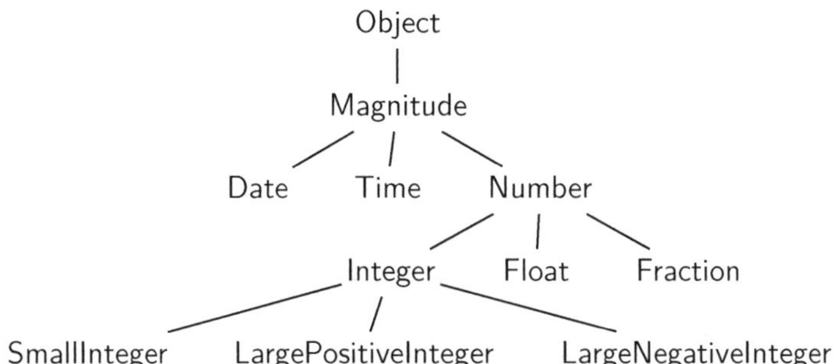

Classes `Magnitude` and `Number` resemble μSmalltalk's versions, but Smalltalk-80's Numbers respond to more messages than μSmalltalk's `Numbers`. Classes `Float` and `Fraction` are likewise similar in both languages. And in Smalltalk-80, these classes are supported by more forms of literals: Smalltalk-80 provides floating-point literals, and its Integer literals may be arbitrarily long. (The class of an integer literal is determined by its magnitude and sign.)

Like many languages, Smalltalk-80 supports mixed arithmetic; for example, Smalltalk-80 code can add a fraction to an integer, answering a fraction. But the class of the result is not determined by a static type system or even by the classes of the receiver and argument; instead, an arithmetic method conventionally answers an object of the *least general* class that can *represent* the result. Under this convention, the class of a result depends on the *value* of a receiver or an argument, not just its class. For example, 10 raisedTo: 2 answers a SmallInteger, but 10 raisedTo: 20 answers a LargePositiveInteger. SmallInteger is considered less general than LargePositiveInteger, which is considered less general than Float. That is why 10 raisedTo: 20 does not answer a Float.

The implementations of the Number operations exploit the continue-after-failure semantics of Smalltalk-80's primitives. For example, the definition of + on SmallInteger uses primitive 1 to do the addition, but if the primitive fails, e.g., because the addition overflows, the succeeding statements automatically change over to large-integer arithmetic. The changeover is effected by the simple coercion asLargeInteger:

```
+ aSmallInteger
  <primitive 1>
  ↑self asLargeInteger + aSmallInteger

asLargeInteger
  self negative
    ifTrue: [↑self asLargeNegativeInteger]
    ifFalse: [↑self asLargePositiveInteger]
```

Smalltalk-80's Collection classes

Smalltalk-80's Collection hierarchy looks a bit different from the `Collection` hierarchy in μSmalltalk. The μSmalltalk hierarchy is derived from the one in Tim

Budd's (1987) *Little Smalltalk*. The Smalltalk-80 collection hierarchy looks, in part, like this:

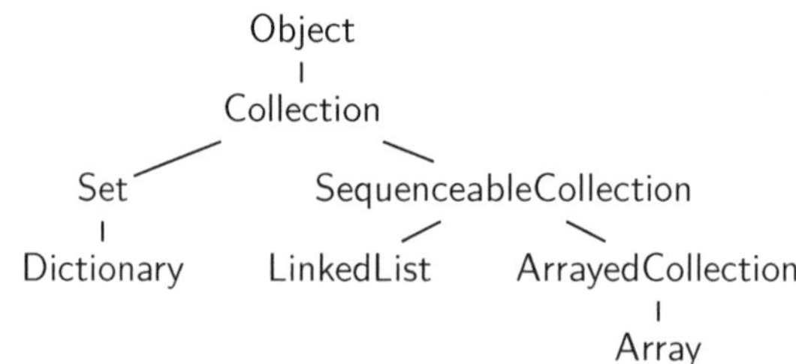

Both the Smalltalk-80 and the μSmalltalk collection hierarchies use iteration (`do:`) as the fundamental operation.

Collection protocols and the message cascade

In μSmalltalk, when `add:` is sent to a collection, the collection answers itself. This protocol supports an idiom that is common in object-oriented languages, which is to modify a collection by sending it a sequence of messages. For example,

```
((((List new) add: 1) add: 2) add: 3)    // uSmalltalk
List:new():add(1):add(2):add(3)          -- Lua
(new List).add(1).add(2).add(3)          // inspired by C++
```

This idiom applies to all sorts of mutable abstractions. But in Smalltalk-80, the `add:` message doesn't work with this idiom: `add:` answers the object just added, *not* the collection receiving the message. What gives?

It turns out that the idiom of sending a sequence of messages to a mutable abstraction is so useful that Smalltalk-80 provides special syntax for it: the *message cascade*. A receiver can be followed by a *sequence* of messages, separated by semicolons, and each message is sent in sequence to the same receiver. In Squeak Smalltalk, for example, the idiom works like this:

```
OrderedCollection new add: 1; add: 2; add: 3; yourself
```

This statement sends a cascade—a sequence of four messages—to the object answered by OrderedCollection new. The answer from the cascade is the answer from the last message. In this example, that's yourself, which causes the receiver to answer itself: a list containing the elements 1, 2, and 3.

Reflection

In Smalltalk-80, aspects of a running image are themselves exposed as objects. These objects can be used by the image to manipulate itself; the ability of a program to manipulate itself is sometimes called *reflection*. Reflection makes it possible to implement class browsers, compilers, debuggers, garbage collectors, and so on in the same language used to write applications. μSmalltalk offers a taste of reflection in the form of methods like `class` and `addSelector:withMethod:`, but a full Smalltalk system offers much more.

For example, given a class object, you can add or remove methods, query for particular methods, and call methods by name. You can compile or decompile code associated with methods. You can add or remove methods. You can change the superclass and add or remove subclasses. You can get the names of all the instance variables, which you can also add and remove. You can get information about the representations of instances. And so on.

Even the "active contexts" (stack frames) used to implement message send are represented as objects. This means, for example, that a debugger or trace routine can visit all active contexts and display values of local variables and instance variables, all using reflection.

10.13 Objects and classes as they really are

While most popular object-oriented languages organize objects into classes, classes aren't required. Object-oriented programming without classes is demonstrated most beautifully by the Self programming language. In Self, an object is a collection of named *slots*; a slot holds one object. Sending a slot name to an object answers the value of the object in the slot, or if the slot holds a special "method object," it answers the result of running the method. An object is created by giving the names and contents of its slots. An object may also be created by *cloning* another object, called the *prototype*. Cloning is a shallow copying operation; it creates a new object whose slots hold the same objects as the original. Self's model of object-orientation has been adopted by JavaScript, and it is also used in Lua.

Among popular object-oriented languages that do use classes, many are hybrids. A hybrid language often includes primitive types that act like abstract data types, not like objects; the classic example is the `int` type found in C++ and Java. And in a hybrid language, a class may act as a static type, not just as a factory for making objects. In such a hybrid, a class behaves more like one of Molecule's abstract data types than like one of Smalltalk's classes. For example, in Modula-3 and C++, the arguments to methods have static types, and a class method can see the representation of any argument of the class. But the method interoperates only with objects of the class (or its subclasses); Smalltalk's flexible, behavioral subtyping ("duck typing") is lost.

One popular language that offers *both* forms of data abstraction is Java. A Java interface corresponds nicely to a Smalltalk protocol. And as long as the types of methods are written entirely using interfaces, Java supports object-oriented programming much in the style of Smalltalk, with behavioral subtyping—different implementations of an interface interoperate with one another. But the moment the type of a method's argument is written using a Java class, that class acts as an abstract data type, not as a factory that builds objects which answer a given protocol. The method gains access to the representation of the argument, but it loses the ability to interoperate: it works only with instances of the specified class (or of one of its subclasses).

10.14 Summary

Smalltalk helped object-oriented languages take over the world. Object-orientation seems very effective for certain types of problems, including simulation, graphics, and user interfaces. Although classes, subclasses, and objects were first introduced in Simula 67, the compelling case for these ideas was made by Smalltalk. Many of Smalltalk's programming-environment ideas were adopted by Apple, and for years Apple's devices were programmed primarily using the object-oriented language Objective C, a relative of Smalltalk. (Apple eventually replaced Objective C with Swift, which adds functional-programming ideas to the mix.) The wild ideas that Alan Kay thought might "amplify human reach" are now central to mainstream programming.

An object is a bundle of operations that share state. When one of the operations is invoked, an implementation is chosen dynamically, and it can be different for different executions of the same code. The bundle of operations and their behaviors are specified by a *protocol*, which describes an abstraction. In a context expecting such an abstraction, any object that responds to the protocol may be used, regardless of the class used to manufacture the object. This property of object-oriented programming is called *behavioral subtyping* or *duck typing*.

In a pure object-oriented language, an operation has access only to the representation of the object on which it is defined; each argument is treated abstractly, through an interface or protocol. An operation that wishes to look at the representation of an argument must somehow extend the argument's interface—perhaps simply by defining additional methods, like μSmalltalk's predefined numeric classes, or perhaps by using double dispatch, like the large-integer classes in the exercises. In a hybrid language like Java or C++, the abstraction presented by an argument may be compromised: a class may act not only as a factory that builds new objects but also as an abstract data type. This sort of hybrid gains the ability to inspect an argument's representation directly, but it loses the ability to implement the argument's abstraction with a representation that is independent of its original class. The distinction between class as object factory and class as abstract type is subtle, and in popular object-oriented languages, it can be hard to untangle.

10.14.1 Key words and phrases

ABSTRACT CLASS A CLASS used only to define METHODS, not to create INSTANCES. Other classes INHERIT from it.

ABSTRACTION FUNCTION A function, used conceptually but not necessarily written in code, that maps the values of an object's INSTANCE VARIABLES to the abstract thing the object represents.

ANSWER Smalltalk's term for the response to a message. Corresponds to a "return value" in other languages. Smalltalkers sometimes refer to an *action* "to answer," which is analogous to the action "to return" found in other languages.

AUTOGNOSTIC PRINCIPLE Cook's (2009) term for a defining principle of object-oriented languages: an OBJECT has access only to its own REPRESENTATION, and it can access other objects only through their public interfaces or PROTOCOLS.

BEHAVIORAL SUBTYPING A principle that says that if an object answers the same PROTOCOL as another object, and if it behaves in the same way, it may be considered to have the same *type* as the other object. Called DUCK TYPING by Ruby programmers, because "if it walks like a duck..."

BLOCK An OBJECT much like a `lambda` abstraction, which is activated by sending it a MESSAGE. It has no instance variables. A block is a first-class value—an object with the same privileges as any other object. Smalltalk blocks are used as continuations to implement conditionals, loops, and exceptions.

CLASS A specification for making OBJECTS. In Smalltalk, a class is also itself an object.

CLASS METHOD A method that responds to messages sent to a class, rather than to instances of that class. Used most often to create or initialize instances of the class, as with the message `new`.

COLLECTION One of several Smalltalk classes whose objects act as containers for other objects. Predefined collections include dictionaries, sets, lists, and arrays. A collection can be defined by just a handful of methods, of which the most important is the `do:` method, which iterates over the objects contained in the collection. The collection then inherits a large number of useful methods from class `Collection`.

COMPLEX METHOD A METHOD that wishes to inspect the representation of one or more ARGUMENTS, not just the RECEIVER.

DATA ABSTRACTION The practice of characterizing a data type by its operations and their specifications, not by its REPRESENTATION.

DELEGATION An implementation technique in which a METHOD is implemented by sending its MESSAGE to another object. For example, if a large integer is represented by a sign and a magnitude, the `isZero` method on large integers might be implemented by sending the `isZero` message to the object that represents the large integer's magnitude.

EXPOSE THE REPRESENTATION Because Smalltalk methods are AUTOGNOSTIC, no method can ever inspect the representation of an argument—all a method can do with an argument is send messages to it. But an argument may define methods that *expose* the representation. The most extreme example is to define a "getter" and "setter" method for every instance variable. This kind of exposure makes it easy to implement COMPLEX METHODS, but it destroys DATA ABSTRACTION.

INHERITANCE The mechanism by which a CLASS definition is combined with the definition of its SUPERCLASS to specify how objects of the class are made. Class definitions may be combined by SINGLE INHERITANCE or MULTIPLE INHERITANCE.

INSTANCE When object O is made from the specification given by class C, O is called an *instance* of C.

INSTANCE VARIABLE Part of the state of a Smalltalk OBJECT. An object's instance variables are accessible only to that object's own METHODS.

MAGNITUDE A quantity like a date, a time, or a number, of which it can be said that one precedes another, but that might not support arithmetic.

MESSAGE A combination of a message name, which is used to select a METHOD, and actual parameters. Sent to an OBJECT. The name is called a MESSAGE SELECTOR.

MESSAGE NOT UNDERSTOOD The error that occurs when an object receives a MESSAGE that is not in its PROTOCOL.

MESSAGE PASSING Smalltalk's central control structure. Message passing sends a MESSAGE to an OBJECT. The message includes actual parameters, which are also objects. The receiver of the message first selects, and then invokes, a METHOD, the result of which is ANSWERED in reply to the message.

MESSAGE SELECTOR The name that, together with arguments, constitutes a MESSAGE.

METHOD Code that is executed in response to a MESSAGE. Sometimes called an INSTANCE METHOD. Like a function, a method takes formal parameters and returns a result. A method has access to the INSTANCE VARIABLES of its RECEIVER, but not to the instance variables of any of its arguments. An object's methods are determined by its CLASS.

METHOD DISPATCH The algorithm used to determine what METHOD is evaluated in response to a MESSAGE. A form of DYNAMIC DISPATCH. In Smalltalk, method dispatch begins with the class of the RECEIVER, looking for a method with the same name as the message. If no such method is found, method dispatch continues with the receiver's superclass, and so on all the way up to class `Object`. If method dispatch fails, it does so with a MESSAGE NOT UNDERSTOOD error.

MULTIPLE INHERITANCE Describes a language in which a CLASS may INHERIT from more than one SUPERCLASS. When different superclasses provide conflicting definitions, e.g., of the same method, the conflict must be resolved somehow. Multiple inheritance has had passionate advocates, but the success of Java has weighted the scales in favor of SINGLE INHERITANCE, and much of the passion has died down.

NUMBER In μSmalltalk, a machine integer, rational number, floating-point number, or arbitrary-precision integer. Machine integers are primitive, and arbitrary-precision integers are left as an exercise. Rational numbers and floating-point numbers are predefined.

OBJECT The unit of DATA ABSTRACTION in Smalltalk. An object encapsulates mutable state represented as INSTANCE VARIABLES and code represented as METHODS. Only an object's own methods have access to its instance variables.

OPEN RECURSION When a method sends a message to `self`, the message may dispatch to a method defined by a SUBCLASS. If the message being sent has the same name as the method from which the message is sent, what looks like a "recursive call" may not be a recursive call. This ability of message passing to "intercept" or "override" the apparently recursive call is called *open recursion*. The phrase "open recursion" is also used to describe the more general phenomenon of a message dispatching to a subclass method, even when the message name and method name are different.

When open recursion is used extensively, as in the implementation of arithmetic, for example, understanding the sequence of actions taken by an algorithm requires you to piece together many methods, which can be difficult.

OVERRIDE When a class defines a method that is also defined in a SUPERCLASS, every instance of that class uses the new definition, not the superclass definition. The superclass definition is said to be *overridden*. Overriding is sometimes called REDEFINING the superclass method.

PRIVATE METHOD A method that is to be invoked only by other methods of the same CLASS, or of its SUBCLASSES. It is part of the class's private PROTOCOL.

In Smalltalk, the private method is purely a programming convention, as it is also in Python. In object-oriented languages with static type systems, the type system usually provides a mechanism to make a method private.

PROTOCOL The set of MESSAGES to which an OBJECT can respond, together with the rules that say what actual parameters are acceptable and how the object behaves in response.

RECEIVER In MESSAGE PASSING, the OBJECT to which a message is sent. A message need not have any actual parameters, but it is always sent to a receiver.

REFLECTION A feature of full Smalltalk whereby methods, usually defined on class `Class` or class `Object`, provide information about the implementations of classes or objects, or enable a Smalltalk program to alter itself. One simple example is the method `subclass:instanceVariableNames:`, which can be sent to any class object to create a new subclass of that class. Smalltalk-80 has many other reflective methods: all instances of a class, all instance variables of an object, and so on. μSmalltalk provides a cheap, plastic imitation of reflection, limited to such methods as `class`, `addSelector:withMethod:`, `compiledMethodAt:`, and a few others.

REPRESENTATION INVARIANT A property that holds among all the INSTANCE VARIABLES of an OBJECT, and which the object's METHODS rely on. Representation invariants must be established and maintained by an object's own methods and by the methods of its subclasses.

`self` A keyword used within a METHOD to refer to the RECEIVER of a MESSAGE. When a message is sent to `self`, METHOD DISPATCH begins with the class of the receiver, not the class in which the method is defined. In some object-oriented languages, "`self`" is written "`this`."

SINGLE INHERITANCE Describes a language in which a CLASS INHERITS from exactly one SUPERCLASS. Contrasted with MULTIPLE INHERITANCE. Smalltalk uses single inheritance.

SUBCLASS A class that INHERITS from a SUPERCLASS. A class may have many subclasses or none. And a subclass of a subclass is also called a subclass.

`super` A special keyword that bypasses the normal METHOD DISPATCH algorithm and dispatches directly to a method defined in the SUPERCLASS of the class in which `super` appears.

SUPERCLASS A class named in a class definition, from which the defined class inherits INSTANCE VARIABLES and METHODS. Except for the primitive class `Object`, every class has a unique superclass. Class `Object` has no superclass. To confuse matters slightly, a superclass of a superclass is sometimes also called a superclass.

10.14.2 Further reading

Smalltalk was invented to help create a computing experience that might deserve to be called "personal." Smalltalk was part of a flood of inventions that emerged from the Xerox Palo Alto Research Center (PARC): the one-person computer; the bitmapped display; the user-interface elements that we now call windows, menus, and pointing; the use of abstract data types in systems programming; and many other delights that we have long since taken for granted. PARC's Smalltalk group wanted to create a software system that would make the computer "an amplifier for the human reach," not just a tool for building software systems. Alan Kay's (1993) account of those heady days is well worth your time.

Smalltalk-80 is described by the "blue book," by Goldberg and Robson (1983), which is so called because of its predominantly blue cover. The blue book introduces the language and class hierarchy. It also presents five chapters on simulation and five chapters on the implementation and the virtual machine on which it is based. The blue book strongly influenced the design of μSmalltalk, especially its blocks. The "red book" (Goldberg 1983) describes the Smalltalk-80 programming environment and its implementation. A "green book" describes some of the early history of Smalltalk (Krasner 1983), and Ingalls (2020) describes the evolution of the language and its implementation from Smalltalk-72 onward.

Smalltalk was the subject of an August 1981 special issue of Byte magazine (*Byte* 1981). The issue includes twelve articles on the system, written by the people who built it. Topics range from design principles to engineering details, with plenty of examples, plus a description of the programming environment. A narrow, deep introduction to the Smalltalk-80 language and programming environment is presented by Kaehler and Patterson (1986), who develop a single, simple example—the towers of Hanoi—all the way up to an animated graphical version.

If you want to use a Smalltalk system, Ingalls et al. (1997) describe Squeak, a free, portable implementation of Smalltalk that is written in Smalltalk itself. To get started, you will want help with the integrated programming environment, which is otherwise overwhelming; consult Black et al. (2009). Or you could try Pharo (Ducasse et al. 2016), a fork that looks better to modern eyes.

If you want something simpler than Smalltalk-80 but more ambitious than μSmalltalk, Budd (1987) describes "Little Smalltalk," which is nearly identical to Smalltalk-80, but which lacks some extras, especially graphics. Budd's book is easier reading than the blue book, and interpreters for Little Smalltalk are available.

No book tells you everything you need to know to become an effective Smalltalk programmer. You must master the class hierarchy, and to gain mastery, you must read and write code. As you write, be guided by Beck (1997), who discusses coding style; Beck's excellent book will help you make your Smalltalk code idiomatic.

Object-oriented programming predates Smalltalk; the first object-oriented language was Simula 67, which introduced objects, classes, and inheritance (Dahl and Hoare 1972; Birtwistle et al. 1973). As its name suggests, Simula 67 was designed with discrete-event simulation in mind. Simula 67 inspired the designers of CLU, Smalltalk, and C++, among others.

Object-oriented languages without classes are rare. The first such language, and still one of the simplest and most innovative, is Self (Ungar and Smith 1987). Another such language, whose semantics is admittedly cluttered with strange behaviors and corner cases, is JavaScript. (Part of the clutter is a `class` keyword, which JavaScript acquired in 2015. Think of `class` as defining a function that creates an object with prototypes and slots.) Underneath the clutter is a language with good bones, which come from Scheme and from Self; for a view of the good parts, see Crockford (2008). And object-oriented programs can be written in a language without objects, provided the language has associative arrays and first-class functions. This idea and the corresponding programming techniques are described in a nice tutorial by Ierusalimschy (2016, chapter 21).

Object-oriented programming has become so popular that many, many programming languages identify as object-oriented or include object-oriented features. C++ (Stroustrup 1997) adds object-oriented features—and many others besides—to C. Objective C also extends C with objects; its object-oriented features look much more like Smalltalk than like C++ (Cox 1986). Objective C was, for many years, the language most often used to write software for Apple products. Modula-3 (Nelson 1991) extends Modula-2 with objects. Modula-3 inspired the development of the scripting language Python (van Rossum 1998) and the general-purpose application language Java (Gosling, Joy, and Steele 1997). Another scripting language, Ruby (Flanagan and Matsumoto 2008), is more directly inspired by Smalltalk.

Many statically typed object-oriented languages, including C++, Modula–3, and Ada 95, mix object-oriented ideas with ideas from abstract data types. Such mixtures can be hard to understand. For a clear, deep analysis of abstract data types, objects, the differences between them, and mixtures thereof, consult Cook (2009). Cook analyzes each set of ideas separately, then applies both to a couple of popular languages, including both Java and Smalltalk. And for a foundational view of these two kinds of abstraction, consult Reynolds (1978).

To understand any language that claims to be both statically typed and object-oriented, you can precede Cook's analysis with a simpler question: Is subtyping distinct from subclassing? If not, then the designer has traded some of the openness and expressivity of object-oriented programming for some other good, like a simple type system. But there are type systems that can handle open languages, even those as flexible as Smalltalk. For example, Graver and Johnson (1990) describe a type system for Smalltalk in which subtyping and subclassing are carefully distinguished. This type system is the basis for an optimizing Smalltalk compiler (Johnson, Graver, and Zurawski 1988).

Behavioral subtyping is described formally by Liskov and Wing (1994), who propose that any definition of subtyping should meet this criterion: if type τ' is considered a subtype of τ, then any property that is provable about objects of type τ must also be true of objects of type τ'. Liskov and Wing provide two definitions of subtyping that meet the criterion.

While inheritance helps build open, extensible systems, it can compromise modularity. Because a subclass can mutate all of a class's representation and can send to any of its private methods, it must understand everything that is going on in the class, lest it violate the class's invariants. Stata (1996) presents the problem and proposes a new programming-language mechanism which expresses the interface between a class and its subclasses, restoring modular reasoning.

Object-orientation continues to inspire the design of new languages. Eiffel, which is described in the excellent book by Meyer (1992), is designed to support a particular object-oriented design methodology (Meyer 1997). Grace (Black et al. 2012) is designed especially for teaching novices. Swift is a successor to Objective C for programming Apple devices (Buttfield-Addison, Manning, and Nugent 2016). Of the languages above, only Objective C, Python, and Ruby share with Smalltalk the property of being dynamically typed; the others are statically typed, or, in the case of Grace, optionally typed. Smalltalk itself can be extended with type checking (Johnson, Graver, and Zurawski 1988).

The object-oriented ideas popularized by Smalltalk were quickly adopted into Lisp. The Flavors system (Cannon 1979; Moon 1986) was developed for MIT's Lisp Machine as a "non-hierarchical" approach to object-oriented programming: a "flavor" takes the place of a class, and a new flavor can be defined by combining several existing flavors. Flavors influenced CommonLoops, a substrate that can be used to absorb ideas from Flavors and from Smalltalk into Common Lisp (Bobrow et al. 1986), and eventually the Common Lisp Object System, an object-oriented extension of Lisp usually called CLOS (Bobrow et al. 1988).

10.15 Exercises

The exercises are arranged by the skill or knowledge they call on (Table 10.36 on the following page). More than in other chapters, the exercises call on knowledge of μSmalltalk's large initial basis. Highlights include new numeric classes and an enhancement to the interpreter.

- Exercises 37 to 39 are the most ambitious exercises in this chapter. You will implement a classic abstraction: full integers of unbounded magnitude. The project is divided into three stages: natural numbers, signed large integers with arithmetic, and finally "mixed arithmetic," which uses small machine integers when possible and transparently switches over to large integers when necessary. These exercises will boost your object-oriented programming skills, and you will understand, from the ground up, an implementation of arithmetic that should be available in every civilized programming language.

Table 10.36: Synopsis of all the exercises, with most relevant sections

Exercises	*Sections*	*Notes*
1	10.1	Using shape classes.
2 to 5	10.1	Defining new shapes and new canvases.
6 and 7	10.1	Creating new classes from scratch (for random numbers, see also §10.4.6).
8 and 9	10.3.4	Messages to `super`: their use for initialization, and their semantics.
10	10.4.1	Equality and object identity.
11 and 12	10.4.2	Redefinition of existing methods using the protocol for all classes: print methods for pictures (§10.4.5); pictures with floating-point coordinates (§10.4.6).
13 to 15	10.4.2	New methods on existing classes: identify metaclasses (§10.11.4), condition on `nil`, hash.
16	10.6	Conditionals as dynamic dispatch: the implementation of class `False`.
17 to 31	10.4.5, 10.7	Modifying existing collections and defining new collections.
32 and 33	10.4.6, 10.7.1, 10.8.2	Make class `Char` a magnitude (§10.4.2); define new magnitudes.
34 to 39	10.4.6, 10.8	Numbers and arithmetic: reasoning about overflow; arithmetic between different classes of numbers; arbitrary-precision arithmetic.
40 and 41	10.10.1, 10.11.2	Method dispatch: understanding its semantics; improving its implementation using a method cache.
42	10.11.2	Object-oriented profiling: finding hot spots by measuring what objects receive what messages.

- Smalltalk's method dispatch might seem inefficient. But many call sites dispatch to the same method over and over—a property that clever implementations exploit. In Exercise 41, you implement a simple *method cache* and measure its effectiveness. The results will surprise you.

10.15.1 Retrieval practice and other short questions

A. In the expression `(c location: 'East)`, what is the receiver? What is the message selector? What is the argument?

B. In the expression `(c location: 'East)`, what is the role of the colon after the word `location`? If the colon were missing, what would go wrong?

C. Why does class `CoordPair` have two protocols (a "class" protocol and an "instance" protocol)? What can you do with the messages in the class protocol? What can you do with the messages in the instance protocol?

D. In a language like C++, `new` signifies a syntactic form. But in Smalltalk, `new` isn't special. When the Smalltalk expression `(List new)` is evaluated, what happens?

E. In the expression `(c location: 'East)`, `c` is an object of class `Circle`, and class `Circle` doesn't define a `location:` method. So when the expression is evaluated, what happens? How does it work?

F. What objects can the message `class` be sent to? What objects can the message `superclass` be sent to?

G. Once a class is defined, can you go back and add, change, or remove methods? How?

H. Message `ifTrue:` is sent to a Boolean, but message `whileTrue:` is sent to a block. Why the difference?

I. In the `drawPolygon:` method implemented on class `TikzCanvas`, what does the expression in square brackets evaluate to? When the resulting object is sent to `coord-list` as an argument to the `do:` message, what happens?

J. A μSmalltalk list is just one form of *collection*—there are others. All collections understand messages that are analogous to the μScheme list functions `map`, `app`, `filter`, `exists?`, and `fold`. What is the Smalltalk analog of each of these list functions?

K. When message `at:ifAbsent:` is sent to a keyed collection, why is the second argument a block?

L. In Smalltalk, every number is a magnitude, but not every magnitude is a number. What's an example of something can you do with a `Number` that you can't do with a `Magnitude`? What's an example of an abstraction that is a magnitude but not a number?

M. How is the message `isNil` implemented without a conditional test?

N. The `Magnitude` protocol offers six relational operators plus operations `min:` and `max:`. But no individual magnitude class has to implement all of them. What operations have to be implemented by subclasses of `Magnitude`, like `Integer` or `Fraction`? And how do things work with the other `Magnitude` operations, which aren't implemented by the subclass?

O. Study how `return` is used in the implementations of methods `isEmpty` and `includes:` on class `Collection`. Each of these methods has a body, which contains one or more nested blocks, one of which contains a `return`. When the `return` is evaluated, what evaluation or evaluations are terminated?

P. To iterate over a list in μScheme, we have to ask the list how it was formed—is it empty or nonempty? Iteration in Smalltalk doesn't have to ask such questions. How is list iteration accomplished instead?

Q. Method `=` on class `Fraction` needs to know the numerator and denominator of both the receiver and the argument. How does the method get the numerator and denominator of the receiver? How does it get the numerator and denominator of the argument?

R. In the semantic judgment $\langle e, \rho, c_{\mathtt{super}}, F, \xi, \sigma, \mathcal{F}\rangle \Downarrow \langle v; \sigma', \mathcal{F}'\rangle$, components e, ρ, ξ, and σ have their familiar roles. What is the role of the component $c_{\mathtt{super}}$?

S. In the semantic judgment $\langle e, \rho, c_{\mathtt{super}}, F, \xi, \sigma, \mathcal{F}\rangle \uparrow \langle v, F'; \sigma', \mathcal{F}'\rangle$, what are the roles of the two frames F and F'? In particular, what happens if those two frames are identical?

T. In the evaluation of an expression of the form $\text{SEND}(m, e, e_1, \ldots, e_n)$, suppose that the evaluation of e_1 returns v to frame F'. Are expressions e_2 to e_n evaluated? What rules of the operational semantics determine the answer?

U. A Smalltalk class is also an object, but in the interpreter, it is represented as an ML record. How does such an object know what its class is? What is the name for the class of such an object?

V. A μSmalltalk literal like `1983` evaluates to an object of class `SmallInteger`. But class `SmallInteger` is itself defined using μSmalltalk code, and that code has to be read by the parser! How is this cyclical dependence resolved? Can anything go wrong?

10.15.2 *Using shape classes*

1. *Draw pictures.* By combining `adjustPoint:to:` with `location:`, you can create pictures without ever having to do vector arithmetic—all the arithmetic is encapsulated in the two methods. Using `adjustPoint:to:`, `location:`, and the other methods defined on shapes and pictures, write Smalltalk code to draw each of these pictures:

   (a)

   (b)

   (c)  (The radii of the circles are in the ratio 9 to 6 to 4.)

10.15.3 *New shapes and canvases*

2. *Implement a new shape.* Using `Square` as a model, implement class `Triangle`.

3. *Reuse code by defining and inheriting from a* `Polygon` *class.* The square and triangle are both polygons, and both can be drawn in the same way, only using different points. Define a new, abstract class `Polygon`, which is a subclass of `Shape`, and which includes a method `points`. When sent the `points` message, a polygon should answer a list of symbols that name the control points that should be drawn.

   (a) Implement `Polygon`. Method `drawOn:` should use method `points`, which should be a subclass responsibility.

   (b) Redefine `Square` and `Triangle` to be subclasses of `Polygon`. The new `Square` and `Triangle` classes should define only the `points` method—all other methods should be inherited from `Polygon`.

   (c) As a subclass of `Polygon`, implement the new shape `Diamond`.

   (d) As subclasses of `Polygon`, implement the new shapes `TriangleRight`, `TriangleLeft`, and `TriangleDown`, whose triangles point left, right, and down.

4. *A scalable canvas.* The `startDrawing` method of class `TikzCanvas` establishes the scale that one unit is rendered as "`4pt`," which means four printer's points, or in LaTeX, about $\frac{4}{72}$ of an inch. Change class `TikzCanvas` so that the size of a unit is an instance variable of the class, and add a class method `withUnit:` that can specify the initial scale. Use a symbol, so that you can specify a scale using any of the units LaTeX understands, as in these examples:

```
(TikzCanvas withUnit: '12pt)
(TikzCanvas withUnit: '1cm)
(TikzCanvas withUnit: '0.5in)
```

   The class method `new` will need to be changed, but sending `new` to class `TikzCanvas` should continue to create a canvas with a scale of `4pt`.

5. *A new class of canvas.* In this problem, you replace `TikzCanvas` with a different back end.

   (a) Learn enough PostScript commands to draw pictures containing polygons and ellipses. For a whole picture, you'll need PostScript commands `%!PS`, `scale`, `setlinewidth`, and `showpage`. For polygons, you'll need `newpath`, `moveto`, `lineto`, `closepath`, and `stroke`. You can draw circles using `arc`, `closepath`, and `stroke`; to draw an ellipse, save the context using `gsave` and `grestore`, then use `scale` to adjust the x and y radii and draw a circle.

   (b) To draw PostScript pictures, define a new class `PSCanvas`. It should implement the same protocol as `TikzCanvas`, and it should produce PostScript.

10.15.4 *Creating new classes from scratch*

6. *An object as a source of random numbers.* For random-number generation, define class `Rand`. An object of class `Rand` should have an internal *seed*, which is an integer, and should respond to the following protocol:

   - Class method `new:` creates a new random-number generator with the given seed.
   - Instance method `next` answers the random number and updates the seed.

   To generate the next random number, use the algorithms from page 124.

7. *Strings.* Define a class `SymbolString` which represents a string of symbols.

   (a) Define a `^` method that concatenates a string or a symbol to a string of symbols. Should class `SymbolString` be mutable or immutable?

   (b) Now extend `Symbol` so that `^` is defined on symbols as well. Should class `Symbol` be mutable or immutable?

10.15.5 *Messages to* `super`

8. *Correct initialization of new pictures.* Section 10.3.4 says that sending `new` to a class should answer a newly allocated object whose state respects the private invariants of the class. One such invariant, of class `Picture`, is that instance variable `shapes` refers to a list of shapes. But the definition of `Picture` in Figure 10.4 simply inherits `new` from `Object`, and `new` returns an *uninitialized* `Picture` object. The definition in Figure 10.4 does not include `new` because in such an early example, I did not want to introduce the technique of sending messages to `super`. Define `new` on class `Picture` so it creates a picture with an empty list of shapes, by sending `empty` to `self`. Then change the `empty` class method to use `super`.

9. *Alternative semantics for* `super`. Suppose `super` were implemented like this: when sending message m to `super`, send it to `self`, but start the method search in the superclass of `self`'s class. Compare this implementation with the way `super` is actually implemented, and explain how they are different. Find an example from this chapter in which the incorrect version does the wrong thing.

   You may find it expedient to implement the incorrect version.

10.15.6 Equality

10. *Object identity for keys in collections.* The collection classes compare keys with equivalence (=). What if you really wanted object identity (==)? You don't have to rewrite all the code. Instead, try the following:

    (a) Define a `Wrapped` class that has the following properties:

    ```
    ((Wrapped new: anObject) value)        == anObject
    ((Wrapped new: x) = (Wrapped new: y)) == (x == y)
    ```

    (b) Define a new collection class that inherits from one of the existing classes, but which overrides methods to use wrapped keys.

10.15.7 Method redefinition

11. *Pictures with non-integer coordinates.* The `print` method in the `CoordPair` class sends the `print` message to instance variables `x` and `y`. As long as `x` and `y` are integers, this works fine, but if they are any other kind of numbers, the syntax that μSmalltalk prints won't be recognized by the LaTeX TikZ package. In this exercise you modify both the `Float` and the `CoordPair` classes to support shapes and positions with non-integer values, using LaTeX syntax.

    (a) Redefine the `print` method on the `Float` class so that it prints `self` as an integer part, followed by a decimal point, followed by two decimal digits, as follows:

    718. ⟨*exercise transcripts* 718⟩≡ 720a ▷

    ```
    -> (69 asFloat)
    69.00
    -> ((-3 / 4) asFloat)
    -0.75
    -> ((314 asFloat) / (100 asFloat))
    3.14
    ```

    To redefine `print`, send `addSelector:withMethod:` to class `Float` with two arguments: the literal symbol `'print` and a `compiled-method` expression with the new method definition.

    (b) Establish a new invariant for class `CoordPair`: that the values of instance variables `x` and `y` are always numbers of class `Float`. Modify only methods of class `CoordPair`, not methods of any other class.

    (c) Make sure the public methods of class `CoordPair` work with arguments of *any* numeric class, not just integers or `Float`s.

12. *More informative* `print` *method for pictures.* The `print` method of class `Picture` would be more interesting if it showed the shapes inside the picture, like so:

    ```
    -> pic
    Picture ( <Circle> <Square> <Triangle> )
    ```

    Make it so. (You might wish to study the `print` method for class `Collection`.)

10.15.8 *New methods on existing classes*

The exercises in the next group explore changes, extensions, and additions to the predefined classes. To modify a predefined class, you have two choices:

- Edit the source code of the interpreter.
- Send the class the `addSelector:withMethod:` message, giving it the method name (as a literal symbol) and a compiled method, as in Exercise 11.

The exercises are as follows:

13. *Method* `isMeta` *for all classes.* In a full Smalltalk system, every class answers the message `isMeta`, saying if it is a metaclass. Define as many `isMeta` methods as you need to, then use reflection to update μSmalltalk's predefined classes so that every *class* object responds appropriately to `isMeta`.

14. *Method* `ifNil:` *for all objects.* In a full Smalltalk system, message `ifNil:` can be sent to any object. The message takes one argument, which is a block. The receiver answers itself, unless the receiver is `nil`, in which case it answers the result of sending `value` to the argument block. Define as many `ifNil:` methods as you need to, then use reflection to update μSmalltalk's predefined classes so that every object responds appropriately to `ifNil:`.

15. *Give every object a* `hash` *method.* In μSmalltalk's predefined classes, only objects of class `Symbol` respond to a `hash` message. Using reflection, update the predefined classes so that *every* object responds to the `hash` message with a small integer. Equal objects must hash to equal values.

10.15.9 *Conditional tests via dynamic dispatch*

16. *Conditional operations on class* `False`. Study the implementation of class `True` in Section 10.6. Write the corresponding definition of class `False`.

10.15.10 *Collections*

17. *Pictures as collections.* A `Picture` is, among other things, a collection of shapes. Perhaps it should understand the entire `Collection` protocol?

    (a) Redefine `Picture` to make it inherit from `Collection`. It could inherit directly from `Collection` or from any of `Collection`'s (transitive) subclasses.

    (b) Which is the better design: `Picture` as defined in Section 10.1, or `Picture` as a specialized collection? Justify your answer.

18. *A class* `Interval` *of integer sequences.* An object of class `Interval` represents a finite sequence of integers in arithmetic progression. The sequence takes the form $[n, n+k, n+2\cdot k, \ldots, n+m\cdot k]$ for some $n > 0$, $k > 0$, and $m \geq 0$. An interval is defined by n, m, and k; intervals are immutable. An interval is a collection and answers the same protocol as any other sequenceable collection, except that it lacks `add:`. `Interval`'s class protocol should provide two initializing methods: `from:to:` and `from:to:by:`. Sending `(from:to:by: Interval` n $(n + m \cdot k)$ k`)` should result in an interval containing the sequence shown above; `(from:to: Interval` n $(n + m)$`)` should use $k = 1$.

    `asFloat` $\mathcal{B}$ 650

    Define class `Interval` as a subclass of `SequenceableCollection`.

19. *Using* `Interval` *for array indices.* Use class `Interval` to implement methods `associationsDo:`, `collect:`, and `select:` on arrays, and to re-implement `do:`.

20. *Class method* `withAll:` *for arrays.* Extend class `Array` with an additional class method `withAll: aCollection`, which makes an array out of the elements of another collection. To add a class method using reflection, you send `addSelector:withMethod:` to `Array`'s *metaclass*, which you get by evaluating `(Array class)`.

21. *Methods* `select:` *and* `collect:` *for arrays.* Add implementations of `select:` and `collect:` to class `Array`.

22. *Collection class* `Bag`. Define the collection class `Bag`. An object of class `Bag` is a grocery bag; it's an unordered collection of elements. Unlike a set, a bag may contain the same element multiple times, as in two cartons of milk; bags are sometimes called *multisets*. A bag has the same protocol as `Set`, and it also answers `count:` by telling how many copies of a given object it holds. For example:

    720a. ⟨*exercise transcripts* 718⟩+≡ ◁718 720b▷

    ```
    -> (val B (Bag new))
    -> (B add: 'milk)
    -> (B add: 'milk)
    -> (B add: 'macaroni)
    -> (B includes: 'milk)
    <True>
    -> (B count: 'milk)
    2
    ```

    Iterating through a bag should visit every item:

    720b. ⟨*exercise transcripts* 718⟩+≡ ◁720a

    ```
    -> (B do: [block (x) ('Bagged: print) (space print) (x println)])
    Bagged: milk
    Bagged: milk
    Bagged: macaroni
    nil
    ```

    Choose `Bag`'s superclass so as to require as little new code as possible, but do not change any existing classes.

23. *Arrays that can change size.* Fixed-size arrays are a nuisance. Using the design in Section 9.6.2 as a model, create an `ArrayList` class that inherits from `SequenceableCollection` and that represents arrays with indices from n to m, inclusive. It should also support the following new messages.

    - Class method `new` should create a new, empty array with $n = 1$ and $m = 0$.
    - Instance method `addlo:` should decrease n by 1 and add its argument in the new slot. Instance method `addhi:` should increase m by 1 and add its argument in the new slot. Method `add:` should be a synonym for `addlo:`.
    - Instance method `remlo` should remove the first element, increase n by 1, and answer the removed element. Instance method `remhi` should remove the last element, decrease m by 1, and answer the removed element.

    Each of these operations should take constant amortized time, as should `at:`.

For ideas about representation, look at the implementation of this abstraction using Molecule (Appendix T).

24. *Lists implemented by arrays.* The `ArrayList` class from Exercise 23 could be used to implement `List`.

    (a) Estimate the space savings for large lists, in both the average case and the worst case.

    (b) Write an implementation.

25. *Complete class* `List`.

    (a) Implement `removeLast` for class `List`.

    (b) Implement `removeKey:ifAbsent:` for lists.

26. *Fix* `at:put:` *on class* `List`. If the index is out of range, the `at:put:` method on class `List` silently produces a wrong answer. What an embarrassment! Please fix it.

    (a) Supplement the existing implementation with an explicit range check.

    (b) Throw away the existing code, and in its place devise a solution that delegates the work to classes `Cons` and `ListSentinel`.

    (c) Compare the two solutions above. Say which you like better and why.

27. *Refactor keyed collections.* Increase code reuse in class `KeyedCollection` by introducing a private method `detectAssociation:ifAbsent:` that takes two blocks as arguments. Then use the new method to implement other methods. Explain why this change might be a good thing even if it makes the code harder to understand. *Hint: What about implementations that use hash tables?*

    Aggressive reuse can divide code into many small methods and distribute them over several classes. Understanding a nontrivial computation may then require understanding of each method and its specification, which can be challenging—but each individual method is simple, easy to understand, and easy to test. In light of this observation, argue whether your change to `KeyedCollection` is an improvement.

28. *Hash tables.* Define a class `Hash` that implements a mutable finite map using a hash table. Objects of class `Hash` should respond to the same protocol as objects of class `Dictionary`, except that a `Hash` object may assume that the `hash` message may be sent to any key. A key object answers the `hash` message with an machine integer that never changes, even if the state of the key changes. Choose a suitable μSmalltalk class to inherit from, and use the representation and the invariants from the hash table in Exercise 34, Chapter 9 (page 598).

29. *Binary-search trees.* Define a class `BST` that implements a mutable finite map using a binary search tree. Objects of class `BST` should respond to the same protocol as objects of class `Dictionary`, except that a `BST` object may assume that keys respond to the `Magnitude` protocol.

30. *Constant-time* `at:ifAbsent:` *for arrays.* Class `Array` inherits `at:ifAbsent:` from `SequenceableCollection`. This implementation costs time linear in the size of the array. Without defining any new primitives, build a new implementation that takes constant time:

    (a) Using `removeSelector:`, remove the definition of `at:` from class `Array`, so it inherits `at:` from `SequenceableCollection`.

(b) On class `Array`, implement `at:ifAbsent:` using primitive `arrayAt` and the other methods of class `Array`.

31. *An iterator for locations in shapes.* In Section 10.1, examine the algorithm for drawing polygons and look at what kinds of intermediate data are allocated. Sending `locations:` to an object of class `Shape` allocates an intermediate list of locations, which is used in `drawPolygon:` on class `Tikzpicture`, then immediately thrown away. Eliminating this sort of allocation often improves performance.

Class `Shape` doesn't have to provide a *list* of the locations; it could equally well provide an *iterator*, with this protocol:

> `locationsDo:with: symbols aBlock`
> For each symbol s in the collection `symbols`, send (`aBlock value:` l), where l is the location of the control point named by symbol s. If s does not name any control point, the result is a checked run-time error.

(a) Extend class `Shape` with a `locationsDo:with:` method.

(b) Suppose that `locations:` were eliminated, so that all client code had to use the `locationsDo:with:` method. What other classes would have to change, in what ways, to continue to draw polygons?

(c) Is there a way to change the other classes so that no intermediate list (or other collection) is allocated? If so, explain what other intermediate objects have to be allocated instead. If not, explain why not.

(d) If your answer to the previous part is "yes, the other classes can be changed," then explain whether you prefer the new design or the original, and why.

10.15.11 New magnitudes

32. *Characters as magnitudes.* In full Smalltalk-80, a character is a `Magnitude`, but in μSmalltalk, it's not. Redefine class `Char` to be a subclass of `Magnitude`. To be sure it implements the full protocol for magnitudes, write unit tests.

33. *More magnitudes.* In μSmalltalk, the only interesting `Magnitudes` are `Numbers`. Don't stop at `Char`—define more `Magnitudes`!

(a) Define `Date` as a subclass of `Magnitude`. A `Date` is given by a month, day, and year. Define a `+` method on `Date` that adds a number of days to the date. This method should know how many days are in each month, and it should also know the rules for leap years (Dershowitz and Reingold 1990, 2018).

(b) Define `Time` as a subclass of `Magnitude`. A `Time` object represents a time on a 24–hour clock. Define a `+` method that adds minutes.

10.15.12 Numbers

34. *Arithmetic overflow in* `Float`. As defined in Section U.5.11, floating-point addition might overflow. Re-implement floating-point addition so that it neither overflows nor loses precision unnecessarily. For example, adding 0.1 to 1 should lose no precision. Try these suggestions:

- Make each exponent as small as it can be without overflowing.
- Use the larger of the two exponents.

35. *Arithmetic overflow in* `Fraction`. In class `Fraction`, could redefining < in terms of - reduce the possibility of overflow? Justify your answer.

36. *Mixed arithmetic with integers and fractions.* This problem explores improvements in the built-in numeric classes, to try to support mixed arithmetic.

    (a) Use reflection to arrange the `Fraction` and `Integer` classes so you can add integers to fractions, subtract integers from fractions, multiply fractions by integers, etc. That is, make it possible to perform arithmetic by sending an integer as an argument to a receiver of class `Fraction`. Minimize the number of methods you add or change.

    (b) Use reflection to change the `Integer` class so you can add fractions to integers—that is, use a fraction as an argument to a + message sent to an integer. This requires much more work than part 36(a). You might be tempted to change the + method to test to see if its argument is an integer or a fraction, then proceed. A better technique is to use *double dispatch* (Section 10.8.3, page 666): the + method does nothing but send a message to its argument, asking the argument to add `self`. The key is that the message encodes the type of `self`. For example, using double dispatch, the + method on `Integer` might be defined this way:

    723. ⟨*double dispatch* 723⟩≡
    ```
    (method + (aNumber)
        (aNumber addIntegerTo: self))
    ```

    The classes `Integer`, `Float`, and `Fraction` would all then define methods for `addIntegerTo:`.

    (c) Complete your work on the `Integer` class so that all the arithmetic operations, including = and <, work on mixed integers and fractions. Minimize the number of new messages you have to introduce. You may wish to use reflection to change or remove some existing methods on `Integer` and `SmallInteger`.

    (d) Finish the job by making `Fraction`'s methods answer an integer whenever the denominator of the fraction is 1.

37. *Arbitrary-precision natural-number arithmetic.* An object of class `Natural` represents a natural number *of any size*; the protocol for natural numbers is shown in Figure 10.22 (page 653). Study the discussion of natural-number arithmetic in Appendix B (page S13). Then study the discussion of object-oriented implementations of natural numbers in Section 10.8.5 (page 669). Finally, implement natural-number arithmetic by completing class `Natural`, which is shown in Figure 10.27 (page 670). You might start by implementing = and < using the other methods of the class, which you can do independent of your choice of representation.

38. *Arbitrary-precision signed-integer arithmetic.* Using a sign-magnitude representation, implement large signed integers as described in Section 10.8.3. Define whatever methods are needed to answer not only the large-integer protocol but also the `Integer`, `Number`, `Magnitude`, and `Object` protocols, except for `div:` and `mod:`. Focus on methods `print`, `isZero`, `isNegative`, `isNonnegative`, `isStrictlyPositive`, `negated`, +, *, and `sdiv:`.

    So that small-integer arguments can be passed to large-integer methods, use reflection to add an `asLargeInteger` method to class `SmallInteger`.

39. *Transparent failover from machine-integer arithmetic to arbitrary-precision arithmetic.* Use reflection to change the definition of class `SmallInteger` such that if arithmetic overflows, the system automatically moves to large integers. Furthermore, make arithmetic between small and large integers work transparently as needed, and make small integers respond to the same `sdiv:` and `smod:` messages that large integers respond to.

    You will need the following primitives:

    - Evaluating `(primitive addWithOverflow self aSmallInteger ovBlock)` computes the sum of the receiver and the argument `aSmallInteger`. If this computation overflows, the result is `ovBlock`; otherwise it is a block that will answer the sum.
    - Evaluating `(primitive subWithOverflow self aSmallInteger ovBlock)` computes the difference of the receiver and the argument `aSmallInteger`. If this computation overflows, the result is `ovBlock`; otherwise it is a block that will answer the difference.
    - Evaluating `(primitive mulWithOverflow self aSmallInteger ovBlock)` computes the product of the receiver and the argument `aSmallInteger`. If this computation overflows, the result is `ovBlock`; otherwise it is a block that will answer the product.

    These primitives require a level of indirection; instead of answering directly with a result, they answer a block capable of returning the result. This property is needed to arrange for the proper execution of the recovery code, but it makes the use of these primitives a bit strange. An example may help; this one includes the analog of the Smalltalk-80 code on page 705:

    724. ⟨*example use of primitives with overflow recovery* 724⟩≡

    ```
    (SmallInteger addSelector:withMethod: '+
       (compiled-method (aNumber) (aNumber addSmallIntegerTo: self)))
    (SmallInteger addSelector:withMethod: 'addSmallIntegerTo:
       (compiled-method (anInteger)
          ((primitive addWithOverflow self anInteger
                            {((self asLargeInteger) + anInteger)}) value)))
    ```

    You might be tempted to test your code against a table of factorials, but factorials are computed using only multiplication. Try Catalan numbers, which can be computed recursively using a combination of multiplication and addition.

10.15.13 Method dispatch

40. *Formal semantics for method dispatch.* Judgment form $m \rhd c \,@\, imp$ describes method dispatch (Section 10.10.1). This form isn't described by proof rules, but it is implemented by function `findMethod` in chunk 690b. Using the implementation as a guide, write proof rules for the judgment.

41. *Method cache.* Because Smalltalk does everything with method dispatch, method dispatch has to be fast. The cost of dispatch can be reduced by *method caching,* as described by Deutsch and Schiffman (1984). Method caching works like this: with each `SEND` form in an abstract-syntax tree, associate a two-word cache. One word gives the class of the last object to receive the message sent, and the other gives the address of the method to which the message was last dispatched. When the message is sent, consult the cache;

if the class of the current receiver is the same as the class of the cached receiver, then execute the cached method; no method search is needed. If the class of the current receiver is different, search for a method in the usual way, update the cache, and execute the method.

Method caching saves time if each `SEND` in the source code usually sends to an object of a single class—which research suggests is true about 95% of the time. Adding a method cache made an early Berkeley Smalltalk system run 37% faster (Conroy and Pelegri-Llopart 1982).

(a) Extend the μSmalltalk interpreter with method caches.

- Define a type `classid` whose value can uniquely identify a class. Since the `class` field of each class is unique, you can start with

```
type classid = metaclass ref
```

- Add a field of type `(classid * method) ref` to the `SEND` form in the abstract syntax. This reference cell should hold a pair representing the unique identifier of the last class to receive the message at this call site, plus the method found on that class.
- Change the parser to initialize each cache. As the initial class identifier, define

```
val invalidId : classid = ref PENDING
```

  Value `invalidId` is guaranteed to be distinct from the `class` field of any class.
- Change function `ev` in chunk 689b to use the cache before calling `findMethod`, and to update the cache afterward (when a method is found). Consider defining a function `findCachedMethod`, whose type might be `(classid * method) ref * name * class -> method`.

(b) Add code to gather statistics about hits and misses, and measure the cache-hit ratio for a variety of programs.

(c) Find or create some long-running μSmalltalk programs, and measure the total speedup obtained by caching. (Because the method cache does not eliminate the overhead of tracing, the speedup will be relatively small. You might want to suppress tracing by adding the definition `fun trace f = f ()`.)

(d) If a μSmalltalk program uses the `setMethod` primitive or any of the reflective facilities that copy methods, it could invalidate a cache. Either eliminate the primitive or correct your implementation so that every use of the primitive invalidates caches that depend on the relevant class. Don't forget that changing a method on class C may invalidate not only caches holding C but also caches holding C's subclasses.

Measure the cost of the additional overhead required to invalidate the caches.

10.15.14 *Object-oriented profiling*

42. *Profiling.* Implement a message-send profiler that counts the number of times each message is sent to each class. Use this profiler to identify hot spots in the simulation code from Appendix E.

Afterword contents

Afterword

It's a magical world, Hobbes, ol' buddy... let's go exploring!

Calvin

Congratulations! You now have some solid skills using functions, types, modules, objects, and more. You also have a cognitive framework that you can use to learn new programming languages, and if you're like my students, you'll be pleasantly surprised at how broadly your skills apply. Now you get the dessert menu. As your server, I recommend some tasty treats: languages that are superlative, unusual, or popular. Many are widely recognized as interesting or important, and some are just to my personal taste. Together, they offer a variety of jumping-off points, ranging from younger, less proven ideas to fashionable ideas drawn from the headlines.

TYPEFUL PROGRAMMING

If you like types, try **Haskell**. Haskell is a *pure* functional language: even I/O interactions are represented as values with special `IO` types. And Haskell is pushing new type-system ideas into the mainstream far faster than any other language. By the time this book is published, Haskell will have cool new features I haven't even heard of yet. Start with the basics: *type classes* and *monads* (Lipovača 2011). Definitely try QuickCheck (Claessen and Hughes 2000; Hughes 2016), which uses Prolog-like inference rules to do amazing things with random testing. And don't overlook QuickCheck's `shrink` function—although it's barely mentioned in the original paper, it's a crucial part. After that, explore what Stephanie Weirich and Richard Eisenberg are doing.

Dependent types can express many interesting properties of data. The classic example uses types to keep track of how long a list is, without losing polymorphism. Interesting dependently typed languages include **Idris** and **Agda**. The **Epigram** language is less active, but its papers and tutorials are very good (McBride 2004).

Types are also being used to manage memory: types can enable safe, fast systems programming without (much) garbage collection. Look into **Rust**, and check out earlier work on **Cyclone** (Grossman et al. 2005).

PROPOSITIONS AS TYPES

Early in the twenty-first century, proofs about correctness start with the principle of *propositions as types*.

Propositions in classical logic correspond to types in a functional language (See Table AW.1 on the next page). In logic, symbols A and B represent propositions;

Table AW.1: Elements of classical logic with their counterparts in types

	Proposition	*Type*	
Conjunction	$A \wedge B$	$A \times B$	Pair
Disjunction	$A \vee B$	$A + B$	Sum
Implication	$A \supset B$	$A \to B$	Function
Complement	$\neg A$	—	(no counterpart)
Quantification	$\forall \alpha . A$	$\forall \alpha . A$	Polymorphism
Truth	$\top$	$\mathbb{1}$	Unit
Falsehood	$\bot$	`void`	Uninhabited

in language, A and B represent types. *Derivations* in logic also correspond to derivations in type theory. For example, in logic, $A \wedge B$ is proved by proving both A and B. And in language, a term of type $A \times B$ is introduced using terms of types A and B. The derivations end in analogous steps; and-introduction corresponds to pair-introduction:

$$\frac{T \vdash A \qquad T \vdash B}{T \vdash A \wedge B} \qquad\qquad \frac{\Gamma \vdash e_1 : A \qquad \Gamma \vdash e_2 : B}{\Gamma \vdash (e_1, e_2) : A \times B}.$$

In logic, symbol T represents a *theory,* and it lists all the propositions whose truth is assumed. In language, symbol Γ represents a *typing context,* and it lists all the types whose inhabitation is assumed. (The context gives a variable of each type, and the type is inhabited by the value of that variable.)

As another example, in logic, $A \supset B$ (implication) is proved by assuming A, then using the assumption of A to prove B. In language, a value of type $A \to B$ is created by defining a function that takes a value of type A, then uses the value to produce a result of type B. Again, the derivations end in analogous steps:

$$\frac{T, A \vdash B}{T \vdash A \supset B} \qquad\qquad \frac{\Gamma, x : A \vdash e : B}{\Gamma \vdash \lambda x : A . e : A \to B}.$$

Almost every classical logical connective corresponds to a type constructor, except one: logical complement. Programming-language types correspond to what is called *constructive* or *intuitionistic* logic, which doesn't have complement. Like Prolog (Appendix D), constructive logic concerns itself not with what is true, but with what is provable. And the provable *is* the computable.

- A *type* in a programming language corresponds to a *proposition* in logic.
- A *term* in a programming language corresponds to a *proof* in logic. But caution! For the proof to be good, the term must evaluate to completion. So such proofs are written using languages in which *all* evaluations are guaranteed to terminate. Such languages resemble one that you already know: if `val-rec` and `letrec` are removed from Typed μScheme, then the evaluation of any well-typed expression is guaranteed to terminate.

The propositions-as-types principle has led to a host of automated theorem provers that are also programming languages. In the late 1980s, this idea was popularized by Nuprl (Constable et al. 1985); in the early 2020s, much work is done in **Coq/Gallina**. These systems are generally considered "proof assistants" rather than "programming languages," but the line is blurry; for example, similar proofs can be written in the dependently typed languages **Agda** and **Idris**.

For deep mathematical background on the connections between propositions and types, as well as connections to decidability and models of computation, read Wadler (2015). To use your knowledge of functional programming to start proving theorems for yourself in Coq, tackle *Software Foundations* (Pierce et al. 2016).

MORE FUNCTIONS

Among functional languages, **OCaml** includes some interesting design experiments, and it's cool among systems programmers, financial engineers, and many academics. **Clojure** brings Lisp ideas to the Java Virtual Machine, with interesting support for multithreading (Hickey 2020). There's also Haskell of course, and you ought to play with **Racket**, which pushes Scheme and macros to the limit. Racket isn't just a language or a system; it's a factory for making new languages (Flatt 2012).

MORE OBJECTS

Objects are everywhere. If you know Smalltalk, you almost know **Ruby**, but the programming environment is very different. The difference is this: Squeak Smalltalk gives you a lovely graphical programming environment, but it's not really connected to anything else on your computer. It's like having a fabulous house—on Mars. Ruby gives you the same fabulous language, but right next door. Or you could try **Pharo**, which nicely integrates the Smalltalk language and programming environment into a modern operating system.

Then there are the hybrids. **Objective C** seems most faithful to Smalltalk's vision. If you prefer complexity to simplicity, you're ready for **Python**. Add more static types and you have **Java**, **C#**, **C++**, **Swift**, and many other popular languages.

More interesting languages provide objects with *prototypes* instead of classes. **Self** is the original and a great place to start (Ungar and Smith 1987). Once you have the ideas, you can apply them in **JavaScript**, whose good parts combine ideas from Scheme and Self (Crockford 2008), and in **Lua**, a great scripting language mentioned below.

FUNCTIONS AND OBJECTS, TOGETHER

Lots of designers have put functions and objects together in a single language. **OCaml** was an early player, combining what was then known about objects and functions into a single system. More ambitious efforts include **Scala** and **F#**, each of which integrates an existing object-oriented type system (respectively the Java Virtual Machine and the Microsoft Common Language Runtime) with ideas from functional programming.

FUNCTIONAL ANIMATION

A *functional reactive animation* is a program that implements animation or even interaction using pure functional code. A very nice exemplar is the **Elm** programming language. It runs right in your web browser, and there's a great community.

SCRIPTING

My favorite scripting language is **Lua**. It is lean, fast, and simple—what Scheme might have been if it had used Pascal's syntax, if it had no macros, and if its central data structure were the mutable hash table, not the cons cell. Lua tables work both as arrays and as hash tables, and they also serve as (prototype-based) objects! Lua ships with a nice, simple string-processing library. And Lua is an *embedded* language: it can easily talk to any library written in C, and it can be dropped into any C or C++ program and be used for scripting and control. For example, Lua scripts make up most of the code in Adobe Lightroom. Lua is described by a fine book (Ierusalimschy 2016) and a nice paper about its design and history (Ierusalimschy, de Figueiredo, and Celes 2007).

PARALLEL AND DISTRIBUTED COMPUTATION

If you want programs to run in parallel, and especially if you want programs to run distributed over multiple computers, try **Erlang**. It's got a simple, effective message-passing model of concurrency, plus great ideas about recovering from failure—and if you're distributing computations, you have to worry about failure. And Erlang is easy to pick up; it uses Prolog's syntax and data, but its computational model is a lot like Scheme.

For more message-passing concurrency, but with a very different flavor, try **Go**. Go's primary mission is to "make systems programming fun again," and the concurrency model is sweet.

ONE WEIRD, COOL, DOMAIN-SPECIFIC LANGUAGE

The language **Inform7** is designed for writing interactive fiction, or, as we used to call it, text adventure games (ATTACK DRAGON WITH BARE HANDS and all that). An Inform7 program doesn't even look like a program; it looks like a cross between a manual and a text adventure game. And Inform7 ships with a really interesting interactive programming environment. I'm still wondering exactly what the abstract syntax of Inform7 is—or if it even uses an abstract syntax—but if you have any interest in this domain, you have to try it.

STACK-BASED LANGUAGES

Chapter 3 uses an evaluation stack to implement μScheme+, but the stack is hidden from the programmer. Why not expose it? The classic stack-based language is **Forth**, which gets extraordinary power from a minimal design. A Forth environment can fit in a few kilobytes of RAM, and Forth has been used on many embedded systems. For a nice example, check out the Open Firmware project.

If you like your stacks with a few more data types, write some **PostScript**. Sweep away all the primitives related to fonts and graphics, and you'll find a very nice stack-based language underneath. Even the current environment is represented as a stack, and by manipulating it, you can quickly change the meanings of names *en masse*.

ARRAY LANGUAGES

While John McCarthy was developing his list-based language, Ken Iverson (1962) was developing the array-based language **APL**. (Both later received Turing Awards.) Derived from notation used at the blackboard, APL evolved into an important language at IBM, where it was written by using a special typeball on IBM's Selectric typewriter. At a time when almost all IBM's mainframe business meant programming with punched cards, APL gave IBM a powerful interactive option. APL originated many ideas that were fully developed in functional languages, including maps, filters, and folds. You can also check out Iverson's successor language, **J**, which may look like line noise, but which runs on ordinary computers. Both APL and J enable you to define array functions that are polymorphic not just in the size of an array, but in the number of its dimensions. This behavior can be explained using a modern, static type system of the sort you have mastered (Slepak, Shivers, and Manolios 2014).

LANGUAGES BASED ON SUBSTITUTION

When you instantiate a polymorphic type in Typed μScheme, you have to implement capture-avoiding substitution (Section 6.6.7, page 371). That same substitution is the computational engine behind lambda calculus. Substitution is hard to get right, hard to reason about, and inefficient. So it's astounding how many eminent computer scientists—and uneducated hackers—have designed languages around substitution. Notable examples include TEX (used to typeset this book); Tcl/Tk (used to make GUIs quickly); the POSIX, Bourne, Korn, and Bourne Again shells (used to script Unix systems), and PHP (used to make web pages). Each of these languages does something well, but for general-purpose programming, they are no fun. For Facebook, PHP is so much not fun that Facebook has developed a language called Hack, which embraces legacy PHP code while adding static types—a real language-design feat.

A related language, based more on string rewriting, was TRAC (Mooers 1966); if you're intrigued by text macros, as opposed to syntax macros, it's worth a look. A clone of TRAC, MINT (for MINT Is Not TRAC), shipped as the extension language of Russ Nelson's Emacs clone, Freemacs.

STRING-PROCESSING LANGUAGES

Domain-specific languages for string processing are in decline, but **Icon** is worth looking at: it uses a *string scanning* technique that relies on a backtracking evaluation model just like the one used in Prolog. Unlike regular expressions, string scanning can be extended with custom string-processing abstractions, and they compose nicely with the built-in abstractions.

For historical interest only, I recommend **Awk**, which was important early and for a long time, although it is both dominated and superseded by later languages. The code I once wrote in Awk I now write in Lua.

Also relegated to historical interest is Perl, which has first-class functions like Scheme, multiple name spaces like Impcore, and string processing based on regular expressions. Perl has become unfashionable, but there is plenty of legacy Perl code out there—to which your skills apply.

CONCLUSION

It really is a magical world. Go exploring!

Bibliography

Harold Abelson and Gerald Jay Sussman. 1985. *Structure and Interpretation of Computer Programs*. New York: McGraw-Hill.

Alfred V. Aho, Brian W. Kernighan, and Peter J. Weinberger. 1988. *The AWK Programming Language*. Reading, MA: Addison-Wesley.

Alfred V. Aho, Monica S. Lam, Ravi Sethi, and Jeffrey D. Ullman. 2007. *Compilers: Principles, Techniques, and Tools*, 2nd ed. Boston: Pearson.

Alfred V. Aho and Jeffrey D. Ullman. 1972. *The Theory of Parsing, Translation, and Compiling*. Upper Saddle River, NJ: Prentice Hall.

Hassan Aït-Kaci. 1991. *Warren's Abstract Machine: A Tutorial Reconstruction*. Cambridge, MA: MIT Press.

Lloyd Allison. 1986. *A Practical Introduction to Denotational Semantics*. Cambridge: Cambridge University Press.

ANSI. 1998. *American National Standards for Information Systems, INCITS 319-1998, Information Technology—Programming Languages—Smalltalk*. New York: American National Standard Institute.

Andrew W. Appel. 1989 (February). Simple generational garbage collection and fast allocation. *Software—Practice & Experience*, 19(2):171–183.

Andrew W. Appel. 1992. *Compiling with Continuations*. Cambridge: Cambridge University Press.

Andrew W. Appel. 1998. *Modern Compiler Implementation*. Cambridge: Cambridge University Press. Available in three editions: C, Java, and ML.

Zena M. Ariola, Huge Herbelin, and David Herman. 2011 (May). A robust implementation of delimited control. In *Theory and Practice of Delimited Continuations Workshop*, pages 6–19.

Kenichi Asai and Oleg Kiselyov. 2011 (September). Introduction to programming with shift and reset. Notes for tutorial given at the ACM SIGPLAN Continuation Workshop.

John Backus. 1978 (August). Can programming be liberated from the Von Neumann style?: A functional style and its algebra of programs. *Communications of the ACM*, 21 (8):613–641.

David F. Bacon, Clement R. Attanasio, Han B. Lee, V. T. Rajan, and Stephen Smith. 2001 (May). Java without the coffee breaks: A nonintrusive multiprocessor garbage collector. *SIGPLAN Notices*, 36(5):92–103.

Henry G. Baker. 1978 (April). List processing in real-time on a serial computer. *Communications of the ACM*, 21(4):280–294.

W. Barrett, R. Bates, D. Gustafson, and J. Couch. 1986. *Compiler Construction: Theory and Practice*, 2nd ed. Chicago: SRA.

Joel F. Bartlett. 1988 (February). Compacting garbage collection with ambiguous roots. Technical Report 88/2, DEC WRL, Palo Alto.

Marianne Baudinet and David MacQueen. 1985 (December). Tree pattern matching for ML (extended abstract). Unpublished manuscript, AT&T Bell Laboratories.

Kent Beck. 1997. *Smalltalk Best Practice Patterns*. Upper Saddle River, NJ: Prentice Hall.

Jon Bentley. 1983 (December). Programming pearls: Writing correct programs. *Communications of the ACM*, 26(12):1040–1045. Reprinted by Bentley (2000, chapter 4).

Jon Bentley. 2000. *Programming Pearls*, 2nd ed. Reading, MA: Addison-Wesley.

Jon L. Bentley and Robert Sedgewick. 1997. Fast algorithms for sorting and searching strings. In *Proceedings of the Eighth Annual ACM-SIAM Symposium on Discrete Algorithms, New Orleans, Louisiana, January 5–7, 1997*, pages 360–369.

Jon L. Bentley and Robert Sedgewick. 1998 (April). Ternary search trees. *Dr. Dobb's Journal*.

Nick Benton and Andrew Kennedy. 2001 (July). Exceptional syntax. *Journal of Functional Programming*, 11(4):395–410.

Richard Bird and Philip Wadler. 1988. *Introduction to Functional Programming*. New York: Prentice Hall.

G. M. Birtwistle, O.-J. Dahl, B. Myhrhaug, and K. Nygaard. 1973. *Simula Begin*. New York: Van Nostrand-Reinhold.

Andrew Black, Stéphane Ducasse, Oscar Nierstrasz, Damien Pollet, Damien Cassou, and Markus Denker. 2009. *Squeak by Example*. Square Bracket Associates. Available under a Creative Commons license.

Andrew P. Black, Kim B. Bruce, Michael Homer, and James Noble. 2012. Grace: The absence of (inessential) difficulty. In *Proceedings of the ACM International Symposium on New Ideas, New Paradigms, and Reflections on Programming and Software*, Onward! 2012, pages 85–98.

Andrew P. Black, Stéphane Ducasse, Oscar Nierstrasz, and Damien Pollet. 2010. *Pharo by Example (Version 2010-02-01)*. Square Bracket Associates.

Stephen M. Blackburn, Perry Cheng, and Kathryn S. McKinley. 2004 (June). Myths and realities: The performance impact of garbage collection. *SIGMETRICS Performance Evaluation Review*, 32(1):25–36.

D. G. Bobrow, L. G. DeMichiel, R. P. Gabriel, S. E. Keene, G. Kiczales, and D. A. Moon. 1988 (September). Common Lisp object system specification. *ACM SIGPLAN Notices*, 23(SI).

Daniel G. Bobrow, Ken Kahn, Gregor Kiczales, Larry Masinter, M. Stefik, and F. Zdybel. 1986 (November). Common Loops, merging Lisp and object-oriented programming. *ACM SIGPLAN Notices*, 21(11): 17–29.

Hans-Juergen Boehm and Mark Weiser. 1988 (September). Garbage collection in an uncooperative environment. *Software—Practice & Experience*, 18(9):807–820. As of 2022, this collector continues to be maintained; see `https://www.hboehm.info/gc/`.

George Boole. 1847. *The mathematical analysis of logic*. Cambridge: Macmillan, Barclay, & Macmillan. Project Gutenberg ebook number 36884.

Per Brinch Hansen. 1994 (June). Multiple-length division revisited: A tour of the minefield. *Software—Practice & Experience*, 24(6):579–601.

Frederick P. Brooks, Jr. 1975. *The Mythical Man-Month*. Reading, MA: Addison-Wesley.

Carl Bruggeman, Oscar Waddell, and R. Kent Dybvig. 1996 (May). Representing control in the presence of one-shot continuations. *Proceedings of the ACM SIGPLAN '96 Conference on Programming Language Design and Implementation*, in *SIGPLAN Notices*, 31(5):99–107.

Timothy Budd. 1987. *A Little Smalltalk*. Reading, MA: Addison-Wesley.

W. H. Burge. 1975. *Recursive Programming Techniques*. Reading, MA: Addison-Wesley.

R. M. Burstall, J. S. Collins, and R. J. Popplestone. 1971. *Programming in POP-2*. Edinburgh: Edinburgh University Press.

Rod M. Burstall, David B. MacQueen, and Donald T. Sannella. 1980 (August). Hope: An experimental applicative language. In *Conference Record of the 1980 LISP Conference*, pages 136–143.

Paris Buttfield-Addison, Jon Manning, and Tim Nugent. 2016. *Learning Swift: Building Apps for OS X and iOS*. O'Reilly.

Lawrence Byrd. 1980. Understanding the control flow of Prolog programs. In S.-A. Tarnlund, editor, *Proceedings of the Logic Programming Workshop*, pages 127–138. See also University of Edinburgh Technical Report 151.

Byte. 1981 (August). Special issue on Smalltalk. *Byte Magazine*, 6(8). Can be downloaded from `archive.org`.

Howard I. Cannon. 1979. Flavors: A non-hierarchical approach to object-oriented programming. Unnumbered, draft technical report, variously attributed to the MIT AI Lab or to Symbolics, Inc.

Luca Cardelli. 1987 (April). Basic polymorphic typechecking. *Science of Computer Programming*, 8(2):147–172.

Luca Cardelli. 1989 (February). Typeful programming. In E. J. Neuhold and M. Paul, editors, *Formal Description of Programming Concepts*, IFIP State of the Art Reports Series. Springer-Verlag. Also appeared as DEC SRC Research Report 45.

Luca Cardelli. 1997. Type systems. In Allen B. Tucker, Jr., editor, *The Computer Science and Engineering Handbook*, chapter 103, pages 2208–2236. Boca Raton, FL: CRC Press.

Luca Cardelli, James Donahue, Lucille Glassman, Mick Jordan, Bill Kalsow, and Greg Nelson. 1992 (August). Modula-3 language definition. *SIGPLAN Notices*, 27(8):15–42.

Craig Chambers. 1992 (March). *The Design and Implementation of the SELF Compiler, an Optimizing Compiler for Object-Oriented Programming Languages.* PhD thesis, Stanford University, Stanford, California. Tech Report STAN-CS-92-1420.

Craig Chambers and David Ungar. 1989 (July). Customization: Optimizing compiler technology for SELF, a dynamically-typed object-oriented programming language. *Proceedings of the ACM SIGPLAN '89 Conference on Programming Language Design and Implementation,* in *SIGPLAN Notices,* 24(7):146–160.

C. J. Cheney. 1970. A nonrecursive list compacting algorithm. *Communications of the ACM,* 13(11):677–78.

Koen Claessen and John Hughes. 2000 (September). QuickCheck: A lightweight tool for random testing of Haskell programs. *Proceedings of the Fifth ACM SIGPLAN International Conference on Functional Programming (ICFP'00),* in *SIGPLAN Notices,* 35(9):268–279.

William Clinger, Anne H. Hartheimer, and Eric M. Ost. 1999. Implementation strategies for first-class continuations. *Higher-Order and Symbolic Computation,* 12(1):7–45.

William D. Clinger. 1998 (May). Proper tail recursion and space efficiency. *Proceedings of the ACM SIGPLAN '98 Conference on Programming Language Design and Implementation,* in *SIGPLAN Notices,* 33(5):174–185.

W. F. Clocksin and C. S. Mellish. 2013. *Programming in Prolog,* 5th ed. Springer.

Jacques Cohen. 1988 (January). A view of the origins and development of Prolog. *Communications of the ACM,* 31(1):26–36.

A. Colmerauer, H. Kanoui, R. Pasero, and P. Roussel. 1973 (November). Un systeme de communication homme-machine en Français. Technical Report, Groupe d'Intelligence Artificielle, Université d'Aix-Marseille II.

Thomas J. Conroy and Eduardo Pelegri-Llopart. 1982. An assessment of method-lookup caches for Smalltalk-80 implementations. In *Smalltalk-80: Bits of History, Words of Advice,* chapter 13, pages 239–247. Reading, MA: Addison-Wesley.

R. L. Constable, S. F. Allen, H. M. Bromley, W. R. Cleaveland, J. F. Cremer, R. W. Harper, D. J. Howe, T. B. Knoblock, N. P. Mendler, P. Panangaden, J. T. Sasaki, and S. F. Smith. 1985. *Implementing Mathematics with the Nuprl Proof Development System.* Prentice Hall.

William R. Cook. 2009 (October). On understanding data abstraction, revisited. *OOPSLA 2009 Conference Proceedings,* in *SIGPLAN Notices,* 44(10):557–572.

Brad J. Cox. 1986. *Object-Oriented Programming—an Evolutionary Approach.* Reading, MA: Addison-Wesley.

Marcus Crestani and Michael Sperber. 2010 (September). Experience Report: Growing programming languages for beginning students. *Proceedings of the Fifteenth ACM SIGPLAN International Conference on Functional Programming (ICFP'10),* in *SIGPLAN Notices,* 45(9):229–234.

Douglas Crockford. 2008. *JavaScript: The Good Parts.* O'Reilly.

Ole-Johan Dahl, Edsger W. Dijkstra, and C. A. R. Hoare. 1972. *Structured Programming.* London and New York: Academic Press.

Ole-Johan Dahl and C. A. R. Hoare. 1972. Hierarchical program structures. In *Structured Programming,* chapter 3, pages 175–220. London and New York: Academic Press.

Luis Damas and Robin Milner. 1982. Principal type-schemes for functional programs. In *Conference Record of the 9th Annual ACM Symposium on Principles of Programming Languages,* pages 207–212.

Olivier Danvy. 2006 (October). *An Analytical Approach to Programs as Data Objects.* DSc thesis, BRICS Research Series, University of Aarhus, Aarhus, Denmark.

Olivier Danvy and Andrzej Filinski. 1990. Abstracting control. In *Proceedings of the 1990 ACM Conference on LISP and Functional Programming,* LFP '90, pages 151–160.

Nachum Dershowitz and Edward M Reingold. 1990. Calendrical calculations. *Software—Practice & Experience,* 20(9):899–928.

Nachum Dershowitz and Edward M Reingold. 2018. *Calendrical Calculations,* 4th ed. Cambridge: Cambridge University Press.

L. Peter Deutsch and Daniel G. Bobrow. 1976 (September). An efficient, incremental, automatic garbage collector. *Communications of the ACM,* 19(9):522–526.

Peter Deutsch and Alan M. Schiffman. 1984 (January). Efficient implementation of the Smalltalk-80 system. In *Conference Record of the 11th Annual ACM Symposium on Principles of Programming Languages,* pages 297–302.

Stephan Diehl, Pieter H. Hartel, and Peter Sestoft. 2000 (May). Abstract machines for programming language implementation. *Future Generation Computer Systems*, 2000 (nr. 7):739–751.

Edsger W. Dijkstra. 1968 (March). Letters to the editor: Go to statement considered harmful. *Communications of the ACM*, 11 (3):147–148.

Edsger W. Dijkstra. 1976. *A Discipline of Programming*. Englewood Cliffs, NJ: Prentice Hall.

Edsger W. Dijkstra, Leslie Lamport, A. J. Martin, C. S. Scholten, and E. F. M. Steffens. 1978 (November). On-the-fly garbage collection: An exercise in cooperation. *Communications of the ACM*, 21(11): 966–975.

S. Drew, K. John Gough, and J. Ledermann. 1995. Implementing zero overhead exception handling. Technical Report 95-12, Faculty of Information Technology, Queensland University of Technology, Brisbane, Australia.

Derek Dreyer, Karl Crary, and Robert Harper. 2003 (January). A type system for higher-order modules. *Conference Record of the 30th Annual ACM Symposium on Principles of Programming Languages,* in *SIGPLAN Notices*, 38(1):236–249.

Derek Dreyer, Robert Harper, Manuel M. T. Chakravarty, and Gabriele Keller. 2007. Modular type classes. In *Proceedings of the 34th Annual ACM Symposium on Principles of Programming Languages*, pages 63–70.

Stéhane Ducasse, Dmitri Zagidulin, Nicolai Hess, and Dimitris Chloupis. 2016. *Pharo by Example 5*. Square Bracket Associates. Available under a Creative Commons license.

R. Kent Dybvig. 1987. *The SCHEME Programming Language*. Upper Saddle River, NJ: Prentice Hall.

R. Kent Dybvig, Robert Hieb, and Carl Bruggeman. 1992 (December). Syntactic abstraction in Scheme. *Lisp and Symbolic Computation*, 5(4):295–326.

Sebastian Egner. 2002 (June). Notation for specializing parameters without currying. SRFI 26, in the Scheme Requests for Implementation series.

Matthias Felleisen. 1988. The theory and practice of first-class prompts. In *Conference Record of the 15th Annual ACM Symposium on Principles of Programming Languages*, pages 180–190.

Matthias Felleisen, Robert Bruce Findler, and Matthew Flatt. 2009. *Semantics Engineering with PLT Redex*. MIT Press.

Matthias Felleisen, Robert Bruce Findler, Matthew Flatt, and Shriram Krishnamurthi. 2018. *How to Design Programs: An Introduction to Programming and Computing*, 2nd ed. Cambridge, MA: MIT Press.

Matthias Felleisen and Daniel P. Friedman. 1997 (December). *The Little MLer*. Cambridge, MA: MIT Press.

Robert R. Fenichel and Jerome C. Yochelson. 1969. A LISP garbage-collector for virtual-memory computer systems. *Communications of the ACM*, 12(11):611–12.

Andrzej Filinski. 1994. Representing monads. In *Conference Record of the 21st Annual ACM Symposium on Principles of Programming Languages*, POPL '94, pages 446–457.

Kathi Fisler. 2014. The recurring rainfall problem. In *Proceedings of the Tenth Annual Conference on International Computing Education Research*, ICER '14, pages 35–42.

David Flanagan and Yukihiro Matsumoto. 2008. *The Ruby Programming Language*. O'Reilly.

Matthew Flatt. 2012 (January). Creating languages in racket. *Communications of the ACM*, 55(1):48–56.

Matthew Flatt. 2016 (January). Bindings as sets of scopes. *Conference Record of the 43rd Annual ACM Symposium on Principles of Programming Languages,* in *SIGPLAN Notices*, 51(1):705–717.

Matthew Flatt, Ryan Culpepper, David Darais, and Robert Bruce Findler. 2012. Macros that work together. *Journal of Functional Programming*, 22:181–216.

Matthew Flatt and Matthias Felleisen. 1998 (May). Units: Cool modules for HOT languages. *Proceedings of the ACM SIGPLAN '98 Conference on Programming Language Design and Implementation,* in *SIGPLAN Notices*, 33(5):236–248.

Christopher W. Fraser and David R. Hanson. 1995. *A Retargetable C Compiler: Design and Implementation*. Redwood City, CA: Benjamin/Cummings.

Daniel P. Friedman and Matthias Felleisen. 1996. *The Little Schemer*, 4th ed. MIT Press.

Daniel P. Friedman, Christopher T. Haynes, and Eugene E. Kohlbecker. 1984. Programming with continuations. In P. Pepper, editor, *Program Transformation and Programming Environments*, pages 263–274. Springer-Verlag.

Emden Gansner and John Reppy, editors. 2002. *The Standard ML Basis Library*. New York: Cambridge University Press.

Martin Gasbichler and Michael Sperber. 2002. Final shift for call/cc: Direct implementation of shift and reset. In *Proceedings of the Seventh ACM SIGPLAN International Conference on Functional Programming (ICFP'02)*, pages 271–282.

Jeremy Gibbons and Geraint Jones. 1998 (September). The under-appreciated unfold. *Proceedings of the 1998 ACM SIGPLAN International Conference on Functional Programming*, in *SIGPLAN Notices*, 34(1):273–279.

A. Goldberg. 1983. *Smalltalk-80: The Interactive Programming Environment*. Reading, MA: Addison-Wesley.

Adele Goldberg and David Robson. 1983. *Smalltalk-80: The Language and Its Implementation*. Reading, MA: Addison-Wesley.

James Gosling, Bill Joy, and Guy Steele. 1997. *The Java Language Specification*. The Java Series. Reading, MA: Addison-Wesley.

Paul Graham. 1993. *On Lisp: Advanced Techniques for Common Lisp*. Upper Saddle River, NJ: Prentice Hall. May be downloadable from `http://www.paulgraham.com/onlisp.html`.

Justin O. Graver and Ralph E. Johnson. 1990. A type system for Smalltalk. In *Conference Record of the 17th Annual ACM Symposium on Principles of Programming Languages*, pages 136–150.

David Gries. 1981. *The Science of Programming*. Springer-Verlag.

Ralph E. Griswold and Madge T. Griswold. 1996. *The Icon Programming Language*, 3rd ed. San Jose, CA: Peer-to-Peer Communications.

Dan Grossman, Michael Hicks, Trevor Jim, and Greg Morrisett. 2005 (January). Cyclone: A type-safe dialect of C. *C/C++ Users Journal*, 23(1).

Dirk Grunwald and Benjamin G. Zorn. 1993 (August). CustoMalloc: Efficient synthesized memory allocators. *Software—Practice & Experience*, 23(8):851–869.

David R. Hanson. 1996. *C Interfaces and Implementations*. Reading, MA: Addison-Wesley.

Robert Harper. 1986 (September). Introduction to Standard ML. Technical Report ECS–LFCS–86–14, Laboratory for the Foundations of Computer Science, Edinburgh University, Edinburgh.

Robert Harper. 2011. Programming in Standard ML. Book draft licensed under Creative Commons. Best sought from Harper's home page at Carnegie Mellon University.

Robert Harper and Mark Lillibridge. 1994 (January). A type-theoretic approach to higher-order modules with sharing. In *Conference Record of the 21st Annual ACM Symposium on Principles of Programming Languages*, pages 123–137.

Robert Harper and Christopher Stone. 2000. A type-theoretic interpretation of Standard ML. In Gordon Plotkin, Colin Stirling, and Mads Tofte, editors, *Proof, Language and Interaction: Essays in Honour of Robin Milner*. Cambridge, MA: MIT Press.

Robert W. Harper. 2012. *Practical Foundations for Programming Languages*. Cambridge: Cambridge University Press.

Brian Harvey and Matthew Wright. 1994. *Simply Scheme: Introducing Computer Science*. Cambridge, MA: MIT Press.

Christopher T. Haynes, Daniel P. Friedman, and Mitchell Wand. 1984. Continuations and coroutines. In *Proceedings of the 1984 ACM Symposium on LISP and Functional Programming*, pages 293–298.

Greg Hendershott. 2020. Fear of macros. URL `http://www.greghendershott.com/fear-of-macros/`. Tutorial from the author's web site.

Peter Henderson. 1980. *Functional Programming: Application and Implementation*. Englewood Cliffs, NJ: Prentice Hall.

Matthew Hertz and Emery D. Berger. 2005 (October). Quantifying the performance of garbage collection vs. explicit memory management. *OOPSLA '05 Conference Proceedings*, in *SIGPLAN Notices*, 40(10):313–326.

Rich Hickey. 2020 (June). A history of Clojure. *Proceedings of the ACM on Programming Languages*, 4(HOPL).

Robert Hieb, R. Kent Dybvig, and Carl Bruggeman. 1990 (June). Representing control in the presence of first-class continuations. *Proceedings of the ACM SIGPLAN '90 Conference on Programming Language Design and Implementation*, in *SIGPLAN Notices*, 25(6):66–77.

J. Roger Hindley. 1969. The principal type scheme of an object in combinatory logic. *Transactions of the American Mathematical Society*, 146:29–60.

Ralf Hinze. 2003. Fun with phantom types. In Jeremy Gibbons and Oege de Moor, editors, *The Fun of Programming*, chapter 12, pages 245–262. London: Palgrave Macmillan.

C. A. R. Hoare. 1972. Proof of correctness of data representations. *Acta Informatica,* 1: 271–281.

C. A. R. Hoare. 2009 (August). Null references: The billion dollar mistake. Presentation delivered at QCon.

C. A. R. Hoare, I. J. Hayes, He Jifeng, C. C. Morgan, A. W. Roscoe, J. W. Sanders, I. H. Sørensen, J. M. Spivey, and B. A. Sufrin. 1987 (August). Laws of programming. *Communications of the ACM,* 30(8): 672–686. Corrected in September 1987.

C. J. Hogger. 1984. *Introduction to Logic Programming.* London: Academic Press.

John E. Hopcroft and Jeffrey D. Ullman. 1979. *Introduction to Automata Theory, Languages and Computation.* Reading, MA: Addison-Wesley.

Jim Horning, Bill Kalsow, Paul McJones, and Greg Nelson. 1993 (December). Some useful Modula-3 interfaces. Research Report 113, Digital Systems Research Center, Palo Alto, CA.

Paul Hudak, John Hughes, Simon L. Peyton Jones, and Philip Wadler. 2007. A history of Haskell: Being lazy with class. In Barbara G. Ryder and Brent Hailpern, editors, *Proceedings of the Third ACM SIGPLAN History of Programming Languages Conference (HOPL-III),* pages 1–55.

John Hughes. 1989 (April). Why functional programming matters. *The Computer Journal,* 32(2):98–107.

John Hughes. 1995. The design of a pretty-printing library. In Johan Jeuring and Erik Meijer, editors, *Advanced Functional Programming, LNCS,* volume 925, pages 53–96. Springer Verlag.

John Hughes. 2016. Experiences with QuickCheck: Testing the hard stuff and staying sane. In *A List of Successes That Can Change the World—Essays Dedicated to Philip Wadler on the Occasion of His 60th Birthday,* pages 169–186. Springer.

Galen C. Hunt and James R. Larus. 2007 (April). Singularity: Rethinking the software stack. *SIGOPS Operating Systems Review,* 41(2):37–49.

Graham Hutton and Erik Meijer. 1996 (January). Monadic parser combinators. Technical Report NOTTCS-TR-96-4, University of Nottingham.

Jean D. Ichbiah, Bernd Krieg-Brueckner, Brian A. Wichmann, John G. P. Barnes, Olivier Roubine, and Jean-Claude Heliard. 1979 (June). Rationale for the design of the Ada programming language. *SIGPLAN Notices,* 14(6b):1–261.

Roberto Ierusalimschy. 2016 (August). *Programming in Lua,* 4th ed. Lua.org.

Roberto Ierusalimschy, Luiz H. de Figueiredo, and Waldemar Celes. 2007 (June). The evolution of Lua. In *Proceedings of the Third ACM SIGPLAN Conference on History of Programming Languages,* pages 2-1–2-26.

Dan Ingalls, Ted Kaehler, John Maloney, Scott Wallace, and Alan Kay. 1997 (October). Back to the future: The story of Squeak—a practical Smalltalk written in itself. *OOPSLA '97 Conference Proceedings,* in *SIGPLAN Notices,* 32(10):318–326.

Daniel Ingalls. 2020 (June). The evolution of Smalltalk: From Smalltalk-72 through Squeak. *Proceedings of the ACM on Programming Languages,* 4(HOPL).

Kenneth E. Iverson. 1962. *A Programming Language.* New York: John Wiley & Sons.

Ralph E. Johnson, Justin O. Graver, and Lawrence W. Zurawski. 1988. TS: An optimizing compiler for Smalltalk. In Norman Meyrowitz, editor, *OOPSLA'88: Object-Oriented Programming Systems, Languages and Applications: Conference Proceedings,* pages 18–26.

Mark S. Johnstone and Paul R. Wilson. 1998 (October). The memory fragmentation problem: Solved? *Proceedings of the First International Symposium on Memory Management,* in *SIGPLAN Notices,* 34(3):26–36.

Mark P. Jones. 1993 (November). Coherence for qualified types. Technical Report YALEU/DCS/RR-989, Yale University, New Haven, CT.

Mark P. Jones. 1999 (October). Typing Haskell in Haskell. In *Proceedings of the 1999 Haskell Workshop.* Published in Technical Report UU-CS-1999-28, Department of Computer Science, University of Utrecht. Additional resources at `http://www.cse.ogi.edu/~mpj/thih`.

Richard Jones, Antony Hosking, and Eliot Moss. 2011. *The Garbage Collection Handbook: The Art of Automatic Memory Management.* Chapman & Hall/CRC.

Richard Jones and Rafael Lins. 1996. *Garbage Collection: Algorithms for Automatic Dynamic Memory Management.* New York: Wiley. Reprinted in 1999 with improved index and corrected errata.

Ted Kaehler and Dave Patterson. 1986. *A Taste of Smalltalk.* New York: W. W. Norton and Co.

Gilles Kahn. 1987. Natural semantics. In *Proceedings of the Symposium on Theoretical Aspects of Computer Science (STACS), LNCS,* volume 247, pages 22–39. Springer-Verlag.

Samuel N. Kamin. 1990. *Programming Languages: An Interpreter-Based Approach*. Reading, MA: Addison-Wesley.

A. C. Kay. 1993 (March). The early history of Smalltalk. *SIGPLAN Notices*, 28(3):69–95.

Richard Kelsey, William Clinger, and Jonathan Rees. 1998 (September). Revised^5 report on the algorithmic language Scheme. *SIGPLAN Notices*, 33(9): 26–76.

Brian W. Kernighan and Dennis M. Ritchie. 1988. *The C Programming Language*, 2nd ed. Englewood Cliffs, NJ: Prentice Hall.

Oleg Kiselyov. 2012 (August). An argument against call/cc. URL `http://okmij.org/ftp/continuations/against-callcc.html`. Referenced in August 2015.

Donald E. Knuth. 1965 (December). On the translation of languages from left to right. *Information and Control*, 8(6):607–639.

Donald E. Knuth. 1973. *Fundamental Algorithms*, 2nd ed., volume 1 of *The Art of Computer Programming*. Reading, MA: Addison-Wesley.

Donald E. Knuth. 1974 (December). Structured programming with **go to** statements. *ACM Computing Surveys*, 6(4):261–301.

Donald E. Knuth. 1981. *Seminumerical Algorithms*, 2nd ed., volume 2 of *The Art of Computer Programming*. Reading, MA: Addison-Wesley.

Donald E. Knuth. 1984. Literate programming. *The Computer Journal*, 27(2):97–111.

Andrew Koenig. 1994. An anecdote about ML type inference. In *Proceedings of the USENIX 1994 Very High Level Languages Symposium*, VHLLS'94, page 1. Berkeley, CA: USENIX Association.

Peter M. Kogge. 1990. *The Architecture of Symbolic Computers*. New York: McGraw-Hill.

Eugene Kohlbecker, Daniel P. Friedman, Matthias Felleisen, and Bruce Duba. 1986. Hygienic macro expansion. In *Proceedings of the 1986 ACM Conference on LISP and Functional Programming*, LFP '86, pages 151–161.

Robert A. Kowalski. 1974. Predicate logic as a programming language. *Proc. IFIP 4*, pages 569–574.

Robert A. Kowalski. 1979. *Logic for Problem Solving*. New York: North Holland. As of 2022, available from Kowalski's site at Imperial College London.

Robert A. Kowalski. 1988 (January). The early years of logic programming. *Communications of the ACM, CACM*, 31(1):38–43.

Robert A. Kowalski. 2014. *Logic for Problem Solving, Revisited*. Books on Demand.

Glenn Krasner, editor. 1983. *Smalltalk-80: Bits of History, Words of Advice*. Boston: Addison-Wesley Longman.

P. J. Landin. 1966. The next 700 programming languages. *Communications of the ACM*, 9(3):157–166.

Peter J. Landin. 1964 (January). The mechanical evaluation of expressions. *Computer Journal*, 6(4):308–320.

Konstantin Läufer and Martin Odersky. 1994 (September). Polymorphic type inference and abstract data types. *ACM Transactions on Programming Languages and Systems*, 16 (5):1411–1430.

Xavier Leroy. 1994 (January). Manifest types, modules, and separate compilation. In *Conference Record of the 21st Annual ACM Symposium on Principles of Programming Languages*, pages 109–122.

Xavier Leroy. 1999 (September). Objects and classes vs. modules in Objective Caml. URL `http://pauillac.inria.fr/~xleroy/talks/icfp99.ps.gz`. Invited talk delivered at the 1999 International Conference on Functional Programming (ICFP).

Xavier Leroy. 2000 (May). A modular module system. *Journal of Functional Programming*, 10(3):269–303.

Henry Lieberman and Carl Hewitt. 1983 (June). A real-time garbage collector based on the lifetimes of objects. *Communications of the ACM*, 26(6):419–429.

Miran Lipovača. 2011. *Learn You a Haskell for Great Good!: A Beginner's Guide*. San Francisco: No Starch Press.

Barbara Liskov. 1996. A history of CLU. In Thomas J. Bergin, Jr. and Richard G. Gibson, Jr., editors, *History of Programming languages—II*, pages 471–510. New York: ACM.

Barbara Liskov and John Guttag. 1986. *Abstraction and Specification in Program Development*. Cambridge, MA: MIT Press/McGraw-Hill.

Barbara Liskov, Alan Snyder, Russell Atkinson, and Craig Schaffert. 1977 (August). Abstraction mechanisms in CLU. *Communications of the ACM*, 20(8):564–576. Republished in *Readings in Object-Oriented Database Systems*, S. Zdonik and D. Maier, Morgan Kaufman, 1990.

Barbara Liskov and Stephen Zilles. 1974 (March). Programming with abstract data types. *Proceedings of the ACM SIGPLAN Symposium on Very High Level Languages,* in *SIGPLAN Notices,* 9(4):50–59.

Barbara H. Liskov and Alan Snyder. 1979 (November). Exception handling in CLU. *IEEE Transactions on Software Engineering,* SE-5(6):546–558.

Barbara H. Liskov and Jeannette M. Wing. 1994 (November). A behavioral notion of subtyping. *ACM Transactions on Programming Languages and Systems,* 16(6):1811–1841.

Chi-Keung Luk, Robert Cohn, Robert Muth, Harish Patil, Artur Klauser, Geoff Lowney, Steven Wallace, Vijay Janapa Reddi, and Kim Hazelwood. 2005 (June). Pin: Building customized program analysis tools with dynamic instrumentation. *Proceedings of the ACM SIGPLAN '05 Conference on Programming Language Design and Implementation,* in *SIGPLAN Notices,* 40(6):190–200.

Luc Maranget. 2007. Warnings for pattern matching. *Journal of Functional Programming,* 17(3):387–421.

Luc Maranget. 2008. Compiling pattern matching to good decision trees. In *Proceedings of the 2008 ACM SIGPLAN Workshop on ML,* pages 35–46.

Simon Marlow, Tim Harris, Roshan P. James, and Simon Peyton Jones. 2008 (June). Parallel generational-copying garbage collection with a block-structured heap. In *ISMM '08: Proceedings of the 7th International Symposium on Memory Management.*

Moe Masuko and Kenichi Asai. 2009. Direct implementation of shift and reset in the MinCaml compiler. In *Proceedings of the 2009 ACM SIGPLAN Workshop on ML,* pages 49–60.

Conor McBride. 2004. Epigram: Practical programming with dependent types. In *International School on Advanced Functional Programming,* pages 130–170. Springer.

Conor McBride and Ross Paterson. 2008 (January). Applicative programming with effects. *Journal of Functional Programming,* 18(1):1–13.

John McCarthy. 1960 (April). Recursive functions of symbolic expressions and their computation by machine, part I. *Communications of the ACM,* 3(4):184–195.

John McCarthy. 1962. *Lisp 1.5 Programmer's Manual.* Cambridge, MA: MIT Press.

Sandi Metz. 2013. *Practical Object-Oriented Design in Ruby: An Agile Primer.* Reading, MA: Addison-Wesley.

Bertrand Meyer. 1992. *Eiffel: The Language.* London: Prentice Hall International.

Bertrand Meyer. 1997. *Object-Oriented Software Construction,* 2nd ed. Englewood Cliffs, NJ: Prentice-Hall.

Todd Millstein, Colin Bleckner, and Craig Chambers. 2004. Modular typechecking for hierarchically extensible datatypes and functions. *ACM Transactions on Programming Languages and Systems,* 26(5): 836–889.

Robin Milner. 1978 (December). A theory of type polymorphism in programming. *Journal of Computer and System Sciences,* 17:348–375.

Robin Milner. 1983. How ML evolved. *Polymorphism—The ML/LCF/Hope Newsletter,* 1(1).

Robin Milner. 1999 (May). *Communicating and Mobile Systems: The π-Calculus.* Cambridge: Cambridge University Press.

Robin Milner and Mads Tofte. 1991. *Commentary on Standard ML.* Cambridge, MA: MIT Press.

Robin Milner, Mads Tofte, Robert Harper, and David MacQueen. 1997. *The Definition of Standard ML (Revised).* Cambridge, MA: MIT Press.

Marvin L. Minsky. 1963 (December). A Lisp garbage collector algorithm using serial secondary storage. Technical Report Memo 58, Project MAC, MIT, Cambridge, MA.

John C. Mitchell and Gordon D. Plotkin. 1988 (July). Abstract types have existential type. *ACM Transactions on Programming Languages and Systems,* 10(3):470–502.

Calvin N. Mooers. 1966 (March). TRAC, a procedure-describing language for the reactive typewriter. *Communications of the ACM,* 9(3):215–219.

David A. Moon. 1986 (October). Object-oriented programming with flavours. In *Proceedings of the ACM Conference on Object-Oriented Programming Systems, Languages, and Applications,* pages 1–8.

George C. Necula, Scott McPeak, and Westley Weimer. 2002 (January). CCured: Type-safe retrofitting of legacy code. *Conference Record of the 29th Annual ACM Symposium on Principles of Programming Languages,* in *SIGPLAN Notices,* 37(1):128–139.

Greg Nelson, editor. 1991. *Systems Programming with Modula-3.* Englewood Cliffs, NJ: Prentice Hall.

Nicholas Nethercote and Julian Seward. 2007a. How to shadow every byte of memory used by a program. In *Proceedings of the 3rd International Conference on Virtual Execution Environments,* VEE '07, pages 65–74.

Nicholas Nethercote and Julian Seward. 2007b. Valgrind: A framework for heavyweight dynamic binary instrumentation. *Proceedings of the ACM SIGPLAN '07 Conference on Programming Language Design and Implementation,* in *SIGPLAN Notices,* 42(6):89–100.

Nils J. Nilsson. 1980. *Principles of Artificial Intelligence.* Tioga/Morgan Kaufman.

James Noble, Andrew P. Black, Kim B. Bruce, Michael Homer, and Mark S. Miller. 2016. The left hand of equals. In *Proceedings of the 2016 ACM International Symposium on New Ideas, New Paradigms, and Reflections on Programming and Software,* Onward! 2016, pages 224–237.

Kristen Nygaard and Ole-Johan Dahl. 1981. The development of the SIMULA languages. In Richard L. Wexelblat, editor, *History of Programming Languages I,* pages 439–480. New York: ACM.

Martin Odersky, Lex Spoon, and Bill Venners. 2019. *Programming in Scala,* 4th ed. Walnut Creek, CA: Artima Press.

Martin Odersky, Martin Sulzmann, and Martin Wehr. 1999. Type inference with constrained types. *Theory and Practice of Object Systems,* 5(1):35–55.

Melissa E. O'Neill. 2009 (January). The genuine sieve of Eratosthenes. *Journal of Functional Programming,* 19(1):95–106.

Derek C. Oppen. 1980 (October). Prettyprinting. *ACM Transactions on Programming Languages and Systems,* 2(4):465–483.

David Lorge Parnas. 1972 (December). On the criteria for decomposing systems into modules. *Communications of the ACM,* 15 (12):1053–1058.

Laurence C. Paulson. 1996. *ML for the Working Programmer,* 2nd ed. New York: Cambridge University Press.

Nigel Perry. 1991. *The Implementation of Practical Functional Programming Languages.* PhD thesis, Imperial College, London.

Simon Peyton Jones, Dimitrios Vytiniotis, Stephanie Weirich, and Mark Shields. 2007. Practical type inference for arbitrary-rank types. *Journal of Functional Programming,* 17(1):1–82.

Benjamin C. Pierce. 2002. *Types and Programming Languages.* Cambridge, MA: MIT Press.

Benjamin C. Pierce, Arthur Azevedo de Amorim, Chris Casinghino, Marco Gaboardi, Michael Greenberg, Cătălin Hriţcu, Vilhelm Sjöberg, and Brent Yorgey. 2016 (May). Software foundations. URL `https://www.cis.upenn.edu/~bcpierce/sf/`. Version 4.0.

Rob Pike. 1990 (July). The implementation of Newsqueak. *Software—Practice & Experience,* 20(7):649–659.

Gordon D. Plotkin. 1981 (September). A structural approach to operational semantics. Technical Report DAIMI FN-19, Department of Computer Science, Aarhus University, Aarhus, Denmark.

François Pottier and Didier Rémy. 2005. The essence of ML type inference. In Benjamin C. Pierce, editor, *Advanced Topics in Types and Programming Languages,* chapter 10, pages 389–489. Cambridge, MA: MIT Press.

François Pottier and Yann Régis-Gianas. 2006 (March). Towards efficient, typed LR parsers. In *ACM Workshop on ML,* pages 155–180.

Todd A. Proebsting. 1997 (June). Simple translation of goal-directed evaluation. *Proceedings of the ACM SIGPLAN '97 Conference on Programming Language Design and Implementation,* in *SIGPLAN Notices,* 32(5):1–6.

Norman Ramsey. 1990 (April). Concurrent programming in ML. Technical Report TR-262-90, Department of Computer Science, Princeton University.

Norman Ramsey. 1994 (September). Literate programming simplified. *IEEE Software,* 11(5):97–105.

Norman Ramsey. 1999. Eliminating spurious error messages using exceptions, polymorphism, and higher-order functions. *Computer Journal,* 42(5):360–372.

Norman Ramsey. 2005 (September). ML module mania: A type-safe, separately compiled, extensible interpreter. In *ACM SIGPLAN Workshop on ML,* pages 172–202.

Norman Ramsey, João Dias, and Simon L. Peyton Jones. 2010. Hoopl: A modular, reusable library for dataflow analysis and transformation. *Proceedings of the 3rd ACM SIGPLAN Symposium on Haskell (Haskell 2010),* in *SIGPLAN Notices,* 45(11): 121–134.

Norman Ramsey, Kathleen Fisher, and Paul Govereau. 2005 (September). An expressive language of signatures. In *Proceedings of the Tenth ACM SIGPLAN International Conference on Functional Programming (ICFP'05),* pages 27–40.

Jonathan Rees and William Clinger. 1986 (December). Revised[3] report on the algorithmic language Scheme. *SIGPLAN Notices*, 21(12):37–79.

E. Reingold and R. Reingold. 1988. *PascAlgorithms: An Introduction to Programming*. Scott, Foresman.

John Reynolds. 1972 (August). Definitional interpreters for higher-order programming languages. In *Proceedings of the 25th ACM National Conference*, pages 717–740. Reprinted in *Higher-Order and Symbolic Computation*, 11(4):363–397, 1998.

John C. Reynolds. 1974. Towards a theory of type structure. In *Colloque sur la Programmation, Paris, France, LNCS*, volume 19, pages 408–425. Springer-Verlag.

John C. Reynolds. 1978. User-defined types and procedural data structures as complementary approaches to data abstraction. In David Gries, editor, *Programming Methodology*, Texts and Monographs in Computer Science, pages 309–317. New York: Springer.

John C. Reynolds. 1993 (November). The discoveries of continuations. *Lisp and Symbolic Computation*, 6(3/4):233–248.

John C. Reynolds. 1998 (December). Definitional interpreters for higher-order programming languages. *Higher-Order and Symbolic Computation*, 11(4):363–397. Reprinted from the proceedings of the 25th ACM National Conference (1972).

E. S. Roberts. 1986. *Thinking Recursively*. New York: John Wiley & Sons.

Eric S. Roberts. 1989 (March). Implementing exceptions in C. Technical Report Research Report 40, Digital Systems Research Center, Palo Alto, CA.

J. Alan Robinson. 1965 (January). A machine-oriented logic based on resolution principle. *Journal of the ACM*, 12(1):23–49.

J. Alan Robinson. 1983. Logic programming—past, present and future. *New Generation Comput. (Japan)*, 1 (2):107–124. QA 76 N 48.

J. S. Rohl. 1984. *Recursion via Pascal*. Cambridge: Cambridge University Press.

Raúl Rojas. 2015. A tutorial introduction to the lambda calculus. `http://arxiv.org/abs/1503.09060`.

Colin Runciman and David Wakeling. 1993 (April). Heap profiling of lazy functional programs. *Journal of Functional Programming*, 3(2):217–246.

David A. Schmidt. 1986. *Denotational Semantics: A Methodology for Language Development*. Reading, MA: Allyn and Bacon.

Tom Schrijvers, Simon Peyton Jones, Martin Sulzmann, and Dimitrios Vytiniotis. 2009 (August). Complete and decidable type inference for GADTs. *Proceedings of the Fourteenth ACM SIGPLAN International Conference on Functional Programming (ICFP'09)*, in *SIGPLAN Notices*, 44(9):341–352.

Kevin Scott and Norman Ramsey. 2000 (May). When do match-compilation heuristics matter? Technical Report CS-2000-13, Department of Computer Science, University of Virginia.

Robert Sedgewick. 1988. *Algorithms*, 2nd ed. Addison-Wesley.

Manuel Serrano and Hans-Juergen Boehm. 2000 (September). Understanding memory allocation of Scheme programs. *Proceedings of the Fifth ACM SIGPLAN International Conference on Functional Programming (ICFP'00)*, in *SIGPLAN Notices*, 35(9): 245–256.

Alex Shinn, John Cowan, and Arthur A. Gleckler. 2013. Revised[7] Report on the algorithmic language Scheme. Technical Report, R7RS Working Group 1. URL `https://small.r7rs.org/attachment/r7rs.pdf`.

Justin Slepak, Olin Shivers, and Panagiotis Manolios. 2014. An array-oriented language with static rank polymorphism. In *23rd European Symposium on Programming (ESOP 2014)*, pages 27–46.

Frederick Smith and Greg Morrisett. 1999 (March). Comparing mostly-copying and mark-sweep conservative collection. *Proceedings of the First International Symposium on Memory Management (ISMM'98)*, in *SIGPLAN Notices*, 34(3):68–78.

Elliott Soloway. 1986 (September). Learning to program = learning to construct mechanisms and explanations. *Communications of the ACM*, 29(9):850–858.

Michael Sperber, R. Kent Dybvig, Matthew Flatt, Anton van Straaten, Robby Findler, and Jacob Matthews. 2009. Revised[6] Report on the algorithmic language Scheme. *Journal of Functional Programming*, 19 (Supplement S1):1–301.

Mike Spivey. 1990 (June). A functional theory of exceptions. *Science of Computer Programming*, 14(1):25–42.

Raymie Stata and John V. Guttag. 1995 (October). Modular reasoning in the presence of subclassing. *OOPSLA '95 Conference Proceedings*, in *SIGPLAN Notices*, 30(10):200–214.

Raymond Paul Stata. 1996. *Modularity in the Presence of Subclassing*. PhD thesis, Massachusetts Institute of Technology.

Guy Lewis Steele, Jr. 1977 (October). Debunking the "expensive procedure call" myth or, procedure call implementations considered harmful or, LAMBDA: The ultimate GOTO. In *Proceedings ACM Annual Conference,* pages 153–162.

Guy Lewis Steele, Jr. 1984. *Common Lisp: The Language.* Digital Press.

Guy Lewis Steele, Jr. 2017. It's time for a new old language. In *Proceedings of the 22nd ACM SIGPLAN Symposium on Principles and Practice of Parallel Programming,* PPoPP '17, page 1. A recording of Steele's talk can likely be found on the Web.

Guy Lewis Steele, Jr. and Gerald Jay Sussman. 1976 (March). Lambda: The ultimate imperative. Technical Report AIM-353, Massachusetts Institute of Technology.

Guy Lewis Steele, Jr. and Gerald Jay Sussman. 1978 (May). The art of the interpreter or, the modularity complex (parts zero, one, and two). Technical Report AIM-453, Massachusetts Institute of Technology.

L. Sterling and E. Shapiro. 1986. *The Art of Prolog.* Cambridge, MA: MIT Press.

Joseph E. Stoy. 1977. *Denotational Semantics: The Scott-Strachey Approach to Programming Language Theory.* Cambridge, MA: MIT Press.

Christopher Strachey and Christopher P. Wadsworth. 2000 (April). Continuations: A mathematical semantics for handling full jumps. *Higher Order Symbol. Comput.,* 13(1-2):135–152. Oxford monograph from 1974 republished in a special issue of *HOSC* devoted to Christopher Strachey.

Bjarne Stroustrup. 1997. *The C++ Programming Language,* 3rd ed. Reading, MA: Addison-Wesley.

Gerald Jay Sussman and Guy Lewis Steele, Jr. 1975 (December). Scheme: An interpreter for extended lambda calculus. MIT AI Memo No. 349, reprinted in *Higher-Order and Symbolic Computation* 11(4):405–439, Dec 1998.

Mads Tofte. 2009 (August). Tips for computer scientists on Standard ML (revised). Linked from `http://www.itu.dk/people/tofte`.

D. S. Touretzky. 1984. *LISP: A Gentle Introduction to Symbolic Computation.* New York: Harper & Row.

Jeffrey D. Ullman. 1997. *Elements of ML Programming, ML97 Edition.* Englewood Cliffs, NJ: Prentice Hall.

David Ungar. 1984 (May). Generation scavenging: A non-disruptive high performance storage reclamation algorithm. *Proceedings of the ACM SIGSOFT/SIGPLAN Symposium on Practical Software Development Environments,* in *SIGPLAN Notices,* 19 (5):157–167.

David Ungar and Randall B. Smith. 1987. Self: The power of simplicity. *OOPSLA '87 Conference Proceedings,* in *SIGPLAN Notices,* pages 227–242.

Peter Van der Linden. 1994. *Expert C Programming: Deep C Secrets.* Englewood Cliffs, NJ: Prentice Hall Professional.

Guido van Rossum. 1998. A tour of the Python language. In R. Ege, M. Singh, and B. Meyer, editors, *Proceedings. Technology of Object-Oriented Languages and Systems, TOOLS-23,* page 370. Silver Spring, MD: IEEE Computer Society.

David Vengerov. 2009. Modeling, analysis and throughput optimization of a generational garbage collector. In *Proceedings of the 2009 International Symposium on Memory Management (ISMM '09),* pages 1–9.

Dimitrios Vytiniotis, Simon Peyton Jones, and Tom Schrijvers. 2010. Let should not be generalised. In *Proceedings of the 5th ACM SIGPLAN workshop on Types in Language Design and Implementation (TLDI '10),* pages 39–50.

Dimitrios Vytiniotis, Simon Peyton Jones, Tom Schrijvers, and Martin Sulzmann. 2011 (September). OutsideIn(X): Modular type inference with local assumptions. *Journal of Functional Programming,* 21(4-5):333–412.

Philip Wadler. 2003. A prettier printer. In Jeremy Gibbons and Oege de Moor, editors, *The Fun of Programming,* chapter 11, pages 223–244. London: Palgrave Macmillan.

Philip Wadler. 2015 (November). Propositions as types. *Communications of the ACM,* 58(12):75–84.

Philip Wadler and Stephen Blott. 1989 (January). How to make *ad-hoc* polymorphism less *ad hoc.* In *Conference Record of the 16th Annual ACM Symposium on Principles of Programming Languages,* pages 60–76.

Daniel C. Wang, Andrew W. Appel, Jeff L. Korn, and Christopher S. Serra. 1997 (October). The Zephyr Abstract Syntax Description Language. In *Proceedings of the 2nd USENIX Conference on Domain-Specific Languages,* pages 213–227.

David H. D. Warren. 1983 (October). An abstract Prolog instruction set. Technical

Report 309, Artificial Intelligence Center, Computer Science and Technology Division, SRI International, Menlo Park, CA.

R. L. Wexelblat, editor. 1981. *History of Programming Languages*. New York: Academic Press.

Robert Wilensky. 1986. *Common LISPcraft*. New York: W. W. Norton.

Paul R. Wilson. 1992 (September). Uniprocessor garbage collection techniques. In *Proceedings of the International Workshop on Memory Management*, volume 637 of *LCNS*, pages 1–42. Springer-Verlag.

Paul R. Wilson, Mark S. Johnstone, Michael Neely, and David Boles. 1995 (September). Dynamic storage allocation: A survey and critical review. In Henry Baker, editor, *Proceedings of International Workshop on Memory Management, LNCS*, volume 986. Springer-Verlag.

Terry Winograd. 1972. *Understanding Natural Language*. New York: Academic Press.

P. H. Winston and B. K. P. Horn. 1984. *Lisp Second Edition*. Reading: Addison-Wesley.

Patrick H. Winston. 1977. *Artificial Intelligence*. Reading, MA: Addison-Wesley.

Niklaus Wirth. 1971 (April). Program development by stepwise refinement. *Communications of the ACM*, 14(4):221–227.

Niklaus Wirth. 1977 (November). What can we do about the unnecessary diversity of notation for syntactic definitions? *Communications of the ACM*, 20(11):822–823.

Niklaus Wirth. 1982. *Programming in Modula-2*. Berlin: Springer.

Robert S. Wolf. 2005. *A Tour through Mathematical Logic*. Mathematical Association of America.

Andrew K. Wright. 1995 (December). Simple imperative polymorphism. *Lisp and Symbolic Computation*, 8(4):343–355.

William A. Wulf, R. L. London, and Mary Shaw. 1976 (December). An introduction to the construction and verification of Alphard programs. *IEEE Transactions on Software Engineering*, 2(4):253–265.

Hongwei Xi and Frank Pfenning. 1998 (May). Eliminating array bound checking through dependent types. *Proceedings of the ACM SIGPLAN '98 Conference on Programming Language Design and Implementation*, in *SIGPLAN Notices*, 33(5):249–257.

Benjamin Zorn. 1993 (July). The measured cost of conservative garbage collection. *Software—Practice & Experience*, 23(7):733–756.

Key words and phrases

Concept index

Colophon

This book was typeset by the author using XƎLaTeX and the Noweb system for literate programming. The main text font is Source Serif Pro by Frank Grießhammer. The code font is Input by David Jonathan Ross. The math font is Computer Modern by Donald Ervin Knuth.

C code was indexed by Libclang via the Rtags tool. ML code was indexed by MLton. Bridge-language code was indexed by modified versions of the interpreters described in the book.